PIBA Personal Injury Handbook

Third Edition

PIBA Personal Injury Handbook

Third Edition

Frank Burton QC
12 King's Bench Walk

Charles Cory-Wright QC
39 Essex Street

Simon Levene
12 King's Bench Walk

Philip Mead
Old Square Chambers

Published by
Jordan Publishing Limited
21 St Thomas Street
Bristol BS1 6JS

Whilst the publishers and the author have taken every care in preparing the material included in this work, any statements made as to the legal or other implications of particular transactions are made in good faith purely for general guidance and cannot be regarded as a substitute for professional advice. Consequently, no liability can be accepted for loss or expense incurred as a result of relying in particular circumstances on statements made in this work.

© The Contributors 2007

All rights reserved. No part of this publication may be reproduced, stored in a retrieval system, or transmitted in any way or by any means, including photocopying or recording, without the written permission of the copyright holder, application for which should be addressed to the publisher.

Crown Copyright material is reproduced with kind permission of the Controller of Her Majesty's Stationery Office.

British Library Cataloguing-in-Publication Data

A catalogue record for this book is available from the British Library.

ISBN 978 1 84661 054 7

Typeset by Letterpart Ltd, Reigate, Surrey

Printed in Great Britain by Antony Rowe Limited

FOREWORD

This is the third edition of the PIBA Handbook. It contains an updated, accessible and authoritative analysis of many areas of personal injury law and practice. Although it has been produced by barristers who are members of the Personal Injury Bar Association – now over 1500 strong – it is intended for a wide variety of reader who is interested in personal injury law.

The reader will find that each chapter has been written by someone with direct practical knowledge of the particular subject. This edition is produced at an important time for practitioners. In particular, we can see how the development of our understanding and use of periodical payments has so far been gradual. The issue of indexation, as at the date of writing, remains controversial. However it is resolved, we are likely to remain some way away from a situation in which settlement of future loss by an award of periodical payments rather than by a lump sum has become 'the norm' – the expectation of, for example, the Department of Constitutional Affairs in its guidance on the subject at the time of the introduction of the new regime. Other subjects which have seen considerable changes in recent years, and which are dealt with thoroughly in this new edition, include the law and practice of claims involving the Motor Insurers Bureau and the role of Rehabilitation as a feature of the constructive management of claims. There is also a chapter dealing directly with recent developments with regard to ADR and mediation. This is a subject of considerable and increasing importance to all practitioners. We are concerned not just with a semi-formal process such as mediation but with the many different ways of achieving consensual settlement without leaving the decision to the Courts which fall under the umbrella of 'ADR'. No competent practitioner can afford to have anything other than a clear understanding of how such processes work. The chapter in this book will help to provide that clarity.

When the first edition of this Handbook was published the then President of our Association, Lord Justice Beldam, wrote that it could 'play an important part in maintaining respect for the law'. In so far as it may have helped the reader more fully to understand an area of law which is intended to provide fair and accurate compensation for those who have suffered injury, I hope the book has satisfied that ambition. In the second edition, Lord Justice Otton, his successor as our President, said that the book was of 'inestimable value'. Although literally true, no doubt, that might be putting things a bit high, although the very reasonable price of the book at least can readily be measured! Its value to the individual reader will vary but I am sure that everyone will find it a very useful source of reference and guidance.

I am extremely grateful to those distinguished members of our Association who have devoted so much time to producing it. I am sure you will find that their efforts have been worthwhile.

William Norris QC
Chairman, Personal Injury Bar Association
39 Essex Street Chambers

LIST OF CONTRIBUTORS

Peter Andrews QC
7 Bedford Row

Charles Bagot
Hardwicke Building

Edward Bishop
1 Chancery Lane

Frank Burton QC
12 King's Bench Walk

His Honour Judge Andrew Collender QC

Charles Cory-Wright QC
39 Essex Street

Lee Evans
Farrar's Buildings

Emily Formby
Hardwicke Building

John Foy QC
9 Gough Square

Caspar Glyn
Cloisters

Christopher Goddard
9 Gough Square

Nicholas Heathcote-Williams QC
12 King's Bench Walk

Andrew Hogarth QC
12 King's Bench Walk

Christopher Hough
Doughty Street Chambers

Jeremy Hyam
1 Crown Office Row

Matthias Kelly QC
39 Essex Street

Sarah Lambert
1 Crown Office Row

Mr Justice Langstaff QC

William Latimer-Sayer
Cloisters

John Leighton Williams QC
Farrar's Buildings

Simon Levene
12 King's Bench Walk

Michael Lewer QC

Patrick Limb
Ropewalk Chambers

Simon McCann
Deans Court Chambers

Philip Mead
Old Square Chambers

Stephen Miller QC
1 Crown Office Row

Michael de Navarro QC
2 Temple Gardens

Sonia Nolten
2 Temple Gardens

Richard Nussey
Farrar's Buildings

Robin Oppenheim QC
Doughty Street Chambers

Martin Porter QC
2 Temple Gardens

James Rowley QC
Byrom Street Chambers

Martin Spencer QC
Hailsham Chambers

Simon Thorp
Park Lane Chambers

Nina Unthank
2 Temple Gardens

Robert Weir
Devereux Chambers

Philippa Whipple
1 Crown Office Row

CONTENTS

Foreword v
List of Contributors vii
Table of Statutes xxxvii
Table of Statutory Instruments xliii
Table of Cases xlv

Part 1
Liability

Chapter 1
Duty of care 3
Employers 3
Employee on loan 3
Self-employed workers 4
Road users 4
Other parties 5
Balancing the duties of care 5
Foreseeability 6
'Nervous shock' 7

Chapter 2
Foreseeability 9
Duty of care 9
The standard of foresight 10
Class of person 11
Kind of damage 12
   The kind of accident 13
   Kind of injury 16
Extent of damage 18
Breach of duty 18
Causation and damage 19
Conclusion 20

Chapter 3
Causation 21
Introduction 21

Some troublesome aspects of the 'but for' test	22
Causally irrelevant facts	22
Alternative sufficient causes	22
When the 'but for' test does not provide the answer	24
The circumstances in which the 'but for' test for causation leads to difficulty	24
Bonnington Castings Ltd v Wardlaw	26
McGhee v National Coal Board	29
Wilsher v Essex Area Health Authority	30
Fairchild v Glenhaven Funeral Services Ltd	32
The effect of the decisions in Bonnington Castings, McGhee, Wilsher and Fairchild	35
The de minimis exception	36
Loss of a chance	38
Intervening causes	39

Chapter 4
Contributory negligence — **41**

The statutory provision	41
The background to the statute	41
The nature of the claimant's failure	42
The availability of the defence	42
Where there are multiple defendants	43
The requirements of pleading and proof	43
The standard of care	44
The objective test	46
Its application generally	46
Its application to children	47
Its application in rescue or emergency situations	48
The just and equitable test	49
Blame	49
Causation and causative potency	51
The decision	52
The 1945 Act and its application to different torts	53

Chapter 5
Expert evidence: the duties and liabilities of an expert — **55**

Introduction	55
The duties of an expert	56
Format of the expert's report	58
Single joint experts	59
The meeting of experts	60
The liabilities of an expert	60
The duties of those instructing an expert	63
The different types of experts in personal injury and clinical negligence cases	64
Medical expert evidence	64
Non-medical expert evidence	65

Confidentiality and privilege 65
Duties of the court 68

Chapter 6
Recovering damages for psychiatric injuries 69
Introduction 69
Recognisable psychiatric illness 71
Primary victims 71
Secondary victims 72
   A close tie of love and affection 73
   Physical and temporal proximity 73
   The means of perception 75
Involuntary participant 75
Rescuers 76
Employees 79
Bystanders 80
The Law Following Frost 81
The aftermath revisited 85
Duty of care owed by primary victims 87
Proposals for reform 88

Chapter 7
Employer's statutory liabilities 91
The scope of this chapter 91
The principal health and safety Regulations 91
Origin in European Directives 94
   Practical effect of direct effect 95
   Where a Directive is not implemented 95
Codes of Practice and Guidance 96
   Codes applicable 97
Regulation: general 97
   Liability 97
      Who is covered? 98
      What is covered and where 98
      When there is liability 98
   General defences: causation and contribution 98
The Management Regulations 99
   Overview 99
   Is there liability for breach? 100
   Content of the Regulations 100
   Points to note 101
   Cases 101
Health and Safety (Display Screen Equipment) Regulations 101
   What is covered? 101
   Where? 101
   Who is protected? 102
   Who is regulated? 102
   Content of the Regulations 102

Points to note	102
Manual Handling Operations Regulations	103
What is covered?	103
Where?	103
Who is protected?	103
Who is regulated?	103
Content of the Regulations	103
Points to note	104
Points from cases	104
Provision and Use of Work Equipment Regulations	105
What is covered?	105
Where?	106
Who is protected?	106
Who is regulated?	106
Content	106
Regulation 4	107
Regulation 5	107
Regulation 11	108
Points to note	108
Points from cases	108
Personal Protective Equipment at Work Regulations	109
What is covered?	109
Where?	109
Who is protected?	109
Who is regulated?	109
Content	110
Points to note	110
The Workplace (Health, Safety and Welfare) Regulations	111
What is covered?	111
Who is covered?	111
Who is regulated?	111
Content	112
Points to note	114
The Construction (Health, Safety and Welfare) Regulations	115
What is covered and where?	115
Who is covered?	115
Who is regulated?	115
Content of the Regulations	116
Points to note	117
Cases	117
Lifting Operations Regulations 1998	117
What is covered?	117
Where?	117
Who is regulated?	117
Contents of the Regulations	118
Points to note	118
Working Time Regulations	119
What is covered?	119

Who is covered?	119
Who is regulated?	119
Content	119
Points to note	120
Procedural implications of the various Regulations	121
General points from the case-law	121

Chapter 8
The European dimension to personal injury practice — **125**

Introduction	125
The reach and application of European law	125
The scope of European regulation	125
Sources of European law	127
Rights and remedies under EU law	128
Interpretation	128
Direct effect	129
Effective remedies	131
Liability of the State for failure to implement a Directive	132
Case-law of the European Court of Justice and the English courts applying European principles in the field of personal injury	133
European Court of Justice	133
English appellate case-law applying European principles	136
Foreign accidents	137
The Brussels Regulation	137
Secondary European legislation governing foreign personal injury claims	141
Package holidays	141
Road traffic accidents	142

Part 2
Damages

Chapter 9
General damages — **147**

Introduction	147
Judicial Studies Board Guidelines	148
The Guidelines and costs	151
Heil v Rankin	152
Updating awards	153
Updating awards made after 23 March 2000	153
Updating awards made before 23 March 2000	154
Individual factors affecting general damages	154
Pain and suffering	154
Loss of amenity	155
Pre-existing condition	156
Acceleration	157
Multiple injuries	157
Fear of impending death	159

Loss of expectation of life	159
Gender	160
Age	160
Death of claimant	160
Means of the claimant	161
Claimant's previous lifestyle	161
Circumstances of the accident	161
Loss of congenial employment	162
Loss of leisure	162
Loss of enjoyment of holiday	162
Note	163
General damages in Fatal Accidents Act claims	163
Appeals against awards of general damages	164
Appendix	164
Checklist for general damages	164

Chapter 10
Multipliers for future loss and expenditure — 167

Using the Tables	171
Calculating loss of earnings	173
Lifetime losses	174
Loss of pension	175
One-off future losses	175
Multipliers for fixed periods	176
Combining the Tables	176
Fatal accident cases and the multiplier	176
The alternative approach	179

Chapter 11
Loss of earnings — 183

The straightforward claim	183
Evidence	184
Expert evidence	185
Ancillary benefits	187
Self-employment	187
Partnership/directors	188
Future losses	188
Periodical payments	189
The multiplicand	190
The multiplier	191
Adjustments for contingencies	192
Handicap on the labour market	195
Loss of chance	195
Delay entering the job market	198

Chapter 12
Loss of pension   199
The conventional approach   199
   Wider principles   199
   Conventional approach in practice following Wells v Wells   199
   Conventional approach – binding on pensions   200
A modern but nevertheless 'conventional' approach   201
Overview of types of pension claims   201
The basic Ogden multipliers   202
   Solution to Type 1 cases using the Ogden Tables   202
     Worked example using basic Ogden multipliers   202
   Solution to Type 2 cases using the Ogden Tables   203
   The multiplier   203
   The multiplicand   204
   Further adjustment   204
The evidential framework   206
   Additional receipt of pension/incapacity pension   208
Miscellaneous   210
   Widow's pension   210
   Alternative occupational pension   210
   Tax allowances and relief   211
   Personal pension plans   212
   Hybrid personal/employer-funded schemes   212
   Average life expectancy short of retirement   213
   Death in service benefits   213
Worked Type 2 example including alternatives of widow's pension and
    death in service benefits   213
   Basic facts   213
   The pension trustees' questionnaire   214
   Example Schedule   215

Chapter 13
Damages for care   219
Part 1: The principles underlying an award for care   219
   Introduction   219
   The principles applied in awards for care   220
   The essential principles   221
   The basis of the claim   222
     The claimant's need for care   222
     Care provided by the tortfeasor   224
   Less serious cases   225
   The evaluation of gratuitous care   226
     The approach   226
   Adopting the commercial rate and discounting   228
     Adopting the commercial rate   228
     The appropriate discount to the commercial rate   229
     Is there a conventional discount?   229
     Awarding more than the commercial rate   231

Lump sum damages and periodical payments	232
The traditional approach – lump sum damages	232
Periodical payments	232
The substantive law	232
Practice and procedure	233
Periodical payments and index linking	234
General points	235
No recovery for care and carer's loss of earnings	235
Interim payments to fund care	236
Interest on care	236
Who has title to the award?	236
The effect of contributory negligence	236
Early advice	236
Differing approaches in different cases	237
The Working Time Regulations 1998	238
Part 2: The provision of care by health authorities and local authorities and recoupment of the cost of care	239
Introduction	239
Provision of care by the National Health Service	240
The relevance of the availability of NHS accommodation and care	241
Provision of care by social services/local authorities	242
The National Assistance Act 1948 and the National Health Service and Community Care Act 1990	242
Section 21 – residential accommodation/care	243
Recoupment of costs of accommodation/care provided under s 21	243
Section 29 – services including home care	244
Recoupment of costs of care provided under Section 29	245
The Health and Social Services and Social Security Adjudications Act 1983	245
What means may be taken into account for charges under s 17	246
The decision in Avon CC v Hooper	247
The National Health Service Act 1977	247
Recoupment of the costs of care under The National Health Service Act 1977	248
The Children Act 1989	248
Provision of accommodation/care	248
Recoupment – children in need	249
Some general points on recoupment	249
Liaison between local health authorities and local authorities	250
Protection from claims for recoupment	251
Indemnities	251
Claims under the National Assistance Act 1948	252
Claims made under s 17 of the Health and Social Services and Social Security Adjudications Act 1983	252
Generally	253

The relevance of the availability of Local Authority/Social Services Accommodation and Care	253
The argument for taking local authority provision into account	253
The approach of the courts	254
Crofton v NHSLA	254
The decisions in Sowden v Rudge and Drury v Crookdale	257
Sowden v Lodge	258
Drury v Crookdale	259
The applicable test – 'best interests' or 'reasonable requirements'	259
The 'reasonable requirements' test	259
The application of the 'reasonable requirements test in practice : the approach of the courts post Sowden	260
Godbold v Mahmood	260
Walton v Calderdale Healthcare NHS Trust	261
Freeman v Lockett	261
Part 3: Claims for care in fatal cases	263
The present law	263
Evaluating the care of children in fatal cases	266

Chapter 14
Valuing aids and equipment — 269

Introduction	269
The test for recovery	269
Types of aids and equipment	270
The purpose of aids and equipment	272
The need for evidence	273
Medical evidence	273
Occupational therapy	273
Care	273
Accommodation	274
Speech and language therapy / assistive communication	274
Physiotherapy	274
Orthotics/prosthetics	274
Information technology	275
Witness evidence	275
Overlap with other claims	275
Care claims	275
Accommodation claims	276
Standard items	276
Travel and transport	276
Holidays	277
Contingency awards	278
State provision	278
Component parts of a claim	278
The assessment of past loss	279
The assessment of future loss: conventional lump sum	280
General principles	280
One-off items of future loss	280

Ongoing items of expense or loss	281
Delayed recurrent expenses and losses	282
Broad brush or global assessments	283
The assessment of future loss: periodical payments	283
The averaging method	283
The exact method	284
Responding to claims for aids and equipment	284
Worked examples	286
Example 1: A straightforward calculation using average annual expenditure	286
(i) Claimant's schedule	286
(ii) Defendant's counter-schedule	287
Example 2: A more complex calculation using periodic multipliers and discount factors	290
(i) Claimant's schedule	290
Example 2 (i) – Schedule of future aids and equipment	290
(ii) Defendant's counter schedule	294
Example 2 (ii) – Counter-schedule of future aids and equipment	294

Chapter 15
Housing — 301
Heads of claim	301
Adaption of existing accommodation	301
When are adaptions reasonably necessary?	301
Betterment of the property	302
Local authority grants and assistance	302
New accommodation	303
The problem of valuation	303
The solution	304
Test of reasonable necessity	304
Application of the formula	305
Deductions from the Roberts v Johnstone claim	306
More than one move	307
Ancillary costs	308
Running costs	308
Maintenance costs	309
Council tax	309
Utility bills	309
Insurance	309
Evidence	309
Local authority/housing association accommodation	310
Accommodation expert	311
Medical evidence	312
Care implications	313

Chapter 16
Recoupment of damages   **315**
Introduction   315
The basic framework   316
Cases in which the Act applies   316
Excluded compensation payments   317
Fatal Accident Act claims   317
Relevant benefits   318
Listed benefits are to be disregarded   318
Excluded benefits   319
Statutory sick pay   319
The 'relevant period'   319
CRU certificates   320
Defendant's liability   320
Offsetting   320
Examples of heads of compensation within Sch 2   321
    Gratuitous care   321
    Pension contributions   321
    Business rent   322
    Examples of heads of compensation outside Sch 2   322
    Interest on damages   323
    Interim payments   324
    Contributory negligence   324
    Judgments   324
    Part 36 Payments   324
    Reviews and appeals   326
       Reviews   326
       Appeals   327
    Variations of certificates   328

Chapter 17
Mentally incapable claimants and the Court of Protection   **329**
Introduction: The Mental Capacity Act 2005   329
The new measures   330
The core principles and overriding objectives of the new regime   330
Best interests   331
    The new definition of a person who is mentally incapable and for whom a special court procedure is appropriate – sections 2 and 3 of the Act.   331
    The principal functions of the new Court of Protection and likely practice   332
Protection from civil liability: general authority to act   333
Independent mental capacity advocates   334
Codes of Practice   335
The Public Guardian   335
Applications to the Court of Protection   335
The Court of Protection Rules 2007   336
Litigation friend   336

Directions 337
Appeals 337
Fees and costs 337
Fees and costs in the new Court of Protection 337
Fees relating to deputies and their supervision 337
    Fees relating to the new Court Reporting Service 339
The legal costs of applying to and attending court 339
The continuation of existing practice: a tentative review 339
The new definition of incapacity anticipated 341
Compromise and settlement 345
The litigation friend and the CPR 346
Potential heads of damage 347
Limitation and mentally incapable claimants 347

Chapter 18
Interest **349**
The statutory framework 349
Rates of interest 350
    General damages 350
    Special damages 350
    Tax 352
The effect of interim payments on interest 353
Delay 354
Relevance of payments by volunteers 355
Interest and social security benefits 356
Repayment of interest following reduction of award on appeal 356
Procedure 356

Chapter 19
Provisional damages **359**
Introduction 359
The legal framework 359
Procedural requirements 361

Chapter 20
Interim payments **363**
Introduction 363
    Definition and availability 363
    The Civil Procedure Rules on interim payments 363
    The preconditions 364
The requirements in detail 364
    Judgment and/or liability admitted 364
        If the action proceeded to trial, the claimant would obtain
            judgment for substantial damages 365
Two or more defendants 366
Judgment for 'substantial damages' 367
    Amount of interim payment/discretion 367
Social security benefits 369

Adjustment	369
Repayment	370
Variation or discharge	370
Payment as between defendants	370
Timing, tactics and mode of application	371
Timing/tactics	371
Mode of application	372
At the hearing	373
Interim payment by instalments	373
Other matters	373
Children/patients	373
Part 36 payments	374
Appeal	374

Chapter 21
Periodical payments — 375

Statutory provisions	375
Policy behind periodical payments	377
Advantages and disadvantages	377
The court's approach	382
Form of Order	383
Is there a need to consider life expectancy?	387
Security of payments	388
Security into the far future	392
The appropriate index	393
Variable orders	394
Agreements for variable orders	396
Assignment and charge of right to receive payments	398
Part 36 offers	399
Appeals	402
Interim payments	402

Chapter 22
Criminal injuries compensation — 405

Introduction	405
Sources of information: 'common law' Scheme	406
Sources of information: the 1996 and 2001 tariff Schemes	406
Guides	407
Who can recover	407
Living victims	407
Dead victims	407
'Criminal injury'	408
Crime of violence	408
Secondary victims	409
Eligibility: absolute bars	410
Eligibility: discretionary bars	411
Attributability	412
How much can be recovered?	413

The tariff injury award	413
Multiple injuries	414
Loss of earnings	414
Compensation for special expenses	414
Fatal cases	415
Multipliers for future loss	416
Deduction of benefits and other payments	416
Making a claim	417
Appeals to CICAP	417
Preparation of case before hearing	418
Procedure at the hearing	419
Medical evidence	420
Re-opening cases for medical deterioration	421
Further appeals	421
The future	421

Chapter 23
Rehabilitation 423

The Rehabilitation Code, early intervention and medical Treatment in Personal Injury Cases	426
1. Introduction	426
2. The claimant's solicitors duty	427
3. The insurer	428
4. Assessment	429
5. The assessment process	429
6. The assessment report	430
7. Recommendations	431

Part 3
Procedure

Chapter 24
Limitation: resume and update 2006 435

Policy and history	435
The primary limitation period	436
Negligence, nuisance and breach of statutory duty	438
'Consists of or includes damages in respect of personal injuries to the plaintiff or any other person'	439
Date of knowledge: Limitation Act 1980, s 11(4), s 14	442
'The date on which he first had knowledge of the following facts . . .' (s 14(1))	442
Significance: s 14(1)(a)	445
Significance and the 'injury in question'	450
Attributability: s 14(1)(b)	454
Identity: s 14(1)(c) and (d)	459
Constructive knowledge: s 14(3)	461
'Medical or other appropriate expert advice' (s 14(3)(b))	468
The proviso (s 14(3))	470

Limitation Act 1980, s 33: discretion, prejudice and 'all the
    circumstances of the case'   472
  The position 1979–2006 prior to Horton v Sadler   472
  Horton v Sadler   473
The exercise of discretion   473
  Prejudice   474
  Discretion generally   477
    Section 33(3)(a): 'The length of and reasons for the delay on the
      part of the Plaintiff'   479
    Section 33(3)(b): 'The extent to which having regard to the delay the
      evidence adduced or likely to be adduced by the Plaintiff or
      the Defendant is or is likely to be less cogent than if the
      action had been brought within the time allowed by
      Section 11'   481
    Section 33(3)(c): 'The conduct of the Defendant after the cause of
      action arose including the extent (if any) to which he
      responded to requests reasonably made by the Plaintiff for
      information or inspection for the purposes of ascertaining
      facts which were or might be relevant to the Plaintiff's cause
      of action'   482
    Section 33(3)(d): 'The duration of any disability of the Plaintiff
      arising after the date of the accrual of the cause of action'   482
    Section 33(3)(e): 'The extent to which the Plaintiff acted promptly
      and reasonably once he knew whether or not the act or
      omission of the Defendant, to which the injury was
      attributable, might be capable at that time as giving rise to an
      action for damages'   483
    Section 33(3)(f): 'The steps if any taken by the Plaintiff to obtain
      medical, legal or other advice and the nature of any such
      advice he may have received'   484
  'All the circumstances of the case'   484
Procedure   485
Special time limits   487

Chapter 25
Medical examinations   **489**
The purpose of a medical examination   489
The commissioning of a medical report   491
  Timing of the report   493
  Single joint expert   494
  Single expert   496
The requirement that a party undergo medical examination   497
Refusal to undergo medical examination   499
  General   499
  Refusal by the claimant to undergo examination   500
  Refusal by the claimant to undergo medical tests   500
  How is the test of reasonableness applied?   501

Imposing conditions	502
Attending with a companion	502
Attending with another doctor present	504
Refusal by a defendant	504
Mutual exchange	505

Chapter 26
Surveillance evidence — **507**

Introduction	507
The status, admissibility and disclosure of video evidence	508
The purpose of video evidence	511
When to use video evidence	512
By the claimant	512
The advantages	512
The disadvantages	513
By the defendant	513
The advantages	514
The disadvantages	515
Tactics for meeting video evidence	516
By the claimant	516
Anticipatory tactics	516
After disclosure of video evidence	517
The defendant	518
Video evidence under the CPR and costs issues	519
The impact of the Human Rights Act 1998	522
Conclusion	525

Chapter 27
Pre-action Protocols and the fast track — **527**

The overriding objective	527
The Protocols	529
Background to the Protocols – the court's approach	529
The Protocols in action	529
The Personal Injury Protocol	529
Specimen letters	530
The letter of claim	530
The defendant's letter	531
The scope of an admission	531
The Defendants' Guide	532
Disclosure of documents	532
Suggested documents	532
Schedule of damages	532
Joint selection of, and instructions to, experts	533
Consequences of unreasonable rejection of an expert	533
Medical notes	533
Permission to rely upon an expert	534
Amendments to reports	534
Exploiting the rules	534

Clarifying the expert's report	534
Rehabilitation	535
Alternative disputes resolution	535
Resolution of Issues	535
The Pre-action Protocol for the Resolution of Clinical Disputes	536
The structure of the Protocol	536
The aim of the Protocol	536
The status of the Protocol	536
Obtaining the healthcare records	536
Time limit for compliance	537
The letter of claim	537
Status of the letter of claim	538
Issuing after the letter of claim	538
Offers to settle	538
The defendant's response	538
The Guide to the Defendant's Response	538
Experts	539
Alternative disputes resolution	539
The Pre-action Protocol for Disease and Illness at Work Claims	539
Pre-action disclosure and inspection	541
The application	541
Inspection	541
The tracks	542
Part 27 – the small claims track	542
Part 28 – the fast track	542
Part 29 – the multi-track	542
Starting the action	543
The Claim Form Guide	543
The Practice Direction	543
The Particulars of Claim	544
The Guide to the Particulars of Claim	544
Statement of truth	545
Defending the action	545
Time limits	545
The contents of the defence	545
Disputing the valuation	546
Statement of Truth	546
The medical report	546
The Schedule of Special Damages	547
Reply	547
Allocation	547
Allocation factors of particular importance in the fast track	548
Fast track directions	549
Variation of directions	550
Failure to comply with directions	550
The pre-trial checklist	551
Fixing the trial	551
A typical timetable	551

Standard disclosure 551
   The duty of search 552
   The disclosure statement 552
   Miscellaneous disclosure points 553
   Taking the initiative 554
Interlocutory applications 554
   The procedure for making an application 554
   Requirements of the Application Notice 555
   Default judgment 555
   Setting aside default judgment 555
   Summary judgment 555
   Summary judgment procedure 556
   Interim payments 556
   Deduction of benefits 557
Experts 557
   Oral evidence 558
   The experts' meeting 558
Provisional damages 559
Costs: reasonableness and proportionality 559
   Fast track costs 559
   Fixed costs in road traffic accidents 560
   Conditional fee agreements 560
   Small claims costs 561
Appeal 561
   Procedural appeals 561

Chapter 28
Proceedings involving children **563**
The Litigation Friend 563
   No Litigation Friend 563
   Proceedings against children 564
   Appointment of Litigation Friend without court order 565
   Appointment of Litigation Friend by court order 566
   Replacement of Litigation Friend by court order 568
   Default proceedings where the child is the defendant 569
Compromise of claims involving children 571
   Settlement after commencement of action 572
   Settlement of claim prior to proceedings being brought 573
   Costs on settlement 575
   Court approval and the Fatal Accidents Act 1976 578
How money recovered is dealt with 580
What happens when a child reaches full age 582

Chapter 29
Offers to settle **585**
Introduction 585
The nature of a Part 36 Offer 585
The relevant period 586

Acceptance	586
Costs consequences of acceptance of an offer	587
Effect of the acceptance of a Part 36 offer	588
Withdrawal of Offers	588
When may an Offer be made?	588
Form and Content	589
General	589
Time when a Part 36 offer is made	590
Clarification	590
Deduction of benefit	590
Calculation of the amount of the recoverable benefit and the complication of contributory negligence	590
In what circumstances will a Court give effect to a non complying offer?	591
Future pecuniary loss claims	591
Costs consequences following judgment	592
Unjust to make the order	593
Provisional Damages	593
Transitional provisions	593

Chapter 30
Compensation for victims of uninsured or unidentifiable users of motor vehicles

	595
Introduction	595
The framework of European Union law	595
The framework	595
The Second Directive	595
The Third Directive	596
Interpretation of domestic law and other implementing measures, in accordance with the Directives if possible	596
UK State's failure to implement Directives	597
Consequences of failure to implement Directives	598
Directive of Direct Effect	598
Even if Directive not of direct effect	599
Illustration	599
Compulsory motor insurance in English law	600
The general rule	600
Exceptions to the general rule	601
Vehicles covered by deposit or used by certain public bodies	601
Liability which is or should be the subject of employers' liability insurance	601
Illustration	602
'Liability caused by, or arising out of, the use of the vehicle on a road or (from 3 April 2000) other public place'	602
'Liability'	602
'Caused by, or arising out of'	603
'Use'	603
'Road'	603

'Or other public place'	604
Insured, uninsured and unidentifiable users	604
The uninsured driver/user	605
Section 151 of the Road Traffic Act 1988	605
The Uninsured Drivers Agreements, the Article 75 insurer and the MIB	608
The Uninsured Drivers Agreements	608
'Article 75 insurer'	608
No 'Article 75 insurer'	608
The Uninsured Drivers Agreement 1988	609
Deductions	609
Conditions Precedent	609
Notice to whom?	610
The 'rule of meaningful degree'	611
The 'new procedure'	611
Reasonableness	612
Exclusions	612
The Uninsured Drivers Agreement 1999	613
Deductions	613
Conditions Precedent	613
The 'rule of meaningful degree' and the 'new procedure'	616
Reasonableness	616
Concessions in Revised Guidance Notes	616
Exclusions	617
Compliance by the claimant with Road Traffic Act 1988, ss 151 and 152 and the Uninsured Drivers Agreements	619
Claimant's only safe course	619
Claimant, having failed to comply, setting aside his own procedural steps and then complying	619
Limitation	619
Waiver or estoppel from reliance on condition precedent	619
European Directives & Human Rights Act 1998	620
Service of proceedings	620
Authority of Road Traffic Act insurer/Article 75 insurer/MIB to act on behalf of D	620
Authority from D or the court	620
Conflict of interest	621
Joinder of Road Traffic Act insurer/Article 75 insurer/ MIB	621
Interim payment	622
Recovery from D by Road Traffic Act insurer/Article 75 insurer/MIB	622
Under Road Traffic Act 1988, s 151	622
Under the Uninsured Drivers Agreements	622
But what if there is no judgment on quantum?	622
The 'untraced' ie unidentifiable driver/user	622
The Untraced Drivers Agreement 1996	623
Conditions Precedent	623
Reasonableness	624

Exclusions	624
Untraced Drivers Agreement 2003	625
Exclusions	627

Chapter 31
Fatal accident claims — 631

Introduction	631
Actions under the 1934 Act: actions for the benefit of the deceased's estate	632
Actions under the Fatal Accidents Act 1976	634
Bereavement	636
Loss of dependency	637
The multiplicand	639
The multiplier	642
Periodical payments	645
Apportionment	646
Funeral expenses	647
Benefits resulting from death	647
Contributory negligence	648
Interest	648
Actions under the Human Rights Act 1998	649

Chapter 32
Alternative dispute resolution — 653

Introduction: the purpose and structure of this chapter	653
Alternative dispute resolution and the CPR	654
The position pre CPR	654
The position post CPR	654
Definition of ADR in the CPR	655
Round table meetings	655
Mediations	656
How to negotiate	657
Introductory comments: a personal view	657
Flexibility and adaptability	657
The twin purpose of negotiations	657
Principles applicable to both round table meetings and mediations	658
Start of the meeting: dealing with any preliminary matters	658
Any discussion of legal/factual issues first	658
Authorities and instructions	659
The negotiations themselves	659
The starting point	659
Stages in the negotiation	659
Illustration	662
Costs sanctions for failure to negotiate	663
Introductory comments	663
The rules: CPR, r 44.3	665
The principles in the rules summarised	665

Halsey	666
Daniels	667
The trial	667
The costs issues at trial	668
The Court of Appeal's ruling	669
Conclusions	670

Part 4
Costs

Chapter 33
Costs

Costs	**675**
Introduction	675
The general rule	675
Entitlement to assessment and recovery	676
Exercise of discretion	677
Conduct of the parties	678
Effect of specific costs orders	679
Silence as to costs	681
Time for complying	681
Award of Costs: the court's discretion	681
Costs against non-parties – Aiden Shipping Co Ltd v Interbulk Ltd	681
Materials for exercising discretion	682
General principles	682
Failure to recover damages	683
Separate issues	683
Relevance of legal aid/LSC funding	683
Late amendment	683
Inflated claims: relevance of financial limits	684
Failure to mediate	684
Costs following allocation or re-allocation	684
Cases where costs orders are deemed to have been made	685
Courts' powers in relation to misconduct	685
Appeal against an order for costs	685
Guiding rules in particular circumstances: Interim hearings	686
Protective Costs Orders	686
Costs capping	687
Lockley orders	687
Counterclaim and set off	688
Part 20 proceedings	689
(i) General principles	689
Discontinuance of Part 20 claims	689
Multiple parties	689
(i) Co-defendants	689
(ii) Joint tortfeasors	690
Part 36 offers and Part 36 payments	690
Security for costs	690
Transfer of Proceedings	690

Costs of setting aside judgment	690
Varying an order for costs	691
Appeals and orders for costs	691
Security for costs of appeal	691
Appeals against orders for costs only	691
Fixed costs	692
Summary assessment of costs	693
Fast track costs	695
Basis of Assessment	696
Detailed assessment	697
Interest on costs	698

Chapter 34
Wasted costs and costs against non-parties 699

Wasted costs	699
Overview	699
A Statutory jurisdiction, s 51(6) of the Supreme Court Act 1981	699
The rules applicable to the statutory jurisdiction	700
Application in practice	702
Circumstances in which a wasted costs order is appropriate	704
Hopeless cases	706
Relevance of public funding; impecunious claimant; conditional fees	707
Reliance on counsel	707
Privilege	708
The second and third stages of the three-stage test	709
Amount of costs	709
B Inherent jurisdiction	709
C Section 51(1) and (3)	710
D CPR, r 44.14	710
Costs against non-parties	712
Generally	712
Jurisdiction	712
The Civil Procedure Rules	712
Principles	713
Application in practice	717

Chapter 35
Conditional fee agreements 719

The common law	719
The indemnity principle	719
Maintenance	719
Champerty	720
Statutory provisions	720
Requirements of primary legislation	722
General observations	722
Collective conditional fee agreements	723
Duties of legal advisers	724

The success rate	725
Fixed success fee	725
Road traffic accidents	725
Employers' liability	726
Employers' liability disease litigation	727
Success fees generally	727
Regulations	729
Conditional Fee Agreements Regulations 2000	730
Enforceability	730
After 1 November 2005	732
CFA Lite	733
Retrospective agreements	733
Assessment of costs	734
Disclosure of agreement	735
ATE insurance	735
Tribunals	736
Sources of information	736
Appendix 1	
CFA for use between solicitors and counsel on or after 1 November 2005	737
What is covered by this agreement	738
What is not covered by this agreement	738
Notes:	739
The solicitors firm acting for the client	741
Counsel's risk assessment	742
Ready reckoner	743
Appendix 2	
Standard terms and conditions posted on the APIL and PIBA websites and treated as annexed to the conditional fee agreement between solicitor and counsel for use after 1 November 2005	744
Part one: conditions precedent	744
Papers provided to Counsel	744
Solicitor's Compliance with Statute	744
Part two: obligations of counsel	744
To act diligently	744
Inappropriate Instructions	744
Part three	
Obligations of the solicitor	745
Part four	
Termination	747
Termination by Counsel	747
Termination by the Solicitor	747
Automatic Termination	748
Client becoming under a Disability	748
Counsel taking Silk	748
Part five	
Counsel's fees and expenses	748
Counsel's Normal Fees	748

Counsel's Success Fee	749
Counsel's Expenses	749
Part six	
Counsel's entitlement to fees	749
(A) If the Agreement is not Terminated	749
Definition of 'success'	749
Part 36 Offers and Payments	750
Failure	750
Errors and Indemnity for Fees	750
Adjudication on disagreement	751
(B) On Termination of the Agreement	751
Termination by Counsel	751
Termination by the Solicitor	752
Automatic Termination and Counsel taking silk	752
Challenge to fees	752
Return of Work	752
Part seven	
Assessment and payment of costs/fees	753
Costs Assessment	753
Solicitor's Obligation to pay	753
Interest	754
Challenge to Success Fee	754
Disclosing the reasons for the success fee	754
Reduction on Assessment	754
Agreement on Fees	755

Part 5
Human rights

Chapter 36
Human rights

Introduction	759
The key Convention rights	759
Article 6	760
Article 8	762
Article 2	763
Article 3	764
Article 1 Protocol 1	765
Article 14	766
The structure of the HRA 1998	766
Direct or indirect impact on legislation	766
Duty on public authorities	767
Claim for damages against public authorities	768
Not retroactive	770
Impact of the HRA on substantive law	770
Law of negligence	770
Nuisance claims	772
Inquests	773

Other claims under s 7	775
Impact of the HRA on procedural law	777
Ordinary case management decisions	777
Bringing more than 1 action	777
Limitation	778
Service	778
Amendment	779
Strike out/stay	779
Right to go to trial	780
Enforcing a foreign judgment	781
Evidence improperly obtained	781
Disclosure	782
Capacity	782
Funding	783
Index	**785**

TABLE OF STATUTES

References are to paragraph numbers.

Access to Justice Act 1999	33.8, 33.26, 33.39, 35.11, 35.15, 35.22, 35.36, 35.60
s 11	33.39
s 28	35.11, 35.22
s 29	35.75
s 30	35.23, 35.36
s 31	33.8, 35.62
s 119(1)	35.13
Administration of Justice Act 1965	18.10
Administration of Justice Act 1982	9.43, 11.7, 13.157, 31.5, 31.6, 31.7
s 1(1)(a)	9.43
s 1(1)(b)	9.43
s 3(1)	13.157
s 5	11.7
Care Standards Act 2000	13.74
Carers (Recognition and Services) Act 1995	13.74
Carers and Disabled Children Act 2000	13.74
Carriage by Air Act 1961	24.146
Carriage of Passengers by Road Act 1974	24.146
Children Act 1989	13.74, 13.86, 13.107, 13.108, 13.109, 13.110, 13.111, 13.112, 13.113, 13.114
s 17	13.109
s 17(7)	13.110
s 17(8)	13.110
s 17(11)	13.109
s 20	13.109
s 20(1)	13.109
s 29	13.110
s 29(1)	13.111
s 29(4)	13.111
Chronically Sick and Disabled Persons Act 1970	13.74, 13.103, 13.107, 13.109, 13.124, 15.7
s 2	13.93, 13.95, 13.124, 13.131
s 2(1)(e)	15.7
Civil Evidence Act 1995	10.7
s 1(1)	11.17
s 10	10.7
Civil Jurisdiction and Judgments Act 1982	8.33, 8.35
s 41	8.35
s 41(6))	8.35
Civil Jurisdiction and Judgments Act 1991	8.33
Civil Liability (Contribution) Act 1978	31.49, 33.46
s 4	33.46
Companies Act 1981	
s 51	33.8
s 51(1))	33.18
Companies Act 1985	24.144
s 33	24.144
s 651	24.144
Congenital Disabilities (Civil Liability) Act 1976	4.10
s 1(2)	4.10
Consumer Protection Act 1987	8.4, 8.25, 24.5, 24.7, 24.146
s 1(1)	8.4, 8.26
s 4(1)(e)	8.25, 8.26
s 11A)	24.7
County Courts Act 1984	18.1, 18.5, 18.34, 18.36, 19.3, 19.11, 21.66, 33.79
s 51	19.3, 19.11, 21.66
s 69	18.1, 18.34, 18.36
s 69(2)	18.1
s 74	33.79
Courts Act 2003	13.48, 13.51, 13.52, 17.80, 21.2, 21.7, 31.39
s 100	13.48, 13.52, 17.80, 21.2, 21.7
s 101	13.48, 17.80, 21.2
Courts and Legal Services Act 1990	34.56, 35.11, 35.15, 35.76, 35.77
s 4	34.56
s 51	34.56, 34.57
s 58	35.10, 35.12, 35.15, 35.52
s 58(1)	35.12
s 58(3)(c)	35.52
s 58B	35.11
s 58B(6)	35.13
Criminal Injuries Compensation Act 1995	16.7, 22.1
Crown Proceedings Act 1947	36.10, 36.43
s 10	36.10
Damages Act 1996	10.8, 10.9, 12.3, 13.48, 13.51, 13.52, 13.57, 14.29, 18.7, 21.2, 21.7, 21.15, 21.17, 21.38, 21.42, 21.51, 21.77, 31.12, 31.39
s 1	10.8, 10.9, 14.29
s 1(1)	10.10
s 1(2)	10.9, 10.10
s 2	21.2, 31.39
s 2(1)	13.52, 21.7, 31.39

Damages Act 1996—*continued*
s 2(1)(b)	21.17
s 2(2)	21.7
s 2(3)	13.52, 21.7
s 2(3))	21.38
s 2(4)	13.52, 21.38, 21.43, 21.46, 21.77
s 2(4)(b)	21.40, 21.43
s 2(4)(c)	21.45
s 2(5)(d)	26.27
s 2(6)	21.15
s 2(8)	13.52, 13.57, 21.51, 21.56
s 2(9)	13.52, 13.57, 21.15, 21.51
s 2A(2)	21.43
s 2A(5)	21.94
s 2B	13.52, 26.27
s 3	31.12
s 4	21.42
s 6	13.52, 21.39
s 7	31.39

Disabled Persons (Services, Consultation and Representation) Act 1986   13.74

Employment Rights Act 1996	7.20
s 230	7.20
European Communities Act 1972	8.4

Factories Act 1961   7.54, 7.67, 7.72, 7.78, 7.89
s 29	7.78
s 63	7.78

Fatal Accidents Act 1959
s 2	13.159

Fatal Accidents Act 1976   4.10, 9.58, 10.7, 10.28, 13.152, 13.153, 13.154, 13.157, 18.13, 20.45, 24.6, 27.58, 27.101, 28.80, 28.81, 28.82, 28.83, 28.84, 28.85, 28.86, 28.87, 29.5, 31.2, 31.5, 31.9, 31.10, 31.11, 31.12, 31.13, 31.14, 31.15, 31.16, 31.17, 31.18, 31.19, 31.20, 31.21, 31.22, 31.23, 31.24, 31.25, 31.26, 31.27, 31.28, 31.29, 31.30, 31.31, 31.32, 31.33, 31.34, 31.35, 31.36, 31.37, 31.38, 31.39, 31.40, 31.41, 31.42, 31.43, 31.44, 31.45, 31.46, 31.47, 31.48, 31.50, 36.59

3(3)	31.32
s 1(1)	31.10, 31.12
s 1(2)	31.16
s 1A	31.5, 31.14
s 2	31.40
s 2(3)	28.83, 36.65
s 3	31.17
s 3(2)	31.18
s 3(3)	13.165, 31.31
s 4	13.157, 13.158, 13.159, 13.160, 13.162, 13.165, 31.32, 31.44, 31.45
s 5	4.10, 31.47
s 8	13.14, 13.20

Financial Services and Markets
Act 2000	13.52, 21.40
s 213	13.52, 21.40
Foreign Limitation Periods Act 1984	24.148

Health and Safety at Work etc
Act 1974	7.2, 7.86
s 16	7.14
s 47	7.27

Health and Social Care (Community Health and Standards)
Act 2003	13.80
s 150	13.80
Health and Social Care Act 2001	13.74, 13.89, 13.100
s 53	13.89
s 57	13.100

Health and Social Services and Social Security Adjudications
Act 1983   13.74, 13.86, 13.95, 13.96, 13.97, 13.98, 13.121, 13.122, 13.123, 13.132, 15.7
s 17	13.97, 13.98, 13.101, 13.103, 13.105, 13.106, 13.107, 13.108, 13.116, 13.123, 13.124, 13.125, 13.132, 15.7
s 17(1)	13.116
s 17(2)	13.107, 13.108

Health Services and Public Health
Act 1968	13.87
s 45	13.87

Housing Grants, Construction and
Regeneration Act 1996	15.6, 15.7
s 23(1)	15.6
s 30	15.7
s 51	15.7

Human Fertilisation and Embryology
Act 1990	17.18

Human Rights Act 1998   24.4, 26.15, 26.41, 26.42, 30.65, 30.66, 30.72, 30.73, 30.98, 31.2, 31.32, 31.48, 31.49, 36.1, 36.2, 36.3, 36.4, 36.5, 36.6, 36.7, 36.8, 36.9, 36.10, 36.11, 36.12, 36.13, 36.14, 36.15, 36.16, 36.17, 36.18, 36.19, 36.20, 36.21, 36.22, 36.23, 36.24, 36.25, 36.26, 36.27, 36.28, 36.29, 36.30, 36.31, 36.32, 36.33, 36.34, 36.35, 36.36, 36.37, 36.38, 36.39, 36.40, 36.41, 36.42, 36.43, 36.44, 36.45, 36.46, 36.47, 36.48, 36.49, 36.50, 36.51, 36.52, 36.53, 36.54, 36.55, 36.56, 36.57, 36.58, 36.59, 36.60, 36.61, 36.62, 36.63, 36.64, 36.65, 36.66, 36.67, 36.68, 36.69, 36.70, 36.71, 36.72, 36.73, 36.74, 36.75, 36.76, 36.77, 36.78, 36.79, 36.80, 36.81, 36.82, 36.83, 36.84, 36.85, 36.86, 36.87

s 3	36.31, 36.40, 36.68, 36.69
s 3(1)	36.29, 36.32
s 4	36.32
s 4(4)	36.30
s 6	31.49, 36.33, 36.50
s 6(1)	31.49, 36.36, 36.37
s 6(3)(a)	36.35
s 6(3)(b)	36.34

Table of Statutes

Human Rights Act 1998—*continued*
s 7   31.49, 36.39, 36.45, 36.50, 36.54, 36.58, 36.60
s 7(1)(a)   31.51
s 7(5)   31.51, 36.39
s 8   31.49, 31.51
s 8(3)   31.51

Income and Corporation Taxes Act 1988   21.51
s 833(2)   21.51

Judgments Act 1838   33.79
s 17   33.79

Law Reform (Contributory Negligence) Act 1945   3.46, 4.1, 13.66, 31.47
s 1   4.11, 13.66
s 1(1)   3.46, 4.1, 31.47
s 4   4.1, 4.3, 4.8
Law Reform (Miscellaneous Provisions) (Scotland) Act 1940
s 3   31.49
Law Reform (Miscellaneous Provisions) Act 1934   10.7, 18.4, 18.5, 29.5, 31.2, 31.47
s 1(2)(c)   31.2
s 3   18.4
s 3(1A)   18.4
Law Reform (Miscellaneous Provisions) Act 1971   24.2
Law Reform (Personal Injuries) Act 1948
s 2(1)   16.1
s 2(4)   13.81, 13.82, 13.127, 14.24
s 2(5)   13.159
Legal Aid Act 1988   28.92, 33.39, 33.63
s 17(1)   33.39
Limitation Act 1623
s 7   24.1
Limitation Act 1963
s 7(5)   24.70
Limitation Act 1975
s 2D   24.93
Limitation Act 1976
s 11   31.11
Limitation Act 1980   4.11, 17.53, 17.65, 17.91, 17.95, 24.4, 24.5, 24.6, 24.10, 24.11, 24.13, 24.16, 24.48, 24.90, 24.91, 24.98, 24.126, 24.128, 24.138, 24.147, 30.69, 30.70, 36.67, 36.69
s 2   24.11, 24.12, 24.13, 36.67
s 5   24.13
s 9   24.147
s 10   4.11
s 11   24.6, 24.10, 24.11, 24.12, 24.13, 24.14, 24.35, 24.41, 24.108, 24.118
s 11(1A)   24.147
s 11(4)   24.16
s 11(5)   24.6

Limitation Act 1980—*continued*
s 11A   24.5
s 12   24.108
s 12)   24.6
s 14   24.16, 24.28, 24.35, 24.37, 24.40, 24.41, 24.47, 24.48, 24.51, 24.76, 24.83, 24.85, 24.86, 24.87, 24.88, 24.89, 24.90, 24.139, 30.70
s 14(1)   24.17
s 14(1)(a)   24.23, 24.34, 24.40
s 14(1)(b)   24.19, 24.40, 24.43, 24.44, 24.88
s 14(1)(c)   24.52, 24.57, 24.78
s 14(1A)   24.5
s 14(2)   24.24, 24.34, 24.40, 24.42, 24.73
s 14(3)   24.30, 24.32, 24.42, 24.57, 24.58, 24.62, 24.70, 24.71, 24.73, 24.84, 24.85
s 14(3)(b)   24.74, 24.75, 24.76, 24.78
s 14(3)(c)   24.57
s 14(3)(d)   24.74
s 14A   24.48, 24.51
s 28(6)   24.9
s 33   24.11, 24.16, 24.37, 24.70, 24.90, 24.91, 24.92, 24.94, 24.96, 24.98, 24.99, 24.100, 24.101, 24.102, 24.103, 24.105, 24.107, 24.109, 24.112, 24.123, 24.138, 24.139, 24.141, 24.143, 30.69
s 33(3)   24.97, 24.107, 24.108, 24.110
s 33(3)(a)   24.113, 24.128, 24.137
s 33(3)(b)   24.100, 24.118
s 33(3)(c)   24.121
s 33(3)(d)   24.125
s 33(3)(e)   24.128, 24.132
s 33(3)(f)   24.133, 24.136
s 35   24.5, 36.69
s 35(5)   36.69
s 38   17.65, 17.91, 24.13, 24.15
s 38(2)   24.126, 24.128
s 39   24.145
Local Authority Social Services Act 1970   13.95, 13.116
s 7(1)   13.95, 13.116

Mental Capacity Act 2005   17.1, 17.2, 17.3, 17.7, 17.9, 17.10, 17.11, 17.12, 17.13, 17.14, 17.15, 17.16, 17.17, 17.18, 17.19, 17.20, 17.25
s 1   17.6
s 2   17.9
s 3   17.10
s 4   17.7
s 16   17.15, 17.19
s 27   17.18
s 35   17.22
s 49   17.29, 17.48
s 51   17.31
s 57   17.27
s 58   17.28
s 68   17.4
Mental Health Act 1983   13.87, 13.108, 13.112, 15.37, 17.14, 17.54, 17.60, 17.65, 17.66, 17.91, 24.9
s 1   17.54

Mental Health Act 1983—*continued*
 s 1(2) 17.54
 s 28 17.65
 s 94(2) 17.65, 17.66
 s 98 17.60
 s 117 13.87, 13.112, 15.37
Merchant Shipping Act 1995 24.146
 s 183 24.146
 s 190 24.146

National Assistance Act 1948 13.74, 13.84,
 13.86, 13.87, 13.88, 13.94, 13.95,
 13.103, 13.107, 13.112, 13.120,
 13.122, 13.123, 13.127, 13.138,
 13.139, 13.150, 13.152, 15.37
 s 21 13.93, 13.97, 13.103, 13.107, 13.123,
 13.132, 13.133, 13.136, 13.143,
 13.145, 13.151, 15.37
 s 21(1) 13.88, 13.138, 13.139
 s 21(1)(a) 13.89
 s 21(2A) 13.89
 s 22 13.97, 13.112, 13.123, 13.127
 s 22(1) 13.90
 s 22(5) 13.91
 s 29 13.93, 13.94, 13.95, 13.96, 13.97,
 13.103, 13.123, 13.127, 13.131,
 13.132, 13.133, 13.150, 13.151,
 13.152
 s 29(1) 13.96
National Health Service Act 1946 13.75
National Health Service Act 1977 13.74,
 13.75, 13.81, 13.86, 13.87, 13.107,
 13.108
 s 1 13.79
 s 1(2) 13.76
 s 2 13.79
 s 3(1) 13.77
 s 21 13.87
 s 23 13.75, 13.79
 s 63) 13.78
 s 64) 13.78
 s 65) 13.78
 s 80 13.77, 13.78
National Health Service and
 Community Care Act 1990 13.84,
 13.86, 13.87, 13.127
 s 46 13.87
 s 47 13.87
 s 47(1) 13.127
NHS and Community Care Act 1990
 s 47 13.100
Nuclear Installations Act 1965 24.146

Occupiers' Liability Act 1984 2.26

Powers of Criminal Courts Act 1973
 s 35 16.7
Protection from Harassment
 Act 1997 24.147
 s 3 24.147

Road Traffic Act 1988 20.18, 30.1, 30.6, 30.9,
 30.15, 30.19, 30.25, 30.27, 30.28,
 30.30, 30.32, 30.33, 30.35, 30.40,
 30.42, 30.44, 30.45, 30.46, 30.47,
 30.48, 30.55, 30.56, 30.66, 30.67,
 30.77, 30.82, 30.83
 s 143 30.25
 s 144 30.27, 30.56, 30.66
 s 145 30.25
 s 145(4)(a) 30.28, 30.30
 s 148 30.44
 s 148(2) 30.44
 s 148(5) 30.44
 s 151 20.18, 30.15, 30.16, 30.32, 30.33,
 30.35, 30.44, 30.45, 30.46, 30.48,
 30.66, 30.82
 s 151(4) 30.48
 s 151(7) 30.83
 s 151(8) 30.9, 30.77
 s 152 30.66, 30.69
 s 152(1)(a) 30.48, 30.55
 s 152(1)(c) 30.48
 s 152(2) 30.48
 s 192(1) 30.40

Social Security (Recovery of Benefits)
 Act 1997 16.2, 20.31, 29.22
 s 1 16.5, 16.6, 29.22
 s 1(2) 16.6
 s 3 16.4, 16.13
 s 3(2) 16.13
 s 3(4) 16.13
 s 4(1) 16.4
 s 6 16.41, 20.31
 s 7 16.15
 s 7(4) 16.15
 s 7(6) 16.15
 s 8 16.16, 16.24, 16.26, 16.28, 16.31, 16.43
 s 10 16.35
 s 11 16.40
 s 12(3) 16.41
 s 15 16.24
 s 16 16.26
 s 17 16.4, 16.10
Social Security Act 1989 16.1
Social Security Act 1998 16.3
Social Security Administration
 Act 1992 16.1, 16.9
 s 103 16.9, 16.16
 s 104 16.9, 16.16
 s 105 16.9
Solicitors Act 1974 35.16, 35.76
 s 57 35.16, 35.76
 s 58(5) 35.16
Supreme Court 1981
 s 35A 18.1
 s 35A(2) 18.1
Supreme Court Act 1981 18.5, 18.34, 19.3,
 19.11, 20.2, 21.66, 27.58, 33.3,
 34.1, 34.2, 34.3, 34.5, 34.29, 34.30,
 34.34, 34.35, 34.37
 s 18 34.32
 s 32(5) 20.2
 s 32A 19.3, 19.11, 21.66, 27.58

Supreme Court Act 1981—*continued*		Supreme Court Act 1981—*continued*	
s 35A	18.34	s 58(3)(c)	34.48
s 51	34.3, 34.29, 34.37, 34.46, 35.62		
s 51(1)	33.3, 34.1, 34.29, 34.30, 34.34, 34.35, 34.43	Taxation of Chargeable Gains Act 1992	18.17
s 51(3)	34.1, 34.47	s 51(2)	18.17
s 51(6)	34.1, 34.2, 34.4, 34.5, 34.7, 34.29, 34.30	Terrorism Act 2000	30.98
		s 1	30.98
s 53	34.6		
s 58	34.48	Vaccine Damage Payments Act 1979	16.7

TABLE OF STATUTORY INSTRUMENTS

References are to paragraph numbers.

Access to Justice Act 1999
(Commencement No 10)
Order 2003, SI 2003/1241   35.62

Civil Procedure (Amendment No 2)
Rules 2003, SI 2003/1242   35.62
Civil Procedure (Amendment No 3)
Rules 2005, SI 2005/2292   33.38
Civil Procedure (Amendment No 4)
Rules 2004, SI 2004/3419   20.7, 28.79
Civil Procedure Rules 1998   28.2
Civil Procedure Rules 1998,
SI 1998/3132   5.1, 9.16, 14.3, 23.3, 24.8, 25.1, 26.4, 27.2, 30.74, 32.4, 33.1, 34.1
   r 8(1)(b)   5.31
   r 11(2)   28.83
   r 12   27.94, 27.95, 28.31, 28.32, 33.56
   r 13   27.96
   r 14   28.34, 28.35, 28.44, 33.56
   r 16   11.2, 18.34, 18.35, 19.10, 27.53, 27.56, 27.61, 27.63
   r 19   30.79
   r 21   28.3, 28.4, 28.5, 28.6, 28.7, 28.8, 28.9, 28.10, 28.13, 28.14, 28.16, 28.18, 28.19, 28.20, 28.21, 28.25, 28.26, 28.27, 28.28, 28.36, 28.39, 28.46, 28.47, 28.53, 28.54, 28.70, 28.74, 28.75, 28.79, 28.86, 28.88, 28.89, 28.100, 28.101, 28.102, 28.103
   r 22   27.64
   r 23   27.92, 27.93, 27.98, 28.21
   r 24   20.13, 20.14, 27.97, 27.98
   r 25   18.21, 20.1, 20.3, 20.4, 20.5, 20.7, 20.8, 20.11, 20.17, 20.18, 20.21, 20.22, 20.23, 20.32, 20.33, 20.36, 20.38, 20.43, 20.44, 20.45, 20.46, 20.49, 20.53, 27.49, 27.100, 30.82, 33.48
   r 26   25.7, 25.8, 27.50, 27.51, 27.52, 27.69, 27.70, 27.71
   r 27   20.10, 20.20, 25.7
   r 28   27.74, 27.75, 27.79, 27.82
   r 29   34.17
   r 31   5.48, 26.5, 27.48, 27.84, 27.86, 27.87, 27.88
   r 32   28.23
   r 33   26.7, 26.9

Civil Procedure Rules 1998,
SI 1998/3132—*continued*
   r 35   5.3, 5.4, 5.5, 5.12, 5.15, 5.19, 5.20, 5.23, 5.33, 5.39, 5.46, 5.50, 25.1, 25.5, 25.17, 25.18, 25.28, 25.42, 27.27, 27.74, 27.78, 27.88, 27.104, 27.108
   r 35(10)(3)   5.30
   r 36   16.28, 16.30, 21.77, 21.78, 21.80, 21.81, 21.82, 21.83, 26.27, 27.109, 28.50, 29.3, 29.14, 33.31
   r 36.23   16.27
   r 36(1)   33.21
   r 36(4)   33.31
   r 38   20.33, 33.31
   r 39   28.51
   r 40   33.40, 33.51
   r 41   19.12, 21.4, 21.5, 21.10, 21.15, 21.18, 21.24, 21.25, 21.30, 21.56, 21.71, 21.78
   r 44   20.2, 26.33, 26.34, 26.39, 26.54, 27.110, 28.78, 32.36, 32.38, 32.39, 32.48, 33.3, 33.4, 33.10, 33.11, 33.13, 33.15, 33.25, 33.26, 33.30, 33.31, 33.32, 33.49, 33.52, 33.70, 33.79, 34.1, 34.6, 34.30, 34.31, 34.32, 34.33
   r 45   27.113, 28.78
   r 46   27.111, 33.40, 33.66, 33.67, 33.68, 33.69
   r 47   28.64, 33.75, 33.76, 34.33
   r 47(1)   33.74
   r 48   28.63, 28.64, 28.65, 33.9, 33.19, 33.76, 33.77, 34.4, 34.5, 34.6, 34.10, 34.12, 34.28, 34.36, 34.37
   r 51   28.65
   r 52   24.139
   r 53   5.48
Community Legal Service (Costs)
Regulations 2000   33.16
   reg 5   33.16
Construction (Health, Safety and
Welfare) Regulations 1996,
SI 1996/1592   7.3
Control of Substances Hazardous to
Health Regulations 2002,
SI 2002/2677   7.78

Electricity at Work Regulations 1989,
SI 1989/635   7.3

European Communities (Rights
  against Insurers)
  Regulations 2002, SI 2002/3061   8.43

Health and Safety
  Manual Handling Operations
    Regulations 1992,
    SI 1992/2793   7.37
    reg 4(1)   7.41
    reg 4(1)(b)(ii)   7.43
Health and Safety (Display Screen
  Equipment) Regulations 1992,
  SI 1992/2792   7.3, 7.31
Health and Safety (Miscellaneous
  Amendments)
  Regulations 2002, SI 2002/2174   7.37

Lifting Operations and Lifting
  Equipment Regulations 1998,
  SI 1998/2307   7.3

Management of Health and Safety at
  Work and Fire Precautions
  (Workplace) (Amendment)
  Regulations 2003, SI 2003/2457   7.3
Management of Health and Safety at
  Work Regulations 1999,
  SI 1999/3242   7.3
Manual Handling Operations
  Regulations 1992   7.3, 8.27

National Assistance (Residential
  Accommodation) (Disregarding
  of Resources) (England)
  Regulations 2001, SI 2001/3067
  reg 21   13.92, 13.103

Package Travel, Package Holidays and
  Package Tours
  Regulations 1992, SI 1992/3288
    reg 2(1)   8.41
    reg 15(1)   8.40
    reg 15(2)   8.41
Personal Protective Equipment at
  Work Regulations 1992, SI
    1992/2966   7.3
    reg 1(1)   7.59
    reg 4(1)   7.62
    reg 5(2)   7.60
    reg 7(1)   7.65, 8.30
    reg 10(1)   7.64
Personal Protective Equipment
  Regulations 2002, SI 2002/1144   7.59
Provision and Use of Work Equipment
  Regulations, SI 1998/2306   7.3
    reg 3(3)   7.47
    reg 5   7.51
    reg 6(1)   8.28
    reg 11   7.51, 7.52

Social Security (Recovery of Benefits)
  Regulations 1997, SI 1997/2205
    reg 8(1)(c)   16.26
    reg 8(2)   16.26

Working Time Regulations 1998,
  SI 1998/1833   7.3
Workplace (Health, Safety and
  Welfare) Regulations 1992,
  SI 1992/3004   7.3
    reg 4(1)   7.67
    reg 12   7.72
    reg 12(2)(a)   7.78

TABLE OF CASES

References are to paragraph numbers.

A (1), B (2) and others v A Teaching Hospital NHS Trust [2003] EWHC 1034	33.38
A and B v United Kingdom (1998) 1 EHRR 82	34.27
A Health Authority v X and others [2001] 2 FLR 673	36.80
A J Fahani v Merc Property Ltd (1999) Times May 19	34.8
A v B NHS Hospitals Trust (Lawtel, 17 June 2004, Document No AM0200683)	11.32, 13.152, 14.13
A v Hoare [2006] 1 WLR 2320	36.67
A v Iorworth Hoare [2006] EWCA Civ 395	24.12
A v UK (Human Rights: Punishment of Child) [1998] 2 FLR 959, [1998] Fam Law 733; sub nom A v UK (1999) 27 EHRR 611, ECHR	36.23
A v X & B (Non party) [2004] EWHC 447	36.81
Aaron v Shelton [2004] EWHC 1162 (QB)	33.12
ABTA v CAA [2006] EWHC 13	8.41
Ackbar v C F Green & Co Ltd [1975] QB 582, [1975] 2 All ER 65	24.13, 24.37
Adams v Bracknell Forest Borough Council [2004] UKHL 29, [2005] 1 AC 76, [2004] 3 All ER 897, [2004] ELR 459, [2005] PIQR 11	24.16, 24.30, 24.42, 24.69, 24.74, 24.81, 24.105
Adams v London Improved Motor Coach Builders Ltd [1921] KB 495	33.9, 35.5
Admiralty Commissioners v SS Amerika [1917] AC 38	31.1
Adoko v Hussein Jemal (1999) *The Times*, July 8	27.6
AEI Rediffusion Music Ltd v Phonographic Performance Ltd [1999] 1 WLR 1507, [1999] 2 All ER 299, [1999] CPLR 551, CA	33.5
Afzal v Ford Motor Co Ltd [1994] 4 All ER 720, [1994] PIQR P418, (1994) *The Times*, 6 July, CA	33.28
Aiden Shipping Co Ltd v Interbulk Ltd [1986] AC 965, [1986] 2 WLR 1051, [1986] 2 All ER 409, HL	33.17, 34.34
Airey v UK (1979) 2 EHRR 305	36.85
Alan Jackson v Marley Davenport Limited [2004] EWCA Civ 1225	5.50
Alan Phillips Associates v Dowling & Ors 12 January 2007, CA (Civ Div)	34.45
Alcock v Chief Constable of South Yorkshire Police [1992] 1 AC 310	1.22, 6.4, 36.55
Allen v Bloomsbury Health Authority [1993] 1 All ER 651	24.15
Alltrans Express Ltd v CVA Holdings Ltd [1984] 1 WLR 394, [1984] 1 All ER 685, CA	33.24, 33.55
Almond v Leeds Western Health Authority [1990] 1 Med LR 370	15.5, 15.13, 15.16
Anderson v Davis [1993] PIQR Q87	11.56
Anderton v Clwyd County Council (No 2) [2001] CP Rep 110, QBD, [2002] EWCA Civ 933, [2002] 1 WLR 3174, [2002] 3 All ER 813, CA	36.68
Anderton v Clywyd, Phelps v Hillingdon London Borough Council [2001] AC 619	24.16
Andrews v Freeborough [1967] 1 QB 1	9.33
Andrews v Reading BC [2004] EWHC 970	36.51
Andrews v Schooling [1991] 3 All ER 723	20.12, 20.14
Anufrijeva v Southwark LBC [2004] QB 1124	36.15, 36.23
Appleby v Walsall Health Authority [1999] Lloyd's Rep Med 154	24.22
Arafa v Potter [1994] PIQR Q73, [1995] IRLR 316, CA	9.10, 9.13, 9.14
Arkin v (1) Borchard Lines Ltd (2) Zim Israel Navigation Company Ltd & others [2005] EWCA Civ 655	34.38, 34.50
Arnold v Central Electricity Generating Board [1998] AC 228	24.4
Arrow Nominees v Blackledge TLR 7.7.2000	36.71

Arthur J S Hall & Co (a firm) v Simons; Barratt v Ansell (trading as Woolf Seddon (a firm)); Harris v Scholfield Roberts & Hill (a firm) [2002] 1 AC 615, [2000] 3 All ER 673, HL 5.24, 36.41
Ashingdane v UK (1985) 7 EHRR 528 36.8
Ashworth v Peterborough United Football Club Ltd SCCO 10 June 2002 35.72
Aspinall v Sterling Mansell Ltd [1981] 3 All ER 866 25.63
Aston Cantlow PCC v Wallbank [2004] 1 AC 546 36.34
Atack v Lee [2005] 1 WLR 2643 35.32, 35.35
ATH v MS [2002] EWCA Civ 792, [2003] QB 965 [2003] PIQR Q1 10.34, 13.65, 13.159, 13.164, 13.168
Atkinson v Anor v Seghal [2003] EWCA Civ 697 6.71
Atkinson v Oxfordshire Health Authority [1993] 4 Med LR 18 24.123
Auty v National Coal Board [1985] 1 WLR 784, [1985] 1 All ER 930, (1985) 129 SJ 249, CA 11.39, 12.1, 14.30
Avery v London and North Eastern Railway Company [1938] AC 606 28.84
Avon County Council v Hooper [1997] 1 All ER 532, [1997] 1 WLR 1605, [1997] 25 BMLR 26, CA 13.103, 13.73, 13.104, 15.7
Awwad v Geraghty & Co [2001] QB 570 35.8

B v (1) Richard Pendelbury, (2) Associated Newspapers [2002] EWHC 1404 34.8
B v B [2001] 1 FLR 843 34.7, 34.8
Bahai v Rashidian [1985] 1 WLR 1337 34.53
Baig v City and Hackney Health Authority [1994] 5 Med LR 221 24.115, 24.121
Bailey v IBC Vehicles Ltd [1998] 3 All ER 570, (1998) 142 SJLB 126, [1998] 2 Costs LR 46, (1998) *The Times*, 9 April, CA 33.9
Bailey v Warren [2005] PIQR P15 17.68
Baker v Bolton (1808) 1 Camp 493 31.1
Baker v Hopkins. [1959] 1 WLR 966 6.39
Baker v Willoughby [1970] AC 467, [1970] 2 WLR 50, [1969] 3 All ER 1528, HL 3.7, 3.8
Ball v Street [2005] EWCA Civ 76, [2005] PIQR P342 7.47, 7.53, 7.57, 8.31
Bank or Baroda v Panessar [1987] Ch 335 33.72
Bankamerica Finance Ltd v Nock [1988] AC 1002 33.44
Barber v RJB Mining (UK) Ltd [1999] ICR 679 7.95
Barber v Somerset County Council [2004] 1 WLR 1089, [2004] 2 All ER 385, [2004] UKHL 13, HL 2.34
Barclays Bank Ltd v Fairclough Building Ltd [1995] QB 214 4.8
Barnes v Nayer *The Times*, December 19, 1986, CA 4.52
Barnett v Kensington and Chelsea Hospital Management Committee [1969] 1 QB 428 3.4
Baron v Lovell [1999] CPLR 630, [2000] PIQR P20, CA 5.17, 27.108, 27.118
Barrand v British Cellophane plc (1995) *The Times*, February 16 24.104
Barrett v LB of Enfield [2001] 2 AC 550 36.41
Bartlett v Barclays Bank Trust Co Ltd (No 2) [1980] 2 All ER 92 33.71
Base Metal Trading Ltd v Ruslan Borisovich Shamurin [2003] EWHC 2606 33.21
Base Metal Trading Ltd v Shamurin (No 3) [2003] EWHC 2602 (Comm) 33.12
Bassie v Merseyside Fire and Civil Defence Authority [2005] EWCA Civ 1474 7.72
Bater v Newbold (1991) Lexis, 30 July 1991 24.120, 24.127
Bates v Leicester Health Authority [1998] Lloyd's Rep Med 93 24.22, 24.68, 24.81
Baugh v Delta Water Fittings Ltd [1971] 1 WLR 1295; [1971] 3 All ER 258 25.55
Baxter v Woolcombers (1963) 107 SJ 553 4.24
BCCI v Ali (No 3) [1999] 4 All ER 83 25.20
Beck v Ministry of Defence [2003] EWCA Civ 1043, [2003] CP Rep 62, [2004] PIQR 1, (2003) 100(31) LSG 31 5.50, 25.27, 25.40
Begum v Barnet & Chase Farm Hospital [2005] EWHC 3383 21.43
Bell v Todd [2002] LR Med 12 13.123
Bennett v Greenland Houchen & Company [1999] PIQR P120 24.13
Bensaid v UK (2001) 33 EHRR 205 36.14
Bensusan v Freedman SCCO 20 August 2001 35.41
Bentley v Bristol and Western Health Authority (No 2) [1991] 3 Med LR 1 24.89
Bentley v Bristol and Western Health Authority [1991] 2 Med LR 359 24.134
Beoco v Alfa Laval Ltd [1995] QB 137 33.27
Bermuda International Securities Limited v KPMG (a firm) [2001] EWCA Civ 269, [2001] CP Rep 73, [2001] CPLR 252, [2001] Lloyds Rep PN 392, CA 27.47
Besterman v British Motor Cab Co Ltd [1914] 3 KB 181 33.45

Bhamjee v Forsdick (No 2) [2003] EWCA Civ 1113, [2004] 1 WLR 88, [2003] BPIR 1252,
 [2003] All ER (D) 429 (Jul), CA 36.76
Bier v Mines de Potasse d'Alsace [1978] QB 708 8.36
Biesheuvel v Birrell [1999] PIQR Q40 14.21, 15.21, 15.26, 15.35
Biguzzi v Rank Leisure plc [1999] 1 WLR 1926 27.7
Billings (A C) & Sons Ltd v Riden [1958] AC 240, [1957] 3 All ER 1, HL 4.17, 4.20
Birch v Hales Containers Ltd [1996] PIQR P307 26.12
Birkett v Hayes [1982] 1WLR 816 18.6
Bishop v Hannaford 21 December 1988, unreported 14.24
Black v Yates [1992] QB 526, [1991] 3 WLR 90, [1991] 4 All ER 722, QBD 28.47
Blair v Michelin Tyre 25 January 2002, unreported 14.42
Blake v Galloway [2004] EWCA Civ 814, [2004] 3 All ER 315, [2004] 1 WLR 2844, (2004)
 101(29) LSG 30 4.41
Blamire v South Cumbria HA (1993) PIQR Q1 10.37
Bolton v Stone [1951] AC 850, [1995] ICR 502, [1995] PIQR P169, CA 1.14, 1.15, 2.5, 2.7, 2.8
Bonnington Castings Ltd v Wardlaw [1956] AC 613, [1956], 2 WLR 707, [1956] 1 All ER
 615, HL 3.14, 3.16, 3.19, 3.21, 3.22, 3.43, 3.44
Booth v Britannia Hotels Limited [2002] EWCA Civ 579 26.41
Booth v Warrington Health Authority [1992] PIQR P137 5.42, 5.43
Bordin v St Mary's NHS Trust [2000] Lloyd's Rep Med 287 31.30
Botham v Khan [2004] EWHC 2602 34.33
Bourhill v Young [1943] AC 92 6.4
Bowen-Jones v Bowen-Jones [1986] 3 All ER 33.71
Bradley v Hanseatic Shipping Co Limited [1986] 2 Lloyd's Rep 34 24.142
Brady v Wirral Health Authority 25 June [1996] CCATF 95/1502/C 24.45, 24.112, 24.121
Brandon v Ostborne, Garrett & Co [1924] 1 KB 548 4.31
Brasserie du Pecheur SA v Federal Republic of Germany; R v Secretary of State for
 Transport ex parte Factortame Ltd and others [1996] ECR I-1029, [1996] QB 404 7.11,
 8.18, 8.20
Brawley v Marcxynski (No 2) [2002] EWCA Civ 1453 33.73
Breeze v John Stacey & Sons Ltd (1999) *The Times*, July 8 27.7
Brennan v Eco Composting Ltd [2006] EWCA 3153 29.8
Bretton v Hancock [2005] EWCA Civ 404 30.55
Brian Anthony Jones v The Chief Constable of Bedfordshire Police 30 July 1999,
 unreported, CA 34.18
Briggs v Pitt-Payne and Lias [1999] Lloyd's Law Rep 1 24.27, 24.30
Brightman v Johnson (1985) *The Times*, December 16 9.5
Brindle v Commissioner of Police for the Metropolis Unreported 1.10
Briody v St Helens and Knowsley Area Health Authority [1999] Lloyd's Rep Med 185 24.121
Bristow v Grout (1987) *The Times*, November 9 24.25, 24.43
Bristow v Judd [1993] PIQR Q117 18.23
British and Commonwealth Holdings plc v Quadrex Holdings Inc [1987] QB 842 20.12
British Cash and Parcel Conveyors Limited v Lamson Store Service Company Limited
 [1908] 1 KB 1006 35.3
British Transport Commission v Gourley [1956] AC 185, [1956] 2 WLR 41, [1955]
 3 All ER 796, HL 10.37, 11.4, 12.2
Broadley v Guy Clapham & Co [1994] 4 All ER 439, [1994] 17 BMLR 56, CA 24.19, 24.45
Brooks v J & P Coates [1994] ICR 158 24.25
Brown v Bennett (2002) 1 WLR 713 34.1
Brown v Grosvenor Building Contractors Ltd [2006] All ER (D) 133 7.83
Brown v Merton Health Authority (Teaching) [1982] 1 All ER 650 15.2
Brown v MoD [2006] EWCA Civ 546 12.2
Brown v Roberts [1965] 1 QB 1 30.39
Bryce v Swan Hunter Group plc [1988] 1 All ER 659 1.17, 3.45
Bubbins v United Kingdom 17 March 2005 36.20
Buck v English Electric Co Ltd [1977] 1 WLR 806, [1978] 1 All ER 271, [1977] ICR 629,
 QBD 24.115
Buckler v Sheffield Forest Borough Council LTL 21/6/04, CA 24.116
Bull v Devon Health Authority [1993] 4 Med LR 117 24.9
Bullock v London General Omnibus Company and Others [1907] 1 KB 264, CA 33.43
Burgess v Florence Nightingale Hospital for Gentlewomen and Anor [1955] 1 QB 349,
 [1955] 1 All ER 511, [1955] 2 WLR 533 31.23
Burgess v Plymouth City Council [2005] EWCA Civ 1659 7.72

Burns v Davies (unreported) 7 August 1998, QBD	13.43
Bush v Philip (No 2) [1989] CLY 1065	9.56
Butt v Nizami [2005] EWHC 159	35.37
Byrne v Sefton Health Authority [2002] EWCA Civ 1904	34.7, 34.33
C v D [2004] All ER(D) 92	24.12
C v Middlesbrough Council [2004] EWCA Civ 1746, [2005] 1 FCR 76, [2004] All ER (D) 339 (Dec), CA	24.12
Cachia v Faluyi [2001] 1 WLR 1966	36.65
Cala Homes (South) Ltd v Alfred McAlpine Homes East Ltd [1995] FSR 818	5.8
Callery v Gray (No 2) [2001] 1 WLR 2142	35.75
Callery v Gray [2001] EWCA Civ 1117, [2001] 1 WLR 2112, [2001] 3 All ER 833, [2001] 2 Costs LR 163, CA	35.29, 35.38
Cambridge v Callaghan [1998] RTR 365	30.55
Cambridge Water Co v Eastern Counties Leather [1994] 2 AC 264	4.53
Cameron v Network Rail Infrastructure Ltd [2007] 1 WLR 163	36.39
Campbell and Cosans v United Kingdom (Application 7511/76) (1980) 3 EHRR 531	31.51
Campbell v McFarland & Omagh UDC [1972] NI 31	30.55
Campbell v MGN Ltd [2005] UKHL 61, [2005] 4 All ER 793, [2005] 1 WLR 3394, [2006] IP & T 54, [2005] 42 LS Gaz R 23, [2005] NLJR 1633, 21 BHRC 516, [2006] EMLR 1	35.21
Campbell v Mylchreest [1999] PIQR Q17	13.63, 20.25, 20.27
Candolin v Pohjola [2005] ECR I-5745	8.19
Caparo Industries plc v Dickman and Others [1990] 2 AC 605, [1990] 2 WLR 358, [1990] 1 All ER 568, HL	1.1, 2.2, 2.14
Capital & Counties plc v Hampshire County Council [1997] QB 1004	2.4
Capital Bank v Strickland [2005]2 All ER 544	29.13
Capital Counties plc v Hampshire County Council [1997] QB 1004	1.11
Capps v Miller [1989] 2 All ER 333, [1989] 1 WLR 839, [1989] RTR 312, CA	3.46, 4.5
Carlisle v Associated British Ports (1987) Lexis, 18 November 1987	24.142
Carlson v Townsend [2001] EWCA Civ 511; [2001] 3 All ER 663	25.39
Cartledge v E Jopling & Sons Ltd [1963] AC 758, [1963] 1 All ER 341, HL	24.2, 24.8
Cassell v Riverside Hospital Health Authority [1992] PIQR Q168	11.34, 14.2, 14.5, 15.2
Caswell v Powell Duffryn Associated Collieries Limited; Trevell v Lee [1955] 1 WLR 113	4.52
Catholic Care (Diocese of Leeds) v Young [2006] EWCA Civ 1534	24.12, 24.30, 24.42, 24.73
Chadwick v British Railways Board [1967] 1 WLR 912, 111 SJ 562; sub nom Chadwick v British Transport Commission [1967] 2 All ER 945	1.23, 6.41
Chan U Seek v Alvis Vehicles Ltd [2003] EWHC 1238	36.72
Chapman v Hearse, Baker v Willoughby [1970] AC 467	3.13
Chapman v Lidstone 3 December 1982 (unreported)	15.9
Charles v Gillian Radford & Co [2003] EWHC 3180 (Ch)	34.7, 34.33
Chilton v Surrey County Council & Foakes [1999] EWCA Civ	27.4
Christopher Greatorex (Claimant) v (1) John Simon Greatorex (First Defendant) (2) Motor Insurers' Bureau (Second Defendant/Part 20 Claimant) (3) Haydon Pope (Part 20 Defendant) [2000] 1 WLR 1970	6.74
Clare v Perry [2005] EWCA Civ 39	2.27
Clark v Vedel [1979] RTR 26 CA	30.44
Clarke v Kato, Smith and General Accident Fire and Life Assurance Corporation plc [1999] PIQR P1	8.10
Clarke v Rotax Aircraft Equipment Ltd [1975] 3 All ER 794, [1975] 1 WLR 1570, [1975] ICR 440, 119 Sol Jo 679, CA	11.50
Clarke v South Yorkshire Transport Ltd [1998] PIQR Q104, 107	9.60
Clenshaw v Tanner [2002] EWHC 184 (QB); [2002] EWCA Civ 1848	16.11
Clough v Tameside and Glossop Health Authority [1998] 1 WLR 1478	5.43
Coad v Cornwall and Isles of Scilly Health Authority [1997] 1 WLR 189, [1997] 8 Med LR 154, CA	24.113, 24.118, 24.121
Codd v Thomsons Tour Operators Limited (CA 7 July 2000, B2/1999/1321, unreported)	8.40
Collier v Williams. [2006] 1 WLR 1945	36.68
Collins v Tesco Stores Ltd [2003] EWCA Civ 1308, LTL, 24/7/2003	24.28, 24.31
Coloroll Pension Trustees Ltd v Russell [1995] ICR 179	7.8
Commission v Germany (C-191/95) [1999] All ER (EC) 483, [1999] 2 CMLR 1265, (1998) The Times, October 10, ECJ	8.21
Commission v UK [2006] 3 CMLR 1322	8.21

Conry v Simpson [1983] 3 All ER 369	24.142
Cook v Consolidated Fisheries Ltd [1977] ICR 635, CA	11.50
Cook v Lewis [1951] SCR 830	3.40
Cook v Square Deal Ltd and others [1992] ICR 262, CA; [1992] PIQR P33, CA	1.4
Cooke & Rippin v Prushki Formerly in Kemp & Kemp, A2-011, October 1992	9.33
Cooke v United Bristol Health Care; Sheppard v Stibbe; Page v Lee [2003] EWCA Civ 1370, [2004] 1 All ER 797, [2004] 1 WLR 251, 78 BMLR 1, [2003] 43 LS Gaz R 32, Times, 24 October, 147 Sol Jo LB 1237, [2003] All ER (D) 258 (Oct)	10.10, 11.38, 12.3, 14.29, 14.30, 21.54
Cookson v Knowles [1979] AC 556, [1978] 2 WLR 978, [1978] 2 All ER 604, [1978] 2 Lloyds Rep 315	10.2, 10.4, 10.5, 10.29, 14.29, 14.30, 31.34, 31.48
Cooper v Carillon plc [2003] Lawtel, 2 December	4.20
Cooper v P& O Stena Line Ltd (1999) *The Times*, February 8	33.72
Cooper v Williams [1963] 2 QB 567	28.85
Copeland v Smith [2001] 1 WLR 1371	24.74, 24.79
Copps v Miller [1989] 1 WLR 839	4.38
Coram (A Minor) v Cornwall & Isles of Scilly HA 16 April 1996, APIL Newsletter, Vol 6, issue 4, p 15	26.23
Corbett v Barking Health Authority [1991] 2 QB 408	10.31, 31.34
Corbin v Penfold Metalising [2000] Lloyd's Rep 247	24.116
Cormack and Cormack v The Excess Insurance Company Ltd (2000) *The Times*, March 30	34.45
Cornell v Green [1998] CLY 1485	10.35
Corr v IBC Vehicles Ltd [2006] EWCA Civ 331	2.32
Corsacov v Moldova 4 April 2006 (Application 18944/02)	36.23
Cosgrove v Baker Unreported, 14 December 1979, CA	25.73
Cosgrove v Pattison Unreported; RCJ, 27 November 2000	25.33
Costanzo v Comune di Milano [1989] ECR 1839, [1990] 3 CMLR 239	8.14
Costello v Chief Constable of Northumbria [1999] ICR 730	1.10
Cotswold Developments Construction Ltd v Williams [2006] IRLR 181	7.20
Cotton v Derbyshire Dales District Council 10 June 1994, CA, unreported	2.23
Cottrell v Redbridge Healthcare NHS Trust (2001) 61 BMLR 72	14.3, 14.42
Coward v Comex (1988) (unreported), noted Kemp & Kemp M2-232	31.29
Craigola Mertha Co v Swansea Corporation [1928] 1 Ch 31	5.21
Cranfield v Bridgegrove Ltd [2003] EWCA Civ 656, [2003] 3 All ER 129, [2003] 1 WLR 2441, [2003] CP Rep 54	36.68
Craze v Meyer-Dunmore Battlers' Equipment Co [1936] 2 All ER 1150	4.6
Cressey v E Timm & Son Limited and E Timm & Son Holding Limited [2006] PIQR P9	24.56
Crocker v British Coal Corporation (1986) 29 BMLR 159	24.59
Crofton v NHSLA [2007] EWCA Civ 71	13.6, 13.72, 13.92, 13.103, 13.128
Cronin v Redbridge 19 May 1987, unreported	19.9
Crouch v King's Healthcare NHS Trust [2005] 1 WLR 2015	29.27
Cummings v Clark [1991] (unreported) QBD	15.23
Cumper v Pothecary [1941] 2 KB 58	29.2
Cunningham v Harrison [1973] QB 942, [1973] 3 All ER 463, [1973] 3 WLR 97, 117 Sol Jo 547, CA	11.8, 13.9
Curi v Colina 29 July 1988, unreported	19.8
Curtis v Birley [2005] 25 February 2005, unreported	28.78
Cutter v Eagle Star Insurance Co Ltd; Clarke v Kato [1998] 4 All ER 417, [1998] 1 WLR 1647, HL	30.40, 30.41, 30.42
D v East Berkshire Community Health NHS Trust [2005] UKHL 23, [2005] 2 AC 373, affirming D v East Berkshire Community Health NHS Trust [2003] EWCV Civ 1151, [2004] QB 558	36.10, 36.45, 36.58
Dale v British Coal Corporation (No 1) [1992] 1 WLR 964	24.139
Daly v General Steam Navigation Ltd [1981] 1 WLR 120	13.38
Daniels v the Commissioner of Police for the Metropolis [2005] EWCA Civ 1312; (2005) *The Times*, October 28	32.35
Daniels v Walker (Practice Note) [2000] 1 WLR 1382, CA	5.17, 25.31, 25.33, 25.35, 25.77, 26.42, 36.63
Darby v National Trust [2001] EWCA Civ 189, [2001] PIQR P27, (2001) 3 LGLR 29, (2001) *The Times*, 23 February	2.23
Darker v Chief Constable of West Midlands Police [2001] 1 AC 435	36.41

Das v Ganju [1999] PIQR P260, [1999] Lloyds Rep Med 198, (1999) 96(19) LSG 28, CA 24.15, 24.116, 24.134
Davie v Edinburgh Magistrates 1953 SC 34 5.7
Davies v Inman [1999] PIQR Q26, CA 11.8, 13.64, 18.2, 18.30
Davies v Mann (184) 10 M&W 546 4.2
Davies v Reed Stock & Company Limited (1984) Lexis, 26 July 1984 24.54
Davies v Swan Motor Co Ltd [1949] 2 KB 291 4.7
Davis v City and Hackney Health Authority [1991] 2 Med LR 366 24.60, 24.61
Davis v Jacobs and Camden and Islington Health Authority [1999] Lloyd's Law Rep Med 72 24.113, 24.132
Davis v Taylor [1974] QB 207 11.55
Deerness v John R Keeble & Son (Brantham) Ltd [1983] 2 Lloyd's Rep 260, [1983] Com LR 221, HL 24.96
Dempsey v Johnstone [2003] EWCA Civ 1134 34.16, 34.19, 34.23
Derby Resources AG v Blue Corinths Marine Co Ltd (The Athenian Harmony) (No 2). [1998] 2 Lloyd' 18.27
Desouza v Waterlow [1998] PIQR P87 CA 30.48
Devine (A Minor) v Northern Ireland Housing Executive [1992] NI 74 4.25
Devine v Franklin [2002] EWHC 1846 (QBD) 27.115
Devonport v A V Wright (Builders) Limited (1985) Lexis, 23 April 1985 24.27
Dews v National Coal Board [1988] AC 1, HL 12.35
Dexter v Courtaulds Ltd, [1984] 1 WLR 372 18.15
Dietz v Lennig Chemicals Limited [1969] 1 AC 170 17.76, 28.41
Dillenkoffer and others v Germany ECR I-4845, [1996] 3 CMLR 469 8.20
Dillon v Twin State Gas and Electric Co 1932 85 NH 449, 163 3.7
Dimond v Lovell [2000] 2 WLR 1121 13.17
Dobbie v Medway Health Authority [1994] 1 WLR 1234, [1994] 4 All ER 450, [1994] 5 Med LR 160, CA 24.11, 24.19, 24.26, 24.38, 24.45, 24.104
Dobbie v United Kingdom 28477/95 24.4
Dodd v Rediffusion (West Midlands Ltd) [1980] CLY 635 18.15
Dodson v Peter H Dodson Insurance Services [2001] 1 Lloyd' 30.48
Doleman v Deakin, Kemp & Kemp A5-005 9.33
Dolman v Rowe [2005] EWCA Civ 715 20.28, 20.29
Donachie v Chief Constable of Greater Manchester Police [2004] EWCA Civ 405 2.32
Donelan v Donelan [1993] PIQR P205 4.35
Donnelly v Joyce [1974] QB 454 13.6, 13.9, 18.30
Donoghue v Stevenson [1932] AC 562, (1932) 48 TLR 494, (1932) 101 LJPC 119 2.2, 2.11
Donovan v Cammell Laird [1949] 2 All ER 82 4.20
Donovan v Gwentoys Ltd [1990] 1 All ER 1018, [1990] 1 WLR 472, HL 24.102, 24.137
Dooley v Cammel Laird & Co Ltd [1951] 1 Lloyd's Rep, 271 6.29
Dorrington v Lawrence 9 November 2001, unreported 14.42, 15.21
Dorset Yacht Co v Home Secretary [1970] 1 AC 1004 3.49
Doughty v North Staffordshire Health Authority [1992] 3 Med LR 81 24.115, 24.131
Doughty v Rolls-Royce [1992] ICR 538 7.9
Doughty v Turner Manufacturing Company [1964] 1 QB 518 2.19, 2.20
Drinkwater v Kimber [1952] 2 QB 281 4.3
DT v Dr Rohatgi & others (Lawtel, 21 July 2004, Document No AM0200647) 14.13
Ducharme v Davis [1984] 1 WLR 699 4.28
Dugmore v Swansea National Health Trust [2002] EWCA Civ 1755 7.78
Duke v GEC Reliance Ltd (formerly Reliance Systems) [1988] AC 618, [1988] 2 WLR 359, [1988] 1 All ER 626, [1988] ICR 339, [1988] IRLR 118, HL 7.8, 8.10
Duncan v British Coal Corporation [1997] 1 All ER 540 6.45, 6.46
Dunnett v Railtrack plc (in railway administration) [2002] EWCA Civ 303; [2002] 1 WLR 2434 32.33, 33.29
Dunthorne v Bentley [1996] RTR 428 30.38
Durau v Evans [1996] PIQR Q18 9.39, 9.60
Dymocks Franchise Systems (NSW) Pty Ltd v Todd [2004] UKPC 39, [2004] 1 WLR 2807, [2005] 4 All ER 195, PC 34.38, 34.39, 34.47
Dyson Appliances Ltd v Hoover Ltd [2003] EWHC 624 (Ch), [2003] 2 All ER 1042, [2004] 1 WLR 1264, [2003] CP Rep 45, [2003] TLR 159, (2003) *The Times*, 18 March 33.13
Dyson Ltd v Hoover Ltd [2002] EWHC 2229 29.10

E (an Alleged Patient), Re; Sheffield City Council v E and S [2004] EWHC 2808 (Fam),
    [2005] Fam 326, [2005] 2 WLR 953, [2005] 1 FLR 965, FD 17.71
Eagle v Chambers (No 2) [2004] EWCA Civ 1033 13.83
EC Commission v United Kingdom: C-300/95 [1997] ECR I-2649, ECJ 8.25
Eden v West & Co [2002] EWCA Civ 991, [2003] PIQR Q2 11.9
Edginton v Clark [1964] 1 QB 367 33.41
Edmeades v Thames Board Mills Ltd [1969] 2 QB 67; [1969] 2 All ER 127, CA 25.47
Edwards v UK (2002) 35 EHRR 487 36.19
Eidi v Service Dowell Schlumberger SA [1990] CLY 2961 24.55
Eileen Corr (Administratrix of the Estate of Thomas Corr, Deceased) v IBC Vehicles Ltd
    [2006] 3 WLR 395; 2 AER 929; 2006 (ICR) 1138 6.61
Elli Christofi v Barclays Bank plc [1999] EWCA Civ 27.3
English v Emery Reimbold & Strick Ltd; DJ & C Withers (Farms Ltd) v Ambic
    Equipment Ltd; Verrechia v Commissioner of Police of the Metropolis (Practice
    Note) [2002] EWCA Civ 605, [2002] 1 WLR 2409, [2002] UKHRR 957, [2002]
    3 All ER 385, CA 5.51, 33.33, 36.75
European Commission v Italy (Case C-63/86) [1988] ECR 29, ECJ 8.21
European Communities v UK Advocate General Case C-127/05, delivered 18 January
    2007 7.97
Evans v London Hospital Medical College (University of London) and Others [1981]
    1 WLR 184, [1981] 1 All ER 715, QBD 5.23
Evans v Pontypridd Roofing Ltd [2001] EWCA Civ 1657, [2002] PIQR Q661   13.6, 13.32, 13.35,
    13.36
Evans v Secretary of State for Environment [2001] PIQR P33, Times Law Reports, 9
    December 2003 30.10, 30.23, 30.87
Excelsior Commercial and Industrial Holdings v Salisbury Hamer and Johnson [2002]
    EWCA Civ 879 29.34

F (Mental Patient: Sterilisation) [1990] 2 AC 1, [1989] 2 WLR 1025, [1989] 2 All ER 545,
    2 WLR 1025, *sub nom* F (Sterilisation: Mental Patient), Re [1989] 2 FLR 376, HL   17.66
Faccini Dori v Recreb [1994] ECR I-3325 8.12
Fairchild v Glenhaven Funeral Services Ltd [2002] UKHL 22, [2003] 1 AC 32   3.14, 3.16, 3.32,
    3.33, 3.41, 3.43, 3.44, 3.46, 10.40
Fairhurst v St Helen's and Knowsley Health Authority [1995] PIQR Q1 13.41
Farmer v Outokumpu Stainless Ltd Lawtel LTL 31/8/2006 6.73
Farraj and another v King's Healthcare NHS Trust and another [2006] EWHC 1228 (QB)   2.11,
    24.15
Farrell v Avon Health Authority [2001] All ER (D) 17 6.65
Farthing v North East Essex Health Authority [1998] 9 Med LR 38 24.112
Farthing v North Essex District Authority [1998] Lloyd's Rep Med 37 24.121
Faulkner v Keffalinos (1971) 45 AJLR 80 3.3
Fenech v East London Health Authority [2000] Lloyd's Rep Med 35 24.67
Ferguson v John Dawson & Partners (Contractors) Ltd [1976] 1 WLR 1213, [1976]
    3 All ER 817, [1976] IRLR 346, [1976] 2 Lloyd's Rep 669, CA 1.6
Field v Leeds City Council (2000) Times Law Report 5.11
Fifield v Denton Hall Legal Services [2006] EWCA Civ 169 7.36
Findlay v Railway Executive [1950] 2 All ER 550 33.55
Firth v Geo Ackroyd Junior Ltd [2000] Lloyds Law Rep Med 312, [2001] PIQR Q4   13.122, 15.7
Fish v Woolcock [1994] 5 Med LR 230 13.62
Fitzgerald and Others v Williams [1996] 2 All ER 171 33.48
Fitzgerald v Ford [1996] PIQR Q72, CA 13.41, 13.47, 13.50
Fitzgerald v Lane [1989] 1 AC 328, [1988] 3 WLR 356, [1988] 2 All ER 961, [1990] RTR
    133, HL 3.14, 3.40, 4.11
Fitzgerald v Williams [1996] 2 All ER 171 8.18
Fitzhugh Gates (a firm) v Elaine Sherman [2003] EWCA Civ 886 34.26
Flannery v Halifax Estate Agencies Ltd (t/a Colleys Professional Services) [2000] 1 WLR
    377, [2000] 1 All ER 373, (1999) 11 Admin LR 465, CA 5.51
Flora v Wakom (Heathrow) Ltd [2006] EWCA Civ 1103 11.32, 13.55, 21.15, 21.49, 21.54
Flower v Ebbw Vale Steel [1936] AC 206 4.15
Flynn v Scougall [2004] EWCA Civ 873, [2004] 3 All ER 609, [2004] 1 WLR 3069   29.2, 29.13
Fookes v Slaytor [1978] 1 WLR 1292 4.14

Forbes v Wandsworth Health Authority [1997] QB 402, [1996] 7 Med LR 175, [1999]
 PIQR P77 24.19, 24.47, 24.62
Ford v GKR Construction Ltd & others [2000] 1 WLR 1397 26.38
Forskringaktieselskapet Vesta v Bukher [1989] AC 852 4.8
Forward v Hendricks [1997] 2 All ER 395 24.93
Foster v British Gas plc [1991] 2 AC 306, [1991] 2 WLR 1075, [1991] ICR 463, HL 7.9, 8.13
Foster v Mall Builders Limited (1983) Lexis, 17 March 1983 24.54
Foster v Tyne and Wear County Council [1986] 1 All ER 567, CA 11.52
Fowell v National Coal Board (1986) *The Times*, May 28 24.76, 24.88
Francis v Porch Kemp & Kemp, A3-003 9.38
Freeman v Lockett [2006] EWHC 102 (QB) 13.131, 13.135, 13.148, 13.152
French v Chief Constable of Sussex [2006] EWCA Civ 312 6.64
Froggatt v Chesterfield and North Derbyshire Royal Hospital NHS Trust [2002] All ER
 (D) 218 (Dec) 6.70
Froom v Butcher [1976] QB 286, [1975] 3 WLR 379, [1975] 3 All ER 520, CA 4.5, 4.39, 4.42
Frost v Chief Constable of South Yorkshire Police [1999] 2 AC 455, [1998] 3 WLR 1509,
 [1999] 1 All ER 1, HL 1.19, 1.23, 2.31, 6.1, 6.4
Furness v Midland Bank (10 November 2000, CA, unreported) 7.72
Fytche v Wincanton Logistics plc [2004] UKHL 31, [2004] 4 All ER 221, [2004] ICR 975,
 [2004] IRLR 817, [2004] 31 LS Gaz R 25, Times, 2 July, 148 Sol Jo LB 825, [2004]
 All ER (D) 07 (Jul) 7.7, 7.59, 7.65, 7.97, 8.30

Galbraith's Curator ad litem v Stewart (No 2) [1998] SLT 1305 4.26
Galt v British Railway Board (1983) 133 NLJ 870 6.32
Gammell v Wilson [1982] AC 27, [1981] 1 All ER 578, HL 10.39, 31.43
Garbutt v Edwards [2006] 1 WLR 2907 35.61
Gardner v Moore [1984] AC 548 30.35
Garrard v AE Soutbey & Co and Standard Telephones and Cables [1952] 2 QB 174 1.4
Gaskin v UK (1990) 12 EHRR 36 36.82
Gaynor v Central West London Buses Ltd [2006] EWCA Civ 1120 35.14
General Accident Fire and Life Assurance Corporation v Foster [1972] 3 All ER 877, CA 33.16
General Cleaning Contractors v Christmas [1953] 2 All ER 1110 4.20
General Medical Council v Meadow & A-G. [2006] EWCA Civ 1390, [2007] 1 All ER 1 5.27
General Mediterranean Holdings SA v Patel [2000] 1 WLR 272 5.48
General of Berne Insurance Co v Jardine Reinsurance Management Ltd [1998] 2 All ER
 301 33.7
George v Pinnock [1973] 1 WLR 118, [1973] 1 All ER 926, CA 15.8
George v Stagecoach South East London and Kent Bus Co Ltd [2003] EWCH 2042 (QB),
 [2003] All ER (D) 522 (Jul) 11.8
Gerrard v Staffordshire Potteries [1995] ICR 502, [1995] PIQR P169, CA 1.14, 1.16, 2.9
Ghaidan v Mendoza [2004] 2 AC 557 36.27, 36.31
Giambrone v Sunworld Holidays Ltd [2004] PIQR Q4 13.28
Giles v Thompson [1994] 1 AC 142, [1993] 2 WLR 908, HL; [1993] 3 All ER 321, CA 34.32,
 13.16, 34.42, 34.46, 35.3
Gillespie v McFadden McManus Construction Ltd [2003] EWCH 2067 4.20
Ginty v Belmont Building [1959] 1 All ER 414 7.24
Glasgow Corporation v Muir [1943] AC 448, 454 2.5
Glass v UK [2004] Lloyd's Rep Med 76 [2004] 39 EHRR 15 36.57, 36.61
Glasscock v London Tilbury & Southend Railway [1902] 18 TLR 295 4.20
Globe Equities Ltd v Globe Legal Services Ltd *sub nom* Globe Equities v Kotrie and
 Others, TLR 14 April 1999 33.18, 34.30, 34.35
Godbold v Mahmood [2005] EWHC 1002 (QB), [2005] Lloyds Rep Med 349, [2005] All
 ER (D) 251 (Apr) 13.144, 21.14
Godfrey v Gloucester Royal Infirmary [2003] Lloyd's Rep Med 398 24.15
Goldborough v Thompson and Crowther [1996] PIQR Q86 11.52
Golden v Lerch Bros (1938) 203 Minn 211 3.45
Golder v UK (1975) 1 EHRR 524 36.8
Goldfinch v Scannell [1993] PIQR Q 143, [1996] CLY 2124 14.19, 15.22, 18.33
Goodchild v Greatness Timber Company Limited [1968] 2 All ER 255 24.25
Goode v Martin [2001] EWCA Civ 1899, [2002] 1 WLR 1828, [2002] 1 All ER 620, CA 36.69
Gorringe v Calderdale Metropolitan Borough Council [2004] 2 All ER 326, [2004] UKHL
 15, [2004] 1 WLR 1057, [2004] PIQR P521, [2004] RTR 443 1.8
Gough v Farrer 24 July 1998 (unreported) 35.7

Gough v Thorne [1966] 1 WLR 1387, [1966] 3 All ER 398, 110 SJ 529, CA   4.25, 4.26, 4.29
Grant v Sun Shipping Company [1948] AC 549   4.19
Gray v Going Places Leisure Travel Ltd (2005) CA (Civ) 7/2/2005   34.9
Green v Building Scene Ltd [1994] PIQR 259   2.6
Green v Chelsea BC [1954] 2 QB 127   4.20
Green v North Essex HA unreported, QBD, 21 December 1998   15.44
Green v Yorkshire Traction Co Ltd [2001] EWCA Civ 1925   7.53
Greenfield v Flather; *sub nom* Greenfield v Irwin (A Firm) [2001] EWCA Civ 113, [2001] 1 WLR 1279, [2001] Lloyds Rep Med 143, [2001] 1 FLR 899   24.15
Gregg v Scott [2005] UKHL 2, [2005] 2 AC 176, [2005] 4 All ER 812, [2005] 2 WLR 268, 82 BMLR 52, Times, 28 January, 149 Sol Jo LB 145, [2005] 5 LRC 408, [2005] All ER (D) 269 (Jan)   3.47
Gregory v Ferro (GB) Limited [1995] 6 Med LR 321   24.18, 24.45, 24.121
Gregory v Kelly [1978] RTR 426   4.48
Griffin v Mersey Regional Ambulance [1998] PIQR P34   4.32
Griffin v South West Water Services Ltd [1995] IRLR 15, ChD   7.9, 8.14
Griffiths v British Coal Corporation [2001] EWCA Civ 336, [2001] 1 WLR 1493, [2001] PIQR Q11, 60 BMLR 188,   16.17, 16.21
Griffiths v Vauxhall Motors Ltd [2003] EWCA Civ 412, [2003] All ER (D) 167 (Mar)   7.52
Grobbelaar v Sun Newspapers (1999) *The Times*, August 12; CA   25.5
Guerra v Italy (1998) 26 EHRR 357   36.48
Guidera v NEI Projects (India) Limited (unreported) 30 January 1990, CA   24.32, 24.89
Gundry v Sainsbury [1910] 1 KB 645, CA   33.8, 35.1
Gupta v Kitto (1998) *The Times* November 23   33.20
Gurtner v Circuit [1968] 2 QB 587, CA   30.79

H & Y v Various Defendants [2006] EWCA Civ 395   24.12
H v S [2002] 3 WLR 1179, [2003] QB 965   31.30, 31.34
H West & Son Ltd v Shephard [1964] AC 326   9.46, 9.50
Haggar v de Placido [1972] 1 WLR 716   13.8
Haines v Airedale NHS Trust (unreported) 2 May 2000   14.5, 15.44
Hajigeorgiou v Vasiliou, [2005] EWCA Civ 236   5.50
Hale v London Underground Ltd [1993] PIQR Q30   9.53
Haley v London Electricity Board [1965] AC 778   4.22
Halford v Brookes [1991] 3 All ER 559, [1991] 1 WLR 428, CA   24.19, 24.88, 24.134
Halford v UK (1997) 24 EHRR 523   36.13
Hall v Avon Area Health Authority (Teaching) [1980] 1 WLR 481; [1980] 1 All ER 516, CA   25.67
Hallam-Eames v Merrett Syndicates [1995] 2 CL 304, [1995] 7 MED LR122   24.47, 24.48, 24.49
Halsey v Milton Keynes General NHS Trust [2004] EWCA Civ 576, [2004] 1WLR 3002   32.35, 33.29, 36.74
Hamilton v Al Fayed (2000) *The Times*, October 13, CA   34.33
Hamilton v Al Fayed (No 2) [2002] EWCA Civ 665, [2003] QB 175, [2002] 3 All ER 641   34.38
Hammond v Metropolitan Police Commissioner [2004] EWCA Civ 830, [2005] PIQR P1   7.58, 8.29

Hardy v MIB [1964] 2 QB 745 CA   30.35
Harley v McDonald (2001) 2 WLR 1749   34.1
Harrhy v Thames Trains Ltd [2003] EWHC 2120 (QB)   6.63
Harrington v Pinkney [2001] 1 Lloyd's Rep 520, CA   30.48
Harris v Brights Asphalt Contractors [1953] 1QB 617   13.82
Harris v Empress [1984] 1 WLR 212   31.28, 31.29, 31.38, 31.40
Harrison v MOD [1993] CLY 3929   4.17
Harrow LBC v Qazi [2004] 1 AC 983   36.12
Hart v Griffiths-Jones [1948] 2 All ER 729   31.43
Hart v Pretty unreported, QBD, 18 April 2005   15.44
Hartley v Birmingham District Council [1992] 2 All ER 213   24.99, 24.120
Hatton v Sutherland [2002] 2 All ER 1   2.33
Hatton v UK (2003) 37 EHRR 611 [2004] 2 AC 42   36.49
Haward v Fawcetts [2006] UKHL 9   24.51
Hawkes v London Borough of Southwark Judgment of 20 February 1998, unreported, CA   8.27
Hawley v Luminar Leisure Plc and Ors [2006] EWCA Civ 30, CA   29.7
Hay v Hughes [1975] QB 790, [1975] 1 All ER 257, [1975] 2 WLR 34, CA   9.58, 13.156, 13.166

Hayden v Hayden [1992] 1 WLR 986, [1993] 2 FLR 16, [1992] 4 All ER 681, [1992] PIQR
   Q111, CA   13.159, 13.161, 13.165, 13.166, 13.169, 31.46
Headford v Bristol and District Health Authority [1995] 6 Med LR 61, [1995] PIQR P180   18.3, 24.9
Hearnshaw v English Steel Corporation Ltd [1971] 11 KIR 306   9.55
Heaton v West 12.12.2002 unreported   15.23, 15.35
Heil v Rankin [2001] QB 272, [2000] 2 WLR 1173, [2000] 3 All ER 138, CA   9.16, 9.17, 9.18, 9.22, 9.24
Henderson v Temple Pier Co Limited [1998] 1 WLR 1540   24.74, 24.78, 24.88
Hendy v Milton Keynes Authority [1992] 3 Med LR 114   24.115
Henser-Leather v Securicor Cash Services [2002] EWCA Civ 816   7.65
Heranger (Owners) v SS Diamond (Owners) [1939] AC 94   4.15
Hertsmere Primary Care Trust v Estate of Rabinda-Anandh decd [2005] EWHC 320   29.28
Hicks v Chief Constable of the South Yorkshire Police [1992] PIQR P63   9.42, 9.43
Hill v Chief Constable of West Yorkshire Police [1989] AC 53, [1988] 138 NLJ 126   1.10, 2.4, 36.10, 36.57
Hill v West Lancashire Health Authority (1996) PMILL (April)   25.64
Hilton International v Noel Martin-Smith 5 October 2000, QBD (unreported)   16.32, 16.43
Hind v York [1998] PIQR P235   24.47
Hinz v Berry [1970] 2 QB 40   6.7
Hobin v Douglas [1998] CLY 1431, (1998) The Independent, October 26   18.16
Hodgson & Others v Imperial Tobacco Limited [1998] 1 WLR 1056   34.1, 34.20, 34.30, 34.35, 35.28
Hodgson v Trapp [1989] AC 807, [1988] 3 All ER 870, [1988] 3 WLR 1281, [1989]
   2 LS Gaz R 36, HL   10.2, 13.127, 13.131, 14.29, 14.31, 16.1, 16.10, 16.11
Hogg v Doyle (Unreported) Kemp Vol 2 A2–006/1   13.47
Hollins v Russell [2003] EWCA Civ 718, [2003] 1 WLR 2487   34.48, 35.52
Holmes v Alfred McAlpine Homes (Yorkshire) Ltd [2006] AllER (D) 68 (Feb)   35.65
Holmes v SGB Services plc [2001] EWCA Civ 354   27.4
Hone v Going Places Leisure Travel Limited [2001] EWCA Civ 947   8.40
Hopkins v MacKenzie [1995] 6 Med LR 26   24.8
Hopwood v Rolls Royce [1947] 176 LT 514   4.20
Horne-Roberts v Smithkline Beecham [2002] 1 WLR 1662   24.5
Horton v Sadler [2006] UKHL 27, [2006] 2 WLR 1346   24.4, 24.91, 24.95, 24.100, 24.120, 24.130, 24.132, 24.137, 36.67
Horton v Taplin Contracts Ltd, *sub nom* Horton v Caplin Contracts Ltd [2002] EWCA
   Civ 1604, [2003] ICR 179, (2002) 146 SJLB 256, (2002) *The Times*, November
   25, CA   7.52
Hotson v East Berkshire Health Authority [1987] AC 750   3.14
Housecroft v Burnett [1986] 1 All ER 332, [1985] 135 NLJ 728, CA   9.33, 13.6, 13.27, 13.35
Howarth v Whittaker [2003] Lloyd's Law Rep Med 235   15.7
Howe v David Brown Tractors (Retail) Limited [1991] 4 All ER 30   24.13
Howell v West Midlands Passenger Transport Executive [1973] 1 Lloyd's Rep 199   24.84
HSS Hire Services Group plc v BMB Builders Merchants Ltd & anor [2005] EWCA Civ
   626, [2005] 1 WLR 3158, [2005] 3 All ER 486, [2005] All ER (D) 351 (Mar), CA   29.17
Hua Lien, The [1991] 1 Lloyd's Rep 309, 328   2.3
Hubbard v LS & L Health Authority [2002] Lloyd   36.63
Huck v Robson [2002] EWCA Civ 398, [2002] 3 All ER 263, [2003] 1 WLR 1340, CA   29.18
Hughes v Lord Advocate [1963] AC 837, [1963] 2 WLR 779, [1963] 1 All ER 705   2.16, 2.17, 2.20, 4.26
Hunt v RM Douglas Roofing [1988] 3 All ER 823   33.79
Hunt v Severs [1994] 2 AC 350, [1994] 2 WLR 602 reversing Hunt v Severs [1993] QB 815   13.6, 13.10, 13.15, 13.21, 13.25, 13.26, 13.50, 13.65, 13.83, 14.2, 18.30
Hunter v Canary Wharf Ltd [1997] AC 655, [1997] 2 FLR 342, [1997] 2 All ER 426, [1997]
   2 WLR 684, HL; [1996] 1 All ER 482, [1996] 2 WLR 348, [1995] NPC 155, CA   36.47
Hurst v Leeming [2002] EWHC 1051 (Ch), [2003] 1 Lloyd's Rep 379   32.33, 33.29
Hyde and Southbank Housing Association v Kain (1989) *The Times* August 30, CA   33.51

Ichard v Frangoulis [1977] 1 WLR 556   9.56
ICI Ltd v Shatwell [1965] AC 656   4.43
Internav Ltd; Nordstern Allegmeine Versicherungs AG v Katsamas (1999) *The Times*,
   June 8, CA   33.18

Table of Cases

Irshad Ali v Courtaulds Textiles Limited [1999] 8 Lloyd's Rep Med 301	24.18, 24.20, 24.47, 24.50, 24.66
Irving v Metropolitan Police Cmr [2005] EWCA Civ 1293	33.44
Jackson v Marley Davenport Limited [2004] EWCA Civ 1225; [2004] 1 WLR 2926	25.43
Jackson v Mirror Group Newspapers Ltd (1994) *The Times*, March 29, CA	25.55
James v Baily Gibson [2002] EWCA Civ 1690	36.72
Jameson v Central Electricity Generating Board [2000] 1 AC 455	31.12
Janardan v East Berkshire Health Authority (1990) Kemp & Kemp, A4-001	9.5
Jassim v Grand Metropolitan Information Services Ltd 18 January 1999, CA, unreported	25.50
JD v East Berks Community NHS Trust [2004] QB 558	36.44
Jefford v Gee [1970] 2 QB 130, [1970] 1 All ER 1202, CA	18.10, 18.11, 18.14, 18.15, 18.16
Jeffrey v C & B Speciality Packaging UK Limited [1999] 9 CL 49	24.82
Jeffrey v Kent County Council, [1958] 3 All ER 155	28.86
Jennifer Joseph v Boyd & Hutchinson (a firm) 13 January 1999 Ch D, unreported	34.15
Jennings v Mather [1902] 1 KB 1	9.23
Jennings v Norman Collision (Contractors) Ltd [1970] 1 All ER 1121	4.51
Jobling v Associated Dairies [1981] QB 389, [1980] 3 All ER 769, [1980] 3 WLR 704, 124 Sol Jo 631	3.8
John Booth v Simon White [2003] Lawtel, 18 November	4.35
Johns v Martin Simms [1983] 1 All ER 127	4.20
Johnsey Estates (1990) Ltd v Secretary of State for Environment Transport and the Regions [2001] EWCA Civ 535	33.33
Johnson v British Midland Airways [1996] PIQR Q8	9.58
Johnson v Ribbons [1977] 1 WLR 1458	33.41
Johnson v Tennant Bros Ltd. (1954) unreported	3.46
Jolley v London Borough of Sutton [1998] 1 WLR 1546; reversed at [2000] 1 WLR 1082	2.20, 2.25, 2.26, 2.29
Jones v Bennett [1976] 1 Lloyd's REP484	24.89
Jones v Caradon Catnic Ltd [2005] EWCA Civ 1821	35.17
Jones v G D Searle & Co Limited [1978] 3 All ER 654	24.135
Jones v Liverpool Health Authority [1996] PIQR P 251	24.47
Jones v Livox Quarries [1952] 2 QB 608	4.17, 4.18, 4.20, 4.47
Jones v University of Warwick [2003] EWCA Civ 151, [2003] 1 WLR 954, [2003] 3 All ER 760, [2003] PIQR P23, CA	26.51, 36.4, 36.35, 36.79
Jordan v UK (2001) 37 EHRR 52	36.19
K R v Bryn Alyn [2003] 3 WLR 107	24.59
Kalfelis v Schroder [1988] ECR 5565	8.36
Kampelmann v Landschaftsverband Westfalen-Lippe: Cases C-253/96 to 258/96 [1998] IRLR 333, ECJ	7.9
Kandalla v British Airways Board [1981] QB 158	31.20
Kearsley v Klarfeld [2005] EWCA Civ 1510	27.62
Keeley v Pashen [2004] EWCA Civ 1491	30.35, 30.48
Keen v Tayside Contracts [2003] Scot CS 55	6.63
Keenan v UK (2001) 33 EHRR 38	36.18
Kellar v Williams [2004] UKPC 30	35.64
Kelly v Bastible [1997] 8 Med LR	24.101
Kenning v Eve Construction [1989] 1 WLR 1189	5.31
Kent v British Railways Board [1995] PIQR Q42, CA	11.24
Kent v Griffiths and Others [2001] QB 36, [2000] 2 WLR 1158, [2000] 2 All ER 474, CA	36.42
Keown v Coventry Healthcare Trust [2006] EWCA Civ 39	2.28, 2.29
Kerby v Redbridge Health Authority Kemp & Kemp, O5-004, 25 April 1997	9.33
Kerry v Keighley Electrical Eng Co [1940] 3 All ER 399	4.16
Kesslar v Moore and Tibbits [2004] EWCA Civ 1551	36.70
Kew v Bettamix Ltd [2006] EWCA Civ 1535	24.74
Khan v Ainslie [1993] 4 Med LR 319	24.46, 24.82
Khan v Duncan (unreported) 9 March 1989	18.13, 31.48
Kidd v Grampian Health Board [1994] SLT 265	24.115
Kiliç v Turkey ECtHR Application No 22492/93, 28 March 2000	31.51
Kilroy v Kilroy [1996] PNLR 67	34.15
King v RCO Support Services [2000] EWCA Civ 314	7.43
King v Smith [1955] PIQR P49	4.50

King v Sussex Ambulance NHS Trust [2002] ICR 1413   1.12
King v Telegraph Group Ltd [2004] EWCA Civ 613   33.38, 35.66
Klass v Germany (Application 5029/71) (1978) 2 EHRR 214, ECtHR   31.51
Knight v Clifton [1971] Ch 700   33.21
Knight v Sage Group CA; unreported, 28 April 1999, Lawtel AC9500203   25.27
Knipe v British Railways Board [1972] 1 Lloyd's Rep 122   24.84
Knott v Newham Healthcare NHS Trust [2002] EWHC 2091 (QBD), [2002] All ER (D)
   216 (Oct)   15.26
Kobler v Austrian Republic [2003] ECR I-10239   8.20
Koonjul v Thameslink Healthcare Services [2000] PIQR P123, [2000] TLR 2   7.43
KR v Bryn Alyn Community (Holdings) Limited [2003] 3 WLR 107, [2003] QB 1441   24.12,
   24.107, 24.120

L v Barry May Haulage [2002] PIQR Q35   31.46
Lacey v Harrison (1992) *The Times*, April 22   25.48, 25.50
Lahey v Pirelli Tyres [2007] EWCA Civ 91   29.10
Lamey v Wirral Health Authority [1993] QBD, unreported   15.22
Lane v The Shire Roofing Company (Oxford) Ltd [1995] PIQR P417   1.6
Lane v Willis; Lane v Beath (Executor of Estate of George William Willis) [1972] 1 WLR
   326; [1972] 1 All ER 430, CA   25.48, 25.49, 25.52
Langford v Hebran [2001] EWCA Civ 361, [2001] PIQR Q13   11.57, 31.25
Langley v Dray [1998] PIQR P314   1.10, 4.31
Laszczyk v NCB [1954] 1 WLR 1426   4.20
Lau Ho Wah v Yau Chi Biu [1985] WLR 1203   11.53
Law Debenture Trust Group v (1) Terence Malley & (2) Pensions Ombudsman (1999)
   Lawtel, 23 July   26.2, 26.28, 26.47
Lawal v Northern Spirit Ltd [2004] EWCA Civ 208   33.12
Lawrence v Chief Constable of Staffordshire [2000] TLR 562, (2000) *The Times*, 25
   July, CA   18.7
Lawrence v Pembrokeshire County Council [2007] PIQR P1   36.45, 36.58
Lawrence v South East London HA Kemp & Kemp, O1-001   31.42
Lay v South West Surrey Health Authority [1989] CA (unreported)   15.26
Laycock v Lagoe (1997) 40 BMLR 82, [1997] PIQR P 518   25.65
Laycock v Morrison Formerly reported in Kemp & Kemp, D 4-019   9.45
LE Cattam Ltd v A Michaelides & Co [1958] 1 WLR 717   33.41
Le Compte, Van Leuven and De Meyere v Belgium (1982) 4 EHRR 1, ECHR   36.6
Leadbitter v Hodge Finance Limited [1982] 2 All ER 167   24.54, 24.74
Letang v Cooper [1965] 1 QN 232   24.11
Lewis v Avidan [2005] EWCA Civ 670   7.72
Lewis v Denye [1939] 1 KB 540   4.15
Lewis v Osborne 4 July 1995 (unreported)   9.58
Liddell v Middleton [1996] PIQR P36   4.51
Lim Poh Choo v Camden and Islington Area Health Authority [1980] AC 174, [1979]
   2 All ER 910, [1979] 3 WLR 44, 123 Sol Jo 457, HL   10.2, 11.2, 12.2, 13.83, 14.30, 14.31
Lister v Hesley Hall Limited [2001] 1 AC 215   24.12
Litster v Forth Dry Dock & Engineering Co Ltd (in Receivership) [1990] 1 AC 546, [1989]
   2 WLR 634, [1989] 1 All ER 1134, [1989] ICR 341, [1989] IRLR 161, HL   8.10
Liverpool Roman Catholic Archdiocesan Trust v Goldberg (No 2) [2001] 4 All ER 950   5.11
Livingstone v Rawyards Coal Co [1880] 5 App Cas 25   10.2, 11.1
Loader v Lucas Kemp & Kemp, para O1-003   31.42
Locke v Camberwell Health Authority (1991) 1 Med LR 249   34.21
Lockley v National Blood Transfusion Service [1992] 2 All ER 589   33.39
London Ambulance Service National Health Service Trust v Swain CA, unreported, 12
   March 1999   12.28
Long v Tolchard and Sons Ltd [2001] PIQR P18   24.113
Longden v British Coal Corporation [1998] AC 653 HL   12.3, 12.4, 12.25
Lopez Ostra v Spain (1994) 20 EHRR 277   36.48
Lough v First Secretary of State [2004] 1 WLR 2557   36.16, 36.25
Lowles v Home Office [2004] EWCA Civ 985   7.72
Lowther v Chatwin [2003] PIQR Q84   16.19
Lucas v Barking, Havering and Redbridge Hospitals NHS Trust [2003] EWCA Civ 1102,
   [2003] 4 All ER 720, [2004] 1 WLR 220, 77 BMLR 13, [2003] 37 LS Gaz R 34,
   [2003] NLJR 1204, Times, 28 August, [2003] All ER (D) 379 (Jul)   5.48

Lye v M C Tleycra & Co [2005] 19 April 2005, unreported	28.80
M v Leeds HA [2002] PIQR Q46	15.22, 15.24
M'Kew v Holland & Hannen & Cubitts (Scotland) Ltd 1970 SC (HL) 20	3.13, 3.14
MacCartney v Oversley House Management [2006] ICR 510	13.70
MacDonald v Taree Holdings Ltd (2000) *The Times*, December 28	33.61
Malcolm v Broadhurst [1970] 3 All ER 508	1.21
Mallett v McMonagle [1970] AC 166, [1969] 2 WLR 767, [1969] 2 All ER 178, HL	10.5, 12.2, 14.29, 14.30, 31.19
Marc Rich & Co v Bishop Rock Marine [1996] 1 AC 211	1.1
March v E & M H Stramare Pty Ltd, (1991) 171 CLR 506 HC of A	3.13
Marcic v Thames Water Utilities Ltd [2003] UKHL 66	36.50
Margolis v Imperial Tobacco Ltd [2000] MLC 204	24.113
Marinari v Lloyds Bank [1996] QB 217	8.36
Marion Henry v BBC [2005] EWHC 2503 (QB)	33.38
Maronier v Larner [2003] QB 620	36.77
Marren v Dawson Bentley & Co [1961] 2 QB 135	24.8
Marrinan v Vibart [1963] 1 QB 234, [1962] 2 WLR 1224, [1962] 1 All ER 869, CA; affirming [1963] 1 QB 234, [1962] 2 WLR 1224, [1962] 1 All ER 869, QBD	5.23
Mars v Teknowledge *The Times*, 8 July 1999	27.112, 33.13, 33.78
Marshall v Martin (1987) Lexis, 10 June 1987	24.125
Marshall v Southampton and South West Hampshire Area Health Authority (Teaching) (Case 152/84) [1986] ECR 723, [1986] QB 401, [1986] 2 WLR 780, [1986] 1 CMLR 688, [1986] ICR 335, [1986] IRLR 140, [1986] 2 All ER 584, ECJ	7.9, 8.12
Marshall v Southampton Area Health Authority (No 2) [1993] ECR I-4367; [1994] QB 126	7.27, 8.19
Marston v British Railways Board and Andrew [1976] ICR 124	24.87
Marvin Sigurdson v British Columbia Electric Railway Company [1953] AC 291	4.47
Masterman-Lister v Brutton & Co and Jewell & Home Counties Dairies [2002] EWCA Civ 1889; [2003] PIQR P310	17.61
Matthews v Metal Improvements [2007] EWCA Civ 215	29.35
Matthews v Ministry of Defence [2003] UKHL 4, [2003] 1 AC 1163, [2003] 2 WLR 435, [2003] UKHRR 453, [2003] 1 All ER 689, HL	36.6, 36.7, 36.9, 36.10, 36.43
Matthews v Tarmac Bricks and Tiles Ltd [1999] CPLR 463, (1999) 96(28) LSG 26, (1999) *The Times*, 1 July, CA	25.36, 27.75
Mayer v Harte [1960] 1 WLR 770	33.44
Maylen v Morris 21 January 1988, unreported	15.13
Maylon v Plummer [1964] 1 QB 330	31.23
McAll v Brooks [1984] RTR 99	13.16
McCafferty v Metropolitan Police District Receiver [1997] 1 WLR 1073	24.26, 24.29, 24.115
McCann v Shepard [1973] 2 All ER 881	9.46
McCann v UK (1995) 21 EHRR 97	36.19
McClaren v Harland & Wolf Limited. [1991] SLT 85	24.115
McCook v Lobo [2002] EWCA Civ 1760	7.81
McDermid v Nash Dredging Co Ltd [1987] AC 906	1.4
McDermott International Inc v Hardy (1995) *The Times*, December 28	28.47
McDonald v Horn [1995] ICR 685	33.5
McDonnell v Congregation of Christian Brothers Trustees [2003] UK HL 63	24.4
McFarlane v Corus [2006] CSOH 38 (Ct of Session)	7.43
McFarlane v EE Caledonia Ltd [1994] 2 All ER 1	1.23, 6.15
McFarlane v Tayside Health Board [2002] 2 AC 59	24.15
McGahie v Union of Shop Distributive and Allied Workers [1966] SLT 74	24.13
McGhee v National Coal Board [1973] 1 WLR 1	3.13, 3.14, 3.21, 3.24, 3.25, 3.26, 3.27, 3.28, 3.32, 3.33, 3.36, 3.37, 3.38, 3.43
McGhie v British Telecommunications plc [2005] EWCA Civ 48	24.106
McGinley and Egan v UK (1999) 27 EHRR 1	36.82
McGlinchey v UK [2003] Lloyd's Med Rep 264	36.22, 36.38, 36.59
McGuigan v Tarmac Ltd CLY 2003 324	34.33
McKay v Borthwick (1982) SLT 265	4.39
McKenna v British Aluminium Ltd (2002) Env LR 30	36.48
McKenzie v Bonar Yarns and Fabrics Ltd [2006] CSOH 23	7.43
Mckew v Holland & Hannen & Cubitts [1969] 3 All ER 1621, 1623G	2.42
McLoughlin v O'Brian [1983] AC 410, [1982] 2 WLR 982, [1982] 2 All ER 298, HL	6.4, 22.19

McManus v Manning Marine [2001] EWCA Civ 1668 24.35
McMullen v NCB [1982] ICR 148 4.20
McMylor v Firth Rixson plc [2002] EWCA Civ 1863 11.3
McPhilemy v Times Newspapers [2002] 1 WLR 934, (1999) *The Times*, May 26 27.57, 29.33
McWilliams v Sir William Arrol Co Ltd [1962] 1 WLR 295, (1962) 106 SJ 218, (1962) SC
    70, HL 3.4
Medcalf v Weatherill Medcalf v Mardell; *sub nom* Medcalf v Weatherill & anor [2002]
    UKHL 27, [2003] 1 AC 120, [2002] 3 WLR 172, [2002] 3 All ER 721, [2002] Costs
    LR 428, HL 34.15, 34.23
Mehmet v Perry [1977] 2 All ER 529 9.58
Mellors v Perry [2003] EWCA CIV89 24.71
Mettaloy Supplies Ltd (in liquidation) v MA (UK) Ltd [1997] 1 All ER 418 34.45
Michael Steven Vaughan v (1) Jones (2) Fowler (3) Fowler [2006] EWHC 2123 34.51, 34.55
Middleton v South Yorkshire Transport Executive Kemp & Kemp, G4-001 9.51
Midland Marts Ltd v Hobday [1989] 1 WLR 1143 33.72
Mighell v Reading, Evans v MIB & White v White [1999] PIQR P101 CA 8.17, 30.17, 30.22
Miller v Jackson [1977] QB 966, [1977] 3 All ER 338, [1977] 3 WLR 20, CA 2.7
Miller v London Electrical Manufacturing Company Limited [1976] 2 Lloyd's Rep 284 24.25
Mills v British Rail Engineering Ltd [1992] PIQR Q 130 13.27
Mirza v Birmingham Health Authority 31 July 2001, unreported, 1998 A No 04592 24.22
Mitchell v Inverclyde [1998] SCLR 191 7.43
Mitchell v Mulholland (No 2) [1972] 1 QB 65 14.30
Moeliker v Reyrolle & Co [1977] 1 WLR 132 11.50
Mohammed Butt v Christi Nizami [2006] EWHC 159 33.8
Mold v Hayton, Newsom [2000] MLC 207 24.113
Molloy v Shell UK Limited [2001] EWCA Civ 1272 26.36
Moon v Garrett [2006] EWCA Civ 1121 7.80
Morrell v Owen (1993) *The Times* December 14 2.10
Morris v Breaveglen Ltd [1993] ICR 766, CA; [1993] PIQR P294 1.4
MS v Sweden (1999) 28 EHRR 313, ECHR 36.80
Mullard v Ben Line Steamers Ltd [1970] 1 WLR 1414 4.20
Murphy and Another v Young & Co's Brewery and Another [1997] 1 WLR 1591 34.41
Murphy v Young & Co's Brewery Limited [1997] 1 All ER 518, [1997] 1 WLR 1591 33.18, 34.45
Mustard v Morris Formerly in Kemp & Kemp, I2-106, 604 9.35
Myatt v NCB [2007] 1 WLR 554 35.54, 35.57, 35.58, 35.59

Nance v British Columbia Electric Railway Co Ltd [1951] AC 601, [1951] 2 All ER 448,
    95 Sol Jo 543, PC 1.7
Napper v National Coal Board Lexis, 1 March 1990 24.74
Nash v Eli Lilly [1993] 4 All ER 383, [1993] 1 WLR 782, 14 BMLR 1, CA *sub nom* [1991]
    2 Med LR 169, (1991) *The Times*, 13 February, QBD 24.18, 24.21, 24.30, 24.45, 24.57,
    24.60, 24.62, 24.66, 24.74, 24.76, 24.77, 24.83, 24.88, 24.89, 24.101,
    24.110, 24.142
Nash v Powerhouse Retail [2000] All ER (D) 110 7.43
Nash v Southmead Health Authority [1993] PIQR Q156, [1994] 5 Med LR 74 13.41, 18.28
National Justice Compania Naviera SA v Prudential Assurance Co Ltd (aka 'The Ikarian
    Reefer') [1993] 2 Lloyd's Rep 68 5.1, 25.21
National Justice Compania Naviera SA v Prudential Assurance Co Ltd (No 2) (1999)
    Times October 15, CA 34.57
National Union of Teachers v St Mary's Church of England Junior School [1997] IRLR
    242 8.14
Nawaz v Crowe Insurance Times Law Reports, 11 March 2003, CA 30.48
Nayler v Beard [2001] 2 FLR 1346 36.83
Naylor v Preston Area Health Authority [1987] 1 WLR 958, [1987] 2 All ER 353, CA 24.15,
    25.75
NCB v England (1954) AC 403 4.49, 4.51
Nelson v Nelson [1997] 1 All ER 970, [1997] 1 WLR 233, [1997] PNLR 413, CA 34.15
Newman v Folkes and Dunlop Tyres Ltd [2002] PIQR, [2002] Q13 13.45
Newton v Cammell Laird & Co Limited [1959] 1 WLR 415 24.60, 24.70
Nicholls v National Coal Board [1976] ICR 266, CA 11.50
Nicholls v Rushton Times Law Reports 19 June 1992 6.9
Nicholson v Atlas Steel Foundry and Engineering Co Ltd [1957] 1 All ER 776, [1957]
    1 WLR 613, 1957 SC (HL) 44, HL 3.19

Nixon v Chanceoption Developments [2002] EWCA Civ 558	7.82
Nizami v London Clubs Management Ltd [2004] EWHC 2577 (QB)	16.18
Nordstern Allgemeime Versicherungs AG v Internav Ltd (1999) Times June 8, CA	34.46
North Glamorgan NHS Trust v Walters [2002] EWCA 1792	6.69
Norton v Corus UK Ltd [2006] EWCA 1630	24.74
Nykredit Mortgage Bank Plc v Edward Erdman Group Ltd (No 2) [1997] 1 WLR 1627	18.4
O'Brien v Harris (unreported), 22 February 2001	14.18, 14.42, 15.25
O'Byrne v (1) Aventis Pasteur MSD Ltd (2) Aventis Pasteur SA [2006] EWHC 2562	24.5
O'Connell v Jackson [1972] 1 QB 270	4.38
O'Driscoll v Dudley Health Authority [1998] Lloyd's Rep Med 210	24.18, 24.21, 24.22, 24.45, 24.47, 24.67
O'Neill v DSG Retail [2002] EWCA Civ 1139	7.43, 7.97
O'Neill v O'Brien Times Law Reports, 21 March 1997, CA	30.68
Oades v Park Kemp & Kemp, F5-025 [1994] CLY	11.65
Oakes v Hopcraft CA 27/7/200	24.48
Oates v Harte Reade [1998] PNLR 458	24.13
Obembe v City and Hackney Health Authority (1989) Lexis, 9 June 1989	24.133
Ogunsanya v Lambeth Area Heath Authority (1985) Lexis, 3 July 1985	24.46, 24.141
Ogur v Turkey (2001) 31 EHHR 912	31.50
Ogwo v Taylor [1988] AC 431 [1988] AC 431	1.11
Orchard v SEE Board [1987] QB 565	34.20
Osman v United Kingdom (2000) 29 EHRR 245, 5 BHRC 293; *sub nom* Osman v UK [1999] 1 FLR 193, ECHR	5.26, 36.10, 36.18, 36.38, 36.41
Ostick v Wandsworth Health Authority [1995] 6 Med LR 338	24.47
Overseas Tankship (UK) Ltd v Morts Dock Engineering Co Ltd (The Wagon Mound No 1) [1961] 1 AC 388; [1961] All ER 404; [1961] 2 WLR 126	2.8, 2.12, 2.18, 2.38, 2.40
Overseas Tankship (UK) Ltd v The Miller Steamship Co Pty (The Wagon Mound No 2) [1967] AC 617	2.8, 2.22, 2.37
Owen v Brown [2002] EWHC 1135	15.44
Owen v Martin [1992] PIQR Q151	31.28
Owens v Brimmell [1977] QB 859	4.35, 4.45
Owusu v Jackson [2005] QB 801	8.33
Oyston v Royal Bank of Scotland plc [2006] EWHC 90053	35.17
Ozgür Gündem v Turkey (2001) 31 EHRR 5	31.51
P (a child) v Mid Kent Area Healthcare NHS Trust [2002] 1 WLR 210	5.16
Pacheco v Brent and Harrow Area Health Authority (1984) Lexis, 17 April 1984	24.27
Page v Plymouth Hospitals NHS Trust [2004] EWHC 1154 (QB), [2004] PIQR Q68	12.3, 17.89
Page v Sheerness Steel Company [1996] PIQR Q26	12.3, 15.41
Page v Smith [1996] 1 AC 155	1.19, 1.21, 2.30, 2.31, 2.32, 6.4, 6.59, 6.67
Painting v University of Oxford [2005] EWCA Civ 161	26.35
Palfrey v GLC [1985] ICR 437	16.12
Palmer v Durnford Ford [1992] 1 QB 480	5.23
Palmer v Marks & Spencer [2001] EWCA Civ 1528	7.72, 7.97
Palmer v Tees HA [2000] PIQR P1	36.42
Paris v Stepney Borough Council [1951] AC 367, [1951] 1 All ER 42, HL	1.18, 2.10, 4.22
Parkhouse v Northern Devon Healthcare NHS Trust [2002] Lloyd's Rep Med 100	14.18, 14.23, 14.24, 14.42, 15.24
Parry v Cleaver [1970] AC 1, [1969] 2 WLR 821, [1969] 1 All ER 555, HL	12.24, 12.25, 12.34, 12.35, 13.131
Parry v Clwyd Health Authority [1997] PIQR P1	24.22, 24.63
Parry v North West Surrey Health Authority (unreported), 29 November 1999	14.2, 14.42
Patel v Wright & Midas [2005] EWHC 347	12.3
Patterson v Ministry of Defence (1986) 29 July (unreported), [1987] CLY 1194	19.8
Pattison v Hobbs (1985) *The Times*, November 11	24.15
Peet v Mid Kent Healthcare NHS Trust [2002] 1 WLR 210	25.34
Pendennis Shipyard Ltd v Margrathea (Pendennis) Ltd (1997) *The Times* August 27	34.45
Penney, Palmer and Cannon v East Kent Health Authority [1999] MIC 126, CA	26.23
Pennington v Surrey County Council [2006] EWCA Civ 1493	7.52
Percy v Church of Scotland [2006] 2 AC 28 [2006] 2 AC 28, [2006] ICR 134	8.10
Performance Cars v Abraham [1962] 1 QB 33	3.7
Perotti v Collyer-Bristow [2003] EWCA Civ 1521, [2004] 2 All ER 189, CA	36.85

Perrett v Collins [1998] PNLR 77, [1998] 2 Lloyds Rep 255, CA 1.9
Persaud (Luke) v Persaud (Mohan) [2003] EWCA Civ 394 34.13, 34.16
Pessos Compania Naviera SA v Belgium (1995) 21 EHRR 301 36.25
Petroleo Brasiliero SA v Petromec Inc [2005] EWHC 2430 34.47
Phelps v Hillingdon BC [2001] 2 AC 619 36.41
Phillips v Rafiq & MIB [2007] EWCA Civ (judgment awaited) 30.66
Phillips v Symes [2004] EWHC 2330 (Ch) 5.25
Phonographic Performance Ltd v AEI Rediffusion Music Ltd [1999] 1 WLR 1507, [1999]
　　2 All ER 299, CA 26.33
Pickett v British Rail Engineering (1978) 3 WLR 955 10.2
Pickett v MIB [2004] EWCA Civ 6, [2004] 1 WLR 2450 4.35, 30.48, 30.56
Pickford v Imperial Chemical Industries plc [1998] 3 All ER 462, [1998] 1 WLR 1189, HL 7.33
Piggott v Aulton [2003] PIQR P22 24.95
Pilmore v Northern Trawlers Limited [1986] 1 Lloyd's Rep 552 24.120, 24.127
Pinnington v Crossleigh Construction [2003] EWCA Civ 1684 14.13, 15.21
Pirie v Ayling SCCO Reference 0207520, 18 February 2003 35.73
Pitts v Hunt [1991] 1 QB 24 4.35
Poplar Housing and Regeneration Community Association Ltd v Donoghue [2001]
　　EWCA Civ 595, [2002] QB 48, [2001] 3 WLR 183, [2001] UKHRR 693, [2001]
　　4 All ER 604, CA; *sub nom* Donoghue v Poplar Housing and Regeneration
　　Community Association Ltd [2001] 2 FLR 284, CA 36.34
Preston and others v Wolverhampton Healthcare NHS Trust and others [2000] ECR
　　I-3201, [2000] 2 CMLR 837 8.18
Pretty v UK (2002) 35 EHRR 1 36.14
Price v Price [2004] PIQR P6 36.64
Price v UK (2002) 34 EHRR 53 36.22
Price v United Engineering Steels Limited [1998] PIQR P407 24.104
Pritam Kaur v S. Russell & sons Limited [1973] QB 336 24.8
Procura Della Repubblica v X [1996] ECR I-6609, [1997] 1 CMLR 399 8.21

Quinn v Birch Bros (Builders) Ltd [1966] 2 QB 370, CA 1.6, 2.43

R (Addinell) v Sheffield City Council 27 October 2000 36.82
R (Amin) v Secretary of State for the Home Department [2003] UKHL 51, [2004] 1 AC
　　653, [2003] 3 WLR 1169, [2004] UKHRR 75, [2003] 4 All ER 1264, 15 BHRC
　　362, HL 36.52
R (D) v Home Secretary [2006] 3 All ER 946 36.53
R (Factortame Ltd) v Transport Secretary (No 8) [2002] EWCA Civ 932 34.38
R (KB) v Mental Health Appeal Tribunal [2003] 2 All ER 31.51
R (Khan) v Secretary of State for Health [2003] EWCA Civ 1129, [2004] 1 WLR 971,
　　[2003] 4 All ER 1239, CA 36.87
R (Middleton) v West Somerset Coroner [2004] UKHL 10, [2004] 2 AC 182, [2004]
　　2 WLR 800, [2004] UKHRR 501, [2004] 2 All ER 465, HL 36.53
R (on the Application of Brewins) v Canterbury and Costal Primary Care Trust [2003]
　　EWHC 3354 13.119
R (on the application of Goodson) v Bedfordshire and Luton Coroner (Luton and
　　Dunstable Hospital NHS Trust, interested party) [2005] 2 All ER 791, [2005]
　　EWHC 2931 (Admin) 33.37, 36.54
R (on the application of Heather) v Leonard Cheshire Foundation [2002] 2 All ER 936 36.34
R (on the application of Kehoe) v Secretary of State for Work and Pensions [2005]
　　UKHL 48, [2006] 1 AC 42 36.6, 36.10
R (on the Application of Spink) v Wandsworth Borough Council [2004] EHWC 2314
　　(Admin) 13.124
R (ota Corner House Research) v Secretary of State for Trade & Industry [2005] EWCA
　　Civ 192 33.36
R (Takoushis) v Coroner for Inner North London [2005] EWCA Civ 1440 36.54
R v Button and Tannahill, [2005] EWCA Crim 516 26.49
R v CICAP, ex parte August [2001] QB 774 22.18
R v CICB, ex parte A [1999] 2 WLR 974 22.39
R v CICB, ex parte Clowes [1987] 3 All ER 854 22.18
R v CICB, ex parte Ince [1973] 3 All ER 808 22.21, 22.22
R v CICB, ex parte K (Minors) and Others [1999] 1 WLR 13.159, 13.163

R v CICB, ex parte K [1998] 1 WLR 1458	22.23
R v CICB, ex parte Lain [1967] 2 QB 864	22.40
R v CICB, ex parte Staten [1972] 1 All ER 1034	22.20
R v CICB, ex parte Thomas [1995] PIQR P99	22.21
R v CICB, ex parte Thompstone [1984] 3 All ER 572	22.21
R v CICB, ex parte Warner [1987] QB 74	22.17
R v Criminal Injuries Compensation Board ex parte Barrett [1994] PIQR Q44	31.37, 31.41
R v Criminal Injuries Compensation Board ex parte K [1999] QB 1	31.46
R v East Sussex County council, the Disability Rights Commission (interested party) ex p A, B (by their Litigation Friend the Official Solicitor), X, Y [2003] EWHC 167 (Admin)	1.13
R v Edward Grant [2005] EWCA Crim 1089	26.49
R v Henn and Darby [1981] AC 850	8.9
R v Her Majesty's Treasury ex parte British Telecommunications plc [1996] QB 615	7.11
R v International Stock Exchange ex parte Else Ltd [1993] QB 534	8.9
R v Liverpool City Council ex parte Horne [1997] PNLR, 95, DC	34.15, 34.24
R v Lord Chancellor ex parte Child Poverty Action Group [1999] 1 WLR 349	33.35
R v LSC ex parte Alliss 25 September 2002 (unreported)	36.85
R v Manchester City Council ex parte Stennet [2002] UKHL 34	13.112
R v Miller (Raymond) [1983] 3 WLR 1056	33.9
R v North East Devon Health Authority, ex parte Coughlan [2001] QB 213	13.118, 13.125
R v North Humberside Coroner ex parte Jamieson [1995] QB 1	36.53
R v Powys CC ex parte Hambridge [1998] 1CCLR 458	13.107
R v Secretary of State for Transport ex parte Factortame Ltd [1996] ECR I-1029, [1996] QB 404	8.18, 8.20
R v Secretary of State for Transport, ex parte Factortame (No 2) [2002] EWCA Civ 932, [2002] 3 WLR 1104	5.11
R v Stockton on Tees BC ex parte W [2000] ELR 93, CA	13.114
R(A) v Lord Saville of Newdigate [2002] 1 WLR 1249	36.18
Rahman v Arearose Ltd [2001] QB 351, [2000] 3 WLR 1184, CA	3.18, 3.48, 3.49
Rahman v West Pennine Health Authority (2002) QBD unreported	15.37
Rall v Hume [2001] EWCA Civ 146, [2001] 3 All ER 248, [2001] CP Rep 58, [2001] CPLR 239, (2001) 98(10) LSG 44, (2001) 145 SJLB 54, CA	26.8, 26.50
Rand v East Dorset Health Authority [2000] Lloyd's Rep Med 181	16.11
Ratcliff v GR McConnell & W Jons [1999] PIQR P170	4.36
Re Campbell, Kemp & Kemp, E1-014	9.11
Re Freudiana Holdings Ltd (1995) Times, December 4, CA	34.53
Re Harry Boodhoo, Solicitor [2007] EWCA Crim 14	34.15
Re Homes Assured: Sampson v Wilson [2002] 1 Costs LR 71	34.33
Re Land and Property Trust Co Ltd [1991] 1 WLR 601	33.54
Re P (Lawtel, March 2004, Document No AM0200602)	14.13
Re Stathams (Wasted Costs Order: Banks v Woodhall Duckham Ltd & Others [1997] PIQR 464	34.15
Re Wiseman Lee (solicitors) (wasted costs order) (No 5 of 2000) 19 March 2001, CA	34.12
Re Workvale Limited No [1992] 2 All ER 627	24.94
Read v Harries [1993] PIQR Q25	18.25
Redrow Homes v Wright [2004] EWCA Civ 469	7.90
Reeves v Commissioner of Police for the Metropolis [1999] 3 WLR 363	4.37
Reg v Horsham DC ex parte Wenman [1994] 4 All ER 681	34.24
Regan v Williamson [1976] 1 WLR 305, [1976] 2 All ER 241, (1975) 120 SJ 217	9.58, 13.167
Reid Minty (A Firm) v Taylor [2001] EWCA Civ 1723, [2002] 2 All ER 150, [2002] 1 WLR 2800, CA	29.33, 33.72
Reid v PRP Architects [2006] EWCA Civ 1119	7.45
Rhodes v Ford [2005] EWCA Civ 440	20.28
Rialis v Mitchell (Unreported), 6 July 1984	13.142
Richardson v Watson [2006] EWCA Civ 1662	24.96, 30.69
Ridehalgh v Horsefield, and Watson v Watson (Wasted Costs Orders), [1994] 3 WLR 462, [1994] 3 All ER 848, [1994] 2 FLR 194, [1994] Ch 205 (CA)	34.14
Ritchie Smith v Manchester Awards 1994 Journal of Personal Injury Litigation 103	11.52
Roach v Yates [1938] 3 KB 256	13.8
Roberts v Johnstone [1989] QB 878, [1988] 3 WLR 1247, (1988) 132 SJ 1672, CA	13.64, 15.1, 15.9, 15.10, 15.11, 15.12, 15.14, 15.15, 15.16, 15.17, 15.18, 15.19, 15.20, 15.35, 15.36, 18.30, 21.27, 21.28

Roberts v Roberts (1960) *The Times*, March 11 — 14.2
Roberts v Winbow [1999] PIQR P77, CA — 24.18, 24.27, 24.45, 24.121
Robertson v Forth Road Bridge 1995 SC 364 — 6.51
Robertson v Lestrange [1950] 1 All ER 950 — 31.25
Robertson v Ridley [1989] 1 WLR 872 — 7.70
Robin Ellis Ltd v Malwright Ltd (1999) BLR 81; 15 Const LJ 141 — 25.43
Robinson v St Helens Metropolitan Borough Council [2002] EWCA Civ 1099, [2002] ELR 681, [2003] PIQR P128, (2002) 99(39) LSG 39, [2002] All ER (D) 388 (Jul), CA — 24.16, 24.105
Roche v UK [2005] All ER (D) 212 (Oct) — 36.10
Roe v Minister of Health [1954] 2 QB 66 — 2.10, 2.39
Rollinson v Kimberley Clark Ltd [1999] CPLR 581, (1999) *The Times*, 22 June, CA — 25.36, 27.108
Rolls-Royce v Doughty [1987] ICR 932 — 8.14
Ronald Stothard (widower & administrator of the estate of Christine Stothard deceased) v Gateshead Health Authority Lawtel Document No AM0200402 — 31.9
Rondel v Worsley [1969] AC 191 — 5.23
Rose v Express Welding Limited (1986) Lexis, 21 January 1986 — 24.94
Rose v Ford [1937] AC 826, [1937] 3 All ER 359, 157 LT 174, HL — 9.46
Rothwell v Chemical & Insulating Co Ltd; Re Pleural Plaques Litigation *sub nom* Grieves v FT Everard & Sons, Re Pleural Plaques Litigation [2006] EWCA Civ 27, [2006] All ER (D) 187 (Jan), CA reversing Grieves v Everard & Sons [2005] EWHC 88 — 6.67, 9.29, 24.33
Rowbotham v the Royal Masonic Hospital [2003] PIQR 1 — 24.47
Rowe v Kingston Upon Hull City Council [2003] ELR 771 — 24.16
Royal Bank of Canada v Secretary of State for Defence [2003] EWHC 1479 — 33.29
Royal Bank of Scotland v S of S for Defence (Unreported) 14 May 2003 — 32.33
Royal Institute of Chartered Surveyors v Wiseman Marshall [2000] PNLR 649 — 34.13
Rubens v Walker [1946] SC 215 — 14.27
Rylands v Fletcher (1868) LR 3 HL 330, HL — 4.53, 36.48

S (a child) v H [2004] 10 June 2004, unreported — 28.78
S (a minor) v Birmingham Health Authority [2001] Lloyd's Rep Medical 382 — 5.17
Saif Ali v Sydney Mitchell & Co (a Firm) [1980] AC 198, [1978] 3 WLR 849, [1978] 3 All ER 1033, HL — 34.15
Samaroo v Secretary of State for HO [2001] UKHRR 1150 — 36.16
SAMCO v York Montague Ltd [1997] AC 191 — 3.3
Samways v London Tilbury & Southend Railway [1902] 18 TLR 295 — 4.18
Sanderson v Blythe Theatre Co [1903] 2 KB 533 — 33.43
Sarra v Sarra [1994] 2 FLR 880 — 34.54
Sarwar v Alam [2002] 1 WLR 125 — 35.56
Savage v South Essex Partnership NHS Foundation Trust TLR 16 February 2007 — 36.57
Sayers v Harlow UDC [1958] 1 WLR 623 — 4.31
Scammell v Dicker LTL [2001] 1 WLR 631, [2001] NPC 1, (2001) 98(7) LSG 41, CA — 29.2, 29.12
Schneider v Eisovitch [1960] 2 QB 430, [1960] 1 All ER 169, [1960] 2 WLR 169 — 13.8
Scholes v Home Secretary (2006) HRLR 44 — 36.53
Schott Chem v Bentley [1990] 3 WLR 397 — 20.15
Scott v Harrogate Borough Council 20 January 2003, unreported, Harrogate County Court — 28.73
Scuriaga v Powell [1979] 123 SJ 406 — 24.46, 24.124
Searby v Yorkshire Traction [2003] EWCA Civ 1856 — 7.97
Secretary of State for Health v R (ex parte Watts) [2004] 2 CMLR 1273 — 8.2
Secretary of State for Social Security and the Chief Adjudication Officer v Percival White [1993] 17 BMLR 68 — 13.79
Seymour v Williams [1995] 1 FLR 862 — 24.12
Shade v Compton Partnership [2000] Lloyd's Rep PN 81 — 24.13
Shah v Singh [1996] PNLR 84, CA — 34.15
Shaher v British Aerospace Flying College Ltd [2003] SLT 791 — 31.51
Shapland v Palmer [1999] 1 WLR 2068 — 24.95
Sharratt v London Central Bus Co Ltd and other appeals (The Accident Group Test Cases), Hollins v Russell and other appeals [2003] 28 LS Gaz R 30, [2003] EWCA Civ 718, [2003] 4 All ER 590, [2003] 1 WLR 2487, [2003] NLJR 920, Times, 10 June, 147 Sol Jo LB 662, [2003] All ER (D) 311 (May) — 35.71

Shaw v Skeet & Others [1996] 7 Med LR 371 25.67
Sherlock v Chester City Council [2004] EWCA Civ 210 4.20, 7.23, 7.30
Shirley v Caswell [2000] Lloyd's Rep PN 955 33.25
Silverton v Goodall [1997] PIQR P451, CA 30.17, 30.55
Simmons v British Steel plc [2004] UKHL 20, [2004] ICR 585 2.32, 6.59
Sindell v Abbott Laboratories 26 Cal 3d 588, 607 P 2d 924 (1980) 3.46
Skitt v Khan [1997] 8 Med LR 105 24.47, 24.112, 24.117
Slade v Caulfield [2004] 17 September 2004, unreported 28.78
Smart v East Cheshire NHS Trust [2003] EWHC 2806, (2003) Lawtel, 2 December, (2003)
    80 BMLR 175, QBD 33.38
Smith (Michael John) v West Lancashire Health Authority [1995] PIQR P514 24.47
Smith v Central Asbestos Company Limited [1973] AC 518 24.60, 24.70, 24.84
Smith v Kvaerner Cementation Foundations Ltd [2007] 1 WLR 370 36.76
Smith v Lancashire Health Authority [1995] PIQR 514 24.19
Smith v Leech Brain & Co Ltd [1962] 2 QB 405 2.36
Smith v Leicester Health Authority [1997] 36 BMLR 23, [1998] Lloyd's Rep Med 77 24.64,
24.121
Smith v Littlewoods Organisation Ltd [1987] 1 AC 241 2.4, 3.49
Smith v Liverpool CC [2006] EWHC 743 24.16
Smith v Manchester Corpn [1974] 17 KIR 1 10.17, 11.50, 11.53, 11.54, 16.20, 9.51
Smith v NHSLA [2001] Lloyd's Rep Med 90 24.47, 24.59
Smith v Notaro Ltd (unreported) 5 May 2006, CA 7.84
Smith v Notaro Ltd 5 May 2006, CA 7.97
Smith v WH Smith & Sons Ltd [1952] 1 All ER 528 33.40
Smith v White Knight Laundry Ltd [2002] 1 WLR 616, [2001] 3 All ER 862, [2001]
    EWCA Civ 660 24.144
Smiths Dock Limited v Edwards et al [2004] EWHC 1116 35.40
Snell v Farrell [1990] 2 SCR 311, 72 DLR (4th) 289 3.11
Sniezek v Bundy (Letchworth) Ltd [2000] PIQR P213, CA 24.18, 24.21, 24.50, 24.124
Soering v UK (1989) 11 EHRR 439 36.4
Sowden v Lodge, Crookdale v Drury [2004] EWCA Civ 1370, [2005] 1 All ER 581 13.6, 13.66,
13.128, 13.135, 13.137, 13.138, 13.139, 13.141, 13.144, 15.37
Sowerby v Charlton [2005] EWCA Civ 1610, [2006] PIQR P15 27.15
Spargo v North Essex District Health Authority [1997] PIQR P235, [1997] 8 Med LR 125,
    (1997) 37 BMLR 99 24.18, 24.19, 24.45, 24.50
Spence v Wilson (No 2) (1998) *The Times*, May 18 16.21
Spencer-Franks v Kellogg, Brown and Root [2005] SC (D) 28/12 7.58
Spittle v Bunney [1988] 3 All ER 1031, [1988] 1 WLR 847, (1988) 132 Sol Jo 754, CA 13.166,
18.24
St Helen's MBC v Barnes [2006] EWCA Civ 1372 30.70
Stanley v Saddique [1992] QB 1, [1992] 1 All ER 529, [1991] 2 WLR 459, CA 13.159, 13.160,
13.161, 13.163, 13.165, 31.45
Stansbie v Trotman [1948] 2 KB 48 3.49
Stanton v Callaghan [1999] 2 WLR 745 5.22, 5.24
Stanton v Youlden [1960] 1 WLR 543 31.43
Stapley v Gypsum Mines Ltd [1953] AC 663 2.42, 4.47
Stark v Post Office [2000] EWCA Civ 64, [2000] ICR 1013 7.51, 7.53, 7.57, 7.97, 8.28, 8.31
Starr v National Coal Board [1977] 1 WLR 63; [1977] 1 All ER 243, CA 25.51, 25.56
Staveley Iron and Chemical Company Ltd v Jones [1956] AC 672 4.40, 7.24
Steeds v Peverel Management Services Ltd [2001] EWCA Civ 419, [2001] All ER (D) 370
    (Mar), (2001) *The Times*, 16 May 24.116, 24.130
Stephen v Riverside Area Health Authority [1990] 1 Med LR 261 24.26, 24.31, 24.46, 24.83
Stephens v Doncaster HA Kemp & Kemp, A1-004 9.25
Stevens Associates v The Aviary Estate TLR 2 February 2001 36.66
Stevens v Gullis and Pile (third party) [2000] 1 All ER 527 5.14, 27.108
Stevens v Nash Dredging and Reclamation Company Limited (1982) Lexis, 27 July 1982 24.55
Stilton v Stilton & MIB [1993] PIQR P135 4.35
Stoczni Gdanska SA v Latvian Shipping Co & ors [2001] *The Times* May 8 33.22
Stokes v Guest, Keen & Nettlefold (Bolts and Nuts) Ltd [1968] 1 WLR 1776 1.17, 2.10
Stovin v Wise [1996] AC 923 2.4
Stringman v McArdle [1994] 1 WLR 1653, [1994] PIQR P230, (1993) *The Times*, 19
    November, CA 20.24
Stubbings v United Kingdom (Applications 22083/93, 22095/93) (1996) 23 EHRR 213,
    [1997] 3 FCR 157, [1997] 1 FLR 105 24.4, 24.11, 36.67

Stubbings v Webb and Another [1993] AC 498, [1993] 2 WLR 120, [1993] 1 FLR 714,
 [1993] 1 All ER 322, HL; reversing [1992] QB 197, [1991] 3 WLR 383, [1992]
 1 FLR 296, [1991] 3 All ER 949, CA 24.11, 24.38, 24.39, 36.67
Sullivan v Boone 1939 205 Minn 437 3.4
Summers v Tice 2 P 2d 1 (1948) 3.40
Sutherland v Hatton; *sub nom* Jones v Sandwell MBC; Hatton v Sutherland; Barber v
 Sutherland CC; Bishop v Baker Refractories Ltd; Somerset CC v Barber;
 Sandwell MBC v Jones; Baker Refractories Ltd v Bishop [2002] EWCA Civ 76,
 [2002] 2 All ER 1, [2002] ICR 613, [2002] PIQR P21, CA 2.34
Symphony Group plc v Hodgson [1994] QB 179, [1993] 3 WLR 830, [1993] 4 All ER
 143, CA 33.18, 34.19, 34.34, 34.39, 34.40

T.G.A. Chapman Ltd v Christopher (1997) *The Times* July 21, CA 34.45
Tait v Pearson (1996) PIQR Q92 10.38
Tanfern Limited v Cameron-MacDonald [2000] 1 WLR1311 24.139
Tatlock v G P Worsley & Co Limited (1989) Lexis, 22 June 1989 24.136
Tattersall v Drysdale (1935) 2KB 174 30.48
Taylor v O'Connor [1971] AC 115 14.30
Taylor v Pace Developments Limited [1991] BCC 406 34.43
Taylor's Application, In Re [1972] 2 QB 369, [1972] 2 WLR 1337, [1972] 2 All ER 873, CA 28.29,
 28.47
TGA Chapman Ltd and another v Christopher and another [1998] 2 All ER 873 34.39
Thai Trading Co v Taylor [1998] QB 785 35.8
Tharros Shipping Co Ltd v Bias Shipping Ltd [1994] 1 Lloyd's Rep. 533 33.72
Theakston v Matthews (1998) *The Times* April 13 33.40
Thomas Johnson Coker v Barkland Cleaning Co TLR, 6 December 1999, CA 25.26
Thomas v Brighton HA [1996] PIQR Q44 15.12, 15.23
Thomas v Plaistow [1997] PIQR P540, (1997) 94(17) LSG 25, (1997) *The Times*, 19
 May, CA 24.127
Thomas v Times Book Co Ltd [1966] 1 WLR 911, [1966] 2 All ER 241, ChD 33.41
Thompson v Brown Construction (Ebbw Vale) Limited [1981] 1 WLR 744 24.96, 24.130, 24.132,
 24.140
Thompson v Fraser [1986] 1 WLR 17 33.54
Thompson v Hampshire County Council (2004) *The Times*, October 14 1.8
Thompson v Price [1973] 1 QB 838, [1973] 2 WLR 1037, [1973] 2 All ER 846 31.32
Thompson v South Tees Area Health Authority 10 April 1990, unreported, QBD 15.24
Thompstone v Tameside and Glossop Acute Services NHS Trust [2006] EWHC 2904 (QB) 10.10,
 11.32, 13.55, 21.15, 21.56
Thornley v Lang [2003] EWCA Civ 1484 35.24
Thrul v Ray [2000] PIQR Q71, CA 13.107, 14.2, 14.4
Tilby v Perfect Pizza Limited SCCO 28 February 2002 35.74
Tindale v Dowsett Engineering Construction Ltd (unreported), Mustill J, 2 December
 1980 9.55
Tinnelly & Sons Ltd v UK (1998) 27 EHRR 249 36.3
Tinsley v Sarkar [2004] EWCA Civ 1098 20.28
Tinsley v Sarkar [2005] EWHC 192 (QB), [2006] PIQR Q1 13.153, 15.37, 15.45
Tolstoy-Miloslavsky v Aldington [1996] 1 WLR 736, [1996] 2 All ER 556, CA 34.20, 34.21, 34.52
Tomlinson v Congleton Borough Council [2003] UKHL 47 2.26, 2.29
Toole v Bolton Metropolitan Borough Council [2002] EWCA Civ 588 4.20, 7.24, 7.65
Topp v London Country Bus (South West) Ltd [1993] 3 All ER 448, [1992] RTR 254,
 [1992] PIQR P206, (1991) *The Times*, 3 December 9.58, 13.169
TP and KM v UK (2002) 34 EHRR 2, [2001] 2 FLR 549, [2001] Fam Law 590, ECHR 36.44,
 36.58
Tranmore v TE Scudder Limited Transcript, 28 April 1998, CA 6.24
Traynor v Donovan [1978] CLY 2612 4.38
Tricker v Hoban [1994] QBD, unreported 15.47

U v Liverpool City Council [2005] 1 WLR 2657 35.39
United Kingdom v EU Council [1996] ECR I-5755; [1996] 3 CMLR 671 8.21, 8.23, 8.24
Urquhart v Fife PCT [2007] CSOH 02 7.43
US Govt v Montgomery (No 2) [2004] 4 All ER 289 36.78
Uttley v Uttley [2002] PIQR P12 26.11, 26.13, 26.40

Van Colle v Chief Constable of Hertfordshire Police [2006] 3 All ER 963 36.39, 36.57
Van Hoffen v Dawson [1994] PIQR P101 20.14, 20.43
Various Claimants v Bryn Alyn Community (Holdings) Ltd [2003] EWCA Civ 383 29.14
Vasiliou v Hajigeorgiou [2005] EWCA Civ 235 25.27, 25.40
Ved v Caress 9 April 2001, unreported 14.42
Vellino v Chief Constable of Greater Manchester [2002] 1 WLR 218 1.10
Vernon v Bosley (No 1) [1997] 1 All ER 577 5.10
Volute, The [1922] 1 AC 129 4.47
Vujnovic v Secretary of State for the Home Department [2003] EWCA Civ 1843, [2003]
    All ER (D) 317 (Dec), CA 36.86

W & Ors v Essex County Council & Anor [2000] 2 WLR 601, [2000] 53 BMLR 1 6.62, 6.73
W (a child) v P [2004] 20 May 2004, unreported 28.78
W v Essex CC [2001] 2 AC 592 36.41
Wadey v Surrey County Council [2001] 1 WLR 820 16.21, 18.31
Wagner v International Railway Company [1921] 232 NY 176 6.38
Wagstaff v Colls [2003] EWCA Civ 469 34.7
Wailes v Stapleton Construction and Commercial Services Ltd [1997] 2 Lloyd's Rep 112 33.72
Wainwright v Home Office [2003] UKHL 53, [2004] 2 AC 406, [2003] 3 WLR 1137, [2004]
    UKHRR 154, [2003] 4 All ER 969, HL, affirming [2001] EWCA Civ 2081, [2002]
    QB 1334, [2002] 3 WLR 405, [2003] 3 All ER 943, CA 36.14, 36.40, 36.56
Wake v Page [2001] RTR 291 30.72
Walker v Northumberland County Council [1995] ICR 702, [1995] 1 All ER 737 2.10, 6.63
Walkin v South Manchester Health Authority [1995] 1 WLR 1543, [1995] 4 All ER
    132, CA 24.15, 24.37
Walkley v Precision Forgings [1979] 2 All ER 548 24.92, 24.93
Wall v Lefevre [1998] 1 Fam LR 605 34.13
Wallersteiner v Moir (No 2) [1975] QB 373, [1975] 2 WLR 389, [1975] 1 All ER 849, CA 35.6
Walsh v Allessio [1996], unreported, QBD, Manchester 15.41
Walters v North Glamorgan NHS Trust [2002] EWCA Civ 1792, [2003] PIQR P232,
    [2002] All ER (D) 87 (Dec), CA 36.42
Walton v Calderdale Healthcare NHS Trust [2005] EW1053 (QB) 13.146
Wandsworth London BC v Michalak [2003] 1 WLR 617 36.27
Ward v Newalls Insulation Company [1998] PIQR Q41 11.23
Ward v The Leeds Teaching Hospitals NHS Trust [2004] EWHC 2106 6.66
Warriner v Warriner [2002] EWCA Civ 81, [2002] 1 WLR 1703, [2003] 3 All ER 447, CA 10.10,
  21.54
Waters v Metropolitan Police Commissioner [2000] 1 WLR 1607 36.41
Watson v McEwan [1905] AC 480 5.23
Watson v Powles [1968] 1 QB 596, [1967] 3 All ER 721, [1967] 3 WLR 1364, 111 Sol Jo
    562, CA 11.2, 11.39
Watson v Willmott [1991] 1 QB 140, [1990] 3 WLR 1103, [1991] 1 All ER 473 9.48, 13.165
Webb v Emo Air Cargo Ltd [1993] ICR 175 7.8, 8.10, 31.34
Welch v Albright and Wilson [1993] unreported, QBD, Birmingham 15.12
Wells v Wells; Thomas v Brighton HA; Page v Sheerness Steel Co plc [1999] 1 AC 345,
    [1998] 3 WLR 329, [1998] 3 All ER 481, [1998] PIQR Q56, HL, reversing Wells v
    Wells; Thomas v Brighton Health Authority; Page v Sheerness Steel Co plc [1997]
    1 WLR 652, [1997] 1 All ER 673, CA 10.3, 10.41, 11.40, 12.1, 12.2, 12.18, 13.49, 13.50,
  13.51, 14.29, 14.30, 14.31, 15.1, 15.12, 15.19, 18.7
Welsh v Robson Road Haulage Limited Court of Appeal, 17 May 1995, unreported 15.39
West v Shephard [1964] AC 326 9.32
Westwood et al v Post Office [1974] AC 1 4.20
White v ESAB Group (UK) Limited (2002) PIQR Q76 10.33
White v Glass (1989) *The Times*, February 18 24.94
White v Revell [2006] EWHC 90054 (8 September 2006) 35.55
White v White [2001] UKHL 9, [2001] 1 WLR 481, [2001] 2 All ER 53, HL 30.8, 30.17, 30.48,
  30.56
White v White and MIB [2001] PIQR P281 8.10, 8.17
Whitehead v Avon County Council (1995) *The Times*, May 3; (1996) PMILL, Vol 9 25.69
Whitehouse v Jordan [1981] 1 WLR 241 5.28
Whitfield v North Durham Health Authority [1995] 6 Med LR 32 24.18, 24.45, 24.103, 24.111,
  24.116, 24.121
Whitfield v North Durham Health Authority [1995] PIQR P 361 24.92

Whittaker (deceased) v BBA Group Kemp & Kemp in the report, K3-007   9.43
Whittles (a firm), Joan Greenhoff v J Lyons & Co Ltd 30 June 1998, CA, unreported   34.15
Whitwood v Drinkall [2003] EWCA Civ 1547   28.40
Wigg v British Railways Board (1986) *The Times*, February 4   6.32
Wiggins v Richard Read (Transport) Ltd (1999) *The Times*, January 14, CA   33.18
Wilding v Lambeth, Southward and Lewisham Area Health Authority (1982) Lexis, 10 May 1982   24.120
Wilkinson v Downton [1897] 2 QB 57, [1895-9] All ER Rep 267, QBD   36.56
Willemse v Hesp [2003] EWCA Civ 994   10.38
Willett v North Bedfordshire Health Authority [1993] PIQR Q166   14.5, 15.15
William McFarlane v Ferguson Shipbuilders Limited 16 March 2004, Ct of Session   7.43
Williams v Ashley (1999) SJ Vol 143, 1144   4.38
Williams v Devon County Council [2003] EWCA Civ 365, (2003) *The Times*, March 18, CA   16.29, 29.26, 29.35
Williams v Giannini 8 May 1998 (unreported)   30.55
Willson v Ministry of Defence [1991] 1 All ER 638, [1991] ICR 595   19.6, 19.7, 21.67
Wilsher v Essex Area Health Authority [1988] AC 1074, 1988 1 All ER 871, [1988] 2 WLR 557   3.14, 3.26, 3.27, 3.28, 3.32, 3.33, 3.36, 3.43
Wilson v Banner Scaffolding Limited (1982) *The Times*, June 22   24.94
Wilson v First County Trust Ltd (No 2) [2004] 1 AC 816   36.9, 36.40
Wilson v Kerry [1993] 1 WLR 963   33.54
Wise v Kaye [1962] 1 QB 638, [1962] 1 All ER 257, [1962] 2 WLR 96, CA   9.49
Wisely v John Fulton (Plumbers) Ltd; Wadey v Surrey County Council [2000] 1 WLR 820, [2000] 2 All ER 545, 2000 SLT 494, (2000) 144 SJLB 197, HL   16.4
Withers v Perry Chain Co Ltd [1961] 1 WLR 1314, [1961] 3 All ER 676, (1961) 105 SJ 648, CA   1.18
Woodhouse v Consignia plc [2002] 1 WLR 2558   36.63, 36.72
Woodings v BT plc 7 February 2003, City of London County Court (unreported)   27.115
Woodrup v Nicol [1993] PIQR, Q104   13.83, 14.19
Woods v Attorney General (1990) Lexis, 18 July 1990   24.31
Worrall v Powergen plc [1999] PIQR Q103   12.20
Wright v British Railways Board [1983] 2 AC 773, [1983] 3 WLR 211, [1983] 2 All ER 698, HL   9.12, 9.17, 18.6
Wright v British Railways Board [2001] QB 272, [2000] 2 WLR 1173, [2000] 3 All ER 138, CA   9.21
Wright v Lodge [1993] 4 All ER 299   2.42
Wright v Romford Blinds and Shutters Ltd [2003] EWHC 1165 (QB), [2003] All ER (D) 331 (May)   7.58
Wright v Sullivan [2006] 1WLR 172   20.28

X (Minors) v Bedfordshire County Council [1995] 2 AC 633   2.4
X v Bedfordshire CC [1995] 2 AC 633   36.44
X v Germany No 7544/76 14 EcomHR   34.27

Yachuk v Oliver Bais Co [1949] AC 386   4.27
Yates v Thakenham Tiles Limited [1995] PIQR 135   24.127
YM v Gloucestershire Hospitals NHS Foundation Trust; Kanu v King's College Hospital Trust [2006] EWHC 820   21.44, 21.45
Yorkshire Traction v Searby [2003] EWCA Civ 1856   7.52
Young (suing as executrix of Young) v Western Power Distribution (South West) plc [2003] EWCA Civ 1034, [2003] 1 WLR 2868   24.4, 24.92, 36.67
Young v Charles Church (Southern) Ltd (1997) 39 BMLR 146, CA   6.31
Young v G L C & Massey [2004] UKHL 29   24.31
Young v Percival [1975] 1 WLR 17   14.30
Younger v Dorset & Somerset Strategic Health Authority Lawtel LTL 25/8/2006: (2006) Lloyd's Rep Med 489   6.9

Z v Finland (1997) 25 EHRR 371   36.80
Z v UK [2001] 2 FLR 612, (2001) 10 BHRC 384, [2001] Fam Law 583, ECHR   36.7, 36.10, 36.22, 36.42, 36.44, 36.58

Part 1
LIABILITY

Chapter 1

DUTY OF CARE

1.1 For a duty of care to arise in common law negligence, a three-part test must be satisfied. There must be sufficient proximity between the parties, it must be just, fair and reasonable to impose a duty of care, and injury to the claimant must be reasonably foreseeable: See *Caparo Industries plc v Dickman*.[1] The three-part test is a flexible test in that there is a large degree of overlap between the parts which provide a useful structure to simplify the problem of identifying whether or not there is a duty of care: see *Marc Rich & Co v Bishop Rock Marine*.[2]

EMPLOYERS

1.2 An employee of workmen clearly satisfies the proximity test and the just, fair and reasonable test so far as his employees are concerned. Thus, the third element of reasonable foreseeability of injury is the important test which needs to be satisfied in order to establish that in the particular circumstances the employer owes a duty of care to his employees. To establish liability it is then necessary to prove breach of the duty and that the breach caused personal injury.

1.3 There may be a duty of care implied in a contract of service between an employer and an employee, but the precise scope is unclear and most commentators consider that the tortuous duty is more extensive.

EMPLOYEE ON LOAN

1.4 Where an employee is loaned to another employer, the temporary employer may so take over the control of how the employee does his work that the employee becomes part of the temporary employer's organisation and the temporary employer is thus liable to the employee: See *Garrard v AE Soutbey & Co and Standard Telephones and Cables*.[3] However, if an employer has delegated to another party one of his duties to his employees, such as the duty to provide and operate a safe system of work, that delegation does not allow the employer to escape liability if the duty has not been properly performed: see

---

[1] [1990] 2 AC 605.
[2] [1996] 1 AC 211.
[3] [1952] 2 QB 174; [1992] 2 QB 174.

McDermid v Nash Dredging Co Ltd,[4] and also *Morris v Breaveglen Ltd*.[5] In such situations it may well be that both the employer and the temporary employer owe a duty of care to the employee. Although the duty may exist and be non-delegable, it is a question of fact and degree as to whether there has been a breach: see *Cook v Square Deal Ltd and others*[6] where the employee was injured by a defective floor in Saudi Arabia and could not recover against his employer who was based in England.

SELF-EMPLOYED WORKERS

1.5 A self-employed worker will satisfy the proximity and 'just, fair and reasonable' tests in respect of those who might be affected by his actions in carrying out his work. Again, the test of foreseeability is the vital third element.

1.6 Where a self-employed worker is engaged by an 'employer', if it is a genuine labour-only sub-contract, the common law duties of an employer to his employee are not owed to the self-employed worker: see *Quinn v Birch Bros (Builders) Ltd*.[7] The true status of the worker will be examined so that a builder's labourer 'on the lump' can be held to be an employee: see *Ferguson v John Dawson & Partners (Contractors) Ltd*.[8] The element of control is important, but not decisive, and the question of element of control is important in determining whether the worker is an employee to whom a duty of care is owed: see *Lane v The Shire Roofing Company (Oxford) Ltd*.[9]

ROAD USERS

1.7 A duty of care is owed by road users, whether drivers or pedestrians, to other road users: see *Nance v British Columbia Electric Railway Co Ltd*.[10]

1.8 However, no duty is owed to road users by the highway authority to provide road markings or warning signs on a road: see *Gorringe v Calderdale Metropolitan Borough Council*.[11] Nor is there liability in respect of the layout of the highway: see *Thompson v Hampshire County Council*.[12] The removal of ice and snow from the highway is subject to a statutory duty, but does not give rise to a common law duty.

---

[4] [1987] AC 906.
[5] [1993] ICR 766, CA; [1993] PIQR P294.
[6] [1992] ICR 262, CA; [1992] PIQR P33, CA.
[7] [1966] 2 QB 370, CA.
[8] [1976] 1 WLR 1213.
[9] [1995] PIQR P417.
[10] [1951] AC 601.
[11] [2004] 2 All ER 326, HL.
[12] (2004) *Times*, October 14.

OTHER PARTIES

1.9 Air passengers are owed a duty of care by the airline, although special rules in respect of limitation and damages may apply. A passenger in an aircraft on a test flight was owed a duty of care by the authorities who certified the airworthiness of the aircraft: see *Perrett v Collins*.[13]

1.10 The police do not owe a duty of care to members of the public to prevent crime: see *Hill v Chief Constable of West Yorkshire*;[14] *Costello v Chief Constable of Northumbria*.[15] The police may put themselves in a degree of proximity which could give rise to a duty of care, but where there was police surveillance it was not just, fair and reasonable to impose a duty in respect of an attempted murder: see *Brindle v Commissioner of Police for the Metropolis*.[16] No duty of care was owed to an escaping prisoner: see *Vellino v Chief Constable of Greater Manchester*.[17] However, an escaping driver owes a duty of care to the pursuing police driver: see *Langley v Dray & MT Policies at Lloyd's*.[18]

1.11 A fire brigade does not owe a duty of care to the owner of premises: see *Capital Counties plc v Hampshire County Council*.[19] In contrast, the owner of premises may owe a duty of care to a firefighter who comes to premises to fight a fire that was caused by the owner of the premises: see *Ogwo v Taylor*.[20]

BALANCING THE DUTIES OF CARE

1.12 More than one duty of care may apply to a particular situation. It arises most obviously in the provision of public services. In such circumstances it may be necessary to weigh up the competing duties, balancing the risk of injury against the task in hand. In *King v Sussex Ambulance NHS Trust*[21] the ambulance service's duty to its employee was balanced with the duty of care owed to its patients. An ambulanceman was required to carry a patient down steep stairs in circumstances which carried with them a foreseeable risk of injury. The moving of the patient was not an emergency, but was urgent. The ambulance service was not liable for injuries sustained whilst carrying the patient using a hazardous method where the only alternative way to remove the patient was by demolishing a window and using the fire brigade. The essential premise was that what is reasonable in the circumstances has to be evaluated with regard to the social utility of the operation, a public authority's duties to the public and to the public service employee.

---

[13] 2 Lloyd's Rep 255, CA.
[14] (1988) 138 NLJ 126.
[15] [1999] ICR 730.
[16] Unreported.
[17] [2002] 1 WLR 218, CA.
[18] [1998] PIQR P314, CA.
[19] [1997] QB 1004, CA.
[20] [1988] AC 431.
[21] [2002] ICR 1413.

1.13 A further example arose in *R v East Sussex County council, the Disability Rights Commission (interested party) ex p A, B (by their Litigation Friend the Official Solicitor), X, Y*.[22] Contrary to the requests of the adult patients' parents, the local authority refused to provide care staff to manually lift and move the patients who suffered from profound physical and learning disabilities. The local authority owed duties to both their employees and to patients. They had to make an assessment on the impact on the employee care assistant and the impact on the patient.

FORESEEABILITY

1.14 The test of foreseeability is flexible. It contains two distinct elements: the incidence of risk and the degree of severity of risk created. This is not always identified in the reported cases. The difficulty arises in making the judgment between the risk that is so small that a reasonable man would disregard it and the risk, which although small, would not be disregarded. In *Bolton v Stone*,[23] the chance of the cricket ball hitting someone in the road was a risk of such small magnitude that it could be disregarded. In *Gerrard v Staffordshire Potteries*[24] the risk of a ceramic fragment flying up into the eye of a worker when glaze was applied by compressed air was held to be sufficiently great to found liability.

1.15 In *Gerrard*, there had never been a previous injury, but the risk was of permanent damage to eyesight. In *Bolton v Stone*, the road was an ordinary side road giving access to private houses in Cheetham Hill, Manchester. If the cricket ground had abutted the M6, where a ball could shatter a windscreen and cause multiple collisions, the decision might have been different.

1.16 The fact that the event has not occurred previously may have evidential force but is not decisive: see, for example, *Gerrard v Staffordshire Potteries*.

1.17 Foreseeability is often said to be an objective test, but this can be misleading. The objective test is the degree of knowledge to be expected of the ordinary prudent employer: see *Stokes v Guest Keen & Nettlefold (Bolts and Nuts) Ltd*.[25] It may well be necessary to consider whether the proposed defendant has or should have specialist knowledge of technical or scientific matters. A large corporation with a research department, medical officers and safety officers will be expected to know more than a smaller concern. Access to trade publications or trade knowledge may be a relevant matter. Reports from the Chief Inspector of Factories may help to set the standard: see *Bryce v Swan Hunter Group*.[26]

---

[22] [2003] EWHC 167 (Admin).
[23] [1951] AC 850.
[24] [1995] ICR 502, CA; [1995] PIQR P169.
[25] [1968] 1 WLR 1776.
[26] [1988] 1 All ER 659.

1.18 Where an employer knows, or ought to have known, that an employee has a vulnerability to injury, whether it be, for example, a weakened back or sensitive skin, then the employer is under a duty to take extra precautions: see *Paris v Stepney Borough Council*.[27] The duty does not necessarily extend to providing complete protection; it is a question of what is reasonable in balancing the risk. It may be sufficient to warn the employee of the risks. There is no duty to provide alternative work, or to dismiss the employee: see *Withers v Perry Chain Co*.[28]

'NERVOUS SHOCK'

1.19 To succeed in a claim for damages for 'nervous shock' it is necessary to prove that the claimant has suffered a recognised psychiatric illness: see *Page v Smith*[29] and *Frost v Chief Constable of South Yorkshire*.[30]

1.20 The law on this topic has undergone recent clarification and some of the earlier cases will need to be treated with care. A key to understanding the topic is to divide the claimants into categories of 'primary victims' and 'secondary victims'.

1.21 A primary victim is someone who is involved in an accident, for example the occupant of a car involved in a collision or a factory worker present at an explosion. A duty of care arises if the defendant can, or should, foresee that his conduct will expose the victim to a risk of personal injury, whether physical or psychiatric. Where the primary victim has suffered physical injury, the defendant will be bound to compensate the claimant if psychiatric injury results, even if psychiatric injury was not foreseeable; this is the 'eggshell skull' rule: see *Malcolm v Broadhurst*.[31] Where there is physical injury, there must be foreseeability of psychiatric injury in a person of reasonable fortitude. Once the duty has arisen it is no defence to the claim that the victim was predisposed to psychiatric illness, or that the psychiatric illness takes a rare form or is of unusual severity: see *Page v Smith*.

1.22 A secondary victim is a person who was no more than a passive and unwilling witness of injury to others. In order to show sufficient proximity to establish a successful claim, the secondary victim must show a close tie of love and affection to the immediate victim, closeness in time and space to the incident or its aftermath, and perception by sight or hearing or its equivalent of the event or its aftermath: see *Alcock v Chief Constable of West Yorkshire*.[32] Seeing a disaster on television was not sufficiently proximate: see *Alcock v Chief Constable of West Yorkshire*.

---

[27] [1951] AC 367.
[28] [1961] 1 WLR 1314, CA.
[29] [1996] AC 155, HL; [1995] PIQR P329, HL.
[30] [1999] 2 AC 455.
[31] [1970] 3 All ER 508.
[32] [1992] 1 AC 310.

1.23 Rescuers are a rather particular hybrid. They were not put in peril by the accident itself, but come to render assistance in the immediate aftermath. They do not have a close tie of love or affection with the victims and so do not qualify for compensation under the secondary victim definition. Where they put themselves in physical danger or reasonably believed that they had put themselves in danger, they will establish a duty of care and will be compensated for psychiatric damage: see *Frost v Chief Constable of South Yorkshire*; *Chadwick v British Railways Board*;[33] *McFarlane v EE Caledonia Ltd*.[34]

---

[33] [1967] 1 WLR 912.
[34] [1994] 2 All ER 1, CA.

Chapter 2

FORESEEABILITY

2.1 The concept of reasonable foreseeability dominates the law of negligence. It is used in determining the existence of a duty of care, breach of a duty and the damages that are recoverable. This chapter considers how far it has become a sufficient, as well as a necessary, condition, and what exactly has to be foreseen, in order to establish liability in tort for personal injuries.

DUTY OF CARE

2.2 The modern tripartite test for the determination of a duty of care consists of (i) foreseeability, (ii) proximity and (iii) consideration of whether it is fair, just and reasonable to impose a duty.[1] 'Proximity' is often used as an umbrella term to encompass all the circumstances in which a duty of care can arise in tort. In this sense foreseeability has been a cornerstone of proximity since the seminal words of Lord Atkin in *Donoghue v Stevenson*[2] that:

> '... you must take reasonable care to avoid acts or omissions which you can reasonably foresee would be likely to injure your neighbour'.

2.3 Whilst foreseeability is always a necessary requirement to generate a duty of care, it is usually sufficient as the only requirement in situations where physical harm is foreseen.[3] Thus in most personal injury cases, reasonable foreseeability of personal injury is the only requirement. It is unnecessary to consider the other elements of the tripartite test in the normal running down or accident at work case.

2.4 There are exceptions to this general rule. In cases of pure omission, mere foresight of physical injury is insufficient to impose a duty. Unless there has been an assumption of responsibility, there is no duty to assist a drowning person. In cases where there is a power but no duty to act, liability is denied on grounds of insufficient proximity[4] or more exceptionally because it is not just and reasonable to impose a duty[5] even though damage from failure to act is

---

[1] *Caparo Industries v Dickman* [1990] 2 AC 605 at 617–618 per Lord Bridge.
[2] [1932] AC 562.
[3] See *The Hua Lien* [1991] 1 Lloyd's Rep 309, 328.
[4] See, eg, *Capital & Counties plc v Hampshire County Council* [1997] QB 1004, *Stovin v Wise* [1996] AC 923.
[5] See, eg, *Hill v Chief Constable of West Yorkshire* [1989] AC 53, *X (Minors) v Bedfordshire County Council* [1995] 2 AC 633.

reasonably foreseeable. In such cases there is no positive duty to act. Where, however, by reason of the proximity of the relationship between the parties or assumption of responsibility by one party, there is a duty to take positive steps (for instance, to prevent the wrongdoing of a third party), the normal test of foreseeability is applied.[6]

THE STANDARD OF FORESIGHT

2.5 'Reasonable foresight' consists of more than merely foreseeing the *possibility* of a particular occurrence. A defendant is expected to foresee and guard against only the reasonable and *probable* consequences of a failure to take care.[7] A classic illustration of this point is *Bolton v Stone*.[8] In that case it was foreseeable that a cricket ball might hit someone passing the cricket ground, but the risk was very small. The House of Lords held that foreseeing the possibility of injury was insufficient and that the reasonable man was only expected to take 'precautions against risks which are reasonably likely to happen'.[9]

2.6 In a modern industrialised society the risk, meaning the possibility, of physical injury is ubiquitous and inescapable. If the risk of being struck by a cricket ball is 'extremely small' or 'negligible', then it amounts to one of the many risks ordinarily to be expected in modern life. Such risks do not normally create a cause of action for anyone suffering an accidental injury.[10]

2.7 Contrast *Bolton v Stone* with *Miller v Jackson*,[11] another cricketing case. What distinguishes the two decisions is the degree of foresight of injury. In *Bolton v Stone*, because only six balls in 28 years had been hit into the road, the risk was foreseeable but not likely. In *Miller v Jackson* because six to nine balls per season were hit into the housing estate, the risk of injury was not merely foreseeable but likely.

2.8 At one time *Bolton v Stone* was erroneously thought to require foresight of injury being more likely than not to occur. It is now well established that the probability required to impose a duty of care is that of a 'real risk'. This was defined by Lord Reid in *Overseas Tankship (UK) Ltd v The Miller Steamship Co Pty (The Wagon Mound No 2)*[12] as 'one which would occur to the mind of a reasonable man . . . and which he would not brush aside as far-fetched'. In that case the Miller Steamship Co owned two vessels, which were moored at a wharf and were undergoing repairs involving oxy-acetylene welding. The *Wagon Mound*, a vessel chartered by Overseas Tankship,

---

[6] See *Smith v Littlewoods Organisation Ltd* [1987] AC 241.
[7] See *Glasgow Corporation v Muir* [1943] AC 448, 454.
[8] [1951] AC 850.
[9] Ibid per Lord Oaksey, 863.
[10] See *Green v Building Scene Ltd* [1994] PIQR 259 at 269 per Staughton LJ.
[11] [1977] QB 966.
[12] [1967] AC 617, 643.

carelessly allowed oil to overflow and drift around the wharf and vessels. The oil caught fire and damaged the wharf and vessels. It was held by the Board that as, on the trial judge's findings, the chief engineer of the *Wagon Mound* ought to have known that there was a real risk that the oil would catch fire,[13] there was sufficient probability of damage by fire for a duty to avoid such damage to exist. This is to be contrasted with the opposite finding of fact in *The Wagon Mound No 1*[14] (in which the wharf owners sued the charterers of the *Wagon Mound*) that an engineer could not reasonably have been expected to know that oil spread on water was capable of catching fire. As a result, in that case no liability was established.

2.9 Whether a risk is sufficiently serious so as to amount to a 'real risk' depends on the facts of each case. A small risk may nonetheless be a real risk.[15]

2.10 Reasonable foreseeability is an objective test in which events are seen through the eyes of the reasonable man who is imputed with all the facts which the defendant knew or ought to have known at the time of the event. He does not have the benefit of hindsight. Hence a defendant is not liable if at the time an operation is carried out, it is not known that the anaesthetic could be contaminated by disinfectant and cause paralysis.[16] The standard of care is to a large degree a function of what ought to have been foreseen and so is very flexible. For instance, if an employer knows that an employee has a particular vulnerability, such as having only one eye, the employer ought to foresee the likelihood of a more severe injury and take additional precautions.[17] Similarly, organisers of a disabled persons' sports event will be under a more onerous duty in respect of safety measures than if it were an able-bodied event.[18] If the defendant has knowledge and experience, which is higher than that to be expected of a reasonable man acting in his position or capacity, then he is judged by that enhanced standard of foresight.[19]

CLASS OF PERSON

2.11 A duty of care in negligence is not owed to the world, but only to one's neighbours, ie 'persons who are so closely and directly affected by my act that I ought reasonably to have them in contemplation as being affected' by one's act

---

[13] 'Serious damage to ships or other property was not only foreseeable but very likely', per Lord Reid 643C–D.
[14] *Overseas Tankship (UK) Ltd v Morts Dock and Engineering Co Ltd (The Wagon Mound No 1)* [1961] AC 388.
[15] *Gerrard v Staffordshire Potteries* [1995] PIQR P169.
[16] See *Roe v Minister of Health* [1954] 2 QB 66, the court 'must not look at the 1947 accident with 1954 spectacles' per Denning LJ.
[17] See *Paris v Stepney Borough Council* [1951] AC 376. This has so far been the route to a finding of liability in the stress at work claims, see, e g *Walker v Northumberland County Council* [1995] 1 All ER 737.
[18] See *Morrell v Owen* (1993) *The Times* December 14.
[19] See *Stokes v Guest, Keen & Nettlefold (Bolts and Nuts) Ltd* [1968] 1 WLR 1776.

or omission.[20] A claimant can only recover if he shows himself to be within the category of victims which was reasonably foreseeable. Another way of putting this is to say that there must be proximity in time, space and relationship between the claimant and the tortfeasor. Generally, if a person is within the range of physical danger then he is a foreseeable claimant. Thus in *Farraj v King's Healthcare NHS Trust and Cytogenic DNA Services Ltd*[21] Mrs Farraj had claimed damages against the Trust for the wrongful birth of her disabled son. Cytogenic had conducted testing on a foetal tissue sample, but had not informed anybody that the sample was poor and another should be obtained. Cytogenic argued that it offered a limited service for a modest fee, that there was no relationship between it and Mrs Farraj, and that it owed Mrs Farraj no duty of care. The High Court held that there was a sufficient relationship of proximity between Cytogenic and Mrs Farraj to found a duty of care because it was reasonably foreseeable that recipients of test results would rely, whether directly or indirectly, on the skill and care of those conducting the tests. That was so even though Mrs Farraj did not know of the existence of Cytogenic, but merely that someone would be carrying out such tests.

KIND OF DAMAGE

2.12 Duties of care in tort do not exist in the abstract.

> 'But there can be no liability until the damage is done. It is not the act but the consequences on which tortious duty is founded. Just as (as it has been said) there is no such thing as negligence in the air, so there is no such thing as liability in the air.'[22]

2.13 Thus in every case it is necessary to analyse whether a duty was owed to the particular claimant to protect him against the damage he has in fact suffered.

> 'The essential factor in determining liability is whether the damage is of such a kind as the reasonable man should have foreseen.'[23]

2.14 In a different context (recovery of damages for pure economic loss), Lord Bridge said:

> 'It is never sufficient to ask simply whether A owes B a duty of care. It is always necessary to determine the scope of the duty by reference to the kind of damage from which A must take care to save B harmless.'[24]

---

[20] *Donoghue v Stevenson* op cit 580.
[21] [2006] EWHC 1228 QB.
[22] *The Wagon Mound No 1* op cit at 425.
[23] Ibid at 426.
[24] *Caparo Industries plc v Dickman* op cit at 627.

2.15 The concept of 'kind of damage' can be analysed in terms of:

(1) the kind of accident or occurrence;

(2) the kind of injury

in fact suffered.

The kind of accident

2.16 The kind of accident or occurrence must be reasonably foreseeable.[25]

2.17 If the kind of accident is foreseeable, it matters not that the precise manner of its occurrence is unforeseeable. Thus in *Hughes v Lord Advocate*[26] liability was established when paraffin lamps were left unguarded by a hole in a road and boys dropped one down the hole causing an explosion in which one of them suffered burn injuries. A burning accident was foreseeable, although the precise way in which it happened (ie an explosion) was not.[27]

2.18 In contrast, in *The Wagon Mound (No 1)*, on the facts found, pollution damage to the wharf from the spillage of oil was foreseeable but the ignition of the oil was not. Hence the defendants owed no duty to the wharf owners in respect of damage to the wharf caused when the spilt oil was unexpectedly set on fire. Damage by fire, which was unforeseeable, was a different kind of damage to damage by spoiling.

2.19 More controversially, the Court of Appeal has held that an accident occurring from an explosion caused by the chemical reaction of an asbestos sheet being dropped in a cauldron of molten liquid was a different kind of accident to one caused by the sheet being dropped and splashing molten liquid.[28] Arguably both were burning accidents. Yet the former was held not to be foreseeable; although the latter was, the danger of such splashing had passed when the asbestos sheet became completely submerged.

2.20 One might possibly reconcile *Hughes* with *Doughty* by saying that in that in the former case the known source of danger was the same, viz the paraffin lamp, whereas in the latter case the explosive nature of asbestos was a different and unknown danger from that of splashing hot liquid. The matter is complicated, however, by *Jolley v London Borough of Sutton*. In this case a boat on the local authority's land was potentially dangerous to children playing on it because it was rotten; the authority accepted that the risk of children suffering injury as a consequence of its rotten state was foreseeable, and that it would have been negligent in failing to remove the boat had an accident of that kind occurred. The accident that did occur, however, was that two teenage boys

---

[25] *Hughes v Lord Advocate* [1963] AC 837.
[26] Ibid.
[27] Ibid at 856.
[28] *Doughty v Turner Manufacturing Company* [1964] 1 QB 518.

propped the boat up with a car jack in order to work under it, and one was injured when the boat collapsed. The cause of the accident was not the rotten condition of the boat, but the inadequate manner in which it had been jacked and propped up. The Court of Appeal held that there was no liability because the accident which occurred was of a different kind to the accident which was foreseeable.[29]

2.21 However, the House of Lords reversed that judgment.[30] Per Lord Steyn, the foreseeable risk posed by a rotten boat was that children 'would meddle with the boat at risk of some physical injury'.[31] An abandoned boat, whether damaged or not, was an allurement to teenage boys, and to draw a comparison between one form of meddling and another was fallacious.

2.22 Lord Hoffmann proposed a broader test. He cited Lord Reid in *The Wagon Mound (No 2)*, who had said that a reasonable man would neglect a risk of an extremely small magnitude 'only if he had some valid reason for doing so, eg that it would involve considerable expense to eliminate the risk'.[32] Here, the council had admitted that it should have removed the boat, thereby showing that 'if there were a wider risk, the council would have had to incur no additional expense to eliminate it'. In the light of the minimal cost of prevention, therefore, the council would be entitled to ignore the risk only if it was both different in kind and 'so remote that it could be brushed aside as far-fetched'.[33]

2.23 Contrast this approach with *Darby v National Trust*.[34] Mr Darby drowned in a pond at one of the Trust's properties. Visitors frequently swam in the pond, a fact of which the Trust was aware, but nothing was done to discourage this save for a notice in the car park which stated, among other information, 'bathing and boating not allowed'. The Court of Appeal found that there was no duty to erect warning notices to prevent swimming, finding that the pond, although murky, cold and deeper towards the middle than at the edges, was 'entirely typical' of ponds in general and, citing *Cotton v Derbyshire Dales District Council*,[35] there was no need to warn adults of sound mind of an obvious hazard.

2.24 There was, however, an admitted risk of contracting Weil's Disease, a risk that the Trust admitted required a notice. The claimant submitted that the cost and expense of such a sign would not have been great and that, had it been in place, it would have prevented Mr Darby from going into the pond and drowning. The Court of Appeal rejected this argument: 'Unpleasant though Weil's Disease, I have no doubt, is, it was not the kind of risk or damage which

---

[29] [1998] 1 WLR 1546.
[30] [2000] 1 WLR 1082.
[31] Ibid at 1085.
[32] Ibid at 642.
[33] Ibid at 1092.
[34] [2001] EWCA Civ 189.
[35] 10 June 1994, CA, unreported.

Mr Darby suffered, and any duty to warn against Weil's Disease cannot, in my judgment, support a claim for damages resulting from a quite different cause.'[36]

2.25 The Court of Appeal did not consider that its ruling was inconsistent with *Jolley* as the risk was different in kind, but did not appear to have regard for Lord Hoffmann's comment that the risk must be different in kind *and* vanishingly remote. The authors would suggest that a risk of drowning in this, or any, pond clearly cannot be wholly unforeseeable, and that had the Court of Appeal adopted Lord Hoffmann's broader approach it would have been bound to find that the risk was foreseeable and that the cost of prevention involved no additional steps to the ones which would have been required to prevent against Weil's Disease.

2.26 The answer may lie in the fact that Jolley, unlike Darby, was a child. Is the House of Lords moving towards a separate, more stringent test of foreseeability in cases where children are involved? The decision of the House of Lords in *Tomlinson v Congleton Borough Council* would seem to suggest that this is so.[37] Tomlinson was a trespasser who broke his neck when diving into shallow water at a flooded former sand quarry, which was a popular beauty spot. Noting that the statutory duty owed to trespassers under the Occupiers' Liability Act 1984 relates only to dangers caused by 'the state of the premises', the court found that no duty was owed because the quarry was an ordinary open stretch of water which was 'shallow in some places and deep in others, but that is the nature of lakes'.[38] Lord Hoffmann took the view that diving was an activity that involved an inherent risk, to which Tomlinson had fallen victim by failing to execute his dive properly or to choose an appropriately deep part of the lake. It could not be said that the risk could be attributed to the state of the premises, for 'otherwise any premises can be said to be dangerous to someone who has chosen to use them for some inherently dangerous activity'.[39] He felt that 'it would be extremely rare for an occupier of land to be under a duty to prevent people from taking risks which are inherent in the activities they freely choose to undertake upon the land'.[40] This judgment would seem to sit ill with the decision in *Jolley* save for the perhaps significant and repeatedly emphasised fact that Tomlinson was an adult and a 'person of full capacity'.[41]

2.27 Recently, in *Clare v Perry*[42] the Court of Appeal rejected a claim where the claimant was injured after she deliberately jumped off a wall, albeit there was a foreseeable risk of an accidental fall from the wall. The claimant's deliberate act was a different kind of accident from that which the defendant occupier should have guarded against. Once again the claimant was an adult not a child, a point stressed by Mance LJ.

---

[36] Para 22.
[37] [2003] UKHL 47.
[38] Ibid para 26.
[39] Ibid para 27.
[40] Ibid para 45.
[41] Ibid para 26.
[42] [2005] EWCA Civ 39.

2.28 The matter has been revisited, albeit indirectly, in *Keown v Coventry Healthcare Trust*.[43] Keown, a trespassing child aged 11, had climbed up – and fallen off – the outside of a fire escape on the defendant Trust's land. There was nothing inherently wrong with the fire escape, but its structure made it possible to scale it from the outside. The Court of Appeal was asked to consider whether there had been any breach of the statutory duty owed to trespassers under the Occupiers Liability Act 1984, and in particular whether this amounted to a 'danger due to the state of the premises' within the meaning of s. 1(1)a of that Act. The Court, in accepting the Defendant's submission that the danger was created not by the state of the premises but by the decision to pursue a particular activity, considered *Tomlinson* and remarked that it 'would conclude the question in [the Defendant's] favour if the Claimant was an adult. Does it make any difference that the Claimant was a child?'[44] The answer – surely relevant too from the perspective of foreseeability of harm in negligence – was that 'premises which are not dangerous from the point of view of an adult can be dangerous for a child but it is a question of fact and degree....The injury suffered by a toddler crawling into an empty and derelict house could be injury suffered by reason of danger due to the state of the premises where injury suffered by an adult in the same circumstances might not be. But it would not be right to ignore a child's choice to indulge in a dangerous activity in every case merely because he was a child.' The judge had found that the Claimant not only appreciated that there was a risk of falling but also that what he was doing was dangerous and that he should not have been climbing the exterior of the fire escape. In the circumstances, it could not be said that the Claimant did not recognise the danger, and the risk arose not out of the state of the premises, which were as one would expect them to be, but out of what the Claimant chose to do.

2.29 Only time will tell whether *Keown* has the effect of closing the gap opened up by *Jolley* and *Congleton* and whether the apparent distinction between children and adults in foreseeability cases becomes explicit.

Kind of injury

2.30 For many years it appeared that a distinction might be drawn between physical injury and psychiatric damage as being two separate kinds of damage. However, after the decision of the House of Lords in *Page v Smith*[45] it seems that personal injuries, whether to the body or the mind, are an indivisible kind of damage. Lord Lloyd delivered the majority decision in that case and said:

> 'Once it is established that the defendant is under a duty of care to avoid causing personal injury to the plaintiff it matters not whether the injury in fact sustained is physical, psychiatric or both.'[46]

---

[43] [2006] EWCA Civ 39.
[44] [2006] EWCA Civ 39, at para 11.
[45] [1996] AC 155.
[46] Ibid 190D–E.

2.31 It should be noted that the ratio decidendi of *Page v Smith* was limited to circumstances in which the claimant was within the foreseeable range of the risk of physical injury (a 'primary victim'). Different control mechanisms still apply to secondary victims, ie those who suffer psychiatric injury but are outside the foreseeable range of physical injury. In such cases, the requirement of witnessing a traumatic or 'shocking' event, of close ties of affection with the primary victim and of foreseeability of psychiatric injury remain.[47]

2.32 In 'primary victim' personal injury cases, however, the *Page v Smith* approach has been and will probably continue to be applied.[48] Foresight of the 'kind of accident' rather than the 'kind of injury' will remain as the main control mechanism in all such psychiatric harm cases. Thus in *Corr v IBC Vehicles Ltd*[49], where an employee suffered physical injuries as a result of an accident at work and subsequently developed a depressive illness and committed suicide 6 years later, his employers were held liable for financial losses flowing from his suicide. The Court of Appeal, reversing the first instance decision of Nigel Baker QC, held that the Claimant did not need to establish that at the time of the accident the deceased's suicide was reasonably foreseeable as a kind of damage separate from psychiatric and personal injury. His depression had been foreseeable, and the medical evidence was that the suicide had flowed from that condition.

2.33 Nevertheless it is accepted that particular problems of foreseeability arise in cases involving psychiatric damage, and especially in so-called 'stress at work cases', in which it is alleged that an employee has developed a psychiatric condition as a result of the stresses of his occupation. Although injury which takes the form of psychiatric illness is no different in principle, for a primary victim, than physical injury or illness, the causes of mental illness 'will often be complex and depend on the interaction between the patient's personality and a number of factors in the patient's life. It is not easy to predict who will fall victim, how, why or when.'[50]

2.34 Accordingly the Court of Appeal in *Hatton v Sutherland* [2002] 2 All ER 1 formulated a number of 'practical propositions' to cases where complaint is made of psychiatric illness brought about by stress at work. The threshold question is whether psychiatric harm to the particular employee was reasonably foreseeable. So far so uncomplicated. However foreseeability in such cases will

---

[47] *Frost v Chief Constable of South Yorkshire Police* [1998] 3 WLR 1509.
[48] See, for example, *Donachie v Chief Constable of Greater Manchester Police* [2004] EWCA Civ 405, and *Simmons v British Steel plc* [2004] UKHL 20. In the latter case S suffered an accident at work and occasioned physical injury. However he was angry at the way that he was treated following the accident and as a consequence developed a psychiatric injury. There was a finding that the anger was caused by the accident and that anger had in turn caused the psychiatric injury; hence there was a sufficient causal connection between the accident and the depression which S had suffered. The court held that the starting point was that S was a primary victim in respect of whom physical injury of some kind was foreseeable, and indeed had happened. S brought himself within *Page* and could recover for the psychiatric illness.
[49] [2006] EWCA Civ 331
[50] *Hatton v Sutherland* [2002] 2 All ER 1, at page 5.

depend upon 'what the employer knows (or ought reasonably to know) about the individual employee. Because of the nature of mental disorder, it is harder to foresee than physical injury, but may be easier to foresee in a known individual than in the population at large...An employer is usually entitled to assume that the employee can withstand the normal pressures of the job unless he knows of some particular problem or vulnerability.'[51] Factors likely to be relevant include the nature of the job and whether the particular individual is subject to unreasonable pressures compared to others in the same or similar jobs but (per Hale LJ) the employer is generally entitled to take what he is told by the employee at face value and is not required to make searching enquiries ether of him or of his medical advisers. In summary, and in order to trigger a duty to take steps, 'the implications of impending harm to health arising from stress at work must be plain enough for any reasonable employer to realizse that he should do something about it.'

2.35 The House of Lords, overturning on the facts the decision in one of the consolidated appeals in *Hatton*, has offered a reminder that the Court of Appeal's guidance is no more than guidance, and that every case will depend on its own particular facts.[52] Further judicial refinements to Hale LJ's guidance seem likely.

EXTENT OF DAMAGE

2.36 Failing to foresee the extent of damage is immaterial. If it was foreseeable that a worker would be burnt by a splash of molten metal, then he can recover for the unforeseeable cancer that ensues.[53] A tortfeasor will be liable in respect of unforeseeable predispositions and latent conditions, once he foresees some physical injury, because he must take his victim as he finds him (the 'egg-shell skull' principle).

BREACH OF DUTY

2.37 Though foreseeability may be sufficient to impose a duty of care, other factors come into play in considering whether there has been a breach of duty. Notwithstanding that a real risk is foreseen, it is not negligent to fail to eliminate it if in all the circumstances a reasonable man would think it right to neglect to do so.[54] This involves a weighing of the magnitude of the risk and potential harm against the difficulty of eliminating it and the benefit of the activity.

---

[51] Ibid. at page 43. The tests formulated by Hale LJ were not the subject of the subsequent appeal to the House of Lords, reported under the name of *Barber v Somerset County Council* [2004] 2 All ER 385.
[52] Ibid. at page 406.
[53] *Smith v Leech Brain & Co Ltd* [1962] 2 QB 405.
[54] *The Wagon Mound No 2* op cit per Lord Reid 643.

CAUSATION AND DAMAGE

2.38 Since the decision of the Privy Council in *The Wagon Mound No 1*[55] reasonable foreseeability has been the touchstone for determining causation and remoteness of damage. The statement that 'the essential factor in determining liability is whether the damage is of such a kind as the reasonable man should have foreseen'[56] applies just as much at this stage of the analysis as at the duty stage. The components which constitute a duty of care, viz foreseeability of a 'kind of damage' and a 'class of claimant', are mirrored in the elements of causation and remoteness of damage.

2.39 The rationale underlying this congruence of test appears to be the acceptance of the principle that the extent of a tortfeasor's liability should reflect his blameworthiness. If the defendant's carelessness consisted of failing to prevent one kind of damage, he should not be held liable if the claimant suffers a different kind of damage. The concept that breach and damage should specifically coincide has sometimes been called the privity of fault doctrine but is better known as the risk principle.[57] In short, the principle is that if the damage suffered was not within the risk generated by the breach of duty it should not be recoverable.[58]

2.40 The principle is justified not by a logical necessity that the test for duty must match the test for damage, but by 'current ideas of justice or morality': see *The Wagon Mound No 1*.[59] The tort of negligence exists to penalise those who failed to act as they should have done. If damage of a particular kind could not have been foreseen, it is unreal to expect the defendant to have taken preventative measures to avoid it.

2.41 Although the application of the foreseeability test to both duty and causation may appear to favour defendants, its effect depends crucially upon how broadly or narrowly the categories of 'kind of accident' are defined. Furthermore, harshness to the claimant is counterbalanced by the 'take your victim as you find him' principle. For instance, the risk of a person scratching their finger merits minor preventative measures. The risk of paralysis merits extensive preventative measures. But if a person suffers a rare reaction to a scratch which results in paralysis, the defendant is liable for the full extent of the injury. Under the risk principle, the defendant ought to be penalised for the minor injuries which were foreseeable (eg a scratch) as a result of failing to take minor preventative measures. Instead he is penalised for failing to take the extensive measures when there was no real risk to justify them. This

---

[55] Op cit at 426.
[56] Ibid.
[57] Glanville Williams provided the classic exposition of this concept in his article *The Risk Principle* 77 LQR 179.
[58] In *Roe v Minister of Health* [1954] 2 QB 66, 85 Denning LJ said 'the extent of his liability is to be found by asking the one question: is the consequence fairly to be regarded as within the risk created by the negligence?'
[59] Op cit at 422 per Viscount Simonds.

inconsistency illustrates the underlying tension between the conflicting objectives of tort law: on the one hand to compensate the victim for all the injury suffered, and on the other to penalise the defendant only to the extent that he has been at fault.

2.42 Just as foreseeability is constrained by other criteria (eg proximity) when the question is whether a duty of care exists and whether a breach of that duty has occurred, so it is with causation. Take the case of fresh intervening acts. Of course, if these were not reasonably foreseeable, causation by the original negligent act is unlikely to be established. However, even where a fresh intervening act is a foreseeable consequence of the original negligent act, it may nonetheless prevent recovery. Thus it is foreseeable that negligently parking a car on a dual carriageway will lead to a collision, but where that collision is due to the reckless driving of a lorry colliding into the defendant's parked car, there is no causation attributable to the defendant.[60] Similarly, the claimant's act may be reasonably foreseeable, but if it is so unreasonable as to eclipse the wrongdoing of the defendant, no liability will attach.[61] The rationale is that causation is a function of blameworthiness as well as simple causative potency.[62]

CONCLUSION

2.43 One is driven to the conclusion that, although reasonable foreseeability is a necessary condition of recovery of damages, it is not a sufficient condition. Though it is, doubtless, a subtle instrument, the law requires other tools to achieve 'justice or morality' in the face of the countless variants of fact that the cases reveal. 'Although the foreseeability test is a handmaiden of the law, it is by no means a maid-of-all-work.'[63]

---

[60] See *Wright v Lodge* [1993] 4 All ER 299.
[61] See *Mckew v Holland & Hannen & Cubitts* [1969] 3 All ER 1621, 1623G.
[62] These are the two values employed by the courts in assessing contributory negligence see: *Stapley v Gypsum Mines Ltd* [1953] AC 663.
[63] Per Salmon LJ in *Quinn v Burch Bros (Builders Ltd)* [1966] 2 QB 370, 394.

Chapter 3

CAUSATION

INTRODUCTION

3.1 Causation is the link in the chain of legal reasoning between breach of duty and damage; the tests used to establish causation attempt to define and confine the circumstances in which an event, amounting to a breach of duty, may be said to be the cause of another event, the damage suffered by the claimant. The standard or default test for proof of causation in tort is the 'but for' test. If a claimant is able to establish on the balance of probabilities that 'but for' the defendant's breach of duty, he would not have suffered injury, then he will have sufficiently proved the causation of that injury. In most circumstances if a claimant is unable to prove causation using this test, then the claim will fail for want of proof of causation. In most instances cause and effect are so obviously and intimately linked that the 'but for' test produces what is obviously the correct conclusion. However, there are a number of commonly encountered factual situations in which the 'but for' test may present difficulties.

3.2 While the simple 'but for' test may be adequate to establish whether or not a defendant is liable to compensate a claimant in simple circumstances, there are circumstances in which it provides an unsatisfactory answer to the question of causation. In circumstances in which there is only one tortfeasor, in circumstances in which there is only one potential cause and in circumstances in which the effect of a particular action is reasonably obvious to a doctor, if not to a layman, no difficulties will arise and no injustice will be caused to either a claimant or a defendant by the use of the 'but for' test for causation. It is when there are multiple tortfeasors, when there is more than one potential cause and when the manner in which an injury is caused is not known to the most experienced of doctors, that causation becomes problematic. In industrial disease claims these complications are frequently present, sometimes individually, but often a single case will present all of these complications. The result is that many of the leading cases on causation are industrial disease cases, but it is a mistake to assume that the principles which are found in those cases are not equally applicable to other types of claim.

SOME TROUBLESOME ASPECTS OF THE 'BUT FOR' TEST

Causally irrelevant facts

3.3 In order for a fact to be considered to be causally relevant, it is not sufficient to establish that it was a result of the actions of the defendant, it must also be connected to the reason why the defendant was in breach of duty. Thus, if a doctor negligently advises a mountaineer that his knee is sufficiently recovered to allow him to resume climbing, it is not sufficient to establish causation to say that 'but for' the doctor's advice the mountaineer would have remained in his hotel and would not have been killed in a climbing accident. If the climber fell because his knee failed him, then there is a connection between the doctor's breach of duty and the damage suffered, but this necessary connection is not present if the mountaineer is carried away by an avalanche.[1] In the Australian case of *Faulkner v Keffalinos*[2] Windeyer J said, 'But for the first accident the plaintiff might still have been employed by the appellants and therefore would not have been where he was when the second accident happened; but lawyers eschew this kind of but for or sine qua non reasoning about cause and consequence.' The American Restatement of the Law of Torts[3] gives as an example a defendant who negligently hands a child a loaded rifle. That he was in breach of a duty owed to the child does not mean that the defendant will be liable to compensate a child who drops the gun on his foot and fractures some bones; the injury is not connected with the reason why the defendant was negligent, the handing of a loaded, rather than an unloaded, gun to the child.

3.4 The same is true of omissions; there must be connection between the breach of duty and the damage, it is simply insufficient to prove that both are present. A train driver may be said to have been negligent if he fails to warn road users that he is approaching an unmanned crossing, but that is causally irrelevant if the claimant strikes the 68th carriage of the train.[4] A doctor may be negligent in failing to diagnose arsenic poisoning, but causation will not be established if the claimant was certain to die in any event.[5] An employer may be said to be negligent in failing to provide a safety harness, but if the claimant would not have worn it, then the failure to provide it is causally irrelevant.[6]

Alternative sufficient causes

3.5 This is the academic's favourite topic, but happily one which detains a practitioner but rarely, as the factual assumptions necessary to raise the issue seldom arise; indeed, the standard example is somewhat far fetched. If a man is falling from the top of the Empire State Building but is shot dead as he passes

---

[1] See Lord Hoffmann in *SAMCO v York Montague Ltd* [1997] AC 191 at 213.
[2] (1971) 45 AJLR 80 at 86.
[3] 2d ss 281.
[4] *Sullivan v Boone* 1939 205 Minn 437.
[5] *Barnett v Kensington and Chelsea Hospital Management Committee* [1969] 1 QB 428.
[6] *McWilliams v Sir William Arrol* [1962] 1 WLR 295.

the windows of the 20th floor, who has caused his death? Is it the man who pushed him off the top of the skyscraper, or is it the man who shot him dead before he reached the ground? The 'but for' test produces the answer that neither is liable.[7]

3.6 If the tortious act is an omission, the 'but for' test may produce the same unacceptable result. A driver may be said to have been negligent in failing to apply the brakes on his car. If we also know that the brakes were ineffective as a result of the tortious act of the owner of the car, can it be said that either breach of duty caused the injury suffered by the pedestrian? The mechanical application of the 'but for' test again produces the result that neither caused the injury.

3.7 If it was possible to define some principle which encompasses all such extraordinary sets of circumstances, it would cause widespread unemployment amongst academic writers. Despite the considerable volume of theoretical answers to these conundrums, such difficulties are usually decided on the basis of judicial instinct, which simply reveals the lack of any underlying principle. However, some general considerations can be identified.

(i) Very close connection in time between the events. In an American case a child fell from a bridge and on his way to certain death, or at least very serious injury, struck a power cable which had been negligently left un-insulated, and was electrocuted.[8] That the child was falling to almost certain death led the court to award only nominal damages against the power company. If the original fall had been a tortious event then the balance of the damages payable would be paid by that tortfeasor. The same answer would result in the man who pushed the victim from the top of the Empire State Building being found liable.

(ii) Longer intervals of time. If a driver on his way to the airport is killed as a result of the negligence of another driver is it an answer to say that he would have died when the plane he was seeking to catch crashed killing all aboard? The answer is 'no', but the reason is based not on the fact that the second event, being killed in a plane crash, is a hypothetical event, it is probably based on wider policy considerations; the claimant must be left with a cause of action against someone, and he would have no cause of action arising out of the plane crash.

(iii) The same is not true if the claimant does have a cause of action in respect of the second event. In *Baker v Willoughby*[9] the claimant suffered an injury to his leg as a result of the tort of one defendant and this injury left him crippled. Later he was shot in the leg as a result of which his leg was amputated. His initial injury had resulted in a reduction in his earnings. Was the original tortfeasor liable to continue to compensate him after his

---

[7] Taken from *Hall's Principles of Criminal Law* (an American textbook).
[8] The facts of *Dillon v Twin State Gas and Electric Co* 1932 85 NH 449, 163.
[9] [1970] AC 467.

leg had been amputated? The 'but for' test applied mechanically produces the result that neither tortfeasor is liable to compensate the claimant for his loss of earnings after his leg was amputated. The House of Lords concluded that the original tortfeasor continued to be liable for the partial loss of earnings after the leg was amputated and that the subsequent tortfeasor was responsible for any additional loss of earnings. The same solution has been applied to cases of property damage. In *Performance Cars v Abraham*[10] the claimant's car was damaged in an accident, but before it had been repaired the same part was damaged in a subsequent accident. The first tortfeasor was responsible for the damage.

3.8 Naturally occurring events. These cases do not deal with the need to ensure that someone is liable to the claimant but are concerned solely with the extent of that liability. In *Jobling v Associated Dairies*,[11] the claimant was injured at work and lost earnings as a result. He subsequently developed a back condition which would have lead to the same loss of earnings. If the solution in *Baker v Willoughby* had been applied then the claimant would have been able to claim for part of his loss of earnings even after the onset of the illness. The House of Lords decided otherwise, drawing a distinction between tortious and non-tortious subsequent events.

3.9 Simultaneous events. If the two events occur at the same time then causation is established in respect of both. Thus if two persons walk towards the scene of a gas leak with lit candles, the 'but for' test will produce the answer that neither are liable for the explosion which occurs. Common sense however prevails, and both are liable for the whole of the damage because it is impossible to separate the causative effect of their individual actions in any sensible fashion.

When the 'but for' test does not provide the answer

3.10 These small wrinkles aside, the but for test serves as the sole and satisfactory test for causation in most cases. However, it does not always provide a sensible or acceptable solution. The cases in which the result is not satisfactory are, almost without exception, cases in which medical knowledge is imperfect with the result that it is impossible for a claimant to succeed using the 'but for' test of causation.

The circumstances in which the 'but for' test for causation leads to difficulty

3.11 The circumstances in which the 'but for' test for causation provides results which are unacceptable has been the subject of considerable academic and judicial discussion over many years, not only in the United Kingdom but in

---

[10] [1962] 1 QB 33.
[11] [1982] AC 794, [1981] 3 WLR 155, [1981] 2 All ER 752.

almost all legal systems. In *Snell v Farrell*,[12] Sopinka J, delivering the judgment of the Supreme Court of Canada, said:

> 'The traditional approach to causation has come under attack in a number of cases in which there is concern that due to the complexities of proof, the probable victim of tortious conduct will be deprived of relief. This concern is strongest in circumstances in which, on the basis of some percentage of statistical probability, the plaintiff is the likely victim of the combined tortious conduct of a number of defendants, but cannot prove causation against a specific defendant or defendants on the basis of particularised evidence in accordance with traditional principles. The challenge to the traditional approach has manifested itself in cases dealing with non-traumatic injuries such as man-made diseases resulting from the widespread diffusion of chemical products, including product liability cases in which a product which can cause injury is widely manufactured and marketed by a large number of corporations.'

3.12 Also in Canada, McLachlin J, the present Chief Justice of Canada, writing extra-judicially[13] voiced a similar concern. She said:

> 'Tort law is about compensating those who are wrongfully injured. But even more fundamentally, it is about recognising and righting wrongful conduct by one person or a group of persons that harms others. If tort law becomes incapable of recognising important wrongs, and hence incapable of righting them, victims will be left with a sense of grievance and the public will be left with a feeling that justice is not what it should be. Some perceive that this may be occurring due to our rules of causation. In recent years, a conflation of factors have caused lawyers, scholars and courts to question anew whether the way tort law has traditionally defined the necessary relationship between tortious acts and injuries is the right way to define it, or at least the only way. This questioning has happened in the United States and in England and has surfaced in Australia. And it is happening in Canada. Why is this happening? Why are courts now asking questions that for decades, indeed centuries, did not pose themselves, or if they did, were of no great urgency? I would suggest that it is because too often the traditional "but-for", all-or-nothing, test denies recovery where our instinctive sense of justice – of what is the right result for the situation – tells us the victim should obtain some compensation.'

3.13 In Australia in *March v E & M H Stramare Pty Ltd*, Mason CJ, sitting in the High Court of Australia, did not 'accept that the 'but for' (causa sine qua non) test ever was or now should become the exclusive test of causation in negligence cases,' and he added:[14]

> 'The "but for" test gives rise to a well known difficulty in cases where there are two or more acts or events which would each be sufficient to bring about the plaintiff's injury. The application of the test "gives the result, contrary to common sense, that neither is a cause": Winfield & Jolowicz on Tort, 13th ed (1989), p 134. In truth, the application of the test proves to be either inadequate or troublesome in

---

[12] [1990] 2 SCR 311, 72 DLR (4th) 289.
[13] 'Negligence Law – Proving the Connection', in *Torts Tomorrow, A Tribute to John Fleming*, eds Mullany & Linden, (1998), p 16.
[14] (1991) 171 CLR 506 HC of A.

various situations in which there are multiple acts or events leading to the plaintiff's injury: see, eg *Chapman v Hearse, Baker v Willoughby* [1970] AC 467; *McGhee v National Coal Board; M'Kew v Holland & Hannen & Cubitts (Scotland) Ltd* 1970 SC (HL) 20 (to which I shall shortly refer in some detail). The cases demonstrate the lesson of experience, namely, that the test, applied as an exclusive criterion of causation, yields unacceptable results and that the results which it yields must be tempered by the making of value judgments and the infusion of policy considerations.'

3.14 The major cases in which the courts have considered the application of a different principle of causation are *Bonnington Castings v Wardlaw, McGhee v National Coal Board, Fitzgerald v Lane* and *Fairchild v Glenhaven*. In these cases the courts have responded to the perceived injustice to claimants which results from the use of 'but for' test for causation by establishing a series of tests for proof of causation which differ from the standard 'but for' test. These authorities have become inextricably bound up with the decision of the House of Lords in *Wilsher v Essex Area Health Authority* and, albeit to a lesser extent, the decision of the House of Lords in *Hotson v East Berkshire Health Authority*. *Wilsher*, which in reality is a simple application of the 'but for' test for causation, is considered in this section, but the possibility of putting such a case as the 'loss of a chance' is considered in para **3.47**.

3.15 These cases can cause a great deal of confusion unless it borne in mind that they provide answers to quite different questions. It is now apparent that there are at least three causation difficulties dealt with by this group of authorities and the cases fall into three groups, each providing an answer to a specific causation problem. There are those dealing with a situation in which there was more than one potential type of cause for an injury,[15] there are those in which there was only one type of cause for an injury, but in which some part of the causative link occurred in circumstances in which the claimant established a breach of duty on the part of a defendant, and part occurred in circumstances in which there was no breach of duty,[16] and there are those in which it was impossible for the claimant to identify which tortfeasor caused the injury from which he suffers.[17]

Bonnington Castings Ltd v Wardlaw

3.16 In the United Kingdom the House of Lords departed from the standard 'but for' test for the first time in *Bonnington Castings Ltd v Wardlaw*[18] by concluding that establishing that a breach of duty materially contributed to the injury was sufficient proof of causation. In *Fairchild v Glenhaven Funeral*

---

[15] Wilsher v Essex Area Health Authority [1988] AC 1074; Hotson v East Berkshire Health Authority [1987] AC 750.
[16] Bonnington Castings Ltd v Wardlaw [1956] AC 613; Nicholson v Atlas Steel Foundry and Engineering Co Ltd [1957] 1 WLR 613; McGhee v National Coal Board [1973] 1 WLR 1.
[17] Fairchild v Glenhaven Funeral Services Ltd [2002] UKHL 22, [2003] 1 AC 32; Sindell v Abott Laboratories 26 Cal 3d 588, 607 P 2d 924 (1980); Summers v Tice 199 2 P 2d 1 (1948); Cook v Lewis [1951] 1 DLR 1.
[18] [1956] AC 613, [1956] All ER 615.

Services Ltd,[2] Lord Rodger traced the origins of the material contribution principle back through the authorities to 1859. This was a considerable tour de force of legal research but it must be said that although the principle can be traced back so far, for very many years it had gone unnoticed. Mr Wardlaw was employed in a foundry where he was exposed to silica dust in the course of his employment. As a result of inhaling silica dust he developed silicosis, a fibrosis of the lung caused by silica dust. The evidence at the trial of the action established that the silica dust which he had inhaled came from two sources. In respect of the first source, which produced the majority of the silica dust which he inhaled, he was unable to prove that his employers were in breach of the duties which they owed to him. However, in respect of the second, but more minor, source of the silica dust, he was able to prove that his employers were in breach of the duty which they owed him. It was contended on behalf of the employers that Mr Wardlaw had failed to establish that he had a cause of action against them, as he was unable to prove that he had suffered damage as a result of their breach of duty. The House of Lords concluded that it was sufficient for the proof of causation, and thus that he had a cause of action, if he was able to establish that the dust he had inhaled as a result of the employer's breach of duty materially contributed to the disease from which he suffered. It should be noted that this case simply establishes that the claimant has established what may be termed 'liability' causation in such circumstances, it does not establish what damage the employer is liable for.

3.17 Lord Reid said:[19]

'It would seem obvious in principle that a pursuer or plaintiff must prove not only negligence or breach of duty but also that such fault caused or materially contributed to his injury, and there is ample authority for that proposition both in Scotland and in England.'

3.18 Later in his speech Lord Reid gave his reasons for reaching a conclusion in favour of the pursuer when he said:[20]

'The medical evidence was that pneumoconiosis is caused by a gradual accumulation in the lungs of minute particles of silica inhaled over a period of years. That means, I think, that the disease is caused by the whole of the noxious material inhaled and, if that material comes from two sources, it cannot be wholly attributed to material from one source or the other.[21] I am in agreement with much of the Lord President's opinion in this case, but I cannot agree that the question is: which was the most probable source of the respondent's disease, the dust from the pneumatic hammers or the dust from the swing grinders? It appears to me that the source of his disease was the dust from both sources, and the real question is whether the dust from the swing grinders materially contributed to the disease. What is a material contribution must be a question of degree. A contribution

---

[19] [1956] AC 613 at 620.
[20] At 621.
[21] Note the similarity of the reasoning with that of Laws LJ in *Rahman v Arearose* [2001] QB 351, [2000] 3 WLR 1184, where the same reason was advanced to justify an apportionment of the damages between the defendants.

which comes within the exception de minimis non curat lex is not material, but I think that any contribution which does not fall within that exception must be material. I do not see how there can be something too large to come within the de minimis principle but yet too small to be material.'

3.19 The following year in *Nicholson v Atlas Steel Foundry and Engineering Co Ltd*,[22] the House of Lords heard an appeal the facts of which were very similar to that in *Bonnington Castings Ltd v Wardlaw*, and followed their earlier decision. The one distinction between the two cases is that Mr Nicholson had died of pneumoconiosis as a result of his exposure to dust during his employment with the defenders, a circumstance which may be relevant when issues of apportionment of damages between the tortious and non-tortious causes are before a court.[23] Viscount Simonds LC, who had also heard the earlier appeal in *Bonnington Castings*, gave reasons for his conclusion which were firmly based on policy grounds, policy grounds which have formed the basis for many of the subsequent decisions. He said:[24]

'if the statute prescribes a proper system of ventilation by the circulation of fresh air so as to render harmless, so far as practicable, all fumes, dust and other impurities that may be injurious to health, generated in the course of work carried on in the factory, and if it is proved that there is no system or only an inadequate system of ventilation, it requires little further to establish a causal link between that default and the illness, due to noxious dust, of a person employed in the shop. Something is required as was held in Wardlaw's case. I was a party to that decision and would not in any way resile from it. But it must not be pressed too far. In the present case there was, in my opinion, ample evidence to support the appellants' case.'

3.20 His conclusion as to the result was most clearly expressed in a passage in which he said:[25]

'where an injury is caused by two (or more) factors operating cumulatively, one (or more) of which factors is a breach of duty and one (or more) is not so, in such a way that it is impossible to ascertain the proportion in which the factors were effective in producing the injury or which factor was decisive, the law does not require a pursuer or plaintiff to prove the impossible, but holds that he is entitled to damages for the injury if he proves on a balance of probabilities that the breach or breaches of duty contributed substantially to causing the injury. If such factors so operate cumulatively, it is, in my judgment, immaterial whether they do so concurrently or successively.'

---

[22] [1957] 1 All ER 77, [1957] 1 WLR 613.
[23] Normally in a case involving pneumoconiosis one would expect the damages to be apportioned as it is a divisible injury. However, death is probably regarded as a single indivisible injury and each defendant is liable for the whole of the damages resulting from the death.
[24] At p 618.
[25] [1957] 1 WLR 613 at 619–620, 1957 1 All ER 776.

McGhee v National Coal Board

3.21 In *McGhee v National Coal Board*,[26] the House of Lords was confronted with a similar, but subtly different, causation problem. Mr McGhee worked in a brickworks and had been exposed to brick dust. As a result of his exposure to brick dust, he contracted dermatitis. He was unable to establish that the exposure to brick dust was in breach of any duty owed to him by the defendants while he was actually at work in the factory. However, he was able to establish that the defenders were in breach of the duty they owed to him by failing to provide showers for his use, with the result that he cycled home while still coated in brick dust. The case differed from *Bonnington Castings* in that the medical evidence did not establish that all the brick dust contributed to the dermatitis. However, the medical evidence did establish that the effect of brick dust on the skin was cumulative in the sense that the longer that brick dust remained on the workman's skin the greater was the chance of his developing dermatitis. The House of Lords was unwilling to draw a distinction between making a material contribution to the injury and materially increasing the chance of an injury. Lord Reid said:[27]

> 'Nor can I accept the distinction drawn by the Lord Ordinary between materially increasing the risk that the disease will occur and making a material contribution to its occurrence. There may be some logical ground for such a distinction where our knowledge of all the material factors is complete. But it has often been said that the legal concept of causation is not based on logic or philosophy. It is based on the practical way in which the ordinary man's mind works in the everyday affairs of life. From a broad and practical viewpoint I can see no substantial difference between saying that what the defender did materially increased the risk of injury to the pursuer and saying that what the defender did made a material contribution to his injury.'

3.22 The distinction between making a material contribution to an injury and materially increasing the chance of an injury occurring is a critical one in circumstances in which medical knowledge is imperfect and where there is more than one defendant exposing a claimant to a noxious substance. If the claimant suffers from a disease which is of a cumulative nature, such as asbestosis or silicosis, it can be said that all the defendants materially contributed to that disease and thus that the claimant, relying on *Bonnington Castings Ltd v Wardlaw*, has established that he has a cause of action. However, if the disease is not of a cumulative nature, each defendant will not have materially contributed to the disease which has occurred, they will simply have increased the risk that the disease will occur.

3.23 The acceptance by the courts that a material increase in the risk is sufficient to prove causation is crucial in mesothelioma cases. While asbestosis may be a condition towards which all of a number of defendants have contributed, by each causing a part of the whole, the same may not be true of mesothelioma. It is possible that this disease is caused by only one of a given

---

[26] [1973] 1 WLR 1.
[27] At p 5.

number of defendants, and that the others, while in breach of the duty which they owed to the claimant, may not have caused him any damage. Thus it cannot be said that each contributed towards the total injury suffered; it may be that only one of them actually caused it. However, as we know that the chance of developing the disease increases with the amount of dust inhaled, each defendant can be said to have materially increased the risk that a given claimant will suffer from the disease.

3.24 In such circumstances, only if a claimant is able to use the test for causation established in *McGhee* will he be able to sufficiently prove causation, as the McGhee test holds that a material increase in the risk is sufficient for proof of causation.

Wilsher v Essex Area Health Authority[28]

3.25 The plaintiff had been born prematurely and was admitted to the special baby care unit of a hospital. He developed retrolental fibroplasia (RLF) as a result of which he became blind in one eye and the sight in his other eye was severely damaged. The evidence at trial established that there were a number of potential medical causes for RLF, one of which was excess oxygen. The trial judge concluded that it was impossible to decide which of the potential causes for RLF had in fact caused it in this particular child's case. However, the evidence at trial did establish that the defendant had been in breach of the duty which they owed to the child. The device which should have monitored the level of oxygen in the claimant's blood had been negligently placed into a vein instead of being placed into an artery, with the result that it did not monitor the oxygen levels properly. The trial judge applied the test in *McGhee*, concluded on the basis of this evidence that the defendant's negligence materially increased the chance of the claimant suffering from RLF, and found in his favour. The trial judge did not conclude that excess oxygen was the cause of the claimant's RLF; he decided no more than that the failure to insert the monitor correctly had increased the risk that the claimant would suffer RLF.

3.26 The Court of Appeal recognised that *Wilsher* differed from *McGhee*. In *McGhee* there had only been one potential cause for the dermatitis from which Mr McGhee suffered, brick dust, whereas in *Wilsher* there were a number of potential causes for the claimant's RLF, only one of which, excess oxygen, was attributable to the defendant's breach of duty. Despite this distinction, the Court of Appeal was willing to apply the principles established in *McGhee* to such a situation.

3.27 The House of Lords disagreed with the Court of Appeal's view. However, instead of choosing to do no more than to distinguish *Wilsher* from *McGhee* on the basis which the majority of the Court of Appeal had

---

[28] [1988] AC 1074, 1988 1 All ER 871, [1988] 2 WLR 557.

recognised was present, they went further. Lord Bridge in his opinion, with which the other members of the House of Lords agreed, concluded that:[29]

> 'The conclusion I draw from these passages is that *McGhee v National Coal Board* [1973] 1 WLR 1 laid down no new principle of law whatever. On the contrary, it affirmed the principle that the onus of proving causation lies on the pursuer or plaintiff. Adopting a robust and pragmatic approach to the undisputed primary facts of the case, the majority concluded that it was a legitimate inference of fact that the defenders' negligence had materially contributed to the pursuer's injury. The decision, in my opinion, is of no greater significance than that and to attempt to extract from it some esoteric principle which in some way modifies, as a matter of law, the nature of the burden of proof of causation which a plaintiff or pursuer must discharge once he has established a relevant breach of duty is a fruitless one.'

3.28 Later in his opinion[30] Lord Bridge did deal with the distinction which the Court of Appeal had recognised between *Wilsher* and *McGhee*, that in the former there were a number of alternative independent causes any one of which may have caused the injury, whereas in *McGhee* there was only one 'agent', brick dust. He approved without reservation a passage from the dissenting judgment of Sir Nicholas Browne-Wilkinson V-C in the Court of Appeal in which he had drawn attention to this distinction. The Vice Chancellor had said:

> 'To apply the principle in *McGhee v National Coal Board* [1973] 1 WLR 1 to the present case would constitute an extension of that principle. In the *McGhee* case there was no doubt that the pursuer's dermatitis was physically caused by brick dust: the only question was whether the continued presence of such brick dust on the pursuer's skin after the time when he should have been provided with a shower caused or materially contributed to the dermatitis which he contracted. There was only one possible agent which could have caused the dermatitis, viz., brick dust, and there was no doubt that the dermatitis from which he suffered was caused by that brick dust. In the present case the question is different. There are a number of different agents which could have caused the RLF. Excess oxygen was one of them. The defendants failed to take reasonable precautions to prevent one of the possible causative agents (e g excess oxygen) from causing RLF. But no one can tell in this case whether excess oxygen did or did not cause or contribute to the RLF suffered by the plaintiff. ... To my mind, the occurrence of RLF following a failure to take a necessary precaution to prevent excess oxygen causing RLF provides no evidence and raises no presumption that it was excess oxygen rather than one or more of the four other possible agents which caused or contributed to RLF in this case. The position, to my mind, is wholly different from that in the *McGhee* [1973] 1 WLR 1, case where there was only one candidate (brick dust) which could have caused the dermatitis, and the failure to take a precaution against brick dust causing dermatitis was followed by dermatitis caused by brick dust. In such a case, I can see the common sense, if not the logic, of holding that, in the absence of any other evidence, the failure to take the precaution caused or contributed to the dermatitis. To the extent that certain members of the House of Lords decided the question on inferences from evidence or presumptions, I do not consider that the

---

[29] [1988] AC 1074 at p 1091.
[30] At p 1092.

present case falls within their reasoning. A failure to take preventative measures against one out of five possible causes is no evidence as to which of those five caused the injury.'

3.29 If, as Lord Bridge had concluded, materially increasing the risk of an event occurring was not sufficient for proof of causation it inevitably presented claimants with a difficulty in one large class of claim, claims for damages arising from the development of mesothelioma, an asbestos cancer. If the actions of two defendants did not combine to create an injury, but were alternative causes for the injury, it ceased to be sufficient for proof of causation to show that a defendant had materially increased the risk of an injury. It followed that unless a claimant was able to show that a particular defendant had caused the injury on the balance of probabilities, then the claimant's claim would fail for want of proof of causation.

3.30 Medical science was able to establish that mesothelioma was the result of asbestos exposure. However, there were two main theories how it caused the disease to start. The first was that mesothelioma is the result of all the fibres of asbestos inhaled by a person acting together to produce the genetic changes in a cell which result in the development of a mesothelioma. The legal consequence of this hypothesis was that all of those who tortiously exposed a claimant to asbestos dust were concurrent tortfeasors, and each was liable for the whole of the injury which resulted.

3.31 The alternative hypothesis, that it was a single fibre, which could have come from only one of the tortfeasors, is just as likely to be correct. Instead of being concurrent tortfeasors the courts had to consider the causation problem caused by alternative tortfeasors, from among whom the claimant was unable to identify which had actually caused his injury.

Fairchild v Glenhaven Funeral Services Ltd

3.32 In *Fairchild v Glenhaven Funeral Services Ltd*,[31] the courts were confronted with the need to decide whether Lord Bridge's view of *McGhee* in *Wilsher* was correct. If it was correct, then it followed that the claimants, on the facts of the cases before the court, would all fail to prove causation against all of the defendants before the court. If Lord Bridge's view was incorrect, and proving an increase in the risk of injury was sufficient for proof of causation, there remained an important distinction between the cases under appeal and *McGhee*. In all of the three appeals there were several tortfeasors and it was necessary for the courts to consider whether the presence of more than one tortfeasor was a distinction between *McGhee* and the cases under appeal which made a difference to the result.

3.33 The House of Lords heard three appeals at the same time, each of which raised the same causation issue. All three workmen had developed mesothelioma as a result of their exposure to asbestos dust. In each case there

---

[31] [2002] UKHL 22, [2003] 1 AC 32, [2002] 3 All ER 305.

were several potential defendants, each of whom had exposed the workman to asbestos dust. In some of the appeals it was only possible to bring before the court those responsible for a small part of the exposure. In *Fairchild* itself the claimant had sued two defendants each of whom were responsible for half of the exposure, but had failed to establish liability against one of them, as neither was responsible for the majority of the exposure. The Court of Appeal followed the view of *McGhee* provided by Lord Bridge in *Wilsher* and decided that the claimants, who were able to establish that each defendant had materially increased the risk of injury, were unable to establish causation on that basis. An unnoticed consequence of the Court of Appeal's decision would have been that in a case in which there were two defendants, one responsible for the majority of the exposure and the other the minority, the claimant would establish causation against the majority exposer, the side effect of which was that the majority exposer would fail to establish a claim for a contribution against the minority exposer.

3.34 The House of Lords could in such circumstances have reached one of three conclusions. They could have concluded that the claimant failed against all defendants, unless the claimant was able to prove on the balance of probabilities that a particular defendant was responsible for the mesothelioma suffered. They could have concluded that the claimant succeeded against all of the exposers in full for the whole of the damage which he had suffered. They could have concluded that the claimant succeeded against each tortfeasor, but only in proportion to the chance of the development of the mesothelioma each defendant had created. The defendants chose not to argue for the third of these possible outcomes.

3.35 The decision is remarkable for its very frank recognition that the result adopted was adopted for policy reasons. Lord Hoffmann said in his opinion:[32]

> 'My Lords, as between the employer in breach of duty and the employee who has lost his life in consequence of a period of exposure to risk to which that employer has contributed, I think it would be both inconsistent with the policy of the law imposing the duty and morally wrong for your Lordships to impose causal requirements which exclude liability.'

3.36 The House of Lords first had to decide whether Lord Bridge's conclusion in *Wilsher*, that *McGhee* did not lay down any rule of law which allowed causation to be sufficiently proved by proving a material increase in the risk of injury, was correct. They examined not only the speeches in *McGhee*, but also the summary of the arguments advanced before the House of Lords and the Inner House of the Court of Session in *McGhee*. Having done so, they were firmly of the view that *McGhee* did in fact establish a legal principle that a material contribution to the risk of injury was sufficient for the proof of causation. Lord Bingham said:[33]

---

[32] At para 64.
[33] [2003] 1 AC 32 at para 21.

'This detailed review of *McGhee* permits certain conclusions to be drawn. First, the House was deciding a question of law. Lord Reid expressly said so, at p 3. The other opinions, save perhaps that of Lord Kilbrandon, cannot be read as decisions of fact or as orthodox applications of settled law. Secondly, the question of law was whether, on the facts of the case as found, a pursuer who could not show that the defender's breach had probably caused the damage of which he complained could none the less succeed. Thirdly, it was not open to the House to draw a factual inference that the breach probably had caused the damage: such an inference was expressly contradicted by the medical experts on both sides; and once that evidence had been given the crux of the argument before the Lord Ordinary and the First Division and the House was whether, since the pursuer could not prove that the breach had probably made a material contribution to his contracting dermatitis, it was enough to show that the breach had increased the risk of his contracting it. Fourthly, it was expressly held by three members of the House (Lord Reid at p 5, Lord Simon at p 8 and Lord Salmon at pp 12–13) that in the circumstances no distinction was to be drawn between making a material contribution to causing the disease and materially increasing the risk of the pursuer contracting it.'

3.37 In his conclusion, with which three of the other four Law Lords agreed he said:[34]

'As is apparent from the conclusions expressed in paragraph 21 above, I cannot for my part accept this passage in Lord Bridge's opinion as accurately reflecting the effect of what the House, or a majority of the House, decided in *McGhee*, which remains sound authority. I am bound to conclude that this passage should no longer be treated as authoritative.'

3.38 There remained two issues to be dealt with, whether the distinction between a case with one tortfeasor and a case with two tortfeasors was a distinction which should prevent the *McGhee* test being used, and the identification of the circumstances in which the favourable test for proof of causation could be applied.

3.39 The House of Lords saw the first of these issues as a moral one. Lord Nicholls put it most strongly when he commented:

'Any other outcome would be deeply offensive to instinctive notions of what justice requires and fairness demands.'

3.40 It is perhaps not surprising that the issue was seen as a moral one, for the alternatives were either that a claimant who had been able to prove that one, or the other, or both of two tortfeasors had killed the deceased, failed against both or succeeded against both. Although the earlier decision of the Court of Appeal in *Fitzgerald v Lane*[35] addressed a similar issue, this was the first time a court in the United Kingdom had been faced with the two hunters problem. Final appeal courts in a number of countries had addressed the same legal and

---

[34] [2003] 1 AC 32 at para 22.
[35] In the Court of Appeal [1987] QB 781. The subsequent appeal to the House of Lords was on a different point.

moral issues raised by the two hunters question before and produced differing results. Their decisions however, differed not in the answer they provided, but only in the way in which the correct result should be reached. Some, such as the courts in Canada[36] and in California,[37] had decided to reverse the burden of proof, requiring a defendant in such a situation to exonerate himself; others had simply imposed liability on all those in breach of duty. Typically the other courts had addressed the issue when confronted with cases involving two hunters. The facts in those cases in their simplest form involved an injury from a single shotgun pellet which could only have been fired by one of two negligent hunters, but it was impossible for the claimant to identify which of the negligent hunters had fired the guilty pellet. After a review of such cases from a number of Commonwealth, American and European jurisdictions,[38] the House of Lords concluded that in such circumstances both defendants were liable to the claimant, despite the fact that only one of them had caused the injury.

3.41 The House of Lords were concerned to define the circumstances in which the new and generous test for causation should be used. The three cases before the House of Lords in *Fairchild* were cases of mesothelioma, a disease for which there is no other cause apart from asbestos dust.

3.42 It is probable that the same principle may be applied to other forms of industrial disease. In a lung cancer claims there are invariably two possible causes for the development of lung cancer, one is the presence of asbestos and the other is tobacco smoke. It is suggested that the first question to be answered is whether the cause was asbestos or tobacco smoke and that the correct causation test is that described in Wilsher, the balance of probabilities test. Once this is established then the Fairchild principles may be applied if there is more than one tortfeasor.

The effect of the decisions in *Bonnington Castings*, *McGhee*, *Wilsher* and *Fairchild*

3.43 Each of these four difficult cases deals with a different causation issue. The questions which they deal with and the answers they provide to them are:

(a) When there is only one tortfeasor, when the condition in question is cumulative, and the evidence establishes that the tortious exposure to a substance materially contributed to the condition's severity, then each tortfeasor against whom breach of duty is proved is liable to the claimant, who will have established against each of them a complete cause of action. See: *Bonnington Castings Ltd v Wardlaw*.

---

[36] *Cook v Lewis* [1951] SCR 830, [1952] 1 DLR 1.
[37] *Summers v Tice* 2 P 2d 1 (1948).
[38] Lord Rodger started with Justinian's Digesta. He then turned to 'slightly more modern' authorities including Cook v Lewis (Supreme Court of Canada) Summers v Tice (Supreme Court of California) and B v Bayer Nederland BV (Hoge Raad, 9 October 1992, NJ 1994, 535).

(b) When there is only one tortfeasor, when the condition in question is not of a cumulative nature, but the evidence establishes that each tortious exposure to the substance materially increased the chance that the claimant will suffer from the condition, then the tortfeasor against whom breach of duty is proved is liable to the claimant, who will have established against him a complete cause of action. See: *McGhee v National Coal Board.*

(c) When there is more than one cause or agent which is capable of causing a condition, then it is necessary for the claimant to prove on the balance of probabilities which agent did cause the disease in his case. See: *Wilsher v Essex Area Health Authority.*

(d) When the condition which is not of a cumulative nature, is proved to be caused by a given substance and the tortious actions of more than one defendant increased to a material extent the chance that a person will suffer from that condition, then the claimant has established a cause of action against all defendants. See: *Fairchild v Glenhaven Funeral Services Ltd.*

The de minimis exception

3.44 The judgments in *Bonnington Castings Ltd v Wardlaw* and *Fairchild v Glenhaven Funeral Services Ltd* establish that a claimant will fail to prove liability against a defendant if that defendant's contribution to the totality of his exposure to dust is de minimis. In a passage from *Bonnington Castings Ltd v Wardlaw*, which was cited with approval in *Fairchild*, Lord Reid said: 'A contribution which comes within the exception de minimis non curat lex is not material, but anything which does not fall within that exception must be material.'

3.45 Neither decision offers any guidance on how modest a level of exposure will amount to de minimis and, as a result, it is difficult to offer any guidance on the level of exposure which a court will consider is within this exception. It is possible to find cases in which the share of the total exposure to asbestos dust for which a defendant is responsible was very modest; *Bryce v Swan Hunter Group plc*[39] is an example of such a case, but the point does not appear to have been argued by the defendants in that case.[40]

3.46 In the absence of any authority, it is impossible to do more than to provide some parameters derived from the few authorities that there are. Taking as an illustration a case of exposure to asbestos dust the following points on the de minimis principle may be made:

---

[39] [1988] 1 All ER 659, [1987] 2 Lloyd's Rep 426.
[40] The only case in which it appears to have been argued is *Golden v Lerch Bros* (1938) 203 Minn 211.

(a) A very large number of very small exposers. In some industries the workmen move from employer to employer with great frequency. In such situations each employer may only be responsible for a few per cent of the claimant's total exposure to asbestos dust. In *Fairchild* some members of the House of Lords commented favourably on the decision of the Supreme Court of California in *Sindell v Abbott Laboratories*,[41] in which liability had been imposed in proportion to the market share the defendant companies had of the total market for the negligently manufactured drug. Liability in that case was imposed on manufacturers whose share of the total market was only 1 or 2%. Those favourable comments may mean that a smaller share of exposure will be sufficient to establish liability causation when there are many similar small exposers.

(b) The only circumstance in which courts frequently consider how small a contribution has to be in order to be classified as de minimis is when assessing degrees of contributory negligence. The statutory provision in the Law Reform (Contributory Negligence) Act 1945, s 1(1), enjoins the court to reduce the damages awarded *'to such extent that the court thinks just and equitable having regard to the claimant's share in the responsibility for the damage'*. The test is therefore broadly similar to the causative requirements for determining whether a defendant is liable at all. It is difficult to find cases where a finding of contributory negligence was made, in which there is a finding of under 10%. In *Capps v Mille*,[42] the trial judge had concluded that:

> 'The Court of Appeal has indicated that one should not make apportionments of contributory negligence for percentages less than 10%, that is to say, that there should only be a reduction of the plaintiff's damages where his responsibility is significant, 10% or above.'

The Court of Appeal did not agree that there was any such rule, but provided no other guidance and then proceeded to assess contributory negligence in that case at 10%. The rule quoted by the trial judge may have been taken from the earlier, but unreported, decision of the Court of Appeal in *Johnson v Tennant Bros Ltd*.[43] In that case, when considering whether a defendant was liable at all, the Court of Appeal came to the conclusion that less than 10% should be regarded as de minimis. However, the authority of this old and unreported decision must be doubtful.

(c) De minimis in this context probably means exposure which is both de minimis in both relative terms and in quantitative terms. Thus in a asbestos disease claim a degree of exposure which is substantial in real terms, even if it is small in terms of the overall exposure, is likely to be

---

[41] 26 Cal 3d 588, 607 P 2d 924 (1980).
[42] [1989] 1 WLR 839.
[43] (1954) unreported, CA transcript 329.

regarded more severely than an exposure which is modest both in percentage terms and in real terms. To do otherwise would be to deprive a serious breach of duty of any effect.

(d) A conclusion that the causative potency of a defendant's conduct should be regarded as de minimis, not only prevents a claimant succeeding in a claim against that defendant, it also has the effect that he cannot be sued for a contribution by other tortfeasors. The probability is that the court will not close its eyes to this consequence. Where there are several tortfeasors each responsible for only a small part of the overall causative potency, but the totality of that for which they are collectively responsible is substantial, the court is likely to impose liability on them, for to do otherwise would deprive the remaining defendants of a right to claim a contribution from them.

LOSS OF A CHANCE

3.47 If a claim fails to meet the balance of probabilities criteria it is possible to redefine the damage which is claimed in the hope that by doing so it will produce a valid claim for damages. To use the illustration given by Lord Nicholls in *Gregg v Scott*[44] if the negligence of a surgeon reduces the chance of survival from 42% to 25% the claimant will inevitably fail to establish that his death was, on the balance of probabilities, caused by the negligence of the treating doctor. If the damage may be defined in terms of the chance lost the claimant has established on the balance of probabilities that he has lost a 17% chance of survival. This manner of putting the claim bears a striking similarity to the success of many claimants in personal injury actions who are able to claim damages for the loss of the chance of some more favourable life event if the tort had not occurred, a chance of promotion perhaps. To some it appears that by denying the prospect of any compensation to a person who has lost a substantial part of his chance of life the court is acting unfairly and that such a conclusion saves the doctor from the consequences of his own neglect. In *Gregg v Scott* the House of Lords faced a case in which the claimant attempted to define his claim in terms of the chance which he had lost. By a majority of 3-2 the House of Lords declined to take this course and concluded that a claim for loss of such a chance could not be advanced. The reasoning of the majority differs but the distinction drawn between *Gregg v Scott* and the recovery for loss of a chance in a PI case is between issues of causation, whether the injury was caused by the tort, and issues relevant to the assessment of damages, how much loss flows from the tort. The debate as to whether the result reached is an unjust one was dealt with by contrasting the position of a claimant who may prove his case on little more than the balance of probabilities, but who will never the less recover the full award of damages. Whether this is a just result will continue to be debated, but in some cases the fact that an injustice is done to the defendant who pays 100% of the damages

---

[44] [2005] 2 AC 176, [2005] 2 WLR 268.

for causing a 60% chance seems a poor argument for causing an injustice to a different group who recover nothing for a loss of a 40% chance. The debate will continue with those who advocate an apportionment of damages in all such cases maintaining that that is the solution which prevents injustice in all cases. The loss of the chance of a favourable outcome cannot serve as a substitute for proof on the balance of probabilities.

INTERVENING CAUSES

3.48 When lawyers spoke Latin the phrase was 'novus actus interveniens'. There comes a time when the causative effect of an action is regarded as being exhausted and that time will come the sooner if there is another significant event between the breach of duty and the occurrence of the damage. If the 'but for' test is applied mechanically the result would be to impose liability on the initial tortfeasor, but there are many situations in which some subsequent event will serve to extinguish or reduce the initial tortfeasor's responsibility. In *Rahman v Arearose*[45] Laws LJ described novus actus as a device used by the courts to ensure that the correct final result was achieved. When this will occur is largely a matter for the judgment of the court and as a result the manner in which novus actus is applied in common situations can be unpredictable. If a lorry is overturned as a result of the negligence of its driver, it may be that another driver some time later will collide with the overturned lorry as a result, in part at least , of his own inattention. Sometimes the initial tortfeasor is held liable for all subsequent events, sometimes he is not. The reason for reaching one conclusion or the other is usually described in terms of common sense; when a judge uses common sense to reach a result it makes it difficult to derive any principle which serves as a universal touchstone.

3.49 It is possible to suggest some of the factors which will be used in order to determine whether or not novus actus will be used to reduce or extinguish the liability of a tortfeasor.

(i) If the subsequent action is the reason why a defendant is in breach of duty novus actus is unlikely to provide a defence, even if the subsequent act is itself a criminal offence. The decorator who fails to shut a front door cannot rely on novus actus to extinguish his liability for a theft which occurs because he has left the door open.[46]

(ii) The more extreme or the more untoward the subsequent events are, the more likely it will be that they are regarded as breaking the chain of causation. Reverting to the example of the overturned lorry, the worse the driving of the second vehicle involved, the longer the time lapse between the first breach of duty and the intervening act and an assessment of the

---

[45] [2001] QB 351.
[46] See *Stansbie v Trotman* [1948] 2 KB 48 at 52. *Dorset Yacht Co v Home Secretary* [1970] 1 AC 1004 at1030 and *Smith v Littlewoods Organisation Ltd* [1987] 1 AC 241 at 249.

relative degrees of lack of care of the parties will all be important criteria in determining whether or not the second event extinguishes the liability of the first tortfeasor.

(iii) The shorter the period of time available to the alleged intervener, the less likely it is that his action will amount to a novus actus. The colloquial expression 'agony of the moment' is not to be elevated to the status of a legal principle, but is simply a description of a set of circumstances which are not considered to be sufficiently blameworthy to extinguish the liability of the initial tortfeasor.

(iv) Medical treatment made necessary by the actions of the initial tortfeasor seldom acts as a novus actus; in order for it to do so the blameworthiness of the medical adviser or surgeon will need to be relatively great.[47]

---

[47] The editor of *Prosser and Keaton on Torts* (5th edn) says at p 309, 'It would be an undue compliment to the medical profession to say that bad surgery is no part of the risk of a broken leg'. See also *Rahman v Arearose Ltd* [2001] QB 501.

Chapter 4

CONTRIBUTORY NEGLIGENCE

THE STATUTORY PROVISION

4.1 The Law Reform (Contributory Negligence) Act 1945, ('the Act') provides:

'S 1(1) Where any person suffers damage as the result partly of his own fault and partly of the fault of any other person or persons, a claim in respect of that damage shall not be defeated by reason of the fault of the person suffering the damage, but the damages recoverable in respect thereof shall be reduced to such extent as the court thinks just and equitable having regard t the claimant's share in the responsibility for the damage ...

S 4 ... fault means negligence, breach of statutory duty or other act or omission which gives rise to liability in tort or would, apart from this Act, give rise to the defence of contributory negligence'.

THE BACKGROUND TO THE STATUTE

4.2 Prior to 1945, contributory negligence, if proved, provided a complete defence to a claim. There was no general power for a court to divide responsibility. If a claimant had the 'last opportunity' to avoid the consequences of the fault of another and, by his blameworthy act or omission, failed to take that opportunity, he could not recover anything.[1]

4.3 The effect of the 1945 Act was to remove an obstacle in the way of a claimant: the Act did not create any right of action.[2] Section 4 of the 1945 Act provides that the act or omission constituting contributory negligence must be such fault on behalf of a claimant as would have given rise to a defence of contributory negligence before 1945. In practice, pre-1945 cases rarely have relevance to modern cases on contributory negligence.

---

[1] *Davies v Mann* (184) 10 M&W 546.
[2] *Drinkwater v Kimber* [1952] 2 QB 281 at 288.

THE NATURE OF THE CLAIMANT'S FAILURE

4.4 If a tortfeasor (T) alleges contributory negligence against a claimant (C), he (T) does not have to show that C owed him (T) a duty of care. C's fault for purposes of contributory negligence amounts to his failure to look after his own interests.

4.5 A finding of contributory negligence is made when the claimant's own negligence contributed to the damage of which he complains. Therefore, in those cases where the claimant would have sustained the same injury even if he had taken all reasonable care for his own safety (such as by wearing a seat belt) his damages will not be reduced.[3]

4.6 However, the defence applies both to those situations where the claimant's own fault contributes to the *extent* of his injuries (such as by not wearing a seat belt) and also where his own fault contributes to the *occurrence of the incident* which itself inflicts the injuries[4] (such as failing to heed a warning instruction). If a court makes a finding of causative negligence, it will only be to the extent that is 'just and equitable' to do so.

4.7 In assessing the appropriate degree of fault on a claimant, two considerations are of paramount importance, namely blameworthiness and causative potency. Making such assessments will depend on the facts of each case and will often involve a comparison with the act or omission of the alleged tortfeasor.[5]

THE AVAILABILITY OF THE DEFENCE

4.8 Contributory negligence is only a defence to a claim which falls within the definition of fault, as set out in s 4 of the 1945 Act. Essentially, it is only available as a defence to tortious claims. If a claimant makes a claim in contract and alleges only duties which are the same as would arise in tort, eg an implied duty to take reasonable care, contributory negligence will be an available defence.[6] However, if the relevant breach of contract relates only to a strict contractual duty, the 1945 Act will be inapplicable. The Law Commission has recommended that the defence should be more widely available in claims for breach of contract.[7]

4.9 A claimant's damages may also be reduced if he is vicariously responsible for the failure of another person, eg a servant, to look after his (the claimant's) interests.

---

[3] *Froom v Butcher* [1976] QB 286; *Capps v Miller* [1989] 2 All ER 333, CA.
[4] *Craze v Meyer-Dunmore Battlers' Equipment Co* [1936] 2 All ER 1150 at 1151.
[5] *Davies v Swan Motor Co Ltd* [1949] 2 KB 291.
[6] *Barclays Bank Ltd v Fairclough Building Ltd* [1995] QB 214: see also 76 BLR 1; *Forskringaktieselskapet Vesta v Bukher* [1989] AC 852.
[7] Law Commission Report No 215.

4.10 Similarly, statute may provide that damages may be reduced even if the claimant is not personally at fault. Examples are claims by dependants of a deceased person[8] or claims arising from pre-natal injury to babies[9] where damages may be reduced by reason of the fault of the deceased or the mother, respectively.

WHERE THERE ARE MULTIPLE DEFENDANTS

4.11 If a claimant sues more than one tortfeasor, the issue of contributory negligence requires the court to contrast the claimant's conduct with the totality of the tortious conduct of all the tortfeasors, rather than with each tortfeasor's fault to the extent that it contributed to the damage.[10] Section 1 also suggests that for the totality of multiple tortfeasors' tortious conduct to be considered, they do not all have to be joined in the action by the claimant. The relevant facts, however, have to be pleaded and proved. It would be open to any tortfeasor joined in the action to issue an additional claim against other tortfeasors who were not already joined. Such a tortfeasor would have a longer period of limitation in which to sue those other tortfeasors than the claimant would have.[11]

4.12 The above consideration may be important particularly in relation to the court's consideration of blameworthiness and causative potency. For a claimant it may be important that seriously blameworthy conduct by a particular tortfeasor is considered even if the particular tortfeasor is not worth suing.

THE REQUIREMENTS OF PLEADING AND PROOF

4.13 If contributory negligence is to be asserted, the party alleging it should always have in mind the following:

- the burden of specifically pleading it;

- the legal burden of proof; and

- the evidential burden of proof.

4.14 No matter how strong the allegation of contributory negligence, the court cannot act upon such an allegation unless it is pleaded.[12]

---

[8] Fatal Accidents Act 1976, s 5.
[9] Congenital Disabilities (Civil Liability) Act 1976, s 1(2).
[10] *Fitzgerald v Lane* [1989] AC 328, HL.
[11] Limitation Act 1980, s 10.
[12] *Fookes v Slaytor* [1978] 1 WLR 1292.

4.15 Once contributory negligence is pleaded, the legal burden of proof at trial rests upon the person alleging it. It is up to that party to establish it by direct evidence or inference from the facts of the case. This is so in relation to both (a) fault and (b) the causative effect of that fault.[13]

4.16 The evidential burden of proof is often a very important feature. Whilst a claimant against whom contributory negligence is alleged does not have to prove a negative in order to rebut an allegation of contributory negligence, a party alleging contributory negligence may (and frequently does) prove the same in cross-examination of the claimant or the claimant's witness.[14]

THE STANDARD OF CARE

4.17 The standard of care in contributory negligence is judged by what is reasonable in the circumstances.[15] Contributory negligence does require foreseeability of harm to oneself from a particular type of behaviour and such a finding will be made whenever a claimant ought reasonably to have foreseen that if he did not act prudently he might suffer injury.[16]

4.18 The test of what amounts to reasonable care and whether or not it was exercised must be approached broadly.[17] The concept of reasonable care is objective and the claimant must take such care as is necessary to avoid those accidents which fall into the general class, as opposed to simply that particular accident.[18] It follows that, except in relation to the failure of a person with special training or skill, the evidence of an expert is unlikely to assist the court.

4.19 A reasonable claimant must also be prepared for the fact that others may not exercise reasonable skill and care in their conduct. In *Grant v Sun Shipping Company*,[19] Lord du Parcq stated: 'A prudent man will guard against the possible negligence of others, when experience shows such negligence to be common.'

4.20 However, as can be seen from the following examples, it is necessary for the claimant's conduct to be judged in the context of his or her work or the circumstances of the incident:

---

[13] *Flower v Ebbw Vale Steel* [1936] AC 206 at 221; *Lewis v Denye* [1939] 1 KB 540 at 554; *Heranger (Owners) v SS Diamond (Owners)* [1939] AC 94.
[14] *Kerry v Keighley Electrical Eng Co* [1940] 3 All ER 399 at 402.
[15] *AC Billings & Son v Riden* [1958] AC 240; *Harrison v MOD* [1993] CLY 3929.
[16] *Jones v Livox Quarries* [1952] 2 QB 608.
[17] *Jones v Livox Quarries* [1952] 2 QB 608.
[18] *Samways v London Tilbury & Southend Railway* [1902] 18 TLR 295.
[19] [1948] AC 549 at 567.

(a) Where a claimant has been thrown off guard by the conduct of the defendant and reasonably induced into believing that he may work in safety, less care will be expected of him.[20]

(b) In *Toole v Bolton MBC*[21] the Court of Appeal held that it is unusual for there to be a '*marked*' finding of contributory negligence in a case involving breach of statutory duty.

In *Toole* the local authority instructed its staff to wear heavy duty gloves when removing hypodermic needles from its premises. Mr Toole did not wear the heavy duty gloves that were provided, but wore rubber gloves, and sustained a needle prick injury. However, the trial judge held that the heavy duty gloves, had they been worn, would not have prevented the needle prick injury.

The Court of Appeal held that Mr Toole could not be held contributory negligent by failing to take a precaution that in itself was a breach of duty by its employer – not wearing the heavy duty gloves that were themselves inadequate.

The Court of Appeal held that Mr Toole was faced with the situation of having to decide what to do in order to protect the public and his colleagues. It was said to be wholly unreasonable to place any criticism in those circumstances on an employee who was faced with an unpleasant and medically dangerous task.

(c) Recent case-law suggest that, in some situations, an employee is entitled to presume that his employer has complied with the statutory duties. In a case where a person who was carrying a board fell down a hole in the ground that was inadequately covered, the Court of Appeal held that an employee is entitled to assume that his employer had properly covered the hole.[22] The Court of Appeal stated that where there had been a breach of statutory duty by an employer, it was important to ensure that the employee's recourse was not taken away or significantly reduced by a finding of contributory negligence. To place too strict a duty on an employee diminished the aim of the statutory duty that was imposed on the employer. The true question to consider is whether the employee has been negligent and whether he should have foreseen the danger.[23] It was not reasonably foreseeable that an assumption that the cover was adequate would result in an injury.

(d) A court should be reluctant to conclude that an employee ought to have realised that his employer's breach of duty placed him in danger.[24] Of course, each case will turn on its facts but the court should be mindful of the purpose of the statutory provisions.

---

[20] *Glasscock v London Tilbury & Southend Railway* [1902] 18 TLR 295.
[21] [2002] ECWA Civ 588.
[22] *Cooper v Carillon plc* [2003] Lawtel, 2 December. See also *Westwood et al v Post Office* [1974] AC 1.
[23] See, also, *Jones v Livox Quarries* [1952] 2 QB 608.
[24] *Gillespie v McFadden McManus Construction Ltd* [2003] EWCH 2067.

(e) Where a claimant had no choice but to work in a particular manner and was not free to avoid the danger, the court will be reluctant to make a finding of contributory negligence.[25]

(f) The courts have for some time emphasised that not all errors will amount to contributory negligence. A momentary lapse of concentration, such as would affect a prudent employee whilst at work, will rarely be regarded as contributory negligence.[26]

(g) The court should bear in mind that the statutory provisions are often aimed at preventing accidents from an employee's inattention.[27]

(h) Where a claimant carried out work in the manner which the defendant expected of him (but which was dangerous) there is unlikely to be a finding of contributory negligence.[28]

(i) Where a claimant acts in contravention of the applicable regulations or health and safety guidance, but does so on the instruction of his supervisor or manager there is unlikely to be a finding of contributory negligence.[29]

(j) However, if the claimant was doing an act against the defendant's advice or in contravention of accepted practice, an award of contributory negligence will usually be made.[30]

THE OBJECTIVE TEST

Its application generally

4.21 The test as to whether or not a person is in beach of his duty to another is objective; likewise the test for purposes of contributory negligence is objective.

4.22 Where the claimant has a physical or mental disability the test of 'reasonable care for one's own safety' must be assessed by reference to the claimant's particular circumstances, infirmity, knowledge and capacity for understanding risk, etc.[31] The degree of care expected by a court from a person who has a serious injury or mobility difficulties will be different to the degree of

---

[25] *Green v Chelsea BC* [1954] 2 QB 127; *AC Billings v Riden* [1957] AC 240.
[26] *Donovan v Cammell Laird* [1949] 2 All ER 82; *Hopwood v Rolls Royce* [1947] 176 LT 514.
[27] *Sherlock v Chester City Council* [2004] EWCA Civ 201; Lawtel 26 February. *Johns v Martin Simms* [1983] 1 All ER 127, at 130. *Mullard v Ben Line Steamers Ltd* [1970] 1 WLR 1414.
[28] *General Cleaning Contractors v Christmas* [1953] 2 All ER 1110.
[29] *Laszczyk v NCB* [1954] 1 WLR 1426.
[30] *McMullen v NCB* [1982] ICR 148.
[31] *Paris v Stepney BC* [1951] AC 367.

care expected from a person without such injury. Thus, the courts have held that a blind person is only required to take such care for his own safety as his disability enables him to do.[32]

4.23 Likewise, in some cases a court will conclude that the claimant has a mental or intellectual disability which is so serious that the degree of care expected of him will only be that of which he is capable given his disability. Whether a claimant is so disabled will be a matter for the circumstances of each case.[33]

4.24 However, for those persons who would not be classified as mentally or physically disabled by a court the 'normal' objective test applies, irrespective of their varying degrees of intelligence or dexterity.[34]

Its application to children

4.25 A finding of contributory negligence can be made by a court against a child claimant. As a matter of law there is no age below which a child is immune from a finding of contributory negligence. Instead, the courts have adopted a variation of the objective test. It is important to remember that behaviour which would amount to contributory negligence for an adult will not necessarily be so for a child. Instead, a court will ask whether the child claimant took reasonable care for his safety by reference to the degree of care which may reasonably be expected of a child of that age.[35]

4.26 Whilst the age of a child will be an important factor in deciding the issue of contributory negligence, it is not the only factor to be considered. Other factors include:

(a) the particular danger to which the child was exposed and the capacity of the child to appreciate the risk;

(b) the child's knowledge of the perils to which the defendant's negligence had exposed him;

(c) the child's intellectual level;

(d) all the circumstances of the case.[36]

---

[32] *Haley v London Electricity Board* [1965] AC 778 at 806, 809.
[33] See *Charlesworth & Percy on Negligence* (9th edn, 1997), para 3-47.
[34] *Baxter v Woolcombers* (1963) 107 SJ 553.
[35] *Gough v Thorne* [1966] 3 All ER 398; *Devine (A Minor) v Northern Ireland Housing Executive* [1992] NI 74.
[36] *Galbraith's Curator ad litem v Stewart (No 2)* [1998] SLT 1305; *Gough v Thorne*, op cit; *Hughes v Lord Advocate* [1963] AC 837.

4.27 A child, however, may have special knowledge and this may be relevant to the issue of contributory negligence. In one case,[37] the knowledge of a 9-year-old child of the explosive qualities of petrol could (if proved) have given rise to a finding of contributory negligence. Likewise, where the child has been a victim in a road traffic accident and claims damages, inquiries will often be made by the defendant as to what road safety training the child had received. The law does, of course, recognise the propensity of children, even when trained, to have lapses of concentration or moments of impetuousness.[38]

4.28 However, it is the actions of the child, and not those of the parents, which will determine whether an allegation of contributory negligence is established. For instance, in the case of a 3-year-old child who was injured in a car accident whilst not wearing a seat belt, the courts have held that the child was too young to be expected to appreciate the risk of injury from such a failure and any negligence on the part of the parents could not be imputed to the child.[39]

4.29 A forensic difficulty facing those representing child claimants injured when young is that any delay in bringing the case to court will inevitably mean that the child's awareness of dangers will have moved on rapidly since the date of the accident. The court, therefore, has the difficult task of trying to asssess the child at the date of the accident and apply the standard expected of a child of that age.[40]

Its application in rescue or emergency situations

4.30 In determining whether a rescuer has taken all reasonable care for his safety, the court will pay particular attention to the risk of danger and the level of urgency which was required. The courts have frequently refused to make a finding of contributory negligence where a rescuer had to act in the 'agony of the moment', even when it also accepted that with hindsight the injury sustained could have been avoided if he had acted differently.

4.31 The relevant test seems to be that, provided the rescuer acted reasonably in the context of the emergency situation or dilemma, his conduct will not be regarded as amounting to contributory negligence.[41] Such an assessment will depend upon all the circumstances of the case. However, despite the level of urgency and danger, the law still requires a rescuer to have taken care for his safety.[42]

4.32 In the case of ambulance drivers and other persons in emergency services vehicles, the question of contributory negligence will be decided by reference to

---

[37] *Yachuk v Oliver Bais Co* [1949] AC 386.
[38] *Yachuk v Oliver Bais Co* [1949] AC 386.
[39] *Ducharme v Davis* [1984] 1 WLR 699.
[40] *Gough v Thorne* [1966] 3 All ER 398 at 400.
[41] *Sayers v Harlow UDC* [1958] 1 WLR 623; *Brandon v Ostborne, Garrett & Co* [1924] 1 KB 548.
[42] *Langley v Dray* [1998] PIQR P314.

the nature of their employment and the unusual demands which were placed upon them (such as responding to an emergency call).[43]

THE JUST AND EQUITABLE TEST

Blame

4.33 As has already been stated, the Act requires the court when contributory negligence has been proved to reduce an injured person's damages to such degree as is just and equitable. This involves consideration of the relative blameworthiness of the tortfeasor and the injured person, as well as the causative effect (or potency) of their respective actions.

4.34 The following are commonly cited examples of contributory negligence.

4.35 A finding of contributory negligence will be made in those cases where a claimant sustained injuries in a road traffic accident as a result of accepting a lift from a driver whom he knew to be intoxicated.[44] However, the law does not require a passenger to question a driver as to how much alcohol he has consumed.[45] A finding of contributory negligence will be made even where the claimant's capacity to assess the reasonableness of his conduct has been impaired by his own intoxication, provided that he knew, or ought reasonably to have known, of the driver's intoxicated state.[46] In cases where the owner of an uninsured car allows it to be driven in a clearly dangerous manner by another, the injured owner may be contributory negligent for not withdrawing his consent to being driven in it and by not asking to get out.[47]

4.36 Likewise, a person who sustained injuries as a result of ignoring warning signs and climbing over a fence into an open-air swimming pool (which was closed to the public) was found contributory negligent.[48]

4.37 In another case, the House of Lords held that there can be a finding of contributory negligence against a person who commits suicide where the defendant has been negligent. An example of such a case would be suicide by a prison inmate. However, such a finding will only be made in the case of a person who was of sound mind at the time of the suicide and not in the case of a person who was classified by the prison authorities as being a suicide risk.[49]

---

[43] *Griffin v Mersey Regional Ambulance* [1998] PIQR P34.
[44] *Owens v Brimmell* [1971] QB 859; *Donelan v Donelan* [1993] PIQR P205.
[45] *John Booth v Simon White* [2003] Lawtel, 18 November.
[46] *Pitts v Hunt* [1991] 1 QB 24; *Stilton v Stilton & MIB* [1993] PIQR P135.
[47] *Pickett v MIB* [2004] 1 WLR 2450.
[48] *Ratcliff v GR McConnell & W Jons* [1999] PIQR P170.
[49] *Reeves v Commissioner of Police for the Metropolis* [1999] 3 WLR 363, see Lord Jauncey at p 375.

4.38 A claimant who is a passenger in a car is, of course, expected to wear a seat belt. Likewise, a motorcyclist is required to wear a crash helmet.[50] However, it is important to note that if the claimant's injuries would have been exactly the same had he been wearing a seat belt (eg burn injuries from a car crash) or a crash helmet[51] (eg a broken leg) the allegation of contributory negligence will not be made out.[52] There is, however, confusion at present as to whether those riding pedal cycles should be held contributory negligent for failing to wear a cycle helmet.[53]

4.39 Whilst the personal views of a claimant as to the health and safety benefits of taking such care (such as wearing a seat belt) are irrelevant[54] the courts do accept that there are some circumstances in which a claimant will not be expected to take such precautions. For instance, if the claimant suffers from a genuine medical condition which would have been aggravated by him wearing a seat belt or helmet,[55] he will not be expected to do so and, similarly, members of the Sikh community are not required to wear crash helmets.

4.40 In some cases, policy considerations will play a significant part in decisions regarding contributory negligence. For instance, where contributory negligence is alleged by an employer who is guilty of a breach of statutory duty, a court is likely to pay particular regard to the underlying purpose of the statutory provision. Often the purpose of such a provision will be to protect employees against the consequences of their own inattention or excessive haste.[56]

4.41 Whilst considering the issue of contributory negligence, it is also important to remember that in some situations the accident and injuries will have been caused solely by the claimant's own acts or omissions. In those cases, the claimant will fail to recover any damages. For example, where a person voluntarily enters into a dangerous game or activity with another (eg throwing missiles) there will be no breach of duty if the accident occurred within the understandings or conventions of the game.[57] In such circumstances the court will view there to have been implied consent by the injured party to the risk of injury. However, in order to persuade a court that it is not liable for the accident, an employer will have to establish that it took all proper precautions, such as training the claimant and the provision of suitable equipment, etc.

4.42 A person against whom contributory negligence is alleged may himself have been under a statutory obligation to take some relevant precaution. The existence of such an obligation may be highly relevant to the question of

---

[50] *Copps v Miller* [1989] 1 WLR 839 at 848E.
[51] *O'Connell v Jackson* [1972] 1 QB 270.
[52] *Traynor v Donovan* [1978] CLY 2612.
[53] For a case which suggests that there is no such need, see *Williams v Ashley* (1999) SJ Vol 143, 1144.
[54] *Froom v Butcher*, op cit.
[55] *McKay v Borthwick* (1982) SLT 265.
[56] *Stavely Iron Co Ltd v Jones* [1956] AC 627 at 648.
[57] *Blake v Galloway* [2004] 1 WLR 2844.

whether a person is to be blamed for the accident and his injuries. The most obvious example of such an obligation is that of wearing a seat belt whilst a passenger in a car.[58]

4.43 Likewise in the industrial context, an employee may be under a duty to act or refrain from acting in a particular way. In this context, general obligations imposed by statute or regulations upon unskilled or semi-skilled employees are not usually particularly important. However, specific statutory obligations imposed upon persons of particular skill are important when considering blame.[59]

Causation and causative potency

4.44 In many cases the issue of causation will present no problems for a court, such as where a workman puts his hand into part of a moving machine. In such a case the issues will simply be the extent of his blame and the level of contributory negligence.

4.45 Outside the straightforward cases, the question of proof of causation must be addressed.[60] Seat belt cases again present a good example of the various issues to consider. It would be wrong to assume that a person who is known not to have worn a seat belt and who has suffered serious injury in a motor accident should, therefore, accept a deduction for contributory negligence. A checklist of factors reveals that such an assumption should not be made. These factors would include:

- what bodily movement does a seat belt normally restrain?

- what were the claimant's precise bodily injuries and would they have been prevented or reduced in extent if he had worn a seat belt?

- what were the movements of the vehicle during the accident?

- what were the claimant's movements likely to have been in relation to the vehicle's structure?

- was the passenger space reduced by any distortion of the vehicle body (which would have caused personal injury of a type that the seat belt, if worn, could not have prevented)?

4.46 These factors, essentially, relate to whether there was a link (and if so, to what extent) between the claimant's behaviour which is alleged to constitute contributory negligence and his injury.

---

[58] *Froom v Butcher* [1976] 1 QB 286 (which was decided before the need to wear seat belts was made compulsory by Parliament).
[59] *ICI Ltd v Shatwell* [1965] AC 656 (shotfirer).
[60] *Owens v Brimmell* [1977] QB 859.

4.47 Whilst there is no logical or scientific test which can be applied to the issue of causation, it is clear that:

(a) the general principles applicable to determining whether the claimant's own fault contributed to his injury are the same as those principles governing whether the defendant caused those injuries;[61]

(b) it matters not whether the operative fault of the claimant occurred prior or subsequent to the wrongdoing of the defendant;[62]

(c) common-sense principles should be used to judge cause and effect, on the facts of each case;[63]

(d) causes which are too remote must be discarded.[64]

The decision

4.48 The decision as to the just and equitable apportionment of fault is not a process of precise arithmetic, nor that of simply adding together percentages. It requires a broad and common-sense approach.[65]

4.49 The decision as to apportionment has been described as the exercise of 'a discretion'.[66] This, however, merely appears to be an indication that a trial judge (having found the relevant facts in relation to blameworthiness and causative potency) is likely to have a range of percentages within which he can properly make his finding. Experience of actual decisions indicates that the trial judge's decision is often based upon a feel for the particular case.

4.50 Against this background it is not surprising that, so long as the judge places his decision on fault somewhere within an arguable range, his decision will not be reversed on appeal. In general, if there is evidence capable of supporting the first instance decision, it will be upheld.[67] An appeal court will also take into account that, unlike the trial judge, it did not observe the claimant and the other witnesses give their evidence.

4.51 However, in the following instances the appeal court will interfere:

(a) if the first instance decision is 'seriously wrong';[68]

---

[61] *Jones v Livox Quarries*, op cit.
[62] *The Volute* [1922] 1 AC 129.
[63] *Stapley v Gypsum Mines* [1953] AC 663; *Marvin Sigurdson v British Columbia Electric Railway Company* [1953] AC 291 at 299.
[64] *Stapley v Gypsum Mines*, ibid at 681.
[65] *Gregory v Kelly* [1978] RTR 426 at 431H.
[66] *NCB v England* (1954) AC 403 at 420.
[67] *King v Smith* [1955] PIQR P49 at P54.
[68] *Jennings v Norman Collision (Contractors) Ltd* [1970] 1 All ER 1121 at 1127.

(b) if the trial judge failed to consider a material factor or, alternatively, based his conclusion on an irrelevant matter;

(c) if there is a 'wide difference of view' between the appeal court and the first instance court;[69] or

(d) if the decision is plainly 'wrong in principle'.[70]

THE 1945 ACT AND ITS APPLICATION TO DIFFERENT TORTS

4.52 In actions which are based on breach of statutory duty or nuisance, contributory negligence is a defence.[71] It has also been held that contributory negligence can be a defence to a claim of trespass to the person or other torts involving intentional harm to the person.[72]

4.53 However, it should not be assumed that contributory negligence is available as a defence to all torts. It is doubtful whether it applies to a claim under *Rylands v Fletcher*.[73] Although the assimilation of liability under *Rylands v Fletcher* with nuisance[74] leaves the position uncertain.

---

[69] *NCB v England*, op cit at 420.
[70] *Liddell v Middleton* [1996] PIQR P36 at P41.
[71] *Caswell v Powell Duffryn Associated Collieries Limited; Trevell v Lee* [1955] 1 WLR 113 at 122, respectively.
[72] *Barnes v Nayer, The Times*, December 19, 1986, CA.
[73] (1868) LR 3 HL 330.
[74] *Cambridge Water Co v Eastern Counties Leather* [1994] 2 AC 264.

Chapter 5

EXPERT EVIDENCE: THE DUTIES AND LIABILITIES OF AN EXPERT

INTRODUCTION

5.1 The rules relating to the use of experts in litigation were overhauled by the Civil Procedure Rules 1998 (CPR). The central tenet of the Part 35 reforms was that experts should have at the forefront of their minds their status as independent, objective voices, whose function is to report to the court and not to associate themselves too closely – at the risk of losing independence or objectivity – with any party to the litigation itself. That said, the requirement that an expert act independently long pre-dated the CPR, having been noted most famously in *The Ikarian Reefer*.[1]

5.2 The current rules relating to experts are set out in Part 35 of the CPR, supplemented by a Practice Direction. A Code of Guidance on Expert Evidence has been produced by the CPR Working Party and is printed in the White Book after the Practice Direction.

5.3 The CPR starts with r 35.1, which requires expert evidence to be restricted to that which is *'reasonably required'* to resolve the proceedings. One key aim of the reforms was to cut down the numbers of experts involved in any particular case. This aim is furthered by r 35.4 which prevents any party from calling an expert or relying on an expert's report without the court's permission, and r 35.7 which permits the court to direct that evidence on a particular issue is to be given by one expert only. The *'single joint expert'* is a true innovation of the CPR, and is considered in more detail below. He is not a court-appointed expert, but is instructed by the parties jointly. Plainly, there are cases where the issues requiring expert assistance are narrow, and a single joint expert is appropriate; but there are others where the issues are of a degree of complexity which make it impractical to appoint a single joint expert.

5.4 The CPR only extends to an expert 'who has been instructed to give or prepare evidence for the purpose of court proceedings' (r 35.2). This exposes what is a critical difference between the expert engaged to *advise* the parties at the early stages of litigation, and the expert engaged to *report* his views to the

---

[1] *National Justice Cia Naviera SA v Prudential Assurance Co Ltd (The Ikarian Reefer)* [1993] 2 Lloyd's Rep 68.

court. If parties instruct experts at an early stage before the permission of the Court has been obtained, they run the risk of not recovering the expert's costs if permission is subsequently refused.

5.5 Unless an expert's report is disclosed, it cannot, without the court's permission, be used at trial, nor can the expert be called (r 35.3).

THE DUTIES OF AN EXPERT

5.6 Only the role of the expert who reports to the court in the course of litigation (and is an *expert witness*, as opposed to the expert who *advises*) is circumscribed by the CPR. There may be some personal injury actions where different experts will fulfil each of the two roles; but the great likelihood in such actions is that the same expert, who joins the team at the pre-litigation stage as an adviser, will subsequently become the expert witness and so will have to comply with the CPR requirements. Thus, all experts must be aware of their obligations as court experts from the moment that they are consulted, because the scope of those obligations will necessarily inform and guide the expert in the stance that he takes even in the pre-litigation advisory stage.

5.7 It has always been the position that an expert should be independent and objective. An expert's functions were described by Lord President Cooper in *Davie v Edinburgh Magistrates*:[2]

> 'Their duty is to furnish the judge with the necessary scientific criteria for testing the accuracy of their conclusions, so as to enable the judge or jury to form their own independent judgment by the application of these criteria to the facts proved in evidence.'

5.8 *The Ikarian Reefer*[3] provided what remains the authoritative statement on the duties and functions of an expert witness (expressly endorsed by Lord Woolf in his Final Report):[4]

> '1. Expert evidence presented to the court should be and should be seen to be the independent product of the expert uninfluenced as to form or content by the exigencies of litigation.
> 2. An expert witness should provide independent assistance to the court by way of objective unbiased opinion in relation to matters within his expertise. An expert witness in the High Court should never assume the role of advocate.
> 3. An expert witness should state the facts or assumptions on which his opinion is based. He should not omit to consider material facts which detract from his concluded opinion.

---

[2] 1953 SC 34.
[3] [1993] 2 Lloyd's Rep 68 at 81, and see also Laddie J in *Cala Homes (South) Ltd v Alfred McAlpine Homes East Ltd* [1995] FSR 818.
[4] See Access to Justice, Final Report, by Lord Woolf MR, available on the website of the Department for Constitutional Affairs, at Section III, paras 25–29.

4. An expert witness should make it clear when a particular question or issue falls outside his area of expertise.
5. If an expert opinion is not properly researched because he considers that insufficient data is available, then this must be stated with an indication that the opinion is no more than a provisional one.
6. If, after exchange of reports, an expert witness changes his view on a material matter ... such change of view should be communicated to the other side without delay and when appropriate to the court.
7. Where expert evidence refers to photographs, plans, calculations ... or other similar documents, these must be provided to the opposite party at the same time as the exchange of the reports.'

5.9 Although Cresswell J's findings were successfully appealed to the Court of Appeal, Stuart-Smith L J spoke of the lower court's guidance on expert evidence in the following terms:

'... the judge gave an admirable résumé of the duties and responsibilities of expert witnesses. We have no hesitation in endorsing it. We should, however, add one word of caution in relation to paragraph 4: that an expert should make it clear when a particular question or issue falls outside his expertise. It is evident that in this case the Judge was concerned to confine each expert to his area of expertise; but it is not always possible to do so and ... when he is assessing the significance of certain evidence, must be entitled to weigh the probabilities and this may involve making use of the skills of other experts or drawing on his general ... knowledge.'[5]

5.10 In the ill-fated case of *Vernon v Bosley (No 1)*,[6] both the judge at first instance and the Court of Appeal were highly critical of the expert psychiatric evidence that was given on both sides. The Court of Appeal made the following broad points:[7]

(a) True objectivity is hard to achieve in the field of psychiatry; a court appointed expert would be more helpful, but this is only possible if the parties agree.

(b) Using treating clinicians as experts makes it harder for them to be objective. It also denies the judge access to some documents (eg the letter of instruction) on the ground of privilege.

(c) Daily attendance at court can jeopardise detachment.

(d) It is likely to be easier for an expert holding current NHS appointments or a chair in medicine to maintain detachment than one whose principal professional activity is medico-legal work.

---

[5] [1995] 1 Lloyd's Rep 455 at 496.
[6] [1997] 1 All ER 577.
[7] At 611–613.

5.11 There is conflicting guidance about whether a person can give evidence for a party with whom he is connected. In *Field v Leeds City Council*[8] it was held that an expert employed by a local authority could give expert evidence for the local authority (in relation to a housing disrepair claim). However, in *Liverpool Roman Catholic Archdiocesan Trust v Goldberg (No 2)*,[9] evidence given by a friend and colleague of the defendant was held to be inadmissible, on the ground that there would be an appearance of bias. In *R v Secretary of State for Transport, ex p Factortame*,[10] the Court of Appeal doubted the conclusion in the *Goldberg* case, and indicated that although it is always desirable that an expert should have no interest in the outcome of the proceedings, this is not a mandatory precondition. If an expert does have an interest, the other side should be alerted to it and the matter considered in the course of case management, with the judge weighing the alternatives available.[11] Expert evidence from a connected person is not, therefore, automatically inadmissible, but parties to litigation are well-advised to recruit truly independent experts wherever possible.

FORMAT OF THE EXPERT'S REPORT

5.12 The evidence of the expert is to be given in a written report which must be addressed to the court, unless the court directs otherwise (r 35.5 and para 2.1 of the Practice Direction). His report must contain certain information set out at rule 35.10 to be read with para 2.2 of the Practice Direction:

'2.2 An expert's report must:
(1) give details of the expert's qualifications,
(2) give details of any literature or other material which the expert has relied on in making the report,
(3) contain a statement setting out the substance of all facts and instructions given to the expert which are material to the opinions expressed in the report or upon which those opinions are based;
(4) make clear which facts stated in the report are within the expert's own knowledge;
(5) say who carried out any examination, measurement, test or experiment which the expert has used for the report, give the qualifications of that person, and say whether or not the test or experiment has been carried out under the expert's supervision;
(6) where there is a range of opinion on matters dealt with in the report –
    (a) summarise the range of opinion, and
    (b) give reasons for his own opinion;
(7) contain a summary of the conclusions reached;
(8) if the expert is not able to give his opinion without qualification, state the qualification; and

---

[8] (2000) Times Law Report, January 15.
[9] [2001] 4 All ER 950.
[10] [2002] 3 WLR 1104.
[11] Per Lord Phillips MR at para 70.

(9) contain a statement that the expert understands his duty to the court, and has complied and will continue to comply with that duty.'

5.13 An expert's report, in common with a witness statement, must be verified by a statement of truth which should, in the case of an expert's report, say:

'I confirm that insofar as the facts stated in my report are within my own knowledge I have made clear which they are and I believe them to be true, and that the opinions I have expressed represent my true and complete professional opinion.' (Practice Direction, paras 2.3 and 2.4)

5.14 The sanction for failure to comply with these and other requirements imposed by the court on the expert may be severe. In *Stevens v Gullis and Pile (third party)*,[12] a defendant's expert, whose report did not comply with the CPR and who had failed to comply with various directions made by the court, was debarred from giving evidence with the consequence that judgment was entered for the claimant. The Master of the Rolls in that case commented that the witness had 'demonstrated that he had no conception of these requirements' referring to the overriding objective and the other requirements of the CPR.

SINGLE JOINT EXPERTS

5.15 The expert instructed as a joint single expert under rr 35.7 and 35.8 is under the same obligations as any other expert. Any questions he has about his role, or his instructions, may be addressed to the court under r 35.14.

5.16 It is inappropriate for the parties to confer with a single joint expert without the involvement of the other party or his representative: *P (a child) v Mid Kent Area Healthcare NHS Trust*,[13] which confirmed that a single joint expert should not attend a conference with one party.

5.17 It may be difficult to decide whether a single joint expert is appropriate. In *Daniels v Walker*,[14] the parties had agreed to instruct a joint care expert in a high value claim, and the defendant then sought permission to adduce its own expert evidence. The Court of Appeal allowed that application. Guidance was given for the correct use of expert evidence in most cases as follows.[15] The first step is the joint commissioning of expert evidence on a particular issue; this may often also be the last step. If a party wishes to obtain further information, for reasons which are not fanciful, subject to the discretion of the court, then that party should be entitled to obtain that evidence; in cases of modest value it would be appropriate to put questions to the expert who has prepared a report; in more substantial cases, it would be appropriate to obtain a further report (or

---

[12] [2000] 1 All ER 527.
[13] [2002] 1 WLR 210.
[14] [2000] 1 WLR 1382.
[15] See paras 1.27 to 1.33 of the judgment of Lord Woolf.

reports); lastly, a decision should then be taken, after a meeting of experts has taken place, as to what evidence should be called. *Daniels v Walker* should be considered alongside the earlier case, *Baron v Lovell*[16] where a judge's direction that medical evidence as to the claimant's personal injuries should be given by the claimant's expert alone was upheld; and a subsequent case, *S (a minor) v Birmingham Health Authority*,[17] where a district judge's restriction to a single joint expert was overturned as inappropriate at the early stages of a complex clinical negligence case.

THE MEETING OF EXPERTS

5.18 The norm is now for experts of the same discipline to be invited to discuss their views at an experts' meeting, the purpose of which is to:

'(a) identify and discuss the expert issues in the proceedings; and
(b) where possible, reach agreed opinion on those issues.' (CPR.35.12(1))

5.19 Somewhat paradoxically, r 35.12(2) goes on to allow the court to 'specify the issues which the experts must discuss'. The current practice is for the court to specify that the experts must, following a discussion, prepare a statement for the court showing those issues on which the experts agree, and those on which they disagree, with a summary of reasons for disagreeing. The meeting itself is 'without prejudice'. Although an agreement between the experts will not bind a party unless that party has expressly agreed to be bound by the agreement (r 35.12(5)), in reality a party will have great difficulty in advancing any argument inconsistent with a position agreed by its expert at the joint meeting.

5.20 An expert may now be questioned by any other party to the litigation (and, if he is a single joint expert, by those instructing him) (r 35.6). Any failure by the expert to answer those questions may lead to a disallowance of his costs, or worse, to the instructing party not being able to rely on his evidence at trial (r 35.6(4)) and his answers are treated as part of his report (r 35.6(3)).

THE LIABILITIES OF AN EXPERT

5.21 Does the expert witness have immunity from proceedings if his opinion turns out to be wrong? Clearly, as with any professional man, an expert witness owes a duty of care or a contractual duty of a like nature to those who instruct him and also the court.[18] To this extent, negligence in the preparation and production of a report may well be actionable. At present, it appears that the expert will, however, enjoy immunity from suit in relation to his evidence at trial.

---

[16] [2000] PIQR P20.
[17] [2001] Lloyd's Rep Medical 382.
[18] *Craigola Mertha Co v Swansea Corporation* [1928] 1 Ch 31 at 38.

5.22 This area was reviewed by the Court of Appeal in *Stanton v Callaghan*,[19] a case involving the alleged negligence of a surveyor in the preparation of a report, following an expert's meeting, on the basis of which the claim was subsequently settled. Chadwick LJ said:

> 'What, then, is the position in relation to expert reports? It seems to me that the following propositions are supported by authority binding in this court:
>
> (i) an expert witness who gives evidence at a trial is immune from suit in respect of anything which he says in court, and that immunity will extend to the contents of the report which he adopts as, or incorporates in his evidence;
> (ii) where an expert witness gives evidence at a trial the immunity which he would enjoy in respect of that evidence is not to be circumvented by a suit based on the report itself; and
> (iii) immunity does not extend to protect an expert who has been retained to advise as to the merits of a party's claim in litigation from a suit by the party by whom he has been retained in respect of that advice, notwithstanding that it was in contemplation at the time when the advice was given that the expert would be a witness at the trial if that litigation were to proceed.'

5.23 Those propositions were all based on existing case law.[20] The new point before the Court of Appeal, on which there was no existing authority, was whether an expert is immune from suit by the party who has retained him in respect of the contents of a report which he has prepared for the purpose of exchange prior to trial, in circumstances where he does not in the event give evidence at the trial, either because the trial doesn't take place or because he is not called as a witness. On that point, Chadwick LJ said:

> 'It is of importance to the administration of justice, and to those members of the public who seek access to justice, that trials should take no longer than is necessary to do justice in the particular case, and that, to that end, time in court should not be taken up with the consideration of matters which are not truly an issue. It is in that context that experts are encouraged to identify, in advance of the trial, those parts of their evidence on which they are, and those on which they are not, in agreement. Provision for a joint statement, reflecting agreement after a meeting of experts has taken place, is made by Ord. 38, rule 38 [now CPR r 35.12]. In my view, the public interest in facilitating full and frank discussion between experts before trial does require that each should be free to make proper concessions without fear that a departure from advice previously given to the party who has retained him will be seen as evidence of negligence. That, as it seems to me is an area in which public policy justifies immunity. The immunity is needed in order to avoid the tension between a desire to assist the court and fear of the consequences of the departure from previous advice.'

5.24 *Stanton v Callaghan* should be treated with some caution, because the Court of Appeal drew on the position of lawyers (barristers and solicitors)

---

[19] [1999] 2 WLR 745.
[20] See *Rondel v Worsley* [1969] AC 191; *Evans v London Hospital* [1981] 1 WLR 184 at 191; *Marrinan v Vibart* [1963] 1 QB 234; and *Watson v McEwan* [1905] AC 480. See also *Palmer v Durnford Ford* [1992] 1 QB 480.

involved in litigation in reaching its conclusions in relation to other experts. Subsequent to that decision, the House of Lords has reviewed the immunity of advocates from suit in *Arthur JS Hall and Co v Simons*[21] and has concluded that the general principles of tort law and professional negligence should apply in full to advocates. Lord Hoffmann referred to the decision of the Court of Appeal in *Stanton*, and rejected the analogy of the lawyer who owes a duty of care to the client and the expert witness whose only duty is to tell the truth to the court. His Lordship considered that any justification for the immunity of an expert would be as an example of the traditional witness immunity.[22]

5.25 *Phillips v Symes*[23] has recently confirmed this normal rule that witnesses enjoy immunity from suit in respect of their evidence, but the judge in that case went on to hold that this rule can be departed from to join an expert witness as a respondent for costs purposes, where his evidence caused significant expense to be incurred, and did so in flagrant and reckless disregard of his duties to the court. This draconian punishment of an expert witness must be reserved for the most serious cases, and required an express warning to the expert witness in question.

5.26 The validity of any rule of immunity from suit must be considered afresh in light of the European Convention on Human Rights. Article 6 provides that:

> 'In the determination of his civil rights and obligations ... everyone is entitled to a fair and public hearing within a reasonable time by an independent and impartial tribunal established by law.'

Any rule of immunity from suit for professionals potentially impacts on an individual's right to have his complaint against the professional determined. The European Court of Human Rights has acknowledged that there are valid public policy grounds for excluding access to the courts in certain cases but has indicated that the domestic courts should be free to evaluate the public policy considerations for and against exclusion in any given case.[24]

5.27 The Court of Appeal has recently considered whether the scope of the expert's immunity from suit should extend to disciplinary proceedings brought against the expert by his or her professional body, in *General Medical Council v Meadow & A-G*.[25] The court concluded that there was no basis upon which that immunity should extend beyond the ambit established in case law, and that in the result the expert in question, Sir Roy Meadow, was liable to disciplinary proceedings by the GMC in respect of statistical evidence during the course of a criminal trial, which turned out to be flawed.

---

[21] 20 July 2000.
[22] See the 18th heading of his Lordship's speech.
[23] [2004] EWHC 2330 (Ch).
[24] *Osman v UK* [1999] BHRC 239.
[25] [2006] EWCA Civ 1390, [2007] 1 All ER 1.

THE DUTIES OF THOSE INSTRUCTING AN EXPERT

5.28 Issues arise relating to the duties of those who instruct experts. The initial instruction of an expert is primarily undertaken by the solicitor, but the final draft of an expert's report is frequently achieved in, or as a result of, a conference or consultation. For no other reason than self-preservation while under cross-examination, the opinions in the final report ought to be the expert's rather than counsel's. This is particularly true in the light of the CPR and the emphasis on the overriding duty being to the court. But although Lord Wilberforce said in *Whitehouse v Jordan*[26] that:

> 'whilst some degree of consultation between experts and legal advisers is entirely proper, it is necessary that expert evidence presented to the court should be and should be seen to be the independent product of the expert, uninfluenced as to form or content by the exigencies of litigation'.

5.29 There is little express guidance in the Code of Conduct for the Bar of England and Wales as to the extent to which it is either permissible or desirable for counsel to have had a hand in the drafting of the expert's report. What happens, not infrequently, is that an expert's preliminary view is modified, having heard or seen the client and having discussed the matter in conference. Suggestions may well be made, but the safest course will be to allow the expert to go away and draft his own amendments.

5.30 Particular care now needs to be taken by a solicitor or barrister who 'suggests' amendments to an expert's report; not only because of the renewed emphasis in the CPR on the expert's role as an independent reporter to the court, but also and more specifically, given the effect of r 35(10)(3), dealt with below under *Confidentiality and Privilege*.

5.31 What of the expert's report which, while on the face of it, favourable to the defendant's case, is accompanied by a letter to the solicitor which identifies serious weaknesses in the defence or a potentially fruitful line of cross-examination which might cause embarrassment to the expert? In *Kenning v Eve Construction*,[27] Michael Wright QC (sitting as a Deputy High Court Judge) had to deal with an interlocutory application relating to the accidental disclosure of a covering letter which identified possible (but as yet unpleaded) negligent causes for an accident. He held that he had:

> '... come to the conclusion that where...the effect of these two documents taken together is that the expert witness is in fact saying effectively: 'On the matters contained in the Statement of Claim it may be that the defendant had a complete answer but there are these other two matters which are not pleaded, but in respect of which I think the defendant is in very grave difficulty', then it seems to me that the solicitor who instructs him only complies with the requirement of Order 25, rule 8(1)(b) [automatic directions under old rules for disclosure of expert evidence]

---

[26] [1981] 1 WLR 241.
[27] [1989] 1 WLR 1189.

if the whole of the expert's opinion is disclosed because only if the whole of the opinion is disclosed, has the substance of his evidence been communicated to the other parties.'

5.32 The CPR does not expressly deal with such a situation. In practice, experts continue to submit reports for disclosure under cover of a letter which gives their 'real' views on the merits of the case – and that practice is a good one in that it ensures that each party has a proper appreciation of the strength of its case, which will often allow negotiations with a view to settlement to take place. But the spirit of the CPR is plainly that the expert should state in his report any particular feature which he considers to be significant, whether or not that feature arises on the case as it is pleaded or not.

5.33 Finally, those instructing an expert are at liberty to put questions to the other side's expert or a single joint expert (r 35.6). CPR, r 35.6(2)(c) states that the purpose of such questions must be for clarification only, and the costs of asking those questions and having them answered is in the first place borne by the questioning party (para 5.3 of the Practice Direction). A copy of the questions is to be sent to the other parties to the litigation (para 5.2 of the Practice Direction).

THE DIFFERENT TYPES OF EXPERTS IN PERSONAL INJURY AND CLINICAL NEGLIGENCE CASES

5.34 In personal injury litigation, two different types of expert may need to be commissioned.

Medical expert evidence

5.35 Since injury and its consequences are part of every action, expert medical evidence will be required to establish the nature of the injury and the prognosis for the future. Paragraph 4.3 of the Practice Direction to Part 16 states:

'Where the Claimant is relying on the evidence of a medical practitioner the claimant must attach to or serve with his particulars of claim a report from the medical practitioner about the personal injuries which he alleges in his claim.'

5.36 The report must be 'about the personal injuries'. This is plainly a requirement to provide evidence as to the present condition and prognosis rather than legal causation of the injury. At its simplest, this will involve a description of the original injury or injuries and their natural consequences. However, the requirement to provide medical evidence is only mandatory where the party is relying on the evidence of a medical practitioner and there may be cases of trivial injury where no medical evidence is necessary if some other evidence, eg photographs exists.

5.37 Problems may, and often do, arise where there is a real issue as to whether the injuries complained of at trial are the true consequence of the accident, or are the result of some pre-existing condition, 'functional overlay/psychogenic illness' or, more rarely, feigned.

Non-medical expert evidence

5.38 It is impossible to predict in general terms the situations which may give rise to a need for non-medical expert evidence. Specialists are available in road traffic accident reconstructions, although doubts have been expressed by the courts about their worth. There are also firms or companies which specialise in industrial accidents and building-site injuries. For an expert's evidence to be credible and helpful to the court, the expert must reflect upon the contentions being advanced by both sides – it may be that the expert will decide that the defendant is still negligent even on its own version of the facts.

5.39 Permission is now required to produce any expert's report or to call any expert to give evidence at trial (r 35.4). Generally, the courts have demonstrated a reluctance to involve experts save where necessary. Accident reconstruction experts, health and safety experts, employment experts, and many other sub-specialisms which had emerged under the old regime may not be accepted nowadays, except where it can be shown that the evidence of such people will be valuable to the judge and the expense of their involvement can be justified. If permission is not given to rely on expert evidence, the cost of any advice or report already obtained from that expert will generally be irrecoverable from the other side, even if the case succeeds.

CONFIDENTIALITY AND PRIVILEGE

5.40 Confidentiality, or perhaps more accurately privilege, presents a problem of considerable practical importance. Until disclosed, one party's expert report is privileged from disclosure to any other party. That does not stop the expert being called as a witness for another party, if he is not being called by the party who commissioned the report; but the original report itself remains privileged from disclosure.

5.41 What of the factual statements, letters or documents upon which the expert has relied in reaching his conclusion? It is often the case that an expert engaged by one or other party unwittingly discloses the existence of a statement which he has seen but upon which the commissioning party does not intend to rely.

5.42 There is at present conflicting authority on whether that document is privileged or not. *Booth v Warrington Health Authority*[28] was a clinical negligence case in which midwives gave statements which were disclosed to an

---

[28] [1992] PIQR P137.

expert consultant obstetrician who referred to them in his report. The report was disclosed to the other side. Tucker J held that, in the absence of some unequivocal act of waiver, the incorporation of part of the witnesses' statement into an expert's report was not sufficient to amount to a waiver of privilege. *Booth v Warrington* was based on a long line of authority and academic comment, which tended to protect one party's right of privilege save in cases where a waiver of privilege had quite clearly taken place.

5.43 *Clough v Tameside and Glossop Health Authority*[29] was also a clinical negligence case. The defendants had disclosed an expert's report which referred to an earlier statement from the doctor involved in the treatment of the claimant in the case. Bracewell J reviewed the authorities, including *Booth v Warrington*, and concluded that privilege in the doctor's statement had been waived. She said:

> 'For my part, I can appreciate a clear distinction between material supplied to an expert by an instructing solicitor as part of the background documentation in the case upon which an expert opinion is sought, and on the other hand, communications between solicitor and expert which fall outside that category. In the first instance, I am persuaded that the privilege is waived.'

She went on:

> 'It is only by proper and full disclosure to all parties, that an expert's opinion can be tested in court, in order to ascertain whether all appropriate information was supplied and how the expert dealt with it. It is not for one party to keep their cards face down on the table so that the other party does not know the full extent of information supplied. Fairness dictates that a party should not be forced to meet a case pleaded or an expert opinion on the basis of documents he cannot see. Although civil litigation is adversarial, it is not permissible to withhold relevant information, or to delete or amend the contents of a report before disclosure, as was submitted by counsel for the defendants to be the practice of some firms of solicitors.'

5.44 The correctness of the decision in *Clough* was doubted in *Bourns Inc v Raychem Corporation and Latham & Watkins*,[30] a decision of the Court of Appeal in a patents case, which restores the position to where it was pre-*Clough*:

> 'Service of a witness statement, whether it be a statement of an expert or a witness to fact, waives privilege in that statement. As stated in *Marubeni* [viz. *Marubeni Corporation v Aristides A Alafouzos*] mere reference to a document does not waive privilege in that document: there must at least be a reference to the contents and reliance' (per Aldous LJ).

---

[29] [1998] 1 WLR 1478.
[30] CA, 30 March 1999.

5.45 Lord Justice Swinton Thomas added, in a very short concurring judgment, that he expressly reserved for future consideration whether, even on its own facts, *Clough* was correctly decided.

5.46 These decisions should be read alongside r 35.10, which states as follows:

> '(3) The expert's report must state the substance of all material instructions, whether written or oral, on the basis of which the report was written.
> (4) Instructions referred to in paragraph (3) shall not be privileged against disclosure but the court will not, in relation to those instructions-
>   (a) order disclosure of any specific document; or
>   (b) permit any questioning in court, other than by the party who instructed the expert,
>
> unless it is satisfied that there are reasonable grounds to consider the statement of instructions given under paragraph (3) to be inaccurate or incomplete.'

5.47 As to what are *'material instructions'*, para 1.2(8) of the Practice Direction tells us that:

> 'the statement should summarise the facts and instructions given to the expert which are material to the opinions expressed in the report or upon which those opinions are based.'

5.48 There is a point of real principle at stake here: instructions to an expert undoubtedly fall under the head of legal professional privilege as a matter of law, and the CPR is merely a procedural code which does not affect substantive legal rights. At least one High Court judge has refused to allow the CPR to encroach on substantive legal rights, by holding that CPR 48.7(3) of the CPR – which purports to permit disclosure of privileged documents in the context of wasted costs orders – was ultra vires and unenforceable (Toulson J in *General Mediterranean Holdings SA v Patel*).[31] The Court of Appeal in *Lucas v Barking, Havering and Redbridge Hospitals NHS Trust*[32] reacted in a similar way to CPR, r 31.14 which provides, subject to CPR, r 53.10(4), that a party may inspect 'any document mentioned in an expert's report which is not already disclosed in the proceedings'; the Court expressed the view, without full argument, that this provision did not confer absolute rights and could not be taken to abrogate legal professional privilege or public interest immunity

5.49 In the same case the Court of Appeal considered the ambit of CPR 35.10(4). It was held that there must be some concrete fact giving rise to reasonable grounds for believing that the statement of instruction was inaccurate or incomplete, before the Court will order specific discovery.[33] A broad definition of 'instructions' was applied, being 'any material supplied by

---

[31] [2000] 1 WLR 272.
[32] [2004] 1 WLR 220 at paras 25 and 44.
[33] Per Laws LJ at paras 42–44.

the instructing party to the expert as the basis on which the expert is being asked to advise'.[34] Overall, the Court of Appeal appeared keen to preserve substantive law rights of privilege.

5.50 In *Alan Jackson v Marley Davenport Limited*[35] the Court of Appeal confirmed that CPR, r 35.10(4) does not extend to the traditional privilege that attaches to earlier reports and drafts. But an earlier decision which lies unhappily alongside *Marley Davenport* is that of *Beck v MoD*.[36] Here, the Court of Appeal granted permission to the defendant to instruct a replacement expert on condition and prognosis, on condition that the first expert's report was disclosed. The decision contains no discussion at all about privilege in the earlier report, the defendant in that case having been willing to disclose the first report as the price of obtaining permission for the replacement expert. The Court of Appeal upheld the decision of *Beck* in *Hajigeorgiou v Vasiliou*,[37] citing it as an example of how the court could control the conduct of litigation and discourage expert shopping, while maintaining that it did not abrogate legal professional privilege. *Hajigeorgiou* also confirmed that *Beck* only applied in those cases where the court's permission for a second or replacement expert was required, which on the facts of that case it was not, as the original direction giving permission had identified experts only by their field of expertise and not by name.

DUTIES OF THE COURT

5.51 The court is obliged to give reasons for preferring the views of one expert over another. Failure to do so may of itself be sufficient to mount an appeal.[38] The Court of Appeal in *English v Emery Reimbold & Strick Ltd*[39] has suggested that to request addition reasons from the trial judge, at the permission to appeal stage, is a sensible cost-saving measure.

---

[34] Per Waller LJ at para 34.
[35] [2004] EWCA Civ 1225.
[36] (2003) *The Times*, July 21.
[37] [2005] EWCA Civ 236.
[38] See *Flannery v Halifax Estate Agencies Ltd* [2000] 1 WLR 377.
[39] [2002] EWCA Civ 605.

Chapter 6

RECOVERING DAMAGES FOR PSYCHIATRIC INJURIES

INTRODUCTION

6.1 In *Frost v Chief Constable of South Yorkshire Police*,[1] Lord Steyn stated:

> '[T]he law on the recovery of compensation for pure psychiatric harm is a patchwork quilt of distinctions which are difficult to justify'.[2]

This comment remains as applicable to the law today as it was when first made. This chapter considers claims for psychiatric injury in the form of nervous shock suffered by those who have themselves been endangered by negligent conduct and by those who have suffered nervous shock as a result of others being killed or injured. It is the case that psychiatric injury can arise in other situations as a result of negligent conduct. One such area which has been the subject of much recent authority is that of 'stress at work' but this is outside the scope of this chapter.

6.2 It is well established that where a claimant suffers a physical injury and also develops a recognisable psychiatric illness as a result of the event that caused that physical injury damages are to be awarded in respect of such illness and, apart from the usual evidential and causation hurdles, no particular difficulties arise. The problem arises where the claimant suffers psychiatric harm but does not suffer physical injury. In this situation the claimant's claim will fail unless he can show that he is suffering from a recognised psychiatric illness. Emotional stress, for example, will not suffice as a basis for a claim.

6.3 Lord Bingham, has said (in the Foreword to NJ Mullany and PR Handford, *Tort Liability for Psychiatric Damage* (1993), p viii) that liability for psychiatric illness is:

---

[1] [1998] 3 WLR 1509. Otherwise referred to as *White v Chief Constable of South Yorkshire Police* [1999] 2 AC 455. At first instance there were six claimants one of whom was Mr Frost. Mr Frost did not appeal to the Court of Appeal but the case is reported in that court under his name. In the House of Lords Mr Frost's name did not feature as he had not appeared in the Court of Appeal and Mr White took on the role of case naming claimant. The All England reports reported the case at [1999] 1 All ER at p 1 under the name of White. The law reports reported the case at the last loose part for 1999. In the law reports it is headed *White v Chief Constable of South Yorkshire* on appeal from *Frost v Chief Constable for South Yorkshire* but is indexed by the law reports as *Frost*.
[2] Op cit at 1547.

'... one of the most vexed and tantalising topics in the modern law of tort. For what kinds of mental damage will a claim lie? And in what circumstances? These deceptively simple questions have lead to a welter of authority in a number of different jurisdictions. Underlying the cases has been the judges' concern that unless the limits of liability are tightly drawn the courts will be inundated with a flood of claims by claimants ever more distant from the scene of the original mishap. So fine distinctions have been drawn and strict lines of demarcation established.'

6.4 At present, it can safely be said that all the important principles in our Jurisdiction in relation to liability for 'nervous shock' are contained within the following authorities: *Bourhill v Young*,[3] *McLoughlin v O'Brian*,[4] *Alcock v Chief Constable of South Yorkshire Police*,[5] *Page v Smith*[6] and *Frost v Chief Constable of South Yorkshire Police* [1998].[7]

6.5 The law on this topic is controversial. Lord Hoffmann observed in the *Frost* case, that the search for some unifying principle was called off in *Alcock*.[8] Also in *Frost*, Lord Steyn referred to the need for limitations to be imposed on the class of claimants entitled to recover, the imperfect justice that inevitably results and to some of the relevant policy considerations in this areas of the law.[9]

6.6 The dissenting speech of Lord Goff in *Frost* represents a powerful view contrary to the majority and a strong critique of the leading speech of Lord Lloyd in *Page*. A lack of judicial unanimity is a particular feature of this corner of the law. There is also controversy in the academic world. Mullany and Handford, in their scholarly treatise, *Tort Liability for Psychiatric Damage* (1993), advocate abolition of the special rules limiting recovery for damages for psychiatric harm. This suggestion was considered and rejected by the Law Commission, primarily for fear of the floodgates being opened. The contrary view that there should be no recovery in tort for pure psychiatric injury is cogently expressed by Professor J Stapleton in her paper 'In Restraint of Tort' who considered that no reasonable boundaries for the cause of action could be established. She describes the law relating to liability for psychiatric illness as:

'... the area where the silliest rules now exist and where criticism is almost universal'.

Again, the Law Commission has rejected such an extreme proposition.

---

[3] [1943] AC 92.
[4] [1983] 1 AC 410.
[5] [1982] 1 AC 310.
[6] [1996] 1 AC 155.
[7] [1998] 3 WLR 1509.
[8] Op cit at 1557D.
[9] Op cit at 1539C, 1543D–1544F, 1457C–F.

RECOGNISABLE PSYCHIATRIC ILLNESS

6.7 The term 'nervous shock', dating as it does from Victorian authorities, is now medically and legally discredited. In *Hinz v Berry*,[10] Lord Denning used the alternative phrase 'recognisable psychiatric injury' and the Law Commission also adopted that phrase.[11]

6.8 Lord Bridge said in *McLoughlin*:[12]

> 'The first hurdle which a claimant claiming damages of the kind in question must surmount is to establish that he is suffering, not merely grief, distress or any other normal emotion, but a positive psychiatric illness.'

6.9 Lord Steyn usefully analysed this distinction and its basis in *Frost*.[13] Mere anxiety will not suffice – see the Court of Appeal decision in *Nicholls v Rushton*[14] and the recent decision of Recorder Blohm in *Younger v Dorset & Somerset Strategic Health Authority*[15].

6.10 Any 'recognisable psychiatric illness' will suffice, but expert medical evidence will generally be required to establish that the claimant has suffered such a condition.

PRIMARY VICTIMS

6.11 In the normal way of a negligence action foresight of harm must be established. The nature of the harm that must be foreseen depends upon whether the claimant is a primary or secondary victim.

6.12 In *Alcock*,[16] Lord Oliver said of cases in which damages are claimed for recognisable psychiatric injury:

> 'Broadly they divide into two categories, that is to say, those cases in which the injured claimant was involved, either mediately or immediately, as a participant, and those in which the claimant was no more than the passive and unwilling witness of injury caused to others.'

6.13 Lord Lloyd, in *Page*,[17] said that, in all claims relating to recognisable psychiatric injury, it is essential to make this distinction between primary and

---

[10] [1970] 2 QB 40.
[11] Law Commission Paper No. 249, *Liability for Psychiatric Illness*.
[12] Op cit at 431H.
[13] Op cit at 1539D.
[14] (1992), *The Times*, 19 June.
[15] Lawtel LTL 25/8/2006: (2006) Lloyd's Rep Med 489.
[16] Op cit at 407D–E.
[17] Op cit at 197E.

secondary victims. This issue must be considered at the outset so as to determine whether the three main requirements of such claims have been fulfilled (see below).

6.14 Whether or not a claimant is a primary or secondary victim is dependent upon the facts of the relevant incident. If, in that incident the claimant is, or reasonably believes that he (or she) is within the range of foreseeable physical injury, then he or she is a primary victim. If he is not or does not believe himself to be within the range of foreseeable injury but suffers injury as a result of the sight or perception of the death, injury or imperilment of another, then he is a secondary victim.

6.15 *Page* establishes that a primary victim may recover damages for a recognisable psychiatric illness suffered in circumstances where the defendant should reasonably have foreseen that his or her conduct might cause the claimant physical or psychiatric injury, whether or not the foreseeable physical injury does in fact occur. Where the claimant is not actually in danger, but because of the sudden or unexpected nature of events, reasonably believes that he or she is and the defendant should reasonably have foreseen that a person of ordinary fortitude in the claimant's position would have done so, the claimant is also a primary victim and can recover for psychiatric injury in the absence of physical injury (*McFarlane v EE Caledonia Ltd*).[18]

SECONDARY VICTIMS

6.16 A secondary victim is a person who suffers a reasonably foreseeable, recognisable psychiatric illness, as a result of another person's death, injury or imperilment. In short, the secondary victim is the unwilling witness who is shocked by events that physically endanger others; he or she is not himself or herself physically endangered.

6.17 In the Consultation Paper, 'Liability for Psychiatric Illness', that preceded the Law Commission report, the Commission said[19]

> '... once such secondary victims were entitled to claim, the law inevitably had to face up to the difficulty of where to draw the line which demarcates those secondary victims who can claim from those who cannot. It is this case problem that continues to bedevil the law ...'.

6.18 It is now clear that in secondary victim cases a single unifying test for liability of foreseeability of recognisable psychiatric injury is not the present law. A secondary victim cannot recover damages for negligence unless he or she can satisfy three main requirements:

---

[18] [1994] 2 All ER 1.
[19] Law Commission, No 137, para 2.13.

(a) that he or she had a close tie of love and affection with the person killed, injured or imperilled;

(b) that he or she was close to the 'accident' in time and space;

(c) that he or she directly perceived the 'accident' rather than, for example, hearing about it from a third person.

See *McLoughlin*,[20] and *Alcock*[21] and *Frost*.[22] These three requirements are now considered in turn.

A close tie of love and affection

6.19 A claimant must establish a close tie of love and affection to the immediate victim. Such a tie may be present in family relationships or those of close friendship, but the closeness of the tie must be proved in each case by the claimant, although it may be rebuttably presumed in the case of a spouse, parent or child and possible fiancé(e) (see *Alcock*[23]).

6.20 That such a tie is a prerequisite to liability is rooted in the concepts of proximity and reasonable foreseeability, which are central to the issue of liability in negligence. Proximity within the neighbourhood principle is the more likely to be established where a close tie of love and affection with the person killed, injured or imperilled is established. Further, the threshold of foreseeability is likely to be crossed in the case of those who have a close tie of love and affection with the person killed, injured or imperilled whereas customary phlegm or fortitude in the ordinary person is likely so to place the threshold of foreseeability that the tortfeasor in breach of duty to a primary victim owes no duty of care to a secondary victim (see *Bourhill*[24] and *Frost*[25]).

Physical and temporal proximity

6.21 To recover for recognisable psychiatric injury as a secondary victim a claimant must be close to the accident in time and space. This requirement has been extended to include cases where the claimant perceives the immediate aftermath of an accident.

6.22 What constitutes the immediate aftermath is a matter of some difficulty. In *Alcock*, Lord Jauncey made plain that he thought it unwise to essay a definition of what constituted the immediate aftermath. However, in the same case, Lord Ackner[26] made clear that it should be narrowly construed.

---

[20] Op cit Lord Wilberforce at 481A–419B and 422A–422H.
[21] Op cit Lord Ackner at 402G–H and Lord Jauncey at 419H–420C.
[22] Op cit Lord Steyn at 1543C–G and Lord Hoffmann at 1548W–1552B.
[23] Op cit Lord Keith at 397C–E, Lord Ackner at 402H–404G and Lord Jauncey at 422C–H.
[24] Op cit Lord Porter at 117.
[25] Op cit at 400H–401A.
[26] Op cit at 400H–401A.

6.23 Notwithstanding the warning of Lord Jauncey, the following pointers may assist in the determination of what constitutes the 'immediate aftermath':

(a) The immediate aftermath is always spoken of as the aftermath of the event; this is to be distinguished from the aftermath of the emergency created by the event.

(b) Whilst there is no set time limit as to how much time may pass following the accident for the immediate aftermath itself to have passed, the period of two hours allowed in *McLoughlin* probably marks the outer limit of the aftermath doctrine. In *Alcock*, three of their Lordships understood the time in *McLoughlin* to have been one hour!

(c) Another way of assessing whether the immediate aftermath has passed is to determine what stage after the accident itself has been reached – for example, are the emergency services present; is some form of order being restored?

(d) A distinction should be drawn between the shock of the news – that is not to be compensated – and the shock of the experience of the primary event.

(e) It should be established what (if anything) the secondary victim saw of the primary victim and in what condition the latter was then found to be.

6.24 In the Court of Appeal decision of *Tranmore v TE Scudder Limited*[27] there has in effect been a restatement that the 'immediate aftermath' doctrine is to be narrowly construed. The claimant's son was killed in an accident on a demolition site caused by the negligence of the defendant employer. The claimant arrived at the site two hours later and was told that his son was trapped in a collapsed building. After a further two hours, he was informed that his son was dead. He did not see his son's body on site, but did see something of the rubble or machinery under which his son had been buried without knowing where, in fact, he was located. He suffered psychiatric injury as a result of his experience and brought an action against the defendant.

6.25 The Court of Appeal unanimously dismissed the claimant's appeal, in respect of which the issue was whether there existed the proximity in time and space necessary to make the claimant a person to whom the defendant owed a duty of care. To differing degrees, each of the five factors identified in (a)–(e) appears to have influenced the court. In particular, the claimant did not go to the site for two hours after the accident had happened, and even during the brief period when he was in the collapsed building, his son was buried in rubble two floors above him. No part of his son's body was seen until he visited the mortuary 24 hours later. Throughout his presence at the scene the emergency services were in attendance. Taken together, such factors were decisive.

---

[27] Transcript, 28 April 1998, CA.

The means of perception

6.26 To recover damages for recognisable psychiatric damage as a secondary victim the damage must be proved to have been shock induced (see *Alcock*[28]).The shock must come through the sight or hearing of the event or its immediate aftermath. The question whether communications via a simultaneous broadcast would be sufficient to ground recovery was left open by Lord Wilberforce in *McLoughlin*.[29] However, in *Alcock* the House ruled that watching what was broadcast live of Hillsborough on the television did not equate to being within sight or hearing of the disaster.

6.27 A psychiatric illness induced by mere knowledge of a distressing fact (concerning the fate of primary victim) is not compensable. Perception by the claimant of the distressing event is essential (*Alcock*[30]).

INVOLUNTARY PARTICIPANT

6.28 The 'involuntary participant' was identified as a category by Lord Oliver. In particular, he analysed in (*Alcock*[31]) the cases as falling into two separate categories: those of participants and witnesses.

6.29 The authority taken as establishing the former category is the decision of Donovan J in *Dooley v Cammel Laird & Co Ltd*, but this is a very special case.[32]

6.30 Mr Dooley, a crane driver, was the unwitting hand who caused the accident – a load fell into the hold of a ship. In the event, there was no injury to the men below, but nothing turned on that. Rather, it was held that 'nervous shock' was a reasonably foreseeable consequence of witnessing an accident to another as it was proved that the claimant had been put in the position of thinking that he was about to be or had been the involuntary cause of another's death or injury. The phrase 'unwilling participant' is used as synonymous with the 'involuntary cause of …'.

6.31 In describing this category, Lord Oliver also spoke of the claimant as being 'mediately' involved. The use of the word 'mediately' does not cover cases of participation in the aftermath. Rather, 'mediately' means to form a connecting link or transitional stage, to act as an intermediary. For example, it covers the situation where a workman gives a scaffolding pole to a colleague that he then raises and hits an electricity wire whereby he is electrocuted (see *Young v Charles Church (Southern) Ltd*[33]).

---

[28] Op cit Lord Ackner at 400F and 401F.
[29] Op cit at 422H–423B.
[30] Op cit Lord Keith at 398C and Lord Ackner at 401B.
[31] Ibid at 407D.
[32] [1951] 1 Lloyd's Rep, 271; Lord Jauncey at 420F.
[33] Transcript, 24 April 1997, CA; also reported at (1998) 39 BMLR 146.

6.32 Two other cases are sometimes taken as more recent applications of the proposition illustrated by *Dooley*. In the first case, *Galt v British Railway Board*,[34] the claimant train driver rounded a bend and saw two men on the track and thought they had been killed. He suffered a myocardial infarction. It is perhaps to be doubted, therefore, whether this was a case involving psychiatric injury at all. In the second case, *Wigg v British Railways Board*,[35] a railway guard negligently gave the claimant train driver a signal to start the train, leading to the death of another. The claimant got out to help. He was in fact treated as a rescuer.

6.33 Before turning to rescuers, it should be noted that in *Dooley*, the case against the employer (the second defendant) succeeded after the relevant regulations. The case was not, therefore, authority for the proposition that an employee is in any special position where the tortfeasor is his employer (see below). Lord Oliver did not say that liability arose because the employer was in breach of its duty of care at common law qua employer.

RESCUERS

6.34 Rescue cases are also regarded as being in a special category. However, the category of rescuer is established in the law of negligence generally, not just when considering liability for recognisable psychiatric illness. If a rescuer, the claimant is not concerned with arguments of contributory negligence, *novus actus interveniens* or *volenti non fit injuria*.[36]

6.35 The question arose in *Frost* whether rescuers were in a special category to whom a duty of care is owned in relation to psychiatric injury. *Frost* also related to the Hillsborough disaster. Police officers who had tended to the victims of the disaster brought claims for post-traumatic disorder arising from their participation in the disaster. It was claimed that they were rescuers and thus primary victims. They also contended that there was a special duty owed to them as employees.

6.36 In the Court of Appeal,[37] Henry LJ argued in favour of a broad definition of a rescuer saying:

> '... that public policy favours a wide rather than a narrow definition, to ensure that those brave and unselfish enough to go to the help of their fellow men will be properly compensated if they suffer damage as a result'.

---

[34] (1983) 133 NLJ 870.
[35] (1986) *The Times*, February 4.
[36] *McLoughlin*, op cit per Lord Wilberforce; cf *Frost*, op cit Lord Hoffmann at 1555F.
[37] [1997] 3 WLR 1194 at 1220D.

6.37 Rose LJ set the criteria for determination of the question of whether a person who suffered psychiatric injury should recover as a rescuer where otherwise they did not fulfil the secondary victim criteria by reference to a number of factors, namely:

> '... the character and extent of the initial accident caused by the tortfeasor; whether that incident has finished or is continuing; whether there is any danger, continuing or otherwise, to the victim or to the claimant; the character of the claimant's conduct, in itself and in relation to the victim; and how proximate, in time and place, the claimant's conduct is to the incident'.[38]

6.38 In the House of Lords the majority favoured a narrow definition of a rescuer and confirmed that, in claims for psychiatric damage, central to the concept of rescue is the notion of extricating someone from a situation of danger (see *Wagner v International Railway Company*[39]). Accordingly, to recover under the rescue principle a claimant must prove that he or she is:

(a) exposed to danger; and

(b) engaged in a rescue as defined by law.

6.39 Being exposed to danger includes those who are primary victims, as for example in *Baker v Hopkins*.[40] Lord Oliver clearly had such cases in mind when he dealt with rescuers in *Alcock*[41] and *McLoughlin* in the Court of Appeal.[42]

6.40 Rescue then is to be defined by reference to peril. Once the primary victim is removed from the place where he or she is in peril or the peril has passed matters have moved to a more remote stage. What is done for treatment of the primary victim where he or she is alive goes to the fact of injury. If the victim is dead, activities such as standing by the bodies in the mortuary and the setting up of the mortuary go to the fact of death as distinct from the circumstances in which it came about.

6.41 The law as now enunciated may be compared with the decision identified by Lord Wilberforce as establishing the category of 'rescuer' in this field, namely the decision of Waller J (as he then was) in *Chadwick v British Railways Board*.[43] Mr Chadwick had worked through the night tending to those injured in the Lewisham train disaster; that had involved him going into the carriages where the dead and injured were trapped.

6.42 Some had interpreted *Chadwick*[44] as being a case where the claimant was held entitled to recover because of the horror of the whole event; similarly in

---

[38] Ibid at 1203G.
[39] [1921] 232 NY 176, Cardozo J at 180.
[40] [1959] 1 WLR 966.
[41] Op cit at 408B–D; Lord Jauncey at 421A–C.
[42] [1981] 1 QB CA per Griffiths LJ at 623A.
[43] [1967] 1 WLR 912.
[44] Ibid per Waller J at 918A–B.

Frost.[45] Others had interpreted that authority on the basis that liability was founded on the risk of personal injury to which the claimant submitted himself (see *McLoughlin*[46] and *McFarlane*[47]).

6.43 The majority of the House of Lords in *Frost* preferred the latter interpretation. As Lord Hoffmann put it:

'... there is no authority which decides that a rescuer is in any special position in relation to liability for psychiatric injury'.[48]

6.44 The speech of Lord Steyn affords particular guidance. He said:

'[ChadwickI] is not authority for the proposition that a person who never exposed himself to any personal danger and never thought that he was in personal danger can recover pure psychiatric injury as a rescuer. In order to recover compensation for pure psychiatric harm as rescuer it is not necessary to establish that his psychiatric condition was caused by the perception of personal danger. And Waller J rightly so held. But in order to contain the concept of rescuer in reasonable bounds for the purposes of the recovery of compensation for pure psychiatric harm the Claimant must at least satisfy the threshold requirement that he objectively exposed himself to danger or reasonably believed that he was doing so'.[49]

6.45 It should also be noted that at the Court of Appeal stage of *Frost* there was also heard the case of *Duncan v British Coal Corporation*.[50] In that case, it was held that a mining supervisor who gave mouth-to-mouth resuscitation to a colleague fatally injured in a mining accident for over two hours was not a rescuer because he had arrived some four minutes after the relevant accident.

6.46 The decision in *Duncan v British Coal Corporation*, and in particular Rose LJ[51] reflects, therefore, a restrictive view; similarly the decision in *McFarlane*. They emphasise that temporal and physical proximity is required where a victim is said to have functioned as a rescuer.

6.47 The latter decision also emphasises that a 'function' test may usefully be applied when determining whether a given claimant is a rescuer. In *McFarlane*, merely handling some blankets was not enough to warrant the conclusion that the claimant was a rescuer; as Lord Griffiths put in *Frost*:

'... trivial or peripheral assistance will not be sufficient'.[52]

---

[45] Op cit per Rose LJ at 1202H–1203A.
[46] Op cit per Griffiths LJ at 622H, CA.
[47] Per Stuart-Smith LJ at 10F.
[48] At 1555F.
[49] At 1546H–1547D.
[50] [1997] 1 All ER.
[51] At 554A.
[52] At 1514F.

6.48 As to the position of the professional rescuer, provided he or she is a rescuer as defined above, it is settled by *Frost* that such a rescuer is in no better or worse position than the volunteer rescuer. In short, as with physical injury, there is no 'fireman's rule' regarding liability for psychiatric illness.

EMPLOYEES

6.49 It was argued in *Frost* that although the claimants lacked a relationship with the primary victims of the disaster, they did have a relationship analogous to that of employment with the defendants. Technically, a police officer is a constable not 'employed' by the police authority, but it was conceded in *Frost* at trial that the relationship of the chief constable with his officers was analogous to that of an employer to his employees with the concomitant rights and duties.

6.50 The argument, that found favour with the majority in the Court of Appeal, was that by reason of that quasi employment relationship, the claimants did not need to fulfil the three main requirements that a secondary victim claimant must ordinarily fulfil to recover, and, particularly relevant in the *Frost* case, the criterion of a close tie of love and affection with the person killed, injured or imperilled. It was contended that the relationship put them in a different and altogether easier position when considering the question of duty to that of spectators at the match even though what they saw and did at the match may have been the same. They were owed a duty of care as claimants who were directly involved in the incident caused by their employers' negligence which resulted in the injury or imperilment of another.

6.51 This argument had earlier been made in the Scottish case of *Robertson v Forth Road Bridge*.[53] Lord Hope's rejection of this argument[54] in the Inner House of the Court of Session was rejected by the Court of Appeal in *Frost* but accepted by the House of Lords.

6.52 As Lord Hoffmann put it, the argument really assumed what it needed to prove. He said:

> 'The liability of an employer to his employees for negligence, either direct or vicarious, is not a separate tort with its own rules. It is an aspect of the general law of negligence. The relationship of employer and employee establishes the employee as a person to whom the employer owes a duty of care. But this tells one nothing about the circumstances in which he will be liable for a particular type of injury. For this one must look to the general law concerning the type of injury which has been suffered.'[55]

He then considered whether the employment relationship should be a reason for allowing an employee to recover damages for psychiatric injury in

---

[53] 1995 SC 364.
[54] Ibid at 370D–374B.
[55] Ibid at 1552E–H.

circumstances in which he would otherwise be a secondary victim and not satisfy the *Alcock* control mechanisms asking the rhetorical question:

> 'Why should the policemen, simply by virtue of the employment analogy and irrespective of what they actually did be treated different [sic] from first-aid workers or ambulance men?'

He concluded that, in line with authority, it would not be fair to permit recovery on such grounds.[56]

6.53 It is now clearly established that the existence of the relationship of employment does not dispose of the need to satisfy the criteria the law has laid down that must be met in secondary victim cases.

BYSTANDERS

6.54 Whether a mere bystander (that is a person who witnesses the death, injury, or imperilment of the immediate victim, but has no close tie of love and affection with him or her) may in any circumstances recover damages for psychiatric injury is not certain (see *McLoughlin*[57] and *Alcock*[58]).

6.55 That an accident may be sufficiently catastrophic that without more a duty of care is owed to witnesses of that accident is not (yet) the law. Three of their Lordships in *Alcock* touched on this issue: Lord Keith described such a case as 'difficult' but did not rule it out if the circumstances of the catastrophe were 'particularly horrific';[59] Lord Ackner would not rule it out and gave an example of a petrol tanker careering out of control into a school in session and bursting into flames;[60] and Lord Oliver would not exclude it, speaking of 'circumstances of such horror as would be likely to traumatise even the most phlegmatic bystander'.[61]

6.56 Notwithstanding the events at Hillsborough and their scale, it was not suggested in *Alcock* that what occurred there was a sufficiently or particular horrific disaster for that alone to entitle the claimants to recover.[62]

6.57 This issue arose in *McFarlane*. It would be difficult to imagine circumstances more horrific than the destruction by an oil fire storm of the Piper Alpha oil rig out of which event that case arose. Stuart-Smith LJ

---

[56] *Alcock*, op cit at 1552H–1554G.
[57] Op cit Lord Wilberforce at 422C–D.
[58] Op cit Lord Ackner at 403E and Lord Oliver at 416C.
[59] At 397E.
[60] At 403E.
[61] At 416B–C.
[62] See 392F, 9393E, 398C and 399A.

expressed clear misgivings about the courts involving themselves in assessing degrees of horror as reactions to such events are entirely subjective. Accordingly he concluded:

> 'In my judgment both as a matter of principle and policy the court should not extend the duty to those who are mere bystanders or witnesses of horrific events.'[63]

THE LAW FOLLOWING *FROST*

6.58 At the Personal Injuries Bar Association's Annual Lecture 2004, Lord Phillips MR presented an informative paper entitled 'Liability for Psychiatric Harm'. The then Master of the Rolls summarised the law, as it appeared to be firmly established after *Frost*:

(1) A claimant exposed by a negligent act or omission to the risk of physical injury can recover if the act or omission causes him psychiatric injury, even if this were not reasonably foreseeable. It is not clear whether recovery depends on showing that the injury resulted from fear for his own safety rather than shock at seeing others injured.

(2) A rescuer who exposes himself to danger can recover whether the psychiatric injury is caused by fear for his own safety or horror at what he sees.

(3) All others who sustain psychiatric injury as a result of reaction to the fate of others are subject to the following control mechanisms: first, there must be a close relationship between the person killed or injured and the claimant. Secondly, the claimant must be in close proximity to the accident, or come upon the aftermath of the accident. Thirdly, the psychiatric injury must result from sudden shock. Finally, the psychiatric injury must be caused by seeing or hearing the accident or its aftermath, rather than being told about it.

6.59 The fundamental importance of the distinction between a primary and secondary victim was highlighted in the Scottish case of *Simmons v British Steel plc*[64] Mr Simmons sustained a head injury during the course of his employment with the defendant. Following the accident Mr Simmons also experienced an exacerbation of a pre-existing skin condition, and he developed a change in his personality which resulted in a severe depressive illness. The Lord Ordinary had found that Mr Simmons had become angry after the accident and that it was his anger that led to the exacerbation of the skin condition and to the depressive mental illness. The approach taken by the House of Lords was that since Mr Simmons actually suffered physical injuries

---

[63] At 14E.
[64] [2004] ICR 585.

as a result of the defendant's fault and negligence, the starting point was that he was a primary victim in terms of Lord Lloyd's analysis in *Page*.[65] It was, therefore, immaterial whether his psoriasis and his depressive illness sprang not from the accident itself but from his anger at the happening of the accident. It was held that where a claimant suffers physical injuries in an accident for which a defendant is found to be liable it is unnecessary applying *Page* to ask whether the psychiatric injury from which he has also been suffering was reasonably foreseeable. No distinction needs to be made between the initial physical injuries and the subsequent mental state.

6.60 The duty of care owed by the defendant extended to the psychiatric injuries as well as to the physical consequences. The defendant must take its victim as it finds him or her, so the aggravation of the psoriasis and the anger which led to the depressive illness could both be assumed to fall within the scope of its liability so long as there was a causal connection between the symptoms and the accident.[66] In *Simmons* it was found that although there were several causes of Mr Simmons' anger, the anger at the happening of the accident could not be dismissed under the *de minimis principle*. On the evidence the anger had materially contributed to the exacerbation of the psoriasis, therefore, the causal connection was established and Mr Simmons was entitled to payment of damages in full.[67]

6.61 In *Eileen Corr (Administratrix of the Estate of Thomas Corr, Deceased) v IBC Vehicles Ltd*[68] the Court of Appeal held that it is not necessary to prove reasonable foresight of suicide to establish liability. Having been categorised as a primary victim, it was sufficient that depression was a foreseeable consequence of the defendant's negligence – the mere fact that the extent of that depression, leading to suicide, might not be foreseeable did not preclude the defendant being held liable for the losses resulting from his death.

6.62 It was acknowledged in *W & Ors v Essex County Council & Anor*[69] that the categorisation of those claiming to be primary or secondary victims is not closed. In *W*, the House of Lords considered an appeal from the decision of the Court of Appeal to uphold a decision to strike out claims by foster parents for damages for psychiatric illness caused by the negligence of the defendant. The foster parents had four children of their own. The defendant placed a known sexual abuser in their home for care. The children were sexually abused by the known sexual abuser. The parents claimed that the defendant was negligent for placing a known sexual abuser in their home when the defendant had been told that the parents were unwilling to accept any child who was known or suspected of being a sexual abuser. The House of Lords allowed the appeal against the strike out. It was held *inter alia* that the concept of primary and secondary victims is still being developed in different factual situations and that

---

[65] Op cit Lord Rodger of Earlsferry at 55.
[66] Op cit Lord Hope of Craighead at 21.
[67] Op cit at 27.
[68] [2006] 3 WLR 395; 2 AER 929; 2006 (ICR) 1138.
[69] [2000] 2 WLR 601 at 243 F–J.

it was not conclusive from the authorities that the parents were prevented front being primary victims if the psychiatric injury flowed from the feeling that they brought the abuser and the abused together or from feeling responsibility for not detecting the abuse earlier. The concept of the unwilling participant discussed in *Alcock* was considered.[70]

6.63 Whether an employee is a primary or secondary victim calls for carefully analysis of the facts. The claimant in *Harrhy v Thames Trains Ltd*[71] was employed by the defendant as a manager of senior train drivers. The day after a serious train accident at Paddington the claimant was requested to attend the scene of the accident as the defendant's representative. The claimant had to enter the carriages and was required to view corpses, thereafter, he developed depression coupled with a form of post traumatic stress disorder. The claimant submitted that his case was analogous to *Walker v Northumberland County Council*[72] in which a senior social worker suffered a nervous breakdown as a result of overwork, a fact which he reported to his employer. Mr Walker was subsequently put back to work under a heavy workload and suffered further psychiatric injury. The judge held that he was entitled to recover for the second breakdown but not the first. The defendant in *Harrhy* argued *inter alia* that the claimant had not fulfilled the control mechanisms applicable to psychiatric injury contained in *Alcock* and that in accordance with the law as it had developed in *Frost* and in *Keen v Tayside Contracts*[73] the claim was bound to fail. Mackay J held that the High Court Master was correct to allow the claim to proceed. He found that the law relating to psychiatric injury was still being developed and it was open to a trial judge to decide whether to follow the approach in *Walker* or *Keen*. Mackay J commented that:

> 'it was far from his mind certain as to whether *Walker* survives the examination it received in *Frost*. The only one of their Lordships who dealt with it at any length was Lord Hoffmann who appears for his part either to have approved of it, or at least not to have disapproved of it, on the basis that Mr Walker was a primary victim [as his mental breakdown was caused by the strain of doing the work which his employer had required him to do]. If that is the right analysis then the claimant in *Harrhy* argues that his mental breakdown too was one which was "caused by the strain of doing work which his employer had required him to do.'[74]

6.64 In *French v Chief Constable of Sussex*[75] claims by police officers for psychiatric injuries suffered following an armed raid which resulted in a fatal shooting were struck out. None of the officers concerned had witnessed the shooting. The stress and psychiatric injuries were caused by the criminal and disciplinary proceedings brought against the officers arising out of the handling of the raid. The officers alleged that there were serious systemic failures in the training provided for the conduct of such raids. The Judge held

---

[70] See discussion above and *Alcock* [1992] 1 AC at 408F.
[71] [2003] EWHC 2120 (QB).
[72] [1995] 1 All ER 737.
[73] [2003] Scot CS 55.
[74] [2003] EWHC 2120 (QB) at 11.
[75] [2006] EWCA Civ 312.

that they did not qualify as secondary victims and that this was not a stress at work case as the stress and psychiatric injuries were not in the context of this case foreseeable.

6.65 Recent cases have considered shock induced as a result of the negligence of health authorities. In *Farrell v Avon Health Authority*,[76] employees at the defendant's hospital negligently told the claimant that his newborn baby had died. The claimant was given a dead baby to hold. In fact, his baby was still alive and he had mistakenly been given someone else's dead baby to hold. It was held that the claimant was a primary victim and he was able to recover damages for the psychiatric injury that he suffered as a result of the defendant's negligence.

6.66 In *Ward v The Leeds Teaching Hospitals NHS Trust*,[77] HHJ Hawkesworth QC ruled in favour of the Defendant holding that the diagnostic criteria for a finding of post traumatic stress disorder required a shocking event of a particularly horrific nature and the death of a loved one in hospital did not meet that description unless accompanied by circumstances that were exceptional in some way so as to shock or horrify.

6.67 In the context of disease litigation, the majority decision of the Court of Appeal in *Rothwell v Chemical & Insulating Co Ltd*[78] is of considerable interest. In the context of conjoined appeals concerning the Pleural Plaques Test Litigation, the court had to consider the position of one particular Appellant, Mr. Grieves, who had suffered a recognisable psychiatric illness, in the form of a depressive illness, which was alleged to have been caused by the defendant's breach of duty in exposing him to asbestos. It was argued on behalf of Mr Grieves that he should recover because the psychiatric injury was a foreseeable consequence of the breach of duty. Alternatively, because physical injury was a foreseeable consequence of breach of duty, recovery could be made for psychiatric injury in accordance with the decision of the House of Lords in *Page v Smith*.

6.68 The first submission was rejected on the basis that there was no evidence that employees of reasonable fortitude would be likely to suffer psychiatric injury on learning that exposure to asbestos carries with it a risk of developing serious disorders. In *Page*, the majority of the House of Lords held that where the Defendant can reasonably foresee that his conduct will expose the claimant to risk of personal injury, he was a primary victim and could recover for a recognised psychiatric injury without satisfying further control mechanisms or establishing a further particular duty in relation to psychiatric injury. The majority in the present appeals has limited the potential scope of the ruling in *Page*. In reliance upon the decision of the United States Supreme Court in *Norfolk & Western Railway*[79], which postulated a 'zone of danger' test, the

---

[76] [2001] All ER (D) 17.
[77] [2004] EWHC 2106.
[78] [2006] EWCA Civ 27.
[79] (2003) 538 US 135.

Court of Appeal held that the test in *Page* could not properly be extended so as to render a Defendant who negligently exposed a Claimant to the risk of contracting a disease liable for free-standing psychiatric injury caused by the fear of contracting a disease (para 90). The Court of Appeal also rejected the submission that Mr Grieves could recover because he was an employee and his employer had breached its duty of care to him. There was no evidence that the employer had caused a foreseeable risk of psychiatric injury in an employee of reasonable fortitude (para 94). The Court of Appeal was not prepared to extend recovery to a case where such injury was not reasonably foreseeable in an employee of reasonable fortitude (para 100).

THE AFTERMATH REVISITED

6.69 In *North Glamorgan NHS Trust v Walters*[80] a mother sued for psychiatric injury suffered as a result of the death of her son, which was attributable to clinical negligence by the defendant. The facts were that the claimant who was sleeping in the same room as her son in hospital awoke to find her son experiencing a major epileptic seizure. The claimant was negligently assured that the child was unlikely to have suffered any permanent harm and the child was moved to another hospital to undergo a liver transplant. In fact, the child had suffered irreparable brain damage. At the new hospital the claimant was told that her son had suffered brain damage and was on a life support machine. The next day she was told that her son could never hope to have any quality of life so she agreed that the life support machine should be switched off. Her child died in her arms. Medical experts agreed that the mental breakdown, diagnosed as pathological grief reaction, which she subsequently suffered was as a result of her experiences over the last two days of her son's life. It was accepted that the claimant was a secondary victim and that her experience over the last two days of her son's life constituted the witnessing of a single horrifying event. Interestingly, Clarke LJ commented that had it been necessary he would have been prepared to take an incremental step advancing the frontiers of liability on the facts of the case.

6.70 In *Froggatt v Chesterfield and North Derbyshire Royal Hospital NHS Trust*[81] a woman was wrongly told that she had cancer and was given an unnecessary mastectomy. Her husband was successful in claiming damages for psychiatric injury as a result of seeing the scar after the operation. Her son was awarded damages for psychiatric injury suffered as a result of being told that his mother suffered from cancer. The husband and son were held to be secondary victims. The events were accepted as being part of the aftermath of the negligent act.

---

[80] [2002] EWCA 1792.
[81] [2002] All ER (D) 218.

6.71 The concept of the aftermath was again considered in *Atkinson v Anor v Seghal*.[82] The claimant's daughter had been severely injured when she was hit by a car. She died shortly after the accident at 7.40 pm. The claimant who was out looking for her daughter, who was late returning home, arrived at the police cordon and was told by the police that her daughter was dead. The claimant visited the mortuary at 9.15 pm and on confirmation that the body was that of her daughter she fell to her knees and sobbed uncontrollably. She saw her daughter's disfigured face and head. The claimant suffered an extreme reaction and developed a psychiatric condition. The expert evidence was that the circumstances surrounding the death made a material contribution to the claimant's psychiatric illness. At first instance, the recorder dismissed the claim for damages for nervous shock. He found that:

(i) on the basis of the authorities in *McLoughlin* and *Alcock* the claimant could not succeed as there could be no claim based on shock being told of death;

(ii) the events at the mortuary were not part of the immediate aftermath of the accident;

(iii) the shock that caused the psychiatric disorder resulted solely from what the claimant had been told by the police officer at the cordon; and

(iv) the shock suffered was the inevitable reaction to the fact that her daughter was dead, and the fact that she was told of the death at the scene rather than elsewhere had not materially contributed to the psychiatric disorder.

The claimant appealed on the following grounds:

(i) the recorder had taken too restrictive an approach to what constituted events giving rise to the shock and the recorder was wrong to exclude consideration of what occurred at the mortuary in determining whether her claim should succeed as it was the whole of what the claimant had seen and was told that caused her psychiatric disorder; and

(ii) there was no evidence to support the recorder's findings that the psychiatric illness suffered occurred solely due to what she had been told.

6.72 The *North Glamorgan* decision was considered and it was held that an event might be made up of a number of components. It was further held that as long as events retained a sufficient proximity to the event, they could be considered to be in the aftermath. In this case, the aftermath extended from the moment of the accident until the moment the claimant left the mortuary. It was found that the recorder had artificially separated the mortuary visit. The visit was not simply to identify her daughter's body but was also to complete the story so for as the claimant was concerned. On the second ground it was held

---

[82] [2003] EWCA Civ 697.

that the recorder's conclusions could not be supported on the evidence. The conclusion that she would have suffered psychiatric illness in any event was not supported by the evidence.

6.73 In *W & Ors v Essex County Council & Anor*, it was accepted that the concept of the immediate aftermath of an incident had to be assessed in the particular factual situation. In *W* the incidents of abuse had happened in a 4-week period before discovery by the parents. It was found that in the circumstances of the case it was arguable that such a time period could be sufficient to constitute the aftermath. A recent example of the extent to which determination of the immediate aftermath is a question of fact and degree is provided by the first instance decision of Recorder Hill in *Farmer v Outokumpu Stainless Ltd*.[83]

DUTY OF CARE OWED BY PRIMARY VICTIMS

6.74 The question of whether as a matter of policy a primary victim of self-inflicted injuries owes a duty of care towards a secondary victim who suffers psychiatric illness as a result of those injuries was considered in *Christopher Greatorex (Claimant) v (1) John Simon Greatorex (First Defendant) (2) Motor Insurers' Bureau (Second Defendant/Part 20 Claimant) (3) Haydon Pope (Part 20 Defendant)*.[84] The claimant was a fire officer who attended a scene of a road traffic accident in the course of his duties. The driver of one of the cars involved in the accident was the claimant's son (the first defendant). The first defendant had suffered a head injury and was unconscious for about an hour. The claimant suffered long-term severe post traumatic stress disorder as a result of attending to his son at the scene and thereafter brought an action against his son in which he claimed damages for psychiatric injury. The son was convicted of driving without due care and attention, without insurance and for failing to provide a specimen. It was found that following *Frost* rescuers should no longer be regarded as coming within a special category and for a rescuer to recover compensation for pure psychiatric injury suffered as a rescuer the claimant had to satisfy the threshold requirement that he objectively exposed himself to a danger or reasonably believed that he was doing so. However, the claimant was not required to prove that his psychiatric injury was caused by the perception of personal danger. *Frost* had clearly established that a rescuer seeking to recover damages for purely psychiatric injury was to be regarded as a secondary victim having no special status. As the claimant here was not in any danger nor in fear of danger his claim as a rescuer had to fail. As to whether the claimant satisfied the requirements to claim as a secondary victim, the first and third requirements were conceded on the facts. Cazalet J found that the second requirement was also satisfied. It was the fact that the claimant was a close relative and not that he was a rescuer that brought him within the category of persons prima facie entitled to claim damages.

---

[83] Lawtel LTL 31/8/2006.
[84] [2000] 1 WLR 1970.

6.75 Cazalet J also considered the question of whether the claimant's son owed the claimant a duty of care in this situation. There was no reported English decision on the question whether a victim of self-inflicted injuries owes a duty of care to a third party not to cause him psychiatric injury but the weight of the Commonwealth authorities to which the judge was referred supported the submission that there was no duty of care in such a situation. The judge considered that policy considerations should come into play. The first *Alcock* requirement has the effect that claims arising out of this situation will be between close relatives. It was considered that the suffering of a close relative for self induced or natural reasons was an inherent part of family life and as such there would have to be a good reason for extending the law to provide a remedy in this situation where it would otherwise be found that there was no duty of care owed by a primary victim of self-inflicted injuries. It was considered to be undesirable to allow a cause of action for psychiatric illness where one family member either witnessed another family member having an accident or found another family member shortly after an accident. It was especially undesirable that there was a possibility that such a claim could be met by a defence of contributory negligence by the claimant (for example, a drunken wife who falls over and hits her head and whose husband suffers psychiatric injury for fear of her life may argue that the husband was guilty of contributory negligence for driving her to drink). The fact that it is established law that family members have the same right as others to make a claim for physical injury within the family does not mean that they should have the right to make a claim for a different kind of harm in respect of which others have no right to claim under the control mechanisms set out in *Alcock*. It was held that as a matter of policy a primary victim does not owe a duty of care to a third party in circumstances where his self-inflicted injuries caused that third party psychiatric injury.

PROPOSALS FOR REFORM

6.76 Our law in this area remains unsatisfactory. In *McLoughlin* Lord Scarman called for legislative reform[85] but such has not yet been promulgated. The Law Commission Consultation Paper (No 137), 'Liability for Psychiatric Illness', usefully poses a number of questions which as yet remain unanswered on the authorities. For example, in cases of simultaneous television, there is the instance given by Nolan LJ in the Court of Appeal of a publicity seeking organisation arranging for the simultaneous broadcast of a balloon trip made by a number of children where, whilst filming and transmitting pictures of the event, the cameras show the balloon suddenly burst into flames.[86]

6.77 The Law Commission, in their report, has recommended legislative reform designed to remove what it considers to be some unwarranted

---

[85] Para 2.38.
[86] Ibid Lord Oliver at 418D–E.

restrictions that presently apply in relation to liability for negligently inflicted psychiatric illness. It has recommended the *removal* of certain preconditions to liability in secondary victim cases:

(a) that the illness must be 'shock' induced;[87]

(b) that the illness must not result from the death, injury, or imperilment of the defendant him or herself;[88]

(c) that the claimant must be close to the accident in time and space;[89]

(d) that he or she directly perceived the accident rather than, for example, hearing about it from a third person.[90]

6.78 The Law Commission recommended the *retention* of the rule that a secondary victim must have had a close tie of love and affection with the person killed, injured or imperilled. The close tie would be assumed in the relationships of spouse, parent, child, brother or sister and cohabitant. For other relationships, the claimant would have the opportunity of proving the existence of a close tie of love and affection.[91]

6.79 The Law Commission considered the issue in *Greatorex*[92] in its report which gives weight to the argument that to create a duty of care in the case of self-inflicted harm would place an undesirably restrictive burden on a person's self-determination. To preserve respect for the claimant's right of self determination, the report recommends that legislation should provide for such a duty to exist where the defendant has negligently harmed himself but not when he has chosen to harm himself.

---

[87] Para 5.33.
[88] Para 5.43.
[89] Para 6.16.
[90] Para 6.16.
[91] Para 6.27.
[92] Paras 5.34–5.44.

Chapter 7

EMPLOYER'S STATUTORY LIABILITIES

THE SCOPE OF THIS CHAPTER

7.1 This chapter is intended as a handy overview of the most important statutory liabilities to which employers are subject. Employers may be liable at both common law, and by statute. Earlier chapters deal with important principles of the former. As to the latter, this chapter will not provide a detailed insightful analysis of the provisions and case law nor will it recite the provisions of the various Regulations in detail (for which the reader should see standard texts such as *Munkman on Employers' Liability*). It is intended to provide a quick synopsis of the main features, which it will try to place both in context and, in respect of each liability, in a similar format for easy cross-reference. It should enable the reader quickly to see (or to check) whether there is indeed liability under statute for the wrongs the claimant complains of. It will draw attention to some problem areas, and available arguments: and perhaps stimulate an idea or two. It may perhaps be of use alongside the Regulations, where frequently the detail of the text may obscure the clarity of the provision.

THE PRINCIPAL HEALTH AND SAFETY REGULATIONS

7.2 The principal Regulations affecting the health and safety of employees (though made under the Health and Safety at Work etc Act 1974) now derive from a group of EC Directives, which were implemented in 1992 in the UK. Those Directives, each of which could be described as a 'daughter' Directive of the 'parent' Framework Directive on Health and Safety at Work, then gave rise to what was colloquially known as 'the six-pack', since it consisted of six linked sets of Regulations. Time has moved on; the old Factories Act legislation has been reduced to being history (though sometimes informative when the recent Regulations have to be interpreted), and there are now more than six major Regulations covering the main fields of liability.

7.3 The principal relevant Regulations are now:

- Management of Health and Safety at Work Regulations 1999[1] ('the Management Regulations');

---

[1] SI 1999/3242, as amended by SI 2003/2457: there is now liability for breach of its provisions

- Health and Safety (Display Screen Equipment) Regulations 1992[2] (the 'Display Screen Equipment Regulations');

- Manual Handling Operations Regulations 1992;[3]

- Provision and Use of Work Equipment Regulations 1998[4] ('PUWER');

- Personal Protective Equipment at Work Regulations[5] ('the PPE Regulations');

- Workplace (Health, Safety and Welfare) Regulations 1992[6] ('the Workplace Regulations').

These form the current versions of the original six, to which have been added (amongst other Regulations covering more esoteric subjects[7]):

- Construction (Health, Safety and Welfare) Regulations 1996[8] ('the Construction Regulations');

- Lifting Operations and Lifting Equipment Regulations 1998[9] ('LOLER'); and

- Working Time Regulations 1998.[10]

7.4 Each set of Regulations, except the Construction Regulations and LOLER,[11] gives effect in domestic law to a European Directive.[12] Each adopts the same standard *approach* to the protection of health and safety, rather than enacting detailed provisions which are individual to specific situations. This approach is now enshrined in the revised Management of Health and Safety at

---

when there was not before. This implements much of the 'Framework Directive' (EC Directive 89/391) which is the parent for the 'daughter' Directives from which the other Regulations mentioned in this chapter mainly derive.

[2] SI 1992/2792, implementing the Display Screen Equipment Directive 90/270.
[3] SI 1992/2793, implementing the Manual Handling Directive 90/269.
[4] SI 1998/2306, implementing the Work Equipment Directive 89/655.
[5] SI 1992/2966, implementing the Personal Protective Equipment Directive 89/656.
[6] SI 1992/3004, implementing the Workplace Directive 89/654.
[7] This chapter has to be selective, for even in a work the size of *Munkman* it is impossible to do justice to the totality of the Regulations. It might be debatable whether some Regulations – such as the Noise at Work or Electricity at Work Regulations (SI 1989/635) – should be covered in addition to those on which the text centres, but economy of treatment and space demands a rigorous selectivity. For those other Regulations see eg *Redgrave's Health and Safety*; *Munkman on Employers' Liability*, or the *Encyclopedia of Health and Safety Law*.
[8] SI 1996/1592.
[9] SI 1998/2307.
[10] SI 1998/1833, implementing the Working Time Directive 93/104.
[11] Though these adopt the same basic approach, they are made under the HSWA 1974 alone.
[12] They implement Council Directives 89/391/EC (the 'Framework' Directive) (MHSWR); 89/654/EC (Workplace); 89/655/EC (PUWER); 89/656/EC (PPE); 90/267/EC (Manual Handling), and 90/270/EC (Display Screen).

Work Regulations, reg 4, incorporating Sch 1 to the Regulations. It requires a hierarchy of measures to be adopted. Thus the general principles of prevention are:

(a) avoiding risks;

(b) evaluating the risks which cannot be avoided;

(c) combating th(os)e risks at source;

(d) adapting the work to the individual, especially as regards the design of workplaces, the choice of work equipment and the choice of working or production methods[13] with a view, in particular, to alleviating monotonous work and work at a predetermined work-rate and to reducing their effect on health;

(e) adapting to technical progress;

(f) replacing the dangerous by the non-dangerous or the less dangerous;

(g) developing a coherent overall prevention policy which covers technology, organisation of work, working conditions, social relationships[14] and the influence of factors relating to the working environment;

(h) giving collective protective measures priority over individual protective measures; and

(i) giving appropriate instructions to employees.

7.5 One matter is not stated in the list which is nonetheless emphasised by all the Regulations: the need to monitor.

7.6 These principles add text to, but do not significantly differ from, the principles which English law has adopted progressively over the last forty years – the obligation to workers to make work safer by (a) designing out dangers; (b) collective protection: taking steps to prevent the danger affecting anyone likely to be affected (eg by guards on machines); (c) protecting an individual (eg by gloves, goggles etc); (d) providing remedies in case the collective or personal protection should be insufficient (eg washing facilities; first-aid); (e) informing staff so that they know of risks, and how to avoid them; and (f) checking, or monitoring, to ensure that these measures are sufficient and are working properly.

---

[13] Thus far, this sounds like the traditional 'system of work' head of employers' common law liability – but see what follows, which invites action.

[14] This is capable of bringing 'stress' claims clearly within the Management Regulations and, for that matter, within the other relevant Regulations which derive from the same European Framework Directive.

7.7 Lord Walker, in *Fytche v Wincanton Logistics*,[15] appears to accept this: he specifically noted that:

> '... the identification and assessment of risk is one fundamental principle underlying the legislation ... another fundamental principle is that where possible risk should be avoided (by organisational measures) rather than reduced (by protective measures) and that means of collective protection are to be preferred to means of individual protection (such as personal protective equipment)'.[16]

ORIGIN IN EUROPEAN DIRECTIVES

7.8 There are two consequences of the European origin of these various Regulations: (a) as to the interpretation of the domestic Regulations, and (b) the possible direct effect of the Directives.

(a) *Interpretation:* The applicable principle is now well established: ' ... it is for a United Kingdom court to construe domestic legislation in any field covered by a Community Directive so as to accord with the interpretation of the Directive as laid down by the European Court of Justice, if that can be done without distorting the meaning of the domestic legislation' (*Duke v GEC Reliance Systems Ltd*.[17] The ECJ itself has emphasised[18] that the courts must utilise 'the full extent of their discretion' in interpreting and applying domestic provisions in conformity with Community law.

(b) *Direct effect:* Health and safety Directives are said to have vertical, not horizontal, direct effect. This means that they may be directly enforced by an individual against a state authority, but not against a fellow private citizen or company.[19]

7.9 'State authority' has a wide scope. It extends not only to the executive or the legislature, but also to the civil administration of the state (such as a local authority). Not only that, a health authority is an emanation of the state (*Marshall v Southampton and South West Hampshire Area Health Authority (Teaching)*[20]). British Gas[21] has been held to be an emanation of the State, as has South West Water[22] – though not, it seems, Rolls-Royce[23]. The test whether a given body is a state authority as expressed by the House of Lords in *Foster v British Gas*[24] is a two-fold one – the organisation said to be an emanation of the

---

[15] [2004] UKHL 31.
[16] Para 47.
[17] [1988] ICR 339 at 352G, per Lord Templeman. See also Lord Keith in *Webb v Emo Air Cargo Ltd* [1993] ICR 175.
[18] In *Coloroll Pension Trustees Ltd v Russell* [1995] ICR 179 at para. 29 of the judgment.
[19] In this latter case, enforcement is indirect only (ie by the interpretation route, if possible).
[20] [1986] QB 401, ECJ.
[21] *Foster v British Gas* [1991] QB 405, ECJ.
[22] *Griffin v South West Water Services* [1995] IRLR 15.
[23] *Doughty v Rolls-Royce* [1992] ICR 538.
[24] [1991] 2 AC 306.

state must (1) be made responsible, pursuant to a measure adopted by the state, for providing a public service under the control of the state, and (2) have for that purpose special powers beyond those which result from the normal rules applicable in relations between individuals.[25] However, it is arguable that this is too narrow a test, since the ECJ has since then in *Kampelmann v Landschaftsverband Westfalen-Lippe*[26] stated the applicable test as satisfied if *either* part of the two-fold requirement is satisfied.

Practical effect of direct effect

7.10 Accordingly, any public authority (eg local authority, health authority, most – but not all – schools), and any privatised utility which retains special powers beyond the normal in order to provide a public service is subject not only to the aforementioned Regulations but also to European Directives relating to health and safety, and any body which satisfies one of the tests may be so subject. Where a Directive goes beyond, or departs from the Regulations, a claimant may rely upon the Directive itself,[27] provided that the requirements of the Directive are clear, unconditional and sufficiently precise.

Where a Directive is not implemented

7.11 Where both a Regulation cannot be interpreted to accord with the Directive, and the defendant is not a state authority, an injured person still may have a remedy. However, this is against the state itself (the action is brought against the Attorney-General), for failing in its duty properly to implement the Directive concerned in domestic law. Three conditions must be met where a Directive gives a wide discretion to a Member State: (1) the rule of law infringed must be intended to confer rights on individuals; (2) the breach must be sufficiently serious; and (3) there must be a direct causal link between the breach of the obligation resting on the state and the damage sustained by the injured party (*Brasserie du Pecheur SA v Federal Republic of Germany; R v Secretary of State for Transport ex parte Factortame Ltd and others*[28]). Where the Directive gives a limited margin of discretion to the Member State, these conditions appear unnecessary.[29]

---

[25] See at 313, per Lord Templeman. *Doughty v Rolls-Royce* [1992] ICR 538, CA, has confirmed that both these requirements are necessary.
[26] Cases C-253/96 to 258/96, reported at [1998] IRLR 333, ECJ, at para 46 of the judgment.
[27] The wording is to be found in the *Encyclopaedia of Health and Safety* (Sweet & Maxwell), or in *Redgrave*. NB beware the frequently open-natured text of the European Directives, which may promise more than can actually be delivered!
[28] [1996] QB 404, ECJ at 499, para 51 judgment.
[29] P 498, ibid; para 45, 46 judgment. An example is where a directive requires a member state to take 'all measures necessary' to achieve a particular result, yet the domestic legislation fails to do so (see para 46, judgment). Where a Directive is *incorrectly* transposed, it is unclear whether the conditions apply where the discretion of the member state is limited: see *R v Her Majesty's Treasury ex parte British Telecommunications plc* [1996] QB 615, at 655A–D.

CODES OF PRACTICE AND GUIDANCE

7.12 The legislative approach in the UK is to reduce primary legislative text to its bare essentials. Traditional English wisdom had been that Regulations alone were compulsory, and that Guidance published alongside the regulations was advisory only, entitled perhaps to respect but not to slavish obedience.[30]

7.13 The Health and Safety at Work etc Act (HSWA) 1974 provides for such a split between primary Regulation and required practice, but also creates a hybrid between 'Regulation' and 'guidance'. Codes of Guidance may be approved by the Health and Safety Commission (these are known by the acronym: ACOP). These are intended to provide for detailed and flexible reaction to recent developments in Health and Safety. The HSWA 1974, s 16 provides, in respect of criminal proceedings, that if the prosecution prove a failure to observe any provision of an ACOP which appears relevant to any matter which it is necessary to prove to establish a contravention of a requirement or prohibition in the Regulations, then the contravention is to be taken as proved 'unless the Court is satisfied that the requirement or prohibition was in respect of that matter complied with otherwise than by way of observance of that provision of the Code'.

7.14 *Limitations* – Section 16 applies (a) to criminal proceedings, and (b) in respect of an ACOP only. However, if observance of an ACOP is necessary to avoid criminal liability (unless the protection aimed at by the Regulation is conferred in some other way which is at least equally satisfactory) a civil court is highly likely to regard the provisions of an ACOP as being equally compelling in an action for damages.[31] Accordingly, the relevant provision of the ACOP should be pleaded if a claimant intends to rely on it.

7.15 The HSE[32] have been seeking a change in the law such that a person owing a duty will be taken to have satisfied the law on the specific issues addressed by the ACOP if he complies with the provisions of that ACOP. This is likely to impact on common law as well as statutory liability: if a person is complying with Regulations in the way he conducts his operations, why should the law hold him negligent in so doing?

7.16 Checking the relevant Code is thus very important for both claimant and defendant. Beware: the full text is not in every textbook.[33]

---

[30] Such guidance may however fix an employer with constructive knowledge of risks – e g HSE Guidance Note MS10 relating to 'Beat Conditions, Tenosynovitis' dealing with the particular health risks of frequent and repeated movements of the forearm hand and wrist.

[31] There is also a good 'European' reason for this – many of the provisions in the directives are assigned by domestic law to ACOPs rather than to the regulations themselves (e g the ACOP attached to the Workplace Regulations).

[32] 'The Role and Status of ACPs – a statement by HSE', available from HSE Information Centre, published spring 1996.

[33] It is in the *Encyclopedia of Health and Safety at Work*. Halsbury Vol 20 contains the central provisions only.

Codes applicable

7.17 Codes of Guidance (NB *not* ACOPs, but guidance pure and simple) exist for the:

- Management Regulations;

- Display Screen Equipment Regulations;

- Manual Handling Operations Regulations;

- PUWER;[34]

- PPE Regulations.

There is *both* an ACOP and 'mere' guidance attached to the Workplace Regulations.[35]

7.18 It is an open question whether the presence of both ACOP and 'mere' guidance in relation to the Workplace Regulations dilutes the force of the latter. The better view is that it does not do so: (a) it has been possible to make ACOPs since the HSWA 1974, yet this has not prevented civil courts giving weight to 'mere' guidance; and (b) where authoritative guidance is given, the reasonable prudent employer must be expected to pay careful heed to it.

REGULATION: GENERAL

Liability

7.19 Liability depends upon:

- **WHO** is covered by the Regulations;

- **WHAT** is covered;

- **WHERE** is covered; and

- **WHEN** it is covered.

These are not as obvious as one might expect.

---

[34] Though the guidance is still that prepared for the 1992 Regulations – the substance of those was largely unaffected by the introduction of the 1998 Regulations.
[35] The provisions of the Code and the ACOP are interleaved with each other.

Who is covered?

7.20 Throughout the Regulations, there are some specific provisions for the self-employed, others for employers and those in control of work. Sometimes those in charge of premises where work is carried out are regulated. However, there is a potential problem as to those protected. The Regulations are made under the HSWA 1974, ss 52 and 53 of which define 'work' as 'work as an employee or self-employed person'. 'Worker' thus might seem to cover both categories, but the Directives apply to 'workers', who are defined as 'any person employed',[36] and thus may be confined to employees. In some situations, therefore, where a Regulation is not specific as to those whom it is intended to protect, an employer may be able to argue that only employees are covered.

What is covered and where

7.21 Essentially, all *work* is covered, including that on offshore installations and in territorial waters, but not on ships. However, the place where it is carried out may not be: many a workplace and much display screen equipment is not covered – see below.

When there is liability

7.22 As to *when*, all Regulations are in full effect on and after 1 January 1997. If it becomes relevant to know what was replaced by the Regulations, regard must be had to earlier texts[37] – but some have full, others partial, effect at differing dates before that. See below.

General defences: causation and contribution

7.23 The statutory duties are designed to secure health and safety. Thus the fact that an employee seeking their protection is guilty of negligence, and that negligence itself is causative of an accident which he suffers, does not necessarily excuse the employer (or other person liable). The law of occupational liability is sophisticated, in that it may see the actions of the person which cause his own injury as being themselves caused by the fault of others – the person who causes himself harm may be a 'victim of the system'. Thus in *Sherlock v Chester Council*,[38] Latham LJ pointed out (at para 30) that:

> '... both common law and the regulations which I have identified have as part of their purpose the objective of ensuring that both employer and employee have

---

[36] Council Directive 89/391 (the 'Framework Directive'). The word 'employed' may have a wider connotation than that in domestic use (under Employment Rights Act 1996, s 230), but is arguably well reflected by the definition of 'worker' contained in Regulations such as the Working Time Regulations 1998, as amended: see *Cotswold Developments Construction Ltd v Williams* [2006] IRLR 181.
[37] Such as the first two editions of this work.
[38] [2004] EWCA Civ 210.

taken stock of a situation where an appropriate work practice has to be identified so as to ensure that each has in mind the relevant risk and the necessary measures to obviate or reduce it'.

7.24 Unless the fault of the employee was co-extensive with that of the employer, the employer would be liable, though there might be a finding of contributory fault.[39] But it should be remembered that in *Toole v Bolton Metropolitan Borough Council*,[40] Buxton LJ said:

> 'It is not usual for there to be marked findings of contributory negligence in a breach of statutory duty case',

and that Lord Tucker said in *Staveley Iron and Chemical Company Ltd v Jones*[41] that:

> 'In Factory Act cases the purpose of imposing the absolute obligation is to protect the workmen against those very acts of inattention which are sometimes relied upon as constituting contributory negligence so that too strict a standard would defeat the object of the statute.'

7.25 In summary, where it appears that a statutory duty has been broken, the employer will have an uphill task in escaping all liability.

THE MANAGEMENT REGULATIONS

Overview

7.26 The Management Regulations generalise and rationalise the *approach* to preventative health and safety: see the references to reg 4 and Sch 1 at **7.4** above. The order in which health and safety measures are placed: prevention first (ie prevent a danger arising at all, perhaps by job or plant design) and protection second (both collective and mechanical, as by guarding, and personal, as by personal protective equipment) is adopted throughout the Regulations, as is to be expected given the common derivation of those Regulations from Directives which share a common parent. Its influence goes far further, however. It informs the common law of employer's liability.[42]

---

[39] As Pearson J said in *Ginty v Belmont Building* [1959] 1 All ER 414, at 424A: 'If there is some fault on the part of the employer which goes beyond or is independent of the wrongful act of the employee, and was a cause of the accident, the employer has some liability.'
[40] [2002] EWCA Civ 588.
[41] [1956] AC 672 at p 648.
[42] Take dermatitis or destructive stress at work – how do you establish the approach an employer should, and the courts will, take to it? The answer is: (1) assess whether the job involves particular exposure to, say, dangerous oils or to stresses and strains (this will involves considering the degree of risk shown eg by the HSE publication on Stress at Work); (2) take preventive measures, by trying to design machinery so that it does not spew out oil, and design unnecessary stresses out of the job or prevent them arising (eg avoid making the last redundancy; be careful with profit-related pay; ensure that time is used efficiently rather than counter-productively); (3) take protective measures (eg rubber gloves; stress management training or an EAP); (4) provide for immediate protective measures if the oil does get on the

Is there liability for breach?

7.27 Until 1 April 2004, breach of a duty specifically imposed by the Regulations did *not* confer a right of action in civil proceedings.[43] It follows that neither did a contravention of the ACOP. However:

(a) failure to follow a provision was relevant to the issues of negligence/breach of statutory duty otherwise arising, whether under the original Regulations of 1992 and 1999 (which may remain relevant for a while yet) and remains so even in the amended form, which permits such liability upon an employer only. An 'employer' is still not liable for work under his control which is performed by those who are not his employees.[44]

(b) as to cases arising before the change in the law, where the defendant is a public authority, the Directive will apply – and Community law demands that there be an effective sanction for any breach.[45] Given that the purpose of the legislation is to protect employees, it is arguable that for domestic law to provide for criminal penalties alone is not an effective sanction.

Content of the Regulations

7.28 The Regulations principally require:

- the making of *suitable and sufficient* risk assessments[46] both of the risks to employees and to others, insofar as they arise out of or in connection with the conduct by the employer of his undertaking;

- that these risk assessments adopt the principles of prevention outlined above;

- appropriate health surveillance;

- the appointment of competent persons to help an employer with health and safety arrangements;

- procedures for serious danger;

- the informing of employees as to risks to their health and safety;

---

skin (washing facilities, emollient creams) or the stressful event is suffered (stress counselling), but always in the context of; (5) advice and information (telling the employee why rubber gloves are needed; how certain conflicts at work are to be resolved e g by prioritising); and (6) monitoring the results (to ensure that the advice is heeded, is sufficient etc.) and reviewing the measures if it is not.

[43] Reg 22 of the 1999 Regulations before amendment, excepting these Regulations from the general rule in HSWA 1974, s 47, that Regulations impose civil liabilities.

[44] Reg 22 Amended Regulations – amended by SI 2003/2457.

[45] *Marshall v Southampton and South-West Hampshire Area Health Authority (No 2)* [1994] 1 AC 530.

[46] Reg 3.

- the provision of adequate health and safety training;

- co-operation with other employers sharing the same workplace; and

- they impose a duty *on employees* to use machinery, equipment etc. in accordance with the training and instruction given to him. Defendants should plead clearly any allegation that the Claimant has breached this duty.

Points to note

7.29 Risk assessments required of an employer by the Management Regulations need to be recorded where the employer has more than five employees.[47] Claimants should get, and defendants give, discovery of them.

Cases

7.30 *Sherlock v Chester City Council*:[48] Where a risk assessment would have identified the need for a long, flexible piece of fascia board being cut on a powered saw table to be supported, on a run-off table or by another workman, and the operative lost his thumb and finger in the saw, the failure to make such an assessment was in part causative of the accident:

> 'The purpose of a risk assessment in a case such as this is to ensure that what may appear to be obvious is in truth obvious, in the sense that both parties have appreciated the risk. I say both parties, because it also provides the opportunity for an employer to ensure that he has taken appropriate steps to protect his employee' (per Latham LJ at para 25).

HEALTH AND SAFETY (DISPLAY SCREEN EQUIPMENT) REGULATIONS[49]

What is covered?

7.31 Workstations involving VDUs and peripherals are covered, but portable workstations (eg laptops) are covered only if in 'prolonged use' (undefined), and display screens on board a means of transport are not covered.

Where?

7.32 Anywhere that the VDU/workstation is used for work. Workers' homes are covered if homework is done.

---

[47] Reg 3(6).
[48] [2004] EWCA Civ 210.
[49] SI 1992/2792.

Who is protected?

7.33 A person who *habitually* uses display screen equipment as a *significant* part of his *normal* work, whether self-employed or an employee.[50] The words in italics are undefined.[51]

Who is regulated?

7.34 Employers.

Content of the Regulations

7.35 An employer must:

- assess the risks, and reduce them to the lowest level practicable;

- plan for breaks in the pattern of work;

- provide free eye tests;

- give health and safety training and information; and

- ensure that a workstation meets detailed requirements set out in a Schedule to the Regulations, on such as absence of glare, flexible and adjustable arrangement of seats, work surfaces, and keyboards, adjustable chairs, sufficient suitable lighting, suitable software, operator posture etc.

Points to note

7.36

- Two useful diagrams of layout and operator posture accompany the Schedule.

- Annex B to the Guidance records that work related upper limb disorders are liable to be caused by a combination of factors, including prolonged static posture of the back, neck and head, awkward positioning of the hands and wrists (eg because of inappropriate work height), high workloads and tight deadlines. This 'requires a risk reduction strategy which embraces proper equipment, furniture, training, job design and work planning'. This injunction may be relied on to cross-examine experts, and help persuade a court as to causation.

---

[50] Eg news sub-editors, air traffic controllers, secretaries; possibly airline check-in clerks, some receptionists.
[51] Eg in *Pickford v Imperial Chemical Industries plc* [1998] 3 All ER 462, [1998] 1 WLR 1189, HL, a typist who the judge found had not suffered from 'telegraphist's cramp' claimed to have been typing for 75% of the time she spent at work. Other evidence suggested 50%. How such a case would fall is uncertain under these Regulations (which were not relied on directly).

- In *Fifield v Denton Hall Legal Services*,[52] the Court of Appeal endorsed the judge's approach of seeing whether the injuries complained of were work-related, then asking whether there were breaches of the Regulations, and then asking whether those breaches caused the injuries. Such an analytical step-by-step approach is liable to favour the claimant.

MANUAL HANDLING OPERATIONS REGULATIONS[53]

What is covered?

7.37 Any 'manual handling operation' (defined to include transporting, supporting, lifting, putting down, pushing, pulling, carrying or moving a load by hand *or bodily force*; a load includes a person or animal).

Where?

7.38 Anywhere at work, except on board ship.

Who is protected?

7.39 An employee. (A self-employed person must protect himself in the same way.)

Who is regulated?

7.40 Employers (and the self-employed in respect of themselves). Employees must make full and proper use of any system of work provided by their employer to reduce the risk of injury.

Content of the Regulations

7.41 The kernel of the Regulations is in reg 4, which reflects the approach of the Management Regulations (see above) in setting out a hierarchy of measures. An employer must, by reg 4(1):

(a) *so far as is reasonably practicable* avoid the need for manual handling operations (eg by mechanisation);

(b) where this is not reasonably practicable, the employer must:
 (i) assess the operations;
 (ii) take appropriate steps to reduce the risk of injury to his employees from those operations to the lowest level reasonably practicable;

---

[52] [2006] EWCA Civ 169.
[53] SI 1992/2793 as amended by SI 2002/2174.

(iii) provide his employees with general indications and, where reasonably practicable, precise information on the weight of each load and the heaviest side where the centre of gravity in not positioned centrally.

Points to note

7.42

- There are diagrams in the Code of Guidance which provide guidelines for the weights which may be raised and lowered safely. They are worth studying – they demonstrate how much more can be lifted/carried at waist height than elsewhere, and how much more close to the body than far away. Lifting, bending, repeating the task and being a woman all go to increase the risk significantly.

- The Regulations use the phrase 'as far as reasonably practicable'. The Directive[54] requires the employer to take 'appropriate measures' although it envisages there are occasions when this may be impossible.[55] Reasonable practicability normally involves balancing financial considerations against that which may be done in the light of present knowledge and perceived risk. There may be room for the Directive to have a purposive interpretative effect here, or even direct effect against a state authority.

- The Directive requires instruction and training in methods of handling. This may often be vital.[56] Yet the Regulations do not implement this requirement in terms. Where the Directive is not directly effective, there is room to argue that the employer who fails to provide such instruction/training is nonetheless culpable, at least at common law, by virtue of other provisions: the Management Regulations, regs 10 and 13, and HSWA 1974, s 2 (though there is no cause of action created by breach of the latter). The Guidance Note (not an ACOP) does mention training, and the Regulations talk of an obligation to take 'appropriate steps' to reduce the risk of injury.

Points from cases

7.43

- The definition of 'handling' makes reference to 'load', so the use of manual force to push and pull a lawnmower (*Mitchell v Inverclyde*[57]), or a hand-grinder (*McFarlane v Ferguson Shipbuilders*[58]) or to manipulate a

---

[54] Art 3.
[55] Art 3(2).
[56] Eg in a 'nurse's lifting' case.
[57] [1998] SCLR 191.
[58] 16 March 2004, Ct of Session.

buffing machine (*McFarlane v Corus*[59]) were not manual handling operations. These operations might, though, involve breaches of other Regulations – such as PUWER (see *McFarlane v Corus*). However, moving grit from a pile to spread on an icy yard is within the Regulations: *King v RCO Support Services*.[60]

- If it is shown that the operation is one to which the Regulations apply, it is then incumbent on the employer to show that he has taken all reasonably practicable steps to avoid risk of injury: *McKenzie v Bonar Yarns*.[61]

- Although the test to identify risk is not probability of injury, but foreseeable possibility of it, risk has to be identified in the context of the operation being conducted: *Koonjul v Thameslink Healthcare*.[62]

- Where an employee operates a risky system which is that adopted in the past, without adverse comment, there should be no contributory fault: *Nash v Powerhouse Retail*.[63]

- Even though it might seem that an action is instinctive, or could not easily be avoided by training, an employer must take into account that his employees will not always behave with a full and proper concern for their own safety, and a failure to train is prima facie a breach of reg 4(1)(b)(ii). Thus an experienced man carrying a microwave who twisted and turned on hearing his name called, suffering a flexion and rotation injury to his spine, succeeded: *O'Neill v DSG Retail*.[64]

PROVISION AND USE OF WORK EQUIPMENT REGULATIONS

What is covered?

7.44 All work equipment, including machinery, appliances, apparatus, and tools – ie a tractor, lawn-mower, ladder, portable drill, and butcher's knife are all covered, *as is display screen equipment*. In 1998, drive shafts, many power presses and mobile work equipment such as fork lift trucks were added to the list.

---

[59] [2006] CSOH 38 (Ct of Session).
[60] [2000] EWCA Civ 314.
[61] [2006] CSOH 23. This Scottish case sets out a model approach to the application of the Regulations.
[62] [2000] PIQR P123, CA.
[63] 28 January 2000, Crane J.
[64] [2002] EWCA Civ 1139; the same provision was successfully relied on by the claimant in the 'nurses' lifting' case of *Urquhart v Fife PCT* [2007] CSOH02.

Where?

7.45 At work,[65] anywhere except on board ship (but including offshore installations).

Who is protected?

7.46 Employees and the self-employed.

Who is regulated?

7.47 Employers, the self-employed in respect of equipment they use themselves, and a person who has to any extent control of work equipment[66] in connection with carrying on a business, trade or undertaking (he is liable however only to the extent of that control[67]).

Content

7.48 PUWER replaced many piecemeal provisions relating to different industries and processes. Both general duties and duties specific to particular equipment are imposed.

7.49 There are general duties:

- to take into account working conditions and risks when selecting equipment;

- to ensure that equipment is suitable for the use that will be made of it, and is properly maintained; and

- to provide adequate information, instruction and training.

7.50 Specific requirements cover:

- protection from dangerous parts;

- maintenance operations;

- parts and materials at high or very low temperatures;

---

[65] Use of a defective lift at the end of a days work in order to leave the premises is within the Regulations: *Reid v PRP Architects* [2006] EWCA Civ 1119, even though the person was leaving, and thus not 'at' work.

[66] This expressly includes a person at work who supervises or manages the use of equipment, someone who has control of equipment, and someone who has control of the way equipment is used at work (reg 3(3)) but do not apply to work equipment which is hired out by such a person for another to use – see, on this point, the factual dispute in *Ball v Street* [2005] EWCA Civ 76 and how its resolution led to judgment for the claimant on appeal.

[67] Where a person lends equipment to another – not on hire – he may well retain control over its maintenance in an efficient state: *Ball v Street* [2005] EWCA Civ 76.

- control systems and controls;

- isolation from power sources;

- stability of equipment;

- lighting;

- warnings and markings.

7.51 The most important regulations in practice are reg 4 (suitability of the equipment for purpose), reg 5 (maintenance, which imposes a strict obligation[68]) and reg 11.

Regulation 4

7.52 Assessment of 'suitability' involves an assessment of the extent of the risk presented by the alleged defect: *Yorkshire Traction v Searby*.[69] Nor is equipment unsuitable where it is merely mishandled by an employee: *Griffiths v Vauxhall Motors*,[70] or deliberately used to injure the claimant by a co-employee: *Horton v Taplin Contracts*.[71] The regulation is concerned with the physical condition of the equipment on the assumption it will be properly operated by properly trained and instructed personnel – thus where a fireman's hand was trapped in the pinch point of a jack that he had not been adequately trained to use, there was no breach of reg 4 as the judge at first instance, but rather a culpable failure under reg 11.[72]

Regulation 5

7.53 'Maintained' must be read by reference to earlier cases under the Factories Act as imposing a strict obligation (*Stark v Post Office*:[73] the fact that the stirrup, part of the front brake of a bicycle, unforeseeably broke in two, with one part lodging in the front wheel and throwing the rider off did not defeat liability, and *Ball v Street*[74]) but apparently not so strict that it is absolute: *Green v Yorkshire Traction*,[75] where the fact that a bus step became wet in use through passengers stepping out of the rain onto it did not amount to a failure to maintain the bus.

---

[68] *Stark v Post Office* [2000] EWCA Civ 64.
[69] [2003] EWCA Civ 1856.
[70] [2003] EWCA Civ 412.
[71] [2002] EWCA Civ 1604.
[72] *Pennington v Surrey County Council* [2006] EWCA Civ 1493.
[73] [2000] EWCA Civ 64.
[74] [2005] EWCA Civ 76.
[75] [2001] EWCA Civ 1925.

Regulation 11

7.54 This requires a hierarchy of protection from dangerous parts of machinery (replacing the Factories Act 1961, s 14). Measures must be taken which are

> '... effective (a) to prevent access to any dangerous part of machinery or to any rotating stock-bar; or (b) to stop the movement of any dangerous part of machinery or rotating stock-bar before any part of a person enters a danger zone'.

7.55 The measures are (by para (2)):

> '(a) the provision of fixed guards enclosing every part of a dangerous part or rotating stock-bar where and to the extent that it is practicable to do so, but where or to the extent that it is not, then
> (b) the provision of other guards or protection devices where and to the extent that it is practicable to do so, but where or to the extent that it is not, then
> (c) the provision of jigs, holders, push sticks or similar protection appliances used in connection with the machinery where and to the extent that it is practicable to do so, but where or to the extent that it is not, then supervision.'

7.56 There are minimum standards that guards and protection devices must satisfy.

Points to note

7.57

- Words such as 'maintaining in an efficient state' (PUWER, reg 5) echo words used under earlier legislation. The question is – efficient for what purpose? (The suggested answer is – for protecting health and safety: this would seem to be endorsed by *Stark v Post Office*;[76] and is specifically endorsed by the Court in *Ball v Street*.[77])

Points from cases

7.58

- See the cases mentioned in relation to regs 4 and 5 above.

- The width of the definition has proved fertile ground for ambitious arguments. What one is working *on* must be kept distinct from what one is working *with: Spencer-Franks v Kellogg, Brown and Root*.[78] Thus in *Hammond v Metropolitan Police Commissioner*[79] it was argued that a

---

[76] [2000] EWCA Civ 64.
[77] [2005] EWCA Civ 76, para 37.
[78] [2005] SC (D) 28/12.
[79] [2004] EWCA Civ 830.

wheel nut on a van was work equipment when it was being worked on: held, it was the subject of the work, not the equipment to do it – it was someone else's work equipment other than that of the claimant.

- If an employer fails to prevent equipment being used for an unsafe purpose, when it has a perfectly reasonable safe use for which it was supplied, he will be in breach: *Wright v Romford Blinds*.[80]

PERSONAL PROTECTIVE EQUIPMENT AT WORK REGULATIONS[81]

What is covered?

7.59 Equipment intended to be worn or held by a person at work which protects him against a risk or risks to his health and safety. This includes accessories or additions designed for that purpose, and includes clothing intended to protect against the weather.[82]

7.60 'Ordinary working clothes which do not specifically protect the health and safety of the wearer' are *not* included, nor is equipment for playing competitive sports, nor equipment used for protection whilst travelling by road such as crash helmets and leathers.[83]

Where?

7.61 Anywhere at work, except on board ship, but including work within territorial waters and on offshore installations.

Who is protected?

7.62 Every employee, and every self-employed person, must provide himself with suitable protective equipment.[84]

Who is regulated?

7.63 Employers, and the self-employed in respect of themselves.

---

[80] [2003] EWHC 1165.
[81] These Regulations made in 1992 relate to those at work. Regulations made in 2002: SI 2002/1144 prescribe standards for the equipment itself, and this work is not concerned further with them.
[82] Reg 1(1). But note the decision in *Fytche v Wincanton Transport* [2004] UKHL 31, where safety boots provided to meet the danger of objects dropping on the foot, and not specifically designed to protect against the weather, were not supplied in breach of the Regulations where there was a small hole in the sole which admitted water, causing frostbite, in icy weather.
[83] Reg 5(2).
[84] Reg 4(1).

Content

7.64 The Regulations impose duties on employers to:

- provide suitable personal protective equipment;[85]

- ensure compatibility with other such equipment;[86]

- assess the suitability of the equipment, and keep this assessment under review;[87]

- maintain and replace protective equipment;[88]

- provide information, instruction and training;[89] and

- ensure proper use.[90]

Points to note

7.65

- Equipment which is to be supplied will often be specific to the needs of the job, to meet the risks of it: thus body armour should have been supplied to a person employed to collect cash (*Henser-Leather v Securicor Cash Services*[91]) and gloves impervious to pin-prick to someone employed to pick up and dispose of used syringes (*Toole v Bolton*[92]).

- Reg 7(1) requires that personal protective equipment be maintained 'in an efficient state, in efficient working order and in good repair'. According to Lord Hoffmann (in the majority in *Fytche v Wincanton*[93]) this is not an absolute concept, but must be construed by reference to what it is that makes the equipment PPE – thus an employer must make sure that it continues to provide protection against the risks which it was designed to combat, not necessarily that it combats risks which it was not intended to protect against. (Lord Hope, in the minority, would have seen it as being appropriate for the conditions in which it was to work at providing protection.[94])

---

[85] Reg 4.
[86] Reg 5.
[87] Reg 6.
[88] Reg 7.
[89] Reg 9.
[90] Reg 10(1).
[91] [2002] EWCA Civ 816.
[92] [2002] EWCA Civ 588.
[93] [2004] UKHL 31.
[94] See also para 29.

THE WORKPLACE (HEALTH, SAFETY AND WELFARE) REGULATIONS

What is covered?

7.66 Non-domestic premises used as a place of work and accessible places therein, together with access corridors, lobbies, stairs, roads etc, but *not* on or in a ship, a construction site, nor agricultural or forestry workplaces away from the undertaking's main buildings.[95] Offshore installations for mineral extraction are *not* covered. (This is not because work in those locations is unregulated, but because there are Regulations specific to them, which are beyond the scope of this chapter: the policy of producing general rules for all work in all places has its limits!)

Who is covered?

7.67 Certainly employees. Probably (but arguably not) anyone else within the workplace. The hesitation arises because the Regulations apply to workplaces, rather than to people, but provide (by reg 4(1) that an employer is under a duty in respect of 'any workplace ... which is under his control and *where any of his employees work* ...'. Yet the overall objective is the promotion of health and safety, and the Factories Act 1961, which these Regulations originally replaced in large part, covered those working who were not the employees of the factory owner.

Who is regulated?

7.68 Employers, and every person who 'has, to any extent, control of a workplace ...'. in connection with a 'trade, business or other undertaking (whether for profit or not)' so far as matters are within his control.

7.69 Use of the words 'other undertaking' may suggest an *eiusdem generis* construction. It may thus be arguable whether this covers entities such as a health trust, a hospital, a school, a charity, or a sportsground.[96]

7.70 A second problem arises from this definition. What is the liability of an unincorporated association for work done by an employee of 'the association'? Regulation 4(2) refers to a 'person' who has control. Can such an association be a 'person', or, if not, how is it to be made liable?[97]

---

[95] Except for requirements as to sanitary conveniences, washing facilities and drinking water, which apply 'so far as is reasonably practicable'.

[96] It is suggested that it does – for in the directive the expression is 'undertaking or establishment'. A wide definition is given to 'undertaking' in other areas of European law where the protection of employees is concerned, eg in relation to the Acquired Rights Directive (77/187/EC) [1977] OJ L61/26. Here, the purpose is the protection of employees, wherever they may work, except domestically, and defining 'other undertaking' as part of a restrictive class analogous to 'trade and business' would be potentially antagonistic to this.

[97] Thus, cases such as *Robertson v Ridley* [1989] 1 WLR 872 relating to the liability of committee members of an unincorporated association may require reconsideration in this context.

Content

7.71 The Regulations impose duties in respect of:

- the maintenance of the workplace, and devices and systems therein;[98]

- temperature (indoors);[99]

- lighting;

- cleanliness and waste materials;

- room dimensions and space;

- workstations and seating (note the potential overlap with the Display Screen Regulations);

- the condition of the floor and traffic routes;

- falls or falling objects;

- windows (and their cleaning), doors, skylights, ventilators;

- organisation of traffic routes;

- doors and gates;

- escalators and moving walkways;

- sanitary conveniences;

- washing facilities;

- drinking water;

- accommodation for clothing and facilities for changing; and

- rest and meals facilities.

7.72 What is proving of the greatest practical importance (with emphasis added) are:

(a) *Regulation 5*:

---

[98] Reg 6.
[99] Reg 7.

- '(1) the workplace and the equipment, devices and systems to which this regulation applies shall be maintained (including cleaned as appropriate) in an *efficient* state, in *efficient* working order, and in *good repair*.'
- 'Where appropriate the *equipment, devices and systems* to which this regulation applies shall be subject to a *suitable* system of maintenance'.[100]

(b) *Regulation 12*:
- '(1) Every floor in a workplace and the surface of every *traffic route* in a workplace shall be of such construction that the floor or surface of the traffic route is *suitable* for the purpose for which it is used.'[101]
- (2) 'Without prejudice to the generality of paragraph (1), the requirements in that paragraph shall include requirements that –
    (i) the floor, or surface of the traffic route, shall have no hole or slope, or be uneven or slippery so as, in each case, to expose any person to a risk to his health or safety;
    (ii) every such floor shall have effective means of drainage where necessary.'
- (3) 'So far as is *reasonably practicable,* every floor in a workplace and the surface of every traffic route in a workplace shall be kept free of obstructions and from *any article or substance* which may cause a person to *slip, trip or fall.*'[102]

7.73 The construction of the floor must be *suitable*. This is not a lower standard than 'sound', and it clearly has a wider application, relating to the expected use.

---

[100] These provisions have not been interpreted as imposing strict liability. Thus in *Lewis v Avidan* [2005] EWCA Civ 670, where a concealed pipe unexpectedly burst and flooded a floor, there was held no failure to maintain.

[101] Construction is given a wide meaning – thus in *Lowles v Home Office* [2004] EWCA Civ 985, it was at fault where there was an unmarked 2-inch step on entry to a Portacabin, between two sets of doors and with no clear warning on the outside door of its presence.

[102] 'Any article' is a broad phrase. Thus a child's lunch-box container which was left by her desk in a classroom, and over which a cleaner tripped, constituted a breach – *Burgess v Plymouth City Council* [2005] EWCA Civ 1659; as did even a thin film of dust on the floor causing a fireman to slip during exercises – *Bassie v Merseyside Fire and Civil Defence Authority* [2005] EWCA Civ 1474. The duty is not absolute: there must be a sufficient risk to make the presence of the article etc. such as to render the floor unsuitable. The existence of a small risk posed by a water-bar about 9mm high across a door threshold did not render a floor unsuitable – *Palmer v Marks & Spencer* [2001] EWCA Civ 1528, nor did a few drops of water lying on stairs where the risk created by it was very small, and instructions to mop up such a spillage would be an 'incantation' because it was so rare – *Furness v Midland Bank* (10 November 2000, CA, unreported). These cases demonstrate that 'risk' for the purpose of identifying a breach of the Regulations is not to be judged by the happening of an accident, despite the intention of the directive arguably being to ensure that compensation is available for any accident at work which happened because of the actual state of the premises, equipment etc. English law at least remains wedded to the idea of fault, and risk, though pays some homage to earlier jurisprudence under the Factories Act 1961 which took a strict line for the benefit of the injured workman.

7.74 For holes, slopes, unevenness and slipperiness, so far as the construction of the floor is concerned, the standard is whether they expose a person to a risk of injury.

7.75 For holes there is no breach where adequate measures have been taken to prevent a person falling in the hole.

7.76 In assessing the risk to health and safety of slopes account must be taken of any handrail provided.

7.77 Keeping the floor free of obstructions, articles and substances which may cause persons to slip, trip or fall is subject to a requirement of *reasonable practicability*.

Points to note

7.78 Various provisions are made by the Directive which are not by the Regulations, in particular:

- In the Directive[103] 'technical maintenance' of the workplace and of equipment and devices therein is required of every employer. There is no obvious counterpart in the Workplace Regulations 1992.

- Annex 1 to the Workplace Directive lays down as a 'minimum' that 'buildings which house workplaces must have a structure and solidity appropriate to the nature of their use'. There is no obvious counterpart in the Workplace Regulations 1992.

- The same applies to loading ramps (Workplace Directive, Annex 1, para 14.3) which must, as far as possible, be safe enough to prevent workers falling off them, and to the requirement of the Directive that there must be first-aid rooms in undertakings large enough (para 19).

- PUWER and the Workplace Regulations both fall short of the requirement in the Annex to Directive 89/655 (Use of Work Equipment Directive)[104] as to the necessity for workers to have safe means of access to, and the ability to remain safely in, all the areas necessary for production, adjustment and maintenance operations. (Yet this was an important aspect of the Factories Act 1961 – see s 29 – which the Workplace Regulations largely replaced.)

- Claims for slipping on snow and ice at the factory gate have gone both ways under the Factories Act 1961, and the case-law should now no longer be relied on. In commenting on reg 12(2)(a) (above) the ACOP (note: this *is* an ACOP) provides two apparently contradictory paragraphs: para 93, which says

---

[103] Art 6 of Directive 89/654 [1989] OJ L393/1 (Workplaces).
[104] [1989] OJ L393/13.

'... surfaces ... which are likely to get wet ... should be of a type which does not become unduly slippery ... Floors ... should be ... kept free from slippery substances ...'

on the one hand, and para 96 on the other, which provides:

'Arrangements should be made to minimise risks from snow and ice, This may ...' (note that word, which does not connote obligation) '... involve gritting, snow clearing and closure of some routes, particularly outside stairs, ladders and walkways on roofs ...'.

- There is no equivalent to the former s 63 of the Factories Act 1961 (requiring the elimination of dangerous fumes).[105] Escape from the smoke of smokers is not specifically provided for (though there can be no doubt of its danger) except that rest areas must be available for the use of non-smokers. Yet any risk assessment nowadays must surely take account of the risks at the workplace of one person's smoke injuring another.

THE CONSTRUCTION (HEALTH, SAFETY AND WELFARE) REGULATIONS

What is covered and where?

7.79 'Construction work' (including building work or repair, renovation, redecoration, maintenance and some specialised cleaning processes; site preparation; demolition; and the installation of the mains supply and telecommunications services) is covered – but a construction site 'set aside for purposes other than construction work' is not covered. This may engage the surprising philosophical question: how is a construction site to be defined as such if no construction is intended thereon?

Who is covered?

7.80 Both employees, and the self-employed, at work. (But note, the work need not itself be that of construction.[106])

Who is regulated?

7.81 Employers, and anyone who controls the way in which construction work is carried out (insofar as the duties relate to matters within his control). The relevant control is of the construction work, not eg as occupier of the site.[107]

---

[105] But see the COSHH Regulations 2002 (SI 2002/2677) which cover many such fumes, and under which liability seems to be strict – see *Dugmore v Swansea National Health Trust* [2002] EWCA Civ 1755.
[106] *Moon v Garrett* [2006] EWCA Civ 1121 – a delivery man injured on site could claim.
[107] *McCook v Lobo* [2002] EWCA Civ 1760.

Content of the Regulations

7.82 The Regulations cover:

- making and keeping the place of work safe;[108]
- falls and falling objects;[109]
- fragile materials;
- stability of structures;
- demolition and dismantling;
- explosives;
- cofferdams and caissons;
- the prevention of drowning;
- traffic routes;
- doors and gates;
- vehicles;
- fire risks;
- emergency procedures;
- welfare facilities;
- fresh air;
- temperature and weather protection;
- lighting;
- plant and equipment;
- training and inspection.

---

[108] Reg 5(1) – perhaps the most important of the regulations in practice, which is qualified by 'as far as is reasonably practicable'.
[109] See *Nixon v Chanceoption Developments* [2002] EWCA Civ 558.

Points to note
7.83

- Making and keeping the place of work safe does not impose absolute obligations: *Brown v Grosvenor Building Contractors Ltd*.[110]

- There are specific and detailed provisions[111] setting out requirements to which guard-rails, working platforms, personal suspension equipment, ladders, the means of arresting falls and welfare facilities should conform.

- Liability may often be linked with that under the Manual Handling Operations Regulations where it involves carrying loads on site: see the case mentioned below.

Cases

7.84 In *Smith v Notaro Ltd*[112] the fact that there was safe access by one route for goods to be carried into a house under construction did not entitle the occupier of a building site to succeed in his defence of a claim where a delivery man chose to use planks laid on soft earth instead, which suddenly sank, causing him to injure his back. Lack of training in the risks of taking such an access route also exposed the defendant to liability under the Manual Handling Operations Regulations.

LIFTING OPERATIONS REGULATIONS 1998

What is covered?

7.85 Lifting equipment provided for use *or used*[113] by an employee at work.

Where?

7.86 Anywhere in Great Britain, and those places outside Great Britain to which the HSWA 1974, ss 1–59 and 80–82 apply,[114] but there is limited application to ships' work equipment.[115]

Who is regulated?

7.87 Employers, self-employed persons in respect of lifting equipment they use at work, and any person who has to any extent control of (i) lifting

---

[110] [2006] All ER (D) 133, CA.
[111] In Schedules to the Regulations.
[112] 5 May 2006, CA.
[113] Cf PUWER, the provisions of which relate only to equipment provided for work.
[114] As provided by the Health and Safety at Work etc Act 1974 (Application outside Great Britain) Order 1995, SI 1995/263.
[115] For this, see regs 3(6)–(10).

equipment, (ii) a person at work who uses *or* supervises *or* manages the use of lifting equipment, *or* (iii) the way in which the lifting equipment is used. Such a person is liable to the extent of his control.[116]

Contents of the Regulations

7.88 The Regulations provide:

- for the strength and stability of lifting equipment;

- that lifting equipment for persons is (so far as reasonably practicable) such as to prevent them being crushed, trapped, or stuck and such as to prevent falls;

- that lifting equipment be positioned so as to reduce any risk of loads striking a person, drifting, falling freely, or being released unintentionally;

- that falls down shafts are prevented by suitable devices;

- that lifting machinery is clearly marked with a safe working load;

- that lifting operations are properly and competently planned, appropriately supervised and carried out in a safe manner;

- that lifting equipment is thoroughly examined before use, and where it is exposed to conditions in which it may deteriorate is examined every six months (if used to lift people) or every 12 months (for other lifting equipment).

Points to note

7.89

- Records have to be kept of EC declarations of conformity relating to the equipment. These should be available on disclosure.

- If equipment is borrowed by one employer from another it may not be used unless accompanied by 'physical evidence that the last thorough examination required' by the Regulations has been carried out. This phrase is pregnant with possibilities.

- The information to be contained in a report of a thorough examination is scheduled (in detail) to the Regulations.

- The previous legislation, especially that under the Factories Act 1961, imposed a strict liability for any breach. Since the policy expressly stated

---

[116] Reg 3.

in legislation is to maintain or improve the standards of safety, it is strongly arguable that no less should be the practical result when applying these (replacement) Regulations.

WORKING TIME REGULATIONS[117]

What is covered?

7.90 Work by an employee or worker under a contract whereby he undertakes to do or perform personally any work or services for another party to the contract whose status is not that of client or customer of any profession or business undertaking carried out by the worker.[118] However, there are a number of excluded areas of work, especially domestic service, sea-fishing, transport, other work at sea, doctors in training, and the uniformed services where the demands of the job inevitably conflict with provisions of the Regulations, and what is known as 'unmeasured working time'.[119]

Who is covered?

7.91 Broadly speaking, those performing work as defined above.

Who is regulated?

7.92 Employers (ie those with whom workers, as defined above, contract). Note that many of the provisions are not mandatory, as under PUWER etc, but are drafted as entitlements which the worker may elect to take.

Content

7.93

- Except where the worker has agreed beforehand in writing, the employer must take 'all reasonable steps' to ensure that he works[120] no more than an

---

[117] Amended – with doubtful effect – by the Working Time (Amendment) Regulations 1999. The effect is doubtful because it merely replicates the wording of the original Directive and, thus, should mean no difference in practice from that which the 1998 unamended Regulations provided.

[118] The meaning of 'worker' has been subject of a number of decisions, which broadly recognise him as in effect a labour-only sub-contractor, as opposed to a professional or a person with a number of business clients – see eg *Redrow Homes v Wright* [2004] EWCA Civ 469 for an appellate consideration.

[119] For a full statement of the eclectic mix of exceptions, reference must be had to Part III of the regulations. 'Unmeasured working time' covers those who can decide for themselves what hours they work, as is the case for managing executives or others with autonomous decision-making powers, family workers, and workers officiating at religious ceremonies. It is otherwise undefined.

[120] Work includes time on call, except when it can be spent at the worker's family home. Thus those on call, at the place where they work, will be at work despite doing nothing economically productive except waiting for something to happen.

average of 48 hours per week, averaged over a 17-week period (or, if he has worked for less time in total, over the period since he began to work).[121]

- A night worker[122] may not work more than an average of 8 hours in 24, averaged over a 17-week period.[123]

- An adult worker is entitled to an uninterrupted rest period of no less than 24 hours in each 7-day period, additional to the 11 consecutive hours of daily rest.[124]

- Where daily work time is more than 6 hours, the adult worker is entitled to a work-break which, in the absence of agreement, is to be not less than 20 minutes. Where a young worker's working time is more than 4.5 hours, he is entitled to a break of no less than 30 minutes.[125]

- Annual leave of 4 weeks' paid holiday must be provided in any leave year beginning after 23 November 1999.[126]

- Where the pattern of work may put an employee at risk – e g because it is at a predetermined work-rate or is monotonous[127] – there must be 'adequate rest breaks'.[128]

Points to note

7.94 The importance may be to set a standard of normal working hours beyond which the employer may have to justify that it is reasonable to ask any employee to work. Because the Regulations are expressly health and safety Regulations, it may be assumed that there is some risk – dependent on the activity – from working hours which are in general longer than 48 hours per week.

7.95 However, the hours of work beyond the statutory figures may be exceeded by a number of agreements, in respect of which there are complicated provisions beyond the scope of this text. Moreover, the entitlement to refuse to work in excess of the weekly hours limit is part of the worker's contract of

---

[121] Reg 4. There are record-keeping requirements, considerably watered down since the original Regulations by amendments in 1999, which provide a cross-check.
[122] Someone who works during night-time, ie between 11 pm and 6 am, unless otherwise agreed: but no such agreement may prevent the hours 12 midnight-5 am being night-time.
[123] Reg 6.
[124] Reg 10.
[125] Reg 11.
[126] Reg 12.
[127] This adopts almost word for word the principles of accident prevention set out in the Management Regulations at reg 4(1) and Schedule 1: see text above.
[128] Reg 13.

employment, such that he may refuse to work the excess hours, and cannot be compelled to do so, nor subject to discipline or disadvantage for refusing: *Barber v RJB Mining (UK) Ltd.*[129]

PROCEDURAL IMPLICATIONS OF THE VARIOUS REGULATIONS

7.96

- Pleadings should contain reference to the relevant Directive where appropriate.

- Pleadings should also refer to any relevant paragraph of any ACOP.

- Defendants should plead any competing interpretation of the Regulations or Directive. They should continue to plead to practicability or reasonable practicability as previously.

- Defendants should consider any breach by an employee of the duties imposed upon him, either by way of defence or (more likely) contribution.

- Disclosure should include risk assessments.

- Documents will be generated in making health and safety arrangements, providing information and making arrangements for training, and prescribing practices for dealing with dangerous procedures.

- Maintenance in an efficient state may be difficult to establish without proper records.

- Experts are open to cross-examination against the information provided or suggested by the Codes of Guidance. Consultation with major employers occurred in the process of making the Directives (in 1989, so far as the first six were concerned), so that knowledge of the essentials should be established in any employer large enough to have a dedicated human resource department.

GENERAL POINTS FROM THE CASE-LAW

7.97 It is possible to divine certain themes which run through the case law across the various Regulations.

- Information and training, where required by the Regulations (as it almost always is) is important, and may found liability. It cannot be argued easily

---

[129] [1999] ICR 679, Gage J.

that a failure to train is simply that, and has no impact on avoiding risks that should be obvious to an experienced man – the courts have tended to assume that if a man is trained, or informed as to the risks of what he is doing, then he will heed the advice and modify what he is doing, or is prepared to do, accordingly. If, so modified, he would probably not have suffered as he did, then liability is made out (subject only to contributory fault for obvious risks). Thus, in *O'Neill v DSG Retail*[130] where a man carrying a heavy and awkward load turned quickly and instinctively on being called, such that two discs in his spine herniated, it was no answer for the Defendant to say that training would have made no difference – it would have alerted him to the need to avoid sudden reactions to such calls; in *Smith v Notaro Ltd*[131] where a man used a barrow on planks laid on earth to gain access to a house being built, where he could just have easily used the solid path, and the planks foreseeably sank in the soft earth beneath them causing him to fall, training would have alerted him specifically to the need to use a stable means of access.

- 'Risk' is to be judged prospectively, not retrospectively. The very fact that there has been an accident must logically mean that before it occurred there was some risk of it happening – but if it can be seen only in retrospect, there is insufficient of a risk to require application of the protective Regulations. Thus, in *Palmer v Marks & Spencer*[132] a water-bar across the threshold of a door caught the heel of an employee. It was so low as not to pose a 'risk' against which the Regulations should guard. Similarly, in *Searby v Yorkshire Traction*[133] there was held insufficient of a risk to render protective screens in buses so necessary as to make the bus unsuitable for use in a night-time urban area without one.

- The definition of 'suitability' which Lord Hoffmann adopted in *Fytche v Wincanton Logistics plc*[134] permits extrapolation to 'suitability' as used in the other Regulations – 'being appropriate for the risks and the conditions'.

- The courts tend not to hold obligations as imposing strict liability, despite the more definite language of the European Directive on which the Regulation in question is based, since the Regulations talk of 'so far as reasonably practicable'. However, where it can be shown that the Regulation replicates a provision of former legislation, under which there was absolute/strict liability, the courts adopt the same approach to the current Regulations – see *Stark v Post Office*.[135] In Commission of the *European Communities v UK Advocate General*[136] Mengozzi has given his

---

[130] [2002] EWCA Civ 1139.
[131] 5 May 2006, CA.
[132] [2001] EWCA Civ 1528.
[133] [2003] EWCA Civ 1856.
[134] [2004] UKHL 31, ICR 975, para 13.
[135] [2000] EWCA Civ 64.
[136] Case C-127/05, delivered 18 January 2007.

Opinion that the Health and Safety Framework Directive requires an employer to take all necessary measures to ensure the health and safety of workers in every aspect related to this work. This is essentially a preventive measure, involving anticipating and assessing risks and preventing harm arising. It does not create an absolute liability for the occurrence of risks that were not foreseeable and preventable: but it does not mean that if 'reasonably practicable' is used to excuse an employer from doing that which is technically feasible to eliminate risk, this is contrary to the Directive. We wait to see what the ECJ will decide.

Chapter 8

THE EUROPEAN DIMENSION TO PERSONAL INJURY PRACTICE

INTRODUCTION

8.1 The aim of this chapter is to provide (1) an introduction to the laws of the European Union which have a direct impact on personal injury practice; (2) a summary of the European constitutional principles which apply in the English courts when European law is sought to be invoked; (3) an overview of the case law of the European Court of Justice and the appellate English courts on the application of European law in the field of personal injury; and (4) a brief description of the relevant European legislation which may apply in relation to foreign accidents and cases with a transnational element.

THE REACH AND APPLICATION OF EUROPEAN LAW

The scope of European regulation

8.2 Personal injury practice and European law intersect in three principal areas: product liability and product safety; health and safety at work; and accidents in other EU Member State jurisdictions. The Treaty of Rome of 1957 set out to establish a common market, and to that end sought to establish four freedoms, namely the free movement of capital, goods, services[1] and persons. Product standardisation and harmonisation is integrally linked to the achievement of the free movement of goods, incorporating the need for the protection of consumers at the same time.[2] Equally, with the increased free movement of individual tourists, the EU has intervened to set minimum rules on motor insurance in relation to road traffic accidents which occur in European Union countries[3] and concerning package holidays.[4] Thirdly, as a

---

[1] A recent series of cases from the European Court of Justice indicates that the freedom to receive services under the EU Treaty may encompass the freedom to receive medical treatment abroad, even where such treatment is publicly funded: see for example Case C-157/99, *Geraets-Smits*, [2001] ECR I-5473, [2002] 2 CMLR 21; and Case C-385/99, *Muller-Faure* [2003] ECR I-4509, [2004] 2 CMLR 33, considered in *Secretary of State for Health v R (ex parte Watts)* [2004] 2 CMLR 1273. The European Court of Justice has now given a preliminary ruling, see Case C-372/04, judgment of 16 May 2006.
[2] See Art 30 EC Treaty (Consolidated Version, incorporating the Amsterdam Treaty amendments) (formerly Art 36), also Arts 152 and 153 (formerly Arts 129 and 129a).
[3] See Directives 72/166, OJ 1972 L103/1; 84/5, OJ 1984 L8/17; 90/232, OJ 1990 L129/33; 2000/26/EC, OJ 2000 L181/65; and 2005/14/EC, OJ 2005 L149/14. See further para **8.40** below.
[4] Directive 90/314, OJ 1990 L158/59. See further para **8.42** below.

consequence of the amendments introduced by the Single European Act of 1986, the EU has been granted express competence to legislate to improve health and safety standards in the working environment.[5]

8.3 European legislation,[6] in the form of Directives, covers such areas of interest as: the protection of workers from risks related to the exposure to chemical, physical and biological agents at work;[7] major accident hazards of certain industrial activities;[8] protection of workers from exposure to metallic lead and its ionic compounds at work;[9] protection of workers from the risks related to exposure to asbestos at work;[10] protection of workers from the risks related to exposure to noise at work;[11] measures to encourage improvements in safety and health of workers at work (the framework Directive);[12] minimum safety and health requirements for the workplace;[13] minimum safety and health requirements for use of work equipment by workers at work;[14] minimum safety and health requirements for use by workers of personal protective equipment at the workplace;[15] minimum safety and health requirements for manual handling of loads where there is a risk particularly of back injury to workers;[16] minimum safety and health requirements for work with display screen equipment;[17] protection of workers from risks related to exposure to carcinogens at work;[18] minimum safety and health requirements at temporary or mobile construction sites;[19] the minimum requirements for the provision of safety signs at work;[20] improving safety and health protection of workers involved in mineral

---

[5] Previously Art 118a EC Treaty, now see Arts 136 and 137 for the reformulated legal basis under the EC Treaty. Mention should also be made of the separate competence in health and safety matters under the Treaty establishing the European Atomic Energy Community in the field of nuclear energy: see Directive 96/269/Euratom OJ 1996 L159/1.

[6] The official European website EUR-Lex, which contains a directory of all current legislation in force with cross references to cases decided by the European Court of Justice in relation to individual acts of European secondary legislation, may be found at http://europa.eu.int/eur-lex/en/index.html. Earlier legislation is available by searching the CELEX website, a hypertext link is available on the EUR-Lex site.

[7] Directive 80/1107, OJ 1980 L197/12; Directive 88/364, OJ 1988 L179/44; Directive 90/679, OJ 1990 L268/71, amended by Directive 93/88, OJ 1993 L268/71; Directive 98/24, OJ 1998 L131/11; also Commission Directive 96/94, OJ 1996 L338/86; Directive 2000/54/EC, OJ 2000 L262/21.

[8] Directive 82/501, OJ 1982 L230/1, amended by Directive 87/216, OJ 1987 L85/36; see also Directive 96/82, OJ 1986 L10/13, as amended by Directive 2003/105/EC, OJ 2003 L345/97.

[9] Directive 82/605, OJ 1982 L247/12.

[10] Directive 83/477, OJ 1983 L263/25, as amended by Directive 91/382, OJ 1991 L206/16, Directive 98/24, OJ 1998 L131/11, and Directive 2003/18/EC, OJ 2003 L97/48.

[11] Directive 2003/10/EC, OJ 2003 L42/38 (which repeals earlier legislation).

[12] Directive 89/391, OJ 1989 L183/1; see also Directive 91/383, OJ 1991 L206/19, concerning workers with a fixed duration or temporary employment relationship.

[13] Directive 89/654, OJ 1989 L393/1.

[14] Directive 89/655, OJ 1989 L393/13, as amended by Directive 95/63/EC, OJ 1995 L335/28 and Directive 2001/45/EC, OJ 2001 L195/46.

[15] Directive 89/656, OJ 1989 L393/18.

[16] Directive 90/269, OJ 1990 L156/9.

[17] Directive 90/270, OJ 1990 L156/14.

[18] Directive 2004/37/EC, OJ 2004 L158/50 (which repeals earlier legislation).

[19] Directive 92/57, OJ 1992 L245/6.

[20] Directive 92/58, OJ 1992 L245/23.

extraction;[21] minimum safety and health requirements for work on board fishing vessels;[22] on the protection of young people at work;[23] the minimum health and safety requirements regarding the exposure of workers to vibration;[24] to electromagnetic fields;[25] and to artificial optical radiation;[26] liability for defective products;[27] the safety of toys;[28] on general product safety;[29] and in relation to machinery.[30]

8.4 Generally, the United Kingdom does implement its European obligations into domestic law in an appropriate manner. However, it is often difficult to identify that a particular piece of legislation has been passed in order to comply with an obligation under EU law, from the title or provisions of the Act or statutory instrument concerned. The clearest indication that a national rule or regulation has been passed as a result of European law arises from a reference in the enabling power to the European Communities Act 1972, and/or in the explanatory note in a statutory instrument. One notable exception to this practice is the express reference in the Consumer Protection Act 1987, s 1(1), to the product liability Directive.[31]

8.5 It is important to understand the underlying rationale behind EU legislation, not only in order to recognise when there may be a European issue, but also because the purpose of the legislation may in fact incorporate more than one Treaty objective. At the heart of much EU legislation is the fundamental principle of establishing an internal market without national barriers to trade.

Sources of European law

8.6 The Treaty of Rome of 1957 has been amended by various Treaties of Accession of new Member States, the Single European Act, the Treaty of Maastricht and the Treaty of Amsterdam. The legal competence of the EU to enact legislation in the field of personal injury has expanded over time, however, the new Treaty rights and legal bases under which the EU institutions may act have largely been general in character, establishing frameworks or programmes for action on the European level and not granting any significant rights actionable by an individual claimant. It is in secondary legislation that most concrete rights and obligations are to be found. In the context of personal injury rights and obligations, the most important legislative instrument is the Directive.

---

[21] Directive 92/91, OJ 1992 L348/9; Directive 92/104, OJ 1992 L404/10.
[22] Directive 93/103, OJ 1993 L307/1.
[23] Directive 94/33, OJ 1994 L216/12.
[24] Directive 2002/44/EC, OJ 2002 L177/13.
[25] Directive 2004/40/EC, OJ 2004 L159/1.
[26] Directive 2006/25/EC, OJ 2006 L114/38.
[27] Directive 85/374, OJ 1985 L210/29; as amended by Directive 99/34, OJ 1999 L 141/20.
[28] Directive 88/378, OJ 1988 L187/1.
[29] Directive 2001/95/EC, OJ 2002 L11/4 (which repeals earlier legislation).
[30] Directive 98/37, OJ 1998 L 207/1.
[31] See further Case C-300/95, referred to below at para 8.25.

8.7 Directives are essentially binding EU agreements which require the Member States to introduce into their domestic laws legislative provisions which implement the agreed standards set out in the Directive on or before a particular deadline set in the Directive.[32] Since Directives require implementation, they are not, accordingly, the intended principal source of rights and/or remedies for the individual. If a Directive has been correctly implemented, then the individual will rely on national rules and regulations, to be interpreted in the light of the general principles of European law as established by the European Court of Justice.

RIGHTS AND REMEDIES UNDER EU LAW

8.8 The principal and orthodox application of European secondary legislation involves consideration of domestic provisions which implement obligations usually contained in a European Directive. There is a duty to interpret such national implementing provisions in accordance with the relevant European obligation (see para 8.9). This is the most likely circumstance in which practitioners will need to consider the application of European law. Where national legislation fails adequately to implement European law, there may be occasions when a Claimant may rely directly on European law ('direct effect') (see para 8.11), or may claim damages for inadequate implementation of European law (see 8.20). The provision of remedies for the breach of directly effective rights is a matter falling within the sphere of the procedural autonomy of national law subject to certain minimum European requirements (described at para 8.18).

Interpretation

8.9 Although the legislative text of any Directive is drafted in English, it is necessary to recall that the text of the Directive will also have been translated into the other official languages of the European Union. Since no linguistic text takes precedence over any other, it is important not to interpret the meaning of the text in accordance with English canons of interpretation. The European style of interpretation is rather more relaxed, and seeks out the broad purpose without reference to fine and precise analysis of the particular word. Thus a word which is tolerably clear in English may have a different meaning when taking into consideration the need for uniform interpretation of EU law by reference to all of the EU languages, and in the light of the legislative intent and context of the measure in question.[33]

---

[32] See Art 249(3) EC Treaty (formerly Art 189(3)).
[33] See Lord Diplock in *R v Henn and Darby* [1981] AC 850 at 906; *R v International Stock Exchange ex parte Else Ltd* [1993] QB 534, at 545D–F (Sir Thomas Bingham MR). The minutes of the meeting of the Council of Ministers at which a measure was adopted are not admissible as an aid to interpretation: see Case C-402/03, *Skov* [2006] 2 CMLR in respect of interpretation of the product liability directive 85/374.

8.10 The English courts have recognised the duty upon the national judge to interpret national implementing legislation in a purposive manner in the light of a European obligation, in circumstances which may depart from a strict or literal interpretation, where it is possible so to do.[34] This may include, for example, the insertion of extra words in a statutory instrument.[35] However, there is a limit to the lengths to which the national courts will apply such interpretative flexibility, and they will not go so far as to distort the meaning of words in a national measure.[36] The duty to apply a purposive interpretation to national legislation to give effect to a European obligation contained in a Directive covers both national legislation passed in order to implement the European law in question as well as pre-existing legislation passed without reference to Europe.[37]

Direct effect

8.11 The question of direct effect will generally only arise where there has been a failure by the Member State properly to implement the obligations contained in a Directive, in circumstances where it is not possible for a national court to interpret any national measure in a purposive manner to comply with European law. Where there has been a total or partial failure of implementation, or a wrongful implementation of a Directive, an individual may rely directly on any provision of the Directive which is sufficiently clear, precise and unconditional and which is capable of conferring on the individual a particular right. Where Directives are concerned, the time for implementation laid down in the Directive must also have expired.[38]

---

[34] Case 106/89, *Marleasing* [1990] I ECR 4135; [1992] 1 CMLR 305; see in particular para 8 of the judgment which states: 'It follows that, in applying national law, whether the provisions in question were adopted before or after the directive, the national court called upon to interpret it is required to do so, as far as possible, in the light of the wording and the purpose of the directive in order to achieve the result pursued by the latter and thereby comply with the third paragraph of Article 189 of the Treaty.' In *White v White and MIB*, [2001] PIQR P281 the House of Lords held that the Marleasing principle did not apply to the 1998 MIB Agreement which had not been embodied in legislation, but was contained in a private contract, albeit that one of the parties to the contract was part of the State.

[35] *Litster v Forth Dry Dock & Engineering Co Ltd* [1990] 1 AC 546.

[36] *Duke v GEC Reliance Ltd* [1988] AC 618. See *Clarke v Kato, Smith and General Accident Fire and Life Assurance Corporation plc* [1999] PIQR P1 at 9 where Lord Clyde stated: 'The adoption of a construction which departs boldly from the ordinary meaning of the language of the statute is, however, particularly appropriate where the validity of legislation has to be tested against the provisions of European law. In that context it is proper to strain to give effect to the design and purpose behind the legislation, and to give weight to the spirit rather than the letter. In this way the Court may implement the requirement formulated by the European Court of Justice in *Marleasing* [para 8 of the European Court judgment is cited]. But even in this context the exercise must still be one of construction and it should not exceed the limits of what is reasonable.'

[37] *Webb v Emo Air Cargo Ltd* [1993] ICR 175 at 186–7; for a graphic example, see *Percy v Church of Scotland* [2006] 2 AC 28, [2006] ICR 134. For a summary of the European Court's case law on the duty to interpret national law sympathetically with European obligations, see, most Case C-212/04, *Adeneler* [2006] 3 CMLR 867 at 915-6.

[38] For recent examples in the field of health and safety, see Case 303/98, *SIMAP*, [2000] ECR I-7963, [2001] 3 CMLR 932 and Cases C-397 to 403/01, *Pfeiffer and others*, [2004] ECR I-8835, [2005] 1 CMLR 1123.

8.12 Directly effective rights and obligations may only be enforced by an individual against an organ or 'emanation of the State'. That is to say, directly effective rights may be applied 'vertically' but not horizontally. If a Directive has not been properly transposed into national law, a Directive cannot be used to impose on another private individual an obligation which the State has failed to incorporate into its domestic legal order.[39] The rationale behind the doctrine of vertical direct effect of Directives is a form of estoppel, namely that the State in all its manifestations may not take advantage of its own wrong for the failure to transpose all the provisions of a Directive into national law after the expiry of the due date for implementation.[40]

8.13 An 'emanation of the State' is a term of art defined by the European Court of Justice. In Case C-188/89, *Foster v British Gas plc*,[41] the European Court held that 'a body, whatever its legal form, which has been made responsible, pursuant to a measure adopted by the State, for providing a public service under the control of the State, and has for that purpose special powers beyond those which result from the normal rules applicable in relations between individuals' is a body against which the directly effective provisions of a Directive may be enforced.

8.14 The jurisprudence of the European Court has also been applied to tax authorities,[42] police authorities,[43] health authorities,[44] and local or regional authorities.[45] The English courts have held an emanation of the state to include British Gas prior to privatisation,[46] the governing body of a voluntary aided school,[47] and a water undertaker[48] (but not a private company wholly owned by the state[49]).

8.15 The fact that the particular emanation of the State against whom an individual may wish to enforce a particular directly effective right had no responsibility for the implementation of the Directive, and was not therefore in any sense to blame, cannot exculpate that body from applying the provisions of the Directive. This may most readily be seen in the context of employment law where state bodies have been obliged to comply with rights granted under European discrimination law which obligations did not apply to the private sector until correct implementation.[50]

---

[39] Case C-91/92, *Faccini Dori v Recreb* [1994] ECR I-3325; see also Cases C-397 to 403/01, *Pfeiffer and others*, [2004] ECR I-8835, [2005] 1 CMLR 1123.
[40] Case 152/84, *Marshall v Southampton and South West Hampshire AHA* [1986] ECR 723, [1986] QB 401.
[41] [1990] ECR I-3313, [1991] QB 405.
[42] Case 8/81, *Becker* [1982] ECR 53, [1982] 1 CMLR 499.
[43] Case 222/84, *Johnston* [1986] ECR 1651, [1987] QB 129.
[44] See *Marshall*, above.
[45] Case 103/88, *Costanzo v Comune di Milano* [1989] ECR 1839, [1990] 3 CMLR 239.
[46] [1991] 2 AC 306.
[47] *National Union of Teachers v St Mary's Church of England Junior School* [1997] IRLR 242.
[48] *Griffin v South West Water Services Ltd* [1995] IRLR 15.
[49] *Rolls-Royce v Doughty* [1987] ICR 932.
[50] See *Marshall*, above.

8.16 One particular difficulty has appeared in the application of the doctrine of direct effect, as a result of the findings of the European Court of Justice in the case of *Francovich*.[51] In that case, Italy had completely failed to bring into effect national laws establishing a guarantee fund responsible for the payment of a minimum level of protection for employees in relation to claims outstanding against an employer at the time of the insolvency of the employer. The European Court held that the provisions of the relevant Directive were sufficiently clear, precise and unconditional to grant directly effective rights insofar as the identity of the persons entitled to the guarantee were concerned and the content of the guarantee. However, the European Court also held that since Italy had a discretion when implementing the directive as to the nature and identity of the fund, which may or may not be a wholly publicly funded body, the individual applicants could not enforce any directly effective rights as against the State.[52] The *Francovich* case was subsequently applied by the European Court in the Spanish case of *Wagner Miret*.[53]

8.17 The European case law was followed and applied by the Court of Appeal in *Mighell v Reading and the Motor Insurers Bureau*.[54] Schiemann LJ, with whose judgment Swinton-Thomas LJ agreed, held that the Second Directive on Motor Insurance (84/5/EEC) did not have direct effect since there was a discretion provided to the Government when seeking to fulfil its obligations to implement the Directive whether by using the MIB or in some other way. Hobhouse LJ preferred to hold that the MIB was a private law body and could not constitute an emanation of the State.[55]

Effective remedies

8.18 Whilst a Member State does not possess any particular discretion when implementing the substantive obligations contained in a Directive, the form and method of implementation are left open for the Member State to choose. The discretion of the Member State as to how to implement the provisions of a Directive is only circumscribed to a limited extent. In principle, the question of what remedy shall be applicable is a question for the procedural autonomy of each Member State, subject to two qualifications prescribed by the European Court of Justice. Firstly, any remedy provided to implement a directly effective European right shall be no less generous than any equivalent national remedy (the principle of non-discrimination);[56] and secondly, no condition attaching to

---

[51] Joined Cases C-6/90 and C-9/90, [1991] ECR I-5357, [1993] 2 CMLR 66.
[52] At paras 10–27, see pages 5407–5413 and 109–113 respectively.
[53] Case C-334/92, [1993] ECR I-6911, [1995] 2 CMLR 49.
[54] [1999] PIQR P101.
[55] The primary argument before the House of Lords was put on the basis of the interpretation of the MIB Agreement: see *White v White and MIB*, [2001] PIQR P281, discussed above at footnote 35.
[56] First articulated in Case 33/76, *Rewe* [1976] ECR 1989. For an English example, see *Fitzgerald v Williams* [1996] 2 All ER 171; also Case C-78/98, *Preston and others v Wolverhampton Healthcare NHS Trust and others*, [2000] ECR I-3201, [2000] 2 CMLR 837.

a remedy should be framed so as to render it extremely difficult or virtually impossible in practice for an individual to obtain an effective remedy.[57]

8.19 Litigation in this area of interest to the personal injury lawyer has concerned limitation periods (both in terms of non-discrimination and effectiveness),[58] and ceilings on compensation/denial of entitlement to interest.[59]

Liability of the State for failure to implement a Directive

8.20 The *Francovich* case[60] is better known for the landmark ruling of the European Court of Justice that a Member State may be liable in damages for a failure properly to implement a Directive into national law, which failure has caused the claimant loss and damage. This is really a longstop remedy if all else fails. The European Court has held that the principles governing the entitlement to damages for a failure of a Member State to comply with its obligations under European law are identical to the principles governing the non-contractual liability of the institutions of the European Union.[61] As a result of the ruling of the European Court in the *Kobler* case,[62] an injured party may claim damages as a result of a breach of European law caused by the decision of a court of final instance in accordance with the principles established in *Francovich*. In summary, in order to establish *Francovich* liability, it is necessary to prove a sufficiently serious breach of a rule of European law. Where Directives are concerned, a failure to adopt the provisions into national law in due time will constitute a sufficiently serious breach.[63] The rule in question must be intended to confer rights on individuals, and there must be a direct causative link between the breach and any damage suffered.[64]

---

[57] Case 199/82, *San Giorgio* [1983] ECR 3595, applied in Case C-213/89, *R v Secretary of State for Transport ex parte Factortame Ltd* [1990] ECR I-2433, [1990] 3 CMLR 375, and Joined Cases C-46/93 and 48/93, *Brasserie du Pecheur v Germany* and *R v Secretary of State for Transport ex parte Factortame Ltd* [1996] ECR I-1029, [1996] QB 404, and Case C-78/98, *Preston*, cited above.

[58] See for example Case C-231/96, *EDIS* [1998] ECR I-4951, [1999] 2 CMLR 995; the *Preston* case, cited above; also Case C-34/02, *Pasquini*, [2003] ECR I-6515, [2004] 1 CMLR 1451; Case C-63/01, *Evans*, [2003] ECR I-14447, [2004] 1 CMLR 1487.

[59] See Case 271/91, *Marshall v Southampton AHA (No 2)* [1993] ECR I-4367; [1994] QB 126; Joined Cases C-279-281/96, *Ansaldo Energia* [1998] ECR I-5625, [1999] 2 CMLR 776; Case C-63/01, *Evans*, above. A recent case in respect of road traffic liability has used the principle of effectiveness to overturn a national decision which was found to have a disproportionate effect on the injured victim: Case C-537/03, *Candolin v Pohjola* [2005] ECR I-5745.

[60] Joined Cases C-6/90 and C-9/90, [1991] ECR I-5357, [1993] 2 CMLR 66.

[61] Joined Cases C-46/93 and 48/93, *Brasserie du Pecheur v Germany* and *R v Secretary of State for Transport ex parte Factortame Ltd* [1996] ECR I-1029, [1996] QB 404. See the jurisprudence under the former Article 215(2) EC Treaty, now Art 288(2).

[62] Case C-224/01, *Kobler v Austrian Republic*, [2003] ECR I-10239.

[63] Joined Cases 178, 179, 188-190/94, *Dillenkoffer and others v Germany* [1996] ECR I-4845, [1996] 3 CMLR 469.

[64] See further Case C-424/97, *Haim*, [2000] ECR I-5123, [2002] 1 CMLR 11; Case C-224/01, *Kobler*, above and Case C-63/01, *Evans*, above.

CASE-LAW OF THE EUROPEAN COURT OF JUSTICE AND THE ENGLISH COURTS APPLYING EUROPEAN PRINCIPLES IN THE FIELD OF PERSONAL INJURY

European Court of Justice

8.21 Several propositions may be extracted from the case-law of the European Court of Justice in relation to the interpretation of European health and safety legislation:

(i) Former Art 118A of the EC Treaty[65] was to be interpreted broadly and accordingly the same principle applied to any Directives passed thereunder (*UK v EC Council*[66]);

(ii) Health and safety measures under former Art 118A should not be subordinated to purely economic considerations (*UK v EC Council; ex parte Bectu*[67]);

(iii) Policy considerations, in particular the imposition of burdens on small and medium size enterprises, concern issues of proportionality (and therefore the legality of European law) and are not concerned with the obligation to correctly implement the provisions of Directives into domestic law (*UK v EC Council; ex parte Bectu*);

(iv) Former Art 118A of the EC Treaty[68] permits national law to go beyond the provisions of a Directive where the Directive provides for minimum standards and such national standards do not hinder the implementation of the Directive (*UK v EC Council; Societá Italiana Petroli*[69]);

(v) Where Member States implement provisions of a Directive, such domestic legislation may be subject to the application of general provisions of EC law such as proportionality (*Societá Italiana Petroli*);

(vi) When assessing implementation into national law and compliance with a Directive, the European Court will look to the substance of national law (*Commission v Germany*[70]);

(vii) Member States are not able to rely on pre-existing domestic law which does not address the particular provision in the Directive (*Commission v Italy*[71]);

---

[65] As noted earlier (see footnote 5 above), the legal basis under the EC Treaty has been reformulated. It is considered that the general principles described will continue to apply.
[66] Case C-84/94, [1996] ECR I-5755, [1996] 3 CMLR 671.
[67] Case C-173/99, [2001] ECR I-4881. See also Case C-484/04, *Commission v UK* [2006] 3 CMLR 1322.
[68] Now contained and repeated in Art 137 EC Treaty.
[69] Case C-2/97, [1998] ECR I-8597, [2001] CMLR 27.
[70] Case C-5/00, [2002] ECR I-1305.
[71] Case C-49/00, [2001] ECR I-8575.

(viii) Member States are not allowed a discretion when implementing a Directive into national law where no discretion is provided for or stipulated in the Directive (*ex parte Bectu*; *Commission v Germany*);

(ix) Any exception to the provisions of a Directive specified in a Directive shall be narrowly construed (*Dietrich*[72]);

(x) Where provisions of a Directive are vague, there is a broad discretion permitted to Member States when implementing such provisions into national law (*Procura Della Repubblica v X*[73]).

8.22 Set out below in greater detail are particular cases with a United Kingdom connection.

8.23 Case C-84/94, *United Kingdom v EU Council*[74] concerned a challenge to the Working Time Directive which it was argued had been adopted without due regard to the powers of the EC Treaty. Directive 93/104[75] concerning the organisation of working time had been adopted under Art 118a of the EC Treaty, the legal basis for the adoption of health and safety directives. The European Court held that:[76]

> 'There is nothing in the wording of Art 118a to indicate that the concepts of "working environment", "safety" and "health" as used in that provision should, in the absence of other indications, be interpreted restrictively, and not as embracing all factors, physical or otherwise, capable of affecting the health and safety of the worker in his environment, including in particular certain aspects of the organisation of working time. On the contrary, the words "especially in the working environment" militate in favour of a broad interpretation of the powers which Art 118a confers upon the Council for the protection of the health and safety of workers. Moreover, such an interpretation of the words "safety" and "health" derives support in particular from the preamble to the Constitution of the World Health Organisation to which all the Member States belong. Health is there defined as a state of complete physical, mental and social well-being that does not consist only in the absence of illness and infirmity.'

8.24 *Ex parte Bectu* was a reference for a preliminary ruling from the High Court to the European Court of Justice in respect of a claim brought by the applicant trade union that the United Kingdom had failed properly to comply with its obligations under the Working Time Directive when implementing those provisions into domestic law. The European Court held that the United Kingdom was not entitled to derogate from a particularly important principle of Community social law when there were no derogations provided for in the Directive. The court held that Directive 93/104 was broad in its scope and was not subject to any preconditions for entitlement to be paid annual leave. The

---

[72] Case C-11/99, [2000] ECR I-5589.
[73] Joined Cases C-74 and 129/95, [1996] ECR I-6609, [1997] 1 CMLR 399.
[74] [1996] ECR I-5755; [1996] 3 CMLR 671.
[75] OJ 1993 L307/18.
[76] At 5800 and 710–1 respectively, para 15.

United Kingdom had argued in that case that the conditions for entitlement to be paid annual leave laid down in implementing regulations struck a fair balance between the objectives of the Directive and the need to avoid imposing excessive constraints on small and medium size undertakings. The European Court held however that the improvement of workers' safety, hygiene and health at work is an objective which should not be subordinated to purely economic considerations and stated, by reference to the judgment in the case of *United Kingdom v EC Council*, that the Directive had already taken account of the effects which the organisation of working time may have for smaller or medium size undertakings, which was one of the preconditions specified in Art 118A of the Treaty. The United Kingdom was therefore not entitled as a matter of its discretion to further rely on such considerations when implementing the provisions of European law into domestic legislation.

8.25 Case C-300/95, *Commission v United Kingdom*[77] concerned infraction proceedings brought by the EC Commission for failure adequately to implement Art 7(e) of the product liability Directive[78] into national law. Article 7(e) provides producers with a defence if the state of scientific and technical knowledge at the time the product was put into circulation was not such as to enable the existence of the defect in the product to have been discovered. The Commission contended that s 4(1)(e) of the Consumer Protection Act 1987 effectively weakened the strict liability regime as set out by the Directive. The European Court dismissed the Commission's application.

8.26 The European Court held[79] that the defence set out in Art 7(e) is not directed at the practices and safety standards in use in the industrial sector in which the producer is operating, 'but, unreservedly, at the state of scientific and technical knowledge, including the most advanced level of such knowledge, at the time when the product in question was put into circulation'. Such an objective state of knowledge referred not to that which the producer knew or could have been apprised, but was that knowledge of which the producer is presumed to have been informed. The knowledge must have been accessible at the time when the product was put into circulation.[80] In assessing whether the Directive had been correctly implemented by the United Kingdom, the European Court paid particular note to the fact that s 1(1) of the 1987 Act made express reference to the Directive. The European Court considered that there was nothing in the material produced to the Court to suggest that the courts in the United Kingdom would not interpret s 4(1)(e) in the light of the wording of the Directive.[81]

---

[77] [1997] ECR I-2649; [1997] 3 CMLR 923.
[78] Directive 85/374, OJ 1985 L210/29.
[79] At 2670 and 940 respectively, paras 26–29.
[80] It would appear to be accepted by the European Court that the precise meaning of Art 7(e) on this point is unclear, since the court considers that it may be necessary for national courts to refer further questions of interpretation under Art 177 EC Treaty (now Art 234). Cf the Opinion of AG Tesauro at paras 21–24.
[81] At 2672 and 941 respectively, para 38.

English appellate case-law applying European principles

8.27 The first case at appellate level to deal with the interaction of European law and breach of statutory duty in respect of the provisions contained in the series of Regulations designed to implement the 'six-pack' health and safety Directives was *Hawkes v London Borough of Southwark*,[82] which concerned the application of the Manual Handling Operations Regulations 1992. Aldous LJ stated that in construing the words 'reasonably practicable' it was reasonable to consider that Parliament had in mind when enacting the 1992 Regulations the construction of the words by reference to the established jurisprudence dating back to 1938. It does not appear from the judgment that the Court of Appeal were invited to adopt a purposive construction of the words, nor were their Lordships taken to the provisions of the Manual Handling Directive.[83]

8.28 In *Stark v The Post Office*,[84] it was necessary for the Court of Appeal to interpret the words 'maintained in an efficient state, in efficient working order and in good repair' contained in reg 6(1) of the Provision and Use of Work Equipment Regulations 1992. The defendant sought to argue that the words in the implementing legislation should be interpreted by reference to the lower standard contained in Arts 3 and 4 of Directive 89/655.[85] Waller LJ referred to established domestic authority without reference to the European legislation and concluded that the words laid down an absolute obligation in line with consistent case-law. His Lordship considered that the Directive imposed minimum standards, and that it was not contrary to European law to apply higher standards.[86]

8.29 *Hammond v Commissioner of Police of the Metropolis*[87] is a recent example of purposive interpretation of national provisions in the light of the underlying European legislation. The Court of Appeal held that the domestic provisions construed in the light of the relevant Directive did not give rise to an interpretation of the phrase 'work equipment' which extended beyond the tools of the trade to include equipment upon which the employee was working which caused the injury.

8.30 *Fytche v Wincanton Logistics plc*[88] concerned the interpretation of the Personal Protective Equipment at Work regulations 1992, in particular the meaning of the phrase in reg 7(1) 'maintained ... in an efficient state, in efficient working order and in good repair'. There was no issue but that the

---

[82] Judgment of 20 February 1998, unreported, CA (CCRTF 97/0501 CMS2).
[83] Directive 90/269, OJ 1990 L156/9.
[84] [2000] ICR 1013.
[85] Directive 89/655, OJ 1989 L393/13.
[86] Paras 2.19 and 2.20 of *Redgrave's Health and Safety* (3rd edn, 1998), where it was observed that the purpose of European harmonisation was to maintain and improve health and safety standards, such that it was 'virtually inconceivable' that a national court would be required to apply lower standards when interpreting national implementing provisions, were cited with approval (at 1019).
[87] [2005] PIQR P1.
[88] [2005] PIQR P61.

1992 Regulations fulfilled the minimum requirements laid down in Directive 89/656. The dispute concerned the interpretation of implementing legislation which went beyond the particular requirements of the Directive, necessitating a determination of the meaning and interpretation of the national provisions without conclusive reference to the underlying European provisions.[89]

8.31 The effect of the determination in the *Fytche* case was considered in *Ball v Street*.[90] The Court of Appeal considered that it was bound by *Stark v Post Office*, and that the result in *Fytche* in relation to the regulation of personal protective equipment, namely an interpretation of the words which was limited by the context in which the particular obligation arose, could not be transposed to the broader area of the regulation of work equipment generally.

FOREIGN ACCIDENTS

8.32 Two areas are covered in this section: (1) an outline of the harmonised rules of private international law which determine which courts have jurisdiction to hear claims with a transnational element; and (2) particular substantive rules introduced by the European legislature which apply in respect of certain categories of foreign accident, where it may be possible for an English claimant to sue in England and Wales when the accident took place abroad, namely package holiday claims and foreign road traffic accident claims.

The Brussels Regulation[91]

8.33 The first question which applies in any litigation with a foreign element is whether the English courts have jurisdiction.[92] The Brussels Regulation[93] (which replaces the earlier regime under the Brussels Convention[94]) provides

---

[89] Their Lordships split 3:2 over the point in issue, with both the speeches of the minority and the majority making reference to the Directive.
[90] [2005] PIQR P 342.
[91] For a comprehensive and up-to-date view on jurisdiction, see Briggs A and Rees P, *Civil Jurisdiction and Judgments* (4th edn, 2005) LLP; and Layton A and Mercer H, *European Civil Practice*, (2nd edn, 2004); also Dicey, Morris & Collins, *The Conflict of Laws*, (14th edn, 2006).
[92] The preliminary question as to whether there is a more profitable forum than the United Kingdom will not frequently arise, since perhaps with the exception of Ireland, English levels of damages are generally towards the top of the European league table, when considered in conjunction with rules on costs. For a survey of the different European jurisdictions and the quantification of personal injury damages, see Bona M and Mead P (eds), *Personal Injury Compensation in Europe* (2003), Kluwer and xpl law, and Bona M, Mead P and Lindenbergh S (eds) *Fatal Accidents & Secondary Victims* (2005), xpl law.
[93] Council Regulation (EC) No. 44/2001 on jurisdiction and the recognition and enforcement of judgments in civil and commercial matters (see Vol 2 of the White Book, paras 5-214 and following).
[94] Incorporated into English law by the Civil Jurisdiction and Judgments Act 1982, Schedule 1 (see White Book Vol 2, para 5-7 at 5-48). Denmark is not a party to the Brussels Regulation regime and the provisions of the Brussels Convention therefore have continuing limited application. The EFTA States (Iceland, Norway and Switzerland) are parties to the Lugano Convention which in many respects replicates the regime under the Brussels Convention: see

harmonised rules on jurisdiction and judgments across the European Union.[95] The purpose behind the Regulation 44/2001 regime is to prevent multiplicity of litigation in the different Member States, and the risk of conflicting judgments. The rules under Regulation 44/2001 are mandatory. Accordingly, national concepts such as the question of forum conveniens do not apply when determining which is the appropriate forum to bring proceedings under the harmonised European rules.[96]

8.34 Regulation 44/2001 provides a hierarchy of rules by which jurisdiction is determined. Where a claim falls within one category which gives jurisdiction to the courts of a Member State, then it is unnecessary to consider other potential jurisdictional bases under the Regulation. The following Articles under the Regulation may be of application in determining jurisdiction against a European domiciled Defendant in respect of a personal injury claim:

(1) Article 22: Claims which have as their object rights in rem in immovable property or tenancies of immovable property;[97]

(2) Article 24: Claims where the Defendant has entered an appearance;

(3) Articles 8 to 14: Claims arising out of a contract of insurance;

(4) Articles 15 to 17: Claims arising out of a consumer contract;[98]

---

the Civil Jurisdiction and Judgments Act 1991 and Schedule 1 inserting a Schedule 3C into the 1982 Act (see Vol 2 of the White Book, para 5-162 and following).

[95] In force on 1 March 2002.

[96] See for example Case C-281/02, *Owusu v Jackson* [2005] QB 801, where the European Court of Justice held that the doctrine of forum non conveniens could not be applied in proceedings involving an English domiciled defendant to stay proceedings in favour of Jamaica, where the other co-defendants were domiciled.

[97] Exclusive jurisdiction is granted to the courts of the Member State where the land is situated, and in certain circumstances the Member State of the domicile of both parties.

[98] 'Section 4 – Jurisdiction over consumer contracts.
Article 15.
1. In matters relating to a contract concluded by a person, the consumer, for a purpose which can be regarded as being outside his trade or profession, jurisdiction shall be determined by this Section, without prejudice to Article 4 and point 5 of Article 5, if:
(a) it is a contract for the sale of goods on instalment credit terms; or
(b) it is a contract for a loan repayable by instalments, or for any other form of credit, made to finance the sale of goods; or
(c) in all other cases, the contract has been concluded with a person who pursues commercial or professional activities in the Member State of the consumer's domicile or, by any means, directs such activities to that Member State or to several States including that Member State, and the contract falls within the scope of such activities.
2. Where a consumer enters into a contract with a party who is not domiciled in the Member State but has a branch, agency or other establishment in one of the Member States, that party shall, in disputes arising out of the operations of the branch, agency or establishment, be deemed to be domiciled in that State.
3. This Section shall not apply to a contract of transport other than a contract which, for an inclusive price, provides for a combination of travel and accommodation.
Article 16.
1. A consumer may bring proceedings against the other party to a contract either in the courts

(5) Articles 18 to 21: Claims arising out of a contract of employment;[99]

(6) Article 2: In respect of Defendants domiciled in the jurisdiction;

(7) Article 5(3): Claims where the harmful event occurred within the jurisdiction;

(8) Article 6(1): Claims in respect of more than one Defendant, where a co-Defendant is domiciled within the jurisdiction.

8.35 The principal rule for determining jurisdiction under Regulation 44/2001 is the domicile (not nationality) of the Defendant. Article 2(1) states 'Subject to this Regulation, persons domiciled in a Member State shall, whatever their

---

of the Member State in which that party is domiciled or in the courts for the place where the consumer is domiciled.

2. Proceedings may be brought against a consumer by the other party to the contract only in the courts of the Member State in which the consumer is domiciled.

3. This Article shall not affect the right to bring a counter-claim in the court in which, in accordance with this Section, the original claim is pending.

Article 17.

The provisions of this Section may be departed from only by an agreement:

1. which is entered into after the dispute has arisen; or

2. which allows the consumer to bring proceedings in courts other than those indicated in this Section; or

3. which is entered into by the consumer and the other party to the contract, both of whom are at the time of conclusion of the contract domiciled or habitually resident in the same Member State, and which confers jurisdiction on the courts of that Member State, provided that such an agreement is not contrary to the law of that Member State.'

[99] 'Section 5 — Jurisdiction over individual contracts of employment

Article 18

1. In matters relating to individual contracts of employment, jurisdiction shall be determined by this Section, without prejudice to Article 4 and point 5 of Article 5.

2. Where an employee enters into an individual contract of employment with an employer who is not domiciled in a Member State but has a branch, agency or other establishment in one of the Member States, the employer shall, in disputes arising out of the operations of the branch, agency or establishment, be deemed to be domiciled in that Member State.

Article 19

An employer domiciled in a Member State may be sued:

1. in the courts of the Member State where he is domiciled; or

2. in another Member State:

(a) in the courts for the place where the employee habitually carries out his work or in the courts for the last place where he did so, or

(b) if the employee does not or did not habitually carry out his work in any one country, in the courts for the place where the business which engaged the employee is or was situated.

Article 20

1. An employer may bring proceedings only in the courts of the Member State in which the employee is domiciled.

2. The provisions of this Section shall not affect the right to bring a counter-claim in the court in which, in accordance with this Section, the original claim is pending.

Article 21

An employer domiciled in a Member State may be sued:

1. which is entered into after the dispute has arisen; or

2. which allows the employee to bring proceedings in courts other than those indicated in this Section.'

nationality, be sued in the courts of that Member State'. Domicile is defined in the Civil Jurisdiction and Judgments Act 1982 at s 41[100] in relation to individuals, and in Article 60 of the Brussels Regulation in respect of corporations and associations. The special provisions governing insurance claims, consumer claims and employment claims all provide for the possibility to sue the Defendant in the jurisdiction of the defendant's domicile (Arts 9(1)(a), 16(1), and 19(1) respectively). In addition, special rules permit the claimant to choose defined alternative jurisdictions.[101] The most beneficial rules are those in respect of consumer contracts which permit the courts of the domicile of the claimant consumer to hear a claim (see Art 16(1)).

8.36 Article 5(3) provides in relation to tortious claims (that is, in respect of those claims which fall outwith the special categories of claim identified above in the hierarchy of rules) that the courts of the Member State where the harmful event occurred have jurisdiction. Tort has been defined by the European Court as being 'all actions which seek to establish the liability of the Defendant and which are not relating to contract within the meaning of Article 5(1)'.[102] The place where the harmful event occurred may be the place where the damage occurred or the place where the event giving rise to the damage occurred. In *Bier v Mines de Potasse d'Alsace*[103] there was a release of polluting chemicals from a French factory into the river Rhine. Damage was suffered by Dutch market gardeners in the Netherlands. The European Court of Justice held that it was permissible to bring proceedings in either France or the Netherlands in accordance with Art 5(3). The fact that an injured claimant continues to suffer loss in the United Kingdom, due to say loss of earnings, as a result of injury or an accident suffered in another Member State does not found jurisdiction in the English courts.[104]

8.37 Finally, Art 6(1) permits a foreign domiciled defendant to be joined in proceedings where there is an English defendant. This will be particularly appropriate where there is a risk of conflicting decisions or findings of fact, in relation to connected disputes. This may be the most useful means of securing English jurisdiction over foreign European-based defendants under Regulation 44/2001. However, the English courts will be astute to protect a foreign defendant who has been joined to an English domiciled defendant merely to obtain jurisdiction where there is no realistic claim in a connected cause of action against the English defendant.

---

[100] Section 41 provides that an individual is domiciled in the United Kingdom if he is resident in the United Kingdom and the nature and circumstances of his residence indicate that he has a substantial connection with the United Kingdom. Where an individual has been resident in the United Kingdom for 3 months or more, it is presumed that he fulfills the requirement of substantial connection, unless the contrary is proved (s 41(6)).
[101] For the complicated provisions in relation to road traffic claims see further para 8.42 below.
[102] See Case 189/87, *Kalfelis v Schroder* [1988] ECR 5565.
[103] Case 21/76, [1978] QB 708.
[104] See Case C-220/88, *Dumez* [1990] ECR I-49; Case C-364/93, *Marinari v Lloyds Bank* [1996] QB 217.

8.38 Article 27 of the Regulation states that where proceedings involving the same cause of action and between the same parties are brought in the courts of different Member States, any court other than the court first seised shall of its own motion stay its proceedings until such time as the jurisdiction of the court first seised is established. Where the jurisdiction of the court first seised has been established, any other court must decline jurisdiction in favour of the court first seised. Article 28 grants a power to courts seised in related actions to stay proceedings pending the outcome of the litigation pending in the court first seised.

8.39 Where there has been a judgment in a court of a Member State, Art 33 permits such judgment to be recognised in the English courts. This allows claimants to rely upon issue estoppel and cause of action estoppel without having to relitigate facts and matters which have already been decided by a court of competent jurisdiction.

Secondary European legislation governing foreign personal injury claims

Package holidays

8.40 Directive 90/314[105] is one of the few examples of European legislation which grants European citizens substantive rights when they travel abroad. The Directive has been implemented into English law by the Package Travel, Package Holidays and Package Tours Regulations 1992.[106] The importance of the Directive is that it removes the need for injured claimants to sue foreign defendants under foreign law in foreign jurisdictions. The Directive and implementing regulations impose a liability on package tour organisers for any failure to perform the obligations under the contract.[107] Thus, it is normally the case that the company who organises or sells a package holiday will have an English domicile, and the applicable law (including limitation) will be English law.

8.41 The Directive and Regulations only apply to package holidays, that is the pre-arranged combination of two out of three components, namely transport; accommodation; and tourist services not ancillary to transport or accommodation and accounting for a significant proportion of the package; sold at an inclusive price as a service, where the service covers a period of more than 24 hours or includes overnight accommodation.[108] There is a limited

---

[105] OJ 1990 L158/19.
[106] SI 1992/3288, as amended. See *Holiday Law* by Grant D and Mason S, (3rd edn), Sweet & Maxwell (2003), also *Travel: Law and Litigation* by Saggerson A (2004) xpl law.
[107] See Regulation 15(1) and (2). In most cases it will be necessary to demonstrate a failure by the service provider providing services in accordance with the provisions of the contract to exercise reasonable skill and care. See for example *Hone v Going Places Leisure Travel Limited* [2001] EWCA Civ 947 and *Codd v Thomsons Tour Operators Limited* (CA 7 July 2000, B2/1999/1321, unreported).
[108] See Regulation 2(1); also Case C-237/97, *AFS Intercultural Programs Finland* [2000] 1 CMLR 845 which held that the provision of accommodation with a family as part of a student

defence available where any injury is solely attributable to the consumer, or a third party unconnected with the provision of the services contracted for and any failure to perform the obligation under the contract is unforeseeable or unavoidable, or occurs in circumstances of force majeure.[109]

Road traffic accidents

8.42 Directive 2000/26/EC on the approximation of the laws of the Member States relating to insurance against civil liability in respect of the use of motor vehicles and amending Council Directives 73/239/EEC and 88/357/EEC[110] establishes a particular regime for the settlement (not litigation) of personal injury claims arising from road traffic accidents. The principal purpose of the Directive is to provide special provisions for the protection of injured persons entitled to claim compensation for injury, loss and damage resulting from a road traffic accident taking place in another Member State by the use of a vehicle insured and normally based in a Member State (Art 1(1)). The Directive introduces four new elements: a direct right of action against insurers (Art 3); the establishment of a system of claims representatives in the state of domicile of the injured party responsible for settling claims in that State (Art 4); a system of information centres in order to provide information concerning the identity of the insurer and the insurer's claims representative (Art 5); and the establishment of compensation bodies who shall pay compensation where there is a default by the insurer in defined circumstances (Art 6).

8.43 The obligation under Art 3 providing for a direct cause of action has been implemented by the European Communities (Rights against Insurers) Regulations 2002[111] which came into force on 19 January 2003, a day earlier than the prescribed date under the Directive. The statutory instrument, although short, provides a dense formulation for the provision of the entitlement to a direct cause of action, by reg 3. Regulation 3 defines the class of claimants who may sue,[112] by reference to the type of vehicle involved, and the place of the accident (being on a road or other public place in the United Kingdom). The Regulations assist foreign claimants by permitting them to sue UK insurers in respect of UK accidents caused by UK drivers. The Regulations do not however assist UK residents in respect of road traffic accidents occurring abroad.[113]

8.44 The picture becomes more confusing when the issue of jurisdiction is concerned. As noted above, Regulation 44/2001 makes particular provision for the jurisdiction of courts in relation to claims concerning insurance and therefore deals with the appropriate courts who may hear direct actions against

---

exchange programme was outside the scope of the Directive. For a recent judgment on the meaning of a package holiday, see *ABTA v CAA* [2006] EWHC 13 Admin (judgment of Goldring J of 16 January 2006).
[109] See reg 15(2).
[110] OJ 2000 L181/65 (the Fourth Motor Insurance Directive).
[111] SI 2002/3061.
[112] Namely, residents of an EU Member State or Iceland, Norway or Liechtenstein.
[113] Indicating under implementation of the Directive.

road traffic insurers. However, a recital inserted into the Fourth Motor Insurance Directive by the Fifth Motor Insurance Directive[114] states that 'injured parties may bring legal proceedings against the civil liability insurance provider in the Member State in which they are domiciled' by virtue of Art 11(2) when read in conjunction with Art 9(1)(b) of Regulation 44/2001. In the author's opinion, this is an incorrect reading of the Regulation,[115] and a legally incorrect[116] mechanism for asserting the interpretation contended for. Injured parties may in particular cases be able to bring proceedings direct against the insurer in their country of domicile by virtue of other provisions in the Regulation (for example because the insured defendant tortfeasor is also domiciled in the jurisdiction), but it is considered incorrect as a general rule to conflate the status of 'beneficiary' as defined under Art 9(1)(b) of the Brussels Regulation with 'injured party' which the provision in the Fifth Directive appears to do, so as to permit any injured claimant to bring proceedings direct against the insurer in the courts of the domicile of the injured claimant.[117]

---

[114] See Art 5(1) of Directive 2005/14/EC amending Council Directives 72/166/EEC, 84/5/EEC, 88/357/EEC and 90/232/EEC and Directive 2000/26/EC relating to insurance against civil liability in respect of the use of motor vehicles (OJ 2005 L149/14).

[115] For an analysis of the detailed provisions of the Regulation as it applies to road traffic claims, see Bona M and Mead P (eds), *Personal Injury Compensation in Europe* (2003), Kluwer and xpl law, pp 627 and following.

[116] It is questionable whether a Directive (which requires implementation) can amend a Regulation which is directly applicable and does not require implementation to take effect in national law. A recital in a Directive does not have any substantive effect on its own and could not bind the European Court in any interpretation of Arts 9 and 11 of Regulation 44/2001.

[117] Care should accordingly be taken when interpreting the detailed insurance provisions of Regulation 44/2001 rather than relying without more on the interpretation contained in the Fifth Directive.

Part 2
DAMAGES

Chapter 9

GENERAL DAMAGES

INTRODUCTION

9.1 Damages for non-pecuniary loss, or general damages, are awarded to a claimant for the pain, suffering and loss of amenity caused by physical or mental injury. In theory, 'pain', 'suffering' and 'loss of amenity' are separate elements, but in practice 'pain and suffering' is a term of art. Such damages are conventional sums, and in assessing them the court will have regard to the overall seriousness of the claimant's loss of amenity, rather than to each individual symptom.

9.2 The English system for the assessment of general damages runs on a tariff, and the ultimate source of the tariff is the courts. The courts' decisions are to be found in a number of well-known sources,[1] and these decisions have been collated into a set of guidelines (see 'Judicial Studies Board Guidelines', below). Perhaps the starting-point for a study of the tariff should be the maximum damages to be awarded for the worst of injuries: in theory, all other injuries should file themselves in order of severity behind such awards.

9.3 The upper limit for general damages for pain suffering and loss of amenity is now about £275,000. Cases of maximum severity present special problems of management and quantification, which are dealt with elsewhere in this volume. The victim may have suffered quadriplegia, paraplegia or hemiplegia,[2] or very severe brain damage with a consequent total dependency on others and a requirement of constant care. The victim may be in pain, and may have insight into his condition. Advances in medical science have led to an increase in such 'total wreck' claims during recent years.

9.4 In the worst cases the claimant will have a degree of insight into his condition (which increases the 'suffering'). There may be some ability to follow basic commands, recovery of eye opening and return of sleep and waking patterns and postural reflex movement. There will be little, if any, evidence of meaningful response to environment, little or no language function, double incontinence and the need for full-time nursing care. The level of the award within the bracket will be affected by the degree of insight, life expectancy, and

---

[1] Eg *Kemp & Kemp* (Sweet & Maxwell); Butterworths Personal Injury Law Service; Personal Injury and Quantum Reports; Current Law (monthly parts and annual volumes); and online services such as Lawtel.
[2] Quadriplegia = paralysis of all four limbs (otherwise known as tetraplegia). Paraplegia = paralysis of the lower limbs. Hemiplegia = paralysis of one side of the body.

the extent of the physical limitation. The top of the bracket will be appropriate only where there is significant effect on the senses. Where there is a persistent vegetative state and/or death occurs very soon after the injuries were suffered and there has been an awareness by the injured person of his or her condition, the award will be solely for loss of amenity and will fall substantially below the bracket.

9.5 As an example of an award at the very top of the range, see *Janardan v East Berkshire Health Authority*[3] in which McCullough J awarded the claimant general damages of £115,000 for devastating injuries, compounded by the fact that his intelligence, understanding and other mental faculties were all normal. This award (made in May 1990) would be worth £242,000 at today's rates. Another example is *Brightman v Johnson*,[4] in which Tudor Price J awarded the claimant in £95,000 for equally terrible injuries: this award would be worth £263,000 today.

JUDICIAL STUDIES BOARD GUIDELINES

9.6 In 1992 the Judicial Studies Board published for the first time its 'Guidelines for the Assessment of General Damages in Personal Injury Cases'. 'It proved' (said the Rt Hon Sir Thomas Bingham MR in his introduction to the second edition) 'a runaway success'. It is now in its eighth edition, published in September 2006. The Judicial Studies Board had been seeking a way of standardising awards of general damages:

> '... whilst no two cases are ever precisely the same, justice requires that there be consistency between awards. The solution to this dilemma has lain in using the amount of damages awarded in reported cases as guidelines or markers and seeking to slot the particular case into the framework thus provided. That is easier stated than done, because reports of the framework cases are scattered over a variety of publications and not all the awards appear, from the sometimes brief reports, to be consistent with one another.'

9.7 The Judicial Studies Board meets regularly to review the level of general damages for a wide range of injuries, and to revise the bands of awards in the light both of inflation and of recent awards. In their introduction to the 1996 edition the Editors said that:

> 'The purpose of this guide is not to preach but rather to reflect the approach adopted by those who assess damages.'

9.8 In his introduction to the first edition, Lord Woolf said:

---

[3] (1990) *Kemp & Kemp*, A4-001.
[4] (1985) *The Times*, December 16.

'Especially in the case of appellate judges, it is important that they are kept up to date as to the value of the most common categories of awards. It is so easy for an appellate judge to lose touch with the current tariff . . .'

9.9 What is the status of the Judicial Studies Board *Guidelines*? They do not pretend to be exhaustive either of all categories of injury, or of all injuries within any given category. As Lord Woolf MR says in his introduction to the 1996 edition, 'Usually it will be the starting off point rather than the last word on the appropriate award in any particular case'.

9.10 Their great merit is they have ironed out the irregularities in the 'real world' cases reported in *Kemp & Kemp* and elsewhere. This does not mean that the court can ignore reported cases, but the *Guidelines* put them in context. Sometimes the *Guidelines* will be all that is needed, but sometimes a party will argue for a higher or lower award than they suggest, by reference to reported cases. It might be said that the *Guidelines* give the basic injury, stripped of many of the surrounding circumstances that will enhance an award. (Wall J, sitting in the Court of Appeal in *Arafa v Potter*,[5] spoke of 'having looked at the comparable cases in Kemp & Kemp and Current Law, and having checked them against the Judicial Studies Board Guidelines'. He found no discrepancies between these three sources.)

9.11 Take, for example, a case in which the claimant has suffered the total loss of one eye. The range of damages in the *Guidelines* is quite tight: £32,000 to £38,175, with the note that 'the level of the award within the bracket will depend on age and cosmetic defect'. If the claimant can satisfy the court that in his case the loss of an eye has had graver consequences than usual, the award will be at the top of the bracket, or even above the bracket. See, for example, *Re Campbell*,[6] in which the 25-year-old female claimant suffered severe alkaline burns to both eyes, leading to the loss of sight in one eye and permanent cosmetic deformity. In the light of all the surrounding circumstances[7] she was awarded £30,000, which is worth £45,500 at today's rates. (See 'Individual factors', below.)

---

[5] [1994] PIQR Q73.
[6] *Kemp & Kemp*, E1-014.
[7] The applicant was in hospital for 10 days and subsequently had one major and various minor operations. Despite this extensive treatment she lost the sight in her right eye with no prospect of restoration. She was left permanently cosmetically deformed. She underwent a significant change in temperament, manifested in panic attacks, loss of confidence, sleeplessness and depression. The applicant, who had been developing a career in drawing and design, was dismissed from her job at the time of the attack and various subsequent jobs due to her unsightly appearance. Her prospects of employment in her chosen career were extremely limited. Her loss of sight and the onset of constant headaches had restricted her social activities, and she gave up participation in squash, tennis and horse training. Due to her limited lifestyle the applicant became extremely depressed. This and the pain she had suffered caused the applicant to have a stressful pregnancy. Her disability was permanent and the side effects were continuing.

9.12 The intention of the *Guidelines* was to provide a snapshot of what courts were awarding for common categories of injuries. Clearly, the *Guidelines* cannot exclude reliance on reported authorities. In *Wright v British Railways Board*,[8] Lord Diplock said:

> 'Non-economic loss constitutes a major item in the damages. Such loss is not susceptible of measurement in money. Any figure at which the assessor of damages arrives cannot be other than artificial and, if the aim is that justice meted out to all litigants should be even-handed instead of depending on idiosyncrasies of the assessor, whether jury or judge, the figure must be "basically a conventional figure derived from experience and awards in comparable cases".
>
> My lords, given the inescapably artificial and conventional nature of the assessment of damages for non-economic loss in personal injury actions and of treating such assessment as a debt bearing interest from the date of service of the writ, it is an important function of the Court of Appeal to lay down guidelines both as to the quantum of damages appropriate to compensate for various types of commonly occurring injuries and as to the rates of "interest" from time to time appropriate to be given in respect of non-economic loss and of the various kinds of economic loss. The purpose of such guidelines is that they should be simple and easy to apply though broad enough to permit allowances to be made for special features of individual cases which make the deprivation caused to the particular Claimant by the non-economic loss greater or less than in the general run of cases involving injuries of the same kind. Guidelines laid down by an appellate court are addressed directly to judges who try personal injury actions; but confidence that trial judges will apply them means that all those who are engaged in settling out of court the many thousands of claims that never reach the stage of litigation at all or, if they do, do not proceed as far as trial, will know very broadly speaking what the claim is likely to be worth if 100 per cent liability is established.
>
> The Court of Appeal, with its considerable case-load of appeals in personal injury actions and the relatively recent experience of many of its members in trying such cases themselves, is, generally speaking, the tribunal best qualified to set the guidelines for judges currently trying such actions, particularly as respects non-economic loss . . .
>
> A guideline as to quantum of conventional damages or conventional interest thereon is not a rule of law nor is it a rule of practice. It sets no binding precedent; it can be varied as circumstances change or experience shows that it does not assist in the achievement of even-handed justice or makes trials more lengthy or expensive or settlements more difficult to reach. But though guidelines should be altered if circumstances relevant to the particular guideline change, too frequent alteration deprives them of their usefulness in providing a reasonable degree of predictability in the litigious process and so facilitating settlement of claims without going to trial.
>
> As regards assessment of damages for non-economic loss in personal injury cases, the Court of Appeal creates the guidelines as to the appropriate conventional figure by increasing or reducing awards of damages made by judges in individual cases for various common kinds of injuries. Thus so-called "brackets" are

---

[8] [1983] AC 773, 777.

established, broad enough to make allowance for circumstances which make the deprivation suffered by an individual plaintiff in consequence of the particular kind of injury greater or less than in the general run of cases, yet clear enough to reduce the unpredictability of what is likely to be the most important factor in arriving at settlement of claims. "Brackets" may call for alteration not only to take account of inflation, for which they ought automatically to be raised, but also it may be to take account of advances in medical science which may make particular kinds of injuries less disabling or advances in medical knowledge which may disclose hitherto unsuspected long-term effects of some kinds of injuries or industrial diseases ...'

9.13 An unfortunate dictum of the Court of Appeal in the early days of the *Guidelines* nearly got them off on the wrong foot. In *Arafa v Potter*[9] the court said:

'We have been referred to the guidelines of the Judicial Studies Board. They are not in themselves law; they form a slim and handy volume which anyone can slip into their briefcases on their way to the county court or travelling on circuit. But the law is to be found elsewhere in rather greater bulk. In this Court we ought to look to the sources rather than the summary produced by the Judicial Studies Board.'

9.14 This passage seems to have been over-used in the next two years, because in his October 1996 introduction to the *Guidelines*, Lord Woolf MR said:

'I am aware of the dicta of one member of the Court of Appeal in the case of *Arafa v Potter*. If the dicta was [sic] intended to suggest that the Court of Appeal should not regard this book as a source from which an approximate figure for damages can be obtained, I profoundly disagree. The other member of the Court in fact referred to this book in the course of his judgment as a check as to what the correct bracket of damages should be. He was entitled to do so. Unless Court of Appeal judges as well as judges at first instance have regard to the guidelines continued in this book, its purpose will be defeated.[10] As in the past so in the future it should be used not only because it is convenient to do so, but because due to the way in which it is compiled and because of its extensive use, it is the most reliable tool which up to now has been made available to courts up and down the land as to what is the correct range of damages for common classes of injuries.'

THE GUIDELINES AND COSTS

9.15 In his 1996 introduction, Lord Woolf said that the *Guidelines*:

'... will help judges to determine whether the attitude to damages which the parties are adopting is reasonable. This will be important in determining issues as to costs.'

---

[9] [1994] PIQR Q73.
[10] A claim that could be made for most things.

9.16 Although the Civil Procedure Rules 1998 (CPR) encourage early settlement by the making of realistic offers and counter-offers, it is hard to see how a claimant who has fairly beaten a payment into court could be penalised as to costs, and a judge who has just made such an award is unlikely to be impressed by a defendant who tries to point out that the award should have been within the *Guidelines*. We know of no case in which the point has arisen.

HEIL V RANKIN

9.17 On 23 March 2000 the Court of Appeal gave judgment in *Heil v Rankin*[11] in which a number of claimants successfully argued that the tariff for general damages should be increased. The Court took as its starting point Lord Diplock's remarks in *Wright v British Railways Board* (cited above at **9.12**) and the Law Commission's recommendations.[12] Their conclusion[13] was:

> 'We are satisfied that it is in the case of the most catastrophic injuries that the awards are most in need of adjustment and that the scale of adjustment which is required reduces as the level of existing awards decreases. At the highest level, we see a need for awards to be increased by in the region of one third. We see no need for an increase in awards which are at present below £10,000.'

9.18 Although some years have now passed since *Heil v Rankin*, and hundreds of reported awards have been made under the increased tariff, it is still necessary to know how to update an old award in line with the court's decision. This is dealt with under 'Updating awards' below.

9.19 The difficulty lies in applying the sliding scale of uplifts. The Court of Appeal assumed that the highest award of general damages was about £150,000. If a case is worth £10,000, there will be no uplift. If a case was worth £150,000, its value on 23 March 2000 would rise by a third to £200,000. There is a formula to calculate the uplift as at that date. Let us call the award 'A': the formula is £A + [£A-10,000/420,000 × £A]. The steps to work out this formula are:

- Subtract £10,000 from A

- Divide the result by 420,000

- Multiply the result by A

- Add A to the result

---

[11] [2000] 2 WLR 1173.
[12] Consultation Paper (No 140) 'Damages for Personal Injury: Non-Pecuniary Loss' (January 1996). This was followed by the publication of the Commission Report (No 257), printed on 19 April 1999.
[13] Para 88.

9.20 A practical application of this is shown in 'Updating awards' below.

UPDATING AWARDS

9.21 In *Wright v British Railways Board* the House of Lords made it clear that it was the duty of the judge to assess general damages in the 'money of the day' as at the date of trial and not in the values which obtained at the date of the injury. When assessing damages in the light of earlier reported awards, those earlier awards must be updated in line with inflation, as measured by the Retail Price Index (RPI) (this is the basis on which awards have been increased in this chapter). The RPI is published widely: it can be found in 'Facts & Figures', Kemp & Kemp, Butterworths Personal Injury Litigation Service, and online. Current Law publishes the current index figure each month.

9.22 When updating the value of a reported award, it is important to note first whether the award was made before or after 23 March 2000 – the date of the Court of Appeal's judgment in *Heil v Rankin* (see above):

- If the award was made *after* that date, update in line with inflation from the date of the award to date.

- If the award was made *before* that date, it is necessary to do three things:
    - update for inflation from the date of the award to 23 March 2000;
    - apply the uplift (if any) recommended by the Court of Appeal. If, after updating for inflation to 23 March 2000 the award is worth less than £10,000, there will be no uplift;
    - update for inflation from 23 March 2000 to date.

Table A11 in 'Facts & Figures 2006' performs these calculations for you.

Updating awards made *after* 23 March 2000

9.23 To calculate the present value of an earlier award, multiply the award by the current index figure, and then divide it by the index figure for the month in which the award was originally made – eg:

In November 2001 the CICB [Criminal Injuries Compensation Board] awarded the applicant in *Re Mather*[14] £25,000 for a serious fracture of the ankle. The retail price index for that month was 173.60. To find the value of the award as at May 2006, when the RPI stood at 197.70:

[197.70 × £25,000] ÷ 173.60 = £28,470

---

[14] *Kemp & Kemp*, 17-002.

Updating awards made *before* 23 March 2000

9.24 The formula for doing this is given under *Heil v Rankin* above. It is helpful to remember that on 23 March 2000 the RPI stood at 168.40.

9.25 Take as an example *Stephens v Doncaster HA*,[15] in which Buxton J awarded £120,000 for quadriplegia on 16 June 1995. The steps are:

- To update this award from 16 June 1995 (when the RPI was 149.80) to 23 March 2000: [168.40 × £120,000] ÷ 149.80 = £134,900. This gives the value of the award on the date of the *Heil* judgment.

- Applying the *Heil* uplift:
  - Subtract £10,000 from £134,900 to give £124,900
  - Divide £124,900 by 420,000 to give 0.2973
  - Multiply 0.2973 by £134,900 to give £40,117
  - Add £134,900 to £40,117 to give £175,017

- Update for inflation from the date of *Heil* to today's date: [197.70 × £175,017] ÷ 168.40 = £205,468

9.26 Subscribers to Lawtel's online service can use their Inflation Calculator, which performs the calculation for them.

INDIVIDUAL FACTORS AFFECTING GENERAL DAMAGES

9.27 The claimant's age and a brief description of his injuries must be pleaded in the Statement of Case: it is not sufficient simply to refer to medical evidence. Each element of the injury should be pleaded: where an orthopaedic injury has caused post-traumatic stress disorder and may lead to degenerative osteoarthritic changes, each of these three elements should be raised in the pleading.

Pain and suffering

9.28 The phrase is a term of art, although the elements are separable. Pain is a part of most injuries, but a claimant will be compensated even where he suffers pain and no other injury – e g in anaesthetic awareness cases.

9.29 Can a claimant recover damages for an asymptomatic condition? In *Rothwell v Chemical & Insulating Co Ltd*[16] the Court of Appeal had to consider pleural plaques, a condition of which it said:

---

[15] *Kemp & Kemp*, A1-004.
[16] [2006] EWCA Civ 27.

'Pleural plaques undoubtedly constitute a physiological change in the body... For present purposes their relevant feature is that, save in the case of about 1% which no-one has suggested has significance, they are symptomless, have no adverse effect on any bodily function and, being internal, have no effect on appearance. In short, ignoring the 1%, no one is any the worse physically for having pleural plaques.'

9.30 The court held (Smith LJ dissenting) that pleural plaques were not a compensatable injury, and that it followed that anxiety secondary to pleural plaques was not compensatable either. This decision is currently under appeal to the House of Lords. It has important implications for certain other conditions, such as asymptomatic asbestosis.

9.31 The courts can make substantial awards for pain and suffering, even where the claimant survives for only a relatively short period. This is particularly so in the case of the asbestos-related condition mesothelioma, and extremely painful cancer that is invariably fatal, usually within about 18 months of diagnosis, but often within a very few months. The range of damages given in the Judicial Studies Board's Guidelines is £47,850 to £74,300, with the comment:

'The duration of pain and suffering accounts for variations within this bracket. For periods of up to 18 months, awards in the bottom half of the bracket may be appropriate; for longer periods of four years or more, an award at the top end.'

Loss of amenity

9.32 Loss of amenity can exist without pain or suffering in cases of unconsciousness, and in theory general damages can be awarded wherever the injured person is unconscious between the time of the injury and the time of death (but see 'Fear of impending death', below). Where the deceased did not die immediately, general damages are assessed in the same way as in any other personal injury case. In coma cases, or cases of persistent vegetative state, damages at the very top of the tariff will not be awarded, because the element of pain and suffering is not present:

'An unconscious person will be spared pain and suffering and will not experience the moral anguish which may result from knowledge of what has in life been lost or from knowledge that life has been shortened. The fact of unconsciousness is therefore relevant in respect of and will eliminate those heads or elements of damage which can only exist by being felt or thought or experienced. The fact of unconsciousness does not, however, eliminate the actuality of the deprivation of the ordinary experiences and amenities of life which may be the inevitable result of some physical injury.'[17]

---

[17] Lord Morris of Borth-y-Gest in *West v Shephard* [1964] AC 326, 349.

9.33 There are a number of reported cases, but following the Court of Appeal's guidance in *Housecroft v Burnett*[18] the pre-1985 authorities are not reliable. See, however:

- **Kerby v Redbridge Health Authority.**[19] Ognall J awarded general damages of £750 (worth £950 today) to the estate of a newborn child who lived in a coma for 3 days before dying.

- **Cooke & Rippin v Prushki.**[20] The deceased suffered diffuse brain injury and tetraplegia in a car accident. Although he was able to sit up out of bed for short periods, he never fully regained consciousness, and died 3 months later. General damages of £9,000 were awarded in October 1992, worth £12,800 today.

- **Andrews v Freeborough.**[21] The claimant remained deeply unconscious for almost a year before dying of injuries she sustained in a car crash. So far as it was possible to say, she did not suffer at all. Damages of £2,000 were awarded in November 1965 (worth £27,300 today).

- **Doleman v Deakin.**[22] The deceased was unconscious for a period of 6 weeks up to his death. An award of £1,500 (worth about £2,000 today) was upheld by the Court of Appeal in January 1990.[23]

Pre-existing condition

9.34 In the majority of personal injury cases, the claimant's previous state of health is irrelevant to the assessment of general damages; there will, nevertheless, be cases in which a claimant is already ill, or suffering from injury, at the time of the accident. In clinical negligence claims (with the exception of those concerning the birth of handicapped children) one is almost invariably obliged to take a pre-existing condition into account. In a simple case – for example, mis-diagnosis as malignant of a benign tumour, leading to excision and adjuvant therapy over a prolonged period – the pre-existing condition may not affect general damages greatly. In a more complicated case – eg the late diagnosis of a malignant tumour – there may well be disagreement about whether the claimant has suffered any significant injury at all.

9.35 In *Mustard v Morris*[24] the claimant was a diabetic suffering from an arterial insufficiency leading to increasing pain in the right leg. As a result of

---

[18] [1986] 1 All ER 332.
[19] *Kemp & Kemp*, O5-004, 25 April 1997.
[20] Formerly in *Kemp & Kemp*, A2-011, October 1992.
[21] [1967] 1 QB 1.
[22] A5-005.
[23] It is not possible to be certain about the current value, because the date of the original award is not known.
[24] Formerly in *Kemp & Kemp*, I2-106, 604, now referred to only in the Law Commission's Consultation Paper 'Damages for Personal Injury: Non-Pecuniary Loss' (No 140) at 2.32 n 127.

the defendant's negligence he lost his left leg above the knee. The defendant argued that the claimant was already seriously unfit at the time of the incident, and that the damages for an impaired claimant should be higher than those for a healthy one. The Court of Appeal described this submission as misconceived, saying:

> 'An argument to the contrary might well be made. To impose upon a man who, though natural causes, has been made ill to a certain extent, very grave injuries such as were sustained in this Plaintiff and which reduce his capacity to bear natural ill health, is in my judgment more likely to increase than reduce damages.'[25]

9.36 Cases of clinical negligence raise problems not usually found in conventional personal injury claims. For example, the claimant's presenting condition may have been aggravated, either through the natural process of the disease, or as a direct result of the negligence, but it will be necessary to consider the extent to which medical science could have helped the patient in any event. There may have been a number of breaches of duty-for example, a road traffic accident, followed by negligence on the part of the casualty officer treating the claimant, and these separate causes of action may have different causative effects.

Acceleration

9.37 Care is needed where the claimant's injury has accelerated a pre-existing condition, whether or not that condition was causing symptoms at the date of the injury. Reported cases commonly state that the accident 'accelerated the onset of symptoms from a previous wrist injury by some three years', or 'accelerated active symptoms in the lumbar spine, not present before, by about five years'. The starting-point for calculating such damages is generally taken to be the injury itself, first quantified as though it were permanent, and then discounted to reflect the shorter period of pain and suffering for which the defendant himself was responsible.

Multiple injuries

9.38 The courts are concerned with the overall level of disability caused by the claimant's injuries, and will not usually make a separate award in respect of each injury. This can lead either to a rounding-up or a rounding-down. It is clear that the closer to the top of the tariff, the less difference further handicap makes to the award. For example, in *Francis v Porch*[26] the claimant suffered paraplegia, severe brain injury and complete blindness. The Judicial Studies

---

[25] Watkins LJ. (The author has had an extreme case of a young autistic girl who was blind and deaf: her only known sources of pleasure were tactile, and in particular she appeared to derive particular pleasure from smearing herself with her own excrement. As a result of the defendant's negligence, the lower part of her body was permanently scarred, interfering even with this limited degree of amenity. How should the conventional damages for such scarring be adjusted in such a case?).

[26] *Kemp & Kemp*, A3-003.

Board *Guidelines* suggest a figure of £155,250 for complete blindness alone, and for paraplegia £188,250 to £235,000. The court approved a settlement of her claim for general damages in the sum of £137,500 (worth £238,000 today).[27]

9.39 At a lower level, the Court of Appeal gave guidance in the case of *Durau v Evans*:[28]

> 'To a limited extent, in a case where there are multiple injuries, the figures in the Judicial Studies Board table can help but I accept Mr Murphy's criticism of them that, where one has a multiplicity of injuries, it is necessary to take an overall view. The off-setting process may mean it is not possible to derive a great deal of benefit from that particular source. One then looks to see if anything can be gained from looking at a comparable award, if one is to be found, in another case. Even that may not prove to be a particularly fruitful source of inquiry. It may be necessary, if it be possible, to select what may be the most serious head of injury to see if a comparable award can be found in relation to that and, if so, build on it to allow for the other heads of injury which have been sustained by the Plaintiff in the instant case.'

9.40 Sometimes it is not difficult to grasp the overall effect of injuries. Where, for example, both legs have been injured, one looks at the effect on mobility; if an arm and a leg are injured, the total effect on independence and the ability to work may provide clear parallels with other cases. What is not so straightforward is the cumulative effect of two entirely unrelated injuries – a shortened leg and an increased risk of developing epilepsy, for example, or a whiplash injury and a facial scar. The only practical advice is to adopt the Court of Appeal's approach, and start with the more serious injury, taking a step back after alighting on a figure, to see whether the award reflects the overall gravity of the injuries.

9.41 The Criminal Injuries Compensation Board (CICB) has its own tariff for injuries, and where an applicant has suffered more than one injury his award of general damages is calculated[29] as:

- the tariff amount for the highest rated injury;

- plus 10% of the tariff amount for the second highest rated injury;

- plus 5% of the tariff value of the third highest rated injury (para 26).

---

[27] Would it have been any different if she had not been blind? Suppose she had been blinded in a later, separate, accident? Would she have been entitled to a tariff award for such an injury? Presumably so.
[28] [1996] PIQR Q18.
[29] Para 26 of the 1996 Scheme; para 27 of the 2001 Scheme.

Fear of impending death

9.42 In *Hicks v Chief Constable of the South Yorkshire Police*,[30] the Court of Appeal refused to award damages to the estates of three of the victims of the Hillsborough football stadium disaster, saying that the evidence of pain suffered by the victims in the few seconds between the onset of asphyxia, and the knowledge and fear of impending death, could not be distinguished from the deaths themselves:

> 'In the case of the Hillsborough disaster, as the situation worsened, many many hundreds of people in pens 3 and 4, I have no doubt, suffered acute feelings of fear and horror without sustaining either physical injury or psychiatric injury. Such persons will have spent some 30 minutes of acute mental anguish but no more. No action lies in respect thereof. Others, although they survived, will have suffered injuries. If those injuries resulted in pain and suffering that pain and suffering including fear for future consequences constitutes a recoverable head of damage, but the preceding mental anguish not caused by injury does not thereby become compensatable. In the case of death, the estate can recover for pain and suffering including if it be the case awareness of shortened expectation of life caused by the injuries which led to death and, if such is the case, pain and suffering caused by other injuries which have nothing whatever to do with death . . .
>
> There remains in my judgment for consideration only such pain as may have occurred in the few seconds between the onset of asphyxia and unconsciousness and the knowledge and fear of impending death which may have occurred in those few seconds. It is in my view possible to infer that both would probably have been suffered to some extent by all three deceased, but can damages be awarded? If so, such damages could in my view only amount to a small nominal conventional sum. In my view, however, when unconsciousness and death occur in such a short period after the injury which causes death no damages are recoverable. The last few moments of mental agony and pain are in reality part of the death itself for which no action lies under the 1934 Act.'[31]

Loss of expectation of life

9.43 General damages are not awarded to compensate for a shortened life: see Administration of Justice Act 1982, s 1(1)(a) – though they may be awarded where the claimant's knowledge that his life has been shortened causes particular distress: see s 1(1)(b):

> 'If the injured person's life has been reduced by the injuries, the court, in assessing damages in respect of pain and suffering caused by the injuries, shall take account of any suffering caused or likely to be caused to him by awareness that his expectation of life has been so reduced.'[32]

---

[30] [1992] PIQR P63.
[31] Parker LJ at P66, 67.
[32] In *Hicks v Chief Constable of the South Yorkshire Police* [1992] PIQR P63, 67, Lord Justice Parker said 'In [asbestosis] cases apprehension for the future is an allowable head but this comes from knowledge that the injury suffered will or may lead to death in the future'. (See also *Whittaker (deceased) v BBA Group* (*Kemp & Kemp*, K3-007) for an example of such an award.)

Gender

9.44 In most claims the gender of the claimant will be irrelevant, though in cases of scarring (especially facial scarring) women are commonly awarded significantly higher damages than men: in fact, this probably does no more than reflect the evidence about the subjective effects of the scarring on men and women. In younger women, the possible effect of hip, pelvic, and low back injuries on childbirth and child care should also be considered. For no easily-discernible reason, the loss of marriage prospects[33] is thought to be a greater blow to a woman than to a man.

Age

9.45 Age is relatively unimportant to damages for loss of amenity, though damages for pain and suffering may be higher if the claimant is young: a fit and active woman in her early 20s who suffers a permanent back injury will be awarded more than a woman in her 40s. Damages for the very old may be slightly lower, but there are few reported cases to substantiate this. An example is *Laycock v Morrison*[34] in which the 79-year-old claimant was awarded general damages worth £9,000 for loss of the senses of taste and smell (an award worth about £14,000 today): the Judicial Studies Board Guidelines suggest a figure of £22,650.

Death of claimant

9.46 If a claimant dies relatively soon after the accident, or before trial, the court can take this fact into account when assessing general damages: see *H West & Son Ltd v Shephard*,[35] in which Lord Morris, dealing with the factors to be taken into account in the assessment, said 'the length of the period of life during which the deprivations will continue will be a relevant factor'. The Court of Appeal took this into account in *McCann v Shepard*,[36] a case in which the claimant died prematurely between the date of the trial and the appeal. The original award had been £20,000. The claimant appealed, and the defendant cross-appealed once it heard of his death. Evidence of the death was admitted, and taken into account by the Court of Appeal in reducing the award to £15,000.

9.47 Not too much can be read into *McCann*, however. The Court of Appeal did not decide whether the original award had been correct (at a time when it was thought that the claimant had a normal life expectation): it therefore cannot be said that there had been a 25% reduction to take the death into account. It simply dealt with the matter de novo, and made a fresh award of £15,000 taking all the factors, including the death, into account.

---

[33] Or, presumably, loss of the prospect of cohabitation (more or less permanent) with a member of either sex.
[34] September 1990. Formerly reported in *Kemp & Kemp*, D 4-019.
[35] [1964] AC 326. See also *Rose v Ford* [1937] AC 826.
[36] [1973] 2 All ER 881.

9.48 In *Watson v Willmott*[37] the deceased survived by only a few months the death of his wife in the car crash before taking his own life as a result of severe depression. Garland J said:

> 'Robert Watson then suffered a most unhappy period until he ended his own life. It is true that during that time he attempted to build some sort of social life and to find congenial female companionship. These efforts were tentative and transient. It is an invidious task to measure total despair in terms of money and the court should, in my view, be cautious. Robert Watson lived four months after his wife's death and I think an appropriate award would be £3,500 [worth £6,000 at today's rates].'

Means of the claimant

9.49 It is irrelevant that an award will mean more or less to a claimant (because of his wealth)[38] or nothing at all (because he is in a persistent vegetative state).

Claimant's previous lifestyle

9.50 There are numerous reported authorities in which sportsmen have been awarded higher damages than the tariff would suggest, to take account of their prowess:

> 'If there is loss of amenity apart from the obvious and normal loss inherent in the deprivation of the limb-if, for instance, the Plaintiff's main interest in life was some sport or hobby from which he will in future be debarred, that too increases the assessment.'[39]

9.51 The claimant in *Middleton v South Yorkshire Transport Executive*[40] was a teacher of physical education, who greatly enjoyed sports. She suffered a fracture of the left femur and a paralysed left arm: the trial judge awarded her £37,500 (worth £87,900 today), identifying £7,500 of that figure (£15,600 today) as being in respect of her reduced ability to take part in the sporting activities she both taught and had previously enjoyed. It is clear from the report that this £7,500 did not overlap with either her claim for lost earnings or a *Smith v Manchester Corporation* award.

Circumstances of the accident

9.52 These may be relevant for a number of reasons: the accident may be painful, or terrifying; the circumstances might cause psychological or psychiatric harm; it might be more difficult for the claimant to adjust to the

---

[37] [1991] 1 QB 140.
[38] *Wise v Kaye* [1962] 1 QB 638.
[39] *West v Shephard* [1965] AC 326, 365.
[40] 28 January 1986. *Kemp & Kemp*, G4-001.

injury because it was inflicted suddenly. In cases of medical negligence, the circumstances are less likely to be traumatic in themselves, however serious the actual injury.

Loss of congenial employment

9.53 'It is now well recognised that [loss of congenial employment] is a separate head of damage',[41] although a court may reflect it in an increased award of general damages. These damages are available when a claimant has to give up a job of which he was particularly fond. For example, in *Hale v London Underground Ltd*[42] the claimant, who was 39 at the date of the accident and 46 at trial, had to give up being an active firefighter, a job which had provided him with great satisfaction. He had taken a job as a fire prevention officer, which he did not enjoy as much, and he missed his old work. The judge bore in mind the claimant's age, and the fact that he might in the future find a job that provided greater satisfaction, and awarded £5,000. This appears to be more or less the tariff for awards under this head.

9.54 A claim for damages for loss of congenial employment must be specifically pleaded. The claimant must establish that he has suffered 'a real loss . . . not mitigated by any enjoyment from his present work'.

Loss of leisure

9.55 Damages for loss of leisure may be claimed when a claimant has to work longer hours to earn the same income, though the court is more likely to take account of the loss of leisure in the global award of general damages. *Tindale v Dowsett Engineering Construction Ltd*[43] was a case in which the judge made a separate award (£1,250, worth about £3,600 today) under this head to a claimant who worked 10 hours a week longer for two years in order to earn the same income.[44] In pleading such a claim, particulars should give the nature of the work, the number of extra hours worked, and when they were worked – evenings, weekends, instead of a holiday, etc.

Loss of enjoyment of holiday

9.56 If a claimant's holiday is interrupted by an accident, or he misses his annual holiday, moderate damages can be awarded, although again these may simply be included in the global general damages[45] (as in *Ichard v Frangoulis*,[46] where the court held that the loss of a holiday was something to be taken into account, not as a separate item of damage, but in estimating general damages

---

[41] Otton J in *Hale v London Underground Ltd* [1993] PIQR Q30.
[42] [1993] PIQR Q30.
[43] Unreported, Mustill J, 2 December 1980 (transcript on Lexis).
[44] See also *Hearnshaw v English Steel Corporation Ltd* [1971] 11 KIR 306.
[45] These damages are not assessed on the same basis as those awarded in contractual 'holiday disputes'.
[46] [1977] 1 WLR 556.

for an injury). For an example of a separate award see *Bush v Philip (No 2)*.[47] The claimant, aged 15 at the date of the accident and 17 at the date of trial, was involved in a road traffic accident at the start of a cycling holiday. He was taken to hospital but not detained, and as a result he missed the first week of his holiday. Damages worth £500 at current rates were awarded.

Note

9.57 The court need not make a separate award for each of the above factors (eg the circumstances of the accident, loss of congenial employment, loss of leisure, loss of enjoyment of holiday), if it takes them into account in the global award for general damages.

GENERAL DAMAGES IN FATAL ACCIDENTS ACT CLAIMS

9.58 Apart from awards for bereavement,[48] there are two possible awards in claims under the Fatal Accidents Act 1976:

- In *Hay v Hughes*[49] Lord Edmund-Davies said 'it may some time have to be considered whether Mr McGregor is not right in saying:[50] " . . . it may be argued that the benefit of a mother's personal attention to a child's upbringing, morals, education and psychology, which the services of a housekeeper, nurse or governess could never provide, has in the long run a financial value for the child, difficult as it is to assess".'

- In *Mehmet v Perry*,[51] Brian Neill QC held that a widower and his orphaned children were entitled to damages for the loss of the deceased's personal care and attention over and above damages for loss of housekeeping services, but that such damages should be relatively low, so as not to overlap with damages for loss of housekeeping, etc.
    — Sedley J took this up in *Lewis v Osborne*,[52] in which he awarded the claimant £40,000 to compensate her for the distracted and distressing early childhood that she endured as a result of the loss of her mother:

    'In sum, what has happened is that the courts, fixed with binding early authority that injury in the legislation means pecuniary loss, have been striving to do justice in terms of contemporary perceptions by expanding the

---

[47] [1989] CLY 1065.
[48] No award for deaths before 1 January 1983. For deaths between 1 January 1983 and 31 March 1991, the award is £3,500. For deaths between 1 April 1991 and 31 March 2002, the award is £7,500. For deaths since 1 April 2002, the award is £10,000.
[49] [1975] QB 790.
[50] In *McGregor on Damages* (13th edn, 1972), para 1232.
[51] [1977] 2 All ER 529.
[52] 4 July 1995 (unreported). See *Kemp & Kemp*, M4-071/1. See also *Topp v London Country Bus (SW) Ltd* [1992] PIQR P206, 222 and *Johnson v British Midland Airways* [1996] PIQR Q8.

meaning of pecuniary as a surrogate for the now forbidden task of giving a neutral meaning to injury. Thus in *Regan v Williamson*[53] Watkins J (as he then was), following Lord Edmund-Davies' dictum, held that services is to be given a generous interpretation, with the consequence that the valuation of such services may be in some measure expanded.'

9.59 Those representing claimants in Fatal Accidents Act cases should consider including in the schedule a claim, eg 'an award of £... for the infant AB for the loss of her father's personal attention to her upbringing, morals, education and psychology, which the services of a housekeeper, nurse or governess could never provide'.

APPEALS AGAINST AWARDS OF GENERAL DAMAGES

9.60 In *Clarke v South Yorkshire Transport Ltd*,[54] the Court of Appeal summarised its functions and limitations on hearing appeals against awards of general damages. After quoting with approval Lord Justice Kennedy's remarks in *Durau v Evans* (see 'Multiple injuries' above), Lord Justice Mantell went on to say:

'I would add that in my judgment an appeal court should always be "slow to interfere with the trial judge's assessment, even though it may seem that such assessment falls outside the Judicial Studies Board Guidelines, or is out of kilter with other roughly comparable cases. After all, the trial judge will have seen the Plaintiff and, sometimes, as in this, have had the advantage of visiting the Plaintiff's home and seeing film of her getting about both in the home and outside. The trial judge will have been in the best position to make a judgment as to the effect upon the Plaintiff's life of the injuries and the consequent disabilities.'

APPENDIX

Checklist for general damages

9.61 This list cannot pretend to be exhaustive, but it should spur a client to think of ways in which he has been affected by his injuries, which would not necessarily occur to his legal advisers. Except where they are obvious, the effects will need to be supported by medical evidence. The claimant's solicitors should take care to cover all the significant effects of the injuries in the claimant's witness statement.

1 The injuries
   The claimant should deal with the injuries, the process of recovery, and the existing state of disability.

2 Pain

---

[53] [1976] 1 WLR 305.
[54] [1998] PIQR Q104, 107.

General damages

    a   Is it continuous or intermittent?
    b   How severe is it?
    c   How disabling is it?
    d   What treatment (if any) helps (eg painkillers, an orthopaedic mattress, TENS machine)?

3   Suffering
    a   Fear
    b   Worry
    c   Embarrassment
    d   Distress at awareness of accelerated death
    e   Distress at the effect of the injury on the claimant's family

4   Loss of amenity
    a   Mobility
        i   Climbing ladders
        ii   Climbing stairs
        iii   Getting out of bed
        iv   Getting into and out of chairs
        v   Getting into and out of the bath
        vi   Getting on and off the lavatory
        vii   Kneeling
        viii   Running
        ix   Sitting
        x   Sleeping (turning over in bed)
        xi   Squatting
        xii   Standing
        xiii   Walking on uneven ground
        xiv   Walking on a slope
        xv   Walking – distance
    b   Personal hygiene
        i   Grooming
        ii   Dressing
        iii   Bathing
        iv   Showering
    c   Housework
        i   Cleaning windows
        ii   Cooking
        iii   Dusting
        iv   Gardening
        v   Hoovering
        vi   Ironing
        vii   Painting and decorating
        viii   Putting objects into cupboards or on high shelves
        ix   Shopping
        x   Washing up
        xi   Washing floors
        xii   Washing
        xiii   Other DIY tasks
    d   Other personal functions
        i   Sexual dysfunction

ii   Lifting children

5   Work
   a   Inability to work at all
   b   Restricted ability to work shorter hours, or different work, or both
   c   Able to work with the help of special equipment
   d   Loss of enjoyment of work
   e   Loss of holiday
   f   More hours' work to earn the same pay

6   Support for other heads of claim – e g
   a   Care: help with activities listed in this checklist
   b   Housing
   c   Aids and appliances
   d   Help with shopping
   e   Greater reliance on motorised transport, or on public transport
   f   Medical treatment

7   Sports and hobbies
   a   Cannot get out on trips, visits to the cinema, family visits, holidays, etc
   b   Active hobbies such as swimming, cycling, aerobics, etc: did the claimant perform sports at a high level?
   c   Other hobbies

Chapter 10

MULTIPLIERS FOR FUTURE LOSS AND EXPENDITURE

10.1 Multipliers are used to calculate all future loss, for example:

- loss of earnings;

- loss of pension;

- additional living expenses;

- the cost of surgery;

- aids and appliances, their replacement and upkeep.

10.2 The objective of any award of damages in personal injuries litigation is to achieve as nearly as possible full compensation for the claimant for the injury sustained.[1] To achieve that objective the court seeks to award such sum as is notionally required to be laid out in the purchase of an annuity which will provide an annual amount equivalent to the loss for the whole period of the loss: per Lord Oliver in *Hodgson v Trapp*.[2] The basis of the calculation is an assumed annuity. The court makes an assumption about how the award will be invested.[3] Lord Fraser of Tullybelton in *Cookson v Knowles*[4] put it thus:

> 'The assumed annuity will be made up partly of income on the principal sum awarded, and partly of capital obtained by gradual encroachment of the principal.

---

[1] *Livingstone v Rawyards Coal Company* (1980) 5 AC 25 at p 39 per Blackburne J, quoted with approval by Lord Scarman in *Lin Poh Choo v Camden Health Authority* (1980) AC 174 at page 187, and also in *Pickett v British Rail Engineering* (1978) 3 WLR 955 at 979.

[2] (1989) AC 804: 'Essentially what the Court has to do is to calculate as best it can the sum of money which will on the one hand be adequate, by its capital and income, to provide annually for the injured person a sum equivalent to his estimated annual loss over the whole of the period during which that loss is likely to continue, but which, on the other hand, will not, at the end of that period, leave him in a better financial position than he would have been apart from the accident. Hence the conventional approach is to assess the amount notionally required to be laid out in the purchase of an annuity which will provide the annual amount needed for the whole period of loss': per Lord Oliver at 826E–F.

[3] 'How the plaintiff, or the majority of plaintiffs, in fact invest their money is irrelevant': Lord Lloyd of Berwick in *Wells* (1998) 3 WLR 329 at p 342.

[4] (1979) AC 556 at 576G.

The income element will be at its largest at the beginning of the period and will tend to decline, while the capital element will tend to increase until the principal is exhausted.'

10.3 In the past the multipliers which were generally adopted in practice were based on the assumption that the principal sum of damages would earn 4.5% as a rate of return. Falling interest rates and severe shifts in the value of stocks and shares led to that being questioned. The House of Lords in *Wells v Wells*[5] transformed the position. These were three appeals where each of the plaintiffs had been seriously injured and each case involved a substantial future loss claim. In the Court of Appeal[6] it was held that a discount rate of 4% to 5% should be assumed and that a claimant could be expected to invest his or her damages prudently. Thus was born the concept of the 'prudent investor'.

10.4 This concept of 'the prudent investor' came from Lord Fraser of Tullybelton in *Cookson v Knowles*.[7] He put it thus:

> 'The proper measure of the award . . . is a sum which, prudently invested, would provide her with an annual equity in amount to the support that she has probably lost through the death of her husband, during the period that she would probably have been supported by him.'[8]

However, the exercise was and is a notional one as is apparent from a later passage in the judgment:

> 'I have referred to the "assumed" annuity because of course the widow may not choose to apply her award in the way I have mentioned; it is for her to decide and she may invest it so as to make a profit or she may squander it but the Defendant's liability should be calculated on the basis of an assumed annuity.'[9]

10.5 In assessing the damages to be awarded in personal injury litigation no account is taken of inflation. This was, formerly, on the basis that in times of high inflation the rate of interest that can be earned by prudent investment in fixed interest securities tends to be high as investors seek to protect their capital and also to obtain a positive rate of interest (after having allowed for the rate of inflation).[10] Today it is because the claimant is assumed to invest in Index Linked Government Stock (ILGS), which guarantees a fixed rate of return over and above inflation.

10.6 In September 1994 the Law Commission[11] recommended that a practice of discounting for the accelerated receipt of payment by reference to returns on

---

[5] *Wells v Wells, Thomas v Brighton Health Authority, Page v Sheerness Steel plc* (1998) 3 WLR 329.
[6] (1997) PIQR Q1.
[7] (1979) AC 556.
[8] P 576G.
[9] P 577D.
[10] See Lord Fraser of Tullybelton in *Cookson v Knowles* at p 577A–B and Lord Diplock in *Mallett v McMonagle* (1970) AC 166 at p 176C–D.
[11] Law Com No 224.

ILGS should be adopted. Its reasoning was that ILGS constituted 'the best evidence of the real return on any investment where the risk element is minimal, because they take account of inflation, rather than attempt to predict it as conventional investments do'. The Commission recommended that there should be legislative provision requiring courts when determining the return to be expected from investment of the sum awarded for damages for personal injuries to take account of the net return on ILGS. The Commission also recommended that the ILGS rate should be used unless the parties, by evidence, demonstrated that some other rate of return was more appropriate in any individual case.

10.7 On 23 March 1995 the Lord Chancellor's Department welcomed the report and said that it was the government's intention to implement the Law Commission's recommendations. This led to s 10 of the Civil Evidence Act 1995 which rendered the actuarial tables admissible in evidence:

Admissibility and proof of Ogden Tables

(1) The actuarial tables (together with explanatory notes) for use in personal injury and fatal accident cases issued from time to time by the Government Actuaries Department are admissible in evidence for the purpose of assessing, in an action for personal injury, the sum to be awarded as general damages for future pecuniary loss.
(2) They may be provided by the production of a copy published by Her Majesty's Stationery Office.
(3) For the purposes of this section –
   (a) 'Personal injury' includes any disease and any impairment of a person's physical or mental condition; and
   (b) 'Action for personal injury' includes an action brought by virtue of the Law Reform (Miscellaneous Provisions) Act 1934 or the Fatal Accidents Act 1976.'

10.8 Section 1 of the Damages Act 1996 provides:

(1) In determining the return to be expected from the investments of a sum awarded as damages for future pecuniary loss in an action for personal injury the Court shall, subject to and in accordance with rules of Court made for the purposes of this section, take into account such rate of return (if any) as may from time to time be prescribed by an order made by the Lord Chancellor.
(2) Sub-section (1) above shall not however prevent the Court taking a different rate of return into account if any party to the proceedings shows that it is more appropriate in the case in question.
(3) An order under sub-section (1) above may prescribe different rates of return for different classes of case.
(4) Before making an order under sub-section (1) above the Lord Chancellor shall consult the Government Actuary and the treasury; and any order under that sub-section shall be made by statutory instrument subject to annulment in pursuance of a resolution of either House of Parliament ...

10.9 On 25 June 2001, the Damages (Personal Injury) Order 2001 was finally made, pursuant to s 1 of the Damages Act 1996. Through it, the Lord Chancellor set the discount rate at 2.5%, based upon the average gross redemption yield based upon ILGS for 3 years up until 8 June 2001. The rate was to apply to all cases, emphasising the importance of certainty and the avoidance of complexity. The courts retain under s 1(2) of the Damages Act 1996 the power to adopt a different rate in cases with exceptional circumstances, sufficient to justify a departure from the norm.

10.10 Although at the time of writing, ILGS give a rate of return of around 1.5%, the rate remains set at 2.5% for the time being. It is, of course, open to the Lord Chancellor to review the rate at any time. Attempts have been made to persuade the Courts to apply a different rate. All have been rebuffed. In *Warriner v Warriner* [2002] EWCA Civ 81 Dyson LJ said at para 33:

> 'We are told that this is the first time that this court has had to consider the Act, and that guidance is needed as to the meaning of "more appropriate in the case in question" in section 1(2). The phrase "more appropriate", if considered in isolation, is open-textured. It prompts the question: by what criteria is the court to judge whether a different rate of return is more appropriate in the case in question? But the phrase must be interpreted in its proper context, which is that the Lord Chancellor has prescribed a rate pursuant to section 1(1) and has given very detailed reasons explaining what factors he took into account in arriving at the rate that he has prescribed. I would hold that in deciding whether a different rate is more appropriate in the case in question, the court must have regard to those reasons. If the case in question falls into a category that the Lord Chancellor did not take into account and/or there are special features of the case which (a) are material to the choice of rate of return and (b) are shown from an examination of the Lord Chancellor's reasons not to have been taken into account, then a different rate of return may be 'more appropriate'.'

The Court of Appeal in *Cooke v United Bristol Health Care*[12] was faced with an attempt to use revised multiplicands with stepped increases over time to reflect the faster rise in care costs in comparison with RPI. The court rejected the approach. Laws LJ at para 30 said:

> 'Once it is accepted that the discount rate is intended in any given personal injury case to be the *only* factor (in the equation ultimately yielding the claimant's lump sum payment) to allow for any future inflation relevant to the case, then the multiplicand cannot be taken as allowing for the same thing, or any part of it, without usurping the basis on which the multiplier has been fixed. And it must be accepted that the discount rate was so intended: by the House in *Wells*, by Parliament in the Act of 1996, and by the Lord Chancellor in making his order under the Act. Mr Hogg's attempt to treat his calculation of the multiplicand as a 'separate issue' from the discount rate, and counsel's submissions supporting that position, are in the end nothing but smoke and mirrors. It follows that the substance of these appeals constitutes an illegitimate assault on the Lord Chancellor's discount rate, and on the efficacy of the 1996 Act itself.'[13]

---

[12] (2003) EWCA Civ 1370.
[13] However, differential rates for future care are common, particularly where the claimant has a

10.11 The multiplier for future losses is therefore to be found in the 2.5% column in the appropriate Table. The Sixth Edition of these Tables recommends in the Introductory Notes a number of significant adjustments to the basic multipliers.

USING THE TABLES

10.12 The Tables deal with five categories of loss:

(a) Tables 1 and 2: Losses for life (based on a normal life expectation).

(b) Tables 3–14: Loss of earnings to retirement age.

(c) Tables 15–26: Loss of pension.

(d) Table 27: One-off future losses (eg an operation that the claimant will undergo in 10 years' time, or a wheelchair that he will buy in 5 years).

(e) Table 28: Losses that will occur annually over a fixed period.

10.13 It is important to note that Tables 1–26 are based on Tables of Mortality: that is, they take into account the chances of a person dying at any particular age. Not all workers will live to retirement age. These tables are based on *average* mortality: they include smokers and non-smokers, the overweight and the underweight, and diabetics, epileptics, and hypertensives as well as those who have never had a day's illness in their life.

10.14 When calculating future loss of earnings, the Notes to the Tables recommend that the basic multiplier be adjusted to take into account certain contingencies; these are:

(a) whether the claimant was able-bodied or disabled at the time of the accident;

(b) whether the claimant was in or out of work at the time of the accident; and

(c) the claimant's level of education (essentially, degree-level, A-level, and low or no qualifications).

The Notes contain four tables (A to D) to enable the parties to adjust the multipliers appropriately:

---

substantial life expectancy and the likelihood of escalating care costs. An index different to RPI may be used: see: *Thompstone v Thameside & Glossop Acute services NHS Trust* [2006] EWHC 2904 (QB), albeit in the context of periodical payments, as opposed to a lump sum award.

- Table A applies to able-bodied men.
- Table B applies to disabled men.
- Table C applies to able-bodied women
- Table D applies to disabled women.

It must be borne in mind that this method is appropriate only where there are no special factors affecting the figures in any particular case. If, for example, the claimant suffers from a condition which would have made her give up work by the age of 50 in any event, Table 10 would not be appropriate. This was accepted in *Wells*:

> 'Mr Havers conceded there is room for a judicial discount when calculating the loss of future earnings, when contingencies may indeed affect the result.[14]
>
> I do not suggest that the Judge should be a slave to the tables. There may well be special factors in particular cases. But the tables should now be regarded as a starting point, rather than a check. A Judge should be slow to depart from the relevant actuarial multiplier on impressionistic grounds, or by reference to "a spread of multipliers in comparable cases" especially when the multipliers were fixed before actuarial tables were widely used.'

10.15 The House of Lords in *Wells* did, however, reject the common practice of capping the multipliers. Lord Lloyd said:

> 'The purpose of the award is to put the Plaintiff in the same position, financially, as if he had not been injured. The sums should be calculated as accurately as possible, making just allowance, where this is appropriate, for contingencies. But once the calculation is done, there is no justification for imposing an artificial cap on the multiplier. There is no room for a judicial scaling down.'[15]

10.16 Referring to the then common practice of imposing a 'judicial discount', Lord Lloyd went on to say:[16]

> 'There is no purpose in the Courts making as accurate a prediction as they can of the Plaintiff's future needs if the resulting sum is arbitrarily reduced for no better reason than the prediction might be wrong. A prediction remains a prediction. Contingencies should be taken into account where they work in one direction, but not where they cancel out. There is no more logic or justice in reducing the whole life multiplier by 15 or 20% on an agreed expectation of life than there would be in increasing it by the same amount.'

---

[14] Page 346.
[15] Page 332.
[16] Page 346.

CALCULATING LOSS OF EARNINGS

10.17 Let us take, for example, a 35-year-old male who left school with no qualifications. At the time of the accident he was in work earning £20,000 net pa, and was able-bodied. But for the accident, he would have retired at the age of 65. Select Table 9 ('Multipliers for loss of earnings to pension age 65 (males)'):

(a) In the 2.5% column we find the appropriate 'basic multiplier', which is 20.53.

(b) Table A gives a discount factor of 0.89 for able-bodied men who are in work.

(c) If the claimant will never work again, the multiplier to be applied to his continuing annual loss of earnings is therefore [20.53 x 0.89] or 18.27.

(d) His claim for loss of earnings is [18.27 x £20,000] = £365,400.

If the claimant is now disabled by the accident, but has a residual earning capacity of, say, £10,000, one calculates how much he is *now* expected to earn, and deducts it from what he *would* have earned but for the accident:

(a) Once again, Table 9 gives a 'basic multiplier' of 20.53.

(b) Because the claimant is now disabled, turn to Table B. If he is still out of work, the discount factor is now 0.20, and the multiplier becomes [20.53 x 0.20] = 4.10.

(c) He can now be expected to earn [4.10 x £10,000] = £41,000.

(d) His future loss of earnings is therefore [£365,400 – £41,000] = £324,400.

Using this approach, there is no need for a *Smith v Manchester Corpn* award, because the discount factor of 0.20 takes into account that he is disabled, and that his disability puts him at a disadvantage on the labour market.

If the claimant is disabled but has now returned to work, the Tables can be used to calculate the value of his disability on the labour market:

(a) Suppose that the same claimant was earning £20,000 a year before the accident, and that after an 18-month absence he has returned to work at the same salary.

(b) Table 9 gives a 'basic multiplier' of 20.53. If the claimant were able-bodied, he could be expected to earn [0.89 × 20.53 x £20,000] = £365,400.

(c) Because the claimant is now disabled, Table B adjusts the Table 9 figure to give the following likely future earnings: [0.39 × 20.53 x £20,000] = £160,134.

(d) His future loss of earnings is therefore [£365,400 – £160,134] = £196,266.

This is a significant increase on past *Smith v Manchester Corpon* awards. It is likely that considerable attention will be paid in the future to the nature of the claimant's disability: clearly, an injury that would disable a scaffolder might have no effect at all on a solicitor's earning capacity. The Tables quote the 2005 Labour Force Survey puts the issue helpfully:

> 'Do you have any health problems or disabilities that you expect will last more than a year? . . . Does this health problem affect the KIND of paid work that you do... or the AMOUNT of paid work that you might do?'

10.18 Variations:

(a) Where the claimant will only be out of work for a few years, use Table 28 ('Multipliers for pecuniary loss for term certain'). Whatever the claimant's age, suppose that he will be out of work for a further 5 years. Table 28 gives a figure of 4.7. (This figure should be reduced slightly for mortality and for contingencies other than mortality.)

(b) Where the claimant will retire slightly earlier or later than expected. In the case of the illustration above, suppose that the scaffolder would retire at the age of 67. Treat him as a 32-year-old (ie deduct 2 from his present age) and use Table 9.

LIFETIME LOSSES

10.19 As we said in para 13 above, the Tables take account only of average mortality. Where there is nothing known about a claimant's life expectation, the courts will tend to assume that it is normal. It is therefore important for both parties to check the claimant's life expectation in any case where there is a significant claim for future losses.

10.20 Where the loss or expenditure will continue for the entire lifetime of the claimant (eg care costs), Table 1 or 2 should be used in the absence of such evidence. For a 34-year-old woman, Table 2 ('Multipliers for pecuniary loss for life (females)') gives a multiplier at 2.5% of 28.80.

10.21 Even where the claimant's life expectation is normal, it may not be appropriate to take the 'whole life' multiplier. A claimant who services his own car, or does all the gardening, may not be physically capable of doing this into extreme old age. There is no one way of calculating such losses. Some litigants will use Ogden Tables 13 and 14 (which are for losses to age 75); others discount the 'whole life' figures in Tables 1 and 2.

10.22 Variations:

(a) Suppose that the claimant suffered from epilepsy before the accident, and the parties' experts agree that this would have shortened her life by 5 years in any event. In such a case, treat the claimant as 5 years older: the lifetime multiplier for a 39-year-old woman is 27.25.

(b) Sometime the claimant's life will have been more drastically shortened. In the case of a child with cerebral palsy with, say, a life expectation of another 20 years, Table 28 gives a multiplier of 15.78 for a 20-year period.

Loss of pension

10.23 The loss of pension calculation is dealt with elsewhere in this book. However, the multipliers to be selected for pension loss are set out at Tables 15 to 26 of the Ogden Tables. The same principles apply as in relation to the calculation of future loss and expenditure. The Tables give guidance to the calculation of multipliers were the claimant retires at an age not shown in any of the Tables – eg 58, or 67, or 71.

One-off future losses

10.24 If in the future the claimant will have a single large item of future expense – for example, a hip replacement, or the purchase of a wheelchair – use Table 27. For example:

> The Claimant is aged 25. She will need a hip replacement in 10 years' time, and this replacement will need revision 20 years later. Both operations will cost £8,000. Table 27 gives a discount factor of 0.7812 for losses that will occur in 10 years, and a factor of 0.4767 for losses in 30 years. The claim is therefore (0.7812 × £8,000) + (0.4767 × £8,000) = £10,064.

In 'Facts & Figures' Table A3 gives multipliers to enable one to calculate *eg* the cumulative cost of:

- a wheelchair every five years to the end of the claimant's life;

- wheelchair batteries that will need replacing every two years; or

- an adjustable bed that will need replacing every 15 years.

10.25 Sometimes, a claim is calculated on the basis of the annual cost of purchasing an item. Suppose, for example, that a wheelchair costing £3,000 will have to be replaced every 6 years, and the claimant is expected to live for another 20 years:[17] [£3,000 ÷ 6] = £500, so there is a claim for £500 a year. The appropriate multiplier for a 20-year period is 15.78,[18] so the claim is [15.78 × £500] = £7,890. The parties should check this against the following approach:

- The first wheelchair is to be bought immediately, at £3,000.

- The second wheelchair is to be bought in year 6, at [0.8623 × £3,000] = £2,587.

- The third wheelchair is to be bought in year 12, at [0.7436 × £3,000] = £2,231.

- The fourth wheelchair is to be bought in year 18, at [0.6412 × £3,000] = £1,924.

- Using this approach, the total cost is [£3,000 + £2,587 + £2,231 + £1,924] = £9,742.

The latter approach is considerably more accurate, but may be too cumbersome for smaller items. There is, however a table (Table A3 in the 2006 edition of 'Facts and Figures') which helps to calculate regularly-recurring expenses.

Multipliers for fixed periods

10.26 Where there is a known period of loss – e g the claimant's life expectation is reduced to 10 years, or the claimant will need physiotherapy for a further 5 years, Table 28 should be used.

COMBINING THE TABLES

10.27 Suppose, for example, the claimant is 50 years old. He will have to retire at 60 because of his injuries, but would otherwise have worked to the age of 65. In such a case, find the appropriate multiplier for loss of earnings for a 60-year-old (Table 9), and discount it by 10 years using Table 27. Example:

> The multiplier for loss of earnings for a 60-year old who would have worked to the age of 65 is (say) 4.58. Because the claimant will not incur this loss for another 10 years, the figure must be multiplied by 0.7812. [0.7812 × 4.58] = 3.58.

Fatal accident cases and the multiplier

10.28 There is an important difference between personal injury claims where the claimant is alive, and those where the claimant is dead:

---

[17] The claimant's life expectation can either be established by the doctors, or (for normal life expectation) it can be found in 'Facts and Figures'.
[18] Table 28.

(a) Where the claimant is alive, there is a claim for past losses, and then there is a claim for future losses based on the claimant's age at the date of trial.

(b) In a claim under the Fatal Accidents Act 1976, the multiplier is calculated as at the date of death. This multiplier will then usually be divided into two parts: losses to the date of trial, and future losses. The multiplier for losses to the date of trial will be the actual number of years that have passed since the death. Future losses will be the residue of the multiplier. Say, for example, the deceased died 5 years ago, and the multiplier for the dependency claim is 17.46. The multiplier for future losses will be 12.46.

10.29 This difference is based on the House of Lords majority decision in *Cookson v Knowles*,[19] in which Lord Diplock stated the general principle thus:

> '... as a general rule in fatal accident cases the damages should be assessed in two parts, the first and less speculative component being an estimate of the loss sustained up to the date of trial, and the second component an estimate of the loss to be sustained thereafter[20] ...'

10.30 Lord Fraser said that damages in a fatal accident claim ought to be assessed as at the date of death as opposed to the date of trial. However, in doing so he believed he was achieving the same objective as that achieved in a personal injury case:

> 'In strict theory I think there is no doubt that they should be assessed as at the date of death just as in theory they are assessed at the date of injury in a personal injury case.'[21]

He noted that in the appeal before the House the total multiplier awarded was 11. The Court of Appeal had deducted 2.5 from that in respect of the 2.5 years which had passed from the date of death to the date of trial. The Court of Appeal used the resulting figure of 8.5 as a multiplier for damages after the trial (future loss). Lord Fraser recognised that this was a departure from the conventional method:

> 'In doing so they departed from the method that would have been appropriate in a personal injury case and counsel for the appellant criticised the departure as being unfair to the appellant... [But nevertheless] in a fatal accident case the multiplier must be selected once and for all as at the date of death, because everything that might have happened to the deceased after that date remains uncertain.'[22]

10.31 *Cookson* has been criticised by the Law Commission and the Ogden Committee. The Commission felt that the *Cookson* approach had the result that claimants were under compensated, particularly where there was a significant gap between death and trial. This was shown particularly clearly in *Corbett v*

---

[19] (1979) AC 556.
[20] Page 569G.
[21] Page 574.
[22] Page 576D.

Barking Health Authority.[23] In that case the claimant sought damages arising from the loss of his mother at the time of his birth. By the date of trial he was 11 years and 6 months old. The trial judge awarded him a total overall multiplier of 12, assessed as at the date of his mother's death. This meant that for the remaining 6½ years of his dependency he had multiplier of only 0.50 years, with the balance being special damage. Purchase LJ said:

> 'It was common ground that either 12 or 13 would have been the appropriate multiplier to cover 18 years dependency in "normal standard circumstances". Not to make a meaningful adjustment because during 11½ of the 18 years of dependency upon which the discounts would normally be applied but which no longer contain uncertainties would be illogical.'[24]

He recognised that the position which had arisen was 'bizarre' because the future dependency of a normal healthy young man (with 6.50 years of future dependency) was being discounted to 6 months, and he recognised that the trial Judge had fixed a multiplier 'which was demonstrably too low'. Nevertheless, he felt bound by the authorities then available to reject the submission that the multiplier should be calculated from the date of trial:

> 'In my judgment, in a case such as the present, the correct approach must be to calculate the multiplier from the date of death but in so doing account must be taken of the removal of many of the "uncertainties" surrounding the provision and receipt of the dependency during the period involved. Accordingly, the discount from the 18 year period to take into account those uncertainties will itself be reduced.'[25]

10.32 The Court of Appeal increased the multiplier to 15. This is an unsatisfactory approach, and is firmly rooted in the facts of the particular case. It does not address the wider question of whether *Cookson* disadvantages claimants in Fatal Accidents Act cases.

10.33 *Cookson* remains binding authority despite widespread criticism. In *White v ESAB Group (UK) Limited*,[26] Nelson J felt bound to apply the House of Lords' approach when assessing future dependency, and took the multiplier as at the date of death:[27]

> 'There is in my judgment a clear distinction to be drawn between guidelines as to discretion or changing economic circumstances and decisions in principle. I am satisfied...that the "date of death calculation" rule is a rule of principle or law, rather than a guideline. This Court is therefore bound by that rule ...
>
> When Lord Lloyd said that the Ogden tables should now be regarded as a starting point rather than a check and that a judge should be slow to depart from the

---

[23] [1991] 2 QB 408.
[24] Page 427E.
[25] Page 428B–C.
[26] (2002) PIQR Q76.
[27] The claimant was given leave to appeal, but the claim was compromised.

relevant actuarial multiplier ... he was dealing ... with the general approach ... in personal injury cases. As the decisions in Cookson and Graham emphasized the difference between the calculation of multipliers in personal injury and fatal cases, it cannot be assumed that the House of Lords in Wells intended this part of their judgment to apply to Fatal Accidents Act claims as well as Personal Injury claims.'

10.34 The Court of Appeal in *ATH v MS*[28] approved this approach. It is likely that the courts will continue to apply *Cookson* unless and until the House of Lords overturns its own decision.

THE ALTERNATIVE APPROACH

10.35 The multiplier/multiplicand approach described above should be adopted where the court is satisfied, on the balance of probabilities, that the claimant will suffer a quantifiable for an ascertainable period of time. In such a case, a 'lump sum' approach is inappropriate (*Cornell v Green*[29]). This approach is not always appropriate – eg where it is uncertain what the claimant would have done had the accident not occurred, or where the claimant's future earning capacity is unclear.

10.36 In cases where there is some uncertainty, but where there is confidence that a loss will be suffered for a significant period of time at some stage, the appropriate solution is to use the multiplier and multiplicand approach. If it is clear that the individual's working life will be shorter than the norm, the court can reduce the multiplier appropriately. In cases where there are numerous uncertainties, the multiplier/multiplicand approach may be inappropriate and the court may be persuaded to award a single lump sum instead in respect of future or even past loss.

10.37 An example of this was *Blamire v South Cumbria HA*,[30] in which Steyn LJ considered that:

> '... the judge took the view that the conventional measure was inappropriate. He had ample material to take that view. First, there was uncertainty as to what the Plaintiff would have earned over the course of her working life if she had not been injured ... The second aspect was the uncertainty as to the likely future pattern of her earnings, and here the uncertainties were very great. Bearing in mind that the burden rested throughout on the Plaintiff, it is in my judgment clear that on the materials before him, the judge was entitled to conclude that the multiplier/multiplicand measure was not the correct one to adopt in this case ... He had in mind that there was no perfect arithmetical way of calculating compensation in such a case. Inevitably one is driven to a broad brush approach. The law is concerned with practical affairs and as Lord Reid said in *British Transport*

---

[28] (2002) EWCA Civ 792.
[29] [1998] CLY 1485.
[30] (1993) PIQR Q1.

Commission v Gourley (1956) A.C. 165 at page 212, very often one is driven to making a very rough estimate of the damages.'[31]

10.38 This approach was reaffirmed in *Tait v Pearson*.[32] More recently, in *Willemse v Hesp*,[33] the claimant was left with modest brain damage and a severe psychological reaction. The Court of Appeal found that the judge at first instance had erred in law by adopting a fixed multiplier approach. In the light of the claimant's uncertain intentions regarding his future employment, it was considered that a 'lump sum' assessment was appropriate. This approach does involve guesswork and is a departure from the court's usual 'evidence driven' approach.

10.39 The broad brush approach advocated in cases such as *Blamire* is still the exception rather than the rule. In *Gammell v Wilson*[34] (a 'lost years' claim), Lord Scarman said:

> 'If sufficient facts are established to enable the court to avoid the fancies of speculation, even though not enabling it to reach mathematical certainty, the court must make the best estimate it can. In civil litigation it is the balance of probabilities which matters . . .'

10.40 In *Fairchild v Glenhaven Funeral Services Ltd & Ors*,[35] Lord Hoffmann cautioned against the 'judicial instinct' approach:

> 'Then there is the role of common sense. Of course the causal requirements for liability are normally framed in accordance with common sense. But there is sometimes a tendency to appeal to common sense in order to avoid having to explain one's reasons. It suggests that causal requirements are a matter of incommunicable judicial instinct. I do not think that this is right. It should be possible to give reasons why one form of causal relationship will do in one situation but not in another.'[36]

10.41 Lord Lloyd in *Wells v Wells* urged caution before departing from the actuarial approach to future loss:

> 'A judge should be slow to depart from the relevant actuarial multiplier on impressionistic grounds, or by reference to "a spread of multipliers in comparable cases.'

It follows that a very careful assessment needs to be made in any case where the claimant's future employment prospects are uncertain, as to whether the standard multiplier/multiplicand approach, is appropriate. If there is evidence

---

[31] (1993) PIQR Q1, at Q5–6.
[32] (1996) PIQR Q92.
[33] (2003) EWCA Civ 994.
[34] (1982) AC 27 at 78.
[35] (2002) 3 WLR 89, (2002) 3 All ER 305.
[36] Para 53.

by which future contingencies can be assessed, the multiplier/multiplicand method remains the appropriate way of quantifying future loss.

Chapter 11

LOSS OF EARNINGS

11.1 Where, as a result of personal injury, a person suffers a loss of earnings, the claimant is entitled to recover any net loss of earnings from the tortfeasor. It is one of the more straightforward applications of the fundamental measure of tortious damages that compensation should put the claimant, as far as possible, back into the position as if the wrongdoing had not occurred.[1]

11.2 Somewhat surprisingly, as recently as 1967 it was thought wrong to make itemised awards.[2] However, the modern approach is for separate heads of claim (confirmed by the House of Lords in *Lim*,[3] and now part of the Civil Procedure Rules 1998 (CPR), which require service of a schedule of past and future loss of earnings[4]).

11.3 The period of unemployment for which compensation is sought must be supported by the medical evidence (both the medico-legal evidence obtained for the purpose of the claim and/or the treating doctors, and including the General Practitioner who may have measured the claimant's capacity to work by issuing sick-notes). It is highly unusual (but not unheard of[5]) for the court to accept a claimant's own evidence of his ability to work, except for modest claims.

THE STRAIGHTFORWARD CLAIM

11.4 In many cases, the calculation is straightforward. Where a claimant has been in steady employment prior to the accident, he is entitled to recover the net earnings[6] he would have received had the accident not occurred. His losses are assessed at the date of trial.

11.5 The claimant is entitled to recover the net earnings he would have received, which includes overtime, pay-rises, promotions and perks. Evidence is required to establish these benefits, although in most cases the court will be prepared to rely on the Average Earnings Index to establish pay rises in line with inflation.

---

1 *Livingstone v Rawyards Coal Co* [1880] 5 App Cas 25.
2 *Watson v Powles* [1968] 1 QB 596.
3 *Lim v Camden Health Authority* [1980] AC 174.
4 CPR, r 16.4.2.
5 *McMylor v Firth Rixson plc* [2002] EWCA Civ 1863.
6 *British Transport Commission v Gourley* [1956] AC 185.

11.6 Where raised by defendants, the claimant should also give credit for the 'cost of earning'. This is usually raised where a parent requires childcare if he or she is going to work: the defendant will seek against the loss of earnings for the cost of that childcare. A defendant is also entitled to ask for credit for the cost of travel to and from work (although examples are rare).

11.7 The defendant is also entitled to credit where the claimant has saved living expenses through his free maintenance in a public institution[7] can be set off against his claim for loss of earnings. Such savings are not usually great: a claimant will still be liable for his rent, mortgage and council tax while he is in hospital, though there will be a saving on such items as food, heating etc.

EVIDENCE

11.8 The following evidence is commonly obtained to support a claim for loss of earnings:

(a) A reasonable spread of pre-accident pay-records. Three months is typical, but a wider spread may be necessary if the claimant's income fluctuates, or if the period of unemployment covers a period where the claimant was likely to have received pay-rises or promotions.

(b) Where the claimant is self-employed, copies of the accounts, Inland Revenue returns and tax bills should be obtained. The claimant who seeks to claim a higher rate of pay than he was declaring in his accounts is unlikely to succeed, and will certainly not succeed unless he makes a clean breast of it to the Revenue.

(c) In the absence of pay-records, a letter from the employer, or copies of bank statements to prove the payments, will usually suffice.

(d) Evidence from the employer of any pay-rises or bonuses to which the claimant would have become entitled.

(e) In some situations, it is very helpful to have evidence of co-workers' incomes to act as comparators. Examples of situations where this evidence is helpful include work where there is a high level of overtime or a particularly high level of pay in a specialised field.[8] It is important to choose realistic comparators.

(f) In many cases, the employer continues to pay the employee, but on the basis that the injured employee agrees to reclaim such payments from the tortfeasor.[9] If payments do not carry this obligation, the claimant is not

---

[7] Administration of Justice Act 1982, s 5: this credit applies only to claims for loss of earnings.
[8] See *George v Stagecoach* [2003] EWCH 2042 per Mackay J.
[9] *Davies v Inman* [1999] PIQR Q26.

entitled to claim loss of earnings as he has suffered no loss: any compensation would represent double recovery.[10]

(g) Evidence from the employer of possible promotions or career developments (see below in relation to the loss of the chance of employment).

(h) In the absence of other evidence about pay-rises, the claimant can rely on the Average Earnings Index, which can be found (with instructions for use) in the annual publication 'Facts & Figures'.

(i) Parties are also entitled to rely on the New Earnings Survey (also in 'Facts & Figures') which gives the rates of pay for a wide range of occupations.

11.9 The absence of such evidence is not catastrophic, but will, inevitably, lead to a discount. In *Eden v West & Co*,[11] the Court of Appeal allowed the claimant's appeal from an order refusing compensation on the basis of the inadequate evidence, but limited the claimed sum of £11,500 (which represented a year's income) as follows:

> 'In my judgment, this claim can only be approached on a global basis. I would award the sum of £5,000 for the period of six months during which the medical evidence shows that the appellant was unfit for work. I have regard to all of the uncertainties which would arise thereafter. However, I would add to that sum, to cover the period of recuperation contemplated by the doctors in the second six months, the sum of £1,000.'

11.10 The disadvantage of inviting the court to take a robust approach to assessing losses in the absence of evidence is that there is a risk that any shortfall may be made up through professional negligence proceedings for under-settlement.

EXPERT EVIDENCE

11.11 CPR Part 35 permits the use of experts if 'reasonably required to resolve the proceedings'. The use of employment consultants to assess potential earnings and residual earning capacity has reduced in recent years.

11.12 In general, the courts seem reluctant to allow expert evidence in relation to loss of earnings, and particularly unwilling to allow both parties to obtain their own evidence, as opposed to joint instruction. Easy access to the New Earnings Survey, which provides reliable information on the range of incomes of a wide range of jobs, supplemented by newspaper advertisement of available work, and the actual rates of pay, renders some reports redundant. This is

---

[10] *Cunningham v Harrison* [1973] QB 942.
[11] [2002] EWCA Civ 991, [2003] PIQR Q2.

particularly the case where the claimant has been in regular, steady employment with a predictable pre-accident earning capability.

11.13 However, an expert may be of real assistance where the claimant:

(a) is a child, or in the course of education, training or retraining;

(b) is young, with likely career changes and or career development;

(c) is a professional, a high flyer, or high earner;

(d) had a pre-accident disability;

(e) in the context of rehabilitation: for example, specialist charitable groups sometimes have invaluable data on the efforts that can be made to help the disabled to get back to work – the Royal National Institute for the Blind and Action for Blind are two such organisations.

11.14 It is of obvious importance to ensure that the expert has all of the expert evidence, as well as a full employment record, and medical history. Witness statements in relation to plans and projects are of value. In the case of a child, school records should be sought.

11.15 Where the claimant is self-employed, a partner in a business or a company director, it may be necessary to instruct a forensic accountant to help predict future growth of business, and lost profits. It is also worth remembering that certain business expenses may include benefits to the self-employed – an allowance for the use of home as office, telephone bills and car and entertainment expenses may mean the claimant's loss is greater than the profits figures shown in the accounts.

11.16 The other area of expert evidence which is of real benefit is from statisticians.[12] As will be seen below; the use of the Retail Price Index to calculate loss of earnings produces a steady erosion of the value of the claimant's compensation, as wage-inflation is higher than price inflation (Average Earnings Index v Retail Price Index).

11.17 Similarly, research has established that the courts consistently undervalue the employment consequences of residual disability and displacement caused by disability, with the result that claimants are under-compensated. This issue is to be addressed in the 2007 edition of the Ogden Tables. The courts have proved reluctant to admit evidence of this research, but the introduction to the Tables is admissible as evidence by virtue of the Civil Evidence Act 1995.[13]

---

[12] *Touchstone.*

[13] Section 1(1). The actuarial tables (together with explanatory notes) for use in personal injury and fatal accident cases issued from time to time by the Government Actuary's Department are admissible in evidence for the purpose of assessing, in an action for personal injury, the sum to be awarded as general damages for future pecuniary loss.

ANCILLARY BENEFITS

11.18 In addition to the paid salary, many jobs include other benefits, perks or free or subsidised benefits or services which form part of the total employment package. These can include:

(a) a company car, plus petrol, servicing and insurance;

(b) free or subsidised accommodation, including payment of the household utilities bills (the police and armed forces often benefit from this);

(c) in-store discounts for shop workers;

(d) health insurance (often extending to the family);

(e) subsidised meals (including luncheon vouchers);

(f) free goods or services;

(g) share options;

(h) subsidised travel (or loans to buy season tickets) – though if the travel was only to and from work, there will be no loss if the claimant is no longer working.

11.19 The value of these benefits to members of the Armed Forces, and to anyone who has the benefit of a company car.

SELF-EMPLOYMENT

11.20 Where the claimant is self-employed, the documents required to support the claim include:

(a) accounts;

(b) Inland Revenue returns;

(c) work sheets;

(d) order books;

(e) receipts; and

(f) invoices.

11.21 Although certain business expenses may include benefits to the self-employed, it is difficult for a claimant to argue that he had personally benefited from expenses that ought to be 'wholly, exclusively and necessarily' incurred to enable him to earn his living.

PARTNERSHIP/DIRECTORS

11.22 In general, where the claimant is a member of a partnership, his loss of earnings is limited to the share of the profits (calculated by looking at the accounts, tax returns and any partnership agreement).

11.23 If the partnership includes 'silent partners' (most typically, a spouse), the court will look at the reality of the situation. If the claimant was the only person contributing to the business, and there was, for example, a non-working/contributing spouse as a nominal partner, the 'actual' or 'real' loss is 100% of the business profits. The only deduction that would be appropriate would be if the spouse made any contribution to the profitability of the business (see *Ward v Newalls Insulation Company*[14]).

11.24 This does not apply to *all* husband and wife partnerships: if both are contributing partners, the injured claimant's losses are limited to the extent of his interest (see *Kent v British Railways Board*[15]).

11.25 If the claimant is a director, the 'earnings' may be suppressed to avoid higher rates of tax, but supplemented by interest rates on director's loans, dividends on share-holdings and so on. These should be disclosed in company returns and Inland Revenue forms, and not only on a P60.

FUTURE LOSSES

11.26 In straightforward cases the calculation of future earnings for an employee is simply a continuation of the approach adopted in respect of past losses. It has long been recognised that this is an imprecise exercise. In *Lim*, Lord Scarman observed:

> '... there is really only one certainty: the future will prove the award to be either too high or too low ... Knowledge of the future being denied to mankind, so much of the award as is to be attributed to future loss and suffering, in many cases the major part of the award, will almost certainly be wrong.'

11.27 In the past, the court has calculated a lump sum based on a multiplier and multiplicand. The future is likely to see an increasing use of periodical payments (introduced in April 2005), although it is too early to say to what extent this will be so.

---

[14] [1998] PIQR Q41.
[15] [1995] PIQR Q42.

PERIODICAL PAYMENTS

11.28 In his speech in *Wells*, Lord Steyn described the lump sum system as a 'major structural flaw'. He went on:

> '... the lump sum system causes acute problems in cases of serious injuries with consequences enduring after the assessment of damages. In such cases the judge must often resort to guesswork about the future ... The solution is relatively straightforward. The court ought to be given the power of its own motion to make an award for periodic payments rather than a lump sum in appropriate cases.'[16]

11.29 The solution proposed by Lord Steyn is now in place. The Department of Constitutional Affairs define the advantages of Periodical Payments as follows:

> 'Periodical payments generally have a number of potential advantages over lump sums:
>
> The lump sum system is based on predictions about the future life expectancy of a claimant which are inevitably uncertain and almost always lead to over-compensation or under-compensation. In contrast, periodical payments ensure that people receive appropriate compensation for as long as it is needed.
>
> Periodical payments should also avoid the need for argument about life expectancy during the litigation. This is often unpleasant and stressful for the claimant. It will not be necessary to assess life expectancy to decide the value of periodical payments that will meet the claimant's future needs (an actuarial judgment on life expectancy will still be relevant to the issue of how payments are to be funded by the defendant; but this should not form part of the litigation or concern the claimant).
>
> There will be greater security for claimants, who will be able to plan for the future without the anxiety of the award running out if they live longer than expected.
>
> Claimants will not have to bear the risks associated with investing and managing a lump sum award. These risks will fall on defendants, who are generally far better able to bear them.
>
> This should remove the need for claimants to obtain detailed financial advice on the investment and management of the award, but equally the system will provide greater flexibility for defendants to choose how to fund the payments, provided the needs of the claimant as ordered or agreed are met.'

11.30 The mechanism for calculating the periodical payment is now similar to calculating the multiplicand. Instead of the traditional 'top-down' approach used for structured settlements, requiring uncertain assumptions about life expectancy and investment, it is intended that where a periodical payments

---

[16] [1998] 3 WLR 329 at 351.

order is made or agreed, a 'bottom-up' approach will be adopted, which focuses instead on calculating claimant's continuing annual loss of earnings.

11.31 Under the 'bottom-up' approach, the various heads of damages (in particular, loss of earnings and costs of care, but, with the consent of the parties, other heads of damage) are considered to estimate the annual needs of the claimant. The order for periodical payments then simply provides for the claimant to be paid the appropriate amounts for the duration of his or her need (usually life), escalating in line with the Retail Price Index (RPI) unless the court orders otherwise. This avoids speculative estimates or disputes about life expectancy, as payments will be based on the claimant's annual needs and will be payable for as long as necessary.

11.32 The major disadvantage is whether the courts fix the growth of periodical payments to RPI or use some other index. The courts have recognized in a series of judgments that to link to RPI leads to a steady shortfall in the value of the claim[17]. The solution has been found in *Thompstone* in which the court accepted that care costs should be linked to a index known as ASHE 6115, which was held to most closely reflect the changes in the earnings of carers employed by the Claimant in that case.

THE MULTIPLICAND

11.33 The multiplicand is the claimant's net annual loss of earnings assessed at the date of trial. In the case of a catastrophically injured claimant with no residual earning capacity, the calculation is relatively straightforward. The claimant's net annual loss of earnings is taken as at the date of trial and multiplied by the appropriate multiplier, reflecting the claimant's future working life.

11.34 It is unusual for future losses to include significant changes in the level of the multiplicand (see 'Loss of chance' below), though where the court is satisfied that the claimant's income would have risen in real terms it may either use two or more multiplicands or (more usually) set a 'career average' that is higher than what the claimant would be earning at the date of trial: see, for example, *Cassell v Riverside Health Authority*.[18]

11.35 There is good evidence[19] that the multiplicand should be increased to reflect the true rate of growth in income from:

---

[17] *Thompstone v Tameside & Glossop NHS Trust* 2006 EWHC 2904: *Flora v Wakom (Heathrow)* 2006 EWCA Civ 1103 and *A v B Hospital NHS Trust*.
[18] [1992] PIQR Q168.
[19] 'Court awards of damages for loss of future earnings: An empirical study and an alternative method calculation' 2002 Journal of Law and Society, Lewis et al; 'Methods for calculating damages for loss of future earnings' 2002 Journal of Personal Injury Litigation 151–165.

(a) Age-related earnings growth: People tend to earn more as they gain experience and qualifications. Evidence in support of this is found in the Labour Force Surveys, and is routinely put before the courts in the United States.

(b) Economy-related growth, which is probably in the region of 1–2% per annum.

The failure to reflect these two factors causes systematic and significant under-compensation for claimants.

11.36 Further problems arise in relation to the claimant with a residual earning capacity. Evidence shows that the courts are over-optimistic in relation to the residual earnings, and fail to allow for the depressing effect of injury upon earnings. Both disability and displacement increase the risk of non-employment,[20] and the courts fail to reflect the true employment disadvantage arising from injury (particularly where a lump sum is awarded for handicap on the labour market). The 6th edition of the Ogden Tables was published in May 2007, and incorporates research that establishes that the most important factors influencing future loss of earnings are:

(a) whether the claimant is able-bodied or disabled;

(b) whether the claimant is presently in work; and

(c) the claimant's educational qualifications.

11.37 By way of example, a 35-year-old male claimant who has been disabled by his accident, and who is currently out of work, is likely to have a multiplier that is between a quarter and a third that of an uninjured man with similar qualifications who is in work. (See 'The multiplier' below.)

THE MULTIPLIER

11.38 Unless an order is made for periodical payments or a structured settlement, damages are paid in the form of a single lump sum payment. If the period of loss is taken to be 10 years, and the annual loss £10,000, the court does not award the mathematical loss of £100,000. The court knows there will be inflation (which will decrease the real value of the £100,000), but assumes that the claimant will invest the damages (which will increase its value in real terms). These two contingencies, the effect of accelerated payment, and the effect of inflation, have opposing influences on how the multiplier is calculated.

---

[20] Walker and Thompson 1996; Rohm 1991.

'Inflation and acceleration are built into the multiplier, and the mechanism for doing that requires that a rate of interest be arrived at as the notional return to be earned on the lump sum over the period in question. This rate of interest is what is known as the discount rate.'[21]

11.39 The problem was to establish the annual rate of return a claimant could expect *over and above the rate of inflation*. For many years, the courts adopted a discount rate of 4.5%, despite actuarial evidence that this was an inappropriate rate. In a long line of cases, from *Watson v Powles*[22] to *Auty v National Coal Board*,[23] the courts rejected the use of actuarial evidence, other than as a form of cross-check.

11.40 The situation was transformed by the working party chaired by Sir Michael Ogden, producing 'Actuarial Tables with explanatory notes for use in Personal Injury and Fatal Accident Act cases':[24]

'The tables should now be regarded as the starting point, rather than a check ... A judge should be slow to depart from the relevant actuarial multiplier on impressionistic grounds.'[25]

11.41 In 2001 the Lord Chancellor fixed the discount rate at 2.5%, based on the return on index-linked government stocks (ILGS) – a stock designed to give a fixed yield *over and above the rate of inflation*. There is clear evidence that this discount is now too high: the current real rate of return on ILGS is nearer 1.8%. The courts have proved reluctant to reconsider this fresh evidence.

11.42 Any disadvantage to the claimant is probably eliminated by the availability of investment advice producing higher returns than the very safe ILGS, but claimants are reasonably entitled to argue that they did not chose to become investors, and are entitled to seek the safest homes they can for their money.

ADJUSTMENTS FOR CONTINGENCIES

11.43 The figures in the Ogden Tables themselves (as opposed to the Introductory Notes) are based on average life expectations, discounted by the appropriate percentage (currently 2.5%) for early receipt. Note that the Tables take no account of any other factors eg:

(a)   reduced life expectation;

---

[21]   *Cooke v United Bristol Health Care* [2003] EWCA Civ 1370 per Laws LJ.
[22]   [1968] 1 QB 596.
[23]   [1985] 1 WLR 784.
[24]   The group is now under the chairmanship of Robin de Wilde QC following the retirement of the much-respected Sir Michael Ogden. It is hoped that this change will not undermine the high status of the Tables.
[25]   *Wells v Wells* [1999] 1 AC 345 per Lord Lloyd at 379.

(b) any time that the claimant was likely to spend out of work as a result of ill-health in any event;

(c) the period of any search for work; and

(d) there may be other factors that affect a particular claimant's occupation: the onus will be on the defendant to establish any further discounts.

11.44 Research[26] shows that adjusting multipliers in the light of economic activity, geography and the dangers of the job (as was recommended in the Ogden Tables up to the 5th edition) tends not to give an accurate result. It recommends looking at the amount of time that a particular claimant would have been expected to spend in work if he had not been injured, and (if he still has an earning capacity) the amount of time he can now expect to spend in work. The figures in the Ogden Tables are still discounted, but the factors will be different. The key factors are disability, unemployment and education.[27] Once the appropriate basic figure has been found in the numbered Table (*e.g.* Table 9 for loss of earnings for males to retirement age 65), the figure is discounted by multiplying it be a figure found in one of four tables in the Introductory Notes:

- Table A: Males – not disabled

- Table B: Males – disabled

- Table C: Females – not disabled

- Table D: Females – disabled

The basic deduction for contingencies other than mortality involves a two-part test.

11.45 First, the court should assess the value of the earnings the claimant would have received had not suffered the injury. The multipliers in Ogden Tables 3 to 14 (multipliers for loss of earnings) are reduced to allow for the fact that the average 'working life expectancy'[28] is likely to be slightly shorter on average than the expected period to retirement. The reason is the modest chance that a Claimant will die before retirement age. So, for example, the average manual worker of 50, expecting to retire at 65, will actually spend less than 15 years in work. There is also a risk of periods of non-employment and absences from work because of sickness, and this is taken into account in the following paragraphs.

---

[26] Haberman and Bloomfield 'Work time lost to sickness, unemployment and stoppages: measurement and application', Journal of the Institute of Actuaries 117, 533–595.

[27] Once the figure are adjusted for educational attainment, all other factors are, in most cases, relatively insignificant and may be dispensed with.

[28] Ie the average time spent in employment until retirement age.

11.46 Next, the court assesses the situation after the injury for which the claimant is to be compensated. Has he any residual earning capacity?

11.47 To return to the example above, let us assume that the lumberjack was out of work at the time of the accident, and left school with three GSCEs.

- Having established the basic multiplier of 20.57, a table (Table A) gives discount factors according to whether the claimant was in or out of work, and able-bodied. Since he was able-bodied, but was out of work, the relevant discount figure is 0.81.

- Other tables provide that for an able-bodied male who was out of work at the time of the accident, a further adjustment of –0.03 should be made.

- The multiplier to be applied to the claimant in his pre-injury state is therefore [0.81 – 0.03] × 20.57 = 16.04. If the claimant has a nil earning capacity as a result of the accident, this is the multiplier to be applied to his pre-accident earnings. If he was earning £10,000 a year net before the accident, his claim for loss of earnings is [16.04 × £20,000] = £160,400.

11.48 If the claimant (who is still out of work following the accident), has a residual earning capacity of £5,000 a year net it is necessary to value his earnings to retirement age. The process is repeated:

- The starting point is 20.57.

- The claimant is now disabled and out of work, and the first table gives a discount figure of 0.24.

- He still only has GCSEs, and he is out of work, so the second table gives us –0.01.

- The multiplier is [0.24 – 0.01] × 20.57 = 4.73.

- His residual earning capacity to the age of 65 is [4.73 × £5,000] = £23,650.

- Subtract what he would have earned from what he will earn: [£160,400 – £23,650] = £136,750. This is his claim for loss of future earnings.

11.49 This compares with [19.60 × £5,000] = £98,000 if the claim is calculated according to the fifth edition of the Tables.

HANDICAP ON THE LABOUR MARKET

11.50 In the 1970s, a cluster of cases[29] confirmed that the court would award damages to the claimant who suffers injury, but who continues to be employed, often by the same employer at the same rate of pay. Where there is a 'real risk' that the employment will come to an end, and the injured claimant has to look for work the court will award a lump sum for his handicap on the labour market.

11.51 How is this figure arrived at? In *Moeliker v Reyrolle*, Browne LJ said:

> 'It is impossible to suggest any formula for solving the extremely difficult problems involved in ... the assessment. A judge must look at all the factors which are relevant ion a particular case and do the best he can.'

11.52 Experience suggests that most awards tend to be between 6 months and 24 months' net earnings,[30] although higher awards have been made.[31]

11.53 Where a claimant is earning more after the accident than he was before, the *Smith v Manchester* award is based on his current income.[32]

11.54 Since adjustments in Tables A to D in the 2007 edition of the Ogden Tables take disability into account, it is likely that the courts will make fewer *Smith v Manchester* awards in the future – though there will still be cases where although it is clear that there will be a loss of earnings, precise calculation would be too speculative.

LOSS OF CHANCE

11.55 In *Davis v Taylor* [1974],[33] the court was asked to assess the chance of the claimant resuming a relationship with her husband. Lord Reid held:

> 'Where the question is whether a certain thing is or is not true – whether a certain event did or did not happen – then the Court must decide one way or the other. There is no question of chance of probability. Either it did or did not happen. But the standard of civil proof is a balance of probabilities. If the evidence shows a balance in favour of it having happened, then it is proved that it did in fact happen
> ...

---

[29] *Smith v Manchester Corpn* [1974] 17 KIR 1; *Clarke v Rotax Aircraft* [1975] 1 WLR 1570; *Nicholls v National Coal Board* [1976] ICR 266; *Moeliker v Reyrolle & Co* [1977] 1 WLR 132; *Cook v Consolidated Fisheries* [1977] ICR 635.
[30] See *Ritchie Smith v Manchester Awards* 1994 Journal of Personal Injury Litigation 103.
[31] *Foster v Tyne and Wear* [1986] 1 All ER 567; *Goldborough v Thompson and Crowther* [1996] PIQR Q86.
[32] *Lau Ho Wah v Yau Chi Biu* [1985] WLR 1203.
[33] [1974] QB 207.

You can prove that a past event happened, but you cannot prove that a future event will happen and I do not think that the law is so foolish as to suppose that you can. All that you can do is to evaluate the chance, sometimes it is virtually 100%: sometimes nil. But often it is somewhere in between. And if it is somewhere in between I do not see much difference between a probability of 51% and a probability of 49%.'

11.56 In *Anderson v Davis* [1992][34] the trial judge assessed the claimant's chance of being promoted to principal lecturer, and reduced the uplift by 66.7% as there was an identified formidable competitor and the prospects of promotion were 'far from certain'. The judge held:

'Where the question for the judge is one of past facts, then mere balance of probability wins the day. Where the question is one of what might have been in a hypothetical state of facts then, to the extent that a chance of the event necessary to an award of damages falls significantly below 100 per cent, the award should be discounted in my view.'

11.57 A more sophisticated model was approved by the Court of Appeal in *Langford v Hebran*.[35] The facts were as follows: in 1994, when he was aged 27, Robert Langford sustained a whiplash and left shoulder injuries in a road traffic accident. The agreed medical evidence concluded that his residual symptoms would prevent him from working as a bricklayer, and would hamper his continued development and success as a kick-boxer.

11.58 The timing of the road accident came at a catastrophic stage in Mr Langford's kick-boxing career. In February 1994, he had won the amateur world light-heavyweight championship, following which he had turned professional. He had won his first professional fight and had a walkover in the second. At the time of the trial in October 1999, he had found part-time work as a car valet, earning £80 pw gross. It was conceded that a fairer reflection of his residual earning capacity was a salary of £160 pw gross, substantially below his earnings as a bricklayer and professional kick-boxer. His claim included a claim for damages for his lost chance of earnings as a successful professional kick-boxer.

11.59 The claim was advanced on the basis of a 'basic loss' calculated as follows:

(a) It was assumed that his kickboxing career would last until he was 36. During that time, he would work for 26 weeks a year as a bricklayer, and fight five fights in the rest of the year (three in Britain, two in the USA);

(b) at the age of 36, he would stop kick-boxing and work as a bricklayer until the age of 60;

---

[34] [1993] PIQR Q87.
[35] [2001] EWCA Civ 361.

(c) in addition to this basic loss, he claimed an uplift for the lost chance of various opportunities. The claim was advanced by:
- identifying the opportunities;
- evaluating the chance of each opportunity being realised;
- calculating the likely benefit to the claimant of having realised the particular opportunity; and
- calculating the mathematical consequences of the above conclusions.

11.60 The four stages of opportunity for the claimant were held to be:

- winning either the British or European title as a professional kick-boxer;

- following this success, to move to the USA where the claimant would win a state/regional title, but not become world champion;

- winning the world championship for one year; and/or

- holding on to the world championship for two years before becoming a professional instructor in the USA, earning $350,000 pa.

11.61 By contrast, the defendant invited the judge to take a 'broad-brush' approach to quantifying the future loss of earnings as a kick-boxer, and suggested a global award of £42,000. The defendant discouraged the court from considering so many uncertain possibilities.

11.62 Both the trial judge and the Court of Appeal preferred the claimant's approach, which produced a fairer result than the jury figure proposed by the defendant. However, the Court of Appeal accepted that the trial judge had erred in his calculation of the lost chance, and was persuaded to do its best on the material before it. The Court of Appeal concluded that there were:

> '... real chances, not fanciful ones, of [Mr Langford] achieving further fame and fortune at each of the four stages of success.'

11.63 The chances were assessed as:

(a) Winning the British/European title: 80%. The court calculated the annual increase on the 'basis loss' and added 80% of this uplift to the past and future losses.

(b) Moving to the USA: 66%. The next stage was to calculate the uplift on the basic loss and the first stage of winning the British/European title (to avoid duplication). 66% of this 'second-stage uplift' was awarded (although, in fact, there was no future loss).

(c) Winning the world championship: 40%. The third stage was to take the aggregate of the basic loss, stage 1 and 2 uplift and to calculate the further uplift that would be received if Mr Langford won the world championship. This uplift was reduced to 40% of the further sum to allow for the lost chance.

(d) Retaining the world championship: 20%. The final stage was to take the aggregate of all the previous stages, calculate the further uplift and then reduce this to 20% of the sum. In fact, the calculation of this fourth stage uplift was to increase future losses by £1,191,048, which was reduced to 20% of the sum claimed.

11.64 The court then applied a 'litigation risk' discount of 20%, limited to future losses (see para 33 of the judgment). Overall, the calculations provided an uplift on the basic loss for past and future loss of earnings of £295,430, considerably in excess of the 'jury' broad-brush approach of £42,000 suggested by the defendant.

DELAY ENTERING THE JOB MARKET

11.65 Sometimes a young person's injuries will delay his degree or A-level results by a year, but will have no long-term ill-effects. Where this happens, damages can be awarded to compensate for the loss of earnings. See, for example, *Oades v Park*:[36] by reason of his injuries, the claimant was forced to defer his university entry by one year, which would have a knock-on effect on his subsequent career in the computing industry, in which he could expect a starting salary of £10,000. During the enforced year off he earned approximately £1,700 net. For the loss of the chance of a year's earnings the judge awarded £3,500.

---

[36] Kemp & Kemp, F5-025 [1994] CLY.

Chapter 12
LOSS OF PENSION

THE CONVENTIONAL APPROACH
Wider principles
12.1

- Pension loss is a head of future pecuniary loss like any other and not an esoteric subject outside the routine assessment of damages.

- The much, but unfairly, criticised previous leading case of *Auty v National Coal Board*.[1] embodied no abstruse method but only the then conventional approach.

- As the conventional approach has shifted following *Wells v Wells*,[2] so must the assessment of pension loss, away from the old method in *Auty*, into line with the present application of the conventional approach.

- While it is beyond the scope of this chapter, there is no reason why future pension shortfall cannot be taken by way of periodical payments.

Conventional approach in practice following *Wells v Wells*

12.2 The conventional approach:

- assesses damages for personal injuries net of tax;[3]

- takes no account of future inflation, setting the multiplicand at date of trial and ignoring the particular avenues of investment open to an individual claimant;[4]

- adopts a rate of discount to be set by the Lord Chancellor (at the time of writing taken to be 2.5% pa[5]);

---

[1] [1985] 1 WLR 784, [1985] 1 All ER 930, CA.
[2] [1998] 3 WLR 329, HL.
[3] *British Transport Commission v Gourley* [1956] AC 185, HL.
[4] *Mallett v McMonagle* [1970] AC 166, HL (NI) 175B–176D. *Lim Poh Choo v Camden and Islington Area Health Authority* [1980] AC 174 HL 193B-194B; upheld on this point in *Wells v Wells* [1998] 3 WLR 319 – per Lord Lloyd 334A, Lord Steyn 353C and Lord Clyde 361E.
[5] *Wells v Wells* above – eg per Lord Lloyd 344A.

- no longer makes *judicial* discounts, using the Ogden Tables now as a starting point rather than a check, being slow to depart from the relevant actuarial multiplier on impressionistic grounds or previously decided multipliers.[6] Where there is agreed life expectancy, an arithmetical multiplier is to be taken over that life expectancy;[7]

- refuses to make pseudo-findings of *future fact* on the balance of probabilities, but reflects future chances by assessing the damages based upon an *assumption* which aims at doing justice in monetary terms balancing the favourable and adverse contingencies.[8] Sometimes all the contingencies are taken into account when the assumptions are articulated. On other occasions the assumption is taken at the nearest convenient starting point and then varied further for contingencies;[9]

- involves doing one's very best;[10] making the best use of such tools to assist the process as are available;[11] and now that detailed calculations and tables founded on a reasonably reliable basis are available, taking full advantage of them.[12]

Conventional approach – binding on pensions

12.3 Given the cornerstones of the conventional approach, first instance decisions before *Wells* based on *Auty* as binding authority were clearly correct.[13] The wider ratio of those cases (that the conventional approach, whatever its current form determined in other cases, applies to pension loss) remains intact following *Wells*. Discount rates covering future losses are governed by the Damages Act 1996 as amended. If it is wrong to attempt to adduce evidence to value future nursing care by reference to a different index or set of criteria,[14] it is wrong for the same reasons to obtain evidence from the markets of its view of the value of an annuity to generate a sum to make up the loss: this is to substitute the view of the markets about investment return against inflation for that set by the Lord Chancellor and is another form of impermissible collateral attack on the conventional discount rate.[15] Encouragement to obtain a quotation on the financial markets to make good the loss and

---

[6] *Wells v Wells* above – per Lord Lloyd 347D–E.
[7] *Wells v Wells* above – per Lord Lloyd 345H–347F.
[8] *Mallett v McMonagle* [1970] AC 166 HL (NI) 173F, 174D and 176E-F; *Wells v Wells* above – per Lord Hope 356F–357A.
[9] For a modern example of the application of *loss of chance* principles to pension loss (rather than *balance of probabilities*) see *Brown v MoD* [2006] EWCA Civ 546.
[10] *Wells v Wells* above – per Lord Lloyd 332H-333A and Lord Clyde 361A.
[11] *Wells v Wells* above – per Lord Hope 357E.
[12] *Wells v Wells* above – per Lord Clyde 364C.
[13] *Page v Sheerness Steel Company* [1996] PIQR Q26, Q38 Dyson J. *Longden v British Coal Corporation* [1995] PIQR Q48, Q50 – CA noting Douglas Brown J's unchallenged decision on that score.
[14] *Cooke v United Bristol Health Care* [2003] EWCA Civ 1370.
[15] Similar attacks at first instance on different points have failed in *Patel v Wright & Midas* [2005] EWHC 347 and *Page v Plymouth Hospitals NHS Trust* [2004] EWHC 1154.

to proffer it as the measure of damage should be ignored.[16] One might as well suggest that nursing care beginning at some future date to run until the end of a claimant's life[17] be valued by reference to the cost of a deferred annuity; or, without any change in the logic, the cost of immediate nursing care to a simple annuity; or loss of earnings . . . all of which is not the law as it stands.

A MODERN BUT NEVERTHELESS 'CONVENTIONAL' APPROACH

12.4 The concept of using the Ogden Tables as a universally adopted basis for the calculation of future recurring losses and expenses over any future tracts of time commended itself to the House of Lords in *Wells*.[18] Indeed, the House of Lords used the Ogden Tables in relation to pensions to solve the question of how much discount should be given from an already paid ill-health retirement lump sum in *Longden v British Coal Corporation*.[19] While the first edition of the Ogden Tables had just been published at the time of the Court of Appeal's decision in *Auty*, it had not gained the widespread acceptance which took over a decade in coming, and the judges in *Auty* did their best, perhaps not fully understanding the nature of actuarial evidence, using the English Life Tables based upon Past Expectation of Life and the Bacon and Woodrow Arithmetical Discount Tables. It should go without saying in the light of the adjustments to the conventional approach enunciated so clearly in *Wells*, that the time has come to move on from *Auty,* using the Ogden Tables 'to do one's very best'.[20]

OVERVIEW OF TYPES OF PENSION CLAIMS

12.5 There are two broad types of claim.

- *Type 1*: Where the claimant is young without an established working history; where the position is insecure; or where there are major uncertainties. In such cases the best one can do is to evaluate a notional claim using the Ogden Pension Tables as at the date of compulsory

---

[16] Indeed, with respect, one should not follow even encouragement from one as experienced as Beldam LJ in *London Ambulance Service National Health Service Trust v Swain* (CA, unreported, 12 March 1999) (a two-judge court.) The encouragement was clearly obiter and the point neither argued nor necessary for decision. It is unfortunate that this case is still referred to in the JSB Civil Bench Book; and practitioners should beware that courts influenced by that publication may come from a different starting point.
[17] An exact analogy for a future loss of pension claim and the same method can be used in such cases.
[18] Above – per Lord Clyde 364B–C.
[19] [1998] AC 653 and vide infra.
[20] See footnote 9 above; but this must be subject to practicalities e g taking into account all the minute changes in tax relief and state pension entitlements at different ages will render calculations so unwieldy, difficult and tedious that, in the context of necessarily imperfect assumptions, the exercise is not worth the attempt. See the worked example below.

retirement which can then only be discounted dramatically with a broad brush given the flavour of the case. This chapter is not really concerned with this type; but with Type 2 cases, where much greater precision is possible.[21]

- *Type 2*: Where the claimant is in long-term secure employment with a good-quality pension scheme and where there are multiple options for voluntary early retirement, ill-health retirement and death-in-service benefits. In these cases, if one is to do one's best following *Wells* and make proper compensation, a more subtle approach is required with an appreciation of the monetary effects of early/ill-health retirement or death in service.

THE BASIC OGDEN MULTIPLIERS

12.6 There is now widespread familiarity with the concept of earnings multipliers and life multipliers which are applied to a current multiplicand to generate a lump sum providing a steady stream of income for the period up to the assumed date of retirement or death, with the fund extinguished at that point. A pension's multiplier is a multiplier to be applied again to a present multiplicand to provide a stream of payments from the assumed date of retirement until the assumed date of death. It already includes an actuarial discount for the chance of early death over the whole period and an arithmetical discount from the date of expected retirement to the date of calculation.

Solution to Type 1 cases using the Ogden Tables

Worked example using basic Ogden multipliers

12.7 Male, 23, in service for 2 years prior to road accident when he lost a leg, compulsory retirement age at 65, and now unfit for work. Pension would have been based on the formula (very common):

Length of service (maximum 40 years) × 1/80 × final year's pensionable pay.

On ill-health retirement, length of service enhanced by 5 years or to 15 years whichever is the greater (again a common type of term.)

Pensionable pay £10,000 pa

Pension if retired at 65

40 years × 1/80 × £10,000 =   £5,000 pa[22]

Pension now payable

---

[21] Nevertheless, see the text at para 12.17 below.
[22] Bearing in mind increased personal allowances for those over 65, any tax at this sort of level is tiny. See examples below for help in calculating deductions for tax.

15 years × 1/80 × £10,000 =   £1,875 pa

Annual loss   £3,125

Multiplier (Ogden Table 21
at age 23 at 2.5% pa discount)   x 5.10

Current value capitalised   £15,937
annual loss

12.8 Adjustment after such a basic calculation will vary depending on the nature of the job and the likelihood of a sustained career. A police-officer or firefighter with 2 years' service is much more likely to have a long-term career than a private soldier (even if he hopes for promotion) where average length of service for raw recruits is very low. There are always exceptional cases, however, and care should be taken to examine the evidence.

Solution to Type 2 cases using the Ogden Tables

12.9 Type 2 cases are those where there is a likelihood of a sustained career.

Now	Retirement	Death
	Period of life multiplier	
Period of earnings multiplier		
		Period of pension multiplier

The multiplier

12.10 If one refers to the linear diagram of multipliers above the following relationship becomes broadly apparent:

Earnings Multiplier + Pension Multiplier = Life Multiplier

At any given age, whatever the age of retirement, the sum of the earnings multiplier and the pension multiplier is the life multiplier. (It might be objected that multipliers for loss of earnings have to be qualified by contingencies other than mortality; and it should be borne in mind that when using the Ogden Tables to calculate loss of earnings, allowance is made for the possibility (or probability) that a claimant would not in any event have worked uninterruptedly to his 65th birthday. In a case of long term secure employment, which is in point in type 2 cases, the main ingredient of this discount is for *early retirement* rather than any interruption in the employment itself. Hence the relationship is sound as a *starting point* for assessing loss of pension. The Guidance Notes to the Tables suggest how to take this into account in calculating pension loss but this chapter argues for a simpler approach as is developed below. See also Chapter 11, 'Loss of earnings', 'Adjustment for contingencies'.)

12.11 The relationship can be rearranged to yield a simple but powerful formula in the calculation of pension loss:

> Life Multiplier − Earnings Multiplier = Pension Multiplier

12.12 The Ogden Tables already take into account mortality so that contingency is satisfied if the Tables are used as the starting points for the life and earnings multipliers. Unless there is medical evidence showing that the claimant has a reduced life expectancy, there is no justification following *Wells* for tinkering with the life multiplier. The major contingency on the earnings multiplier is the age of retirement. If, when deciding the earnings multiplier the judge considers only the contingencies as to length of service (leaving contingencies as to *wage* eg promotion etc for consideration when setting the earnings multiplicand − more logical after all), whatever the process of balancing the contingencies from the basic Ogden earnings multiplier, those very same contingencies are substantially taken into account in the case of a claimant with long-term secure employment if the pension multiplier uses the actual earnings and life multipliers assessed on other heads of loss. A *tailored* pension multiplier can be reached by simply taking the earnings multiplier in the case away from the life multiplier in the case. This is not an entirely *bespoke* multiplier but better than an *off the peg* Ogden multiplier for the starting point.

The multiplicand

12.13 Having established the best starting point for the pension multiplier, the multiplicand needs to be tailored to fit with the multiplier: the correct length of service to be taken in the formula for the calculation of the pension itself must match the assumption for length of service in the multiplier. The potential problem can easily be solved. If the judge in setting the earnings multiplier and using the Ogden Tables articulates the 'assumption' as to age at retirement, we will know in turn the correct assumption as to the length of service in order to fix the multiplicand under a final salary scheme. Even if the assumption is not specifically articulated, it can be estimated with reasonable precision using the Ogden tables in reverse.

Further adjustment

12.14 It would be a mistake to think that there will be *no scope at all* for adjustment on the facts of each case after the above method has been followed; but it provides more than the best starting point in a Type 2 case.

12.15 There can be no scope for *further* adjustment for a contingency which has *already* been taken into account in setting the multiplier and the multiplicand. The length of service was set as a fair assumption, already considering the risks of falling under a bus, unrelated ill-health, redundancy, liquidation of the company etc when the multiplier for loss of earnings was set. If that is the *prediction* for the major head of damage on earnings, one should not be doubtful in one's very doubts and discount again when assessing pension loss for identical risks. The same goes for pensionable pay if the multiplicand has been carried forward from the loss of earnings claim.

12.16 Adjustment may be necessary, however, if the various contingencies have not been compartmentalised between multiplier and multiplicand quite as clearly as hoped. If the judge provides for the prospects of promotion by enhancing the multiplier rather than the multiplicand everything will be thrown out of line. As already discussed, the job may not involve long-term secure employment. The quality of the pension scheme may be poor so that there is no entitlement to early retirement/ill-health pension before the date of compulsory retirement. In all those circumstances one can revert to using the Ogden Pension Tables, but remembering that much greater adjustment will be needed with a broad brush. By way of contrast, sometimes there are identifiable chances of an improved pension which can be used to offset any temptation to discount (and may lead a claim for an additional *loss of chance* of increased pension if the multiplicand has not already taken that factor into account[23]).

12.17 Nevertheless, the logic can be extended even to Type 1 cases to get to the best starting point. If, for instance, the assumption/prediction of 7 years' service in the Army for a new recruit was good enough to govern the claim for loss of earnings (balancing the claimant's contention for full service with that of the Ministry of Defence for only 3 years), why should it not represent the best starting point also for loss of pension, leading to a moderate arithmetical claim calculated from the tailored multiplier applied to the multiplicand carried forward? The advice in *Wells*, not to depart from the starting point on *impressionistic* grounds, should lead to this figure standing untouched unless there is some logical reason, based on evidence and capable of articulation, to depart from it.[24]

12.18 At any rate, adjustments in earlier reported cases are not part of their *ratio* but on their own facts as part of the conventional approach to the assessment of damages which tries to reflect the chances, good and bad. It is a mistake to pick a previous decision and purport to apply it to a current case on a *pro rata* basis comparing the number of years before retirement. In any event,

---

[23] See footnote 9 for an example case.
[24] In this instance there would probably have to be a small uplift rather than a deduction for contingencies – although a slim chance, the claimant may have completed full service to entitle him to payment of an immediate pension on retirement (rather than waiting to age 55), which would increase the loss from the starting point considerably, and the contingency deserves to be incorporated in the assessment to reach a fair result. The point illustrates the wider one – adjustment is quite possible, indeed obligatory, *if* some logical reason can be articulated. No logical reasoning = no tinkering.

in recent years we have all got better at refraining from unreasoned discounts;[25] and earlier decisions are apt to over-discount in line with the times.

12.19 In the current climate, there may be some doubt as to whether an advantageous final salary pension scheme will remain open even to existing members in some occupations (particularly outside of the public sector) right up to normal retirement. Some adjustment may be reasonable if there is evidence to show that a replacement money purchase scheme is likely to be less valuable overall. While there have been a few high profile cases, a court is unlikely to want to discount for the slim chance of fraud on the pension scheme.

THE EVIDENTIAL FRAMEWORK

12.20 Much of the evidence going to the assumptions required for pension loss calculation is assembled in relation to the heads of loss other than pension. Nevertheless, the following matters are relevant and can be stored on a standard draft for ease of completion and to ensure a methodical approach.

(1) claimant's age at date of calculation;

(2) claimant's life multiplier at date of calculation (using the Ogden Tables as a starting point,[26] only to be adjusted in the light of cogent evidence, when that evidence may give a life expectancy and an arithmetical multiplier from Table 28 should then be used);

(3) the *assumption* for age at retirement if the accident had not occurred and hence length of service;

(4) the *assumption* as to wage at retirement and hence *pensionable pay*;

(5) claimant's attitude to any possible commutation of periodical payments to a tax-free lump sum;

(6) spouse's age;

(7) spouse's life multiplier (using similar considerations as for the claimant's life multiplier).

---

[25] As Lord Clyde observed in *Wells v Wells* above: 'If each of the elements has individually achieved the best approximation possible to the proper compensation for each particular aspect of the claim, then the total figure should correspondingly represent the best assessment possible for the total claim. If at the conclusion of the exercise the judge is uneasy at the total result he should not seek to make any overall adjustment in either direction to the total award to meet his unease; he should return to reconsider each element in the calculation and secure that there is no need for revision at that level.' 395C–D.

[26] *Worrall v Powergen plc* [1999] PIQR Q103.

12.21 The pension fund trustees should then be invited to answer a questionnaire (which can again be stored as a standard draft) and to provide the main terms of the scheme which are usually within an Explanatory Booklet for Employees.[27]

(1) What is the formula for pension entitlement under the final salary scheme?

(2) What constitutes 'pensionable pay' under the scheme as distinct from overall earnings?

(3) What entitlement is there to a lump sum?

(4) If the lump sum is a commutation of entitlement to periodical payments, how is it calculated and with what effect upon annual pension?

(5) When did the claimant's pensionable service commence?

(6) Has there been any 'pension's holiday' in respect of the claimant's service?

(7) What are the provisions for:
    (a) Voluntary early retirement?
    (b) Ill-health early retirement?
    (c) Any payments under the pension scheme on redundancy?
    (d) Preservation of pension on voluntary resignation?
    (e) Benefits on death in service or otherwise?
    (f) Widow's pension?

(8) In the case of a claimant who has already retired, what is the current value of the actual entitlement to pension and, if a commuted lump sum has been paid, when and how much?

12.22 The trustees can be invited to show a worked example based upon the present-day value of the assumptions contended for, so as to make clear how the calculation is to be done in the event of alternative assumptions requiring calculation at a later date.

12.23 Answers to the above questions coupled with the explanatory booklet should be more than sufficient in most cases. The problem with calculating pension loss is, and always has been, not so much a difficulty in doing the arithmetic once the correct evidence has been obtained, but in making sure that there is a sufficient breadth of evidence so that when the assumptions upon which the damages are to be awarded are articulated by the Judge the figures are easily available and converted. If there is any difficulty in understanding the information from the trustees then, at a relatively late stage just prior to trial,

---

[27] In fact, the explanatory booklets of very many schemes are now on the internet. Using a search engine such as Google usually leads straight to the booklet and enough information to forget the time-consuming approaches to the trustees. Sometimes the website even has a tool to calculate the pension for you.

when the issues between the parties are delineated, the trustees can be invited to fill in a questionnaire which can be tailored to meet the competing contentions of the parties and the possible middle ground.

Additional receipt of pension/incapacity pension

12.24 In many cases a claimant will be able to exercise an early or ill-health retirement option following an accident and obtain periodical payments and/or a lump sum prior to normal retirement. The House of Lords' decision in *Parry v Cleaver*[28] is the leading authority and the following propositions from it are sound:

- Additional receipts of pension are not to be deducted from other heads of loss.[29]

- After the date of normal retirement, credit must be given for any payments under the scheme. Whether labelled as *retirement* or *incapacity/injury*, the pensions are of one and the same kind.[30]

- No credit is to be given for periodical payments prior to the date of normal retirement, not even from the later pension loss claim itself.[31]

12.25 The first two propositions have never been challenged, nor were they in the case of *Longden v British Coal Corporation*.[32] However, while the third proposition was clearly the ratio of *Parry v Cleaver* it arose essentially from the monetary result of the case as against any detailed discussion of the issues involved. It was challenged in *Longden* but upheld. *Parry v Cleaver* did not involve the commutation of periodical payments to a lump sum. In *Longden* the House of Lords decided that the proportion of the lump sum which represents the period after normal retirement should be deducted.[33]

12.26 This is only logical bearing in mind the diagram set out above. We could again apply our formula but rearranged to give us a close approximation to the correct proportion to be deducted:

Deductible proportion = pension multiplier ÷ life multiplier

12.27 Strictly, however, the multipliers should be taken *as at the date when the lump sum was actually paid,* not at trial/settlement, but using the 'assumptions' found or contended for in the trial to fix the end point of the earnings multiplier. The strict formula to apply but using multipliers taken from the Ogden Tables at the date of actual retirement/receipt of the lump sum is:

---

[28] [1970] AC 1, HL.
[29] Ibid per Lord Reid at 20G–21A.
[30] Loc cit.
[31] Vide infra.
[32] [1998] AC 653 HL.
[33] Ibid 672D–F.

Deductible proportion = [life multiplier *minus* earnings multiplier to the date of the retirement assumption] ÷ [life multiplier]

12.28 This will ensure internal consistency and that the same contingencies are taken into account in the same fashion, but may not be worth the candle for most people unless there is a long delay between retirement and trial.

- *Longden* appears in the speech of Lord Hope to have been narrowly decided: that part of the lump sum attributable to the commutation of the post normal retirement pension is to be deducted. Neither in the speeches nor in the cases for the applicant and the respondent in the House of Lords is the nature of that lump sum set out explicitly; but the reasoning of Lord Hope suggested it was a commutation of future entitlement. In previous editions of this Handbook I have argued that, following this logic, *Longden* suggests that if the lump sum is not a strict commutation but paid compulsorily under the scheme, there should be no deduction of any part. Paid in a *different accounting period* and containing no element attributable to the period of loss, I posed the question, 'What can there be to deduct?' and suggested that, while litigation would have to decide the point definitively, the better view was not to deduct any part. However, going back to the British Coal Staff Superannuation Scheme current at the date of the plaintiff's retirement in *Longden* (1986), it is clear that the lump sum at that time was not a formal commutation at all but paid compulsorily as part of the terms of the scheme.[34] It appears that the plaintiff's fall-back position in *Longden* (as to partial deduction of the lump sum) was not as narrow as I had previously thought: it effectively encompasses *all* early pension lump sums as being on account of a stream of future payments *whether or not expressly calculated as such* under the terms of the scheme. In the light of the actual scheme in *Longden*, I must now reverse my previous advice and suggest that credit should be given using the *Longden* formula for all early lump sum payments.[35]

- In *London Ambulance Service National Health Service Trust v Swain*,[36] Beldam LJ upheld an increase in the credit for an already paid lump sum to bring its monetary value up to that at the date of trial, applying the tables using the then prescribed rate of 3% (now 2.5%), not the Court Special Investment Account rate, for which the appellants contended, or any other rate. The case is mentioned by commentators[37] without any significant caveat and some, at least, should be provided. The problem is that this approach to the early lump sum, uplifting its value from the date of receipt to the date of trial or settlement, has no foundation in the

---

[34] Based on 3x annual pension, without reduction (*commutation*) in the later pension.
[35] The author is grateful to Maurice Faull Esq, Partner in Charge of Litigation Support at Hilton Sharp & Clarke, Chartered Accountants, 30 New Road, Brighton for pointing out to me my earlier mistake; and for other helpful comments on the draft for this edition of the Handbook.
[36] CA, unreported, 12 March 1999.
[37] Eg JSB Civil Bench Book and Kemp & Kemp.

reasoning[38] or arithmetical result[39] in *Longden* itself, where the point was not argued. Beldam LJ gave no reason for his decision but one can be provided from the way the appellants put their case: the loss of pension lump sum is a *future* loss, to be calculated at the date of trial in monetary values current at that date in line with first principles; where a payment has been made in the past to defray that loss it should be updated to the trial date to compare like with like. Readers will have to form their own conclusion bearing in mind footnotes 38 and 39.

MISCELLANEOUS

Widow's pension

12.29 The method used in *Auty* can be adapted for use with our more modern tools.

12.30 The widow's pension is usually expressed as a proportion of the claimant's entitlement – often a half. If we add on to the claimant's pension multiplier, as already evaluated, the extent by which the wife's life multiplier exceeds the claimant's life multiplier *but reduced by the proportion of the widow's entitlement*, we have a combined pension multiplier for the couple, what I call an Adjusted Joint Life Pension Multiplier.[40]

Alternative occupational pension

12.31 It was conceded in *Auty* that where a claimant is able to obtain alternative pensionable work, the value of the additional pension should be offset. The eventualities of the alternative position are likely to be very different from those of the original. If so, it is not possible simply to subtract the alternative pension from the figures in the original calculation. Rather, a quick calculation in reverse gives the credit to be allowed, discounted back to date of trial, and then in turn adjusted for eventualities if necessary. Often the claimant is unemployed at trial but with some residual earning capacity. The chance of obtaining alternative pensionable employment should be taken into account in the overall adjustment for eventualities, but there will usually be little or no chance of an injured claimant obtaining work with entitlement to a much-coveted and increasingly rare (because expensive) *final salary* pension.

---

[38] There is no suggestion anywhere that the lump sum already received should be uplifted to the date of trial for early receipt. One of the main lines of thought of Lord Hope, when considering that the claimant cannot fairly be expected to give credit for early receipt of ill health retirement pension against later claims for loss of pension, is that it is unreasonable to expect the claimant, who requires the income to live on in one accounting period, to invest the payments he receives to abide a loss in a different accounting period. Similarly, most people use rather than reinvest a lump sum when they receive it, and all the more so when they have been forced into ill health retirement with a claim pending at common law.

[39] In *Longden,* there was no uplift on the figure of £1,630 (16% of £10,185.91 lump sum received) on account of early receipt. Albeit the point was not argued, the monetary result was an essential part of the ratio of *Longden.*

[40] See the worked example below.

Only this type of alternative pension stands to be offset from *pension* loss, like for like: a money purchase pension is a benefit in kind to be taken into account when calculating loss of earnings.[41]

Tax allowances and relief

12.32 As in any personal injuries action the damages must be computed net of tax. It should be remembered that Personal Allowances are increased for those between 65 and 74 years and slightly increased again at 75. There is an income limit (total income) before the higher allowance is gradually whittled down. Very few claims for loss of *final salary* pension will qualify and recourse will then have to be made to the detailed provisions in any given tax year. While the old Married Couple's Allowance remains for those who qualified (with one or other 65 when abolition occurred) in April 2000, it has no longer any relevance for claims for loss of future pension. The age for women's entitlement to State pension will rise gradually from 2010 to age 65 by 2020.

Higher Personal Allowances

	2006/2007
Single person	
- aged 65-74	£7,280
- aged 75+	£7,420
Additional age-related allowance reduced by ½ of income over	£20,100

State Retirement Pension

	2006-2007
Claimant (Category A)	£84.25 per week or £4,381 pa
Non-contributing spouse/adult dependant	
– extra	£50.50 per week or £2,626 pa

12.33 The tax deductions fall, in line with first principles, to be taken from the top slice of tax. A little care is required to get details from the claimant of other sources of income. For most it will be an entitlement to the basic State pension only, hence the inclusion of its current levels in the information above. The total income as it should have been is to be netted down and then the netted down total of the actual income subtracted to leave the total net annual loss. Handy conversion charts for incomes in retirement have appeared since the 2004 edition of the PNBA 'Facts and Figures Tables for the Calculation of Damages'; but the work is often published towards the end of a tax year and the table may be out of date when carrying out a calculation.

---

[41] Cf money purchase/personal pensions – vide infra.

Personal pension plans

12.34 There can be no claim for losses under personal pension plans, which are *money purchase* schemes, converted into an annuity with the option of a tax free lump sum at the date of retirement. There is no formula for fixing the value of the pension but rather only speculation on the performance of the fund against inflation. More importantly, it is not *future remuneration* for *past work*, in the form of insurance, following *Parry v Cleaver*. Rather it is easily distinguished as the proceeds of an *investment* by the individual of *remuneration already received*. One might as well claim the lost investment proceeds of speculation with the same money on the Stock Exchange, but not under a pension's umbrella (or gold bars under the bed), as attempt to shoe horn a claim for loss of personal pension into *Parry v Cleaver*. The claimant should simply receive his loss of earnings *before* contributions into the fund. The loss of tax relief is a quite separate matter and if properly proved can be used to reduce the tax payable on the loss of *earnings* claim – it has nothing to do with loss of *pension*.

Hybrid personal/employer-funded schemes

12.35 Such schemes are *money purchase* plans but linked to an employer, perhaps instigated by and with contributions from him. Again there is no identifiable formula for fixing the value of the pension which depends upon the performance of the fund. Similarly, the scheme is essentially an investment of remuneration albeit *at source*. The only sensible solution in line with principle is to calculate the loss of earnings before deduction of the employee's contributions (but taking into account tax relief) and to value the employer's contributions as current (tax-free) benefits in kind. The scheme is an *investment*, as against a vehicle for payment of *future remuneration* in retirement within the spirit of *Parry v Cleaver*. There is no conflict with *Dews v National Coal Board*,[42] which can easily be distinguished as dealing with a classical final salary scheme.

12.36 Again, even weighty encouragement to obtain a quotation on the financial markets to make good either or both aspects of the supposed loss should be politely ignored. No other head of personal injury damage is calculated by reference to how the *financial markets* assesses the cost of making good the loss by *their criteria* in a lump sum investment, rather than the *court* assessing it using the *current prescribed discount rate* (and standard rules such as the inclusion of current benefits in kind as part of the claim for loss of earnings). In fact, once the fog clears and the simplicity of the obvious answer is appreciated, the temptation to rush to the financial adviser can easily be overcome.

---

[42] [1988] AC 1, HL.

Average life expectancy short of retirement

12.37 Unless medical evidence practically rules out survival beyond normal retirement age, the chance that the claimant may survive is an eventuality which calls for compensation under the conventional approach. The medical evidence should address the longest realistic life expectancy and a calculation carried out to that date but then heavily discounted against the flavour of the medical evidence for its improbability.

Death in service benefits

12.38 Quite apart from the pension payments under a final salary scheme, although unrelated to pension and to be paid prior to normal retirement, there is often death in service benefit. This has nothing to do with a claim for pension itself but certainly stands to offset any temptation to discount further for the risk of mortality. In fact, if the Ogden Tables are used as the starting point and mortality is thereby taken into account, the loss of death in service benefit is a separate loss that stands to be compensated and was in fact compensated in *Auty*. Those not entitled to *death in service benefits* have to provide for themselves by purchasing *term life assurance* at the cost of a regular premium. Provision for death in service benefits therefore amounts to another benefit in kind, which can be added on to the loss of earnings claim, as the *term* is usually for the term of the wage loss.[43] Some evidence will be required as to the size of the benefit in kind ie the sort of premium that would be required each year to produce the lump sum envisaged under the scheme in the event of death.

WORKED TYPE 2 EXAMPLE INCLUDING ALTERNATIVES OF WIDOW'S PENSION AND DEATH IN SERVICE BENEFITS

Basic facts

12.39 Male aged 40, married, previously worked as an established company accountant in industry (basic pay plus contractual overtime – £25,000 pa gross) but now, following brain injury, capable only of low grade clerical work (basic pay with no available overtime – £10,000 pa gross) with the same company who are a secure and sympathetic employer. The claimant is very likely to have remained as an employed company accountant with them and is now likely to remain with them as a clerk. No impairment of life expectancy. Unconnected constitutional condition was/is likely to become increasingly troublesome and may force retirement between 55 and 65.

---

[43] Some schemes also provide for a lump sum on death in early retirement and multipliers longer than the earnings multiplier may be appropriate.

The pension trustees' questionnaire

	Question	Answer
1	What is the formula for pension entitlement under the final salary scheme?	Pension = length of service (years subject to an overall maximum of 40 years) $\times 1/80 \times$ final year's pensionable pay
2	What constitutes *pensionable pay* under the scheme as distinct from overall earnings?	Basic pay and contractual overtime pay only, without reference to bonus payments and additional voluntary overtime.
3	What entitlement is there to a lump sum?	3 × gross annual pension tax free on top of the annual entitlement.
4	If the lump sum is a commutation of entitlements to periodical payments, how is it calculated and with what effect upon annual pension?	Not applicable
5	When did the claimant's pensionable service commence?	Aged 22½
6	Have there been *pension holidays* in respect of the claimant's service?	None

Question		Answer
7	(a) Voluntary early retirement?	At 55 without penalty (subject to the company's approval which has never yet been known to be withheld).
What are the provisions for —	(b) Ill-health early retirement?	At any age without penalty (but with the approval of the company medical officer) with an ill-health enhancement of 5 years' additional service on top of actual years service or up to 20 years' total service, whichever is the higher.
	(c) Payments under the scheme on redundancy?	Not applicable.
	(d) Preservation of pension on voluntary resignation?	Pension preserved with previous employer; or value transferable to new employer's final salary scheme; or value transferable into a personal pension plan.
	(e) Benefits on death in service or otherwise?	2 × final year's pensionable pay
	(f) Widow's pension?	Not applicable
8	In the case of a claimant who has already retired, what is the current value of the actual entitlement to pension and, if a commuted lump sum has been paid, when and how much?	Not applicable[44]

Example Schedule

12.40

Claimant's age:	40
Claimant's life multiplier:	25.61 (Ogden Table 1)
Assumption for age at retirement in keeping with the earnings multiplier	62½

---

[44] This is far too much information in most cases; but these pretty common terms go to show that the value of the pension is pretty secure and there should be no undue rush to discount for contingencies.

Earnings multiplier: 16.5 (carried forward from future loss of earnings claim where based on Ogden Table 9 for retirement at 65 – 18.05 – but discounted for the chance of early retirement based on general contingencies and the constitutional condition).

Claimant's pension multiplier: 25.61 – 16.5 = 9.11, say 9 after minor adjustment for risks

Length of service: 62.5 – 22.5 = 40 years

[If appropriate, expand to include widow's pension – see below for additional working*]

Annual income retiring as company accountant[45]

40 years × 1/80 × £25,000 =	12,500	
State retirement pension £84.25 × 52 weeks	4,381	
Annual gross income	16,881	16,881
Less higher personal allowance[46]	–7,280	
Taxable income	9,601	
Tax on 1st £2,150 @ 10%		–215
Tax on balance (£7,451) @ 22%		–1,639
		–1,854

---

[45] General templates in Word for this and the following tables are available to be downloaded at www.piba.org.uk along with the papers delivered by the author at the PIBA Annual Conference 2006.

[46] The example calculation assumes the Higher Personal Allowance and entitlement to State Retirement Pension (tax year 2006/7) strictly only available at age 65 (even though the loss begins at 62½) throughout the period given the closeness to that age. This is balanced to some extent by also ignoring the slightly increased allowance at 75.

Loss of pension

Net income				15,027

Annual income retiring as clerk

40 years × 1/80 × £10,000 = 5,000

State retirement pension
£84.25 × 52 weeks   4,381

Annual gross income	9,381	9,381	
Less higher personal allowance	−7,280		
Taxable income	2,101		
Tax on 1st £2,150 (£2,101) @ 10%		−210	
Tax on balance (£0) @ 22%		0	
		−210	
Net income			−9,171

Annual net loss in retirement		5,856
Claimant's [or *Adjusted Joint Life* – see below**] pension multiplier:		× 9
Total current capitalised value of lost annual pension		52,704

Loss of lump sum at the assumed age of 62 ½

As company accountant:	3 ×	12,500	37,500	
Less as clerk	3 ×	5,000	−15,000	
Loss at 62 ½			22,500	
Discount over 22½ years to age 40 (table 27)			× 0.5735	
Total current value of loss of lump sum				12,904
Total				£65,608

Adjustment for any other contingencies not already included …

Additions incorporating widow's pension
[Insert in the preamble at * and use multiplier in the calculation at **]

Wife aged:	35	
Wife's life multiplier: [Ogden table 2]	28.51	
Less Claimant's life multiplier:	−25.61	
Widow's survival multiplier:	2.9	
Widow's entitlement[47]:	x ½	
Widow's adjusted survival multiplier:	1.45	
Add back Claimant's pension multiplier:	9	
Adjusted joint life pension multiplier	10.45	

If the figures are adjusted in the above calculation to use an Adjusted Joint Life Pension Multiplier, it makes £5,856 × 1.45 difference ie £8,491 on to the schedule, which is well worth the little effort required.

Loss of death in service benefits

As an accountant:	2 x 25,000	50,000	
Less as a clerk	2 x 10,000	−20,000	
Loss of term life assurance to the value of		30,000	
Equivalent to benefit in kind of annual premium:		100	
Earnings multiplier		x 16.5	
Total			£1,650

---

[47] In a pension scheme where the lump sum is a commutation, unlike this example, the widow's proportion is usually expressed as a fraction of the claimant's pre-commutation entitlement. In other words, when commuting the retiring employee only commutes part of the pension during his/her own lifetime, and not on the joint lives of both. In those circumstances the widow's entitlement should be adjusted upwards as a true proportion of the post-commutation multiplicand – a point for purists only ...

Chapter 13

DAMAGES FOR CARE

13.1 For convenience I have divided this chapter into three parts. The first deals with the principles upon which awards for care are made; the second with the provision of care by the National Health Service and social services/local authorities and the recoupment of the costs of such care; the third with care in fatal cases. The practitioner needs to be aware of the extent to which the provision of the first two subjects interact since the provision of publicly funded care may have a considerable effect on the extent to which a claim for the costs of care will succeed. The third traditionally stands alone, although the principles underlying the award are essentially the same whether the claimant is injured or a dependant.

PART 1: THE PRINCIPLES UNDERLYING AN AWARD FOR CARE

Introduction

13.2 Care is usually the largest head of damage in claims for damages for serious personal injuries. It has developed into a substantial head as public awareness of the need for care has increased. A decline in the 1980s and early 1990s in the provision of publicly funded care encouraged privately funded care which led to considerable growth in the numbers of private carers and then increasing specialisation in different types of care. In the field of serious personal injuries litigation the care expert has become the norm and such expertise is no longer limited to assessing the type of care and hours of care required but needs to encompass an understanding of the operation of the Working Times Regulations, services such as care provided by local authorities and what charges local authorities may level for such services. Since the early 1990s the public call for the provision of care has imposed huge financial burdens on local authorities who may well seek to recover their outlay where possible.

13.3 Judicial input on principles has been relatively small. This is hardly surprising. In most cases the issues are factual and cases have to be decided on evidence. Care experts invariably agree that care is needed and adopt an approach of valuing care by costing it by reference to commercial hourly rates. This approach has been accepted by the courts leaving only issues of type of care appropriate, hours of care necessary, hourly rate and, where appropriate, multiplier to be decided. Decisions on principle are few. Recently, there has been an increasing number of cases concerned with extent to which the availability of residential and other care from or the funding for care by local authorities may be relevant to claims for accommodation and care. The practitioner needs to keep up with developments in this field if the interests of claimants and defendants are properly to be protected.

13.4 The need for care is not reserved to serious cases (see *Giambrone*, discussed below at paras **13.36–13.39**). It may exist in any case where as a result of injury or disease a claimant needs care (nursing or domestic) over and above that which he would normally require. Care may be provided professionally or by family or friends.

13.5 The cost of care and the cost to the country of providing benefits, especially for those suffering lasting effects of injuries, has prompted an interest in rehabilitation as a means of improving the quality of life of those injured and reducing the ongoing costs of injuries, one of which may be the need for care. Both claimants and defendants and/or their insurers benefit from rehabilitation and it is to be expected that in the not too distant future pre-action protocols will include an obligation on parties to investigate rehabilitation. At present rehabilitation is voluntary, although in serious cases it is frequently sought by claimants and/or encouraged and funded by insurers.

The principles applied in awards for care

13.6 The need for care is part of the claim for loss of amenity. Entitlement to damages to pay for necessary and reasonable expenditure on care is obviously just. However, the principle upon which awards for care are made is of uncertain validity. The historical development of this head of claim is not one of logical progression but one of the common law struggling to do justice in the face of logic. The leading cases are *Donnelly v Joyce*;[1] *Housecroft v Burnett*;[2] *Hunt v Severs*;[3] *Evans v Pontypridd Roofing Ltd*[4]. More recently *Sowden v Rudge, Drury v Crookdale* and *Crofton v NHSLA* have considered the extent to which the provision of and availability of accommodation, care and funding from local authorities ought to be taken into account in assessing awards for residential and other care.

13.7 The cost of paid care has been recoverable for many years, but gratuitous care by family or friends raises different issues. The early view was that there could be no recovery for gratuitous care. A claimant had to prove his loss, mitigate his loss and give credit for benefits received (apart from the established exceptions of financial benevolence and insurance moneys): a claimant who received gratuitous care either suffered no loss under that head, or had mitigated that loss or had to give credit for gratuitous care as a benefit. Thus gratuitous family care went uncompensated.

---

[1] [1974] QB 454.
[2] [1986] 1 AER 332.
[3] [1994] 2AC 350.
[4] [2002] PIQR Q661.

13.8 In *Roach v Yates*[5] an award was made for gratuitous care was but in *Schneider v Eisovitch*[6] Paull J held that before there could be recovery it had to be shown not only that the sums were necessary and reasonable but that the claimant undertook to pay the sum awarded to the provider. It became the practice for claimants to enter into commercial agreements with family carers thus removing the gratuitous element: see eg *Haggar v de Placido*.[7]

13.9 It was this unseemly state of affairs that greeted the Court of Appeal in *Cunningham v Harrison*[8] and *Donnelly v Joyce*,[9] decisions by different divisions of the Court of Appeal on successive days. In *Cunningham* the claimant had made an agreement to pay: Lord Denning MR said this should not be necessary and that the claimant husband should hold the award for care on trust and pay it to his caring wife. In *Donnelly* Megaw LJ set out to correct the unseemliness by holding that the claimant's loss was not the expenditure of money to buy the care but the existence of the need for the care, thus rendering irrelevant whether or not the care had to be paid for.

13.10 In the context of the provision of care, few would quarrel with the result. The reasoning in *Donnelly* was reiterated in *Housecroft*. But the importance of *Housecroft* rests on the guidelines given by O'Connor LJ, on how the award should be calculated. In *Hunt v Severs* Lord Bridge disapproved some of the reasoning in Donnelly, particularly the relevance of who provided the care, and decided that no claim could be made for care provided by the tortfeasor. Both *Housecroft* and *Hunt v Severs* are dealt with in greater detail below.

The essential principles

13.11 The following main principles represent the present law:

(a) Care, whether paid for by a claimant or provided gratuitously, is a recoverable head of damage.

(b) Where professional care has properly been employed, then the costs, if reasonable, may be recovered.

(c) The basis of a claimant's claim for gratuitous care is his need for care. It is his need for care that constitutes the loss.

(d) Where care has been provided gratuitously, eg by family or friends, then:
   (i) where the relative has reasonably given up work in order to care, he or she should not be the worse off as a result;
   (ii) the ceiling would be the commercial rate;

---

[5] [1938] 3 KB 256.
[6] [1960] 2 QB 430.
[7] [1972] 1 WLR 716.
[8] [1973] QB 942.
[9] [1974] QB 454.

(iii) the award should enable a claimant to make reasonable recompense for the care provided.

(e) Who provides the care is a relevant, or at least not an irrelevant, consideration:
   (i) where care is provided by the NHS a claimant has no claim – see Part 2;
   (ii) where care has been or will be provided by social services/local authorities, a claimant may claim the cost to the extent that he has to pay for such care – see Part 2;
   (iii) where gratuitous care is provided by the tortfeasor, a claimant has no claim.

(f) Care may be valued by way of a lump sum or by a multiplier/multiplicand approach, depending on the facts of the case.

(g) The claimant holds sums awarded for gratuitous care on trust for the carer(s).

The basis of the claim

The claimant's need for care

13.12 In Donnelly Megaw LJ said at pp 461–462:

> 'We do not agree with the proposition inherent in counsel for the Defendant's submission, that the Plaintiff's claim, in circumstances such as the present, is properly to be regarded as being, to use his phrase, "in relation to someone else's loss", merely because someone else has provided to, or for the benefit of, the plaintiff – the injured person – the money, or the services to be valued as money, to provide for needs of the plaintiff directly caused by the defendant's wrongdoing. The loss is the plaintiff's loss. The question from what source the plaintiff's needs have been met, the question who has paid the money or given the services, the question whether or not the plaintiff is or is not under a legal or moral liability to repay, are, so far as the defendant and his liability are concerned, all irrelevant. The plaintiff's loss, to take this present case, is not the expenditure of money to buy the special boots or to pay for the nursing attention. His loss is the existence of the need for those special boots or for those nursing services, the value of which for purposes of damages – for the purpose of the ascertainment of the amount of his loss – is the proper and reasonable cost of supplying those needs. That, in our judgment, is the key to the problem. So far as the defendant is concerned, the loss is not someone else's loss. It is the plaintiff's loss.'

13.13 This reasoning has not gone without criticism. The Scottish Law Commission in their report *Damages for Personal Injuries* (1978) criticised *Donnelly* and rejected the argument that the loss was the claimant's stating:

> 'The loss is in fact sustained by the person rendering the services, a point vividly illustrated in cases where he has lost earnings in the course of rendering those services. We suggest, therefore, that it is wrong in principle, in cases where services

have been rendered gratuitously by another to an injured person, to regard the latter as having in fact suffered a net loss.'

13.14 The Commission recommended legislation to attend to the problem and in Scotland s 8 Part II of the Administration of Justice Act 1992 now allows such a claim unless it is agreed or contemplated that no payment should be made.

13.15 In Australia the reasoning has been rejected in a number of states: for references see the speech of Lord Bridge in *Hunt v Severs* at pp 364H–365D. In *Hunt v Severs*[10] Lord Bridge rejected the proposition that the source from which the claimant's needs had been met was irrelevant stating at p 361E:

> '. . . I do not find this reasoning [ie *Donnelly*] convincing. I accept the basis of the plaintiff's claim for damages may consist in his need for services but I cannot accept that the question from what source that need has been met is irrelevant.'

Hardly, when coupled with his views on the Australian authorities, a strong endorsement of the reasoning in *Donnelly*.

13.16 The *Donnelly* reasoning has not been confined to care in personal injury actions. In *McAll v Brooks*[11] it was applied to enable a claimant whose motor car had been damaged in an accident to recover the cost of hire paid under agreement by a third party: the claimant's loss was held to be the need for the use of a motor car, the Court of Appeal, considering itself bound by *Donnelly*. In *Giles v Thompson*[12] Lord Mustill thought the question of what the position would have been if the use of a substitute car really had been free by no means easy but left the decision for another case.

13.17 In *Dimond v Lovell*,[13] the question did arise. The claimant was provided a replacement motor car free by way of hire whilst his own motor car underwent repair. The hire agreement did not comply with the Consumer Credit Act and was therefore unenforceable against him so that, in effect, the replacement vehicle was provided gratuitously.

13.18 The House of Lords, upheld the Court of Appeal's decision that the claimant had suffered no loss and the cost of the hire was not recoverable from the defendant, overruling *McAll*. The House did not, however, overrule *Donnelly*.

13.19 The facts of *Dimond* are far removed from the facts of *Donnelly* and *Dimond* is probably best seen as a case confined to claims for the cost of ' free' replacement motor vehicles where policy considerations differ considerably from those that arise in connection with gratuitous care. Thus the issue ruled

---

[10] [1994] 2AC 350.
[11] [1984] RTR 99.
[12] [1994] 1 AC 142.
[13] [2000] 2 WLR 1121.

on in *Donnelly*, whether one defines loss, whether in terms of expenditure or need for expenditure, remains unresolved by the House of Lords.

13.20 Since no one queries the merit of providing compensation for those who have provided care gratuitously, legislation such as s 8 of the Administration of Justice Act 1992, may provide the answer.

Care provided by the tortfeasor

13.21 In *Hunt v Severs* an attempt was made to take *Donnelly* to its logical conclusion. If it was the claimant's need for care that fell to be compensated and the source of the care was irrelevant, the fact that the carer was the tortfeasor was also irrelevant. The Court of Appeal[14] accepted this argument, rejecting the defendant's argument (or rather that of his insurers) that, damages being compensatory, a claimant was entitled to either the value or the performance of the services but not both since both would mean double recovery. Sir Thomas Bingham MR, giving the judgment at p 831, described such services as 'adventitious benefits' in the same category as services rendered voluntarily by a third party, charitable gifts or insurance payments, stating that for considerations of public policy they should not be regarded as diminishing the claimant's loss.

13.22 The House of Lords held that the source from which the claimant's needs were met was not always irrelevant, that dicta to the contrary in *Donnelly* were wrong, that damages being compensatory a claimant should recover no more and no less than he has lost and that public policy could not justify any requirement that a tortfeasor should compensate a claimant twice over for the same loss. Thus there was no recovery for care provided by the tortfeasor.

13.23 Lord Bridge at p 361E, after stating that he did not find the reasoning in *Donnelly* convincing (see above), observed:

> '... I cannot accept that the question from what source that need has been met is irrelevant. If an injured plaintiff is treated in hospital as a private patient he is entitled to recover the cost of that treatment. But if he receives free treatment under the National Health Service, his need has been met without cost to him and he cannot claim the cost of the treatment from the tortfeasor. So it cannot, I think, be right to say that in all cases the plaintiff's loss is "for the purposes of damages ... the proper and reasonable cost of supplying (his) needs".'

13.24 He further observed that the absurdity of the argument that a claimant could recover the cost of the tortfeasor's care was brought home when the tortfeasor was not insured when, if the cost of his care were recoverable, he would have to pay for his own services.

13.25 Kemp & Kemp under the editorship of the late David Kemp QC suggested that the difficulty posed by *Hunt v Severs* might be resolved by a

---

[14] [1993] QB 454.

return to pre-*Donnelly* days and that the claimant should enter into a bona fide agreement with the tortfeasor for the provision of care and then recover the cost 'as special damage'. But difficulty may arise in establishing the bona fides or reasonableness of such an agreement. In *Housecroft* O'Connor LJ at p343 c said:

> '... I am very anxious that there should be no resurrection of the practice of plaintiffs making contractual agreements with relatives to pay for what are in fact gratuitous services rendered out of love. Now that it is established that an award can be made in the absence of such an agreement, I would regard an agreement made for the purposes of trying to increase the award as a sham.'

13.26 These words were uttered before the decision in *Hunt v Severs*. But in *Hunt v Severs*, Sir Thomas Bingham in the Court of Appeal was equally disapproving of contracts of this nature.

Less serious cases

13.27 In *Mills v British Rail Engineering Ltd*,[15] Dillon LJ at p137 said:

> 'In principle it must be, in my judgement, a matter for an award only in recompense for care by the relative well beyond the ordinary call of duty for the special needs of the sufferer. The basis, as explained by O'Connor LJ in his judgement in *Housecroft v Burnett*, is that the court will make an award to enable the sufferer or his estate to make reasonable recompense to the relative who has cared so devotedly. So it must be indeed only be in a very serious case that an award is justified – where, as here, there is no question of the carer having lost wages of her or his own to look after the patient.'

13.28 Dillon LJ's view was thereafter cited as authority for the proposition that it was only in a very serious case that an award could be made. This view was disapproved by the Court of Appeal in *Giambrone v Sunworld Holidays Ltd*,[16] when it upheld awards ranging from £120 to £275 for care, mostly by parents of children who contracted gastro-enteritis and similar illnesses on holiday.

13.29 The court was clearly concerned to keep awards at modest levels in this type of case. Brooke LJ stated:

> '... I consider that any award for gratuitous care in excess of £50 per week at present day values in a case in which a child suffering from gastro-enteritis receives care from her family (so that there is no question of the cost of substitute care) should be reserved for cases more serious than these. This sum represents, in my judgement, a fair and proportionate balance, in cases of the type I have described in paras [28] to [30] above, between consideration that some payment ought to be made for the unpleasant additional burden placed on the family carer and the consideration that the care is being rendered in a family context and that the remuneration on this account should be relatively modest.'

---

[15] [1992] PIQR Q130.
[16] [2004] PIQR Q4.

13.30 Brooke LJ also noted that although Dillon LJ had used the phrase 'well beyond the ordinary call of duty' in the passage cited above he had also used the milder phrase 'beyond what a [wife] would anyway have been doing for her husband' and that it was the latter test that the Court of Appeal had applied. As can be seen, Brooke LJ contented himself with the word 'additional'.

The evaluation of gratuitous care

The approach

13.31 In *Housecroft* O'Connor LJ appears to have had in mind modest awards. He referred to 'some monetary acknowledgement', 'a present, or series of presents', and the need to look at the award as a whole in cases where the relative has not given up paid employment to care. However, in serious cases modest awards have not been typical. Courts have not looked at the award for care in the context of the award for loss of amenity as a whole.

13.32 There is no set formula for the calculation of the value of care. Each case will depend on its own facts. This was made clear in O'Connor LJ in *Housecroft* and affirmed by May LJ in *Evans v Pontypridd Roofing Ltd*.[17]

13.33 In *Housecroft* O'Connor LJ said at p 342h:

> 'Where the needs of an injured plaintiff are and will be supplied by a relative or friend out of love or affection (and in cases of little children where the provider is under a parental duty) freely and without regard to monetary reward, how should the court assess the "proper and reasonable cost"? There are two extreme solutions: (i) assess the full commercial rate for supplying the needs by employing someone to do what the relative does; (ii) assess the cost at nil, just as it is assessed at nil where the plaintiff is cared for under the national health scheme ... the reason why a nil assessment is made where the plaintiff is to be looked after under the national health service is because no expense will be incurred in supplying the needs ... It follows that in assessing the "proper and reasonable cost of supplying the needs" each case must be considered on its own facts, but it is not to be assessed regardless of whether it will be incurred.'

13.34 And at p 343d:

> 'Once it is understood that this an element in the award to the plaintiff to provide for the reasonable and proper care of the plaintiff and that a capital sum is to be available for that purpose, the court should look at it as a whole and consider whether, on the facts of the case, it is sufficient to enable the plaintiff, among other things, to make reasonable recompense to the relative. So in cases where the relative has given up gainful employment to look after the plaintiff, I would regard it as natural that the plaintiff would not wish the relative to be the loser and the court would award sufficient to enable the plaintiff to achieve that result. The ceiling would be the commercial rate. In cases like the present I would look at the award of £108,550, remembering that there is in that sum a sum of £39,000 over and above the sum required to provide the expected outgoings, and ask: is this

---

[17] [2001] EWCA, [2002] PIQR Q661.

sufficient to provide for the plaintiff's needs, including enabling her to make some monetary acknowledgement of her appreciation of all that her mother does for her ? I would also ask: is it sufficient for this plaintiff should her mother fall by the wayside and be unable to give as she gives now ?

The court is recognising that part of the reasonable and proper cost of providing for the plaintiff's needs is to enable her to make a present, or series of presents, to her mother. Neither of the extreme solutions is right. The assessment will be somewhere in between, depending on the facts of the case.'

13.35 In *Evans v Pontypridd Roofing Ltd*[18] the Court of Appeal declined to set a standard discount to be applied in each case. May LJ said at Q69:

'In my judgement, this court should avoid putting first instance judges in to too restrictive a straight-jacket, such as might happen if it was said that the means of assessing a proper recompense for services provided gratuitously by a family carer had to be assessed in a particular way or ways. Circumstances vary enormously and what is appropriate and just in one case may not be so in another. If a caring relation has given up remunerative employment to care for the claimant gratuitously, it may well be appropriate to assess the proper recompense for the services provided by reference to the carer's lost earnings. If the carer has not given up gainful employment, the task remains to assess proper recompense for the services provided. As O'Connor LJ said in *Housecroft v Burnett*, regard may be had to what it would cost to provide the services on the open market. But the services are not in fact being bought in the open market so that adjustments will probably need to be made. Since, however, any such adjustments are no more than an element in a single assessment, it would not in my view be appropriate to bind first instance judges to a conventional formalised calculation. The assessment is of an amount as a whole. The means of reaching the assessment must depend on what is appropriate to the individual case. If it is appropriate, as I think it is in the present case, to have regard to what it would cost to buy the services which Mrs Evans provides in the open market, it may well also be appropriate to scale them down. But I do not think that this can be done by means of a conventional percentage, since the appropriate extent of the scaling down and the reasons for it may vary from case to case.'

13.36 The evaluation of past non-continuing care and short periods of care clearly raises different problems from the evaluation of care for life. In *Giambrone HH* Judge Macduff, sitting as a Deputy High Court Judge, applying *Evans v Pontypridd Roofing Ltd*, rejected the approach of taking the commercial cost and discounting (which, however, he said might well be appropriate for more serious cases) and assessed the value of care very much as one would assess damages for pain suffering and loss of amenity. The Court of Appeal upheld his approach. By contrast, as noted above, in *Evans v Pontypridd Roofing Ltd* May LJ considered the extent of the care provided justified assessing the value of care by reference to a discounted commercial rate, thereby confirming the practice which has been followed for many years in more serious cases.

---

[18] [2001] EWCA, [2002] PIQR Q661 at Q69.

13.37 In serious cases, the following principles have frequently been applied by consent:

(a) Where commercial care has properly been engaged the costs are recoverable in full, subject to reasonableness.
(b)
  (i) Where family/friends have provided care the hours spent caring are assessed and the appropriate rate applied. Evidence of hours spent, rate applicable and the consequent calculations, is invariably provided by nursing experts.
  (ii) However, the rates nursing experts employ being commercial rates on which the professional carer will likely have to pay income tax, national insurance and other costs associated with employment, the calculated figures are usually discounted to allow for these factors and the fact that the care is gratuitous.

Adopting the commercial rate and discounting

Adopting the commercial rate

13.38 In *Daly v General Steam Navigation Ltd*[19] Ormrod LJ said:

'... in trying to assess what is fair compensation in an internal family situation, it is not necessarily at all reliable to have regard to market values of housekeepers or other comparable people. It introduces a wildly artificial concept if one resorts to that and talks about compensating the husband in this case at the rate of a daily woman at so many hours a week. It simply does not represent reality at all'.

13.39 By contrast, in *Housecroft* Kilner Brown J, at first instance, thought the commercial cost of care as the only yardstick by which to measure the cost of family care and that the trial judge had to have the assistance of costed figures for the appropriate type of assistance. On appeal, O'Connor LJ observed at p 343b:

'Very often we find rates being agreed and, as is shown by the approach of the judge in the present case, regard is had to what it would cost to buy the services in the open market, but it is scaled down.'

13.40 Given that the approach adopted by the judge at first instance in *Housecroft* was to take as his starting point commercial rates and that O'Connor LJ was obviously aware of the practice of starting with commercial rates and then 'scaling down', it is relevant that instead of expressly adopting the trial judge's approach he adopted reasonable recompense as the criterion of assessment. The same approach was adopted by May LJ in *Evans*. But the practice of discounting commercial rates has been endorsed by he Court of Appeal on many occasions.

---

[19] [1981] 1 WLR 120, at p 130.

The appropriate discount to the commercial rate

13.41 In practice, and bearing in mind that in most care cases a significant amount of care has been or will be provided, discounts have usually varied from 25% to 33.3%. In *Nash v Southmead Health Authority*[20] the deduction was one-third. In *Fairhurst v St Helen's and Knowsley Health Authority*[21] the deduction was 25%. In *Fitzgerald v Ford*[22] Stuart–Smith LJ took a straightforward approach and deducted 25%, pointing out at p 78:

> '£109,397 is the gross cost of employing a carer. Obviously that is not the relevant figure. It should be the net cost, which, after a reduction of 25% for tax and national insurance comes to about £82,000.'

Is there a conventional discount?

13.42 There is no conventional discount to be applied to a care award when the care is provided gratuitously by a family member. In Evans May LJ stated there was no scientific basis for a strictly mathematical approach to answer the question of what discount was appropriate nor was the exercise amenable to such an answer. In short, it again all depends on the circumstances of the case. Discounts of 25% to 33.3%, stem from the days when deductions for income tax and national insurance were looked at broadly in such percentages. But over the years income tax has reduced, although national insurance has increased. More significantly, tables are now readily available to calculate the incidence of income tax and national insurance. See, for example, the very helpful table G1 'Net equivalents to a range of gross annual income figures' published in 'Facts and Figures'. Reference to Table G1 in the 2006 edition reveals the following for the tax years 2000–2007 for an employed person.[23] The third column is the author's calculation:

Year	Gross Income	Net income	% deduction for Income Tax and National Insurance
2000/2001	£10,000	£8,342	15.68%
	£15,000	£11,742	21.72%
	£20,000	£15,142	24.29%
2001/2002	£10,000	£8476	15.24%
	£15,000	£11,876	20.82%
	£20,000	£15,276	23.62%

---

[20] [1993] PIQR Q156.
[21] [1995] PIQR Q1.
[22] [1996] PIQR Q72.
[23] The figures for 2000/2001 are for a married person. Since then marriage has not been a relevant consideration. All figures are for the employed as opposed to the self-employed.

Year	Gross Income	Net income	% deduction for Income Tax and National Insurance
2002/2003	£10,000	£8,509	14.91%
	£15,000	11,909	20.6%
	£20,000	£15,309	23.55%
2003/2004	£10,000	£8,458	15.42%
	£15,000	£11,808	21.28%
	£20,000	£15,158	24.21%
2004/2005	£10,000	£8,508	14.92%
	£15,000	£11,858	20.94%
	£20,000	£15,208	23.96%
2005/2006	£10,000	£8,566	14.33%
	£15,000	£11,916	20.56%
	£20,000	£15,266	23.66%
2006/2007	£10,000	£8,620	13.8%
	£15,000	£11,970	20.2%
	£20,000	£15,320	23.4%

13.43 These figures show that the percentage deductions for income tax and national insurance (NI) vary considerably with the annual gross figure but the percentage deductions remain relatively constant for each. If income tax and NI were the only relevant considerations for discounting then deductions of 25% to 33% would be excessive for smaller annual sums. But one must remember other matters to be considered such as expenses that go with employment and, not least, the gratuitous element. In *Burns v Davies*[24] O'Connell J said:

> '... the discount arises partly because that person pays no income tax and does not suffer any other deductions on the sum awarded but also because the care is provided out of love and affection and in the convenience of the family home where commercial considerations are not so relevant. It is clear that individual cases depend on individual facts, and such a discount is not compulsory'.

13.44 Then after pointing out that the mother had provided care in very difficult circumstances, at great cost to herself although she had not had to give up work, that there had been no uplift claimed for unsocial hours and that there was some substance in the suggestion that she had done work equivalent to two nurses he continued:

---

[24] Unreported, judgment given 7 August 1998.

'The task of the court ... is to assess a fair valuation of the care provided. Given the features which I have mentioned, in my judgement the appropriate discount which should be applied to the figure of past care is a discount of 20%. I take this figure, which is lower than the conventional 33% or 25%, bearing in mind first the high quality of the care provided and second the basic rate of tax applicable at the present time.'

13.45 In *Newman v Folkes and Dunlop Tyres Ltd*[25] Garland J did not discount the commercial rate in a case where a claimant was obsessive, potentially violent and could demand attention at any time of day or night. On appeal,[26] Ward LJ, upholding the trial judge pointed out the difficulty of employing professional carers to deal with irregular demands for care, that rates for unsocial hours were said to be two-and-a-half times higher than the ordinary rates which the judge had taken, and, citing May LJ in Evans held that there was 'such a broad margin of matters to take into account that the matter had to be looked at in the round'.

13.46 Whether or not there should be a discount and if so at what rate will therefore depend on the facts of each case, will include consideration of what deductions a commercial carer would face and take into account matters such as the nature and extent of the care, who provides it and when it is provided. It should be noted, however, that in *Evans* the Court of Appeal said of the trial judge's discount of 25%:

'In my judgment Mr Purchas' submissions do not persuade me that the judge's assessed discount in the present case of 25% was wrong. I am not persuaded that the reasons for making a discount which may be regarded as normal should result in a deduction greater than 25%. There were no grounds in the present case for making a discount which was greater or less than normal.'

Awarding more than the commercial rate

13.47 In *Hogg v Doyle*,[27] Turner J assessed a wife's care at 1.5 times her net income as a nurse on the basis that she was doing work (24-hour care of a tetraplegic) the equivalent of at least two paid carers. He was upheld on appeal. But in *Fitzgerald v Ford* (supra) the Court of Appeal allowed an appeal against an evaluation of care based on 1.5 times loss of the carer's earnings, Stuart-Smith LJ stating at p 77:

'... there is no principle involved in *Hogg v Doyle*. It is a case on its own facts. In particular, there is no principle that, simply because a member of the family gives up full – time paid work where they probably work eight hours a day for five days a week, when they become a full–time carer being available to help if need be throughout the 24 hours, they should be paid at the rate of 1.5 of their earnings, or, indeed, any more than their loss of earnings. In many cases, the actual nursing or physical assistance may only take a few hours distributed throughout the day or

---

[25] [2002] PIQR, [2002] Q13.
[26] [2002] EWCA Civ 591.
[27] (Unreported) Kemp Vol 2 A2–006/1.

night. For the rest of the time it will be spent in preparation and cooking of meals, shopping, laundry, jobs concerned with the maintenance of the house, all of which have to be done for the carer and any other members of the family in any case. In addition time will be spent on going out on visits or acts of companionship, conversation or mutual occupation.'

Lump sum damages and periodical payments

13.48 Historically, future care has been is calculated as a once and for all lump sum. The introduction of periodical payments by consent under the Damages Act 1996 had no impact on this practice since the provision was, in practice, disregarded. The introduction of periodical payments, which may now be imposed by the court under the amendments to the Damages Act 1996, introduced by ss 100 and 101 of the Courts Act 2003, have yet to become a daily feature of claims for future care in personal injuries and clinical negligence actions. I discuss them below.

The traditional approach – lump sum damages

13.49 Assessing the appropriate lump sum for future care employs the multiplier/multiplicand approach, the multiplier representing the period of the loss, frequently dependent on life expectancy, and the multiplicand being the annual valuation of the care to be provided. Where there is no reduction in life expectancy then reference to the Ogden Tables will produce the appropriate multiplier for the claimant's age. Where life expectancy is agreed or decided by the judge as a fixed period then an arithmetic multiplier is appropriate: see *Wells v Wells*. Split multipliers will be appropriate where the need for care will change: the need for care in a seriously injured claimant will almost certainly increase towards the end of life, but it may also increase earlier with events such as pregnancy and the need to care for children.

13.50 Medical evidence on life expectancy is essential if a reduction or increase in normal life expectancy is to be argued. Lord Bridge's view in *Hunt v Severs* (above) at p 365G that life expectancy is not exclusively a medical question and that even where doctors agreed life expectancy, some discount for 'life's manifold contingencies' was appropriate was not followed by the House of Lords in *Wells v Wells*. Similarly the approach of Stuart-Smith LJ in *Fitzgerald v Ford* (above) at p 80 where he suggested that because of the uncertainties involved in the exercise the court should take the mean period or '50% chance' figure between the competing periods contended for. *Wells v Wells* makes clear that actuarial figures should be the starting point and only departed from where justified by the evidence.

Periodical payments

The substantive law

13.51 This is not the place to discuss in detail the substantive law on periodical payments now contained in ss 2, 4 and 5 of the Damages Act 1996 as substituted by ss 100–101 of the Courts Act 2003 but the practitioner dealing with a claim for future care must be aware of them. Care was a head of damage for which Lord Steyn in *Wells v Wells* thought periodical payments especially appropriate.

13.52 The Courts Act 2003 s 100 substitutes a new section for Damages Act 1996 s 2(1). Periodical payments apply only in respect of **awards for future pecuniary loss in respect of personal injury.** Although the court retains the power to order periodic payments by consent, **consent is no longer necessary**. The **court has a duty to consider whether or not to order periodic payments** in respect of **all or part of the award,** and, where appropriate may make such an award. But there are **restrictions** on the court's power. In particular, such an order may not be made unless the court is satisfied that **continuity of payment under the order is reasonably secure** (s 2(3)). By s 2(4) continuity of payment is reasonably secure if protected by a guarantee given under s 6 of the Schedule to the Act, is protected by a scheme under s 213 of the Financial Services and Markets Act 2000 (which requires insurers to close match assets and liabilities), or the source of payment is a government or health service body. By s 2(8) orders for periodical payments are to be treated as providing for the amount of payments to vary by reference to the retail prices index unless this section is disapplied or modified (s 2(9)). Finally, by way of summary of the essentials, under a new s 2B, the Lord Chancellor is given power to make an order enabling courts to vary orders for periodical payments, where the original order permits a party to apply for variation.

Practice and procedure

13.53 The Act left a lot of the detail to be filled in by Civil Procedure Rules. Such detail is now provided by CPR 41.4 – 41.10 which set out procedures to be followed and criteria to be taken into consideration. Each party may in its statement of case state whether it considers periodical payments or a lump sum is more **appropriate for all or part** of the award for damages. In the absence of such a statement the court may order a party to make such a statement (CPR 41.5). The court will then consider and indicate to the parties "as soon as practicable" whether an order for periodical payments or lump sum is likely to be appropriate (CPR 41(6)). It is envisaged that this will be at case management. In reaching its decision the court, in time honoured tradition, is to have regard to "all the circumstances of the case" but in particular to the form of award which best meets the claimant's needs, having regard to the factors set out in the practice direction (CPR 41.7).

13.54 Practice Direction 41B specifies the following factors:

(a) the scale of the annual payments, after allowing for any negligence;

(b) the form of award preferred by the claimant including:
 (i) the reasons for the claimant's preference; and
 (ii) the nature of any financial advice received by the claimant; and

(c) the form of award preferred by the defendant including the reasons for the defendant's preference.

Periodical payments and index linking

13.55 The new regime of periodical payments has had little effect so far not least because it is considered that tying the payments to the Retail Prices Index ('RPI') will not enable those payments to keep pace with increasing care costs and because of the difficulties of finding an insurance company providing annuities tied to any index other than the RPI. In practice awards of periodical payments have been rare and confined to NHS clinical negligence cases, where the payment is government funded, and claims involving the Motor Insurers' Bureau, but even in such cases awards had been tied to the RPI. Two recent cases, *Flora v Wakom (Heathrow)*[28] and *Thompstone v Tameside and Glossop Acute Services NHS Trust*,[29] have moved the arguments forward in this field.

13.56 In *Flora* the defendants sought to strike out that part of the claimant's case where he contended that the index by reference to which periodical payments should be increased should be an index other than RPI. The defendants argued that such a claim had no reasonable prospects of success and that the court should refuse the claimant permission to call expert evidence in support of his contention. Sir Michael Turner's firmly rejected these submissions and was upheld in the Court of Appeal.

13.57 In *Thompstone* Swift J had to rule on two issues

(a) whether an order for periodical payments for future care should be varied by reference to the RPI pursuant to s 2(8) of the Damages Act 1996 or whether such an order should be modified under s 2(9);

(b) following determination of (a) whether the award should be by way of periodical payments or a lump sum.

13.58 The claimant contended for an order for periodical payments for future care, that indexation to the RPI was inappropriate and that one of the following indices/measures should be adopted:

(a) the Average Earnings Index ('AEI');

(b) the Annual Survey of Hours and Earnings 50 median ('ASHE 50 median');

(c) the Annual Survey of Hours and Earnings: Occupational Earnings for Care Assistants and Home Carers ('ASHE 6115').

---

[28] [2006] EWCA Civ 1103.
[29] [2006] EWHC 2904 QB.

13.59 The defendant argued that distributive justice/affordability, which Swift J regarded as essentially the same on the facts of the case (either impact on the public by way of increased insurance premiums or reduction in resources where government funding is concerned), militated against allowing variation. Swift J rejected this argument and, as in *Flora*, held that the courts should award full compensation. After detailed expert evidence she concluded that such periodical payments should be indexed by reference to the 75th percentile of ASHE 6115 and held that periodical payments were appropriate for the case. She rejected the RPI: it was not a tool for measuring growth in earnings; historically earnings had grown at a significantly faster rate than RPI and indexing care costs by reference to the RPI would inevitably lead to under-compensation. She considered both the AEI and ASHE data as reliable and authoritative but considered the most serious disadvantage of the AEI would be the systematic over-compensation likely to result from its use. To a lesser extent the ASHE median could result in over-compensation on the facts of the case. She preferred ASHE 6115 to the ASHE median because it could more sensitively track changes in the care market, and the 75th percentile as it most closely appeared to fit the average hourly rate likely to be paid in the case.

13.60 *Thompstone* is under appeal and other cases are in the pipeline. The probabilities are that it will be some time before periodical payments become the established basis of funding care, assuming that claimants wish to fund their care by that means. While indices or measures other than the RPI may be appropriate for the calculation of future care, the lack of annuity providers will prevent such returns being provided in non-government funded and MIB cases. Many claimants retain the traditional preference for a lump sum and/or consider that with proper investment advice they can obtain a return on their award that will outweigh the benefits of periodical payments.

13.61 Those representing claimants will need to ensure that future care contingencies are properly catered for – see, for example, O'Connor LJ in *Housecroft* at p 342h: 'Is it sufficient for this plaintiff should her mother fall by the wayside?' A periodical payments order may not be varied unless the original order so provides. Where serious deterioration or significant improvement may occur, parties must be alive to the need to ensure the original order contains a variation provision.

General points

No recovery for care and carer's loss of earnings

13.62 Where a carer gives up work to care then the claimant cannot recover the carer's loss of income as well as the value of care. No one can do two jobs at once: see *Fish v Woolcock*.[30]

---

[30] [1994] 5 Med LR 230.

Interim payments to fund care

13.63 Where a care claim is inevitable it is only sensible, where this can be achieved, for interim payments to be obtained to set up any necessary regime and go some way to taking the burden of caring from the family who might otherwise not cope satisfactorily. Interim payments are ultimately a matter for the discretion of the court but a court is not likely to reject such a request where reasonably made. In *Cambell v Mylchreest* [1999] PIQR Q17, CA, an interim payment was sought expressly to set up a regime of part home care for a severely injured claimant cared for in a home. The defendants resisted on the basis that to make such an award would interfere with the 'level playing field' which ought to exist between the parties. The Court of Appeal held the request reasonable.

Interest on care

13.64 Past care attracts interest as special damage: see *Roberts v Johnstone* [1987] QB 878 and *Davies v Inman* [1999] PIQR Q26.

Who has title to the award?

13.65 In *Cunningham* Lord Denning MR said a claimant held the award on trust for the carer. In *Housecroft* O'Connor LJ at p 343d considered this obiter and thought it inconsistent with *Donnelly* – the loss was the claimant's loss. In *Hunt v Severs* Lord Bridge at p 363C adopted Lord Denning's view. More recently, in *ATH v MS* [2003] PIQR Q1 the Court of Appeal in a claim brought under the Fatal Accidents Act, followed *Hunt v Severs*, holding that damages for care could only be awarded on the basis that they were used to reimburse the voluntary carer for services already rendered and were available to pay for such services in the future. The court ordered that the award be brought in to court for further directions. It is worth noting, however, that in this case there was already a trust set up for the benefit of two of the dependants.

The effect of contributory negligence

13.66 The argument that a claimant will not be able to fund the care he seeks because contributory negligence will reduce the award necessary for the funding was rejected by the Court of Appeal in *Sowden v Lodge*,[31] where the court pointed out that under the s 1 of the Law Reform (Contributory Negligence) Act 1945 contributory negligence does not defeat the claim but 'the damages recoverable ... shall be reduced to such extent as the court thinks just'.

Early advice

13.67 In cases involving tetraplegia, paraplegia and serious brain damage, there is no substitute for early advice. Not only will this assist in overall valuation of the claim but it can be of inestimable value to a claimant. From a defendant's

---

[31] [2004] EWCA Civ 1370.

point of view, an early assessment not only assists in valuation, so necessary for the insurer's reserve, but enables a defendant to have some reasoned input into suggestions for care.

Differing approaches in different cases

13.68 Different types of case will dictate different approaches to care. For example:

(a) In a typical case of a broken leg or arm, most claimants do not think of claiming for care. Yet almost inevitably someone has to provide support and care and may lose income as a result. In such cases no report ought to be necessary to value the care, which can be done by reference to any loss of income and/or the British Nursing Association rates for carers set out in Facts & Figures unless the defendant is resisting the claim.

(b) In serious spinal injury cases, the level of lesion is often crucial to the level of care needed. Here a report is essential. In such cases sometimes care is evaluated by a nursing expert and an occupational therapist deals with aids, equipment and therapies. But an appropriately qualified expert may cover both.

(c) Brain damage cases may form a separate category. In catastrophic brain damage cases the claimant may have many of the problems of a tetraplegic or paraplegic. But not infrequently a brain damaged claimant may be able to live in the community. Such a claimant may well need not clinical care but supervision which may need to be constant or near constant. A new class of carer variously called an enabler, support worker, or coach has emerged. Sadly, the demands such patients make frequently result in carers moving on and the need for new carers to be recruited. This needs to be allowed for in costing such care. Again a report is essential and it is important that it is obtained from someone who understands the problems that brain damage can cause. Sometimes an assessment with attendance at a specialist hospital/unit to evaluate needs is appropriate.

(d) Case managers, whose expertise lies in organising and implementing systems of care, have become an established feature. They may have more relevance in brain damage than spinal injury cases but each case will depend on its facts. Good ones are in short supply.

(e) Care reports frequently cost on the basis of two or more carers, it being said that in practice a system of two or more alternating carers is more practical and more reliable. In more demanding cases this is frequently so. With the introduction of restrictions on working hours, two or more carers are frequently the norm. The live-in housekeeper willing to be on call for 24 hours a day may well become a thing of the past.

(f) Resident carers need to be housed and even daytime carers need space. It is therefore sensible in serious cases to ensure that the expert architect and care expert (and other experts with related expertise) discuss the options before any decisions are made. Too frequently claimants needing care move home only to realise too late that the new home is unsuitable. Where both care and housing are required, a concerted approach is essential.

(g) Too frequently care reports are updated only at the last minute and/or the initial recommendation for care has either not been implemented or has been varied with no revised costings available. Care experts are always too busy. Make sure that the up-to-date situation is appraised well before trial.

The Working Time Regulations 1998[32]

13.69 The employment of carers is subject to the Working Time Regulations 1998 as amended. In summary they provide that working time, which includes overtime, shall not exceed an average of 48 hours for each seven days, that a night worker's normal hours of work shall not exceed an average of eight hours for each 24 hours and that a night worker whose work involves special hazards or heavy physical or mental strain shall not work for more than eight hours in any 24-hour period, that every adult (young ie aged 15–18) worker has an uninterrupted rest period of not less than 11(12) hours in any 24-hour working day and 24 (48) hours in each seven day working period, that adult workers are entitled to a rest break of not less than 20 minutes where their daily working time exceeds six hours and young workers a rest break of not less than 30 minutes where their daily working time exceeds 4½ hours. In addition the Regulations make provision for paid leave. There are limited exceptions to some of these provisions.

13.70 These provisions implement European Directives and in addition to being applied in employment tribunals have been the subject of review by the European Court. The whole of the time when an employee is required to be on the premises and on call counts as 'working time' regardless of whether the employee is actively engaged on duty : see *MacCartney v Oversley House Management*.[33]

13.71 It can easily be seen that these provisions have a significant effect on the employment of carers. The days of the 24-hour resident carer are over.

---

[32] For a helpful article on the subject see Anthony Seys-Llewellyn QC 'The Single Resident Carer – An endangered Species?' [2006] JPIL Issue 3/06.
[33] [2006] ICR 510.

PART 2: THE PROVISION OF CARE BY HEALTH AUTHORITIES AND LOCAL AUTHORITIES AND RECOUPMENT OF THE COST OF CARE

Introduction

13.72 This is a developing field where there are many statutory provisions, some imposing duties and some providing powers for the provision of care. It is also a field where the statutory provisions overlap, are regularly changed and where guidance notes published by the Secretary of State attempt to explain the provisions and steer local authorities through the maze. Recently, the Court of Appeal expressed its dismay at the complexity and labyrinthine nature of the relevant legislation and guidance as well as (in some respects) its obscurity.[34] It is a field where the demarcation of responsibilities between health authorities and local authorities is blurred in practice, where local authorities' practices differ and where local authorities are still testing the water. It is an area of law and practice where significant developments have taken place in recent years and where we may expect further developments not least by way of legislation, since government has indicated an intention to implement the Law Commission's recommendation that tortfeasors should fund the care of those they injure.[35] What follows should, therefore, be regarded merely as an introduction to the topic, a tentative dipping of a toe into the water. There can be no substitute for going to the relevant source.

13.73 Publicly funded care is provided usually by a health authority or a local authority. In general terms clinical care is the responsibility of the NHS and social care is the responsibility of the social services /local authorities but there are grey areas. The decision of the Court of Appeal in *Avon County Council v Hooper*[36] that a local authority was entitled to recover the costs of residential care provided for an injured child, prompted concern amongst insurers that they would be called upon to pay for care hitherto provided for the most part free-of-charge, and amongst claimants that they would be called on to reimburse local authorities for care provided and hence needed to protect themselves from such liabilities. Since *Avon* a number of cases have highlighted the issues and problems that may arise with publicly funded care. Where publicly funded care falls to be considered it is crucial to discover who has funded the care, and if by both health and local authorities, in what proportions and under what statutory provisions. NHS services have, for the most part, to be provided free of charge. So far as local authority services are concerned, some statutes enable the local authority to recover its outlay or a contribution thereto : others do not.

13.74 The main statutes dealing with the provision of services including accommodation and care are:

---

[34] Per Dyson LJ in *Crofton v NHSLA* [2007] EWCA Civ 71 at para 111.
[35] Law Commission Report: Damages for Personal Injury: Medical Nursing and other Expenses (Law Com No 262) paras 2.8–2.10.
[36] [1996] 1 WLR 1605, 1997 25 BMLR 26.

- National Health Service Act 1977;

- National Health Service Act (Primary Care) Act 1997;

- Health and Social Care Act 2001;

- Children Act 1989;

- National Assistance Act 1948;

- National Health and Community Care Act 1990;

- Chronically Sick and Disabled Persons Act 1970;

- Health and Social Services and Social Security Adjudications Act 1983;

- Disabled Persons (Services, Consultation and Representation) Act 1986;

- Carers (Recognition and Services) Act 1995;

- Carers and Disabled Children Act 2000;

- Care Standards Act 2000;

- Health and Social Care Act 2001.

Provision of care by the National Health Service

13.75 The Secretary of State, who acts by health authorities, is responsible for arranging and funding a range of services to meet the needs of people who require continuing physical or mental health care. The obligation to provide these services (hospital and other accommodation and facilities for, inter alia, care and after-care) stems from The National Health Service Act 1946 and is now contained in ss 1–7 of the National Health Service Act 1977 as amended. Under s 23 of the 1977 Act the Secretary of State may arrange for such services to be provided by any person or body including voluntary organisations.

13.76 Provision of services under the NHS is, in the main, free. Section 1(2) of the 1977 Act provides:

> 'The services so provided shall be free of charge except in so far as the making and recovery of charges is expressly provided for by or under any enactment, whenever passed.'

13.77 Section 80 provides:

> 'Regulations may provide for the making and recovery of charges in respect of facilities designated by the regulations as facilities provided in pursuance of paragraph (d) or paragraph (e) of Section 3(1) above.'

13.78 Regulations have been made under s 80 enabling charges for goods for expectant mothers. Other statutory provisions have enabled charges to be made for such as medical prescriptions, dental treatment and the provision of spectacles. Sections 63–65 inclusive enable charges to be made in very limited circumstances namely for accommodation not needed on medical grounds (s 63); to charge part of the costs of maintenance where resident patients are in remunerative employment (s 64); and for private patients (s 65). But there is no general provision at present enabling a health authority to recover for accommodation, treatment and residential care as such.

13.79 The above sections do not authorise the Secretary of State to charge patients for NHS services provided pursuant to his duty whether under s 1 or s 23. For him to do so would be an abdication of his responsibilities under s 1 and ultra vires. Hence in *Secretary of State for Social Security and the Chief Adjudication Officer v Percival White*[37] an attempt to deduct state benefits from the cost of care in a private nursing home contracted under s 23 ('a hospital' within s 2) failed.

13.80 Recently, there has been an important change in respect of NHS hospital and ambulance services. Section 150 of the Health and Social Care (Community Health and Standards) Act 2003, which came into force on 28 January 2007, provides that any person who has made a compensation payment in respect of an injury to another person will be liable to pay relevant NHS charges for treatment and ambulance services provided to that person. This legislation may be the first step in implementing the Law Commission's proposals (see footnote 37 ante). It does not affect the assessment of damages as between the claimant and the tortfeasor but will impose extra liabilities on tortfeasors and their insurers.

The relevance of the availability of NHS accommodation and care

13.81 Section 2(4) of the Law Reform (Personal Injuries) Act 1948 as amended provides:

> 'In an action for damages for personal injuries . . . there shall be disregarded, in determining the reasonableness of any expenses, the possibility of avoiding those expenses or part of them by taking advantage of facilities available under the National Health Service Act 1977 . . .'

13.82 The subsection prevents a defendant arguing that a claimant is being unreasonable in employing private medical care where such care is available to him under the NHS. It does not enable a claimant using or intending to use NHS facilities to recover the costs of medical care. This was first made clear by Slade J in *Harris v Brights Asphalt Contractors*[38] when he said at p 635:

---

[37] [1993] 17 BMLR 68.
[38] [1953] 1QB 617.

'I do not understand section 2(4) to enact that a plaintiff shall be deemed to be entitled to recover expenses which he will never incur.'

13.83 This view was adopted by Lord Scarman in *Lim Po Choo v Camden and Islington Area Health Authority*;[39] and in *Housecroft* O'Connor LJ stated[40] that the reason why a nil assessment is made when the claimant is looked after by the NHS is because no expense will be incurred. See also: *Lord Bridge in Hunt v Severs*;[41] *Woodrup v Nicol*;[42] and *Eagle v Chambers (No 2)*.[43]

13.84 There is therefore no obligation on a claimant to avail himself of NHS treatment and care. He may do so if he wishes or intend to do so and, if he does, he cannot claim for what has been provided or will be provided free of charge. But if he prefers to have private treatment or care he is entitled to claim the reasonable costs of such treatment or care.

Provision of care by social services/local authorities

13.85 Social services legislation, sometimes contained in NHS Acts, makes provision for community social services for the injured and those in poor health. The duty or power, as the case may be, to provide such services which may include care and accommodation.is vested in local authorities who may have a duty or power to charge for these services.

13.86 Examples of such provisions may be found in the National Assistance Act 1948 as amended, The National Health Service Act 1977 as amended, the Health and Social Services and Social Security Adjudications Act 1983 and the Children Act 1989. The local authority's entitlement to contribution depends on the statutory provision under which the service is provided. Relevant criteria frequently include:

(i) the status of the person to whom the service is provided, eg an adult, a child under 16, a child aged 16–18, a beneficiary under a trust, or a patient under the Mental Health Acts.

(ii) means, which in the case of a child may include the means of the parents;

(iii) whether the means derive from an award of damages for personal injuries.

The National Assistance Act 1948 and the National Health Service and Community Care Act 1990

13.87 The present structure of provision is contained in the National Assistance Act 1948 and the National Health Service and Community Care

---

[39] [1980] AC 174 at pp 187E–188D.
[40] At p 342J.
[41] At p 361E.
[42] [1993] PIQR, Q104, 114.
[43] [2004] EWCA Civ 1033.

Act 1990. Under s 47 of the 1990 Act the disabled have a right to have their needs assessed and where need is established to have a right to receive residential accommodation and/or care under various statutory provisions listed in s 46 of the Act[44] which include Part III of the 1948 Act which in turn contains ss 21–29. Sections 21 and 229 are the most frequently employed sections for the provision of accommodation and care by local authorities.

Section 21 – residential accommodation/care

13.88 Section 21(1) of the National Assistance Act 1948 as amended provides as follows:

> '... a local authority may with the approval of the Secretary of State and to such extent as he may direct make arrangements for providing
>
> (a) residential accommodation for persons aged 18 or more who by reason of age, illness, disability or any other circumstances are in need of care and attention which is not otherwise available to them.'

13.89 Section 21(2A) of the Act, inserted by s 53 of the Health and Social Care Act 2001, provides that in determining for the purposes of s 21(1)(a) whether care and attention are otherwise available to a person, a local authority shall disregard so much of the person's resources as may be specified in, or determined in accordance with, regulations made by the Secretary of State for the purpose.

Recoupment of costs of accommodation/care provided under s 21

13.90 Section 22(1) provides:

> '... where a person is provided with accommodation under this Part of this Act the local authority providing the accommodation shall recover from him the amount of the payment which he is liable to make in accordance with the following provisions of this section.'

The section goes on to provide that the recipient of accommodation under the section shall be liable to pay for that accommodation at a standard rate, less what he needs for his personal requirements (a fixed sum prescribed by the minister) or such lesser sum as he can afford.

13.91 Importantly, s 22(5) specifies that in assessing a person's means to pay, the local authority shall give effect to regulations made by the minister for the purposes of the subsection. The relevant regulations are the National

---

[44] Part III of the National Assistance Act 1948, S 45 of the Health Services and Public Health Act 1968, s 21 of and Sch 8 to the National Health Service Act 1977; and s 117 of the Mental Health Act 1983.

Assistance (Assessment of Resources) Regulations 1992 as amended,[45] the Income Support (General) Regulations 1987 and the National Assistance (Residential Accommodation) (Disregarding of Resources) (England) Regulations 2001.

13.92 In *Crofton v NHSLA* the Court of Appeal concluded obiter that the effect of reg 21 of the National Assistance (Residential Accommodation) (Disregarding of Resources) (England) Regulations 2001 and para 19 of Sch 4 to the National Assistance (Assessment of Resources) Regulations 1992 was that, when assessing entitlement to local authority-funded accommodation, for the purposes of calculating the claimant's capital, where the claimant's damages derived from an award for personal injuries and were administered by the Court of Protection, that capital should be disregarded. The court was less sure about the position of income deriving from that capital but concluded it too should be regarded.

Section 29 – services including home care

13.93 Whereas s 21 is tied to accommodation, s 29 is of much wider application. Its scope has been defined by s 2 of the Chronically Sick and Disabled Act 1970 and ministerial guidance. By these provisions local authorities have a duty to provide advice and support for the needy which extends to the provision of care or the payment for care in their own homes. The relevant provisions are as follows.

13.94 Section 29 National Assistance Act 1948 provides:

> '(1) A local authority may, with the approval of the Secretary of State and to such extent as he may direct in relation to **persons ordinarily resident in the area** of the local authority shall make **arrangements for promoting the welfare** of persons to whom this section applies...'

13.95 Section 2 of the Chronically Sick and Disabled Person Act 1970 ('CSDPA 1970') provides:

> '(1) Where a local authority having functions under section 29 of the National Assistance Act 1948 are satisfied in the case of any person to whom that section applies who is ordinarily resident in their area that it is **necessary in order to meet the needs** of that person for that authority to make arrangements for all or any of the following matters, namely –
>
> (a) the provision of practical assistance for that person in his home...then,[46]... it shall be the duty of the authority to make those arrangements in exercise for their functions under the said section 29.'

---

[45] At the time of going to press there are some 32 amendments applying variously to England, Wales and Scotland, updating annual allowances, identifying benefits to be disregarded in assessment etc.

[46] Subject to the provisions of s 7(1) of the Local Authority Social Services Act 1970 (which

13.96 Directions were given by the Secretary of State on 17 March 1993 in App 2 to Local Authority Circular (LAC(93)10). Paragraph 2 provides:

> 'The Secretary of State hereby approves...and directs local authorities to make arrangements under section 29(1) of the Act ...for all or any of the following purposes –
>
> (a) to provide a social work service and such **advice and support** as may be needed for people **in their own homes or elsewhere;**...'

Recoupment of costs of care provided under Section 29

13.97 In the case of s 21, specific provision for recoupment was made by s 22. No such provision was contained in the 1948 Act for services provided under s 29. However, s 17 of the Health and Social Services and Social Security Adjudications Act 1983 confers a discretion on local authorities to recover charges from persons to whom services are provided inter alia under s 29. That discretion is subject to the direction and guidance of the Secretary of State. The mechanism for the recoupment of the costs of care provided under s 29 is therefore via s 17 of the 1983 Act which is dealt with below.

The Health and Social Services and Social Security Adjudications Act 1983

13.98 Section 17 of the Health and Social Services and Social Security Adjudications Act 1983 provides as follows:

> **'Provision and Recoupment**
>
> (1) Subject to subsection (3) below, an authority providing a service to which this section applies may recover such charge (if any) for it as they consider reasonable.
>
> (2) This section applies to services provided under the following enactments: [The provisions listed include welfare arrangements for the blind and infirm, welfare of old people, services provided under Schedule 8 (which include care and after care) and meals and recreation for old people.]
>
> (3) If a person –
>
> (a) avails himself of a service to which this section applies and
> (b) satisfies the authority providing the service that his means are insufficient for it to be reasonably practicable for him to pay for the service the amount which he would otherwise be obliged to pay for it,
>
> the authority shall not require him to pay more for it than it appears to them that it is reasonably practicable for him to pay.'

---

requires local authorities in the exercise of certain functions, including functions under s 29, to act under the general guidance of the Secretary of State).

13.99 Guidance on the exercise of this discretion was issued by the Department of Health in *Fairer Charging Policies for Home Care and other non-residential Social Services* (2003). This states there is no presumption that local authorities will charge but, where they do, they retain a **'substantial discretion in the design of charging policies'**. It offers detailed guidance on which resources should be taken into account. It states savings and capital may be taken into account. In particular savings may be taken into account to calculate a tariff income on the same basis as in CRAG (see below).

13.100 Section 57 Health and Social Care Act 2001 provides for those needing services pursuant to assessment under s 47 of the NHS and Community Care Act 1990 to receive **direct payments to secure the provision of those services**.

13.101 The Community Care, Services for Carers and Children's Services (Direct Payments) (England) Regulations 2003 makes provision for the determination of those direct payments. Under reg 5 the local authority has to determine 'having regard to the prescribed person's means what amount or amounts (if any) it is reasonably practicable for him to pay'.

What means may be taken into account for charges under s 17

13.102 This is an area that justifies the description 'labyrinthine'. The publication *Direct Payments Guidance Community Care Services for Carers and Children's Services (Direct Payments) Guidance England 2003*, issued by the Department of Health, identifies 'Fairer Charging Policies' as offering the relevant guidance. Further detailed guidance may be found in *Charges for Residential Accommodation Guidance* (CRAG) LAC(99)9.

13.103 In *Crofton v NHSLA* the Court of Appeal, as noted above, reasoned that the effect of reg 21 of the 2001 Regulations and para 19 of Sch 4 to the Assessment of Resources Regulations was that for the purposes of calculating the claimant's capital, where the claimant's damages derived from an award for personal injuries and were administered by the Court of Protection both that capital and income deriving from it would be disregarded. It found it striking that there was no like provision in the National Assistance Act 1948 or the Chronically Sick and Disabled Persons Act 1970 but refused to infer from this difference that Parliament had in mind different policies for provision under s 21 and s 29 of the National Assistance Act. The court reasoned that the Fairer Charging Policy stated that forms of capital other than a main residence should not be taken into account and CRAG should be applied. Paragraph 6.028 of CRAG states that the value of funds held in trust or administered by a court and that derive from a payment for personal injury is a capital asset that is disregarded indefinitely. Thus, so far as s 17 of the 1983 Act and therefore s 29 of the National Assistance Act were concerned capital deriving from an award of personal injuries and held in trust or administered by the court, and income deriving from that capital, fell to be disregarded. Although the decision was limited to capital administered by the Court of Protection, the reasoning would apply it to such payments held in trust as well.

The decision in *Avon CC v Hooper*

13.104 In *Avon CC v Hooper*[47] a child born in 1978 was brain-damaged at birth as a result of negligence for which a health authority was liable. The child was cared for by the local authority in a Cheshire home from 1981 until his death in 1991. The child's claim had been the subject of an action against the health authority and the agreed settlement had included the cost of future care and an indemnity to the child's estate for any sums the claimant (ie the local authority) might lawfully recover from the estate for care from 1981 to November 1989. The local authority was held entitled to recover from the deceased child's estate the costs of care provided to the child but recovery was limited to the six-year period preceding the issue of the writ in 1991.

13.105 The case decided that a local authority could recover charges under s 17 retrospectively provided the local authority acted reasonably (Hobhouse LJ said it was implicit in the section that the local authority had to act reasonably), the charge was reasonable, and the defendant had the means to pay.

13.106 No question of recovery for future loss arose and it would seem implicit in *Avon* that the indemnity was regarded as part of the child's means. The case is concerned solely with the right of recovery under s 17. It does not deal with obligations of the respective authorities qua authorities to fund care. It just happened to be that the health authority was the tortfeasor.

13.107 Section 17 does not apply to all care services provided by local authorities. The services to which it applies are set out in s 17(2). In *R v Powys CC ex parte Hambridge*[48] it was held that s 17(2) applied also to services provided under the Chronically Sick and Disabled Persons Act 1970. But in *Thrul v Ray*[49] a claim for an indemnity against the cost of accommodation failed on the basis that the accommodation provided under s 21 of the National Assistance Act 1948, which was not caught by s 17(2). Services provided under s. 29 of the Act are referred to expressly in s 17(2).

The National Health Service Act 1977

13.108 Schedule 8, para 2 to the National Health Service Act 1977 enables a local social services authority, with the Secretary of State's approval, to make arrangements for the prevention of illness and for the care and after care of persons suffering or who have been suffering from illness, in particular by the provision of residential accommodation. The power extends to the care of persons suffering from mental disorder who are received into guardianship under Part II or Part III of the Mental Health Act 1983.

---

[47] [1996] 1 WLR 1605; [1997] 25 BMLR 26.
[48] [1998] 1CCLR 458.
[49] [2000] PIQR Q44.

Recoupment of the costs of care under The National Health Service Act 1977

Section 17(2) of the 1983 Act applies s 17 to services provided under Sch 8 of the 1977 Act.

The Children Act 1989

Provision of accommodation/care

13.109 This Act, in addition to reforming the law relating to children, deals with the provision of services by local authorities for children in need, children's homes, fostering etc. In particular:

(a) Section 17 imposes on local authorities a duty to safeguard and promote the welfare of *children* within their area and, so far as is consistent with that duty, to promote the upbringing of such children by their families by providing services appropriate to their needs. Such services may include assistance in kind or cash. For these purposes local authorities have specific duties and powers set out in Part 1 of Sch 2 to the Act. A child is taken to be in need if it is unlikely to achieve a reasonable standard of development without the provision of services by a local authority or is disabled as defined by s 17(11), which states:

> '...a child is disabled if he is blind, deaf or dumb or suffers from mental disorder of any kind or is substantially and permanently handicapped by illness, injury or congenital deformity or such other disability as may be prescribed ...'

Part I Sch 2 to the Act provides (paras I(1) and (3)) that local authorities shall take steps to identify the extent to which children in their area are in need, maintain a register of disabled children, and that they may assess their needs at the same time as any assessment of needs is made under other Acts.[50] Schedule 2 (para 6) provides that local authorities shall provide services designed to minimise the effect of disabilities on disabled children and give them the opportunity to live lives as normal as possible. Where children in need are living with their families, para 8 provides that local authorities shall make provision inter alia for home help and recreational activities and assistance with travelling and holidays.

(b) Section 20 imposes a duty on local authorities to provide accommodation for children within their area who are in need for a variety of reasons. In particular under s 20(1) they have a duty to provide accommodation:

> 'for any child who appears to require accommodation as a result of –

---

[50] Identified as: the Chronically Sick and Disabled Persons Act 1970, the Education Act 1981, the Disabled Persons Services, Consultation and Representation Act 1986, and any other enactment.

(c) the person who has been caring for him being prevented (whether or not permanently, and for whatever reason) from providing him with suitable accommodation or care.'

Recoupment – children in need

13.110 Recoupment is dealt with by s 29 and Part III of Sch 2 of the Act. Section 17(7) provides that assistance provided may be subject to a condition as to repayment and s 17(8) provides that before giving assistance or imposing conditions the local authority 'shall have regard to the means of the child concerned and each of its parents'.

13.111 Under s 29(1) the local authority may recover the reasonable cost – 'such charges for the service as they consider reasonable' and under s29(2) 'where a person's means are insufficient for it to be reasonably practicable for him to pay the charge, they shall not require him to pay more than he can reasonably be expected to pay.' Section 29(4) provides that where the child is under 16, recoupment may be sought from each of the parents, where the child has reached the age of 16 from the child himself and where the service has been provided for a member of the child's family, from the family member.

Some general points on recoupment

13.112 Sometimes a local authority has the option of providing care under more than one statute. Which statute it employs may affect its right of recovery. Alert local authorities seek to provide care under provisions giving them the right to recoup their outlay. But sometimes they have no choice. An example of the latter may be seen in *R v Manchester City Council ex parte Stennet* and other appeals,[51] where the House of Lords held that s 117 of the Mental Health Act 1983 (which imposes on local authorities an obligation to provide accommodation by way of after care to discharged mental patients) imposed a freestanding obligation to provide such care and did not give the local authority the option of providing care under the National Assistance Act 1948 for which they could charge under s 22 of that Act.

13.113 By this decision the House of Lords upheld the reasoning in the earlier case of *Richmond London Borough Council ex parte Watson*.[52]

13.114 An attempt to defeat the local authority's right of recoupment failed in *R v Stockton On Tees BC*.[53] The facts were simple: 78-year-old Mrs Stephenson lived in sheltered accommodation, and was in receipt of various benefits and home support provided four times per day by the local authority. In addition she received care from her daughter who had given up work to help her. To compensate her daughter for her lost income Mrs Stephenson paid her £45 per

---

[51] [2002] UKHL 34.
[52] [2000] 58 BMLR 219, [2001] QB 370.
[53] QBD Admin [2004] EWHC 2228.

week. In 2003 the Secretary of State for Health issued local authorities guidance on charging policies for home care identifying costs which should be disregarded by the local authority when seeking recoupment. The guidance provided that allowance should not be made for costs of funding care where that care was provided by a family member (the 'family member rule'). The local authority followed the guidance and when assessing Mrs Stephenson's means made no allowance for the £45 she paid her daughter for care.

13.115 Keith J held the local authority was not acting unreasonably. He also held that the family member rule did not breach Art 8(1) of the European Convention of Human Rights: the rule did not deny the disabled person the choice of being cared for by a family member but of having payment made to the family member.

13.116 The validity of recoupment may also be relevant. Local authorities actions are subject to guidance issued by the Secretary of State.[54] Disregard of such guidance in setting a recoupment policy may prevent recoupment. It is also important to consider whether a local authority's policy in relation to charging is reasonable. It will be remembered that in *Avon* when dealing with s 17 of the 1983 Act Hobhouse LJ said there was an overriding criterion of reasonableness which governed the local authority's exercise of the power given it by s 17(1). Unreasonable exercise of a power may prevent recoupment.

13.117 Where local authorities have provided care in the past, or it is envisaged they will provide care in the future, the possibility of recoupment must always be considered and the claimant's interests protected by a claim for the cost of past and/or future care. Where local authority care has or will be provided it will obviously be to a defendant's advantage to show that there is no right to recoupment.

Liaison between local health authorities and local authorities

13.118 Health authorities and local authorities liaise on the provision of care and health authorities sometimes contribute to the cost of care provided both by local authorities and other bodies to whom the provision of NHS services has been delegated. In *R v North East Devon Health Authority, ex parte Coughlan*[55] a patient rendered tetraplegic in a road traffic accident, was assured by her health authority that she had a home for life at Mardon House, a purpose-built facility for the severely disabled. The health authority then decided to close Mardon House and transfer her care to the local authority. The Court of Appeal held:

(a) nursing care for the chronically sick was not always the sole responsibility of the NHS but could, in appropriate cases be provided as a social service

---

[54] Local Authority Social Services Act 1970, s 7(1).
[55] [2001] QB 213.

by the local authority, with the patient then liable to meet the cost of that care according to the patient's means;

(b) a health authority could lawfully transfer to a local authority responsibility for care where that care could properly be described as social care;

(c) where a patient's needs were primarily health needs the health authority should not transfer care to the local authority.

13.119 In the result the court, on judicial review, held the health authority had acted unlawfully in seeking to transfer her care and quashed the decision to close the home. The case sets out considerations relevant to whether care should be provided by the health authority or local authority. On the other hand, the fact that a local authority provides care does not mean that care was necessarily to be classed as 'social care'. Each case has to be considered on its own facts. Of particular relevance is whether the care required is clinical, therapeutic or psychiatric or merely incidental to a need for accommodation. Hence in *R (on the Application of Brewins) v Canterbury and Costal Primary Care Trust*[56] whilst poor health was the cause of the claimant's need for care, the court held her care was not such as required therapeutic intervention by registered staff or psychiatric care, but was incidental to her need for accommodation and therefore properly the province of the local authority so that the cost was recoverable by the local authority subject to means.

13.120 In essence, the need for care by clinicians, medical care properly so called, is a matter for the NHS, but social care is a matter for local authorities. *Ex parte Coughlan* is a reminder of the need to ensure that where a claimant's care is provided by the NHS, the NHS should be asked to provide an assurance that it will continue to provide that care and not seek to transfer responsibility for that care to the local authority. Where no such assurance is available then consideration should be given to claiming the cost of such care.

Protection from claims for recoupment

13.121 Attempts by local authorities to recoup have inevitably led to claimants seeking to protect themselves against such a call. Thus claimants, in addition to claiming the cost of such care, have taken precautions such as claiming indemnities and placing awards into trust and have asserted that the attempt to charge is ultra vires or unreasonable.

Indemnities

13.122 In *Avon* the court was concerned with past care and the health authority had agreed to indemnify the patient or his estate as part of the settlement. The case is not authority for the proposition that a claimant is

---

[56] [2003] EWHC 3354.

entitled to be indemnified against liability for the costs of future care provided by a local authority. Indemnities are awarded by way of declaration and although claimants frequently seek such declarations as part of their claim, authority to date is against such entitlement. A declaration is a discretionary remedy. In *Firth v Geo Ackroyd Junior Ltd*[57] it was held that awarding a declaration would infringe the principle that in personal injuries actions (and subject to provisional damages) damages had to be awarded on a once and for all basis. It remains to be seen whether the introduction of periodical payments will enable the courts to take a different view over the exercise of discretion in this field.

Claims under the National Assistance Act 1948

13.123 We have already seen that recoupment for services provided under s 21 of the National Assistance Act 1948 depends on fixed guidelines and regulations. The effect of the National Assistance (Assessment of Resources) Regulations 1992 as amended, the Income Support (General) Regulations 1987, and the National Assistance (Residential Accommodation) (Disregard of Resources) (England) Regulations 2001 is that payments for damages for personal injuries held in trusts and compensation for personal injuries administered by the court are to be disregarded for the purposes of s 22 of the Act as is income from capital administered by the court (see *Bell v Todd*[58]). In *Crofton* the Court of Appeal held that capital deriving from a payment for personal injuries and income deriving from that capital were to be disregarded for the purposes of s 17 of the 1983 Act and thereby for care provided under s 29 of the 1948 Act. The first resort of a claimant receiving accommodation/services under the 1948 Act and who is not a patient should be to ensure, if so advised, that his award is ring-fenced by a Personal Injuries Trust. Since there may be disadvantage to an individual claimant in having such a trust it is essential that specialist advice be sought on whether such a trust is appropriate.

Claims made under s 17 of the Health and Social Services and Social Security Adjudications Act 1983

13.124 The right under s 17 is to require 'the person availing himself of the service', to pay subject to means. Prima facie the person to whom these words apply is the recipient of the service and the section would not therefore appear to give a direct right of recovery against anyone else, eg a tortfeasor. That was said to have been the advice given to Avon CC in Avon. Recently in *R (on the Application of Spink) v Wandsworth Borough Council*,[59] Richards J held that the local authority was entitled to have regard to parental resources when deciding whether it was necessary to make arrangements under s 2 of the Chronically Sick and Disabled Persons Act 1970 Act to meet the needs of their two disabled children but left open for future decision whether s 17 of the 1983

---

[57] [2001] PIQR Q4.
[58] [2002] LR Med 12.
[59] [2004] EHWC 2314 (Admin).

Act empowers an authority to charge the parent of a disabled child for a service provided to the child on the basis that the parent 'avails himself' of the service so provided.

Generally

13.125 Claims made by a local authority under s 17 are subject to the 6-year limitation period: hence the limited recovery in *Avon*. Such claims would also be subject to defences such as waiver and estoppel, so that if a local authority with full knowledge of the facts had made clear that a service was to be free and the service had been accepted on that basis they ought not to be able to recover their outlay. See also *R v ex parte Coughlan* (above).

The relevance of the availability of Local Authority/Social Services Accommodation and Care

13.126 The increasing cost of providing care together with the duties placed on local authorities to provide care have led defendants' insurers to argue that claimants already in receipt of NHS or local authority funded care should continue with such funding or rely on such provision for the future. Similarly health authorities have argued that claimants should rely on local authority funded care and vice versa.

The argument for taking local authority provision into account

13.127 This runs on these lines.

(a) Section 2(4) of the Law Reform (Personal Injuries) Act 1948 provides that in an action for damages for personal injuries there shall be disregarded, in determining the reasonableness of any expenses, the possibility of avoiding those expenses or part of them by taking advantage of facilities available in the National Health Service. No comparable provision exists so far as facilities provided by local authorities. By implication, therefore, the availability of facilities provided by local authorities has to be taken into account.

(b) Damages are compensatory. Where a local authority is willing to provide for a claimant's need, that need has been met and no longer calls for compensation.

(c) So far as a local authority has a duty to provide care then should an award for private care be made there is the potential for double recovery: in *Hodgson v Trapp*[60] it was held the statutory benefits of attendance and mobility allowances had to be brought into account to mitigate damages awarded under those heads, otherwise there would be double recovery.

---

[60] [1989] AC 807.

(d) Under provisions such as s 47(1) of the National Health Service and Community Care Act 1990 local authorities have a duty to assess the needs of the disabled in their areas and under provisions such as s 29 of the National Assistance Act 1948, supplemented by regulations and ministerial guidance, they have a duty to provide the disabled with services. A claimant is therefore entitled to call for and be provided with the services he needs.

(e) Although under some statutory provisions such as s 22 of the National Assistance Act 1948 local authorities may charge for what they provide, compensation for injuries taken by way of personal injuries trusts or administered by the court is disregarded when assessing means. Thus where claimants are entitled to receive local authority services free or at a reduced rate of charge, it is reasonable to expect them to do so.

(f) Claimants have an obligation to employ local authority provision by way of mitigation of loss.

The approach of the courts

13.128 The point has been considered twice by the Court of Appeal in recent years, seemingly for the first time in *Sowden v Rudge; Drury v Crookdake*[61] and, more recently, in *Crofton v NHSLA*.[62]

Crofton v NHSLA[63]

13.129 The claimant suffered a serious brain injury as a result of clinical negligence. At first instance the total award on a full liability basis[64] was assessed at £3,494,882 of which future care costs were assessed at £1,387,525, representing £122,602 pa less a continuing local authority contribution of £68,018 pa, to both of which the judge applied a lifetime multiplier of 25.42. Thus, taking into account the local authority contribution had the effect of reducing the value of the claim by £1,729,017.50 (£68,018 x 25.42).

13.130 There was no appeal against the finding that it was reasonable for the claimant to live in private residential accommodation as opposed to continuing to live in supervised accommodation, 'Meadowbank', where carers were provided by SeeAbility and paid for by the local authority. In the course of evidence it emerged that, regardless of any award of damages to the claimant, the local authority would continue to contribute £68.018 pa. towards the cost of care. His care expert accepted in cross-examination that as a case manager she would consider it her duty to encourage an application to be made to the local authority for direct payments for care. In the result the judge held it was

---

[61] [2004] EWCA Civ 1370.
[62] [2007] EWCA Civ 71.
[63] [2007] EWCA Civ 71.
[64] Liability had been compromised on the basis that the claimant would receive 67.5% of damages assessed on the basis of full liability.

not unjust that the local authority payment should be brought into account. Not to do so would give rise to the possibility of double recovery.

13.131 The Court of Appeal upheld the trial judge on this point. Dyson LJ giving the judgement of the court made the following observations:

'88. Once the judge decided that the Council would make such direct payments, it seems to us that he was bound to hold that they should be taken into account in the assessment of damages. This point needs to be made because there is much to be said for the view that the tortfeasor should pay, and that the state should be relieved of the burden of funding the care of the victims of torts and that its hard-pressed resources should be concentrated on the care of those who are not the victims of torts. ... It does not seem right, particularly where the care costs are very large, that they should be met from the public purse rather than borne by the tortfeasor.

89. Longmore LJ (in Sowden) referred to the 'instinctive feeling that, if no award for care is made because it will be provided free by the local authority, the defendant and his insurers will have received an undeserved windfall'. The counter-argument is that, if the claimant does not have to give credit for benefits that he will receive from the state as a result of his personal injury, then on the law as it currently stands, he will make double recovery. To satisfy the "instinctive feeling", a change in the law would be necessary.

90. Such a change raises what is essentially a political question and, therefore, a matter for Parliament. Historically, the state provided many services to the victims of tortious accidents without charge and made no attempt to recoup the cost of those services from the tortfeasors. Recently, there has been an important change in respect of NHS hospital and ambulances services. Part 3 of the Health and Social Care (Community Health and Standards) Act 2003 (which came into force in January 2007) provides that any person who has made a compensation payment in respect of an injury to another person will be liable to pay relevant NHS charges for treatment and ambulance services provided to that person. This legislation does not affect the assessment of damages as between the claimant and the tortfeasor. We do not know whether this legislation signals a general change in the attitude of the legislature to the responsibilities of tortfeasors to pay for the costs presently imposed upon the public purse. We say only that we can see no good policy reason why the care costs in a case such as this should fall upon the public purse. We can see no good policy reason why damages which are about to be awarded specifically for the provision of care to the claimant, needed only as a result of the tort, should be reduced, thereby shifting the burden from the tortfeasor to the public purse. We recognise that the mechanism by which these ends could be achieved with justice might be complex and difficult. But, as we say these are policy issues and are a matter for Parliament.

91. It is trite law that a claimant is entitled to recover the full extent of his loss. That involves asking what the claimant would have received but for the event which gave rise to the claim and which he can no longer get; and what he has received and will receive as a result of the event which he would not have received but for the event. The question then arises whether the latter sums must be deducted from the former in assessing the damages: *Parry v Cleaver* [1970] AC *1*, 13. In *Hodgson v Trapp* [1989] 1 AC 807, 891 Lord Bridge said that it was "elementary" that if in consequence of the injuries he has

> sustained a claimant enjoys receipts to which he would not otherwise have been entitled, then prima facie those receipts are to be set against the aggregate of his loss and expenses in arriving at the measure of damages. To this basic rule there are certain well established exceptions, none of which is of application in the present case.
>
> 92. In principle, payments by third parties which a claimant would not have received but for his injuries have to be taken into account in carrying out the assessment of damages unless they come within one of the established exceptions. It is not suggested that direct payments made by a local authority in the exercise of its statutory functions to make care arrangements under section 29 NAA and section 2 CSDPA may not in principle be taken into account. If the court is satisfied that a claimant will seek and obtain payments which will enable him to pay for some or all of the services for which he needs care, there can be no doubt that those payments must be taken into account in the assessment of his loss. Otherwise, the claimant will enjoy a double recovery. . . .
>
> 96. We would accept that there may be cases where the possibility of a claimant receiving direct payments is so uncertain that they should be disregarded altogether in the assessment of damages. It will depend on the facts of the particular case. But if the court finds that a claimant will receive direct payments for at least a certain period of time and possibly for much longer, it seems to us that this finding must be taken into account in the assessment. In such a case, the correct way to reflect the uncertainties to which Tomlinson J[65] referred is to discount the multiplier....'

13.132 The decision was on the provision of care under s 29 not s 21 of the National Assistance Act and different considerations apply to each. Dyson LJ pointed out at para 77:

> 'The section 21 and section 29 regimes are quite different. In relation to the assessment of means for the purposes of making a contribution to the cost of accommodation and care provided pursuant to section 21, the ring-fencing of damages and income arising from damages is provided for by statute and statutory instrument. The section 29 framework is different: the local authority is given a discretion to decide what to charge by section 17 of HASSASSA[66]. There are no provisions corresponding with the Assessment of Resources Regulations. The discretion is asserted and guidance is given as to how it should be exercised in the Fairer Charging Policy.'

13.133 It is not obvious that different recoupment criteria ought to apply in the case of s 21 accommodation and s 29 care. The same principles ought to apply to both. In fact *Crofton* decided that where capital derived from a payment in respect of personal injuries and the capital was administered by the court or held in trust, both capital and income deriving from it were ring-fenced from recoupment claims for accommodation under s 21 and care under s 29.

---

[65] In *Freeman v Lockett* (see below).
[66] Health and Social Services and Social Security Adjudications Act 1983.

13.134 It is important to note that in para 92 Dyson LJ confined his observation that local authority contributions should be taken into account to where 'a claimant will seek and obtain (such) payments'. He did not go further and state that a claimant had an obligation to seek such payments towards the cost of care. The whole tenor of the judgement is that fairness dictates that the tortfeasor not the local authority should have to pay. The case should not be regarded, therefore, as authority for the proposition that in every case a claimant has an obligation to seek a local authority contribution towards the costs of his care. The claimant in Crofton was recovering only 67.5% of the value of his claim. It was inevitable therefore that there would be a shortfall in monies to provide for all the care he claimed. In such circumstances it is not surprising that the evidence was that a case manager could reasonably be expected to seek a contribution towards the cost of care from the local authority.

13.135 On the subsidiary issues arising in *Crofton* the court considered that the question of continuing provision by the local authority should be remitted for further consideration by the trial judge. The point was not one which the parties had considered in advance of the trial, had not been addressed by detailed evidence and there was uncertainty about cuts that the local authority might make. Dyson LJ said at para 108:

> 'In our view, the judge was wrong to apply the agreed whole-life multiplier to the direct payments. The uncertainties to which he referred at paragraph 17 of his judgment and to which Tomlinson J referred in *Freeman v Lockett* should have led him to conclude that a substantial discount to the multiplier was necessary. It is by no means far-fetched to suggest that, at some time in the future, the ministerial policy of ring-fencing personal injury damages and/or the Council's approach to that policy will change.'

The decisions in Sowden v Rudge and Drury v Crookdale

13.136 These decisions were made in a very limited context. The Court of Appeal was not called upon to decide whether the availability of local authority care *had* to be considered. That question was not put before the court for decision. At the outset of his judgement Pill LJ said:

> 'I have to say, however, that as the cases have developed and concessions have been made, the resolution of the appeals does not involve consideration of some of the points of law of general importance which may have been contemplated. Both cases turn primarily on the application of the law to the facts of the case though an issue as to the test to be applied by the judge when considering the adequacy of the proposed provision for the claimant does arise in the case of *Sowden*.'

and

> '... it is not disputed that

a) a judge is entitled to hold on appropriate evidence that the statutory provision for care and accommodation meets the claimant's reasonable requirements. In such circumstances the tortfeasor may not be required to pay for care and accommodation.
b) statutory provision for care and accommodation, augmented by payments on behalf of the tortfeasor for further care, may, on appropriate evidence, meet the reasonable requirements of a claimant.'

At para 13 he said:

'It is ....conceded on behalf of the claimants in these cases that, if the compensatory principle requires only accommodation and care provided by the local authority under Section 21 of the 1948 Act, damages cannot be awarded as if they were not so provided.'

13.137 Thus the claimants accepted that the court was entitled to take into account the availability of care provided by the local authority, to decide such care met the claimant's reasonable requirements and, if the court so decided, could not award damages to enable care to be purchased privately. *Sowden* and *Drury v Crookdale* did not decide that a court *had to* take into account the availability of local authority services when deciding what care was appropriate. They are merely decisions on the facts that local authority accommodation and care met Louise Sowden's reasonable requirements and that private accommodation and care met Philip Crookdale's reasonable requirements. But they helpfully set out matters that may well fall for consideration in deciding whether or not local authority provision meets a claimant's reasonable requirements.

13.138 The facts of *Sowden* and *Crookdale* were straightforward. Both claimants were adult patients. In both the court considered the effect of s 21(1) of the National Assistance Act 1948 (duty of the local authority to provide residential accommodation for disabled adults).

Sowden v Lodge

13.139 Louise Sowden received catastrophic brain damage in a road traffic accident in 1992 when she was 13 years old. She had very limited understanding. She required continuing care and support. Following the accident she had spent her time in institutions and no longer had any contact with her parents. The issue before the court was whether she should be housed privately or in sheltered residential accommodation funded by the local authority pursuant to s 21(1) of the National Assistance Act 1948 with a top-up arrangement for extra facilities she needed. Andrew Smith J held the test was what was *in her best interests*. The Court of Appeal held that topped up local authority residential accommodation was reasonable but remitted the case for further rehearing on the extent of the top up.

Drury v Crookdale

13.140 Philip Crookdale sustained serious head injuries when knocked off his bicycle in 2000. He was married and had been living with his wife, their daughter and her two children. Again the issue was whether he was entitled to recover damages to enable him to live in his own home or whether he should live in a residential home with funding from the local authority. Owen J at first instance applied the *reasonable requirements test* and appears easily to have been convinced that Mr Crookdale reasonably required his own accommodation. He gave four reasons:

(a) Mr Crookdale was entitled to have as natural a family life as possible: but the local authority had no duty to accommodate Mrs Crookdale and the children;

(b) he required a bungalow in close proximity to Mrs Crookdale's home: but the local authority had 'some margin of appreciation' in what accommodation it provided and there could be no certainty that provision by the local authority in discharge of its duty would match what he reasonably required;

(c) he was entitled to make long-term arrangements for his accommodation: but the local authority could meet its duty with a series of short term placements;

(d) his freedom of choice as to his domestic arrangements would inevitably be circumscribed by being dependent on the local authority for his accommodation, for example if Mrs Crookdale decided to move away from the area.

His approach and reasoning were upheld on appeal.

The applicable test – 'best interests' or 'reasonable requirements'

13.141 In reaching its decisions in *Sowden* and *Drury v Crookdale*, the Court of Appeal rejected the 'best interests' test adopted by Andrew Smith J in *Sowden* in favour of the reasonable requirements applied by Owen J. in *Drury v Crookdale* but considered the difference was of no consequence on the facts of the case.

The 'reasonable requirements' test

13.142 The test was put forward by Stephenson LJ in *Rialis v Mitchell*[67] namely:

> '... (not) whether other treatment is reasonable but whether the treatment chosen is reasonable.'

---

[67] (Unreported), 6 July 1984.

13.143 In Sowden Pill LJ said at para 41:

> 'In general terms, the approach is to compare what the claimant can reasonably require with what a local authority, having regard to the uncertainties which almost invariably are present, are likely to provide in the discharge of their duty under section 21. If the second falls significantly short of the first, as Owen J found in *Crookdale* it did, the tortfeasor must pay, subject to the argument raised in both cases that Section 21 provision augmented by contribution by the tortfeasor meets the reasonable requirements. If it is the statutory provision which meets the claimant's reasonable requirements, as assessed by the judge, the tortfeasor does not have to pay for a different regime. I accept that in making the comparison a court may have regard to the power to compel a local authority to perform its duties.'

The application of the 'reasonable requirements test in practice : the approach of the courts post Sowden

13.144 Owen J's reasoning in *Drury v Crookdale* was upheld on appeal and provides guidance for those having to consider whether the claimant's reasonable requirements would be met. Since *Sowden* and *Drury v Crookdale* judges have in general been reluctant to find that a claimant's reasonable needs may be met by local authority provision as the following cases illustrate.

Godbold v Mahmood[68]

13.145 Mitting J refused to find it reasonable that when the claimant would have to move from his present home he would be housed by a local authority, the London Borough of Waltham Forest ('LBWF'). He gave the following reasons:

(a) LBWF's eligibility criteria were unknown;

(b) there was no evidence of the resources LBWF considered relevant in setting their criteria;

(c) there was no evidence of the extent to which LBWF discharged its statutory duty;

(d) local authorities had shown some reluctance to fulfil that duty as shown by cases in the Administrative Court;

(e) even if LBWF accepted an obligation to provide accommodation, it was wholly unclear whether such accommodation would be acceptable to the claimant or those responsible for his care;

(f) there was no evidence of the type of accommodation LBWF regarded as suitable nor what they would usually expect to pay;

---

[68] [2005] EWHC 1002 (QB) 20 April 2005, Mitting J.

(g) he had no confidence that the duty currently imposed under s 21 of the 1948 Act by ministerial direction would exist when the claimant's needs came to be considered – ministerial directions could be changed or withdrawn at any time;

(h) it was notorious that the burden of providing for the elderly and disabled on local authorities was increasing and it was not beyond question that local authorities might persuade a future Secretary of State that the burden was unsupportable.

13.146 For these reasons he held the defendants had failed to discharge the burden on them of showing that the privately funded option was unreasonable. Note that reasons (d), (g) and (h) are of general application.

Walton v Calderdale Healthcare NHS Trust[69]

13.147 The claimant, a 10-year-old girl, suffered from dyskinetic cerebral palsy as a result of perinatal asphyxia. The issues were how she should be compensated for care after she reached the age of 19, in particular whether her care would be provided by the local authority and whether the burden of proof on this issue was on the claimant or the defendant. The claimant wished her post-age 19 care to be funded by periodical payments: the defendant argued that credit against such payments should be given for the extent to which the local authority would contribute towards that care.

13.148 Silber J held the onus was on the defendants and that they had failed to discharge that onus but he added that even if the onus had been on the claimant she might well have discharged it as there was a strong prospect that by the time the claimant was aged 19 and thereafter local authorities might well be means-testing such benefits: he added he did not decide the case on that point. Again the reason is of general application.

Freeman v Lockett[70]

13.149 Tomlinson J held it would be unreasonable to require the claimant to rely on local authority rather than private provision for care. The judgement contains some strong observations on the reasonableness of requiring the claimant to depend on local authority provision.

13.150 The claimant had received serious high level spinal injuries in a road traffic accident and was wheelchair dependent. She was intellectually intact and described as intelligent and strong minded. She had been provided with domiciliary care funded by the local authority under s 29 of the National Assistance Act 1948. The judge reviewed the applicable statutory provisions and ministerial guidance. He clearly found the defendants' argument that she

---

[69] [2005] EW1053 (QB), Silber J.
[70] [2006] EWHC 102 (QB) 7 February 2006, Tomlinson J.

should continue to rely on domiciliary care paid for under s 29 of the 1948 Act distasteful both in general principle and on the facts of the case. Prior to dealing with the statutory provisions and guidance he made the following observations:

'I would have expected the purpose of an award of damages against a tortfeasor would in these circumstances be to relieve the victim of his negligence of the necessity to resort to state funding of his or her care, thereby incidentally relieving the state of the necessity to fund the care of that victim and ensuring that the state's limited and hard pressed resources are available to fund care in the case of those whose injury has not come about as the result of actionable fault of another who is by statute required to purchase insurance against the risk of his negligently injuring persons.'

and

'Here the claimant has told the court with conviction that she does not wish to be beholden to local authority for a substantial part of the money which she requires in order to fund her care, pointing not least to the frustrations which all of us know inevitably attend resort to or communication with institutions which must of necessity operate through a large and inevitably changing staff and by reference to procedures which in order to be fair must sometimes seem inflexible or unnecessarily bureaucratic ... The point is that the claimant, quite reasonably, would prefer to have no further dealings with them. Furthermore I recoil from the notion that a failure to avail oneself of a state benefit could in the circumstances be characterised as an unreasonable failure to mitigate loss. I should have thought such conduct was praiseworthy and moreover calculated to contribute to the sense of wellbeing of the person concerned.'

13.151 Having reviewed the legislation and guidance he noted that councils who decide to charge for services retain substantial discretion in the design of charging policies. He thought it was not easy to discern any clear Parliamentary intention on the question of whether direct payments made to assist with domiciliary care were intended to be for the benefit of the wrongdoer and concluded that, if anything, the indication was the other way. He noted too that while there were political and other considerations which would constrain Hertfordshire County Council's approach to the future discharge of its functions there were few tangible legal constraints; that local authorities were entitled to take their resources into account when drawing up eligibility criteria and there was no legal impediment to a local authority altering the basis of its assessments of need. Indeed, he concluded that the possibility of a reduction in the level of publicly-funded services was obvious to any moderately informed person and it was difficult to know what the future held. He thought it unfair to impose such uncertainty and the need to bear such risk on the claimant. On the contrary it was entirely reasonable for the claimant to keep control over her own funding for the future. Given the future uncertainties he considered he was not in a position to assess the care the claimant would receive from the council in the future. He considered *Sowden* strictly had no application since it concerned s 21 not s 29 of the 1948 Act.

13.152 Tomlinson J's detailed reasons accord with those of Mitting and Silber JJ. In *A v B Hospitals Trust* Lloyd Jones J on similar facts also took the view that there was no principled basis upon which he could estimate what provision would be made by the local authority in the future. However, in *Crofton*, as we have seen, the Court of Appeal did find a principled basis upon which to take into account future local authority provision under s 29 of the National Assistance Act 1948 namely where a claimant would seek and obtain such funding and where the funding was known. In *Crofton* Dyson LJ pointed out that in making his observations Tomlinson J was influenced by the fragility of the policy from which the right to receive direct payments derived. But Dyson LJ accepted at para 96 that there may be cases where the possibility of a claimant receiving direct payments was so uncertain that they should be disregarded altogether in the assessment of damages, adding that it would depend on the facts of the particular case. The court remitted the question of continuing provision for further consideration, observing that inter alia the uncertainties to which Tomlinson J referred in *Freeman v Lockett* should have led him to conclude that a substantial discount to the multiplier was necessary and that it was by no means far-fetched to suggest that, at some time in the future, the ministerial policy of ring-fencing personal injury damages and/or the council's approach to that policy would change.

13.153 Thus far the approach of the courts has, in general, been to regard a claimant's preference for privately-funded care as reasonable in the absence of compelling evidence to the contrary, the onus being on the defendant to prove his case. But where there is such compelling evidence the court will act on it. Thus in *Sowden* it could be said that given the absence of any family support and her history of institutional care it was reasonable for institutional care to continue. Likewise in *Tinsley v Sarkar*[71] Leveson J ruled that it was not reasonable that that a mentally damaged claimant with a long history of alcohol and drug abuse, little insight and no prospect of living independently should recover for private care rather than be supported at public expense in a purpose built rehabilitation centre run by the Brain Injury Rehabilitation Trust, a charity.

PART 3: CLAIMS FOR CARE IN FATAL CASES

The present law

13.154 When parents die, children may have to be cared for. Sometimes nannies are employed, sometimes the surviving parent or, not uncommonly, grandparents take over. The child who was dependent on its deceased parent(s) for care has lost that dependency. How should that loss be calculated?

13.155 At common law the answer would be straightforward: assess the amount of loss of care, value it, then bring into the reckoning the value of any benefits resulting from the death.

---

[71] [2005] EWHC 192 (QB) 18 February 2005.

13.156 The essential decision to be made would be whether the substitute care resulted from the death, in which case it is to be brought into account, or whether it resulted from the decision of the substitute carer, motivated by generosity or otherwise, to undertake the care. In *Hay v Hughes*[72] surrogate care provided by a grandmother was held not to be a benefit resulting from the death but the result of generous action on her part so that it did not have to be brought into account, leaving the surviving children entitled to recover the costs of care.

13.157 But the position is complicated, if not confounded, by the Fatal Accidents Act 1976 as substituted by s 3(1) of the Administration of Justice Act 1982. The original s 4 of the 1976 Act provided:

> 'In assessing damages in respect of a person's death in an action under this act, there shall not be taken into account any insurance money, benefit, pension or gratuity which has been or will or may be paid as a result of the death.'

13.158 Section 4 as substituted provides:

> 'In assessing damages in respect of a person's death in an action under this act, benefits which have accrued or will or may accrue to any person from his estate or otherwise (my italics) as a result of his death shall be disregarded.'

13.159 In the original s 4 of the 1976 Act (which replaced s 2 (1) of the Fatal Accidents Act 1959 which in turn had replaced s 2(5) of the Law Reform (Personal Injuries) Act 1948), the word 'benefit' is sandwiched in the phrase 'insurance money, benefit, pension or gratuity' and it is not difficult to see it as being intended to cover financial benefits. The substituted s 4 refers simply to 'benefits'. How then should one deal with the benefit of substitute care provided following death? Should it be regarded as replacing the loss in whole or part, so that there is no loss or only a partial loss to claim for? Or is replacement care a benefit to be disregarded under s 4? There have been four decisions of the Court of Appeal on the point: *Stanley v Saddique*;[73] *Hayden v Hayden*;[74] *R v CICB ex parte K (Minors) and Others*;[75] and *ATH v MS*.[76] *Stanley v Saddique* and *Hayden v Hayden* are not easy to reconcile. *Ex parte K* and *ATH v MS* have come down on the side of *Stanley v Saddique*.

13.160 In *Stanley v Saddique* the Court of Appeal held that 'benefit' in s 4 should be construed broadly: it was not restricted to pecuniary benefit but included benefit accruing to a claimant as a result of his absorption into a new family unit. Purchas LJ at p 467B thought decisions based on whether the benefit resulted from the death or from generosity were divided by 'a thin and very artificial line' and accepted that Parliament must have intended to widen

---

[72] [1975] QB 790.
[73] [1992] QB 1, [1991] 2 WLR 459.
[74] [1992] 1 WLR 986.
[75] [1999] 1 WLR.
[76] [2003] PIQR Q1.

the scope of benefits to be deducted in what had become a field where common law rules of damages had largely been replaced over the years by artificial concepts. Therefore, the replacement care, which in *Saddique* was argued to be an improvement on the original care, was to be disregarded.

13.161 In *Hayden v Hayden*[77] the majority in the Court of Appeal held that each case of dependency had to be decided on its own facts and that whether substitute care was a 'benefit resulting from the death' was itself a question of fact. *Stanley v Saddique* was considered to be as a decision on its own facts. In *Hayden* a mother was killed in a collision caused by her husband's negligence. The husband defendant gave up work to care for their dependant child. At p 999H Sir David Croom-Johnson concluded on the evidence that:

> 'No reasonable judge or jury would regard the defendant, in doing what he did, as doing other than discharge his parental duties, many of which he had been carrying out in any event and would be expected to continue to do so',

and that the continuing services of the father were not a benefit to be disregarded in any event.

13.162 Parker LJ observed at p 1000H:

> '... in cases in which it is shown that the services of the father are in every respect as good as, or even better than the services previously provided by the mother it is, again on the face of it difficult to see that the child has suffered a recoverable loss. He will or she will of course have been deprived of the mother's love and affection but it is not and could not be suggested that this sounds in damages',

and at p 1004H:

> 'In my judgement before one gets to section 4 it must first be established what injury has been suffered by the child. What it has prima facie lost, is the services provided by the mother but the fact that they were provided by the mother is irrelevant. If in fact those services were replaced without interval of time up to date of trial by as good or better services it is in my view at least open to a judge or jury to conclude that the child has lost nothing up to that date. But if the replacement services can be discontinued it is of course exposed to the risk that such services may be discontinued and that risk must be quantified.'

13.163 In *Re K* Brooke LJ and Rougier J came down on the side of *Stanley v Saddique*. Brooke LJ considered *Stanley v Saddique* could not properly be regarded as a decision on its own facts (as it had been considered in *Hayden*) and noted that two of the three judges in *Hayden* (McCowan LJ who dissented and Sir David Croom-Johnson) considered the court bound by *Stanley v Saddique*. He regarded *Hayden* as a decision based on its own facts.

---

[77] [1992] 1 WLR 986.

13.164 The reasoning in *Saddique* was followed by the Court of Appeal in *ATH v MS*.[78]

13.165 While it is clear that authority favours *Stanley v Saddique* the position is far from satisfactory and resolution of the problem must rest with the House of Lords. The point is important and has a run on effect on s 3(3) of the 1976 Act. Section 3(3) provides that remarriage or prospects of remarriage of a widow are to be disregarded in assessing damages payable to her in respect of the death of her husband. Section 3(3) is silent on the position of widowers and children. Remarriage and prospects of remarriage remain relevant considerations when assessing the loss of dependencies by widowers and children. Where a widow remarries is the care provided by the stepfather a 'benefit' within s 4 following *Stanley v Saddique* or does it result from remarriage not death following *Hayden v Hayden*? In *Watson v Willmott*,[79] which preceded *Stanley v Saddique*, Garland J held that an infant's dependency on his mother for non–pecuniary benefits ended when he was adopted and his adoptive mother provided similar services and that his pecuniary dependency on his natural father was reduced by the value of the dependency provided by the adoptive father.

Evaluating the care of children in fatal cases

13.166 In *Hay v Hughes* (above) the cost of employing a nanny was taken as the yardstick for evaluating care of children. *Spittle v Bunney*[80] refined the approach on stating a diminishing multiplicand was appropriate to allow for the fact that as a dependant child grew older, less care would be required. This approach remains valid where a nanny will be employed. But it is inappropriate where no nanny will be employed (see Sir David Croom-Johnson in *Hayden v Hayden* (above) at p 998B). In such cases it is submitted there is no reason why the approach in *Housecroft* should not be followed but with the following qualification.

13.167 The courts have recognised that there is something extra about the quality of a mother's care. This was stressed by Tasker Watkins J in *Regan v Williamson*[81] when he said at p 309:

> 'I am . . . of the view that the word "services" has been too narrowly construed. It should at least, include an acknowledgement that a wife and mother does not work to set hours and, still less, to rule. She is in constant attendance save . . . when at work. During those hours she may well give the children instruction on essential matters to do with their upbringing and, possibly, with such things as their homework. This sort of attention seems to be as much of a service, and probably more value to them than the other kinds of service conventionally so regarded.'

---

[78] [2003] QB 965.
[79] [1991] QB 140.
[80] [1988] 1 WLR 847.
[81] [1976] 1 WLR 305.

13.168 Making allowance for these extra services he increased his valuation of services from £12.50 per week to £20 per week. Tasker Watkins J allowed for that something extra by increasing the weekly multiplicand. It is equally permissible to award a single lump sum under this head. In *ATH v MS* the Court of Appeal reduced lump sum awards of £5,000 and £7,000 for children aged 11 and 7 respectively at the date of death to £3,500 and £4,500.

13.169 In *Topp v London Country Bus (South West) Ltd*[82] in addition to an award for loss of a deceased mother's household services, awards were made for loss to the daughter of her mother's care and advice and for loss to the husband of his wife's individual care and attention but the claims had been accepted in principle by the defendants. Thus even if *Hayden v Hayden* were ultimately to prevail provided the mother was a good mother some award would appear appropriate for those services which only a mother can give even though the quality of the replacement care is highly satisfactory.

---

[82] [1992] PIQR P206.

Chapter 14

VALUING AIDS AND EQUIPMENT

INTRODUCTION

14.1 Claims for aids and equipment tend to arise in cases involving claimants who are catastrophically injured, such as amputees, those with severe spinal cord injuries, or those who suffer severe brain injuries. However, they are not limited to such cases. Indeed in many instances where there is a significant injury which causes ongoing impairment of day-to-day function, eg a soft tissue back injury or a non-union limb fracture, it may be appropriate to consider whether or not there are any aids or equipment that could be of benefit to the claimant. In this chapter we look at the sorts of claims that can be made under this head of damages; the principles governing recoverability; and how best to respond to such claims. Practical illustrations are provided and example schedules and counter-schedules are set out.

THE TEST FOR RECOVERY

14.2 A claim for a particular aid or appliance is treated in the same way as a claim for any other item of special damage: the claimant bears the burden of proving that the item in question is reasonably needed by reason of his injuries.[1]

14.3 Whilst there is no specific definition of 'reasonableness', an item does not need to be the cheapest available.[2] The reasonableness of a particular item will depend upon the facts of a case. How this works in practice is usually determined by considering a number of factors, such as:

- whether the medical evidence supports the need for the item claimed;[3]

---

[1] *Roberts v Roberts* (1960) *The Times*, March 11; *Rialas v Mitchell* (CA, 6 July 1984, unreported); *Cassell v Riverside Hospital Health Authority* [1992] PIQR Q1; *Hunt v Severs* [1993] QB 815; *Wells v Wells* [1999] 1 AC 345; *Parry v North West Surrey Health Authority* (unreported, 29 November 1999), QBD; *Thrul v Ray* [2000] PIQR Q71, CA; *Sowden v Lodge* [2004] EWCA Civ 1370.
[2] *Rialas v Mitchell* (CA, unreported, 6 July 1984).
[3] A claimant will not be able to claim for an item of equipment that would have been necessary in any event due to pre-existing injuries (see eg *Taylor v Weston AHA* [2003] All ER (D) 50 (Dec)) or that the medical expert considers will provide little or no benefit (see eg *Cottrell v Redbridge Healthcare NHS Trust* (2001) 61 BMLR 72).

- whether the cost of the item is proportionate to the benefit it will bring;[4]

- whether the benefit sought can be achieved by other less expensive means.

14.4 Generally speaking it will be much easier to claim an item of equipment that has a clearly identifiable medical or therapeutic benefit. Likewise, items which enable a claimant to lead a more independent or normal life are likely to be allowed. However, it may not be so easy to recover items which are not essential, but would improve the claimant's 'quality of life'.[5]

TYPES OF AIDS AND EQUIPMENT

14.5 There is an enormous range of products on the market designed to assist the disabled. New products are constantly being developed and it is important to try to keep up to date with advancements. Of course, the particular items of equipment which might be appropriate for an individual claimant will depend heavily upon the nature and extent of the injuries sustained. Whilst it is impossible to draw up an exhaustive list of the available aids and appliances, it is possible to group them into a number of broad categories. Common types of aids and equipment include those relating to:

- Mobility/handling – eg wheelchairs, walking sticks, prosthetic limbs, crutches, hoists, stair lifts, hand/grab rails, ramps etc.

- Personal care/hygiene – eg special baths/showers, body driers etc.

- Washing/toileting/continence – eg Clos-o-mat toilets,[6] incontinence pads, potty chairs, increased use of washing machine/tumble dryer etc.

- Bed/sleep – eg special beds, orthopaedic pillows, pressure-relieving mattresses, waterproof mattress protectors etc.

---

[4] The principle of proportionality is firmly enshrined in civil litigation by virtue of its inclusion in Part 1 of the Civil Procedure Rules 1998 (CPR) and the definition of the overriding objective. Although proportionality is not a concept which often features explicitly in judgments dealing with the assessment of damages, it is inherent to the assessment of 'reasonableness'. If the cost of an item were grossly disproportionate to the benefit it would bring, it is likely to be held unreasonable for the claimant to recover damages for that item. For example, where the medical evidence supports the need for a walking stick, the provision of such an item is unlikely to be contested; but, the claimant would not be entitled to recover the cost of commissioning a custom made jewel-encrusted walking stick in order to suit his tastes.

[5] This is a controversial area. In certain cases involving serious injuries some judges may be minded to allow items which have little or no therapeutic benefit as long as they result in a demonstrable improvement to the claimant's 'quality of life'. However, it should be noted that other judges have gone out of their way to emphasise that the object of the award of damages is to make provision for that which is reasonably necessary to replace that which has been lost and is not to improve the claimant's quality of life: see, for example, *Thurl v Ray* [2000] PIQR Q44.

[6] A combination of a conventional WC and a bidet which flushes, washes and dries in one operation.

- Seating – eg high backed chairs, riser/recliner chairs, perching stools etc.

- Eating/feeding – eg feeding machines, feeding chairs, Diody cups, electronic can openers, special cutlery etc.

- Dressing/clothing – eg special shoes, eye patches, orthotics etc.

- Employment – eg special chairs, VDU screens, adapted keyboards etc.

- Domestic – eg lightweight vacuum cleaners, perching stools, gardening cushions etc.

- DIY/home maintenance/gardening – eg lightweight ladders, specially adapted tools, gardening cushions etc.

- Accommodation – eg ceiling hoists, lifts, air conditioning units, specially adapted kitchen units etc.

- Travel and transport – eg specially adapted vehicles, scooters, hand controls, AA membership etc.

- Sight/sound – eg special glasses, hearing aids, big-buttoned telephones etc.

- Safety and security – eg alarm systems, emergency pull cords, entry phones, intercoms, close circuit TV cameras etc.

- Pain management – eg heat pads, TENS machine, back massagers etc.

- Speech and communication – eg voice boxes, picture books, computers, software, speech synthesisers etc.

- Education – computers, large print books, electronic page turners etc.

- Therapy – exercise bicycles, parallel bars, multi-gyms, hydrotherapy pools[7] etc.

- Information technology – environmental controls,[8] computers, infrared remote controls etc.

---

[7] Please note that, save in exceptional circumstances, it will be difficult to justify the cost of a private hydrotherapy pool: *Cassell v Riverside Health Authority* [1992] PIQR Q1. Cf *Haines v Airedale NHS Trust* (unreported, 2 May 2000), QBD, per Bell J, where the evidence did support the need for a hydrotherapy pool at the claimant's home and *Willett v North Bedfordshire Health Authority* [1993] PIQR Q166 where the property included a swimming pool, which was not necessary to the claimant's needs. The cost of buying that property was nevertheless held to be reasonable and recoverable.

[8] Environmental controls are specialist pieces of equipment designed to enable severely disabled people to control their immediate surroundings eg by operating things such as telephones, intercoms, door release systems, alarms, TVs and many other appliances. Such systems commonly work by sending either a radio or infrared signal to special receivers connected to

- Holidays – lightweight suitcases, trolley bags etc.

- Entertainment – digital TV and hard disc recorder,[9] MP3 players, large screen televisions etc.

- Sundry – increased use of washing machines/tumble dryers, increased use of toiletries, tissues and washing powder etc.

THE PURPOSE OF AIDS AND EQUIPMENT

14.6 The reasons for providing aids and equipment vary widely from case to case. It is possible to anticipate many of the usual aims by considering the broad categories of appliances listed above. However, perhaps the most frequent objectives are to:

- increase the claimant's level of independence, mobility and ability to carry out everyday activities;

- assist the claimant's learning/education or return to work;

- improve the claimant's ability to communicate with others and/or interact with his environment;

- reduce the claimant's care needs (and the burden on his carers);

- ensure that the claimant obtains sufficient amounts of nutrition, sleep and exercise;

- ensure the claimant's safety and security;

- reduce levels of boredom and provide new leisure activities;[10] and

- reduce the claimant's level of pain and discomfort.

---

the item of equipment that needs to be controlled. They can be controlled by a single switch or series of switches and there are many different types of switches available depending on the claimant's physical abilities.

[9] Where a person has incontinence problems, some experts will argue that it is reasonable to allow facilities for pausing live television so that programmes are not missed, particularly live sporting events. Where manual dexterity is a problem, hard disc recorders can be useful to avoid the need to manipulate videos or DVDs.

[10] For example, where a claimant previously spent his leisure time playing football but can no longer play due to an ankle injury, it may be necessary for him to find other activities to fill his free time (which may be more expensive and require aids and equipment to facilitate them).

THE NEED FOR EVIDENCE

Medical evidence

14.7 Generally speaking, it is important for all claims in respect of aids and equipment to have a proper foundation in the medical evidence and to be supported by the medical expert responsible for commenting upon the relevant aspect of the claimant's condition and prognosis. In cases involving multiple experts, it is usual for different experts to comment upon the reasonableness of aids and equipment that are pertinent to their area of expertise. For example, an orthopaedic surgeon would usually comment upon the reasonableness of purchasing an orthopaedic bed; a pain expert would be the appropriate expert to comment upon the purchase of a TENS machine; and an ENT surgeon or an audiological physician might comment upon the need for hearing aids.

Occupational therapy

14.8 Any significant claim for aids and equipment should be supported by specific expert evidence from an occupational therapist.[11] Such experts are trained in the assessment of a claimant's needs and the provision of suitable aids and equipment. The expert will usually be able to suggest makes and models of equipment, and provide details of suppliers. The report should also suggest appropriate replacement intervals and any associated maintenance, repair or insurance costs. Often copy leaflets or brochures describing the items of equipment that are recommended will be attached as an appendix to any report. It should be noted that not all occupational therapists have experience in the same areas. Care should be taken to ensure that any occupational therapist instructed has experience of assessing the needs of people who have suffered similar injuries. Particular areas of specialism include brain injuries, spinal injuries, amputees, burn injuries, blindness, deafness and orthopaedic injuries.

Care

14.9 Sometimes an expert will have sufficient expertise to be able to comment upon both the claimant's care needs and his aids and equipment needs. In cases where it might not be proportionate to instruct separate care and occupational therapy experts, a composite report can be obtained. Such a report may cover the claimant's past and future care needs; any need for aids and equipment; any

---

[11] Where there is a limited claim for past aids and equipment, e g a claim for a single orthopaedic bed and mattress, it would not be proportionate to instruct a separate care expert or occupational therapist to confirm the reasonableness of these purchases. In such circumstances, it is usually sufficient to support the need for these items by asking the medical expert whether it was reasonable for the claimant to have bought the items in light of his injuries. When acting for a claimant it may also be helpful to ensure that the background to any such claim is set out in the claimant's witness statement, e g explaining that when discharged from the hospital it was the treating doctor who suggested that the claimant bought an orthopaedic bed.

travel and transport needs; any DIY/decorating/gardening needs; and any miscellaneous expenses eg window cleaning, car servicing and dog walking.

Accommodation

14.10 In cases involving severe injuries, the claimant's home may have to be adapted or a new home bought in order to meet his needs: see Chapter 15, Housing.

Speech and language therapy / assistive communication

14.11 Where the claimant has difficulty speaking or communicating, it will be necessary to instruct an expert in Speech and Language Therapy. Such experts should be able to comment generally upon the equipment that might be available to assist with communication such as computers, picture books and speech synthesisers. However, there are a few experts (often coming from a background in Speech and Language Therapy) who specialise solely in the provision of assisted communication devices and can provide a specific report regarding the items of assistive technology equipment that might be relevant in a particular case.

Physiotherapy

14.12 Physiotherapists will often be able to recommend certain aids and equipment that are designed to help the provision of physiotherapy; improve muscle tone, muscle bulk and flexibility; and facilitate the practising of certain exercises. Examples of such items include physiotherapy mats, physiotherapy rolls, physiotherapy balls, physiotherapy benches, walking frames, special tricycles, multi-gyms and weights. In appropriate cases, a separate therapy room might be justified where this equipment is kept and the claimant can perform his exercise routine.

Orthotics/prosthetics

14.13 Specialist experts will need to be instructed in order to consider the applicability of specialised footwear or false body parts (in particular, limbs). Such items are usually bespoke and need to be made for the individual claimant. Multiple items might need to be provided in order to cover different types of usage including formal, informal and sporting activities. The potential value of such claims, in particular for prosthetic limbs, should not be under-estimated as they can run into hundreds of thousands of pounds in their own right.[12] In these cases, arguments often centre upon the reasonableness of

---

[12] See, for example, *DT v Dr Rohatgi & others* (Lawtel, 21 July 2004, Document No AM0200647) in which £215,000 was claimed for future prosthetics; *A v B NHS Hospitals Trust* (Lawtel, 17 June 2004, Document No AM0200683) in which the claimant recovered future prosthetics costs of £265,300); and *Re P* (Lawtel, March 2004, Document No AM0200602) in which the claimant was awarded £484,755 for future prosthetics.

state provision and whether or not the claimant should be entitled to recover the cost of obtaining prosthetics privately.[13]

Information technology

14.14 There are a growing number of experts who specialise in making suggestions as to how information technology can be used to enhance a claimant's interaction with their environment. Such experts are very useful in catastrophic cases, eg those involving cerebral palsy, where poor limb control may prevent the claimant from performing everyday tasks including opening doors, opening curtains and operating electrical equipment such as televisions. Sophisticated environmental controls[14] can be successful in restoring a degree of independence and enabling the claimant to undertake everyday tasks without needing to rely upon a carer. However, some caution should be exercised regarding the myriad of items that are sometimes advanced by such experts since they may include standard items that the claimant might have bought in any event (see below).

Witness evidence

14.15 Where there has been significant expenditure on past aids and equipment, this should be fully set out in the relevant witness statements, ie the statement(s) prepared on behalf of the claimant and/or the litigation friend. When acting for a claimant, it is also worthwhile taking instructions regarding any items recommended by the expert evidence. Sometimes claimants will already have bought some of the items suggested or may not be keen to use them, in which case it is better to know this before the schedule of loss is prepared or the claim gets to trial.

OVERLAP WITH OTHER CLAIMS

Care claims

14.16 There is often an interaction between the claims for care and aids and equipment. The provision of certain items, eg hoists and powered electric chairs, may significantly reduce the need for 'hands-on' care. Likewise, adapting a vehicle so that the claimant can drive it herself may significantly reduce her dependency on others. It is therefore sensible for the experts of each discipline to see and comment upon each other's reports. In substantial cases or those in which there is a dispute, it may also be useful to see the experts of each discipline in conference to consider how the evidence of each expert impacts upon the claim overall.

---

[13] See eg *Pinnington v Crossleigh Construction* [2003] EWCA Civ 1684.
[14] For a definition of environmental controls see note 8 above.

Accommodation claims

14.17 Claims for accommodation (which are usually supported by architects) may also overlap with the claim for aids and equipment. Generally speaking, the architect will tend to have the greater experience of the relevant cost of installing new aids and equipment into the home. However, it should be checked that each expert appreciates what the other is saying. For example, where a therapy room is recommended in order to house the claimant's physiotherapy equipment, it is important that the expert considering the accommodation claim takes this into account when searching for suitable properties. Likewise, the care expert may be recommending a live-in carer in which case an additional room for the carer will be required. Again, in any significant claim, it is often useful for the accommodation expert to be seen in conference together with the care expert and occupational therapist.

Standard items

14.18 It should be noted that there are a growing number of first instance cases in which judges have held that various household items are standard, everyday items for which damages should not be recoverable. The argument is that the claimant probably would have bought such an item in any event (and therefore the cost of the item should not be met by the defendant). No doubt over time the list of standard items will evolve, however, the following items have been held not to be recoverable in recent first instance cases:[15] mobile telephone, TV, video, cooker, fridge/freezer, washing machine, dishwasher, microwave, Walkman, radio, computer, laptop, scanner and lawnmower. Of course, even though an item might be a standard everyday item, if a more expensive version of the item needs to be bought – eg a lightweight lawnmower – then the additional cost over and above the normal cost of the item can be claimed.

TRAVEL AND TRANSPORT

14.19 The claimant's condition may render it necessary for him to buy or adapt a car or other vehicle. In the absence of injury, most claimants would probably have owned a vehicle paid for out of their earnings. However, a claim can be made for any reasonable additional cost caused by the injuries. In *Woodrup v Nicol*[16] the Court of Appeal held that a car ought to be treated as a wasting asset, in the same way as a piece of equipment such as a special bed, which might be expected to wear out periodically. Therefore the correct approach was to calculate the figure which would buy the car (the purchase price – plus adaptation expenses less any money that would have been spent in any event), and add to that a surplus which, when invested, would enable the claimant to replace the car as many times as necessary (which may require expert evidence)

---

[15] See, for example, *Parkhouse v Northern Devon Healthcare NHS Trust* [2002] Lloyd's Rep Med 100; *O'Brien v Harris* (unreported, 22 February 2001), QBD; *Knott v Newham Healthcare NHS Trust* [2002] EWHC 2091, QB.

[16] [1993] PIQR Q104. See also *Goldfinch v Scannell* [1993] PIQR Q 143.

within the period to be covered (usually the claimant's life expectancy), taking into account the likely 'trade-in' value of the car.

14.20 Allowance must be made for the facts that:

- a larger car is likely to be required for a disabled person (the running costs of which are likely to be greater than those of a smaller car[17]);

- a disabled person's vehicle is likely to require replacement more frequently because a premium has to be placed on reliability, which of course diminishes with the age of the vehicle; and

- more miles are likely to be covered, since the disabled person may not be able to walk or to use public transport, both of which are cheaper.

14.21 A claimant with severe disability will be vulnerable if the car breaks down. It may therefore be reasonable to allow for the car to be changed more frequently than for an able-bodied person and to provide for breakdown recovery insurance.[18] Claimants who have not driven for some time by reason of an accident may have lost confidence on the road as a result, and a claim may reasonably be made for refresher driving lessons or cognitive behaviour therapy. Likewise, claimants who have to learn to drive again using special aids and equipment may claim for the cost of attending special mobility centres where they are given expert training suited to their individual needs. The increased cost of insuring the claimant's vehicle for his carers may also be recoverable.[19]

HOLIDAYS

14.22 It should be noted that disabled people might be subject to additional expenses arising from the need to take aids and equipment with them when they travel, particularly when going abroad. Examples of additional holiday charges include additional cost of ground floor wheelchair-friendly accommodation, the cost of extra flights and accommodation for carers, additional hire-charge costs (when hiring a larger adapted vehicle when away), extra baggage charges and increased travel insurance. Assuming he has suitable expertise to comment upon this area, the expert instructed to report upon the claimant's aids and equipment needs should be asked to cover the likely increased annual holiday costs caused by the claimant's disability.

---

[17] These can be obtained from the AA's running tables, set out in PNBA's Facts & Figures.
[18] Cf *Biesheuvel v Birrell* [1999] PIQR Q40 at Q79 where Eady J did not accept on the facts that the rescue recovery service was specifically related to the claimant's disability.
[19] *Biesheuvel v Birrell* [1999] PIQR Q40. Please note that this may be significant additional cost, especially where it is anticipated that the claimant's carers will be under the age of 25.

CONTINGENCY AWARDS

14.23 It should be noted that in some cases, claims have been advanced for 'contingency awards' in respect of aids and equipment and/or information technology that might not be available now, but may become available in the future. The argument is that new devices are being developed all the time and it is impossible to predict what products might be available in the future. In the case of *Parkhouse v Northern Devon Healthcare NHS Trust*[20] *the parties' respective information technology experts agreed in their joint statement that* a sum of £100,000 should be allowed to cover technical aids that were not currently available but might become available in the future. Notwithstanding the agreement reached between the experts, this claim was rejected by Mr Justice Gage (as he then was), on the basis that it was almost 'pure speculation'.

STATE PROVISION

14.24 The reasonable cost of providing aids and equipment will usually be recoverable even if the aids and equipment claimed are available free on the NHS or from social services.[21] This is because the Law Reform (Personal Injuries) Act 1948, s 2(4) provides that when determining the reasonableness of any expenses incurred the possibility of avoiding those expenses or part of them by taking advantage of facilities available under the National Health Service is to be disregarded. But where it can be established that the claimant would *actually* make use of free state provision these costs will not be recoverable from the defendant since no loss would actually be incurred.[22] In these circumstances, it is not sufficient that there is no evidence that the items claimed could not be obtained on the NHS or from social services. The burden is on the defendant to prove on the balance of probabilities that the aids and equipment in question are not only available but would be obtained by the claimant.[23]

COMPONENT PARTS OF A CLAIM

14.25 Before attempting to assess the value of a claim for aids and equipment, it is important to recognise that there may be a number of additional expenses arising out of the purchase of any single item. These knock-on or associated

---

[20] [2002] Lloyd's Rep Med 100.
[21] *Bishop v Hannaford* (21 December 1988, unreported), Otton J (as he then was); *Parkhouse v Northern Devon Healthcare NHS Trust* [2002] Lloyd's Rep Med 100; *Eagle v Chambers (No 2)* [2004] EWCA Civ 1033. See also *Pennington v Crossleigh Construction* [2003] EWCA 1684 in respect of a claim for prosthetics.
[22] By analogy with medical expenses see eg *Woodrup v Nicol* [1993] PIQR Q104.
[23] *Eagle v Chambers (No 2)* [2004] EWCA Civ 1033.

expenses should not be forgotten as, when added up, they often exceed the original capital sum. The different elements of a claim for aids and equipment might include the following:

- the capital cost of the item in question;

- cost of repairs;

- cost of installation, maintenance and servicing;

- cost of insurance;

- replacement batteries or other components;

- associated aids and appliances that are used in conjunction with the item in question;

- replacement costs;

- spare or duplicate items;[24]

- additional cost due to increased wear and tear caused by use of the item.

14.26 Take, for example, the claim for a powered wheelchair. In order to ensure smooth and efficient running, the wheelchair will require regular maintenance. There is likely to be an annual charge for insurance. Associated items of expenditure might include waterproof capes, attendant controls or pressure-relieving cushions. The replacement costs will depend upon the lifespan of the wheelchair in question. It may be still be appropriate to claim the cost of a manual chair in case the powered wheelchair breaks down. Further, extra costs may be incurred by reason of increased wear and tear on carpets, and the need to widen doorways to allow easy access.

THE ASSESSMENT OF PAST LOSS

14.27 Past loss relates to all expenses incurred before trial. Whilst it is often not seen in these terms, most items of past aids and equipment are usually bought in mitigation of the claimant's loss (eg improving mobility, restoring independence or reducing pain and suffering etc). The general rule is that any reasonable expense incurred by the claimant in an effort to minimise his losses may be recovered. The question of whether or not an item was reasonably necessary is an objective test, assessed as at the date that the loss was

---

[24] For example, it may be necessary to have the same item at home and at school/college/work.

incurred.[25] All the circumstances are taken into account and it is important to assess the reasonableness of the claimant's actions on the basis of the information then available. Subsequent knowledge gleaned with the benefit of hindsight is ignored.[26] If, for example, a claimant bought a particular item of equipment on the advice of his treating therapist which actually worsened his condition, as long as the chain of causation is not broken the defendant will remain liable for the expenses incurred as well any deterioration in his condition caused by the use of the equipment.[27]

THE ASSESSMENT OF FUTURE LOSS: CONVENTIONAL LUMP SUM

14.28 See also Chapter 10, Future loss.

General principles

14.29 In theory, the same principle for the recovery of past expenses and losses applies to the assessment of future expenses and losses, ie the claimant is entitled to recover any aids and equipment (and associated expenditure) reasonably needed by reason of his injuries. In practice, however, the quantification of future expenses and losses is more complex as account must be taken of accelerated receipt, replacement intervals and uncertainties.[28] Generally speaking, when considering a claim for future aids and equipment, much uncertainty is removed by experts predicting when certain items will be needed and how long they will last for. The multiplicand will usually be the cost of the item in question or the averaged annualised loss. As regards accelerated receipt, the present-day value of the loss in question is calculated in accordance with the discount rate set by the Lord Chancellor under s 1 of the Damages Act 1996 (the present rate is fixed at 2.5%). The appropriate multiplier is then calculated by using the 2.5% column of the Ogden Tables, now in their 5th edition. Technically, the claimant need not prove that the loss will in fact be incurred on the balance of probabilities; as long as there is more than a fanciful or speculative chance that the item will be needed, damages will be recoverable.

One-off items of future loss

14.30 Where there is a particular item of equipment that will be needed at some point in the future, it is fairly straightforward to calculate the loss by

---

[25] *Morgan v T Wallis* [1974] 1 Lloyd's Rep 165. This case concerned the recoverability of past medical expenses but, by analogy, the principles are equally applicable to a claim for past aids and equipment.
[26] *Rubens v Walker* [1946] SC 215; *Morgan v T Wallis* [1974] 1 Lloyd's Rep 165.
[27] *Rubens v Walker* [1946] SC 215.
[28] As regards the general theory behind assessment of future expenses and losses, particularly regarding the traditional multiplier/multiplicand method of assessment, see further *Mallett v McMonagle* [1970] AC 166; *Cookson v Knowles* [1979] AC 556; *Hodgson v Trapp* [1989] AC 807; *Wells v Wells* [1999] 1 AC 345; and *Cooke v United Bristol Health Care* [2003] EWCA Civ 1370.

obtaining the current day value of the item[29] and discounting for: (i) accelerated receipt; and (ii) the chance that such loss might not be incurred (or might have been incurred in the absence of the injuries in any event). Take, for example, the case of a claimant who has a 50% chance of needing a stair lift at home in 10 years' time by reason of a back injury. Assuming the cost of the stair lift is £5,000 (including delivery and installation) the loss (excluding any ongoing maintenance, repair or servicing charges) is calculated as follows:

£5,000 × 0.7812[30] × 50%[31] = £1,953.

Ongoing items of expense or loss

14.31 The theory, behind compensating for ongoing future loss is to award a lump sum that is of sufficient size to meet the claimant's annual needs arising from his injuries until those needs come to an end (usually on the claimant's death), but no more.[32] Continuing losses and expenses or those that are likely to persist over a period of time are calculated using the conventional multiplier/multiplicand approach. In practice there are three main methods of assessment:

- calculating the average annual loss and multiplying this sum by the appropriate multiplier for the period of the loss: this is most appropriate for small items, and items that need replacing frequently;

- computing a specific periodic multiplier for each item that needs replacing: this is most appropriate for large items that need replacing infrequently; or

- computing individual discount factors for each item of equipment and any subsequent replacements and performing a number of separate calculations.

---

[29] Current day figures are used since future inflation is ignored: *Mallet v McMonagle* [1970] AC 166; *Taylor v O'Connor* [1971] AC 115; *Mitchell v Mulholland (No 2)* [1972] 1 QB 65; *Young v Percival* [1975] 1 WLR 17; *Cookson v Knowles* [1979] AC 556; *Lim Poh Choo v Camden and Islington Area Health Authority* [1980] AC 174; *Auty v NCB* [1985] 1 WLR 784; *Wells v Wells* [1999] AC 345; *Cooke v United Bristol Health Care* [2003] EWCA Civ 1370.

[30] The discount factor for a term certain of 10 years, Table 27, Ogden Tables 5th edn at a discount rate of 2.5%.

[31] The chance that the stair lift will be required.

[32] *Taylor v O'Connor* [1971] AC 115; *Lim Poh Choo v Camden and Islington Area Health Authority* [1980] AC 174; *Hodgson v Trapp* [1989] AC 807; *Wells v Wells* [1999] AC 345. In *Hodgson v Trapp* [1989] AC 807 at 826D Lord Oliver of Aylmerton elegantly expressed the law as follows: 'Essentially what the court has to do is to calculate as best it can the sum of money which will on the one hand be adequate, by its capital and income, to provide annually for the injured person a sum equal to his estimated annual loss over the whole of the period during which that loss is likely to continue, but which, on the other hand, will not, at the end of that period, leave him in a better financial position than he would have been apart from the accident.'

14.32 When adopting the averaging method of assessment, the appropriate multiplier is usually the lifetime multiplier (or the lifetime multiplier minus one where the capital costs are claimed in Year 1 as well). Appropriate periodic multipliers and discount factors are provided in PNBA's 'Facts & Figures' or can be calculated using a computer programme such as 'Computing Personal Injury Damages' or the 'Personal Injury Toolkit'. Where a periodic multiplier is used and immediate purchase of the item is necessary, 1.00 may be added to the multiplier.

14.33 The appropriate method for calculating a particular item of future loss depends upon the facts of the individual case and the head of loss being claimed. The easiest and most commonly used method of assessment is probably the averaging method which is illustrated by the first worked example at the end of this chapter. This method of assessment lends itself well to regular or annualised loss such as additional insurance costs. However, whilst it is more time consuming, calculating specific periodic multipliers and/or discount factors for each item of loss arguably generates a more accurate assessment (see the second worked example at the end of this chapter). Such a calculation tends to be more appropriate for irregular expenses. Where necessary, different methods of calculation can be mixed and matched in the schedule or counter-schedule so that the most appropriate method of assessment is used to calculate each element of the claim.

Delayed recurrent expenses and losses

14.34 Where an item of expense/loss may not occur for some time but when it does will recur on either a regular or irregular basis, the calculation of that loss is performed in the same way as for ongoing or periodic items of expense/loss but an additional discount is made to take account of accelerated receipt in relation to the period before the loss starts. For example, it may be that as a result of an accident a female claimant will require a custom made knee support from the age of 50. The current cost of the knee support is £500. From age 50 the knee support will require replacement annually for the rest of the claimant's life. If the claimant is aged 20 at the date of trial, a discount needs to be made for 30 years' accelerated receipt. The calculation is as follows:

£500[33] × 23.22[34] × 0.4767[35] = 10,647.76

14.35 As mentioned above, where the delayed loss is irregular or varies in amount, it may be more accurate to use a periodic multiplier or to apply the exact discount factors instead of using a lifetime multiplier.

---

[33] Current cost of the knee support.
[34] Lifetime multiplier for a female aged 50 taken from Table 2 of the Ogden Tables, 5th edn, at a discount rate of 2.5%.
[35] The discount factor for a term certain of 30 years taken from Table 27 of the Ogden Tables, 5th edn, at a discount rate of 2.5%.

Broad brush or global assessments

14.36 Although it is not a common way of valuing claims for future aids and equipment, where there are numerous imponderables which prevent an accurate assessment of loss being made, the court may be inclined to make a broad brush or global assessment instead of using the conventional multiplier/multiplicand approach.

THE ASSESSMENT OF FUTURE LOSS: PERIODICAL PAYMENTS

14.37 Since 1 April 2005 the court has had the power to make an award for future pecuniary loss wholly or in part by way of periodical payments. Periodical payments will be particularly useful in cases where there is an issue in respect of the claimant's life expectancy or there are significant ongoing expenses and a concern that the money might run out if damages were awarded on a conventional basis. Given the irregular expenditure involved in replacing aids and equipment (especially since it is impossible to know exactly when an item will come to the end of its working life), periodical payments may not be thought best suited to this head of loss. Often claimants may prefer to have a lump sum which gives them more flexibility. Where a decision has been taken not to capitalise the claim for future aids and equipment, there are likely to be two main approaches to the calculation of periodical payments in respect of aids and equipment.

The averaging method

14.38 Take the example of a powered wheelchair, the costs for which are as follows:

(i) capital cost of chair £5,000;

(ii) cost of accessories (annual cost) – £200;

(iii) annual cost of maintenance/servicing – £100;

(iv) annual cost of insurance – £100;

(v) annual cost of tyres – £100.

14.39 The initial capital costs total £5,500 and these can be claimed as a one-off payment in Year 1. If the wheelchair needs replacing every 5 years, the averaged annual replacement costs are £1,000. Therefore the total annual payment required to cover the wheelchair from Year 2 onwards £1,000 plus £500 = £1,500. The claim can thus be set out in the following table.

Item	Year 1	Year 2	Year 3	Year 4	Year 5	Year 6
Powered wheelchair & accessories etc	5,500	1,500	1,500	1,500	1,500	1,500

The exact method

14.40 Taking the same example of the powered wheelchair above, if the claimant had a short life expectancy and died in Years 2, 3, 4 or 5 after trial the defendant would have paid over the odds. Therefore the defendant may wish to contend for a more accurate method of assessment with varying periodical payments as set out in the table below.

Item	Year 1	Year 2	Year 3	Year 4	Year 5	Year 6
Powered wheelchair	5,000	0	0	0	0	5,000
– accessories	100	100	100	100	100	100
– maintenance / servicing	100	100	100	100	100	100
– insurance	100	100	100	100	100	100
– tyres	100	100	100	100	100	100
Total	5,500	500	500	500	500	5,500

14.41 The level of detail that the courts will require when calculating periodical payments for aids and equipment remains to be seen. In practice the averaging method is likely to commend itself to courts and practitioners alike particularly in complex claims because it is easier to have one level of ongoing payment rather than payments which vary almost randomly from year to year. Indeed it must be remembered that replacement intervals are usually based upon guidelines given by manufacturers but an item bought will almost certainly require replacement either before or after the average depending upon the degree of use, how well it is looked after and a number of other variable factors. It should also be borne in mind that many aids are designed for heavy continuous use in hospital, and they may last longer when used relatively infrequently – once or twice a day – by a single user in a home environment.

RESPONDING TO CLAIMS FOR AIDS AND EQUIPMENT

14.42 When defending claims for aids and equipment, a number of points should be considered, including:

- whether the item claimed is supported by the medical evidence;[36]

- whether the claimant has the necessary capacity to use and benefit from the aid, appliance or item of equipment claimed;[37]

- whether the claimant and/or the litigation friend understands the need for and actually wants the aid, appliance or item of equipment claimed;[38]

- whether the aid, appliance or item of equipment is a standard household item or might have been bought in any event;[39]

- whether the capital cost of the aid, appliance or item of equipment claimed is reasonable;

- whether the cost of the aid, appliance or item of equipment is proportionate to its cost;

- whether the replacement interval time of the aid, appliance or item of equipment claimed is reasonable;

- whether the claimant would take advantage of aids and equipment available from the state instead of being the items privately;

- whether credit should be given for the (less expensive) items that the claimant might have bought in any event; and

---

[36] See, for example, the case of *Cottrell v Redbridge Healthcare NHS Trust* (2001) 61 BMLR 72 in which the claim for the past cost of a reclining chair was disallowed on the basis that the medical experts in their joint report had agreed that such a chair was unnecessary.

[37] See, for example, *Dorrington v Lawrence* (9 November 2001, unreported), QBD, Hooper J disallowed a claim for a computer and £600 worth of software because the claimant already had a computer which he didn't use and it was unclear whether the claimant had the capacity to make use of the software that was recommended.

[38] See for example, in *Blair v Michelin Tyre* (25 January 2002, unreported), HHJ Marr-Johnson sitting as a judge of the QBD the trial judge rejected the claim for a second wheelchair because the claimant did not seem keen on it and it 'might seldom, if ever, be used'.

[39] Some items such as TVs, videos, mobile phones, cookers, washing machines and dishwashers may be considered normal everyday household items which the claimant may well have bought in any event. See, for example, *Parkhouse v Northern Devon Healthcare NHS Trust* [2002] Lloyd's Rep Med 100 in which Gage J disallowed the claims for a lawnmower, a washing machine, a microwave, a dishwasher, a TV and video as these were commonplace normal items of household equipment. In *O'Brien v Harris* (22 February 2001, unreported), QBD Pitchford J disallowed claims for a Walkman, radio, computer, scanner, software and stylewriter because the same were either purchases for recreation and hobbies which would have been incurred in an alternative form in any event or purchases which would have been made irrespective of the accident. A laptop was disallowed as a standard item not related to the claimant's injuries in *Knott v Newham Healthcare NHS Trust* [2002] EWHC 2091, QB (this case was subsequently appealed to the Court of Appeal but not on this issue). In *Parry v North West Surrey Health Authority* (29 November 1999, unreported), QBD Penry-Davey J disallowed the cost of a mobile telephone since the claimant probably would have had one in any event. See also *Ved v Caress* (9 April 2001, unreported), QBD where HHJ Chapman disallowed the cost of an automatic transmission because he held that the claimant, who was a professional woman, would probably have bought an automatic car in any event.

- whether the item would have been needed in any event due to pre-existing injuries/symptoms or by reason of the natural ageing/degenerative process.[40]

14.43 In any significant claim, it is worthwhile having access to independent expert evidence. However, much depends upon the reasonableness of the expert instructed by the claimant. To this end sequential disclosure of expert reports can avoid the need to instruct further experts and therefore save costs.

14.44 A further point worth noting is that there can sometimes be duplication in the claims advanced for aids and equipment and the claims made under other heads. For example, accommodation claims may have built into them a sum for increased running costs and household bills, but such an allowance is also often included under aids and equipment or miscellaneous expenses. The claimant's schedule of loss (and supporting expert reports) should be carefully scrutinised for potential overlap of claims and double-recovery of heads of damage.

WORKED EXAMPLES

14.45 Following are example extracts of claims for aids and equipment taken from schedules in two different cases, together with the defendant's response.

Example 1: A straightforward calculation using average annual expenditure

(i) Claimant's schedule

DESCRIPTION OF ITEM	CAPITAL COST (£)	REPLACE-MENT INTERVAL (YEARS)	ANNUAL (£)
Power Glide Wheelchair	2,500.00	5	500.00
Insurance for wheelchair			49.50
Servicing/ maintenance			100.00
Stair lift	5,000.00	10	500.00

---

[40] See eg *Taylor v Weston AHA* [2003] All ER (D) 50 (Dec) in which Pitchers J held that the costs of a manual wheelchair were not recoverable in light of the claimant's pre-existing Crohn's disease.

DESCRIPTION OF ITEM	CAPITAL COST (£)	REPLACEMENT INTERVAL (YEARS)	ANNUAL (£)
Servicing/maintenance			200.00
Walk-in shower/bath	4,500.00	15	300.00
Reclining chair	1,500.00	8	187.50
Grab rails	200.00	10	20.00
Shower chair	50.00	10	5.00
Perching stool	40.00	8	5.00
Long-handled cutlery	10.00	5	2.00
	13,800.00		**1,869.00**

The claim is therefore £13,800 plus (an annual amount of £1,869 × a lifetime multiplier of 20) = **£51,180**

(ii) Defendant's counter-schedule

ITEM	CLAIM (£)	DEF (£)	COMMENT
Power Glide Wheelchair	2,500 plus 500 annually	2,000 plus 250 annually	The need for the wheelchair is agreed, but it can be bought more cheaply for £2,000. Further, it only needs replacing every 8 years, making the annual cost £250.
Insurance for wheelchair	49.50 annually	49.50 annually	Agreed.
Servicing/maintenance	100 annually	100 annually	Agreed.

ITEM	CLAIM (£)	DEF (£)	COMMENT
Stair lift	5,000 plus 500 annually	Nil	The defendant relies upon the expert evidence of Mr Orthopod that this item would have been needed in any event by reason of the claimant's pre-existing degenerative changes.
Servicing/ maintenance	200 annually	Nil	See above.
Walk-in shower/bath	4,500 plus 300 annually	2,250 plus 150 annually	The defendant relies upon the expert evidence of Mr Orthopod that there was a 50% chance that the claimant might have needed this item in any event. 50% of the claim is therefore allowed. The replacement interval of 15 years is agreed.
Reclining chair	1,500 plus 187.50 annually	Nil	The defendant denies that this item is necessary and/or contends that it would have been needed in any event.
Grab rails	200 plus 20 annually	Nil	These have been installed by the local authority and are unlikely to need replacing.
Shower chair	50 plus 5 annually	25 plus 2.5 annually	The defendant relies upon the expert evidence of Mr Orthopod that there was a 50% chance that the claimant might have needed this item in any event. 50% of the claim is therefore allowed. The replacement interval of 15 years is agreed.
Perching stool	40 plus 5 annually	40 plus 5 annually	Agreed.

ITEM	CLAIM (£)	DEF (£)	COMMENT
Long-handled cutlery	10 plus 2 annually	Nil	This claim is not supported by the medical evidence and no allowance is made.
	13,800 plus 1,868 annually = 51,180	4,315 plus 557 annually = 12,113	Since the capital costs are claimed separately, and no servicing / maintenance or insurance would be needed until the second year, the appropriate multiplier is the lifetime multiplier minus 1. Using the defendant's lifetime multiplier of 15, the total allowed under this head is 4,315 plus (an annual amount of £557 × a lifetime multiplier of 14) = £7,798

Example 2: A more complex calculation using periodic multipliers and discount factors

(i) *Claimant's schedule*

Example 2 (i) – Schedule of future aids and equipment

Item	Price	INITIAL CAPITAL COSTS Years to 1st purch	Dis-count factor	Capital cost (A)	REPLACEMENTS Years to Replace't	Multi-plier	Replace't costs (B)	RECURRING/ANNUAL COST Recur-ring cost	Multi-plier	Recurring costs (C)
MOBILITY/HANDLING										
Quickie II wheelchair	£3,500.00	0	1	£3,500.00	5	6.26	£21,910.00			
~ Insurance								£49.50	33.31	£1,648.85
~ New tyres / repairs								£93.33	33.31	£3,108.82
Waterproof capes								£116.20	33.31	£3,870.62
Portable ramps	£265.00	0	1	£265.00	10	2.94	£779.10			
PowerTec F45 wheelchair	£7,000.00	2	0.9518	£6,662.60	5	5.89	£41,230.00			
~ Insurance for powered wheelchair								£49.50	33.31	£1,648.85
~ Servicing / Maintenance								£200.00	33.31	£6,662.00

Valuing aids and equipment

Item	INITIAL CAPITAL COSTS				REPLACEMENTS			RECURRING/ANNUAL COST		
	Price	Years to 1st purch	Discount factor	Capital cost (A)	Years to Replace't	Multiplier	Replace't costs (B)	Recurring cost	Multiplier	Recurring costs (C)
~ Battery replacement								£200.00	33.31	£6,662.00
Portable hoist	£2,360.00	0	1	£2,360.00	10	2.94	£6,938.40			
~ Servicing								£100.00	33.31	£3,331.00
~ Slings (x2)	£336.00	0	1	£336.00	10	2.94	£987.84			
WASHING/TOILETING/CONTINENCE										
Leckey toilet chair	£700.00	5	0.8839	£618.73						
Chailey toilet seat	£400.00	0	1	£400.00	5	6.26	£2,504.00			
SEATING										
Tilt-rite multi-adjustable chair	£1,300.00	0	1	£1,300.00	5	6.26	£8,138.00			
Portable table	£64.00	0	1	£64.00	10	2.94	£188.16			
BED/SLEEP										

Item	INITIAL CAPITAL COSTS				REPLACEMENTS				RECURRING/ANNUAL COST		
	Price	Years to 1st purch	Discount factor	Capital cost (A)	Years to Replace't	Multiplier	Replace't costs (B)	Recurring cost	Multiplier	Recurring costs (C)
Theraposture bed	£3,500.00	10	0.7812	£2,734.20	10	2.16	£7,560.00			
Overhaul/maintenance of bed								£100.00	33.31	£3,331.00
Permaflow mattress	£200.00	0	1	£200.00	2	16.25	£3,250.00			
Sheepskin covers (x 2)	£100.00	0	1	£100.00				£100.00	33.31	£3,331.00
Mattress protectors (x 2)	£40.00	0	1	£40.00				£40.00	33.31	£1,332.40
ACCOMMODATION EQUIPMENT										
Overhead track hoist	£5,700.00	0	1	£5,700.00	12	2.76	£15,732.00			
~ Servicing / Maintenance								£256.80	33.31	£8,554.01
~ Slings	£336.00	0	1	£336.00	2	16.25	£5,460.00			
Adjustable height wash basin	£1,972.00	0	1	£1,972.00						
Acquanova bath	£6,647.70	0	1	£6,647.70	10	2.94	£19,544.24			

Valuing aids and equipment

	INITIAL CAPITAL COSTS				REPLACEMENTS			RECURRING/ANNUAL COST		
Item	Price	Years to 1st purch	Discount factor	Capital cost (A)	Years to Replace't	Multiplier	Replace't costs (B)	Recurring cost	Multiplier	Recurring costs (C)
~ Servicing / Maintenance								£110.00	33.31	£3,664.10
Clos-O-Mat toilet	£2,545.00	0	1	£2,545.00	15	1.83	£4,657.35			
~ Servicing / Maintenance								£115.00	33.31	£3,830.65
Apres body drier	£394.06	0	1	£394.06	15	1.83	£721.13			
Alarm, sensors etc.	£1,500.00	0	1	£1,500.00	10	2.94	£4,410.00			
~ Servicing / Maintenance								£100.00	33.31	£3,331.00
Intercom system	£600.00	0	1	£600.00	10	2.94	£1,764.00			
PHYSIOTHERAPY EQUIPMENT										
Garden play equipment	£300.00	0	1	£300.00						
~ Delivery, say	£100.00	0	1	£100.00						
~ Servicing / Maintenance								£68.00	33.31	£2,265.08
Physiotherapy rolls and wedges	£200.00	0	1	£200.00						

INITIAL CAPITAL COSTS | REPLACEMENTS | RECURRING/ANNUAL COST

Item	Price	Years to 1st purch	Discount factor	Capital cost (A)	Years to Replace't	Multi-plier	Replace't costs (B)	Recurring cost	Multi-plier	Recurring costs (C)
Symmetrikit Sleep System	£1,000.00	0	1	£1,000.00						
Totals				£39,875.29 (A)			£145,774.22 (B)			£56,571.37 (C)

Total Claim is (A) + (B) + (C) = **£242,220.88**

(ii) *Defendant's counter schedule*

Example 2 (ii) – Counter-schedule of future aids and equipment

INITIAL CAPITAL COSTS | REPLACEMENTS | RECURRING/ANNUAL COST

Item	Price	Years to 1st purch.	Discount factor	Capital cost (A)	Years to Replace't	Multi-plier	Replace't costs (B)	Recurring cost	Multi-plier	Recurring costs (C)
MOBILITY/ HANDLING										
Quickie I wheelchair	£2,500.00	0		1 £2,500.00	8	3.76	£9,400.00			

Valuing aids and equipment

	INITIAL CAPITAL COSTS				REPLACEMENTS			RECURRING/ANNUAL COST		
Item	Price	Years to 1st purch.	Discount factor	Capital cost (A)	Years to Replace't	Multiplier	Replace't costs (B)	Recurring cost	Multiplier	Recurring costs (C)
~ Insurance								£49.50	27.07	£1,339.97
~ New tyres / repairs								£75.00	26.07	£1,955.25
Waterproof capes								£116.20	27.07	£3,145.53
Portable ramps	£265.00	0	1	£265.00	10	2.65	£702.25			
Force G55 wheelchair	£4,500.00	5	0.8839	£3,977.55	5	4.77	£21,465.00			
~ Insurance								£49.50	27.07	£1,339.97
~ Servicing / Maintenance								£200.00	26.07	£5,214.00
~ Battery replacement								£200.00	26.07	£5,214.00
Portable hoist	already provided			nil	10	2.65	£5,300.00			
~ Servicing								£100.00	26.07	£2,607.00
~ Slings (x2)	already provided			nil	10	2.65	£795.00			

WASHING/TOILETING/CONTINENCE

	INITIAL CAPITAL COSTS				REPLACEMENTS				RECURRING/ANNUAL COST		
Item	Price	Years to 1st purch.	Discount factor	Capital cost (A)	Years to Replace't	Multiplier	Replace't costs (B)		Recurring cost	Multiplier	Recurring costs (C)
Leckey toilet chair	700	10	0.7812	546.84							
Chailey toilet seat	suitability not established										
SEATING											
Tilt-rite multi-adjustable chair	£750.00	0	1	£750.00	5	5.65	£4,237.50				
Portable table	£35.00	0	1	£35.00	10	2.65	£92.75				
BED/SLEEP											
Theraposture bed	would have needed in any event										
Overhaul/maintenance of bed	N/A										
Permaflow mattress	N/A										
Sheepskin covers (x 2)	N/A										

Valuing aids and equipment

	INITIAL CAPITAL COSTS			REPLACEMENTS				RECURRING/ANNUAL COST		
Item	Price	Years to 1st purch.	Dis-count factor	Capital cost (A)	Years to Replace't	Multi-plier	Replace't costs (B)	Recur-ring cost	Multi-plier	Recurring costs (C)
Mattress protectors (x 2)	N/A									
ACCOMMODATION EQUIPMENT										
Overhead track hoist	£5,000.00	0	1	£5,000.00	12	2.15	£10,750.00			
~ Servicing / Maintenance								£150.00	26.07	£3,910.50
~ Slings	£250.00	0	1	£250.00	2	14.67	£3,667.50			
Adjustable height wash basin	suitability not established									
Acquanova bath	£6,647.70	0	1	£6,647.70	10	2.65	£17,616.41			
~ Servicing / Maintenance								£110.00	27.07	£2,977.70
Clos-O-Mat toilet	not reasonably necessary									

Item	INITIAL CAPITAL COSTS				REPLACEMENTS			RECURRING/ANNUAL COST		
	Price	Years to 1st purch.	Discount factor	Capital cost (A)	Years to Replace't	Multiplier	Replace't costs (B)	Recurring cost	Multiplier	Recurring costs (C)
~ Servicing / Maintenance	N/A									
Apres body drier	£394.06	0	1	£394.06	15	1.65	£650.20			
Alarm, sensors etc.	suitability not established									
~ Servicing / Maintenance	NA									
Intercom system	£600.00	0	1	£600.00	15	1.65	£990.00			
PHYSIOTHERAPY EQUIPMENT										
Garden play equipment	not reasonably necessary									
~ Delivery, say	not reasonably necessary									
~ Servicing / Maintenance	not reasonably necessary									

Valuing aids and equipment

	INITIAL CAPITAL COSTS				REPLACEMENTS				RECURRING/ANNUAL COST		
Item	Price	Years to 1st purch.	Discount factor	Capital cost (A)	Years to Replace't	Multi-plier	Replace't costs (B)	Recurring cost	Multi-plier	Recurring costs (C)
Physiotherapy rolls and wedges	£200.00	0	1	£200.00						
Symmetrikit Sleep System	duplicates system already has									
Totals				£21,166.15			£75,666.60			£27,703.91
				(A)			(B)			(C)

Total Claim is (A) + (B) + (C) = <u>£124,536.67</u>

Chapter 15

HOUSING

HEADS OF CLAIM

15.1 There are three principal heads of claim:

(1) *Adaption of existing accommodation:* Where existing accommodation can be adapted to meet the reasonably necessary requirements of the claimant, then the cost can be recovered as an item of special damage, subject to allowance for any betterment or diminution in value of the property.

(2) *New accommodation:* Where existing accommodation is inadequate and there is a net capital cost in purchasing accommodation, then under the *Roberts v Johnstone* formula, the claimant is entitled to recover 2.5% of the net capital expended, representing the lost interest on the forced investment, and any associated ancillary costs.[1] This may not always reflect the true loss to the claimant, as will be seen below.

(3) *Increased running costs:* In either case there may be a claim for the increased running costs of the home. These are claimed on the conventional multiplier/multiplicand basis.

ADAPTION OF EXISTING ACCOMMODATION

When are adaptions reasonably necessary?

15.2 Recovery for adaptions to the claimant's home will only be recoverable if they are reasonably necessary and are not merely to replace lost amenity that will be covered by an award of general damages for loss of amenity. Therefore, the claimant who is wheelchair bound following an accident and cannot use existing accommodation without having all the doors widened will recover for such costs. The claimant who spends money having raised flower beds built in the garden for therapeutic reasons, risks not recovering such expenditure on the basis that it is a claim for loss of amenity.[2] Such a claim could be justified if the claimant were a keen gardener before the accident and in order to garden from a wheelchair raised flower beds were necessary. Similarly, the Court of Appeal

---

[1] *Roberts v Johnstone* [1989] QB 878, CA; *Wells v Wells* [1999] 1 AC 345.
[2] An example of where this common claim for wheelchair bound claimants was disallowed is *Brown v Merton Health Authority (Teaching)* [1982] 1 All ER 650, CA.

in *Cassell v Riverside Health Authority* may have allowed the claim for a swimming pool if there had been evidence that it was necessary to care for the claimant.[3] The only evidence before the court was that this was the best means for Hugo Cassell to get exercise and enjoyment. It was disallowed on this basis.

15.3 The dividing line between necessity and amenity is always a question of fact and degree. The evidence relating to proposed adaptions must always be scrutinised and presented by reference to the criterion of reasonable necessity.

Betterment of the property

15.4 It is axiomatic that the cost of a particular adaption will not be recoverable if its function is to improve the property, rather than meet the claimant's changed requirements as a result of injury. However, there are many adaptions to accommodation that have both consequences. For instance, a conservatory added to the property may be necessary for the wheelchair-bound claimant because the medical evidence demonstrates that much more time will be spent indoors, and there is a need to provide some sheltered access to the garden environment. Equally, a conservatory built on to an existing property in an appropriate context may add value to the property.

15.5 In the event of betterment, a deduction must be made from the claim for the value of betterment.[4] In the converse situation, the loss of value of the property should be added to the claim for the cost of adaptions.

Local authority grants and assistance

15.6 Disabled facilities grant from the local housing authority may be available to fund the adaption of accommodation.[5] The grant is mandatory for certain types of adaptions (such as the provision of access to and from the house and within the house to the claimant's bedroom).[6] Beyond this there is a general discretionary power to provide assistance.[7] Local authorities may provide assistance in the form of grants or loans if they consider them to be the most appropriate form of assistance.[8] Disabled facilities grant is cash-limited.

---

[3] [1992] PIQR Q168 at Q181.

[4] A working example is provided by *Almond v Leeds Western Health Authority* [1990] 1 Med LR 370 at 373.

[5] Part I of the Housing Grants, Construction and Regeneration Act 1996. See 'Delivering Adaptations: a good practice guide' issued by the Office of the Deputy Prime Minister and the Department of Health (November 2004).

[6] Housing Grants, Construction and Regeneration Act 1996, s 23(1) and Annex B of 'Delivering Adaptations: a good practice guide'.

[7] Regulatory Reform (Housing Assistance) (England and Wales) Order 2002 (SI 2002/1860), art 3. The Order is accompanied by guidance: ODPM Circular 05/2003 Housing Renewal, chapter 3 and annex B.

[8] ODPM Circular 05/2003, para 3.4. In such cases, the local authority should bear in mind the determined means test used for the mandatory grants and consider using the same test (para 3.5-6).

The maximum amount of mandatory grant that can be given is £25,000 in England and £30,000 in Wales,[9] but the amount of discretionary assistance is not cash-limited.[10]

15.7 It should be noted that grant aid for disabled facilities is means tested.[11] This means that it will not be usually available to a claimant after settlement. However, it is common for claimants in the absence of an interim payment to apply for a disabled facilities grant to fund essential works. It should be borne in mind that the local housing authority can impose a condition requiring the claimant to take reasonable steps to pursue his or her claim for damages and to repay the grant out of the proceeds of the claim. If a condition is imposed upon the grant, the claimant comes under a duty to repay the local housing authority, subject to a discretion vested in the local housing authority to waive a claim or accept a lesser amount.[12] Where the local social services department have provided top-up assistance for equipment, such as hoists and the like, such financial assistance should be included in the claim.[13] Any settlement should make provision for the recoupment. The Court has no power to order the defendant to indemnify the claimant generally against such contingent liability,[14] so actual liability to a third party must be demonstrated.

NEW ACCOMMODATION

The problem of valuation

15.8 A difficulty is posed where the injured claimant is forced to buy new and more expensive housing: namely, to value the increased cost, while taking account of the enhanced capital asset, which the claimant's estate will retain. It is settled law that an award cannot be made for the whole of the cost of the new home, because at the end of his life the claimant will still have the capital asset.[15] However, this asset will not be realised while the claimant lives in it. Further, given that awards are made on the assumed basis that the claimant will only move once (about which see **15.26** below), any award is based on the assumption that the enhanced value will only be realised at death.

---

[9] Disabled Facilities Grants and Home Repair Assistance (Maximum Amounts) (amendment No 2) Order 2001 (SI 2001/4036); Disabled Facilities Grants and Home Repair Assistance (Maximum Amounts) (Amendment) Order 2002 (WSI No 837 (W99)).
[10] Regulatory Reform (Housing Assistance) (England and Wales) Order 2002/1860.
[11] Housing Grants, Construction and Regeneration Act 1996, s 30 and 'Delivering Adaptations: a good practice guide', Annex B, paras 4–8.
[12] Housing Grants, Construction and Regeneration Act 1996, s 51 and 'Delivering Adaptations: a good practice guide', Annex B paras 59–64.
[13] Chronically Sick and Disabled Persons Act 1970, s 2(1)(e); Health and Social Services and Social Security Adjudications Act 1983, s 17; *Avon County Council v Hooper and another* [1997] 1 WLR 1605. See also 'Delivering Adaptations: a good practice guide', Annex B para 65.
[14] See *Firth v Geo Ackroyd Jnr Ltd* [2000] Lloyds Law Rep Med 312 at 321; *Howarth v Whittaker* [2003] Lloyd's Law Rep Med 235 at [32].
[15] *George v Pinnock* [1973] 1 WLR 118 at 124H–125A, CA.

15.9 One way of measuring the loss is to calculate the additional expense to the claimant of the additional capital expenditure (eg mortgage interest on that sum).[16] This used to be the approach, but the Court of Appeal held in *Roberts v Johnstone*[17] that this was inappropriate.

15.10 An alternative is to calculate the loss of investment income on the additional capital expenditure. This is the solution provided by *Roberts v Johnstone*.

The solution

15.11 In *Roberts v Johnstone*, the Court of Appeal held:

> '... [T]hat where the capital asset in respect of which the cost is incurred consists of house property, inflation and risk element are secured by the rising value of such property particularly in desirable residential areas, and thus the rate of 2% would appear to be more appropriate than that of 7% or 9.1% which represents the actual cost of a mortgage loan for such a property.
>
> We are reinforced in this view by the fact that in reality in this case that the purchase was financed by a capital sum paid on account on behalf of the defendants by way of interim payments, and thus it may be appropriate to consider the annual cost in terms of lost income and investment, since the sum expended on the house would not be available to produce income. A tax-free yield of 2% in risk-free investment would not be a wholly unacceptable one.'[18]

15.12 It was held by the House of Lords in *Wells v Wells* that the rate of 2% was not appropriate. The correct rate is the same as the discount rate used for the calculation of multipliers for future loss, namely the net rate of return on index linked government stock (ILGS). The House of Lords in *Wells* decided then that the appropriate rate of return to take was 3%.[19] It is now 2.5%.[20] It should be noted that it is not open to argue that the rate applied should be greater than 2.5% on the basis that property prices will not keep pace with inflation.[21]

Test of reasonable necessity

15.13 As with all such claims it is necessary to show that the move to special accommodation is reasonably necessary. This means that 'it is for the plaintiff

---

[16] *George*, op cit at 123BVF; *Chapman v Lidstone*, 3 December 1982 (unreported), referred to in *Johnstone*, op cit at 891F–H.
[17] Op cit, at 891H–893A.
[18] Per Stocker LJ at 892F–893A.
[19] *Wells*, above, at 380F–381A.
[20] See Lord Chancellor's statement, 27 July 2001.
[21] *Thomas v Brighton HA* [1996] PIQR Q44 at Q55–56 (first instance, subsequently reported as *Wells v Wells*). See also *Welch v Albright and Wilson*, [1993] unreported, QBD, Birmingham, where Kay J refused to vary the *Roberts v Johnstone* formula because of then recent slump in house prices.

to satisfy the judge on the balance of probabilities that the move is appropriate and necessary in the light of the injuries and disabilities sustained'.[22]

Application of the formula

15.14 Generally, the claimant is entitled to recover as follows:

(a) The cost of the new property less the net market value of the property sold at the rate of 2.5% for the period of the life multiplier.

(b) The costs of adapting the new accommodation are recoverable as items of special damage. Where such work enhances the value of the property, such added value should be subtracted from the sum claimed.[23] Where such work diminishes the value of the property, then the diminution in value should be added to the sum claimed.

15.15 There is first instance authority to suggest that where the works of adaption enhance the capital value, those works are not recoverable as special damage in full, but only as an item subject to the *Roberts v Johnstone* formula. In *Willett v North Bedfordshire Health Authority*, Hobhouse J (as he then was) treated the provision of a bedroom for a second carer as a capital payment as subject to the formula and not recoverable as a cost thrown away.[24] However, this is not consistent with the general approach set out above. Further, it potentially significantly undervalues a claimant's claim since the cost thrown away is immediately incurred while the enhanced value of the property is only realisable on sale.

15.16 Fennell J was persuaded in *Almond v Leeds Health Authority* to award a further head of loss, namely the value of the betterment caused by the works recovered at the rate of 2% per annum under the *Roberts v Johnstone* formula,[25] which he had deducted from the costs thrown away claim.[26] This is justifiable, if there has been no addition to the claim for the net capital cost of the accommodation to reflect the added value of the property.

15.17 It follows that where the value of the new property is enhanced by the works of adaption, this increase in value should be added to the cost of the new property for the *Roberts v Johnstone* calculation in addition to subtracting the amount of any betterment.[27]

---

[22] *Almond v Leeds Western HA* [1990] 1 Med LR 370 at 373 per Fennell J. An example of where the evidence did not met that test is *Maylen v Morris*, CA, 21 January 1988, unreported where the medical and accommodation experts gave equivocal support for the claim for new accommodation for a paraplegic.
[23] *Roberts v Johnstone* , supra, at 893C–G.
[24] [1993] PIQR Q166 at Q172–3.
[25] This would now be 2½%.
[26] Op cit at 373.
[27] See Law Commission Report (1999) No 262 at para 4.27, which in effect replicates this position albeit in the context of a case where the claimant does not move. In that situation, it is suggested by the Law Commission that the approach should be to take the increased value of

15.18 If the value of the new property is diminished by the adaption, it is arguable that in addition to adding the diminution of value claim to the costs thrown away, the decrease in value should be deducted from the cost of the new property for the purposes of the *Roberts v Johnstone* calculation.[28]

15.19 In *Wells v Wells*, the Court of Appeal confirmed that where new accommodation has been purchased before trial and mortgage interest payments made the claim for such past costs, as well as future costs, is subject to the *Roberts v Johnstone* formula and consequently interest payments to date of trial are not recoverable as such.[29] This finding was not appealed to the House of Lords.

15.20 There should be no deduction from the claim where any element of betterment is not due to factors related to the claimant's need. Hence, in *Willett*, one coincidental advantage of the property purchased was that it had a swimming pool. Hobhouse J refused to discount the award under the *Roberts v Johnstone* formula to reflect the value of the unnecessary pool, since he found that the price paid was within the purchase price bracket for properties which it was reasonable to purchase.[30]

Deductions from the *Roberts v Johnstone* claim

15.21 Where the claimant is not an owner-occupier, credit must be given for any move that the claimant would have made or any rental costs that would have been incurred but for the accident. A typical example would be the young tetraplegic who is living at home and now requires an adapted bungalow and who but for the accident would have bought a starter home at some point.[31] The housing expert should be instructed to provide a valuation of an appropriate starter home which can then be deducted from the capital cost of the new accommodation in such cases. The life multiplier may have to be split to take into account when a starter home and any subsequent homes would have been bought.

---

the property referable to the works of improvement at the appropriate discount rate to produce an annual loss and any wasted costs as a capital sum less the increased value of the property. It is suggested by the Report authors that this is an application of the *Willett* approach. This is doubtful as Hobhouse J (as he then was) did not allow for the wasted cost as well.

[28] See Law Commission Report (1999) No 262 at para 2.46 and para 4.33.
[29] *Wells v Wells* [1997] 1 WLR 652, CA.
[30] Op cit at Q173-4.
[31] See *Biesheuvel v Birrell* [1999] PIQR Q40 at Q72 where Eady J accepted discounts on a staged basis on the assumption that for his injury the claimant would have 'traded up' over time. See also *Pinnington v Crossleigh Construction* [2003] EWCA Civ 1684 at [26]-[34] for an example of the approach as to what property would have been purchased by the claimant in the uninjured scenario. In some circumstances, where the claimant's earning power was such in the uninjured scenario the amount that would have spent on accommodation may completely offset the cost of adapted property: see *Dorrington v Lawrence* 13 November 2001 unreported Hooper J.

15.22 Similarly, where the claimant would otherwise have married and have made contributions to the capital cost of the matrimonial home, the pro rated cost should be deducted from the capital cost of the new accommodation.[32]

15.23 Where the claimant is a child whose parents buy new accommodation, credit should be given for the housing expenses that would have been incurred[33] in any event. There is an argument that in such circumstances the parents should be entitled to recover the full capital cost since there is no financial windfall to the claimant's estate. However, although Collins J raised the point in *Thomas v Brighton Health Authority,* neither party pursued it before him or on appeal.[34]

15.24 Conversely, there is some authority to suggest no deduction should be made where a child claimant purchases the property and the parents save rent or mortgage costs thereby.[35] However, the basis of this principle is not clear and does not appear to be uniformly followed in practice. It may be that the proper deduction for saved housing expenses by third parties who care for the claimant is for there to be a set off against any gratuitous care award. In practice, given the practical difficulties of funding a capital purchase of accommodation, many parents in this position make either a capital contribution to the purchase price or a rental contribution, where they retain their own property.

15.25 It is not clear where the claimant obtains a windfall profit due to increased property prices where he or she purchases a property as result of injuries prior to trial, whether the claimant is required to give credit for it. In most situations, any windfall will be marginal because of the *Roberts v Johnstone* formula and the need to account for the property that would have been purchased.[36]

More than one move

15.26 If the circumstances arise and the evidence justifies a further move, the cost can be recovered.[37] However, it should be noted that while most people will move several times in their life, no claim is usually put forward for future moves. It is assumed that the claimant once having purchased special accommodation will remain there for life. Consequently the claim should

---

[32] *Goldfinch v Scannell* (26 March 1992, unreported, QBD, Latham QC sitting as a deputy High Court judge); *Lamey v Wirral Health Authority* [1993] QBD, unreported, Morland J, Kemp & Kemp B3-011; *M v Leeds HA* [2002] PIQR Q46 at Q56.

[33] *Cummings v Clark* [1991] (unreported) QBD, Judge J (as he then was); *Heaton v West* 12.12.2002 unreported, Aylen QC sitting as a deputy High Court Judge.

[34] Op cit at Q55; See Law Commission Report (1999) No 262 at paras 4.18–4.19.

[35] *Thompson v South Tees Area Health Authority* (10 April 1990, unreported, QBD, Middlesborough, French J); *Parkhouse v North Devon Healthcare NHS Trust* [2002] Lloyds Law Rep Med 100 at 103; *M v Leeds HA* [2002] PIQR Q46 at Q56–7.

[36] *O'Brien v Harris* (22.2.01) unreported, QBD, Pitchford J at [213]–[215].

[37] *Almond*, supra at 373; *Lay v South West Surrey Health Authority* [1989] CA (unreported). Such a claim was disallowed in *Knott v Newham Healthcare NHS Trust* [2002] EWHC 2091 QB at [74].

envisage all likely future events, such as increased number of carers or children with an appropriate credit for accelerated receipt, although this will always be subject to challenge on the ground of remoteness of damage.[38]

Ancillary costs

15.27 A typical claim will include some or all of the following:

- VAT on works;

- architect's and surveyor's design and supervision fees;

- quantity surveyor's fees;

- structural engineer's fees;

- local authority fees (these may be waived by some authorities);

- legal fees;

- estate agent's commission;

- removal costs;

- surveyor fees;

- mortgage valuation fees;

- stamp duty.

15.28 Some of these costs (local authority fees, legal fees and the like) will be open to attack by the defendant on the basis that they would have been incurred in any event. The riposte may be that some costs would have been lower if a cheaper property had been built – eg stamp duty and conveyancing charges.

RUNNING COSTS

15.29 In most cases the move to specially adapted accommodation will involve increased running costs that can be annualised and claimed as an item of future loss on the usual basis.

---

[38] In *Biesheuvel v Birrell* see note 31 above at Q72 Eady J accepted a proposal for future accommodation which would be large enough to house a family in the event that the claimant had one without any apparent discount for accelerated receipt or for the fact that the claim was necessarily a contingent one.

Maintenance costs

15.30 This covers all those maintenance activities that the claimant formerly did and cannot now do. There is a potential overlap with any claim for DIY and gardening now done by others: defendants should check for this. There will also be claims for maintenance of special equipment, such as Clos-o-mat toilets, hoists and the like. These should be separately itemised. Again, there is a potential overlap with any claim for aids and equipment, both in terms of maintenance and costs thrown away.

Council tax

15.31 Any special features provided for the claimant which enhance the value of the property will be disregarded for the purposes of banding a property for council tax purposes. There will normally be a claim for increased council tax as result of living in a property in a higher valuation band, even allowing for the reduced council tax paid by the disabled.[39]

Utility bills

15.32 The bigger a house the higher the utility bills – especially if there are resident carers. A tetraplegic will normally find it necessary to heat the house to a higher temperature than the able-bodied and will be in the home for more of the time.

Insurance

15.33 Building and contents insurance will also be increased if the property is larger and there is valuable special equipment in the house.

EVIDENCE

15.34 Evidencing in support of an accommodation claims will generally come from an architect specialising in the housing needs of the disabled. The views of other experts should also be sought – eg the doctors, the care experts, and experts in aids and equipment. It is important for the claimant to check that the medical experts support the recommended housing regime, and that the care, aids and appliances are consistent with it. The most appropriate time for the claimant to ensure that the expert evidence is putting forward a coherent plan is in conference before drafting a schedule of loss, and certainly before any accommodation scheme is put into place. Defendants too should canvass the views of all their experts before the counter schedule is drafted. A general attack on the claimant's proposals is less likely succeed than an alternative set of proposals supported by experts.

---

[39] See the Council Tax (Regulations for Disabilities) Regulations 1992 and the Council Tax (Additional Provisions for Discount Disregards) Regulations 1992.

15.35 It is often necessary for tactical and practical reasons for a claimant to buy new accommodation before trial. This is particularly so where the claimant's proposed care regime cannot be put into place without new accommodation and it is desired to test out such a regime. There may be a tension between where the claimant and his family wish to live and where the most economical accommodation can be found.[40] In such circumstances, it is important for the claimant to recognise that the capital cost of any new accommodation will have to come out of the claimant's general fund. This is because compensation is only for the loss of investment income and not the initial capital cost. Therefore, the claim must be carefully examined to ensure that the proper evidential basis for the claim is there before a scheme is put into place. Such a scheme may have profound implications for other parts of the claimant's claim and will deplete the capital fund.

15.36 Depletion of the capital fund caused by the way in which accommodation costs are awarded has particular ramifications where a periodical payments order is sought by the claimant. The claimant's legal advisers should check that there will be enough money left to buy a property over and above the periodical payments. This has led some to question whether a periodical payments order requires the *Roberts v Johnstone* formula to be revisited in order to ensure that heads of damage which would otherwise be the subject of a periodical payments order are not placed in the capital fund calculated by multiplier-multiplicand method to subsidise the immediate capital costs of purchase. The difficulty is that no one has yet to come up with an alternative that does not result in a windfall to the claimant or his or her estate on sale of the property.[41]

LOCAL AUTHORITY/HOUSING ASSOCIATION ACCOMMODATION

15.37 Where the claimant is living (or may eventually live) in local authority accommodation pursuant to s 21 of the National Assistance Act 1948, an issue arises as to the extent of the defendant's liability to fund accommodation.[42] Where the claimant is already in local authority or housing association non-residential accommodation, the claimant will be entitled to a claim on the basis of new private accommodation, unless it can be shown that any adaption of that property to meet the claimant's accommodation needs can meet his

---

[40] In *Biesheuvel v Birrell*, see note 31 above at Q74 Eady J was persuaded to award the capital cost of more expensive accommodation under the *Roberts v Johnstone* formula local to where the claimant's family and friends were, even though adequate and cheaper accommodation could have provided elsewhere; *Heaton v West*, supra.

[41] See the earlier debate recorded in the Law Commission report No 262, paras 4.2–4.17.

[42] *Sowden v Lodge* [2004] EWCA Civ 1370. Different considerations arise under section 117 of the Mental Health Act 1983: see *Tinsley v Sarkar* [2005] EWHC 192 QB at [107]–[129].

long-term accommodation needs and restore the claimant to the position as nearly as possible to the position he or she would have been in but for the tort.[43]

ACCOMMODATION EXPERT

15.38 There are several different disciplines that will need to be covered. It is not always possible to embrace all the necessary areas within one expert report, although it would be unusual to seek to call more than one expert or be given permission to call more than one expert. An estate agent or chartered surveyor in general practice will usually be the most sensible person to instruct as to the identification and acquisition of property rather than an architect. Valuation calls for different skills and local knowledge of the area may be invaluable. Most importantly, the accommodation expert must be a specialist architect or chartered building surveyor experienced in the construction of schemes for the disabled. It is striking how often solicitors instruct experts without such first hand experience who then assess a scheme by reference to an out of date body of literature. The assessment of the increased running costs of adapted accommodation is best dealt with by a chartered building surveyor. The appropriate course is to agree joint instruction of a local estate agent or chartered surveyor to deal with the question of valuation evidence. Whether the principal accommodation expert can be made the subject of joint instructions must depend on the extent to which any accommodation scheme is likely to be controversial and a matter of disputed opinion.

15.39 Without any accommodation expert evidence, the court will take a broad brush approach, provided the medical evidence is in place.[44] Similarly, it is not adequate to rely on a 'catch all' rehabilitation expert, unless there is only a very small claim for minor adaptions to a property.[45]

15.40 The expert should be asked to consider any list of properties produced by an estate agent critically to assess suitability and value (which is not necessarily the asking price). The other relevant experts must support any adaption scheme. Further, the nature of the scheme must be addressed to the needs and wishes of the individual claimant. There is no point including in a claim a piece of equipment or adaption that the claimant will never use.

15.41 Conversely, defendants should recognise that claimants do not always fall into neat categories of need. For instance, it may be wrong to assume that a head injured claimant does not require a conservatory whereas a tetraplegic

---

[43] *Rahman v West Pennine Health Authority* (2002) QBD unreported McCombe J at [15]–[25] where the judge preferred a 'new build' scheme to adaption of housing association stock given the imponderables on the evidence as it stood.
[44] See, for example, *Welch*, supra.
[45] See for example *Welsh v Robson Road Haulage Limited* (Court of Appeal, 17 May 1995, unreported).

would.[46] It is essential that the defendant's expert visit the claimant at home and make his own assessment of the claimant's real housing needs. Without this, the defendant's expert is vulnerable in cross-examination.

15.42 The costing of works should be the result of a tendering process (where the works are contemplated before trial). Careful selection of the best tender may not necessarily result in the cheapest tender being accepted. Often the costs incurred by a claimant are challenged by reference to the *Quarterly Review of Building Tender Prices* produced by the Building Cost Information Service (BCIS) of the Royal Institution of Chartered Surveyors. However, this may be quite misleading as BCIS does not provide costings for this type of scheme. A challenge is best most mounted through a close examination of all the tender and contract documentation if the works have already been carried out or an actual costing.

15.43 An interim payment based on an estimate obtained by the defendant may be appropriate where there is agreement about the scope of the works to be done and the defendant suspects that the claimant could do the works on a cheaper basis, and will do so, rather than for the cost claimed in the schedule. This would prevent the claimant from pocketing the difference. A tied interim payment can be used to real effect in this context particularly where it is connected to the claim for future care.

MEDICAL EVIDENCE

15.44 For the claim to stand up at trial there must be cogent medical evidence from the lead medical expert that the claimant needs rehousing (or needs the adaptions). Many claims have failed or been substantially reduced because the accommodation expert has proposed (and sometimes implemented) a scheme that the medical experts think is over-elaborate or can only be justified in 20 or 30 years' time. Not only should the medical expert support the principle of an accommodation scheme, but the detail needs to be supported. Expensive individual items, such as a claim for a hydrotherapy pool[47] or an environmental control system,[48] must be supported by evidence of actual need. A defendant

---

[46] Examples of head injured claimants recovering such items where the defendants have contested the need: *Page v Sheerness Steel plc* [1996] PIQR Q26 at Q42–3, upheld on this point by the Court of Appeal in *Wells*, supra; *Walsh v Allessio* [1996], unreported, QBD, Manchester, Gage J.

[47] In *Haines v Airedale NHS Trust*, unreported, QBD, 2 May 2000, Bell J awarded a hydrotherapy pool where the physiotherapy evidence is that it would be of benefit to the claimant. He declined to discount the award for the cost of sporting activities that would have been engaged in or to treat the claim as one for lost amenity. A similar award was made in *Hart v Pretty*, unreported, QBD, 18 April 2005, HHJ Taylor in a spinal injury case. A contrasting decision was reached by Thomas J in *Green v North Essex HA*, unreported, QBD, 21 December 1998 where he disallowed a claim for pool at home on the basis that a spa tub would suffice and there was sufficient provision at school.

[48] See *Eagle*, supra at [102]. It does not appear that any medical evidence was led in that case as to need and therefore, it is unsurprising that the claim was rejected.

may be able to eliminate individual items that have no medical basis (such as a Clos-o-mat toilet for a claimant who is independent in using the toilet).[49] Such an exercise will also have implications for a claim for aids and equipment.

15.45 In some cases there will be significant dispute between the doctors whether the care implications of the claimant's injuries are such that it will not be possible for him to be cared for in his own adapted home. There may be significant 'quality of life' issues about whether the claimant's reasonable needs for care would be better met in a group living scheme or a care home, particularly in child and adult brain injury cases.[50] It is important that such issues are fully canvassed with the medical experts to assess whether or not a care regime in the claimant's own home is realistic.

CARE IMPLICATIONS

15.46 The participation of the parties' care experts will often be crucial in determining the extent of any accommodation claim. It is essential to explore the implications of accommodation on care. For instance, a seriously head-injured claimant who lives with her family but requires round-the-clock care at home from two resident carers is plainly going to have to provide appropriate accommodation for the carers. There may need to be special storage for bulky items of equipment.

15.47 Care experts will differ in their views about what accommodation requirements are necessary to attract and retain carers of quality. The minimum requirements are usually their own separate bed/sitting room with separate washing, toilet and cooking facilities. In *Tricker v Hoban*, it was observed by the judge:

> 'The evidence on this [type of accommodation] is simply that the carers will require space. The carers will inevitably be around probably most of the time, even though they are not directly involved in the care. The one thing that governs the case entirely is the quality of the carers that are going to be obtained and employed and to stint upon the space that is made available to them is, in my judgment, going to militate against getting the right sort of person.'[51]

15.48 If the case for live-in carers is weak, this may affect the claim for new accommodation, and the claim may fail.[52] It is therefore important in such cases for both sides to examine closely the justification for new accommodation. This will be particularly important for a claimant who proposes to spend money on new accommodation before trial.

---

[49] See *Owen v Brown* [2002] EWHC 1135 (QB) at [116], [118] where the judge allowed a claim for body drier for a teraplegic because it had medical support, but disallowed a claim for automatic garage doors.
[50] *Tinsley v Sarkar* [2005] EWHC 192 (QB).
[51] *Tricker v Hoban* [1994] QBD, unreported, Wolton QC sitting as a deputy High Court judge).
[52] See for example, *Welsh*, above, note 45.

15.49 Where the care regime will change in due course, leading to a need for more accommodation, it is important that this is factored into the claim for future accommodation. For instance, a young tetraplegic may be quite capable of managing without live-in carers in the early years, but may require such care in the future. From the claimant's perspective, it will be important to present a united front between medical, care and accommodation experts that this future need should be met now. A challenge to this should focus on persuading the court that this is just a speculative medical possibility rather than a substantial chance: the defendant can then either oppose the claim completely or argue for a discount. In any event, there should be a discount for the accelerated receipt of damages for a need that will not occur for many years. The accommodation, medical and care experts should be asked to estimate how great the risk is, when it will come about, and what the accommodation consequences will be, if and when it does.

Chapter 16

RECOUPMENT OF DAMAGES

INTRODUCTION

16.1 For more than 50 years the treatment of benefits received by a claimant in a personal injuries action has been controlled to some extent by statute. From 1948 to 1990 claimants had to give credit for one half of specified benefits received over a five-year period.[1] Benefits not falling within the statutory scheme were deducted from the claimant's damages in full.[2] From 3 September 1990 to 5 October 1997, the statutory scheme originally contained in the Social Security Act 1989, and then in the Social Security Administration Act 1992, required defendants to deduct listed benefits from a claimant's damages and pay them back to the state. The deductions were made from all elements of the claimant's damages, including general damages. This came to be regarded as unfair. On 21 June 1995, the House of Commons Social Security Committee provided a report on the Statutory Recoupment Scheme. The Committee concluded that:

> 'The Government have passed too great a burden to the individual ... some of the cases which we have encountered we believe are revolting to the ordinary man's sense of justice. In our view the present system operates in a way which is ... contrary to public policy ... we cannot accept that the general taxpayer should be reimbursed out of damages awarded for an individual's pain and suffering ... or future loss of earnings ... by allowing recovery from total settlement rather than simply from loss of earnings, we believe that injured parties have been most unfairly treated.'

16.2 This perceived unfairness led to the implementation of the Social Security (Recovery of Benefits) Act 1997 ('the Act'), which came into force – with retrospective effect – on 6 October 1997. Defendants remain liable to pay relevant benefits received by a claimant back to the state, but they can only set off against the claimant's damages those benefits which correspond to claims made by the claimant. In this way, a claimant's general damages are 'ring-fenced'.

16.3 Although it is theoretically possible that practitioners will encounter cases involving court orders or agreements to pay compensation made before 6

---

[1] Law Reform (Personal Injuries) Act 1948, s 2(1).
[2] *Hodgson v Trapp* [1989] 1 AC 807.

October 1997, the remainder of this chapter will address the law as it stands as defined by the Act and accompanying Regulations.[3]

THE BASIC FRAMEWORK

16.4 When a defendant – or 'compensator' as he is known within the terms of Act[4] – receives notification that a compensation claim is to be made, he must apply to the Compensation Recovery Unit (CRU – the body established by the Department for Work and Pensions to administer the statutory recoupment scheme) and obtain a Certificate of Recoverable Benefits (known popularly as a 'CRU certificate'). The CRU certificate sets out any 'listed benefits'[5] that have been received by the claimant over the 'relevant period'.[6] The claimant's claim for damages is then assessed in the normal way, disregarding the fact that the claimant has received any listed benefits.[7] When the compensation payment is made, the defendant must pay the entire amount of benefits set out on the CRU certificate to the CRU. The defendant may also – subject to certain conditions – be able to deduct some or all of the benefits on the CRU certificate from the compensation payment he makes to the claimant. In summary, the defendant can offset certain benefits against certain claims, but not – for example – against the claimant's general damages. He can only deduct like from like. There will be no alteration to the calculation to take account of any actual or prospective award for contributory negligence. Moreover, a claimant is entitled to interest on his full damages whether or not a defendant is entitled to offset a sum equivalent to benefits received by a claimant.[8]

CASES IN WHICH THE ACT APPLIES

16.5 By s 1 of the Act, the statutory scheme applies to cases where:

'(a) a person makes a payment (whether on his own behalf or not) to or in respect of any other person in consequence of any accident, injury or disease suffered by the other, and
(b) any listed benefits have been, or are likely to be, paid to or for the other during the relevant period in respect of the accident, injury or disease.'

16.6 By s 1(2) of the Act, the 'payment' referred to in s 1 includes payments made 'in pursuance of a compensation scheme for motor accident' (ie MIB cases).

---

[3] Social Security (Recovery of Benefits) Regulations 1997 as amended by paras 148–152 of Sch 7 to the Social Security Act 1998 ('the Regulations').
[4] Section 4(1).
[5] Ie any of the benefits set out in column 2 of Sch 2 to the Act.
[6] As defined by s 3. Essentially, the period is a maximum of five years from the accident or injury in question, or, in the case of a disease, five years from the date benefit was first claimed.
[7] Section 17.
[8] *Wadey v Surrey County Council* [2000] 1 WLR 820.

EXCLUDED COMPENSATION PAYMENTS

16.7 Schedule 1 to the Act (together with reg 2 of the Regulations) specifies certain types of compensation payments that are excluded from the scheme. Under the former legislation small payments of £2,500 or less were excluded from the scheme. Schedule 1 to the Act makes provision for Regulations to introduce a small payment exemption, but so far no such exemption has been created. Practitioners should consult the Act and the Regulations for a full list of exempt payments. The following are examples that are more likely than others to be encountered in practice:

- payments made to or for the injured person under s 35 of the Powers of Criminal Courts Act 1973;

- payments made from certain discretionary or specified trusts;

- insurance payments paid under the terms of a contract of insurance entered into before the accident;

- redundancy payments;

- payments for costs;

- payments under the Vaccine Damage Payments Act 1979;

- awards of compensation under the Criminal Injuries Compensation Act 1995 or by the Criminal Injuries Compensation Board (CICB) under the Criminal Injuries Compensation Scheme 1990 or any earlier scheme;

- compensation payments in accordance with the NCB Pneumoconiosis Compensation Scheme;

- any payment made to the injured person in respect of sensorineural hearing loss (where the loss is less than 50 dB in one or both ears).

FATAL ACCIDENT ACT CLAIMS

16.8 The recoupment scheme does not apply to Fatal Accidents Act claims, as the damages for dependency do not fall within the categories of damages against which benefits can be offset.[9]

---

[9] See below under 'Offsetting'.

RELEVANT BENEFITS

16.9 The benefits covered by the Act are:

- disability working allowance;

- disablement pension payable under s 103 of the Social Security Administration Act 1992;

- incapacity benefit;

- income support;

- invalidity pension and allowance;

- jobseeker's allowance;

- reduced earnings allowance;

- severe disablement allowance;

- sickness benefit;

- statutory sick pay paid before 6 April 1994 (see further below);

- unemployability supplement;

- unemployment benefit;

- attendance allowance;

- care component of disability living allowance;

- disablement pension increase payable under s 104 or s 105 of the 1992 Act;

- mobility allowance;

- mobility component of disability living allowance.

LISTED BENEFITS ARE TO BE DISREGARDED

16.10 Pursuant to s 17 of the Act, all of the benefits listed above are to be disregarded when assessing a claimant's damages. This is true in respect of both past and future losses, and operates to exclude the common law principle set out by the House of Lords in *Hodgson v Trapp*.[10] A claimant will not therefore have to give credit for listed benefits received after the relevant period has ended.

EXCLUDED BENEFITS

16.11 Non-listed benefits may still fall to be deducted in accordance with *Hodgson v Trapp* principles. Thus, housing benefit was deducted from a claimant's claim in *Clenshaw v Tanner*.[11] However, invalid care allowance received by parents who claimed in respect of a failure by doctors to inform them that their daughter was going to be born with Down's syndrome was not deducted from their damages.[12]

STATUTORY SICK PAY

16.12 In the Notes to Schedule 2 to the Act, it is stated that any reference to statutory sick pay '(a) includes only 80% of payments made between 6 April 1991 and 5 April 1994 and (b) does not include payments made on or after 6 April 1994'. Therefore, any statutory sick pay paid after 6 April 1994 is outside the statutory scheme set up by the Act. It should presumably therefore be open to a defendant to deduct statutory sick pay received by a claimant in full without having to pay the equivalent amount back to the CRU. At common law, it would seem to be established that statutory sick pay is to be deducted from the claimant's damages.[13] A claimant who has claimed his loss of earnings net of sick pay should check that the defendant does not also deduct sick pay.

THE 'RELEVANT PERIOD'

16.13 The 'relevant period' (ie the period of time over which benefits are to be taken into account under the statutory scheme) is defined by s 3 of the Act. The period begins on the day following an accident or injury, or, in disease cases, the date that a listed benefit is first claimed in consequence of the disease.[14] The period ends five years after the relevant period begins or the date on which a compensation payment is made in final discharge of a claim, whichever comes first.[15]

---

[10] [1989] 1 AC 807.
[11] [2002] EWCA Civ 1848.
[12] *Rand v East Dorset Health Authority* [2000] Lloyd's Rep Med 181.
[13] *Palfrey v GLC* [1985] ICR 437.
[14] S 3(2) and (3).
[15] S 3(4).

CRU CERTIFICATES

16.14 The defendant must apply for a certificate within 14 days of notification of a claim. The Secretary of State then sends an acknowledgement. When ready to make an offer of compensation, the defendant must return the acknowledgement and apply for a CRU certificate. Having received the certificate the defendant becomes liable to pay the full amount of recoverable benefits to the CRU immediately before making the compensation payment to the claimant. The technical requirements and obligations regarding certificates are set out in ss 4 and 5 of the Act.

DEFENDANT'S LIABILITY

16.15 It is important to understand that whether or not the compensator is entitled to offset any listed benefits set out on the CRB, he must make full payment of all the listed benefits to the CRU. Section 7 provides that the Secretary of State can enforce payment by 'execution issued from the County Court ... as if it were payable under an order of that Court'.[16] A properly signed certificate is 'conclusive evidence' that the amount set out is recoverable.[17]

OFFSETTING

16.16 The compensator may reduce the compensation which it pays to the victim under s 8 of the 1997 Act. The reduction is allowed against damages paid for three heads of loss:

- past loss of earnings;

- past care costs;

- past mobility costs.

In each case 'past' means compensation within the relevant period: ie to the date of payment of the full compensation or five years, whichever is shorter. Only certain listed benefits may be set off against each head. They are set out in Sch 2 to the 1997 Act. The table showing which benefits may be set off against which heads of loss is as follows:

---

[16] Section 7(4).
[17] Section 7(6).

Head of Compensation	Benefit
Compensation for earnings lost during the relevant period	Disability working allowance Disablement pension payable under section 103 of the 1992 Act Incapacity Benefit Income support Invalidity pension and allowance Jobseeker's allowance Severe disablement allowance Sickness benefit Statutory sick pay Unemployability supplement Unemployment benefit
Compensation for cost of care incurred during the relevant period	Attendance allowance Care component of disability living allowance Disablement pension increase payable under section 104 or 105 of the 1992 Act.
Compensation for loss of mobility during the relevant period.	Mobility allowance Mobility component of disability living allowance.

EXAMPLES OF HEADS OF COMPENSATION WITHIN SCH 2

Gratuitous care

16.17 In *Griffiths v British Coal Corporation*[18] the Court of Appeal upheld the judgment of Mr Justice Turner, holding that the phrase 'compensation for cost of care incurred during the relevant period' in the context of Sch 2 includes care rendered gratuitously by family members or friends. Thus attendance allowance, for example, can be set off against a claim for gratuitous care.

Pension contributions

16.18 In *Nizami v London Clubs Management Ltd*,[19] McKinnon J held that an award for loss of pension (calculated by reference to the amount of pension contributions that formed a part of the claimant's earnings when he was working) amounted to 'compensation for earnings lost', and the defendant was therefore able to offset benefits against the award.

---

[18] [2001] 1 WLR 1493.
[19] [2004] EWHC 2577 (QB) (unreported).

Business rent

16.19 Where a self-employed claimant had to close her business due to an accident, an award for business premises rent liability fell within the head of 'compensation for earnings lost', and the defendant could offset benefits against the award.[20]

Examples of heads of compensation outside Sch 2

16.20 In the Guidance on the CRU scheme issued by the Department for Work and Pensions, there is a list of heads of loss which are not thought to fall within the lost earnings, costs of care or loss of mobility categories. The DWP are keen to stress that the list is 'not definitive', and that it does not 'purport to be an interpretation of the law'. However, the list may provide helpful guidance for practitioners. The full list is:

- Accommodation, special
- Amenities of life, loss of
- Benefits associated with injured person's work, loss of
- Bereavement
- Cleaner, cost of
- Congenial employment, loss of
- Court of Protection fees
- Diet, special
- Expectation of life, loss of
- Financial interest, loss of
- Future care
- Future earnings, loss of
- Future mobility
- Gardener, cost of
- General damages
- Guide dog

---

[20] *Lowther v Chatwin* [2003] PIQR Q84.

- Hospital visits other than for treatment

- Housekeeping capacity, loss of

- Investment advice

- DIY, loss of ability to carry out

- Labour market, disadvantage on (*Smith v Manchester*)

- Leisure, loss of

- Marriage prospects, loss of

- Marriage, breakdown of, and associated losses

- Medical expenses (not included in cost of respite or nursing care and attendance)

- Motor car, loss of use of

- Paid help

- Pension rights, loss of

- Privacy, loss of

- Second home on breakdown of marriage

- Society, loss of

- Special appliances (except as mentioned in loss of mobility)

- Specific enjoyment, loss of[21]

Interest on damages

16.21 Interest on heads of damage falling within the Sch 2 forms a part of those damages. The compensator can therefore offset benefits against such interest.[22] Moreover, a claimant is entitled to be awarded interest on damages notwithstanding receipt of listed benefits which may reduce partially or completely the amount of compensation he actually receives from the defendant.[23]

---

[21] From 'DWP Advisers Z1 – Recovery Benefits and NHS Charges' – last updated August 2005 (http://dwp.gov.uk/advisers/z1/.)

[22] *Spence v Wilson (No 2)* (1998) *The Times*, May 18 and *Griffiths v British Coal Corporation* [2001] 1 WLR 1493.

[23] *Wadey v Surrey County Council* (2001) 1 WLR 820, HL.

Interim payments

16.22 The statutory scheme applies to interim payments.

Contributory negligence

16.23 There is no provision in the Act for reducing the sum a defendant is obliged to pay to the state to take account of contributory negligence. Thus a defendant will remain liable to pay 100% of the benefits to the CRU even if a claimant is awarded only 50% of his damages. This can cause particular difficulties when calculating, making and assessing the effects of a Part 36 payment.[24]

Judgments

16.24 Where a case goes to full trial and judgment is given, s 15 of the Act requires the judge to specify the sums awarded for each head of damage listed in Sch 2, namely past loss of earnings, past care and past mobility. No such requirement is imposed if the order is made by consent. However, judges will not be required to make s 8 calculations. They will have to consider the s 8 calculation once costs are put in issue on Part 36 payments (see below).

Part 36 Payments

16.25 Although the statutory scheme is reasonably simple to state, difficulties can arise (and have arisen) when defendants attempt to protect their position by means of Part 36 payments into court.

16.26 Section 16 of the Act provides that regulations may make provision for cases in which payments into court are made, and reg 8 of the Regulations deals with some technical aspects of making Part 36 payments, including rules about the treatment and timing of payments. The defendant must, for example, confirm to the claimant that the payment has been calculated in accordance with s 8,[25] and the liability to pay the sum to the CRU does not arise until the defendant is informed that the money has been paid out of court 'to or for the [claimant]'.[26]

16.27 Of more interest – and complexity – to practitioners are the provisions of r 36.23 of the Civil Procedure Rules 1998 (CPR) and the accompanying Practice Direction, which govern the defendant's obligations when making a Part 36 payment and the treatment by the courts of such payments with respect to costs.

16.28 A defendant must, when making a Part 36 payment, state in the payment notice the amount of gross compensation, the name and amount of any benefit

---

[24] See further below.
[25] Reg 8(1)(c).
[26] Reg 8(2).

by which that gross amount is reduced in accordance with s 8 and that the sum paid in is the net amount after deduction of the amount of benefit.[27] By CPR, r 36.23(4), a claimant is deemed to have failed to better a Part 36 payment if he 'fails to obtain judgment for more than the gross sum specified in the Part 36 payment notice'. Although these provisions appear reasonably straight forward, difficulties can arise in practice, particularly if a claimant's damages are reduced by reason of contributory negligence and/or heads of claim are reduced by reason, for example, of a pre-existing medical condition that would have prevented the claimant from working after a certain date in any event.

16.29 Both these problems were encountered by the Court of Appeal in *Williams v Devon County Council*.[28] In that case the judge awarded the claimant £34,587.58 (including interest) but reduced her damages by one third for contributory negligence, leaving a sum of £23,058.39. The defendant had made a Part 36 payment of £10,000 and had included in the payment notice a total of £15,669.91 being the sum set out on the CRU certificate, making a total payment of £25,669.91. The defendant argued that the claimant had failed to beat the Part 36 payment. The judge agreed and awarded the defendant its costs from the date of the payment. The claimant appealed and the Court of Appeal took the opportunity to provide guidance on the proper approach to Part 36 payments in theses circumstances. After the deduction for contributory negligence, the claimant's damages included £15,738.91 for pain, suffering, loss of amenity (and various other awards that did not appear as heads of compensation in Sch 2 to the Act) and it was only the remainder of the award – some £7,319.48 – against which the defendant could legitimately offset the benefits set out on the CRU certificate. Thus, the claimant was in fact better off in terms of the money he actually received than he would have been if he had accepted the Part 36 payment. The judge's decision was therefore wrong.

16.30 What the defendant should have done, but did not do, was set out on the payment notice exactly how the payment was calculated, giving details of what was allowed for general and other protected damages, what had been allowed for loss of earnings and setting out what benefits had been set off against what heads of loss. This, said the Court of Appeal, was, in effect, the obligation on defendants imposed by CPR, r 36.23(3).[29] If the exercise is carried out properly by the compensator, 'resulting in an appropriate payment for general damages, then the process of calculation of the Part 36 payment equiparates to the way in which damages would be awarded were the matter to go to trial'.[30] The failure to set out this detail meant that the Part 36 payment was not a proper or effective payment.

16.31 The court went on to anticipate future difficulties in circumstances where, for example, a defendant underestimates the claim for general damages but overestimates the claim for loss of earnings, resulting in a larger sum being

---

[27] CPR, r 36.23(3).
[28] [2003] EWCA Civ 365.
[29] See also the requirements set out in 36 PD.10.3, 10.4 and 10.5.
[30] Judgment para 27.

set off against the claimant's claim than would be legitimate under s 8. In these situations the court thought that 'the touchstone' would be that 'the claimant is entitled to the full value of his general damages claim ... It is for the compensator to make a proper assessment of the general damages figure and ensure that the Part 36 payment at least provides the claimant with that sum'.[31]

16.32 In *Hilton International v Noel Martin-Smith*,[32] the defendant paid £6,000 into court expressed to be in addition to deductible benefits of £40,124.58. The claimant accepted the payment. The defendant later successfully appealed the certificate, reducing it to nil, and the CRU paid the sum of £40,124.58 back to the defendant. The claimant claimed the sum from the defendant, and the judge acceded to the application. On appeal, Pitchford J upheld the judge's decision, relying on reg 11 of the Regulations, which required the compensator to pay the sum back to the claimant. The defendant should have paid in only the £6,000, and not added the sum equivalent to the benefits received. Had that been done, then the claimant would have had no claim in respect of the sum paid back to the defendant by the CRU.

16.33 The lesson from both the cases above would seem to be that defendants must set out exactly how they have calculated the payment into court, ensuring that the claimant knows the amount that is offered by way of damages that are ring-fenced. Only then will the defendant be in a position to take advantage of a Part 36 payment that is greater than the sum received by a claimant at trial.

Reviews and appeals

16.34 There are two ways in which the content of a CRU certificate can be challenged: review and appeal.

Reviews

16.35 Reviews are governed by s 10 of the Act. Any party may apply for a review at any time. The basis of an application for review is:

> 'the certificate ... was issued in ignorance of, or was based on a mistake as to a material fact or that a mistake has occurred in its preparation.'

16.36 On review, the certificate may be varied up or down. This is a change from the old law which only allowed reduction on review. If the certificate is reviewed down, then the effect for the parties is a refund. It will only be reviewed upwards if the DWP considers that the person who applied for the certificate gave the DWP 'incorrect or insufficient information'. The CRU has issued guidance notes which suggest that variations upwards will only occur where the claimant has supplied fraudulent information, but the Act allows for upwards variations where the insurer has made errors in providing information to the CRU.

---

[31] Judgment para 29.
[32] 5 October 2000, QBD, Pitchford J (unreported).

Appeals

16.37 The practical effect of the introduction of the Act was to increase the burden on insurers, so that benefits paid to a claimant were to be paid back to the Secretary of State irrespective of whether a defendant could offset those benefits against the claimant's claim. Appeals are decided by an Appeals Tribunal (AT), and after the introduction of the new statutory regime a number of appeals were consolidated and heard by a special tribunal of Social Security Commissioners (TSSC) to decide whether or not a AT was entitled to decide that a benefit had been wrongly awarded to a victim of accident, injury or disease.

16.38 In the first of the appeals – *Yorkshire Repetition Castings Ltd v Secretary of State for Social Security* – the TSSC said that:

> 'The real issue is whether Parliament intended to impose on compensators a liability that they had not previously had, to recompense the Secretary of State for benefits that ought not to have been paid because either the relevant accident or disease had not caused the relevant disablement or because the claimant had not been as disabled or incapable as the adjudicating authority had found.'

16.39 The TSSC answered the question in favour of compensators, deciding that an AT was entitled to come to a conclusion 'that is inconsistent with the award of benefit'.

16.40 Appeals are governed by s 11 of the Act. They can only be brought after the compensation has been paid and the CRU recoupment satisfied in full. Provisional damages awards also trigger the right to appeal. Any party can appeal. The grounds of appeal are:

> '... any amount, rate or period specified in the certificate is incorrect ... or listed benefits which have been paid otherwise than in respect of the accident ... in question have been brought into account'.

It would be a mistake for practitioners to assume that appeals are unlikely to succeed. Indeed, the Appeals Service's 'Annual Report and Accounts 2003-2004' estimated that 70% to 80% of all appeals against CRU certificates were successful.

16.41 The procedure for appeals is set out in the Social Security and Child Support (Decisions and Appeals) Regulations 1999. There is a strict time limit of one month after the date on which a compensator discharges his liability under s 6 of the Act. There is limited scope for appealing out of time. The AT consists of one legally qualified representative and – usually – one medical expert. Compensators can request that appeals be dealt with on paper, otherwise there will be an oral hearing which will be informal with no strict rules of evidence. Under s 12(3) the AT is obliged to take note of any previous order made by the Court, and this would presumably apply to a consent order as well as one made after a disputed trial. Medical reports and full medical records should be available, together with any video evidence that may have been obtained.

16.42 An appeal from the AT on a point of law lies to the Social Security Commissioner.

Variations of certificates

16.43 Once the appeal or review has taken place, if the certificate has been varied the CRU can either claim excess benefits from the compensator or refund the excess paid to the compensator. If the CRU makes a refund to the compensator, then the compensator is bound to recalculate the section 8 deduction and pass the extra sums on to the claimant.[33]

---

[33] Reg 11 of the Regulations. See also *Hilton International v Noel Martin-Smith*, 5 October 2000, QBD, Pitchford J (unreported).

Chapter 17

MENTALLY INCAPABLE CLAIMANTS AND THE COURT OF PROTECTION

INTRODUCTION: THE MENTAL CAPACITY ACT 2005

17.1 The Mental Capacity Act 2005 makes major changes to the existing law and practice for mentally incapable claimants and to the structure and powers of the Court of Protection. The new act provides a detailed statutory framework that is designed to empower and protect vulnerable people who are unable to make their own decisions. It seeks to make clear who can take the decisions that matter on their behalf, in what circumstances and how to put the decision making into practice. The new Court of Protection, as a court of record enjoying the powers of the High Court, will combine the personal welfare and healthcare jurisdiction currently exercised by the Family Division of the High Court with the property and financial decision-making jurisdiction of the former Court of Protection.

17.2 The Act is designed to signal innovatory and wide-ranging provisions for persons who are proved to lack mental capacity, to make significant changes to the current law and practice where decisions need to be made on behalf of others in respect of personal welfare as well as financial matters, and to establish a system of court appointed deputies with authority to make decisions on behalf of others who lack capacity.

17.3 The Mental Capacity Bill was introduced into the House of Commons on 17 June 2004 and, after a stormy passage, received the Royal Assent on 7 April 2005.

17.4 By s 68, the Act comes into force in accordance with provision made by order of the Lord Chancellor. To date no formal provision has been made, but the Department of Constitutional Affairs (DCA) is stated to be working towards an implementation in April 2007, with a likely commencement date of 1 April. The new Court of Protection and the Office of the Public Guardian are expected to come into being on that date. The Court of Protection Rules 2007 and the new fee policy are expected to commence at the same time.

THE NEW MEASURES

17.5 The Act introduces reforms that include:

(1) a new definition of mental incapacity: 'a person lacks capacity in relation to a matter if at the material time he is unable to make a decision for himself in relation to the matter because of an impairment of, or disturbance of the mind or brain';

(2) the assessment process for mental capacity will be regulated by a series of guideline principles;

(3) the overhaul of the present receivership system and the appointment of deputies;

(4) the overhaul of enduring powers of attorney, to be replaced by lasting powers of attorney;

(5) the appointment of independent mental capacity advocates;

(6) the creation of a superior court of record with the same powers, rights, privileges and authority as the High Court, to be called the Court of Protection, that will have substantially enhanced powers and responsibilities for those who lack mental capacity;

(7) the preparation of codes of practice by the Lord Chancellor for the guidance of assessing whether a person has capacity, of persons acting in connection with the care or treatment of another, of donees of lasting powers of attorney, of court-appointed deputies, and others;

(8) the making of new Court of Protection Rules for the practice and procedure of the new court;

(9) the appointment of a new statutory official, the Public Guardian, to support the work of the new Court of Protection;

(10) the creation of a Public Guardian Board that will scrutinise and review the way in which the Public Guardian discharges his functions and to make recommendations to the Lord Chancellor.

THE CORE PRINCIPLES AND OVERRIDING OBJECTIVES OF THE NEW REGIME

17.6 Section 1 of the Act lays down a series of five key principles:

(1) a person must be assumed to have capacity unless it is established, on the balance of probabilities, that he lacks capacity;

(2) a person is not to be treated as unable to make a decision unless all practicable steps to help him to do so have been taken without success;

(3) a person is not to be treated as unable to make a decision merely because he makes an unwise decision;

(4) an act done, or a decision made, under the Act for or on behalf of a person who lacks capacity must be done, or made, in his best interests;

(5) before the act is done, or the decision is made, regard must be had to whether the purpose for which it is needed can be as effectively achieved in a way that is less restrictive of the person's rights and freedom of action.

BEST INTERESTS

17.7 Any act done or decision made on behalf of someone who lacks mental capacity must be in their best interests. By s 4 of the Act, when determining what is in a person's best interests, specific regard must be had to the likelihood of a person having capacity in relation to the matter in the future; to the need to encourage his self-participation; to his past and present wishes and feelings as far as reasonably ascertainable; to the views of others closely connected with the person, including a court-appointed deputy; and whether the purpose for which any act or decision is needed can be as effectively achieved in a manner less restrictive of the person's freedom of action.

17.8 The Act makes clear that when deciding whether a person lacks capacity or not, and if so, when determining what are in his or her best interests, these issues should not be established merely on the basis of age or appearance or on the basis of the person's condition or an aspect of behaviour that might lead others to make unjustified assumptions about capacity or best interests.

The new definition of a person who is mentally incapable and for whom a special court procedure is appropriate – sections 2 and 3 of the Act.

17.9 The new definition is unequivocally issue specific. By s 2 of the Act, a person lacks capacity in relation to a matter if at the material time he is unable to make a decision for himself in relation to the matter because of an impairment of, or a disturbance in, the functioning of the mind or brain.[1] It matters not if the impairment or disturbance is permanent or temporary.

17.10 By s 3 of the Act, a person is unable to make a decision for himself[2] if he is unable to:

---

[1] The 'diagnostic' test.
[2] The 'functional' test.

(1) understand the information relevant to the decision;

(2) retain that information;

(3) use or weigh that information as part of the process of making the decision;

(4) communicate his decision (whether by talking, using sign language or any other means).

17.11 A person is not to be regarded as unable to understand the information relevant to a decision if he is able to understand an explanation of it given to him in a way that is appropriate to his circumstances (using simple language, visual aids or other means).

17.12 The fact that a person is able to retain the information relevant to a decision for a short period only does not prevent him from being regarded as able to make the decision.

17.13 The information relevant to the decision includes information about the reasonably foreseeable consequences of (1) deciding one way or another, or (2) failing to make the decision.

The principal functions of the new Court of Protection and likely practice

17.14 The exercise of the new powers and responsibilities will include the following:

(1) to determine whether or not a person has the capacity to make a particular decision;

(2) to make declarations concerning the lawfulness or otherwise of any act done or yet to be done in relation to a person;

(3) to make single, one-off, orders; for example an order authorising the execution of a statutory will or an order for the sale of a house and the investment of the net proceeds of sale;

(4) to appoint a deputy to take individual decisions in relation to the matter or matters in which a person lacks the mental capacity to make the decision;

(5) to grant persons, not automatically entitled, to make application to the court;

(6) to exercise an appellate jurisdiction under the Mental Health Act 1983.

17.15 By s 16, the new Court of Protection is empowered to make decisions on behalf of a person's personal welfare or his property and affairs where that person lacks capacity. It will be able to make declarations as to whether a person has, or lacks, capacity to make a specified decision, has the capacity to make decisions on specified matters and the lawfulness, or otherwise, of any act done or yet to be done in relation to that person.

17.16 Where a person, who has not made a lasting power of attorney, lacks the capacity to make a decision about his or her personal welfare or about his property and financial affairs, the court may appoint a 'deputy' to make that decision for him. This will not be a receiver with a new name. When deciding whether it is in the person's best interests to appoint a deputy, the new Court of Protection must have regard to the principles that (1) a decision by the Court is to be preferred to the appointment of a deputy to make decisions; and (2) the powers conferred on the deputy should be as limited in scope and duration as possible.

17.17 The Court of Protection (via the Office of the Public Guardian) will, in the future, supervise the court-appointed deputies. Two supervision regimes are envisaged, 'light touch' and 'close supervision.'

17.18 Personal welfare includes place of residence, contact with specified persons, and the giving or refusing of consent for healthcare treatment. However, family matters and relationships are specifically excluded from the definition of personal welfare. Section 27 makes clear that decisions about marriage or civil partnership, sexual relations, divorce on the basis of two years' separation, adoption consent, parental responsibility and consent under the Human Fertilisation and Embryology Act 1990 on behalf of a person who lacks capacity, fall outside the scope of the Act and that applications on these issues will not permitted.

17.19 The power under s 16 to make decisions for another upon on matters of his property and affairs includes the control and management of his property, the sale or other disposition of his property, the acquisition of property, the carrying on of his profession, trade or business, dissolving a partnership, performing contractual obligations, the discharge of debts, the settlement of his property for his or others benefit, the execution of a will, the exercise of any power, and the conduct of legal proceedings in his name.

PROTECTION FROM CIVIL LIABILITY: GENERAL AUTHORITY TO ACT

17.20 By ss 5 to 8 of the Act those who provide the care and treatment of another without capacity will not incur civil liability for loss or damage, provided that the care is in the best interests of the person concerned and is performed without negligence. The Act envisages that, with basic and sensible precautions, carers and treatment providers will be protected from civil and criminal law liability.

17.21 Special provisions will apply to the approval, and to consultation, in respect of medical research concerning those without mental capacity.

INDEPENDENT MENTAL CAPACITY ADVOCATES

17.22 By s 35 of the Act the Court of Protection, as the appropriate authority, will make reasonable arrangements to enable independent mental capacity advocates to represent and support persons who lack capacity to whom acts or decisions relate in respect of:

(1) the provision of serious medical treatment by the NHS;

(2) the provision of accommodation by the NHS; and

(3) the provision of accommodation by a local authority.

17.23 Independent mental capacity advocates are likely to be appointed to represent persons lacking mental capacity who have no family or friends to support them.

17.24 The functions, powers, responsibilities of independent mental capacity advocates are defined by ss 35 and 36 of the Act. The Court of Protection will be able to make regulations that will supplement the primary legislation for mental capacity advocates. No regulations had been drafted at the date of writing.

17.25 The present Master of the Court of Protection has highlighted some concern that has been expressed about the lack of clarity in the role of the independent advocates:

- why the advocacy service should be limited to NHS treatment or to NHS/local authority accommodation;

- what 'serious medical treatment' actually means;

- how the advocacy service will be organised;

- how existing advocacy providers should be involved in the service;

- what will be the funding constraints on the service provision.

CODES OF PRACTICE

17.26 Guidance on the practical application and effect of the Act will be provided in one or more codes of practice. These will have relevance for the conduct of the donees of a lasting power of attorney, deputies appointed by the court, persons undertaking intrusive research as part of an approved research project, an independent mental capacity advocate, and persons acting in a professional capacity and/or providing services for remuneration.

THE PUBLIC GUARDIAN

17.27 Section 57 of the Act creates a new, statutory office-holder to be known as the Public Guardian. Richard Brook, the former chief executive of MIND, took up the office as chief executive of the PGO and Public Guardian designate in February 2006.

17.28 Section 58 of the Act confers on the Public Guardian important new functions:

(1) to establish and maintain registers of lasting power attorneys and deputies appointed by the court;

(2) to supervise deputies appointed by the court;

(3) to direct a visit by a Court of Protection visitor;

(4) to receive security, reports and accounts; and

(5) to handle complaints.

17.29 By s 49 the new Court of Protection is given with an important power to call for reports from the Public Guardian and from a Court of Protection visitor. It may also require a local authority or NHS body to make reports to deal with any such matter as it directs. Court of Protection rules will specify other matters of practice and procedure in relation to reports.

APPLICATIONS TO THE COURT OF PROTECTION

17.30 Applications for the exercise of its fundamental powers under the Act, for example the appointment of deputies, will not need the preliminary permission of the Court, but all other applications will require such permission in order to proceed. By r 23 of the proposed Court of Protection Rules 2007, the court's permission will be required for every application to start proceedings, except where the application is made by the Official Solicitor, is made by the Public Guardian, concerns a lasting power of attorney, concerns an enduring power of attorney, or relates solely to the exercise of the court's powers in relation to the incapable person's property and affairs.

THE COURT OF PROTECTION RULES 2007

17.31 By s 51, the rules of the new Court may, in particular, make provision for:

(1) the manner and form of commencement of proceedings;

(2) the parties to be notified and to be made parties;

(3) the allocation of business;

(4) the exercise of jurisdiction by officers or other staff of the court;

(5) the appointment of a suitable person, who may be, with his consent, the Official Solicitor, to act on behalf of the person to whom the proceedings relate;

(6) the disposal of an application without a hearing;

(7) proceeding with a hearing in the absence of the person to whom the proceedings relate;

(8) proceedings in private and the exclusion of specified persons when sitting in public;

(9) the admission of evidence and procedure at hearings;

(10) the enforcement of orders and directions made by the new Court.

17.32 The proposed Court of Protection Rules 2007 provide a comprehensive and wide ranging code of practice on all the matters permitted by the Act, including the overriding objective. The Rules match the scope and format of the CPR, but detailed reference to the proposed rules is recommended.

LITIGATION FRIEND

17.33 In addition the new Court of Protection, by Part 8 (rr 47–52) of the proposed Court of Protection Rules 2007, will have the power to appoint a litigation friend at any stage in the proceedings if the relevant person or any other person with sufficient interest lacks the capacity to conduct the proceedings himself. The proposed rules permit litigation friends to act without a court order (on the filing of the appropriate certificate of suitability). The court may also appoint the litigation friend, order that a named person may not act as a litigation friend and order a change of litigation friend. The Rules lay down a procedure where the appointment of a litigation friend comes to an end.

DIRECTIONS

17.34 The President, with the concurrence of the Lord Chancellor, will be able to give directions concerning the practice and procedure of the new Court, supplementing the Rules.

APPEALS

17.35 An appeal, but only with permission, save for an appeal against an order for committal to prison, will lie to the Court of Appeal from any decision of the new Court of Protection.

FEES AND COSTS

17.36 Sections 54 and 55 of the Act make provision for fees and costs. The DCA set out its proposals for the fees of the new Court of Protection in a consultation paper dated 7 September 2006.

FEES AND COSTS IN THE NEW COURT OF PROTECTION

17.37 The new court will be a superior court of record that will assume responsibility both for applications that, at present, come to the present Court of Protection and for personal welfare and healthcare cases that are currently heard by the Family Division of the High Court.

17.38 Under the new regime, all applications will be decided by the judicial members of the Court. The delegation to nominated officers of the public Guardianship Office will cease.

17.39 The proposed application fee is £400 with payment on initial application and on every subsequent application to vary an existing order.

FEES RELATING TO DEPUTIES AND THEIR SUPERVISION

17.40 From April 2007 the power of the Court of Protection to appoint receivers with authority to make financial decisions on behalf of those who lack mental capacity will be replaced with the power to appoint deputies. The deputies will be able to make financial or personal welfare decisions on behalf of a person who lacks capacity to take those decisions.

17.41 When the new Court appoints a deputy, a key function of the Public Guardian will be to act as a regulator, monitoring the deputyship and ensuring that the deputy acts in the best interest of the person who lacks capacity.

17.42 Most deputies are expected to be supervised by a range of activities that reflect the need for 'light' touch supervision, characterised by:

- training and coaching opportunities;

- assistance from an easily accessible customer support and advice service;

- a requirement to provide an annual account or report to the Office of the Public Guardian;

- confirmation of a security bond as directed by the Court;

- the provision of short-term advice on specific questions of concern.

17.43 Where the assessment of the Public Guardian determines that a greater degree of supervision is appropriate, additional activities will be undertaken:

- enhanced support for deputies;

- an initial visit, followed by further visits as required;

- the calling for records and other documents;

- additional financial assessment during the initial period of accounting;

- periodic review by the Office of the Public Guardian.

17.44 The proposed fee on appointment for the initial set up is £125. The proposed annual 'light' supervision fee is £175 and the annual 'close' supervision fee £800.

17.45 The DCA anticipates that the majority of deputy appointments will fall into the 'light' supervision category and that the annual fee of £175 will be significantly lower than the fees currently charged to receivers.

17.46 Applicants and those protected within the jurisdiction of the new Court of Protection will be exempt from payment for fees if they are in receipt of specific means-tested benefits and do not own net capital assets, including any property, above a ceiling of £16,000. A formal application to the Court for exemption will be required.

17.47 Where clients of the Court are not entitled to an automatic exemption, they will be able to apply for the remission of the fee. Remissions will be undertaken on a discretionary basis, dependent on exceptional circumstances or undue financial hardship. Remissions will be considered on evidence of income, expenditure and capital assets. A partial remission would be the starting point and full remission given only if the applicant or party could not pay any part of the fee. Again, a formal application for a remission will be required.

Fees relating to the new Court Reporting Service

17.48 Section 49 of the Act provides for the new Court of Protection to ask for a report on matters relating to a person who lacks capacity, in order to assist in the determination of a case. An impartial report may be sought from the Public Guardian, a Court of Protection visitor, and from other bodies such as local authorities or the NHS wherever the Court decides that this would be helpful.

17.49 The Public Guardian will set up and manage the new, independent Court Reporting Service. A fee will be charged where the Court asks the Public Guardian or a Court of Protection visitor to report. The fee will comprise two elements: the actual cost of preparing the report and an administrative handling charge of £100, payable on completion of the hearing.

THE LEGAL COSTS OF APPLYING TO AND ATTENDING COURT

17.50 The DCA made proposals for the payment of costs in its consultation paper dated 17 July 2006. In summary, the parties to a case should each fund their own costs, but with a wide discretion for the court to order that the costs, including any court fees incurred, are to be paid from the estate of the person who lacks mental capacity.

17.51 The court will also have the power to make costs orders against other parties where they had acted unreasonably or not in the best interests of the person who lacked capacity.

17.52 New rules of court on costs are awaited following the period of consultation, which ended on 6 October 2006.

THE CONTINUATION OF EXISTING PRACTICE: A TENTATIVE REVIEW

17.53 It is not clear, at the time of writing, what part of the existing law, practice and procedure will remain in place with relevance to claims for damages in respect of personal injury. Amendments may be made to the Civil

Procedure Rules (in particular to Part 21) and to the Limitation Act 1980. The following review should be considered with some caution during the period of transaction.

17.54 Personal injury practitioners, however, must continue to make a careful investigation of capacity, at the early stages of the litigation, when acting for any person with serious neurological and/or cognitive damage. If the claimant has been rendered mentally incapable, compliance with special procedural rules is mandatory. The former definition[3] of incapacity is no longer valid. However, a patient or person without mental capacity must be so described in the title of the proceedings. He is obliged, without exception, to pursue his action by, and in the name of, a litigation friend.

17.55 A patient, acting alone and without a litigation friend, whether as the result of his lawyer's self-induced ignorance or otherwise, cannot bring an effective claim or make a binding settlement.

17.56 The victims of catastrophic head injury and acquired brain damage, having suffered unconsciousness, prolonged periods of rehabilitation and, with continuing dementia or loss of cognitive functions, are all likely to come unambiguously within the definition of mental disorder and bring the special patient procedure into play.

17.57 In the course of the preparation of the claim for compensation arising from an accident on behalf of a brain-injured claimant, expert medical evidence on his condition and likely prognosis will be obtained as a matter of routine from a neurologist or a neurosurgeon and/or a psychiatrist. One of these experts may be instructed to give an opinion on the claimant's mental capacity.

17.58 It is not necessary, however, when the original application is made to the Court of Protection for the appointment of a receiver, to present evidence from a specialist medical practitioner. In clear cases, the requisite medical certificate (form CP3) is frequently signed by the patient's general practitioner and this was generally accepted by the Master of the Court of Protection as sufficient proof of mental incapacity and the concomitant patient status. The acceptance by the Master, however, does not bind a court with the power to award compensation and does not ensure the automatic operation of the patient procedure and limitation provisions.

17.59 Note, however, that a registered medical practitioner must sign the form. A certificate from a clinical psychologist, or similar expert, is not acceptable to the Court of Protection.

---

[3] Any claimant, who by reason of mental disorder, as defined by s 1 of the Mental Health Act 1983, is incapable of managing and administering his property and affairs. By s 1(2) of the Act, four categories of mental disorder were specified for the purpose of defining a patient: (1) mental illness; (2) arrested or incomplete development of mind; (3) psychopathic disorder; or (4) any other disorder or disability or mind.

17.60 In cases of emergency, the Court of Protection had jurisdiction to act without conclusive medical evidence of incapacity:

- where the Master has reason to believe that a person may be incapable, by reason of mental disorder, of managing and administering his property and affairs; *and*

- the Master is of the opinion that it is necessary to make immediate provision for the administration of the person's affairs.[4]

THE NEW DEFINITION OF INCAPACITY ANTICIPATED

17.61 The new definition was foreshowed in a careful review of the law and practice by the Court of Appeal in *Masterman-Lister v Brutton & Co and Jewell & Home Counties Dairies* [2002] EWCA Civ 1889; [2003] PIQR P310. The case gives a useful illustration of how the new definition of incapacity may adopted in practice. Following the decision, fewer claimants were likely to be categorised as patients. Practitioners could no longer assume that the former professional security, engendered by the comfortable absence of limitation anxiety, would, without further enquiry necessarily continue to be available. Consultant psychiatrists and neurologists are now tending to say 'not a patient' in borderline cases.

17.62 The facts in *Masterman-Lister* were not unique. The claimant had been seriously injured in a motorcycle accident on 9 September 1980 when aged 17 years. He suffered concussion and anoxic brain damage, being left with little in the way of physical disabilities or impairment of general intellectual function, but permanent disability by reason of an impoverished and unreliable memory, a change in personality and a reduced capacity to organise his life and his affairs. He was unable to return to his former employment as an engineering apprentice and, although he was found a routine job as a clerical assistant, he ceased all work in 1989.

17.63 His parents had consulted solicitors on his behalf. Liability was disputed. In September 1987, after obtaining personal instructions from the claimant, who was then aged 24 years, the solicitors accepted an offer in settlement. Approval was not sought from the court. All the parties believed that the litigation was at an end.

17.64 Since 1992, the claimant had lived alone in a house purchased from the fruits of the litigation, relying on statutory benefits. He was self-caring and able to deal with the ordinary incidents of everyday life. He maintained a bank account and had the use of a credit card. When serious problems arose he was able to recognise their existence and then to seek help from his parents and others. He had kept a detailed diary of his every day life during the relevant

---

[4] Mental Health Act 1983, s 98.

times and had written letters to outside parties, learnt to drive, learnt to type and passed two public examinations (ordinary level general certificates of education).

17.65 In December 1993, the claimant issued proceedings alleging negligence against his former solicitors in their handling of the original claim and, in due course, against the original defendants to the road traffic litigation. The defendants claimed that as more than six/three years had expired since the accident, the action was statute barred. In June 1997, the claimant received an opinion from a consultant in neuro-psychiatric rehabilitation, a registered medical practitioner, that he was, and had been since the head injury at the time of the accident, a patient within the meaning of s 94(2) of the Mental Health Act 1983. The claimant sought to re-open the settlement of his claim on the basis that it had never received the approval of the court. Moreover, he claimed that the subsequent action against his former solicitors was not statute barred because at all material times he was of unsound mind within the meaning of s 38 of the Limitation Act 1980. He asserted that by reason of s 28, no period of limitation had run against him, contending that all times since the accident he had been a patient and under a mental disability.

17.66 The Court of Appeal determined to the contrary. Although the claimant was suffering from mental disorder within the meaning of the Mental Health Act 1983, he was not incapable of managing his affairs and therefore could not be a patient. There was, accordingly, no answer to the plea of limitation. The Court dismissed the claim, holding that:

(1) all adults are presumed capable of managing their property and affairs unless and until the contrary is proved; the burden of proof rests on the party asserting incapacity;

(2) the term 'affairs' is not defined in the Act but it includes only business matters, legal transactions or other dealings of a similar kind; it does not extend to physical care and/or treatment;[5]

(3) capacity is a matter dependent upon time and context; consideration must be given to the individual claimant and to the particular litigation in question rather than the whole of his business affairs; the decision about mental capacity required by the law concerned capacity in relation to the particular transaction that is to be effected, its nature and its complexity; the correct test of mental capacity was closely issue-specific;

(4) what is required is the capacity to understand the nature of the transaction when properly explained by legal advisers or other experts as the circumstances demand;

---

[5] *Re F (Mental Patient: Sterilisation)* [1990] 2 AC 1.

(5) a court has to investigate capacity in relation to a particular transaction and not outcomes in general such as the ability to self care or to manage a bank account, but outcomes can often throw a flood of light on capacity;

(6) a person's ability to manage his property and affairs requires an ability to make and to communicate, and where appropriate, to give effect to all decisions in relation to them;[6]

(7) a person incapable of taking investment decisions about a large compensation-derived fund could not be said for that reason alone to be incapable of pursuing a claim for that compensation, because few people have the capacity to manage all their affairs unaided;

(8) where lack of capacity is demonstrated, the court will then have to determine whether the incapacity is due to mental disorder as defined in the Act;

(9) in the event that there has been lack of capacity but where that was not recognised at the time, any litigation is ineffective and any decisions, including orders of the court, made in the course of that litigation are invalid; however the CPR allow a court to regularise the position retrospectively; it should do so where all the parties acted in good faith and there has been no manifest injustice to anyone subsequently held to have been a patient at the relevant time; the incapacity procedure was not intended to provide a vehicle for reopening litigation which has been apparently properly conducted and had long been understood to be at an end;

(10) where a person is treated by the court as a patient, he is deprived of the important civil right of litigation self-dependence, ie to sue or to defend in his own name, to have the litigation based on his own instructions and to compromise the claim without the need for court approval; this right should not be taken from a person without allowing him the opportunity of establishing his capacity, but there was no mechanism in the CPR for a person labelled a patient to institute a judicial determination of his capacity; the courts should[7] always, as a matter of practice, at the first

---

[6] This formulation by the Court of Appeal reflects the unreported decision at first instance by Boreham J in *While v Fell*, 12 November 1987 who held that to have capacity a party requires (1) the insight and understanding of the fact that they have a problem in respect of which advice is needed; (2) having identified the problem, that it will be necessary to seek an appropriate adviser and then to instruct him with sufficient clarity to enable him to understand the problem and to advise appropriately; and (3) to have sufficient capacity to understand and to make decisions based upon, or otherwise give effect to, such advice as may be received. The whole test of capacity is, per Kennedy LJ, *Masterman-Lister* at 318, related to the individual party and to his or her immediate problems.

[7] Save where the Court of Protection has already intervened to assume jurisdiction over a person's property and affairs pursuant to s 94(2) of the MHA 1983, having considered medical evidence and being satisfied that a person is incapable. Someone who is treated as a patient for

convenient opportunity, investigate the question of capacity whenever there is reason to suggest it may be absent.

17.67 A claimant could be found to be capable for some parts of ongoing litigation but incapable for other, severable parts of the same litigation.

17.68 In *Bailey v Warren* [2005] PIQR P15 (Holland J, Manchester) the claimant had sustained a severe brain injury in a road traffic accident. As a pedestrian, he had been struck by car at night. He had no recollection of the accident. In November 2000 liability was compromised between the parties at 50:50 and judgment entered in December 2001. The court held that for the compromise issue, in which the claimant had been given simple and positive advice by counsel, he enjoyed specific litigation capacity. He was not a patient for the purpose of the settlement.

17.69 His application to set aside the compromise failed. In November 2000 he:

(1) had sufficient insight on the liability issue to know he needed legal advice;

(2) had instructed an appropriate adviser; and

(3) was capable of understanding and making decisions based upon the advice received.

The liability compromise at 50:50 was held to be valid and binding on the parties.

17.70 However, the quantum determination was different. It gave rise to a sophisticated and complex claim for damages, together with an ongoing responsibility for managing the resultant and substantial fund. The court held that, for quantum, he not enjoy specific litigation capacity. Accordingly, he was, and had been, a patient from and at least since his sister's appointment as litigation friend in October 2003. In summary, therefore, he had not been a patient for the purpose of the liability compromise in November 2000, but had been a patient for the quantum claim at least from and since October 2003.

17.71 This picture of differing status in relation to differing issues was neatly summarised in *Sheffield City Council v E* [2005] 2 WLR 953 at 964, para 39:

> 'Someone may have the capacity to litigate in a case where the nature of the dispute and the issues are simple, whilst at the same time lacking the capacity to litigate in a case where either the nature of the dispute or the issues are more complex.'

17.72 The issue-specific approach of the Court of Appeal in *Masterman-Lister* more narrowly defined the meaning of patient than hitherto and did not

---

the purpose of CPR, r 21 and who litigates by a litigation friend is not necessarily and may never be accepted by the Court of Protection as a patient pursuant to s 94(2).

address the general needs of an 'at risk' claimant. On the other hand, with more developed notions of litigation self-determination in an era of care in the community, the law perhaps should be slow to deprive a claimant of his or her human right of self-determination without decisive evidence.

17.73 The Court of Appeal sought to balance the competing claims of paternalistic state intervention by way of protection on the one hand and the self-empowerment of the disadvantaged on the other. In the current judicial climate, empowerment has gained precedence over protection.

17.74 The personal injury practitioner bears a burden of over-reaching responsibility to the injured party that here includes legal, moral and social elements. The prudent course is scrupulously to investigate all marginal cases and to proceed on the basis of medical evidence. If the special code is not adopted, and the claimant later proves that he was a patient, any settlement and other significant decisions will be invalid. On the other hand if the claimant has legal capacity, and is not a patient, he will not be protected from the ordinary impact of limitation. He will not be able to challenge any settlement or to re-open the case at a later date.

17.75 There is no halfway protective category between the competent claimant and the incompetent patient as defined by the Act. This was seen by some observers as an unfortunate gap in the powers of the Court but by others a contrary view is cogently proposed.[8] The legal advisers for the borderline patient claimant should be ready to explore the possibility of protecting the compensation capital by the mechanism of periodical payments, a trust fund or a detailed investment strategy prepared by independent financial advisers.

COMPROMISE AND SETTLEMENT

17.76 No binding compromise or settlement of a patient's claim for damages may be validly concluded, or a defendant's Pt 36 payment into court accepted, unless and until, the approval of the compensation court has been obtained. Without such approval, neither side is obliged to consider the compromise as enforceable.[9]

17.77 On behalf of a claimant without capacity the discrete code of procedure under the CPR Pt 21 must be followed. The assistance of a separate agency, the

---

[8] The PTO Quinquennial Review (1999) observed that attitudes towards how people with mental incapacity should be treated by the public services are markedly different from those that hitherto have prevailed for decades. The Law Commission's four-year study, culminating in the LCD report 'Who Decides' (1999) shows that an intrusive, restrictive and paternalistic approach, no matter how well-intentioned is not wanted by people on the receiving end. Some personal freedoms and a reasonable degree of risk are sought by families that include those with mental incapacity, even while they recognise the need for irreplaceable financial assets to be judiciously protected. The underlining of a claimant's human rights be the Court of Appeal in *Masterman-Lister*, ibid, reflects this changing attitude.

[9] *Dietz v Lennig Chemicals* [1069] 1 AC 170; [1967] 2 All ER 282.

Court of Protection, should be invoked if substantial net sums are to be financially managed. The patient's property and affairs then come under the direct control and supervision of the Court of Protection.

17.78 Interim payments are not exempt from the procedure. Any such payment made on account of damages, by voluntary agreement between the parties, consent order or otherwise, should be approved by an express order of the compensation court.

17.79 Where the proposed settlement or compromise for an incapable claimant includes an order that the damages or part of them be made by periodical payments, the amended PD 21, the amended CPR 41, and the new PD 41B should be followed.

17.80 Note that the former, and short-lived, PD 40C has been replaced by the wholly new practice direction, PD41B, following the implementation on 1 April 2005 of ss 100 and 101 of the Courts Act 2003, the amendments to the CPR (in particular, CPR 41) and the subsidiary orders and rules.

THE LITIGATION FRIEND AND THE CPR

17.81 In any case where the claimant's legal advisers reasonably believe that there is evidence of mental incapacity, the claimant should, prior to the issue of the proceedings, undergo a thorough and careful medical examination and assessment of his mental health and capacity. Thereafter, if the patient criteria are satisfied, the claimant must conduct the action by, and in the name of, an independent third party. Such a person can have no adverse interest in the case and must consent to act as the litigation friend. Without regard to possible issues of human rights, the present CPR permit the action to be started in this way without notice being given to the claimant, and without any independent, judicial determination of capacity.

17.82 The procedural requirements for the litigation friend involvement are provided in clear terms in CPR 21 and supplemented in PD21.

17.83 Any step in an action commenced before a valid litigation friend is involved will have no effect. However, there is a saving provision. Upon application, the court may by specific order retrospectively validate the previous, unauthorised part of the proceedings.

17.84 Unlike an action brought by a child, the court cannot dispense with the requirement for a litigation friend in the case of a patient.

17.85 The litigation friend should file a certificate of suitability when the claim is commenced, stating that he satisfies each of the heads of specified suitability.

17.86 Good practice indicates that the certificate of suitability is also served on the person with whom the claimant resides or in whose care he is living.

POTENTIAL HEADS OF DAMAGE

17.87 A checklist of potential heads of damage for the 'patient–claimant' who is subject to the protection of the Court includes:

(1) the various fees charged by the Court of Protection for its asset management and other allied functions;

(2) the reasonable out-of-pocket expenses of the receiver/deputy, including professional fees if incurred;

(3) the reasonable fees of a professional deputy/receiver;

(4) an allowance for the gratuitous deputy/receivership services provided by a non-professional receiver;

(5) the fees for legal services arising from the representation of the claimant in the Court.

17.88 Both past and prospective fees and expenses should be claimed. Save where the damages are awarded as periodical payments, future loss will be calculated on a multiplier–multiplicand basis.

17.89 The expense of specialist investment advice and management, over and above the Court of Protection fees, are not recoverable.[10]

LIMITATION AND MENTALLY INCAPABLE CLAIMANTS

17.90 A defendant is unable to raise the defence of limitation against a person who is under a mental disability.

17.91 A person under a disability is defined by. s 38 of the Limitation Act 1980:

> '(2) For the purposes of this Act a person shall be treated as under a disability while he is an infant, or of unsound mind.
>
> For the purposes of subsection (2) above a person is of unsound mind if he is a person who, by reason of mental disorder within the meaning of the Mental Health Act 1983 is incapable of managing his own property and affairs.'

---

[10] *Page v Plymouth Hospitals NHS Trust* [2004] EWHC 1154 (QB); [2004] PIQR Q68.

17.92 A person of unsound mind may bring an action for personal injury loss and damage at any time before the expiration of three years, and a professional negligence action at any time before the expiration of six years, from the date when, if at all, he ceased to be under a disability, notwithstanding that the initial chronological period of limitation has expired.

17.93 The effective suspension of the normal three-year period of limitation by reason of continuing mental incapacity allows litigation on behalf of a patient to be commenced many years after the accident or omission that caused the original cerebral injury. Claimants who have suffered catastrophic brain damage leading to mental disorder as a result of peri-natal trauma may begin an action in their third or fourth decades or later without any concomitant anxiety about a limitation defence being effectively deployed against them. The long delay, however, is likely to impact on the prospects of success, remembering that the claimant has the burden of proving his case.

17.94 The absence of limitation pressure may persuade the less astute practitioner to adopt a relaxed approach to the litigation. However, well before the three-year period is allowed to expire, the investigation and determination of capacity should be complete.

17.95 Proceedings in borderline cases should be issued before the expiration of three years from accrual of the cause of action or knowledge as defined by the Limitation Act 1980.

Chapter 18

INTEREST

THE STATUTORY FRAMEWORK

18.1 The provisions applicable to personal injury claims[1] at first instance are s 35A of the Supreme Court 1981 (High Court) and s 69 of the County Courts Act 1984 (County Court). These confer a general power on the court, subject to rules of court, to award interest on debts and damages. Personal Injury claims[2] are particularly favoured with an obligation on the court to award interest unless the court is satisfied that there are special reasons to the contrary: see s 35A(2) and s 69(2). The court can and does find special reasons to the contrary and disallows interest, most notably where there has been unacceptable delay in the bringing and prosecution of an action (see below).

18.2 In the absence of a special reason to the contrary, the court will award interest. As Roch LJ observed in *Davies v Inman*[3] there is a 'presumption that interest is to be awarded on compensation arising from personal injuries'.

18.3 The court awarding the interest is, as the legislation suggests, the court that determines whether there are special reasons to the contrary. Accordingly the Court of Appeal will not, on an interlocutory appeal, tie the trial judge's hands: see *Headford v Bristol & District Health Authority*.[4]

18.4 In the Court of Appeal the relevant statutory provision is still s 3 of the Law Reform (Miscellaneous Provisions) Act 1934. Again personal injury actions are favoured with a requirement that interest will run on damages for personal injuries unless the court is satisfied that there are special reasons to the contrary: s 3(1A). The Court of Appeal has no power to award interst on costs other than that conferred by statute and cannot therefore backdate their order for costs to the date of judgment so as to receive interest on costs between the original judgment and that of the Court of Appeal. There is however power in an appellate court ot order interest on any sums which it orders an unsuccessful Respondent to repay: see *Nykredit Mortgage Bank Plc v Edward Erdman Group Ltd (No 2)*.[5]

---

[1] In this chapter the term personal injury claim should be taken to include an action arising from a fatality.
[2] If worth more than £200 – but what personal injury claim nowadays is not?
[3] [1999] PIQR Q26.
[4] [1995] PIQR P180.
[5] [1997] 1 WLR 1627.

RATES OF INTEREST

18.5 The Supreme Court Act 1981, the County Courts Act 1984 and the Law Reform (Miscellaneous Provisions) Act 1934 all confine the court's power to an award of *simple* interest. There can be no award for compound interest under these sections.

General damages

18.6 General damages are assessed using money values applicable as at the date of trial. The value of the award therefore does not diminish between the date of the accident and the date of the award; there is therefore no corresponding requirement to compensate for the effect of inflation. Interest is awarded to compensate the claimant for being kept out of his money after he has formally demanded it. Since the Court of Appeal's decision *Birkett v Hayes*,[6] the conventional rate awarded on general damages has been 2% pa from the date of service of proceedings. This has therefore been thought to be a reasonable real rate of return even when the courts used to discount future losses by $4\frac{1}{2}\%$. The underlying, though never clearly expressed, philosophy was that the claimant receiving a lump sum for future losses was expected to invest his damages in assets (including equities) to provide the future income. The award of general damages need not be invested; it could be spent. The 2% was to compensate the claimant for being kept out of her money and set down as a rate that should be followed in future cases to bring some certainty.

18.7 As the discount rate moved closer to the general damages rate (first in *Wells v Wells*[7] and subsequently by the Lord Chancellor's exercise of his powers under the Damages Act 1996) a body of opinion[8] argued that they should coincide. The Court of Appeal rejected that argument in *Lawrence v Chief Constable of Staffordshire*.[9] May LJ pointed out that historically the rates had been different and that was because they served different purposes. It was adjudged important that the rate be predictable to facilitate settlements and inexpensive litigation and only susceptible to change if a powerful economic case was made out.

18.8 Personal injury practitioners should expect the rate to remain at 2% for the foreseeable future.

Special damages

18.9 In contrast, the interest on past losses has to compensate the claimant both for being kept out of his money and for the fact that (assuming we stay

---

[6] [1982] 1 WLR 816, which received the approval of the House of Lords in *Wright v British Railways Board* [1983] 2 AC 773.
[7] [1999] 1 AC 345.
[8] Led by David Kemp QC in his book *The Quantum of Damages*.
[9] (2000) *The Times*, July 25.

clear of a deflationary environment) the value of money when judgment is given is less than it was at the time his losses were sustained.

18.10 The appropriate yardstick is the nominal rate at which a risk-free investment can be made. In 1970, when *Jefford v Gee* was decided, this was represented by the interest payable on monies paid into court and placed on a short-term investment account.[10] Subsequently this became the High Court Special Investment Account. This account pays a good rate of interest which is altered by order of the Lord Chancellor relatively infrequently; at the time of writing the rate is 6%, which compares favourably to base rate at 5.25% and benchmark 10-year gilt yields of 4.97%.

18.11 The theory is that the interest should run from the date an individual loss was sustained to the date of judgment. Typically most past losses (such as earnings, care or transport costs) will have been incurred incrementally from the time of accident to judgment. Rather than calculate interest over the whole period for the first week's loss of earnings reducing gradually to no interest for the last week's, the same, or similar,[11] effect can be achieved far more simply by awarding interest at half the short-term investment account rate on all past losses. This was the approach sanctioned by the Court of Appeal in *Jefford v Gee*. Lord Denning MR, giving the judgment of the court, said that:

> 'In *all ordinary cases* we should have thought that it would be fair to award interest on the total sum of special damages from the date of the accident until the date of trial at half the [special account] rate....'[12]

18.12 It is clear from the judgment that the court was greatly influenced in that case by the continuing loss of wages. The claimant had not worked from the date of the accident to the date of trial. In dealing with this, Lord Denning said:

> '*Loss of wages.* This occurred week by week. In principle, the interest should be calculated on each week's loss from that week to the date of trial. But that would mean too much detail. Alternatively, it would be possible to add up the loss every six months and allow interest on the total every six months until trial. That would seem fair, especially as the loss for the initial weeks might be for total incapacity, and afterwards only for partial incapacity, when he could do light work. More rough and ready, the total loss could be taken from accident to trial: and interest allowed only on half of it, or for half the time, or at half the rate.'

18.13 However, the approach, although simple and appropriate in the large majority of cases, should never be applied mechanistically. In claims under the Fatal Accidents Act 1976 damages for bereavement may be awarded: the amount due is fixed as at the date of death, and the full investment account rate from death should therefore be claimed: see *Khan v Duncan*.[13] A claimant who

---

[10] An account that had been created by statute in 1965: Administration of Justice Act 1965.
[11] The effect is the same if neither the size of regular payments nor the interest rates change.
[12] Emphasis added.
[13] Popplewell J, 9 March 1989.

is off work for one year post-accident and sustains all or most of his losses in that period will be selling himself short if he asks only for half rate when he commences proceedings 2 years subsequently: such a claimant should seek interest at the full investment account rate from the mid-point of the period of loss. Conversely, a defendant should decline to pay interest at half rate from the date of the accident where a claimant has kept going at her work for 2 years post accident before a deterioration in her condition causes her to give up work and require care one year prior to trial.

18.14 In *Prokop v DHSS*,[14] May LJ[15] said that the half-rate approach referred to in *Jefford v Gee* is:

> '... only applicable to cases where the special damages comprise more or less regular periodical losses which are continuous from the date of the accident to the date of trial; these are more often than not lost earnings. If there is any general view in any quarter that the interest on special damages is in any event to be calculated at half-rate, when the losses do not continue from accident to trial, then I think that this is wrong and should not hereafter be followed.'

18.15 In *Dexter v Courtaulds Ltd*,[16] the Court of Appeal affirmed the general principle of the half-rate approach for interest upon special damages. Lawton LJ referred to circumstances in which full-rate interest might be appropriate, citing a passage from an unreported decision of Forbes J in *Dodd v Rediffusion (West Midlands Ltd)*[17] in which he explained the half-rate principle as 'a short cut in the mathematics'. Kerr LJ in argument in *Dexter* had said that when the claimant wished to argue that there are special circumstances which exclude the *Jefford v Gee* principle, he should 'say so'.[18] Lawton LJ expressly adopted this view in his judgment, and Fox LJ agreed.

18.16 In calculating interest on damages a judge is free to depart from the *Jefford v Gee* method if another method of calculation would produce a fairer and more accurate figure.[19]

Tax

18.17 The rates paid on the Court Special Account are gross of tax. However, compensation for personal injuries or death, including interest thereon within the award, is not subject to income tax[20] or capital gains[21] tax. This factor adds further to the attractiveness of the rates awarded. It also means that a claimant should never permit any part of his damages or interest thereon to be

---

[14] Op cit.
[15] J May QC had appeared as *amicus curiae* in *Jefford v Gee*.
[16] [1984] 1 WLR 372.
[17] [1980] CLY 635.
[18] By raising the matter in (now) the statement of case, and giving reasons for departing from the half-rate rule.
[19] *Hobin v Douglas* (No 1) [1998] CLY 1431, (1998) *The Independent*, October 26, per Roch LJ.
[20] As not covered by any of the income tax schedules.
[21] Taxation of Chargeable Gains Act 1992, s 51(2).

discharged by any payment out of the taxable interest that has accrued prior to judgment on any monies paid into court. Any such interest should always be paid back to the defendant's solicitors so that any tax liability remains the defendant's. A secondary reason is that although such interest is theoretically calculable, it is hard to be certain what it will be before it arrives.

THE EFFECT OF INTERIM PAYMENTS ON INTEREST

18.18 Obviously a claimant has not been kept out of damages covered by an interim payment from the date of that payment. There is an easy and a difficult approach to the calculations required to adjust interest to take account of interim payments.

18.19 The simple approach is to calculate the interest due to the claimant applying normal principles (so usually half rate) ignoring the interim payment(s) and then to offset against that the interest on the interim payment(s) from the date(s) the payment(s) were made at the *full* short-term investment account rate.

18.20 The complex method is to take the interim payment to have reduced the damages on which the claimant's interest is calculated. If by this method you have reduced the special damages to zero you then start in on the general damages. You then calculate interest on whatever is left at the conventional rates.

18.21 If the interim payments exceed the total amount of the defendant's liability to the claimant then the court, as well as ordering repayment of the excess, may award interest on the overdue amount from the date when he made the interim payment: see Civil Procedure Rules 1998 (CPR), r 25.8(5). It is suggested that the rate is inevitably going to be the full special account rate. It is therefore anomalous to credit the defendant with effectively the special account rate until special damages are exhausted, then 2% pa until general damages are exhausted then 0% until future losses are exhausted and finally the special account rate under CPR, r 25.8(5) on any excess.

18.22 Example: C is injured by D's breach of duty on 1 February 2004. C is unable to work and suffers a net loss of earnings of £10,000 a year. D makes an interim payment of £10,000 on 1 February 2005. The trial is on 31 January 2007, and C is awarded special damages of £30,000.

Simple method:

- Interest on £30,000 at half rate from 1 February 2004 to 31 January 2007: 3 years at 3% pa on £30,000 = £2,700

- Less interest on £10,000 at full rate from 1 February 2005 to 31 January 2007: 2 years at 6% pa on £10,000 = £1,200

- Interest due on specials: £2,700 minus £1,200 = £1,500
  Complex method:

- Interest on £10,000 at half rate from 1 February 2004 to 31 January 2005: 1 year at 3%pa on £10,000 = £300

- Plus interest on £20,000 at half rate from 1 February 2005 to 31 January 2007: 2 years at 3% pa on £20,000 = £1,200

- Interest due on specials £300 + £1,200 = £1,500.

18.23 The Court of Appeal adopted the complex approach in *Bristow v Judd* in preference to the respondent's suggestion of the simple approach. The court declined the invitation of counsel to give general guidance and confined their observations to the facts of that case.

DELAY

18.24 The 'special reason to the contrary' permitting the court not to award interest is usually delay. In cases of unjustifiable delay the reduction in interest over the period of delay is calculated at the full investment account rate: see *Spittle v Bunny*.[22] This is logical for parallel reasons to those discussed for interim payments.

18.25 In *Read v Harries*,[23] 7 years elapsed between the relevant accident and the trial, and delays totaling more than 3 years were caused by the claimant's failure to give her solicitors sufficient information to permit them to formulate her claim. Interest was allowed only to the date (3 years earlier) at which the case would have been tried but for such delay:

> 'Insurers ought to be entitled to close their books in respect of claims within a reasonable period of time; they are prejudiced if they have to keep alive an outstanding claim, which inevitably results in increased costs payable by them to their solicitors which are not recoverable from the claimant.'[24]

18.26 With the advent of the CPR and active case management, such delays are rare, as is docking of interest.

18.27 In a commercial case it was held that where there had been substantial delay by the claimant in bringing an action to trial, and the primary cause of the claimant being deprived of his money was his own conduct, interest should be reduced. Rather than disallow interest for any specific period, however, which led to complications as to the rates applicable to particular periods, the

---

[22] [1988] 3 All ER 1031.
[23] [1993] PIQR Q25.
[24] *Read v Harries* [1993] PIQR Q34.

overall rate which should be applied to the whole period should be reduced: see *Derby Resources AG v Blue Corinths Marine Co Ltd (The Athenian Harmony) (No 2)*.[25]

18.28 Where the claimant in a personal injuries case was a minor, and his next friend delayed bringing proceedings for 17 years, which the judge described as understandable in human terms, the delay was, nevertheless, so unjustifiable forensically as to result in interest on special damages being payable for only 7 years. To have done otherwise would be to have placed a premium on delaying litigation: see *Nash v Southmead Health Authority*.[26]

18.29 The court has a wide discretion on interest, and can either reduce the period over which interest is paid, or the rate, or simply reduce the overall sum.

RELEVANCE OF PAYMENTS BY VOLUNTEERS

18.30 In *Davies v Inman*,[27] a claimant's employers voluntarily continued to pay him sums equivalent to his wages during a period of absence from work following an accident caused by the negligence of an unconnected defendant (under an agreement that the allowance would be refunded by the claimant to the employers from any damages awarded against the defendant.) At trial, only 13 weeks of the total period of 60 weeks absence was found to have been attributable to the accident. The defendant argued that no interest should have been awarded in respect of the loss of earnings, since the employers had made good the claimant's losses, and thus he had not been 'kept out of his money'. The argument was rejected. The Court of Appeal held that the proper approach to interest in such a case was to consider the position of the volunteer-employers who made good the loss by analogy, eg with volunteer-carers. The authorities, such as *Hunt v Severs*,[28] considering *Donnelly v Joyce*,[29] establish that damages are awarded to a claimant to compensate for either the value of the services performed or the amount of money contributed. The employers had a legal right to recover the money from the claimant. They had lost the use of the money. If the claimant were to recover interest on it from the defendants, he would hold it on trust for the employers. There was 'no question' in the light of the court's decision in *Roberts v Johnstone*[30] but that an award of interest on damages which represent the value of voluntary care is a proper order. Moreover, there was a public interest to encourage volunteers.

---

[25] [1998] 2 Lloyd's Rep 425 per Colman J.
[26] [1993] PIQR Q156.
[27] [1999] PIQR Q26.
[28] [1994] PIQR Q60, HL.
[29] [1974] QB 454.
[30] [1989] 1 QB 878.

INTEREST AND SOCIAL SECURITY BENEFITS

18.31 In *Wadley v Surrey CC*,[31] £49,197 of an award of more than £220,000 represented loss offset by state benefits paid to the claimant over a 5-year period. The sum of £49,197 was left out of account by the trial judge for the purpose of calculating interest on special damages. The House of Lords held that the scheme of the Social Security Recovery of Benefits Act 1997 provided, by omitting the express provision to the contrary that had appeared in the predecessor 1989 and 1992 Acts, that not only should state benefits be disregarded from the assessment of damages but also from the assessment of interest. The claimant was entitled to the award of interest upon the special damages in respect of which judgment was given including the sum of benefits which the defendants would eventually have to pay over to the Compensation Recovery Unit (CRU).

18.32 Where an interim payment has been made requiring the payment of certified benefits to the CRU at the time of the interim payment, it is submitted that interest does not run on that repaid amount from the date it is repaid. Since the House of Lords made it clear that state benefits are to be disregarded, this result is achieved by regarding the interim payment as made gross of the CRU.

REPAYMENT OF INTEREST FOLLOWING REDUCTION OF AWARD ON APPEAL

18.33 In *Goldfinch v Scannell*,[32] the defendant appealed against quantum in a case involving a patient. The award of over £470,000 was reduced by some £82,000 on appeal. The defendant had not sought a stay because the money was not paid to the claimant personally, and it would not have been possible to have contended that the money might prove to be irrecoverable. The defendant claimed to be entitled to interest on the £82,000 for the period during which it was wrongly in the hands of the Court of Protection on behalf of the claimant. Ordering the claimant to return the interest in addition to the £82,000, it was held that the defendant had been justified in not applying for a stay, although if the sum had been paid to a personal claimant the outcome might have been different. Defendants who appeal liability or quantum are wise to at least seek a stay to prevent this argument arising.

PROCEDURE

18.34 A claim for interest must be pleaded or it will not be awarded: CPR, r 16.4(1)(b) and (2). The rule requires the claimant to state whether he is claiming under a contract, enactment or some other basis. In personal injury

---

[31] [2000] 1 WLR 820.
[32] [1996] CLY 2124.

cases the claim will be under an enactment and the rule requires that the enactment be specified. Hence the reference in all personal injury pleadings to either s 35A of the Supreme Court Act 1981 or s 69 of the County Courts Act 1984.

18.35 There are further requirements for claims for a specified sum of money to set out a number of dates, rates and amounts. These will not normally concern the personal injury practitioner unless perhaps quantum has been agreed subject to liability prior to the service of the Particulars of Claim. The purpose of r 16.4(2)(b) (which requires greater detail for a specified sum) is that it enables interest to be awarded with a default judgment without a hearing. This will not happen in a personal injury case unless general damages have been agreed by a defendant who then fails to defend.

18.36 The following pleading should suffice for most purposes:

Pursuant to s 69 of the County Courts Act 1984 the claimant is entitled to claim and does claim interest on all damages awarded herein, at the following rates:

1   At 2% from the date of service of proceedings on general damages;
2   At the full special investment account rate on all single losses, from the date that the claimant suffered those losses; and
3   At half the full special investment account rate on all continuing losses, from the mid-point of the period in which the claimant suffered those losses; alternatively
4   At such rates and for such periods as the Court thinks fit.

AND the claimant claims:

(1)   Damages
(2)   Interest

Chapter 19

PROVISIONAL DAMAGES

INTRODUCTION

19.1 The historical rule is that damages are quantified on a lump sum basis, however, there is a potential for injustice to both parties in such a situation. If, for example, the evidence suggests that a deterioration in the condition suffered by a claimant may not on the balance of probabilities come about, but the claimant does in fact go on to suffer a downturn, he is left under-compensated if the original award of damages took no account of this possibility. Equally, a defendant who under a conventional award is ordered to pay in full for the costs associated with a remote chance of a deterioration taking place could rightly say that the claimant had been over-compensated.

19.2 Since 1 July 1985, the courts have had the power to award provisional damages in cases where there is a risk that the claimant's condition will worsen at some point in the future. When such an award is made, the court assesses damages in the normal way on the assumption that the claimant will not suffer the deterioration that might occur. The damages are thus provisional. Should the claimant find himself suffering in from the deterioration that was contemplated, he can return to the court to seek a further award of damages. There is no obligation on the claimant to seek provisional damages, however.

THE LEGAL FRAMEWORK

19.3 The power to award provisional damages is set out in s 32A of the Supreme Court Act 1981,[1] which states:

> '**32A-**(1) This section applies to an action for damages for personal injuries in which there is personal proved or admitted to be a chance that at some definite or indefinite time in the future the injured person will, as a result of the act or omission which gave rise to the cause of action, develop some serious disease or suffer some serious deterioration in his physical or mental condition.
>
> (2) Subject to subsection (4) below, as regards any action for damages to which this section applies in which a judgment is given in the High Court, provision may be made by rules of court for enabling the court, in such circumstances as may be prescribed, to award the injured person.

---

[1] The power of the County Courts to make orders for provisional damages is in exactly the same terms, and is contained within s 51 of the County Courts Act 1984.

(a) damages assessed on the assumption that the injured person will not develop the disease or suffer the deterioration in his condition; and
(b) further damages at a future date if he develops the disease or suffers the deterioration.'

19.4 In a provisional damages case, therefore, there is a two-stage assessment of the award. First, the damages are assessed on the basis that the claimant will not develop the disease or condition, or suffer the deterioration. The court must then specify in its order what the disease or type of deterioration will permit the claimant to return to the court to seek further compensation. Thus, no award of provisional damages can be made unless it is possible to identify what these terms are.

19.5 The court has a discretion as to whether to make an award of provisional damages in cases where there is a 'chance' that the 'serious' deterioration or development might occur. No definition of the words 'chance' or 'serious' is given.

19.6 In the case of *Willson v Ministry of Defence*,[2] Scott Baker J held that there was a three-stage test in a case of provisional damages. As a first stage it is necessary to analyse what the 'chance' of the deterioration is. He held that it was necessary that the likelihood of the deterioration had to be measurable rather than 'fanciful'. Even where the chance is small, provided that it can be quantified it is potentially the case that provisional damages are available. Where it is established that the likelihood of a deterioration is more probable than not, however, this is properly to be taken into account in assessment by way of a conventional award.

19.7 The second stage is to establish whether the deterioration is one which is 'serious'. This is to be considered on a case-by-case basis, although Scott Baker J stated in *Willson* that 'serious deterioration' meant something 'beyond ordinary deterioration'.[3] The factors for consideration include the impact of the change in the condition on the claimant himself, and such matters as the adverse effect on his lifestyle, working capacity and finances. It is a prerequisite for an award of provisional damages that the serious deterioration must be one which is beyond the natural progression of the condition. In the words of Scott Baker J in *Willson*:

'... the section envisages a clear and severable risk rather than a continuing deterioration'.

19.8 The third and final stage of the analysis in a case of provisional damages involves the court considering whether to exercise its discretion. The first and probably primary criterion to be applied is the need to do justice to the parties, as Roch LJ said in *Curi v Colina* (29 July 1988, unreported):

---

[2] [1991] 1 All ER 638.
[3] *Willson v Ministry of Defence* [1991] 1 All ER 638 at 642.

'The section should be confined to those cases where to compensate for the condition for which there is a chance on the basis that it will occur would be unfair to the defendant and to leave the claimant without the opportunity to ask for further compensation should the condition, of which there is a chance, materialise would be unfair to the claimant.'

The second consideration is the ability of such an order to be properly administered. There is little point in making an order for provisional damages unless there is a clear-cut event or time after which there could be no dispute that the deterioration had occurred.[4]

19.9 The range of cases in which it has been held that provisional damages were appropriate is reasonably limited. In *Willson* itself, it was held that provisional damages were not applicable where the condition under consideration was osteo-arthritis, which it was said was a progression of a disease rather than a deterioration. The possible occurrence of epilepsy after a head injury is, however, widely regard as a situation where a provisional award of damages would be applicable, whilst the risk of a serious deterioration in an eye condition that might lead to blindness has also been held to be an appropriate case for such an order.[5]

PROCEDURAL REQUIREMENTS

19.10 Civil Procedure Rules 1998 (CPR) 41 deals with the procedural requirements for an award of provisional damages, including the need for a claimant to plead his wish for such an order:

'41.2(1) The court may make an order for an award of provisional damages if –

(a) the particulars of claim include a claim for provisional damages; and
(b) the court is satisfied that SCA s.32A or CCA s.51 applies.

(Rule 16.4(1)(d) sets out what must be included in the particulars of claim where the claimant is claiming provisional damages)

(2) An order for an award of provisional damages –

(a) must specify the disease or type of deterioration in respect of which an application may be made at a future date;
(b) must specify the period within which such an application may be made; and
(c) may be made in respect of more than one disease or type of deterioration and may, in respect of each disease or type of deterioration, specify a different period within which a subsequent application may be made.

---

[4] See, for example, *Patterson v Ministry of Defence* [1987] CLY 1194 in which the difficulties of proving that causation in the event of pleural thickening were a bar to a provisional award.
[5] *Cronin v Redbridge* (19 May 1987, unreported).

(3) The claimant may make more than one application to extend the period specified under paragraph (2)(b) or (2)(c).'

19.11 The Practice Direction to CPR 16 requires the claimant to state a considerable level of detail as to the claim for provisional damages:

'4.4 In a provisional damages claim the claimant must state in his particulars of claim:

(1) that he is seeking an award of provisional damages under either section 32A of the Supreme Court Act 1981 or section 51 of the County Courts Act 1984,
(2) that there is a chance that at some future time the claimant will develop some serious disease or suffer some serious deterioration in his physical or mental condition, and
(3) specify the disease or type of deterioration in respect of which an application may be made at a future date.'

19.12 It is important to be clear as to the condition or deterioration for which the award is sought, and to state over what period the application for further damages can be made (this can be over the claimant's lifetime). Whilst an extension of the period can be sought, the claimant is limited by CPR, r 41.3(2) to one application for further damages:

'41.3 (1) The claimant may not make an application for further damages after the end of the period specified under rule 41.2(2), or such period as extended by the court.

(2) Only one application for further damages may be made in respect of each disease or type of deterioration specified in the award of provisional damages.

(3) The claimant must give at least 28 days' written notice to the defendant of his intention to apply for further damages.

(4) If the claimant knows –

(a) that the defendant is insured in respect of the claim; and
(b) the identity of the defendant's insurers,

he must also give at least 28 days' written notice to the insurers.

(5) Within 21 days after the end of the 28 day notice period referred to in paragraphs (3) and (4), the claimant must apply for directions.'

19.13 There are also important practical considerations in a provisional damages case. The Practice Direction to CPR 41 emphasises the duty on legal representatives to preserve case files, and specifies the documents to be included.

Chapter 20

INTERIM PAYMENTS

INTRODUCTION

Definition and availability

20.1 An interim payment is a payment on account of any damages, debt or other sum (excluding costs) which the defendant may be held liable to pay to or for the benefit of the claimant.[1]

20.2 The court has no inherent power to award a payment on account of damages. Such power only arises by reason of the provisions of the Supreme Court Act 1981 (which defines an interim payment at s 32(5)) and under the Civil Procedure Rules 1998 (CPR) Part 25. It should be noted that costs are excluded from such payments and are dealt with by a different regime.[2]

20.3 A claimant may make an application for an interim payment at any time after proceedings have been served on the defendant and the time provided for acknowledgement of service has expired.[3]

20.4 The claimant may make more than one application for an interim payment[4] and in many large cases where a substantial delay is likely before trial, multiple applications are relatively common. However, the effect of CPR (and in particular pre-action protocols and case management powers) has had the effect of reducing delay in bringing cases to trial, and courts will be less sympathetic to second and subsequent applications when there is no good reason for such and when the claim can be brought on for trial.

20.5 Under CPR, r 25.6(7) an interim payment can be made by way of instalments as well as by a lump sum – and this may be of increased relevance in light of the new rules on periodical payments.

The Civil Procedure Rules on interim payments

20.6 Interim remedies, which include interim payments, are dealt with at CPR Part 25 and the associated practice directions. The rules are in similar

---

[1] CPR, r 25.1(1)(k).
[2] CPR, r 44.3(8).
[3] CPR, r 25.7(3).
[4] CPR, r 25.6(2).

terms to their predecessors (RSC Order 29) and some of the previous authorities as to how the rules should be applied are still of relevance.

20.7 An amendment to CPR, r 25.7 was provided by the Civil Procedure (Amendment No 4) Rules 2004.[5] This has remedied the anomaly whereby a claimant could not recover an interim payment in a personal injury action against a specific defendant (who might even have admitted liability) if that defendant did not fall within one of the specified categories. Those categories remain in respect of cases involving multiple defendants. There is also an amendment to clarify those categories.

The preconditions

20.8 These are set out in CPR, r 25.7(1). The claimant must establish one of the following:

(i) that the defendant against whom the order is sought has admitted liability to pay damages to the claimant;[6] or

(ii) the claimant has obtained judgment against that defendant for damages to be assessed;[7] or

(iii) the court is satisfied that if the action proceeded to trial, the claimant would obtain judgment for substantial damages against the defendant against whom the interim payment is sought;[8] or

(iv) in a claim where there are two or more defendants and the order is sought against any one or more of them, the court is satisfied that the claimant would obtain judgment for substantial damages against at least one of those defendants. Further, in this category of case the claimant must establish that all of the defendants are within the specified categories.[9]

20.9 The court then has a discretion as to whether to make an order and must decide on the amount to be ordered.

THE REQUIREMENTS IN DETAIL

Judgment and/or liability admitted

20.10 These cases should be relatively straightforward. Note that the admission of liability must be by, or the judgment entered against, the particular defendant against whom the application for an interim payment is made. There

---

[5] SI 2004/3419.
[6] CPR, r 25.7(1)(a).
[7] CPR, r 25.7(1)(b).
[8] CPR, r 25.7(1)(c).
[9] CPR, r 25.7(1)(e).

is no requirement under these provisions that any award is likely to be 'substantial'. However, it should be noted that the provisions do not apply to small claims.[10]

If the action proceeded to trial, the claimant would obtain judgment for substantial damages

20.11 This rule[11] applies only to the defendant against whom an interim payment is sought. There are competing principles here. On the one hand, the court is reluctant to award an interim payment to a claimant who may spend the money, lose at trial and be unable to repay a defendant who has had to pay monies out in advance of trial. On the other hand, many injured claimants lose their employment as a consequence of an accident for which the defendant is ultimately held responsible; they may require care or rehousing; they may be insufficiently supported by benefits or other income; their standard of living may be threatened; the stress of litigation may be increased. It is no part of the court's role to keep an injured claimant from their money. It is against that background that a court must attempt to deal with the issue of whether it is 'satisfied' that the claimant *would* obtain judgment for *substantial* damages.

20.12 There are a number of authorities under the previous rules which suggest that the burden on the claimant is relatively high. Those authorities largely considered the interaction between an application for summary judgment and for an interim payment. The view was expressed that the granting of unconditional leave to defend was inconsistent with an order for an interim payment. Thus, in the case of *British and Commonwealth Holdings plc v Quadrex Holdings Inc*[12] Browne-Wilkinson V-C (as he then was) stated that:

> '... Order 29 ... requires the court, at the first stage, to be satisfied that the Claimant *will* succeed and the burden is a high one; it is not enough that the court thinks it likely that the Claimant will succeed at trial. For myself, I find it an impossible concept that the same court can be simultaneously "satisfied" that the Claimant *will* succeed at trial and at the same time consider that the Defendant has an arguable defence sufficient to warrant unconditional leave to defend.'[13]

In *Andrews v Schooling*[14] the Court of Appeal agreed with this approach.

20.13 It should be noted that the test for summary judgment in CPR is different to that in the previous rules. The court may give summary judgment if it considers that the defendant has 'no realistic prospect of successfully defending' the claim or issue (CPR, r 24.2). Thus, it is arguably easier for the claimant to obtain summary judgment. If the court is satisfied that the claimant 'would obtain Judgement for a substantial sum of money . . .', then it

---

[10] CPR, r 27.2(1)(a).
[11] CPR, r 25.7(1)(c).
[12] [1987] QB 842.
[13] [1989] QB 842 at 865–866.
[14] [1991] 3 All ER 723.

is also likely to find that the defendant has 'no realistic prospect' of a successful defence.[15] It may therefore be advisable to apply for summary judgment at the same time as making an application for an interim payment.

20.14 That having been said, it should be noted that CPR still allows for conditional orders on an application for summary judgment.[16] In those circumstances, the court may well allow the defendant to defend the action but on the condition that an interim payment is made. This is consistent with the approach taken in *Andrews v Schooling*[17] in which Balcombe LJ stated that the issue was:

> 'Are we satisfied that the Claimant will succeed at the trial ... and that the Defence is so shadowy that the Defendant should only be given conditional leave to defend, the condition being an interim payment to the Claimant?'[18]

This is also the case if the court is of the view that the defendant has not put sufficient information before it to establish that it has a full defence on liability.[19]

20.15 On the other hand, if there are complicated factual issues or difficult points of law which may take a substantial time to resolve, the court will be reluctant to make such an order.[20]

20.16 If the case is borderline, a court may well use its case management powers to order an early trial on liability.

TWO OR MORE DEFENDANTS

20.17 This power is now contained in CPR, r 25.7(1)(e). The claimant does not have to show that he would succeed against a specific defendant against whom the interim payment is sought, only that he would obtain judgment for substantial damages against at least one of the defendants.

20.18 However, in any application under this rule, the court must also be satisfied that all of the defendants in the action (and not just the defendant against whom the interim payment is sought) fall into one of the specified categories, these being:

(a) a defendant that is insured in respect of the claim; or

---

[15] See the *White Book* 2006 at para 25.7.27.
[16] CPR, r 24.6 and 24 PD4, 5.
[17] (1991) 3 All ER 723.
[18] [1991] 3 All ER 723 at 726.
[19] See eg *Van Hoffen v Dawson* [1994] PIQR P101.
[20] *Schott Chem v Bentley* [1990] 3 WLR 397.

(b) a defendant whose liability will be met by an insurer under s 151 of the Road Traffic Act 1988 or an insurer acting under the Motor Insurers' Bureau Agreement, or the Motor Insurers' Bureau where it is acting itself; or

(c) a defendant that is a public body.[21]

JUDGMENT FOR 'SUBSTANTIAL DAMAGES'

20.19 This is a requirement for any application under CPR, rr 25.7(1)(c) and 25.7(1)(e). 'Substantial' is not defined. While the CPR do not limit the availability of interim payments to multi-track cases (so that it is arguable that damages totalling less than £15,000 can be deemed as 'substantial' in appropriate cases), applications are rare in fast track cases.

20.20 Small claims are not covered by the interim payment rules.[22]

20.21 It should be noted that CPR, r 25.7(5) requires the court to take into account contributory negligence and any relevant set-off or counterclaim. While that requirement is clearly relevant to the issue of discretion, there appears to be no reason why it should not be taken into account in assessing whether damages are likely to be 'substantial' – for example in a case where the claimant's case is strong on primary liability but contributory negligence is likely to be very high.

Amount of interim payment/discretion

20.22 CPR, r 25.7 provides as follows:

> '(4) The court must not order an interim payment of more than a reasonable proportion of the likely amount of the final judgment.
>
> *(5) The court must take into account –*
>
> (a) contributory negligence; and
> (b) any relevant set-off or counterclaim'.

20.23 There will often be considerable uncertainty as to levels of damages which may ultimately be awarded, and the court must make the best assessment in the circumstances as to the likely levels of damages. The award should not exceed a 'reasonable proportion' of those damages. The reasoning behind this is to avoid a situation where the claimant may be awarded less damages at trial than the interim payment (requiring a repayment under CPR, r 25.8 which they may or may not be able to satisfy).

---

[21] CPR, r 25.7(e)(ii).
[22] CPR, r 27.2(1)(a).

20.24 The Court of Appeal has emphasised that a claimant does not need to show any specific need for an interim payment. Such is clear from the case of *Stringman v McArdle*[23] in which Stuart Smith LJ stated that:

> '... once the threshold conditions ... are satisfied, what the court has to do, if it thinks fit, is to make an interim payment of such amount as it thinks just not exceeding a reasonable proportion of the damages which in the opinion of the court are likely to be recovered by the Plaintiff after taking into account contributory negligence and any set-off or counterclaim. It should be noted that the Plaintiff does not have to demonstrate any particular need over and above the general need that a Plaintiff has to be paid his or her damages as soon as reasonably may be done.'

20.25 Nevertheless, the granting of an order and its amount remains a matter for the discretion of the judge (albeit to be exercised judicially and in accordance with the guidelines set out). The practice direction[24] states (at para 2.1) that an application must be supported by evidence of various matters including 'the items or matters in respect of which the interim payment is sought'. This reflects the views of the Court of Appeal in the case of *Campbell v Mylchreest*[25] to the effect that such information is desirable in order to assist the judge in exercising their discretion.

20.26 In a number of recent cases, defendants have argued that interim payments should not be granted to a claimant due to the fact that it may prejudice the defendant's position at trial. This is based on the proposition that if a claimant (for example) puts in place a specific care regime or moves to specific housing (which the defendant's experts may have contended was unsuitable for him), the defendant will be faced with a *fait accompli* at trial and will find it difficult to argue that such expense is unreasonable. In effect, there will not be a 'level playing field'.

20.27 The Court of Appeal in *Campbell v Mylchreest*[26] recognised that this was a factor to be taken into account by the judge when exercising their discretion, but in that case found that the judge was not likely to be 'seriously affected' by this factor.

20.28 This issue has more recently been dealt with by the Court of Appeal in a number of cases, these being *Tinsley v Sarkar*;[27] *Dolman v Rowe*;[28] *Rhodes v Ford*[29] and *Wright v Sullivan*[30]. In *Dolman* the Court of Appeal recognised that the issue of a 'level playing field' was a relevant factor to take into account. Nevertheless, it formed the view that a judge would be well able to deal with

---

[23] [1994] 1 WLR 1653.
[24] 25 BPD.
[25] [1999] PIQR Q17.
[26] [1999] PIQR Q17.
[27] [2004] EWCA Civ 1098.
[28] [2005] EWCA Civ 715.
[29] [2005] EWCA Civ 440.
[30] [2006] 1WLR 172.

any issues between the parties and, indeed, that a trial of living at home (the necessity of which was disputed) was likely to be 'positively helpful' to the forensic process. It should be noted that in both of the latter cases (in which interim payments were granted), total damages were likely to exceed the sums requested on interim payment, whereas in *Tinsley* the judge's doubts as to whether a care regime would be found to be necessary led to the conclusion that interim payments might well have exceeded a 'reasonable proportion' of the claimant's damages. Further, the medical evidence in this case did not support a suggestion that such an 'experiment' might have assisted the trial judge. The application was refused.

20.29 There is no guidance as to what is a 'reasonable proportion' of damages. Indeed, in *Dolman v Rowe*[31] the Court of Appeal confirmed their view that there should be no judicial guidance on this issue and that it is a matter for the discretion of the judge. In a case where funds are likely to be held in the Court of Protection and not spent immediately, the discretion may be exercised more generously. In that case a total interim payment of approximately £835,000 was approved against a total award (as estimated by the judge at first instance) of over £1,000,000.

20.30 There may, of course, be other factors to take into account in exercising the court's discretion. These may include (for example) the defendant's lack of means; the conduct of the claimant (in particular if there is a clear attempt to gain an unjustified tactical advantage); whether the case can be put on for trial at an early stage. Other relevant matters will depend upon the particular case.

SOCIAL SECURITY BENEFITS

20.31 When a defendant makes an interim payment, whether voluntary or pursuant to a court order, the provisions of the Social Security (Recovery of Benefits) Act 1997, s 6 apply.

ADJUSTMENT

20.32 CPR, r 25.8 provides for a court to make an order adjusting an interim payment, whether such payment was made pursuant to an order of the court or voluntarily. No application is necessary and the court can make an order under the rule when it disposes of the claim or any part of it.[32] The principal scenarios are as follows.

---

[31] [2005] EWCA Civ 715.
[32] CPR, r 25.8(4).

Repayment

20.33 The claimant may discontinue the action, lose on liability or recover less by way of damages than the amount received as an interim payment. In such circumstances, the court may order the claimant to repay all or part of the amount received (or the excess received) to the defendant. CPR, r 25.8(5) makes it clear that the court may also order the claimant to pay interest on the amount to be repaid, from the date the interim payment was paid. Although the rule states that in these circumstances interest 'may' awarded, the accompanying practice direction states that an order for interest on an overpayment 'should' be made.[33] It should be noted that a claimant who has received an interim payment may only discontinue that claim or part of it if the defendant who made the interim payment consents in writing or if the court gives permission.[34]

Variation or discharge

20.34 Where there is judgment in a particular sum for the claimant, the sums payable may be varied (ie reduced downwards) or discharged by the amount of any interim payment. The details must be recorded in the judgment and the final order for payment should set out the total award as well as specifying the amounts and dates of the interim payments.[35]

20.35 It should be noted that where a claimant has invested interim payments received from the defendant and has earned interest, that accrued interest should not be deducted from the sum allowed for interest at the final determination of quantum.[36]

Payment as between defendants

20.36 The court may order a defendant to reimburse, either wholly or partially, another defendant who has made an interim payment.[37] However, such an order will only be made if the defendant claiming to be reimbursed has made a claim for contribution and/or indemnity against the other defendant.[38] Further, if a claim (or part to which the interim payment relates) has not been discontinued or disposed of, the circumstances must be such that a court would have been able to make an order for interim payment under CPR r 25.7.[39]

---

[33] 25 BPD 5.5.
[34] CPR, r 38.2(2)(b).
[35] 25 BPD para 5.2.
[36] *Parry v North West Surrey HA*, (2000) *The Times*, January 5.
[37] CPR, r 25.8(2)(c).
[38] CPR, r 25.8(3)(a).
[39] CPR, r 25.8(3)(b).

TIMING, TACTICS AND MODE OF APPLICATION

Timing/tactics

20.37 The issue is when and what should be sought. In many cases an interim payment may be provided voluntarily before proceedings are commenced and while investigations and/or negotiations are ongoing. However, if no voluntary payment is forthcoming then it will be necessary to issue proceedings.

20.38 The claimant may not then apply for an interim payment before the end of the period for filing of an acknowledgement of service applicable to the defendant against whom the interim payment is sought.[40] It is not necessary to wait until all defendants are served to make the application against a particular defendant.

20.39 If a defendant admits liability in the defence, an application for interim payment may be combined with an application to enter judgment. This simplifies matters, because liability is disposed of.

20.40 If liability is denied, the claimant's representatives must assess both the law and the evidence in order to establish the prospects of success against the requirements described above. It will, for example, be sensible to seek as much evidence as possible in relation to liability, rather than to rely solely upon what the claimant says. The relative strengths of the parties' cases should now be capable of assessment at a much earlier stage than previously (by reason of the relevant pre action protocol), and the claimant's representatives should already have all (or most) of the evidence on liability before proceedings are commenced. Documentation will have been obtained pre-action along with some indication of the defendant's allegations. In a road traffic accident, it would assist to have obtained a police report and to have sought additional statements from witnesses, along with a certificate of conviction (if available). In work related accidents, expert evidence may be required. In essence, the claimant will be seeking to show that he has a very strong case.

20.41 If liability remains in dispute, it would be advisable in most cases to make an application for summary judgment at the same time as the application for interim payment. This can be heard immediately before (but during the same hearing as) the application for an interim payment.

20.42 If a Part 36 offer or payment has been made, then there is no objection to the court being told of such offer/payment.[41] This may well assist in establishing that the defendant does not realistically have a defence.

20.43 Similarly, a defendant wishing to resist an application for an interim payment will have to show that the court cannot be satisfied the claimant will be successful at trial, or that there are difficult factual or legal issues which it is

---

[40] CPR, r 25.6(1).
[41] *Friar v LTE*, (1982) *The Times*, December 4.

not appropriate to assess at such an early stage. In the absence evidence to this effect, a court may well reject the defendant's arguments.[42] Obviously, the defendant will also require witness evidence if it wishes to dispute that the case satisfies CPR, r 25.7.

Mode of application

20.44 Applications for interim payment, like all other interlocutory applications, should be made in accordance with the provisions of CPR Part 23. This must be read in conjunction with CPR, r 25.6 which prescribes different time limits for interim payment applications, and therefore overrides CPR Part 23 to this extent. The time limits are as follows:

- the claimant must give 14 days' notice of the application (evidence to be served with the application);

- if the respondent wishes to object to the application his evidence in reply is to be filed and served seven days before the hearing;

- any evidence in reply from the applicant should filed three days before the hearing.

20.45 The application must be supported by evidence, and the quality and detail of such evidence is usually central to the success or otherwise of the application. Paragraph 2.1 of the Practice Direction lists the matters which must be dealt with by the claimant's evidence:

(1) the sum of money sought by way of interim payment;

(2) the items or matters in respect of which the interim payment is sought;

(3) the sum of money for which final judgment is likely to be given;

(4) the reasons for believing that the conditions set out in CPR r 25.7 are satisfied;

(5) any other relevant matters;

(6) in claims for personal injuries, details of the special damages and past and future loss;

(7) in a claim under the Fatal Accidents Act 1976, details of the person(s) on whose behalf the claim is made and the nature of the claim.

20.46 The claimant's evidence should deal with these matters clearly, thoroughly and in logical order. Those advising defendants should bear in mind

---

[42] See, for example, *Van Hoffen v Dawson* [1994] PIQR P101.

that any evidence challenging the claimant's assertions must be before the court if it is to receive due consideration. It should be noted that the rules allow a party to rely upon matters set out in a Statement of Case, a Reply to Further Information and/or an Application Notice if they are verified by a statement of truth.[43] Nevertheless, a claimant will inevitably require a statement dealing with the matters set out in CPR, r 25.7.

AT THE HEARING

20.47 The claimant goes first. If it becomes apparent that there is a serious dispute as to liability or quantum which was not previously predicted, an outright loss may be avoided by seeking an adjournment of the application to deal with what has unexpectedly arisen.

20.48 Another alternative available to both parties (and often attractive to courts) is to seek an order for a split trial. The trial on liability can then be expedited so that the parties can properly assess their respective positions.

INTERIM PAYMENT BY INSTALMENTS

20.49 CPR, r 25.6(7) provides that the court may order an interim payment in one sum or in instalments. If an order is made for instalments, then the provisions of 25 BPD.3 should be complied with. The order should set out:

(1) the total amount of the payment;

(2) the amount of each instalment;

(3) the number of instalments and the date on which each is to be paid; and

(4) to whom the payment should be made.

20.50 It may be expected that there will be an increase in this type of order given the new provisions for periodical payments.

OTHER MATTERS

Children/patients

20.51 25BPD1.2 provides that the permission of the court must be obtained before making a voluntary interim payment in respect of a claim by a child or patient.

---

[43] CPR, rr 25.6(3), 32.6(2).

Part 36 payments

20.52 A Part 36 offer can be made by reference to an interim payment (also note amended Part 36 from April 2007).

Appeal

20.53 The Court of Appeal have emphasised that as long as a judge takes into account all of the matters referred to above then the granting of an interim payment (and its amount) is a discretionary matter. That having been said, if a claimant can satisfy the requirements of CPR, r 25.7, and if the payment sought is clearly within the damages which are likely to be awarded, then it may be difficult for a judge to justify exercising the discretion against the claimant.

Chapter 21

PERIODICAL PAYMENTS

21.1 The main question that arises in practice is whether to advise (or agree, or seek) an order for part of the damages – or all of them – to be paid by way of periodical payment rather than by lump sum award. This involves understanding whether an award of periodical payments is likely to be more advantageous than one on a lump sum basis, knowing the statutory provisions, and the applicable case-law (which is still developing). However, the power of the court to award interim periodical payments should not be overlooked by concentrating on the form of the eventual award. In any case in which there is no real issue as to liability, but the injuries and their effects may take some time to settle – as is often the case in catastrophic or cerebral palsy claims – an award of interim periodical payments may provide much better for current care costs and interim loss of earnings than does a system of repeated one-off applications for interim payment(s).

STATUTORY PROVISIONS

21.2 Sections 100 and 101 of the Courts Act 2003 inserted a new s 2 into the Damages Act 1996 enabling a court to order that damages for future pecuniary loss in respect of personal injury should take the form wholly or partly of periodical payments.

21.3 In addition to the court ordering such payments, the parties may agree (if they choose to do so) that damages for personal injury other than those in respect of future loss (for example, sums in respect of past loss, or in respect of non-pecuniary loss) should be paid periodically rather than as one lump sum. The court, however, has no power to order any part of a damages award other than that in respect of future loss to be paid in the form of periodical payments.

21.4 Civil Procedure Rules 1998 (CPR), r 41.5 enables the parties to state in their Statements of Case whether they regard periodical payments or a lump sum as likely to be more appropriate for all or part of an award of damages in respect of future loss. Both claimants and defendants will need to consider whether to make such an indication. The relevant considerations are set out below.

21.5 However, if no view is expressed, the court may order the parties to state one; and r 41.6 requires the court to consider and to indicate to the parties as soon as practicable whether periodical payments or a lump sum is likely to be the more appropriate form for all or part of an award of damages. This is likely to be at the first case management conference: be prepared.

21.6 The legislation and practice provides that a court may order either (a) what might be called *'non-variable'* periodical payments or (b) *'variable'* periodical payments. It also distinguishes between orders of a court, and agreements between the parties. This chapter will consider those, and also deal with the need for schedules of loss to take account of the possibility of periodical payments being ordered, appeals from an adverse decision in respect of such payments, Part 36 offers, and the (much overlooked) interim periodical payments which may be of particular use in high value cases where injuries are resolving only slowly.

21.7 The distinction between orders and agreements is important. Section 2(1) of the Damages Act 1996, inserted by the Courts Act 2003, s 100, limits the power of a court to making an award by way of periodical payments in respect of *future pecuniary loss only* unless the parties consent (s 2.2). Moreover, it may not make an order unless satisfied that continuity of payment under the order is reasonably secure (s 2.3).

21.8 An agreement may thus provide for *a greater amount* of the damages to be paid by way of periodical payment. It is also possible by agreement to provide that the insurer of the paying party will purchase a 'with profits' annuity, which has the potential for equalling growth on the Stock Exchange, which is a proxy for growth in the economy and therefore growth in average earnings. Historically, this has been in excess of retail price inflation (which measures the cost of goods and some services). Accordingly, there may be advantages (depending upon the economic circumstances current at the time) in reaching an agreement if not as to the whole then as to part of the payment.

21.9 In one respect, however, agreements are regulated by Statutory Instrument. If the parties agree that a claimant (or defendant) should be entitled to return to court to ask for the terms of a periodical payment agreement to be varied then the agreement must comply with art 9(2) of the Damages (Variation of Periodical Payments) Order 2004, and the person permitted to apply for the terms to be varied must obtain the court's permission before making that application.

21.10 Agreements by which the parties consent to an order for periodical payments have to take account of the provisions of r 41.8 (see 'Form of Order' below). If the parties wish the terms of a settlement to be embodied in a consent order made by the court, the requirements of that rule will also need to be satisfied.

POLICY BEHIND PERIODICAL PAYMENTS

21.11 The policy rationale underlying the introduction of the power to order periodical payments is firstly that the lump sum system can be unsatisfactory, because it is based upon predictions about the future life expectancy of a claimant which are inevitably uncertain and almost always lead to either over-compensation or under-compensation. Secondly, with periodical payments, responsibility for managing the investment of the award transfers from claimants to defendants, who are better able to bear it. A third rationale is that most future losses are periodic in nature (eg loss of future salary; payment of future care costs from month to month). Since the purpose of the law of compensation is to ensure that a victim of an accident is restored to the position in which he would have been if the accident had not occurred, so far as money can achieve it, it may be argued that to be placed in regular receipt of sums in respect of salary, or paid to cover the costs of care, more accurately replicates full restitution than does the payment of one lump sum which may be spent at any time and for any purpose.

Advantages and disadvantages

21.12 The advantages of a periodical payment order are:

(1) There is less risk of over-compensation or under-compensation than with a lump sum system (which is based on predictions about life expectancy which are inevitably inaccurate): actual life expectancy ceases to matter, since the payments will go on for life.

(2) There is no tax to be paid upon the periodical payments when received (whereas income produced by a lump sum is taxable).

(3) Any investment risk is borne by the provider of the payment.

(4) The time, trouble and effort of ensuring that a lump sum is invested so as to produce the required return is, again, borne by the provider of the periodical payment, and not by the injured claimant.

(5) Payment is guaranteed under the Financial Services Compensation Scheme or by the government directly: by comparison, the payment of income from an invested lump sum is not guaranteed. This is important. One recent example of such exposure to the stock market, is of lump sums invested in UK equities in 1999. The collapse of share values in the succeeding two years was severely damaging to such investments, possibly halving their value, yet without recompense.

(6) If the recipient should go bankrupt, sums in respect of his care needs remain payable to him and are not property to which his trustee in bankruptcy is entitled (the position in respect of payments relating to future loss of income is different, however).

(7) Receipt of a periodical payment does not prejudice entitlement to free national or local authority provision in respect of state benefits, local authority residential care, or local authority provided care.

(8) There is no real risk that the sums will run out.

(9) Any claimant who is vulnerable, but not so injured as to be a patient, is protected against unscrupulous third parties (or even well-meaning but irresponsible family and friends): they might take a chunk of a lump sum, but cannot deprive the claimant of his right to go on receiving periodical payments.

(10) Finally, there is no need to engage in the difficulties to which the Ogden Tables can give rise, or to obtain expensive and difficult (and often distressing) evidence as to life expectancy because there is no need to determine what lump sum would be payable.

(11) It might further be added, though more speculatively, it is less likely that the courts will permit the same scope for discounts in respect of heads of loss than the courts have historically done when assessing lump sum compensation.

21.13 The disadvantages are:

(1) The loss of flexibility: in particular, if the whole of provision for future loss is converted into periodical payments, the loss of any ability to meet large capital expenses, or unexpected demands on income (eg for an urgent or new operation or treatment).

(2) Lump sum awards have certainty.

(3) Lump sum awards represent a 'clean break' from the defendant, whereas periodical payments imply an ongoing relationship. Though this may be with an insurer, rather than a personal defendant, the insurer concerned may be regarded with suspicion by the claimant because of its actions earlier in the litigation.

(4) It may be possible to invest a lump sum in a way which produces a higher return than would be produced by Retail Price Index (RPI), which is the default index to be adopted by the courts (though it is likely that the circumstances in which this will be so are limited, and may apply more where a claimant wishes to invest his award in the establishment of a business, purchase of property to let etc).

(5) A lump sum award, though calculated such that every penny of future loss is used up at the exact moment when the claimant's life expires, has the potential of leaving funds for heirs and dependants.

21.14 In *Godbold v Mahmood* [2005] EWHC 1002, [2006] PIQR Q5, Mitting J determined that there should be a periodical payment order for recurring care and related costs, but not for future loss of earnings, in a claim for serious head and orthopaedic injuries by a 58-year-old male road-sweeper. He had become epileptic, and required round the clock supervision. The factors he selected as particularly influential (para 34, judgment) were (1) uncertainty as to the claimant's life expectancy (a heavy smoking habit and epilepsy made it uncertain, (2) because it is easier with a periodical payment order to match expense to income and (3) because the income stream is secure and not dependent on investment returns.

21.15 A number of myths as to the advantages and disadvantages of periodical payment provision need to be debunked:-

(a) It is said that periodic payments afford '**No ability to raise capital**': this is not so, since the presence of a guaranteed income stream of a guaranteed amount, rising with inflation, can be used to afford personal security for a loan, in the same way as mortgages are frequently granted on the expectation of continuing income. However, it is not possible to charge or assign the right to receive periodical payments without the express consent of the court (Damages Act 1996, s 2(6)), and lenders may be reluctant to enter into loans if their ultimate security depends on taking enforcement action against someone who is seriously disabled. It may not be something a disabled person wishes to embark upon.

(b) '**There will be no money to leave to dependants**'. Not so: CPR, r 41.8(2) provides that a court may order part of the award to continue after the claimant's death for the benefit of the claimant's dependants. The purpose is to permit payments to continue to dependants, particularly when they might otherwise have had a Fatal Accident Act claim. This may, in particular, afford opportunities for those suffering from incurable cancers such as mesothelioma to secure provision during their lifetime for the security of their family, knowing that dependants will be provided for, whereas at present a lump sum award to a live claimant, who has only a 'lost years' claim for the period after his death, may afford less total compensation than the potential claim under the Fatal Accident Act where the victim has a spouse, and more so where he has a spouse and dependant family.

(c) '**Once ordered, the amount cannot be varied to meet future developments**'. True only in part. Any development which is anticipated at the date of trial/assessment of damages can be catered for within the periodical payment order. For instance, payments in respect of loss of earnings can be ordered to cease being payable at the intended retirement age; additional payments for education, care, or in the event of deterioration can be built in to the payment structure at the outset. Note that the ability to tailor an award to meet anticipated developments at or about the time that they are anticipated is to be distinguished from the making of a variable order, for which see below. An order which provides at the outset for increases of specified amounts on certain dates (and arguably contingent on certain future events) is not a 'variable order' and is not subject to the restrictions on making such an order.

(d) **'A minimum sum is needed before periodical payments are appropriate'**. Not so. The government guidance is specific that there should be no minimum limit. Everything will depend upon the circumstances. For instance, periodical payments may be more important to meet the needs of a person injured at the age of 90, where even a slight variation in life expectancy could affect the entire award, than they would be for a lifetime award for an injured victim of 16, yet the total amount of future loss if calculated as a lump sum would be small.

(e) **'Periodical payments are bad value because they are not linked to an appropriate index'**. In fact, following *Flora v Wakom (Heathrow) Ltd*,[1] and *Thompstone v Tameside Glossop Acute Services NHS Trust*[2] it is lump sum awards which are likely to be worse value. A lump sum is currently calculated upon assumptions as to the real return on investments (the Lord Chancellor's 'discount rate', reflected by the Ogden Tables at 2.5%). The Lord Chancellor's discount rate assumes a real rate of return over and above inflation as judged by the RPI. Lump sums are calculated on this basis. Thus an RPI index-linked periodical payment should achieve the same overall financial result as that which is assumed for a lump sum award (there is no need to allow for the 'real' return, since this is used only to annuitise a lump sum, reducing the number of 'years' of payment because of the accelerated receipt of one large sum which may be invested). Periodical payments may be paid for as long as the claimant lives, per year, without the claimant having to worry what lump sum is necessary at what investment rate). Current economic thinking is that the discount rate is too high and thus the chance of a lump sum award meeting future expenses is poor. The reality is that if the RPI is an inappropriate index, both patterns of award (periodic or lump sum) suffer from the defect, and formal indexation is no reason for choosing one over the other. However, it is possible to seek an order from the court that the damages or part of them should be indexed by reference to a different index (r 41.8(1)(d); s 2(9) of the Damages Act 1996: the court has a power to order that there should be a different index). This offers the opportunity of making the practical provision for future inflation in costs to which the claimant's unsuccessful argument in *Cooke v United Bristol Healthcare Trust*[3] was directed. The decision in *Flora v Wakom (Heathrow) Ltd*[4] affirms that so far as periodical payments are concerned, although RPI is the default index, the power of the court to depart from it and to specify another index it regards as more appropriate is not limited

---

[1] [2006] EWCA Civ 1103.
[2] [2006] EWHC 2904, Swift J, currently under appeal.
[3] [2004] 1 WLR 251.
[4] [2006] EWCA Civ 1103 (affirming the first instance decision at [2006] PIQR Q7).

to 'exceptional' cases, as is the calculation of a lump sum (see *Warriner v Warriner*;[5] *Cooke*). Thus in any case in which there are substantial ongoing care costs it will be reasonably arguable that a different index should be adopted for periodical payments, which is more likely to preserve the position of the claimant in the future than is a lump sum award which is calculated by incorporating assumptions based on RPI: and such an award is almost certainly preferable to a lump sum one.

(f) **'An order for periodical payments won't pay for necessary accommodation'.** An order can only make provision for *future pecuniary loss*, unless the parties agree otherwise. It does **not** have to order that the *entirety* of future pecuniary loss be paid for periodically (thus, for example, the high cost of accommodation may be met by a capital payment, leaving a lower sum for the balance of future loss).

(g) In general, a claimant will usually benefit more than he will lose from having a periodical payment order made unless the total award is discounted significantly, as in the case of contributory negligence (perhaps over 20%). Certainly, those advising a claimant will need to be careful to provide considered advice, usually supported by expert financial opinion, if the claimant proposes not to take advantage of a periodical payment order. defendants, on the other hand, have probably on balance something to lose by having a periodical payment order imposed. Although the ability to self-fund gives greater flexibility financially to the paying insurer or public body than the previous purchased annuity to provide a structured settlement, the need to be able to provide reasonable continuity of payment into the future, whatever the life expectancy of the claimant, implies that the insurer will need to reserve so as to cover the eventuality that the claimant will live to the greatest age which falls within a reasonable bracket of life expectancy. Over-reserving ties up funds. It seems likely that many general insurers will therefore prefer to purchase annuities (but, at the moment, there are few available on the open market) or will pay a premium by way of lump sum in order to avoid the difficulties of having to over-reserve. The pressures created by the decision in *Flora v Wakom*[6] may increase this tendency.

21.16 Periodical payments are not necessarily the Holy Grail. They need to be seen in context. They are one way of providing for future loss. When advising, you may wish to consider other possibilities which may be as, or more, effective:

- Some future losses may be covered by the ability to return to court given where a provisional damages award is made.

- Some may be susceptible to insurance (eg life insurance of a gratuitous carer).

---

[5] [2002] 1 WLR 1703.
[6] [2006] EWCA Civ 1103.

- Some may be provided in kind (eg by agreement with a defendant insurer, rehabilitation may be available paid for by the insurer).

- Some may be capable of being covered by an indemnity (though this has to be agreed, and cannot at present be ordered by a court).

- In addition, a trust may usefully be established, especially of a 'special needs' type which does not prejudice the continued receipt of free accommodation or care support.

- In respect of housing claims, see also **21.29** below.

No advisor should therefore confine his or her consideration of a client's case (or of the other party's claim) to the simple question: 'Lump sum award or periodical payment order'. Much may still be provided by agreement (despite the restrictions on such agreements where they deal with periodical payments, if they are to be effective in conferring the tax advantages and the security of an order) which cannot be given by the courts, and advisors should always be alert to this.

THE COURT'S APPROACH

21.17 A court is under an obligation to consider whether or not to make an award in the form of periodical payments (Damages Act 1996, s 2(1)(b)).

21.18 The primary criterion is what best meets the claimant's needs: CPR, r 41.7 provides that the court in considering whether to make such an order 'shall have regard to all the circumstances of the case and in particular the form of award which best meets the claimant's needs, having regard to the factors set out in the Practice Direction'.

21.19 The factors set out in Practice Direction PD41B 'include' (note that word: this is not a comprehensive list – the primary criterion is what best meets the claimant's[7] needs):

(i) the scale of the annual payments, taking into account any deduction for contributory negligence.

(ii) the form of award preferred by the claimant including (a) the reason for the claimant's preference; and (b) the nature of any financial advice received by the claimant when considering the form of award; and

(iii) the form of award preferred by the defendant including the reasons for the defendant's preference.

---

[7] Not the defendant's needs: the legislation here clearly favours the claimant.

21.20 There is no provision that the claimant's *preference* is conclusive. It is his needs which the court must consider.

21.21 There is a broad hint here that where there is a substantial deduction by reason of contributory negligence an award of periodical payments may not be appropriate. This would be because the amount would never, in any year, match the need. 50% of a claimant's care needs, for example, will not come near his requirements. The effect of a periodical payment in such an amount is to require him to subsidise current payments, under a periodical order, with other resources (which he may not have). It is here that the flexibility provided by a lump sum may outweigh the benefits of the periodical payment arrangements set out above. However, conversely, if contributory negligence is high (say, 80%), there may still be good reason for awarding a 20% periodical annual payment. Such sums may be regarded by the claimant as 'top-up' provision, in a world in which his basic care and accommodation needs are met, for instance, by the local authority. In such a case, the fact that periodical payments are tax-free and do not affect entitlement to receive free provision from State or local authority sources may tip the balance. Where there is a discount for litigation risk or for contributory fault, but the claimant regards periodical payments as advantageous, this can be achieved by making a periodical payment agreement.

21.22 In determining the 'scale' point, the courts may also weigh up the amount of the annual payment and the period over which payments are likely to be needed.

21.23 Under (ii)(b) above, the description '*the nature of* any financial advice' implies that the advice itself is not to be disclosed, at least at this stage. An earlier draft of the Practice Direction would have required the court to see the financial advice received by a claimant, but perhaps significantly the current PD does not in terms require this. Financial advice is likely to be privileged. In the regime which predated the periodical payment power, the advice of a financial adviser in relation to a proposed infant settlement was, for instance, seen by the court but not by the defendant. In a 'lump sum' case it still is. If, however, financial advice is to be relied upon by a claimant, in seeking to make an Order which is resisted by a defendant, there seems to be no good reason why in principle the advice should not be treated like any other expert advice, and disclosed for the purpose of determining the method by which the payment is to be made. This leaves it open to a defendant to seek to put in contrary advice.

FORM OF ORDER

21.24 Rule 41.8(1) requires a court making an Order for periodical payments to specify:

(a) the annual amount awarded, how each payment is to be made during the year and at what intervals;

(b) the amount awarded for future:
   (i) loss of earnings and other income; and
   (ii) care and medical costs and other recurring or capital costs;
   Note that these two elements have to be separated – thus any schedule of loss, or agreement, should separately identify these two heads.

(c) that the claimant's annual future pecuniary losses, as assessed by the court, are to be paid for the duration of the claimant's life, or such other period as the court orders; and

(d) that the amount of the payments shall vary annually by reference to RPI, unless otherwise ordered.

In addition,

(a) where the court orders that any part of the award shall continue after the claimant's death, for the benefit of the claimant's dependants, the Order must also specify the relevant amount and duration of the payments and how each payment is to be made during the year and at what intervals (CPR, r 41.8(2));

(b) where an amount in respect of future losses is to increase or decrease on a certain date, the Order must also specify (i) the date on which the increase or decrease will take effect, and (ii) the amount of the increase or decrease at current value; and

(c) where damages for substantial capital purchases are awarded under (b)(ii) above, the Order must also specify:
   (i) the amount of the payments at current value;
   (ii) when the payments are to be made; and
   (iii) that the amount of the payments shall be adjusted by reference to RPI unless otherwise ordered.

21.25 The basic payment period is thus a year. Losses for the future are to be calculated by reference to a year. However, r 41.8(1)(a) permits an award, though expressed in terms of 'so much per year', actually to be paid at intervals at less than a year – eg half-yearly, quarterly, monthly or even weekly. The description as to 'how' a payment is to be made will presumably relate to whether by standing order, direct debit, etc. There is no other specific guidance on the meaning of this.

21.26 The distinction between future loss of earnings and other income on the one hand, and care and medical and other costs on the other is important. First, it is likely that loss of earnings as such will be expressed to finish at notional retirement age. The 'default' retirement age may be higher than the previously conventional 65, perhaps as much as 70 since the government has indicated that:

(a) there will be no distinction made between men and women as to normal retirement date;

(b) the emphasis of anti-age discrimination is in permitting people to continue to work despite their age;

(c) increasing longevity has so attenuated pension provision as to make it necessary for workers to continue to work in order to enjoy a reasonable income in later life;

(d) improvements in general health enable them physically to be better able to do so; and

(e) policy statements indicate that retirement age is to become later.

21.27 Although 'other recurring or capital costs' covers accommodation, damages for accommodation give rise to their own problems. Capital outlay is required to purchase a property. In the conventional lump sum order, the capital outlay is in part financed by a capitalisation of the annual payments made under the principle in *Roberts v Johnstone*.[8] This will no longer be possible if a periodical payment order is made for the entirety of future loss. If, however, a court is to be invited to award damages in respect of loss of earnings, care and medical costs and other costs *apart from* accommodation, the value of accommodation over a lifetime must be capitalised in some form. This may require identification of whether evidence as to life expectancy is to be considered: defeating one of the advantages of the periodical payment approach, which is that it operates 'bottom up' rather than 'top down'.

21.28 In any case in which the amount of the lump sum and compensation for past earnings permits it (thus, in large awards such as in many cases of catastrophic injury) there will be less of a problem since a house may be purchased from the capital in respect of those past losses, and payment for the loss of use of the capital (which is the purpose of payments under *Roberts v Johnstone*) made in the usual way. For example, a high-earning claimant who has suffered catastrophic injuries and received past gratuitous care measured in thousands of pounds, and who thus has a substantial special damage claim in respect of past losses of earnings and care, will not find it difficult to purchase a larger property without having to capitalise any part of the future periodical payments due to him. The alteration charges, moving expenses, and the solicitors' and estate agents' costs of purchase and sale of the new and old properties are all one-off expenses in respect of which there will be a claim, which will not be periodicised (or which can be provided for as a first-year

---

[8] [1989] QB 878.

expense within the periodic payments order). In such a case, the additional cost of his new house will produce an annual sum, calculated under *Roberts v Johnstone* at the conventional 2½%. Indeed, the claimant will arguably be better off making such an arrangement than under the lump-sum system, because the amount of the payment for loss of use of his additional capital will be index-linked, unless the defendant persuades the court otherwise: whereas otherwise it will be treated as a flat annual payment, by analogy with a mortgage payment.

21.29 One alternative, however, might be to consider whether a house might be held in trust for the claimant for life, with a reversionary interest to the paying party (or his insurer), on terms that provided for a periodical payment equivalent to a flat rate mortgage: such schemes have been proposed in the past, but thought unattractive, not least because of the administrative burden they impose on a defendant and the difficulty such a defendant may have in ensuring vacant possession of a home which, when the claimant dies, may still be occupied by his partner or family. There is some evidence that recently defendants have been more willing to consider such arrangements.

21.30 The provision that the future pecuniary losses are to be paid for the duration of the claimant's life 'or such other period as the court orders' does not require one single period of time to be specified for all payments. Thus, future educational expenses may be ordered to be payable until the claimant reaches the age of 18, or 19 (or as may be); payment of salary until retirement age (see above); accommodation costs until a hypothetical future date upon which, or by when, it is anticipated that the claimant will be in a residential home and will no longer need his own personal accommodation, etc. Note that under CPR, r 41.8(1), the period for which the losses are to be paid provides an end stop for any particular category of payment. Provision for the increase or decrease of a payment at different times within that period is provided for by r 41.8(3).

21.31 Rules 41.8(3)(a) and (b), provide for increase or decrease in a pre-specified amount on a certain date in the future. They operate by reference to date, not to event. 'Certain date' must in context mean a calendar date, and not a date which can be made certain because it is expressed by reference to the happening of a particular event which, if and when it happens, will occur on a specific day. Note that this does not make the order a 'variable order' subject under the Damages (Variation of Periodical Payments) Order 2005 to restrictive provisions similar to those applying to a further award in the case of provisional damages, which provides for variation upon the happening of a certain, limited, class of future events (see below). It remains an order under which the future pattern of payment is fixed at the outset, by reference to specific dates (hence the description used here of 'non-variable order'). More than one increase or decrease can be specified. The design of a periodical payment order is thus important. It should be tailor-made to fit as closely as possible to the needs of the claimant.

21.32 Paragraph 2.2 of the Practice Direction gives examples of circumstances which might lead the court to make a non-variable order providing for an increase or decrease on a future certain date. The list is not exclusive, merely exemplary. It provides for the increase or decrease to take into account:

(a) a change in the claimant's condition, leading to an increase or reduction in his or her need to incur care, medical or other recurring or capital costs (there may be different dates for different particular costs: for instance, the change from a manually operated to an electronically-driven wheelchair);

(b) when gratuitous carers will no longer continue to provide care (note that this envisages an estimate being made of a future date on which parents or relatives will probably be unable to provide such care. It may also be possible, and occasionally preferable, to provide for this by insuring, eg the life of a principal gratuitous carer, or taking out critical illness cover, although the availability of this depends on market conditions);

(c) the claimant's educational circumstances;

(d) that the claimant would have received a promotional increase in pay (in some jobs, there may also be a decrease as where the anticipated career plan would have provided for the claimant taking a consultancy);

(e) that the claimant will cease earning (this will normally lead to a reduction where the job is pensionable, to the level of pension anticipated pre-injury).

IS THERE A NEED TO CONSIDER LIFE EXPECTANCY?

21.33 The intention of the government in introducing the power to order periodical payments was to lead to a culture change in the way in which payments were calculated, from a 'top down' approach to a 'bottom up' approach.

21.34 A top down approach requires a prediction to be made about the future life expectancy of the claimant. Using this method, the various heads of damages (earnings, care, etc) are used to produce an annual multiplicand, which is then multiplied by a multiplier which is intended to accommodate both inflation on the one hand, and real investment return on the other, the exact numerical value of which is selected by reference to the estimated life expectancy of the claimant. Most structured settlements have in the past been worked out by converting a lump sum produced by such a method into an annuity. The annuity is purchased using the lump sum as a premium. The resulting payments are unlikely to match the original assessment of annual needs.

21.35 Such a system requires an agreement, or a finding of the court, as to the probable life expectancy of the claimant. One of the principal criticisms of the lump sum approach is that whatever figure is derived is unlikely to be right: it may, even, be wildly under or over-stated.

21.36 By contrast, a bottom up approach requires no estimate of life expectancy. The various heads of damages produce an annual figure, as before. The order for periodical payments simply provides for the claimant to be paid that amount on an annual basis for the duration of the specific need to which the payment relates (usually life, though it may be less in respect of future earnings) escalating in line with RPI or an alternative index as specified by the court.

21.37 A further advantage of periodical payments over structured settlements for the defendant is that such payments may be funded in any way in which the defendant chooses, provided the arrangement meets the requirement of reasonable security as defined by the Courts Act (see below): a structured settlement required the purchase of an annuity from a life office providing such a product.

SECURITY OF PAYMENTS

21.38 A court cannot order periodical payments unless it is satisfied that payment is reasonably secure (Damages Act 1996, s 2(3)). If the court is not satisfied of the security of the payments, it may either order a lump sum, or require the party making the payment to use a method which is automatically considered to be reasonably secure by the terms of s 2(4) of the 1996 Act. It is this area which has caused the greatest amount of case-law thus far.

21.39 Continuity of payment is automatically considered to be reasonably secure in three circumstances. First, it is reasonably secure where it is protected by a ministerial guarantee under s 6 of the 1996 Act (no such guarantees have yet been given, but it is possible for this to be done on a case-by-case basis). This covers 'self-funded' payments made from public sector bodies – but note that the Government or Health Service bodies named in the Damages (Government and Health Service Bodies) Order 2005 do not require to be specifically guaranteed under s 6).

21.40 Secondly, by s 2(4)(b), payment is automatically considered reasonably secure if it is protected by a scheme under s 213 of the Financial Services and Markets Act 2000 (ie which attracts statutory protection under the Financial Services Compensation Scheme). This will apply to payments made by authorised insurers, whether they are self-funded, made directly by a liability insurer to the claimant, or payments made by a life insurer under an annuity contract. It should be noted, however, that a defendant liability insurer providing aircraft or shipping insurance is not covered by the FSCS, and direct funding by such an insurer does not qualify as reasonably secure. Nor does the FSCS cover Lloyd's of London policies.

21.41 The FSCS provides compensation to policyholders if they are insured by authorised insurance firms under contracts of insurance issued in the UK, or in some cases (but not all – please note) those issued in the EEA, Channel Islands or Isle of Man. (If an insurer is not issuing a policy in the UK, watch out!) The scheme covers compulsory, general and life insurance and is triggered if an insurance firm goes out of business or into liquidation: continuity of periodical payments is protected to 100% under the scheme, although for the 'ordinary' uninjured insured policyholder the usual figure is 90%, except where insurance is compulsory as in the case of employer's liability or motor insurance.

21.42 A general insurer may prefer to fund payments directly from its own resources rather than purchase an annuity, or may wish to purchase an annuity in its own name and then contract to pass the periodical payments to the claimant. Defendants may find this latter possibility attractive if the payments stand to be varied downward at some later date, or if there is a chance of the reduction of the payments on appeal. Section 4 of the Damages Act 1996 provides for the extension of protection ordinarily afforded to uninjured policyholders to the recipients of periodical payments, even where the policyholder is, for example, the insurer, to 100%, and should be consulted if there is any doubt about security of payment.

21.43 What are *not* covered by s 2(4), and therefore not automatically reasonably secure under s 2(4)(b), are payments which are self-funded by Lloyd's insurers, by the MIB, by the MDU, MPS, or other medical defence organisations, or by private defendants. Such payments do not on the face of it attract statutory protection, and another method of security must be used if such a defendant is to be ordered to provide periodical payments. However, in *Begum v Barnet & Chase Farm Hospital*,[9] Sir Michael Turner took the view that s 2(4) was a 'deeming provision', which meant that any body able to satisfy its provisions need go no further, rather than a conclusive list of those circumstances in which reasonable security was provided. He pointed out that the wording was 'reasonably' secure, which suggests that a court may be satisfied as a matter of judgment that the security offered is sufficient. He also concluded that where an NHS Trust had applied to become a foundation trust, periodical payments ordered to be paid it were nonetheless secure. However, his reasoning may be vulnerable in part: he appears to have assumed that an NHS Trust, foundation or otherwise, would fall within the definition of a 'health service body'. This may ignore the fact that in s 2A(2) it is provided that 'government or health service body' means a body designated as a government body or a health service body by order made by the Lord Chancellor.

---

[9] [2005] EWHC 3383.

21.44 Nonetheless, in *YM v Gloucestershire Hospitals NHS Foundation Trust; Kanu v King's College Hospital Trust*,[10] Forbes J gave detailed and careful consideration to the same question, and concluded that arrangements made between the NHSLA and the parties, and between the NHSLA and the state, had overcome the essential difficulty and that, if necessary, the orders made could be enforced against the NHSLA (payments from which, as will be seen from the list below, are reasonably secure). *This case is important – it concludes with a model form of order which should be adopted wherever an NHS Trust or foundation trust is a paying defendant.*

21.45 Under s 2(4)(c), where the source of the payments is a government or health service body named in the Damages (Government and Health Service Bodies) Order 2005, payment is automatically assumed to be reasonably secure. The government bodies listed are:

- Department for Constitutional Affairs

- Department for Culture, Media and Sport

- Ministry of Defence

- Office of the Deputy Prime Minister

- Department for Education and Skills

- Department for Environment, Food and Rural Affairs

- Department of Health

- Home Office

- Foreign and Commonwealth Office

- Commissioners of Inland Revenue and Commissioners of Customs and Excise

- Department for International Development

- Northern Ireland Office

- Department of Trade and Industry

- Department for Transport

- HM Treasury

---

[10] [2006] EWHC 820.

- Wales Office

- Department for Work and Pensions

- National Assembly for Wales

- Department of Health, Social Services and Public Safety (Northern Ireland)

The health services bodies listed in the 2005 Order are:

- National Health Service Litigation Authority

- In Wales, NHS Trusts

- In Wales, Local Health Boards

- In Northern Ireland, Health and Social Services Boards

- In Northern Ireland, Health and Social Services Trusts

- In Northern Ireland, Health and Personal Social Services Agencies and Special Agencies

Note: Health authorities and healthcare trusts in England are *not* designated bodies, so any periodical payment order must be one met by the NHSLA if it is to be reasonably secure: see *YM v Gloucestershire* above.

21.46 The list in s 2(4) does not exclude consideration of other methods of funding. However, these must be scrutinised by a court, and a court must specify the alternative method of funding in its Order. The criteria set out in the Practice Direction are:

(a) that a method of funding provided for under s 2(4) of the 1996 Act is not possible or there are good reasons to justify an alternative method of funding;

(b) the proposed method of funding can be maintained for the duration of the award or for the proposed duration of the method of funding; and

(c) the proposed method of funding will meet the level of payment ordered by the court.

By application of these criteria, the court must be satisfied overall that the continuity of payment under the order is 'reasonably secure'.

21.47 What amounts to being 'reasonably secure' is not otherwise defined. (An interesting test case might be to explore the extent to which a local authority which is self-insuring is held by a court to offer reasonable security.) However, it seems likely that the courts will take a restrictive view. This is because any appreciation of 'reasonableness' must take into account the view of Parliament that it is reasonable for a periodical payment order to have the backing of the Financial Services Compensation Scheme, not just to the extent of a 90% guarantee, as in the case of an ordinary insured policyholder, but as to 100%, and its decision that the bodies specified under the 2005 Order are Departments of State, and no other public body is specified. Local authorities, which might constitute public bodies for the purposes of European law, are not themselves listed. This suggests that such bodies are not automatically to be regarded as reasonably secure. If so, the standard set is a high one.

SECURITY INTO THE FAR FUTURE

21.48 Where a victim is likely to live beyond the date of the longest currently available index-linked stock (until recently 2035), there may be a further problem with determining whether or not a periodical payment order offers reasonable security. This is because the Financial Services Authority (FSA) regulates the long-term business funds of insurers who provide annuities. Put simply, an insurer must be able to purchase suitable matching assets to cover any liability to make annuity payments. In the case of an annuity linked to RPI, matching assets are provided by purchasing index-linked government stocks. When the longest dated stock expires then unless fresh stocks are issued, there will be no suitable matching asset. To continue to provide for an index-linked annuity beyond that date, significantly greater reserves would have to be tied up. Most life offices providing RPI-linked annuities incorporate a Limited Price Index clause into their policies, the effect of which is to provide that if no suitable matching assets are available in the future the insurer will match the retail price index up to a cap (typically within a range of 1% to 7%: the variation depends upon the age and health of the claimant, and varies from insurer to insurer).

21.49 There is no possibility of close matching the average earnings index, or, for that matter, the Pay Cost Index (PCI) which has been suggested as a potential index in respect of future care costs. Accordingly, it seems difficult to think that reasonable security, at least from an insurer, can easily be assured for an award linked to these indices: although *Flora v Wakom* shows a green light for suggesting other indices, the requirement of reasonable security may yet make it difficult to award where the defendant is not a governmental or health service body.

21.50 The problem may disappear, if the government issues sufficiently long-dated index-linked securities. It may also be that government stocks are issued which are tied to some index other than RPI. At the time of writing this, however, seems unlikely: and thus PCI or National Average Earnings (NAE) indexation (see below) remains problematic and unlikely except against public bodies or the NHSLA.

THE APPROPRIATE INDEX

21.51 Section 2(8) of the Damages Act 1996 provides that an order for periodical payments 'shall be treated as providing for the amount of payments to vary by reference to the Retail Price Index (within the meaning of s 833(2) of the Income and Corporation Taxes Act 1988) at such times, and in such manner as may be determined by or in accordance with Civil Procedure Rules'. However, s 2(9) provides that an Order made by a court for periodical payments may include provision '(a) disapplying sub-section (a) or (b) modifying the effect of sub-section (8)'.

21.52 Thus, the 'default' index is RPI, which measures the cost of goods and services and includes the cost of mortgages. It does not, however, directly measure any increase in average earnings.

21.53 The CPR provides, similarly to the Act, that the amount of payments shall vary annually by reference to RPI, unless the court orders otherwise. In guidance produced in respect of the power to impose periodical payments, the Department of Constitutional Affairs notes that during the passage of the Bill ministers indicated that it was expected that, as before, periodical payments would be linked to RPI in the great majority of cases, but that it would remain open to the courts to adopt a different index (or none) in a particular case if there were exceptional circumstances which justified their doing so.

21.54 Government guidance thus uses the phrase 'exceptional circumstances' which echoes the phrase of the Lord Chancellor which in *Warriner v Warriner*[11] was used to defeat an argument that a different discount rate should be applied in a particularly high value case, since although a high value case was not the norm, it could not be said to be exceptional and in *Cooke v United Bristol Health Care*[12] led to the rejection of a claim to calculate future loss by reference to a rate other than one which allowed for the RPI and impact of tax. However, the Court of Appeal in *Flora v Wakom*[13] declined to regard the power to adopt another index as being exercisable only in exceptional circumstances. Brooke LJ observed:

> 'The fact that these two quite different mechanisms now sit side by side in the same Act of Parliament does not in my judgment mean that the problems that infected the operation of the one should be allowed to infect the operation of the other'

and went on to observe that the governing principle was:

> '... the "100% principle", namely that a victim of a tort was entitled to be compensated as nearly as possible in full for all pecuniary losses' (see para 28).

---

[11] [2002] 1 WLR 1703.
[12] [2003] EWCA Civ 1370.
[13] [2006] EWCA Civ 1103.

21.55 Since the court is concerned with the needs of the claimant, and with compensating as accurately as possible (two underlying reasons for adopting the power to provide for periodical payments) full restitution requires the identification of the most appropriate index. This, however, begs the question as to whether another index can be shown to be clearly more appropriate than the default index of RPI. Evidence would be needed before a court could be persuaded that another index was likely to produce more accurate figures over the lifetime of an award, and provide a more accurate picture of variation in costs so that neither claimant nor defendant is disadvantaged by the shift from RPI to such an index: assertion of this will not suffice. It may well be that the cost of providing care has in the past risen at a rate significantly higher than that of RPI, and arguable that this shows a pattern likely to continue for the foreseeable future. If so, an index linked to earnings rather than prices might be indicated, but views differ whether there is a suitable one: the NAE index may be too broadly based to deal with a small subset of workers, and the NHS PCI may be open to the objection that it includes the earnings of many professional grades which appear to have grown faster than have the lower earnings of those providing care.

21.56 It has been suggested that despite the problem that insufficiently long-dated stocks may be available for the future, and the difficulties for bodies other than health service or public bodies providing reasonable security for the continuity of periodical payments referenced to NAE or PCI in the health service, a court could provide for indexation by reference to RPI plus a fixed percentage uplift beyond it. It is likely that the courts would be hesitant to do this, since s 2(8), and r 41.8 appear to envisage that the link will be to some index, or none, as opposed to a separate reference point (RPI plus) devised by the court itself. However, Baroness Scotland did say in Parliament during the passage of the Act that it would be open to a court to order that periodical payments should be linked to the RPI plus a percentage as a proxy for some other index.[14] However, in *Thompstone v Tameside Glossop Acute Services NHS Trust*[15] Swift J adopted the 75th percentile of ASHE occupational group 6155, published by the ONS, or any comparable group, as the appropriate index, after hearing evidence. This and similar cases are due to be heard soon on appea;.

VARIABLE ORDERS

21.57 At the time when an order is made, provision may be made for the terms to be varied on the occurrence of some future event. This is to be distinguished from a variation of the terms upon a certain future date (which is part of the design of a non-variable periodical payment order).

---

[14] See generally W Norris QC: 'Periodical Payments: Indexation, Variation, Protection and Practice', JPIL, March 2005.
[15] [2006] EWHC 2904.

21.58 The Damages (Variation of Periodical Payments) Order 2005 provides that the court may on the application of one party, with the agreement of all parties, or of its own initiative provide in an Order for periodical payments that it may be varied if there is proved or admitted to be a chance that:

(1) at some definite or indefinite time in the future the claimant will:
   (a) as a result of the act or omission which gave rise to the cause of action, develop some serious disease or suffer some serious deterioration; or
   (b) enjoy some significant improvement in his physical or mental condition, where that condition had been adversely affected as a result of that act or omission.

21.59 In such a case, damages are to be assessed or agreed on the assumption that the disease, deterioration or improvement will not occur. The order:

(a) must specify the disease or type of deterioration or improvement;

(b) may (but does not have to) specify a period within which an application for variation may be made;

(c) may (but does not have to) specify more than one disease or type of deterioration or improvement; and

(d) may, in respect of each, specify a different period within which an application for variation in respect of it may be made.

21.60 In addition, a variable order must provide that a party must obtain the court's permission to apply for it to be varied, unless the court otherwise orders. If the parties can agree a mechanism by which an application for variation can be facilitated, they might invite the court to exercise its power to order 'otherwise', for this would avoid the expense of one party going through the application for permission stage before a substantive hearing for a variation at some future date. Accordingly, claimants and defendants should consider whether an application for permission to apply is strictly necessary in their particular case: if not, they should apply to omit reference to permission in the original variable order at the time it is made.

21.61 Where any period is specified within which an application for permission to vary may be made, an application to extend the period for applying may be made (such an application must, however, be made within the period originally stipulated).

21.62 It is important to note that:

(a) Only one application to vary may be made in respect of each specified disease or type of deterioration or improvement.

(b) The case file documents must be preserved by the legal representatives of the parties (this includes barristers). (They will also be preserved by the court.)

AGREEMENTS FOR VARIABLE ORDERS

21.63 The parties may agree to settle a case upon terms that one will pay the other periodical payments which may be varied if there is agreed to be a chance that at some definite or indefinite time in the future the claimant will (a) as a result of the act or omission which gave rise to the cause of action, develop some serious disease or suffer some serious deterioration, or (b) enjoy some significant improvement, in his physical or mental condition, where that condition had been adversely affected as a result of that act or omission. But note – the terms of such an agreement *must* comply with art 9(2) of the 2005 Order. It must therefore expressly state:

(a) that a party to it may apply to the court for the terms of the variable agreement to be varied;

(b) must specify the disease or type of deterioration or improvement;

(c) may (but does not have to) specify a period within which an application for it to be varied may be made; and

(d) may (but does not have to) specify more than one disease or type of deterioration or improvement and may, in respect of each, specify a different period within which an application for it to be varied may be made.

21.64 If an agreement does *not* comply, the consequence does not seem to be that the agreement itself is an invalid contract, but rather that the court will have no jurisdiction to determine any dispute arising, and this could both deprive the agreement of any real effect and expose his legal advisors to a potential claim!

21.65 Where an agreement provides that a party is permitted to apply for it to be varied, the party so permitted must nonetheless obtain the court's permission to apply for the variation. It is unclear whether the applicant is limited to one application per type of disease or deterioration: the safest course would be to assume that this is so, since in particular the applicant will have to ask the permission of the court to apply for a variation, and implicit in this is the possibility that the application might, for good reason, be refused. It is likely to be regarded as good reason that it is a second application where there is nothing express which permits it; and even if there is, that a consistent regime should apply as between variable orders and variable agreements.

21.66 There is an obvious overlap with the possibility of claiming an award of provisional damages under s 32A of the Supreme Court Act 1981, or s 51 of the County Courts Act 1984. The wording of those provisions plainly formed a model for the provisions applicable to variable periodical payment orders. The 2005 Order provides that a variable order may be made in addition to an order for an award of provisional damages.

21.67 Thus, in a situation in which there is uncertainty about whether an injured party will suffer further deterioration, or develop some further condition (eg epilepsy; syringomyelia; immobility such that a wheelchair is necessary at all times) the parties may:

(a) claim, or agree, a lump sum award;

(b) claim, or agree, a non-variable periodical payment order: if, for instance, deterioration to wheelchair status from partial mobility is anticipated, it can be provided for by a fixed date at which the level of annual payment increases;

(c) claim, or agree, a provisional damages award (subject to the restrictions envisaged in *Willson v Ministry of Defence*:[16] inevitable deterioration does not qualify for an award of provisional damages);

(d) claim or agree an award of provisional damages with a variable order, thus providing that, for instance, the order might be varied in the event that the claimant became wheelchair bound, but was also provisional, by asserting that the damages were assessed upon the footing that there would be no epilepsy, and no syringomyelia; or

(e) ask or consent to the court making a variable order providing that the order for periodical payments may be varied upon the claimant suffering epilepsy, or developing syringomyelia, or becoming totally wheelchair bound (or whatever).

21.68 A principal use of the 'combination' of provisional damages and variable order may be to avoid the problems caused by the inability to claim provisional damages for progressive deterioration. The reasoning in *Willson* (which denied a claim for provisional damages assessed on the footing that osteo-arthritis would not develop to certain specified levels of disability, when it was seen that such a progression was inevitable) arguably does not apply to prevent a variable agreement being made, despite the superficial similarity as to the circumstances in which such an order may be made when compared to the circumstances in which an order for provisional damages may be made.

21.69 Note that variable orders may be made in respect of an improvement in the claimant's condition. It should not be thought that a deterioration will

---

[16] [1991] 1 All ER 638.

inevitably increase damages, and an improvement inevitably decrease them. For instance, a claimant who is in a persistent vegetative state (PVS) who recovers a little from his coma is likely to need greater financial assistance than if he had remained in PVS, as would a claimant who recovers sufficiently from agoraphobia to wish to travel outside his home from time to time, thus requiring transport and company in which to do so. A deterioration may similarly reduce rather than increase costs: someone who is no longer able to care for himself in his own home is a case in point, since such a person might be more cheaply cared for in a residential setting, despite the fact that his overall physical state has deteriorated.

ASSIGNMENT AND CHARGE OF RIGHT TO RECEIVE PAYMENTS

21.70 The right to receive periodical payments may not be assigned nor charged unless the court which made the original order is satisfied there are special circumstances which make this necessary. (This is intended to prevent claimants assigning their right to receive payments in return for a lump sum, and thereby bypassing the power to impose periodical payments.)

21.71 CPR, r 41.10 requires the court to have regard to a number of factors in considering whether to permit an assignment or a charge. Those factors, which are identified in para 4 of the Practice Direction, are:

(a) whether the capitalised value of the assignment or charge represents value for money;

(b) whether the assignment or charge is in the claimant's best interests, taking into account whether those interests can be met in some other way; and

(c) how the claimant would be financially supported following the assignment or charge.

21.72 These provisions are not as restrictive as they might appear at first blush. They do not prohibit a loan being made to the recipient of periodical payments on personal security alone. If the recipient failed to repay, he could be sued, and the lender recover out of the income stream provided for by the periodical payments. What the provisions do, however, restrict is the ability of a claimant to take out a loan which is secured upon the periodical payments rather than unsecured, such that the lender takes priority over other debtors. There is a link, here, with the insolvency provisions relating to periodical payments, which provide that periodical payments in respect of care may not be taken as property of the bankrupt recipient of such payments, although payments in respect of future loss of earnings may be. (This is partly why a distinction must be made in any award of periodical payments as between future earnings on the one hand, and care and other recurring costs on the other.)

PART 36 OFFERS

21.73 Part 36 has been amended by the Civil Procedure (Amendment No 3) Rules 2004, which came into force on 1 April 2005. These rules add a Part 36.2A, which governs the operation of Part 36 in relation to personal injury cases involving a claim for future pecuniary loss. Although Part 36 will be amended significantly following consultation in early 2006, in particular to permit paper offers to count as effectively as cash payments where made by bodies who will be 'good for the money', it is unlikely there will be any great change to the provisions as they impact on periodical payments.

21.74 Where both an offer, and the award by the court, are made in lump sum terms Part 36 operates as it always has done: a straightforward comparison may be made between the offer, and the award. Where, however, the offer is in terms of a lump sum and the award is made in a periodical payment order (or where there is a mixture of the two, or where the offer is to accept periodical payments and the award is a lump sum award) the simplicity of the Part 36 regime will not apply.

21.75 An offer may be made to pay (if made by a defendant) or to accept (if made by a claimant):

(a) the whole or part of the damages for future pecuniary loss in the form of:
    (i) either a lump sum or periodical payments; or
    (ii) both a lump sum and periodical payments; and

(b) the whole or part of any other damages in the form of a lump sum.

21.76 Since a court only has a power to make a periodical payment order in respect of future pecuniary loss, any claim for a lump sum in respect of pain, suffering and loss of amenity, and for past loss, must be made on a lump sum basis: however, such an offer does not require that the lump sum part of an offer stops there. It may provide that, so far as the future is concerned, payment will be made, or accepted, with a mixture of lump sum and periodical payment. Any permutation of capital and income is thus possible.

21.77 A Part 36 offer to which r 36.2A(4) applies must:

(a) state the amount of any offer to pay the whole or part of any damages in the form of a lump sum;

(b) may (but does not have to) state what part of the offer relates to damages for future pecuniary loss to be accepted in the form of a lump sum;

(c) may (but does not have to) state, where part of the offer relates to other damages to be accepted in the form of a lump sum, what amounts are attributable to those other damages;

(d) *must* state what part of the offer relates to damages for future pecuniary loss to be paid or accepted in the form of periodical payments and must specify:
 (i) the amount and duration of the periodical payments;
 (ii) the amount of any payments for substantial capital purchases[17] and when they are to be made; and
 (iii) that each amount is to vary by reference to RPI (or to some other named index, or none); and

(e) *must* state either that any damages which take the form of periodical payments will be funded in a way which ensures that the continuity of payment is reasonably secure in accordance with s 2(4) of the Damages Act 1996, or how such damages are to be paid and how the continuity of their payment is to be secured.

21.78 Note that the list in r 36.2A(5) (set out above) does not require all the details which are required to be set out in an offer by r 41.8. If the parties wish the terms of a settlement to be embodied in a consent order made by the court, the requirements of that rule will also need to be satisfied.

21.79 Where a defendant's offer includes both a lump sum and periodical payments, the claimant may only accept the offer as a whole, and not in part alone. There is no corresponding provision in respect of a defendant's entitlement, or otherwise, to accept the claimant's offer in part.

21.80 If a defendant's offer is to have costs consequences under Part 36, a Part 36 payment of the lump sum element must be made (r 36.2A(2)). Where both a Part 36 offer and a Part 36 payment are made, r 36.2A(3) requires the offer to include details of the payment.

21.81 The time for acceptance of an offer is calculated from the date of the Part 36 offer, not from the date of the payment into court of the lump sum element (this is the effect of r 36.2A(3)).

21.82 Where a periodical payment offer has been made under Part 36, and the claimant fails to obtain a judgment which is 'more advantageous than the Part 36 offer made under (r 36.2A)' then r 36.20(1)(a) provides that a court will order a claimant to pay the defendant's costs incurred after the latest date on which the payment or offer could have been accepted without needing the permission of the court. Similarly, if a judgment against a defendant is more advantageous to the claimant than the proposals contained in a periodical payment Part 36 offer, the court may order interest on the whole or part of the sum of money awarded to the claimant at a rate not exceeding 10% above base rate for some or all the period beginning with the latest date on which the

---

[17] 'Substantial' is undefined but care should be taken to define these purchases or a later variation will not be permitted.

defendant could have accepted the claimant's offer without needing permission of the court, and may order indemnity costs from the same date together with interest on those costs.

21.83 No guidance is given by the rule as to when an offer will be considered 'more advantageous'. In particular, problems are likely to arise if a lump sum award is made where a periodical payment offer was advanced, or vice versa. Similarly, under the unamended r 36.20, where a lump sum offer is made by a defendant, but periodical payments are awarded, it may be difficult to know whether the judgment is more or less advantageous than a defendant's Part 36 offer.

21.84 Considerable thought was given as to whether there should be more detailed guidance or provision by rule as to the costs consequences of Part 36 offers. So many and varied are the possibilities and permutations that no single rule could be clearly applied, and it was decided best to leave the matter to the general discretion of the courts. In most cases it will be clear whether a claimant has, or has not, done better or worse than a relevant Part 36 offer. In those cases where it is less clear, parties may seek to argue that it is necessary to establish what would have been the lump sum if the periodical payments are capitalised, taking into account the probable life expectancy of the claimant. However, this is to introduce evidence of life expectancy which an award of periodical payments is in part designed to avoid.

21.85 Both rr 36.20 and 36.21 allow a court not to make an Order against a party where the court considers it unjust to do so. Part of the consideration of that injustice may be whether it was appropriate for the claimant to ask for periodical payments (or depending on the circumstances, to ask for a lump sum). Thus it seems possible that the cost of evidence as to life expectancy may not be allowed if it is directed merely to a possible argument that a Part 36 offer has or has not been beaten.

21.86 It is not easy to circumvent a broad based application of discretion by the courts in determining whether or not a claimant has, or has not 'beaten' the payment in by, for instance, advancing two Part 36 offers in advance of trial, one consisting of a lump sum alone, the other consisting of a mix. This is because the mix of lump sum and periodical payment element may vary considerably.

21.87 It seems unlikely that the Court of Appeal would be sympathetic to any appeal in respect of the award, or withholding of, Part 36 costs. The general approach is that costs are awarded at the discretion of the trial judge, whose exercise of that discretion should be respected, and there should not be satellite litigation to establish what the award would have been if the award had been differently composed.

APPEALS

21.88 No separate rule deals with appeals in respect of periodical payment orders which are imposed against the wishes of one or both parties.

21.89 Where there is a dispute as to whether a periodical payment order should be made, or a lump sum order instead, the 'default' position would appear to be that periodical payments should be preferred by the court (see e g the comments of Mitting J in *Godbold* (above). This follows from the policy background (set out, for instance, in the DCA guidance, and summarised above). It is incumbent upon the court to consider whether an award can be made in every case involving future pecuniary loss.

21.90 The factors to which the rules, and the Practice Direction, refer are such that the decision whether to order periodical payments or a lump sum is one of discretion. Although it a judicial discretion must meet the requirements of relevance, reason, justice and fairness, this still makes it difficult for the exercise of a discretion to be faulted. Thus, providing that the court has in mind that the central requirement is to meet the needs of the claimant, as opposed to adopt his wishes, it seems unlikely that many appeals will succeed.

21.91 However, if an appeal is made, what happens to financial provision for the claimant in the meantime? The answer seems to be that it is effectively no different from any case in which there is an appeal against an award. Where periodical payments are ordered, there seems to be no good reason why pending the determination of the appeal, any periodical payment falling due should not be paid (unless, that is, a stay is sought if, for instance, there is an appeal against liability). In the case of a lump sum order, again, there seems to be no reason why there should not be at least some payment pending the appeal. However, the principles are bound to be individual to each case. Moreover, defendants may wish to seek an early stay of payment if they intend to satisfy the requirement of reasonable security by purchasing an annuity from a life insurer. Such a purchase demands a lump sum outlay, which once paid is likely to be irrecoverable.

INTERIM PAYMENTS

21.92 Consideration should be given to two aspects relating to interim payments. First, will the award of an interim in one lump sum, as an advance against future losses (e g to buy a house) prejudice the potential to be awarded periodical payments? Secondly, should an application be made for interim payments to be awarded on a periodical basis?

21.93 As to the first, an award of a lump sum interim payment in respect of expenses which have been met by trial, and thus form part of the special damage claim, will not prejudice any award the court can make (though it might affect the amount parties can allocate to periodical payments by agreement). Care needs to be taken, though, if any part of the sum is 'borrowing' against future income payments or care expenses.

21.94 As to the second, s 2A(5) specifically includes an award of interim damages as being within the scope of the damages in respect of which the courts may impose an order. This has potential, especially where the final assessment of damages sensibly needs to be delayed, but provision is needed in the meantime for ongoing care, or to supplement income resources. The advantage of the periodical payment regime is that it can require regular payments, uprated by an appropriate index such as RPI, pending final trial. The 'reasonable security' provisions apply, but are more likely to be easily satisfied for a short-term provision than for a final order. Sensible use of this provision should avoid the need for repeated return visits to the masters' corridor.

Chapter 22

CRIMINAL INJURIES COMPENSATION

INTRODUCTION

22.1 State compensation has been available in Great Britain for victims of crimes of violence since 1964. For claims made before April 1996 the assessment of compensation for eligible applicants was based on common law damages. This link with common law damages was broken for claims received from 1 April 1996 when the Criminal Injuries Compensation Act 1995 placed criminal injuries compensation on a statutory footing and introduced a tariff of awards. The Act also created two new bodies, the Criminal Injuries Compensation Authority (CICA) to administer it, and the Criminal Injuries Compensation Appeals Panel (CICAP) to determine appeals by claimants dissatisfied with the decisions of the CICA.

22.2 When the tariff was devised, the amount of each award was based on the common law levels of damages then current. However, a tariff which set awards for 366 differing injuries by allocating them to 25 compensation levels graded from £1,000 to £250,000, according to the nature of the injury, necessarily provided a blunter and less sophisticated, if more readily understood, approach to compensation than did the common law. The tariff additionally capped the maximum available award at £500,000, and provided for a lower limit of £1,000. The changes in 1996, though radical for quantum for pain and suffering and for financial loss, made relatively few alterations to the rules determining eligibility for an award. Pre-1996 case-law decisions on eligibility are mostly still relevant.

22.3 The social basis of criminal injury compensation was explained by a Home Office minister in a House of Commons debate in January 1999 in this way:

> 'The state is not liable for injuries caused by the acts of others, but we are determined to continue to acknowledge in some way the public sense of responsibility for and sympathy with the blameless victim. Through the criminal injuries compensation Scheme, the state provides a monetary award on behalf of the community ... the Scheme no longer seeks to provide finely judged compensation covering every head of damage that might be awarded in a successful civil suit. [It] represents some extra public recognition of the harm suffered by a blameless victim.'

SOURCES OF INFORMATION: 'COMMON LAW' SCHEME

22.4 The rules which determine when, how much, and how compensation can be paid are set out in documents known as 'Schemes'. They are made by the Home Secretary and have been approved by Parliament.

22.5 Before the creation of the CICA and the introduction of a tariff in 1996, awards were made by the Criminal Injuries Compensation Board. They were made without any statutory basis (*ex gratia*). From 1964 to 1990 there were four successive common law Schemes, the last being the 1990 Scheme. Earlier Schemes remain in effect for claims received during their currency, though the practical effect is that pre-1990 Schemes need only ever be consulted in reopened claims (see **22.44** below); and that is not straightforward as later Schemes have introduced transitional provisions which have modified most of the provisions of earlier Schemes.

22.6 The Board was wound up on 31 March 2000. Claims which remain unresolved mostly involve only the assessment of quantum, usually of high potential value, made on behalf of seriously injured children. Reopened claims will also continue to be assessed under common law Schemes. The 1990 Scheme presently remains effective in some 240 remaining claims.

SOURCES OF INFORMATION: THE 1996 AND 2001 TARIFF SCHEMES

22.7 The first tariff Scheme is known as the 1996 Scheme. It continues to apply to claims received by the CICA from 1 April 1996 to 31 March 2001, and the 1996 injury descriptions and levels and proportions of compensation are retained for those claims.

22.8 For claims received after 31 March 2001, regardless of when the injury was sustained, a second Scheme has been introduced: the 2001 Scheme. The significant changes have been to increase the amounts awarded for compensation levels 7–23 by up to 10%; to increase the number of injury descriptions by 75 (to 441); and in claims for separate multiple injuries to increase the proportions of the tariff amount to 30% and 15% for second and third injuries.

22.9 The effect is that there are two different Schemes concurrently in operation, and the one which applies to any particular claim depends on the date the claim was received by CICA (the date is stamped by CICA on page 1 of the application form on receipt). The 2001 Scheme also introduced other changes and most, though not all, have been imported by transitional provisions into the operation of the 1996 Scheme (two which do not have retrospective effect are the extension of compensation in fatal claims to same sex partners, and the tables for assessing multipliers: see **22.31** and **22.34** below). Paragraph references in this chapter are to the 2001 tariff Scheme, the paragraph numbers of which largely coincide with the 1996 Scheme.

GUIDES

22.10 The CICA is required by para 22 of each Scheme to publish a guide to the operation of the Scheme. It is called a 'Guide to the Criminal Injuries Compensation Scheme'. It explains the procedures for dealing with applications and helpfully sets out the criteria normally applied when decisions on eligibility are made. However it is not a substitute for the Scheme. The guide to the 1996 Scheme was last issued in April 1999 and is a cream-coloured document. The most recent guide to the 2001 Scheme is blue and was issued in January 2004. The CICA publishes other guides as well as leaflets on several topics. Useful guides are a 'Guide to Applicants for Loss of Earnings and Special Expenses', and a 'Guide to Applicants for Compensation in Fatal Cases'. They explain the provisions of paras 30–36 (loss of earnings and special expenses) and 37–44 (fatal cases). Copies of the Scheme guides as well as some of their leaflets are available on the CICA website (cica.gov.uk).

WHO CAN RECOVER

Living victims

22.11 Compensation may be paid to those who have sustained 'a criminal injury' (para 8 of the Scheme) who satisfy the other rules in the Scheme for eligibility (see **22.14** and **22.19–22.23** below).

Dead victims

22.12 If the victim has died in consequence of the injury, and would otherwise have been eligible, compensation in tariff claims, including a dependency, may be paid to 'qualifying claimants' (para 38 of the Scheme). The Schemes in some respects provide more generous compensation, and for a wider class of claimants, than do the Fatal Accidents Acts.

22.13 If the victim has died otherwise than in consequence of the criminal injury and before notification has been given that an award has been accepted, with the exception of a claim for supplementary compensation, the claim dies with the applicant, and no compensation will be paid to the estate (paras 38 and 44 of the Scheme). For the scope of the exception see **22.32** below.

'CRIMINAL INJURY'

22.14 The principal definition of criminal injury (para 8(a) of the Scheme), which applies to some 97% of claims made, is that it means one or more personal injuries sustained in Great Britain being injury 'directly attributable to a crime of violence (including arson, fire raising or an act of poisoning)'. The balance of 3% of claims consists of two other classes of victim who intuitively may not appear to have sustained a criminal injury, though by definition they have done so.

22.15 One is a person who suffers injury 'directly attributable to an offence of trespass on the railway'. This provision usually operates when someone employed on the railways, such as a train driver or guard, has suffered psychological injury by being present and witness to or becoming involved in the immediate aftermath of a railway suicide (see para 9(d) of the Scheme).

22.16 The other is a person who sustains injury in the course of law enforcement activities, which are defined as 'the apprehension or attempted apprehension of an offender or suspected offender, the prevention or attempted prevention of an offence, or the giving of help to any constable who is engaged in any such activity'. This provision benefits not only police officers but also security guards, store detectives and on occasions members of the public. The offence in which the offender is involved does not have to be a crime of violence: shoplifting, car theft, or avoiding arrest are often involved. And compensation is nevertheless recoverable when the injury has been sustained accidentally, so long as the person injured was taking an exceptional risk at the time, which was justified (para 12 of the Scheme).

CRIME OF VIOLENCE

22.17 A 'crime of violence' is not defined in the Schemes (unlike 'criminal injury', which is defined). In *R v CICB, ex parte Warner*,[1] the Court of Appeal emphasised that what matters in deciding whether unlawful conduct amounts to a crime of violence is its nature and not its consequences. Lawton LJ said

> '... (the) submission that what matters is the nature of the crime, not its likely consequences, is well founded. It is for the Board to decide whether unlawful conduct because of its nature, not its consequences, amounts to a crime of violence. As Lord Widgery C.J. pointed out in *Clowes'* case, the meaning of crime of violence is very much a jury point. Most crimes of violence will involve the infliction or threat of force but some may not. I do not think it is prudent to attempt a definition of words of ordinary English which the Board, as a fact finding body, have to apply to the case before them. They will recognise a crime of violence when they hear about it, even though as a matter of semantics it may be

---

[1] [1987] QB 74.

difficult to produce a definition which is not too narrow or so wide as to produce absurd consequences, as in the case of the Road Traffic Act 1972 to which I have referred.'

22.18 Thus not every breach of criminal law is a crime of violence, even though its consequences may be indistinguishable from the effects of what is clearly a crime of violence. Breach of Health and Safety Regulations, dangerous parking of a vehicle (Lawton LJ's example), or theft of an elderly person's possessions can lead to physical or psychological consequences identical to those of assaults, but victims in such cases will not be within the Scheme. On the other hand assaults can be committed recklessly as well as with hostile intent. A pedestrian unintentionally knocked down and injured by a fleeing shoplifter may, nevertheless, recover if it can be properly inferred that the thief was reckless as to the pedestrian's safety. Criminal damage can also be a crime of violence since it can be committed by someone who is reckless as to whether the life of another would be endangered by his acts: see *R v CICB, ex parte Clowes*.[2] Claimants regularly recover compensation if they have been cut and injured by flying glass when standing on the inside of a window or glass door when it is damaged maliciously, or have been injured by a bottle that someone has thrown in a public house intending only to cause damage. Less clear are cases when the victim has been stalked, or has been the recipient of threatening telephone calls, or there has been indecent exposure. Possible tests involve the intent and the proximity of the perpetrator, and whether the circumstances caused the victim to apprehend immediate physical harm (see para 9(a) of the Scheme). There can be difficult problems when sexual abuse is alleged and consent is an issue: see para 9(c) of the Scheme and a helpful discussion in *R v CICAP, ex parte August* [2001] QB 774. It should be borne in mind, however, that a defendant can be found guilty of assault occasioning actual bodily harm where that harm takes the form of psychiatric or psychological injury.

SECONDARY VICTIMS

22.19 When a secondary victim has suffered psychological injury because of the effect of a criminal injury on another person, who has sustained physical injury, the secondary victim may qualify for compensation. The class of victims who may recover is limited by rules set out in para 9(b) of the Scheme, which substantially follow the principles of *McLoughlin v O'Brian*.[3] In particular the Scheme provides that to recover the claimant must have had a close relationship of love and affection, which still subsists, with the person physically injured, and must also either have witnessed and been present on the occasion when the other person sustained physical injury or have been closely involved in the immediate aftermath. The nature of the injury which can be compensated is identified in para 9 as a 'medically recognised psychiatric or psychological illness' and is described in the tariff under the heading 'Mental illness and

---

[2] [1987] 3 All ER 854.
[3] [1983] AC 410.

temporary mental anxiety'. It can attract awards from level 1 to 18, and medical verification (for level 1) or confirmation by psychiatric diagnosis is required.

ELIGIBILITY: ABSOLUTE BARS

22.20 Compensation cannot be recovered in the following circumstances (listed in approximate frequency of occurrence):

(1) For an injury sustained outside Great Britain (para 8 of the Scheme). This excludes Northern Ireland which has its own similar Scheme. 'Great Britain' is given an extended definition. Importantly it includes British ships. It also includes lighthouses off the coast of Great Britain, installations on the continental shelf, the English part of the Channel Tunnel system, and British aircraft and hovercraft: see Notes 1 and 2 to the 2001 Scheme, which differ slightly in respect of the Tunnel from those in the 1996 Scheme.

(2) For a criminal injury sustained before 1 August 1964, which is the date the first Scheme was introduced (para 6 of the Scheme). This provision has been applied in abuse claims which have been submitted very long after the abuse occurred, and in which waiver of the time limit has been sought.

(3) When a previous application for compensation has been lodged by the same claimant in respect of the same criminal injury (para 7(a) of the Scheme). Sometimes this can occur inadvertently, but second applications for the same injury can be lodged by optimistic claimants who hope to obtain an award despite an earlier failed claim, or who hope to take advantage of an increased tariff amount in the later Scheme.

(4) When the injury is attributable to the use of a vehicle, except when the vehicle was deliberately used to inflict or attempt to inflict injury (para 11 of the Scheme).

(5) When the injury was sustained before 1 October 1979 at a time when the victim and assailant were living together as members of the same family (para 7(b) of the Scheme), sometimes referred to as 'the same roof rule'. The reason for the rule, which has been challenged unsuccessfully several times and is presently under challenge again, is that in pre-1979 Schemes recovery was excluded because of the perceived difficulties of proof which would arise in same roof situations, where there were rarely witnesses available. The bar was removed when the 1979 Scheme was introduced on 1 October 1979, but it was not removed retrospectively and the bar has survived with historical effect in all later Schemes. It still arises relatively frequently with adult claimants who say they were abused as children within the home. Whether they were living with their assailant or abuser is a question of fact, and the phrase 'members of the same family' is to be

given its ordinary sensible meaning. In *R v CICB, ex parte Staten* [1972] 1 All ER 1034 the parties were 'living together' though the evidence given was that they slept apart and the wife provided neither cleaning nor cooking for her husband.

(6) When at the time the injury was sustained the victim and any assailant were living in the same household as members of the same family, unless the assailant has been prosecuted in connection with the offence (except when there were practical, technical or other good reasons why a prosecution was not brought); and in the case of violence between adults in the family, the claimant and the assailant had stopped living in the same household before the application for compensation was made and were unlikely to share the same household again (para 17 of the Scheme). A man and a woman living together as husband and wife would be treated as members of the same family.

(7) Unless there is no likelihood that an assailant would benefit if an award were made (para 15(a) of the Scheme). In the case of minors where the risk is that premature death could leave the award to an assailant parent, the likelihood can be circumvented by keeping the money on deposit, through the CICA, until the child is of age and using para 50 of the Scheme to provide that the balance of the award is returned to the CICA upon death before majority. More acute problems arise where the assailant may be able to influence the victim to hand over some or all of the award, where a woman continues to have occasional contact with the boyfriend who injured her, or where a severely disabled child is being cared for by a reformed parent who was party to the assault that maimed the child.

ELIGIBILITY: DISCRETIONARY BARS

22.21 The Schemes are associated with the criminal justice system, and include in their objectives the assisting of blameless victims of violent crime and support for the prosecution of violent offenders. Paragraph 13 (and 14 of the 2001 Scheme) contains five provisions which enable an award to be withheld or reduced when a claimant has fallen short of its requirements. They are explained in some detail in 31 paras in part 4 of the CICA guide to the Scheme, which is available on the CICA website (cica.gov.uk). In summary an award may be withheld or reduced if:

(a) 'the applicant failed to take without delay all reasonable steps to inform the police or other body or person ... appropriate for the purpose, of the circumstances giving rise to the injury'. Until the circumstances of a crime are reported, investigation is delayed, and the circumstances cannot be verified. However a measure of delay is normally accepted in the case of young, elderly or incapacitated applicants.

(b) 'the applicant failed to cooperate with the police or other authority in attempting to bring the assailant to justice'.

(c) 'the applicant has failed to give all reasonable assistance to the CICA or other body or person in connection with the application'. If a claimant does not keep in touch with the CICA nor responds to enquiries, or will not attend a medical examination, it is difficult to resolve fairly any valid claim there may be.

(d) 'the conduct of the applicant before, during or after the incident giving rise to the application makes it inappropriate that a full award or any award at all be made'. It is provocative or reprehensible conduct, something which could fairly be called bad conduct or misconduct, which is taken into account, and not merely conduct amounting to 'contributory negligence': see *R v CICB ex parte Ince*.[4] Paragraph 14 of the 2001 Scheme added a provision which, when conduct is in issue, has allowed consideration to be given to the contribution of excessive consumption of alcohol or illicit use of drugs to the circumstances of the injury.

(e) 'the applicant's character as shown by any criminal convictions (excluding convictions spent ... at the date of application or death), or by evidence available to the claims officer, makes it inappropriate that a full or any award at all be made'. CICA operates a points system for assessing the extent to which an award should be reduced for convictions, and 10 points or over normally lead to CICA withholding any award. The more serious the conviction and sentence, the more points the conviction will attract. The details are set out in paras 19 to 26 of Part 4 of the CICA guide. It is irrelevant that a conviction has no bearing on the occurrence of the injury, or that a conviction is subsequent to the injury (*R v CICB ex parte Thompstone*,[5] and *R v CICB ex parte Thomas*[6]).

ATTRIBUTABILITY

22.22 The Schemes do not use the word 'causation', but provide for payment of compensation when the injury is 'directly attributable' to a relevant event. In *R v CICB ex parte Ince* (above) a widow whose police officer husband had been killed whilst answering an emergency call in his police car, and who made a claim under the 'law enforcement' provisions of the Scheme, had had her claim rejected on the grounds that his death was not directly attributable to the attempted prevention of an offence but to his own act of folly in crossing lights at red. In his judgment Lord Denning said:

---

[4] [1973] 3 All ER 808.
[5] [1984 3 All ER 572.
[6] [1995] PIQR P99.

'In my opinion "directly attributable" does not mean "solely attributable". It means directly attributable in whole or in part, to the state of affairs as PC Ince assumed them to be. If the death of PC Ince was directly attributable to his answering the call for help, it does not cease to be attributable because he was negligent or foolish in crossing the lights. In such a case there are two causes: (i) the call for help; (ii) his negligence or foolishness. His widow can rely on the first, even though the second exists.'

22.23 Although the Schemes make no reference to concepts of foreseeability or remoteness to limit the scope of claims, in cases involving secondary victims in both the English and Scottish courts judges supported the Board by holding that the use of the word 'directly' in the words 'directly attributable' was intended to impose a restrictive limitation on causation, and that proximity in space and time was relevant to whether an injury was directly, as opposed to indirectly attributable to the crime: see *R v CICB, ex parte K*,[7] and *CW v CICB* (available on CICAP website at www.tribunals.gov.uk). Although these cases involved claims by secondary victims, their decisions on the effect of the phrase 'directly attributable' are probably of wider application. (The current tariff rules as to attributability and secondary victims are dealt with at **22.19** above on secondary victims.)

HOW MUCH CAN BE RECOVERED?

22.24 The Schemes describe two principal heads of compensation. A 'standard amount of compensation' is payable for the injury identified in the tariff, and an 'additional amount' of compensation can be recovered for loss of earnings or earning capacity and for special expenses. There are also provisions as to how much can be recovered in fatal cases. The maximum award that may be made cannot exceed the cap of £500,000 and an injury, or the exacerbation of a pre-existing condition, must be sufficiently serious to qualify for the minimum award of £1,000 (paras 24 and 25 of the 2001 Scheme).

THE TARIFF INJURY AWARD

22.25 The award for an injury identified in the tariff attracts the 'standard amount of compensation'. (At the time of going to press, Parliament is considering amending the following rules in respect of victims of the terrorist bombings in London on 7 July 2005.) The amount is set out in a scale of 25 fixed levels of compensation. Claimants whose injuries do not qualify for the minimum award of £1,000 do not receive a tariff award, though lesser sums may be paid if a tariff award of £1,000 or more has been reduced under para 13, para 14 or para 15 of the Scheme. The highest level of 'standard' award is £250,000 for tetraplegia or extremely serious brain damage. If an injury is not identified in the tariff, the CICA can refer the injury to the

---

[7] [1998] 1 WLR 1458.

Secretary of State with a view to it being included and meanwhile an interim award can be made (paras 28 and 29 of the Scheme). However, this provision has been a rarely used. An injury can often be fairly placed in the general category of 'medically recognised illness/condition – not mental illness' which enables standard awards to be made from level 1 to level 17 (£22,000).

22.26 Awards of the standard amount of compensation are ring-fenced to the extent they are not subject to deductions for benefits or insurance payments (paras 45 and 47 of the Scheme). This is a change from common law Schemes where benefits and insurance payments were deductible from the overall total of the award. For deductions generally see **22.36** below.

MULTIPLE INJURIES

22.27 For claims made under the 1996 Scheme an applicant receives the full tariff amount for the highest-rated description of injury, 10% of the tariff amount for the second highest-rated injury, 5% for the third highest-rated injury, and there is no award for any further injuries. These proportions have been increased for claims made under the 2001 Scheme, and for the second and third injuries are now 30% and 15% (para 26 of the 1996 Scheme and 27 of the 2001 Scheme).

LOSS OF EARNINGS

22.28 An 'additional amount' of compensation is available to compensate for loss of earnings or earning capacity. An important qualification is that compensation for loss of earnings or earning capacity is not payable for the first 28 weeks of loss. Paragraphs 31–34 of the Scheme provide a code for assessing past and future loss, which is modelled on the common law approach, and provision is also made for a lump sum award for loss of earnings or earning capacity. There is a cap on the rate of net loss of one-and-a-half times gross average industrial earnings at the time of assessment. There is no provision in the Scheme for the payment of interest on past losses or payments, and no power to pay it. The treatment of future loss and of deductions in tariff claims differs from the approach in a claim in the civil courts for damages, and the Schemes have their own rules for each: see 'Multipliers for Future Loss' and 'Deductions for benefits and other payments' at **22.33–35** and **22.36** below.

COMPENSATION FOR SPECIAL EXPENSES

22.29 There is also an 'additional amount' of compensation available for 'special expenses', as described in paras 35 and 36 of the Scheme, where six heads of recovery are identified. Outside of these, special expenses are not recoverable. An important qualification to all these heads of claim is that 'special expenses' only become payable where the claimant has been incapacitated to the extent of losing earnings or earning capacity for longer than 28 weeks, although once payable they are paid from the date of the injury. The permitted heads of compensation cover:

(i) loss or damage to property or equipment of the claimant used as a physical aid (eg spectacles or false teeth, though the 28-week incapacity qualification precludes recovery of such expenses in many claims);

(ii) the costs of health treatment including private treatment if it and its cost are reasonable (this will include prescription and dental charges);

(iii) the reasonable cost to the claimant of special equipment (eg a wheel chair and hoist);

(iv) the reasonable cost to the claimant of adaptations to accommodation;

(v) the reasonable cost to the claimant of care (including residential care and unpaid care);

(vi) Court of Protection costs.

FATAL CASES

22.30 Where a victim has died in consequence of the injury, compensation is recoverable by a wide class of close relatives identified as 'qualifying claimants', but only funeral expenses may be recovered for the benefit of the estate. The Schemes provide for the payment of a standard amount of compensation at level 13 (£10,000 in the 1996 Scheme, and £11,000 in the 2001 Scheme) to a single qualifying claimant, or where there is more than one qualifying claimant each claimant can be paid a level 10 award, which is half that amount. Additional compensation can be claimed by qualifying claimants who were financially or physically dependent on the deceased victim, and annual payments for children to age 18 for loss of a parent's services are standardised at level 5 (£2,000), but can be increased for other resultant losses. Paragraphs 40 and 41 of the Scheme provide for calculation of a dependency by way of lump sum payment on the lines of a Fatal Accidents Act dependency, though different rules apply to the treatment of benefits (paras 40 and 45 of the Scheme), pensions (para 47), and multipliers (paras 32 and 41).

22.31 Qualifying claimants include not only spouses and partners but also the parents and children ('accepted' as such as well as 'natural', and of any age) of the deceased victim. A spouse can include a former spouse who was financially dependent on the deceased immediately before the death. A partner, who must have lived in the same household as the deceased throughout two years before the date of death, includes a same sex partner. The provision for compensation arising from the death of a same sex partner was introduced by the 2001

Scheme. It is not retrospective and is only available in respect of injuries incurred on or after 1 April 2001(para 83 of 2001 Scheme).

22.32 Supplementary compensation may be paid in the relatively rare cases where the victim has died otherwise than in consequence of the injury but before compensation for financial loss has been awarded. Payment is limited to loss of earnings (except for the first 28 weeks of loss) and special expenses incurred, and is only payable to 'qualifying claimants' who were financially dependent on the deceased (para 44 of the Scheme).

MULTIPLIERS FOR FUTURE LOSS

22.33 *1996 Scheme cases.* Paragraph 32 of the 1996 Scheme refers to Note 3 which includes a summary table illustrating the applicable multiplier for various periods of future loss. The paragraph also includes reference to using actuarial tables (the Ogden Tables). The Note 3 table was prepared when interest rates were higher, and differing multipliers now result depending upon whether one uses the Note 3 table or the Ogden Tables with low interest rates. For short periods the Note 3 table is the more favourable to applicants. Which to use is a matter for individual approach in each case.

22.34 *2001 Scheme cases.* Paragraph 32 of the 2001 Scheme identifies three tables in a new Note 3. The tables are to be referred to when assessing the appropriate multiplier in future loss claims (Table A), the discount to be applied for accelerated receipt of compensation (Table B), and male and female life expectancy (Table C) (which can be relevant in pension calculations and when a whole life claim arises). Adjustments to take account of other relevant factors and contingencies may be made. In 2001 Scheme claims, use of the Ogden tables is no longer available as an alternative to the Note 3 tables when assessing future loss multipliers.

22.35 The CICA has to follow the normal judicial approach to the assessment of general and special damages, though it need not follow the multiplier/multiplicand approach slavishly: *R v Criminal Injuries Compensation Board, ex parte Cummins.*[8]

DEDUCTION OF BENEFITS AND OTHER PAYMENTS

22.36 The treatment of deductions in the Scheme has its own rules which vary from those which apply in a civil action for damages (see paras 45–47 of the Scheme).

(a) Loss of earnings and special expenses claims are reduced by the full value of social security benefits or insurance payments made by way of

---

[8] [1992] PIQR Q81.

compensation for the same contingency, although the reduction only applies to the categories or periods of loss for which the additional or supplementary compensation is payable. This means, for example, that the care element of DLA benefits is not deducted from a loss of earnings claim but would be liable to be deducted from a claim for special expenses for the cost of care. Payments under insurance arrangements personally effected, paid for and maintained by the personal income of the victim are disregarded, save in respect of claims for special expenses for private health treatment, special equipment, adaptations to accommodation, care and Court of Protection costs (para 45(c) of the Scheme).

(b) Compensation paid for loss of earnings and for a dependency is also reduced to take account of pensions accruing as a result of the injury. Pensions are given a wide meaning. They are defined as any payment payable as a result of the injury or death in pursuance of pension or any other rights connected with the victim's employment, and include gratuities and benefits payable by insurance policies paid for by the victim's employers. Only pension payments accruing solely as a result of payments by victim or a dependant are disregarded. Where pensions are taxable only half their value is deducted though they are otherwise deducted in full.

MAKING A CLAIM

22.37 An application for compensation has to be made on the form provided by the CICA, and there is now provision for it to be made online on the CICA website (cica.gov.uk). There is a two-year time limit for applying, with power to waive the limit if it is reasonable and in the interests of justice to do so (para 18 of the Scheme). When a claim is received CICA make enquiries of the police or other appropriate authority to help them reach a decision on eligibility, and of hospitals, doctors and dentists the claimant has attended for treatment, to reach a decision on the appropriate award. The decision is made by a civil servant (a 'claims officer'). It takes the CICA on average eight months to collect the information it needs and reach its decision. If dissatisfied, the claimant can ask for the decision to be reviewed by a more senior claims officer. If still dissatisfied the claimant has 90 days from the date of the review decision to appeal to CICAP. There is power to extend or waive the time limit. Appeals can similarly be made online on the CICAP website (www.tribunals.gov.uk).

APPEALS TO CICAP

22.38 Although there is power in the Scheme to consider and dismiss appeals on paper, in practice all appeals now go to an oral hearing. The time that elapses before an appeal is heard is variable. It depends substantially on the complexity of the case and the time taken by the CICA to prepare it for hearing, and on the availability and cooperation of other parties, not least police witnesses and the applicant and his advisers. The target for hearing a straightforward case is within 6 months of appeal.

PREPARATION OF CASE BEFORE HEARING

22.39 When the CICA has collected the evidence it intends to use at the appeal, it prepares a list of documents (which includes witness statements which have been provided to the CICA) and a hearing summary, which are sent to the claimant or his representative. The summary identifies the issues raised and outlines the case the CICA will make at the hearing. It also contains a list of witnesses who will be invited to attend. Once the documents to be used at the hearing have been agreed the appeal is usually ready to be listed by CICAP. Some matters on which action may be needed in the period before the hearing are:

(a) The list of witnesses may include a convicted or alleged assailant or abuser. In the interests of fairness such persons usually have to be invited to hearings involving eligibility issues. They rarely attend. If an assailant has indicated a wish to attend, and a meeting might cause the claimant distress, CICAP can make arrangements for claimant and witness to be kept apart at the hearing, though CICAP must obviously be given reasonable warning that that is what the claimant wants.

(b) There is no onus on the CICA to search out evidence in a case. It is for a claimant to make out a case at the hearing (para 64 of the Scheme), and if eligibility is in issue the CICA will usually obtain evidence from the police and invite relevant witnesses identified by the police. However witnesses are not compellable, and those invited may well not attend. If it is considered those or other witnesses can support the appeal with oral evidence it is for the claimant to ask or persuade them to attend. If circumstances indicate that evidence exists which supports the claimant's case but it is not of a nature that the claimant can obtain, the claimant should draw its existence to the notice of CICA. Thus in *R v CICB, ex parte A*[9] a rehearing was ordered after a board had rejected an appellant's claim without sight of the report of a contemporaneous medical examination by a police doctor undertaken after an allegation of rape.

(c) If eligibility is not in issue and the hearing is for assessment, the documents will probably comprise only medical (or other expert) reports, possibly GP records, and the CICA's calculations in respect of any claim made for loss of earnings. There is a standard form of directions for financial loss claims (available on CICAP website www.tribunals.gov.uk) which indicates the nature of the documents which should be submitted on behalf of a claimant well in advance of a hearing. If there is any

---

[9] [1999] 2 WLR 974.

dispute about the sums in CICA's calculations, the claimant or his advisers should submit their own calculations or schedule well before the hearing date.

(d) If eligibility is in issue the hearing is likely to be in a city near the location of the incident, but if the only issue is assessment, a city venue convenient for the claimant and his representatives could be provided if requested.

(e) If there is an issue of eligibility as well as reasonably complex matters of assessment to prepare, CICA or CICAP may agree in advance to a split hearing, deciding eligibility first.

(f) If a further witness statement or medical evidence has been obtained, it should be submitted to CICA (or CICAP) at least two weeks before the date of the hearing, so that it can reach the adjudicators, or there is a risk it will not be accepted at a hearing.

(g) Although the Schemes provide that hearings will take place in private, this conflicts with Art 6 of the European Convention on Human Rights which provides that everyone is entitled to a public hearing. If given adequate notice CICAP will arrange a public hearing at a suitable venue (not all venues used are suitable) for any claimant who asks in good time. Also if asked by a claimant the CICAP decision can be published, which is another HRC option, by placing it on the internet.

PROCEDURE AT THE HEARING

22.40 The procedure to be followed at the hearing is a matter for the adjudicators. There are also some rules, contained in paras 72–78 of the Scheme, which assist.

(a) The appeal is a determination of the application afresh, and an award may be refused even if one has been offered initially: see *R v CICB, ex parte Lain*.[10] This can be a risk if there have been further convictions.

(b) The burden of proof, which is on the balance of probabilities, is placed on the claimant (para 64 of the Scheme).

(c) A claimant may bring a legal adviser or friend into the hearing to assist in presenting the claim, or for moral support. However the costs of representation will not be met, though the panel will normally meet the reasonable costs of attendance of the claimant and any witnesses (para 74 of the Scheme).

---

[10] [1967] 2 QB 864.

(d) The panel is not bound by the rules of evidence which prevent a court from admitting any document or other matter or statement in evidence. Hearsay and opinion evidence are commonly accepted from witnesses and the strict rules of evidence applied to the admissibility of documents are not applied.

(e) Hearings take place before two or three panel members (called adjudicators in the Scheme), one of whom is invariably a lawyer, though that is not a requirement of the Scheme. Unlike the Board, which comprised only lawyers, the panel also includes lay and medically qualified members. The CICA presenting officer will also be present. The proceedings are by way of inquiry. They should not be conducted adversarially, and should be as informal as is consistent with the proper determination of what can sometimes amount to serious allegations.

(f) At the start of the hearing the issues are invariably introduced by the chairman. If the hearing is on eligibility the claimant may either be asked to give his own account of relevant events, or he may at once be asked questions about the claim by the CICA's presenting officer. A police officer is usually called as a witness by the CICA. If the issue is assessment it is likely that, after the introduction, the claimant will be asked to give any evidence that may be needed, and if it is not apparent from the papers, asked what compensation is being sought. After evidence and submissions there is likely to be a short interval for the adjudicators to consider their decision, which is then normally given orally.

MEDICAL EVIDENCE

22.41 It is rare for medical witnesses to attend a hearing, and medical evidence is usually taken from reports. The CICA if asked will usually obtain and pay for further reports from treating doctors, but if a report is sought from a non-treating consultant it will probably not be funded by CICA. However the cost of a report can be sought from the panel at the conclusion of the hearing.

22.42 Reports should substantiate the injuries sustained in the incident, and describe their nature and the treatment required. There is seldom a need for a report with a detailed prognosis of the kind seen in personal injury litigation. The tariff is often concerned with the distinction between disabilities in which there has been recovery and those which are permanent or continuing; or between substantial recovery and continuing significant disability. Sometimes an assessment of how long the injury remained disabling is required. These issues can be helpfully addressed in the reports, without the need for a detailed prognosis. Another reason why a detailed prognosis may not be needed is that there is power to reopen a claim (see below). Any significant deterioration (such as supervening epilepsy, or incapacity from osteoarthritis) can be compensated when and if it occurs rather than at a hearing on the basis of a prognosis and probabilities.

22.43 If medical evidence is incomplete at a hearing, or there has been a split hearing with eligibility determined first, and only assessment remains to be decided, a retrospective provision introduced in the 2001 Scheme (para 77) enables adjudicators to adjourn the claim to one of themselves for determination on the papers. If then dissatisfied with the award, the claimant can ask for a further oral hearing. On adjourning a hearing there is power to make an interim payment.

RE-OPENING CASES FOR MEDICAL DETERIORATION

22.44 An award accepted or an adjudicators' decision is normally regarded as final, but where there has been such a change in the victim's medical condition that injustice would occur if the original assessment were allowed to stand, the CICA (to whom application should be made) has power to re-open the claim: see para 57 of the Scheme for details of the evidence required.

FURTHER APPEALS

22.45 A decision by CICAP is final and there is no appeal to the Secretary of State (para 3 of the Scheme). Since its inception however decisions under the Schemes have been challenged by way of judicial review. The change from ex gratia to statutory Scheme has not altered that, and there is now a body of reported case law on the effect of the provisions of the Scheme. A summary and the text of many of the decisions can be found on CICAP's website (www.tribunals.gov.uk).

THE FUTURE

22.46 As part of the changes resulting from the creation of a Tribunals Service, CICAP's sponsoring department changed from the Home Office to the DCA in 2006. This has not had any immediate effect on the substance of the Scheme and is unlikely to affect the nature and route of appeals that can be made from CICAP decisions. The present procedure by way of Judicial Review is unlikely to be altered. The changeover may also lead to the formulation and formalisation of rules of procedure for CICAP appeals, but none have so far been put forward.

Chapter 23

REHABILITATION

23.1 Rehabilitation can take many forms:

- It may improve the claimant's medical condition, whether by surgery, physiotherapy, specialist advice or counselling.

- It may help a dependent claimant to live independently.

- It may reduce the need for care, even if it cannot eliminate it altogether.

- It may get a claimant previously thought unemployable back into work.

- It may suggest a regime of treatment, aids and appliances, and case management that will speed up the recovery progress.

On the other hand, of course, it may do no good at all, and all that may be achieved is the knowledge that the claimant's condition is indeed intractable, unlikely to improve, and likely to call for expensive care and other costs for the rest of his life.

23.2 To an injured person, rehabilitation will usually be of greater concern than compensation. Most litigants would rather get back their health, if they could, even if that meant their damages would be lower. Claimants' lawyers, however, have often pursued compensation at the expense of rehabilitation. In 1999, however, a 'Code of Best Practice on Rehabilitation, Early Intervention and Medical Treatment in Personal Injury Claims' was introduced, as the result of consultation between insurers and personal injury lawyers. All the evidence had gone to show that the earlier rehabilitation was made available, the better a recovery a claimant was likely to make, and the more readily he or she was able to re-integrate into society. The benefits of rehabilitation to both parties are obvious. As the introduction to the Code said:

> 'Solicitors acting for claimants understand that, taking all these matters into account, they can achieve more for the claimant – by making rehabilitation available – than just the payment of compensation. The insurance industry realises that great benefit may be had in considering making funds available for these purposes.'

23.3 The Code promotes 'the use of rehabilitation and early intervention in the claims process so that the injured person makes the best and quickest possible medical, social and psychological recovery':

- It is available irrespective of the severity of the original injury sustained by the claimant.

- It is optional.

- It acknowledges that it only contains one approach to rehabilitation; there may well be others.

- It is compatible with the Personal Injury protocols in the Civil Procedure Rules 1998 (CPR), but following the Code does not relieve either party of its obligations under the CPR.

23.4 The Code (which is set out in full in the annual publication 'Facts & Figures') is written in straightforward English, and the remainder of this Chapter sets out is main provisions.

1. The duty of the claimant's solicitor is to discuss the claimant's needs at the earliest possible stage, with a view to putting rehabilitation proposals to the defendant or its insurer.
    a. The Claimant's solicitor must discuss with the claimant or his family whether there is a role for early intervention, rehabilitation or medical treatment. The earlier this is done, the more likely rehabilitation is to be effective. Is there an immediate need for aids or adaptations?
    b. It is not up to the solicitor to take medical decisions, or to plan rehabilitation: that is for the experts. However, the solicitor needs to be able to put before the insurer enough information to enable the insurer to make an informed decision about the claimant's needs.
    c. All this may be done before any medical evidence has been commissioned.

2. The duty of the Insurer
    a. The insurer has a similar duty to that of the claimant's solicitor to consider whether this Claimant will benefit from rehabilitation and, if it considers that he will, to communicate this to the claimant's solicitor.
    b. If the insurer puts proposals to the claimant's solicitor, the solicitor must discuss them with the claimant or his family, and where appropriate seek advice from the claimant's treating doctors.

3. Nothing in this or any other Code of Practice shall in any way modify the obligations of the insurer under the Protocol to investigate claims rapidly and in any event within three months (except where time is extended by the claimant's solicitor) from the date of the formal claim letter. It is recognised that, although the rehabilitation assessment can be done even where liability investigations are outstanding, it is essential that such investigations proceed with the appropriate speed.

4   The Assessment
    a   Unless rehabilitation needs have already been identified, there should be an independent assessment of the claimant's needs.
    b   The Code defines 'independent assessment' as one carried out by:
        i   One or more of the treating doctors, or
        ii By an appropriate agency that is fully independent of the claimant's solicitor an of the insurers.
    c   The assessment must be carried out by a qualified and experienced doctor, physiotherapist, occupational therapist, or as may be.
    d   The parties should where possible agree the identity of the doctor or agency that will be invited to report. The Claimant's solicitor will send the letter of instruction, and send a copy of the letter to the insurer. The letter of instructions should request a report covering:
        • The claimant's injuries;
        • The claimant's present medical condition;
        • The claimant's domestic circumstances, including mobility, accommodation and employment;
        • Where early intervention or rehabilitation might help;
        • What type of intervention is envisage;
        • The likely cost; and
        • The likely benefit to the claimant in the short term and the medium term.

5   The Assessment Report
    a   The assessment report[1] is wholly without prejudice to the litigation process. It is crucial that the parties understand this. Claimant's solicitors are often suspicious of such cooperation with insurers, but the Code specifically says that 'Neither side can therefore rely on its contents in any subsequent litigation. With that strict proviso, to be confirmed in writing by the individual solicitor and insurer if required, the report shall be disclosed to both parties.' It follows that an expert involved in the rehabilitation process is not a compellable witness should the matter proceed to trial.
    b   The report should be sent to both parties simultaneously. The insurer will pay for it within 28 days of receipt.
    c   Both parties can question the maker of the report, which they should disclose to the other side.
    d   Although the assessment report itself is outside the litigation process, any regime set up as a result of the report falls outside the Code. This means that notes and reports generated by those implementing a rehabilitation regime are governed by the rules relating to disclosure of the claimant's documents and medical records.

6   The Report's recommendations
    a   The insurer is obliged to consider the report's recommendations and decide how much money to make available.

---

[1] Or reports: there may be more than one.

b   The claimant is not obliged to undergo investigation or treatment that he regards as unreasonable.
c   The insurer is not obliged to pay for rehabilitation it regards as 'unreasonable in nature, content or cost'.
d   Such funds as the insurer makes available are to be regarded as an interim payment. When drafting the Schedule, therefore, the claimant must ensure that he includes the cost of the treatment he has undergone, to be set off against the interim payment(s).
e   Once the insurer has paid for rehabilitation it cannot later challenge the reasonableness of the cost.

Conclusions

- There is no limit to the categories of rehabilitation. Rehabilitation may involve medical treatment, case management, aids and appliances, housing adaptations, or a mixture of all of these.

- If it is in the insurer's financial interest to see whether the claimant's condition can be improved, it is no less in the claimant's interest to reclaim as much independence as possible.

- Because the process is without prejudice, the claimant cannot lose by undergoing assessment.

- A claimant who has been through the process described will be in a strong position to argue that he has done all that could reasonably be required of him to improve his condition; the conclusion of a medical expert that his condition is unlikely to improve in the future will have the merit of having been tested by the rehabilitation process. Although the point has yet to be tested, it would in theory be open to insurers to argue that failure to cooperate with the spirit of the Code amounted to a failure to mitigate his losses.

- The Bodily Injury Claims Management Association have produced a detailed Practitioner's Guide to Rehabilitation, which promotes the services of the Claims Management Society of the UK (CMSUK). The Guide is set out as an appendix to this chapter.

THE REHABILITATION CODE, EARLY INTERVENTION AND MEDICAL TREATMENT IN PERSONAL INJURY CASES

1. Introduction

23.5 It is recognised that, in many claims for damages for personal injuries, the claimant's current medical situation, and/or the long-term prognosis, may be improved by appropriate medical treatment, including surgery, being given at the earliest practicable opportunity, rather than waiting until the claim has been settled. Similarly, claims may involve a need for non-medical treatment, such as physiotherapy, counselling, occupational therapy, speech therapy and so forth ('rehabilitation'): again, there is a benefit in these services being provided as early as practicable.

23.6 It is also recognised that (predominantly in cases of serious injury) the claimant's quality of life can be immediately improved by undertaking some basic home adaptations and/or by the provision of aids and equipment and/or appropriate medical treatment as soon as these are needed ('early intervention'), rather than when the claim is finally settled.

23.7 It is further recognised that, where these medical or other issues have been dealt with, there may be employment issues that can be addressed for the benefit of the claimant, to enable the claimant to keep his/her existing job, to obtain alternative suitable employment with the same employer or to retrain for new employment. Again, if these needs are addressed at the proper time, the claimant's quality of life and long-term prospects may be greatly improved.

23.8 Solicitors acting for claimants understand that, taking all these matters into account, they can achieve more for the claimant – by making rehabilitation available – than just the payment of compensation. The insurance industry realises that great benefit may be had in considering making funds available for these purposes.

23.9 The aim of this Rehabilitation Code is therefore to ensure that the claimant's solicitor and the insurer (and the insurer's solicitor or handling agent) both actively consider the use of rehabilitation services and the benefits of an early assessment of the claimant's needs. The further aim is that both should treat the possibility of improving the claimant's quality of life and their present and long-term physical and mental well-being as issues equally as important as the payment of just, full and proper compensation.

23.10 The report mentioned in section 6 of the Code focuses on the early assessment of the claimant's needs in terms of treatment and/or rehabilitation. The assessment report is not intended to determine the claimant's long-term needs for care or medical treatment, other than by way of general indication and comment.

2. The claimant's solicitors duty

23.11 It shall be the duty of every claimant's solicitor to consider, from the earliest practicable stage, and in consultation with the claimant and/or the claimant's family, whether it is likely or possible that early intervention, rehabilitation or medical treatment would improve their present and/or long-term physical or mental well-being. This duty is ongoing throughout the life of the case but is of most importance in the early stages.

23.12 It shall be the duty of a claimant's solicitor to consider, with the claimant and/or the claimant's family, whether there is an immediate need for aids, adaptations or other matters that would seek to alleviate problems caused by disability, and then to communicate with the insurer as soon as practicable about any rehabilitation needs, with a view to putting this Code into effect.

23.13 It shall not be the responsibility of the solicitor to decide on the need for treatment or rehabilitation or to arrange such matters without appropriate medical consultation. Such medical consultation should involve the claimant and/or the claimant's family, the claimant's primary care physician and, where appropriate, any other medical practitioner currently treating the claimant.

23.14 Nothing in this Code shall in any way affect the obligations placed on a claimant's solicitor by the Pre-Action Protocol for Personal Injury Claims ('the Protocol'). However, it must be appreciated that very early communication with the insurer will enable the matters dealt with here to be addressed more effectively.

23.15 It must be recognised that the insurer will need to receive from the claimant's solicitor sufficient information for the insurer to make a proper decision about the need for intervention, rehabilitation or treatment. To this extent, the claimant's solicitor must comply with the requirements of the Protocol to provide the insurer with full and adequate details of the injuries sustained by the claimant, the nature and extent of any, or any likely, continuing disability and any suggestions that may already have been made concerning rehabilitation and/or early intervention. There is no requirement under the Protocol, or this Code, for the claimant's solicitor to have obtained a full medical report. It is recognised that many cases will be identified for consideration under this Code before medical evidence has actually been commissioned.

3. The insurer

23.16 It shall be the duty of the insurer to consider, from the earliest practicable stage in any appropriate case, whether it is likely that the claimant will benefit in the immediate, medium or longer term from further medical treatment, rehabilitation or early intervention. This duty is ongoing throughout the life of the case but is of most importance in the early stages.

23.17 If the insurer considers that a particular claim might be suitable for intervention, rehabilitation or treatment, the insurer will communicate this to the claimant's solicitor as soon as practicable.

23.18 On receipt of such communication, the claimant's solicitor will immediately discuss these issues with the claimant and/or the claimant's family pursuant to his duty as set out above and, where appropriate, will seek advice from the claimant's treating physicians/surgeons.

23.19 Nothing in this or any other Code of Practice shall in any way modify the obligations of the insurer under the Protocol to investigate claims rapidly and in any event within three months (except where time is extended by the claimant's solicitor) from the date of the formal claim letter. It is recognised that, although the rehabilitation assessment can be done even where liability investigations are outstanding, it is essential that such investigations proceed with the appropriate speed.

4. Assessment

23.20 Unless the need for intervention, rehabilitation or treatment has already been identified by medical reports obtained and disclosed by either side, the need for and extent of such intervention, rehabilitation or treatment will be considered by means of an independent assessment.

23.21 'Independent assessment' in this context means that the assessment will be carried out by either:
    a. One or more of the treating physicians/surgeons, or
    b. By an agency suitably qualified and/or experienced in such matters, which is financially and managerially independent of the claimant's solicitor's firm and the insurers dealing with the claim.

23.22 It is essential that the process of assessment and recommendation be carried out by those who have an appropriate qualification (to include physiotherapists, occupational therapists, psychologists, psychotherapists and so forth). It would be inappropriate for assessments to be done by someone who does not have a medical or other appropriate qualification. Those doing the assessments should not only have an appropriate qualification but should have experience in treating the type of disability from which the individual claimant suffers.

5. The assessment process

23.23 Where possible, the agency to be instructed to provide the assessment should be agreed between the claimant's solicitor and the insurer. The instruction letter will be sent by the claimant's solicitor to the medical agency and a copy of the instruction letter will be sent to the insurer.

23.24 The medical agency will be asked to interview the claimant at home (or in hospital, if the claimant is still in hospital, with a subsequent visit to the claimant's home) and will be asked to produce a report, which covers the following headings:

1. The injuries sustained by the claimant

2. The claimant's present medical condition (medical conditions that do not arise from the accident should also be noted where relevant to the overall picture of the claimant's needs)

3. The claimant's domestic circumstances (including mobility, accommodation and employment), where relevant

4. The injuries/disability in respect of which early intervention or early rehabilitation is suggested

5. The type of intervention or treatment envisaged

6. The likely cost

7. The likely short/medium-term benefit to the claimant

23.25 The report will not deal with diagnostic criteria, causation issues or long-term care requirements.

6. The assessment report

23.26 The reporting agency will, on completion of the report, send copies to both the instructing solicitor and the insurer simultaneously. Both parties will have the right to raise queries on the report, disclosing such correspondence to the other party.

23.27 It is recognised that for this independent assessment report to be of benefit to the parties, it should be prepared and used wholly outside the litigation process. Neither side can therefore rely on its contents in any subsequent litigation. With that strict proviso, to be confirmed in writing by the individual solicitor and insurer if required, the report shall be disclosed to both parties.

23.28 The report, any correspondence relating to it and any notes created by the assessing agency will be covered by legal privilege and will not under any circumstances be disclosed in any legal proceedings. Any notes or documents created in connection with the assessment process will not be disclosed in any litigation, and any person involved in the preparation of the report or involved in the assessment process shall not be a compellable witness at court.

23.29 The provision in **23.28** above as to treating the report, etc. as outside the litigation process is limited to the assessment report and any notes relating to it. Once the parties have agreed, following an assessment report, that a particular regime of rehabilitation or treatment should be put in place, the case management of that regime falls outside this Code and paragraph 6.3 does not therefore apply. Any notes and reports created during the subsequent case management will be governed by the usual principles relating to disclosure of documents and medical records relating to the claimant.

23.30 The insurer will pay for the report within 28 days of receipt.

23.31 The need for any further or subsequent assessment shall be agreed between the claimant's solicitor and the insurer. The provisions of this Code shall apply to such assessments.

7. Recommendations

23.32 When the assessment report is disclosed to the insurer, the insurer will be under a duty to consider the recommendations made and the extent to which funds will be made available to implement all or some of the recommendations. The insurer will not be required to pay for intervention or treatment that is unreasonable in nature, content or cost. The claimant will be under no obligation to undergo intervention, medical investigation or treatment that is unreasonable in all the circumstances of the case.

23.33 Any funds made available shall be treated as an interim payment on account of damages. However, if the funds are provided to enable specific intervention, rehabilitation or treatment to occur, the insurers warrant that they will not, in any legal proceedings connected with the claim, dispute the reasonableness of that treatment nor the agreed cost, provided of course that the claimant has had the recommended treatment.

Part 3
PROCEDURE

Chapter 24

LIMITATION: RESUME AND UPDATE 2006

POLICY AND HISTORY

24.1 Since the Limitation Act 1623, which imposed a limitation period of 6 years in respect of causes of action essentially concerned with simple contract and tort, the legislature has recognised as a matter of policy that there should be finality and certainty in litigation. The 1623 Act also recognised that a fixed period of limitation could cause injustice and by s 7 of the Act provided that time would not run against a claimant who suffered under a disability. The 6-year period in which to bring an action based on simple contract or tort survived until the Law Reform (Limitation of Actions, etc) Act 1954, when the period for instituting proceedings with respect to personal injuries was reduced to 3 years. The 1954 Act did, however, abolish the limitation period of one year, then in force, in favour of public authorities as instituted by the Public Authorities Protection Act 1893 and the Limitation Act 1939.

24.2 One effect of the 1954 Act was to aggravate the harshness of limitation law when applied to imperceptible injury where time expired even before the diagnosis of incipient disease was possible. Following criticism of these hard cases[1] the Limitation Act 1963 was enacted which introduced the concept of 'date of knowledge' which allowed a claimant to commence an action after 3 years if it could be demonstrated that material facts of a decisive character were outside his knowledge within the primary 3-year period. The 1963 Act allowed a claim to be initiated with leave if proceedings were started within 12 months of a claimant's date of knowledge. This period was extended to 3 years by the Law Reform (Miscellaneous Provisions) Act 1971.

24.3 The 1975 Limitation Act, following recommendations made by the Report on Limitations of Actions in Personal Injury Claims, Cmnd S630 (1974), invested the court for the first time with a discretion to disapply the primary limitation period if in all the circumstances of a case it was thought equitable to do so. The thinking behind the Committee's recommendations was to empower the court to investigate actual hardship arising from the operation of strict periods imposed both by the primary limitation period and by the claimant's date of knowledge.

24.4 The Limitation Act 1980, in force on 1 May 1981, consolidated all limitation legislation and now contains the total legislative code in respect of

---

[1] Cf *Cartledge v Jopling & Sons Limited* [1963] AC 758.

personal injury actions. Accrued defences that existed before the coming into force of the 1954 Act on 4 June 1954 are not affected by the 1963 and 1975 Acts (see *Arnold v Central Electricity Generating Board*,[2] reaffirmed in *McDonnell v Congregation of Christian Brothers Trustees*.[3] To date, attempts to establish that aspects of the English law of limitation are in breach of convention rights or contrary to the Human Rights Act 1998 have been unsuccessful (see *Stubbings v United Kingdom*,[4] *Dobbie v United Kingdom*,[5] *Young v Western Power Distribution (South West)*[6] and *Horton v Sadler*[7]).

24.5 The Consumer Protection Act 1987, which created a statutory cause of action for damages including those arising out of personal injury due to unsafe products, has caused a further amendment to the Limitation Act 1980, ss 14(1A) and 11A. Actions brought under the Act for damages arising out of the use of unsafe products may be brought within 3 years of the cause of action accruing or 3 years from the date when the claimant knew or could with reasonable diligence have discovered the existence of his cause of action. However, no such action under the Act may be brought after 10 years from when the product in question was last supplied. In *Horne-Roberts v Smithkline Beecham*[8] the Court of Appeal confirmed that s 35 of the Limitation Act applied to a s 11A case and permitted the substitution of the manufacturers of a batch of MMR vaccine outside of the 10-year period on the basis that the claimant had made a mistake in suing, within the 10 years, the wrong defendant (see also *O'Byrne v (1) Aventis Pasteur MSD Ltd (2) Aventis Pasteur SA*[9]).

THE PRIMARY LIMITATION PERIOD

24.6 Section 11 of the Limitation Act 1980 imposes a primary limitation period for actions in respect of personal injuries of 3 years from the date of the accrual of the cause of action, or 3 years from the date of knowledge of the person injured, if later. In cases brought on behalf of an estate following the death of the injured person, the limitation period is 3 years from the date of death or 3 years from the date of the personal representative's knowledge, whichever is later (s 11(5)). In fatal cases brought on behalf of a dependant under the Fatal Accident Act 1976, the dependants have 3 years to initiate an action from the date of death or 3 years from the date of knowledge of the person for whose benefit the action is brought, whichever is later (s 12). Further, in fatal cases under the Fatal Accidents Act 1976 where the action is

---

[2] [1998] AC 228.
[3] [2003] UK HL 63.
[4] (1997) 23 EHRR 213.
[5] 28477/95.
[6] [2003] 1 WLR 2868.
[7] [2006] UKHL 27.
[8] [2002] 1 WLR 1662.
[9] [2006] EWHC 2562.

brought for the benefit of more than one person, the limitation period is to be applied separately to each of the dependants with respect to their dates of knowledge.

24.7 There is no long-stop provision for personal injury actions except those brought alleging a beach of the Consumer Protection Act 1987 which prohibits any claim brought after the expiry of 10 years (s 11A).

24.8 In tort, a cause of action accrues when damage which is more than minimal occurs (see *Cartledge v Jopling*;[10] *Hopkins v MacKenzie*[11]). Time stops running when proceedings are issued and not from when they are served. In calculating the period of limitation, the day upon which the cause of action arose is excluded (*see Marren v Dawson Bentley & Co*[12]). Similarly, pursuant to Civil Procedure Rules 1998 (CPR), r 7.4(2) a claim form must be served within four months *after* the date of issue, which effectively ignores the day of issue in calculating the 4-month period. Conversely, the Particulars of Claim, if not served with the Claim Form, must be served within 14 days. If process cannot be issued because the court office is closed, as on a weekend or on a public holiday, the limitation period is effectively extended until the next date upon which the court is open for business (see CPR, r 2.8(5) and *Pritam Kaur v S. Russell & sons Limited*[13]). The relevant date for the issuing of proceedings is the date entered on the form by the court pursuant to CPR, r 7.2(2). If, however, a claim form is sent by post to the County Court office and it is received before the date of issue the proceedings will be deemed to have been brought on the date of receipt, not the date of issue. CPR 5PD5.1 requires that particulars of the date of delivery of any document delivered at court for filing must be entered on the court record. If a defendant learns that a Claim Form has been issued against him he can serve a notice on the claimant requiring him either to serve the form or to discontinue. If after 14 days from that notice the claimant has not complied the defendant may issue an application to the court, which may dismiss the claim or make any order it thinks fit.

24.9 Time does not run for a minor until the age of 18 is reached, and accordingly a minor has 3 years from the age of 18 to bring an action for personal injury (s 28(6)). Similarly a person suffering from a mental disability within the meaning of the Mental Health Act 1983, and who is thereby incapable of managing and administering his property and affairs, has 3 years to bring a claim after the cessation of the disability (ss 28 and 38(4)). There is therefore no limitation period in respect of a permanently brain-damaged claimant minor or adult who sues in respect of the incident which caused the brain damage, if he is a patient or likely to be one when his minority ends. Such

---

[10] [1963] AC 758.
[11] [1995] 6 Med LR 26.
[12] [1961] 2 QB 135.
[13] [1973] QB 336.

a person may have a claim brought in his name at any time including up to 3 years after his death. (See *Bull v Devon Health Authority*,[14] *Headford v Bristol and District Health Authority*.[15])

NEGLIGENCE, NUISANCE AND BREACH OF STATUTORY DUTY

24.10 Section 11 of the Limitation Act 1980 provides:

'11(1) This section applies to any action for damages for negligence, nuisance or breach of duty (whether the duty exists by virtue of a contract or of provision made by or under a statute or independently of any contract or any such provision) where the damages claimed by the plaintiff for the negligence, nuisance or breach of duty consist of or include damages in respect of personal injuries to the Plaintiff or any other person.'

24.11 The vast bulk of personal injury claims will fall within the scope of this section, as having been caused by negligence, nuisance or breach of duty. The major exception has been held by the House of Lords in *Stubbings v Webb*[16] to be those personal injuries resulting from deliberate assaults including sexual assault and rape. The primary limitation period for such causes of action is 6 years under s 2 of the Limitation Act 1980. This 6-year period is not subject to a claimant's date of knowledge nor is the court invested with any discretion to disapply the period. The European Court of Human Rights held in *Stubbings and others v UK*[17] that the House of Lords decision did not amount to a breach of Arts 6, 8 or 14 of the Convention. This decision raises a significant issue as to what is the appropriate limitation period in that class of action brought against medical practitioners based upon an allegation of failing to obtain consent for treatment. In *Dobbie v Medway Health Authority*[18] the then Master of the Rolls indicated that s 11 of the Limitation Action 1980 did not apply to actions in trespass for which no extension of time in law was permissible. It would appear therefore possible to have a claim with two causes of action, one alleging no consent for medical treatment based on trespass, which would have a limitation period of 6 years, and another based upon negligent treatment, which would have a 3-year period but subject to a date of knowledge provision and a possible extension under s 33 of the Limitation Act 1980. It might have been thought that in cases of so-called unintentional trespass the court would have construed the cause of action as essentially being based in negligence and apply the provisions of s 11 (see *Letang v Cooper*[19]); however the scope for doing so is limited by the court's decision in *Dobbie*.

---

[14] [1993] 4 Med LR 117.
[15] [1995] 6 Med LR 61.
[16] [1993] AC 498.
[17] [1997] 1 FLR 105.
[18] [1994] 4 All ER 450.
[19] [1965] 1 QN 232.

24.12 Claimants in sexual abuse cases can avoid the effects of *Stubbings* if they have a collateral claim based upon negligence. In *Seymour v Williams*[20] a child's claim against an abusive father was held statute barred under s 2 but the common law claim against the mother for failing to protect her child was held to be governed by s 11 and therefore also ss 14 and 33 were applicable. Similarly in *KR v Bryn Alyn Community (Holdings) Limited*[21] the court held that most of the sexual and physical assaults on the inmates of the defendants children's homes fell within the principles of vicarious liability as set out in *Lister v Hesley Hall Limited*[22] and as such the claims against the employers were governed by s 11 even though the claims against the individual perpetrators were governed by s 2. In *Bryn Alyn* the Court of Appeal endorsed the Law Commission's recommendation that claims for personal injury arising from trespass to the person should be included in the core regime governing personal injury within s 11(see para 100 per Lord Justice Auld and Law Com 151.) For cases applying the reasoning in *Bryn Alyn* see *C v D*,[23] *H v N* and *T*[24] and *C v Middlesbrough Council*.[25] In *A v Iorworth Hoare, H & Y v Various Defendants*[26] the Court of Appeal again called for this area of the law to be revisited by the House of Lords as it produced deficiency and incoherence. Further doubt over the limits of the Court of Appeals' reasoning in *Bryn Alyn* was expressed by a differently constituted Court of Appeal in *Catholic Care (Diocese of Leeds) v Young*.[27]

'CONSISTS OF OR INCLUDES DAMAGES IN RESPECT OF PERSONAL INJURIES TO THE PLAINTIFF OR ANY OTHER PERSON'

24.13 Section 38 of the 1980 Act defines personal injuries to include:

> 'Any disease and any impairment of a person's physical or mental condition and "injury" and cognate expressions shall be construed accordingly.'

This definition will *not* include professional negligence actions against solicitors who fail to launch personal injury actions in time or who fail to prevent a claim being struck out for want of prosecution (see Nicholls LJ in *Howe v David Brown Tractors (Retail) Limited*;[28] *Ackbar v Green*;[29] and *McGahie v Union of Shop Distributive and Allied Workers*.[30] However, if such a professional negligence action includes a claim for personal injury in the form of an anxiety

---

[20] [1995] 1 FLR 862.
[21] [2003] 3 WLR 107.
[22] [2001] 1 AC 215.
[23] [2004] All ER(D) 92.
[24] LTL 29 April 2004.
[25] [2004] EWCA Civ 1746.
[26] [2006] EWCA Civ 395.
[27] [2006] EWCA Civ 1534.
[28] [1991] 4 All ER 30.
[29] [1975] QB 582.
[30] [1966] SLT 74.

and stress condition caused by the solicitors' failure to handle a claim properly then the professional negligence action will be a personal injury claim and will be subject to the provisions of s 11 of the Limitation Act 1980. A claimant may not be allowed merely to jettison the personal injury claim in an attempt to obtain a longer period of limitation under s 2 or s 5 of the 1980 Act as in *Bennett v Greenland Houchen & Company*[31] and *Oates v Harte Reade*.[32] However, in *Shade v Compton Partnership*[33] the Court of Appeal said it found the reasoning in *Oates* as 'less than fully satisfactory' and took a more pragmatic view towards severing off a time barred personal injury claim, which was not very substantial, to permit a very substantial economic loss claim based on professional negligence to continue.

24.14 A claimant cannot avoid the provisions of s 11 of the 1980 Act by putting forward a claim as an economic loss of a partnership, firm or company if in fact the true nature of the loss is a loss of income or profit arising out of a personal injury occasioned to a partner or director. In *Howe* (above) the Court of Appeal held than an attempt by the claimant to add his father and his firm to an action so as to claim for the whole of the firm's loss of profit arising from the claimant's inability to work due to a personal injury, if such a claim existed as a matter of law at all, did not avoid the provisions of s 11 because the claim was for damages in respect of personal injuries to the claimant or to *any other person*.

24.15 A similar approach was taken by the Court of Appeal in *Walkin v South Manchester Health Authority*[34] where it was held that a failed sterilisation resulting in an unplanned pregnancy was a claim based on personal injury even if the mother did not bring a claim for the impairment to her health which the pregnancy created or for the pain and suffering of the birth. In *Walkin* the mother's claim was for the economic loss resulting from bringing up the unplanned child. The court held that the unwanted pregnancy was an impairment of the mother's physical condition within the definition of s 38 of the 1980 Limitation Act and damage was said to have occurred at the moment of conception. The court therefore would not allow the claimant to obtain the benefit of a 6-year limitation period by simply jettisoning her own personal claim for personal injury. Different considerations might, however, apply to a failed vasectomy (see *Pattison v Hobbs*;[35] *Naylor v Preston Area Health Authority*;[36] and *Allen v Bloomsbury Health Authority*[37]). In such cases, there obviously is no physical injury to the father when a claim is based upon the economic loss of bringing up a child as a result of a failed vasectomy. However, Auld LJ doubted this proposition and expressed a view that he could see no reason why a failed vasectomy was not a personal injury because it related to

---

[31] [1999] PIQR P120.
[32] [1998] PNLR 458.
[33] [2000] Lloyd's Rep PN 81.
[34] [1995] 4 All ER 132.
[35] (1985) *The Times*, November 11.
[36] [1987] 2 All ER 353.
[37] [1993] 1 All ER 651.

damages in respect of injury not to the claimant but to '*any other person*', namely the 'injury' to the mother. A failure to ascertain whether an unborn child had rubella and which thereby resulted in the birth of a disabled child may give rise to a personal injury cause of action on behalf of a mother on the basis that her continued pregnancy was a personal injury (*Das v Ganju*[38]). *Walkin* was followed in *Godfrey v Gloucester Royal Infirmary*,[39] a case where a mother sued in respect of the death of her daughter due to brain damage which was apparent from birth. The claimant alleged that a pre-natal ultrasound showed abnormalities and she was not properly advised of their significance and therefore elected to continue the pregnancy rather than undergo an abortion. *Walkin* was found to have survived both the House of Lord's decision in *McFarlane v Tayside Health Board*,[40] which held that a claim for the upkeep of a *healthy* child born as a result of a failed vasectomy was invalid, and remarks made upon it in the Court of Appeal in *Greenfield v Flather*.[41] Leveson J held that Mrs Godfrey's claim was in respect of a personal injury and that he was bound by *Walkin*. (See also *Farraj and Farraj v Kings Healthcare NHS Trust*.[42])

24.16 In *Anderton v Clywyd and Phelps v Hillingdon London Borough Council*[43] the House of Lords has held that a failure to mitigate or reduce the constitutional effects of dyslexia amounted to a personal injury. A claimant suffering from dyslexia which is not recognised and dealt with by an educational authority and who subsequently failed to achieve his full potential would have a potential claim 'in respect of personal injuries'. Of particular interest in this respect is that the courts have further held that the injury does not have to amount to a psychiatric condition. A negligent failure to improve the consequences of dyslexia by appropriate treatment causes the continuation of the injury and is analogous to a failure to treat a physical injury (per Lord Hoffmann in *Adams v Bracknell Forest Borough Council*[44]). In *Robinson v St Helens Metropolitan Borough Council*[45] the Court of Appeal confirmed that emotional and psychological upset resulting from a failure to deal with dyslexia was a personal injury even though it fell short of psychiatric injury. Such claims, however, are still frequently held to be statute barred and may often face difficulty in obtaining a s 33 dispensation (see, for example, *Rowe v Kingston Upon Hull City Council*,[46] *Smith v Liverpool CC*[47]).

---

[38] [1999] Lloyd's Rep Med 198.
[39] [2003] Lloyd's Rep Med 398.
[40] [2002] 2 AC 59.
[41] [2001] Lloyd's Rep Med 143.
[42] [2006] EWHC 1228.
[43] [2001] AC 619.
[44] [2004] UKHL 29.
[45] [2002] EWCA Civ 1099.
[46] [2003] ELR 771.
[47] [2006] EWHC 743.

DATE OF KNOWLEDGE: LIMITATION ACT 1980, S 11(4), S 14

24.17 Section 14(1) provides:

'In Sections 11 and 12 of this Act references to a person's date of knowledge are references to the date on which he first had knowledge of the following facts:-

(a) that the injury in question was significant; and
(b) that the injury was attributable in whole or in part to the act of omission which is alleged to constitute negligence, nuisance or breach of duty; and
(c) the identity of the defendant; and
(d) if it is alleged that the sex or omission was that of a person other than the defendant, the identity of that person and the additional facts supporting the bringing of an action against the defendant;

and knowledge that any acts or omissions did or did not, as a matter of law, involve negligence, nuisance of breach of duty is irrelevant.'

'The date on which he first had knowledge of the following facts . . .' (s 14(1))

24.18 The limitation period does not begin to run against a claimant until he has knowledge (i) that his injury was significant, (ii) that it was attributable to an act or omission either on the part of the defendant, or some other person for whom the defendant is liable, (iii) the identity of the defendant, and (iv) where the act or omission is of someone other than the defendant, the identity of that person and the factual basis upon which the defendant is vicariously liable.

A leading authority on what constitutes knowledge is the product liability case of *Nash v Eli Lilly & Co and others*.[48] This action concerned preliminary trials on limitation arising from reactions to the drug Opren such as skin sensitivity, abnormal hair growth and liver and kidney failure. Knowledge for the purposes of the section is now defined by the court as a condition of mind which imports a degree of certainty which might reasonably be regarded as sufficient to justify the claimant embarking upon the preliminaries to the making of a claim such as taking legal or other advice. Knowledge does not therefore mean knowing for certain and may amount to no more than a reasonably firmly held belief which would warrant a claimant taking steps to investigate the claim. Investigating whether the claimant had such a degree of certainty would involve the court looking at not only the intellectual capacity of the claimant to understand information but also considering, as a matter of fact, whether the claimant did comprehend the information obtained. The Court of Appeal in *Nash* also stipulated that time was not suspended or interrupted because an expert opinion contradicted the claimant's firmly held belief that the injury sustained was due to the defendant's act or omission. Providing that a claimant

---

[48] [1993] 1 WLR 782.

has a firm enough belief that the defendant's act or omission did in fact cause his injury then time runs irrespective of what an expert says. Alternatively, if a claimant has a suspended belief but feels the need for confirmation of that belief by an expert then time would not run until the expert's positive opinion was obtained. The Court of Appeal has subsequently reaffirmed the approach in *Nash* by emphasising that all a claimant had to know was the essence of the complaint, not the full details required to plead a case, and that all the court had to inquire into was how far the claimant had knowledge in broad terms of the facts upon which the complaint was based (see also *Whitfield v North Durham Health Authority*;[49] *Gregory v Ferro (GB) Limited*;[50] *Spargo v North Essex District Health Authority*;[51] *O'Driscoll v Dudley Health Authority*;[52] *Roberts v Winbow*;[53] *Irshad Ali v Courtaulds Textiles Limited*;[54] and *Sniezek v Bundy (Letchworth)*[55]).

24.19 *Spargo v North Essex District Health Authority* (above) concerned knowledge of attribution within the meaning of s 14(1)(b). The court sought to distil some of the principles to be found in *Nash* and subsequent cases. Lord Justice Brooke said this:

'What, then, does the law require in order that actual knowledge is established?

This branch of the law is already so grossly over-loaded with reported cases, a great many of which have been shown to us or cited by Counsel, that I see no reason to add to the overload by citation from early decisions. I have considered the judgments of this Court in *Halford v Brookes* [1991] 1 WLR 443; *Nash v Eli Lilly & Co* [1993] 1 WLR 782; *Broadley v Guy Clapham* [1993] 4 All ER 439; *Dobbie v Medway Health Authority* [1994] 1 WLR 1234; *Smith v Lancashire Health Authority* [1995] PIQR 514; and *Forbes v Wandsworth Health Authority* [1996] 7 Med LR 175. From these decisions I draw the following principles:

(i) The knowledge required to satisfy s 14(1)(b) is a broad knowledge of the essence of the causally relevant act or omission to which the injury is attributable;
(ii) 'Attributable' in this context means 'capable of being attributed to', in the sense of being a real possibility;
(iii) A plaintiff has the requisite knowledge when she knows enough to make it reasonable for her to begin to investigate whether or not she has a case against the defendant. Another way of putting this is to say that she will have such knowledge if she so firmly believes that her condition is capable of being attributed to an act or omission which she can identify (in broad terms) that she goes to a solicitor to seek advice about making a claim for compensation;

---

[49] [1995] 6 Med LR 32.
[50] [1995] 6 Med LR 321.
[51] [1997] PIQR P235.
[52] [1998] Lloyd's Rep Med 210.
[53] [1999] PIQR P77.
[54] [1999] 8 Lloyd's Rep Med 301.
[55] [2000] PIQR P13.

(iv) On the other hand, she will not have the requisite knowledge if she thinks she knows the act or omission she should investigate but in fact is barking up the wrong tree: or if her knowledge of what the defendant did or did not do is so vague or general that she cannot fairly be expected to know what she should investigate; or if her state of mind is such that she thinks her condition is capable of being attributed to the act or omission alleged to constitute negligence, but she is not sure about this, and would need to check with an expert before she could be properly said to know that it was.'

24.20 *Ali v Courtaulds Textiles* (above) illustrates a case where a two-judge Court of Appeal determined that time did not run against a claimant in a deafness case until he received an expert opinion that his deafness was noise induced rather than constitutional and due to the ageing process. This was so even though the claimant had been told by a community worker to consult a solicitor, which he did, as he might have a claim against his employers. The Court of Appeal thought that the case fell within category (iv) of the *Spargo* exception.

24.21 However, in *Sniezek v Bundy (Letchworth) Limited* (above) a differently constituted three-judge court doubted *Ali* and reaffirmed that firm belief in attribution which takes a claimant to a solicitor for advice is likely to be regarded as actual knowledge (*O'Driscoll v Dudley Health Authority* affirmed; see Simon Brown LJ, para 10 of his judgment, p 23). Whether a case falls within category (iii) or category (iv) of *Spargo* will require a close factual analysis. Simon Brown LJ said this in *Sniezek*:

'6. Now it seems to me one thing to say that a mere believer in attributability who 'realises that his belief requires expert confirmation' does not have knowledge of that attributability; arguably another to say that a firm believer who, for example, nevertheless wants legal advice (say to reassure him that he has reasonable prospects of success) is not to be regarded as having the requisite knowledge. Why should not time have started running in the case of the latter? Why should he be entitled to his solicitor's reassurance before the three year limitation period ever begins? I do not think that he is and nor do I think that the Court in *Nash v Eli Lilly* were intending to suggest otherwise: and that surely is evidenced from the final sentence in paragraph 5.

7. In short, it seems to me that the real contrast being struck in *Nash v Eli Lilly* is between on the one hand the mere believer whose situation is described in the first passage in the judgment, and on the other hand the firm believer sufficiently certain of his case to have clearly in mind (although always, of course, subject to the taking of appropriate advice and the preparation of evidence) the making of a compensation claim ...

8. Having regard to these considerations and having regard to the underlying purpose of this legislation – to postpone the three year period allowing for the investigation and institution of a specified claim until the claimant knows enough to make it reasonable to set time running – I find it difficult indeed to imagine a case where, having consulted a solicitor with a view to making a claim for compensation, a claimant could still then be held lacking in the requisite knowledge.

9. In short, I adhere to what I said in *O'Driscoll* and in the result confess to some difficulty both with the reasoning and, I have to say, with the result in the subsequent case of Ali. True it is that when Mr Ali went to his solicitor he knew only that his deafness might have been caused by his conditions of work in a cotton mill rather than (as he had earlier assumed) by a natural aging process. That seemed to me sufficient knowledge of attributability given, as stated in the second of the Spargo principles, that in this context a real possibility of establishing causation constitutes attributability. ... Mr Ali, therefore, seems to me to have come strictly within the second category outlined in *Nash v Eli Lilly*; he was someone 'obtaining advice about making a claim for compensation'; he had, indeed, already obtained a legal aid certificate for the purpose, albeit one initially limited to obtaining the necessary ENT report.'

24.22 In summary, time will run against a claimant if he has a firm enough belief to warrant the taking of preliminary steps for the institution of proceedings. If those steps fail at first to confirm his belief but subsequently his belief is confirmed, time will have run from the first date at which he had belief irrespective of the initial non-confirmation. If, however, a claimant has a suspicion or a relatively uncertain belief which requires expert or other opinion to establish whether he has suffered any injury and if so whether it was due to any act or omission of a possible defendant time may not run until that belief is confirmed. In cases concerning injury to the claimant during birth, the court has emphasised that the knowledge in question is the knowledge of the claimant himself and not the knowledge, actual or constructive of his parents (see *Appleby v Walsall Health Authority*,[56] *Parry v Clwyd Health Authority*,[57] *Bates v Leicester Health Authority*,[58] *Mirza v Birmingham Health Authority*[59]). Obviously, however, if the parents discuss the birth with the claimant the claimant may have actual knowledge or the court may impose constructive knowledge (see *O'Driscoll v Dudley Health Authority* above).

24.23 The court, having refused to define 'knowledge', has created a pragmatic theory of knowledge based upon a condition of mind which would warrant the initiation of preliminaries to making a claim. The practical effect of this approach is to require a detailed examination of the claimant's state of mind in the light of the information he has available to him and his intellectual capacity to comprehend it. For actual knowledge, as opposed to constructive knowledge, the test is subjective. The personal characteristics of the claimant, the effects, if any, of the injury upon him, will be relevant in considering what facts were observable and ascertainable by him given his intellect and other characteristics.

Significance: s 14(1)(a)

24.24 'Significant' is defined by s 14(2) in the following terms:

---

[56] [1999] Lloyd's Rep Med 154.
[57] [1997] PIQR P1.
[58] [1998] Lloyd's Rep Med 93.
[59] 31 July 2001, unreported, 1998 A No 04592.

'For the purposes of this section an injury is significant is the person whose date of knowledge is in question would reasonably have considered it sufficiently serious to justify his instituting proceedings for damages against a defendant who did not dispute liability and was able to satisfy a judgment.'

24.25 This test makes even relatively trivial matters significant because it might well be worth suing over minor injuries if a defendant is able to pay damages and does not put liability in issue. The courts have emphasised that significance is to be determined by looking at the first injury and its manifestations not by looking at a subsequent deterioration (see *Bristow v Grout*[60]). The court had taken a similar position under the 1963 Act, see *Goodchild v Greatness Timber Company Limited*,[61] *Miller v London Electrical Manufacturing Company Limited*.[62] In *Miller*, the claimant developed dermatitis in 1967 and needed some time off work but by 1971 the condition had deteriorated to eczema all over his body. The court held that his significant injury ran from the development of the dermatitis and not from the deterioration. Similarly, in *Brooks v J & P Coates*[63] a claimant who had left his place of work at a cotton mill in 1965 because of wheezing, coughing and shortness of breath was fixed with a significant injury at that date and not when a later diagnosis of byssinosis was made in 1979.

24.26 The test of reasonableness was said in *McCafferty v Metropolitan Police Receiver*[64] to be both subjective and objective. The court can examine whether the particular claimant in question subjectively considered the injury sufficiently serious but must also look objectively as to whether he was acting reasonably if he did not regard it as sufficiently serious (see *Stephen v Riverside Area Health Authority*[65]). However, in *Dobbie v Medway Health Authority*[66] the Master of the Rolls indicated that the question of significance was to be directed solely to the quantum of the injury namely whether he would reasonably have accepted it as a fact of life or not worth bothering about. Sir Thomas Bingham stated in *Dobbie*:

'The requirement that the injury of which a Plaintiff has knowledge should be "significant" is, in my view, directed solely to the quantum of the injury and not the Plaintiff's evaluation of its cause, nature or usualness. Time does not run against the Plaintiff, even if he is aware of the injury, if he would reasonably have accepted, as a fact of life, were not worth bothering about. It is otherwise if the injury is reasonably to be considered to be sufficiently serious in the statutory definition: Time then runs (subject to the requirement of attributability) even if the Plaintiff believes the injury to be normal or properly caused.'

---

[60] (1987) *The Times*, November 9.
[61] [1968] 2 All ER 255.
[62] [1976] 2 Lloyd's Rep 284.
[63] [1994] ICR 158.
[64] [1977] 1 WLR 1073.
[65] [1990] 1 Med LR 261.
[66] [1994] 4 All ER 450.

24.27 In *Briggs v Pitt-Payne and Lias*[67] the Court of Appeal emphasised that the assessment as to whether an injury caused by a drug regime was significant did not require a fine analysis of whether the side effects outweighed the beneficial effects of the drug. In *Roberts v Winbow*[68] the court found that time ran against the claimant when he knew that a lesser part of his injuries from a drug regime, namely a Stevens Johnson Syndrome, was caused by the drugs he had been given although he did not know that a more significant injury, namely a oesophageal stricture, was also the result of the medication. Hale LJ noted that the court's approach in emphasising the low threshold of significance was in accord with the Law Commission Report No 151, Consultation Paper on Limitation of Accidents 1998 (see paras 3.38-43, 12-39-41). There are cases where the court has been willing to postpone the running of time where a claimant has adopted a wait-and-see attitude, particularly in back cases where it might be reasonable to wait a little while to see if the back complaint was merely a strain or an ache and might soon settle (see *Devonport v A v Wright (Builders) Limited*[69] and *Pacheco v Brent and Harrow Area Health Authority*[70]).

24.28 Conversely the 'wait and see' approach did not avail the claimant in *Collins v Tesco*.[71] The claimant hurt her shoulder using a metal cage to move stock in 1996. In January 1998, physiotherapist told her that her injury was caused by heavy lifting and proceedings issued in 2001. At trial the court found that the injury was not significant until the meeting with the physiotherapist and the wait and see attitude as to whether the pain would settle was reasonable. The Court of Appeal disagreed and found the injury was significant before that meeting and the claim was statute-barred:

> '13. The test is not an easy one to apply. It is set out in section 14 (2) of the Act ... That definition must be read, in my judgment, and the context of the purpose of the statute. The limitation period for an action such as this is normally one of 3 years. The Act provides relaxations with one of which the Court is concerned. It allows a claimant with a lack of knowledge to bring a claim beyond the 3 year period from when the cause of action arose. At the same time it must be borne in mind that the defendant is entitled to the protection of the limitation defence which the statute provides and that Section must, in my judgment, be read as striking a balance between fairness to a claimant who may lack knowledge and fairness to a defendant who, because of the statute and in the public interest, is entitled to be free of claims unless they are brought within an appropriate time.
>
> 14. In my judgment, an over elaborate approach to the question is inappropriate. A possible elaboration is introduced with the "no risk" litigation contemplated in the section. That does not introduce into the test the consideration of readiness with which particular injured person may resort to litigation. Such elaboration is, in my judgment, inimical to the intention of the statute in this respect. The word "significant" has to be approached in a common sense way, and a common sense

---

[67] [1999] Lloyd's Law Rep 1.
[68] [1999] PIQR P77.
[69] Lexis, 23 April 1985.
[70] Lexis, 17 April 1984.
[71] [2003] EWCA Civ 1308, LTL 24/7/2003.

way based upon the evidence in a particular case. While in some circumstances the effect on a particular Plaintiff may be a factor, the test appears to me to be an objective test as, in my judgment, Lord Justice Geoffrey Lane in effect recognised. If, by introducing the concept of wait and see, the Judge was suggesting that a relevant consideration when considering the significance of the injury is the degree of robustness or stoicism which a claimant has, in my judgment, it is an elaboration which is not appropriate to the test and I would respectfully disagree with this approach. However sympathetic one would wish to be to a claimant who may be slow to resort to the courts and who is prepared to adopt the wait and see attitude as to whether an injury is significant, those factors cannot be crucial to whether an injury is significant, although in some circumstances, they may throw light on whether or not it is.' (Per Lord Justice Pill.)

24.29 The reference to Lane LJ in *Collins* refers to the test that was espoused by him in *McCafferty v Metropolitan Police Receiver* (above):

'. . . it is clear that the test is partly a subjective test, namely: Would this Plaintiff have considered the injuries sufficiently serious? And partly an objective test namely: Would he have been reasonable if he did not regard it sufficiently serious? It seems to me that "the" subsection ... is directed at the nature of the injuries known to the Plaintiff at the time. Taking that Plaintiff with that Plaintiff's intelligence would he have been reasonable in considering the injury not sufficiently serious to justify instituting proceedings for damages.'

24.30 The Court of Appeal in *Nash v Eli Lilly* , above, confirmed the *McCafferty* test and made a distinction between the normal or expected side effects of a drug and the unacceptable consequences which may not have been immediately apparent in any particular plaintiff. The limit of that approach for drug induced injuries was further explained and clarified in *Briggs v Pitt Payne*, above. That the test for significance has a degree of subjectivity within it was confirmed by the Court of Appeal again in *K R V Bryn Alyn*.[72] However, the Court of Appeal in *Catholic Care (Diocese of Leeds) v Young* has now determined that, following the House of Lords decision in *Adams v Bracknell Forest BC*,[73] a case concerning s 14(3) of the Act, that the test is objective. Where though the injury itself may result in the claimant being inhibited in bringing proceedings as in sexual abuse cases that was a factor to be taken into account.

24.31 Applying the so-called McCafferty Test in *Young v G L C & Massey*[74] had the effect of postponing for 3 years the claimant's state of knowledge. Mr Young sustained what was thought to be a minor whiplash injury to his neck in April 1981 which required some time off work at regular intervals during the 3 years after the accident. In May 1984, however, he was declared permanently unfit for his work as a foreman. Owen J found it reasonable for that particular claimant not to sue prior to May 1984 because he reasonably

---

[72] [2003] 3 WLR 107.
[73] [2004] UKHL 29.
[74] Owen J, 19 December 1986 CL 87/2328.

did not think it worthwhile or proper to do so. In *Woods v Attorney General*[75] Macpherson J indicated that a claimant should not necessarily be considered as essentially litigious and willing to issue proceedings for the slightest of injuries. In *Stephen v Riverside Area Health Authority*[76] Auld J felt it reasonable that a claimant did not sue in respect of erythema and anxiety because she did not consider this sufficiently serious to warrant proceedings, and that the knowledge of how significant the injury was only came later when she knew that the overdose of radiation she had been subjected to might cause her cancer. These cases need, however, to be considered in the light of the limits imposed by the Court of Appeal in *Collins v Tesco*.

24.32 In other cases, particularly in clinical negligence actions and disease cases, a claimant may not have knowledge that an injury is significant until he is informed of that fact by a medical practitioner. In *Guidera v Nei Projects (India) Limited*[77] a steel erector was exposed to asbestos between 1932 and 1953 but did not issue proceedings until 12 January 1987. In 1976 the claimant was referred to a chest physician because of an abnormal X-ray but when asked whether he had been exposed to asbestos, indicated that he had not and this was because he had forgotten about the exposure because it was so long ago. In 1982, he told his physician that he had in fact been exposed to asbestos, who then advised to apply for benefit which required examination by the Pneumoconiosis Medical Panel. The Panel told him in February 1983 that there was no evidence to diagnose asbestosis so the claimant instructed his trade union to take no further action. In June 1983 he was advised to re-apply to the Panel but did not do so because he did not think he had any good grounds for succeeding. McCullough J at first instance found the claimant did not know he had a significant injury because of the negligent decision of the Panel in 1983. The judge, however, did fix the claimant with constructive knowledge because he failed to act on the chest physician's advice to re-apply to the Panel. However, the judge indicated that had such advice been followed, it would inevitably have caused further delay and in fixing him with a date of knowledge of 12 January 1984, he held that the defendant had failed to prove that the Writ was issued out of time. The Court of Appeal in *Guidera* overturned the trial judge's finding on constructive knowledge and fixed the claimant with a date of knowledge in 1976. They did so on the basis that if he had answered the chest physician's questions properly in 1976, she would have told him that he had a significant injury caused by asbestosis. Accordingly, it was held unreasonable within the meaning of s 14(3) to fail to answer the doctor's enquiry properly.

24.33 In *Grieves and 9 others v F T Everard & Sons and British Uralite plc*,[78] the court confirmed that pleural plaques constituted an injury and time would accordingly run from the date of knowledge when a claimant knew that he had the pleural plaques and would not be postponed until he developed a more

---

[75] Lexis, 18 July 1990.
[76] [1990] 1 Med LR 261.
[77] CA, (1990) *The Independent*, February 19.
[78] [2005] EWHC 88.

serious asbestos induced injury such as asbestosis or mesothelioma. However, in the same test cases in *Rothwell v Chemical Insulating Company Ltd*[79] the Court of Appeal held that pleural plaques were not an actionable injury. This case is subject to further appeal.

Significance and the 'injury in question'

24.34 In some cases where an initial injury has occurred before a later more serious injury or deterioration, the courts have circumvented the low threshold of significance within s 14(2) by permitting time to run from the later manifestations on the basis that the latter constituted 'the injury in question' within s 14(1)(a). The two classes of cases where this has been considered are disease and sexual abuse actions.

24.35 In *McManus v Manning Marine*[80] the claimant developed vibration white finger in his left hand in the 1980s and made a claim to the Department of Social Security (DSS) in 1992. His condition was due to working in the ship building industry including a short period with the defendants in 1989 and 1990. The claimant was told in 1993 that his condition would deteriorate. His application to the DSS was rejected in September 1982. The claimant resumed employment from August 1993 to November 1999 with the defendants. His condition did worsen and spread to both hands. He issued proceedings in September 2002. At first instance, the judge held, conventionally, that the claimant's claim was statute-barred, his date of knowledge being in 1992. The Court of Appeal reversed this decision, stating that 'the injury in question' was the injury for which the action was brought, namely the exacerbation of his condition since 1993. The question, therefore, with respect to significance, was when was this exacerbation significant? In the Court of Appeal, it became common ground that the judge should have not have dismissed the claim in respect of any exacerbation within the 3-year period from 2 December 1996 to the 2 December 1999 (when proceedings were issued) as this would have been in time because the tort was a continuing one. Lady Justice Hale said this:

> '12. In my judgment, the Judge did take the wrong approach to this question. Section 14 (1) clearly refers back to Section 11 which refers to an action for "damages in respect of personal injuries". When, therefore, Section 14 (1)(a) talks about "the injury in question" it must mean the injury in respect of which the action is brought. This appellant is not bringing an action in respect of any injury that he may have suffered in the 2 very short periods of employment with this respondent before 1993. This action is in respect of exacerbation since then. The respondent accepts that there was a continuing cause of action arising day by day as and when the appellant continued to be affected by any negligence or breach of duty which may eventually been proved against the respondent.

---

[79] [2006] All ER (D) 187.
[80] [2001] EWCA Civ 1668.

13. I conclude that the Judge must have approached this matter wrongly. He should have asked himself when, within the meaning of the Act, did this claimant know that the injury in question, that is the exacerbation of his condition in this employment, was significant?'

24.36 The case was remitted back for a final hearing on both liability and limitation. No authorities were cited in the judgment. This case is of interest because the court is not saying that the initial injury was insignificant (the claimant went to a solicitor and made a claim for benefit) but that the exacerbation was the significant injury in question. The claimant was, therefore, permitted to abandon part of his personal injury as statute-barred, but was able to continue to sue in respect of the exacerbation. This case is perhaps best understood as one where a fresh injury is caused during the post-1992 employment and where a fresh cause of action was arising daily (Keene LJ).

24.37 The second class of case to adopt this approach was in the sexual abuse action in *K R V Bryn Alyn*.[81] This case concerned a consolidated action by 14 claimants for damages arising out of physical and sexual abuse suffered by them when residents at children's homes run by the defendant. The abuse was substantial and included buggery and unlawful sexual intercourse with respect to some of the children. The Court of Appeal found, however, that the so-called impact injuries of the initial assaults were not significant within the meaning of s 14 and were not, in any event, the 'injury in question'. The significant injury in question was the long-term psychiatric harm created by the abusive experiences rather than the immediate assaults. At first instance, the court had found that all claims were statute-barred but a s 33 discretion was exercised. The Court of Appeal's decision is remarkable because none of the claimants, except one, sought to challenge the judge's findings with respect to their date of knowledge on their cross-appeals. It was not until the Court of Appeal had started to write its judgment that it effectively took the point of its own motion:

> '26. As we have said, when this Court began to hear this Appeal, only MCK challenged that ruling and then only contingently on the success of her Appeal as to liability in negligence and on the success of the second defendant's Cross-Appeal on the Section 33 point. However, after hearing all the original submissions on Appeal, having reserved judgment and having begun to write it, we began to feel unease at the Judge's concentration for the purpose of determining the date of knowledge under Section 14, on the immediate effects of the abuse which, for the reasons we have given, appeared not to be the injuries for which they sought damages. We consider that the true question for the judgment for us was, as Croom-Johnson J put it in *Ackbar v C F Green & Co* [1975] QV582,587, in the slightly different context of whether a claim consisted of or included damages for personal injuries, "what is the action all about?", a test approved and applied by Stuart Smith LJ in *Harvey Brown Tractors (Retail) Limited* [1991] 4 All ER 30,6 and Auld J in *Walkin v South Manchester Health Authority* [1995] 1LLR1543,1152B-G.

---

[81] [2003] QB 1441.

27. This case was all about long-term post-traumatic, psychiatric injury.'

24.38 The claimants, no doubt, accepted that the trial judge's findings that the children has sustained a significant injury as soon as they were assaulted. This was in accordance with authority (see, for example, the Master of the Rolls Sir Thomas Bingham' judgment in *Dobbie v Medway Health Authority*[82]). Further, Lord Griffith, in *Stubbings v Webb*,[83] had stated:

> 'I have the greatest difficulty in accepting that a woman who knows she has been raped does not know that she has suffered a significant injury. ... In my view, the same applies to a young person who knows that he or she has been assaulted on a regular basis, or has been buggered or masturbated or fondled in an inappropriate way. Of course the realisation of the extent of the injury may grow with time, as may the injury itself; but in every case, I conclude that these unhappy victims had the relevant knowledge before they had left the community.'

24.39 The Court of Appeal, however, held in *Bryn Alyn* that Lord Griffiths' remarks were obiter and revisited the Court of Appeal's judgment in *Stubbings v Webb* particularly where it had stated (at p 208):

> 'Recognition that these acts have caused her serious long-term mental impairment could reasonably be seen by the Plaintiff as importing a new order of gravity. To distinguish between the immediate impairment of the Plaintiff's mental condition caused by these acts, apparently minor and transient, and a much more serious long-term impairment of the Plaintiff's mental condition, the attributability of which to the Webbs' conduct was appreciated later, is not, in my judgment, to defeat the intention of the legislature but to promote it.'

24.40 The Court of Appeal in *Bryn Alyn* went on to state that the issue as to whether each claimant had the required knowledge was a fact sensitive question requiring a determination of the individual's history, circumstances, nature, severity and duration of the abuse and its physical and mental effects. The court expressed the view that such an exercise would lead to a finding that the immediate injury caused by the abuse was of such a disabling character as to prevent the claimant from obtaining knowledge within the 3 year period after their majority. The court found that it was not until the receipt of a psychiatric report that the injury was known to be significant:

> '41. Application of the Section 14(2) meaning of "significant" to child victims of abuse is often the more difficult because many of them, as in the case of these claimants, come to it already damaged and vulnerable because of similar ill-treatment in other settings. For some, such behaviour is unpleasant, but familiar ... some victims of physical abuse may believe, to some extent, they deserved it and, in the case of serious sexual abuse unaccompanied by serious physical injury of any permanent or disabling kind, it is not surprising, submitted Mr Owen, that they did not see the significance of the conduct in Section 14(2) terms, and simply tried to make the best of things.

---

[82] [1994] 1WLR 1234.
[83] [1993] AC 498.

42. However artificial it may seem to pose the question in this context, Section 14 requires the Court, on a case by case basis, to ask whether such an already damaged child would reasonably turn his mind to litigation as a solution to his problems. The same applies to those, as in the case of many of these claimants who, subsequently abused, progress into adulthood and a twilight world of drugs, further abuse and violence and, in some cases, crime. Some would put the abuse to the back of their mind: some might, as a result or a symptom of an as yet undiagnosed development of psychiatric illness, block or suppress it. Whether such a reaction is deliberate or unconscious, whether or not it is a result of some mental impairment, the question remains whether and when such a person would have reasonably seen the significance of his injury so as to turn his mind to litigation in the sense require of Section 14(1)(a) and (2) to start the period of limitation running. At this stage the Section 14(1)(b) issue of actual or constructive knowledge of attributablity becomes more of a live issue than it would have been at, or shortly after the abuse, because in some cases it might only be after the intervention of a psychiatrist that a claimant realises that there could have been a cause or link between the childhood abuse and the psychiatric problems suffered as an adult, an argument accepted by the Court of Appeal, but which Lord Griffiths found difficult to accept in *Stubbings v Webb*.'

24.41 As indicated, the court found that the initial injuries were not significant within the meaning of the section and the claimants could sue for both the impact injury and the later psychiatric consequences:

'57. The narrow question to which the courts are confined when a Section 14 issue arises is as to the knowledge of the claimant at any material time for the purpose of starting a limitation period. If, as provided by Section 11, an action for negligence, nuisance or breach of duty "includes" a claim for damages for personal injury which, at the material time, he knew to be "significant" so as to bring it within the limitation period, he may proceed with that claim. He may also proceed with any other claim for damages arising out of the same cause of action – whether previous or subsequent to the injury of which he had significant knowledge, and whether or not for personal injury. But where an action includes a claim for damages for personal injury which he did not, within the limitation period, know to be significant, that claim would be statute-barred unless the action "includes" another claim for damages for personal injuries of which he first had significant knowledge within the period. Thus in the same action, Section 14 depending on the circumstances, may preserve or bar the recoverability of damages for the later of two injuries however late the date of knowledge of it, or enable recovery for the earlier of the two injuries which, but for the claim for the second, would have been statute-barred.

58. Thus here, if the Judge correctly found in the case of any claimant that he or she had the requisite knowledge within 3 years after the majority, that knowledge would operate to bar not only the claim for damages for the immediate injuries caused by the abuse, but also the long-term psychiatric injury of which he or she first acquired knowledge must later. If the Judge was wrong in that finding, the operative date of knowledge would be that of the long-term psychiatric abuse which, within the limitation period, would enable the claim for both the earlier immediate injuries caused by the abuse and the long-term psychiatric injuries. It is thus necessary to consider the case of each claimant individually against the general conclusion of the Judge, at paragraph 30 of his judgment, that "a young

person who knows that he or she has been assaulted on a regular basis, who has been buggered, masturbated or fondled in an inappropriate way" has the relevant knowledge and that each of these claimants had it "before they left the community".'

24.42 This approach in sexual abuse cases concerning children as laid down in *Bryn Alyn* was followed in the subsequent case of *H V N and T*.[84] *Bryn Alyn* was, however, subject to substantial reinterpretation by a differently constituted Court of Appeal in *Catholic Care (Diocese of Leeds) v Young*.[85] Following the House of Lords decision in *Adams v Bracknell Forest BC*[86] that the test in s 14(3) of the Act was objective, the Court of Appeal in *Catholic Care* found that the same test applied to the construction of reasonableness within s 14(2). This meant that the intelligence, personal history and all the personal characteristics of the claimant were not relevant in determining whether it was reasonable for the claimant to consider that his injury was sufficiently serious to institute proceedings. The so-called Adams approach did, however, permit the court to take into account whether the injury was one which, as in sexual abuse cases, had the effect of inhibiting the claimant from starting proceedings.

24.43 The Court of Appeal's approval of the principles in *Bristow v Grout* supra (see paras 37–40 of the judgment), suggests that the extension of the 'injury in question' approach for other cases of deterioration or aggravation, may be limited. *McManus* (ibid) appears not to have been considered by the Court of Appeal in *Bryn Alyn*.

Attributability: s 14(1)(b)

24.44 Section 14(1)(b) provides:

> '... that the injury was attributable in whole or in part to the act or omission which is alleged to constitute negligence, nuisance or breach of duty ...'

24.45 The concept of attributability has generated a great deal of case-law. In *Dobbie v Medway Health Authority*,[87] the Court of Appeal reviewed a number of leading authorities on attribution and attributability and came to conclusions that have resulted in bringing forward claimants' dates of knowledge *closer* to the act or omission giving rise to the injury. Mrs Dobbie was admitted for a biopsy on a lump in her breast on 27 April 1973 and the surgeon considering that the lump was pre-cancerous carried out a left mastectomy without microscopic examination and allegedly without the claimant's consent. On 14 May 1973 it was found that the lump was in fact benign and the claimant was told this on 11 June 1973. The claimant developed a significant psychiatric reaction to the loss of her breast but did not issue proceedings until 1989 following hearing about a similar case reported in a

---

[84] LTL 29 April 2004.
[85] [2006] EWCA Civ 1534.
[86] [2004] UKHL 29.
[87] [1994] PIQR P353.

newspaper and on a local radio. The trial judge found that time ran against the claimant as soon as she was informed about the laboratory analysis of the lump and the Court of Appeal concurred with that view. The court held first, that attribution meant 'capable of being attributed to' and not caused by. Secondly, the court emphasised that the claimant did not need to know that the defendant's act or omission was capable of being attributed to fault because that was specifically excluded on the clear words of the statute indicating that knowledge that any act or omission as a matter of law involved negligence, nuisance or breach of duty was irrelevant. Thirdly, the court confirmed that all that the claimant needed for knowledge was a broad understanding of the essence of the act or omission and confirmed the reasoning in *Nash v Eli Lilley & Co*[88] and *Broadley v Guy Clapham & Co.*[89] Earlier authorities that indicated that knowledge of detailed acts or omissions such as would be necessary to draft particulars of negligence were not correct. The court concluded that Mrs Dobbie knew within hours of the operation that she had suffered a significant injury, and knew from the beginning that the injury was capable of being attributed to an act or omission of the Health Authority. What she did not know was whether the act or omission was blameworthy, but knowledge of fault did not stop time beginning to run. (For cases which have followed *Dobbie* see *Whitfield v North Durham Health Authority*;[90] *Gregory v Ferro (GB) Limited*;[91] *Brady v Wirral Health Authority*;[92] *Spargo v North Essex District Health Authority*;[93] *O'Driscoll v Dudley Health Authority* [94] *Roberts v Winbow*.[95])

24.46 Attributability must, of course, relate even in general terms to the act or omission complained of, that is it must be causally relevant.

- In *Ogunsanya v Lambeth Health Authority* the claimant was rendered paraplegic following a gallstone operation which resulted in extensive internal bleeding. The cause of the paraplegia was thought to be attributable to a low dose of subcutaneous heparin which caused the bleeding. It was not until a medical report from a neurologist indicating that the paraplegia was due to a delay in treating the bleeding that attributability was established.

- Similarly in *Scuriaga v Powell*[96] time was held not to run against the claimant in respect of a claim arising out of a failure to terminate a pregnancy, until she received a medical report indicating that it was a lack of care on the part of the surgeon which had caused the failure. The treating surgeon had in fact told the claimant that his failure to terminate

---

[88] [1993] 4 All ER 383.
[89] (1993) *The Times*, July 6.
[90] [1995] 6 Med LR 32.
[91] [1995] 6 Med LR 321.
[92] 25 June 1996 CCATF 95/1502/C.
[93] [1997] PIQR 235.
[94] [1999] Lloyd's Rep Med 210.
[95] [1999] PIQR P77.
[96] (1979) 123 SJ 406.

the pregnancy was due to a structural defect in her which she believed until a medico-legal expert contradicted it.

- In *Khan v Ainslie*[97] a claimant's blindness was thought by him to have been caused when his medical practitioner administered eye drops which resulted in him experiencing pain. Nearly 6 years later he finally received a medical opinion indicating that the cause of his blindness was in fact delay in treating his condition of glaucoma. The receipt of this report was held to be the date of attributability and the claimant's date of knowledge.

- In *Stephen v Riverside Health Authority*,[98] although a claimant suspected she was at an increased risk of cancer following an overdose of radiation, she was not fixed with actual knowledge until nearly 8 years later when in conference with her own counsel and her medical expert she learned that the overdose might not have been in the order of only 30 roentgen, as claimed by the defendant, but could possibly have been in the order hundreds or thousands of roentgen. This case was of added interest in that the claimant herself had some experience of radiology having been an unqualified radiographer 24 years before her own x-rays. The judge found that that in itself was not sufficient to constitute making her an expert to set off against the chorus of negligent expert advice she had received until that stage concerning attribution.

24.47 It remains, therefore, important to realise that attributability may be delayed in cases where it is by no means clear whether the persisting problems a claimant has are extensions of a pre-existing condition or whether in fact there has been a medical mishap.

- In *Forbes v Wandsworth Health Authority*,[99] the Court of Appeal held, in a clinical negligence action, that there must be knowledge of some causative link between the treatment or lack of it and the claimant's condition. Mr Forbes was operated on in 1982 for a by-pass; the operation failed and a second operation was carried out the next day. The operation was unsuccessful and the claimant was told that he needed to have his leg amputated to prevent gangrene and this was done on 5 November 1982. Subsequently, the claimant obtained a report in 1992 which alleged that the practitioners had been negligent not to perform the second operation sooner. The defendant contended that all that was needed was knowledge that there was a period of time between the first and second operations, that the second operation was not successful and as a result the claimant had his leg amputated. The Court of Appeal found, however, that the claimant did not know that the loss of his leg was capable of being attributed to the act or omission of the defendant until the receipt of an opinion by a vascular surgeon. The court held that in many medical negligence cases the claimant would not know that his injury was

---

[97] [1993] 4 Med LR 319.
[98] [1990] 1 Med LR 261.
[99] [1999] PIQR P77.

attributable to the omission of the defendant until he also learned that there had been negligence. That, however, did not mean that there was no distinction between causation and negligence, the first being relevant to s 14 and the second irrelevant.

- A similar approach was taken in the case of *Smith (Michael John) v West Lancashire Health Authority*.[100] Mr Smith injured his right hand on 12 November 1981 and attended hospital for emergency treatment where a diagnosis of any uncomplicated fracture to the ring finger was made. In January 1982, an operation was necessary as the conservative treatment had not worked. In 1989, Mr Smith was dismissed from his job as a labourer due to loss of function in the right hand. In 1991, an expert medical report said that there had been a failure in November 1981 to treat the finger properly which had resulted in degenerative changes which now meant loss of function in the hand. The Court of Appeal held that the claimant did not have the requisite knowledge on which to found his claim until 1991, because although he was aware that the first treatment had not worked that did not imbue him with a knowledge of an omission on the part of the treating physicians. (See also *Ostick v Wandsworth Health Authority*,[101] *Hallam-Eames v Merrett Syndicates*;[102] *Hind v York*.[103])

- In *Irshad Ali v Courtaulds Textiles Limited*[104] the Court of Appeal allowed an appeal in a deafness case holding that the claimant did not know whether his deafness was due to the ageing process or to industrial noise until an expert informed him of that fact.

- For other cases where knowledge of attributability has been postponed because it was unclear whether the persisting problems facing a claimant were extensions of a pre-existing condition or due to a medical mishap see *Jones v Liverpool Health Authority*;[105] *O'Driscoll v Dudley Health Authority*;[106] *Rowbotham v the Royal Masonic Hospital*;[107] *Skitt v Khan*;[108] and *Smith v NHSLA*.[109]

24.48 Similar principles were adopted by the Court of Appeal in *Oakes v Hopcraft*,[110] a case of professional negligence concerning a medical expert's alleged incompetence which led to an under-settlement of a personal injury claim. The court was concerned with the provisions of s 14A of the Limitation

---

[100] [1995] PIQR P514, CA.
[101] [1995] 6 Med LR 338.
[102] [1995] 2 CL 304.
[103] [1998] PIQR P235.
[104] [1999] 8 Lloyd's Rep Med 301.
[105] [1996] PIQR P 251.
[106] [1999] Lloyd's Rep Med 210.
[107] [2003] PIQR 1.
[108] [1997] Med LR 105.
[109] [2001] Lloyd's Rep Med 90.
[110] CA 27/7/200.

Act 1980 but applied the principles derived from personal injury cases under s 14 and as also set out in the case of *Hallam Eames v Merrett Syndicate*.[111] In *Hallam*, Hoffmann LJ had emphasised the need for the causal relevance of the act or omission (pp 125–6):

> '... If all that was necessary was that a plaintiff should have known that the damage was attributable to an act or omission of the defendant, the statute would have said so. Instead, it speaks for the damage being attributable to "the act or omission which is alleged to constitute negligence". In other words, the act or omission of which the plaintiff must have knowledge must be that which is causatively relevant for the purposes of an allegation of negligence.'

24.49 In Oakes v Hopcraft Clarke LJ considered in detail *Hallam-Eames v Merrett Syndicates*, and other personal injury authorities and concluded:

> '52. ... If one asks what is it that the claimant is essentially complaining about, it is that the defendant failed to diagnose her condition correctly and to advise her that the accident had caused a severe traction injury to the brachial plexus and damage to the radial artery and that her condition would not improve. It was only when she knew both what injuries had been caused by the accident and, importantly, that they would not improve so that she would not (as it were) get better, that to my mind it can fairly be held that she knew that the omission of the defendant to give her that advice caused her damage. The damage was the loss she sustained because she settled for too little. The claimant could not know that she had settled for too little as a result of any failure on the part of the defendant until she knew that she would not get better because it was that fact, namely that her condition would not improve, which essentially caused the settlement to be too low. That is because the essential reason that the settlement is said to have been too low is that it did not include anything to compensate her for not being able to work in future as a result of the accident.'

24.50 The decision of the Court of Appeal in *Spargo v North Essex District Health Authority*[112] has been referred to, and quoted from, in detail above. In *Sniezek v Bundy*,[113] also referred to above, the court in considering the question of attributability discussed the difficulties which can arise concerning the last sub-category of point (iv) in *Spargo*, namely knowledge that required expert confirmation, and doubted whether the decision in *Ali v Courtauld* had been correct in this respect.

24.51 In *Haward v Fawcetts*[114] the House of Lords, in a s 14A case concerning an action in negligence against an accountant, indicated that its observations on knowledge and attributability applied equally to s 14 and it approved *Halford, Hendy, Nash, Spargo, Broadley* and *Hallam-Eames*.

24.52 In summary, attributability will be established when the essence of the case against the defendant is known by a claimant so that the act or omission

---

[111] [1995] 7MED LR122.
[112] [1997] PIQR P235.
[113] [2000] PIQR P123.
[114] [2006] UKHL 9.

complained of is possibly capable of being attributed to the defendant in broad terms; there is no need for the degree of precision which a pleaded Particulars of Claim would require. In some circumstances often arising out of negligence and omissions in clinical cases attributability may be postponed until a cause or connection between the injury and the act or omission said to constitute negligence is established. This is not the same as knowledge of fault which is not required. In such cases attributability may be delayed until an expert opinion establishes a cause or connection between the injury and the act or omission. Difficulties may arise in determining whether in any particular case the extent (whether certainty or otherwise) of the belief of attribution is sufficient to start the running of time and/or the effect of a belief remaining uncertain until expert confirmation.

Identity: s 14(1)(c) and (d)

24.53 Under s14(1)(c) and (d) the claimant must know:

'(c) The identity of the defendants;
(d) If it is alleged the act or admission was that of a person other than a defendant, the identity of that person and the additional facts supporting the bringing of an action against the defendant'.

24.54 Thus the final fact that a claimant must know for his date of knowledge to be established is the identity of the defendant (and, where the defendant is alleged to be vicariously liable for another's act or omission, the identity of that other and the factual basis upon which the defendant is said to be so liable). These provisions are designed to deal with cases where a claimant cannot ascertain immediately who was responsible for the injury, such as in a road traffic accident where a driver might fail to stop, or where there might be a complex division of labour and division of responsibility on a building site and it is not clear which sub-contractor was responsible for a particular act of negligence. In addition, where a third party is blamed in a defence, the claimant may have an extended period of time to sue on the basis of not knowing before then that the third party was responsible (see *Davies v Reed Stock & Company Limited*;[115] *Foster v Mall Builders Limited*;[116] and *Lead Bitter v Hodge Finance Limited*[117]).

24.55 Similar problems can arise where the precise legal identity of a defendant is difficult to ascertain because of a complex corporate structure which might have connected companies with similar names. Time may not run until the claimant had knowledge of the actual name of his employer in such

---

[115] Lexis, 26 July 1984.
[116] Lexis, 17 March 1983.
[117] [1982] 2 All ER 167.

circumstances (see *Simpson v Norwest Holst Southern Limited*;[118] *Eidi v Service Dowell Schlumberger SA*;[119] and *Stevens v Nash Dredging and Reclamation Company Limited*[120]).

24.56 In *Cressey v E Timm & Son Limited and E Timm & Son Holding Limited*,[121] the Court of Appeal affirmed *Simpson v Norwest Holst Southern Limited*. The claimant had worked as a fork-lift truck driver for the second defendant but his pay slips were in the name of an associated company, the first defendants, who he believed he was employed by. The claimant was injured on 2 December 2000 and sued the first defendant within time on 27 November 2003. The claim form was not, however, served in time and a second claim form against both companies was issued on 30 March 2004. The second defendant alone sought to strike out the second claim. The court confirmed the first instance decision that the claimant did not know, within the 3-year period prior to 30 March 2004, who the identity of his employers were, the earliest possible date being 30 April 2000 when the solicitors learnt of the existence of the second defendant (per Lord Justice Rix):

> '28. On the particular facts of this case, I do not think that the right answer is hard to reach. It is likely that in most cases in an accident at work, the employee will there and then have knowledge of the identity of his employer, and therefore, the defendant. However, in a minority of cases, where the identity of the employer is uncertain, as in Simpson, or even wrongly stated to the employee, as here, the date of knowledge may well be postponed. How long it will be postponed by will depend on the facts of such cases. In general I do not believe it can be postponed for long: only as long as it reasonably takes to make and complete the appropriate enquiries. But if such enquiries are met by mis-information or a dilatory response, again as in Simpson, then it is not possible to be dogmatic about the right conclusion. In Simpson, the Court only had to cover a period of about 2 weeks after the accident and therefore did not have to go further into the facts.
>
> In the present case, I agree with the submission that the facts are in their way stronger than in *Simpson*.'

24.57 In *Nash v Eli Lilly*[122] the Court of Appeal indicated that a claimant might be fixed with constructive knowledge in respect of the names of different companies in a group structure as the law applicable to the operation of such corporations provides for information as to the true position of the individual members of the corporate structure:

> 'It is also a clear requirement of Section 14(1)(c) that the Plaintiff must have knowledge of the identity of the defendant. However, in a case of corporate entity, such as those with which these appeals are concerned, the law as applicable to the operation of such corporations may be expected to provide, and do provide, that

---

[118] [1980] 1 WLR 968.
[119] [1990] CLY 2961.
[120] Lexis, 27 July 1982.
[121] [2006] PIQR P9.
[122] [1993] 4 All ER 383.

the true position of the individual members of the corporate structure are ascertainable. These details as facts would therefore fall within Section 14(3)(c).'

Constructive knowledge: s 14(3)

24.58 Section 14(3) provides:

'For the purposes of this section a person's knowledge includes knowledge which he might reasonably have been expected to acquire:-

(a) from facts observable or ascertainable by him; or
(b) from facts ascertainable by him with the help of medical or other appropriate expert advice which it is reasonable for him to seek;

but a person shall not be fixed under this sub-section with knowledge of a fact ascertainable only with the help of expert advice so long as he has taken all reasonable steps to obtain (and, where appropriate, to act on) that advice.'

24.59 This important subsection may provide a good deal of protection to prospective defendants. A claimant is required to act reasonably in using information he has and in obtaining information which he could get to establish knowledge of (i) the significance of his injury, (ii) to whom the injury might be attributed and (iii) the identity of the defendants. When a court is examining a claimant's date of knowledge it will first inquire as to what the actual claimant's knowledge was and then, if necessary, ask what the claimant could reasonably have known if he had applied his mind to the matter and if he had sought assistance. If both his actual and his constructive knowledge, as fixed by the court, are within the 3-year period prior to the issue of proceedings, then his action will not be time barred. The subsection, therefore, requires that the claimant is both mentally active in comprehending the facts of his accident and injury and also physically active in obtaining expert and other advice and opinions. It is for the claimant to establish that his actual date of knowledge is within time but if a defendant contends for an earlier constructive date of knowledge then the evidential burden may shift to the defendant to establish that fact (see *Crocker v British Coal Corporation*;[123] *Smith v NHSLA*;[124] *K R v Bryn Alyn*[125]).

24.60 In construing what is reasonable, the courts initially adopted the same approach used in construing whether a claimant reasonably felt his injury was significant. This was to qualify the objective criteria of reasonableness with the particular qualities of the actual claimant (see *Davis v City and Hackney Health Authority*[126]). Thus in *Nash v Eli Lilly*[127] it was held:

---

[123] (1986) 29 BMLR 159.
[124] [2001] Lloyd's Rep Med 90.
[125] [2003] 3 WLR 107.
[126] [1991] 2 Med LR 366.
[127] [1993] 4 All ER 383.

'The standard of reasonableness in connection with the observations and/or the effort to ascertain are therefore finally objective but must be qualified to take into consideration the provision and circumstances and character of the Plaintiff . . . In considering whether or not the inquiry is, or is not, reasonable the situation, character and intelligence of the Plaintiff must be relevant.'

(See also Widgery LJ's judgment in *Newton v Cammell Laird & Co Limited*[128] and the House of Lords decision in *Smith v Central Asbestos Company Limited*[129] per Lord Reid at 530.)

24.61 This approach is illustrated in *Davis v City & Hackney Health Authority* (above) where a claimant suffering from cerebral palsy had an actual date of knowledge of attribution fixed on the receipt of the medico-legal report nearly 23 years after his birth and approximately 2 years outside the primary limitation period. Jowitt J had to consider whether that actual date of knowledge ought to be replaced with the constructive date of knowledge based upon the claimant's failure to take legal advice earlier than he did. The judge held that, taking into account the claimant's age, his disability and his dependence upon his parents, who had discouraged him from making a claim, the claimant had not acted unreasonably in delaying.

24.62 However, in *Forbes v Wandsworth Health Authority*,[130] the Court of Appeal emphasized the primarily objective nature of the test to be applied in s 14(3). Mr Forbes received surgery in 1982 for a heart bypass operation which was unsuccessful so a second operation was carried out the next day. That operation was also unsuccessful and the claimant's leg had to be amputated. He later received in October 1992 a medical opinion alleging negligence against the surgeon for not performing the second operation sooner than it was. Proceedings were issued on 10 December 1992. Part of the delay was due to the implicit trust the claimant had for his doctor. The judge said that the claimant's claim was not statute-barred as he had neither actual nor constructive knowledge until 1992. The Court of Appeal agreed with the judge on actual knowledge as the claimant did not know, until he was told by an expert, that the loss of his leg was capable of being attributed to an act or admission of the defendant. The Court of Appeal did, however (Roch LJ dissenting), fix him with constructive knowledge, saying that it was reasonable to allow the claimant 12–18 months (only) to get over the shock of the amputation, take stock of his situation and then take advice. The court therefore considered that the claimant had constructive knowledge in 1984. The court went on to express the view that the claimant's individual characteristics were not relevant to s 14(3) and doubted *Nash v Eli Lilly* on this point (Roch LJ dissenting, holding that *Nash* was binding). Stuart-Smith LJ had considered the quotation from Purchas LJ as quoted above in *Nash v Eli Lilly*, but said this (p 19/20):

---

[128] [1959] 1 WLR 415.
[129] [1973] AC 518.
[130] [1997] QB 402.

'... I have difficulty in seeing how the individual character and intelligence of the Plaintiff can be relevant in an objective test ... it does not seem to me that the fact that the Plaintiff is more trusting, incurious or indolent, resigned or uncomplaining by nature can be a relevant characteristic, since this too undermines any objective approach.'

24.63 Lord Justice Evans agreed, stating that the claimant's situation is relevant but not his character and intelligence. *Forbes* was followed in *Parry v Clywyd Health Authority*.[131]

24.64 However, the difficulties of having two conflicting Court of Appeal decisions soon arose. In *Smith v Leicester Health Authority*[132] the Court of Appeal considered the conflicting decisions in *Nash* and *Forbes* and felt free to decide which to follow. They opted for the objective *Forbes* approach:

'We are prepared to accept, for the purposes of this Appeal, that the proper approach to this question is "What would the reasonable man have done, placed in the situation of the Plaintiff?" and that the answer in each case must depend on its own facts ... we accept that the Plaintiff's individual characteristics which might distinguish her from the reasonable woman should be disregarded. Therefore her fortitude, a lack of any bitterness at becoming a tetraplegic and the determination and devotion she has shown to making herself as independent and a useful member of her family and society as she can, which has surpassed what might be expected, are to be put on one side.'

24.65 The court in *Smith* did, however, state that *Forbes* was not authority for the proposition that when a patient is severely disabled following an operation they have 12–18 months to decide whether to investigate the claim. The court in *Smith* reversed the first instance decision on constructive knowledge and found that the claim was not statute-barred. Whether it is reasonable for a claimant to seek advice was held to depend on the facts and circumstances in each case, excluding the character traits of the individual claimant.

24.66 However, in *Ali v Courtaulds Textiles Limited*[133] the Court of Appeal relied on *Nash v Eli Lilly* to find that:

'The temporal and circumstantial span of reasonable enquiry will depend on the factual context of the case and subjective characteristics of the individual (claimant) involved.'

24.67 In *Fenech v East London Health Authority*[134] the claimant experienced severe perineal pain following the birth of her child in 1960. This pain continued and was apparent after sexual intercourse but she did not mention that fact to her male GP due to embarrassment. Investigation of her hips eventually found a needle fragment in the perineum in 1991 and she was told

---

[131] [1997] PIQR P1.
[132] (1997) 36 BMLR 23.
[133] [1999] Lloyd's Rep Med 301.
[134] [2000] Lloyd's Rep Med 35.

about this in 1994. She issued proceedings on 24 January 1997. The court fixed the claimant with constructive knowledge by the early 1960s. Lord Justice Brown stated:

> 'For my part I think it unnecessary on the present Appeal to attempt any final reconciliation of the authorities or solution of the difficulties presented by the Section. It is sufficient to recognise that some degree of objectivity at least must be required determining when it is reasonable for someone to seek advice – otherwise the proviso could never apply save only when a person acts out of character – and to conclude, as I do, that on any sort of objective approach ... this claimant should have sought medical advice on her injury long before she did, indeed in the early 1960's at latest.' (See also *O'Driscoll v Dudley Health Authority*.[135])

24.68 In *Bates v Leicester Health Authority*[136] Dyson J after reviewing the disparity between Nash and Forbes approached the question of constructive knowledge:

> '... by asking what knowledge it was reasonable to expect to be acquired by a Plaintiff of average intelligence and without unusual personal characteristics. The personal characteristics which I believe the Court of Appeal in Forbes were saying should be left out of account were personality traits such as those mentioned at the end of the passage that I quoted from the judgment of Stuart-Smith LJ (trusting, incurious, indolent, resigned and complaining). I do not think that the Court of Appeal was saying that in applying the objective test, one should ignore the fact that as in the present case, a Plaintiff has great difficulty in communication, and that the potential source of knowledge is a parent who is trusted and is heavily relied upon by the Plaintiff in all the important areas of her life. As Evans LJ said, (in Forbes): "the reasonable man must be placed in the situation that the Plaintiff was".'

24.69 The conflict between the authorities received the House of Lords' attention in the case of *Adams v Bracknell Forest Borough Council*.[137] The House determined that *Forbes* should be preferred over *Nash* and the test was objective. Mr Adams suffered from severe dyslexia and sued an education authority for negligent failure to ameliorate his condition whilst at school between 1977 and 1988. He issued proceedings in 2002 after having spoken to an Educational Psychologist at a social event in 1999. At first instance the judge found he did not have constructive knowledge and the Court of Appeal rejected the defendant's appeal. The defendant's further appeal to the House of Lords was however successful. The test for constructive knowledge was found to be objective. There was no evidence in Mr Adams' case to support the judge's finding that the claimant because of his dyslexia could not reveal his problems to his doctor nor was it established that extreme reticence about the problem of dyslexia was standard behaviour for dyslexics. The claimant was found to be of normal intelligence and there was no reason why the normal expectation that a person suffering from a significant injury should not be

---

[135] [1998] Lloyd's Rep Med 210.
[136] [1998] Lloyd's Rep Med 93.
[137] [2005] 1 AC 76.

curious about its origins should not apply to dyslexics. Constructive knowledge was fixed well before the 3-year period immediately prior to the start of proceedings.

24.70 The route which led Lord Hoffmann to this decision was partially based on the recognition that the court did have a discretionary power to extend the primary limitation period. Lord Hoffmann noted the subjective element in the test as set out in *Newton v Cammell Laird* and *Smith v Asbestos*, but preferred the reasoning of the Court of Appeal in *Forbes*:

> '45. I find this reasoning persuasive. The Court of Appeal did not refer to the decisions of the 1963 Act which had taken a more subjective view. While it is true that the language of Section 7(5) of the 1963 Act was not materially different from that of Section 14(3) of the 1980 Act, I think that the Court of Appeal in Forbes was right in saying the introduction of the discretion under Section 33 had altered the balance. As I said earlier, the assumptions which one makes about the hypothetical person to whom a standard of reasonableness is applied will be very much affected by the policy of the law in applying such a standard. Since the 1975 Act, the postponement of the commencement of the limitation period by reference to the date of knowledge is no longer the sole mechanism for avoiding injustice to a Plaintiff who could not reasonably be expected to have known that he had a cause of action. It is, therefore possible to interpret Section 14(3) with a greater regard to the potential injustice for the defendant if the limitation period should be indefinitely extended.
>
> 46. I, therefore, think that Lord Reid's dictum in Smith v Central Asbestos Co Limited [1973] AC518, 530 that the "test is subjective" is not a correct interpretation of Section 14(3). The same is true of the dictum of Purchas LJ in Nash v Eli Lilly & Co [1993] 1WLR782, ...
>
> 47. It is true that the Plaintiff must be assumed to be a person who has suffered the injury in question not some other person. But, like Roch LJ in Forbes [1997] QB 402, 425 I do not see how his particular character or intelligence can be relevant. In my opinion, Section 14(3) requires one to assume that a person who is aware that he has suffered a personal injury, serious enough to be something about which he would go and see a solicitor if he knew he had a claim, will be sufficiently curious about the causes of the injury to seek whatever expert advice is appropriate.'

24.71 Baroness Hale, although concurring with the decision, took 'a slightly different view' and emphasised that she would not want to rule out that a claimant's personal characteristics may be relevant to what knowledge can be imputed to him under s 14(3). Baroness Hale reviewed the leading authorities and the Law Commission Report 151 and expressed the opinion that:

> '88. I wonder, therefore, how much difference there is in practice between the two approaches. We are not here concerned with knowledge that the claimant might reasonably have been expected to acquire from facts observable or ascertainable by him. We are concerned with knowledge that he might reasonably be expected to acquire with the help of medical or other advice which it is reasonable for him to seek. The question is when is it reasonable to expect a potential claimant to seek

such advice? Objectively, it will be reasonable to seek such advice when he has good reason to do so. This will depend upon the situation in which the claimant finds himself, to include the consequences of the accident, illness or other injury which he has suffered. Rarely, if ever, will it depend upon his personal characteristics. If, faced with the situation in which it is reasonable to seek advice, a person fails to do so, then the fact that he was reluctant to make a fuss, or embarrassed to talk to his doctor, while understandable, does not take him outside this sub-section.

89. Mr Forbes was faced with the amputation of his leg after an unsuccessful by-pass operation. This was clearly a significant and unexpected injury connected with the medical treatment he had been receiving. It is not clear why he took no further action at the time, although in the end he did so reluctantly later. But it was reasonable to expect him to seek a second opinion then and there. Mrs Fenech was faced with years of pain after giving birth to her first child, when she was told that the needle used to stitch up an episiotomy had broken. She was embarrassed to talk about these matters, even to her doctor. But of course it was reasonable to expect her to do so. In contrast, Miss Smith underwent numerous operations during her childhood because of her Spina Bifida, one of which resulted in her becoming tetraplegic. There was no reason for her to think that this was anything other than a consequence of her disability (another example is *Mellors v Perry* [2003] EWCA CIV89, where the claimant had endured a childhood of renal problems with three kidney transplants but had no reason to think that this was anything other than a consequence of her congenital disability).

91. In my view, all the cases to which we have been referred are explicable on the basis that the law expects people to make such enquiries or seek such professional advice as they reasonably can when they have good reason to do so. Their motive for not doing so will generally be irrelevant. But I would not want to rule out that their personal characteristics may be relevant to what knowledge can be imputed to them under Section 14(3). There is a distinction between those personal characteristics which affect the ability to acquire information and those which affect one's reaction to what one does now. A blind man cannot be expected to observe things around him, but he may sometimes be expected to ask questions. It will all depend upon the circumstances in which he finds himself. As McGee & Scanlan have suggested, in an attempt to reconcile the authorities, a factor or attribute which is connected with the ability of the claimant to discover facts which are relevant to an action, should be taken into account; but a factor in his make-up which has no discernable effect upon his ability to discover relevant facts should be disregarded: see "Constructive knowledge within the Limitation Act (2003) 22 Civil Justice Quarterly 248, and 260. They go on to suggest that qualifications, training and experience may have such an affect whilst intelligence may not. It will all depend upon the facts of the case.'

24.72 Lord Walker also expressed caution about any simple formula put forward to cover every case that might occur (see paras 76–78).

24.73 The test for constructive knowledge within s 14(3) is accordingly objective. However, this will require the court to consider the objective situation in which the claimant finds himself in, including the effects of the injury itself. If the injury itself would reasonably inhibit him from seeking advice then that is a factor which must be taken into account (per Lord Hoffmann para 41

Adams above). The test should be by reference to the norms of the behaviour of persons in the situation in which the claimant finds himself (per Lord Scott, *Adams* supra). For example if a brain injury to the frontal lobe, not sufficient to make a claimant a patient, inhibits the claimant from making decisions, being able to concentrate or being able to comprehend information, that would be relevant to what was objectively reasonable for him to discover. If, however, the same claimant was constitutionally stoical, or forbearing, or too embarrassed to ask questions, that would not be relevant. Lady Hale, however, might go further and include those pre-accident characteristics which affect one's ability to discover and comprehend facts. To this extent a pre-accident subjective characteristic may be pertinent as in the case of the blind man.[138]

24.74 Given the claimant's situation he will be fixed with facts that are observable and ascertainable by him. In the *Opren* litigation certain claimants were fixed with knowledge which they had been exposed to and comprehended from newspaper and television coverage of the drugs' withdrawal and its possible side effects (see the cases of Eaton and Higgins in *Nash v Eli Lilly*). A claimant may also be fixed with knowledge which would have been easily ascertainable from a witness to his accident. In *Napper v National Coal Board*,[139] an action brought by a son in 1988 in respect of his father's death in a coal mining accident in 1957 was dismissed at statute-barred on the basis that the statement taken in 1985 from a material witness could reasonably have been taken much earlier. In *Leadbitter v Hodge Finance Limited*,[140] the claimant was also fixed with a constructive date of knowledge by the court as to when he ought, through his solicitors, have learned of the identity of a further defendant by ascertaining facts from a full police report. A claimant is most likely to be fixed with facts ascertainable with the help of his solicitor. In determining when such facts might have been available the date when it was reasonable for a solicitor to have been consulted will be evaluated. In *Henderson v Temple Pier Co Limited*[141] a claimant was fixed with constructive knowledge in circumstances where her solicitor acted dilatorily in acquiring the name of the owner of a ship upon which she slipped as this did not require any particular expertise and the proviso in s 14(3)(d) did not apply (see below). *Henderson* was followed in *Copeland v Smith*.[142] Examples of the court making findings of finding constructive knowledge after the House of Lords decision in *Adams v Bracknell Forest BC*[143] in vibration white finger cases are *Kew v Bettamix Ltd*[144] and *Norton v Corus UK Ltd*.[145]

---

[138] In *Catholic Care (Diocese of Leeds) v Young* [2006] EWCA Civ 1534 the Court of Appeal adopted this reasoning to the construction of s 14(2) concerning knowledge of whether an injury was reasonably significant. There is, therefore, currently a consensus that the test in construing reasonableness is the same in both subsections.
[139] Lexis, 1 March 1990.
[140] [1982] 2 All ER 167.
[141] [1998] 1 WLR 1540.
[142] [2001] 1 WLR 1371.
[143] [2004] UKHL 29.
[144] [2006] EWCA Civ 1535.
[145] [2006] EWCA 1630.

'Medical or other appropriate expert advice' (s 14(3)(b))

24.75 Section 14(3)(b) refers specifically to:

> '... facts ascertainable by him with the help of medical or other appropriate expert advice which it is reasonable for him to seek'.

24.76 In *Fowell v National Coal Board*,[146] the Court of Appeal held, obiter, that a claimant's solicitor was not an expert in the meaning of this subsection. Hidden J, at first instance, in *Nash v Eli Lilly*[147] concluded after detailed analysis of *Fowell* that there was no binding authority on the point as to whether solicitors came within the ambit of s 14(3)(b) but he doubted whether in most ordinary circumstances they did. Hidden J did emphasise however, that (at P182):

> ' ... suffice it to say that I am satisfied for the purposes in Section 14, a Plaintiff's knowledge of facts include knowledge which he might reasonably have been expected to acquire from facts ascertainable by him through the services of a Solicitor'.

24.77 The Court of Appeal in *Nash v Eli Lilly* saw no reason to depart from Hidden J's approach but also emphasised (at P344–400):

> 'Of course, as advice from the Solicitor as to the legal consequences of the act or omission is not relevant, his contribution can only consist of factual information. Moreover, where constructive knowledge is under consideration through the channel of the Solicitor this can only be relevant where it is established that the Plaintiff ought reasonably to have consulted a Solicitor at all. Thus it is for the defendant to establish not only that a Solicitor whom the Plaintiff might consult but have the necessary knowledge but also that it was reasonable to expect the Plaintiff to consult him.'

24.78 In *Henderson v Temple Pier & Co Limited*, above, the Court of Appeal decided that advice given by a solicitor could only fall within s 14(3)(b) if it related to a matter of fact on which expert advice was required. In that case the obtaining of the identity of the owners of the ship upon which the claimant fell was a relatively simple matter not requiring expert advice (per Bracewell J 1545):

> 'Having given her Solicitors general responsibility for the conduct of her claim, actions are taken and knowledge is acquired on behalf of the Plaintiff. If Solicitors fail to take appropriate steps to discover the person against whom that action should be brought, she cannot take refuge under Section 14(1)(c) because on the face of it the occupier of the St. Katherine and the gangway was knowledge which she might reasonably have been expected to acquire from facts obtainable or ascertainable by her. Even if the Solicitor is to be regarded as an appropriate expert, the facts were ascertainable by him without the use of legal expertise. The

---

[146] (1986) *The Times*, May 28.
[147] [1991] 2 Med LR169 at 182.

proviso is not intended to give an extended period of limitation of the person whose Solicitor acts dilatorily in acquiring information which was obtainable without particular expertise.'

24.79 In *Copeland v Smith & Goodwin*, decided four and a half months after *Henderson*, the latter was applied and the claimant was, in principle, to be fixed with the action and inaction of her legal advisors.

24.80 It is of course frequently the case that experts are only instructed after a solicitor is instructed. The type of solicitor that is instructed may well, therefore, be relevant. Invidious as it may seem, a claimant who consults a specialist firm in personal injury with expertise in spinal, brain injury or disease work might be fixed with an earlier date of constructive knowledge than one who seeks the advice of a non-specialist.

24.81 Whether it is reasonable for a claimant to seek the advice of a solicitor or another expert will also depend on the precise circumstances of the case (see *Adams v Bracknell Forest Borough Council* above). In *Bates v Leicester Health Authority*[148] a claimant was born with tetraplegia due to cerebral palsy in 1968. The claimant alleged his birth had been mis-managed. His parents told him that he could not sue the hospital. In 1993 he instructed a solicitor after his care worker suggested, following his father's death, that he might have a claim. The judge found that the claimant did not have actual knowledge of an omission of failing to intervene in the birth until receipt of an expert's report in 1994. The court also refused to fix the claimant with constructive knowledge as the defendant had not demonstrated that if the claimant had pressed his parents it would have made any difference to the knowledge he received. Relevant to this claimant's particular situation was his difficulty in communication and his substantial reliance on his parents.

24.82 In *Khan v Ainslie*[149] Waterhouse J refused to fix the claimant with constructive knowledge in respect of the cause of his blindness in the circumstances where his solicitor had received a negative medical opinion. Given the tenor of that report, the solicitors had not acted unreasonably in failing to put supplementary questions to the medical expert. Similarly, in *Jeffrey v C & B Speciality Packaging UK Limited*[150] the Court of Appeal allowed a claimant's appeal against the finding of constructive knowledge by the trial judge who found that a claimant, in a deafness case, should have made further enquiries of medical staff who provided him with the results of his hearing test. The claimant was told that a natural cause of his tinnitus was being investigated by his consultant. The Court of Appeal found that it was not reasonable to require the claimant to go behind this until 1991 when concern was expressed in a further report over his hearing loss.

---

[148] [1998] Lloyd's Rep Med 93.
[149] [1993] Med LR 319.
[150] [1999] 9 CL 49.

24.83 Section 14 does not define who is an expert but singles out, appropriately, medical experts who can range from a general practitioner to treating hospital physicians or medico-legal experts instructed by his solicitors. In *Nash v Eli Lilly* (above) the Court of Appeal held that certain claimants would be fixed with the knowledge of their GPs provided that it was reasonable for the claimant to have sought the advice of the doctor and reasonable to ask him what information the doctor had concerning the drug and its negative side-effects. In *Stephen v Riverside Health Authority*[151] a claimant with a limited knowledge of radiography was held not to be an expert in her own case particularly when much medical expertise directly conflicted with her own suspicions concerning the possible consequence of a radiation overdose.

24.84 If a claimant fails to take expert advice but relies on non-expert opinion he may nevertheless escape being fixed with constructive knowledge that would have been available from an expert if his action in going to non-experts was reasonable. In *Smith v Central Asbestos Limited*[152] the House of Lords indicated that workmen had acted reasonably in relying on erroneous advice given by their Works Manager. Similarly in *Howell v West Midlands Passenger Transport Executive*[153] the Court of Appeal held that the claimant in her circumstances had acted reasonably in relying on the opinions of unqualified people. Both these cases arose under the 1963 Act and concerned advice over a matter of law which is no long relevant under the 1980 Act. However, the cases do indicate the approach the Court is likely to take, as it did in *Knipe v British Railways Board*[154] where it was considered reasonable that a claimant took advice from his trade union.

The proviso (s 14(3))

24.85 Section 14(3) concludes as follows

> '... but a person shall not be fixed under this sub-section with knowledge of a fact ascertainable only with the help of expert advice so long as he has taken all reasonable steps to obtain (and, where appropriate, to act on) that advice'.

24.86 This proviso helps the claimant who instructs an expert who through oversight or incompetence, or even in the case of a treating doctor on therapeutic grounds, fails to provide the claimant with relevant facts concerning significance, attribution or identity.

24.87 This principle is well illustrated in the case of *Marston v British Railways Board*[155] where an engineer had been instructed by the claimant's solicitors to examine a hammer which had caused Mr Marston's carotid artery to be severed when a chip from the hammer flew off whilst he was striking a metal sett. Both

---

[151] [1990] Med LR 261.
[152] [1973] AC 518.
[153] [1973] 1 Lloyd's Rep 199.
[154] [1972] 1 Lloyd's Rep 122.
[155] [1976] ICR 124.

Mr Marston, before his death, and other employees believed that the hammer was in fact new. The expert reported that the hammer was satisfactory in terms of its hardness, but he failed to mention the fact that the hammer was neither new nor in good condition. At the trial, one expert thought the hammer fractured because of poor manufacturing while another thought it was due to previous misuse. The fact that the hammer was in poor condition did not emerge until cross-examination of the claimant's experts. Croom-Johnson J held that the claimant, the widow, was not to be fixed with the knowledge of the hammer's defect, because all reasonable steps had been taken to obtain that knowledge which the expert had not in fact revealed.

24.88 The proviso itself would rarely avail a claimant who relies upon a solicitor's advice not to pursue a witness or avenue of enquiry and, thereby, fails to uncover some relevant knowledge, because as indicated a solicitor is normally not an expert within the meaning of s 14(1)(b) (*Fowell v National Coal Board, Nash v Eli Lilly, Hallford v Brooks, Henderson v Temple Pier Co Limited* above). If, of course, a solicitor in possession of relevant knowledge advises a claimant that he has no case in law, that is entirely irrelevant on the clear wording of the section and time will continue to run against a claimant with the relevant knowledge of significance, attributability and identity.

24.89 In *Jones v Bennett*,[156] Widgery LJ held that the claimant had constructive knowledge from the date when it was reasonable for her to seek advice. That case concerned the claimant's inability to pay for her solicitor's advice so no detailed advice was given. Many other cases, however, have indicated that the date of constructive knowledge would, in fact, be when the advice was actually received or was likely to have been received following the instruction of the solicitor or of an expert (see *Guidera v NEI Projects (India) Limited*;[157] *Nash v Eli Lilly* above; *Bentley v Bristol & Western Health Authority (No 1)*[158]). This approach appears to be eminently reasonable because frequently when a report is commissioned from an expert, substantial time will elapse before the report is produced and delivered to the solicitors and its details are disclosed to the actual claimant.

24.90 The tenor of recent authorities is towards fixing a claimant with both an earlier date of actual knowledge and an earlier date of constructive knowledge. This process has led to an increasing reliance on the provisions of s 33 of the Limitation Act 1980.

---

[156] [1976] 1 Lloyd's Rep 484.
[157] CA Independent 1921990.
[158] [1991] 3 Med LR 1.

LIMITATION ACT 1980, S 33: DISCRETION, PREJUDICE AND 'ALL THE CIRCUMSTANCES OF THE CASE'

24.91 The court has a power in personal injury actions to allow a statute-barred claim to proceed if it appears equitable having regard to the respective prejudices likely to be suffered by each party. The discretion within s 33 of the Limitation Act 1980 to disapply a period of limitation is entirely unfettered. In most personal injury actions there is no 'out of time' long-stop beyond which a case is statutorily too stale and this includes those classes of cases where the claimant has an irresistible claim over against negligent legal advisers who permitted a claim to become statute barred.

The position 1979–2006 prior to *Horton v Sadler*[159]

24.92 The major class of action excluded from s 33 discretion between 1979 and 2006 were those governed by the rule in *Walkley v Precision Forgings*,[160] where a second writ has been issued because the first writ was never served or lawfully renewed, or where the first action was struck out for want of prosecution or was otherwise discontinued (see *Whitfield v North Durham Health Authority*;[161] *Young v Western Power Distribution (South West)*[162]). Unless in such cases it could be established that the date of knowledge occurred within 3 years prior to the issue of the second writ, this class of case was held to be statute-barred as the court had no power to apply the provision of s 33 of the 1980 Act.

24.93 This was because the House in *Walkley* held that the prejudice to the claimant was caused not by the provisions of the Limitation Act (then s 2D of the 1975 Act) but by the failure to prosecute the first action. The result of *Walkley* was to produce a series of cases where the courts strained to distinguish it on unprincipled grounds. Exceptions to the rule first arose where the initial action having been brought in time was discontinued due to misrepresentation or improper conduct on the part of the defendant (per Lord Diplock in *Walkley*, *Deerness v John Keeble & Sons (Brantham) Limited*;[163] *Forward v Hendricks*;[164] see also *Re: Philip Powis Limited*[165]).

24.94 A further class of exceptions occurred where an invalid writ had been issued such as against a company in compulsory liquidation so that the writ was wholly ineffective. If subsequent leave was given to issue proceedings then

---

[159] [2006] UKHL 27.
[160] [1979] 2 All ER 548.
[161] [1995] PIQR P 361.
[162] [2003] 1 WLR 2868.
[163] [1983] 2 Lloyd's Rep 260.
[164] [1997] 2 All ER 395.
[165] [1997] 2 BCLC 481.

s 33 of the 1980 Act was permitted to apply (*Wilson v Banner Scaffolding Limited*;[166] *Rose v Express Welding Limited*;[167] *Re Workvale Limited No 2*;[168] *White v Glass*[169]).

24.95 Neither did the rule in *Walkley* apply if a different party was sued in the second action (*Shapland v Palmer*[170]) or when the first action was against the estate of a deceased but no personal representatives had been appointed and the second action was against a named personal representative (*Piggott v Aulton*[171]).

Horton v Sadler

24.96 The anomalies which *Walkley* created were swept away in *Horton* by the House of Lords departing from its previous decision in *Walkley*, as affirmed in *Deerness v Keeble* and *Thompson v Brown*, by invoking its Practice Statement on Judicial Precedent.[172] The House found that *Walkley* was simply wrong as a matter of statutory construction because the claimant was prejudiced by the Limitation Act in the second action. *Walkley* was said have conflated the first action, where there was no prejudice caused by the Act as it was brought in time, with the second action where the claimant clearly was prejudiced. The House also said the decision had created distinctions not based on principle and restricted the Act's discretion which on proper construction was entirely unfettered (see Lord Bingham, paras 22–28). The principles in Horton were applied in *Richardson v Watson*[173] by the Court of Appeal who permitted a second action against the MIB to proceed through the exercise of a s 33 discretion.

THE EXERCISE OF DISCRETION

24.97 In exercising its discretion the court looks at:

(a) the balance of prejudice to each party;

(b) the six specific factors contained in s 33(3); and

(c) 'all the circumstances of the case' (s 33(3)).

24.98 There are very many cases involving the application of s 33 of the Limitation Act 1980 and they cannot be treated as precedents because of the

---

[166] (1982) *The Times*, June 22.
[167] Lexis, 21 January 1986.
[168] [1992] 2 All ER 627.
[169] (1989) *The Times*, February 18.
[170] [1999] 1 WLR 2068.
[171] [2003] PIQR P22.
[172] [1966] 1 WLR 1234.
[173] [2006] EWCA Civ 1662.

varied factual circumstances they give rise to and because judicial conceptions of discretion and equity vary. Certain principles, however, do arise and some of the following illustrations indicate the current judicial attitude to both questions of prejudice and discretion.

Prejudice

24.99 In *Hartley v Birmingham District Council*[174] Parker LJ became one of the first appellate judges to make some general observations on the nature of s 33 prejudice, although like other appellate judges before him he refused to lay down guidelines. In *Hartley*, the claimant issued a writ only a matter of hours out of time but no s 33 discretion was granted at first instance notwithstanding the minimal delay. Parker LJ held that in all or nearly all cases the prejudice in terms of refusing or allowing an action to proceed was equal and opposite because the stronger on liability the claimant's case was the greater the prejudice to him was if the claim was barred and the greater the prejudice would be to a defendant if the limitation period was disapplied. Alternatively, the weaker the claimant's case was the less the claimant would be prejudiced by being shut out because his claim was likely to fail and equally the defendants would suffer less prejudice in that they would be likely still to be able to defeat what was by definition a weak case.

24.100 This line of reasoning led the court to express the view that the most important question concerning prejudice was evidential prejudice as specified in s 33(3)(b) which dealt with the effect of the delay on the defendant's ability to defend the case on its merits. The court went on to state that if it was legitimate to consider, as it was, whether a claimant had a claim over against his solicitors, it was also legitimate to consider whether the defendant was insured. The court expressed the opinion that suing one's previous solicitors always created prejudice because the original wrong-doer may know very little about the weaknesses of the claimant's case particularly on quantum whereas the previous solicitor could well be appraised of them. Further, the court indicated that if the delay resulted in a windfall defence only and did not seriously affect the evidence then the power within s 33 would generally be exercised in the claimant's favour. This case was approved in 2006 by the House of Lords in *Horton v Sadler*.

24.101 Approximately a year after *Hartley* a differently constituted Court of Appeal remarked in *Nash v Eli Lilly*[175] that Lord Justice Parker's remarks were not of universal application. In *Nash*, the court emphasised that if a claimant's claim lacked merit then there might well be significant prejudice in allowing an action to proceed particularly where the claimant was legally aided and where a defendant would be put to great expense in defeating an unmeritorious claim. In those circumstances the claimant was in a position to extract a nuisance value settlement. Such considerations are likely to be more relevant to high cost complex pharmaceutical or product liability actions or clinical claims where

---

[174] [1992] 2 All ER 213.
[175] [1993] 4 All ER 344.

public funding is still available. In *Nash*, several claimants were denied s 33 dispensations primarily on the weakness of their case on the merits (eg *Eastern, O'Hara and Jenkins*). In *Kelly v Bastible*[176] the Court of Appeal held that whereas *Hartley* could permit a claim under s 33 where a short delay occurred which did not affect the defence and where there had been early notification of the claim it did not preclude insurers from relying on any evidential points which demonstrated prejudice. The proper approach in such a case should be to consider the insurer and the insured as forming a composite whole when considering prejudice.

24.102 In *Donovan v Gwentoys Limited*,[177] the House of Lords determined that prejudice which occurred before the expiry of the limitation period was a relevant matter for the Court to consider in deciding whether to grant a s 33 dispensation. The date of a letter before action in this context can be an important matter. In *Donovan*, the defendants were not put on notice as to the nature of the claimant's claim until more than 5 years from the date of her accident. The claimant, being a minor, had an extended period of limitation but even so issued proceedings five and a half months outside her primary limitation period.

24.103 Economic prejudice arising out of changes in the payment of damages in clinical negligence actions which arose due to restructuring of the National Health Service (NHS) with effect from 1 January 1990 might also constitute prejudice within a s 33 application. In *Whitfield v North Durham Health Authority*[178] the trial judge accepted that if the claim had been prosecuted in time damages would have been paid by Medical Defence Organisations but because the claim was brought late the Health Authority would need to fund any claim with respect to damages below £300,000. The trial judge took the view that any patients who might have to wait for treatment because a claimant was awarded damages would be probably willing to do so. The Court of Appeal reversed the trial judge's exercise of his discretion in allowing the case to proceed and found that an assumption of altruism on the part of patients who may be kept waiting longer for the treatment was something which was too speculative for the judge properly to consider.

24.104 In *Dobbie v Medway Health Authority*,[179] the claimant's case was not allowed to proceed following a 16-year delay on a number of grounds including one that the surgeon and hospital would be prejudiced by having the action hanging over them indefinitely. In the Court of Appeal, Beldam LJ remarked that he could not see how Damoclean sword type prejudice could apply to a doctor who did not know that any action was being contemplated against him. The fact that a defendant has had a number of claims brought against him in the past for example concerning industrial deafness which have been settled or compromised does not mean that a defendant may not be prejudiced by the

---

[176] [1997] 8 Med LR.
[177] [1990] 1 WLR 472.
[178] [1995] 6 Med LR 32.
[179] [1994] PIQR P353.

delay in any particular case (*Price v United Engineering Steels Limited*;[180] *Barrand v British Cellophane plc*[181] disapproving *Buck v English Electric Company Limited*[182]).

24.105 In cases concerning failures to deal with the effects of dyslexia the House of Lords in *Adams v Bracknell Forest Borough*[183] endorsed the Court of Appeal's remarks on the exercise of s 33 discretion made in *Robinson v St Helens Metropolitan Borough Council*[184] which emphasised the need for proportionality (per Sir Murray Stuart-Smith at P139):

> '32. ... These cases are very time consuming to prepare and try and they inevitably divert resources ... Under Section 33 the onus is on the Claimant to establish that it would be equitable to allow the claim to proceed having regard to the balance of prejudice.
>
> 33. The question of proportionality is now important in the exercise of discretion, none more so than under section 33. Courts should be slow to exercise their discretion in favour of a claimant in the absence of cogent medical evidence showing a serious effect on the claimant's health or enjoyment of life and employability. The likely amount of an award is an important factor to consider, especially if, as is usual in these cases, they are likely to take a considerable time to try.'

24.106 Such an approach was applied in *McGhie v British Telecommunications plc*.[185]

24.107 In *KR v Bryn Alyn Community Holdings Ltd*[186] the Court of Appeal was concerned with the exercise of discretion to cases of long standing psychiatric injury from sexual and physical abuse in children's homes. The court recognised that given the width of discretion available only general guidance could be given but derived a number of principles from the decided cases:

- The discretion is fettered only to the extent that s 33 provides a non-exhaustive list of circumstances to which to have regard.

- The matter is not determined simply by assessing comparative scales of hardship: rather the overall question is one of equity, namely whether it would be equitable to disapply the limitation period having regard to the balance of prejudice.

- An appellate court should not intervene save where the judge was so plainly wrong that his decision exceeded the ambit within which

---

[180] [1998] PIQR P407.
[181] (1995) *The Times*, February 16.
[182] [1997] 1 WLR 806.
[183] [2004] UKHL 29.
[184] [2003] PIQR P128.
[185] [2005] EWCA Civ 48.
[186] [2003] QB 1441.

- In multiple claimant cases each claim should be considered separately.

- The claimant has a heavy burden in showing that it would be equitable to disapply the limitation period and the dispensation is an exceptional indulgence to be granted only where equity demands it.

- Depending on the evidence and the issues generally the longer the delay the more likely and greater will be the prejudice to the defendant.

- Where a judge is minded to grant a long extension he should take meticulous care to give his reasons.

- A judge should not decide the matter on any one circumstance in s 33(3) but he should conduct a balancing exercise taking all the relevant circumstances into account.

- Where feasible a judge should decide the matter as a preliminary issue so as to avoid the decision on liability affecting the reasoning on limitation. If limitation is decided at trial it should be done before determining the substantive issues.

- In cases such as sexual abuse actions the date of knowledge test will extend time to favour claimants and therefore limited weight should be given to the reasons for the delay.

- In assessing the cogency of the claimant's evidence the judge should bear in mind that the more cogent the claimant's evidence the greater the prejudice to the defendant in depriving him of the limitation defence. What is of paramount importance is the effect of the delay on the defendant's ability to defend the case.

Discretion generally

24.108 Section 33(3) provides:

> 'In acting under this section the court shall have regard to all the circumstances of the case and in particular to:
>
> (a) the length of, and reasons for, the delay on the part of the plaintiff;
> (b) the extent to which having regard to the delay the evidence adduced or likely to be adduced by the plaintiff or the defendant is or is likely to be less cogent than if the action had been brought within the time allowed by section 11 . . . or as the case may be by section 12;
> (c) the conduct of the defendant after the cause of action arose, including the extent (if any) to which he responded to requests reasonably made by the

plaintiff for information or inspection for the purpose of ascertaining facts which were or might be relevant to the plaintiff's cause of action against the defendant;

(d) the duration of any disability of the plaintiff arising after the date of the accrual of the cause of action;

(e) the extent to which the plaintiff acted promptly and reasonably once he knew whether not the act or omission of the defendant, to which the injury was attributable, might be capable at that time of giving rise to an action for damages;

(f) the steps, if any, taken by the plaintiff to obtain medical, legal or other expert advice and the nature of any such advice he may have received.'

24.109 The six factors contained within s 33 are exemplary only, and not exclusive, and cannot be analysed in isolation from each other. Trial judges tend, however, to look at each factor in turn in exercising their discretion.

24.110 In *Nash v Eli Lilly*[187] the Court of Appeal indicated that it would be very slow to interfere with the exercise of discretion under this section but would do so where a judge either took into account factors which he should have ignored or ignored factors which he should have taken into account. The court expressed the view that, provided that it was relevant, the judge may take into account a factor not specifically listed in the sub-paragraphs of s 33(3) but alternatively, if it was established that he failed to take into account any of the matters mentioned in s 33(3) which were relevant to the carrying out of the balancing exercise then his judgment would be susceptible to attack.

24.111 A powerful illustration of intervention by the Court of Appeal with the exercise of discretion is found in the case of *Whitfield v North Durham Health Authority*,[188] where the court allowed the defendant's appeal against the exercise of the discretion in the claimant's favour. In analysing the judge's exercise of his discretion, the Court of Appeal said, first, that the judge ought to have taken into account that it was by mere oversight that the practitioner sued was excluded from the first writ which had been issued and accordingly it was relevant to consider whether the claimant should have such a windfall advantage from the incompetence of her own first solicitors. Secondly, the court indicated that the judge gave way to inappropriate speculation as discussed above. Thirdly, the court felt that the claimant should not for this purpose be treated as separate from her advisers, and any delay by the legal advisers was a relevant matter in considering the defendant's prejudice. Fourthly, the court indicated that the trial judge had given insufficient weight to the prejudicial effect of a doctor having to rely on his powers of recollection with the increasing passage of time.

24.112 Waite LJ said this:

---

[187] [1993] 4 All ER 383.
[188] [1995] 6 Med LR 32.

'The outcome of the balancing exercise under Section 33 is not to be determined on comparative scales of hardship (although hardship can never be irrelevant in a jurisdiction where all circumstances are to be taken into account). The overriding question is one of equity. Would it be equitable for the action to be allowed to proceed on the balance of prejudice weighted with due regard to all the circumstances and specific facts mentioned in the section? In determining such a question there can be no severance of the Plaintiff's conduct from that of her advisers.'

(See also *Brady v Wirral Health Authority*;[189] *Skitt v Khan and Wakefield Health Authority*;[190] *Farthing v North East Essex Health Authority*.[191])

24.113 For a case where the Court of Appeal interfered with the exercise of discretion to the benefit of the claimant see *Davis v Jacobs and Camden and Islington Health Authority*.[192] See also *Long v Tolchard and Sons Ltd*;[193] *Coad v Cornwall and Isles of Scilly Health Authority*;[194] *Margolis v Imperial Tobacco Ltd*;[195] *Mold v Hayton, Newsom*.[196]

Section 33(3)(a): 'The length of and reasons for the delay on the part of the Plaintiff'

24.114 The reference to delay here is to delay since the expiry of the limitation period.

24.115 Cases of extreme delay of over 20 years have been allowed to proceed but principally when they involve the contraction of insidious diseases due to exposure to substances arising out of allegations of negligence concerning a system of work rather than from a specific injury in a particular accident. (See *Buck v English Electric*[197] and *McClaren v Harland & Wolf Limited*.[198]) Generally speaking, however, the shorter the delay the more likely the court is to allow an action to proceed. In *Hendy v Milton Keynes Authority*[199] a 9-day delay which gave rise to no evidential prejudice was excused by the court in respect of an action for damages arising out of injury sustained during a hysterectomy. Even when there has been extensive delay and prejudice the court on occasions does allow a claim to proceed. In *Doughty v North Staffordshire Health Authority*[200] an action was brought some 25 years after the removal of a port wine stain on the claimant's face and some 13 years after the claimant's date of knowledge. The judge found the delay was due to discouraging advice

---

[189] Judgment, 25 June 1996 CCRTF 90/ 1502/C.
[190] [1997] 8 Med LR.
[191] [1998] 9 Med LR 38.
[192] [1999] Lloyd's Law Rep Med 72.
[193] [2001] PIQR P18.
[194] [1997] 1 WLR 189.
[195] [2000] MLC 204.
[196] [2000] MLC 207.
[197] [1977] 1 WLR 806.
[198] [1991] SLT 85.
[199] [1992] 3 Med LR 114.
[200] [1992] 3 Med LR 81.

and problems with legal aid. The action was allowed to proceed notwithstanding the fact the treating surgeon had had a stroke and was unable to testify (see also *Kidd v Grampian Health Board*[201] and *Baig v City and Hackney Health Authority*[202]). The court is obviously influenced by what is an acceptable reason for the delay and the claimant's prospects are enhanced if there is no direct criticism of the claimant himself as occurred in *McCafferty v Metropolitan Police District Receiver*.[203] Mr McCaffery was a policeofficer who had delayed in bringing an action because of a combination of his liking his job, feeling insecure with respect to his tenure and his desire to preserve good relations with his employer. Similarly, cases where a claimant's initial minor injury has triggered a severe exacerbation are likely to be looked upon favourably.

24.116 The position is otherwise where there has been no development and no good reason for the delay as in *Buckler v Sheffield Forest Borough Council*.[204] In *Das v Ganju*[205] inaccurate and misleading advice given by lawyers was held not to be a fault attributable to the claimant and in the absence of substantial prejudice to the Defendants a claim was allowed to proceed in respect of the birth of a child suffering from rubella syndrome. In *Corbin v Penfold Metalising*[206] a judge was held to be wrong to attribute to the Claimant the solicitors delay and the court held there was no such rule (see also *Whitfield v North Durham Health Authority* ibid and *Steeds v Peverel Management Services Ltd*[207]). However In Horton v Sadler supra Lord Carswell expressed doubt as to whether *Das* and *Corbin should be* construed so as to prevent the court from taking into account the failings of the claimant's solicitors. Lord Carswell's speech stated that the claimant must bear responsibility for delays which have occurred whether caused by him or his solicitors (para 53b).

24.117 In *Skitt v Khan*[208] the relative poverty of a claimant during his lifetime was held not to be a good enough reason for a failure to obtain a medical report.

24.118 In *Coad v Cornwall and Isles of Scilly Health Authority*[209] the Court of Appeal held that in considering the length of and reasons for the delay the test was a subjective one and ignorance of legal rights was a factor to be considered.

---

[201] [1994] SLT 265.
[202] [1997] 5 Med LR 221.
[203] [1997] 1 WLR 1073.
[204] LTL 21/6/04, CA.
[205] [1999] Lloyd's Med 198.
[206] [2000] Lloyd's Rep 247.
[207] (2001) *The Times*, May 16.
[208] [1997] 8 Med LR 165.
[209] [1997] 1 WLR 189.

Section 33(3)(b): 'The extent to which having regard to the delay the evidence adduced or likely to be adduced by the Plaintiff or the Defendant is or is likely to be less cogent than if the action had been brought within the time allowed by Section 11'

24.119 Again the delay referred to in this subparagraph is delay since the expiry of the limitation period.

24.120 This consideration was stated in *Hartley v Birmingham District Council, KR v Bryn Alyn* and *Horton v Sadler* to be the most significant matter in the exercise of the Court's discretion. Few cases are likely to be allowed to proceed where the defendants establish significant evidential prejudice such as the death of a witness or the destruction of written or other evidence. (See *Bater v Newbold*;[210] *Wilding v Lambeth, Southward and Lewisham Area Health Authority*;[211] and *Pilmore v Northern Trawlers Limited*.[212])

24.121 Accordingly, clinical negligence actions primarily based upon expert opinion where the written medical and nursing notes have been preserved are more likely to be allowed to proceed if time barred than those which raise issues concerning consent and warning as to risks which will turn upon oral recollection. In *Baig v City and Hackney Health Authority*[213] the trial judge refused to allow a statute-barred action to proceed partly on the basis that it would not be possible to have valuable recollections of the warnings given with respect to an operation performed some 17 years earlier. (See also *Farthing v North Essex District Authority*;[214] *Smith v Leicester Health Authority*;[215] *Gregory v Ferro (GB) Limited*;[216] *Brady v Wirral Health Authority*;[217] *Whitfield v North Durham Health Authority*;[218] *Roberts v Winbow*;[219] *Coad v Cornwall*;[220] *Briody v St Helens and Knowsley Area Health Authority*.[221])

---

[210] Lexis, 30 July 1991.
[211] Lexis, 10 May 1982.
[212] [1986] Lloyd's Rep 552.
[213] [1994] 5 Med LR 221.
[214] [1998] Lloyd's Rep Med 37.
[215] [1998] Lloyd's Rep Med 77.
[216] [1995] 6 Med LR 320.
[217] Judgment, 25 June [1996] CCRTF 90/1502.C.
[218] [1995] 6 Med LR 32.
[219] [1999] PIQR P77.
[220] [1997] 1 WLR 189.
[221] [1999] Lloyd's Rep Med 185.

Section 33(3)(c): 'The conduct of the Defendant after the cause of action arose including the extent (if any) to which he responded to requests reasonably made by the Plaintiff for information or inspection for the purposes of ascertaining facts which were or might be relevant to the Plaintiff's cause of action'

24.122 Refusals by potential defendants, insurers or solicitors to deal with a claim quickly or at all will not stop running against a claimant. However, if such activity can be shown to have slowed down the progress of the claim such behaviour might be relevant for the exercise of the court's discretion.

24.123 In *Atkinson v Oxfordshire Health Authority*,[222] the court held that it had been required to exercise its discretion under s 33 it would have done so in the claimant's favour because a large part of the delay was a failure by the defendant to tell the claimant's mother precisely what had happened during an operation to evacuate a tumour on the claimant which had resulted in injury to him.

24.124 A similar approach was adopted by the court in *Scuriaga v Powell*[223] where the claimant was told that a failed abortion was due to structural defect in her rather than a practitioner's own negligence. In *Sniezek v Bundy (Letchworth)*[224] the defendants obstructed pre-action disclosure in a case where the claimant's action for exposure to chemical dust became statute barred. The Court of Appeal upheld the exercise of the judge's discretion partly based upon the defendant's behaviour.

24.125 In *Marshall v Martin*[225] the Court of Appeal held that the defendant's conduct need not be discreditable or unsatisfactory and the fact that the defendant had made an interim payment would be relevant in considering how that operated on the claimant's mind in respect of a belief that the case was likely to be settled.

Section 33(3)(d): 'The duration of any disability of the Plaintiff arising after the date of the accrual of the cause of action'

24.126 Disability here refers to unsoundness of mind pursuant to the definition contained in s 38(2) of the Limitation Act 1980 as the only other form of disability namely infancy cannot arise after the accrual of a cause of action.

24.127 Dicta which treated disability within the meaning of this subsection as a physical disability as in *Bater v Newbold*[226] and *Pilmore v Northern Trawlers*

---

[222] [1993] 4 Med LR 18.
[223] [1979] 123 SJ 406.
[224] [2000] PIQR P213.
[225] Lexis, 10 June 1987.
[226] Lexis, 30 July 1991.

Limited[227] are wrong, see the Court of Appeal's decision in *Yates v Thakenham Tiles Limited*[228] and *Thomas v Plaistow*.[229]

24.128 Nevertheless such physical disability not amounting to disability within the meaning of s 38(2) of the Limitation Act 1980 is frequently relevant when considering the reasons for the delay in s 33(3)(a) and in considering all the circumstances of the case.

Section 33(3)(e): 'The extent to which the Plaintiff acted promptly and reasonably once he knew whether or not the act or omission of the Defendant, to which the injury was attributable, might be capable at that time as giving rise to an action for damages'

24.129 One of the major reasons for recommending a discretionary power to disapply the limitation period was to mitigate the effect that ignorance of the law should not stop time running against a claimant. Once, however, a claimant has personal knowledge that he has a cause of action upon which he can sue the court will inquire into how expeditiously the action was progressed before the issue of proceedings.

24.130 The claimant will be fixed with the action and behaviour of his lawyers as well as himself (*Thompson v Brown*,[230] *Horton v Sadler* above) but not necessarily blamed for his lawyer's delays (see *Steeds v Peverell Management* above).

24.131 In *Doughty v North Staffordshire Health Authority*[231] the court was willing to excuse the delay of the claimant's lawyers and exonerated the claimant from any personal blame in respect of failing to insist that her lawyers prosecuted the claim more quickly.

24.132 In *Davis v Jacobs and Camden and Islington Health Authority*[232] the Court of Appeal was of the view that in construing s 33(3)(e) the court was concerned only with the conduct of the claimant (at p 86 col 2). This would appear to run contrary to the speech of Lord Diplock in *Thomas v Brown* and Lord Carswell in *Horton v Sadler*.

24.133 In *Obembe v City and Hackney Health Authority*[233] parents sued in 1988 for alleged malpractice occurring at the birth of their son in 1979. They included a claim for damages in respect of themselves which was statute-barred

---

[227] [1986] 1 Lloyd's Rep 552.
[228] [1995] PIQR 135.
[229] [1997] PIQR P540.
[230] [1981] 2 All ER 296.
[231] [1992] 3 Med LR 81.
[232] [1999] Lloyd's Law Rep Med 72.
[233] Lexis, 9 June 1989.

and the court rejected the contention put forward that because they had 21 years to sue in respect of their son that was a reasonable excuse for not bringing their own action earlier.

Section 33(3)(f): 'The steps if any taken by the Plaintiff to obtain medical, legal or other advice and the nature of any such advice he may have received'

24.134 Negative legal or medical advice is frequently a problem for claimants and can delay the prosecution of an action because of difficulties over negligence or causation. In some publicly funded cases it led to the discharge of the certificate. (See *Bentley v Bristol and Western Health Authority*;[234] *Halford v Brooks*;[235] *Das v Ganju*.[236])

24.135 The wording of the subparagraph indicates that it is relevant for the court to consider what the advice was. In *Jones v G D Searle & Co Limited*[237] the defendants wanted to know what previous legal advice had been given in a case where the claimant claimed that new developments in science had made previous advice, which was negative, out-dated. The defendants sought leave to administer an interrogatory to ascertain whether the prior advice was favourable or not, but the claimant said that that would amount to offend against legal professional privilege. The Court of Appeal found that giving the answer to the interrogatory, which limited itself to seeking to know whether the previous advice was negative or not, did not have the consequence that Counsel's Opinions were liable to discovery.

24.136 In *Tatlock v G P Worsley & Co Limited*[238] the defendants sought disclosure of the contents of an allegedly negative medical report together with correspondence with medical experts which meant that a claim was not proceeded with earlier than it was. The Court of Appeal held that s 33(3)(f) did not override the rules of legal professional privilege save in the restricted sense of a requirement for a claimant to indicate the nature of the advice only. As a matter of tactics and evidence the claimant might need to waive privilege if he was to rely effectively on the contents of the documents in issue.

'All the circumstances of the case'

24.137 As indicated in *Donovan v Gwentoys Limited*[239] the House of Lords stipulated that although s 33(3)(a) and (b) required the court to look at the delay after the expiry of the limitation period the injunction to look at all the circumstances of the case allowed the court to consider what prejudice had occurred within the primary limitation period. The court is also likely to

---

[234] [1991] 2 Med LR 359.
[235] [1991] 1 WLR 428.
[236] [1999] Lloyd's Rep Med 198.
[237] [1978] 3 All ER 654.
[238] Lexis, 22 June 1989.
[239] [1990] 1 All ER 1018.

consider the strength of the claimant's case, the likely size of the award, the strength of the defendant's case on the merits, whether a claimant is legally aided or not, whether a defendant is insured, whether there is an alternative remedy such as a good claim over against the claimant's solicitors or perhaps the possibility of a judgment being satisfied by the Motor Insurers' Bureau (see *Horton v Sadler* above, paras 52–55).

PROCEDURE

24.138 A district judge or a master in addition to a judge is empowered to exercise discretion under s 33 of the Limitation Act 1980 pursuant to CPR, r 2.4. If the defendants believe that they have an extremely strong case they may issue an application to strike out the claimant's claim but this is unlikely to be successful if the claimant has any arguable merit at all. The normal procedure adopted is to issue an application to determine the limitation issue at an interlocutory hearing. If, however, it is desirable to call evidence or where there is a need for extensive discovery of documents it is better to have a preliminary trial on the issue of limitation. Any such preliminary trial may take place immediately before the trial of the main action or it may be at an earlier date. If the preliminary trial requires a rehearsal of many or most of the issues likely to be raised in the main trial then there is no great saving in costs by having the preliminary issue on limitation tried on a different date to the substantive hearing. However in *Bryn Alyn* (P) the Court of Appeal emphasised that limitation issues should be decided as preliminary issues if practicable. If the limitation issue is tried at the main trial it should be done before determining the substantive issues.

24.139 A pertinent distinction between having an interlocutory trial and having a trial on limitation immediately before the trial of the main action was thought at one stage to be that if a claimant failed on an interlocutory hearing leave was required to appeal to the Court of Appeal, but if a claimant failed at trial of the preliminary limitation point immediately before the substantive hearing no leave was required. However, the Court of Appeal in *Dale v British Coal Corporation (No 1)*[240] stipulated that whatever procedure is adopted a judge's determination is deemed to be a final one and at the time of that ruling pursuant to the then RSC Rules no leave was required. Under the CPR provisions the distinction between an interlocutory and a final Order is not pertinent to the issue of permission as permission is now required pursuant to CPR, r 52.3. The destination of an appeal is now determined by the Destination of Appeals Order 2000 as amended by Civil Procedure (Modification of Enactment) Order 2003 and Practice Direction 52PD. The general principle is that an appeal lies to the next level of judge in the court's hierarchy. However the normal rule will not be followed in a case where the Court's decision is a final one in multi-track claims. In these cases s 14 and s 33

---

[240] [1992] 1 WLR 964.

appeals would lie to the Court of Appeal (see *Tanfern Limited v Cameron-MacDonald*.[241] This does not apply to those cases not in the multi-track.

24.140 The onus of persuading the court to disapply the primary limitation period lies on the claimant (*Thompson v Brown Construction (Ebbw Vale) Limited*[242]).

24.141 Practitioners have been divided as to whether the proper pleading practice is for a claimant to particularise the facts and circumstances which he intends to rely on in seeking to persuade the court to exercise s 33 in his favour in the Particulars of Claim or whether it should be pleaded in a reply following the defendant raising limitation in the defence. While the onus is on the claimant to persuade the court, the fact that limitation is not a bar to a case but (rather) a defence suggests that there is no need to anticipate the defence, and that it might be preferable to wait and see if the defendant takes the point (see *Ogunsanya v Lambeth Area Heath Authority*).[243] Alternatively in a clear case where the claimant is obviously out of time it may be sensible for the claimant to plead the particulars intended to be relied upon for a s 33 dispensation so to assist the court in fulfilling the overriding objective and clarifying the issues between the parties pursuant to the spirit of the CPR. A limitation defence must be pleaded and if a s 33 application is required and has not been pleaded in the Particulars of Claim there must be a reply.

24.142 Appeals to the Court of Appeal are not infrequent as the number of cases referred to illustrates. Because, however, the discretion of the judge is unfettered the Court of Appeal has indicated that it will be slow to overturn a first instance decision recognising that judgments over what is equitable in all the circumstances will necessarily lead to a variation of judicial opinion (*Conry v Simpson*[244]). Where, however, the judge has failed to exercise his discretion at all or has exercised it erroneously or on wrong principles the Court has not infrequently reversed a trial judge's decision. The Court of Appeal will not interfere merely because its own discretion might have been exercised in a different way (*Bradley v Hanseatic Shipping Co Limited*;[245] *Carlisle v Associated British Ports*[246]). In *Nash v Eli Lilly*[247] Lord Justice Purchas stated:

> 'Subject to acting judicially the discretion of the Court is unfettered. The specific matters set out in sub-section (3) are exemplary not definitive. Thus the Court of Appeal will be very slow to interfere with the exercise of that discretion under this section: See Conry v Simpson [1983] 3All ER 369. Where, however, it is established that the judge either took into account factors which he should have ignored or ignored factors which he should have taken into account, or was plainly wrong,

---

[241] [2000] 1 WLR1311.
[242] [1981] 1 WLR 744.
[243] Lexis, 3 July 1985.
[244] [1983] 3 All ER 369.
[245] [1986] 2 Lloyd's Rep 34.
[246] Lexis, 18 November 1987.
[247] [1993] 4 All ER 383 at 402.

then this court is under a duty to interfere and in appropriate cases to substitute a decision based upon its own discretion. On the other hand, provided that it is relevant to the circumstances of the case, the judge may take into account a factor not specifically mentioned in the sub-paragraphs of sub-section (3), but on the other hand, if it is established that the judge failed to take into account any of the matters in sub-paragraph (3) which were relevant to the carrying out of the balancing exercise, then his judgment is susceptible to attack. It should however be mentioned that a judge is not under a duty specifically to refer to each and every fact which he has found and upon which he has exercised his discretion.'

24.143 In *Bryn Alyn* (above) the Court of Appeal confirmed this approach by indicating that a judge's s 33 discretion could only be disturbed if it was outside the ambit of reasonable disagreement. This included the exercise of wrong principles, taking into account irrelevant factors, ignoring relevant factors or making a decision that was plainly wrong. If the appeal court intervened on any such ground the matter should be treated as at large and the discretion exercised afresh.

24.144 Where a claimant restores a dissolved company to the Register in order to bring proceedings under s 651 of the Companies Act 1985 the restoration order should not usually include a provision that the period of dissolution should not count for limitation purposes. In *Smith v White Knight Laundry*[248] the Court of Appeal held that such an order that the period of dissolution was to be discounted should only be made where notice of the restoration was served on all parties that could be expected to oppose it, the court was satisfied that it had all the evidence that the parties would wish to adduce for an application under s 33 and any such application was bound to succeed. Otherwise, as will be the case in most proceedings the claimant should seek relief under s 33 in the normal manner.

SPECIAL TIME LIMITS

24.145 Section 39 of the 1980 Limitation Act provides a saving for those periods of limitation prescribed in other statutes:

'This Act shall not apply to any action or arbitration for which a period of limitation is prescribed by or under any other enactment (whether passed before or after the passing of this Act) . . .'

24.146 Accordingly, practitioners should be alert to the different time limits imposed by many statutes governing transport such as ss 183 and 190 of the Merchant Shipping Act 1995 (2-year limitation period), the Carriage by Air Act 1961 (2-year limitation) the International Transport Convention Act 1983 (3-year period but a 5-year long-stop), the Carriage of Passengers by Road Act 1974 (3-year period but with a long-stop of 5 years), the Consumer

---

[248] [2002] 1 WLR 616.

Protection Act 1987 (3-year period but with a 10-year long-stop), the Nuclear Installations Act 1965 (30- or 20-year long-stops depending on the circumstances).

24.147 Claims brought under s 3 of the Protection from Harassment Act 1997 are specifically excluded from the personal injury limitation regime by s 11(1A) of the Limitation Act 1980 and accordingly have a 6-year period as a statutory cause of action pursuant to s 9 of the 1980 Act.

24.148 Under the Foreign Limitation Periods Act 1984 a foreign limitation period may be imposed with respect to a tort committed overseas but litigated in England.

Chapter 25

MEDICAL EXAMINATIONS

25.1 This chapter only deals with the expert evidence of medical experts and their examinations. Chapter 5 deals with expert evidence more generally, and practitioners should refer to both chapters when considering expert medical evidence. Other considerations may apply to non-medical experts, although Civil Procedure Rules 1998 (CPR), r 35 covers all expert evidence. Neither does this chapter deal with medical reports gathered as part of the rehabilitation process nor the considerations parties involved in or considering rehabilitation as part of the resolution of an injury claim should bear in mind. This is not to suggest that rehabilitation should form less than an increasingly important part of all practitioners thinking and planning around a claim.

25.2 The first consideration is whether medical evidence is required at all. It will be a rare case where it is not, but CPR 16PD.4 states:

> '4.3 Where the claimant is relying on the evidence of a medical practitioner the claimant must attach to or serve with his particulars of claim a report from a medical practitioner about the personal injuries which he alleges in his claim.'

25.3 From a pleading point of view, what is vital is that the injuries be set out in the Particulars of Claim, then, if relied upon, the medical report must be attached,[1] but in a minor and wholly resolved injury such report may not be required.

25.4 However, the rest of this chapter addresses the vast majority of claims in which such a report will be required and will form the bedrock of evidence upon which the quantum of any claim is based or forms the foundation for an attack on such claims by the defendant.

THE PURPOSE OF A MEDICAL EXAMINATION

25.5 The purpose of the medical report (and the role of the expert) is primarily to assist the court, not the requisitioning party: Part 35 makes it clear that the expert's duty is to the court, not the party who has instructed him.[2] Furthermore, the court has a positive duty, pursuant to CPR, r 35.1, to restrict

---

[1] There may be occasions when a medical report is not attached to the pleadings, but relied upon at a later date, but this is outside the scope of the present chapter.
[2] CPR, r 35.3.

expert evidence to that which is reasonably required to resolve proceedings. The court has the power to exclude expert evidence, in whole or part if deemed not to be so required.[3]

25.6 This has been interpreted by the courts in a number of ways. It is almost always the case in a personal injury action that some medical evidence will be allowed, but often this will be restricted to one expert discipline only, so care must be taken when choosing that discipline.

25.7 Of course, the expert evidence allowed will depend on the track to which the claim is allocated. A small track claim, currently a personal injury claim with a value of less than £1,000,[4] has the strictest rules relating to expert evidence (see CPR Part 27 in general and CPR, r 27.5 in particular). An expert report will often not be allowed at all, or will be less formal than in other tracks. The payment to an expert is limited to £200.

25.8 The fast track is slightly less restrictive, but the court will first ask if any expert evidence is required, then if it is, whether a single joint expert will suffice and only then consider each party instructing its own. A claim can only remain in the fast track if oral expert evidence is limited to one expert per party in no more than two disciplines (CPR, r 26.6(4)(b)). This may seem generous, but a road traffic accident with a liability expert, orthopaedic expert and psychiatric expert would no longer be fast track even if damages were less than £15,000.

25.9 Often in the smaller injury case, particularly if limitation is looming, the expert who is able to produce a report in a short period of time appeals to the instructing party but, at a later stage in the litigation process, this can lead to parties being constrained to the evidence of an accident and emergency consultant, rather than an orthopaedic consultant or rheumatologist who may be more appropriate.

25.10 The judge dealing with the case management of a claim is rarely the trial judge, yet great influence on the outcome of a claim is in the hands of the court when restricting or allowing the parties to instruct experts. It is unusual, except in the larger cases, for more than one medical expert to be allowed per party and although the fast track directions anticipate no more than two experts per party for a claim within that regime, this is the exception rather than the rule.

25.11 A survey conducted in December 1999 reported that experts' workloads were down by 35% and 65% of experts had been appointed as joint experts. The number of experts attending to give oral evidence at trial had reduced by 30%.

25.12 Therefore, the purpose of the medical examination and the accompanying report are vitally important for informing the court as to the nature and severity of a claimant's injuries, the prognosis, and any needs arising

---

[3] *Grobbelaar v Sun Newspapers* (1999) *The Times*, August 12; CA.
[4] CPR, r 26.6.

from the sequelae of the injury. Often the paper report will be all that is before the court, oral evidence being dispensed with.

25.13 Medical examination should be carried out by someone with the relevant expertise who restricts the content of the report to matters within his expertise, save where it is necessary to consider the extent to which, if at all, the material injury affects other clinical assessments; eg a psychiatrist should not give an opinion upon orthopaedic matters but is entitled to comment upon the extent to which reported orthopaedic sequelae may have affected the psychological condition upon which the report has been sought.

25.14 The examination should be confined to medical matters and should not, for example, include observations as to the honesty or evasiveness of the person being examined unless these are based upon sound clinical findings, eg responses to tests and examination which are illogical or inconsistent with the alleged injury.

25.15 Sometimes an expert will comment on disparity of findings on examination and observation, eg: 'On examination the claimant was unable to stand or sit without my assistance and could not walk without the use of a stick but I watched her from my consulting room window as she ran to catch a bus with no seeming disability and without using her walking stick'. But unless the observation is clear, speculation is to be discouraged.

25.16 Unless there are special reasons, it is preferable that the examination for the medico-legal report is not by any doctor who has treated the claimant and should be by a doctor who is in current clinical practice and not retired. If the expert has retired, as a rule of thumb their currency as an expert will last only about 2-3 years post-retirement, except for someone with exceptional expertise who has striven to remain abreast of current events and developments in their former area of practice.

THE COMMISSIONING OF A MEDICAL REPORT

25.17 Considerable care must be taken when instructing a medical expert. CPR, r 35.10(3) says that the expert's report must state the 'substance of all material instructions, whether written or oral, on the basis of which the report was written'.

25.18 This does not mean that the letter of instruction is automatically to be disclosed (see CPR, r 35.10(4)) but the instructions are not privileged so that, if necessary, the court can consider the statement of instructions. Often medical experts will include a paragraph in their report setting out the ambit of their instructions, which can save argument at a later date.

25.19 It is important to note that all material instructions must be stated – written or oral. A 'side' letter or a telephone call giving instructions not contained in the main letter of instruction does not escape the rule of materiality.[5]

25.20 If an expert interviews witnesses to prepare his report, the notes of the interviews should be annexed to the report and are not privileged, *BCCI v Ali (No 3)*.[6] If the medical expert refers to any peer journals or textbooks in support of conclusions reached, either the references should be attached to the report or they should be clearly cited and copies provided for court and other parties if required.

25.21 Often, if a medical expert is jointly instructed, the parties will agree the letter of instruction. If there are matters upon which either party wishes the doctor to give a view, which is not agreed by the other, then a second letter can be written containing those particular instructions and, if they are matters within the experts' field, they must be dealt with.

The guidance given to experts by Cresswell J in *National Justice Compania Naviera SA v Prudential Assurance Co Ltd (aka 'The Ikarian Reefer')*[7] has largely been incorporated into CPR Part 35 and the 'Code of Guidance on Expert Evidence: A Guide for experts and those instructing them for the purpose of court proceedings' (set out in the Practice Direction to CPR Part 35):

- Expert evidence presented to the court should be, and should be seen to be, the independent product of the expert.

- An expert witness should provide independent assistance to the court by way of objective, unbiased opinion in relation to matters within his expertise. An expert should never assume the role of an advocate.

- An expert witness should state the facts or assumptions on which his opinion is based. He should not omit to consider material facts which could detract from his concluded opinion or be selective about the facts on which he relies.

- An expert should make it clear when any matter falls outside his field of expertise.

- If there is insufficient data or research an expert must make it clear that his report is provisional.

---

[5] While disclosure of instructions is rare, it can happen. A solicitor's entire letters of instruction were ordered to be disclosed in *Salt v Consignia plc* Current Law, December 2002; 420.
[6] [1999] 4 All ER 83.
[7] [1993] 2 Lloyd's Rep 68.

- If, after exchanging reports, the expert changes his view for any reason such change of view must be communicated to the other party.

- All material before the expert must be provided to the other party.

25.22 If a medical expert is not familiar with the Code and does not know the Expert's Declaration, nor append it automatically to his report, then the instructing party may wish to think carefully about their choice of expert. It may be that the area in which medical expertise is being sought is sufficiently unusual in the litigation field that the expert, truly a medical expert, has little or no medico-legal experience. However, if the field is more common, the lack of experience may suggest an alternative expert should be considered.

25.23 Increasingly experts in common fields (such as orthopaedics, psychiatry, plastic surgery etc) are members of the Expert Witness Institute and have been on medico-legal training courses and will readily give those intending to instruct them a breakdown of their instructions with percentage instructions for claimant, defendant and single joint and also details of appearances in court.

Timing of the report

25.24 The time at which a report is commissioned can be important. Often, with the pre-action protocol applying automatically to fast track cases and in spirit to all cases, instruction will be well before issue of proceedings is contemplated. This can mean that a first report deals with the particular aftermath of an accident, with a later report giving a better view on long-term prognosis or, indeed, analysis of the impact of any previous medical history.

25.25 It is not uncommon for an initial general report to be superseded at the agreement of the parties by a more specialist report when the nature of the injury, or the primary issues between the parties, becomes clearer. The early report need not, however, be wasted. Even if the expert is abandoned, the report, in particular its expert independent view of the claimant at an early stage after the accident, can be incorporated or adopted as valuable history into a later report.

25.26 The parties do run a risk producing early expert reports. If the court subsequently decides the instruction was unnecessary (even as late as at trial) or refuses to give permission to rely on the evidence at an earlier CMC, the commissioning party will fail to recover the cost of commissioning that expert.[8]

25.27 While a medical report must be served with the pleadings, it is possible to serve a preliminary report, if time is short and further reports are awaited. In *Knight v Sage Group*[9] the judge rejected a defendant's submission that a GP report served with proceedings was not a proper report so as to comply with

---

[8] *Thomas Johnson Coker v Barkland Cleaning Co*, TLR, 6 December 1999, CA.
[9] CA; unreported, 28 April 1999, Lawtel AC9500203.

CPR, r 6.1(5) and (7) but did rule that two psychiatric reports, which the claimant did not want to disclose, must be served so as to comply with the rule and defeat the defendant's application to strike out. The claimant was reluctant to disclose these privileged reports. The Court of Appeal agreed, allowing the GP report as a preliminary report, rather than CPR compliant medical report, and giving the claimant three months to file further medical evidence. This was felt to be a better balance of discretion and court intervention. The court's approach is usefully contrasted with the approaches of the Court of Appeal in the more recent cases of *Beck v Ministry of Defence* and *Vasiliou v Hajigeorgiou*.

Single joint expert

25.28 It is important to understand the status of the expert being instructed. It may be that the expert is a single joint instruction. This is an expert imposed by the court or agreed by the parties to produce one report on any particular field (see CPR, r 35.7). If the expert is jointly instructed, not only do both parties have a right to an involvement in the letter of instruction, but neither party can withhold disclosure of the final report. Indeed, it is good practice for an expert to send a copy to each party at the same time.

25.29 While both parties then have the right to ask questions, the report itself cannot be rejected. Even if one party wishes to abandon the joint expert and seek its own evidence, an application to the court will be required with reasons (other than the view that the expert has not given evidence supportive to the party seeking redress).

25.30 It can be most useful in such instances to obtain a 'desktop' report from the expert with which the party hopes to replace the joint report. This 'desktop' report can be obtained without examination of the claimant (useful if the protesting party is the defendant) and can give the expert's reasons for disagreeing with the conclusions expressed in the joint report. It is also important to make any such application in a timely fashion – the better the new expert can fit into any timetable already given by the court, the better the chances of successfully persuading the court to allow the evidence. Any case managing judge will be cautious of superseding the role of the trial judge and, if a convincing argument can be raised showing a genuine area of dispute in the medical evidence, should be persuaded to allow the new expert to be called.

25.31 The Court of Appeal in *Daniels v Walker*[10] set out a now common approach to dealing with the instruction of experts. The instruction of a single joint expert is a first, not a last, step. Once instructed, and the report received, questions should be asked by both parties. If one party remains unhappy with the report, then an application for its own expert can be made (the process suggested in para 25.25 is recommended). The objection to the single joint expert can be made having attempted to seek answers to questions sought, and

---

[10] [2000] 1 WLR 1382.

if problems and issues remain, and are deemed by the court to be more than merely fanciful the dissenting party's application will have a better prospect of success.

25.32 Proportionality was also referred to by the Court of Appeal as an important consideration. Clearly the higher the value case the greater the chance that an application for a second expert will succeed. However, proportionality is not merely the overall size of quantum. Even in a relatively modest claim the issue between the medical experts upon which a second view is sought could be the primary issue between the parties and represent the dispute between the parties upon which adjudication is sought. In such an instance, it will be more proportionate to seek a second report that, say, in a case where a small part of the overall quantum sum is general damages for pain and suffering and therefore the effect of a different medical view will be merely a few hundred pounds while argument centres on a care claim or some other issue.

25.33 Since *Daniels v Walker* Mr Justice Neuberger, in *Cosgrove v Pattison*,[11] considered the factors to be taken into account when considering an application to permit a further expert to be called after the instruction of a single joint expert. He listed the factors as:

'(1) the nature of the issue or issues; (2) the number of issues between the parties; (3) the reason the new expert is wanted; (4) the amount at stage and, if it is not purely money, the nature of the issues at stake and their importance; (5) the effect of permitting one party to call further expert evidence on the conduct of the trial; (6) the delay, if any, in making the application; (7) any delay that the instructing and calling of the new expert will cause; (8) any other special features of the case; and, finally, and in a sense all embracing, the overall justice to the parties in the context of the litigation.'

25.34 The opinion of a single joint expert must be clear and expressed to both parties. Therefore, it is inappropriate for a single joint expert to attend a conference with only one party present. The Court of Appeal in *Peet v Mid Kent Healthcare NHS Trust*[12] suggested there may never be circumstances in which such a one sided conference would be appropriate but quoted with approval the protocol for expert evidence prepared by the Academy of Experts which states at para 17.13:[13]

'A single joint expert should not attend any meeting or conference that is not a joint one, unless all the parties have first agreed in writing [or the court has directed that such a meeting may be held] and who is to pay the experts' fees for the meeting.'

---

[11] Unreported; RCJ, 27 November 2000.
[12] [2002] 1 WLR 210.
[13] Paragraph 19.9 at the time of the *Peet* judgment. Phrase in square brackets added since the judgment.

25.35 It should also be noted that *Daniels v Walker* makes it clear that obtaining written reports does not automatically lead to a direction allowing the makers of the reports to be called at trial. This is a separate secondary question for the procedural judge to consider and may need to be subject to specific application. Parties often overlook the need for permission to call medical experts at trial. It should also be remembered, that the experts are called for cross-examination on their reports, rather than to give evidence in chief. The trial judge may well expect the issues to be aired in court to be clearly defined, even set out in skeleton arguments before trial.

25.36 It is not acceptable for a solicitor to instruct an expert shortly before trial without first checking the expert's availability for any trial date (*Rollinson v Kimberley Clark*[14]). If, once a trial date is set, an expert is not able to attend trial, the court will need to know why before it will consider vacating that date (*Matthews v Tarmac Bricks and Tiles Ltd*[15]). Such explanation will need to be more than a bare 'the expert is unavailable' or 'the expert is on holiday'. Details of when the expert was booked, when the problems were known and when the expert first informed the party of his unavailability will all be required.

25.37 Indeed, since it is now a requirement to give notice to the expert of the dates by which steps in the action must be taken, including the trial date, within seven days of the making of any time order it must be expected that successful late applications for the vacation of a trial date due to unavailability of an expert will become ever rarer.

Single expert

25.38 If the expert was instructed pursuant to the personal injury pre-action protocol (either the defendant agrees to a choice of expert when given notice or does not respond within the required time) then while the defendant will be deemed to have agreed to that choice of expert, the expert is jointly selected, not a single joint expert. This means that the claimant, having commissioned the report, is not obliged to disclose either the letter of instructions nor the report, if it is disappointing.

25.39 Of course, the defendant will know the report has been commissioned and will know the rejected expert was likely to have been disappointing to the claimant, but the defendant cannot require disclosure.[16]

25.40 If the parties have their own expert on any discipline, even if permission is given to rely on the report of a named expert, disclosure cannot be compelled. If the expert is not named, simply the discipline considered by the court, then the party can substitute one expert for another (*Vasiliou v Hajigeorgiou*[17]). However, if the court has given permission for a named expert

---

[14] (1999) *The Times*, June 15, CA.
[15] TLR, 1 July 1999, CA.
[16] *Carlson v Townsend* [2001] EWCA Civ 511; [2001] 3 All ER 663.
[17] [2005] EWCA Civ 235; [2005] 3 All ER 17.

and, in the event, the party seeks to rely on the evidence of another expert, the court can, and usually will, make it a condition of giving permission to 'switch' experts that the first report be disclosed as well (*Beck v Ministry of Defence*[18]). The purpose of this is to restrict 'expert shopping' and reflect the court's overall desire to control expert evidence. If the party remains reluctant to disclose the first report, then it will usually have to forego the switch of experts, but that may be a price considered worth paying if the first report is highly prejudicial.

25.41 These cases all deal with experts whose reports have never been disclosed – that is the parties seek to change experts prior to disclosing the first report. Different considerations may apply if the first report has been disclosed and the party wishes to switch experts without disclosing a second report.

25.42 Once a report has been disclosed, either party can rely on it, so if a party later chooses to abandon an expert, perhaps due to an unfavourable second report, the other party can use the disclosed report (CPR, r 35.11). If the later report represents a change of opinion on the part of the expert, the party must disclose that report, albeit unfavourable, if it wishes still to rely on the medical expert, since the entirety of the expert's view on relevant matters must be before the court. If the party seeks to abandon reliance on that expert upon receipt of the unfavourable report, it may be compelled to disclose it as a condition of relying on further medical evidence in the same discipline.

25.43 It is inappropriate and unethical for any party's advisers to write reports or to tell the experts the views they are allowed to hold: *Robin Ellis Ltd v Malwright Ltd*.[19] However, it is appropriate for an expert to attend a conference or meeting prior to finalising a report and earlier draft reports – prepared for conference or otherwise – remain privileged. It is only the final complete report that the expert is required to disclose and the party cannot be compelled to disclose earlier drafts (*Jackson v Marley Davenport Limited*[20]).

THE REQUIREMENT THAT A PARTY UNDERGO MEDICAL EXAMINATION

25.44 Difficulties with a claimant consenting to examination rarely occur where he is being examined by his own expert or an expert jointly instructed by both parties, although occasionally a claimant will refuse to attend a particular doctor for a further examination. In these circumstances it is wise to seek an alternative expert both for the further report and for trial as all reports should be up-to-date when the case is heard.

25.45 Problems can, however, arise when a claimant, having issued proceedings in respect of personal injuries:

---

[18] [2003] EWCA Civ 1043.
[19] (1999) BLR 81; 15 Const LJ 141, Judge Bowsher QC.
[20] [2004] EWCA Civ 1225; [2004] 1 WLR 2926.

(a) refuses to undergo a medical examination by the doctor nominated by the defendant or the court; or

(b) objects to medical tests or further investigations required by the defendant's doctor; or

(c) seeks to impose conditions on such examination, eg being accompanied by a friend or having his/her own doctor present.

25.46 Such reluctance is sometimes with just cause: proposed investigations may be invasive, be considered unnecessary by the claimant's own medical expert and/or may carry an element of risk. Sometimes the objection is simply that the consulting room is geographically inconvenient, particularly where the claimant is significantly disabled. The party requesting the examination is always required to pay reasonable travelling costs, and if a particular expert is wanted despite being some distance from the claimant's home, those travelling costs should include over night accommodation or perhaps paying for a private car to drive the claimant to avoid over complicated journeys on public transport.

25.47 Essentially, the claimant brings the case, and is required to take reasonable steps to comply with the defendant's request that he be examined. The dicta in *Edmeades v Thames Board Mills Ltd*[21] laid down the general principle that if a claimant unreasonably refuses to submit to a medical examination on behalf of a defendant in circumstances which would prevent the just determination of the cause, the court will exercise its inherent jurisdiction to grant a stay in the proceedings until the claimant submits to such examination.

25.48 The cases of *Lacey v Harrison*[22] and *Lane v Willis*[23] (see below) are examples where a stay has been granted by the Court in circumstances where a claimant has refused to submit to examination. However, 'if the proposed examination is unpleasant, painful or risky the court will be reluctant to order a stay unless the interests of justice imperatively require' such examination. The court has the power to stay an action either on application or pursuant to its inherent jurisdiction set out in CPR, r 3.1(2).

25.49 The *Lane v Willis* considerations were important factors in the *Beck* decision as to whether to allow the defendant to reject one expert and instruct another. Quite apart from the issues of expert shopping (the main concern of the court) the inconvenience to the claimant was another important factor.

---

[21] [1969] 2 QB 67; [1969] 2 All ER 127, CA.
[22] (1992) *The Times*, April 22.
[23] [1972] 1 WLR 326.

REFUSAL TO UNDERGO MEDICAL EXAMINATION

General

25.50 The granting of a stay is in the discretion of the Master or District Judge and has been very broadly and diversely exercised.[24] Failure after the action has been stayed to submit himself for examination exposes the claimant to the risk of his claim being stayed or struck out.[25] See *Jassim v Grand Metropolitan Information Services Ltd*[26] and *Lacey v Harrison*.

25.51 The onus is on the party making the application for the stay (usually the defendant) to show that it is reasonable and in the interests of justice for such a stay to be made (*Starr v National Coal Board*)[27] and, in particular, that he cannot properly prepare his claim without the examination and subsequent report and is thereby prejudiced by the claimant's refusal which is preventing the just determination of the claim.

25.52 The test laid down in *Lane v Willis; Lane v Beath (Executor of Estate of George William Willis)*[28] was that of 'reasonableness': the reasonableness of the claimant in refusing to be examined by a particular doctor, and the reasonableness of the defendant in insisting upon examination by a doctor unacceptable to the claimant. In the exercise of its discretion the court must balance:

(a) the claimant's rights not to have his/her personal liberty invaded; with

(b) not unfairly restricting the defendant's right to defend himself in the litigation as he and his advisers think fit, which includes the freedom to choose the witnesses that he will call.

25.53 In determining the balance, the court must consider whether the proposed medical examination is:

(a) of a reasonable character? and

(b) 'reasonably required'?

25.54 In *Lane,* the claimant was injured in a motor accident and claimed he had suffered bruising, nervous shock and a depressive anxiety. He was examined by the defendant's neurologist but thereafter the gravity of the neurological injury was enlarged upon in an amended statement of claim. The claimant submitted to two further examinations by the defendant's neurologist but refused to submit to a psychiatric examination. The Court of Appeal held

---

[24] See the wide range of powers conferred by CPR, r 3.1(2)(m).
[25] CPR, r 3.4(2)(c).
[26] 18 January 1999, CA, unreported.
[27] [1977] 1 All ER 243 at 249, per Scarman LJ.
[28] [1972] 1 WLR 326; [1972] 1 All ER 430, CA (examination of plaintiff by named psychiatrist).

that in view of the substantial difference between the injuries as originally pleaded and as pleaded in the amended statement of claim, the request for psychiatric examination was reasonable.

25.55 Other examples include *Jackson v Mirror Group Newspapers Ltd*[29] (stay ordered where issue of claimant's disfigurement arose in defamation claim), and *Baugh v Delta Water Fittings Ltd*[30] (in the absence of any concrete basis for requiring an examination, a stay was refused in a Fatal Accidents Act claim brought by a window).

25.56 A stay should not be ordered if the party can show some substantial ground for this refusal, such as the particular medical expert is likely to conduct his examination or make his report unkindly or unfavourably (see *Starr v National Coal Board*).[31] In an application for a stay, therefore, each party should file detailed witness statements dealing with the issues and the factors in favour of or against the granting of the stay.

Refusal by the claimant to undergo examination

25.57 A claimant may object to examination in general, or may object to a particular doctor. The claimant will usually have to show reasonable objections to a particular doctor, rather than the general principle of examination. He must at least be able to show some substantial ground on which he or his legal advisers have formed the opinion that the doctor in question lacks the proper qualifications or is likely to conduct his examination and to make his reports unkindly or unfairly (per Cairns LJ in *Starr*).[32]

25.58 Objections based on allegations of bias, however, should be approached with great care particularly now that all experts have a duty to the court not their reporting party.

Refusal by the claimant to undergo medical tests

25.59 Doctors are not normally permitted to carry out tests unless they are for therapeutic purposes in the course of investigation and treatment, and the General Medical Council (GMC) and the Royal Colleges give specific guidance on this point, eg the Royal College of Radiologists deems it an act of professional misconduct to perform radiological examinations other than for clinical reasons. Yet frequently doctors require claimants to undergo tests and investigations purely for the purposes of preparing their reports. Parties should co-operate in trying to minimise such requests for x-rays and MRI scans.

---

[29] (1994) *The Times*, March 29, CA.
[30] [1971] 1 WLR 1295; [1971] 3 All ER 258.
[31] [1977] 1 WLR 63; [1977] 1 WLR 63; [1977] 1 All ER 243, CA, see below, 'Refusal by the claimant to undergo examination'.
[32] Ibid at p 256.

25.60 Often while treating hospitals have a relatively efficient system for disclosing medical notes, obtaining original X-rays can be difficult – hence the desire on the part of the reporting expert to test again. This should be discouraged. However, an expert asking for something such as a diagnostic MRI scan can assist a claimant who has been on a long NHS waiting list, since insurers will often pay for the scan to move the litigation forward, and its results can then be used by the treating doctors.

25.61 If a claimant refuses to undergo a test which the defendant's doctor wishes to carry out, eg a lumbar spine x-ray, the defendant must apply for a stay of the proceedings until the request is complied with. A court must then balance the claimant's personal liberty against the defendant's right to defend the case. A number of factors will be taken into consideration, including:

(a) the amount of pain or discomfort involved;

(b) the risk of injury to health;

(c) whether similar tests have recently been carried out elsewhere and whether the films and results are available for inspection such as x-rays CT and MRI scans; and

(d) the extent to which the result of the test is likely to assist the court in the determination of the medical issues between the parties.

25.62 In view of the latter requirement, the appropriate time for such application is at a case management conference.

How is the test of reasonableness applied?

25.63 A claimant is likely to succeed where his objection is that the medical examination will involve him in some element of risk or discomfort. In *Aspinall v Sterling Mansell Ltd*,[33] the claimant allegedly suffered from industrial dermatitis. The defendant's doctor wished to carry out a patch test which carried a small but identifiable risk of the recurrence of this condition. The court held that by reason of that risk the claimant's objection was reasonable.

25.64 By way of contrast, in *Prescott v Bulldog Tools*,[34] a case concerning industrial deafness, the defendant's doctors wished to carry out three tests on the claimant's ears to determine the aetiology and extent of the deafness. These tests comprised a water test, an x-ray of the inner ear and piercing of the ear drum with a very fine needle. The claimant's objections were principally that he had already been examined by the defendant's doctors on four occasions. The court held that both the defendant's requests and the claimant's refusal were reasonable but that with regard to the second and third of the proposed tests, which were both uncomfortable and invasive, the claimant's objection

---

[33] Ibid.
[34] Ibid.

outweighed the reasonableness of the defendant's request, whereas with regard to the water test, the defendant's request carried the day.[35] In so doing Webster J outlined a three-stage approach:

(i) was the request made by the defendant reasonable?

(ii) was the claimant's refusal reasonable? and

(iii) balancing on the one hand the defendant's need for further information, against the refusal of the claimant on the other, and the grounds which each had, what conclusion should the court reach?

25.65 In *Laycock v Lagoe*,[36] the Court of Appeal dismissed the defendant's appeal against a refusal to stay an action unless the claimant submitted to an MRI scan. The Court of Appeal reduced the test to two stages:

(i) do the interests of justice require the test which the defendant proposes? If the answer is in the negative the enquiry need go no further. If, however the answer is in the affirmative, then

(ii) the court should go on to consider whether the party who opposes the test has put forward a substantial reason for the test not being undertaken; 'a substantial reason being one that is not imaginary or illusory'.

Imposing conditions

Attending with a companion

25.66 It may sometimes be legitimate for a claimant to be accompanied to a medical examination by a companion. Sometimes it is a condition placed by the claimant upon an examination; in other circumstances, the court may require that the claimant be permitted to have a friend present, as a condition of granting a stay.

25.67 It is, however, a difficult area where the companion is perceived by the doctor to be checking up on him or there to intercept perceived unfairness, eg trick questions or rigorous physical examination: see *Hall v Avon Area Health Authority (Teaching)*.[37] If, therefore, a claimant wishes a companion, a court before imposing such a condition, even if the request is reasonable, requires a good or substantial reason for it. Normally, a court will not restrict a claimant's right to be accompanied to a physical examination and it is well-recognised that claimants suffering from brain injury should be

---

[35] See too *Hill v West Lancashire Health Authority1* (1996) PMILL (April) where the 'balance of reasonableness' test was applied in an application for the infant claimant to undergo an MRI scan and the defendant's application was refused.

[36] 18 July 1997, CA: Beldam & Kennedy LJJ.

[37] [1980] 1 WLR 481; [1980] 1 All ER 516, CA. The court held it was unreasonable for a claimant to have his own medical expert to be present to be able to testify to the inaccuracy of the other expert's report should this issue arise.

accompanied to assist in the provision of coherent answers. Any claimant 'under a disability' will not be expected to attend unaccompanied. The need for this and the claimant's vulnerability are self-evident.[38]

25.68 Problems often arise where claimants with psychiatric/psychological conditions, request a companion and are refused. In *Hall,* Stephenson LJ observed that:

> 'If the plaintiff was in a nervous state or confused by a serious head injury, or if the defendants' nominated doctor had a reputation for a fierce examining manner ... it might be reasonable for her solicitors to insist, for her, on such a condition.'

25.69 In *Whitehead v Avon County Council*,[39] an orthopaedic surgeon reporting to the defendant, described the claimant's 'illness behaviour' and 'gross psychological problem'. He recommended she be seen by a psychiatrist and the claimant, a psychiatric nurse, agreed on condition that she was accompanied by a friend who was herself a nurse and a qualified psychologist. The defendant refused and obtained a stay. The claimant relied upon an affidavit from her psychiatrist who had examined her in the presence of this friend. The psychiatrist maintained this was a common and acceptable practice but the defendant's expert contended that this would impede and detract from the quality of his own examination, and that it was not in any case his practice to work in that way. The stay was upheld and the claimant appealed to the Court of Appeal.

25.70 In his judgment, Otton LJ reviewed the case-law and set out guidelines. These are:

(a) There can be no objection in principle to a friend or relative being present, citing the example of a nervous plaintiff when it would be preferable to have some other person present (see *Hall*[40]).

(b) Nonetheless, the insistence of the defendants' experts on seeing the plaintiff alone was 'in accordance with established clinical practice, albeit not universally followed'.

(c) Where (as in the instant case) both the defendant and plaintiff are being 'reasonable' in their respective request and refusal, the issue was to be determined by 'the exercise of judicial discretion, in which all relevant factors should be weighed up and a balance struck between the interest of the parties'.

(d) A court should be slow to restrict a defendant's choice of expert when he has 'a sound reputation ... and is not eccentric'.

---

[38] See the observations of Buckley J in *Shaw v Skeet & Others* [1996] 7 Med LR 371 that it was entirely reasonable to have a parent present at an examination of an infant.
[39] (1995) *The Times*, May 3; (1996) PMILL, Vol 9, p 19; Nourse, Millett and Otton LJJ.
[40] [1980] 1 WLR 481; [1980] 1 All ER 516, CA.

Attending with another doctor present

25.71 Sometimes the nominated companion is the claimant's. If objected to, the test is as with a non-medical companion and remains a matter for the court's discretion. Often the sensible compromise is for the parties to agree to a joint examination where both parties' experts attend. This has the added advantage of enabling the respective experts to reach agreement or to identify those issues on which they cannot agree, and is very much in keeping with the spirit of the CPR.

REFUSAL BY A DEFENDANT

25.72 Although the claimant may be submitting to examination or tests against his own will, it must be borne in mind that he has the ultimate decision whether or not to continue the action. On occasion, however, a defendant, without a counterclaim, may be compelled to submit to medical examination without such choice.

25.73 This is an unusual situation which was considered by the Court of Appeal in *Cosgrove v Baker*.[41] This claim arose out of a road traffic accident where the defendant's motor car had suddenly crossed onto the wrong side of the road and struck the claimant's van. The defendant relied upon 'inevitable accident' by reason of having without prior warning suffered a heart attack leading him to lose consciousness and control of his car. Initially the defendant objected to any medical examination but before the Court of Appeal, on appeal from Milmo J. it was submitted that the defendant was prepared to undergo medical examination on condition that no questions should be asked during that examination which might relate to the issue of liability. The Court of Appeal affirmed Milmo J's decision that the defendant submit himself to medical examination within 28 days on the basis that it 'is now the well-established rule that a court can order a party in a personal injury action to submit to a medical examination', per Roskill LJ.

25.74 In *Cosgrove* the defendant's medical condition was crucial to his defence because unless he could show he had a heart attack, he would be held liable. In *Lacey* on the other hand, the defendant's medical condition went to his recollection of events not to the facts of the accident. By examination, the claimant was therefore seeking to pre-empt evidential findings by establishing that on medical grounds the defendant could not realistically be expected to have recall of the material events. The defendant's refusal may therefore seem more reasonable. Given the court's wide discretion under CPR if such circumstances arose again a less draconian sanction that the strike out of the

---

[41] Unreported, 14 December 1979, CA, 744; Roskill & Templeman LJJ.

defence (as ordered in *Lacey*) may now be more appropriate such as disclosure of medical records or Part 18 requests for information.

MUTUAL EXCHANGE

25.75 The practice of sequential disclosure whereby the defendants' medical evidence could be prepared in full awareness of the manner in which the claimant pleaded his case, was ruled unacceptable in a series of decisions including *Naylor v Preston Area Health Authority*.[42] Thereafter, the rule was for mutual and simultaneous exchange of reports on a fixed date.

25.76 The pre-action protocols and exercise of case management powers post CPR, however, has made considerable inroads into the principle established in *Naylor*. It is now common for Masters and District Judges to order sequential disclosure, particularly of medical evidence where liability is not in dispute, requiring the claimant to disclose and append all of his quantum reports to the Schedule of past and future loss.

25.77 This can be to the parties' advantage if agreement can be reached as to joint instruction of a single expert on such issues as accommodation, employment, speech therapy and so on. Courts will often require the defendant to ask questions of a claimant's expert before considering an application for its own expert, as directed in *Daniels v Walker*, which, of course, requires sequential disclosure.

25.78 While this may seem to place the claimant at a disadvantage, the ability to ask questions of each party's experts, and the joint expert discussion means that initial unfairness, and the defendant's ability to comment on the claimant's evidence, is usually ironed out.

---

[42] [1987] 1 WLR 958; [1987] 2 All ER 353, CA.

Chapter 26

SURVEILLANCE EVIDENCE

INTRODUCTION

26.1 Reliance upon surveillance evidence remains a commonly used tactic in personal injury litigation. Normally this consists of images covertly recorded with a concealed camera. Sometimes photographs are used or eye witness accounts given in witness statements although these have much less immediate impact and are more easily disputed or explained away. Defendants seek to demonstrate that restrictions imposed on a claimant by relevant symptoms are being exaggerated or fabricated. The aim is to limit the claim and undermine the claimant's credibility if inconsistencies are exposed. To a lesser extent, claimants also make use of 'a day in the life' type recordings to indicate the level of ongoing disability in cases of catastrophic injury. This is much less often controversial and most of this chapter is concerned with covertly obtained surveillance evidence relied upon by a defendant to undermine a claimant's case.

26.2 The use of covert surveillance has been recognised as a legitimate course to pursue on appropriate occasions in the investigation of personal injury claims: see for instance *Law Debenture Trust Group v (1) Terence Malley & (2) Pensions Ombudsman.*[1]

26.3 Advances in technology have made obtaining and presenting such evidence much easier in the digital age. Concealing a video camera used to necessitate a large container, such as a briefcase, due to the size of the recorder. The diminishing size of cameras now enables them to be attached to a tie pin or contained in a mobile telephone. Surveillance evidence is still commonly referred to as 'video evidence', as it will be in this chapter, although many inquiry agents now provide their surveillance on DVD. Few courts are equipped to deal with this format. Special arrangements well before trial will be necessary.

26.4 This chapter will look at:

(a) the status, admissibility and disclosure of video evidence;

(b) the purpose of video evidence;

---

[1] (1999) Lawtel, 23 July, Ch D Alliot J.

(c) when to use video evidence;

(d) tactics for meeting video evidence;

(e) video evidence under the Civil Procedure Rules 1998 (CPR) and costs issues;

(f) the impact of the Human Rights Act (HRA) 1998.

THE STATUS, ADMISSIBILITY AND DISCLOSURE OF VIDEO EVIDENCE

26.5 A video-tape, DVD or digital recording are all documents within the extended CPR definition in r 31.4. Therefore a party seeking to rely upon video evidence is subject to all the rules as to disclosure and inspection in CPR Part 31.

26.6 Importantly, if disclosure of video evidence is made by the defendant in accordance with CPR Part 31, the claimant will be taken to admit the authenticity of the recording unless notice is served that the claimant wishes the document to be proved at trial. This is unusual, except where there are allegations that a recording has been 'edited'. It should not be and the entire recording should be disclosed. Few claimants challenge the authenticity of the recording. The much more routine response involves claimants seeking to minimise the impact of video evidence by demonstrating that what is shown is not inconsistent with the stated case or is explicable in some other way. The two most frequently arising areas are disputes about admissibility concern the timing of disclosure of video evidence and the manner of obtaining it.

26.7 CPR, r 33.6 governs the procedure for the admissibility of evidence and the need for notice to the other parties of an intention to rely upon a particular piece of evidence. The normal rule (CPR, r 33.6(3)) is that evidence is not receivable at trial unless notice has been given. There is a mandatory notice period of no less than 21 days (CPR, r 33.6(7)). As discussed below, the court retains a discretion in CPR, r 33.6(3) to admit evidence where there has not been the requisite notice. The court also has wide case management powers in CPR, r 3.1 which have been used to extend and shorten time limits and attach conditions to orders admitting late evidence. Similar obligations of disclosure apply to recordings relied upon by claimants, but the emotional and legal problems created by covert surveillance do not arise in that situation.

26.8 The case of *Rall v Hume*[2] gave important guidance on the post-CPR approach to the introduction of video evidence. The case reiterated the status of video evidence, being a document like any other. It set out the

---

[2] [2001] EWCA Civ 146.

proper starting point for approaching video evidence, namely that a defendant should be permitted to adduce it and cross-examine upon it unless this amounts to trial by ambush:

> 'In principle, as it seems to me, the starting point on any application of this kind must be that, where video evidence is available which, according to the Defendant, undermines the case of the Claimant to an extent that would substantially reduce the award of damages to which she is entitled, it will usually be in the overall interests of justice to require that the Defendant should be permitted to cross-examine the plaintiff and her medical advisers upon it, so long as this does not amount to trial by ambush.'

26.9 *Rall* also confirmed the procedure for disclosing and proving video evidence. Some defendants (and claimants) still consider incorrectly that a formal application is routinely necessary to introduce video evidence and that witness statements from the inquiry agents are always necessary to prove the evidence at trial. An application is not necessary where the evidence is disclosed in accordance with the standard or ongoing duty of disclosure and where the evidence is not served late, ie in breach of CPR, r 33.6. Witness statements are not necessary unless the claimant serves notice disputing the authenticity of the recording and requiring it to be proved at trial.

26.10 *Rall* also indicates the flexible approach to be taken to case management in order to achieve justice. So as not to lose a trial date by reason of the additional court time necessary to show video evidence, the Court of Appeal directed that the defendant have permission to cross-examine on footage totalling no more than 20 minutes running time. The court also directed that some footage arguably breaching the claimant's right to respect for her private and family life (Art 8 of the European Convention on Human Rights) be excluded. This is discussed in greater depth at the end of this chapter.

26.11 Defendants have always been keen to delay service of video evidence until the claimant has 'pinned his colours to the mast' in his witness statement and an updated schedule of loss (now requiring a statement of truth). The aim is to cause the maximum damage to the claimant's credibility if the recordings are inconsistent with the claimant's contemporaneously stated case. There is also the desire to avoid a claimant wriggling out of the impact of video evidence where he has not given an inconsistent account in a signed document around the same date as the recording (or post-dating it). 'Withholding relevant material in an attempt simply to ambush a claimant is no longer permissible'*:* per Hallett J in *Uttley v Uttley*.[3] There is therefore a tension between the desire to disclose after the claimant's case has crystallised and the duty to disclose in accordance with the rules. *Rall* underlines the duty to raise intended reliance upon video evidence at the first opportunity after a decision has been made to rely upon it:

---

[3] [2002] PIQR P12. An appeal to the High Court Judge from a QB Master's case management decision.

'It is therefore necessary in the interests of proper case management and the avoidance of wasted court time that the matter be ventilated with the judge managing the case at the first practicable opportunity once a decision has been made by a Defendant to rely on video evidence obtained. Such a duty lies upon the Defendant under CPR 1.3 which requires the parties to help the court to further the overriding objective under CPR 1.1(2) . . .'

26.12 The historical discretion of special reasons to permit non-disclosure of surveillance evidence before trial is now likely to be very rarely sought and very rarely granted: for the historical position see the line of cases reviewed by the Court of Appeal pre-CPR in *Birch v Hales Containers Ltd*[4] and carefully analysed by Deidre Goodman in the previous edition of this handbook. The ambush at trial runs contrary to the 'cards on the table' approach propounded in the post-CPR era requiring each party to set out its case and disclose its evidence early. Even in *Birch v Hales*, Evans LJ noted the 'movement in favour of a greater requirement on the defendants both to disclose and make available for inspection video recordings before the hearing'. This 'cards on the table' approach is now the general rule as indicated by cases such as *Rall*. This post-CPR ethos requires disclosure of surveillance before trial save in quite exceptional cases or when the surveillance is only obtained at or after trial.

26.13 This does not mean that video evidence need always be disclosed as soon as it is to hand. On appeal in *Uttley v Uttley*,[5] Hallett J (in the QBD) upheld the Master's ruling that the defendant's decision not to disclose video evidence until after the claimant had served an updated witness statement and schedule of loss did not prevent its use at trial. The judge reiterated that the CPR were designed to promote disclosure of all relevant material within a reasonable time so that the parties and their advisers might prepare for trial. Nevertheless, in the circumstances of the case, the defendant's desire to withhold the video evidence until receipt of the claimant's updated witness statement was legitimate to enable the defendant to engage in effective cross-examination. The key was that there should not be disclosure so late as to amount to an ambush at trial. A factor in the decision was the claimant's lengthy delay in serving the updated statement. The videos would have been served earlier had the statement been served when it should have been.

26.14 Quite often surveillance evidence is fairly inconclusive: it is rare for a case to collapse entirely when a recording is disclosed. However, on occasions it can be devastating to a claimant's credibility, for instance where a loss of earnings claim for life is presented and a video shows the claimant back at work. Nevertheless, surveillance evidence needs to be used with care as it can rebound on the defendant if the claimant's medical expert is able to state authoritatively that the claimant's demeanour is consistent with the injury or symptoms of which complaint is made.

---

[4] [1996] PIQR P307.
[5] Op cit.

26.15 The disclosure that covert surveillance has taken place often causes considerable upset and anxiety to claimants. They often view it as distasteful and with good reason where allegations of 'malingering' prove to be without foundation. The other allied area in which concern and dispute can arise is the manner in which recordings are obtained, for instance where it is alleged that the Human Rights Act 1998 has been infringed by recording a claimant in his or her home (see 'The Impact of the Human Rights Act' below).

THE PURPOSE OF VIDEO EVIDENCE

26.16 Defendants' insurers are generally enthusiastic about obtaining surveillance evidence, despite the substantial costs which can be involved. Many view it as a routine part of the defence to higher value claims. Even where malingering is not demonstrated, surveillance can be used to balance the picture of how a claimant is coping with his disability thereby going some way towards assisting the court in the assessment of all major heads of damages. In the larger claims, attention is focused not so much on general damages for pain, suffering and loss of amenity but upon the much larger heads of claim for past and future loss of earnings, care needs, domestic assistance, accommodation requirements and so forth.

26.17 Moreover, if malingering can be demonstrated, this has the additional advantage of seriously throwing into doubt the claimant's credibility as a witness on other issues including matters of liability.

26.18 Sometimes, video evidence is specifically aimed at liability issues, eg to show that a claimant was prepared to drink and drive on occasions subsequent to the accident and therefore had probably been prepared to do so on the occasion in question.

26.19 Increasingly, video evidence has come to be seen by defendants as an essential weapon in their armoury particularly where the claim carries a significant damages potential. The complexity of many back-injury claims, for example, where claimants additionally allege severe or almost complete incapacity by reason of Chronic Pain Syndrome, Fibromyalgia and/or Somatoform Disorders, takes the medical evidence outside the expertise of the orthopaedic and neurological experts alone into the realm of psychology, psychiatry and pain management. Many insurers (and some medical experts) view such conditions with circumspection and as a matter of course include surveillance evidence in their defence specifically to exclude malingering or unmask it. Although the present climate is one where the rules and rule makers are increasingly pressing alternative dispute resolution and early compromise, many insurers challenge such claims as a matter of course. Indeed, this attitude has become more rather than less entrenched with conditional fee agreements (CFAs) becoming the norm. The recoverability of success fees and insurance premiums make the stakes higher when settling claims. Equally, defendant insurers know that adverse costs will be recoverable against a claimant proceeding under an insured CFA.

26.20 For a claimant, 'a day in the life' video evidence can be useful in an appropriate maximum severity case in demonstrating the claimant's condition and needs, particularly in support of a care regime.

WHEN TO USE VIDEO EVIDENCE

By the claimant

26.21 In catastrophic injury cases, video evidence can be used where it is difficult, in writing, to describe the reality of the claimant's condition. Video evidence can give a graphic illustration of how the injuries and their sequelae have affected every aspect of the claimant's daily life and that of his family. Such recordings must not be over done and care should be taken to make sure that the recording is balanced not biased.

26.22 Properly prepared, with professional input, such recordings can assist in the presentation of the case and make an impact on the quantification of the claim or hasten a sensible settlement proposal by insurers.

The advantages

26.23 These include:

(a) The provision of a valuable insight into a day in the life of a catastrophically injured claimant with a clear demonstration of the daily difficulties encountered in mobility and in coping with the normal tasks of dressing, eating, exercise, etc, as well as the demands the handicap place on his carers.

(b) Assistance in persuading the court as to the appropriateness of a particular therapy or item of equipment, where this is disputed by the defendant: see for instance *Coram (A Minor) v Cornwall & Isles of Scilly HA*,[6] (installation of hydrotherapy pool).

(c) Assistance in demonstrating to the court certain technical procedures: in *Penney, Palmer and Cannon v East Kent Health Authority*,[7] demonstrating the process for screening smear tests.

(d) Where a claimant is grievously injured, avoiding the need for him to attend court. This is particularly so where the claimant is not capable of

---

[6] 16 April 1996, Tucker J reported in APIL *Newsletter*, Vol 6, issue 4, p 15.
[7] [1999] MIC 126, CA, Lord Woolf MR Lord Justice May and Lady Justice Hale.

preparing a witness statement or of giving oral evidence. Where a claimant can attend court, live evidence is preferable, even if supplemented by a video.

(e) Where it is anticipated that the claimant will be unlikely to survive until the date of trial, either by reason of the accident injury or otherwise.

(f) Disclosure of the video can be accompanied by a claimant's CPR Part 36 offer to settle the claim for a specified sum. This may be the necessary prompt for a sensible compromise of the claim.

The disadvantages

26.24 Editing of videos may, even unwittingly, present a distorted picture and this should be avoided. Wherever possible, therefore, a claimant should attend court in person and expand upon the matters shown in the video if called upon to do so. Live evidence-in-chief (with the opportunity for cross-examination) will carry more weight than a video alone. This also allows the defendant to cross-examine upon the video and thus pre-empt adverse comment that the portrayal of the claimant is not accurate.

By the defendant

26.25 As set out above, many insurers view surveillance evidence as routine in high-value claims. It is suggested that a more focused approach is likely to avoid the considerable expense in cases where it is very unlikely to assist. Carefully considered instructions to inquiry agents and provision of relevant information will avoid the production of unreliable or irrelevant recordings. Video evidence is likely to be of assistance where it is believed the claimant is malingering or exaggerating the effect of the injury, or not giving credit for alternative earnings or earning capacity when maintaining a claim for loss of earnings. It is also useful in providing a realistic picture of the likely care, assistance, equipment, therapy and accommodation requirements where significant ongoing claims are made under these heads.

26.26 The suspicion of malingering is likely to arise in the following situations:

(a) Where there is an unresolved conflict on the findings of respective medical experts. A typical case is where a claimant has suffered a back injury and where the medical reports of one or both sides may comment upon the absence of organic findings supporting a complaint of disability which appears to be disproportionate to the apparently relatively minor nature of the original injury.

(b) Where the medical records, in particular those pre-accident, raise doubts as to whether certain symptoms and an alleged incapacity are entirely attributable to the accident. Using again the example of a back injury, claimants frequently deny any previous back problems whereas pre-accident general practitioner notes will show a number of consultations for back pain. Although the cross-examination opportunities from this inconsistency are self-evident, video evidence may be the clincher and avoid the expense of a trial and result in a settlement well within the insurer's reserve.

The advantages

26.27

(a) Video evidence throws the extent of the claimant's disability into sharp focus. It may have a significant impact upon the level of damages by demonstrating whether the apparently functional disability is genuine or whether the claimant is malingering or exaggerating. At the very least, damages will be lower and adverse costs orders may be made (see further below under CPR and costs orders).

(b) It may assist in a contested liability claim by casting doubt on the claimant's credibility.

(c) It assists in assessing the appropriate level of a Part 36 payment into court.

(d) It encourages early settlement as a claimant is unlikely to want to take his chances at trial in the face of cogent surveillance evidence. Offers before issue are also taken into account and pressure can be applied at this early stage (CPR, r 36.10).

(e) Where the claimant has not been entirely frank but does nonetheless have a genuine injury in respect of which damages will be awarded, early disclosure of video evidence may induce him to enter into earlier settlement than would otherwise be the case, with a resultant saving of costs (as well as damages).

(f) Even where a claimant is entirely honest, the knowledge that there is a video is unnerving and may render the claimant more amenable to settlement offers.

(g) Equally, CPR, r 36.21 contains punitive interest provisions on damages and costs, for defendants who proceed after receipt of a claimant's Part 36 offer, only to find that a larger sum is awarded at trial. There is, therefore, every incentive for defendants to make an attractive offer at an early stage of proceedings, and a video may tip the balance as to whether or not the claimant will accept this.

(h) Such an offer combined with a video may also create difficulties for the claimant's legal advisers operating under a conditional fee agreement (CFA) or legal expenses insurance policy (LEI).

(i) The insurers funding the costs of the claimant's claim and the claimant's advisers may also be reluctant to proceed to a trial with the added risk of surveillance evidence and in the teeth of a Part 36 payment accompanied by a video. If not beaten, such a Part 36 payment (or pre-issue Part 36 offer) will result in an order to pay the defendant's costs since the last date for acceptance of the offer (CPR, r 36.20).

(j) It is, therefore, essential for these advisers to view any such video with considerable care and seek the views of the claimant and the relevant experts so that a balanced decision can be made.

(k) It can be used retrospectively and advantageously even after the case has been fought and lost. There are a few examples of this in existing case-law. The ability of the courts in certain circumstances to revisit periodical payments orders and vary them both upwards *and downwards*[8] may well result in a greater use of post-settlement/judgment surveillance, perhaps many years after the conclusion of the claim. This is likely to be a developing area in the use of surveillance in coming years.

The disadvantages

26.28

(a) Despite a general improvement in the methods adopted by inquiry agents and the Association of British Investigators 'Code of Ethics',[9] some practitioners and judges still view all covert surveillance with a certain amount of distaste. However, cases such as *Law Debenture Trust Group v (1) Terence Malley & (2) Pensions Ombudsman* (see the introduction) have recognised that covert surveillance is a legitimate tactic in appropriate cases. It is suggested that this must be correct. The success of an exaggerated or fraudulent claim would be an affront to justice. Surveillance evidence is an important part of the checks upon personal injury claims. However, such evidence is rightly the subject of criticism where shady practices are used or where the CPR are flouted by attempts at ambush via late disclosure.

(b) When dubious tactics of inquiry agents (eg letting down tyres to see if a claimant will attempt to change a car wheel or trespass into a claimant's home) come to light and the claimant is shown to be genuine, a court will almost invariably regard all the claimant's claims more benevolently than

---

[8] The power in s 2B of the Damages Act which provides that the Lord Chancellor: may by order enable a Court which has made an order for periodical payment to vary the order in specified circumstances (otherwise than in accordance with Section 2(5)(d)). The Damages (Variation of Periodical Payments) Order 2004 sets out provisions which enable the court in limited circumstances to provide in an order for periodical payments that it may be varied (see also CPR PD 41B para 5). Claimants and defendants need to consider carefully whether such provisions should be included at the time of the original order.

[9] See www.theabi.org.uk/visitor/ethics.htm.

otherwise would be the case. The defendant may well find that the final award is higher than expected, outweighing the benefits of obtaining expensive surveillance evidence.

(c) Surveillance which does not have a real impact on a claimant's credibility can seriously backfire and result in a higher award than would otherwise have been made. If it only goes to reinforce the medical experts' views then it will hardly assist the defendant. Defendants routinely 'bury' unhelpful surveillance and do not reveal its existence. There is an argument that the mere existence of surveillance evidence makes it disclosable, whether or not the defendant seeks to rely upon it although this remains a moot point. If correct, this could significantly up the stakes for defendants in obtaining speculative surveillance, which if unhelpful, could actually strengthen a claimant's case.

(d) If the defendant receives a very lengthy tape containing one or two moments which suggest the claimant has greater capacity than claimed, considerable thought needs to be given to the overall impact of the evidence. The defendant may wish to fast forward the tape to the few 'damning' moments, the court will consider the whole tape in the round; on balance such a video may be supportive not undermining of the claim.

(e) Similarly, an allegation of malingering (an allegation amounting to fraud which must be pleaded) which is held to be unfounded may well result in an indemnity costs order. Accordingly, considerable care should be taken in commissioning and placing reliance upon such surveillance.

(f) Many claimants find knowledge that they have been subject to surveillance shocking and distasteful. It can worsen some conditions; particularly stress related conditions or injuries with a psychiatric component. Therefore, a defendant may have some useful surveillance but find the cost of obtaining it is an increase in the overall claim as the claimant's condition worsens.

(g) Evidence which breaches the Art 8 Convention right to respect for private and family life may be inadmissible unless the interests of a fair trial (Art 6 right to a fair trial) demand that it is admitted in evidence. Inappropriate methods will at the very least result in adverse costs orders. This is discussed in more depth below.

TACTICS FOR MEETING VIDEO EVIDENCE

By the claimant

Anticipatory tactics

26.29 There are a number of ways in which being forewarned of video surveillance is to be forearmed:

(a) The shock and anxiety often experienced by claimants on discovering that they have been the subject of covert video surveillance, can to some extent be diffused if in cases where this is likely to happen, the claimant's legal advisers warn him in advance at an early stage in the litigation that the defendant is likely to embark on this investigation. The claimant should be encouraged to report any suspicions to his solicitors so that, where appropriate, objections as to methods can be made to the defendant in open correspondence and an application for disclosure of evidence made early in the proceedings, either at a case management conference or by application under CPR Part 23.

(b) In an appropriate case where surveillance is suspected, a claimant should be encouraged to keep a diary; in that way he may be able to point to artful editing of events on a given day.

(c) A counter-attack may be mounted by claiming that the methods employed in obtaining recordings contravenes the claimant's right to respect for private and family life under Art 8 of the Convention on Human Rights (see 'Impact of the Human Rights Act' below).

After disclosure of video evidence

26.29 When confronted by a video, the cardinal rule is not to panic but to make a careful evaluation of the recordings and any supporting documentation. This will give rise to a strategy to deal with the impact of the evidence or to challenge it. The videos should be viewed at a meeting between the claimant and his legal advisers so that they can be objectively analysed, problems arising calmly confronted and the claimant appropriately reassured, or – if the video proves to be his undoing – appropriately advised.

26.30 Questions to consider:

(a) Is the subject of the film actually the claimant and not someone else, eg a twin brother/sister?

(b) Does the video present an accurate picture of the claimant's disability?

(c) Is what is shown consistent with the findings and opinion of the claimant's medical experts? Their views on the videos should be obtained and disclosed, hopefully to undermine the defendant's assertions as to the impact of the videos.

(d) Does the content and action shown accord with those matters described in the claimant's own witness statement and those of other witnesses who have commented upon the claimant's injury and apparent resultant disability? If not, is there a potential explanation, eg a condition which is accepted by the medical experts to be fluctuating. The videos should be viewed with the claimant and the legal advisers present to analyse the content, take instructions and give realistic advice.

(e) Has there been misleading editing? A video might show the claimant moving apparently effortlessly from one strenuous task to another whereas the reality is that there may have been a considerable time lapse between the two activities. If the claimant has been encouraged to keep a diary, this may help with this analysis and rebuttal.

(f) To what extent, if at all, is the claimant's case weakened/strengthened by this evidence?

(g) To what extent has the video infringed the claimant's right to respect for private and family life? (Art 8 of the Convention). This is discussed in more depth below.

(h) Can the credibility of the maker be attacked? Has there been editing? Have dubious methods been employed to obtain the recordings? These issues may give rise to bases to challenge the admissibility or weight to be attached to the evidence.

(i) Is the impact of the video such that the claimant's condition has worsened? While proper preparation by legal advisers, as suggested above, should contain or prevent an adverse reaction, if the claimant's physical (or more usually) mental condition is significantly affected by the fact of surveillance, medical evidence as to this decline may be required.

The defendant

26.31 There is usually little contentious about a 'Day in the Life of [a Claimant]' video and anticipatory tactics beyond awareness that such a video is likely to be made are unnecessary. Upon disclosure, however, if the video appears to present a distorted impression of the claimant's disability, the defendant can:

(a) seek disclosure of the unedited film;

(b) require the maker to attend court;

(c) apply to obtain its own video (this is extremely unusual);

(d) show this to its own quantum witnesses – occupational therapist, physiotherapist, care expert, etc, and obtain their written comments which should then be disclosed to the claimant with a view to this evidence being given orally at trial. It is also useful ammunition at any pre-trial meeting of experts. This is only likely to arise where the claimant himself is competent to give evidence and thus the video can be attacked in the course of cross-examination.

The main risk to a defendant of a 'day in the life' video is that it will tend to support the higher or highest valuation of the claimant's claim (or it would not be disclosed). This is particularly the case if the video deals with levels of care provided or required. To some extent, the defendant's best tactic in an appropriate high value case is to embark (via the Rehabilitation Code) in a joint establishment of the care regime, thereby exercising some checks on the care claims made.

Alternatively, if the defendant's care experts seek to challenge the level of care claimed, careful consideration of the video evidence will be required before a proper assessment of the realistic prospects of success of such a challenge can be made.

VIDEO EVIDENCE UNDER THE CPR AND COSTS ISSUES

26.32 The application of the CPR to the status, admissibility and disclosure of surveillance evidence has been considered earlier in this chapter.

26.33 CPR, r 44.3(4)(a) obliges the court to consider all parties' conduct when deciding about costs so as to reflect the justice of the case. There is a range of different costs orders now available to a judge, as set out in CPR, r 44.3(6), other than the usual order that costs 'follow the event'. These powers have long-since been available[10] but are only now being used more readily.

26.34 The court is obliged to consider conduct before as well as during proceedings (CPR, r 44.3(5)). It is also mandatory to consider whether a claimant who has succeeded in his claim in whole or in part exaggerated his claim (CPR, r 44.3(5)(d)). Curiously, as discussed below, no distinction is made in the rules between conscious and unconscious exaggeration although the courts have found this distinction to be very material.

26.35 The availability of flexible costs orders to meet the particular circumstances enables a defendant to argue, for instance, that there should be a limit placed on the recoverable costs, even where a claimant has beaten the Part 36 payment and is nominally entitled to all his costs. In *Painting v University of Oxford*,[11] video surveillance evidence undermined the claimant's claim and the defendant was granted permission to reduce its payment into

---

[10] It has taken time for the courts to act upon the call to use the powers to make imaginative costs orders provided in CPR, r 44.3. As long ago as February 1999, Lord Woolf MR, in *Phonographic Performance Ltd v AEI Rediffusion Music Ltd* [1999] 2 All ER 299, said: 'I draw attention to the new rules ... From 26 April 1999 the 'follow the event principle' will still play a significant role, but it will be a starting point from which a court can readily depart. This is also the position prior to the new rules coming into force. The most significant change of emphasis of the new rules is to require courts to be more ready to make separate costs orders which reflect the outcome of different issues.'

[11] [2005] EWCA Civ 161.

court from £184,000 to £10,000. The claimant had claimed more than £400,000 in damages but was awarded just over £23,000 at trial, the judge having found intentional exaggeration of the claim. The trial judge awarded the claimant all her costs on the basis that she beat the payment into court. The Court of Appeal allowed the defendant's appeal against the decision holding that the defendant had effectively been the 'winner' and the judge had failed to take into account the absence of any attempt to negotiate by the claimant and the probability that were it not for the exaggeration, the claim would have settled at an early stage. An order was substituted that the claimant recover her costs down to the payment in and thereafter she was ordered to pay the defendant's costs in full.

26.36 In a gross case of fraud, it has been suggested that a claimant should forfeit even the legitimate part of his damages, as well as paying all the defendant's costs. An example is *Molloy v Shell UK Limited*,[12] where the claimant had a legitimate injury but claimed that he could never work again and sought more than £300,000. Days before trial, it was uncovered that he had in fact returned to work 3 years earlier and the trial judge awarded him a little over £18,000. On appeal against the judge's order on costs, Laws LJ observed:

> 'For my part I entertain considerable qualms as to whether, faced with manipulation of the civil justice system on so grand a scale, the court should once it knows the facts entertain the case at all save to make the dishonest Claimant pay the Defendant's costs.'

26.37 The above parts of the rules also provide the basis for a claimant to argue that a defendant should be penalised for improper conduct, e g dubiously obtained surveillance or late disclosure of videos, or raising issues of malingering which failed and which should never have been raised.

26.38 In *Ford v GKR Construction Ltd & others*,[13] the defendant first sought surveillance evidence during an adjournment of several months between the first 2 days of a quantum trial and the subsequent conclusion of the hearing. The judge admitted the surveillance evidence and found that without the video the award would have been substantially greater although the claimant had not been deliberately lying. However, the judge awarded the claimant all of her costs even though she had failed to beat the payment in. He held that the defendants ought to have obtained the evidence earlier; that the late disclosure had prevented the claimant from assessing the merits of the payment in and that she had acted reasonably in the light of the fresh evidence, by trying to negotiate. The Court of Appeal dismissed the defendant's appeal.

26.39 It is suggested that the absence of dishonesty was a very material factor in *Ford* and Judge LJ in that case recognised that the result would have been different in the face of dishonesty. Although at CPR, r 44.3(5)(d) the rules do

---

[12] [2001] EWCA Civ 1272.
[13] [2000] 1 WLR 1397.

not distinguish between conscious and unconscious exaggeration, Longmore LJ highlighted in *Painting* (para 26), that: 'the fact that the exaggeration is intended and fraudulent is, to my mind, a very important element which needs to be addressed in any assessment of costs'. Equally, the issue of whether or not a claimant seeks actively to negotiate, make and respond to offers will be very material in considering costs orders in the light of adverse surveillance evidence. These issues were highlighted as centrally relevant to the exercise of discretion on costs in both the *Ford* and *Painting* appeals.

26.40 Nevertheless, it is not necessary to have something tantamount to a finding of fraud against a claimant before an adverse costs order is made, nor is unreasonable conduct necessarily required. In *Uttley v Uttley*[14] the claimant sued his brother for injuries sustained in a car accident, for which liability was admitted. In November 1999, a payment in of £45,000 gross was made. There was a directions order for the claimant to serve a schedule of special damages by the end of July and subsequently a trial was listed for January 2001. On 18 July the defendant had received some video surveillance showing the claimant apparently making a van delivery and lifting a cooker. The claimant failed to serve his schedule and updated statement, despite repeated requests, until 15 December 2000. The defendant served the surveillance on 20 December. On 17 January the claimant accepted the payment in out of time. The Master ordered the claimant to pay the defendant's costs since 21 days after the payment in. The claimant appealed arguing that it was unjust to have ordered him to pay those post-payment in costs due to the defendant's conduct in withholding the videos. Hallett J, in dismissing the claimant's appeal held that the defendant's conduct was legitimate. The aim was not to ambush the claimant at trial, but to ensure effective use of the video for cross-examination. The effect of CPR, rr 36.20 and 36.21 is that the claimant should pay the defendant's costs from 21 days post-payment in if that payment in was not bettered. The burden is on the claimant to show that this 'usual order' would be unjust. The order is not an expression of disapproval, but an encouragement to settle.

26.41 However, the court should not go too far in penalising a defendant for late disclosure of evidence which unmasks conscious exaggeration. *Booth v Britannia Hotels Limited* [2002] EWCA Civ 579 was a second appeal against a District Judge's order on detailed assessment. The claimant had pursued a claim for more than £600,000 for reflex sympathetic dystrophy (RSD). Five weeks before the quantum trial, the defendant disclosed surveillance evidence of the claimant with full movement inconsistent with RSD. The parties agreed that the claimant could accept an earlier Part 36 payment of just £2,500 with costs on the standard basis. The claimant sought in excess of £82,000 in costs which the defendant claimed was wholly unreasonable in view of the sum recovered. The District Judge awarded 60% of the costs claimed on the basis that the video evidence was disclosed late. The High Court judge dismissed a first appeal on the basis that the defendant had taken a tactical decision to disclose the video evidence at a late stage and therefore had to suffer the

---

[14] Discussed and cited above under 'Disclosure'.

implications. The Court of Appeal allowed the defendant's further appeal holding that there where a claimant pursued a claim for damages for a condition which she knew she had not suffered, there was no reason why the defendant should bear any part of the costs expended in that unreasonable pursuit. The case was remitted for further consideration on the amount of costs recoverable.

THE IMPACT OF THE HUMAN RIGHTS ACT 1998

26.42 The approach of our civil courts to human rights was signposted even before the Human Rights Act (HRA) 1998 which incorporates the European Convention on Human Rights and Fundamental Freedoms ('the Convention'), came into force on 2 October 2000. In *Daniels v Walker*[15] the Court of Appeal held that human rights points must not be taken unnecessarily and should be properly argued and supported by authority if relied upon.

26.43 A detailed analysis of the HRA 1998 and Convention is beyond the scope of this chapter but consideration will be given to the approach taken in relevant cases.

26.44 It was commonly believed that the CPR already contained sufficient powers (particularly that of judicial case management) to ensure that litigants' human rights – especially the competing rights for a fair trial (Art 6) and right to respect for private life (Art 8) – are dealt with adequately so as to avoid a proliferation of challenges. Nevertheless, the courts cannot ignore the interplay between the HRA 1998 and the operation of the CPR, for instance, when approaching video evidence.

26.45 The right to respect for private life does not impose the purely negative obligation that the state should refrain from interfering with the individual. It also imposes a positive obligation: to provide for effective respect to be given to and shown for private life. The obligation should not be thought of as imposing a right to privacy per se. The claimant who is recorded jogging along a public road when meant to be wheelchair-bound cannot complain that his privacy rights have not been protected. It is only if the right to respect for private life has been infringed that a complaint may lie.

26.46 Since Art 8 is a qualified right, the mechanisms for interference by the state with the right can be justified, as long as the principles of legality, necessity, proportionality and purpose are complied with. The courts are expected to interpret all legislation and proceed in a manner compatible with the Convention, even where the dispute is between individuals. As between individual litigants, the considerations are more likely to be framed as the balancing of both parties' rights to a fair trial.

---

[15] [2000] 1 WLR 1382.

26.47 Video evidence will not be excluded merely because it has been covertly obtained. In *Law Debenture Trust Group v Terence Malley (1) and Pensions Ombudsman (2)*,[16] Alliott J held that covert surveillance evidence obtained by the trustees of a pension scheme (used as grounds for refusing an applicant an ill-health early retirement pension) was not a breach of Art 8. Indeed it was a legitimate approach in an appropriate case.

26.48 Equally, video evidence will not be excluded simply because it has been obtained via methods which breach Convention rights, eg filming a claimant in his home, in breach of the right to respect for private and family life in Art 8. Even in criminal proceedings there is no automatic exclusion of unlawfully obtained evidence, so it is logical that the position is no less strict in civil proceedings.

26.49 It is instructive to consider two criminal appeal cases which fall either side of the admissibility line. In *R v Button and Tannahill*,[17] in a murder trial, a judge had admitted covert video evidence of the two accused when they were alone in a room at a police station. It was conceded that the evidence was obtained in breach of Art 8. The defendants appealed arguing that the evidence obtained in breach of Art 8 could not be admitted because in doing so, the court would be repeating the breach and acting in a way incompatible with the Convention, ie open to challenge. This argument failed. The Court of Appeal held that Art 6 right to a fair trial does not prevent a court from admitting evidence obtained in breach of Art 8. The court's obligation is confined to deciding whether, having regard to the way in which the evidence was obtained, it would be fair to admit it. The answer to this test was 'no', in *R v Edward Grant*.[18] The defendant had been recorded in the exercise yard following arrest and the recordings captured telephone calls with his legal representative. It was held that even though there was no prejudice to the defendant, general unlawful acts such as this deliberate violation of a suspect's right to legal professional privilege were so great an affront to the rule of law and justice system so as to render the prosecution abusive.

26.50 Nevertheless, where part of a film is obtained via some breach of the HRA 1998, the answer in civil proceedings may be to allow permission to rely upon a film provided that the objectionable part of the film is edited out. This was the approach taken in *Rall v Hume*[19] discussed above in relation to disclosure. One of the claimant's objections to reliance upon the videos, other than the late disclosure, was that parts of the recordings arguably breached the claimant's Art 8 right to respect for her private and family life. She was shown partly in her own home and in another excerpt inside her child's nursery school. These parts were to be excluded from the footage upon which reliance was allowed.

---

[16] Op cit.
[17] [2005] EWCA Crim 516.
[18] [2005] EWCA Crim 1089.
[19] Op cit.

26.51 However, courts are reluctant effectively to condone improper practices by permitting reliance upon wrongly obtained footage. Where an entire film is obtained in breach of a claimant's right to respect for private life, more difficult considerations apply. The compromise of excluding the objectionable parts does not assist as this would rule out reliance upon the surveillance entirely. The assistance to be drawn from the criminal jurisdiction is discussed above. In civil proceedings, this issue arose in *Jones v University of Warwick*[20] when the claimant was covertly filmed in her own home on two occasions by an inquiry agent engaging in deception by posing as a market researcher. She was claiming a six-figure sum from her employer for a hand injury. The evidence caused the defendant's medical expert to conclude that the claimant's hand functioned entirely satisfactorily.

26.52 The court had to grapple with the competing public interests that, on the one hand, in litigation the truth should be revealed and, on the other, the courts should not acquiesce in, let alone encourage, a party to use unlawful means to obtain evidence. In this case it was common ground that the inquiry agent was guilty of trespass and the recording breached Art 8. The conduct was not so outrageous so as to justify striking out the defence, so a trial would have to take place. The court's decision was influenced by the artificial situation which would be created if the evidence was excluded and the claimant could not be cross-examined upon it. Fresh experts would need to be instructed as they had already seen the videos. The existence of the videos would have to be concealed from the new experts and the trial judge. The court took the view that an appropriate costs order could be used in this or similar cases to express the court's disapproval of such conduct whilst admitting the video evidence so as to do justice. The defendant had to pay the costs of the hearings and appeals relating to the surveillance even though the surveillance was allowed in. The Court of Appeal indicated that the costs of the inquiry agent might not be recoverable in such circumstances. Equally, if the allegations were not made out, it indicated that the trial judge should reflect this in costs, perhaps by ordering the defendant to pay the costs throughout on an indemnity basis:

> 'Excluding the evidence is not, moreover, the only weapon in the court's armoury. The court has other steps it can take to discourage conduct of the type of which complaint is made. In particular, it can reflect its disapproval in the orders for costs which it makes ... We do not pretend that this is a perfect reconciliation of the conflicting public interests. It is not; but at least the solution does not ignore the insurers' conduct.'

26.53 It is also worth noting that where the defendant is a *public body* it may well have separate and distinct obligations in relation to any covert surveillance pursuant to Part II (ss 26–32) of the Regulation of Investigatory Powers Act (RIPA) 2000. Those obligations require, among other things, proper authorisation for such surveillance, such to be given by only upon consideration of both the necessity for and the proportionality of the proposed surveillance.

---

[20] [2003] EWCA Civ 151.

CONCLUSION

26.54 It can be seen that the court's wide case management powers have been used to control the manner in which surveillance evidence is used and to reflect the justice of the situation via appropriate costs orders. The issue is now less about deciding between the extreme positions of admitting versus not admitting the evidence and costs following the event. Much more subtle and creative powers have long since been available and belatedly are being more widely used. The court is better able via its wide discretion (CPR, r 3.1(2)), for instance, to limit issues, limit cross-examination and make imaginative costs orders (CPR, r 44.3(6)) so as actively to manage cases and so as to do justice between the parties when video evidence arises.

Chapter 27

PRE-ACTION PROTOCOLS AND THE FAST TRACK

27.1 This chapter reviews the relevant Protocols (in particular the Personal Injury Protocol) and those rules which have a particular impact upon the Personal Injury Fast Track. The fast track stands as a more formal route than the small claims track but less formal and less expensive than the multi-track. The fast track applies to personal injury cases worth more than £1,000 but less than £15,000.

THE OVERRIDING OBJECTIVE

27.2 Civil Procedure Rules 1998 (CPR), r 1.1 provides the court with an overriding objective of enabling the court to deal with cases justly. CPR, r 1.1(2) sets out a list of the matters that the court has to, insofar as is practicable, take account of:

(a) ensuring that the parties are on an equal footing;

(b) saving expense;

(c) dealing in the case in ways in which are proportionate to:
 (i) the amount of money involved;
 (ii) the importance of the case;
 (iii) the complexity of the issues;
 (iv) the financial position of each party;

(d) ensuring that the case is dealt with expeditiously and fairly;

(e) allotting to it an appropriate share of the court's resources, while taking into account the need to allot resources to other cases.

This is the starting point for every application that the courts consider.

27.3 The overriding objective is an uncertain one. Courts have a wide discretion to apply justice to the facts of individual cases without being bound by other precedent. In *Elli Christofi v Barclays Bank plc*,[1] the Court of Appeal refused leave to amend pleadings resulting in the claimant's case being struck

---

[1] [1999] EWCA Civ.

out. The decision was founded upon the overriding principle including, particularly, reference to saving expense and the importance of sharing the court's time appropriately. This would appear to be a departure from the widely accepted doctrine under the old rules that if another party could be compensated by costs for an amendment then it was likely to be allowed.

27.4 Further, in *Chilton v Surrey County Council & Foakes*,[2] the claimant had mistakenly failed to file an amended Schedule of Special Damages that took the claim from being worth £5,000 to £400,000. The court found that the disclosed medical evidence clearly foreshadowed a large loss of earnings claim and that the defendants should have realised that the claimant had made a mistake by not making such a claim. The amendment was allowed, with time for the defendant to investigate the claim. The Court of Appeal also held that the parties were required to help the court to further the overriding objective. The parties should have cooperated so as to avoid satellite litigation. In *Holmes v SGB Services plc*[3] the Court of Appeal emphasised that the interests of justice in achieving a fair trial did not conflict with maintaining trial dates and that that all of the criteria under CPR, r 1.1 should be taken into account with none of them being accorded undue weight.

27.5 The parties cannot necessarily remain silent in the face of an opponent's error, but that they should cooperate to ensure that the matter is dealt with justly.

27.6 A full Court of Appeal reiterated the need for the parties to cooperate so that the litigation could be conducted justly and economically in *Adoko v Hussein Jemal*.[4]

27.7 On considering an appeal as to a decision to strike out a claimant's case the Court of Appeal in *Biguzzi v Rank Leisure plc*,[5] held that the CPR were a new procedural code and that their whole purpose was that as such the rules were self-contained and rendered earlier authorities irrelevant. This approach may be contrasted with a differently constituted Court of Appeal in *Breeze v John Stacey & Sons Ltd*,[6] who held that the principles to be applied in considering whether to prevent the use of privileged documents that had been disclosed in an exhibit to an affidavit in support of an application to strike out were the same as under cases decided in discovery and that the CPR did not affect the position.

---

[2] 24 June [1999] EWCA Civ.
[3] [2001] EWCA Civ 354.
[4] (1999) *The Times*, July 8.
[5] [1999] 1 WLR 1926, CA.
[6] (1999) *The Times*, July 8, Peter Gibson Judge and Clark LJJ.

THE PROTOCOLS

27.8 The Pre-action Protocol for Personal Injury Claims ('the Personal Injury Protocol') is particularly important in the fast track where compliance should be considered mandatory. There are separate protocols for Clinical Negligence and Industrial Disease. The latter came into force on 8 December 2003.

Background to the Protocols – the court's approach

27.9 The Practice Direction provides that the objectives are to encourage early exchange of information, avoid litigation and support efficient litigation where it is unavoidable. If non-compliance has led to litigation or costs unnecessarily, then sanctions include costs (they may be on an indemnity basis), lower rates of or no interest (against a claimant), and/or a rate of interest not exceeding 10% above base rate (against a defendant) per para 2.3 of the Practice Direction. Compliance with the standards set by the protocols is expected by the courts in fast track cases.

The Protocols in action

27.10 Amendments to the Protocols and Practice Directions have been made since their introduction to stress that penalties for material breaches that affect the other side will still be punished under Para 3.4 of the Protocols Practice Direction. Compliance with the protocols will be taken into account when giving directions and in making any orders as to costs.

THE PERSONAL INJURY PROTOCOL

27.11 The Personal Injury Protocol consists of 6 main parts:

(a) specimen letters;

(b) disclosure of documents;

(c) schedules of damages;

(d) joint selection of, and instructions to, experts;

(e) questions of rehabilitation of the claimant;

(f) resolution of issues.

Specimen letters

The letter of claim

27.12 A practitioner following best practice will already be fulfilling most of the requirements as to the specimen letters which are set out in the protocols. The main purpose of the letter of claim is for sufficient information to be given by the claimant to the defendant so that the defendant can assess liability and put a broad valuation on the risk. The Protocol also encourages early notification before the letter of claim but when they know that a claim is likely to be made or where the claimant is incurring significant expenditure as a result of the accident. This is a useful tactic by the claimant's representative to ensure that the time limits in the protocol are adhered to by the defendant. Two copies should be sent with one to be passed to the defendant's insurer.

27.13 The 'Letter of Claim Guide' provides for the following:

(a) Claimant's full name, address, date of birth and national insurance number.

(b) Claimant's clock or works number (if applicable).

(c) Claimant's employer and name and address.

(d) Date of accident.

(e) Place of accident that is sufficiently detailed to establish location.

(f) A request for the defendant to identity of insurers and warning:
   (i) that the insurers will need to see a copy of the letter as soon as possible;
   (ii) that it may affect insurance cover if they do not send a copy of this letter to their insurers.

(g) A brief outline of the circumstances of the accident so that investigations can be started.

(h) A simple explanation as to why fault is alleged (regulations or statutory instruments).

(i) A brief outline of the claimant's injuries with any financial loss incurred and in road traffic cases in particular the name and address of the treating hospital with the claimant's hospital reference number.

(j) Brief statement of occupation and dates of absence and approximate weekly income, if known.

(k) If the defendant is the employer, then the usual earning details should be requested.

(l) If a police report is to be obtained, the defendant should be informed and invited to contribute half the fee.

(m) If another defendant is involved then a copy of that letter should be attached with the name of the insurers and claim number and if there is a funding arrangement (eg CFA).

(n) The claimant's solicitor should set out that the documents contained in the appropriate parts of the standard disclosure list are relevant to the action (as to standard disclosure lists see below). Disclosure as to these items is not required where the defendant admits liability.

(o) Invite defendant to send a copy to his insurers.

(p) A reply is expected within 21 days (42 days if outside England and Wales). However, the protocol recommends that a Defendant be given 3 months to investigate a claim and respond (although clearly this will not always be possible as in the case of imminent expiry of a limitation period).

The defendant's letter

27.14 Defendants should be aware that they have a strict time limit within which to investigate the claim and to admit or deny liability. Judges will not be sympathetic to the defendant who merely fails to admit liability and gives no reasons for doing so. Failing to deal with correspondence, not asserting a positive case where liability is denied, or filing a bare defence will be to invite costs sanction from the court.

The scope of an admission

27.15 The protocol suggests that defendants will have to be careful when admitting liability in a claim worth less than £15,000 where other claims allege that they have been injured in similar circumstances. If the defendant or a firm of insurers admits liability for one claim, then it is presumed to have admitted for all other claims up to £15,000. The presumption is rebuttable but, nevertheless, it is a trap that insurers and defendants should be wary of. Any admissions in respect of liability should be very carefully worded to apply only to the particular case in which an admission is intended. In *Sowerby v Charlton*[7] the Court of Appeal necessarily endorsed the binding nature of Fast Track admissions in arriving at a conclusion that parties in multi track cases do not need the permission of the court or the other party's agreement to resile from pre-action admissions. Whilst the status of pre-issue admissions in multi track cases has been thrown into disarray the fast track position is apparently preserved.

---

[7] [2005] EWCA Civ 1610.

The Defendants' Guide
27.16

(a) If there is no reply from the defendant or the insurer within 21 days of the letter, then there is no sanction against the claimant for proceeding with the action.

(b) Defendant's insurers have a maximum of 3 months, inclusive of the 21 days, to investigate liability.

(c) If liability is denied, reasons have to be given.

(d) Where liability is admitted, the presumption is that the defendant will be bound by this admission for all claims of a value up to £15,000.

Disclosure of documents

27.17 Where a defendant denies liability, documents which are clearly relevant to the issues between the parties should be enclosed with the letter. The Protocol sets out the relevant test:

> 'Documents in his possession which are material to the issues between the parties, and which would be likely to be ordered to be disclosed by the court, either on an application for pre-action disclosure, or on disclosure during proceedings.'

27.18 If documents are disclosed after the action has been commenced that prompt the claimant to reconsider its case under liability and, perhaps, to discontinue, then a claimant may be able to avoid paying costs or event to recover its wasted costs in pursuing the claim from the defendant as a result of its breaches of the rules.

Suggested documents

27.19 Annex B of the Personal Injury Protocol sets out non-exhaustive lists of documents that should be inserted by the claimant into its pre-action letter. Such lists should guide the defendant as to the type of documents that may be relevant. Defendants should note that it is *not* up to the claimant necessarily to notify them of documents that the claimant considers relevant – the primary duty of disclosure as to relevant documents rests with the defendant in whose possession most of the documents will exist.

Schedule of damages

27.20 The claimant should note that the Protocol provides that a schedule should be provided along with supporting documents as soon as practicable particularly if liability is admitted. It is the clear intention of the Protocol that this schedule is provided before the action is issued. There may be cases where, if a schedule, or at least an indication of the damages, is not provided to the defendant, costs sanctions may apply at a later time.

Joint selection of, and instructions to, experts

27.21 The Protocol sets out the following procedure for the instruction of an expert:

(a) Before any prospective party instructs an expert, the other party must be given a list of the name or names of one or more experts in the relevant specialty whom they consider suitable.

(b) Within 14 days (or if the nomination is in the letter of claim, 35 days), the second party may indicate an objection to one or more such experts and the first party should then instruct a mutually acceptable expert.

(c) If the second party objects to all the listed experts, the parties may then instruct experts of their own choice.

(d) If the second party does not object to an expert nominated, they shall not be entitled to reply upon their own expert evidence within that particular speciality unless:
  (i) the first party agrees;
  (ii) the court so directs;
  (iii) the first party's expert report has been amended and the first party is not prepared to disclose the original report.

Consequences of unreasonable rejection of an expert

27.22 If proceedings are subsequently issued and agreement of experts was not possible, then it is for the court to decide if either party has acted unreasonably. If the court takes the view that either a party put forward experts which it knew or should have known would not be suitable or if the second party rejected experts which it knew or should have known would be suitable, then costs sanctions such as the disallowance on taxation of the medical report will be applied. A party should have a good objective reason in rejecting an expert if it is to avoid penalty. Experience has shown on the fast track of inexorable movement towards the single expert.

Medical notes

27.23 It is for the claimant's solicitor to organise access to relevant medical records. The claimant can no longer simply send the defendant an authority for disclosure and the defendant can no longer, as of right, seek to gain primary access to the notes themselves. Defendants should be cautious of any claimant seeking to assert privilege over any medical records that do not, in reality, merit such a status It would be good practice for the defendants to ask the claimant's representatives to set out whether they have asserted privilege over any notes that have been provided.

Permission to rely upon an expert

27.24 It is clear that, unless the second party objects to a nominated expert, he may not rely on his own expert evidence unless there is agreement or a direction to that effect.

Amendments to reports

27.25 If the first party has caused an amendment to appear on the report, the original must be disclosed to the second party, otherwise the second party may be entitled to rely upon another report. In such circumstances, one can easily envisage the second party being able to apply for a costs sanction against the initial instructing party for causing him to instruct a further expert.

Exploiting the rules

27.26 There is a real tactical advantage in being efficient and proposing to instruct the first expert. The Protocol makes it clear by using the terminology of 'the first party' and 'the second party' that it is not necessarily the claimant's solicitor who can be the first and therefore the original instructing party. The Protocol envisages a situation whereby a defendant writes to the claimant setting out a list of nominated doctors who are then instructed. In this way the organised defendant could take the initiative from the tardy claimant. Therefore, the party for whom the practitioner is acting for should always be the first to nominate experts, thereby shifting the burden of rejection and potential unreasonable conduct to the other side.

Clarifying the expert's report

27.27 The Protocol provides that if either party has written questions on the report relevant to the issues then those questions should be sent via the first party solicitor and the expert should then despatch his replies to both parties separately. Practitioners should note that in the fast track it will be *unusual* for experts to give oral evidence Further, CPR, r 35.6 only allows a party to put written questions to the expert once, within 28 days of the receipt of the report. Therefore, practitioners *must*:

(a) consider a medical report quickly;

(b) instruct one's own expert to comment on the report so that more information can be asked for – strict time limits have to be observed;

(c) note that once litigation commences the scope for questions is narrowed.

The Protocol is more generous.

Rehabilitation

27.28 The parties should consider whether the claimant has reasonable needs which could be met by rehabilitation as soon as possible. The Rehabilitation Code has been added to the Protocol setting out an approach as to identifying the claimant's needs and how to deal with the costs which provides that:

(a) The Claimant's advisors and the insurer being under a duty to consider whether the claimant could benefit from any treatment, rehabilitation or other early intervention;

(b) The parties should communicate about such needs;

(c) The Claimant's advisors should consider with the claimant and his medical advisors any suggestions as to rehabilitation made by the insurer;

(d) Unless already identified by medical reports a rehabilitation report should be obtained from an appropriate independent expert and be paid for by the insurer;

(e) A report or any notes etc used in its preparation cannot be used in the litigation process except as to the case management of any agreed rehabilitation regime or treatment.

Alternative disputes resolution

27.29 The parties should consider whether some form of ADR would be more suitable than litigation and if so agree on the course to be taken. Parties might be required by the court to show evidence that alternative means of resolving the dispute were considered. Although the type of ADR is not prescribed and the protocol recognises that no party can be forced to ADR, the protocol specifically sets out that if these steps are not followed then the court must have regard to such conduct when determining costs.

Resolution of Issues

27.30 The protocol specifically sets out that the courts take the view that litigation is a last resort. Where liability is admitted the claimant should (subject, of course, to limitation) delay issuing for 21 days from (a) disclosure of his medical report to enable a compromise prior to issue of proceedings and (b) service of a schedule of special damages. The making of a Part 36 Offer should be considered and enough information be provided to the other side to enable such an offer to be accepted or rejected. Parties are advised to consider other methods of dispute resolution although no party can be force to enter into any form of alternative dispute resolution.

THE PRE-ACTION PROTOCOL FOR THE RESOLUTION OF CLINICAL DISPUTES

The structure of the Protocol

27.31 The Protocol sets out good practice commitments for healthcare providers and encourages patients and advisers to take a number of steps to ensure that the healthcare provider is aware of their complaints. The Protocol is divided into the following material parts:

(a) obtaining the health records;

(b) the letter of claim;

(c) the defendant's response;

(d) experts;

(e) alternative approaches to settling disputes.

The aim of the Protocol

27.32 The Protocol aims to encourage a climate of openness when something has gone wrong. It provides general guidance and recommends a timed sequence of steps for patients and potential defendants. The Clinical Disputes Forum hopes that it will lead, in the area of medical negligence, to a changing attitude between the claimants and healthcare providers in handling litigation. These objectives reflect concern that, historically in this area of litigation, above all others, claimants feel injustice, not only for the loss that they have suffered, but in the way in which they are treated by the healthcare provider after the medical accident.

The status of the Protocol

27.33 The Protocol is not a comprehensive code but sets out a code of good practice which parties should follow. It has been taken since 1999, however, as setting out mandatory practice for those approaching clinical disputes in the fast track.

Obtaining the healthcare records

27.34 The Protocol provides that the practitioner should:

(a) provide sufficient information to alert the healthcare provider where an adverse outcome has been serious; and

(b) be as specific as possible about the records which are required. Requests for copies of the patient's clinical records should be made using the standard forms that have been in use by both the Law Society and the Department of Health for some time and that are enclosed at Annex B of the Protocol.

Time limit for compliance

27.35 Most importantly, from a practical point of view, the copy records should be provided within 40 days of the request. If the healthcare provider has difficulty in complying with the request then it should state this quickly and set out the action that it is taking. The Protocol expects non-compliance with the 40-day limit to be rare. If the records are not provided within 40 days, then an order for pre-action disclosure can be made to the court. In keeping with the carrot-and-stick approach of the Protocols, the court will have the power to impose costs sanctions for unreasonable delay in providing records. If records are required from a third party, then it is expected that the third party healthcare provider will co-operate.

The letter of claim

27.36 Where the practitioner is seized of enough information to decide that there are grounds for a claim, then they should send, as soon as practicable, a letter of claim to the healthcare provider.

27.37 The 'Letter of Claim Guide' provides for the following:

(a) Claimant's name, address and date of birth.

(b) Dates of allegedly negligent treatment.

(c) Events giving rise to the claim including:
  (i) outline of what happened; and
  (ii) details of other relevant treatments.

(d) Main allegations of negligence and causal link with injuries (a brief outline or, in a more detailed and complex case a detailed list).

(e) Outline of the causal link between the allegations and the injuries.

(f) Client's condition and prognosis.

(g) Request for clinical records (Law Society form if appropriate).

(h) Specify records required.

(i) State what other investigations have been carried out to date.

(j) Likely value of the claim.
  (i) Main heads of damage or in straightforward cases the details of loss.

(k) Optional enclosures:
   (i) an offer to settle without supporting evidence;
   (ii) suggestions for obtaining expert evidence (follow the recommendations in the Personal Injury Protocol);
   (iii) suggestions for meetings, negotiations, discussion or mediation;
   (iv) chronology (this should be provided in more complex cases);
   (v) clinical records, request form and client's authorisation;
   (vi) experts' reports;
   (vii) schedules of loss and supporting evidence.

Status of the letter of claim

27.38 The letter of claim is not intended to have the same formal status as a pleading and sanctions will not necessarily apply, if the Statement of Case is different from the letter of claim.

Issuing after the letter of claim

27.39 The Protocol sets out that proceedings should not be issued until after 3 months from the letter of claim unless there is a limitation problem and/or the patient's position needs to be protected by early issue.

Offers to settle

27.40 The Protocol refers to the full CPR and the fact that a claimant may wish to make an early offer to settle. If an offer to settle is made, this should generally be supported by a medical report which deals with the injuries, condition and prognosis, and by a Schedule of Loss and supporting documentation. The level of detail is dependent upon each case.

The defendant's response

27.41 The bare defence is long dead. Any defendant who delays actions merely by denying the claimant's case without asserting a positive case can expect to be penalised by the courts. The court will expect the defendant to have a case if liability is not admitted. Defence practitioners will be under heavy pressure to investigate fully a case within a comparatively short period and to formulate a case that should be advanced.

The Guide to the Defendant's Response

27.42
   The Guide provides for the following:

(a) Acknowledge letter within 14 days.

(b) Provide requested records and invoice for copying by the claimant and:
   (i) explain if records incomplete or extensive records are held;
   (ii) ask for further instructions; and

(iii) request additional records from third parties.

(c) Within 3 months, provide a reasoned answer:
  (i) if the claim is admitted, say so in clear terms;
  (ii) if part of the claim is admitted, the healthcare provider should make clear which:
    • issues of breach of duty and/or causation are admitted; and
    • which are denied and why;
    • it should be made clear if any admissions will be binding.

(d) If the claim is denied, this should include specific comments of the allegations of negligence and:
  (i) if a synopsis or chronology of relevant events has been provided and is disputed, the healthcare provider's version of those events should be set out;
  (ii) where additional documents are relied upon such as internal protocols, copies should be provided;
  (iii) if the patient has made an offer to settle, the healthcare provider should respond to that offer in the response letter with reasons;
  (iv) the provider may make its own offer to settle at this stage.

(e) If agreement is reached on liability a reasonable time should be agreed to resolve the value of the claim if necessary.

Experts

27.43 The Clinical Protocol deliberately avoids any prescriptive approach to medical experts. It provides that this matter should be left to the parties and their advisers. More economy with regard to experts and a less adversarial expert culture is encouraged.

Alternative disputes resolution

27.44 The Clinical Disputes Protocol concludes by noting that there are alternative approaches to settling disputes in the Clinical Forum such as the NHS Complaints Procedure, Mediation and Arbitration. It does not prescribe that the parties should take any steps. The Protocol carries the same warnings as to failure to consider ADR as the Personal Injury Protocol.

THE PRE-ACTION PROTOCOL FOR DISEASE AND ILLNESS AT WORK CLAIMS

27.45 This Protocol is expressed to apply to such claims which may be complex and unsuitable for the fast track despite their value. Such cases might well include provisional claims in asbestos cases where the initial value will be less than £5,000 but the provisional claim could be multiple six figures or in WRULD cases where questions of breach and causation are complex and require multiple experts on breach and quantum. Practitioners are advised to pay particular attention to setting out matters in the Statement of Case and Allocation Questionnaire in order to persuade the court to remove these comparatively low value but complex claims from the fast track.

27.46 The Protocol does not apply to accidents as such, but where the problem takes the form of an illness or disease. The Protocol is essentially similar to the Personal Injury Protocol with the following additions:

(a) Claimants may request Occupational Records including Health Records and Personnel Records in appropriate cases before sending a latter of claim. Such a request should provide sufficient information to alert the potential defendant where a disease claim is being investigated. Copies should be supplied within 40 days. Unless there are good reasons for not complying with the request which are communicated to the claimant costs sanctions may be visited upon the defendant in any pre-action disclosure application to the courts.

(b) Further records may be necessary and this should be communicated. Third party record holders are expected to cooperate. If a decision is made not to proceed the potential defendant should be told as soon as practicable.

(c) The letter of claim follows the Personal Injury Protocol and a standard form is provided in the Protocols. There are one or two additions in that:
   (i) a chronology should be provided;
   (ii) relevant documents not in the defendant's possession should be identified;
   (iii) if the worker has died then relevant documents will include the death certificate, post mortem report, inquest depositions and if possible the relevant court documents in respect of the will;
   (iv) the defendant should be told if the claim is being pursued against other defendants.

(d) A claim should not be issued until after 3 months from the date of acknowledgement.

(e) The Response is, again, in very similar terms to the Personal Injury Protocol. Extensions of time can be sought but the Protocol sets out that a lapse of many years does not by itself constitute reasonable justification for an extension.

(f) The Disease Protocol, in the same way as the Clinical Negligence Protocol, is less prescriptive about the use of experts understanding that their role is likely to be greater and is likely to touch on breach and damage. Names of experts still should be provided to the other party and the parties are encouraged to agree a single expert. The method of agreeing experts is the same as in the Personal Injury Protocol and, therefore, parties may still exploit the rules by taking the initiative.

(g) If limitation is pressing upon a claimant then proceedings should be issued and this may be followed by an on notice application for directions as to the timetable and form of procedure to be adopted including whether the proceedings should be stayed pending compliance with the Protocol.(h)ADR is treated in exactly the same way as in the Personal Injury protocol set out above.

PRE-ACTION DISCLOSURE AND INSPECTION

27.47 In *Bermuda International Securities Limited v KPMG*[8] the Court of Appeal refused to provide guidance as to the exercise of the discretion leaving it to judges considering the vast range of cases which they will have before them. The rules do set out that which is required. Costs will normally be paid by the applicant although in *Bermuda International Securities* the Court of Appeal upheld the decision that the judge that costs were in the case if there were one and otherwise there would be no order for costs as the application had been unreasonably rejected.

The application

27.48 CPR, r 31.16(3) requires that an applicant must show by evidence that:

(a) the applicant and respondent are likely to be parties to subsequent proceedings; and

(b) if proceedings had started, the respondent's duty, by way of standard disclosure, would extend to the documents sought;

(c) pre-action disclosure is desirable to dispose fairly of the anticipated proceedings or to assist dispute resolution without the need for proceedings or to save costs;

(d) it is clear per CPR, r 31.16(3)(c) that pre-action disclosure does not go beyond what one can obtain under standard disclosure.

Inspection

27.49 CPR, r 25.5(2) provides that an applicant must show by evidence:

(a) if practicable, by reference to any Statement of Case prepared in relation to the proceedings or anticipated proceedings;

---

[8] [2001] EWCA Civ 269.

(b) that the property is or may become the subject matter of such proceedings;

(c) that the property is relevant to the issues that will arise in relation to such proceedings.

THE TRACKS

Part 27 – the small claims track

27.50 Claims that have a financial value of not more than £5,000 (CPR, r 26.6(3)), except where per CPR, r 26.6(1)A it is a personal injury claim where the financial value of the claim is not more than £5,000 and the value of the claim for damages for pain suffering and loss of amenity is not more than £1,000, are allocated to the small claims track.

Part 28 – the fast track

27.51 Per CPR, r 26.6(4) claims with a financial value of not more than £15,000 and for which the small claims track is not the normal track fall into the fast track. CPR, r 26.6(5) provides that the fast track is not the normal track for the following:

(a) that the trial is likely to last for more than one day;

(b) where there will be oral expert evidence at trial in more than two expert fields;

(c) that there will be more than one expert called by any party in any one field.

In the fast track, the trial date – 30 weeks after the allocation notice – is considered inviolable save in exceptional circumstances.

Part 29 – the multi-track

27.52 CPR, r 26.6(6) provides that claims for which the small claims track or fast track is not the normal track will fall to be considered here. In the Practice Direction, it is stated that the hallmarks of the multi-track are the ability of the court to deal with cases of widely differing values and complexity, and the flexibility given to the court in the way it will manage cases in an appropriate way to its particular needs.

STARTING THE ACTION

The Claim Form Guide

27.53 The Claim Form must contain the following:

(a) A concise statement of the nature of the claim (CPR, r 16.2(1)(a)).

(b) Specify the remedy which the claimant seeks (CPR, r 16.2(1)(b)).

(c) If the Particulars of Claim are not contained in or are not served with the Claim Form, the claimant must state on the Claim Form that particulars will follow (CPR, r 16.2(2)).

(d) The representative capacity of the claimant and his capacity must be stated; if the defendant is sued in a representative capacity his capacity must also be stated (CPR, r 16.2(3) and (4)).

(e) A statement of the value of the whole action as to whether it is worth (CPR, r 16.3(2)):
   (i) not more than £5,000;
   (ii) more than £5,000 but not more than £15,000; or
   (iii) more than £15,000; or
   (iv) the claimant should state that he cannot say how much he expects to recover.

(f) In personal injuries the claimant must state whether the claim is worth (CPR, r 16.3(3)):
   (i) not more than £1,000; or
   (ii) more than £1,000.

27.54 In the rules the term 'Claim Form' means, to all intents and purposes what used to be referred to as the 'summons'. Remember to ignore interest, costs, contributory deductions, counterclaims and set offs when calculating the likely value of the action.

The Practice Direction

27.55 The Practice Direction provides that, if it is practicable, the full particulars of the claim should be set out in the Claim Form. If the claimant does not include the Particulars of Claim in the Claim Form, they may be served separately, either at the same time as the Claim Form or within 14 days after service of the Claim Form provided that the service of the Particulars of Claim is not later than four months from the date of issue of the Claim Form. Therefore, the claimant must ensure that the Particulars of Claim are served within the 4-month period of validity of the Claim Form.

The Particulars of Claim

27.56 The rules provide (CPR, r 16.4(1)(a)) that the Particulars of Claim must only include a concise statement of the facts on which the claimant relies. The Particulars can refer to law and documents may be attached to it. No more than a concise statement of the claim is needed. Further, as will be seen below the defendant has to answer each allegation. If a short set of Particulars is drafted, an opportunity to force the defendant's hand is missed. The defendant might only then have to surprise at exchange of witness statements. However, with a properly settled Particulars, the defendant would be hemmed in and either have to meet the pleading head on (which it would have to verify) or be forced to admit liability earlier than otherwise.

27.57 In *McPhilemy v Times Newspapers Ltd*,[9] Lord Woolf said that no more than a concise statement of the facts on which a defendant relied was required – witness statements reduced the need for extensive pleadings.

The Guide to the Particulars of Claim

27.58 As before, interest should be pleaded and the particular statute referred to. Aggravated or exemplary damages and the grounds for claiming such should also be stated. In the annex to the Practice Direction, para 2 sets out that Particulars of Claim must contain the following:

(a) The claimant's date of birth.

(b) Brief details of the claimant's personal injuries.

(c) A schedule of any past and future expenses and losses claimed.

(d) Where medical evidence is relied upon, a report from a medical practitioner about the personal injuries alleged must be attached.

(e) Provisional damages per s 32A of the Supreme Court Act 1981 must be specifically pleaded and:
  (i) it should be stated that there is a chance that at some future time the claimant will develop some serious disease or suffer from serious deterioration in his physical or mental condition; and
  (ii) specify the disease or type of deterioration.

(f) In a fatal accidents claim the following must be stated:
  (i) the action is brought under the Fatal Accidents Act 1976;
  (ii) the dependants on whose behalf the claim is made;
  (iii) the date of birth of each dependant.

(g) Statutory/contractual claim for interest.

---

[9] (1999) *The Times*, May 26, Woolf MR, Judge and May LJJ.

A further advantage in having set out a detailed Claim Form and Particulars of Claim is that the Statement of Case can be used as a source of evidence at the trial itself.

Statement of truth

27.59 As with all other actions issued by Claim Form a statement of truth has to be appended to the Particulars of Claim. Practitioners must note that if no statement of truth is attached then the defendant can apply to strike out the Particulars of Claim and, if the Particulars of Claim are not verified within the specified period, then the Particulars shall be struck out. A lawyer may verify a Statement of Case for a client but in doing so has to explain to the client that it is as if the client had signed it and would be liable thereunder.

DEFENDING THE ACTION

Time limits

27.60 The rules provide that the defence shall be filed 14 days after service of the Particulars of Claim or, by agreement this period may be extended by 28 days. If an extension is given, the defendant must notify the court in writing. It is clear from the rules that an extension of more than 28 days may not be agreed by the parties without reference to the court (normally per CPR, r 3.8(3) – the parties cannot even agree an extension between themselves without recourse to the court). This is a new development and parties cannot seek to oust the court's jurisdiction. Although the new rule might, at first glance, require parties to apply for unnecessary time extensions, the rule has to be seen in the context of the parties having fulfilled the pre-action protocols, which should mean that the defendant will have no difficulties in complying with the time limits.

The contents of the defence

27.61 In personal injury actions, like all other actions, the rules require from the defendant the following:

(a) Specify which of the allegations in the Particulars of Claim are denied (CPR, r 16.5(1)(a)).

(b) If the defendant is to advance a positive case at trial that is different from the claimant's case, it must be stated (CPR, r 16.5(2)(b)).

(c) Specify which allegations the defendant is unable to admit or deny, but which he wishes the claimant to prove (CPR, r 16.5(1)(b)).

(d) Specify which allegations are admitted (CPR, r 16.5(1)(c)).

(e) A defendant who does not deal specifically with an allegation but sets out the case in relation to that issue shall not be taken to have admitted that allegation (CPR, r 16.5(3)).

(f) In respect of damage, a defendant is not taken to admit a claim unless a specific admission is filed (CPR, r 16.5(4)).

(g) Subject to the exceptions, the defendant will be taken to have admitted all other allegations that he has not dealt with (CPR, r 16.5(5)).

27.62 Those acting for defendants must plead any case that will be advanced. For instance, a simple denial of a failure to provide a safe system of work is not enough under the rules. The defendant will now have to set out the particulars of the safe system that it set up and implemented. In *Kearsley v Klarfeld*[10] the Court of Appeal held that a Defendant does not have to plead fraud when it is denied that the Claimant has suffered injury.

Disputing the valuation

27.63 If the defendant disputes the valuation of the claim by the claimant, he must say why he disputes it and put his own valuation on the form (CPR, r 16.5(6)). This will be vital when it comes to the allocation stage.

Statement of Truth

27.64 The defence must be verified in a similar manner to the Particulars of Claim and failure to do so carries the same sanctions (CPR, r 22.1(1)(a)).

The medical report

27.65

(a) The defendant should state whether:
   (i) he agrees;
   (ii) disputes; or
   (iii) neither agrees nor disputes, but has no knowledge of the matters contained in the medical report.

(b) Where the medical report is disputed the defendant should give in his defence his reasons for disputing it.

(c) Where the defendant has obtained his own medical report it should be attached to his defence.

---

[10] [2005] EWCA Civ 1510.

The Schedule of Special Damages

27.66 Where a Schedule of Damages has been served upon the defendant, the defendant should attach a Counter-Schedule and state which of those items he:

(a) agrees;

(b) disputes; or

(c) neither agrees nor disputes, but has no knowledge of it;

(d) where appropriate supply alternative figures of valuation.

Reply

27.67 In the same way as under the old rules, a claimant will be taken to join issue with those matters which are put forward in a defence. However, a claimant can, and should in some cases (such as, for example, where a limitation defence is taken) serve a reply. However, no further pleadings are allowed without the leave of the court after the service of the reply.

Allocation

27.68 The claimant is likely to wish either to move from the small claims track to the fast track or from the fast track to the multi-track. The defendant will be keen to resist such moves.

27.69 On the filing of a defence, the court will serve an allocation questionnaire on each party unless the court dispenses with the need (CPR, r 26.3(1)).

27.70 A stay of one month may be ordered by agreement, request or on the order of the court so that the parties might consider settlement (CPR, r 26.4).

27.71 CPR, r 26.8 provides a list of factors which the court must have regard to when allocating to the appropriate track. These matters include the following:

(a) The financial value, if any of the claim:
   (i) disregarding amounts not in dispute;
   (ii) disregarding any claim for interest;
   (iii) disregarding costs;
   (iv) disregarding any contributory negligence;
   (v) in a case where two or more claimants have made claims against the same defendant using the same Claim Form and the claims are separate from each other, considering the claim of each claimant separately.

(b) The nature of the remedy sought.

(c) The likely complexity of the facts, law or evidence.

(d) The number of parties or likely parties.

(e) The value of any counterclaim or other Part 20 claim and the complexity of any matters relating to it.

(f) The amount of oral evidence which may be required.

(g) The importance of the claim to persons who are not parties to the proceedings.

(h) The views expressed by the parties.

(i) The circumstances of the parties.

27.72 Cases can be subsequently reallocated and further information may be requested. The court does not have to hold an allocation hearing. It is important, therefore, when trying to escape into the next highest level or when trying to push another down a level to put full reasons in the questionnaire and also note that a hearing may be appropriate if the circumstances of the case demand it. If a party disagrees with allocation, then the remedy is either by way of application if there was no hearing or by way of appeal if there was a hearing. The Practice Direction makes it clear that the parties should cooperate in the questionnaires. The wording of the rules as to the £1,000 rules is merely 'that the value of the claim is not more than £1,000'. In cases where there is a doubt over allocation the parties will need to show in the allocation questionnaire why the claim should be valued at more or less than £1,000 (pain suffering and loss of amenity only) or £15,000 (the value of the whole claim excluding interest). If both the claimant and defendant do not file a questionnaire, the usual order provided for in the Practice Direction will be that the claim is struck out.

Allocation factors of particular importance in the fast track

27.73 Paragraph 9 of the Practice Direction sets out those matters which are particularly important when considering allocating a case to the fast track:

(a) The limits placed on disclosure.

(b) The extent to which expert evidence may be necessary.

(c) Whether the trial is likely to last more than one day (5 hours) – this factor is not, however, conclusive of the decision and the court will take into account its powers to control evidence and cross examination when arriving at the time limit.

FAST TRACK DIRECTIONS

27.74 When a case is allocated to the fast track, directions are given that include (CPR, r 28.2):

(a) Fixing the trial date to take place within a period not exceeding three weeks.

(b) The trial date or period will be specified in the allocation notice.

(c) The standard period between directions and trial is 30 weeks.

(d) Directions for the filing and service of further information to clarify the case.

(e) Standard disclosure.

(f) Service of witness statements and expert evidence by mutual and simultaneous exchange.
    (i) directions for a single expert unless there are good reasons;
    (ii) if more than one expert and they are not agreed then direct a discussion and preparation by experts of a joint report as per r 35.12(3).

(g) Expert evidence.

27.75 The court will jealously guard the trial dates and the parties cannot, without the court's permission vary the date for the return of the pre-trial checklist, the trial (or the trial period) (CPR, r 28.4). In *Matthews v Tarmac Bricks & Tiles Ltd*,[11] the Court of Appeal held that it was essential that the parties cooperated in organising a trial date. The old practice of finding a date to fit the convenience of the doctors was not acceptable. An expert had to be prepared to accommodate the court as far as practicable and, if a date was not practicable, reasons had to be given to the court.

27.76 The Practice Direction refers to the expectation of the court that the parties will cooperate. Hearings will, if possible, be avoided.

27.77 The parties are encouraged to file agreed directions. To obtain the approval of the court they have to contain:

- the matters referred to above;

- a timetable by reference to calendar dates;

---

[11] (1999) *The Times*, July 1, Woolf MR, Clarke and Mance LJJ.

- a period or date for the trial not later than 30 weeks later than the date for directions;

- provision for disclosure which can limit disclosure to less than standard disclosure or disclose without list;

- provision for factual and expert evidence. In regard to expert evidence the directions should set out the names of the experts and whether there is permission for oral evidence (this permission for oral evidence is only given where it is necessary in the interests of justice to do so);

- a trial timetable and estimate. The trial should take no more than 5 hours and a timetable should set out time for (taking into account that a judge should generally have read the papers and may dispense with opening submissions) opening submissions (some courts are allowing defendants to make brief opening statements so that the issues are clearly delineated), cross examination, re-examination, submissions, thinking time and judgment, costs and consequential orders;

- the preparation of the bundle.

27.78 Any directions may contain timetables for amendments, Part 18 requests, r 35.6 requests and the use of single experts. The Practice Direction has a useful Appendix that can be used as a template for directions. If the court does not approve the agreed directions it can give its own directions but will take into account the agreed directions.

Variation of directions

27.79 Unless a party applies within 14 days for a variation of the directions or appeals them the court will assume that the party was content and that the directions were correct. An appeal is appropriate if the directions were given at a hearing at which the party was represented. Otherwise an application should be made that the directions be reconsidered. If the parties agree as to a variation of the directions (as long as it does not trespass on the matters under CPR, r 28.4 then a written agreement need not be filed with the court otherwise an application will be required and if by consent an agreed statement of the reasons will still be required.

Failure to comply with directions

27.80 Paragraph 5 of the Practice Direction provides that sanctions can follow non-compliance which can include being deprived from being able to raise or contest an issue. The court will attempt to hold the trial date and, if necessary, will reduce the issues to those which can be tried on that date and penalise the party at fault in respect of any extra costs. Postponement of a trial date is set out as an order of last resort.

The pre-trial checklist

27.81 The parties are sent the checklist for completion and return by the date set out in the Notice of Allocation (usually 8 weeks before the beginning of the trial window), unless the court considers that the case can be listed for trial without one. Directions may be given if the checklist is not returned by the date specified, a party fails to give all the requested information or if the court considers that a hearing is necessary to enable it to give directions in order to complete preparations for trial. The parties should cooperate on filing the checklist and should remember to file a costs estimate at the same time. If a hearing is brought about by the default of a party, they can expect to pay the costs of that hearing.

Fixing the trial

27.82 As soon as practicable after the date for the return of the checklist the Court (CPR, r 28.6) will fix the date for the trial, give directions for the trial (including a timetable and preparation of a bundle) and specify any further steps which the parties should take. The parties should seek to agree such directions At least 3 weeks' notice will be given save in exceptional circumstance. The parties must inform the court immediately a claim is settled whether or not it is then possible to file a draft consent order of their agreement.

A typical timetable

27.83 The Practice Direction sets out a typical case and parties would be well advised to follow those limits if it is proposed to submit agreed Directions. The time is from the date of the allocation notice:

(a) Disclosure: 4 weeks

(b) Exchange of witness statements: 10 weeks

(c) Exchange of Experts' Reports: 14 weeks

(d) Sending out of listing questionnaire: 20 weeks

(e) Filing of listing questionnaire: 22 weeks

(f) Trial: 30 weeks

STANDARD DISCLOSURE

27.84 CPR, r 31.6 provides that standard disclosure requires a party to disclose only:

(a) documents upon which he relies;

(b) documents which:
    (i) adversely affect his own case;
    (ii) adversely affect another party's case;
    (iii) support another party's case;

(c) documents required by a relevant Practice Direction to be disclosed;

(d) a party's duty of disclosure extends only to documents which are or have been in his control.

27.85 This is the normal requirement for disclosure under the fast track. However, there can be provision for no disclosure and for disclosure not by list but merely by provision of copies but in that case either a disclosure statement is necessary or a record that it has been agreed that there will be no disclosure statement.

The duty of search

27.86 CPR, r 31.7(1) provides that a party giving standard disclosure is under a duty to make a reasonable search for documents which must be disclosed. Factors relevant to whether or not a search is reasonable include per CPR, r 31.7(2) the following:

- the number of documents involved;

- the nature and complexity of the proceedings;

- the ease and expense of retrieval of any particular document;

- the significance of any document which is likely to be located during a search;

- if a party has not carried out a search for a category or class of document on the ground that to do so would be unreasonable that must be stated in the disclosure statement and must identify the class or category of document (CPR, r 31.7(3)).

The disclosure statement

27.87 Per CPR, r 31.10 this is a statement which:

(a) sets out the extent of the search which was carried out to locate documents required to be disclosed (CPR, r 31.10(6)(a));

(b) certifies that the party understands the duty to disclose documents (CPR, r 31.10(6)(b);

(c) certifies to the best of the party's knowledge he has carried out that duty (CPR, r 31.10(6)(c);

(d) where a party making a disclosure statement is a company or some such other body, the statement must identify the person making the statement and explain why that person is considered to be an appropriate person to make that statement (CPR, r 31.10(8));

(e) the parties may agree in writing to give disclosure without making a disclosure statement (CPR, r 31.10(8)(b));

(f) the duty of disclosure is a continuing one.

Miscellaneous disclosure points

27.88

(a) CPR, r 31.12 gives the court power to order disclosure, a search for and the inspection of documents.

(b) Documents mentioned in a Statement of Case, witness statement, witness summary or affidavit are, per CPR, r 31.14, documents that may always be inspected whether or not disclosed in a list.

(c) Documents referred to in expert's report are always liable to inspection, save that CPR, r 35.10(4) provides that a court will not order disclosure of any specific document in relation to an expert's instructions unless there are reasonable grounds to consider that the statement of instructions included in the expert's report is inaccurate or incomplete.

(d) CPR, r 31.15 provides for notice to be given before inspection.

(e) If a party asserts a right to withhold inspection of a document, it must make a statement as to the fact that it is asserting the right to withhold inspection and the grounds on which the claim is made.

(f) CPR, r 31.20 provides that, where a document has been inadvertently disclosed and inspected, the document can only be used by the inspecting party with the court's permission.

(g) If a party fails to disclose a document or fails to permit inspection of it, then that party may not rely on that document without the court's permission (CPR, r 31.21).

(h) A court may make an order particularly restricting the use of a document outside of the proceedings in which it is disclosed.

(i) Documents properly disclosed may not be used for other purposes unless it was referred to or read out in a public hearing, or the court gives its permission, or there is an agreement between the parties.

Taking the initiative

27.89 It is clear that the fast track procedure will favour the organised litigator who has set up and implemented efficient systems to deal with litigation. The requirements of the Personal Injury Protocol will probably put the parties and, certainly should put the claimant, in a position in which to litigate speedily once proceedings have been issued. The party who has its evidence ready and has speedily prepared to deal with the issues that will arise in the course of proceedings will be put in a strong position by forcing the pace of the other party. Judges are likely to be much less sympathetic to parties who fail to meet deadlines. This will be particularly true where one party is in a position to meet the deadlines. Defendants and claimants would do well to prepare their witness statements before issue of proceedings in a standard fast track action. If the other party is not prepared, their statements or their case is likely to suffer, especially where the other party is forcing the pace.

INTERLOCUTORY APPLICATIONS

27.90 The organised party in litigation can use interlocutory applications not only to force the less organised party to comply with the directions timeously, but also use them to gain a consistent costs advantage over the opposite party. This is not to suggest that applications should be used frivolously or on minor points. The court will not be impressed if a party fails to cooperate with an opponent and merely applies to the court at every opportunity. The emphasis of the fast track is that the trial date must not be moved. The parties should cooperate to ensure that this does not happen. Courts will use the sanction of the court by way of costs or by excluding evidence to encourage a defendant or claimant to comply with directions.

27.91 A note of caution should be sounded. The practitioner will have to ensure that an application is reasonable. Correspondence evidencing a cooperative approach should be exhibited in any application. The Court of Appeal has already expressed dissatisfaction at unnecessary satellite litigation and a party will be penalised for it.

The procedure for making an application

27.92 Unless an order, rule or Practice Direction permits otherwise, CPR, r 23.3 provides that a party must file an Application Notice at Court. Where the Notice has to be served, it must be served as soon as practicable after filing and, in any event, at least 3 days before the court is to deal with the application. Under CPR, r 23.7(4), where the applicant has failed to serve the Notice at least 3 days before the court, the court can deem that sufficient notice has been given for the circumstances of the case warranted.

Requirements of the Application Notice

27.93 The Notice must state what order is sought and why it is sought. In addition, the Notice can be verified by a Statement of Truth, if the applicant wishes to rely on the matters set out in the Notice as evidence (CPR, r 23.6).

Default judgment

27.94 It is important to remember that in a case where a claimant served the Claim Form, the claimant has to file the Certificate of Service per CPR, r 6.14, or default judgment will not be entered. CPR, rr 12.4–12.10 provide for restrictions on which procedural route to follow when entering judgment. For instance, per CPR, r 12.10(a)(iii), default judgment cannot be entered in a claim against the Crown unless an application is made in order to obtain default judgment.

27.95 However, CPR, r 12.4(1)(b) still provides that one can enter default judgment by filing a form where a claim is for an amount of money to be decided by the court. Further, CPR, r 12.8(1) provides that filing a request for default judgment against one defendant does not prevent the claimant from continuing against the others.

Setting aside default judgment

27.96 The rules provide that the court must set aside default judgment if a judgment was wrongly entered because any of the requirements for default judgment were not met. If the judgment was regular, then the court has a discretion to set aside or vary a judgment in default if the defendant has a real prospect of defending the claim, or if it appears to the court either that there is some good reason why the judgment should be set aside or varied or that the defendant should be allowed to defend the claim per CPR, r 13.3. Please note – and this will be useful for personal injury actions – a matter to which the court must have regard is whether the person seeking to set aside or vary the judgment made an application promptly per CPR, r 13.3(2).

Summary judgment

27.97 Under CPR, r 24.2, a court can give judgment against a claimant or a defendant on *any issue* in the case or in respect of the whole claim without a trial, if it considers that the defendant has no real prospect of successfully defending the claim or issue, or if the claimant has no real prospect of succeeding on the claim or the issue in question. Judgment can be obtained by *either* side. Judgment may be given provided that there is no other reason why the case should go to trial. One should note per CPR, r 24.4(1) that the claimant cannot apply for summary judgment until the defendant in question has filed either an Acknowledgement of Service or a Defence, unless the court grants permission. Practitioners should be ready to use the wider scope of Part 24 to obtain judgments as to particular issues so that the issues can be narrowed or a tactical advantage gained.

Summary judgment procedure

27.98 The normal rule for services of Notices of Applications is varied in respect of summary judgments as follows:

(a) The respondent must be given a period of at least 14 days' notice of the date fixed for the hearing.

(b) The respondent must be given at least 14 days' notice of the issues which it is proposed that the court will decide.

(c) Evidence in support of the application must be filed at the same time and served at the same time as the Application Notice (CPR, r 23.7(3)).

(d) Any written evidence on behalf of the respondent to resist the application must be filed and served at least 7 days before the hearing (CPR, r 24.5(1)).

(e) If the party applying for summary judgment wishes to rely on any written evidence in reply, it must be filed at least 3 days before the hearing (CPR, r 24.5(2)).

(f) One must remember that the court may give judgment on the whole of the claim or on any issue of the claim per CPR, r 24.2 and may give directions for the filing and service of a defence and any other case management directions (CPR, r 24.6).

(g) As is the case under the present rules, the court may impose conditions when it makes any order (CPR, r 3.1(3)).

27.99 Obtaining summary judgment is easier than it used to be. The rules provide both the claimant and the defendant with a powerful tool to narrow the issues before trial and or force earlier settlements. Practitioners acting for either party should always examine their opponents' Statements of Case to establish whether their client would be assisted by the disposal of some issues at an interlocutory stage.

Interim payments

27.100 Per CPR, r 25.6(7), the court may make an order for an interim payment only if:

(a) the defendant has admitted liability to pay a sum of money to the claimant (CPR, r 25.7(1)(a)); or

(b) the claimant has obtained judgment against a relevant defendant for damages or another sum of money apart from costs, to be assessed (CPR, r 25.7(1)(b)); or

(c) the court is satisfied that, if the claim went to trial, the claimant would obtain judgment for a substantial amount of money, apart from costs, against the defendant from whom the interim payment is sought (CPR, r 25.7(1)(c)).

27.101 An application for an interim payment in personal injury work should contain the following:

- the amount of damages or sum of money which the application relates to;

- the reasons for the application;

- details of special damages and past and future loss of earnings;

- in a claim under the Fatal Accidents Act 1976, details of the persons on whose behalf the claim is made and the nature of the claim;

- documents in support of the application should be exhibited including, in personal injury claims, the medical reports.

27.102 The old restrictions on personal injury interim payments were removed in 2005 although the court will consider the ability of the defendant to pay.

Deduction of benefits

27.103 Where there is an application for an interim payment that does not go by consent and the application is one which includes damages which stand to be recouped by the Compensation Recovery Unit and which the defendant is liable to pay recoverable benefits upon, then the defendant should obtain a certificate of recoverable benefits and the order should be reduced in accordance with that certificate.

EXPERTS

27.104 Practitioners must remember that:

(a) experts' evidence to be restricted to what is reasonably necessary (CPR, r 35.1);

(b) no party can call an expert or rely on his evidence without the court's permission (CPR, r 35.4(1));

(c) where permission to rely upon an expert is sought he must identify:

(i) the expert's field; and
(ii) where practicable, the expert himself.

27.105 Practitioners must now be more aware of the specialists whom they instruct. If a psychologist is instructed where a client is suffering from a clinical depression and a psychiatrist should have been instructed, then it is very unlikely that one would be able to obtain the costs of both reports back on assessment of costs.

Oral evidence

27.106 The normal position in the fast track is that experts will not give oral evidence. Therefore, it is of the first importance that practitioners use their opportunities, first under the Protocol to question and, secondly under Part 35.6. If an expert does not answer a proper question, the party relying upon the expert may be prevented from doing so or unable to recover the costs associated with the expert. Unless the other party agrees or the court allows, written questions may only be put once and within 28 days of service of the report.

The experts' meeting

27.107 Part 35.12 sets out the system for the experts' meeting. The Protocol for the Instruction of Experts provides that meetings will be unusual in fast track or small claims cases. The parties and the experts (although predominantly the lawyers) should cooperate to produce an agenda.. The experts should identify the issues and, where possible, reach agreement. A statement should be prepared as to those issues and the basis on which they agree and disagree as well as any further issues not in the agenda that were discussed or action or further meetings that should take place. Unless parties decide otherwise agreements between experts are not binding on them however caution has to be exercised in light of the overriding objective.

27.108 In *Baron v Lovell*,[12] the Court of Appeal held that a defendant who had not kept to the trial timetable should not be allowed to rely upon his own medical expert. The experts were, in any event, close to each other and the defendant's breach of directions put him at the mercy of the court. The same court, in the same sitting, refused to intervene with a judge's order debarring the defendant from calling a crucial witness where that witness had failed to comply with the requirements of r 35.12 (*Stevens v Gullis*). The judgment is a warning to parties that they must ensure that their experts comply with directions. Further, in *Rollinson v Kimberly Clark Ltd*,[13] Peter Gibson LJ held that it was inappropriate to instruct an expert without regard to his availability where the trial was so near. If availability was a problem an alternative expert should be used.

---

[12] 27 July 1999, Woolf MR, Brooke and Walker LJJ.
[13] (1999) *The Times*, June 22.

PROVISIONAL DAMAGES

27.109 If the defendant agrees to the payment of provisional damages, then the payment notice must state the following per CPR, r 36.7(3):

(a) That the sum paid into court is in satisfaction of the claim for damages on the assumption that the further condition/deterioration will not take place.

(b) That the offer is subject to the condition that the claimant must make any claim for further damages within a limited period and that period is specified.

COSTS: REASONABLENESS AND PROPORTIONALITY

27.110 Per CPR, r 44.5(3), the court must have regard to:

(a) the conduct of all the parties including, in particular:
  (i) conduct before, as well as during, the proceedings; and
  (ii) the efforts made, if any, before and during the proceedings in order to try to resolve the dispute;

(b) the amount and value of any money or property involved;

(c) the importance of the matter to all the parties;

(d) the particular complexity of the matter or the difficulty or novelty of the questions raised;

(e) the skill, effort, specialised knowledge and responsibility involved;

(f) the time spent on the case;

(g) the place where and the circumstances in which work or any part of it was done.

Fast track costs

27.111 CPR, r 46.2(1) provides for a fee of £350 for cases up to £3,000, £500 up to £10,000 and £750 up to £15,000. In awarding costs to a claimant, the sum excludes contributory negligence deductions, interest and costs (CPR, r 46.3(3)(a)) and when awarding costs to a defendant, the figure is that specified in the claim for or, if not specified, then the maximum amount that the claimant could reasonably expect to recover (CPR, r 46.3(3)(b)). An additional £250 can be paid to a party's legal representative if it was necessary for him to attend to assist the advocate(CPR, r 46.3).

27.112 The standard practice is either for a summary assessment of costs or, if matter are delayed to a detailed assessment, then the court should, on a rough-and-ready basis, order an amount (less than the full amount) to be paid to the successful party on account (*Mars UK Ltd v Teknowledge Ltd (No 2)*).[14]

Fixed costs in road traffic accidents

27.113 CPR, r 45.7 applies a fixed costs regime where the dispute arises from a road traffic accident, the agreed damages are in respect of personal injury and or damage to property, the total value of agreed damages does not exceed £10,000 and that the small claim track would not have been the appropriate track (ie personal injury damages are more than £1,000 and or property damage alone is more than £5,000).

(a) Fixed recoverable costs are limited to:
  (i) £800 plus;
  (ii) 20% of damages agreed up to £5,000 plus;
  (iii) 15% of damages agreed between £5,000 and £10,000;
  (iv) there is an uplift of 12.5% if the claimant lives and works within prescribed areas and instructs a solicitor in that area.

(b) Disbursements can be recovered for the cost of medical records, medical report, police report, engineer's report or a search of the DVLA.

(c) Insurance costs for or an additional amount if the claimant is a member of an organisation which protects against the risk of meeting the other side's costs.

(d) If the claimant is a child/patient then counsel's fees and appropriate application fees.

(e) A success fee of 12.5% of the recoverable costs.

(f) Exceptional circumstances can justify a further claim for costs outside these limits.

Conditional fee agreements

27.114 The other party should be informed within 7 days of the entering of a conditional fee agreement. In road traffic accidents after 6 October 2003, CPR Part 45 provides for fixed uplifts. A solicitor is entitled to a 100% uplift if the claim concludes at trial or 12.5% is settled at any stage before a trial has commenced and counsel is entitled (in a fast track case) to an uplift of 100% if the claim concludes at trial, 50% if the case settles 14 days or less before the date fixed for the start of the trial and otherwise to 12.5%. In employer liability claims (other than disease) the same uplifts apply except that the 12.5% is

---

[14] (1999) *The Times*, July 8, Jacob J.

doubled to 25% for both solicitors and counsel save in cases where a membership organisation (eg trades union) has undertaken to meet the other sides costs in which case the 25% is increased to 27.5%. Exceptional cases fall outside the ambit of these standard uplifts.

Small claims costs

27.115 In *Woodings v BT plc*[15] the judge allowed the claimant to reclaim costs from the defendant in acoustic shock claims which were valued less than £1,000 as a result of the extent of the technical expert evidence required and the fact that the defendants never cooperated to find an economical solution to the claimant's problem and the fact that expense could have been spared had the defendants acted in a more rational manner. Conversely, in *Devine v Franklin*[16] it was held that a successful claimant who only recovered £795 should have his costs restricted to small claims amounts as he had exaggerated his injuries which had resulted in fast track allocation.

APPEAL

27.116 An appeal lies to the circuit judge on a trial before a district judge unless the party consented to the order. The Notice of Appeal must be served within 14 days after the judgment or order was given or made. The judge's power is limited to the exercise of his discretion – the original judgment has to be one in which no reasonable district judge could have exercised the court's discretion in the way it was done.

27.117 An appeal lies from the circuit judge as the trial judge to the Court of Appeal in the normal way. Permission is required.

Procedural appeals

27.118 In terms of procedure, Woolf MR stated in *Baron v Lovell*[17] that the Court of Appeal would only interfere with a judge's discretion if he was plainly wrong.

---

[15] 7 February 2003, City of London County Court (unreported).
[16] [2002] EWHC 1846 (QBD).
[17] Op cit.

Chapter 28

PROCEEDINGS INVOLVING CHILDREN

28.1 This chapter deals only with claims brought by or against children. It does not deal with claims brought by or against patients.

28.2 The rules relating to claims involving children are largely dealt with in Part 21 of the Civil Procedure Rules 1998 (CPR) and its attendant Practice Direction. The hallmark of the CPR in relation to children is the intention to protect the child as a potentially vulnerable litigant. Therefore, almost any step taken in an action will need to be considered and approved by the court. This should be borne in mind when one is involved in litigation on behalf of or against children.

28.3 A child means a person under 18.[1]

THE LITIGATION FRIEND

28.4 Save where the court makes an order pursuant to r 21.2(3), the child must have a Litigation Friend to conduct proceedings on his behalf.[2] Litigation Friend is the term used whether the child is the claimant or the defendant.

No Litigation Friend

28.5 While is it usual, it is not always necessary for a child to have a Litigation Friend. Rule 21.2(3) specifically provides for the court to make an order permitting a child to conduct proceedings without a Litigation Friend, and r 21.2(4) goes on to provide:

'(4) An application for an order under paragraph (3) –

(a) may be made by the child,
(b) if the child already has a litigation friend must be made on notice to the litigation friend, and
(c) if the child has no litigation friend may be made without notice.'

28.6 However, even where the court has made an order permitting the child to conduct proceedings without a Litigation Friend 'where it subsequently

---

[1] CPR, r 21.1(2)(a).
[2] CPR, r 21.2(1).

appears to the court that it is desirable for a Litigation Friend to conduct the proceedings on behalf of the child, the court may appoint a person to be the child's litigation friend'.[3]

28.7 Paragraph 1.5 of the Practice Direction annexed to r 21 provides that:

'Where ... (2) the child is conducting proceedings on his own behalf, the child should be referred to in the title as "AB (a child)".'

Proceedings against children

28.8 Unless the court has made an order permitting the child to act on his own behalf, then the provisions of r 21.3 apply.

28.9 Rule 21.3(2) provides as follows:

'(2) A person may not without the permission of the court:

(a) make an application against a child ... before proceedings have started, or
(b) take any steps in proceedings except –
 (i) issuing and serving a claim from, or
 (ii) applying for the appointment of a Litigation friend under rule 21.6

until the child ... has a Litigation Friend ...

(4) Any step taken before a child has a Litigation Friend shall be of no effect, unless the court otherwise orders.'

28.10 Rule 21.3 applies to all claims involving children including a Part 20 claim against a child, such as a claim by a defendant against any child for contribution or indemnity.

28.11 This rule must be read in conjunction with the service rules of Part 6.6 of the CPR which deals with the service of documents on children. Rule 6.6(1) sets out in table form the person on whom a document must be served if it is a document which would otherwise be served on a child. Under the heading 'Type of Document', there is a reference to a Claim Form and, where the child is not also a patient, the person to be served is specified as 'one of the child's parents or guardians or if there is no parent or guardian, the person with whom the child resides or in whose care the child is'.

28.12 Presumably, if the would-be claimant has no idea who the child's parent or guardian is or with whom the child resides or in whose care the child is, it would be permissible to serve on the child himself. If personal service is effected the adult living with the child would suffice as the person on whom the documents were served if the child is in their care. It may be prudent to obtain a Court Order prior to service. It may be necessary to seek an extension of time for service of the Claim Form or Part 20 Claim Form if the 4 months for

---

[3] CPR, r 21.2(5).

service is approaching. Primary limitation may on occasion also be an issue (in contrast, of course, to the position the child is the *claimant*).

Appointment of Litigation Friend without court order

28.13 The mechanism of CPR Part 21 expects a Litigation Friend to support the child litigant. If nobody has been appointed by the court then r 21.4(3) provides that a person may act as a litigation friend if he:

> '(a) can fairly and competently conduct proceedings on behalf of the child; and
> (b) has no interest adverse to that of the child; and
> (c) where the child ... is a claimant, undertakes to pay any costs which the child ... may be ordered to pay in relation to the proceedings, subject to any right he may have to be repaid from the assets of the child.'

28.14 A person wishing to act as Litigation Friend must follow the procedure set out in r 21.5(1), namely that he must file a certificate of suitability stating that he satisfies the conditions specified in r 21.4(3).[4] If he is acting for a claimant, he must file the authorisation or certificate of suitability at the time when the claim is made.[5] If he is acting for a child defendant, he must file the certificate of suitability at the time when he first takes a step in the proceedings on behalf of that defendant child.[6] In addition, he must serve the certificate of suitability on every person on whom, in accordance with r 6.6, the Claim Form should be served. If he is acting for a child defendant, then pursuant to r 6.1(4), when he files the certificate of service on behalf of the defendant he should likewise file the certificate of suitability (form N235).[7]

28.15 Further information in respect of the procedural aspects in and about becoming a Litigation Friend is set out in the Practice Direction. Paragraph 2.3(2) of the Practice Direction provides that the person who wishes to act as Litigation Friend must file a certificate of suitability:

(a) stating that he consents to act;

(b) stating that he knows or believes that the claimant or defendant is a child;

(c) stating that he can fairly and competently conduct proceedings on behalf of the child and has no interest adverse to that of the child;

(d) where the child is a claimant, undertaking to pay any costs which the child may be ordered to pay in the proceedings subject to any right he may have to be repaid from the assets of the child; and

(e) which he has signed in verification of its contents.

---

[4] CPR, r 21.5(3).
[5] CPR, r 21.5(4).
[6] CPR, r 21.5(5).
[7] CPR, r 21.5(6).

28.16 By para 2.4, the Litigation Friend must serve a certificate of suitability:[8]

'(1) in the case of a child (who is not also a patient) on one of the child's parents or guardians or if there is no parent or guardian on the person with whom the child resides or in whose are the child is.'

28.17 And by para 2.5

'The litigation friend must file either the certificate of suitability together with a certificate of service of it –

(1) where the litigation friend is acting on behalf of a claimant, when the claim form is issued, and
(2) where the litigation friend is acting on behalf of a defendant, when he first takes a step in the action.'

Appointment of Litigation Friend by court order

28.18 Rule 21.6 sets out the procedure by which a person may become a litigation friend by virtue of a court order. By r 21.6(2):

'An application for an order appointing a Litigation friend may be made by –

(a) a person who wishes to be the litigation friend; or
(b) a party.'

28.19 A person wishing to sue a child or who wishes to pursue a Part 20 claim against a child will want a Litigation Friend appointed and indeed the rules require it to be so unless specifically exempt. If, as defendant, a claim is initiated by a child and there is no Litigation Friend, the defendant should raise this with the court as soon as possible, at the latest by a first CMC but preferably before then by specific application. It should be borne in mind that CPR, r 21.3(4) states that no step taken before a Litigation Friend is in place will be of effect without court order. This therefore may need to be addressed at any application seeking appointment of Litigation Friend by the court. One may question whether proceedings are validly issued or claim commenced without a Litigation Friend, but it would be usual upon review of steps already taken, for the court to confirm such steps as have been taken subject to consideration of any prejudice that may have been suffered by the parties.

28.20 By r 21.6(3):

'Where –

(a) a person makes a claim against a child;
(b) the child has no Litigation Friend;
(c) the court has not made an order that a child can act without a Litigation Friend; and

---

[8] See CPR, r 21.5(6) and r 6.9 (service).

(d) either –
  (i) someone who is not entitled to be a Litigation Friend files a defence or
  (ii) the claimant wishes to take some step in the proceedings,
  the claimant must apply to the court for an order appointing a Litigation Friend for the child.'

28.21 The court has to be satisfied that the Litigation Friend satisfies the criteria set out in r 21.4(3) (above). The application for an order appointing a Litigation Friend must be supported by evidence.[9] Paragraph 3.3 of the Practice Direction provides that the application notice must be served on one of the child's parents or guardians or, if there is no parent or guardian, on the person with whom the child resides or in whose care the child is. Paragraph 3.2 reiterates that the application must be made in accordance with Part 23 and be supported by evidence. In other words, following r 23.6 the application notice must state: (a) what order the applicant is seeking and (b) briefly why the applicant is seeking the order.

28.22 According to para 3.4 of Part 21 of the Practice Direction, the evidence in support of the application must satisfy the court that the proposed Litigation Friend:

(i) consents to act;

(ii) can fairly and competently conduct proceedings on behalf of the child;

(iii) has no interest adverse to that of the child; and

(iv) where the child is a claimant, undertakes to pay any costs which the child may be ordered to pay in relation to the proceedings, subject to any right he may have to be repaid from the assets of the child.

28.23 It is to be noted that if the person seeking the appointment wishes to rely upon matters contained within the application notice itself, then the application has to be verified by a statement of truth. This is in accordance with r 32.6(2) which provides that:

> 'At hearings other than the trial, a party may in support of his application rely upon the matters set out in ... his application, if the statement or application is verified by a statement of truth.'

28.24 Care must be taken to ensure there is no potential for conflict between the child and the person acting as Litigation Friend. It is common for a parent to act as Litigation Friend, but it is important to ensure the Litigation Friend could have no association with the litigation – as defendant or potential witness. For example, if the injury occurred in a road traffic accident and one of the parents were driving, and another a witness, there may be difficulties in either parent being the Litigation Friend.

---

[9] CPR, r 21.6(4).

Replacement of Litigation Friend by court order

28.25 By r 21.7(1), the court may:

'(a) direct that a person may not act as a litigation friend,
(b) terminate a litigation friend's appointment,
(c) appoint a new litigation friend in substitution for an existing one.'

28.26 The application for an order under this paragraph must be supported by evidence (see discussion above).[10] In any event, the court may not appoint a litigation friend unless it is satisfied that the person appointed complies with the conditions specified in r 21.4(3).[11] Paragraph 4 of the Practice Direction provides further information in respect of the court's ability to order a change or prevention of person acting as Litigation Friend. Paragraph 4.2 reiterates that the application must be supported by evidence setting out the reasons for seeking the change or replacement. Further, if there is to be a new Litigation Friend in place of an existing Litigation Friend, the evidence will have to satisfy the court of the matters specified in para 3.4 of the Practice Direction which has been set out above.

28.27 CPR, r 21.8 sets out additional requirements for the appointment of a Litigation Friend by way of court order. The application must be served on every person on which the claim form should be served and also on the person who is currently the Litigation Friend or purporting to act as the Litigation Friend at the time the application is made. So too it must be served on the person who it is proposed should be the Litigation Friend (if this is not the applicant). On application for an order either to appoint or change or prevent a person acting as Litigation Friend the Court may appoint the person proposed or any other person who complies with the condition specified in CPR, r 21.4(3).[12]

28.28 There is nothing in r 21.7(1) which gives a hint as to the circumstances in which the litigation friend's appointment may be terminated. While the rules allow for an application to be made, presumably usually by a defendant but possibly also by the claimant child, the court has the power to change the Litigation Friend of its own initiative pursuant to CPR, r 21.8(4) and CPR, r 3.3(1) and the court's general power to vary or revoke any order which it makes – CPR, r 3.1(7).

28.29 Obviously, if a Litigation Friend dies or goes to prison or himself becomes a patient or there is a risk of prejudice within the proceedings, it would be appropriate for a new Litigation Friend to be appointed. I would suggest that the guide or test should be that the Litigation Friend should only be removed if he is not pursuing the best interests of the child. Allowing for

---

[10] CPR, r 21.7(2).
[11] CPR, r 21.7(3).
[12] CPR, r 21.8(4).

some possible updating of language, I can see no reason why that which was said by Lord Denning in *Re Taylor's Application*[13] should not apply. He said:

> 'I take it to be clear that the father is prima facie the person entitled to be the next friend of his child so as to look after the interests of the child. He is the person entitled to consider his child's case on its own merits. He is not bound to consider the cases of others who may not be as strong as his child's. If he is to be removed, it should only be done if the proposed settlement is so clearly beneficial for his child that he is acting improperly in refusing it. ... The burden is clearly on those who seek to remove a parent to show that he is not acting properly in the interests of his child as its next friend.'

28.30 This was said in the context of the thalidomide litigation where a particular parent did not desire to join the general settlement of that litigation. In modern litigation potential problems may particularly arise between a Litigation Friend and child when settlements are proposed in claims funded by conditional fee agreements. Determination to recover costs or payments made by a Litigation Friend to purchase insurance premiums could create a conflict between the child and Litigation Friend, this is considered further in the costs section below.

Default proceedings where the child is the defendant

28.31 Rule 12.1 of the CPR provides that:

> 'In these rules, default judgment means judgment without trial where a defendant (a) has failed to file an acknowledgement of service or (b) has failed to file a defence.'

28.32 In these circumstances a claimant, whether of a claim or Part 20 proceedings, can normally enter a default judgment. However, this normal default procedure does not apply where the claim involves a child. When the defendant is a child, 'the claimant must make an application in accordance with Part 23'.[14] An application for a default judgment against a child must be supported by evidence.[15]

28.33 Paragraph 4.2 of the Part 12 Practice Direction provides that:

> 'On an application against a child ...
>
> (1) a litigation friend to act on behalf of the child ... must be appointed by the court before judgment can be obtained, and
> (2) the claimant must satisfy the court by evidence that he is entitled to the judgment claimed.'

---

[13] [1972] 2 QB 369.
[14] CPR, r 12.10.
[15] CPR, r 12.10(3).

28.34 Part 14 of the CPR deals with admissions. Rule 14.1(1) provides that:

'A party may admit the truth of the whole or any part of another party's case.'

28.35 Further, by r 14.1(4):

'Where the defendant makes an admission as mentioned in paragraph (3) the claimant has a right to enter judgment except where (a) the defendant is a child ...'

28.36 This is then followed by a specific reference to r 21.10(1), namely that:

'Where a claim is made by or on behalf of a child ... or against a child ... no settlement compromise or payment shall be valid so far as it relates to that person's claim, without the approval of the court.'

28.37 Therefore, even when an admission is made in a claim involving a child, whether the child is the party making the admission or the beneficiary of the admission, that admission will not be binding unless it has received the approval of the court.

28.38 This is contrary to the suggestion of the pre-action protocol, that pre-action admissions made in fast track cases are binding, and indeed overrules the rebuttable presumption in CPR Part 14 that an admission is binding, unless the court allows it to be withdrawn.

28.39 Therefore, although CPR, r 21.10(1) intends to protect the child as litigant, in fact it may mean that parties who have proceeded for some time, indeed perhaps years, dealing with quantum only in reliance on an admission without troubling the court for approval, may find that the defendant changes its mind, withdraws the admission, and possibly leaves the child claimant without remedy.

28.40 The Court of Appeal considered just this situation in *Whitwood v Drinkall*.[16] In this case a then 14-year-old claimant had been injured when her bicycle was in collision with a car. She suffered permanent brain damage. An admission of 80% liability was finalised two years after the accident, before proceedings were issued, and the parties moved on to quantum issues. Two years after that, shortly before the claimant was 18, the defendant withdrew its admission.

28.41 The court held that it was bound by a House of Lords decision in *Dietz v Lennig Chemicals Limited*[17] which dealt with a similar rule under the old Supreme Court Rules. In *Whitwood* the Court of Appeal confirmed that the need for approval covered partial (ie liability issues) as well as complete settlement of the claim. As Lord Justice Simon Brown said, giving the judgment of the court:

---

[16] [2003] EWCA Civ 1547.
[17] [1969] 1 AC 170.

'It inescapably follows ... regrettable though it might seem, the defendants here were entitled to renege on their agreement as they did, for good reason or none, and must therefore succeed upon this appeal.'

28.42 It is right to note Lord Justice Simon Brown made two important comments, as footnotes. First, he said that if an agreement between child and adult party has been reached but not approved by the court, when the child reaches majority, the settlement agreement would be open to be accepted as an offer made by either side, unless the offer was repudiated. Secondly, he said that there may well be an argument of estoppel if a party has relied on a settlement agreement to its material disadvantage that the other party then seeks to repudiate before approval.

28.43 However, the clear message from this case is that if any settlement agreement is reached between parties, one of whom is a child, the court must approve it before it becomes binding. Therefore, the party wishing to benefit from the settlement agreement may well wish to issue proceedings or make an application to seek approval as soon as possible.

28.44 The notes to the White Book (21.0.3) suggest that the purpose of the restriction on entering judgment put in place by CPR, r 14.1(4) is to protect a child who is a defendant – to ensure the scrutiny of the court before a concession is made to the detriment of the weaker party. This may well have been the intention, but as *Whitwood* demonstrates, the rule also has perhaps unforeseen consequences.

COMPROMISE OF CLAIMS INVOLVING CHILDREN

28.45 Court approval is required of any compromise of any claim involving a child in order for it to be effective and binding on the parties.

28.46 Specifically, by r 21.10(1) where a claim is made (a) by or on behalf of a child or (b) against a child, no settlement compromise or payment and no acceptance of money paid into court shall be valid so far as it relates to the claim by, on behalf of or against the child without the approval of the court.

28.47 There are several reasons for the court to require approval of any compromise. They are:

(a) to protect children from any lack of skill or experience on the part of their legal advisers and to ensure the compromise is fair and reasonable (see *Black v Yates*[18] where minors challenged the award of compensation they received in a foreign court);

---

[18] [1992] QB 526.

(b) to protect the defendant by ensuring there is a valid discharge from the child's claim. A child is not bound by a common law contract of compromise out of court therefore, the approval of the court gives the defendant necessary certainty;

(c) to ensure that solicitors acting on behalf of a child are paid their proper costs, and no more. Two problems may arise – first, that a child may be charged too much, and secondly that a solicitor may be tempted to recommend too low a settlement to ensure payment of fees. This second point, in particular, is now a common ethical dilemma faced by all litigants involved in conditional fee claims. The drafting of CPR Part 21 harks back to a time when such a potential conflict was highly unusual;

(d) to ensure the proper investment of money received on behalf of children. By CPR, r 21.12 money is placed under the control of the court. While this requirement may lessen in larger cases where periodical payments and sophisticated investment advice and strategies are in place, the rule provides a considerable measure of protection to children with modest sums in damages, often from their own desire quickly to spend that which would be better invested for their future needs;

(e) to ensure the interests of all dependents entitled to a share of any settlement. This chapter primarily deals with single child claimants, but of course, particularly in Fatal Accident claims, there may be more than one. The court will be interested in all the potential claimants, particularly in a group action such as *McDermott International Inc v Hardy*;[19] or *Re Taylor's Application* (as to which, see discussion above).

Settlement after commencement of action

28.48 In respect of the compromise of actions made after proceedings have been commenced, Part 21 is somewhat silent as to the appropriate procedure by which that court approval is to be obtained. If a claim ends in judgment, that judgment will be the necessary approval of the court. If the case settles at trial, without judgment, the trial judge is on hand and sufficiently seized of the matter to be able to give approval. However, if the case settles after proceedings have been commenced but before trial, an application has to be made pursuant to Part 23 by way of an application notice.

28.49 This application must be supported by evidence sufficient for the court to form a view on the appropriateness of the settlement, which may require explanation of issues of liability and well as quantum. The application should be served on the defendant, since this ought to be an application by consent. If privileged material is disclosed to the judge, such as counsel's advice on merits or quantum, this should not be served on the defendant.

---

[19] (1995) *The Times*, December 28.

28.50 Approval will be required even if the sum accepted was offered by way of a Part 36 payment by the defendant. No child can accept a Part 36 payment without approval of the court and no payment out of any sum shall be made without a court order.[20]

28.51 It is possible for the hearing or part of the hearing to be in private, if appropriate.[21] Whether or not to hold a hearing in private is a matter for the judge conducting the hearing, having regard to any representations which may have been made to him and also having regard to Art 6(1) of the European Convention on Human Rights.[22] It is usual for the child and the Litigation Friend to be present in court. If not present, a cogent explanation will have to be furnished.

28.52 Form CFO Form 320 – request for investment, now largely replaced by Form 212 – must be filled out and handed in to the Court for final completion at the hearing by the Master or District Judge, whether at a trial or compromise at any stage.[23] The child's birth certificate (original or certified copy) must also be brought to court for the judge to examine.

Settlement of claim prior to proceedings being brought

28.53 If a claim is resolved by agreement prior to the start of proceedings, the court's only involvement will be for the purposes of approval. If the sole purpose of the proceedings is to obtain the approval of the court, then the claim must be made using the procedure set out in Part 8 and include a request to the court for approval of the settlement of compromise.[24]

28.54 Rule 21.10(2) provides as follows:

'Where –

(a) before proceedings in which a claim is made by or on behalf of or against a child (whether alone or with any other person) are begun, an agreement is reached for settlement of the claim; and
(b) the sole purpose of proceedings on that claim is to obtain the approval of the court to a settlement or compromise of the claim,

the claim must –

(i) be made using the procedure set out in Part 8 (alternative procedure for claims); and
(ii) include a request for the court for approval of the settlement or compromise.'

---

[20] CPR, r 36.18(1).
[21] CPR, r 39.2(3)(d).
[22] CPR 39PD 1.4 and 1.4A.
[23] CPR 21PD.10.
[24] CPR, r 21.10(2).

28.55 The rules governing a Part 8 Claim Form can be found in CPR Part 8, particularly r 8.2 (as to the contents to the Claim Form).

28.56 In relation to approval in cases involving children the general requirement is repeated in CPR 21PD.6 which also sets out the evidence required when making the application, namely that the application will have to include terms of the settlement or compromise, or have attached to it a draft consent order in practice form N292 and detail information as to whether and to what extent the defendant admits liability, the age and occupation (if any) of the child, the Litigation Friend's approval of the proposed settlement or compromise, the circumstances of the accident, any medical report, a schedule of special damages and future loss, police reports or evidence in criminal proceedings or in an inquest and details of the result of any criminal prosecution. The police reports and evidence is only required if liability is in issue.

28.57 Except in very clear cases, an opinion on the merits of the settlement or compromise given by counsel or solicitor acting for the claimant should be obtained and, as necessary, a copy of instructions on which the advice is based.[25]

28.58 The hearing is usually to be before a Master or a District Judge.[26]

28.59 While it is common, particularly in smaller cases, for a defendant not to be present at an approval hearing some indication from the defendant that agreement has been reached, even if by letter, will be required. If the defendant is not represented it is good practice for the claimant to try to have contact details so that if the court has specific questions or wants to approve a different figure it may be possible to negotiate and achieved compromise without having to adjourn the hearing and attend court at a later date. The precise approach to a settlement hearing will of course depend on many factors, predominantly the size of the damages claim.

28.60 For any settlement or compromise to be approved, the compromise must deal not only with damages but also with costs.

28.61 It is possible for a compromise or settlement to be by way of provisional damages. If this is the case, then the additional information required in a provisional damages claim will be required to present to the court before approval will be obtained (CPR, rr 41.1-41.3 and CPR 41PD.1).

28.62 The parties must have considered whether or not a periodical payment would be appropriate for the claim particularly if a compromise or settlement involves a significant element of future loss. If periodical payment is not thought to be appropriate, the application for approval must explain why. If it

---

[25] CPR 21PD 6.3.
[26] CPR 21PD 6.5.

is, then the necessary elements of the periodical payment will have to be put before the court prior to approval (CPR, rr 41.40–41.10 and CPR 41BPD.1). Separating out any element of damages that is to be paid by way of periodical payment will, of course, affect the availability of funds for immediate payment out rather than investment.

Costs on settlement

28.63 Whether the case settles after proceedings are brought or prior to the commencement of proceedings, CPR, r 48.5 dealing with costs will apply. It applies to any proceedings where the claimant is a child and (a) money is ordered or agreed to be paid to or for the benefit of that child or (b) money is ordered to be paid by him or on his behalf.

28.64 By r 48.5(2), the general rule is that:

'(a) the court must order a detailed assessment of the costs payable by any party who is a child to his solicitor; and
(b) on an assessment under paragraph (a) the court must also assess any costs payable to that party in the proceedings unless –
　(i) the Court has issued a default costs certificate in relation to those costs under rule 47.11; or
　(ii) the costs are payable in proceedings to which Section II of Part 45 applies.'[27]

28.65 Detailed assessment can be avoided as set out in 48PD.2 r 51:

'51.1 The circumstances in which the court need not order the assessment of costs under rule 48.5(3) are as follows:

(a) where there is no need to do so to protect the interests of the child ... or his estate;
(b) where another party has agreed to pay a specified sum in respect of the costs of the child ... and the solicitor acting for the child or patient has waived the right to claim further costs;
(c) where the court has decided the costs payable to the child ... by way of summary assessment and the solicitor acting for the child or patient has waived the right to claim further costs;
(d) where an insurer or other person is liable to discharge the costs which the child or patient would otherwise be liable to pay to his solicitor and the court is satisfied that the insurer or other person is financially able to discharge those costs.'

28.66 Essentially, therefore, costs must be dealt with before any compromise will be approved by the court. They can be dealt with as follows:

---

[27] Fixed recoverable costs in a road traffic accident arising after 6 October 2003.

(a) where an agreement on the amount of costs has been reached *plus* the child's solicitor has agreed to waive the right to claim any further costs from the client;

(b) where the court summarily assesses costs *plus* the child's solicitor waives the right to claim any further costs;

(c) a detailed assessment (which will determine the amount of recoverable costs).

28.67 The important purpose of these rules is to protect the child from having his award of damages fund reduced on the payment of legal costs. Therefore, the usual rule of cost recovery against the client is abrogated. It is most commonly the case that detailed assessment of costs is ordered – as set out in form N292, 'the defendant to pay the claimant's costs to be assessed with permission to request assessment to be dispensed with and the Claimant's solicitor waiving any claim for further costs' which allows for sending a matter off for detailed assessment subject to agreement prior to hearing, so long as any further costs claim by the claimant's solicitor against his client are waived.

28.68 It is possible but less common for the court summarily to assess costs at the compromise hearing. Often time restrictions in listing will mean no time is available for assessment.

28.69 The increased use of conditional fee agreements in cases involving children have led to particular problems arising. It is the Litigation Friend who is required to sign an After the Event insurance policy on behalf of a child and so too it is the Litigation Friend who commonly has to fund the cost of that policy and pay any interest accruing to the insurer if the policy is paid by way of loan. In the usual case, the cost of policy and additional interest is recovered either as costs or from the eventual damages award. The effect of CPR, rr 48.5 and 48.PD.2 section 51 is to prevent this and, potentially, leave a Litigation Friend with an irrecoverable cost.

28.70 Circumvention of the costs rules has been attempted by reliance on CPR, r 21.4(3)(c) setting out the requirements of a Litigation Friend which states:

'... where the child ... is a claimant, undertakes to pay any costs which the child or patient may be ordered to pay in relation to the proceedings, subject to any right he may have to be repaid from the assets of the child'.

28.71 This has been coupled with CPR 21.PD8.2(2):

'The court ... may also direct that certain sums be paid direct to the child... his litigation friend or his legal representative for the immediate benefit of the child or for expenses incurred on his behalf.'

28.72 It has been argued that the payment of the insurance premium and interest is such a benefit for which the Litigation Friend should rightfully recover. An application for these costs is often made at the time of the approval hearing, as an immediate payment out of approved damages.

28.73 While this approach would seem to put the Litigation Friend in conflict with the child, and indeed be an attempt to subvert the purpose of the cost rules, it has found favour with the court on at least one occasion.[28] Although only a District Judge level decision, the conditional fee agreement administrative success fee of 10% and interest on the bank loan to cover expenses (neither of which were recoverable from the defendant in costs) were ordered to be paid to the Litigation Friend from the child's approved damages sum. This decision remains an anomaly, albeit one seized upon with a certain enthusiasm by various funding bodies.

28.74 However, the reluctance of the courts to award costs from the child's damages, yet the ensuing unfairness to the Litigation Friend has led to a redrafting of the rules. There is now a new CPR, r 21.11A which allows a litigation friend who incurs expenses on behalf of a child or patient in any proceedings to recover the amount paid, or payable out of any money recovered, to the extent that it has been reasonably incurred and is reasonable in amount.

28.75 Expenses specifically include both an insurance premium (CPR, r 21.11A(2)(a)) and interest on a loan for an insurance premium (CPR, r 21.11A(b)).

28.76 This rule therefore addresses the exact problem discussed above, while allowing the court to retain a discretion in assessing the reasonableness of both the size of the insurance premium and the interest rate of any loan. It attempts to strike a pragmatic balance between the needs of the child and need for protection of the child against the injustice of penalising the impecunious litigation friend, who without after the event insurance would not be able to assist the child in bringing a claim in the first place.

28.77 Expenses that would normally form part of the assessment of costs are specifically excluded from the new rule.

28.78 The advent of fixed recoverable costs in Road Traffic Accident cases (Section II, CPR, r 45.7) has also lead to some problems. In accidents occurring after 6 October 2003 where the total agreed damages do not exceed £10,000 fixed recoverable costs are in place. Where costs are not agreed, the procedure for issuing costs only proceedings is set out in CPR, r 44.12A. There has been

---

[28] *Scott v Harrogate Borough Council* 20 January 2003, unreported, Harrogate County Court. This case is referred to in *Cook on Costs 2005*, LexisNexis, Butterworths.

some confusion as to whether cases involving children fall into the fixed cost regime or not or whether the need for approval of damages lifts the claims out of the fixed cost provisions.[29]

28.79 The question is now largely academic since amendment to CPR, r 21.10 in force on 1 April 2005 by virtue of SI 2004/3419 adds a new CPR, r 21.10(3):

> 'In proceedings to which Section II of Part 45 applies, the court shall not make an order for detailed assessment of the costs payable to the child or patient but shall assess the costs in the manner set out in that section'

and amends Section II CPR 45 specifically to apply the fixed cost regime to proceedings for approval of settlement pursuant to CRP, r 21.10(2).

28.80 Therefore, from 1 April 2005 at any approval for a compromise of a child's claim falling within the Section II regime expect to deal with the fixed costs at the end of the approval hearing. For claims where the road traffic accident occurred after 6 October 2003 but approval was before 1 April 2005, while there remains some conflicting authority, the only Circuit Judge authority[30] supports fixed costs; therefore, on the basis of this judgment and the amended rules, expect fixed costs to apply too.

Court approval and the Fatal Accidents Act 1976

28.81 Part 21 itself is silent in respect of the Fatal Accidents Act 1976. However, the Practice Direction does deal with it. Paragraph 1.6 of the Practice Direction provides that:

> 'An offer of settlement includes a proposal for a sum to be apportioned to a dependent child under the Fatal Accidents Act 1976.'

28.82 By paragraph 7.3 of the Practice Direction it is provided that:

> 'In order to approve an appointment of money to a dependent child, the court will require the following information:
>
> (1) the matters set out in paragraphs 6.2(1) and 6.2(2) (to what extent the defendant admits liability and the age and occupation of the child) and
> (2) in respect of the deceased
>   (a) where the death was caused by an accident, the matters set out in 6.2(3)(a), (b), (c) above, and [*Note:* This, in fact, should clearly be a reference to paragraph 6.2(4). That information includes the

---

[29] *W (a child) v P* [2004] 20 May 2004 unreported, Oswestry County Court, District Judge Rogers; *S (a child) v H* [2004] 10 June 2004 unreported, Portsmouth County Court, District Judge Wilson; *Curtis v Birley* [2005] 25 February 2005 unreported, Slough County Court, District Judge Fortgang – all held fixed costs did not apply. Contrast with *Slade v Caulfield* [2004] 17 September 2004 unreported, Liverpool County Court, District Judge Wright – held that fixed costs did apply.

[30] *Lye v M C Tleycra & Co* [2005] 19 April 2005 unreported, Nuneaton County Court, HHJ Oliver-Jones QC – refused permission to appeal DJ's decision that fixed costs regime applied.

circumstances of the accident, the medical reports and a schedule of any past and future expenses. Further, the extent and nature of the dependency has to be set out.]
(b) his future loss of earnings, and
(3) the extent and nature of the dependency.'

28.83 The Practice Direction does not say in terms that the application must include the particulars of all dependants upon whose behalf the action has been brought (compare RSC, Ord 18 r 11(2)). However, in practice this has remained the case. It is of some considerable importance because only one action lies in respect of the death which gives rise to the claim and it is vital that all persons with claims to be dependants are covered by the settlement – see Fatal Accidents Act 1976, s 2(3) which provides: 'Not more than one action shall lie for and in respect of the same subject matter or complaint.'

28.84 In *Avery v London and North Eastern Railway Company*,[31] Lord McMillan said:

'The remedy given by the statute is to individuals, not to a class, but it still remains essential that one action only shall be brought and if any individual who has a claim is either not a plaintiff nor mentioned in the particulars as a person on whose behalf the action is brought, so much the worse for that individual. He cannot bring a second action against the wrongdoer.'

28.85 In *Cooper v Williams*,[32] Lord Denning said:

'I am satisfied that, if one of the dependants brings an action under the Fatal Accidents Acts (which is the only action which can be brought) it is the duty of that person (just as it is clearly the duty of an executor or administrator) to take all reasonable steps to see that all those dependants of the deceased person who desire to claim for their losses are informed of the action and named as persons on whose behalf it is brought.'

28.86 The bringing of a claim does not, however, bind the personal representative if seeking to settle part of the claim. It is open to a personal representative to accept a sum for himself alone, but this would not bind any of the dependants and indeed, those dependants who were children would require approval of the court for any compromise to be valid. In *Jeffrey v Kent County Council*,[33] Paull J said, at p 157:

'The conclusion to which I have come is that when the administrator enters into an agreement with the defendant to take a lump sum to cover all the dependants that agreement is not a valid agreement unless (a) each of the dependants who is *sui juris* and desires to claim has approved thereof and (b) the court has sanctioned the agreement as being one for the benefit of each of the dependants who are

---

[31] [1938] AC 606.
[32] [1963] 2 QB 567.
[33] [1958] 3 All ER 155.

infants. ...[34] Where however the administrator has with the approval of any dependant who is *sui juris* entered into an agreement with the defendant that the defendant should pay to that dependant (whom I shall call the settling dependant) a sum of money which is agreed to be sufficient as being proportionate to the injuries suffered by the settling dependant, then the settling dependant is bound by the agreement as he would be if he personally entered into such agreement, but the claim of the other dependants still remain to be settled by the court and the court in judging what is the proper amount to be paid to each of the remaining dependants does not take the sum paid to the settling dependant into account unless the amount so paid affects the loss which has been suffered by any of the other dependants. For instance, if a widow agrees to take a sum of money (not as part of a general lump sum settlement but individually) which the court considers is too small and which does not result in her having these resources behind her which she would otherwise have had for the bringing up of her infant children, the court in deciding the injury which has been suffered by the infant children by the loss of their father may give sums to such infants much larger than the sums which the court would have awarded had the widow received a proper capital sum. Clearly the ability of the widow to support the children in the future may be affected by the fact that she has too small a capital sum at her disposal and that would increase the loss suffered by the children by the death of their father.'

28.87 On the assumption that all relevant claims are validly in front of the court for the approval of the court and accepting that the court has to apportion the sum awarded between the various dependants, it is not possible to specify any detailed rules governing the apportionment beyond saying that in the ordinary case involving a widow and dependant children, the majority of the money is awarded to the widow to spend while bringing up the children. In practice a rough rule of thumb seems to lead to 25% of the claim being invested on behalf of the dependant children with the remaining 75% being kept by the widow to spend during their childhood. Of course, this is merely a rule of thumb and those seeking approval of a Fatal Accident Act compromise must be prepared to address the court on apportionment. The percentage is also likely to change if there is a periodical payment element to the proposed settlement. Another influencing factor could, say, be a house with a very large mortgage. The age of the dependent children will also be an influencing factor.[35]

HOW MONEY RECOVERED IS DEALT WITH

28.88 Part 21 also deals with the question of how money recovered by or on behalf of a child is to be dealt with. Rule 21.11(1) provides that:

'Where in any proceedings

(a) money is recovered by or on behalf of or for the benefit of a child or

---

[34] Now clearly the case as set out in CPR, r 21.10.
[35] For an interesting discussion on the principles see *The Quantum of Damages*, Kemp & Kemp Vol 1, Chapter 29, 29–089 to 29–094.

(b) money paid into court is accepted by or on behalf of a child, the money shall be dealt with in accordance with directions given by the court under this rule and not otherwise.'

28.89 Those directions may provide that the money shall be wholly or partly paid into court and invested or otherwise dealt with.[36]

28.90 The Practice Direction contains fairly detailed rules about these matters. CPR 21PD.8 is headed, 'Control of money recovered by or on behalf of a child'. By para 8.2 the court:

'(1) may direct the money to be paid into the High Court for investment,
(2) may also direct that certain sums be paid direct to the child, his Litigation Friend or his legal representative for the immediate benefit of the child or for expenses incurred on his behalf, and
(3) may direct that applications in respect of the investment of the money be transferred to a local district registry.'

28.91 By para 8.3 of the Practice Direction it is provided that:

'The Master or District Judge will consider the general aims to be achieved for the money in court (the fund) by investment and will give directions as to the type of investment.'

28.92 By para 8.5:

'Where a child is legally aided the sum will be subject to a first charge under s16 of the Legal Aid Act 1988 (the Legal Aid Charge) and an order for the investment of money on the child's behalf must contain a direction to that effect.'

28.93 Paragraph 10 of the Practice Direction is headed, 'Investment on behalf of a child'. Paragraph 10.1 provides that:

'At the hearing of the application for the approval of the agreement, the litigation friend or his legal representative should provide a CFO Form 320 (request for investment) or CFO 212 for completion by the Master or District Judge.'

28.94 By para 10.2:

'On receipt of that form in the Court Funds Office, the investment managers of the Public Trust Office will make the appropriate investment.'

28.95 Lastly, by para 10.3:

'Where an award of damages for a child is made at trial the trial judge may direct

(1) the money to be paid into court and placed in the special investment account and

---

[36] See CPR, r 21.11(2).

(2) the litigation friend to make an application to the Master or District Judge for further investment directions.'

28.96 It should be noted that by para 10.4, if the money to be invested is very small, the court may order it to be paid direct to the Litigation Friend to be put into a building society account or similar for the child's use. In any event, if the money is invested in court, it must be paid out to the child when he reaches full age.[37]

28.97 It is often the case that although the majority of an approved sum will be invested there is an immediate call for some funds to be paid from court. This will need to be dealt with as part of the application for approval. Not only will the amount of money sought for immediate payment need to be clearly set out, the reason for the money to be paid now rather than invested on behalf of the claimant must be explained to the court which has a discretion to approve the sum or not. It is also possible to award a lesser sum.

28.98 The practice of the court will vary. Items of immediate expense such as medical expenses or travel costs are usually allowed. Some judges will allow a small sum even for a relatively frivolous but inexpensive treat for a child to mark the end of the litigation process. Others take a strict view on the need for any payment to match a determined loss. Any larger sum must be referenced to a particular head of damage or immediate need.

28.99 In the county court one District Judge in the district will be appointed the contact point for children with concluded cases. Future applications for payment out of funds are made directly to that judge. Any applications for payment out of funds in Court or for a variation of the investment strategy can be made to the Master or District Judge and dealt with without a hearing, unless the court directs otherwise. For an application to be dealt with on paper full and sufficient explanation of what is to be done, what is required and why will be needed.[38] No particular mechanism for how to make an application is set out in the rules, but a general application form with supporting evidence would be appropriate.

WHAT HAPPENS WHEN A CHILD REACHES FULL AGE

28.100 When a child who is not a patient reaches the age of 18, the appointment of the Litigation Friend ceases.[39] The cessation is immediate and it is so that the court has an accurate record of the appropriate date that the birth certificate is required at the approval hearing.

28.101 By r 21.9(4) it is provided that:

---

[37] See para 10.5.
[38] CPR 21 PD. 12.1.
[39] CPR, r 21.9(1).

'(4) The child ... in respect of whom the appointment to act has ceased must serve notice on the other parties –

(a) stating that the appointment of a litigation friend to act has ceased,
(b) giving his address for service, and
(c) stating whether or not he intends to carry on the proceedings.'

28.102 It is important to note that if the child does not comply with the foregoing subparagraph within 28 days after the date on which the appointment of the Litigation Friend ceases, the court may on application strike out any claim or defence brought by him.[40] Therefore, if you are acting for or involved in a claim with a child who is nearing 18 it would be wise to put in place steps in advance of the 18th birthday so that the other parties are contacted and informed of the child's intentions immediately.

28.103 It should also be noted that the liability of the Litigation Friend for costs continues until:

(a) the person in respect of whom his appointment to act has ceased serves the notice referred to in para (4); or

(b) the Litigation Friend serves notice on the parties that his appointment to act has ceased.[41]

28.104 It may be to the Litigation Friend's advantage to serve notice as soon as possible.

28.105 Paragraph 5 of the Practice Direction spells out the procedure where the need for a Litigation Friend has come to an end. In particular it is provided by para 5.2 that:

'A child on reaching full age must serve on the other parties to the proceedings and file with the court a notice:

(1) stating that he has reached full age
(2) stating that his litigation friend's appointment has ceased
(3) giving an address for service
(4) stating whether or not he intends to carry on with or continue to defend the proceedings.'

28.106 Lastly, it is provided by para 5.3 that:

'If the notice states that the child intends to carry on with or continue to defend the proceedings, he shall subsequently be described in the proceedings as "AB (formerly a child but now of full age)"'.'

---

[40] CPR, r 21.9(5).
[41] CPR, r 21.9(6).

Chapter 29

OFFERS TO SETTLE

INTRODUCTION

29.1 A new Part 36 rule that substantially amends the old rule came into effect on 6 April 2007. As is well known, originally a defendant could protect himself against an adverse order for costs by making a payment into Court. The general civil law then imported the *Calderbank offer* 'without prejudice save as to costs' procedure from the matrimonial jurisdiction. The 1998 CPR provided for both offers and payments into Court and extended the right to make offers to claimants. This was all at the expense of Part 36 becoming long and complicated. The 2007 rewriting of Part 36 has significantly reduced the procedure; primarily by abolishing the payment into Court. Hereafter there will only be offers to settle. However, it should not be thought that the rules are entirely straightforward and there are traps for the unwary. This chapter considers the key provisions of the new Part 36 and references are to its provisions unless the text states otherwise.

THE NATURE OF A PART 36 OFFER

29.2 Part 36.3 states that the party who makes an offer is the *offeror* and the party to whom the offer is made is the *offeree*. The use of these terms would tend to suggest that a Part 36 offer is contractual. Indeed under the pre-2007 rule the normal principles of contract applied to offers. In *Scammell v Dicker*[1] it was held that as the contractual rules applied, an offer could be withdrawn unless accepted. Conversely, it had been held as long ago as 1941 in *Cumper v Pothecary*[2] and applied to the CPR in *Flynn v Scougall*[3] that there was nothing contractual about a payment into court. It was *wholly procedural and has no true analogy to a settlement arranged between the parties out of court, which, of course, does constitute a contract.* In general the 2007 amendments mean that Part 36 generally has ceased to apply the contractual rules and has become much more procedural.

---

[1] [2001] 1 WLR 631.
[2] [1941] 2 KB 58 at 67.
[3] [2004] 1 WLR 3069.

THE RELEVANT PERIOD

29.3 The operation of Part 36 now depends very significantly on this new concept. Under r 36.2(2)(c) an offer must specify a period not less than 21 days within which the Defendant will be liable for the Claimant's costs if accepted. This is unlike a pre-2007 offer where the offeree had 21 days to accept an offer. Now the burden is on the offeror to specify the period for which the offer will carry the costs consequences. If the offer is made not less than 21 days before trial (subject to agreement between the parties, of which more below) that is the relevant period. If made less than 21 days before trial, the relevant period is up to the end of the trial or such other period as the court determines.

ACCEPTANCE

29.4 It is important to distinguish the offeree's right to accept an offer and the Claimant's right to recover costs up to the date of the offer. Subject to exceptions an offer may be accepted at any time unless the offeror serves notice of withdrawal on the offeree (CPR 36.9(2)). The wording of the rule (and the provisions as to withdrawal of an offer, as to which see below) is such that it will not be sufficient in the offer to state that the offer will remain open for a period and will then be withdrawn, but that a second notice of withdrawal will have to be served.

29.5 The exceptions where the court's permission is required to accept an offer are set out in CPR 36.9(3):

- where the claimant wishes to accept the offer of one or more but not all of a number of defendants;

- where the relevant period has expired and further deductible benefits have been paid to the claimant since the date of the offer;

- where an apportionment is required under the renumbered CPR 41.3A. Where a single sum is offered in an action which covers claims under the Fatal Accidents Act 1976 and Law Reform (Miscellaneous Provisions) Act 1934 and/or there are several dependents, the Court will have to apportion the single sum between the claims and dependents. In such a case permission is now required to accept such an offer;

- where the trial has started.

29.6 The second situation is not quite what it seems. In many personal injury claims, the claimant will not accept the offer within the period specified in the offer but will want to do so subsequently. It should not be thought that permission will necessarily have to be obtained. The definition of *relevant period* includes not only the period specified in the offer but also *such longer period as the parties agree*. This means that in such circumstances the parties may agree to extend the relevant period to enable the offeree to accept the offer and therefore it will not be necessary to seek permission to do so. If the offeror will not agree to an extended period, permission will have to be sought.

29.7 It should also be noted that one of the issues raised in *Hawley v Luminar Leisure plc*[4] has been resolved. In that case, after an appeal had been heard but before judgment had been delivered, L purported to accept an offer. It was held that even if an offer was available for acceptance after an appeal had started (which the court doubted) there was certainly an implied term that it would not be available for acceptance after the hearing had ended and the court had reserved judgment. However the Court of Appeal invited the Rules Committee to consider the position, which they did. The result is CPR 36.9(5) which provides that *unless the parties agree, a Part 36 offer may not be accepted after the end of the trial but before judgment is given.* For these purposes an appeal will be treated the same as a trial (see *Hawley*).

29.8 Note also that an offer is not 'accepted' where approval is required if the Claimant is under a disability until the approval is obtained. The effect of this may be seen in *Brennan v Eco Composting Ltd.*[5] C was entitled to interest from the date of approval not from the date of acceptance.

COSTS CONSEQUENCES OF ACCEPTANCE OF AN OFFER

29.9 Except where the offer was made less than 21 days before the start of the trial, if a Part 36 offer is accepted within the relevant period, the Claimant will be entitled to his costs up to the date upon which notice of acceptance was served on the offeror (CPR 36.10). They will be assessed on the standard basis if not agreed. Where an offer is accepted after the expiry of the relevant period, the parties may agree the liability for costs. If they do not, the court will do so. The order will be (unless the court orders otherwise) Claimant's costs up to expiry of the relevant period; and the offeree to be liable for the offeror's costs from the expiry of the relevant period to the date of acceptance.

29.10 It is worth observing that, where an offer is accepted, a costs judge does not have jurisdiction to make a percentage reduction of the assessed costs before embarking on a detailed assessment (see *Lahey v Pirelli Tyres*[6]) but may in appropriate cases disallow sections of the bill of costs. Conversely the court has no discretion to award indemnity costs since the rules provide that an offer is made on the basis that, if accepted, costs would be paid on the standard basis; see the reasoning of Jacob J in *Dyson Ltd v Hoover Ltd.*[7]

---

[4] [2006] EWCA Civ 30.
[5] [2006] EWCA 3153, QBD.
[6] [2007] EWCA Civ 91.
[7] [2002]EWHC 2229, ChD.

EFFECT OF THE ACCEPTANCE OF A PART 36 OFFER

29.11 Where an offer is accepted, the claim will be stayed. This will not affect the power of the court to enforce the terms of the offer and to deal with any question of costs. It is to be noted that under CPR 36.11(6) unless the parties agree otherwise in writing, where an offer by a Defendant to pay a single sum of money is accepted, that sum must be paid to the offeree within 14 days of the date of acceptance or the making of an award for provisional damages or periodical payments. Where payment is not made within 14 days the offeree may enter judgment and take enforcement proceedings.

WITHDRAWAL OF OFFERS

29.12 Contrary to the rule in *Scammell v Dicker* and to general contractual principles, before the expiry of the relevant period, an offer may be withdrawn or its terms changed to be less advantageous to the offeree, only if the court gives permission (CPR 36.3(5)). After expiry of the relevant period and provided the offeree has not served notice of acceptance, CPR 36.3(6) allows the offeror to withdraw the offer or change its terms to be less advantageous to the offeree, without permission of the court. CPR 36.3(6) requires that notice of withdrawal or change in the terms of an offer is achieved by the offeror serving written notice.

29.13 If the offeror wishes to withdraw or reduce his offer within the relevant period and seeks permission, the offeree may well want to accept the offer. In such a situation, the court will have to adjudicate. The Court of Appeal, in *Capital Bank v Strickland*[8], held a judge had an unfettered discretion and that relevant considerations might be availability of the money; the timing of the application or a change in circumstances. In considering the pre-2007 rules the Court of Appeal in *Flynn v Scougall*[9] said that an important consideration will be that not to allow the offeree to accept will be to deprive him of an otherwise unfettered right. Further to allow withdrawal or reduction will need a sufficient change in circumstances.

It may be expected that the post-2007 rules will be interpreted in the same way.

WHEN MAY AN OFFER BE MADE?

29.14 An offer to settle may be made at any time, including before the commencement of proceedings. (r 36.3(2)). An offer made before proceedings were commenced will not need to be repeated after issue as was the pre-2007 position and the court will give full effect to it.

---

[8] [2005]2 All ER 544.
[9] [2004] 1 WLR 3069.

An offer may be made in appeal proceedings. In the pre-2007 decision of *Various Claimants v Bryn Alyn Community (Holdings) Ltd*,[10] the Court of Appeal said that in the absence of a fresh offer the machinery of Part 36 was not available to it, and it would be disinclined to use its discretion by reference to a pre-trial offer. There is no reason to believe the position will now be different.

FORM AND CONTENT
General

29.15 A Part 36 offer is an offer to settle which is made in accordance with CPR 36.2. It must be in writing; state on its face that it is intended to have the consequences of Part 36 and specify the period of not less than 21 days in which the Defendant will be liable for the Claimant's costs if the offer is accepted. In appropriate case there must be further information about future pecuniary loss claims; provisional damages and deduction of benefit.

29.16 The starting point for the practitioner making an offer should be the prescribed form N242A. This may be modified as appropriate but its use will be an essential aide memoire and will mean a judge will be less likely to find the offer did not comply.

29.17 Part 36.2(5) recognises that an offer may be solely in respect of liability. Note in this regard *HSS Hire Services Group plc v BMB Builders Merchants*[11] where in a pre-2007 case the defendant made a Part 36 payment before an order was made for a split trial of liability. The Court of Appeal said that the rationale of Parts 36 and 44 required that the issues of costs should be left until after quantum had been determined so that the overall picture could be assessed.

29.18 Note also *Huck v Robson*[12] where a claimant offered to apportion liability 95:5 in his favour and this was held to be a genuine offer of settlement with the appropriate consequences when he succeeded 100%.

29.19 Any head of damage may be the subject of a Part 36 offer. Subject to consideration of lump sums/periodical payments, offers could be made where appropriate on say loss of earnings, care, aids and equipment; transport; and housing. However Part 36.4 requires that an offer by a Defendant must be an offer to pay a single sum of money and it is suggested that if there are offers under individual heads there must be also a composite offer of a single sum of money in settlement of the whole claim.

---

[10] [2003] EWCA Civ 383.
[11] [2005] EWCA Civ 626.
[12] [2003] 1 WLR 1340.

Time when a Part 36 offer is made

29.20 It is made when served on the offeree. This is an alteration from the pre-2007 rule which was made when received.

Clarification

29.21 Under Part 36.8 the offeree may within 7 days of the offer request clarification. If it is not given within seven days, the offeree (unless the trial has started) can apply for an order that he does. If the court makes an order, it must say when the offer is to be treated as having been made.

Deduction of benefit

29.22 In personal injury claims, following acceptance of an offer, the payment to a Claimant will be a compensation payment as defined by s 1 of the Social Security (Recovery of Benefits) Act 1997. Where there are deductible benefits, the Part 36 offer must state the amount of gross compensation; the name and amount of any benefit by which the gross amount is reduced by recoverable benefit; the net amount after the deduction of benefit (Part 36.15).

29.23 Where a defendant has applied for but not received the Compensation Recovery Unit (CRU) certificate of recoverable benefit, he must clarify the offer within 7 days after receiving the certificate (CPR 36.15(7)).

29.24 This Part (CPR 36.15) has now been altered from the pre-2007 rule in one important consideration. The amended rule (CPR 36.15(8)) provides that a Claimant fails to recover more than the sum offered if he fails upon judgment being entered to recover a sum, once deductible benefits have been deducted, greater than the net amount stated in the notice. The pre-2007 rule looked to gross benefit. One importance of the change is that it means that a defendant must ensure that he calculates the benefit correctly otherwise his offer will not necessarily have the costs effect of the rule.

Calculation of the amount of the recoverable benefit and the complication of contributory negligence

29.25 This problem is highlighted in situations where the compensator has to pay to the CRU more than he is entitled to deduct from the damages to which a claimant is entitled. Such a situation arises because a like-for-like set off may only reduce the particular head of damages to zero and any resulting balance may not be carried over as a general set off. This will arise most acutely where there is a finding of contributory negligence. Although the claimant's award will be reduced by the amount of the contributory negligence, the whole of the benefit must be deducted. So care must be taken in calculating the amounts. If the amounts shown are incorrect the offer will not be effective.

29.26 The complications which may arise can be seen in the pre-2007 case of *Williams v Devon County Council*.[13] The defendant miscalculated the amount of the deductible benefit so it appeared after deduction of one third for contributory negligence that the claimant had not beaten the payment into court. The trial judge awarded the defendant costs from the date of the payment in. The Court of Appeal reversed the costs order on the basis that D should have properly calculated the benefit amount which could be set off and issued a proper notice. It also held it would be unjust to award the Defendant his costs when the notice was wrong.

In what circumstances will a Court give effect to a non complying offer?

29.27 Nothing in Part 36 prevents a party making an offer to settle in whatever way he chooses but if the offer is not made in accordance with Part 36, it will not have the consequences specified in Part 36. The rule as amended excludes the words of the previous Rule that the offer can have the same effect *if the court so orders*. That said it is presumed that it is intended that the court should have a general discretion to give effect to a non-complying offer. Reference is made in Part 36 to CPR 44.3 which gives a court a general discretion as to costs. CPR 44.3(4) provides that in considering what costs order to make it should have regard to all the circumstances, including *(c) any admissible offer to settle made by a party which is drawn to the court's attention (whether or not made in accordance with Part 36)*. The discretion here is probably the same as under Part 36 : as Waller LJ said in *Crouch v King's Healthcare NHS Trust*[14] it was doubtful if there was any difference in exercising the discretion under CPR 44.3(4) and that under CPR 36.1(2).

29.28 An example of where the discretion was exercised in favour of the offeree may be seen in *Hertsmere Primary Care Trust v Estate of Rabinda-Anandh decd*[15] Lightman J allowed the Claimant to rely upon an offer to settle which did not state the time limits. Both parties were represented by lawyers; the Defendant's lawyers appreciated the point immediately and no question arose of the omission misleading the Estate or occasioning any prejudice.

Future pecuniary loss claims

29.29 The majority of personal injury claims will have future pecuniary loss claims. Part 36.5 on the face of it requires an offer to specify in respect thereof whether it is an offer of a lump sum; of periodical payments or a combination of both. CPR 36.5(2) states that the Part 36 costs consequences will not follow an offer unless made in accordance with the rule. In practice, unless periodical payments are offered, the rule is not observed but the costs consequences still follow. It would be unjust if it were otherwise.

---

[13] [2003] EWCA Civ 365.
[14] [2005] 1 WLR 2015.
[15] [2005] EWHC 320, ChD.

29.30 Where an offer is made in this form it must state the amount of any offer to pay the whole or part of any damages in the form of a lump sum. It may also break down a lump sum offer into future pecuniary loss and/or other damages; state what part of the offer relates to future loss to be accepted by lump sum and if any other head is to be accepted by lump sum, what amounts are attributable. It must state the amount of damages for future pecuniary loss to be paid/accepted by periodical payments and must also specify the amount and duration of the periodical payments; particulars of substantial capital purchases and any indexing (RPI or otherwise). Finally it must give funding particulars and security of periodical payments.

Costs consequences following judgment

29.31 Where the claimant fails to obtain judgment more advantageous than defendant's Part 36 offer, then the court unless it considers it unjust to do so will order that the defendant is entitled to:

- costs from the date on which the relevant period expired;

- interest on those costs (nb a change).

29.32 Where the judgment against the defendant is at least as advantageous to the claimant as the proposals in the Part 36 offer then the court unless it considers it unjust to do so will order that the claimant is entitled to:

- interest on the whole or part of any sum (excluding interest) awarded to the claimant for some or all of the period starting at the expiry of the relevant period. It is to be noted that this award of interest is on the whole award and as such includes future loss, which may well make any such interest significant. This is even more so since past loss will presumably already have attracted interest in the normal way and the total award of interest under this rule cannot exceed 10% above base rate which must take into account other interest already awarded. So if loss of earnings had already attracted interest at $\frac{1}{2}$ of 6%; the additional interest on that award under this rule could not exceed 7% above base rate.

- indemnity costs from the expiry of the relevant period;

- interest on those costs at a rate not exceeding 10% above base rate.

29.33 A costs or interest award under this rule is not punitive nor does it indicate any disapproval of the defendant's conduct. It is intended to encourage settlement and to redress the injustice of having to fight the case for longer than was reasonably necessary. See *McPhilemy v Times Newspapers*[16] and *Reid*

---

[16] [2002] 1 WLR 934.

Minty v Taylor.[17] It should therefore be considered as compensatory to award the uplifted interest and it is to be noted that 10% above base rate is the maximum rate which can be awarded.

Unjust to make the order

29.34 Regard in this respect is to be had to all the circumstances including the terms of any Part 36 offer; the stage of the proceedings at which the offer was made; the then available information and how much was provided subsequently. In *Excelsior Commercial and Industrial Holdings v Salisbury Hamer and Johnson*[18] the Court of Appeal declined to issue guidelines and said it was a matter of discretion.

29.35 An example of where it was unjust was considered above in the case of *Williams v Devon County Council*. As was seen above, there the notice of payment was wrongly calculated. It would therefore be *unjust* to deprive a *successful* claimant of costs even though technically she did not better the Part 36 payment. An example of where it was not unjust may be seen in *Matthews v Metal Improvements*.[19] The medical evidence changed and the claimant accepted the offer out of time. Whether the claimant's advisors acted reasonably was not the correct question to ask in deciding whether it was unjust to make the normal order.

Provisional Damages

29.36 Where a claim includes a claim for provisional damages the Defendant may make a Part 36 offer in the normal way (CPR 36.6). The notice must state if he is offering to agree to the making of an award for provisional damages. If he is, the notice must state the offer is on the basis that the claimant will not develop the disease or suffer the deterioration; that the offer is subject to the condition that the claimant must make any claim for further damages within a limited period and what that period is. Where the offeree accepts the offer, he must apply within seven days for an award of provisional damages.

Transitional provisions

29.37 Where a Part 36 offer or payment was made before 6 April 2007, if it would have had the consequences in the pre-amendment rules immediately before that date, it will have the consequences in the post-amendment rules after that date.

29.38 Where a Part 36 offer or payment was made before 6 April 2007, if the permission of the court was required under the pre-amendment rules, permission will still be required.

---

[17] [2002] 1 WLR 2800.
[18] [2002] EWCA Civ 879.
[19] [2007] EWCA Civ 215.

29.39 Where the Part 36 offer or payment was made less than 21 days before 6 April 2007:

- the pre-amendment rules will apply as if not revoked;

- but at the expiry of 21 days from the date of the offer/payment, the new rules apply unless the trial has started.

29.40 Where before 6 April 2007, an offer which complies with the pre-amendment rules was made pre-issue, the court after 6 April 2007will take it into account when making an order for costs.

Chapter 30

COMPENSATION FOR VICTIMS OF UNINSURED OR UNIDENTIFIABLE USERS OF MOTOR VEHICLES

INTRODUCTION

30.1 This chapter deals with compensation for the victims of uninsured and unidentifiable users of motor vehicles under the Road Traffic Act 1988, the Uninsured Drivers Agreements 1988 and 1999, and the Untraced Drivers Agreements 1996 and 2003. It does *not* deal with earlier Road Traffic Acts, Uninsured and Untraced Drivers Agreements, which are now of largely historical significance.

30.2 What follows is of course only a summary and cannot be a substitute for a close study of the relevant provisions and their application to the facts of any particular case.

THE FRAMEWORK OF EUROPEAN UNION LAW

The framework

30.3 The framework is set by the four European Directives on motor insurance, the most important in the present context being the Second and, to a lesser extent, the Third Directives.

The Second Directive

30.4 The Second Directive (84/5/EEC):

(A) requires Member States:
- (i) to make insurance in respect of the liability of users of motor vehicles compulsory up to certain minimum sums; and
- (ii) 'to set up or authorise a body with the task of providing compensation, at least up to the limit of the insurance obligation, for damage to property or personal injuries caused by an unidentified vehicle or a vehicle for which the insurance obligation ... has not been satisfied' (the body providing this safety net of compensation being known as a 'Guarantee Fund'); but

(B) permits Member States:

(i) to '... exclude the payment of compensation by that body in respect of persons who voluntarily enter the vehicle which caused the damage or injury when the body can prove that they knew it was uninsured';

(ii) similarly to exclude the payment of compensation by Insurers or that body in respect of persons who voluntarily entered the vehicle which caused the damage or injury when Insurers or that body can prove that they knew it was stolen; and

(iii) to exclude the payment of compensation by that body in respect of damage to property caused by an unidentified vehicle.

30.5 Part VI of the Road Traffic Act, the Uninsured Drivers Agreements 1988 and 1999, and the Untraced Drivers Agreements 1996 and 2003, are intended to implement the Second Directive.

The Third Directive

30.6 The Third Directive (90/232/EEC) requires Member States:

(A) to ensure that the victims protected by compulsory motor insurance and safety net compensation include passengers, with effect from 31 December 1992.
Amendments were made to the Road Traffic Act 1988 to extend compulsory motor insurance, and therefore safety net compensation, to cover the liability of an employer or fellow employees using a motor vehicle to an employee who is a passenger, in order to implement this;

(B) to ensure that, where there is a dispute between their Guarantee Fund and a Motor Insurer as to which should compensate a victim, one of the two shall be designated as 'responsible for paying compensation to the victim without delay', and then the paying party shall be reimbursed in due course by the non-paying party if and to the extent that the non-paying party is found liable.
The MIB's 'New Procedure' (see below) is intended to implement this.

Interpretation of domestic law and other implementing measures, in accordance with the Directives if possible

30.7 Laws of a Member State, whether passed before or after Directives, are to be interpreted in accordance with Directives, if at all possible: see *Marleasing*.[1]

30.8 In the case of other measures which are intended to implement Directives – eg agreements such as the Uninsured Drivers Agreements 1988 and 1999 and the Untraced Drivers Agreements 1996 and 2003 – although the *Marleasing* principle does not strictly speaking apply, on ordinary English

---

[1] [1990] ECR I-14135.

principles of interpretation, the measures will be interpreted in accordance with the Directives which they are intended to implement, if at all possible: see *White v White*.[2]

UK State's failure to implement Directives

30.9 But, even with favourable interpretation, it is arguable that the UK State has failed to implement the Directives in a number of ways, eg:

(a) in failing to ensure that compulsory motor insurance, and therefore safety net compensation, covers the liability of an employer or fellow employees using a motor vehicle to an employee who is not a passenger – which would appear to be contrary to the Second Directive;

(b) in restricting compulsory motor insurance, and consequently safety net compensation, to liabilities caused by or arising out of, the use of motor vehicles 'on a road or (from 3 April 2000) other public place' – a restriction not mentioned in the Directives, which appear to require motor insurance, and consequently safety net compensation, wherever a motor vehicle is used;

(c) in making the exclusion from safety net compensation in s 151(8) of the Road Traffic Act 1988 and/or the conditions precedent to and/or exclusions from safety net compensation in the Uninsured Drivers Agreements 1999 so extensive and/or demanding that they arguably constitute unwarranted derogations from the protection intended by the Directives;

(d) in implementing the Second Directive by treating 'unidentified vehicle' in the Directive as meaning 'vehicle used by an unidentifiable person' – so that the total absence of compensation for liability for property damage under the Untraced Drivers Agreement 1996 is arguably more extensive than the Directive permits;

(e) in imposing a rigid time-limit for claims under the Untraced Drivers Agreement 1996, and an only slightly more flexible time-limit for claims under the Untraced Drivers Agreement 2003, even for children and patients – which would appear to offend against a cardinal principle of European law, namely that, where a Directive requires a Member State to confer a right (here of safety net compensation), it also requires the Member State to ensure that there is a fair and effective ability to exercise that right;

(f) in making the exclusions from safety net compensation in the Untraced Drivers Agreement 2003, which are similar to those in the Uninsured Drivers Agreement 1999, similarly too extensive.

---

[2] [2001] 1 WLR 481 HL.

30.10 The UK State has certainly failed to implement the Second Directive properly in failing to ensure that compensation under the Untraced Drivers Agreement 1996 includes some allowance for interest and costs: see *Evans v Secretary of State for Environment*.[3]

Consequences of failure to implement Directives

30.11 If a Member State fails to implement a Directive properly, the consequences are as follows.

Directive of Direct Effect

30.12 The Article of the Directive concerned may itself be of direct effect in domestic law, if the Article is sufficiently clear, precise and unconditional.

30.13 But even if the Article is sufficiently clear, precise and unconditional to be of direct effect in domestic law, such effect is in Euro jargon 'vertical' rather than 'horizontal', ie it applies vertically between an individual and the Member State (or any 'emanation of the State'), but not horizontally between individuals.

30.14 A body is an 'emanation of the State' if:

(a) State measures make the body responsible for providing a public service; and

(b) the public service is sufficiently under the control of the State; and

(c) the body has special powers (although this last condition is not essential).

An insurer is plainly an individual and not an emanation of the UK State.

30.15 So, even if the provisions regarding safety net compensation for the victims of uninsured drivers in s 151 of the Road Traffic Act 1988 fail to implement the Second Directive properly, and the relevant Articles of the Directive are of direct effect, a potential Road Traffic Act insurer, as an individual, is still entitled to rely on the offending provisions against a claimant, as another individual.

30.16 Moreover, the protection afforded to victims of uninsured drivers by s 151 of the Road Traffic Act is only the victim's first line of protection. A victim excluded from protection under s 151 can normally look to the protection afforded by the Uninsured Drivers Agreement 1988 or 1999 as a second and last resort.

---

[3] (2003) *The Times*, 9 December 2003.

30.17 Consequently, it is victims who have found themselves excluded from safety net compensation under the Uninsured and Untraced Drivers Agreements, who have concentrated on trying to establish against the MIB:

(i) that the relevant Agreements fail to implement the Directives properly; and

(ii) that the relevant Articles of the Directives are of direct effect; and

(iii) that the relevant Articles bind the MIB, on the ground that the MIB is an emanation of the UK State;

– but so far without complete success: see *Silverton v Goodall*,[4] *Mighell v Reading*, *Evans v MIB* & *White v White*[5] and *White v White*.[6]

Even if Directive not of direct effect

30.18 However, even if the relevant Article of a Directive is not of direct effect, the State itself will be liable to a claimant for any loss which he may suffer as a result of a failure by the State to implement the Directive: see *Francovich*[7] (or, where the State has a wide discretion how to implement the Directive, a grave failure by the State to implement the Directive: see *Factortame (No 4)*).[8]

30.19 So a claimant ('C'), who is excluded from safety net compensation by questionable provisions of the Road Traffic Act 1988, the Uninsured Drivers Agreement 1988 or 1999 or the Untraced Drivers Agreement 1996 or 2003, may have a remedy against the UK State in the UK Courts under *Francovich/Factortame* – if C can establish that the UK State, in enacting or agreeing the questionable provisions, was guilty of a failure or grave failure to implement a Directive, and has thereby caused C loss of safety net compensation.

Illustration

30.20 The Untraced Drivers Agreement 1996 makes no provision for the award of interest or costs, and it was the practice of the MIB when awarding compensation under the Agreement to award no interest and little or no costs.

30.21 In the *Evans* cases, the claimant, after receiving an award from the MIB under the Untraced Drivers Agreement 1996 with no interest and little costs, first sued the MIB, claiming:

---

[4] [1997] PIQR P451 CA.
[5] [1999] PIQR P101 CA.
[6] [2001] 1 WLR 481 HL.
[7] [1991] ECR 1-5357.
[8] [1996] QB 404.

(i) that the absence of provision for payment of interest and costs in the Untraced Drivers Agreement 1996 was contrary to the requirement in Article 1 of the Second Directive that the Guarantee Fund shall pay 'compensation';

(ii) that Article 1 of the Second Directive was sufficiently clear, precise and unconditional to be of direct effect in English law; and

(iii) that it was binding on the MIB on the ground that the MIB was an 'emanation of the State'.

30.22 The Court of Appeal rejected this claim, holding that Art 1 of the Second Directive was too conditional to be of direct effect in English law, see *Evans v MIB*.[9]

30.23 The claimant then sued the UK State under *Francovich/Factortame*, on the ground that the UK State, in agreeing the Untraced Drivers Agreement 1996 without provision for payment of interest or costs, had failed properly to implement the Second Directive's requirement that the Guarantee Fund shall pay 'compensation', and that he had thereby suffered loss of 'compensation'. On a reference from the UK court (*Evans v Secretary of State for Environment*[10]), the EU court held that the Second Directive does require the 'compensation' awarded by the Guarantee Fund to 'take account of the effluxion of time' and to include sufficient award for costs to enable the claimant fairly and effectively to exercise his right to compensation, but that it was for the UK court to decide whether the UK State's failure to implement the Directive properly was sufficiently serious to justify an award of damages under *Factortame* (*Evans v Secretary of State for Environment*[11]).

30.24 In anticipation of this outcome, the UK State has ensured that the Untraced Drivers Agreement 2003 incorporates specific provisions for the payment of interest and costs.

COMPULSORY MOTOR INSURANCE IN ENGLISH LAW

The general rule

30.25 As a general rule, it is compulsory in English law for a user of a motor vehicle on a road or (from 3 April 2000) other public place to be insured in respect of liability for injury, death, or property damage up to £250,000, 'caused by or arising out of the use of the vehicle on a road or (from 3 April 2000) other public place': see Road Traffic Act 1988, ss 143 and 145.

---

[9] [1999] PIQR P101.
[10] [2001] PIQR P33.
[11] (2003) *The Times Law Reports*, 9 December 2003.

Exceptions to the general rule

30.26 The two major exceptions to this general rule are:

Vehicles covered by deposit or used by certain public bodies

30.27 Vehicles which are covered by a deposit of £500,000 with the Accountant General of the Supreme Court, or are being used by certain specified public bodies (a derogation permitted by the First Directive): see Road Traffic Act 1988, s 144.

Liability which is or should be the subject of employers' liability insurance

30.28 It is not compulsory in English law to have motor insurance in respect of the liability for injury or death to an employee in the course of his employment incurred by an employer or fellow employee in the course of his employment (Road Traffic Act 1988, s 145(4)(a)), since this should be the subject of compulsory employers' liability insurance.

30.29 However, this exception can leave an employee claimant unprotected where there should be, but is not, in fact employers' liability insurance, because there is no Employers' Liability Insurers' Bureau.

30.30 So, in order to comply with the Third Directive, in the case of liability to an employee who is a passenger boarding, travelling in or on, or alighting from a vehicle:

(a) since 31 December 1992, the exception from compulsory motor insurance (and consequently safety net compensation) only applies where the liability is *in fact* covered by compulsory employers' liability insurance (Road Traffic Act 1988, s 145(4)(a)); and

(b) since 1 July 1994, this exception ceases to apply, because it has ceased to be compulsory for employers' liability insurance to cover liability to a passenger, see the Employer's Liability (Compulsory Insurance) Exemption (Amendment) Regulations 1992.[12]

30.31 But this still leaves the liability of an employer or fellow employee to an employee who is *not* a passenger outside the scope of compulsory motor insurance (and therefore safety net compensation) – which would appear to be contrary to the Second Directive.

---

[12] SI 1992/3172.

Illustration

30.32 Assume that it is sometime after 1 July 1994, that Albert and Bernard are both employed by Charlie, and that Bernard and Charlie are penniless and uninsured.

If in the course of their employment, Bernard is driving and Albert is a *passenger* in a motor vehicle on a road, and Bernard negligently crashes the vehicle, injuring Albert, Albert's judgment against Bernard and/or Charlie will be satisfied under s 151 of the Road Traffic Act 1988 or, if there is no Road Traffic Act Insurer, under the MIB's Uninsured Drivers Agreement – because Bernard and Charlie's liabilities are liabilities against which motor insurance is compulsory.

But if, in the course of their employment, Bernard is driving a motor vehicle on a road, Albert is *standing* on the road, and Bernard negligently runs over Albert, Albert's judgment against Bernard and/or Charlie will not be satisfied by anyone – since Bernard and Charlie's liabilities are not liabilities against which motor insurance is compulsory and there is no Employers' Liability Insurers' Bureau.

In the latter case, Albert's only remedy, if any, is to sue the UK State under *Francovich/Factortame* for damages for failing properly to implement the Directive.

'Liability caused by, or arising out of, the use of the vehicle on a road or (from 3 April 2000) other public place'

30.33 These words define the limit of compulsory motor insurance in English law, and therefore the limit of safety net compensation under s 151 of the Road Traffic Act 1988, the Uninsured Drivers Agreements 1988 and 1999 and the Untraced Drivers Agreements 1996 and 2003.

'Liability'

30.34 'Liability' is not restricted to liability through inadvertence, such as negligence, but also covers liability for deliberate wrongdoing, such as use of a motor vehicle as a weapon.

30.35 Whilst public policy permits a motor insurer to refuse to indemnify its insured in respect of liability for use of a motor vehicle as a weapon, public policy does not entitle the Motor Insurer or the MIB to refuse safety net compensation under s 151 of the Road Traffic Act 1988 or the Uninsured Drivers Agreements to the victim: see *Hardy v MIB*[13] approved in *Gardner v Moore*,[14] and *Keeley v Pashen*.[15]

---

[13] [1964] 2 QB 745 CA.
[14] [1984] AC 548.
[15] [2004] EWCA Civ 1491.

30.36 The position is different under the Untraced Drivers Agreements 1996, where safety net compensation for the victim of a motor vehicle used as a weapon is specifically excluded (leaving the victim to his remedy under the Criminal Injuries Compensation Scheme).

'Caused by, or arising out of'

30.37 Clearly, the injury, death, or property damage need not actually occur on a road or (from 3 April 2000) other public place for the liability to be compulsorily insurable, and therefore the subject of safety net compensation. The liability need only be '... caused by, or arising out of ...' the use of a vehicle on a road or (from 3 April 2000) other public place. So for example liability for injury, death and/or property damage caused by a motor vehicle smashing into a private house is covered, provided the liability was 'caused by, or arising out of' the use of the vehicle on a public road, e g because it resulted from a loss of control on the road.

30.38 In *Dunthorne v Bentley*,[16] the Court of Appeal gave a wide meaning to 'caused by, or arising out of' the use of a vehicle on a road, in holding that the negligence of D in running across a road from her broken down car to seek help from a friend, thereby causing C to swerve, crash and sustain injury, was a liability 'caused by or arising out of' the use of D's broken down vehicle on a road, and consequently a liability which had to be met by her Motor Insurers.

'Use'

30.39 'Use' means driving, use by an owner/employer through his agent/employee driving in the course of his agency/employment, and any other form of control, operation or management of the vehicle. But a mere passenger opening a car door is not using the vehicle, see *Brown v Roberts*.[17]

'Road'

30.40 'Road' is defined as 'any highway and any other road to which the public has access' in s 192(1) Road Traffic Act 1988.

(a) 'Highway'
   NB that this includes a public bridleway or public footpath.
   So, even before 3 April 2000, if you were knocked down by a motorcyclist on a public footpath, the motorcyclist should have been insured and, if he was not insured, you could obtain compensation from any Road Traffic Act Insurer or, failing that, through the MIB.

(b) 'Any other road to which the public has access'
   Any place which is not a 'highway' may still be a 'road' if:
   (i) it is in the ordinary sense of the word a road:

---

[16] [1996] RTR 428.
[17] [1965] 1 QB 1.

and
(ii) it is a road to which the public both in fact has access and is expressly or implicitly permitted access (Generally, if there are signs prohibiting public access but the public in fact has access, the public is treated as being implicitly permitted access unless the prohibition is enforced),

see *Clarke v Kato*,[18] where the previous authorities are helpfully summarised.

30.41 Efforts by the Court of Appeal to extend the meaning of 'road', and thereby what is compulsorily insurable by D and compulsorily compensatable by Motor Insurers and the MIB, were overturned by the House of Lords in *Clarke v Kato*, which held that only in exceptional circumstances would a car park or part thereof fall within the natural meaning of the word 'road'.

'Or other public place'

30.42 Concern about the restrictive effect of *Clarke v Kato* resulted in the amendment of the Road Traffic Act 1988 to insert after the words 'caused by or arising out of the use of the vehicle on a road' the words 'or other public place' with effect from 3 April 2000.

30.43 But even from 3 April 2000 this leaves liability caused by or arising out of the use of a motor vehicle in a purely private place outside the scope of compulsory motor insurance and therefore safety net compensation in English law. The only remedy, if any, for a claimant who cannot get safety net compensation as a result would appear to be to sue the UK State under *Francovich/Factortame*.

INSURED, UNINSURED AND UNIDENTIFIABLE USERS

30.44 Where C is a victim of an accident for which D has a liability against which motor insurance is compulsory in English law, D may be:

(a) Identifiable and insured
D may be identifiable and insured – in which case clearly there is no problem from an insurance point of view.
Note the often overlooked provisions of s 148 of the Road Traffic Act 1988, under which a motor insurer's contractual obligation to indemnify D is extended by statute.
Under s 148(2) and (5), a motor insurer cannot refuse to indemnify D in respect of a liability against which motor insurance is compulsory, on the grounds of:
(2)(a) the age or physical or mental condition of the person driving;
(i) the condition of the vehicle;

---

[18] [1998] 1 WLR 1647 HL.

(ii) the number of persons that the vehicle carries;
(iii) the weight or physical characteristics of the goods that the vehicle carries;
(iv) the time at which or the areas within which the vehicle is used;
(v) the horsepower or cylinder capacity or value of the vehicle;
(vi) the carrying on the vehicle of any particular apparatus;
(vii) the carrying on the vehicle of means of identification other than a compulsory registration plate; or

(5) acts or omissions after the accident, such as making admissions or failing to report the accident, a prosecution or a claim.

However, an insurer who is compelled to indemnify by s 148(2) is automatically entitled to recoup its outlay from D, and an insurer who is compelled to indemnify by s 148(5) is not prevented by s 148(5) from having a term in its policy entitling it to recoup its outlay from its insured.

(b) Identifiable but uninsured
Alternatively, D may be identifiable but uninsured – an 'uninsured driver' (or more accurately 'uninsured user') – in which case he can be sued (even if he cannot be located and can only be served by alternative means). This is the territory of s 151 of the Road Traffic Act 1988 and the Uninsured Drivers Agreements 1988 and 1999.

(c) Unidentifiable
Alternatively again, D may be unidentifiable – in which case, he cannot be sued and any claim must be made, not through the courts, but direct to the MIB under the Untraced Drivers Agreement 1996 or 2003.
It is very important to understand that 'untraced' means unidentifiable and not merely unlocatable: see *Clark v Vedel*,[19] clause 5 of the Untraced Drivers Agreement 1996 and clause 4 of the Untraced Drivers Agreement 2003.

THE UNINSURED DRIVER/USER

Section 151 of the Road Traffic Act 1988

30.45 Where C is the victim of an accident for which D has a liability against which motor insurance is compulsory in English law, but D, while identifiable, is *uninsured*, s 151 of the Road Traffic Act 1988 is C's first line of protection.

30.46 If C obtains judgment against D in respect of that liability, that judgment must be satisfied by any insurer who is caught by s 151 (a 'Road Traffic Act insurer').

---

[19] [1979] RTR 26 CA.

30.47 Broadly speaking, an insurer is a Road Traffic Act insurer if it has delivered a current certificate of compulsory motor insurance in respect of the offending vehicle at the time of the accident, although the insurance did not cover the offending user D.

30.48 But this is subject to a number of exceptions. The most important are that an insurer will not be a Road Traffic Act insurer in the following circumstances:

(a) Disposal of insurable interest
 If the insured has sold or otherwise disposed of any insurable interest in the vehicle(s) covered under the policy, so that, on a true interpretation of the policy, the policy has ceased to have effect, see *Tattersall v Drysdale*[20] but note *Dodson v Peter H Dodson Insurance Services*.[21]

(b) Cancellation
 If the insurance had been cancelled prior to the accident and in accordance with the procedure in s 152(1)(c) Road Traffic Act 1988.

(c) Declaration of avoidance
 If the insurer obtains a declaration from a court that the insurance is voidable or has been avoided on the ground of material misrepresentation or non-disclosure, in accordance with the time limits and procedure in s 152(2) Road Traffic Act 1988.

(d) Different type of use
 If, even if you substituted D's name for the name(s) of the person(s) insured under the policy, the terms of the policy would still not apply (eg because the type of use to which the vehicle was being put was not a type of use covered by the policy – say the vehicle was being used by D for 'business' purposes but the policy only covered use for 'social, domestic and pleasure' purposes): see Road Traffic Act 1988, s 151(2).
 A sudden spur-of-the-moment use of the vehicle for a criminal purpose may still be incidental to use for 'social domestic and pleasure' purposes, whereas use of the vehicle on a prolonged criminal enterprise is likely to be neither 'business' nor 'social domestic and pleasure': see *Keeley v Pashen*.[22]

(e) Lack of notice of bringing of proceedings
 If the insurer has not had notice of the bringing of C's proceedings against D before or within 7 days of the issue of those proceedings: Road Traffic Act 1988, s 152(1)(a).

---

[20] (1935) 2KB 174.
[21] [2001] 1 Lloyd's Rep 520, CA.
[22] [2004] EWCA Civ 1491.

The requirements of this condition precedent to a Road Traffic Act insurer's liability to satisfy judgment are relatively lax, provided that the potential Road Traffic Act insurer has notice of an unequivocal intention on C's part to bring proceedings:
 (i) notice may be at any time before the issue of proceedings (so that it need not be notice of when or where the proceeds will be brought: see *Desouza v Waterlow*[23]) or within 7 days after the issue of proceedings;
 (ii) notice may be oral: see *Desouza v Waterlow*;
 (iii) an experienced legal secretary working for the potential Road Traffic Act insurers' solicitors was held to be a sufficient person to receive such notice in the case of *Nawaz v Crowe Insurance*;[24] and
 (iv) it seems that the words in the subsection '... the insurer has notice...' mean that the notice may be received by the insurer from any source and not necessarily from C or his agents: see dicta of Buckley LJ in *Harrington v Pinkney*.[25]

(f) **C travelling in/on offending vehicle knowing that it was unlawfully taken**
If C was 'allowing himself to be carried' in or on the offending vehicle and (either before the commencement of the journey or after the commencement of the journey if he could reasonably have been expected to alight) he 'knew or had reason to believe' that the vehicle was stolen or otherwise unlawfully taken: see Road Traffic Act 1988, s 151(4).
Under *Marleasing*, s 151(4) must of course be interpreted in accordance with the European Directives if at all possible. So:
 (i) for authoritative guidance on the meaning of 'allowing himself to be carried', see *Pickett v MIB*[26] (a decision on the identical words in clause 6(1)(e) of the Uninsured Drivers Agreement 1988);
 (ii) in the light of the decision of the House of Lords in *White v White*[27] on clause 6(1)(e), 'had reason to believe' in s 151(4) must be read as meaning 'deliberately turned a blind eye to' and not merely 'had some reason to believe which would have put a reasonable person on enquiry';
 (iii) the onus of proving the passenger's guilty knowledge is on the Road Traffic Act insurer.
Note that s 151(4) only deals with knowledge of theft or other unlawful taking. Under s 151, a passenger victim's knowledge of the non-insurance of the offending vehicle does not exempt a Road Traffic Act insurer from liability (although, if the passenger victim is himself insured under the motor policy, he is likely to be caught under (G) below).

(g) **C insured by policy and causing/permitting use of offending vehicle.**

---

[23] [1998] PIQR P87 CA.
[24] Times Law Reports, 11 March 2003, CA.
[25] [1989] 2 Lloyd's 310 CA.
[26] [2004] EWCA Civ 6.
[27] [2001] 1 WLR 481.

If C was insured by the motor policy and caused or permitted the use of the vehicle which gave rise to the liability: Road Traffic Act 1988, s 151(4). Strictly speaking, this is not an exception to a Road Traffic Act insurer's liability. In this instance, the Road Traffic Act insurer is still liable to satisfy C's judgment, but is entitled to immediate repayment of the same sum by C, and consequently has a defence of set off or 'circuity of action'. This has two important consequences:

(i) Arguably, C's judgment is satisfied under the Road Traffic Act, and there is therefore no unsatisfied judgment remaining to be satisfied under the Uninsured Drivers Agreements, so in these circumstances C has no second line of protection under the Uninsured Drivers Agreements.

(ii) The terms of this 'exception' would appear to be considerably wider than the limited exclusions from safety net compensation permitted by the Second Directive. Again, the UK State may be liable under *Francovich/Factortame* for failure to implement the Directive.

The Uninsured Drivers Agreements, the Article 75 insurer and the MIB

The Uninsured Drivers Agreements

30.49 If C has a judgment against D in respect of a liability against which motor insurance is compulsory in English Law (a 'relevant liability') which does not fall to be satisfied by an indemnifying insurer or a Road Traffic Act insurer, then, if and in so far as the judgment remains unsatisfied for more than 7 days – and subject again to certain exceptions – it will fall to be satisfied by the MIB under the Uninsured Drivers Agreement 1988 or the Uninsured Drivers Agreement 1999.

'Article 75 insurer'

30.50 The liability of the MIB under the Uninsured Drivers Agreements is in turn passed on under the MIB's Articles of Association to any insurer who is an 'Article 75 insurer' (formerly known as a 'Domestic Regulations insurer').

30.51 Article 75 defines an 'Article 75 insurer' but, broadly speaking, an Article 75 insurer is any insurer who was providing motor insurance in respect of the offending vehicle at the time of the accident – or, in the case of a normal 12-month renewable policy, up to 15 days before the accident – notwithstanding that the insurance did not cover the offending user and that for one reason or another the insurer is not a 'Road Traffic Act insurer'.

No 'Article 75 insurer'

30.52 If there is no Article 75 insurer, the liability to satisfy a judgment rests with the central fund of the MIB itself.

The Uninsured Drivers Agreement 1988

30.53 Under the Uninsured Drivers Agreement 1988 – which applies to accidents occurring between 31 December 1988 to 30 September 1999 – the MIB is obliged to satisfy any judgment in respect of a 'relevant liability' to the extent that it remains unsatisfied for more than 7 days, subject to the following principal exceptions.

Deductions

30.54 Under clause 2(3) and (4) of the Agreement, before satisfying any judgment, the MIB is entitled to deduct from the amount, if any, payable in respect of property damage:

(a) the amount of any compensation which the claimant has received or is entitled to receive as a consequence of a claim made by him from any other source in respect of that damage (eg under his own comprehensive motor policy or household policy); and

(b) up to £175 (in addition to (A) above, if applicable).

Conditions Precedent

30.55

(a) Notice of issue of proceedings
Under clause 5(1)(a) of the Agreement, it is a condition precedent to the MIB's liability to satisfy any judgment that:

> 'Notice in writing of the bringing of the proceedings is given within seven days after the commencement of the proceedings –
> (i) to MIB in the case of proceedings in respect of a relevant liability which is either not covered by a contract of insurance or covered by a contract of insurance with an insurer whose identity cannot be ascertained, or
> (ii) to the Insurer in the case of proceedings in respect of a relevant liability which is covered by a contract of insurance with an insurer whose identity can be ascertained;
>
> Such notice shall be accompanied by a copy of the writ, summons or other document initiating the proceedings'.

The requirements of notice under clause 5(1)(a) of the Agreement are much stricter than the requirements of notice under s 152(1)(a) of the Road Traffic Act 1988.
Under clause 5(1)(a), notice must be **in writing**, must be given not before **but only within 7 days after** the issue of proceedings, and **must be accompanied by a copy of the writ, summons or other document initiating the proceedings.**

In *Williams v Giannini*,[28] Tucker J suggested obiter that notice is 'given' for the purpose of clause 5(1)(a) not when it is sent but only when it is received.

In *Cambridge v Callaghan*,[29] the Court of Appeal held:
(i) that it is essential to compliance with clause 5(1)(a) that the notice 'be accompanied by a copy of the writ, summons or other document initiating the proceedings'; and
(ii) that in County Court proceedings, the requisite document was either the sealed summons or the plaint note.

Presumably the requisite document is now the sealed claim form or plaint note.

In *Silverton v Goodall*,[30] the Court of Appeal held that the strict notice requirements of clause 5(1)(a) are not a derogation from the protection intended by the European Directives on Motor Insurance.

Notice to whom?

Notice must be given to the MIB unless the **'relevant liability ... is covered by a contract of insurance with an insurer** whose identity can be ascertained', in which case notice must be given to that insurer.

But the meaning of these words is unclear:
(a) taken literally, they seem to refer to an indemnifying insurer – in which case they will never have any actual application;
(b) yet, if the words are supposed to refer to an Article 75 insurer, they seem inapt.

(b) Providing such information as MIB reasonably requires

Under clause 5(1)(b), there are conditions precedent to the MIB's liability that C provides to the MIB such information as the MIB may reasonably require (in such form as the MIB may specify):
(i) regarding the proceedings: this provision is commonly used by the MIB to require notice of service of proceedings and of entry of judgment on liability; and
(ii) if C is claiming property damage in the proceedings, regarding any insurance cover or insurance or other claim in respect of the property damage.

Clause 5(1)(b) contains no express provision as to the time within which information is to be provided. Presumably, there is an implicit obligation to provide it within a reasonable time.

(c) Demanding particulars of D's motor insurance

Under clause 5(1)(c), it is a condition precedent to the MIB's liability that C has exercised his statutory right to demand particulars of D's motor insurance (or, if required by the MIB to do so, has authorised the MIB to do so).

---

[28] 8 May 1998 (unreported).
[29] [1998] RTR 365.
[30] [1997] PIQR P451.

Again there is no express provision as to the time within which C must comply, but presumably there is an implicit obligation to comply within a reasonable time.

(d) (If required by MIB, and subject to full indemnity from MIB as to costs) Taking all reasonable steps to obtain judgment against another tortfeasor
Under clause 5(1)(d), it is a condition precedent to the MIB's liability that, if so required by the MIB and subject to full indemnity from the MIB as to costs, C has taken all reasonable steps to obtain Judgment against any person other than D who is liable in respect of the same death, injury or property damage.

The 'rule of meaningful degree'

Clause 5(1)(d), together with clause 5(1)(e) below, provides a mechanism by which the MIB enforces its so called 'rule of meaningful degree', namely that the MIB will not satisfy a judgment which C obtains against D, if C can recover under a judgment against any other person liable to any meaningful degree in respect of the same injury, death or damage (and the MIB does not have to satisfy the judgment against that other person).

This rule applies even if, as between D and that other person ('D2'), D is far more, eg 90%, to blame, because:

(i) subject only to any contributory fault on the part of C, D and D2 are each 100% liable to C, and C can therefore recover 100% against D2;

(ii) the fact that D2 can get a judgment for contribution against D will not avail him against the MIB, since a liability for contribution between defendants is not a liability against which insurance is compulsory under the Road Traffic Act and consequently is not a 'relevant liability' in respect of which the MIB must satisfy a judgment under the Uninsured Drivers Agreement: see *Campbell v McFarland & Omagh UDC*[31] and *Bretton v Hancock*.[32]

The 'new procedure'

In order to implement the Third Directive, under the MIB's 'New Procedure', where there is a dispute about liability between the MIB or an Article 75 insurer in respect of D and another Indemnifying or Road Traffic Act or Article 75 insurer in respect of D2 – subject only to the possible need for C to commence proceedings against each D in order to prevent either D acquiring a limitation defence – C's claim must be treated as if there was no such dispute, and the dispute must be referred for resolution by the MIB's Technical Committee.

(e) Assignment of judgment

---

[31] [1972] NI 31.
[32] [2005] EWCA Civ 404.

Under clause 5(1)(e), it is a condition precedent to the MIB's liability that the judgment obtained by C against D (and any judgment obtained by C against D2 above) is assigned to the MIB or its nominee (eg an Article 75 insurer).

This is a mechanism by which the MIB can recoup its outlay from the uninsured user D (and also complete its enforcement of its 'rule of meaningful degree' against any D2).

Reasonableness

Under clause 5(2), the reasonableness of a request by the MIB:
(i) for the supply of information, under clause 5(1)(b); or
(ii) to take any particular step to obtain judgment against D2, under clause 5(1)(d);

may be referred to the Secretary of State for Transport whose decision shall be final.

Exclusions

30.56 Under clause 6(1)(a)–(e), the following are excluded from the MIB's liability to satisfy judgment:

(a) Offending vehicle a Crown vehicle
   A claim where the offending vehicle was a Crown vehicle – unless someone had taken responsibility for ensuring that there was a motor insurance policy in respect of the vehicle, or the liability was in fact covered by a contract of insurance.

(b) Offending vehicle an exempt vehicle
   A claim where the offending vehicle was exempt from compulsory motor insurance under s 144 of the Road Traffic Act 1988 (the vehicles covered by deposit or being used by certain public bodies) – unless there was in fact a motor insurance policy in respect of its use.

(c) Subrogated claim
   A claim in respect of a judgment or part thereof which has been obtained by the exercise of a right of subrogation (eg by a motor insurer who has indemnified C in respect of damage to his car, or a health insurer who has indemnified C in respect of private treatment for his injury).

(d) Claim for damage to C's vehicle when C knew his vehicle was being used without compulsory motor insurance
   A claim in respect of damage to a motor vehicle or loss consequential thereon if at the time of the damage C knew or ought to have known that the vehicle was being used without compulsory motor insurance.

(e) C travelling in/on offending vehicle knowing that it had been unlawfully taken or that it was being used without compulsory motor insurance

A claim where C was allowing himself to be carried in or on the offending vehicle and (either before the commencement of the journey, or after the commencement of the journey if he could reasonably have been expected to alight) he knew or ought to have known that the vehicle was stolen or otherwise unlawfully taken or was being used without compulsory motor insurance.

For authoritative guidance on the meaning of 'allowing himself to be carried', see *Pickett v MIB*.[33]

In *White v White*[34] the House of Lords held that the Uninsured Drivers Agreement 1988 must be interpreted if at all possible in accordance with the Second Directive which it is intended to implement, and consequently that 'knew or ought to have known' in clause 6(1)(e) means 'knew or deliberately turned a blind eye to' and not merely – despite the ordinary meaning of the words – 'knew or ought reasonably to have known'.

In accordance with the Second Directive, the onus of proving this guilty knowledge is on the MIB.

The Uninsured Drivers Agreement 1999

30.57 Under the Uninsured Drivers Agreement 1999, which applies to accidents occurring on or after 1 October 1999, the MIB is obliged to satisfy any judgment in respect of a 'relevant liability' to the extent that it remains unsatisfied for more than 7 days, subject to the following principal exceptions (differences from the Uninsured Drivers Agreement 1988 being in **bold**):

Deductions

30.58 Under clause 16 of the Agreement, the MIB is entitled to deduct up to £300 from the amount, if any, payable in respect of property damage.

30.59 Under clause 17, the MIB is entitled to deduct from the amount payable in respect of **injury, death** or property damage, any compensation which C **has received** from any other source in respect of the same **injury, death** or property damage (eg under his own personal accident insurance, motor policy or household policy) – provided that that compensation has not already been taken into account in the calculation of the award.

Conditions Precedent

30.60 There are a formidable series of conditions precedent to the MIB's liability under the 1999 Agreement. Rearranged roughly in the order in which C is likely to encounter them, they are as follows:

(a) Demanding particulars of D's motor insurance
Under clause 13, C must **as soon as reasonably practicable**:

---

[33] [2004] EWCA Civ 6.
[34] (2001) 1 WLR 481.

(i) exercise his statutory rights to demand particulars of D's motor insurance; and
(ii) **if D fails to give such particulars:**
   (a) **make a formal complaint to the police; and**
   (b) **use all reasonable endeavours to obtain the name and address of the registered keeper of the vehicle**

(or, if required by the MIB to do so, must authorise the MIB to take such steps on his behalf).

(b) Making application to MIB
Under clause 7, C **must make an application under the Agreement in such form, giving such information and accompanied by such documents as the MIB may reasonably require**.
But note that this obligation is not subject to any express time limit.

(c) Notice of issue of proceedings
Under Clause 9, within **14 days** after the commencement of the proceedings, C must give:
(i) notice in writing of the bringing of proceedings;
(ii) a copy of the sealed claim form or other official document providing evidence of the commencement of proceedings;
(iii) **a copy of details of any insurance which C has in respect of the death, injury or property damage claimed;**
(iv) copies of all correspondence in the possession of C, his solicitors or agents, passing between C, his solicitors or agents, and D, his solicitors, insurers or agents, regarding:
   (a) the injury, death or property damage which is the subject of the claim; and
   (b) any insurance which D may have in respect of liability for the same;
(v) copies of the particulars of claim and accompanying medical evidence and schedule (although, if these have not yet been served with the claim form on D, C may provide copies of them to the MIB up to 7 days after service);
(vi) **such other information about the proceedings as the MIB may reasonably specify**.

(d) Notice of service of proceedings
Under clause 10, C must give **notice in writing of the service of the claim form**:
(i) **within 7 days (excluding Saturdays, Sundays, Bank Holidays, Christmas Day and Good Friday) after the date on which:**
   (a) **C receives notification from the court of service of the claim form on D; or**
   (b) **C receives notification from D of service of the claim form on him; or**
   (c) **personal service is effected; or**
(ii) within 14 days after the date on which service is deemed to have occurred under the CPR; whichever of these periods expires first.

(e) Notice of defence, of amendment of particulars of claim, accompanying medical evidence and schedule, and of setting down for trial and trial date, and providing such other information and documents as MIB reasonably requires.
Under clause 11, C must:
  (i) **give notice in writing of the date of the following within 7 days (excluding the days referred to above) after the following:**
    (a) **the filing of any defence;**
    (b) **any amendment to the particulars of claim, accompanying medical evidence or schedule;**
    (c) **setting down for trial or receipt of notification of a trial date;**
    and must supply copies of any defence and any amendment to the particulars of claim, accompanying medical evidence or schedule; and
  (ii) **within a reasonable time of being required to do so, must supply such further information and documents in support of his claim as the MIB may reasonably require.**

(f) Notice of application for judgment
Under clause 12, C **must give notice after the commencement of the proceedings and at least 35 days before any application for Judgment of his intention to apply for Judgment**.
Notice
Notices under clauses 9–12 must be given to the MIB unless the '**relevant liability . . . is covered by a contract of insurance with an Insurer** whose identity can be ascertained', in which case notice must be given to that Insurer.
As under the 1988 Agreement, the meaning of these words is obscure.
Under clause 8, any notice required to be given or documents to be supplied **to the MIB** pursuant to clauses 9–12 shall be sufficiently given or supplied *only if* **sent by fax or registered or recorded delivery post to the MIB's registered office or any Solicitors instructed by the MIB, and delivery shall be proved by production of the sender's fax transmission report or the appropriate postal receipt**.

(g) (If required by MIB, and subject to full indemnity from MIB as to costs) Taking all reasonable steps to obtain judgment against another tortfeasor, and consenting to MIB being joined to proceedings
Under clause 14, C must:
  (i) if so required by the MIB and subject to full indemnity from the MIB as to costs, take all reasonable steps to obtain Judgment against any person other than D who is liable in respect of the same death, injury or property damage;
  (ii) **consent to the MIB being joined to proceedings**.

(h) Assignment of judgment, and undertaking regarding repayment
Under clause 15, C must:

(i) assign to the MIB or its nominee the judgment obtained by C against D;

(ii) **undertake to repay to the MIB any sum paid to him:**
   (a) **by the MIB, if and in so far as the judgment against D is subsequently set aside; and**
   (b) **by any other person by way of compensation or benefit or the same death, injury or property damage (unless already deducted by the MIB under clause 17 above).**

The 'rule of meaningful degree' and the 'new procedure'

30.61 The MIB's 'rule of meaningful degree' and 'new procedure' continue to apply, as described in the section on the Uninsured Drivers Agreement 1988 above.

Reasonableness

30.62 Under clause 19, any dispute as to the reasonableness of any requirement made by the MIB for the supply of information or documents or the taking of any step by C, may be referred by C or the MIB to the Secretary of State for the Environment, Transport and the Regions, whose decision shall be final.

Concessions in Revised Guidance Notes

30.63 In revised Guidance Notes to the 1999 Agreement, the MIB makes the following important concessions in respect of applications made on or after 15 April 2002:

(i) If the MIB application form is sufficiently completed and signed by C, C will be taken to have complied with clause 13(a) (the requirement as soon as reasonably to exercise his statutory rights to demand particulars of D's motor insurance);

(ii) C may serve notice on the MIB of the issue of proceedings under clause 9 by any means of service recognised under the CPR;

(iii) the time for service of notice of service of the proceedings under clause 10 is extended from 7 to 14 days;

(iv) the MIB should be joined as a defendant from the outset (unless there is good reason not to do so). A set form of words should be used when doing so. Once the MIB is a defendant, clauses 9(3) (notice of service of the particulars of claim if the particulars of claim is served after the claim form), 11 and 12 shall not apply;

(v) even if for any reason clause 11 remains effective, the time for giving notices under that clause is extended from 7 to 14 days.

30.64 No doubt, once C has acted in reliance on any of these concessions, the MIB will be estopped from resiling from the concession concerned.

30.65 But, even after these concessions, query whether the conditions precedent in the Uninsured Drivers Agreement 1999, either individually or cumulatively, are not so extensive and/or demanding that:

(i) they are unwarranted derogations from the protection intended by the European Directives; and/or

(ii) reliance on them is contrary to C's Article 6 right under the Human Rights Act 1998 (and, if so, whether the MIB is for this purpose a 'public authority')?

Exclusions

30.66 Under clause 6(1)(a)–(e), the following are excluded from the MIB's liability to satisfy judgment:

(a) Offending vehicle a Crown vehicle
A claim where the offending vehicle was a Crown vehicle – unless someone had taken responsibility for ensuring that there was a motor insurance policy in respect of the vehicle, or the liability was in fact covered by a contract of insurance.

(b) Offending vehicle an exempt vehicle
A claim where the offending vehicle was exempt from compulsory motor insurance under s 144 of the Road Traffic Act 1988 (vehicles covered by deposit, or being used by certain public bodies) – unless there was in fact a motor insurance policy in respect of its use.

(c) Assigned or subrogated claim
A claim by or for the benefit of someone other than the person who suffered the death, injury or property damage, which is made as a result of any **assignment**, right of subrogation, or contractual or other similar right.

(d) Claim for damage to C's vehicle when C knew his vehicle was being used without compulsory motor insurance
A claim in respect of damage to a motor vehicle or loss consequential thereon if at the time of the damage C knew or ought to have known that the vehicle was being used without compulsory motor insurance.

(e) C travelling in/on offending vehicle knowing that it had been unlawfully taken or that it was being used without compulsory motor insurance or for a criminal purpose
A claim where C was allowing himself to be carried in or on the offending vehicle and (either before the commencement of the journey, or after the

commencement of the journey if he could reasonably have been expected to alight) he knew or ought to have known:
(i) that the vehicle had been stolen or unlawfully taken; or
(ii) that the vehicle was being used without compulsory motor insurance; or
(iii) **that the vehicle was being used in the course of or furtherance of a crime;**
(iv) **that the vehicle was being used as a means of escape from or avoidance of lawful apprehension.**

By what appears to be an error of drafting, **there is no provision in the Uninsured Drivers Agreement 1999** comparable to the provision in the Uninsured Drivers Agreement 1988 **that, in the case of a Fatal Accidents Act claim, it is the knowledge of the Deceased not the knowledge of the claimant which counts**, see *Phillips v Rafiq & MIB*.[35]

For the meaning of 'allowing himself to be carried' and 'knew or ought to have known', see the commentary and cases cited in relation to the identical words in Clause 6(1)(e) of the Uninsured Drivers Agreement 1988 above.

Under Clause 6(3), the burden of proving 'knew or ought to have known' in Clause 6(1)(e) is expressly on the MIB – in keeping with the Second Directive; but

Clause 6(3) goes on to provide that, in the absence of evidence to the contrary, **proof by the MIB of any of the following matters shall be taken as proof of C's knowledge of no insurance for the purpose of clause 6(1)(e)(ii):**
(a) that C was the owner or registered keeper of the vehicle or had caused or permitted its use;
(b) that C knew the vehicle was being used by a person who was below the minimum age to hold a licence to drive a vehicle of that class;
(c) that C knew that the person driving was disqualified from driving;
(d) that C knew that the user of the vehicle was neither its owner nor registered keeper, nor an employee of the owner or registered keeper, nor the owner or registered keeper of any other vehicle; and

Under Clause 6(4), **knowledge which C has or ought to have for the purpose of Clause 6(1)(e) includes knowledge of matters of which he could reasonably be expected to have been aware had he not been under the self-induced influence of drink or drugs.**

It is again questionable whether these provisions are consistent with the European Directives or reliance on them is consistent with C's Article 6 right under the Human Rights Act 1998.

---

[35] [2007] EWCA Civ (judgment awaited).

Compliance by the claimant with Road Traffic Act 1988, ss 151 and 152 and the Uninsured Drivers Agreements

Claimant's only safe course

30.67 Clearly, C's only safe course is to comply strictly with the requirements of the Road Traffic Act 1988 and the relevant Uninsured Drivers Agreement.

Claimant, having failed to comply, setting aside his own procedural steps and then complying

30.68 Where C has failed to comply with a condition precedent under the Road Traffic Act or the Uninsured Drivers Agreements, the Courts are normally sympathetic to allowing C to set aside any step in Court procedure which he has taken, if that will enable him then to satisfy the condition precedent and take the procedural step again (even to the extent of setting aside his own default Judgment and discontinuing proceedings in order to commence fresh proceedings with proper notice, see *O'Neill v O'Brien*[36]).

Limitation

30.69 But, if C only issues his second set of proceedings in respect of the same cause of action, albeit with proper notice, outside the limitation period, the second set of proceedings will be vulnerable to a plea of limitation and a possible refusal by the court to exercise its discretion under s 33 of the Limitation Act 1980 to disapply the limitation defence (if D and/or the MIB can show real prejudice, see *Richardson v Watson & MIIB*[37]). This is what gives the notice requirements in s 152 of the Road Traffic Act and under the Uninsured Drivers Agreements teeth.

30.70 However, bear in mind that the limitation period will of course be longer than normal if C was a child or patient at the time of the accident, or has a 'date of knowledge' under s 14 of the Limitation Act 1980 later than the date of the accident, and that proceedings are 'brought' for the purpose of limitation when the claim form is received by the court for issue, although 'started' for other purposes only when the claim form is issued by the court, see *St Helen's MBC v Barnes*.[38]

Waiver or estoppel from reliance on condition precedent

30.71 A Road Traffic Act/Article 75 Insurer/MIB may of course waive or become estopped from relying upon a condition precedent – under the normal principles of waiver and estoppel.

---

[36] (1997) The Times Law Reports, 21 March 1997, CA.
[37] [2006] EWCA Civ 1662.
[38] [2006] EWCA Civ 1372.

30.72 But mere delay on the part of the Road Traffic Act/Article 75 insurer/MIB, without more, cannot constitute waiver of C's non-compliance with a condition precedent, see *Wake v Page*.[39]

European Directives & Human Rights Act 1998

30.73 If all else fails, the European Directives and/or the Human Rights Act 1998 may save C. See above.

Service of proceedings

30.74 It is important to understand that the potential involvement of a Road Traffic Act/Article 75 insurer/MIB does not relieve C of the obligation to serve his proceedings on D (unless the court exercises its power under Civil Procedure Rules 1998 (CPR), r 6.9 to dispense with service).

30.75 C may serve D:

(a) by one of the ordinary means of service on D; or

(b) by service on solicitors appointed by the Road Traffic Act/Article 75 insurer/MIB if the solicitors have confirmed that they have authority from D to accept service on his behalf (or if the Road Traffic Act/Article 75 insurer/MIB has been joined to the action with permission to exercise D's rights, but this will rarely be the case); or

(c) by obtaining and acting under an order for service by an alternative method (eg service on D by way of service on the potentially liable Road Traffic Act/Article 75 insurer/MIB) if it appears to the court that there is a good reason to authorize service by an alternative method (eg that C cannot by reasonable efforts locate D and serve him by ordinary means).

Authority of Road Traffic Act insurer/Article 75 insurer/MIB to act on behalf of D

Authority from D or the court

30.76 A Road Traffic Act/Article 75 insurer/MIB can only act on behalf of D:

(a) If it has obtained authority from D to do so; or

(b) If it has been joined to proceedings against D with the permission of the Court to exercise D's rights.

In either of these circumstances, the insurer/MIB can sign a statement of truth in a statement of case on behalf of D, see PD 22.3.6A.

---

[39] [2001] RTR 291, CA.

Conflict of interest

30.77 Where a Road Traffic Act/Article 75 Insurer/MIB disputes its own liability to satisfy a Judgment against D, eg under s 151(8) of the Road Traffic Act 1988 or Clause 6(1)(e)(ii) of the Uninsured Drivers Agreement 1988 or 1999, it is wrong for the Road Traffic Act/Article 75 Insurer/MIB to obtain authority from D to act on his behalf – save possibly if D gives such authority after being fully informed and taking independent legal advice – since there is a clear conflict of interest.

30.78 In these circumstances, the only safe course for the Road Traffic Act/Article 75 insurer/MIB is not to seek such authority from D, to terminate any such authority already obtained from D, and – if necessary – to apply to the court to be joined to C's action against D 'with permission to exercise D's rights' (to enable it to enter a notice of intention to defend and/or defence on behalf of D and prevent C obtaining judgment on liability in default) 'but without prejudice to its own contention that it is not liable to satisfy any Judgment which C may obtain against D'.

Joinder of Road Traffic Act insurer/Article 75 insurer/ MIB

30.79 If a Road Traffic Act/Article 75 insurer/MIB wants to be joined to C's action against D, it will normally succeed in its application, since it is 'a person liable to be affected in its pocket by the outcome of the proceedings' *Gurtner v Circuit*,[40] and see now CPR, r 19.2(2).

30.80 It may be joined:

(a) simply to exercise its own rights; or

(b) with permission to exercise the rights of D (in which case it has the benefit of being able to enter a notice of intention to defend and/or defence on D's behalf, but must take the burden that service on it will constitute service on D); or

(c) with permission to exercise the rights of D but without prejudice to its contention that it is not liable to satisfy any judgment obtained by C against D (in which case, the same applies).

Both (b) and (c) above are anomalous, but this anomaly is probably now too well-established to be displaced.

30.81 As we have seen, under the Uninsured Drivers Agreement 1999, it is a condition precedent to the MIB's liability that C, if requested to do so by the MIB, consents to the MIB being joined as a party.

---

[40] [1968] 2 QB 587, CA.

Interim payment

30.82 CPR, r 25.7(2) expressly provides that a court may order an interim payment against uninsured D if there is a Road Traffic Act or Article 75 insurer or the MIB standing behind him.

Recovery from D by Road Traffic Act insurer/Article 75 insurer/MIB

Under Road Traffic Act 1988, s 151

30.83 If a Road Traffic Act insurer has to satisfy a judgment for damages, interest and costs obtained by C against D, it has a statutory right to recoup the amount of that judgment from D, see Road Traffic Act 1988, s 151(7) and (8).

Under the Uninsured Drivers Agreements

30.84 If the MIB (or an Article 75 insurer) has to satisfy a judgment for damages, interest and costs obtained by C against D, it is entitled to require – as a condition precedent to paying C – an assignment from C of the judgment against D, which it can then enforce against D, see clause 5(1)(e) of the 1988 Agreement and 15(a) of the 1999 Agreement.

But what if there is no judgment on quantum?

30.85 But normally, of course, the Road Traffic Act/Article 75 insurer/MIB settles C's claim long before judgment on quantum. If it has D's agreement to reimburse it, it can rely on that agreement. Otherwise:

(a) it would appear improper to make the settlement in the form of an agreed judgment on quantum – assuming that the Road Traffic Act/Article 75 insurer/MIB has authority to agree judgment on D's behalf – and then to turn around and seek to enforce that judgment against D;

(b) but it would appear proper for the Road Traffic Act/Article 75 insurer/MIB to take an assignment of C's cause of action against D and then pursue that cause of action against D – provided it has not previously obtained instructions or evidence from D (ie provided that, having run to some extent with hare, it does not then seek to hunt as the hound);

(c) failing that, it is doubtful that the Road Traffic Act/Article 75 insurer/MIB has any restitutionary remedy against D.

THE 'UNTRACED' IE UNIDENTIFIABLE DRIVER/USER

30.86 Where C is the victim of an accident for which D has a liability against which motor insurance is compulsory in English law, but D is *unidentifiable*, C cannot sue D but may make a claim, not through the Courts, but direct to the MIB under the Untraced Drivers Agreement 1996 (for accidents 1 July 1996 – 13 February 2003) or the Untraced Drivers Agreement 2003 (for accidents on or after 14 February 2003).

The Untraced Drivers Agreement 1996

30.87 The Untraced Drivers Agreement 1996:

(a) does not provide compensation for property damage (although this is arguably contrary to the Second Directive, which only permits the exclusion of compensation for property damage where the offending vehicle is unidentified);

(b) makes no provision for the award of interest or costs (although this is contrary to the Second Directive, see *Evans v Secretary of State for Environment*[41]);

(c) does not allow for oral hearings.

30.88 C applies on paper to the MIB. The MIB investigates and determines whether the application is within the terms of the Agreement and, if so, determines liability and, if there is liability, quantum on the same basis as a court would (save that C is not compensated for loss of earnings which he has in fact received, even if he has given an undertaking to his employer to repay them). The MIB then notifies C of its decision. C can either accept the decision or, within 6 weeks, appeal to an Arbitrator, one of a panel of QCs appointed for this purpose by the Lord Chancellor, who will decide the matter afresh, again on the basis of paper submissions.

30.89 The MIB may but is not bound to follow a speedier procedure, under which the MIB makes C an offer: if C accepts the offer, that is the end of the matter; if C does not accept the offer, the matter goes through the full procedure above.

30.90 If C is a child or a patient, the MIB may make the whole or part of any award the subject of a trust.

30.91 C's claim is subject to a number of conditions precedent and exclusions:

Conditions Precedent

30.92

(i) Reporting accident to and cooperating with the police

---

[41] (2003) *The Times*, 9 December 2003.

The accident must be reported to the Police within 14 days or as soon as C reasonably can, and C must cooperate with the Police;

(ii) Strict 3-year limitation period
The claim must be submitted to the MIB in writing within 3 years of the accident (even if C is a child or patient – an inflexible time limit which is arguably contrary to the Second Directive);

(iii) Providing such assistance as MIB reasonably requires
C must give such assistance as is reasonably required by or on behalf of the MIB to enable any investigation to be carried out under the Agreement, including the provision of statements and information in writing or, if required, orally. The MIB may 'request' (presumably this means 'require') C to make a statutory declaration about any relevant facts;

(iv) (If required by MIB, and subject to full indemnity from MIB as to costs) Taking all reasonable steps to obtain judgment against another tortfeasor
At any time before the MIB notifies its decision, C must take all reasonable steps required of him by the MIB to obtain Judgment against any person other than unidentifiable D who may be liable – subject to the MIB indemnifying C in respect of all costs reasonably incurred in complying with this requirement (unless the result of the proceedings contributes to exonerating unidentifiable D);

(v) Assignment of judgment
If required by the MIB, C must assign to the MIB or its nominee any Judgment which C obtains against anyone other than unidentifiable D liable in respect of the same injury or death – subject to the MIB or its nominee undertaking to account to C for any sum received by the MIB or its nominee under the Judgment (after deducting all reasonable expenses in effecting recovery) over and above what is payable to C by the MIB under the Agreement.

Reasonableness

30.93 In the event of a dispute about the reasonableness of a requirement under (iii) or (iv) above, the dispute must be referred to the Secretary of State for the Environment, whose decision shall be final. But in the event of a dispute as to whether the result of any proceedings contributed to exonerating unidentifiable D, that dispute must be referred to one of the Arbitrators, whose decision shall be final.

Exclusions

30.94 The Agreement excludes the following claims:

(i) Offending vehicle used as a weapon

Where the offending vehicle was deliberately used as a weapon – C is left to make his application to the Criminal Injuries Compensation Authority.

(ii) Offending vehicle a Crown vehicle
Where the offending vehicle was a Crown vehicle – unless someone had taken responsibility for ensuring that there was a motor insurance policy in respect of the vehicle.

(iii) C travelling in/on offending vehicle knowing that it had been unlawfully taken or that it was being used without compulsory motor insurance or for a criminal purpose
Where C was allowing himself to be carried in or on the offending vehicle and (either before the commencement of the journey, or after the commencement of the journey if he could reasonably have been expected to alight) he knew or ought to have known:
(a) that the vehicle had been stolen or unlawfully taken; or
(b) that the vehicle was being used without compulsory motor insurance; or
(c) that the vehicle was being used in the course of or furtherance of a crime;
(d) that the vehicle was being used as a means of escape from or avoidance of lawful apprehension.

30.95 For the meaning of 'allowing himself to be carried' and 'knew or ought to have known', see the commentary and cases cited in relation to the identical words in clause 6(1)(e) of the Uninsured Drivers Agreement 1988 above.

30.96 Since the Untraced Drivers Agreement must be interpreted in accordance with the Second Directive which it is intended to implement, the onus of proving 'knew or ought to have known' must be on the MIB.

Untraced Drivers Agreement 2003

30.97 The Untraced Drivers Agreement 2003 is a similar but more detailed scheme. The main differences (in **bold**) are that the Untraced Drivers Agreement 2003:

(a) provides compensation for property damage (subject to a £300 excess, an upper limit, and a number of additional conditions precedent and exceptions);

(b) deducts from any compensation payable under the Agreement the amount of any compensation which C has received from any insurer (eg personal accident, motor or household Insurer) or like person in respect of the same injury, death or damage;

(c) **provides that the MIB may offer compensation on a 'provisional damages' basis and/or by way of periodical payments;**

(d) makes provision for the award of interest and costs (although the costs provisions are in some instances confused and obscure);

(e) allows for oral hearings before the Arbitrator, if requested by C or the MIB; and

(f) contains more detailed conditions precedent and exclusions, in particular:
- Conditions precedent
  - (i) Reporting accident to and cooperation with the police
    C or someone acting on C's behalf must report the accident to the police:
    (a) **within 5 days if it involved any property damage; or**
    (b) **within 14 days if it involved injury or death without any property damage; or**
    if that is not reasonably possible, as soon as reasonably possible, and C must provide satisfactory evidence of the report in the form of an acknowledgment from the relevant police force showing the crime or incident number, and C must cooperate with the police.
  - (ii) Slightly more flexible limitation period
    A claim for property damage must be submitted in writing to the MIB within 9 months of the accident or, in a case where C could not reasonably have been expected to be aware of the property damage, as soon as practicable after he did become or ought reasonably to have become aware of it and in any event no later than 2 years after the accident.
    A claim for injury or death must be submitted in writing to the MIB within 3 years of the accident or, in a case where C could not reasonably have been expected to be aware of the injury, as soon as practicable after he did become or ought reasonably to have become aware of it and in any event no later than 15 years after the accident.
    Note that this may still bar deserving claims, eg by children and patients who know that they have suffered injury but not that they can claim;
  - (iii) Providing such assistance as MIB reasonably requires
    C must **make his application in such form,** provide in support of the application such statements and other information (whether in writing or orally at interview) and give such further assistance as is reasonably required by or on behalf of the MIB to enable an investigation to be carried out under the Agreement, **and must provide the MIB with written authority to take all such steps as may be reasonably necessary to carry out a proper investigation.** If the MIB reasonably requires him to do so before reaching its decision, C must make a statutory declaration about any relevant facts;
  - (iv) (If required by MIB, and subject to full indemnity from MIB as to costs) Taking all reasonable steps to obtain judgment against another tortfeasor
    If C has already commenced proceedings against any person other than unidentifiable D who may be liable in respect of the same injury, death

or damage, C must as soon as reasonably possible notify the MIB of such proceedings and provide the MIB with such further information about them as the MIB may reasonably require. In any event, if reasonably required by the MIB before it reaches its decision (and subject to an indemnity from the MIB in respect of all costs reasonably incurred in complying with this requirement), C must bring proceedings against any such person and cooperate with the MIB in taking such steps as are reasonably necessary to obtain Judgment in those proceedings (or, at the MIB's option, authorise the MIB to do so in C's name), and must provide the MIB with a transcript of any official shorthand or recorded note of the evidence or judgment given in those proceedings;

(v) Assignment of judgment

If reasonably required by the MIB before it reaches its decision, C must assign to the MIB or its nominee any Judgment which C obtains against anyone other than unidentifiable D in respect of the same injury, death **or damage** – subject to the MIB or its nominee undertaking to account to C for any sum received by the MIB or its nominee under the Judgment (after deducting all reasonable expenses in effecting recovery) over and above what is payable to C by the MIB under the Agreement – **and C must also undertake to assign to the MIB or its nominee the right to any compensation which is or may be due from any insurer (such as a personal accident, motor or household Insurer) or like person in respect of the same injury, death or damage.**

Disputes as to requirements

Any dispute between C and the MIB as to a requirement made by the MIB under the Agreement is to be referred to and determined by one of the Arbitrators.

Exclusions

30.98 The Agreement does not exclude claims arising from use of the offending vehicle as a weapon but excludes the following claims:

(i) Offending vehicle a Crown vehicle
Where the offending vehicle was a Crown vehicle – unless someone had taken responsibility for ensuring that there was a motor insurance policy in respect of the vehicle;

(ii) C travelling in/on offending vehicle knowing that it had been unlawfully taken or that it was being used without compulsory motor insurance or for a criminal purpose
Where C was allowing himself to be carried in or on the offending vehicle and (either before the commencement of the journey, or after the commencement of the journey if he could reasonably have been expected to alight) he knew or ought to have known:
(a) That the vehicle had been stolen or unlawfully taken; or

(b) That the vehicle was being used without compulsory motor insurance; or
(c) That the vehicle was being used in the course of or furtherance of a crime;
(d) That the vehicle was being used as a means of escape from or avoidance of lawful apprehension.

For the meaning of 'allowing himself to be carried' and 'knew or ought to have known', see the commentary and cases cited in relation to the identical words in Clause 6(1)(e) of the Uninsured Drivers Agreement 1988 above.

The burden of proving 'knew or ought to have known' is expressly placed on the MIB – in keeping with the Second Directive.

But, as in the Uninsured Drivers Agreement 1999, the Agreement goes on to provide that, in the absence of evidence to the contrary, proof by the MIB of any of the following matters shall be taken as proof of C's knowledge of no insurance:

(a) **that C was the owner or registered keeper of the vehicle or had caused or permitted its use;**
(b) **that C knew the vehicle was being used by a person who was below the minimum age to hold a licence to drive a vehicle of that class;**
(c) **that C knew that the person driving was disqualified from driving;**
(d) **that C knew that the user of the vehicle was neither its owner nor registered keeper, nor an employee of the owner or registered keeper, nor the owner or registered keeper of any other vehicle; and**

That knowledge which C has or ought to have includes knowledge of matters of which he could reasonably be expected to have been aware had he not been under the self-induced influence of drink or drugs.

Query again whether these provisions are consistent with the European Directives or reliance on them is consistent with C's Article 6 right under the Human Rights Act 1998;

(iii) Terrorism
Where the injury, death or damage concerned was caused by or in the course of 'terrorism' within the meaning of s 1 of the Terrorism Act 2000;

(iv) C claiming as mere assignee or by subrogation
Where C is not the person who suffered the injury or damage or a personal representative or dependent of the person who was killed, but is a mere assignee of the claim, or where C is claiming by virtue of a right of subrogation or similar right.

In addition, there are the following specific exclusions in respect of claims for property damage:

(v) Damage to property where offending vehicle unidentified
A claim for damage to property where the offending vehicle is unidentified (an exclusion expressly sanctioned in the Second Directive);

(vi) Damaged property insured against such damage & c already recovered full amount of his loss from insurer
A claim for damage to property where the damaged property was insured against such damage and C has already recovered the full amount of his loss from the Insurer;

(vii) Claim for damage to C's vehicle when C knew his vehicle was being used without compulsory motor insurance
A claim for damage to a motor vehicle if at the time of the damage C knew or ought to have known that the vehicle was being used without compulsory motor insurance.

Chapter 31

FATAL ACCIDENT CLAIMS

INTRODUCTION

31.1 At common law, there was no right of action in respect of the death of another person, this being known as the rule in *Baker v Bolton*.[1] Statute has intervened to ameliorate the injustice of this rule, with the result that the right to damages arising out of a person's death is entirely governed by statute.

31.2 Since October 2000, there have been three main causes of action which can be brought in respect of a person's death:

(1) First, under the Law Reform (Miscellaneous Provisions) Act 1934 (hereafter referred to as 'the 1934 Act'), there is the action which the deceased would have been able to bring on his own account, had he not died, and which survives for the benefit of his estate.[2] Thus where, for example, a person sustains grave injuries as a result of another's negligence causing him great pain and suffering, he would be able to bring an action for damages in respect of such pain and suffering. If, however, he dies before the action is brought, then that right of action survives for the benefit of his estate, and his personal representatives will be able to sue on behalf of the estate for the same damages which the deceased would have been able seek had he not died. Such an action is not consequent upon the death[3] itself, but pre-exists the death and, by virtue of the 1934 Act, survives despite the death.

(2) Secondly, under the Fatal Accidents Act 1976, an action may be brought consequent upon the death itself.[4] This action relates to the losses which arise out of that death, for example the losses to the deceased's wife and children, who may have been dependent on the deceased by virtue of the fact that his death has deprived them of that support which he gave them when he was alive.

(3) Thirdly, since 2 October 2000,[5] the courts have had the power to make awards of damages for certain breaches of the European Convention on

---

[1] Affirmed by the House of Lords in *Admiralty Commissioners v SS Amerika* [1917] AC 38.
[2] See further **31.5–31.9** below.
[3] There being a sole exception in the case of funeral expenses: see s 1(2)(c) of the 1934 Act.
[4] See further **31.10–31.48** below.
[5] The date upon which the Human Rights Act 1998 came into force.

Human Rights (ECHR).[6] Article 2 of the ECHR protects the right to life and it is therefore possible for the courts to award damages for a person's death pursuant to its powers under the Human Rights Act (HRA) 1998. This cause of action is quite separate from, and supplemental to, the causes of action under the 1934 Act and the Fatal Accidents Act 1976 and could cover, for example, damages for bereavement in respect of an adult child.[7]

31.3 In addition to the above, certain specific statutes create rights arising out of death in particular circumstances. For example, the Coal Mining (Subsidence) Act 1991 imposes special liability on the British Coal Corporation for deaths arising as a result of mining subsidence. These minor statutes are beyond the scope of this chapter.[8]

31.4 Each of the above main causes of action will now be considered in turn.

ACTIONS UNDER THE 1934 ACT: ACTIONS FOR THE BENEFIT OF THE DECEASED'S ESTATE

31.5 The 1934 Act, as amended by the Administration of Justice Act 1982, provides:

'1 Effect of death on certain causes of action

(1) Subject to the provisions of this section, on the death of any person after the commencement of this Act all causes of action subsisting against or vested in him shall survive against, or, as the case may be, for the benefit of, his estate. Provided that this subsection shall not apply to causes of action for defamation . . .

[(1A) The right of a person to claim under section 1A of the Fatal Accidents Act 1976 (bereavement) shall not survive for the benefit of his estate on his death.]

(2) Where a cause of action survives as aforesaid for the benefit of the estate of a deceased person, the damages recoverable for the benefit of the estate of that person:—

[(a) shall not include—
  (i) any exemplary damages;
  (ii) any damages for loss of income in respect of any period after that person's death;]
(b) . . .
(c) where the death of that person has been caused by the act or omission which give rise to the cause of action, shall be calculated without reference to any

---

[6] See further **31.49–31.52** below.
[7] A lacuna in the Fatal Accidents Act: see **31.15**(c) below.
[8] For further information, readers are referred to, for example, *Charlesworth & Percy on Negligence* (10th edn) at paras 15–66 et seq.

loss or gain to his estate consequent on his death, except that a sum in respect of funeral expenses may be included.

(3) ...

(4) Where damage has been suffered by reason of any act or omission in respect of which a cause of action would have subsisted against any person if that person had not died before or at the same time as the damage was suffered, there shall be deemed, for the purposes of this Act, to have been subsisting against him before his death such cause of action in respect of that act or omission as would have subsisted if he had died after the damage was suffered.

(5) The rights conferred by this Act for the benefit of the estates of deceased persons shall be in addition to and not in derogation of any rights conferred on the dependants of deceased persons by the Fatal Accidents Acts 1846 to 1908 ... and so much of this Act as relates to causes of action against the estates of deceased persons shall apply in relation to causes of action under the said Acts as it applies in relation to other causes of action not expressly excepted from the operation of subsection (1) of this section.

(6) In the event of the insolvency of an estate against which proceedings are maintainable by virtue of this section, any liability in respect of the cause of action in respect of which the proceedings are maintainable shall be deemed to be a debt provable in the administration of the estate, notwithstanding that it is a demand in the nature of unliquidated damages arising otherwise than by a contract, promise or breach of trust.'

31.6 In relation to actions accruing for the benefit of the estate under the 1934 Act, a distinction must be drawn between those losses of the deceased which, at the time of his death, were future losses and those which were past losses that had already crystallised. Until 1982, both past and future losses could be claimed, including damages for pecuniary losses in the 'lost years', namely the years between the date of death and the date when, but for the negligence, the deceased could have expected to die in any event.[9] However, the cause of action in respect of the lost years was abolished so far as claims on behalf of the estate under the 1934 Act were concerned, by the amendments made to the 1934 Act by the Administration of Justice Act 1982. This had the desirable effect of doing away with the anomaly that there were overlapping claims for future loss of earnings between the claims under the 1934 Act and the claims on behalf of the dependants under the Fatal Accidents Act, where the beneficiaries under those two claims would not necessarily be the same.

31.7 In addition, so far as accrued claims were concerned, the deceased previously had a cause of action in respect of his loss of expectation of life, and claims for this became fixed at the conventional sum of £2,000. This claim was also abolished by the Administration of Justice Act 1982.

---

[9] An injured claimant, whose expectation of life is significantly reduced as a result of his injuries, may still claim damages for his losses in the lost years, typically loss of earnings, although he must give credit for that part of those earnings which he would have spent exclusively on himself, expenses which, ex hypothesi, will never be incurred.

31.8 The result is that claims under the 1934 Act are now effectively confined to two causes of action: first, damages for the deceased's past loss up to the date of his death, including his pain and suffering in the period between the injury and his death, and, secondly, the funeral expenses. Such actions, when brought on their own, are typically brought where the deceased had no dependants, or where the dependants have no valid dependency claim under the Fatal Accidents Act, and the beneficiaries under the deceased's will, or of his estate on intestacy, wish to make a claim for the funeral expenses and the deceased's pain and suffering and loss up to the date of death. In practice, however, claims under the 1934 Act are nearly always joined in claims under the Fatal Accidents Act so as to give the beneficiaries of the estate, who are often also the dependants for the purposes of the 1976, the additional damages representing the deceased's pain and suffering and past loss. The claim for funeral expenses under the 1934 Act and the Fatal Accident Act is identical.

31.9 So far as the claim for the deceased's past losses are concerned, this will include the usual heads of damage seen in a personal injury action: past loss of earnings, the cost of past care including the value of gratuitous care, medical expenses, the cost of equipment, expenses incurred by relatives in visiting the deceased in hospital together with interest calculated in the usual way. In relation to general damages, although these will tend to be limited by virtue of the fact that the pain and suffering was confined to the period between the accident and the death, they may be aggravated by the fact that the deceased was aware of his predicament and the fact that he is dying. This is typically the case in clinical negligence claims where the negligence in question was a failure to diagnose and treat cancer so that, instead of being cured, the deceased suffers inoperable metastases and death. For example, in *Ronald Stothard (widower & administrator of the estate of Christine Stothard deceased) v Gateshead Health Authority*[10] (2002) the deceased was a 33-year-old woman who died of cervical cancer after the defendant negligently failed to detect and treat an abnormal cervical smear. The claim under the 1934 Act comprised £70,708 which included £50,000 in respect of the deceased's pain and suffering, and £20,708 in respect of loss of earnings and interest. The deceased's youngest child was aged only 18 months at the date of her death, and she died knowing that she would not see her child grow up. There have also been many recent cases which have included claims for damages under the 1934 Act in respect of mesothelioma contracted as a result of exposure to asbestos, where the deceased has died after what has often been a long and painful illness.

ACTIONS UNDER THE FATAL ACCIDENTS ACT 1976

31.10 The cause of action arising under the 1976 Act is the principal cause of action in respect of death, and is for the benefit of the deceased's dependants. There have been Fatal Accidents Acts since 1846 ('Lord Campbell's Act') to fill

---

[10] Lawtel Document No AM0200402, decision of HHJ Walton sitting as a Deputy High Court Judge.

the gap left by the common law, and the 1976 Act, as amended by the Administration of justice Act 1982, is the presently applicable statute. Section 1(1) provides:

> 'If death is caused by any wrongful act, neglect or default which is such as would (if death had not ensued) have entitled the person injured to maintain an action and recover damages in respect thereof, the person who would have been liable if death had not ensued shall be liable to an action for damages, notwithstanding the death of the person injured.'

31.11 This section is somewhat confusing as a person reading it might ask himself: isn't this the same as the action under the 1934 Act, ie the action which the deceased could have brought and which survives for the benefit of his estate? The answer is no, it is not the same. However, there is the same threshold hypothetical question which needs to be answered in the affirmative to provide the foundation for the cause of action which is then subsequently explained and defined in the 1976 Act. Thus, it is necessary that the deceased could have sued in respect of the wrongful act, neglect or default if he had not died. The effect of this section is to exclude actions by the dependants where, for whatever reason, the cause of action would have been denied to the deceased. Two examples may be used to illustrate this principle. First, the dependants cannot bring an action under the 1976 Act if, by the time of the deceased's death, the original action he could have brought in respect of the same wrongful act had become statute barred. The usual limitation period for personal injury actions is three years.[11] If a person was injured on, for example, 1 March 2002 and he died as a result of his injuries on 1 April 2005, his dependants would be unable to bring an action under the 1976 Act because the action which the deceased would otherwise have been able to bring had become statute-barred on 1 March 2005, one month before his death.

31.12 The second example is shown by the case of *Jameson v Central Electricity Generating Board*.[12] The deceased (D) contracted occupational disease as a result of the wrongful acts of two joint tortfeasors, A and B. D sued A and settled the action 'in full and final settlement' during his lifetime. After his death, a claim was brought by his dependants under the 1976 Act against B. B sought to join A as a third party. It was held that the settlement by D of the first action against A extinguished his cause of action against B, with the result that D could not have maintained an action against B had he not died and therefore the action under the 1976 Act against B could not be brought by reason of s 1(1).[13]

31.13 Under the 1976 Act, there are three heads of damage: the claim for bereavement, the claim for loss of dependency and the claim for funeral expenses. These will be dealt with in turn.

---

[11] Limitation Act 1976, s 11.
[12] [2000] 1 AC 455.
[13] An award of provisional damages, however, does not bar a subsequent action under the 1976 Act: Damages Act 1996, s 3. The damages are, though, taken into account as appropriate.

Bereavement

31.14 Section 1A of the 1976 Act provides:

'(1) An action under this Act may consist of or include a claim for damages for bereavement.

(2) A claim for damages for bereavement shall only be for the benefit –

(a) of the wife or husband of the deceased; and
(b) where the deceased was a minor who was never married –
   (i) of his parents, if he was legitimate; and
   (ii) of his mother, if he was illegitimate.

(3) Subject to subsection (5) below, the sum to be awarded as damages under this section shall be [GBP10,000].

(4) Where there is a claim for damages under this section for the benefit of both the parents of the deceased, the sum awarded shall be divided equally between them (subject to any deduction falling to be made in respect of costs not recovered from the defendant).

(5) The Lord Chancellor may by order made by statutory instrument, subject to annulment in pursuance of a resolution of either House of Parliament, amend this section by varying the sum for the time being specified in subsection (3) above.'

31.15 There are a number of points to be noted about the action for bereavement:

(a) The action only applies in respect of deaths occurring after 1 January 1983, when the amendment to the 1976 Act came into force.

(b) The figure of £10,000 is the current sum for bereavement set by the Lord Chancellor. Originally, the sum was £3,500, it then rose to £7,500 in respect of deaths on or after 1 April 1991 and it has been £10,000 since 1 April 2002 for deaths on or after that date.

(c) The claim can only be made by spouses (in respect of the death of the other spouse) or by parents in respect of the death of an unmarried minor child (ie a child who has not reached the age of 18). It is clear that the class of people who may actually be bereaved by a death is much wider, for example the parents of an 18-year-old who is killed, or a sibling of a minor who is killed, or grandparents. The restriction of those who may receive compensation for bereavement to this very narrow class is a political decision, and appears difficult to justify given that, for example, the effect on the parents of the death of an 18-year-old is no different to the effect of the death of a 17-year-old. If 17-year-old twins were injured in a car crash as a result of the negligence of a drunken driver, and one twin died on the day before his 18th birthday and the other died on the day after, the parents would recover bereavement damages in respect of the one, but not the other.[14]

Loss of dependency

31.16 The claim for loss of dependency is the main claim under the 1976 Act. In contrast to the claim for bereavement, the class of dependants is very wide and includes spouses, parents, grandparents, brothers, sisters, uncles, aunts, common law spouses.[15]

31.17 The foundation for the dependency claim is s 3 of the 1976 Act which provides:

> **'Assessment of damages**
>
> (1) In the action such damages, other than damages for bereavement, may be awarded as are proportioned to the injury resulting from the death to the dependants respectively.'

31.18 Section 3(2) then provides for the division of the amount recovered among the dependants 'in such shares as may be directed'.

31.19 The approach of the courts to the assessment of the loss caused by the death is similar to the approach used in personal injury actions. Thus, the court does its best to assess what would have happened, but for the death in question, evaluating the evidence as to what the deceased would have done, how his career would have progressed, how long the dependants would have remained dependent etc. However, in *Mallett v McMonagle*[16] Lord Diplock contrasted the fact-finding task of a court in relation past fact, decided on the balance of probabilities, and its task in relation to what will happen or would have happened but for the wrongful act. He said:[17]

> 'But in assessing damages which depend upon its view as to what will happen in the future or would have happened in the future if something had not happened in the past, the court must make an estimate as to what are the chances that a particular thing will or would have happened and reflect those chances, whether they are more or less than even, in the amount of damages which it awards.'

31.20 In relation to future pecuniary loss, the methodology used is the application of multipliers to multiplicands,[18] as in calculating future loss of earnings and the future cost of care in personal injury actions. Often, the best evidence of dependency is that the person claiming was in fact dependent upon

---

[14] Other classes of bereaved in respect of whom the Act has been criticised are common law spouses and the children of deceased parents.
[15] See s 1(2) of the Act.
[16] [1970] AC 115.
[17] At p 176.
[18] But see **31.39** below in relation to the new power of the courts to awards periodical payments.

the deceased at the time of the death and was being maintained by him, but this is not a necessary precondition. Thus, a person may be able to show that there was a reasonable expectation of future maintenance even though that person had not in fact been dependant on the deceased at all during the deceased's lifetime.[19]

31.21 Many of the claims made under the umbrella of loss of dependency include a significant element of hypothesis in that there is inherent uncertainty as to what would have happened if the deceased had not died. For this reason, the courts will often apply percentage reductions to mathematically reached sums to reflect the hypothetical nature of the claim. Sometimes the reduction appears arbitrary, and there is an element of the judge reaching a 'jury' award, that is, putting himself in the position of a jury awarding damages and finding the sum which appears to him to be reasonable compensation, looked at overall as a lump sum, for the loss sustained. Often, therefore, different judges will reach different results in respect of losses which are indistinguishable, and this makes the position of the practitioner difficult in giving reliable advice. Advice in fatal accidents cases should therefore be cautious, and recognise that there will often be a band of reasonable awards, and that the band may, in some cases, be fairly wide, with it being unpredictable where within the band the final award will fall. Judges therefore have a large degree of latitude. The Court of Appeal will, however, interfere if it thinks that a judge has gone unreasonably outside the reasonable band.[20]

31.22 Practitioners should beware of double deductions for uncertainty. This can happen, for example, where the uncertainties have already been catered for in the evidence. Thus, the issue might be whether the deceased would have been promoted, as discussed below at **31.25**. If the chances of promotion have been fully taken into account in reaching the appropriate multiplicands and the appropriate starting dates for their application, there is no justification for any further reduction in relation to the same uncertainties, either in respect of the multiplier or in respect of the final lump sum reached. For the same reason, practitioners should be careful to ascertain what uncertainties have already been taken into account in the medical evidence, for example in relation to the deceased's expectation of life.

31.23 Under the 1976 Act, only the loss which arises out of the *relationship of dependency* will be recoverable. Thus, a person who is within the definition of a dependent may suffer a loss as a result of the death which is not, in reality, a loss associated with the dependency but was, for example, as a result of a business relationship. This was the position in *Burgess v Florence Nightingale*

---

[19] See, for example, *Kandalla v British Airways Board* [1981] QB 158 where the parents of two sisters, both doctors, killed in an air crash were able to prove that they intended to come to England from Iraq where they would have been supported by their daughters.

[20] As happened, for example, in *H v S* [2003] QB 965 where an award of £50,000 for loss of a mother's services was reduced to £37,500 by the Court of Appeal by reference to a bracket established in other cases.

Hospital for Gentlewomen[21] where the deceased wife was the claimant husband's dancing partner. Devlin J held that the value to the husband of his wife as his dancing partner, assessed at £2,500, could not be claimed. That this decision is plainly correct becomes clear when one considers that the loss would equally have been incurred if their relationship had been purely professional and they had not been married at all. Sometimes, though, the benefit will, on analysis, be shown to have derived more from the relationship of dependency even though the benefit was commercial in its nature. Thus, in *Maylon v Plummer*[22] the surviving wife had been employed by her husband's company, the company being merely a corporate vehicle for the husband's services and having no income-generating asset after the husband's death. The salary paid to the wife by the company had exceeded the market value of the work which she performed and it was held that the excess was a benefit derived from her relationship to the deceased as his wife and was therefore claimable as damages under the 1976 Act.

31.24 In making the calculation of loss, the court will often use the multiplier/multiplicand approach. The multiplicand represents the annual amount of the lost dependency and the multiplier represents the period that the dependency would have lasted. Each of these elements of the calculation will now be considered.

The multiplicand

31.25 In a typical case of the death of a husband/father who was earning and supporting his family, the multiplicand will represent the annual amount which was being spent on maintaining the family. The multiplicand need not be fixed at a particular sum. Thus, if the deceased had promotion prospects, then this can be taken into account, with the court assessing the prospects by applying a percentage to the anticipated increase to represent the chance of such promotion. Take, for example, a married man killed at the age of 30 who would have worked to age 65 and was earning £50,000 a year at the time of his death. If it can be established by evidence that he had a 75% chance of a promotion to a salary of £70,000 at age 40 and a 50% chance of further promotion to a salary of £100,000 at age 50, then the court could take as the basis for its dependency multiplicand the figure of £50,000 for the period from death to the date when the deceased would have reached age 40, then £65,000 (ie £50,000 + 75% x £20,000, the value of the promotion) for the period when the deceased would have been aged between 40 and 50, and £80,000 (ie £65,000 + 50% x £30,000, the value of the further promotion) for the remainder of the period representing the deceased's working life.[23] These figures could then also form the basis for the calculation of the lost pension which will often form part of

---

[21] [1955] 1 QB 349.
[22] [1964] 1 QB 330.
[23] This approach was approved by the Court of Appeal in a personal claim in the case of *Langford v Hebran* [2001] PIQR Q13. An example of a claim under the Fatal Accidents Act where the judge took full account of the deceased's prospects of promotion is *Robertson v Lestrange* [1950] 1 All ER 950.

the widow's claim as she would have been supported by the deceased from his pension during the period of his retirement.

31.26 It should be noted though that whilst future anticipated increases for promotions can be taken into account, future increases for inflation can not, as inflation is already taken into account in fixing the multiplier, the discount rate of 2.5% reflecting the return to be expected on investment of a lump sum *after* taking into account inflation and tax.

31.27 Once the basis for the multiplicand (the lost earnings, after deduction of tax and national insurance contributions) is established, the next stage is to ascertain how much of that sum would have been spent on the family and how much on the deceased personally – clearly, the dependency does not include the money which the deceased would have spent on himself. Of course, in any case it would be possible to do an analysis of the finances of the family, showing the cost of household expenses and to calculate the percentage of his income which the deceased spent on the family. However, a useful formula deriving from the case of *Harris v Empress Motors Ltd*[24] is now used by practitioners in the vast majority of cases. Under this formula:

(i) Where the only dependent was the deceased's widow, it is assumed that the deceased would have spent one-third of his net income on himself personally and two-thirds on his wife or on their joint expenses, so that the loss of dependency is taken as being *two-thirds* of the lost net income.

(ii) Where, on the other hand, the dependants were the widow and one or more children, then it is assumed that the deceased would have spent one-quarter of his net income on himself personally and three-quarters on his wife and children or on their joint expenses, so that the loss of dependency is taken as being *three-quarters* of the lost net income.

31.28 There are, though, typically two situations where it may not be appropriate to use the *Harris v Empress* formula but to undertake a fuller assessment of the family finances. First, where the deceased was a relatively low earner, and he had a large family. Here, it may be possible to show that money in the family was so tight that, after providing for the expenses, the deceased had almost nothing left over for himself so that the 25% reduction is inappropriate, and it should be nearer to, say, 10% or 5%. Secondly, where the deceased was a very high earner and had a very expensive hobby, such as flying helicopters. In those circumstances, the defendant might wish to argue that the formula percentages for the deceased's personal expenditure are too low, and that a higher percentage was spent by the deceased on himself and therefore a lower percentage of the deceased's net income was applied to the dependants.[25]

---

[24] [1984] 1 WLR 212. See per O'Connor LJ at pp 216–217.
[25] For further discussion of when the *Harris* formula is inappropriate, see *Owen v Martin* [1992] PIQR Q151 per Parker LJ at pp 155–157.

31.29 A further problem that arises in practice is where the surviving widow was working and continues to work, so that there would have been a notional joint income. In such cases, a useful formula derives from the decision of the Court of Appeal in *Coward v Comex*[26] where it was held that, in applying the conventional percentages laid down in *Harris v Empress*, the court should use the joint income of the husband and wife, and then deduct the whole of the wife's earnings to reach the value of the dependency. Thus, take a deceased husband who was earning £20,000 a year net, and a wife earning £10,000, with no children. Their joint income was £30,000. Applying the conventional percentages, the amount of income spent on the family was £20,000 (£30,000 x 2/3). Then, deducting the wife's income of £10,000, £10,000 is left as the value the dependency upon the deceased.

31.30 Apart from the dependency upon the deceased's income, there may also have been dependency upon the deceased's services, which had monetary value and may form part of the claim. This can arise where the deceased husband was 'useful about the house' and contributed with his services towards decorating, DIY, car servicing etc. However, it most commonly arises where the deceased was a mother looking after children. The surviving husband is then deprived of the 'housekeeping' services of his wife and the children are deprived of the 'nanny' services of their mother. The first question that arises is how those services have been replaced since the death, and will continue to be replaced in the future. If the surviving husband has actually employed a housekeeper/nanny to replace the services of his deceased's wife, then the dependency will be assessed by reference to the actual cost of such a housekeeper/nanny, both as a matter of past loss and as anticipated in the future according to his and the children's needs as they grow older.[27] Often, though, a relative such as a grandparent or aunt will step in and help to look after the children, or the surviving father will carry out the services himself. In those circumstances, the court generally uses the commercial cost of such services, had they been provided commercially, as the starting point. However, a deduction (commonly upwards of 25%) will then be applied to take into account the fact that, had a commercial provider been used, that person would have had to pay tax and national insurance upon his or her earnings, so that it is the net value which properly represents the value of the replaced services by the relative.[28] In such cases, it is now established that the damages obtained in respect of the relative's services are held in trust for the relative(s): see *H v S*.[29] It was held that, if appropriate, the court should take steps to ensure that the trust is enforced for the benefit of the gratuitous carer, but it is not clear how, in practice, the court might do this.

---

[26] Court of Appeal, 18 July 1988.
[27] As in *Bordin v St Mary's NHS Trust* [2000] Lloyd's Rep Med 287.
[28] Thus, in *Bordin's case* (above), as well as a nanny substitute being employed, relatives also assisted in the care of the children and the value of their services was assessed by reference to the commercial rate, less 35%.
[29] [2002] 3 WLR 1179.

31.31 In the case of the death of a spouse, the question of the prospects of remarriage of the surviving spouse may arise. In the case of a widow, this is specifically addressed by s 3(3) of the Fatal Accidents Act 1976 which provides:

> 'In an action under this Act where there fall to be assessed damages payable to a widow in respect of the death of her husband there shall not be taken into account the re-marriage of the widow or her prospects of re-marriage.'

31.32 The result is that the widow will recover full damages even if she has remarried, and the lost income and services of the deceased have been fully replaced by her new husband. This might be considered anomalous. Even more anomalous is that it is only in respect of the *widow's* claim that her marriage or prospects of remarriage are ignored: these must both be taken into account in respect of the claim by other dependants, including the children.[30] It is also to be noted that s 3(3) refers only to a widow's claim, not a widower's claim so it appears specifically to discriminate between men and women in this respect. It remains to be seen whether s 3(3) would survive a challenge under the Human Rights Act 1998. It has further been argued[31] that the wide interpretation of s 4 of the 1976 Act[32] now given by the courts is such that both the prospects of remarriage of a widower and the actual remarriage of a widow or widower should be ignored.

The multiplier

31.33 The other part of the equation in calculating the dependency is the multiplier. This is essentially the number of years that the dependency would have lasted, discounted at the appropriate rate (currently 2.5%). It can be seen that the multiplier will therefore vary according to the facts including the particular relationship of the dependent to the deceased. Thus, where the dependants are the deceased's children, the appropriate multiplier may depend on the child's age, whether he or she would have attended further education and generally what would have happened but for the deceased's death. On the other hand, where the dependent is the deceased's spouse, the multiplier may depend on the ages and respective expectations of life of the couple.

31.34 The calculation of the multiplier, by use of the Ogden Tables, is familiar to all practitioners who deal with personal injury claims. However, there is a crucial difference between fatal accident claims and personal injury claims: in fatal accident claims, the multiplier is calculated *at the date of death* rather than at the date of trial, as in personal injury claims.[33] Having thus reached the multiplier, the time that has elapsed between the death and trial is then deducted so as to give the remaining multiplier for the future. The calculation of the multiplier at the date of death may lead to anomalous results where there

---

[30] See *Thompson v Price* [1973] 1 QB 838.
[31] See, for example, *McGregor on Damages*, 17th edn, para 36-108.
[32] See further **31.44–31.46** below.
[33] See *Cookson v Knowles* [1979] AC 556.

has been a long interval between the death and trial[34] and has been the subject of convincing criticism.[35] However, the approach was affirmed by the Court of Appeal in *H v S*[36] endorsing the reasoning of Nelson J in *White v ESAB Ltd*[37] so that it would appear that any change in the law to a more logical approach of calculating the multiplier as at the date of trial must await either legislation or a decision of the House of Lords.

31.35 The calculation of the multiplier and its application in reaching the value of the dependency can be applied to the illustration at **31.25** above of the 30-year-old man killed. Suppose the trial comes on 2 years after the death. Using the Table 9 of the Ogden Tables, it can be seen that the appropriate multiplier for a 30 year old in relation to loss of earnings to age 65 at 2.5% is 22.81. This then needs to be reduced further to take into account contingencies other than mortality, which will depend on a variety of factors such as geographical location. If, for the sake of argument, a 5% discount is applied, then the resulting multiplier is 21.67. As two years have elapsed, the multiplier for the future is 19.67. The illustration at **31.25** postulated earnings continuing at £50,000 gross to age 40 (a further eight years), £65,000 between 40 and 50 (a further 10 years) and £80,000 between 50 and 65 (the remainder of the period). The calculation of the multiplier for the first period can be carried out using Ogden Table 28 (multiplier for term certain) and the calculation of the multiplier for the second period can be carried out using a combination of Table 28 and Table 27 (discount factors for term certain) so as to allow for the fact that the term does not start for eight years. The resulting multipliers are shown in the following Table:

Period	Multiplier	Discount	Result	5% Discount for factors other than mortality	Result
1. Trial to age 40 (8 years)	7.26	1	7.26	0.36	6.9
2. Age 40 to age 50 (10 years)	8.86	0.8207	7.27	0.36	6.91

---

[34] As in *Corbett v Barking Health Authority* [1991] 2 QB 408.
[35] See, for example, *Kemp & Kemp* at para 29–058 and *McGregor on Damages*, 17th edn at paras 36-053 to 36-055.
[36] [2003] QB 965.
[37] [2002] PIQR Q76.

Period	Multiplier	Discount	Result	5% Discount for factors other than mortality	Result
3. Age 50 to age 65					5.8[38]

31.36 It would be possible to discount the multipliers for periods 1 and 2 further in order to take into account the possibility that the deceased would have died before age 50. Otherwise, the discount for mortality which forms the basis for the Ogden multiplier of 19.61, which is the starting point, is loaded onto the final period when the multiplicand is at its highest, to the disadvantage of the dependants. This can seen when one considers that the multiplier for a term certain of 15 years is 12.54, and the discount for a loss starting in 18 years' time is 0.6412, so that the multiplier for the period from age 50 to 65 would be 8.04 (12.54 x 0.6412) compared to 5.8 in the Table above, showing that the overall loss for mortality from the multiplier is 2.24. Clearly, *some* loading on the final period is appropriate as it is more likely that, if the deceased was going to die anyway before the age of 65, it would have been in the period between age 50 and 65 (the period is longer, and the deceased would have been older), so using a rough estimate, a reasonable apportionment of the loss of 2.24 could be 1 to the final period, and 0.62 for each of the other two. This would reduce the multiplier for the first period to 6.28 (6.9 – 0.62), and the multiplier for the second period to 6.29 (6.91 – 0.62) and increase the multiplier for the final period to 7.04 (5.8 + 1.24).

31.37 From the above, it can be seen that the calculation of the multiplier under the 1976 Act is significantly more complicated than the calculation in a personal injury claim. It is not within the scope of this chapter to consider all the different variables which will affect the multiplier in a particular case. What needs to be remembered is that the claim of each dependent is separate and independent of the claim of the other dependants (although brought in a single action) and so will be influenced by the dependent's individual circumstances such as age, life expectancy, anticipated duration of the dependency etc.[39] There are also the variables relating to the individual circumstances of the deceased such as his age, life expectancy, anticipated date of retirement and the like.

31.38 Once the multipliers are ascertained, they can then be applied as appropriate to the multiplicands. Thus, in the example from **31.25**, the gross

---

[38] Ie the overall multiplier of 19.61, less the two multipliers already used which together amount to 13.81.

[39] See, for example, per Latham J in *R v Criminal Injuries Compensation Board ex parte Barrett* [1994] PIQR Q44 where he said: 'Under the Fatal Accidents Act each individual dependent has his own separate claim which he or she is entitled to have assessed separately. However, in procedural terms it is one claim brought usually by the personal representative of the estate of the deceased, which is then apportioned between the dependants.'

earnings figures needed to be 'netted' down, and then the appropriate *Harris v Empress Motors* discount applied. Assuming that, in the example, there were no children, the discount would be one-third and the value of the dependency would be calculated as follows:

Period	Gross m/cand	Net m/cand	M/er	Total	'Harris' discount	Total
1. Age 32–40	£50,000	£34,802	6.28	£218,557	£72,852	£145,705
2. Age 40–50	£65,000	£43,652	6.29	£274,571	£91,524	£183,047
3. Age 50 to 65	£80,000	£52,501	7.04	£369,607	£123,202	£246,405
Total loss of dependency						£575,157

Periodical payments

31.39 It should be noted that, by virtue of s 7 of the Damages Act 1996, fatal accident claims under the 1976 Act come within the new provisions of s 2 of the Damages Act 1996, as amended by the Courts Act 2003, which came into effect on 1 April 2005. Section 2(1) of the Damages Act 1996 provides:

> '**Periodical payments**
>
> (1) A court awarding damages for future pecuniary loss in respect of personal injury–
>
> (a) may order that the damages are wholly or partly to take the form of periodical payments, and
> (b) shall consider whether to make that order.'

31.40 It is submitted that this is particularly likely to be of use in the case of dependent minor children where there is uncertainty as to whether those children will go into further education and therefore it is uncertain at the date of trial for how long they would have been dependent on the deceased. It is to be noted that this is more than merely adjusting how the overall cake is divided up. If a *Harris v Empress* formula is adopted so that the deduction from the lost wages is only 25% for as long as there are dependent children, increasing to 33% once the children are no longer dependent, the lengthening of the dependency will accordingly have the effect of increasing the size of the cake. The provisions of s 2 and claims for periodical payments instead of a lump sum award are more fully dealt with in Chapter 21.

Apportionment

31.41 As stated,[40] whilst in procedural terms only one action is brought, the action is for the benefit of all the dependants who wish to make a claim under the 1976 Act, and therefore it is necessary for the damages awarded to be apportioned between the dependants. Where one or more of the dependants are under a disability, which will very often be the case where the deceased left dependent children, any settlement in respect of the minor children needs to be approved by the court, which will therefore need to consider the apportionment of the agreed damages and ensure that the children are to receive adequate compensation in respect of their individual claims. In practice, this is rarely a problem as the claim is often indivisible from the widow's claim in that the children will continue to live with their mother and be provided for by her out of the dependency award, and it makes little difference whether she makes such provision from the part apportioned to her from the sums apportioned to the children. However, some caution needs to be exercised as it is not inconceivable that the widow could remarry, and then die herself with the possibility of the stepfather inheriting some or all of the widow's assets including the dependency damages which in reality were earmarked for the children. Although the children will be able to make a claim under the Inheritance Act if they are not adequately provided for, this may involve some considerable loss from the estate by way of costs.

31.42 Despite the above, it is the usual practice for the court to approve an apportionment which gives a moderate lump sum to the minor children, the amount depending on their age and the various other factors. This recognises that it is in fact impossible accurately and scientifically to calculate the dependency of each dependent separately where they are all living in the same household, as this would produce a sum which exceeds the overall lump sum to be paid by the defendant which has been calculated on the conventional basis, and so some paring down is almost always necessary. Also the widow's dependency will almost always be significantly longer than that of the children. Thus, take two examples:

(1) *Lawrence v South East London HA*.[41] Deceased aged 44 at date of death, leaving wife aged 40 and 2 children aged 7 and 4. The total award was £184,104, and apportioned £15,000 to each child and £154,104 to the widow. Of the award, £92,115.68 was in respect of future loss.

(2) *Loader v Lucas*.[42] Deceased aged 24 at date of death, leaving wife aged 22 and two children aged 5 and 3. The dependency award for the future amounted to £149,460 and the children were awarded £15,750 each.

---

[40] See the reference to *R v Criminal Injuries Compensation Board ex parte Barrett* [1994] PIQR Q44 at 31.37 above.
[41] *Kemp & Kemp*, para O1-001.
[42] *Kemp & Kemp*, para O1-003.

Funeral expenses

31.43 The third head of damage under the 1976 Act, after the claims for bereavement and loss of dependency, is the claim for funeral expenses. These are not defined, and it is generally thought that the court will allow such expenses as it considers to have been reasonably incurred. The approach of Mr Benet Hytner QC, sitting as a Deputy High Court Judge in *Gammell v Wilson and Swift Ltd*[43] is commended, where he considered what was reasonable by reference to the customs and mores of the community from which the deceased came. He allowed the cost of a tombstone, preferring the decision of McNair J in *Stanton v Youlden*[44] to that of Streatfield J in *Hart v Griffiths-Jones*[45] but he disallowed the cost of mourning clothes and the wake.

Benefits resulting from death

31.44 Section 4 of the 1976 Act, as amended, provides (in respect of deaths from 1 January 1983) as follows:

> 'In assessing damages in respect of a person's death in an action under this Act, benefits which have accrued or will or may accrue to any person from his estate or otherwise as a result of his death shall be disregarded.'

31.45 In this section, it is the words 'or otherwise' which potentially make the provision extremely powerful. The question is whether those words should be given a restricted meaning or a wide interpretation. The answer to this question was provided by the Court of Appeal in *Stanley v Saddique*[46] where, after the death of his mother and the remarriage of his father, the dependent child was looked after by his stepmother who, in a most un-Cinderella-like fashion, was far more caring than the deceased had been. The question was whether the care which the boy was getting from his stepmother should be taken into account in assessing his loss as a result of his mother's death. Was the care from the stepmother a benefit accruing to the dependent child as a result of his mother death so as to be disregarded in accordance with s 4? The answer from the Court of Appeal was: 'yes'. This was by particular reference to the historical development of the law since 1908 which had introduced various exceptions to the deductibility of benefits from Fatal Accident Act damages and, unless a wide interpretation of the words 'or otherwise' was given, these developments would all have been swept away. As Purchas LJ said:[47]

> 'It seems inconceivable that Parliament would have effected a wholesale repeal of all the long-standing previous statutory exceptions from the deductions of benefits by a side wind of this sort.'

---

[43] See *Kemp & Kemp* at para 29–150.
[44] [1960] 1 WLR 543.
[45] [1948] 2 All ER 729.
[46] [1992] QB 1.
[47] Ibid at p 13F–G.

31.46 This has been followed in *R v Criminal Injuries Compensation Board ex parte K*[48] where the services of a mother, murdered by the father, were replaced by an uncle and aunt, and no deduction was made, and again in *L v Barry May Haulage*[49] where the deceased's mother's services were replaced by the support and services of the father. A different view had been taken by the Court of Appeal in *Hayden v Hayden*[50] but it is submitted that the criticisms of that case by academic writers such as Harvey McGregor and the disinclination of the Courts subsequently to follow it are such that it no longer represents good law. It has been argued that, on the same basis, the remarriage of a husband, whether actual or anticipated, is a benefit resulting from death and so need not be taken into account.[51]

Contributory negligence

31.47 The issue of contributory negligence by the deceased in a claim for damages under the 1976 Act is covered by s 5 which provides that the same reduction in damages for contributory negligence by the deceased applies to the claim by the dependants as would have applied if the action had been brought by the deceased before he died. Section 5 provides:

> 'Where any person dies as the result partly of his own fault and partly of the fault of any other person or persons, and accordingly if an action were brought for the benefit of the estate under the Law Reform (Miscellaneous Provisions) Act 1934 the damages recoverable would be reduced under section 1(1) of the Law Reform (Contributory Negligence) Act 1945, any damages recoverable in an action brought for the benefit of the dependants of that person under this Act shall be reduced to a proportionate extent.'

Interest

31.48 Finally, in relation to the dependency claim, it must be remembered that the award under the 1976 Act consists of elements of both past loss and future loss. Thus, the dependency award will comprise the loss of dependency between the date of death and the date of trial (past loss), and the loss of future dependency. In respect of all awards of past damages, the claimant can and should make a claim for interest. In respect of bereavement damages, it is usual for the court to award interest at the full special investment account rate (currently 6%) from the date of death.[52] In respect of funeral expenses, it is again usual for the court to award interest at the full rate from the date of payment of the funeral director's invoice. However, in respect of the dependency award, where that award has accrued over a number of years between death and trial, the method adopted is usually the same as is used in

---

[48] [1999] QB 1.
[49] [2002] PIQR Q35.
[50] [1992] 1 WLR 986.
[51] See **31.32** above.
[52] As in, for example, *Khan v Duncan*, unreported decision of Popplewell J of 9 March 1989 referred to in *Kemp & Kemp* at para 26–029.

personal injury actions for loss of past earnings, namely to award interest at half the special investment account rate for the period between death and trial.[53]

ACTIONS UNDER THE HUMAN RIGHTS ACT 1998

31.49 The third principal way in which damages can be claimed in respect of death is by way of an action under the Human Rights Act (HRA) 1998, which came into force on 2 October 2000. By s 6 of the 1998 Act, it is unlawful for a public authority to act in a way which is incompatible with a right protected by the European Convention on Human Rights. In the context of a fatal accident, the relevant Convention right is the 'right to life' protected by Art 2. By s 7 of the 1998 Act, a person who claims that a public authority has acted (or proposes to act) in a way which is made unlawful by s 6(1) may bring proceedings against the authority under this Act in the appropriate court or tribunal, or rely on the Convention right or rights concerned in any legal proceedings, if he is (or would be) a victim of the unlawful act. In those circumstances, s 8 of the 1998 Act provides:

'(1) In relation to any act (or proposed act) of a public authority which the court finds is (or would be) unlawful, it may grant such relief or remedy, or make such order, within its powers as it considers just and appropriate.

(2) But damages may be awarded only by a court which has power to award damages, or to order the payment of compensation, in civil proceedings.

(3) No award of damages is to be made unless, taking account of all the circumstances of the case, including
  (a) any other relief or remedy granted, or order made, in relation to the act in question (by that or any other court), and
  (b) the consequences of any decision (of that or any other court) in respect of that act,
  the court is satisfied that the award is necessary to afford just satisfaction to the person in whose favour it is made.

(4) In determining
  (a) whether to award damages, or
  (b) the amount of an award,
  the court must take into account the principles applied by the European Court of Human Rights in relation to the award of compensation under Article 41 of the Convention.

(5) A public authority against which damages are awarded is to be treated
  (a) in Scotland, for the purposes of section 3 of the Law Reform (Miscellaneous Provisions) (Scotland) Act 1940 as if the award were made in an action of damages in which the authority has been found liable in respect of loss or damage to the person to whom the award is made
  (b) for the purposes of the Civil Liability (Contribution) Act 1978 as liable in respect of damage suffered by the person to whom the award is made.

---

[53] See *Cookson v Knowles* [1979] AC 556.

(6) In this section
 court includes a tribunal
 damages means damages for an unlawful act of a public authority and unlawful means unlawful under section 6(1).'

31.50 It is thought that a successful action for damages within this section could have the effect of filling at least some of the gaps left by the Fatal Accidents Act 1976. Thus, for example, if there is a potential action under the 1998 Act for the equivalent to bereavement damages, there is no reason why it should be confined to minor children and spouses, and indeed the jurisprudence of the European Court of Human Rights (ECtHR) show it not to be.[54]

31.51 The following points and limitations to an action for damages under the 1998 Act need to be noted:

(a) The action is confined to situations where Convention rights have been breached by public authorities, but does not extend to breaches by private individuals or companies. The action will therefore be of no use in an ordinary road traffic case, but may be of use where a patient dies as a result of negligence or deliberate act by a NHS Trust which amounts to a breach of Art 2.

(b) The action is available to any person who can show himself to be a victim of the Convention breach. This has been interpreted widely by the ECtHR. The decided cases[55] show that while the court will not allow any member of the general public or general pressure group without a specific connection with the act or proposed act in question to make a claim, if a particular connection can be shown, for example because the claimant falls within a class of persons who are particularly likely to be affected by the alleged breach, then the claim will be entertained. This will encompass grandparents, brothers,[56] sisters, aunts and uncles of the deceased who all suffer bereavement as a result of a death.

(c) By s 7(5) of the 1998 Act, proceedings under s 7(1)(a) must be brought within one year of the act complained of or 'such longer period as the court or tribunal considers equitable having regard to all the circumstances'. This is a potential trap as it is significantly shorter than the usual limitation period for claims under the 1976 Act, ie 3 years form the date of death. There is as yet no jurisprudence showing how the courts might extend the limitation period for claims under the 1998 Act.

---

[54] See, for example, *Ogur v Turkey* (2001) 31 EHHR 912 where the ECtHR awarded non-pecuniary damages of 100,000 French Francs to the mother of the adult deceased who had been killed and the Turkish authorities had failed to conduct an effective judicial investigation into the circumstances of the death.

[55] See, for example, *Campbell and Cosans v United Kingdom* (1980) 3 EHRR 531 and *Klass v Germany* (1978) 2 EHRR 214.

[56] See, for example, *Kiliç v Turkey* ECtHR Application No 22492/93, 28 March 2000.

(d) The court's power to award damages under the 1998 Act is a *discretionary* power: there is no right to an award of damages, even where the claimant can prove that he has suffered 'damage' as a result of a breach of his Convention rights by a public authority. Furthermore, the 1998[57] Act makes it clear that the awarding of damages is a last resort. The concept of 'just satisfaction' is taken from Art 41 of the Convention which provides:

> 'Just Satisfaction. If the Court finds that there has been a violation of the Convention or the protocols thereto, and if the internal law of the High Contracting Party concerned allows only partial reparation to be made, the Court shall, if necessary, afford just satisfaction to the injured party.'

The wording of s 8 gives the court a wide discretion to award damages where it is necessary to do so in order to afford just satisfaction, but deprives the court of that power where an award of damages is not so necessary,[58] for example where a mere finding of breach of a Convention right is thought to be sufficient to give the claimant just satisfaction.

(e) There is no reason to think that the deceased is not a victim for the purposes of the 1998 Act and therefore it may be possible to maintain an action on behalf of the Estate. This happened in *Ozgür Gündem v Turkey*[59] where the deceased had been detained, tortured and killed by the security forces in breach of Arts 2, 3, 5 and 13. The ECtHR awarded non-pecuniary damages of £25,000 for the deceased, to be held by the applicant in trust for the deceased's heirs.

(f) Where the court does decide to award damages, there is no statutory reason why the quantum should be the same as the English domestic statutory bereavement award (currently £10,000) and it is thought that higher awards should be made in accordance with the level of awards made by the ECtHR and particularly also when higher awards are made in Scotland, as in *Shaher v British Aerospace Flying College Ltd*[60] where £20,000 was awarded to each of the parents of a son killed at 19 in a flying accident.

31.52 For a more detailed discussion of the effect of the 1998 Act, see Chapter 36 on human rights.

---

[57] See s 8(3).
[58] See, for example, per Stanley Burnton J in *R (KB) v Mental Health Appeal Tribunal* [2003] 2 All ER at para 28.
[59] (2001) 31 EHRR 5.
[60] [2003] SLT 791.

Chapter 32

ALTERNATIVE DISPUTE RESOLUTION

INTRODUCTION: THE PURPOSE AND STRUCTURE OF THIS CHAPTER

32.1 It is an obvious truism that these days very few personal injury claims ever get to court. This reflects the equally obvious truism (which happens usually also to be true!) that if a case ends up in court that means that at least one party has got it wrong. In other words, almost all cases should settle. Some will settle before they get anywhere near the Bar. However this chapter is concerned with the mechanisms for settlement of those cases in which we at the Bar are instructed, which mechanisms are collectively described as alternative dispute resolution (ADR).

32.3 To many practitioners in other fields the term ADR normally means mediation – whether by choice or under coercion from the court. However those of us who work regularly in the personal injury field are well aware that mediation is not the most common way of settling cases: it is simply one method of ADR to which we resort if the normal methods of one-to-one negotiation (whether in correspondence or at round table meetings) have failed.

32.4 The purpose of the chapter is to be of use to the personal injury practitioner when he or she is either considering the use of, or is undertaking some form of, ADR – in particular a round table meeting or a mediation. As such it is divided into three sections.

- The first section is a summary of the nature of ADR (including the most important types of ADR for present purposes – round table meetings (RTMs) and mediations – and puts ADR in context historically and procedurally; it explains the place that ADR now has within the Civil Procedure Rules 1998 (CPR).

- The second section is less legal and more practical in nature. It is intended to be helpful to personal injury practitioners who are about to undertake settlement meetings and mediations. It summarises my own views as to how best to do this, and is essentially a list of 'do's and don'ts'. As I make clear at the beginning of that section, this is an essentially personal view and I do not claim it as any more than that: I simply hope that the methods that I suggest will be of use to other practitioners.

- The third section deals in detail with a specific aspect of legal procedure which represents a potentially dangerous pitfall for the practitioner, namely the questions of costs sanctions for failure to explore ADR.

ALTERNATIVE DISPUTE RESOLUTION AND THE CPR

The position pre CPR

32.5 Even before the advent of the CPR in 1998, the overwhelming majority of personal injury cases were resolved by settlement, very often before barristers were instructed. The Bar tended only to become involved in cases which appeared likely to be contentious.

32.6 The problem with settlement that led in part to the CPR was with precisely those potentially contentious cases, far too many of them either did not settle at all (notwithstanding that in most instances they would have done had settlement been explored) or settled very late – most likely at the door of the court – resulting both in a huge waste of costs and in delays in justice for those litigants and for others whose cases might have been heard instead.

The position post CPR

32.7 The main effect of the CPR from this point of view was to increase the chances of early settlement of this hard core of cases – the ones which prior to 1998 would have been likely either to fight or only to settle at the last minute. This has been achieved by rules encouraging early negotiation and penalising failure to do undertake such negotiation.

32.8 The importance of ADR is enshrined in the CPR Part 1 (Overriding Objective). Having defined the Overriding Objective in terms that will be familiar to the readers of this work, it goes on at Part 1.4 as follows:

> 'Court's Duty to Manage Cases
>
> 1.4(1) The court must further the overriding objective by actively managing cases.
>
> (2) Active case management includes ...
>
> (e) encouraging the parties to use an alternative dispute resolution procedure if the court considers that appropriate and facilitating the use of such procedure.'

32.9 Different courts give effect to this obligation in different ways: however practitioners are likely to be aware of the fact that some County Courts have instituted their own mediation schemes which are (at least unless the court is satisfied to the contrary) necessary as part of the case management of all cases.

Definition of ADR in the CPR

32.10 The Glossary to the CPR gives a rather wider definition to the phrase 'Alternative Dispute Resolution' than one might at first expect. It is defined as a

> 'collective description of methods of resolving disputes otherwise than through the normal trial process'.

In other words, it is any form of negotiation. This would therefore include without prejudice negotiation in correspondence or by the telephone. It would include Offers made pursuant to Part 36 (which are not within the scope of this chapter). It could also include some form of Early Neutral Evaluation by an independent expert (probably a personal injury lawyer) designed to lead to compromise.

32.11 Most relevant for present purposes however are round table meetings and mediations, and it is fair to say that normally when people refer to ADR they mean one or other of those two.

Round table meetings

32.12 This is the most common method of settling personal injury disputes if such cannot be achieved by correspondence. The precise nature of the meeting will vary from case to case, but the following principles should be borne in mind. (These are, in my view, universal principles – my more personal recommendations as to how to negotiate follow in part two of this chapter.)

- It should always be expressly agreed to be without prejudice.

- It should take place at the right stage of proceedings:
  - late enough for the issues in the case to have been properly articulated and for there to be a sufficient evidential basis (including expert evidence) for resolution of those issues; but
  - not so late as to have resulted in unnecessary costs expenditure on both sides. That is crucial, because one of the main incentives to settle a case is to avoid the exponential increase in costs as trial approaches – whether one's own or (if one ultimately loses) the other side's.

- Normally (but not invariably) it should involve attendance by the lay clients as well the lawyers involved.
  - If the lay client is there, he or she might be present throughout the negotiations, or for some only of them, or for none of them (but available in another room to receive advice and give instructions). This will vary from case to case.
  - I would however say that my experience is that it is almost invariably helpful for everyone to be present at the beginning of the RTM, so as to clear the air and show keen.

- The parties will tend to set out their respective stalls in terms of the issues and then move on to negotiate.
  - Some discussion of the parties views as to the respective merits of their cases is, at least at the outset, inevitable. However in my experience detailed discussion (or assertion) of the parties' respective pleaded cases, except perhaps at the outset in order to get it dealt with, is unproductive.
  - More helpful are attempts by the parties to identify common ground;
  - In any event what is really important is that the meeting doesn't turn into a mini-court hearing.
  - For this reason it is often easier to discuss matters globally rather than by reference to individual issues.

- Even if the meeting does not result in a settlement at the time, often follow up meetings or correspondence (including resulting Part 36 correspondence) can be effective.

Mediations

32.13 A mediation is essentially a RTM chaired by an independent mediator, whose function is to facilitate settlement. Normally he or she will not evaluate the case, at least unless absolutely necessary; but rather assist the parties in resolving matters in circumstances where a RTM without a mediator is likely to be difficult.

32.14 In my experience the general rule is that mediations are not normally necessary in personal injury cases, so long as the parties' representatives are relatively experienced. They do however tend to be used where one or more of the following features is involved

- where there is some fundamental imbalance in bargaining power between the representatives,

- where there is some feature of the case (including, for example, a particular resentment or emotional aspect for one or other of the parties, which makes it more difficult than it might be for the parties be in the same room or to negotiate directly with one another), or

- where it is a multi-party action; often in such cases it is necessary to undertake two or more sets of negotiations simultaneously between different parties: this is something which can be arranged more easily and effectively with the assistance of an expert mediator.

HOW TO NEGOTIATE

Introductory comments: a personal view

32.15 What follows is intended to be no more than a summary of the principles which I use to guide me when I am undertaking negotiations, whether for a claimant of a defendant. As I have said in the Introduction to this chapter, the subject of the strategy for and tactics of negotiations is by nature a very personal one. In this area even more than in court different practitioners may have very different ways of doing things, all of which may be entirely proper in terms of professional ethics and the like. For this reason I am acutely aware of the danger that my way of doing things may not suit, or indeed seem right to, all other practitioners. However, I make no apology for this. If practitioners disagree with some or all of my advice about the tactics of negotiating, all I can say is that these principles have worked thus far for me and I would commend them as a sensible starting point for others.

Flexibility and adaptability

32.16 The whole point about negotiations is that it is not possible until they are concluded to be certain what the other side's true position is. This is why the sensible negotiator will have some flexibility in approach, in order to be able to adapt his or her strategy dependent upon what the other side does or says. It is for precisely this reason that the principles that I set out below should not remotely be regarded as rules: rather they should be seen as the starting point, the default mode, from which any departure needs to be justified by the particular circumstances of the negotiation at that point.

The twin purpose of negotiations

32.17 Always remember that there are two related but in fact quite distinct ends that you should have in mind in any negotiation: ensuring that you achieve a *just result* for your client, and ensuring that you achieve the *best available result* for your client.

It is important to recognise that these two ends are not synonymous.

(i) *Just Result?*
It is obviously important to ensure that any settlement represents a just result for your client: in other words that the amount of that proposed settlement is appropriate (and is one that you can properly advise settlement at).

(ii) *Best Available Result?*
However it is possible to have a just result that is nonetheless not necessarily the best one that was available. Thus the second aim, which is the one that your client (whether claimant or defendant/insurer) may be rather more focused on than you are, is to ensure that you have pushed the other side as far as they are prepared to go. Your client will not thank you

for achieving a just settlement if s/he feels that the other side would have been prepared to pay more / settle for less had they been squeezed. It is in this context that the flexibility of approach and the need to respond to the dynamics of the other side's position become very important.

Principles applicable to both round table meetings and mediations

32.18 The rules of thumb (for that is really what they are) set out below are intended to be applicable both to round table meetings and to mediations. The fact that the negotiation process at mediations is a little more complex and a little less predictable does not affect the principles by which the negotiation should be conducted.

Start of the meeting: dealing with any preliminary matters

32.19 It is a good idea to start by dealing with (so as to allow to be put to one side) any issues that may otherwise get in the way: for example, apologies or other personal notes. This meeting may be the first time that the claimant has ever met anyone representing the defendant. It is important to acknowledge this. If there may be no issue as to liability, an apology on behalf of the defendant (if appropriate) may do more to assist the negotiations than any other single thing.

Any discussion of legal/factual issues first

32.20 The extent to which detailed discussion of the issues in the case will be necessary at any Round Table Meeting or Mediation will vary from case to case. In some cases the issues will be very clear from the Statements of Case, and they will not need to be addressed in detail at the meeting. In other cases one or both parties will feel the need to explore them in detail.

32.21 In my experience what is important about this is that if there is to be any discussion of the issues it should be done at the outset, and before the negotiation proper commences. This is for two related reasons.

32.22 First, it reduces the chances of (i) the parties being at cross-purposes as to the issues during the course of the negotiation itself, and also (ii) of new issues being raised during the negotiations, both of which can create difficulties in the settlement process.

32.23 Secondly, it means that the parties can commence the negotiation process proper having had all these things in mind (and having discussed them and given instructions on the basis of them – see immediately below). In other words, it means that the decisions as to the nature of the negotiations themselves are made both on as informed a basis and as early as possible.

Authorities and instructions

32.24 It is important that by the time the negotiations proper commence you have a clear picture as to your current instructions. (Of course those instructions may change thereafter in response to what the other side says, but that is a different matter.)

32.25 This may well mean having an authority up to (if acting for the defendant) or down to (if acting for the claimant) a certain figure – in other words a 'bottom line'. However, the client may very well not be prepared to give any authority at this stage – preferring rather to await events. Even in that case it is nonetheless important, for a number of reasons upon which I elaborate below, to have a game plan for the negotiations – to have discussed possible bottom lines in advance.

The negotiations themselves

The starting point

32.26 It is perhaps obvious, but important to remember, that there are three things that shape the dynamics of any negotiation:

(i) the parties' respective starting points;

(ii) where they want to move to (ie their intended bottom line); and

(iii) how many steps it takes them to get there.

32.27 It is just as obvious and just as important to bear in mind that those dynamics are also shaped by the fact that neither party knows for sure what the other side's position as to any of these three things is until it declares it. That is of course what gives the uncertainty to the negotiation.

Stages in the negotiation

32.28 Thus, particular points to bear in mind are the following:

Plan strategy in advance

(1) Even if there is no clear instruction at the outset as to what the limit of authority is, it is crucial to have a plan as to your own client's position on each of (i)–(iii) above at the outset. In particular, it is important to decide where to start by reference to where one wants to end up: see below. Bear in mind the need to respond to the other side

(2) That said, it is of course impossible to plan everything in advance, because one's strategy has to depend upon and accommodate the other side's negotiation positions – which may be sophisticated and intelligent or may

be the absolute opposite. This is where the element of flexibility comes in: the advance plan should not be regarded as writ in stone.

Who bids first?

(3) Who makes the first offer? The traditional view has always been that that it is a disadvantage to go first because you are showing your hand before knowing what the other side's opening bid is.

This may often be sound thinking: particularly if you have absolutely no idea what the other side might offer (where, for example, the other side is the defendant, and it has not even articulated a pleaded case by Counter-Schedule yet – as all too often happens). In such circumstances there can be a real concern that one's own offer will concede too much – that one will be 'bidding against oneself'.

However, my experience is that in most cases, at least where the issues are clear and the parties' positions are properly defined, it is a positive advantage to go first – whether you are acting for claimant or defendant – so long as you have a clear strategy as to the negotiation. This is because you are simultaneously (i) controlling the process (rather than simply being responsive), and (ii) sending out the signal that you are prepared to negotiate, at least to some extent. As to the precise extent and the nature of the signal that you give – see 4 and 5 below.

What should the first offer be?

(4) The important point here is, again, that you and your clients need to have a view as to your own answers to all of questions (i) – (iii) at the outset. Where you start should depend upon where you want to end up and a recognition of the effect on the other side of the signals that you give out (i.e. by how much you are prepared to move) in the meantime.

The traditional view has always been that the first offer should be as high (if acting for a claimant) or as low (if acting for a defendant) as feasible – i.e. as close as possible to one's pleaded case.

In my view this traditional view is wrong, unless (again) you have no idea at all as to what the other side's true position is. The point here is that while an offer that is very close to your best case may look initially like a sign of strength, any 'strong' signal that it gives out is immediately lost once you have moved substantially from it by any subsequent offer(s) – which by definition you are likely to have to do if your true bottom line is in fact radically different from your best case.

Thus in my view it is better to start with something much nearer your assessment of the true value of the case – i.e. nearer to your bottom line – and then to make it clear, by any subsequent negotiation (see below) that you are not prepared to move far from it.

(Of course if your bottom line is in fact pretty well the same as your pleaded case then by definition you will not be offering anything at the outset that is radically different from the pleaded case. But the important point there is that you are still determining your opening offer by reference to your bottom line, and not simply by reference to your pleaded case.)

This combination has the double advantage (similar to that which comes from bidding first – see 3 above) that you are showing both (a) a preparedness to compromise but also (b) that you are not being a pushover.

In my experience this, in turn, often engenders a more open and straightforward response from the other side – if they see that you are prepared to be open and straightforward they will do the same.

Subsequent offers: not too many

(5) You do not want to make too many moves from your first offer. If the other side thinks that the process is open-ended it will be harder to get to its bottom line as quickly or as obviously as one would like. Obviously there is no hard and fast rule here, given that one is responding in the context of the individual case and the circumstances of the negotiations, but in my experience two or three subsequent offers are normally enough.

Subsequent offers: not too much movement

(6) On the thinking set out at 4 above you have made your initial offer by reference to your bottom line rather than simply as close to your pleaded case as possible *precisely in order* to reduce the need for substantial movement thereafter. It follows that the second offer should not be substantially different from the first, and should certainly not be anything like as far from your first offer as that was from your pleaded case. The point is that you want to give the clear impression that your first offer was a genuine attempt to settle and not simply a negotiation stance – that your attitude towards accommodation of the other side's case was represented by that offer and is not still to come in any subsequent offers.

Third and subsequent offers: reduce extent of movement

(7) Furthermore, and for similar reasons, each further move should ideally be smaller in amount than the last – to maintain the extent of the movement does not show any particular endgame in mind: the other side must not get the signal that you might be prepared to move indefinitely!

Respond to the other side's stance – movement or otherwise

(8) Finally, and crucially – again, what you do and say must be a response to what the other side does and says. Slavishly following the principles set out above will get you nowhere if you haven't also borne in mind what the significance of the other side's movement (or lack of it) may be.

Thus if, for example, the other side has not moved substantially from their pleaded case, you need to work out whether you think that is because they have a genuine perception that their case is very strong (and possibly ask whether that is right) or whether this is simply a negotiation stance. If you decide that it is the latter, then you also have to decide whether you withdraw from the process or find some other way of convincing them to move their position. My experience is that that can best be achieved by following the principles set out above.

Illustration

32.29 I hope that the following example will demonstrate the principles outlined above.

The figures

Imagine you act for a claimant in a personal injury case, and that the relevant figures (in broad overall terms) are as follows:

- Your Schedule of Loss puts the claim at £1m (inclusive of all heads of damage).

- Your assessment of your best realistic case is £850,000.

- Your assessment of the likely result is in the range of £600,000 – 700,000, say £650,000.

- Your assessment of your worst realistic case is £450,000

- The defendant's Counter-Schedule figure is £300,000
  What are you aiming at?

The first thing to do is to decide on the bottom line – ie what you would advise the claimant to settle at / what instructions he gives you in the light of that advice. Assume the answer is £650,000 – ie the middle of the range of likely results.

Who bids first? What is the offer?

As I have already said the traditional answer is that you want the defendant to bid first. But that gives rise to a possible problem. If you allow that to happen, the defendant's representatives are quite likely (in the absence of any offer from you at all) simply to apply the traditional approach and come in with an offer at say £350,000.

The disadvantage for you in allowing them do that is that you may then be left with rather a difficult choice:

(a) You could come back in kind – ie with an offer in excess of your best realistic case, at say £850,000. However if you do that the gap is then £500,000, and looks unbridgeable; this in turn means that unless the other side makes a very substantial move you are going to have either (i) to call a day to negotiations or (ii) look weak by moving a long way from your first bid

(b) Alternatively you could then apply the principles set out above and offer say £700,000 – in which case, because of the fact that the defendant has gone first the 'negotiation ground' is artificially and uncomfortably low for the claimant – £350,000 as against £700,000, mid-point £525,000.

Therefore, and for the reasons set out above, my view is that it is much better for the claimant to bid first, and to do so with an expressly stated realistic offer of £750k (not £900,000 or even £850,000).

What happens thereafter?

The defendant will react to this privately in one of two possible ways. Either (i) it will take the claimant's opening offer – expressly stated as being intended to be a realistic one rather than a negotiation stance – as just that, and make a sensible offer – say £550,000 – or (ii) it will think (initially at least) that the claimant's opening offer is a sign of weakness and offer something like the £350,000 that might well have been its opening offer had it made one (see immediately above).

The key point in all this is that *either way* you come back on behalf of the claimant with an offer of £700,000 – i.e. only £50,000 less than your opening bid. That will show them that you are not prepared to go substantially below that, whatever approach they have.

Depending on what they do you either go straight to £650,000 after that, or make intermediate offers (say £670,000) in order to see whether they will bite at a higher figure, being prepared to go down to £650,000 thereafter if necessary.

I hope that it is plain that the point of all this is that you have demonstrated quite quickly and effectively that such movement as you are prepared to make was done in the early stage of the negotiations, and that you are unlikely to be moved substantially at any later stage. That is the best way of ensuring that you get the most out of the other side.

COSTS SANCTIONS FOR FAILURE TO NEGOTIATE

Introductory comments

32.30 The growth in importance of ADR since the advent of the CPR was as obvious as it was rapid. This was a reflection both of the modern approach to litigation and of the terms of the CPR. Very soon, anyone dealing with personal injury litigation became aware of the need at least to consider ADR in any particular case. Furthermore nearly all practitioners saw that as a good thing. We welcomed it because settlement without having to go to court, however achieved, must in the huge majority of cases be a good thing for the client, whether claimant or defendant, and (in the case of the latter) whether insurer or government department, in terms of savings both of expense and human emotion. Nonetheless, at times the notion that some form of ADR was a prerequisite in all cases seemed to get out of hand – the cart appeared at times to be pulling the horse.

32.31 It was of course no surprise when the courts began to exercise their new powers of case management in imposing costs sanctions upon the parties in relation to their conduct of cases. By the same token, it should have been no surprise, given the terms of the CPR, that they would do so by reference not simply to the conduct of the trial process, but also by reference to extra-trial aspects of the litigation such as Part 36 Offers and even without prejudice negotiation.

32.32 However it certainly was a surprise to many when the courts gave the appearance of wishing to impose sanctions on a party who had refused to go to ADR simply for that reason; doing so even where that party felt that on the merits it was justified in such refusal because – quite simply – the other side's case was hopeless.

32.33 Such sanctions began to be imposed on 'conduct' grounds pursuant to CPR Part 44.3(4) and (5), even where the successful party justified the refusal to negotiate on the basis of the strength of its case: see for example

- *Dunnett v Railtrack plc*;[1]

- *Royal Bank of Scotland v S of S for Defence*;[2]

- *Hurst v Leeming*.[3]

32.34 Practitioners began to feel uneasily as if they were under pressure to advise a client (claimant or defendant) to go to ADR in every case, and whatever the merits, simply in order to avoid the possibility of costs sanctions for failing to do so even if the case was won. That felt wrong, and the law seemed wrong-headed accordingly.

32.35 If that tide was flowing, it now seems to have turned. This turn was first signalled by the Court of Appeal, in relation specifically to a successful party's refusal to go to mediation so long as that refusal was reasonable, in the judgment of the court given by Dyson LJ in *Halsey v Milton Keynes General NHS Trust*.[4] More recently and more emphatically, the application of that approach to refusal to engage in any sort of negotiation (including responding to repeated Part 36 Offers) was made clear in *Daniels v the Commissioner of Police for the Metropolis*.[5]

32.36 The combined effect of these cases is, quite simply, that a party who refuses to negotiate and is then successful at trial will not be penalised as to costs for its refusal to negotiate *if* the court is satisfied that that refusal was not unreasonable. Whether that was so in any particular case remains of course a

---

[1] [2002] EWCA Civ 303; [2002] 1 WLR 2434.
[2] (Unreported) 14 May 2003.
[3] [2003] 1 Lloyd's Rep 379 (for relevant dicta).
[4] [2004] EWCA Civ 576, [2004] 1WLR 3002.
[5] [2005] EWCA Civ 1312; (2005) *The Times*, October 28.

question of fact. However the welcome feature of all this is the clear statement of principle made by the Court of Appeal that it wishes actively and positively to discourage attempts by the other side's advisors to 'blackmail' a claimant or a defendant with a strong case into a negotiation (and possibly a settlement) that did not reflect the merits.

The rules: CPR, r 44.3

32.37 As always the court's decisions on costs are a matter of discretion. The rules for the exercise of this discretion are now set out in CPR Part 43. This states as relevant as follows (emphasis in italics added).

'44.3 (1) The court has *discretion* as to –

(a) *whether costs are payable by one party to another*;
(b) *the amount of those costs*; and
(c) when they are to be paid.

(2) If the court decides to make an order about costs –

(a) *the general rule is that the unsuccessful party will be ordered to pay the costs of the successful party*; but
(b) *the court may make a different order*.

(4) In deciding what order (if any) to make about costs, *the court must have regard to all the circumstances, including* –

(a) *the conduct of all the parties*;
(b) whether a party has succeeded on part of his case, even if he has not been wholly successful; and
(c) any payment into court or admissible offer to settle made by a party which is drawn to the court's attention (whether or not made in accordance with Part 36).

(5) *The conduct of the parties includes* –

(a) *conduct before, as well as during, the proceedings* and in particular the extent to which the parties followed any relevant pre-action protocol;
(b) whether it was reasonable for a party to raise, pursue or contest a particular allegation or issue;
(c) the manner in which a party has pursued or defended his case or a particular allegation or issue; and
(d) whether a claimant who has succeeded in his claim, in whole or in part, exaggerated his claim.'

The principles in the rules summarised

32.38 The relevant principles for present purposes can, it seems to me, be summarised as follows.

(a) The starting point is the '**general rule**' that the **unsuccessful party pays** the successful party's costs (r 44.3(2)(a)).

(b) In deciding what order to make (and therefore whether to follow the general rule or not) the court must take into account **all the circumstances** (r 44.3(4)).

(c) The circumstances include in particular (but of course are not limited to)
 – the **conduct** of the parties before trial (r 44.3(4)(a)); and
 – any **admissible offers**, whether made by Part 36 or otherwise, that are drawn to the court's attention (r 44.3(4)(c).

(d) Specifically as to that last point, it is worth noting in passing that the reference in r 44.3(4)(c) must be intended to allow for at least the possibility of relevance for those purposes of an *ineffective* Part 36 offer – whether made by a successful claimant or a successful defendant. It cannot be contemplating simply an *effective* Part 36 offer, since in that case the wholly different Part 36 regime would itself be being invoked, and there would be no need to look to Part 44.3 for this purpose of the exercise of discretion on costs.

32.39 However the general question which still arose (and to which the rules themselves give no answer) is as follows: To what extent should the courts regard a successful party's (i) failure to negotiate, or, particularly (ii) refusal to negotiate in the face of requests by the other side to do so, as conduct for the purposes of CPR, r 44.3(4) and (5) that justifies departure from the normal rule on costs?

Halsey

32.40

At para 2 if the judgment of the court in *Halsey* Dyson LJ identified the main issue as follows.

'2 These two appeals raise a question of some general importance: when should the court impose a costs sanction against a successful litigant on the grounds that he has refused to take part in an alternative dispute resolution ('ADR')? There seems to be some uncertainty as to the approach that should be adopted in answering this question: it has been the subject of consideration by courts on a number of occasions.'

The general ratio of the court's ruling was then set out at para 13 and following:

'13 In deciding whether to deprive a successful party of some or all of his costs on the grounds that he has refused to agree to ADR, it must be borne in mind that such an order is an exception to the general rule that costs should follow the event. In our view, the burden is on the unsuccessful party to show why there should be a departure from the general rule. The fundamental principle is that such departure is not justified unless it is shown (the burden being on the unsuccessful party) that the successful party acted unreasonably in refusing to agree to ADR. We shall endeavour in this judgment to provide some guidance as to the factors that should be considered by the court in deciding whether a refusal to agree to ADR is unreasonable.

14 We make it clear at the outset that it was common ground before us (and we accept) that parties are entitled in an ADR to adopt whatever position they wish, and if as a result the dispute is not settled, that is not a matter for the court. ...

16 In deciding whether a party has acted unreasonably in refusing ADR, these considerations should be borne in mind. ... The question whether a party has acted unreasonably in refusing ADR must be determined having regard to all the circumstances of the particular case. We accept the submission of the Law Society that factors which may be relevant to the question whether a party has unreasonably refused ADR will include (but are not limited to) the following: (a) the nature of the dispute; (b) the merits of the case; (c) the extent to which other settlement methods have been attempted; (d) whether the costs of the ADR would be disproportionately high; (e) whether any delay in setting up and attending the ADR would have been prejudicial; and (f) whether the ADR had a reasonable prospect of success.'

32.41 Ultimately the general principles which could be derived from the Court of Appeal's ruling in Halsey, which was of course concerned specifically with failure to *mediate*, were as follows:

(a) that a successful party would not be deprived of its costs because it had refused to mediate, if that **refusal was not unreasonable;**

(b) that the refusal would not be unreasonable if the successful party **reasonably believed that it had a very strong case;**

(c) that the refusal would not be unreasonable where the successful party **reasonably believed that mediation would have had little prospect of success;** and as to that;

(d) the **burden of proof** in relation to such an issue was on the **unsuccessful party** to prove that mediation did have a reasonable prospect of success, rather than on the successful party to disprove it; but

(e) the successful party was **not entitled to rely upon its own unreasonable obduracy** in contesting that.

Daniels

32.42 This was a stark case of its type: it came to the Court of Appeal because (a) the claim was worth a very small amount of money compared with the costs outlay, and (b) the successful defendant had repeatedly made it clear that it was fighting the case on principle, and would not engage in any negotiation.

The trial

32.43 Up to and during the trial it was a typical and uncomplicated, albeit hard-fought, personal Injury action.

- The claimant, who was an experienced horsewoman serving in the Mounted Branch, sued the defendant, her employer, for injuries sustained while on her annual training course, arising out of a fall from her horse.

- The trial was listed for both liability and quantum.

- Quantum was agreed at £7,000 (subject to liability) just before the trial started.

- When informed of this agreement the judge made it very clear that at the end of the case, whatever the result, he would require for the purposes of costs an explanation as to why the case had had to come to trial.

- The trial duly proceeded on liability alone. The claimant failed and her claim was dismissed. (It was common ground at the appeal that the defendant won comprehensively on all of the numerous issues, many of which, as the judge pointed out, depended on his assessment of the claimant's credibility.)

The costs issues at trial

32.44 At the conclusion of the trial the claimant contended that the defendant should not get all of its costs. Her principal arguments for this were:

(a) the size of the claim as compared with the costs expended (which were in total of the order of £50,000) and

(b) the fact that the defendant had refused to negotiate, even in the face of two (rejected) claimant's Part 36 Offers (of less than the ultimately agreed quantum of the claim in the event of a finding of liability), stating rather that it insisted on taking the case to trial on liability.

32.45 The defendant duly gave its reasons (in the form of a memorandum from the Met Police claims handlers) for wishing to take the case to trial rather than seeking to settle on a 'commercial' basis, notwithstanding the limited quantum. These were

(a) that there was historically a claims culture in the Mounted Branch, and that it had very compelling evidence that its robust stance in refusing to settle unmeritorious claims had led to a substantial fall off in such claims and

(b) the fact that this claim was brought in the context of other injury claims being pursued against it by this claimant.

32.46 The judge accepted these reasons as justified, and awarded the defendant its costs in full in the normal way. He stated in terms:

'I have taken the view that the Claimant is very much the author of her own misfortune in this litigation. The ordinary rule of course is that costs must follow the event and I have to have reasons to depart from that.'

He went on to find that there were no such reasons here.

The Court of Appeal's ruling

32.47 The claimant appealed against the judge's order on costs. While she did raise other issues, it was common ground at the appeal that the principal basis of the appeal against the order remained (a) the size of the claim and (b) the defendant's refusal to negotiate at all, and stated insistence on going to trial.

32.48 In his leading judgment Dyson LJ, having stated the background, identified the issues and summarised the terms and effect of CPR, r 44.3. He went on as follows (and it is worth setting out this part of his judgment in full):

'22 I find it difficult to envisage circumstances in which it would ever be right to deprive a successful defendant of some or all of his costs solely on the grounds that he refused to accept a claimant's Part 36 offer. Take the present case, which is in many ways a paradigm case. The claimant alleges negligence and claims damages which are agreed at £7,000. The defendant is strongly of the view that the claim is without foundation and makes no Part 36 payment of offer. The claimant makes a Part 36 offer of £4,000 which the defendant rejects. The claim is dismissed by the judge. In my judgment there is no basis for saying that the defendant's refusal of the claimant's part 36 offer is conduct which should be taken into account by the judge to deprive the defendant of some or all of his costs.

23 The inference to be drawn from Parts 36 and 44.3 is that (notwithstanding the terms of Part 44.3(4)(c)) the mere fact that a successful defendant has refused a claimant's Part 36 offer cannot of itself be a sufficient reason for departing from the general rule and depriving the defendant of costs.

24 Another way of putting the same point is to say that it is only unreasonable conduct by a successful party that may be relied on by a court to deprive him of costs [Dyson LJ then made reference to the facts of *Halsey* and the Court's judgment there in relation mediation and continued].

25 Although no question of mediation has been raised in the present case, in my judgment the same general approach should be adopted. I do not see how an unsuccessful claimant can show that a successful defendant acted unreasonably simply on the grounds that he refused to accept the Part 36 offer.

26 In the course of her submissions [counsel for the claimant] made it clear that this was not in fact how she was putting her argument. Her case is that the court can depart from the general rule where a defendant unreasonably refuses even to enter into negotiations to attempt to settle a case. I would accept this general proposition, but I would emphasise the word "unreasonably". The difficult question is: in what circumstances is a refusal to negotiate unreasonable? This will depend on all the circumstances of the case. ...

28 The fundamental question, therefore, is whether by indicating to a claimant that he has no wish to negotiate at all (as occurred in the present case) a

defendant is acting so unreasonably that he should be deprived of some or all of his costs [Dyson LJ then referred to the Court of Appeal judgment in *Halsey* and in particular passages therein relating to two of the factors there identified as relevant: "the merits of the case" and "the question of whether mediation had a prospect of success", and continued]

30   The first of these factors is particularly germane in the present case. It seems to me to be entirely reasonable for a defendant, especially a public body such as the police, to take the view that it will contest what it reasonably considers to be an unfounded claim in order to deter other, similarly unfounded, claims. It is well known that large organisations often make payments to buy off claims which they consider to be speculative, if not wholly without foundation, in order to avoid the trouble and expense of contesting them. This propensity, coupled with the fact that claims are now funded on a "no win, no fee" basis, may, in part, be responsible for fuelling what has been described in some quarters as a "compensation culture".

31   If defendants, who routinely face what the consider to be unfounded claims, wish to take a stand and contest them rather than make payments (even nuisance value payments) to buy them off, then the court should be slow to characterise such conduct as unreasonable so as to deprive defendants of their costs if they are ultimately successful.

32   As the judge recognised, this may mean (and in the present case did mean) that litigation is sometimes contested whose costs are wholly disproportionate to the sums claimed. The court will always seek to ensure that all litigation is conducted in a reasonable and proportionate manner. But that does not mean that, in a case where costs are necessarily disproportionate to the amount claimed, a defendant is acting unreasonably and should in some way be penalised in costs if he reasonably considers that the claim is without foundation and insists on a trial, any more than it means that a claimant is acting unreasonably and should in some way be penalized for issuing proceedings in respect of a claim, the cost of which is unavoidably out of all proportion to its size.

33   In my view, the judge's exercise if discretion in this case was unimpeachable. He was fully entitled to decide the issue of costs in the way that he did. Claimants who bring unfounded claims may, in certain circumstances, persuade a court to deprive successful defendants of their costs. But they will only succeed on the basis if a refusal to negotiate if that refusal was unreasonable. In the present case the judge was amply justified in holding that the defendants' refusal was not unreasonable.'

Conclusions

32.49 The main point to make about this judgment is that it is not in any sense 'anti-ADR', as some have painted it. It simply gives welcome judicial confirmation of something that all practitioners are aware of: that there are some cases in which it would be reasonable to refuse to engage in negotiation with the other side.

32.50 The trenchancy of the judgment in *Daniels* speaks for itself. It was undoubtedly very welcome news for defendants and their insurers facing wholly unmeritorious claims; the clear effect of the final four paragraphs of Dyson LJ's judgment is a direct attack on the compensation culture and the bringing of unmeritorious claims in the hope of achieving a 'nuisance value' settlement. However, it was also good news for claimants with cast-iron cases who did not wish to be penalised in costs for (reasonably) refusing to negotiate with insurers intent on reducing a claim below its proper level.

Part 4
COSTS

Chapter 33

COSTS

INTRODUCTION

33.1 At the time of implementation of the Civil Procedure Rules 1998 (CPR), Lord Woolf said that the change to the civil procedure relating to costs, in particular the introduction of summary assessment of costs, was one of the most significant in the CPR.[1] This observation has been borne out. With the introduction of CFAs (dealt with in a subsequent chapter), the possibility of costs capping, and the routine summary assessment of costs, it can truly be said that the subject of costs has been one of the most interesting procedural developments post-CPR.

33.2 What follows is a summary of the rules about costs, where still relevant, decisions made under the old rules are cited in this text. Any such authorities must be treated with caution since they pre-date the CPR, which has had a pervasive impact on every area of procedural change. The Rules themselves are accompanied by the Costs Practice Direction to CPR Parts 43–48 which sets out the new costs vocabulary and relevant definitions, as well as creating obligations on the parties, e.g. the provision of costs estimates.

THE GENERAL RULE

33.3 The general rule is that costs are in the discretion of the court which shall have full power to determine by whom, to what extent, and when costs are to be paid.[2] The general rule in the High and County Court is expressly set out in CPR Part 44.

33.4 That general rule is re-stated at CPR, r 44.3(2) as follows:

'(2) If the court decides to make an order about costs –

(a) the general rule is that the unsuccessful party will be ordered to pay the costs of the successful party; but
(b) the court may make a different order.'

---

[1] CPR Costs Regime and the Bar – Seminar 19 July 1999 at Lincoln's Inn.
[2] See Supreme Court Act 1981, s 51(1) and (3) and CPR, r 44.3(1).

33.5 As Hoffmann LJ observed in *McDonald v Horn*,[3] referring to its predecessor Ord 62 r.3, this rule reflects a basic rule of English civil procedure, that a successful litigant has a prima facie right to his costs. This general approach, which goes back at least 130 years, is deeply embedded in the judicial mindset. Despite the rules of the CPR which now allow for costs of separate issues, and Lord Woolf's judicial observations in this regard[4] this general rule is the overriding principle applied to the award of costs.

33.6 CPR Parts 43–48 and the associated Practice Direction set out the specific rules about costs, in particular: the court's discretion and the circumstances to be taken into account when exercising the discretion as to costs (CPR 44.3); the basis of assessment (CPR 44.4); factors to be taken into account in deciding the amount of costs (CPR 44.5); procedure for assessing costs (CPR 44.7); special situations (CPR 44.13); courts' powers in relation to misconduct (CPR 44.14); summary assessment procedure (PD to CPR 47.4); fixed costs (CPR 45); fast track trial costs (CPR 46); procedure for detailed assessment of costs (CPR 47).

ENTITLEMENT TO ASSESSMENT AND RECOVERY

33.7 The 'indemnity principle' has historically been the backbone to an order for the recovery of costs. That principle is that a successful party cannot recover from the unsuccessful party a sum in excess of the successful party's liability to his solicitor. It was considered by the Court of Appeal in *General of Berne Insurance Co v Jardine Reinsurance Management Ltd*[5] May LJ said (at 304):

> 'The principle is simply that costs are normally to be paid in compensation for what the receiving party has or is obliged himself to pay. They are not punitive and should not enable the receiving party to make a profit.'

33.8 Thus in general terms a successful party is only entitled to recover those costs which he is (legally) obliged to pay his solicitor.[6] However, after the introduction of CFAs and the fixed costs rules under CPR Part 45, it is now clear that the indemnity principle is abrogated in respect of certain claims for costs.[7] Furthermore, the abolition of the indemnity principle to all litigation is actively being considered by the Civil Justice Council. Such abolition is likely to require amendment to primary legislation.

---

[3] [1995] ICR 685.
[4] *AEI Rediffusion Music Ltd v Phonographic Performance Ltd* [1999] 1 WLR 1507, CA.
[5] [1998] 2 All ER 301.
[6] *Gundry v Sainsbury* [1910] 1 KB 645; but see the amendment to SCA 1981, s 51 introduced by Access to Justice Act 1999, s 31.
[7] *Mohammed Butt v Christi Nizami* QBD Simon J, Master Hurst, Jason Rowley, 9 February 2006 (fixed costs).

33.9 Although the indemnity principle is overridden in certain cases of legally assisted parties, it is not undermined merely because the successful litigant is a member of a trade union whose claim is being pursued with financial support from his union.[8] Once the client-solicitor relationship is established there is a presumption that the client will be personally liable for the costs. That presumption can, however, be rebutted if it is established that there is an express or implied agreement, binding on the solicitor that the client would not have to pay those costs in any circumstances.[9] In *Bailey v IBC Vehicles*[10] the solicitors for a defendant in a personal injury action which had settled before trial objected to the hourly rate and mark up specified in the bill of costs submitted by the union on Claimant's behalf and requested evidence to prove that there was no breach of the indemnity principle. The request was dismissed but Judge J indicated that in future, due to the growth of conditional fees and the increased interest in challenging such bills of costs, the extension of the client care letter and contentious business agreements, or a brief written explanation should normally be attached to the bill of costs in order to avoid unnecessary litigation. With the introduction of summary assessments of costs, and the potential for obtaining an order for costs at an interim hearing on behalf of a party whose personal liability for costs is contingent on the final outcome of the case, it is thought that some brief explanation of the entitlement to costs[11] should accompany the costs schedule. If the personal liability for costs is contingent upon the final outcome of the case, there may be a strong argument for postponing the summary assessment.[12]

EXERCISE OF DISCRETION

33.10 In exercising its discretion on costs the court is required to have regard to all the circumstances[13] including:

(a) the conduct of all the parties;

(b) whether a party has succeeded on part of his case, even if he has not been wholly successful; and

(c) any payment into court, or admissible offer to settle made by a party which is drawn to the court's attention (whether or not made in accordance with Part 36).

---

[8] See *Adams v London Improved Motor Coach Builders Ltd* [1921] KB 499; followed in *R Miller (Raymond)* [1983] 1 WLR 1056.
[9] See Lloyd J in *R v Miller (Raymond)* [1983] 3 WLR 1056 at 1061.
[10] [1998] 3 All ER 570.
[11] If solicitor and own client costs are claimed then it ought to include sufficient details of base costs and percentage uplift to answer the court's enquiry under CPR, r 48.(2), see CPR, r 48.9.
[12] CPR PD 44.4.4(1)(b).
[13] CPR, r 44.3(4).

CONDUCT OF THE PARTIES

33.11 'Conduct' is defined as including:

(a) conduct before as well as during the proceedings and the extent to which both parties followed any relevant pre-action protocol;

(b) whether it was reasonable for a party to raise, pursue or contest a particular allegation or issue;

(c) the manner in which a party has pursued or defended his case in relation to a particular allegation; and

(d) whether a claimant who has succeeded in his claim, in whole or in part, exaggerated his claim.[14]

33.12 Some commentary is required on these rules. Firstly 'conduct' has been considered in a number of cases and means essentially the unreasonable conduct of the litigation in all its aspects. For example, in *Base Metal Trading Ltd v Shamurin (No 3)*,[15] the defendant succeeded at trial but had raised unsuccessfully issues which had extended the trial by some 14 days. No order for costs was appropriate. In *Lawal v Northern Spirit Ltd*,[16] a litigant in person's offensive language in correspondence was not such as to entitle the Defendant to a reduction in her costs. Secondly, and of importance to a party wishing to raise such an issue, is *Aaron v Shelton*,[17] where it was held that if a losing party considers he should not have to pay all or part of the successful party's costs on the ground of misconduct he must make such application to the trial judge. If he does not do so, it will not then be open to him to make such application to the costs judge on assessment.

33.13 The Costs Practice Direction to Part 44.3 out a non-exhaustive list of orders which the court may make.[18] CPR, r 44.3.8 provides that the court may order an amount to be paid on account *before* the costs are assessed. This power was considered in *Mars v Teknowledge*,[19] where it was held by Jacob J that the court should, on a rough and ready basis, normally order an interim payment of some lesser amount being such sum as that party would almost certainly collect. That case emphasises the principle aim of the CPR regime relating to costs, namely to bring home to the parties at an early stage in the proceedings both the costs and risks of litigation. In practice an interim order for costs payable forthwith may frequently either stay or dispose of proceedings

---

[14] CPR, r 44.3(5).
[15] [2003] EWHC 2602 (Comm).
[16] [2004] EWCA Civ 208.
[17] [2004] EWHC 1162 (QB).
[18] See table below in text.
[19] (1999) *The Times*, 8 July.

altogether. In some cases however the issue of costs may be so complex that the proper course is to adjourn the assessment of costs to a costs judge.[20]

EFFECT OF SPECIFIC COSTS ORDERS

33.14 The Practice Direction to CPR 44.3.8 sets out in tabular form, repeated below, the effect of specific orders which the court may make:

Term	Effect
Costs Costs in any event	The party in whose favour the order is made is entitled to the costs in respect of the part of the proceedings to which the order relates, whatever other costs orders are made in the proceedings.
Costs in the case Costs in the application	The party in whose favour the court makes an order for costs at the end of the proceedings is entitled to his costs of the part of the proceedings to which the order relates.
Costs reserved	The decision about costs is deferred to a later occasion, but if no later order is made the costs will be costs in the case.
Claimant's/defendants' costs in the case/application	If the party in whose favour the costs order is made is awarded costs at the end of the proceedings, that party is entitled to his costs of the part of the proceedings to which the order relates. If any other party is awarded costs at the end of the proceedings, the party in whose favour the costs order is made is not liable to pay the costs of any other party in respect of the part of the proceedings to which the order relates.

---

[20] See, for example, *Dyson Appliances Ltd v Hoover Ltd* [2003] EWHC 624 (Ch) per Laddie J.

Term	Effect
Costs thrown away	Where, for example, a judgment or order is set aside, or the whole or part of any proceedings are adjourned, the party in whose favour the costs order is made is entitled to the costs which have been incurred as a consequence. This includes the costs of: (a) preparing for and attending any hearing at which the judgment or order which has been set aside was made; (b) preparing for and attending any hearing to set aside the judgment or order in question; (c) preparing for and attending any hearing at which the court orders the proceedings or the part in question to be adjourned; (d) any steps taken to enforce a judgment or order which has subsequently been set aside.
Costs of and caused by (an amendment)	Where, for example, the court makes this order on an application to amend a statement of case, the party in whose favour the costs order is made is entitled to the costs of preparing for and attending the application and the costs of any consequential amendment to his own statement of case.
Costs here and below	The party in whose favour the costs order is made is entitled not only to his costs in respect of the proceedings in which the court makes the order but also to his costs of the proceedings in any lower court.
No order as to costs Each party to pay his own costs	Each party is to bear its own costs of the part of the proceedings to which the order relates whatever costs order the court makes at the end of the proceedings.

SILENCE AS TO COSTS

33.15 CPR, r 44.13 (1) provides that:

'Where the court makes an order which does not mention costs (with certain exceptions – permission to appeal, permission for judicial review, and directions on an ex parte application) *no party is entitled to costs in relation to that order.'*

33.16 This rule emphasises the importance to the practitioner of ensuring that the claim for costs is pursued at the hearing. Under Regulation 5 of the Community Legal Service (Costs) Regulations 2000, an order should be made before the judge for the determination of the assisted person's liability to pay costs and for any application by the Respondent for an order for payment by the Legal Services Commission.[21]

TIME FOR COMPLYING

33.17 A party must comply with an order for the payment of costs within 14 days of (i) the date of the judgment or order; or (ii) if detailed assessment is ordered the date of the certificate of the detailed assessment, or in either case, such later date as the Court may specify: CPR, 44.8(a) – (c).

AWARD OF COSTS: THE COURT'S DISCRETION

Costs against non-parties – *Aiden Shipping Co Ltd v Interbulk Ltd*[22]

33.18 In the *Aiden Shipping* case it was held that the discretionary power to award costs (SCA 1981, s 51(1)) was in wide terms; there was no basis to imply a limitation to the effect that costs could only be ordered to be paid by parties to the proceedings. Balcombe LJ in *Symphony Group v Hodgson*[23] set out guiding principles which govern the exercise of discretion where an application is made for a non-party to pay costs of proceedings. It has been held that there is no statutory requirement or authority that 'exceptional circumstances' are a necessary precondition for the exercise of the power,[24] nor that the relationship between a party and non-party need be an unusually close one.[25] A costs order can certainly be made against a non-party to proceedings, particularly where that person has a financial interest in the outcome and his involvement has not

---

[21] See *General Accident Fire and Life Assurance Corporation v Foster* [1972] 3 All ER 877, CA.
[22] [1986] AC 965, HL.
[23] [1994] QB 179.
[24] *Globe Equities Ltd v Globe Legal Services and others* (1999) *The Times,* April 14, CA.
[25] *Wiggins v Richard Read (Transport) Ltd* (1999) *The Times,* January 14, CA.

been justified but has been 'wanton officious intermeddling'.[26] For a fuller discussion of such orders and the principles involved see the chapter on wasted costs hereafter to which reference should be made; there is often an interrelationship between the two.

33.19 Where the court is considering making a costs order in favour of a non-party, that party must be added as a party for the purposes of costs only and must be given an opportunity to be heard.[27]

MATERIALS FOR EXERCISING DISCRETION

General principles

33.20 The discretion to make any order for costs must be exercised judicially in accordance with reason and justice.[28] The old authorities relating to the exercise of discretion as to costs are perhaps still helpful guiding authority. Thus a successful claimant who recovers more than nominal damages should ordinarily have an order for costs against an unsuccessful defendant, subject to the other considerations to which the court is to have regard, in particular proportionality and the conduct of the parties.

33.21 Certainly under the older authorities it was wrong in principle for a Judge to mark his disapproval of the way a successful claimant has conducted litigation by ordering him to pay the defendant's costs. In *Knight v Clifton*[29] it was held that in exceptional circumstances (but only then) the court had jurisdiction to award costs against a wholly successful defendant. This authority must now be seen in the light of the penal sanctions which may be imposed under the CPR where a claimant has done better than he has proposed in a Part 36 offer[30] and the relevance of 'conduct' in exercising the discretion on costs. It has been said that litigants need to be encouraged to be selective as to the points they take and the extent of costs recovery as an incentive to responsible behaviour.[31]

33.22 In deciding what order for costs to make the court is entitled (some would say obliged) to take into account whether a party has succeeded on part of the case even if it is not wholly successful; the other party's reasonableness in raising, pursuing or contesting a particular allegation or issue is not necessarily relevant or a pre-condition to taking that factor into account.[32]

---

[26] *Nordstern Allegmeine Versicherungs AG v Internav Ltd; Nordstern Allegmeine Versicherungs AG v Katsamas*, (1999) *The Times*, June 8, CA, following *Murphy v Young & Co's Brewery plc* [1997] 1 WLR 1591.
[27] CPR, r 48.2(1).
[28] *Gupta v Kitto* (1998) *The Times* November 23, if this principle needs authority.
[29] *Knight v Clifton* [1971] Ch 700, CA.
[30] CPR, r 36(1) and the relevant chapter in this text.
[31] *Base Metal Trading Ltd v Ruslan Borisovich Shamurin* [2003] EWHC 2606 Tomlinson J.
[32] See *Stoczni Gdanska SA v Latvian Shipping Co & ors* (2001) *The Times* May 8 Thomas J.

33.23 In the case of a wholly successful defendant the judge should award him his costs unless there is evidence that he brought about the litigation, or has done something connected with the institution or conduct of the action calculated to occasion unnecessary litigation and expense, or has done some wrongful act in the course of the transaction of which the Claimant complains.[33]

Failure to recover damages

33.24 Damage is of the essence of the tort of negligence. Thus a plaintiff who fails to prove that the defendant's negligence caused damage loses his action. More than nominal damages must be recovered. A claimant who only recovers nominal damages is normally regarded as unsuccessful and liable to pay the defendant's costs.[34]

SEPARATE ISSUES

33.25 A notable change from earlier case law is at CPR, r 44.3(4) which allows the court to assess the extent to which a party has been successful on each of the issues pursued. Where a claimant has succeeded on some issues but lost or abandoned others, the Court of Appeal has held that it was open to the judge to award the claimant a proportion of his costs in relation to those issues on which he had succeeded but the abandoned issues should have been left to the costs judge. Those costs should be disallowed as costs unreasonably incurred in the litigation.[35]

RELEVANCE OF LEGAL AID/LSC FUNDING

33.26 The fact that the successful party has been in receipt of legal aid or is LSC funded is *not* relevant to the exercise of discretion as to costs. The award of costs is determined by the factors prescribed in CPR, r 44.3. The extent to which that party has costs protection is determined by the Access to Justice Act 1999 and the CLS (Cost Protection) Regulations 2000.

LATE AMENDMENT

33.27 The general rule is that where a claimant makes a late amendment, which substantially alters his case and without which the action would fail, a defendant is entitled to his costs down to the date of the amendment.[36] Furthermore, any amendment is almost bound to incur an order for the costs

---

[33] See Atkin LJ in *Ritter v Godfrey* [1920] KB 47.
[34] *Alltrans Express Ltd v CVA Holdings Ltd* [1984] 1 WLR 394 (breach of contract).
[35] *Shirley v Caswell* [2000] Lloyd's Rep PN 955.
[36] *Beoco v Alfa Laval Ltd* [1995] QB 137, CA.

of and occasioned by the amendment. If made near the trial the amendment may even result in the adjournment of the trial and the costs thrown away by the adjournment.[37]

INFLATED CLAIMS: RELEVANCE OF FINANCIAL LIMITS

33.28 Prior to the implementation of the CPR the Court of Appeal had criticised improper inflation of a claim to a sum exceeding the relevant financial limit.[38] The test adopted in that case was whether the claimant could reasonably have expected to recover a sum in excess of the limit. With the raising of the small claims limit to £5,000, and the introduction of a fast track procedure with limitations on recovery of costs for cases less than £15,000 in value, it is thought that a similar test should apply to claimants who artificially inflate a claim in order to oust the prescribed fast track or small claims limits.

FAILURE TO MEDIATE

33.29 With the wide availability of ADR the failure by the parties to mediate can be a reason for disallowing costs. In *Dunnett v Railtrack plc (in railway administration)*,[39] the Court of Appeal showed their displeasure in the failure of the successful party to mediate (Railtrack had turned down mediation on the ground that they had no offers to make and were confident of success on appeal) by disallowing the costs of the appeal. To similar effect was *Royal Bank of Canada v Secretary of State for Defence*.[40] However, failure to mediate has not resulted in any form of penalisation in other cases, for example *Hurst v Leeming*[41] and more recently it seems the Courts have been reluctant to penalise a party for failure to mediate unless it can be demonstrated by the opposing party that the mediation had a reasonable chance of success – see *Halsey v Milton Keynes General NHS Trust*.[42]

COSTS FOLLOWING ALLOCATION OR RE-ALLOCATION

33.30 CPR, r 44.11 deals with allocation and re-allocation costs. Where a claim is allocated to a track and the court subsequently re-allocates that claim to a different track then, unless the court orders otherwise, any special rules about

---

[37] See however the modified approach in *Professional Information Technology Consultants Ltd v Jones* [2001] EWCA Civ 2103.
[38] See *Afzal v Ford Motor Co Ltd* [1994] 4 All ER 720, CA.
[39] [2002] EWCA Civ 303.
[40] [2003] EWHC 1479.
[41] [2002] EWHC 1051 (Ch).
[42] [2004] EWCA Civ 576.

costs applying (i) to the fast track will apply up to the date of re-allocation and (ii) to the second track will apply from the date of re-allocation.

CASES WHERE COSTS ORDERS ARE DEEMED TO HAVE BEEN MADE

33.31 In four specified circumstances under four separate rules which provide for a right to costs, a costs order will be deemed to have been made on the standard basis. Those particular circumstances are set out in CPR, r 44.12, but are in summary:

- Rule 3.7 (Defendant's right to costs where claim is struck out for non-payment of fees);

- Rule 36.3(1) (Claimant's right to costs where he accepts Defendant's Part 36 offer or Part 36 payment;

- Rule 36(4) Claimant's right to costs where Defendant accepts the Claimant's Part 36 offer); and

- Rule 38.6 (Defendant's right to costs where Claimant discontinues).

COURTS' POWERS IN RELATION TO MISCONDUCT

33.32 The courts' powers in relation to misconduct are set out at CPR, r 44.14. These matters are dealt with in the chapter of this book relating to wasted costs.

APPEAL AGAINST AN ORDER FOR COSTS

33.33 Permission to appeal is required to appeal against a summary or detailed assessment of costs. An appeal does not act as a stay, and usually an interim amount may have to be paid until the appeal is determined. The appeal from a detailed or summary assessment by the district judge is to the circuit judge, and from a costs judge or a circuit judge to a High Court judge. Any further appeal is to the Court of Appeal. Appeals are not full re-hearings (unless the appeal judge so orders) and are by way of review – see *Johnsey Estates (1990) Ltd v Secretary of State for Environment Transport and the Regions*.[43] The usual ground of appeal would be lack of reasons supporting a particular aspect of the costs decision, on which issue the leading case is *English v Emery Reimbold v Strick Ltd*.[44]

---

[43] [2001] EWCA Civ 535.
[44] [2002] EWCA Civ 605.

GUIDING RULES IN PARTICULAR CIRCUMSTANCES: INTERIM HEARINGS

33.34 The costs of interim applications are in the discretion of the court and are subject to the same general principles already covered. Unless there is good reason not to do so these costs will be summarily assessed at the conclusion of the application and by reference to schedules of costs of the hearing prepared by both parties.

PROTECTIVE COSTS ORDERS

33.35 In the 'most exceptional circumstances' the court may make an order pre-empting the final outcome of the case in public interest cases. The 'general rule' cited above is a formidable obstacle to any pre-emptive costs order as between adverse parties in ordinary litigation. It is difficult to imagine a case falling within the general principle in which it would be possible for a court properly to exercise its discretion in advance of the substantive decision.[45]

33.36 In public law cases, the recent case of *Corner House Research* has established that a protective costs order will only be made in exceptional cases, and specifically:

(i) the issues raised must be of genuine public importance;

(ii) the public interest requires that those issues should be resolved;

(iii) the applicant has no private interest in the outcome of the case;

(iv) having regard to the financial resources of the applicant and respondent and to the amount of costs that were likely to be involved it is fair and just to make the order; and

(v) if the order was not made the applicant would probably discontinue the proceedings and would be acting reasonably in so doing.[46]

33.37 As may be seen from the above, these are high (if not insurmountable) hurdles for the claimant with any private interest in the outcome. One such example of an unsuccessful claimant seeking a pre-emptive order was *R (Goodson) v HM Coroner for Bedfordshire*,[47] where the claimant having obtained permission to appeal from Richards J failed to obtain a pre-emptive

---

[45] *R v Lord Chancellor ex parte Child Poverty Action Group* [1999] 1 WLR 349.
[46] *R (ota Corner House Research) v Secretary of State for Trade & Industry* [2005] EWCA Civ 192.
[47] [2005] EWHC 2931 (Admin).

costs order in respect of her appeal to the Court of Appeal because she had a private interest in the outcome of the proceedings.[48]

COSTS CAPPING

33.38 There have recently been amendments to CPR, r 3.1 adding a new power for the court to order a party to file and serve an estimate of costs.[49] This power may be used to bolster an application by a party to the proceedings that the costs should be capped at a certain limit. At present the Courts have generally set their face against cost-capping orders, save in exceptional circumstances, or in the context of group litigation.[50] The position was summarised in *Smart v East Cheshire NHS Trust*[51] thus:

> '... the court should only consider making a costs cap order in such cases where the applicant shows by evidence that there is a real and substantial risk that without such an order costs will be disproportionately or unreasonably incurred; and that this risk may not be managed by conventional case management and detailed assessment after trial.'

Where such orders have been made they are (or should be) made prospectively.[52] The rationale for the making of such orders is helpfully outlined by Lord Justice Brooke at paras 78–109 of *King v Telegraph Group*.[53]

LOCKLEY ORDERS

33.39 Where a party has the benefit of LSC (Legal Services Commission) funding the court may, on an interim hearing order that costs awarded to the other party be set off against any damages or costs to which the legally aided party is or may become entitled.[54] Where the LSC funded party is the receiving party of an order for costs no summary assessment may be made. Conversely where the LSC funded party is the paying party it is proper to make a summary assessment of the costs and set off such costs against any award of damages and/or costs to which the legally aided party is or may become entitled. It is worth noting that the Costs Practice Direction to CPR, 44 at 13.10 provides that summary assessment is not by itself a determination of the assisted

---

[48] Although some disquiet has been expressed about the correctness of the Corner House decision in *R (Derek England) v Tower Hamlets LBC and Ors*. [2006] EWCA 1742.
[49] See Civil Procedure (Amendment No 3) Rules 2005, SI 2005/2292.
[50] See, for example, *A (1), B (2) and others v A Teaching Hospital NHS Trust* (the nationwide organ litigation) [2003] EWHC 1034.
[51] [2003] EWHC 2806, QB.
[52] *Marion Henry v BBC* [2005] EWHC 2503, QB.
[53] *King v Telegraph Group* [2004] EWCA (Civ) 613 paras 78–109.
[54] *Lockley v National Blood Transfusion Service* [1992] 2 All ER 589.

person's liability to pay those costs.[55] Properly understood there are three stages to the process of costs orders against state-funded parties. First, a costs order is made either in a specified sum (summary assessment) or to be assessed by way of detailed assessment. Secondly, the determination of the amount the state-funded person shall pay is postponed. The usual order will be 'The amount of the costs payable under s 17(1) of the Legal Aid Act' or 'the amount of costs payable under s 11 of the Access to Justice Act to be determined'. Thirdly, steps are taken to have that determination carried out. Thus at an interim stage, when a costs order has been made in favour of the defendant, a Lockley order in terms that the determination of the liability of the claimant to pay such costs be postponed, save where such costs may be set off against any damages or costs recoverable by him, is still appropriate.

COUNTERCLAIM AND SET OFF

33.40 Where a claimant recovers money on the claim and the defendant recovers on his counterclaim, the general practice is to enter one judgment only for the balance in favour of the claimant if he is the net winner. In such circumstances the usual principles, costs to follow the event, will apply in respect of claim and counterclaim. This will of course be subject to the particular circumstances. Where in a traffic accident both parties were equally to blame and were awarded almost identical sums on the claim and counterclaim, the Court of Appeal made no order on either, as an order in favour of the claimant would have given him an unfair advantage.[56] Further, where a judge struck out part of a defendant's counterclaim and made an award of costs against him, it was, as a matter of principle, wrong for the judge to then make a further order staying proceedings relating to the remainder of the counterclaim until the defendant paid the costs awarded to the claimants[57] CPR, r 40.13 provides that where the court gives judgment both *for* the claimant on his claim and *against* the claimant on a counterclaim, if there is a balance in favour of one of the parties, it may order the party whose judgment is for the lesser amount to pay the balance. In a case to which this rule applies, the court may make a separate order as to costs against each party.[58]

---

[55] See CPR 44.12 and paragraphs 21.1 to 23.17 of the Costs Practice Direction; also s.11 Access to Justice Act 1999 and the provisions made under that Act or regulations made under the Legal Aid Act 1988.
[56] *Smith v WH Smith & Sons Ltd* [1952] 1 All ER 528, CA.
[57] *Theakston v Matthews*, (1998) *The Time,* April 13.
[58] See also CPR, r 46.3 (6) in relation to fast track costs.

PART 20 PROCEEDINGS

(i) General principles

33.41 The court has always had power to make such order as to costs between the respective parties as the justice of the case may require.[59] Where the defendant reasonably brings in a Part 20 defendant and succeeds in the main action, he should usually recover against the claimant his costs of both the action and the Part 20 proceedings including those he has been ordered to pay to the Part 20 defendant, or, in a proper case, the claimant can be ordered to pay the Part 20 defendant's costs directly.[60] A successful Part 20 defendant is normally entitled to an order for costs against an unsuccessful Part 20 claimant even where the Part 20 claimant is legally aided.[61]

Discontinuance of Part 20 claims

33.42 No costs order is deemed to be made where a party discontinues third party or Part 20 proceedings. The Part 20 defendant must seek an order for his costs by application.

Multiple parties

(i) Co-defendants

33.43 Where the claimant has reasonably sued two defendants in the alternative and succeeded against only one of them, the court may in its discretion order the unsuccessful defendant to pay the successful defendant's costs. This may be done:

(a) by an order that the unsuccessful defendant pay the successful defendant's costs direct, a 'Sanderson order',[62] or

(b) by an order that the claimant pay the successful defendant's costs and recover them from the unsuccessful defendant as part of the Claimant's costs of the action, a 'Bullock order'.[63]

33.44 The form of order is in the court's discretion. Where the claimant is insolvent or legally aided a Sanderson order may be preferable. But where the unsuccessful defendant is insolvent the successful defendant is not necessarily entitled to a Bullock or Sanderson order.[64] *Irving v Metropolitan Police Cmr*,[65] has confirmed that Sanderson orders have survived the CPR changes.

---

[59] *Edginton v Clark* [1964] 1 QB 367, CA.
[60] *LE Cattam Ltd v A Michaelides & Co* [1958] 1 WLR 717; *Thomas v Times Book Co Ltd* [1966] 1 WLR 911.
[61] *Johnson v Ribbons* [1977] 1 WLR 1458, CA.
[62] *Sanderson v Blythe Theatre Co* [1903] 2 KB 533, CA.
[63] *Bullock v London General Omnibus Co* [1907] 1 KB 264, CA.
[64] *Bankamerica Finance Ltd v Nock* [1988] AC 1002 and *Mayer v Harte* [1960] 1 WLR 770, CA.
[65] [2005] EWCA Civ 1293.

33.45 Before the court can make either of the above orders it must be satisfied that the claimant acted reasonably in joining both defendants, eg where the claimant was a passenger injured in a vehicle in collision with another. In deciding whether to exercise such discretion the court will look at all the facts which the claimant knew or might reasonably have ascertained when he commenced proceedings.[66]

(ii) Joint tortfeasors

33.46 The Civil Liability (Contribution) Act 1978, which provides for contribution between persons liable in respect of the same damage, by s 4 deprives the claimant of costs where more than one action is unnecessarily brought.

Part 36 offers and Part 36 payments

33.47 Costs orders in connection with Part 36 payments and offers are dealt with in a separate chapter of this book.

Security for costs

33.48 CPR, r 25.12 deals with Security for costs. The general principle is that no person shall be prevented from taking or defending proceedings as a result of his or her impecuniosity. In practice there is unlikely to be any question of security having any part to play in personal injury actions at first instance. Under the old RSC Order 23 rule 1, even where the claimant was ordinarily resident abroad, the court should never exercise its discretion under to order security to be given by an individual claimant resident in a member state of the European Union in the absence of very cogent evidence of substantial difficulty in enforcing a judgment in the member state.[67] If some special situation has arises which might merit a possible application for security then reference should be made to the detailed provisions of the rules.[68]

Transfer of Proceedings

33.49 Subject to any order which may have been made by the original court, CPR, r 44.13(3), (4) provides that once a case is transferred the new court will deal with all questions as to costs, including the costs incurred before transfer.

Costs of setting aside judgment

33.50 A claimant will normally be entitled to the costs of any application to set aside a regular judgment. The court may impose terms as to costs as a condition of setting judgment aside, eg the costs of the application and those thrown away. Where a judgment is irregular, the defendant is normally entitled

---

[66] *Besterman v British Motor Cab Co Ltd* [1914] 3 KB 181.
[67] *Fitzgerald and Others v Williams* [1996] 2 All ER 171, CA.
[68] RSC Ord 23.

to his costs of the application, but different considerations may apply, particularly if the irregularity was not the fault of the claimant.

Varying an order for costs

33.51 As under the old 'slip rule' the court has power under CPR, r 40.12(1) to correct any accidental slip or omission in any judgment or order. Normally an order or judgment will be drawn up by the court. Until it is drawn up the court may recall or vary any order at any time.[69]

Appeals and orders for costs

33.52 By CPR, r 44.13(2), a court dealing with a case on appeal may make orders relating to the proceedings giving rise to the appeal as well as the appeal itself. As a general rule, the successful appellant gets his costs of the appeal and below, and an unsuccessful appellant will have to pay the costs of the appeal. Where the appellant only succeeds in part or has succeeded only on a point not argued below or not raised in his notice of appeal, or has been guilty of objectionable conduct he may well be deprived of some or all of his costs.[70]

Security for costs of appeal

33.53 Security for the costs of an appeal may be ordered where there are special circumstances which in the opinion of the court render it just to order security. While in the case of an individual claimant (as opposed to a company) his impecuniosity is not grounds for an order for security below, the impecuniosity of a claimant is a ground for the award of security in the Court of Appeal: the appellant has already had the case determined after a trial and it is prima facie an injustice to allow an appeal by an impecunious appellant to proceed where the respondent will be unable to enforce an order for costs made in his favour by the Court of Appeal. The Court of Appeal nonetheless retains a discretion.

Appeals against orders for costs only

33.54 Permission to appeal is required to appeal questions of costs only. Permission to appeal may be given to appeal or cross appeal by the court below, or by the Court of Appeal. Permission to appeal is not required where the order for costs against which an appeal is to be made is either against a non-party (*Aiden Shipping* type order)[71] or a wasted costs order against a Legal Representative.[72]

33.55 The first question will be whether the judge had material before him upon which he could exercise his discretion by making the order he did as to

---

[69] *Hyde and Southbank Housing Association v Kain* (1989) *The Times*, August 30, CA.
[70] CPR, r 44.3(5).
[71] *Re Land and Property Trust Co Ltd* [1991] 1 WLR 601, CA.
[72] *Thompson v Fraser* [1986] 1 WLR 17 (CA) followed in *Wilson v Kerry* [1993] 1 WLR 963, CA.

costs. The court will assume that he exercised his discretion unless satisfied that he did not do so. So it will not interfere where he gave reasons which are germane and not based on any false principle, nor where there are also other possible grounds for his discretion. But he must exercise it fairly. To succeed therefore on such an appeal the appellant must (in an area where the judge has a wide discretion) satisfy the court that the judge applied a false principle, or had no materials on which he could reasonably so exercise his discretion. Even where permission to appeal has been given the court will not interfere unless there has been a manifest disregard of principle or misapprehension of the facts.[73] The same principles apply to an appeal to the judge against summary assessment for costs made by the master or district judge.

Fixed costs

33.56 A new system of fixed costs is set out in CPR Part 45, and supplemented by the associated PD, RSC Ord 62[74] and CCR Ord 38.[75] Fixed costs apply where the only claim is a claim for a specified sum of money and:

(i) judgment in default is obtained under CPR, r 12.4(1);

(ii) judgment on an admission is obtained under CPR, r 14.4.(3);

(iii) judgment on an admission on part of the claim is obtained under CPR, r 14.5(6);

(iv) summary judgment is given under CPR Part 24;

(v) the court has made an order to strike out a defence under CPR, r 3.4.(2)(a) as disclosing no reasonable grounds for defending the claims;

(vi) the only claim is a claim where the Court gave a fixed date for the hearing when it issued the claim and judgment is given for the delivery of goods, and in either case the value of the claim exceeds £25.

33.57 RSC Order 62, Appendix 3 to Schedule 1 CPR sets out the fixed costs in the High Court for:

entering judgment in claims for the possession of land and additional costs for service; and taking certain enforcement proceedings.

A new table setting out these costs came into operation on 1 April 2003.

33.58 CCR Ord 38 appendix B to CPR schedule 2 sets out fixed costs in county court cases for:

---

[73] *Findlay v Railway Executive* [1950] 2 All ER 550; *Alltrans Express Ltd v CVA Holdings Ltd* [1984] 1 WLR 394, CA.
[74] CPR Sch 1 appendix 3.
[75] CPR Sch 2 appendix B.

(a) money claims;

(b) claims for the recovery of land; and

(c) claims for the recovery of goods including goods covered under Hire Purchase agreements.

Summary assessment of costs

33.59 The rules on summary assessment embody the main principles underlying the CPR. They serve a threefold purpose:

(i) to ensure that the successful party to an application or hearing is out of pocket in respect of their costs for as short a time as possible;

(ii) to impress upon the parties both the risks and the costs of litigation and thereby encourage settlement; and

(iii) to save the further costs of a detailed assessment.

33.60 The Practice Direction to CPR, 44 para.13.1 sets out the procedure for summary assessment. Generally, any interim application which is disposed of in less than one day will conclude with a summary assessment of costs unless there is good reason not to do so[76] – for example where the paying party can show substantial grounds for disputing the sums claimed for costs that cannot be dealt with summarily or there is insufficient time. Although the general rule applies to cases not lasting more than a day, there is no presumption against summary assessment in cases which last longer – *Q v Q (Family Division: costs: summary assessment)*.[77] It is the duty of the parties and their legal representatives to assist the judge in making a summary assessment of costs and to do so each party who claim costs must prepare a written statement of the costs he intends to claim showing separately in the form of a schedule:

(a) the number of hours to be claimed;

(b) the hourly rate to be claimed;

(c) the grade of fee earner;

(d) the amount and nature of any disbursement to be claimed;

(e) the amount of solicitor's costs to be claimed for attending or appearing at the hearing, and any VAT to be claimed on these amounts.

---

[76] This includes proceedings in the Court of Appeal – see para 14 of the Practice Direction to CPR Part 52 for the circumstances in which it is expected a summary assessment of costs will take place I the Court of Appeal.

[77] [2002] 2 FLR 668.

33.61 The statement of costs must be filed at court and copies of it must be served on any party against whom an order for payment of those costs is intended to be sought. The schedule must be served as soon as possible and in any event not later than 24 hours before the hearing. However, the failure of a party to comply with paragraph 13(5)(2) of the Costs Practice Direction by omitting to file and serve a copy of the statement of costs not less than 24 hours before the date fixed for hearing does not warrant the wholesale disallowance of costs. The court should take the failure into account but must act proportionately. Often allowing a short adjournment for the prejudiced party to consider the schedule, or adjourning the summary assessment to another date will be appropriate.[78]

33.62 The failure by a party to comply with this direction is a matter to be taken into account by the court in deciding what order to make about costs, and about any further hearing or detailed assessment hearing that may be necessary as a result of that failure.

33.63 The court may not make summary assessment of a receiving party who is an assisted person under the Legal Aid Act 1988, a LSC funded client; or of a receiving party who is a child or patient.

33.64 On assessment the court must have regard to all the circumstances including:

(1) conduct before and during proceedings;

(2) any efforts made to resolve the dispute;

(3) the amount or value of any property involved;

(4) the importance of the matter to all parties;

(5) the complexity, difficulty or novelty of the questions raised;

(6) the skill, effort, specialised knowledge and responsibility involved;

(7) the time spent on the case;

(8) the place where and circumstances in which work was done.

33.65 No summary assessment of costs will be made if the parties have agreed the amount of costs payable. In every case where an order for costs is made against a legally represented party (including an agreed order); and the party is not present when the order is made, the party's solicitor must notify his client in writing of the costs order no later than 7 days after the solicitor receives notice of the order.

---

[78] See *MacDonald v Taree Holdings Ltd* (2000) *The Times*, December 28, per Neuberger J.

FAST TRACK COSTS

33.66 CPR Part 46 deals with the amount of costs which the court may award as the costs of an advocate for preparing for and appearing at the trial of a claim in the fast track. The following table shows the amount of fast track trial costs which the court may award (whether by summary or detailed assessment).[79]

Value of the claim	Amount of fast track trial costs which the court may award
Up to £3,000	£350
More than £3,000 but no more than £10,000	£500
More than £10,000	£750

33.67 The court does have power to award more, or less than the prescribed rates under CPR, r 46.3, in particular an additional £250 to a legal representative who attends the trial in addition to the advocate, and the court considers the legal representative's attendance necessary to assist the advocate.[80]

33.68 Where a defendant has made a counterclaim against the claimant, and (a) the claimant has succeeded on his claim; and (b) the defendant has succeeded on his counterclaim, the court will quantify the amount of the award of fast track trial costs to which:

(i) but for the counterclaim, the claimant would be entitled for succeeding on his claim; and

(ii) but for the claim, the defendant would be entitled to for succeeding on his counterclaim, and make one award of the difference, if any, to the party entitled to the higher award of costs.[81]

33.69 Improper or unreasonable conduct by a receiving party may result in the court awarding a party less than would otherwise be payable.[82] Conversely, where the paying party has behaved improperly during the trial the court may award such additional amount to the other party as it considers appropriate.[83]

---

[79] CPR, r 46.2(1).
[80] CPR, r 46.3(2)(b).
[81] CPR, r 46.3(6)(a), (b).
[82] CPR, r 46.3(7).
[83] CPR, r 46.3(8).

Basis of Assessment

33.70 Costs (other than fixed fast track trial costs) are awarded either on the standard or the indemnity basis. The difference between an award under the standard or indemnity basis is now more significant than under the old rules because whereas on an assessment on the standard basis the court must have regard to whether the costs were 'proportionately and reasonably' incurred and 'proportionate and reasonable in amount', the proportionality of the costs is ignored on the indemnity basis.[84]

33.71 There is little guidance on when indemnity costs should be ordered. In *Bowen-Jones v Bowen-Jones*[85] Knox J, declined to reappraise the old cases and adopted the approach of Brightman J in respect of a predecessor to RSC Ord 76:

> 'It is not the policy of the courts in hostile litigation to give the successful party an indemnity against the expense to which he has been put and, therefore, to compensate him for the loss which he has inevitably suffered, save in very special circumstances.'[86]

33.72 Notwithstanding these remarks, a typical case for indemnity costs, would be for example against a contemnor[87] for persistent non-compliance with orders or the rules and Indemnity costs have been awarded against a Defendant who failed to specifically plead that the claimant was a malingerer, such allegation amounting to an allegation of fraud which should have been specifically pleaded.[88] On the other hand over vigorous of a breach of confidence action was held to be different from overt or deliberate dishonesty in its prosecution and not to attract an order for indemnity costs. However the test appears does not necessarily require that there must be misconduct in connection with the litigation whether in its actual conduct, or because of the nature of the underlying action, eg a finding of fraud such as would attract the criticism that the way the claim was conducted lacked moral probity or was deserving of moral condemnation see *Reid Minty (a firm) v Taylor*.[89]

33.73 In *Brawley v Marcxynski (No 2)*[90] costs were awarded on the indemnity basis to a publicly funded party in order to penalise the losing party's unreasonable conduct. There is thus no impediment to an award of indemnity costs even though the only beneficiaries of such award are likely to be the claimant's lawyers.

---

[84] CPR, r 44.4(2).
[85] [1986] 3 All ER.
[86] *Bartlett v Barclays Bank Trust Co Ltd (No 2)* [1980] 2 All ER 92 at 98.
[87] See, eg, *Midland Marts Ltd v Hobday* [1989] 1 WLR 1143.
[88] *Cooper v P& O Stena Line Ltd* (1999) *The Times*, February 8, applying *Bank or Baroda v Panessar* [1987] Ch 335; *Tharros Shipping Co Ltd v Bias Shipping Ltd* [1994] 1 Lloyd's Rep. 533; and *Wailes v Stapleton Construction and Commercial Services Ltd* [1997] 2 Lloyd's Rep 112.
[89] [2001] EWCA Civ 1723.
[90] [2002] EWCA Civ 1453.

DETAILED ASSESSMENT

33.74 Under the CPR detailed assessment replaces what was formerly the taxation of costs. It is governed by CPR Part 47 and the associated practice direction. The general rule is that the costs of any proceedings or any part of the proceedings are not to be assessed by the detailed procedure until the conclusion of the proceedings but the court may order them to be assessed immediately.[91] Proceedings are concluded when the court has finally determined the matters in issue in the claim, whether or not there is an appeal.[92]

33.75 Within 3 months of the judgment, or the event whereby the right to detailed assessment arose a notice of commencement must be served on the paying party by the receiving party, together with the bill of costs. If proceedings are not commenced in time CPR, r 47.8 provides sanctions for delay including the disallowance of all or part of the costs or interest payable. Within 21 days of service of the notice of commencement, the *paying* party must serve points of dispute in relation to the disputed items on the bill or costs. If no points of dispute are served the receiving party may serve a request for a default costs certificate.[93]

33.76 The request for a hearing of the detailed assessment must be made by the receiving party after service of the points of dispute and in any event within three months of the expiry of the period for commencing the assessment proceedings. If such a request is not made the paying party may apply for an order requiring the receiving party to make on failing which costs or interest may be disallowed in whole or in part.[94] An interim costs certificate may be issued by the court at any time after the filing of the request, and will generally include an order that the specified sum be paid.[95] Solicitor and own client costs are, unless the bill is paid out by the Legal Services Commission or pursuant to a conditional fee agreement, assessed on the indemnity basis.[96]

33.77 CPR, r 48.9 provides that on every assessment (whether summary or detailed), of a solicitor's bill to a client where the solicitor and the client have entered into a conditional fee agreement, the client may apply of assessment of the base costs or of a percentage increase on or both. Where the assessment is for base costs they are to be assessed in accordance with CPR, r 48.8(2) as if the solicitor and his client had not entered into a conditional fee agreement. Where the client applies for assessment of a percentage increase, the court may reduce the percentage increase where it considers it to be disproportionate having regard to all the relevant factors as they reasonably appeared to the solicitor or counsel when the conditional fee agreement was made.

---

[91] CPR, r 47(1).
[92] CPR PD 47 1.1(1).
[93] CPR, r 47.9 – see also however the accompanying Practice Direction.
[94] CPR, r 47.14.
[95] CPR, r 47.15.
[96] CPR, r 48.8.

33.78 Even where a detailed assessment is ordered the receiving party ought to apply for an interim payment of costs on account.[97]

Interest on costs

33.79 The statutory interest on a judgment or order for the payment of costs runs from the date of the judgment or order, *not* from the date of the certificate quantifying the same or such other date as may be ordered as the date on which payment is to be made.[98] Interest payable pursuant to s 17 of the Judgments Act 1838 or s 74 of the County Courts Act 1984 on the costs deemed to have been made under CPR, r 44.12 begins to run from the date on which the event which gave rise to the entitlement to costs occurred.[99]

---

[97] See *Mars v Teknowledge* (1999) *The Times,* July 8.
[98] *Hunt v RM Douglas Roofing* [1988] 3 All ER 823.
[99] CPR, r 44.12(2).

Chapter 34

WASTED COSTS AND COSTS AGAINST NON-PARTIES

WASTED COSTS

Overview

34.1 There are several routes via which a legal representative may be made personally liable for the costs of any proceedings in respect of acts or omissions committed in connection with such proceedings. Essentially the jurisdiction is statutory, provided for by s 51(6) of the Supreme Court Act 1981 and it is pursuant to this provision that wasted costs orders within the strict definition of that term are made. The statutory jurisdiction covers both applications against a party's own advisers (which ought to be rare)[1] and against those acting for the opposing party.[2] Additionally the court also has limited jurisdiction to make an order for costs against a legal adviser (probably only a solicitor) personally, arising from the inherent jurisdiction of the High Court. A second, equally limited, area of additional jurisdiction arises under the general jurisdiction of the court as to costs contained in s 51(1) and (3) of the Supreme Court Act 1981, see generally *Hodgson v Imperial Tobacco*.[3] Finally, at the costs stage, there are powers conferred by Civil Procedure Rules 1998 (CPR), r 44.14, which apply where misconduct is alleged on the part of a legal representative.

A Statutory jurisdiction, s 51(6) of the Supreme Court Act 1981

34.2 The power to make a wasted costs order in the High Court and County Court is found in the Supreme Court Act 1981, s 51(6) and (7).

34.3 The Supreme Court Act 1981, s 51 provides:

> "(6) In any proceedings mentioned in sub-section (1)[4] the court may disallow, or, (as the case may be), order the legal or other representative concerned to meet, the whole of any wasted costs or such part of them as may be determined in accordance with the rules of court.

---

[1] *Harley v McDonald* (2001) 2 WLR 1749.
[2] *Brown v Bennett* (2002) 1 WLR 713.
[3] [1998] 1 WLR 1056, 1066.
[4] Subsection (1) refers to 'all proceedings in (a) the Civil Division of the Court of Appeal; (b) the High Court, and (c) any County Court'.

(7) In sub-section (6), "Wasted Costs" means any costs incurred by a party –

(a) as a result of any improper, unreasonable or negligent act or omission on the part of any legal or other representative or any employee of such representative; or
(b) which in the light of any such act or omission occurring after they were incurred, the court considers it unreasonable to expect that party to pay.'

34.4 The CPR contain a codified framework of rules applicable to the exercise of the statutory jurisdiction found in s 51(6), see CPR, r 48.7. Rule 48.7 is itself supplemented both by the Practice Direction to CPR Part 44, applicable to costs applications generally, and specifically by Practice Direction 48, Costs – Special Cases, which as we shall see below appears to lay down both substantive and procedural guidance.

The rules applicable to the statutory jurisdiction

34.5 Rule 48.7 of the CPR provides for the personal liability of legal representatives for costs as follows:

48.7 Personal liability of legal representative for costs – wasted costs orders

(1) This rule applies where the court is considering whether to make an order under Section 51(6) of the Supreme Court Act 1981 (court's power to disallow or (as the case may be) order a legal representative to meet, "wasted costs").
(2) The court must give the legal representative a reasonable opportunity to attend a hearing to give reasons why it should not make such an order.
(3) (revoked).
(4) When the court makes a wasted costs order, it must
   (a) specify the amount to be disallowed or paid, or
   (b) direct a costs judge or a district judge to decide the amount of costs to be disallowed or paid.
(5) The court may direct that notice must be given to the legal representative's client, in such manner as the court may direct –
   (a) of any proceedings under this rule; or
   (b) of any order made under it against his legal representative.
(6) Before making a wasted costs order, the court may direct a costs judge or a district judge to inquire into the matter and report to the court.
(7) The court may refer the question of wasted costs to a costs judge or a district judge, instead of making a wasted costs order.

34.6 The Practice Direction to Part 48 provides:

Section 53 – Personal liability of legal representative for costs – wasted costs orders; Rule 48.7

53.1 Rule 48.7 deals with wasted costs orders against legal representatives. Such orders can be made at any stage in the proceedings up to and including the proceedings relating to the detailed assessment of costs. In general, applications for wasted costs are best left until the end of the trial.

53.2 The court may make a wasted costs order against a legal representative of its own initiative.

53.3 A party may apply for a wasted costs order:

(1) by filing an application notice in accordance with Part 23; or
(2) by making an application orally in the course of any hearing.

53.4 It is appropriate for the court to make a wasted costs order against the legal representative only if:

(1) the legal representative has acted improperly, unreasonably or negligently,
(2) his conduct has caused a party to incur unnecessary costs, and
(3) it is just in all the circumstances to order him to compensate that party for the whole or part of those costs.

53.5 The court will give directions about the procedure that will be followed in each case in order to ensure that the issue is dealt with in a way which is fair and as simple and summary as the circumstances permit.

53.6 As a general rule the court will consider whether to make a wasted costs order in two stages:

(1) In the first stage, the court must be satisfied –
    (a) that it has before it evidence or other material which, if unanswered, would be likely to lead to a wasted costs order being made, and
    (b) the wasted costs proceedings are justified notwithstanding the likely costs involved.
(2) At the second stage (even if the court is satisfied under paragraph (1)) the court will consider, after giving the legal representative an opportunity to give reasons why the court should not make a wasted costs order, whether it is appropriate to make a wasted costs order in accordance with paragraph 53.4 above.

53.7 On an application for a wasted costs order under Part 23 the court may proceed to the second stage described in paragraph 53.6 without first adjourning the hearing if it is satisfied that the legal representative has already had a reasonable opportunity to give reasons why the court should not make a wasted costs order. In other cases the court will adjourn the hearing before proceeding to the second stage.

53.8 On an application for a wasted costs order under Part 23 the application notice and any evidence in support must identify:

(1) what the legal representative is alleged to have done or failed to do; and
(2) the costs that he may be ordered to pay or which are sought against him.

53.9 A wasted costs order is an order:

(1) that the legal representative pay a specified sum in respect of costs to a party; or

(2) for costs relating to a specified sum or items of work to be disallowed.

53.10 Attention is drawn to rule 44.3(A) (1) and (2) which respectively prevent the court from assessing any additional liability until the conclusion of the proceedings (or the part of the proceedings) to which the funding arrangement relates, and set out the orders the court may make at the conclusion of the proceedings.

Application in practice

34.7 Orders can be made at any stage in the proceedings, including proceedings relating to the detailed assessment of costs. That is however subject to the important qualification that proceedings must actually have been commenced. The s 51(6) jurisdiction applies to 'a legal or other representative' and this means a person exercising a right to conduct litigation on behalf of a party. A solicitor who fails to issue proceedings does not fall within that definition because until issue he has no right to conduct the litigation. Accordingly he cannot be sanctioned by a wasted costs order because he falls outside of the wasted costs jurisdiction.[5] This is in accordance with the nature of the wasted costs jurisdiction, which penalises not breaches of duty to a party, but breaches of duty to the court itself. An application can also be made after proceedings have been stayed and need not be raised during the currency of the proceedings, because 'in any proceedings' means 'in connection with' or 'in relation to' the proceedings rather than during the course of such proceedings.[6] In general, applications for wasted costs orders are probably best left until the end of proceedings. This general rule of thumb however can be modified in special circumstances, for example where a party's own counsel concedes that a proposed step in the proceedings is hopeless.[7] It is also open to the court to make a wasted costs order of its own initiative (PD 53.2). Although an oral application in the course of proceedings is possible pursuant to para 53, it is only likely to be sensible if the scope of the application to the costs said to have been wasted is narrow and clear; for example, if an adjournment is necessary because of a solicitor's or counsel's conduct, as regards the costs thrown away by the adjournment.[8]

34.8 The Part 48 Practice Direction sets out detailed provisions which need to be followed on any such application. As a general rule (but apparently not inevitably[9]) there are two stages to the process of obtaining a wasted costs order, whether instigated on the court's own initiative, or on application by a party. At the first stage the court must be satisfied (i) that it has before it evidence or other material which, if unanswered, would be likely to lead to a

---

[5] *Byrne v Sefton Health Authority* [2002] EWCA Civ 1904, *Charles v Gillian Radford & Co* [2003] EWHC 3180 (Ch).
[6] *Wagstaff v Colls* [2003] EWCA Civ 469.
[7] *B v B* [2001] 1 FLR 843.
[8] *Regent Leisuretime Ltd, Amos & Barton v Skerrett, Pearson* [2006] EWCA Civ 1032.
[9] Part 53.7 allows for both stages to be dealt with together on a Part 23 application if the legal representative has had the opportunity to give reasons why the court should not make an order.

wasted costs order being made, and (ii) that wasted costs proceedings are justified notwithstanding the likely costs involved (Practice Direction 53.6 (1) (b)). These are matters warranting serious assessment. A view that a lawyer's conduct needs to be investigated is not the same as there being a prima facie case of improper, unreasonable or negligent conduct. Further, the application must, whether made orally or by application notice, identify the costs sought (PD 53.8). Without details of the costs sought, it is not possible to assess whether or not the tests under 53.6 are likely to be met[10].The party applying for wasted costs needs to bear in mind the proportionality of the costs involved in wasted costs proceedings, see *A J Fahani v Merc Property Ltd*,[11] where more time was spent on the wasted costs proceedings than on the substantive proceedings, and a wasted costs order was refused. On the other hand, it would not be right to prevent the pursuit of a meritorious wasted costs application purely because the costs of defending it would be substantial, see *B v B*.[12] If a party loses its application for wasted costs, then the normal rule will be that costs follow the event. Thus the party seeking wasted costs would in fact end up paying the costs of the party against whom wasted costs were sought in relation to the satellite litigation. This is of particular importance where the wasted costs investigation may have been initiated by the court and subsequently pursued by a party. In some cases consideration should be given to the pursuit of the complaint via an alternative route, such as referral to the Law Society, in particular if the wasted costs hearing is likely to involve complexity of factual material in a case which has not been tried.[13]

34.9 The same judge should ideally hear the wasted costs application as heard the substantive hearing, if practical, and the wasted costs proceedings should follow the substantive hearing as soon as possible, as the longer the time period between hearings the more that needs to explained to the judge. The starting point is that the court that determined a case alone has jurisdiction to make a wasted costs order arising out of it. However it is possible in certain limited circumstances for a court other than the one that had dealt with the proceedings to have jurisdiction. Those circumstances included where it was impracticable for the original judge to deal with the matter or where the parties agreed to another judge dealing with the matter, see *Gray v Going Places Leisure Travel Ltd*.[14]

34.10 The court may direct that notice of any proceedings for wasted costs be given to the legal representative's client in any manner as the court may direct. This assumes that the client is not present at the time. The obligation to give the legal representative in question a reasonable opportunity to attend a hearing to give reasons why the court should not make such an order applies equally where the court of its own initiative, rather than on application, considers that a wasted costs order should be considered, CPR, r 48.7(2).

---

[10] *Regent Leisuretime Ltd, Amos & Barton v Skerrett, Pearson* [2006] EWCA Civ 1032.
[11] (1999) *The Times*, May 19.
[12] [2001] 1 FLR 843.
[13] *B v (1) Richard Pendelbury, (2) Associated Newspapers* [2002] EWHC 1404 QB.
[14] (2005) CA (Civ) 7/2/2005.

34.11 The court will then give directions about the procedure that will be followed in each case in order to ensure that the issues are dealt with in a way that is fair and as simple and summary as circumstances permit (PD 53.5).

34.12 At the second stage, the actual hearing for the application for wasted costs, the legal representative must be given an opportunity to state why a wasted costs order should not be made (CPR, r 48.7(2) and PD 53.6(2)(b)). In practice, it is often directed that the representative against whom an order is sought file written evidence in his or her defence. Once such evidence is received the application may be decided on paper by the court without the necessity and expense of an appearance. The representations of the legal representative must however be considered prior to the making of any order against him or her. The making of such an order first, with provision for the affected representative to make such representations about the order as they deem fit, does not adequately comply with the procedure and should be set aside.[15]

34.13 Appeals from refusals to make wasted costs orders should be embarked upon with extreme caution, see *Wall v Lefevre*,[16] *Royal Institute of Chartered Surveyors v Wiseman Marshall*,[17] *Persaud*.[18]

Circumstances in which a wasted costs order is appropriate

34.14 It is appropriate for the court to make a wasted costs order against the legal representative only if the representative has acted improperly, unreasonably or negligently, his conduct has caused a party to incur unnecessary costs, and it is just in all the circumstances to order him to compensate that party for the whole or part of those costs. The leading explanation of what amounts to conduct justifying the making of a wasted costs order is now more than a decade old and is to be found in *Ridehalgh v Horsefield*.[19] *Ridehalgh* antedates the enactment of the CPR, but the statutory basis for wasted costs was of course not changed by the CPR.

34.15 Improper conduct covers, but is not confined to, conduct which would ordinarily justify disbarment, striking off, suspension from practice or other serious professional penalties. Unreasonable describes conduct which is vexatious, designed to harass the other side, rather than advance the resolution of the case; it makes no difference that the conduct was the product of excessive zeal rather than improper motives. However it is not correct that conduct is *only* unreasonable if it is vexatious or designed to harass the other side.[20] Negligence is not to be construed technically, but to denote failure to act with the competence reasonably expected of ordinary members of the

---

[15] *Re Wiseman Lee (solicitors) wasted costs order) (No 5 of 2000)*, 19 March 2001, CA.
[16] [1998] 1 Fam LR 605.
[17] [2000] PNLR 649.
[18] [2003] EWCA Civ 394.
[19] [1994] Ch 205, CA.
[20] *Jennifer Joseph v Boyd & Hutchinson (a firm)*, 13 January 1999 Ch D, unreported.

profession.[21] There are numerous reported examples covering a myriad of faults and defaults in the conduct of litigation, and although each new case will need to be considered on its own circumstances there is a considerable body of cases which indicate the type of behaviour which is or is not likely to be visited with a wasted costs order. Examples attracting a wasted costs order include: a solicitor who fails properly to instruct his advocate so that not all relevant matters are put before the court on an application to adjourn;[22] delay in the conduct of proceedings even though not leading to their dismissal;[23] a solicitor who learned of fraudulent conduct of his client and whose actions thereafter caused further costs to be wasted;[24] failure to serve notice of discharge or revocation of Legal Aid;[25] failure to agree substantially similar medical evidence in a minor personal injury case, necessitating the attendance at court of two expert witnesses.[26] Falling on the other side of reasonable, a solicitor who commences an action does not thereby warrant that his client has a good cause of action but merely that he has a client who bears the name of a party to the proceedings and who has authorised them;[27] Counsel drafting allegations of fraud does not require admissible evidence of fraud before him/her at the time, but only such material as would lead responsible Counsel to conclude that serious allegations could be based on it.[28] It is neither improper, negligent nor unreasonable for a solicitor or counsel whose client has been slow to provide instructions and who then fails to attend court to conclude that they cannot properly represent him and should withdraw.[29]

34.16 The court in *Ridehalgh* made it plain at four points in its judgment that the threshold was whether the conduct in question was unjustifiable.[30] More recently in *Persaud (Luke) v Persaud (Mohan)*[31] the court was at pains to underline that there needs to be something more than plain negligence, at least where the allegation is that a representative was pursuing a hopeless case, per Peter Gibson LJ, 'it is necessary that there should have been a breach of duty to the court for a legal representative to be made liable by a wasted costs order. That concession seems to me to have been rightly made'.[32] It appears to be moot whether the meaning of 'negligent' as expounded in *Ridehalgh* has in fact been modified so that a breach of duty without more may not be enough and there has to be something akin to abuse of process, or whether the passages in *Medcalf* and *Persaud* which might appear to suggest this are erroneous in that

---

[21] *Ridehalgh* at 232H and 233C, approving the test in *Saif Ali v Sydney Mitchell & Co* [1980] AC 198 at 218, 220.
[22] *Shah v Singh* [1996] PNLR 84, CA.
[23] *Kilroy v Kilroy* [1996] PNLR 67, CA.
[24] *R v Liverpool City Council ex parte Horne* [1997] PNLR, 95, DC.
[25] *Re Stathams (Wasted Costs Order: Banks v Woodhall Duckham Ltd & Others* [1997] PIQR 464.
[26] *Whittles (a firm), Joan Greenhoff v J Lyons & Co Ltd*, 30 June 1998, CA, unreported.
[27] *Nelson v Nelson* [1997] 1 WLR 233, CA.
[28] *Medcalf v Weatherill* [2002] UKHL 27.
[29] *Re Harry Boodhoo, Solicitor* [2007] EWCA Crim 14.
[30] At 226, 231, 236 and 237.
[31] [2003] EWCA Civ 394.
[32] Following from the speech of Lord Hobhouse in *Medcalf*, primarily concerned with the duty owed to a representative's own client.

regard and to the extent that they are inconsistent with *Ridehalgh*, that earlier authority stands.[33] This is perhaps best resolved by the recognition that the wasted costs jurisdiction regulates the lawyer's duty not to his own client nor to the opposing party, but to the court. It is conduct which amounts to a breach of duty to the court which is the prerequisite for a wasted costs order.

34.17 Failure to conduct a case economically or to abide by a Practice Direction will expose practitioners to a risk of wasted costs order.[34] A practitioner ought also to expect that failure to comply with mandatory requirements or even the spirit of the CPR and protocols, may, if there is no reasonable explanation, be visited with a wasted costs order. Such a step is specifically provided for in CPR Part 29 (dealing with case management conferences), in that CPR, r 29.3(2) requires a legal representative familiar with the case and with sufficient authority to deal with any issues that arise to attend case management conferences and pre trial reviews, and the attendant Practice Direction sets out in terms (29 PD 5.2(3)) that where the inadequacy of the person attending or of his instructions leads to the adjournment of a hearing, the court 'will expect to make a wasted costs order'.

Hopeless cases

34.18 A legal representative is not to be held to have acted unreasonably, improperly, or negligently just because he acts for a party whose case is plainly doomed to fail. Courts should rarely if ever assume that a hopeless case is being litigated on the advice of the lawyers; clients are free to reject advice and to insist that their cases be litigated. The lawyer is there to present the case; it is for the judge and not the lawyers to judge it. Legal advisers are expected to continue to make their services available in a hopeless case where the litigant persists in pursuing the claim.[35] A properly conducted case could appear reasonable and then turn out to be hopeless, accordingly care should be exercised in finding that lawyers must have been acting improperly or unreasonably in a hopeless case. But a lawyer cannot lend assistance to a case which is an abuse of process, e.g. to use litigation for procedures or purposes for which they were not intended, or to pursue proceedings for reasons unconnected with success in the litigation of a case known to be dishonest. It is not entirely easy to distinguish by definition between the hopeless case and that which amounts to an abuse of process, but in practice it is not hard to say which it is. Absent abuse of process, or breach of duty to the court, the pursuit of a hopeless case of itself will not found an order (*Persaud*, ibid*)*, even if the legal representative could be said to be in breach of duty to his/her own client or to the Legal Services Commission. If there is any doubt the legal representative is entitled to the benefit of it.

---

[33] *Dempsey v Johnstone* [2003] EWCA Civ 1134.
[34] *Practice Direction (Civil Litigation) Case Management* [1995] 1 WLR 252.
[35] *Brian Anthony Jones v The Chief Constable of Bedfordshire Police*, 30 July 1999, unreported, CA.

Relevance of public funding; impecunious claimant; conditional fees

34.19 The courts must bear prominently in mind the peculiar vulnerability of lawyers representing assisted parties to applications for wasted costs orders because their clients are unlikely to meet any costs liability.[36] It would subvert the benevolent purposes of the Community Legal Service if such representatives were subject to any unusual risk. They for their part must bear prominently in mind that their advice and conduct should not be tempered by the knowledge that their client is not the paymaster and so not in all probability liable for the costs to the other side. An inadequate assessment of the merits of the assisted party's case, or failure to comply with the Bar Council's Guidelines for written opinions in publicly funded cases may be indicative of a breach of duty to the Legal Services Commission, but is not equivalent to a breach of duty to the court.[37]

34.20 Nor is there jurisdiction to make an order for costs against a lawyer solely on the ground that he acted without fee or under a conditional fee agreement.[38] Whether a solicitor is acting for remuneration or not does not alter the existence or nature of his duty to his client and the court, or affect the absence of any duty to protect the opposing party in litigation from exposure to the expense of a hopeless claim. In neither case does he have to impose a pre-trial screen through which a litigant must pass.[39] The existence of a conditional fee agreement should make a legal adviser's position as a matter of law no worse, so far as being ordered to pay costs is concerned, than it would be if there were no CFAs. This is said to be unless, of course, the CFA is outside statutory protection.[40]

Reliance on counsel

34.21 The guidance in *Locke v Camberwell Health Authority*[41] was endorsed. A solicitor does not abdicate his professional responsibility when he seeks the advice of Counsel. He must apply his mind to the advice received. But the more specialist nature the advice sought, the more likely it is that it was reasonable to accept it and act on it. The solicitor is not allowed however to follow Counsel blindly or to ignore the glaringly obvious, see *Tolstoy-Miloslavsky v Aldington*.[42] Nor can a solicitor shelter behind a decision of the Legal Services Commission.[43] Conversely a barrister may not always rely on instructing solicitors to notify him of the times and dates of his cases, see *(Re A Barrister*

---

[36] *Symphony Group Plc v Hodgson* [1994] QB 179 at 194, CA.
[37] *Persaud*, ibid; *Dempsey v Johnstone*, ibid.
[38] *Tolstoy-Miloslavsky v Aldington* [1996] 1 WLR 736 at 746, CA and *Hodgson & Others v Imperial Tobacco* [1998] 1 WLR 1056.
[39] *Orchard v SEE Board* [1987] QB 565, 572–574, CA.
[40] *Hodgson & Others v Imperial Tobacco* [1998] 1 WLR 1056.
[41] (1991) 1 Med LR 249, CA.
[42] [1996] 1 WLR 736 at 747, 749, 751.
[43] *In re Messrs Russell & Russell (solicitors)* 8 August 2003, CA.

(*Wasted Costs Order*) (*No 4 of 1992*)[44] and see *Re A Barrister* (*Wasted Costs Order*) (*No 4 of 1993*).[45] Essentially, every legal representative individually owes a non delegable duty to the court.

Privilege

34.22 If the applicant's privileged communications are germane to an issue in the application, to show what he would or would not have done had the other side not acted in the manner complained of, he can waive privilege; if he declines to do so adverse inferences can be drawn.

34.23 The respondent lawyers are in a difficult position. This is because privilege is not theirs to waive. In the usual case, where waiver will not benefit their client, they should be slow to advise him to waive his privilege, and they may well feel bound to advise their client to seek independent advice before doing so. The client in any event may be unwilling to waive privilege. Accordingly the respondent lawyers are at a grave disadvantage in defending their conduct of the proceedings, unable to disclose what advice and warnings they gave, what instructions they received. It follows that the courts have to make allowance for the inability of the respondent lawyers to tell the whole story. Where there is room for doubt they are entitled to the benefit of it. It is only when, with all allowances made, a lawyer's conduct of proceedings was quite clearly unjustifiable that it could be appropriate to make a wasted costs order.[46] Nor is the court entitled to draw inferences from unseen privileged material, for example in *Dempsey v Johnstone*[47] the Court of Appeal held that the judge below had not been entitled to infer from an extension of legal aid following counsel's advice, that counsel was asserting that there were good prospects of success.

34.24 Clients cannot rely on their legal privilege when they have acted fraudulently and the solicitor cannot connive in the use of such privilege to conceal fraudulent conduct.[48] It is also the case that not only are the respondents not permitted to disclose any privileged facts to the court, but since privilege is that of their client they should not reveal such matters to the lawyers retained to represent them on the application. Thus they should not disclose to their own representatives their client's instructions, advice they gave, instructions to Counsel or his advices, any correspondence or notes or communication with the client, witnesses or experts and so on. For further discussion of what may be disclosed see *Reg v Horsham DC ex parte Wenman*.[49]

---

[44] (1994) *The Times*, March 15, CA (Criminal Division).
[45] (1993) *The Times*, April 21, CA (Criminal Division).
[46] *Ridehalgh* at 237, and *Medcalf v Weatherill*.
[47] [2003] EWCA 1134, approved in *Medcalf*.
[48] *R v Liverpool City Council, ex parte Horne* [1997] PNLR 95, DC.
[49] [1994] 4 All ER 681 at 703, 704.

The second and third stages of the three-stage test

34.25 Even if the conduct of litigation has been improper, unreasonable or negligent, this is not of itself sufficient to give rise to a wasted costs order. Thus a finding of negligence does not mean that a wasted costs order has to be made. Such use of the jurisdiction could result in satellite litigation which was as complex and expensive as the original litigation.

34.26 Obviously the conduct complained of needs to have caused an applicant to incur unnecessary costs. In addition it must be just in all the circumstances to order a legal representative to bear all or part of the unnecessary costs, see *Fitzhugh Gates (a firm) v Elaine Sherman*.[50]

34.27 The jurisdiction is not objectionable on human rights grounds nor does it involve any breaches of Art 6 ECHR, see *X v Germany*,[51] *B v United Kingdom*.[52]

Amount of costs

34.28 A wasted costs order which does not specify the amount of costs to be awarded is said to be fatally flawed and it is not possible to vary or amend the order by adding a figure at a later date.[53] The court when making a wasted costs order must direct that the legal representative pay a specified sum, 48.7(4). But the Practice Direction at 53.9 allows alternatively for the court to specify that costs relating to a particular sum or items of work be disallowed. The court also has power to direct that a costs judge or district judge to inquire into the matter and report to the court before making a wasted costs order. This power of referring to a costs judge or a district judge also allows the court itself to refer the question of wasted costs instead of making a decision thereon and making a wasted costs order itself, CPR, r 48.7(6) and (7).

B Inherent jurisdiction

34.29 In *Ridehalgh* Lord Justice Rose accepted the submission of Leading Counsel that there are only two categories of conduct which can give rise to an order for costs against a solicitor and the court has no power to make an order against solicitors save under the wasted costs provisions of subsections (6) and (7) of s 51 of the Supreme Court Act 1981, *or* under its inherent jurisdiction in relation to breaches of duty to the court (*Ridehalgh* at 227B–E). Examples of conduct falling into the latter category are given as acting without authority or in breach of an undertaking, although acting without instructions in

---

[50] [2003] EWCA Civ 886.
[51] No 7544/76 14 EcomHR.
[52] No 10615/83 38 EcomHR.
[53] *Re Harry Jagdev & Co (Wasted Costs Order) (No 2 of 1999)*, (1999) *The Times,* August 12, CA.

acknowledging service has been held not to amount to conduct justifying a wasted costs order in a s 51(6) application.[54] In practice such cases will usually be brought under s 51(6).

C Section 51(1) and (3)

34.30 The second area of additional jurisdiction, s 51(1) and (3) of the Supreme Court Act 1981, cannot arise where a legal representative is acting only in that capacity in legal proceedings,[55] and is used ordinarily to obtain costs orders against non-parties (see later in this chapter). However the Court of Appeal has held that there is jurisdiction to make a wasted costs order against a firm of solicitors being a non-party acting for a party to proceedings, where a benefit accrued to that firm from the subject matter of the litigation and hence in acting, and where the firm had known that the client was not likely to be able to pay its costs.[56] The original application had been made under all three substantive heads of jurisdiction, namely (i) s 51(6), (ii) the court's inherent jurisdiction, and (iii) under the general jurisdiction provided for by s 51(1) and (3). The judge had made a personal costs order in reliance on s 51(1) and (3), and the firm of solicitors in question were unsuccessful in their appeal against that order. *Globe Equities*, however, concerned a solicitor who had effectively become the client and was the driving force behind the litigation. He was not therefore acting only in the capacity of legal representative.

D CPR, r 44.14

34.31 Rule 44.14, The Court's powers in relation to misconduct, provides as follows:

(1) The court may make an order under this rule where –

(a) a party or his legal representative, in connection with a summary or detailed assessment, fails to comply with a rule, practice direction or court order; or
(b) it appears to the court that the conduct of a party or his legal representative, before or during the proceedings which gave rise to the assessment proceedings, was unreasonable or improper.

(2) Where paragraph (1) applies, the court may –

(a) disallow all or part of the costs which are being assessed; or
(b) order the party at fault or his legal representative to pay costs which he has caused any other party to incur.

(3) Where

---

[54] *Regent Leisuretime Ltd, Amos & Barton v Skerrett, Pearson* [2006] EWCA Civ 1032.
[55] *Hodgson v Imperial Tobacco* [1998] 1 WLR 1056, 1066.
[56] *Globe Equities Ltd v Globe Legal Services Ltd* sub nom *Globe Equities v Kotrie and Others*, (1999) *The Times*, 14 April.

(a) the court makes an order under paragraph (2) against a legally represented party; and
(b) the party is not present when the order is made, the party's solicitor must notify his client in writing of the order no later than 7 days after the solicitor receives notice of the order.

34.32 The Practice Directions supplementing this Part are PD 44 (General rules about costs) and PD 43-48. The supplemental practice direction aimed at this provision provides;–

Section 18 – Court's Powers in relation to misconduct: rule 44.14.

18.1 Before making an order under rule 44.14 the court must give the party or legal representative in question a reasonable opportunity to attend a hearing to give reasons why it should not make such an order.

18.2 Conduct before or during the proceedings which gave rise to the assessment which is unreasonable or improper includes steps which are calculated to prevent or inhibit the court from furthering the overriding objective.

18.3 Although rule 44.14(3) does not specify any sanction for breach of the obligation imposed by the rule the court may, either in the order under paragraph (2) or in a subsequent order, require the solicitor to produce to the court evidence that he took reasonable steps to comply with the obligation.

34.33 There are two points of focus to the CPR Part 44 sanction, firstly the sanction attaches to failures to comply with rules, practice directions or court orders in connection with the assessment procedure itself. Delay in commencing detailed assessment, 'sufficiently beyond that sometimes encountered' can amount to misconduct within this part of the rule.[57] However, the mere failure to initiate assessment within three months of the judgment or order is already penalised by disallowance of interest under r 47.8. The further sanction of disallowance of actual costs either for that breach, or for technical non-compliance in the form of the bill, would not found reasonable justification for the imposition of sanctions for miscounduct under r 44.14.[58] The second part of the rule however applies to 'unreasonable or improper' conduct both during and before the substantive proceedings. There are very few reported decisions of the operation and scope of these powers in practice, but in the light of the inability of the statutory wasted costs jurisdiction to penalise conduct pre issue of proceedings, see *Byrne v Sefton Health Authority*,[59] *Charles v Gillian Radford & Co*,[60] the r 44.14 powers may be of significant import. That they might be called upon to play a role in sanctioning pre trial conduct was considered in *Hamilton v Fayed*.[61]

---

[57] *McGuigan v Tarmac Ltd* CLY 2003 324, *Re Homes Assured: Sampson v Wilson* [2002] 1 Costs LR 71.
[58] *Botham v Khan* [2004] EWHC 2602.
[59] [2002] EWCA Civ 1904.
[60] [2003] EWHC 3180 (Ch).
[61] (2000) *The Times,* October 13, CA.

COSTS AGAINST NON-PARTIES

Generally

34.34 In *Aiden Shipping Co Ltd v Interbulk*[62] it was held that the discretionary power to award costs (Supreme Court Act 1981, s 51(1)) was in wide terms; there was no basis to imply a limitation to the effect that costs would only be ordered to be paid by the parties to proceedings. The Court of Appeal in *Symphony Group plc v Hodgson*,[63] has laid down principles to govern the exercise of discretion where an application is made for a non party to pay costs of proceedings.

Jurisdiction

34.35 An order against a non party may be made under s 51(1) and (3) of the Supreme Court Act 1981. Where a legal representative acts solely in that capacity he is not subject to the s 51(1) and (3) jurisdiction.[64] Section 51(1) and (3) will however operate against a legal representative who in reality is the client.[65]

The Civil Procedure Rules

34.36 CPR, r 48.2 applies to costs orders in favour of or against non-parties. There is as yet no Practice Direction aimed specifically at this issue, but PD Costs, supplementing Parts 43 to 48, applies to all such applications.

34.37 Rule 48.2 provides:

(1) Where the court is considering whether to exercise its power under section 51 of the Supreme Court Act 1981 (costs are in the discretion of the court) to make a costs order in favour of or against a person who is not a party to proceedings:
   (a) that person must be added as a party to the proceedings for the purposes of costs only; and
   (b) he must be given a reasonable opportunity to attend a hearing at which the court will consider the matter further.

(2) This rule does not apply:
   (a) where the court is considering whether to
      (i) make an order against the Legal Services Commission;
      (ii) make a wasted costs order (as defined in 48.7); and
   (b) in proceedings to which rule 48.1 applies (pre-commencement disclosure and orders for disclosure against a person who is not a party).

---

[62] [1986] AC 965, HL.
[63] [1994] QB 179 at 192 to 194, CA.
[64] *Hodgson v Imperial Tobacco* [1998] 1 WLR 1056, 1066.
[65] *Globe Equities Ltd v Globe Legal Services Ltd sub nom Globe Equities v Kotrie and Others* (1999) *The Times*, 14 April.

Principles[66]

34.38 Three recent decisions of the Court of Appeal, and one of the Privy Council, – *Hamilton v Al Fayed (No 2)*,[67] *R (Factortame Ltd) v Transport Secretary (No 8)*[68], *Dymocks Franchise Systems (NSW) Pty Ltd v Todd*[69] and *Arkin v (1) Borchard Lines Ltd (2) Zim Israel Navigation Company Ltd & others*[70] – have made the position much clearer and must be regarded as the starting point. Earlier decisions must now be read with caution and in the light of these.

34.39 Certain principles however can be extracted from earlier authority and remain relevant. The starting point is that an order for the payment of costs by a non-party will always be exceptional, *Symphony Group plc v Hodgson*.[71] What is exceptional is to be judged as in whether a set of circumstances are extraordinary in the context of the entire range of litigation that comes to the courts, *TGA Chapman Ltd and another v Christopher and another*.[72] It will be even more exceptional for an order for the payment of costs to be made against a non-party, where the applicant has a cause of action against the non-party and could have joined him as a party in the original proceedings. Even if the applicant has good reason for not joining the non-party against whom he has a valid cause of action, he should warn him at the earliest opportunity of the possibility that he may seek an order for costs against him. At the very least this will be an opportunity to apply to be joined. A note of caution however, although third party costs orders are said to be 'exceptional', exceptional in this context means no more than outside the run of cases where parties pursue or defend claims for their own benefit and at their own expense.[73]

34.40 The judge should treat any application for such an order with considerable caution, *Symphony Group plc v Hodgson*.[74]

34.41 Each case should be decided on the facts individually so that principles are guidelines rather than fetters, *Murphy and Another v Young & Co's Brewery and Another*.[75]

34.42 An important question will be whether there has been wanton and officious intermeddling in the disputes of others where the meddler has no

---

[66] *Symphony Group Plc v Hodgson* [1994] QB 179.
[67] [2002] EWCA Civ 665.
[68] [2002] EWCA Civ 932.
[69] [2004] 1 WLR 2807, PC.
[70] [2005] EWCA Civ 655.
[71] [1993] 4 All ER 143, CA.
[72] [1998] 2 All ER 873, CA.
[73] *Dymocks Franchise Systems (NSW) Pty Ltd v Todd* [2004] 1 WLR 2807, PC.
[74] [1993] 4 All ER 143, CA.
[75] [1997] 1 WLR 1591, CA.

interest whatever, and where the assistance he renders to one or the other party is without justification or excuse, *Giles v Thompson*,[76] as set out in Murphy (ibid) at 1601D.

34.43 The Court of Appeal[77] has rejected the submission that *Aiden Shipping* was authority for the proposition that the rationale of s 51(1), (3) was to make the person substantially responsible for causing the costs to be incurred to bear them.

34.44 If however a third party:

(1) has a commercial interest in supporting the litigation, such as a trade union, insurer or other trade organisation, so as to render it just that they should be rendered liable; or

(2) has given an express or implied promise of indemnity to the claimant against his liability, if unsuccessful, for the defendant's costs,

it might be right to make an order.

34.45 In the absence of exceptional circumstances this will not extend to making an order against a liquidator[78] or a legal expenses insurer.[79] However, insurers of a negligent defendant who caused an action against the defendant to be defended were held liable both to indemnify the defendant to the limit of the insurance policy and to pay the costs of the action in which negligence was established. The liability for costs flowed from the insurer's decision that the action be defended. The court said, in reality, the insurers were the defendants.[80] Costs were awarded against insurers for similar reasons in a first instance decision decided shortly after *TGA Chapman, Pendennis Shipyard Ltd v Margrathea (Pendennis) Ltd*.[81] Usually however costs will not be awarded against indemnity insurers in a sum which exceeds the limit of the indemnity.[82] Where the interests of a director and his company and his identity and that of the company were essentially one and the same in each case, it would be unjust for the director to escape a personal costs liability by relying on the separate legal personality of the company.[83]

34.46 In *Nordstern Allgemeime Versicherungs AG v Internav Ltd: Same vKatsamas and Another*,[84] considering the current test of maintenance, Waller LJ referred to Lord Mustill's suggestion in *Giles v Thompson*[85] that it

---

[76] [1994] 1 AC 142, 164.
[77] *Taylor v Pace Developments Limited* [1991] BCC 406 at 409, CA.
[78] *Mettaloy Supplies Ltd (in liquidation) v MA (UK) Ltd* [1997] 1 All ER 418, CA.
[79] *Murphy v Young & Co's Brewery Limited* [1997] 1 All ER 518, CA.
[80] *T.G.A. Chapman Ltd v Christopher*, (1997) *Times* July 21, CA.
[81] (1997) *The Times*, August 27.
[82] *Cormack and Cormack v The Excess Insurance Company Ltd* (2000) *The Times*, March 30.
[83] *Alan Phillips Associates v Dowling & Ors* 12 January 2007, CA (Civ Div).
[84] (1999) *The Times*, June 8, CA.
[85] [1994] 1 AC 142, 164.

was for the court to ask whether or not there was wanton and officious intermeddling with the disputes of others where the meddler had no interest, save a financial interest in the result. *Nordstern* makes plain that whilst it was the case that where an agreement fell within the definition of champerty that would form a firm basis for exercising the s 51 jurisdiction against a non-party, the fact that an agreement did not fall within the strict definition of champerty would not lead to the conclusion that the jurisdiction should not be exercised under s 51. The court also rejected a submission that a non-party's liability to pay needs to be secondary, holding that the jurisdiction to order costs against a non-party provided by s 51 is not limited to those cases where a costs order has previously been made against a party to the litigation.

34.47 Since the decisions in *Hamilton* and *Factortame* it is clear that factors such as the absence of agreement by the funder to accept liability for any costs order against the person funded or the fact that the funding is made in the course of business is not enough to render the funder liable. Likewise since *Hamilton* and *Factortame* the modern emphasis is on access to justice, and there have evolved substantial inroads into what historically was considered champertous or improper maintenance. In *Hamilton* the court declined to order that a pure funder pay costs; they were exempt from liability under s 51(3). Pure funders were generally exempt from liability under s 51(3) of the 1981 Act for the costs of the successful unfunded party; the unfunded party's ability to recover his costs had to yield to the funded party's right of access to the courts; the pure funding of litigation was in the public interest provided that its essential motivation was to enable the funded party to litigate what the funders perceived to be a genuine case. Similarly, if funds are provided to a litigant by way of loan with no further involvement by the lender and no interest in the litigation conferred on the lender, a costs order would not ordinarily follow against the lender.[86] On the other hand, those with an interest akin to that of the funded party, who fund litigation when standing to gain a significant profit if the litigation is successful, will ordinarily be required to pay the successful party's costs because they are not facilitating access to justice, but rather gaining access to justice for their own purposes.[87]

34.48 Some assistance as to the proper approach is also to be found *in Hollins v Russell and other cases*.[88] There, in the context of departures from the strict statutory requirements relating to CFAs, the Court of Appeal at paragraph 107 posed the question, 'Has the particular departure from a regulation pursuant to s 58(3)(c) of the 1990 Act or a requirement in s 58, either on its own or in conjunction with any other such departure in this case, had a materially adverse effect either upon the protection afforded to the client or upon the proper administration of justice?' That indicates that in addition to the points made above about who is the real party to the litigation, the approach of the court in this context is concerned to protect the integrity of public justice, but no more, and not by a purely technical matters.

---

[86] *Petroleo Brasiliero SA v Petromec Inc* [2005] EWHC 2430 (Comm).
[87] *Dymocks Franchise Systems (NSW) Pty v Todd* [2004] 1 WLR 2807 (Privy Council).
[88] [2003] EWCA Civ 718.

34.49 Important general guidance can be found in the decision of the Privy Council in the case of *Dymocks Franchise Systems (NSW)*,[89] in which the ultimate question of whether or not to make a third party costs order was said to turn on whether in all the circumstances it was just. It was recognized that this is very much a fact specific jurisdiction with a number of different considerations at play.

34.50 The issue of third party funding was considered as a question of public policy by a specially constituted Court of Appeal in *Arkin v (1) Borchard Lines Ltd (2) Zim Israel Navigation Company Ltd & Others.*[90] In that case the third party funder had not funded the litigation itself, which was facilitated by solicitors and counsel acting under to CFAs. The third party funded a specific and discrete disbursement, namely the ultimately unsuccessful and impecunious claimant's huge experts' fees, in return for a share of the damages recovered in the event that the claim was ultimately successful. Without funding by the third party of the experts, the claimant would have had little realistic prospect of pursuing his claim in any meaningful way because of the lack of any other means of funding experts in his claim (insurance being both unavailable and unaffordable and experts being unable themselves to act under CFA agreements). At first instance Colman J had refused applications by the defendants and Part 20 defendants for their costs to be paid by the third party, finding as a fact that the third party funder had had no control over and had not sought to interfere with the litigation in any way, and conscious of the anticipated strong deterrence to professional funders to provide support for impecunious claimants if they were as a matter of course always liable to costs orders. On appeal, whilst providing some support for the business of professional third party funding where the basis of that funding was not objectionable, the Court of Appeal did hold the third party funder liable for a contribution to the costs of the opposing parties, but only to the extent of the funding provided. This is a pragmatic solution with the benefit for third party funders of setting a cap on their exposure which is within their control. In this way, the funder's outlay on disbursements provides a measure which operates as a ceiling for its liability for costs to the other party.

34.51 It now seems unlikely that a party that funds litigation with a view to some personal financial gain from the outcome of the litigation, can escape all costs liability in the event that the litigation is unsuccessful. The benefits to be derived from funding litigation need not take the form of a benefit from the outcome of the litigation, such as a share in any recovery or avoidance of any judgment. However, neither the provision of funds to annul the bankruptcy of one party, nor the provision of loans to that party by way of option agreements to purchase that party's property, such acts enabling her to fund litigation, were proper grounds for costs orders against the lenders.[91]

---

[89] [2004] 1 WLR 2807.
[90] [2005] EWCA Civ 655.
[91] *Michael Steven Vaughan v (1) Jones (2) Fowler (3) Fowler* [2006] EWHC 2123 (Ch).

Application in practice

34.52 The judge should be alert to the possibility that the application against a non-party is motivated by resentment of the inability to obtain an order for costs against a legally aided litigant.[92]

34.53 An application for payment of costs by a non party should normally be determined by the trial judge. The fact that a trial judge may in the course of his judgment have expressed views on the conduct of a non party constitutes neither bias nor the appearance of bias.[93]

34.54 The procedure for the determination of costs is summary. Subject to any relevant statutory exceptions judicial findings are inadmissible as evidence of the facts upon which they were based in proceedings between one of the parties to the original proceedings and a stranger. The normal rule is that witnesses in proceedings enjoy immunity from any form of civil action in respect of evidence given during those proceedings.[94] The fact that an employee, or even a director or the managing director, of a company gives evidence in an action does not normally mean that the company is taking part in the action (to which it has not been joined), insofar as that is an allegation relied upon by the party who applied for an order for costs against a non-party company.

34.55 It is desirable, both for the respondents and the court, that there should in these cases be a concise statement of the grounds and essential allegations of fact relied upon by the applicant.[95]

34.56 Whilst s 51 of the 1981 Act had been replaced by s 4 of the Courts and Legal Services Act 1990 there was no suggestion in any of the subsequent cases that the change in language had produced any difference in the result.

34.57 An application for costs against a non-party under s 51 does not involve suing the non-party and the jurisdiction of the English court extends to the making of an order for costs against a non-party domiciled outside the jurisdiction where such a non-party, alleged to be the alter ego of a party to the proceedings, had such a connection with those proceedings that an order against him should be made. A non -party domiciled in a state party to the Convention on Jurisdiction and the Enforcement of judgments in civil and commercial matters cannot thus require an applicant for costs to sue him in his home state. Even if an application for costs against a non-party does involve

---

[92] See at 746 also *Tolstoy-Miloslavsky v Aldington* [1996] 1 WLR 736, CA.
[93] See *Bahai v Rashidian* [1985] 1 WLR 1337 at 1342, 1346, CA; but otherwise where he has made findings against the unrepresented non-party; see *Re Freudiana Holdings Ltd*, (1995) *The Times*, December 4, CA.
[94] In *Sarra v Sarra* [1994] 2 FLR 880 an application for an order for costs against an expert witness was refused applying these principles.
[95] *Michael Steven Vaughan v (1) Jones (2) Fowler (3) Fowler* [2006] EWHC 2123 (Ch).

the non-party being sued, the non-party was sued as a third party to proceedings so that Art 6(2) applied as an exception to Art 2.[96]

---

[96] *National Justice Compania Naviera SA v Prudential Assurance Co Ltd (No 2)* (1999) *The Times,* October 15, CA.

Chapter 35

CONDITIONAL FEE AGREEMENTS

THE COMMON LAW

The indemnity principle

35.1 Costs cannot be recovered where there is an express or implied agreement not to charge the client unless the claim is successful. The receiving party cannot receive more in costs from the paying party than he is actually liable to pay his own lawyers. In *Gundry v Sainsbury*,[1] it was said that,

> 'Costs between party and party are given by the law as an indemnity ... they are not a punishment ... nor a bonus.'

35.2 So, where the solicitor enables the client to bring the action by maintaining it, or where the solicitor enters into a champertous agreement with the client whereby he shares the damages with the client, no costs are recoverable.

Maintenance

35.3 This is the financial support of litigation without just cause.

> 'It is directed against wanton and officious meddling with the disputes of others in which the [maintainer] has no interest whatsoever, and where the assistance he renders to one or the other is without justification or excuse'.[2]

35.4 Maintenance is not unlawful. A just case would exist where the maintainer has a legitimate interest in the outcome of the suit as a result of a commercial or financial interest or where social, family or other ties justify the maintainer in supporting the litigation.

35.5 In a trade union case, the member who is the client retains a liability for his solicitors' costs. That he is indemnified by his trade union does not exclude his liability to the solicitors. That would only happen if there was a bargain between the union and the solicitors, or between the member and the solicitors,

---

[1] [1910] 1 KB 645.
[2] Per Fletcher Moulton, LJ in *British Cash and Parcel Conveyors Limited v Lamson Store Service Company Limited* [1908] 1 KB 1006 at P.1014 approved by Lord Mustill when giving the only reasoned speech of the House of Lords in *Giles v Thompson* [1994] 1 AC 142.

that under no circumstances would the member be liable for costs: *Adams v London Improved Motor Coaches Builders Ltd*.[3]

Champerty

35.6 This is maintenance, with the addition that the maintainer acts in return for a share of the proceeds of the litigation. This is unlawful unless permitted by statute. It has always been considered contrary to public policy for lawyers to accept a retainer to conduct litigation on a contingency fee basis: see eg *Wallersteiner v Moir (No 2)*.[4]

35.7 There is a useful exposition of the general principles of law in the context of an unusual agreement to fund personal injury litigation by Mr S Silber QC, as he then was, sitting as a Deputy Judge of the High Court, in *Gough v Farrer*.[5]

35.8 In *Awwad v Geraghty & Co*,[6] the Court of Appeal restated the common law condemnation of contingency and conditional fee agreements to fund legal proceedings unless authorised by statute, saying that they were contrary to public interest and unenforceable. The earlier Court of Appeal decision in *Thai Trading Co v Taylor*,[7] that there were no longer public policy reasons to prevent a lawyer forgoing all or part of his fee if the case was lost, has been reversed.

35.9 Therefore, at common law, the following are all unlawful and unenforceable:

1. Where the lawyer will recover some of the damages (a contingency fee);

2. Where the lawyer will recover normal fees plus an uplift (a conditional fee agreement);

3. Where the lawyer will recover only normal fees if successful but nothing if unsuccessful (a conditional fee agreement without uplift).

STATUTORY PROVISIONS

35.10 Lawful conditional fee agreements were introduced by s 58 of the Courts and Legal Services Act, 1990, which was brought into force on 1 October 1993. A losing litigant was still likely to be liable to pay his opponent's costs and a new kind of 'after the event' ('ATE') insurance came on the market to cover the risk that an unsuccessful party might have to pay the costs of the other side.

---

[3] [1921] 1 KB 495.
[4] [1975] QB 373.
[5] 24 July 1998 (unreported).
[6] [2001] QB 570.
[7] [1998] QB 785.

35.11 From 30 July 1998, conditional fee agreements could be used in all personal injury and clinical negligence claims. In relation to agreements entered into after 1 April 2000, success fees and insurance premiums became recoverable from the paying party, by virtue of s 58B of the Courts and Legal Services Act 1990, as amended by s 28 of the Access to Justice Act 1999. It was as a result of this that insurers increasingly attacked the enforceability of conditional fee agreements, mainly by arguing that the agreement was a breach of the indemnity principle if the precise and detailed requirements of the relevant Regulations were not satisfied.

35.12 Section 58 of the 1990 Act, in its original wording, has been substituted by new wording set out in ss 27 and 28 of the Access to Justice Act, 1999, which now contains the relevant statutory code. Section 58(1) as re-enacted provides that a conditional fee agreement shall not be unenforceable by reason only of the fact that it is a conditional fee agreement providing all the conditions of s 58 are satisfied. If they are not satisfied, the conditional fee agreement is unenforceable.

35.13 A conditional fee agreement is an agreement with a person providing advocacy or litigation services which provides for his fees or expenses to be payable only in specified circumstances (usually that the litigation results in success). If the specified circumstances occur, then a success fee may be provided for and that will be an increase on the normal fee. 'Advocacy services and litigation services' includes any sort of proceedings for resolving disputes (and not just proceedings in court), whether commenced or contemplated: s 58B(6). 'Litigation services' are defined in s 119(1) of the Access to Justice Act as:

> 'any services which it would be reasonable to expect a person who is exercising, or contemplating exercising, a right to conduct litigation in relation to any proceedings, or any contemplated proceedings, to provide.'

35.14 In *Gaynor v Central West London Buses Ltd*,[8] solicitors, in their client care letter, said 'If your claim is disputed by your opponent and you decide not to pursue your claim then we will not make a charge for the work we have done to date.' It was argued that this was a CFA which did not comply with the statute, but the Court of Appeal held that work done before a decision is made not to pursue a claim is not provision of legal services. 'Contemplated proceedings' are those in which it can be said that there is at least a real likelihood that they will be issued.

---

[8] [2006] EWCA Civ 1120.

REQUIREMENTS OF PRIMARY LEGISLATION

35.15 These requirements are unaffected by the 2005 Regulations and are relevant to all CFAs whenever entered into. By section 58 of the Courts and Legal Services Act 1990 as amended by the Access to Justice Act 1999, agreements must:

1. be in writing;

2. relate to proceedings in which a CFA is permissible (this includes personal injury and clinical negligence actions);

3. comply with such requirements, if any, as may be laid down by any relevant statutory instrument; and

4. state the percentage increase which is to be applied to base fees and they must not exceed the percentage laid down in the Conditional Fee Agreement Order 2000, which is 100%.

35.16 The section does not apply if the agreement is a non-contentious business agreement between solicitor and client under s 57 of the Solicitors Act 1974 – s 58(5).

35.17 In *Jones v Caradon Catnic Ltd*,[9] a success fee of 120% was a clear breach of the 1990 Act and the 2000 Order and it rendered the whole agreement unenforceable. In *Oyston v Royal Bank of Scotland plc*,[10] the claimant and his solicitors entered into an agreement which provided for a 100% uplift and a bonus in the event that damages were recovered in excess of a certain amount. There was subsequently a deed of variation that removed the bonus payment, but this could not save the agreement, which was in clear breach of the Act. The deed of variation had only been entered into when it was realised that the CFA had a potentially fatal flaw and it could not be right that a deed of variation could be used to impose a greater burden on the paying party than existed before there was a judgment.

General observations

35.18 Counsel is free to choose whether or not he enters into a conditional fee agreement and the cab rank principle does not apply.

35.19 Matters such as the definition of success, the obligations under the agreement, withdrawal from and termination of the agreement are all subjects for agreement in a solicitor/counsel agreement. A model form for a solicitor/counsel conditional fee agreement has been agreed between the Personal Injury Bar Association and the Association of Personal Injury

---

[9] [2005] EWCA Civ 1821.
[10] [2006] EWHC 90053 (Costs).

Lawyers, and a copy of the latest version, APIL/PIBA 6, is appended to this chapter. The agreement can be varied or redrafted in any way providing it complies with the statutory provisions contained in the Act and Regulations. The Bar Council and the Personal Injury Bar Association recommend that the APIL/PIBA model is used. Any CFA that is materially different from APIL/PIBA 6 must be approved by BMIF if the work is to be covered by Bar Mutual insurance. BMIF r 10.1.1 provides:

> 'BMIF shall indemnify the insured against claims by a solicitor for payment of all or part of a solicitors fees under a conditional fee agreement between the insured barrister and that solicitor only if and to the extent that:
>
> The conditional fee agreement entered into by the barrister and the solicitor is in a form previously approved in writing by the Directors.'

35.20 There is no need for the percentage uplift in a solicitor/counsel agreement to be the same as that in the solicitor/client agreement, and where fixed uplifts (see later) apply it will not always be so. There is now no statutory provision for a cap on the amount that can be recovered by way of a success fee, except that the percentage by which the fees which would be payable if there was not a conditional fee agreement can be increased (ie the success fee) shall not exceed 100% – Conditional Fee Agreement Order 2000, which is not revoked.

35.21 In *Campbell v MGN Ltd*,[11] the House of Lords rejected an argument that a success fee should not be awarded because the litigant could afford to fund the litigation from her own resources, saying that CFAs were open to everyone.

Collective conditional fee agreements

35.22 These are designed for mass providers and purchasers of legal services ('membership organisations'), such as trade unions, motoring organisations and the like. They are governed by s 28 of the Access to Justice Act 1999 and are intended to provide a simplified process for the funding of multiple claims. The organisation enters into a single CCFA with solicitors to govern the way in which cases for its members will be conducted and funded.

35.23 Section 30 of the Access to Justice Act permits prescribed membership organisations to recover as part of a costs order an additional amount that reflects the provision which the organisation has made against the risk of having to meet the liabilities of a member whose case it has underwritten. The additional amount must not exceed 'the likely cost to the member of the body ... of the premium of an insurance policy against the risk of incurring a liability to pay the costs of other parties to the proceedings': Access to Justice (Membership Organisations) Regulations 2005, reg 5. The requirements of a CCFA have been simplified by the 2005 Regulations which will require only

---

[11] [2005] UKHL 61.

that the arrangements must be in writing and contain a statement specifying the circumstances in which the member may be liable to pay the costs of the proceedings.

35.24 In *Thornley v Lang*,[12] it was argued that the trade union member, whose union indemnified his costs under a CCFA, was only personally liable himself on the basis of an individual CFA agreed between him and the solicitors, and that because this did not meet the requirements of the CFA Regulations, which were then in force, (as distinct from the CCFA Regulations) it was unenforceable as between him and the solicitors. It was argued that the CCFA could not make him personally liable. This attempt to defeat the purpose of the CCFA Regulations by invoking the indemnity principle was defeated by the decision of the Court of Appeal that:

> 'The agreement under which the union agreed with their Solicitors that they should represent the Claimant was a CCFA ... the union so agreed with the authority of the Claimant. An alternative view is that the Claimant ratified the agreement reached by the union on his behalf by availing himself of the services of the Solicitors. On either footing, the contract pursuant to which he came under a liability to pay the Solicitors for their services was a CCFA. As such it was not subject to the CFA Regulations'.

DUTIES OF LEGAL ADVISERS

35.25 By para 303(a) of the Code of Conduct of the Bar Council:

> 'A barrister must promote and protect fearlessly and by all proper lawful means the lay client's best interests and do so without regard to his own interests or to any consequences to himself or to any other persons (including any professional client or other intermediary or another barrister)'.

35.26 The barrister must therefore, when advising on a settlement, advise as to the best course of action from the lay client's point of view only.

35.27 Solicitors Practice Rules apply to work done pursuant to a CFA. Under-settling a case would be a breach of the Law Society Rules of Professional Conduct as well as laying the legal representative open to a possible claim for negligence.

35.28 In *Hodgson & Others v Imperial Tobacco Limited*,[13] Lord Woolf said:

> 'Except that a CFA enables Solicitors and Counsel to enter into an agreement which they would not otherwise be able to make, the existence of a CFA does not alter the relationship between the legal adviser and his client. Solicitor or Counsel still owes to the client exactly the same duties as he would owe the client if he had

---

[12] [2003] EWCA Civ 1484 (29 October 2003).
[13] [1998] 1 WLR 1056 at p 1065.

not entered into a CFA. [He] remains under the same duty to his client to disregard his own interests in giving advice to the client and in performing his other responsibilities on behalf of the client. It extends to advising the client of what are the consequences to the client of the client entering into a CFA. The lawyer also still owes the same duties to the Court ... The lawyer, as long as he puts aside any consideration of his own interests, is entitled to advise the client about commencing, continuing or compromising proceedings, but the decision must be that of the client and not of the lawyer. The lawyer has, however, the right, if the need should arise, to cease to act for a client under a CFA in the same way as a lawyer can cease to act in the event of there being a conventional retainer.'

THE SUCCESS RATE

35.29 This is capped at 100% of base costs. The principle that winning cases should pay for losing ones across the whole spectrum of cases seemed to be accepted by the Court of Appeal in *Callery v Gray*.[14] The result is that the legal costs of claimants whose claims fail should fall to be borne by unsuccessful defendants (para 99 of the judgment of the Court of Appeal). When *Callery v Gray* was considered by the House of Lords,[15] the House concluded that it should not interfere in such practice matters which were pre-eminently the responsibility of the Court of Appeal.

Fixed success fee

Road traffic accidents

35.30 By CPR 45.16, the success fee in road traffic accidents which occurred after 6 October, 2003, is fixed for solicitors at 12½% if the case is concluded successfully before trial, and 100% if concluded at trial. Trial means a final contested hearing or contested hearing on any issue tried separately – CPR 45.15(6)(b). In *Watson v Gray* (Liverpool County Court 8/2/2005), HHJ Stewart held that a disposal hearing after judgment in default, which was listed for 10 minutes and which could have been used for the purpose of giving directions, but at which, in fact, the contested quantum of the claim was decided, was a 'final contested hearing'. The disposal did bring the proceedings to an end and so was 'final'. The Judge also suggested (surely correctly) that the words 'or contested hearing of any issue ordered to be tried separately' contemplates cases where liability or limitation is ordered to be tried separately.

35.31 For Counsel, the fixed rates are (in a case allocated to the fast track) 12½% if it is concluded successfully more than 14 days before trial; 50% if 14 days or less before the date fixed for the commencement of the trial; and 100% if concluded at trial. If the case is allocated to the multi-track, the fixed rates are 12½% if it is concluded successfully more than 21 days before the trial;

---

[14] [2001] 1 WLR 2112.
[15] Reported at [2002] 1 WLR 2000.

75% if 21 days or less before the date fixed for the commencement of the trial; and 100% if concluded at trial (CPR 45.17). These uplifts do not necessarily apply if the value of the damages is £500,000 or more, disregarding any contributory negligence (see CPR 45.18 and 45.19 for the detailed provisions relating to assessment in these circumstances).

35.32 In *Atack v Lee*,[16] the Court of Appeal said that it was wrong to apply the new rules to CFAs entered into before 6 October 2003, but on the other hand, it was legitimate to look at the statistical evidence which informed the negotiations which led to the agreed fixed uplifts. The court emphasised, in a case where there was one uplift only agreed (ie not a two or three stage uplift), that the position had to be considered as at the date when the funding arrangement was entered into. Although Atack went to trial on liability, a 100% uplift could not be justified on the facts, adopting that approach. It is submitted that the position ought to be different if a two or three stage uplift is adopted and that 100% uplift can readily be justified because there is a smaller uplift if the case is settled earlier. The writer recommends that the fixed uplift regime is adopted for CFAs relating to road traffic accidents occurring before 6 October 2003 as well as after it.

Employers' liability

35.33 By CPR 45.21, fixed uplifts were applied to any dispute between an employee and employer arising from a bodily injury sustained in the course of employment (ie an employers' liability accident). This does not apply, however, in relation to an injury sustained before 1 October, 2004, or if the injury arises from a road traffic accident.

35.34 In EL accident cases after this date, the fixed success fees for solicitors are 25% if the case is concluded successfully before trial (but 27.5% if there is a prescribed membership organisation liability for costs), and 100% if concluded at trial. For counsel, the fixed success fee in a case allocated to the fast track is 25% if concluded successfully more than 14 days before trial; 50% if 14 days or less before the commencement of the trial; and 100% if concluded at trial. In a case allocated to the multi-track, the fixed success fee is 25% if concluded successfully more than 21 days before trial; 75% if 21 days or less before trial; and 100% if at trial. There is provision for assessment if damages are reasonably expected to be £500,000 or more, disregarding contributory negligence, similar to those in relation to road traffic accidents.

35.35 If these success fees are adopted for employers liability accident claims occurring before 1 October 2004, it might be difficult in practice for them to be effectively challenged since they are to be universally applied to accidents occurring after that date. The observations made above in relation to *Atack v Lee* would apply equally to EL cases.

---

[16] [2005] 1 WLR 2643.

Employers' liability disease litigation

35.36 By CPR 45.24 and 25 there are fixed success fees in relation to employers' liability disease litigation. These fixed uplifts apply where a letter of claim was sent to the defendant containing a summary of the facts on which the claim is based and main allegations of fault on or after 1 October 2005. They are as follows:

1. *Asbestos:* Solicitors 27.5% (30% if the claim falls under s 30 Access to Justice Act 1999) and 100% if the case goes to trial.
   Counsel 27.5% if concluded before 21 days before trial in the case of a multi-track case and 14 days before trial in a fast track case; 75% if concluded within 21 days of a multi-track trial and 50% if concluded within 14 days of a fast track trial; 100% if concluded at trial.

2. *RSI and Stress*: 100% throughout for counsel and solicitors.

3. *All other diseases including VWF and deafness*: Solicitors 62.5% (70% for s.30 claims) if settled before trial and 100% if concluded at trial.
   Counsel : multi-track 62.5% if concluded more than 21 days before trial; 75% if within 21 days of trial; and 100% if concluded at trial. Fast track 62.5% if concluded before trial and 100% if at trial.

4. There is provision for exceptions if damages are more than £250,000.

35.37 In *Butt v Nizami*,[17] Simon J. held that the indemnity principle had no application to the fixed recoverable costs regime of the CPR Part 45 and the receiving party did not have to demonstrate there was a valid CFA between the solicitor and client, but merely had to show compliance with the relevant provisions of CPR.

Success fees generally

35.38 In *Callery v Gray* (supra), Lord Woolf recommended a two stage uplift (now incorporated in the fixed uplifts prescribed by CPR) and the appropriateness of a 100% uplift if the case goes to trial seems to be established by this regime. The rationale is that, if the case goes to a contested trial, it is reasonable to assume that both sides consider they have at least a 50% chance of winning. In *Designer Guild Limited v Russell Williams (Textiles) Limited* (which can be found on www.hmcourts-service.gov.uk), Mr Brendon Keith, Principal Judicial Clerk in the House of Lords, sitting with the Senior Costs Judge, Master Hurst, said on 20 March, 2003:

'There is an argument for saying that in any case which reached trial a success fee of 100% is easily justified because both sides presumably believed that they had an arguable and winnable case.'

---

[17] [2005] EWHC 159.

35.39 In *U v Liverpool City Council*,[18] the Court of Appeal held that the costs Judge had no power to direct that a success fee was recoverable at different rates for different periods of the proceedings and so the costs Judge could not vary the success fee for periods when the risk increased or reduced ie once the appropriate uplift was determined in accordance with a two or three stage CFA, that uplift was to be applied throughout. To the extent that Costs Practice Direction para 11.8(2) suggests otherwise, it is wrong.

35.40 In *Smiths Dock Limited v Edwards et al*,[19] Crane J dismissed an appeal against an assessment of a single stage success fee of 87% in an asbestos case. He took into account the risk that a Part 36 offer and payment in might be made and not be beaten, which would result in the claimant's solicitors not achieving 'success' as it was defined in the agreement. This case must be read in the light of the subsequent fixed uplift regime of the CPR.

35.41 In *Bensusan v Freedman*,[20] a single stage success fee of 20% was assessed in a straightforward, modest value, clinical negligence claim.

35.42 In assessing the amount of any success fee, the Costs Judge cannot use the benefit of hindsight. He must have regard to the circumstances as they reasonably appeared when the funding arrangement was entered into (PD Part 44.11.7). In deciding whether a percentage increase is reasonable, relevant factors to take into account include the risk that no costs will be recovered (usually because the case is lost, but presumably also that a Part 36 offer will not be beaten), the legal representatives' liability for disbursements, and what other methods of financing the costs were available to the receiving party (PD 44.11.8).

35.43 To assist the Court to make a summary assessment of an additional liability, a party seeking such costs must prepare and have available for the Court a bundle of documents which must include a copy of: (1) the notice of the funding arrangement; (2) every estimate and statement of costs filed by him; and (3) the risk assessment prepared at the time when the relevant funding arrangement was entered into and on the basis of which the amount of the additional liability was fixed (PD 44.14.9). A party may not recover any percentage increase if he has not complied with the Practice Direction or a Court order to disclose the reasons for setting the percentage increase at the level stated in the conditional fee agreement.

35.44 The court will not assess any 'additional liability' (by which is meant 'the percentage increase, the insurance premium or the additional amount in respect of provision made by a membership organisation') until the conclusion of the proceedings (PD 44.14.2 and 44.14.5). A party who seeks to recover an additional liability must provide information about the funding arrangements

---

[18] [2005] 1 WLR 2657.
[19] [2004] EWHC 1116 on 13 May 2004.
[20] SCCO 20 August 2001.

to the Court and to the other parties. There is, however, no requirement to specify the amount of the additional liability or how it is calculated until it falls to be assessed (PD 44.19.1).

35.45 Where costs are summarily assessed at an interim application, an order for payment of those costs will not be made unless the court is satisfied that in respect of the costs claimed the receiving party is at the time liable to pay his legal representative an amount equal to or greater than the sum awarded. Such a liability will not usually exist where there is a CFA. The court may direct that any costs, for which the receiving party may not become liable shall be paid into court to await the outcome of the case or shall not become enforceable until further order or it may postpone the receiving party's right to receive payment: see PD44.14.3-4.

35.46 A claimant who has entered into a funding arrangement before starting proceedings must provide information to the Court by filing notice when he issues the claim form, and the information must be served on the other side with the claim form. If the funding arrangement is entered into later, a party must file and serve notice within seven days of entering into the funding arrangement (PD 44.19.2). If the information given is no longer accurate, notice of the change must be given (PD 44.19.3). A party cannot recover any additional liability in respect of a period during which he failed to give the information required (CPR 44.3B(1)(c)).

35.47 Further, a party may not recover from a paying party any proportion of an additional liability which represents a percentage increase relating to the cost to the legal representative of the postponement of the payment of his fees and expenses (ie that proportion of the uplift which relates to the taking of the risk can be recovered from the other side, but not that part which relates to delay in payment) (CPR 44.3B(1)(a)).

REGULATIONS

35.48 The statutory framework set out in the 1990 Act, as amended by the 1999 Act was supplemented by statutory instruments which were intended to provide consumer protection and to regulate the relationship between the client (consumer) and the legal representative. The Regulations have led to a great deal of satellite litigation and, as a result, the Department of Constitutional Affairs instituted a consultation process designed to simplify the Regulatory regime. This has resulted in the Conditional Fee Agreements (Revocation) Regulations 2005 and the Access to Justice (Membership Organisations) Regulations 2005, which together revoke the Conditional Fee Agreements Regulations 2000, the Collective Conditional Fee Agreements Regulations 2000 and the Access to Justice (Membership Organisation) Regulations 2000 for all agreements entered into after 1 November 2005.

35.49 However the revoked Regulations will continue to govern agreements entered into before that date and the following commentary will remain relevant for some time to come

Conditional Fee Agreements Regulations 2000[21]

35.50 These Regulations came into force on 1 April 2000 and apply to CFAs entered into before 1 November 2005. Important changes were made in 2000 regarding the necessary contents of a conditional fee agreement. A conditional fee agreement must be signed by the client and the legal representative unless it is an agreement between a legal representative and an additional legal representative (usually solicitor and counsel).

35.51 The client care requirements for the contents of conditional fee agreements were set out in regs 2, 3 and 4 of the Regulations. They were detailed and had to be complied with.

Enforceability

35.52 After success fees and insurance premiums became recoverable from a paying party on 1 April 2000, insurers attacked the enforceability of CFAs, arguing that a CFA which did not comply with the Regulations was unenforceable by the solicitor against his client and, if the client was not liable to pay any fees under it, there was nothing for the paying party to indemnify and so there was no liability to pay costs. In *Hollins v Russell*,[22] the Court of Appeal gave important guidance on the effect of non compliance with the Regulations. Brooke, LJ, giving the judgment of the court, said that the key question is:

> 'Has the particular departure from a Regulation pursuant to Section 58(3)(c) of the 1990 Act or a requirement in Section 58, either on its own or in conjunction with any other such departure in this case, had a materially adverse effect either upon the protection afforded to the client or upon the proper administration of justice?'

35.53 If the answer is 'Yes', the conditions have not been satisfied. If the answer is 'No', then the departure is immaterial and the conditions have been satisfied. The paying party to the litigation has no legitimate interest in seeking to avoid his proper obligations by seizing on an apparent breach of the requirements which is immaterial in the context of the purposes of the statutory regulation. The court also observed that ATE insurance premiums are recoverable as costs in any proceedings irrespective of whether or not there is a CFA between the receiving party and his legal representatives, and the same will apply to paid disbursements.

---

[21] SI 2000/692.
[22] [2003] 1 WLR 2487.

35.54 There is some uncertainty whether 'materially adverse effect' means that only de minimis departures from the requirements of the Regulations will leave the CFA enforceable or whether something more than that will still enable the CFA to be enforced in a suitable case. See the observations of Dyson LJ in *Myatt v NCB* where he left the issue open.[23]

35.55 In that case the Court of Appeal was concerned with the steps that a solicitor should take to ascertain whether there was before the event insurance which the client could utilise rather than rely on a CFA. It will generally be inappropriate for the solicitor to ask the client simply whether he has an insurance policy which covers the proposed claim, because this is asking the lay client something which the solicitor has the duty to inform the client about pursuant to reg 4(2)(c) of the CFA Regulations 2000. An example of a case where the solicitor did not have to look into the terms and conditions of a policy when the client said that he did not have any cover which would protect his costs position was *White v Revell*.[24] In *Myatt* the court did say that the duty under this Regulation does:

> 'not require solicitors slavishly to follow the detailed guidance given by this court in *Sarwar* [2002] 1 WLR 125. In particular the statement...that a solicitor should normally invite a client to bring to the first interview any relevant policy should be treated with considerable caution. It has no application in high volume low value litigation conducted by solicitors on referral by claims management companies.'

35.56 In *Sarwar v Alam*,[25] the Court of Appeal had held that, in relatively small personal injury claims arising out of road traffic accidents not exceeding about £5,000, a claimant who already possessed before the event legal expenses insurance cover which appeared to be satisfactory for a claim of that size should ordinarily be referred to the relevant before the event insurer rather than incurring the cost of an ATE insurance premium. Where, however, a passenger in a road traffic accident claim might blame the driver, the passenger should not be required to invoke insurance cover provided by his opponent where, for example, the insurers would be entitled to the full conduct and control of any claim and the claimant was denied the opportunity of instructing a suitably qualified solicitor of his own choice. The court said that proper modern practice dictates that a solicitor should normally ask the client to bring copies of motor, household and any stand-alone BTE policy belonging to the client or any spouse or partner living in the same household as the client to determine whether ATE insurance cover is appropriate. The solicitor's enquiries should be proportionate to the amount at stake and the solicitor is not obliged to embark on treasure hunt, seeking to see the insurance policies of every member of the client's family in case by chance they contain relevant BTE cover which the client might use. The solicitor should ordinarily ask the client passenger to obtain a copy of the driver's insurance policy, if reasonably practicable. This

---

[23] [2007] 1 WLR 554 at para 31.
[24] [2006] EWHC 90054 (8 September 2006).
[25] [2002] 1 WLR 125.

was a case governed by the solicitor's client care duty setout in the Solicitors' Costs Information and Client Care Code and the Solicitors' Practice Rules.

35.57 *Myatt v NCB* also established that whether there was a breach which had a materially adverse effect on the protection afforded to the client or on the proper administration of justice was to be determined as at the time of the breach and it is irrelevant whether the breach in fact caused any loss. Therefore it does not help the solicitor who makes inadequate enquiries about the existence of BTE cover, if it turns out that there was in fact no such policy in existence.

35.58 In *Garrett v Halton Borough Council* (decided and reported with *Myatt v NCB*), the Court of Appeal decided that a solicitor who received work from a referrer, who prescribed an after the event insurance product which was to be used, had an interest which should be disclosed to the client when he recommended that insurance product because he had an interest in staying on the referrer's panel and continuing to receive instructions. It was not enough simply to tell the client that the solicitor was on the panel.

35.59 In *Myatt v NCB (No 2)*,[26] the court held that it had jurisdiction to make a costs order against a solicitor where litigation was pursued by the client for the benefit, or to a substantial degree for the benefit, of the solicitor.

After 1 November 2005

35.60 The client care provisions of the 2000 Regulations have been swept away in an attempt to simplify procedure. It has been widely accepted that explanations required to be given by solicitors to clients are at best confusing to the lay client. The new agreements need only recite that the solicitor has complied with the Law Society Professional Rules relating to client care and/or that reg 4 of the Access to Justice Act 1999 (Membership Organisations) Regulations 2005 has been complied with. The current Solicitors' Costs Information and Client Care Code can be found on the Law Society website.[27] There is a new Law Society Code of Conduct but it is not yet in force and is expected to come into force during the first half of 2007. The Law Society have prepared a new simplified solicitor/client standard CFA.

35.61 In *Garbutt v Edwards*,[28] it was decided that a breach of the Solicitors' Code did not make the retainer contract unenforceable, though it may affect what costs are reasonably incurred. This case was decided in the context of a failure to give a costs estimate, but the same reasoning would apply to other breaches of the Costs Information and Client Care Code.

---

[26] Judgment given by the Court of Appeal on 16 March 2007.
[27] www.lawsociety.org.uk/professional/conduct/guidline.
[28] [2006] 1 WLR 2907.

CFA Lite

35.62 Section 31 of the Access to Justice Act, 1999, which amends s 51 of the Supreme Court Act, 1981, was brought into effect by the Access to Justice Act, 1999 (Commencement No 10) Order 2003,[29] and CPR 43.2 was amended by the Civil Procedure (Amendment No 2) Rules 2003.[30] CPR 43.2(3) says:

'2. The costs to which Parts 44 to 48 apply include:

. . .

(3) Where advocacy or litigation services are provided to a client under a conditional fee agreement, costs are recoverable under Parts 44 to 48 notwithstanding that the client is liable to pay his legal representative's fees and expenses only to the extent that sums are recovered in respect of the proceedings, whether by way of costs or otherwise.'

35.63 An agreement in these terms is referred to colloquially as a 'CFA Lite'.

Retrospective agreements

35.64 There is no clear authority on whether retrospective CFA agreements are permissible. An ordinary fee paying agreement can be varied retrospectively providing there is consideration for it. In *Kellar v Williams*[31] there was a fee-paying agreement with solicitors after a costs order was made. The Privy Council held it was quite open to the client and his solicitors to vary the agreement by changing the method of calculating the fees payable, if there was consideration for the change. The paying party could not be ordered to accept the variation if it produced a higher figure for costs because the amendment came into existence subsequent to the costs order and so could be disregarded by the paying party if he wished. This case is often regarded as authority for the proposition (surely reasonable enough) that a variation in a funding agreement cannot be enforced against a paying party if the variation is made after the costs liability is determined, but it makes clear that a funding arrangement can be varied as long as there is consideration.

35.65 In *Holmes v Alfred McAlpine Homes (Yorkshire) Ltd*,[32] a CFA was backdated by six weeks and claimed a success fee. Burnton J held that backdating of an agreement was generally wrong but it was not, on its construction, of retrospective effect. However, the Judge made clear that a CFA can have retrospective effect as long as there was express provision for its application to work done from an identified prior date. This case did proceed on the basis that before the CFA there was an ordinary retainer so that there was consideration because the client was relieved of the obligation to pay costs if the case was lost or to fund it.

---

[29] SI 2003/1241.
[30] SI 2003/1242.
[31] [2004] UKPC 30 (24 June 2004).
[32] [2006] AllER (D) 68 (Feb).

35.66 In *King v Telegraph Group Ltd*,[33] the CFA provided that it covered work done for three weeks prior to the date of the agreement. It was argued that an agreement with retrospective effect was inconsistent with the statutory requirements then in force, although permissible at common law. SCJ Hurst said:

> '88. There is no doubt that, as between the Claimant's solicitors and their client, the CFA may be backdated. This would, in my judgment, be sufficient to satisfy the court that there was a proper retainer between the client and his solicitors before the signing of the CFA, ie the client by signing the CFA is ratifying what has gone before. There seems no doubt therefore that the Claimant is entitled to recover base costs from the date when he instructed his solicitors until the signing of the CFA.
>
> 89. Although there is no prohibition in the legislation against backdating a success fee, such backdating seems to me to fly in the face of the CFA Regulations and the CPR. As Mr Morgan has pointed out the solicitors are placed under a strict duty to explain the position to their client, which they did not do until shortly before the CFA was signed. The solicitors do not assume any risks under the CFA until it is signed (although they may well have been at the normal commercial risk of not being paid prior to that point). The solicitors are under no duty to give notice of funding until the CFA has been signed. It is of great importance that an opposing party should be aware of any additional liability as early as possible...
>
> 90. It seems to me therefore to be quite wrong, and contrary to public policy, to permit the Claimant's solicitors to recover a success fee prior to the signing of the CFA.'

Assessment of costs

35.67 The court will consider the amount of any additional liability separately from the base costs. So, if proportionality is relevant to the assessment of costs, the amount of the success fee will not be taken into account in considering whether the total costs are proportionate (PD 44.11.9).

35.68 In order to maintain income and compensate for lost cases, the following formula can be used if a single stage uplift is agreed.

35.69 If the probability of success is $x\%$, the conditional fee should be $100 \div x$ multiplied by the basic fee. So, for example, if the probability of success is 50%, the calculation is $100 \div 50$, which equals twice the normal fee, ie an uplift of 100%. The following table shows the effect of the uplift.

Chance of success	Percentage uplift
100	nil

---

[33] SCCO Ref: PTH 0408205 & 0408206: 2 December 2005.

Chance of success	Percentage uplift
90	11
80	25
75	33
60	67
50	100 (maximum allowed)

35.70 These figures compensate solely for the uncertainty of outcome. They do not compensate for the outlay of any disbursements which the solicitor may fund, nor for delay in remuneration, and an increase in the uplift is appropriate to take account of these factors, although the other side will not have to pay any proportion of the increase attributable to the delay in payment. Given that the amount of fees lost in an unsuccessful case which goes to trial may well be substantially more than the costs expended on a successful case (which may well settle long before trial), a slightly increased percentage uplift would seem to be justified to balance the books. This principle was recognized in the mediation which led to the fixed uplift regime of the CPR.

DISCLOSURE OF AGREEMENT

35.71 The Court of Appeal in *Hollins v Russell*[34] addressed the issue of whether it was necessary for a receiving party to disclose his conditional fee agreement. It determined that a costs judge should normally exercise his discretion to require the receiving party to disclose the CFA to the paying party, subject to the receiving party's right to rely instead on other evidence under Paragraph 40.14 of the Costs Practice Direction, and subject to redaction, where necessary, of any privileged or confidential information; but that attendance notes or other correspondence should not normally be ordered to be disclosed unless there was a genuine issue as to whether the CFA was enforceable by the client. A genuine issue is one in which there is a real chance that the CFA is unenforceable as a result of failure to satisfy the applicable client care provisions under the 2000 Regulations or, presumably, after 1 November 2005 the Solicitors Practice Rules.

ATE INSURANCE

35.72 The premium for an ATE policy is an 'additional Liability' and notice of funding must be given pursuant to CPR 44.15. The amount of premium recoverable is that which is reasonable. Details of ATE insurance availability

---

[34] [2003] 1 WLR 2487.

and premiums are helpfully set out from time to time in 'Litigation Funding', published by the Law Society. In *Ashworth v Peterborough United Football Club Ltd*,[35] the court considered the reasonableness of a bespoke ATE premium taken out in the course of litigation and considered whether the receiving party had made an adequate search for a premium at reasonable rates.

35.73 In *Pirie v Ayling*,[36] the ATE premium was defined as '20% of damages awarded' and on that basis it amounted to £2,600. It was submitted that the basis of the calculation of the premium was champertous. Senior Costs Judge Hurst rejected this argument, saying it was open to an insurer to calculate and charge premiums on whatever basis best suits its business. However, he did consider what amount might reasonably be payable by the paying party and suggested that the premium of 20% of damages was likely to be unreasonable in all simple road accident cases in which the compensation exceeds about £2,000. He decided at that time that the appropriate premium should be no more than £350 plus IPT.

35.74 In *Tilby v Perfect Pizza Limited*,[37] it was held that deferment of payment for the ATE premium was not a consumer credit agreement which needed the statutory requirements for such an agreement to be met.

35.75 In *Callery v Gray (No 2)*,[38] it was held that Section 29 of the Access to Justice Act should be interpreted so as to permit the recovery of a premium for insuring the risk that the claimant's own costs cannot be recovered.

TRIBUNALS

35.76 Work done in connection with the Criminal Injuries Compensation Scheme and Employment Tribunal cases is deemed to be non-contentious business and solicitors may make a contingency arrangements as a non-contentious business agreement under s 57 of the Solicitors Act 1974. The requirements of the Courts and Legal Services Act 1990, as amended, and the Regulations referred to above do not therefore apply.

SOURCES OF INFORMATION

35.77 Ethical and practical guidance on conditional fee agreements is to be found on the Bar Council website at www.barcouncil.org.uk. APIL/PIBA 6 which is appended to this chapter can also be downloaded from this site. APIL/PIBA 6 is in two parts with an agreement which must be completed in every case and, separately the standard terms. The recommended solicitor/

---

[35] SCCO 10 June 2002.
[36] SCCO Reference 0207520, 18 February 2003.
[37] SCCO 28 February 2002.
[38] [2001] 1 WLR 2142.

client CFA and information for clients can be found on the Law Society website at www.lawsociety.org.uk. Cost cases are reported on www.hmcourts-service.gov.uk.

APPENDIX 1
CFA FOR USE BETWEEN SOLICITORS AND COUNSEL ON OR AFTER 1 NOVEMBER 2005

This agreement forms the basis on which instructions are accepted by counsel from the solicitor to act under a conditional fee agreement and incorporates the standard terms agreed between APIL and PIBA on 31.10.05, which is available on both the APIL and PIBA websites and is incorporated in, but not annexed to this agreement. *Paragraphs ... of the standard terms and conditions have been amended as shown and underlined on the copy annexed hereto.

This agreement is not a contract enforceable at law. The relationship of counsel and solicitor shall be governed by the Terms of Work under which barristers offer their services to solicitors and the Withdrawal of Credit Scheme as authorised by the General Council of the Bar as from time to time amended and set out in the Code of Conduct of the Bar of England and Wales, save that where such terms of work are inconsistent with the terms of this agreement the latter shall prevail.

Csl's Ref:

Sol's Ref:

In this agreement 'Counsel' means: and any other counsel either from Chambers or recommended by counsel in accordance with clause 20 who signs this agreement at any time at the solicitor's request. 'The solicitor means the firm:...........

'The client' means:..........

[*acting by his/her Litigation Friend..........]

'Chambers' means members of chambers at............

The solicitor provided Counsel with instructions, see copy attached, date stamped __/__/__ and the documents listed there.

What is covered by this agreement

- The client's claim for damages for personal injuries against............ suffered on .... until the claim is won, lost or otherwise concluded, or this agreement is terminated,* or part only of proceedings as set out below.
  [If either the name of the opponent or the date of the incident are unclear then set out here as much detail as possible to give sufficient information for the client and solicitor to understand the basis of the claim pursued.]

- Part only of proceedings, specifically:............;

- Any appeal by the opponent(s);

- Any appeal the client makes against an interim order advised by Counsel;

- Negotiations about and/or a court assessment of the costs of this claim.

What is not covered by this agreement

- Any Part 20 claim against the client;

- Any appeal the client makes against the final judgment order;

- Any application under any award of provisional damages that might be obtained in these proceedings or to vary any order for periodical payments that might be obtained in the proceedings.

[NOTE: delete those parts of the proceedings to which the agreement relates or does not relate as appropriate]

The case is likely to be allocated to the *multi-track *fast track and damages are likely to be in excess of *£500,000* £250,000, disregarding any possible reduction for contributory negligence.

DELIVERY OF BRIEF FOR TRIAL: The solicitor agrees to deliver the brief for trial of any issue including the assessment of damages not less than ....weeks *days before the date fixed for hearing.

COUNSEL'S NORMAL FEES are as follows:

Advisory work and drafting: in accordance with counsel's
hourly rate obtaining for such work in this field currently:
(hourly rate) *   £100.00
                                                   [insert hourly
Court appearances:-   rate]

Brief fees for a trial (allowing 5 hours per day in court) whose duration and hours of preparation are estimated as follows:

Time estimate for trial**	Hours of preparation**	Estimated fee*
Up to 2 days	6	£1,600.00
3 to 5 days	12	£3,200.00
6 to 8 days	18	£5,050.00
9 to 12 days	24	£7,650.00
13 to 20 days	30	£11,400.00

Brief fees for interlocutory hearings whose duration and hours of preparation are estimated as follows:

Estimated duration **	Hours of preparation**	Estimated fee*
Up to one hour	2	£300.00
One hour to half a day	3	£450.00
Half a day to one day	4	£650.00

Over one day will be charged as if it were a trial.

Refreshers, estimated at 5 hours in court ** at counsel's hourly rate currently obtaining for such work in this field*:   £500.00

Renegotiating Counsel's fees: to the extent that the hours of preparation set out above are reasonably exceeded then counsel's hourly rate will apply to each additional hour of preparation. If the case is settled or goes short, counsel will consider the solicitor's reasonable requests to reduce his/her brief fee set out above.

Notes:

* The hourly rate and the estimated fees shown above are examples only. It is up to counsel and solicitors to agree rates for each agreement.

** The time estimates for the duration of a trial or interlocutory hearing and for the hours of preparation which are shown above are examples only. It is up to counsel and solicitors to make such estimates or other means of specifying likely fees as they think appropriate for each agreement.

Counsels Success Fees: Case Concludes:

		at trial:	14 or 21 days before date fixed for trial	more than 14 or 21 days before date fixed for trial	Applicable row marked with a tick: ✔
CPR	Track	%	%	%	
Road Traffic Accident Claims (for accident after 6.10.03)					
45.17	Multi Track:	100	75	12.5	
	Fast Tack:	100	50	12.5	
45.18(2); 45.19 (over £500,000)		100	75	More than 20 or less than 7.5	
Employers Liability Claims (for injury sustained after 1.10.04)					
45.21	Multi Track:	100	75	25	
	Fast Tack:	100	50	25	
45.22 (over £ 500,000)		100	75	More than 40 or less than 15	
Employers Liability Disease Claims (when letter of claim sent after 1.10.05)					
45.23 (3)(a) Asbestos	Multi Track:	100	75	27.5	
	Fast Tack:	100	50	27.5	
45.26 Asbestos Over £ 250,000		100	75	More than 40/ less than 15	
45.23(3)(d) RSI & Stress	Multi Track:	100	100	100	
	Fast Tack:	100	100	100	
45.26 RSI & Stress Over £ 250,000		100	100	Less than 75	
45.23(e) Other disease claim	Multi Track	100	75	62.5	
	Fast Track	100	62.5	62.5	
45.26 Other disease claim Over £250,000		100	...	More than 75 or less than 50	
Other Type of PI Claim					

| | Multi Track: | 100 | ... | ... | |
| | Fast Track: | 100 | ... | ... | |

The reasons, briefly stated, for counsel's success fee are that at the time of entry into this agreement:

- the percentage increase is fixed by CPR 45 ...... [specify];

- the percentage increase is fixed by CPR 45 ...... [specify] but CPR 45.18*, CPR 45.22*, or CPR 45.26* applies to this claim;

- the percentage increase sought is consistent with an industry-wide agreement for this type of case reached by representatives of both Claimants and Defendants under the supervision of the Civil Justice Council and there is no special reason to apply a different uplift in this case;

- the percentage increase reflects the prospects of success estimated in counsel's risk assessment which is* not attached to this agreement;

- the length of postponement of the payment of counsel's fees and expenses is estimated at __ year(s), and a further increase of ......% relates to that postponement and cannot be recovered from the opponent.

The success fee inclusive of any additional % relating to postponement cannot be more than 100% of counsel's normal fees in total.

Dated:

Signed by counsel

or by his/her clerk [with counsel's authority]

[Additional counsel*]

Date............... **signed**

Signed by:

Solicitor/employee in Messrs:

The solicitors firm acting for the client

By signing and today returning to counsel the last page of this agreement the solicitor agrees to instruct counsel under the terms of this agreement and confirms that the Conditional Fee Agreement between the solicitor and client complies with ss 58 and 58A of the Courts and Legal Services Act 1990 as amended.

DISCLAIMER: Counsel is not bound to act on a conditional fee basis until both parties have signed this agreement.

Counsel's risk assessment

[To help counsel make a Risk Assessment and give a Statement of Reasons for Conditional Fees in Personal Injury Cases]

1. The Solicitor has agreed with the client a *one-stage uplift, namely ......% or a two-stage uplift, namely........% where the claim concludes at trial; or ......% where the claim concludes before a trial has commenced. The solicitor has*not included an element relating to the postponement of payment of basic charges.

2. The following stages of the proceedings have been completed: *pre-action protocol, statements of case, disclosure, exchange of evidence as to fact, exchange of expert evidence, case management conference(s), other (please specify)............................ Attempts to settle the claim have failed; the defendant's latest offer (if any) was ....; the client's latest offer (if any) was .... (see letter(s) dated .... & ....).

3. Counsel estimates the overall **prospects of success**, taking all risk factors into account, in the region of ....%. This overall assessment is made irrespective of the date for delivery of the brief.

4. Csl's reasons for setting the % increase at the level(s) stated in the agreement are:
    [N.B. The ordinary risks of litigation and facts set out elsewhere in this form are deemed to be incorporated into this statement of reasons and do not need to be repeated here.]

5. **Further considerations**:

Current APIL/PIBA 5 Agreement?	√/x
Case requiring screening?	√/x
Csl has reason to believe the client is/may be, a child or patient	√/x
A leader is likely to be needed	√/x

This Statement of Reasons is to be attached to the CFA?	√/x

6. Csl's **decision**: *Accepted; Rejected &/or advised alternative funding / ADR

7. Csl's note of the **next step** due to be taken (if instructed on conditional fees) & any comment:

Screened by ....on..........................

Signed by screener ....

Signed by Csl...................................... Dated

The ready reckoner is included for use only as a familiar aide-memoire when assessing a one stage uplift from the overall prospects of success:

Ready reckoner

Prospects of 'Success'	% Increase
100%	0%
95%	5%
90%	11%
80%	25%
75%	33%
70%	43%
67%	50%
60%	67%
55%	82%
50%	100%

APPENDIX 2
STANDARD TERMS AND CONDITIONS POSTED ON THE APIL AND PIBA WEBSITES AND TREATED AS ANNEXED TO THE CONDITIONAL FEE AGREEMENT BETWEEN SOLICITOR AND COUNSEL FOR USE AFTER 1 NOVEMBER 2005

Part one: conditions precedent

Papers provided to Counsel

1. The solicitor should have provided counsel with the following documents:

1) a copy of the conditional fee agreement between the solicitor and the client and the Law Society's Conditions as they apply to the claim;

2) written confirmation that 'after the event' or other similar insurance is in place, or a written explanation why it is not;

3) all relevant papers and risk assessment material, including all advice from experts and other solicitors or barristers to the client or any Litigation Friend in respect of the claim, which is currently available to the solicitor; and

4) any offers of settlement already made by the client or the defendant.

Solicitor's Compliance with Statute

2. The solicitor confirms that the conditional fee agreement between the solicitor and the client complies with sections 58 and 58A of the Courts and legal Services Act 1990 and the Conditional Fee Agreements Order 2000.

Part two: obligations of counsel

To act diligently

3. Counsel agrees to act diligently on all proper instructions from the solicitor subject to paragraph 4 hereof.

Inappropriate Instructions

4. Counsel is not bound to accept instructions:

1) to appear at any hearing where it would be reasonable
   (a) to assume that counsel's fees would not be allowed on assessment or

(b) to instruct a barrister of less experience and seniority,(albeit that counsel shall use his/her best endeavours to ensure that an appropriate barrister will act for the client on the same terms as this agreement);

2) to draft documents or advise if a barrister of similar seniority would not ordinarily be instructed so to do if not instructed on a conditional fee basis;

3) outside the scope of this agreement.

Part three
Obligations of the solicitor

5. The solicitor agrees:

1) to comply with all the requirements of the CPR, the practice direction about costs supplementing parts 43 to 48 of the CPR (PD Costs), the relevant pre-action protocol, and any court order relating to conditional fee agreements, and in particular promptly to notify the Court and the opponent of the existence and any subsequent variation of the CFA with the client and of this agreement and whether he / she has taken out an insurance policy or made an arrangement with a membership organisation and of the fact that additional liabilities are being claimed from the opponent;

2) promptly to apply for relief from sanction pursuant to CPR part 3.8 if any default under part 44.3B(1)(c) or (d) occurs and to notify counsel of any such default;

3) to act diligently in all dealings with counsel and the prosecution of the claim;

4) to liaise with or consult counsel about the likely amount of counsel's fees before filing any estimate of costs in the proceedings, and to provide a copy of any such estimate to counsel;

5) to consult counsel on the need for advice and action following:
   (a) the service of statements of case and if possible before the allocation decision; and
   (b) the exchange of factual and expert evidence;

6) to deliver within a reasonable time papers reasonably requested by counsel for consideration;

7) promptly to bring to counsel's attention:
   (a) any priority or equivalent report to insurers;
   (b) any Part 36 or other offer to settle;

(c) any Part 36 payment into Court;
(d) any evidence information or communication which may materially affect the merits of any issue in the case;
(e) any application by any party to have the client's costs capped;
(f) any costs capping order;
(e) any other factor coming to the solicitors attention which may affect counsel's entitlement to success fees whether before or after the termination of this agreement;

8) promptly to communicate to the client any advice by counsel:
   (a) to make, accept or reject any Part 36 or other offer;
   (b) to accept or reject any Part 36 payment in;
   (c) to incur, or not incur, expenditure in obtaining evidence or preparing the case;
   (d) to instruct Leading counsel or a more senior or specialised barrister;
   (e) that the case is likely to be lost;
   (f) that damages and costs recoverable on success make it unreasonable or uneconomic for the action to proceed;

9) promptly to inform counsel's clerk of any listing for trial;

10) to deliver the brief to counsel in accordance with the agreement between the solicitor and counsel;

11) to inform Counsel promptly if the case concludes 14 days before the date fixed for trial if the claim is allocated to the fast-track or 21 days if allocated to the multi-track;

12) if any summary assessment of costs takes place in the absence of counsel, to submit to the court a copy of counsel's risk assessment and make representations on counsel's behalf in relation to his/her fees;

13) to inform counsel in writing within 2 days of any reduction of counsel's fees on summary assessment in the absence of counsel and of any directions given under PD Costs 20.3(1) or alternatively to make application for such directions on counsel's behalf;

14) where points of dispute are served pursuant to CPR part 47.9 seeking a reduction in any percentage increase charged by counsel on his fees, to give the client the written explanation required by PD Costs 20.5 on counsel's behalf;

15) where more than one defendant is sued, the solicitor will write to the 'after the event' insurers clarifying whether and when defendants' costs are to be covered if the claimant does not succeed or win against all of the defendants, and send that correspondence to counsel; and

16) when drawing up a costs bill at any stage of the case to include in it a claim for interest on counsel's fees.

Part four
Termination

Termination by Counsel

6. Counsel may terminate the agreement if:

1) Counsel discovers the existence of any document which should have been disclosed to him under clause 1 above and which materially affects Counsel's view of the likelihood of success and/or the amount of financial recovery in the event of success;

2) Counsel discovers that the solicitor is in breach of any obligation in paragraph 5 hereof;

3) the solicitor, client or any Litigation Friend rejects counsel's advice in any respect set out in paragraph 5(8) hereof;

4) Counsel is informed or discovers the existence of any set-off or counter-claim which materially affects the likelihood of success and/or the amount of financial recovery in the event of success;

5) Counsel is informed or discovers the existence of information which has been falsified or should have been but has not been provided by the solicitor, client or any Litigation Friend, of which counsel was not aware and which counsel could not reasonably have anticipated, which materially affects the merits of any substantial issue in the case;

6) Counsel is required to cease to act by the Code of Conduct of the Bar of England and Wales or counsel's professional conduct is being impugned; provided that counsel may not terminate the agreement if so to do would be a breach of that Code, and notice of any termination must be communicated promptly in writing to the solicitor;

7) A costs capping order is made which counsel reasonably believes may adversely affect the recoverability of his or her normal fees and/or his or her percentage increase:

8) If the opponent receives Community Legal Service funding.

Termination by the Solicitor

7. The solicitor may terminate the agreement at any time on the instructions of the client or any Litigation Friend.

Automatic Termination

8. This agreement shall automatically terminate if:

1)   Counsel accepts a full-time judicial appointment;

2)   Counsel retires from practice;

3)   the solicitors agreement with the client is terminated before the conclusion of the case;

4)   Legal Services Commission funding is granted to the client;

5)   the client dies;

6)   the court makes a Group Litigation Order covering this claim.

Client becoming under a Disability

9. If the client at any time becomes under a disability then the solicitor will:

1)   consent to a novation of his Conditional Fee Agreement with the client to the Litigation Friend and

2)   where appropriate, apply to the Court to obtain its consent to acting under a conditional fee agreement with the Litigation Friend.

Thereafter, the Litigation Friend shall, for the purposes of this agreement, be treated as if he/she was and has always been the client.

Counsel taking Silk

10. If counsel becomes Queen's Counsel during the course of the agreement then either party may terminate it provided he/she does so promptly in writing.

Part five
Counsel's fees and expenses

Counsel's Normal Fees

11.

1)   Counsel's fees upon which a success fee will be calculated (the normal fees) will be calculated on the basis of the figures contained in the agreement between the Solicitor and Counsel.

2) To the extent that the hours of preparation set out in that agreement are reasonably exceeded then counsel's hourly rate will apply to each additional hour of preparation.

3) If the case is settled or goes short counsel will consider the solicitor's reasonable requests to reduce his/her brief fees as set out in the agreement.

4) Counsel's normal fees will be subject to review with effect from each successive *anniversary of / * first day of February from the date of this agreement but Counsel will not increase the normal fees by more than any increase in the rate of inflation measured by the Retail Prices Index.

Counsel's Success Fee

12. The rate of counsel's success fee and reasons will be as set out in the agreement between the Solicitor and Counsel.

Counsel's Expenses

13. If a hearing, conference or view takes place more than 25 miles from counsel's chambers the solicitor shall pay counsel's reasonable travel and accommodation expenses which shall:

1) appear separately on counsel's fee note;

2) attract no success fee; and

3) subject to paragraph 16 be payable on the conclusion of the claim or earlier termination of this agreement.

Part six
Counsel's entitlement to fees

(A) If the Agreement is not Terminated

Definition of 'success'

14.

1) 'Success' means the same as 'win' in the Conditional Fee Agreement between the solicitor and the client.

2) Subject to paragraphs 15, 18 & 21 hereof, in the event of success the solicitor will pay counsel his/her normal and success fees.

3) If the client is successful at an interim hearing counsel may apply for summary assessment of solicitor's basics costs and counsel's normal fees.

Part 36 Offers and Payments

15. If the amount of damages and interest awarded by a court is less than a Part 36 payment into Court or effective Part 36 offer then:

1) if counsel advised its rejection he/she is entitled to normal and success fees for work up to receipt of the notice of Part 36 payment into Court or offer but only normal fees for subsequent work;

2) if counsel advised its acceptance he/she is entitled to normal and success fees for all work done.

Failure

16. Subject to paragraph 17 (1) hereof, if the case is lost or on counsel's advice ends without success then counsel is not entitled to any fees or expenses.

Errors and Indemnity for Fees

17.

1) If, because of a breach by the solicitor of his/her duty to the client, the client's claim is dismissed or struck out:
   a) for non compliance with an interlocutory order; or
   b) for want of prosecution, or
   c) by rule of court or the Civil Procedure Rules; or
   d) becomes unenforceable against the MIB for breach of the terms of the Uninsured Drivers Agreement:
   the solicitor shall (subject to sub paragraphs (3) – (6) hereof) pay counsel such normal fees as would have been recoverable under this agreement.

(2) If, because of a breach by counsel of his/her duty to the client, the client's claim is dismissed or struck out:
   a) for non compliance with an interlocutory order; or
   b) for want of prosecution, or
   c) by rule of court or the Civil Procedure Rules
   counsel shall (subject to sub paragraphs (3) -(6) hereof) pay the solicitor such basic costs as would have been recoverable from the client under the solicitor's agreement with the client.

(3) If, because of non-compliance by the solicitor of the obligations under sub-paragraphs (1), (2), (11), (12) or (13) of paragraph 5 above, counsel's success fee is not payable by the Opponent or the client then the solicitor shall (subject to sub-paragraphs (5) to (7) hereof) pay counsel such success fees as would have been recoverable under this agreement.

(4) No payment shall be made under sub paragraph (1), (2) or (3) hereof in respect of any non-negligent breach by the solicitor or counsel.

Adjudication on disagreement

(5) In the event of any disagreement as to whether there has been an actionable breach by either the solicitor or counsel, or as to the amount payable under sub paragraph (1), (2) or (3) hereof, that disagreement shall be referred to adjudication by a panel consisting of a Barrister nominated by PIBA and a solicitor nominated by APIL who shall be requested to resolve the issue on written representations and on the basis of a procedure laid down by agreement between PIBA and APIL. The costs of such adjudication shall, unless otherwise ordered by the panel, be met by the unsuccessful party.

(6) In the event of a panel being appointed pursuant to sub paragraph (5) hereof:
   a) if that panel considers, after initial consideration of the disagreement, that there is a real risk that they may not be able to reach a unanimous decision, then the panel shall request APIL (where it is alleged there has been an actionable breach by the solicitor) or PIBA (where it is alleged that the has been an actionable breach by counsel) to nominate a third member of the panel;
   b) that panel shall be entitled if it considers it reasonably necessary, to appoint a qualified costs draftsman, to be nominated by the President for the time being of the Law Society, to assist the panel;
   c) the solicitor or counsel alleged to be in breach of duty shall be entitled to argue that, on the basis of information reasonably available to both solicitor and barrister, the claim would not have succeeded in any event. The panel shall resolve such issue on the balance of probabilities, and if satisfied that the claim would have been lost in any event shall not make any order for payment of fees or costs.
   the amount payable in respect of any claim under sub paragraph (1) or (2) or (3) shall be limited to a maximum of £25,000.

(B) On Termination of the Agreement

Termination by Counsel

18.

(1) If counsel terminates the agreement under paragraph 6 then, subject to sub-paragraph 2 hereof, counsel may elect either:
   a) to receive payment of normal fees without a success fee which the solicitor shall pay not later than three months after termination: (**'Option A'**), or
   b) to await the outcome of the case and receive payment of normal and success fees if it ends in success: (**'Option B'**).

(2) If counsel terminates the agreement because the solicitor, client or Litigation Friend rejects advice under paragraph 5(8) (e) or 5(8)(f) counsel is entitled only to **'Option B'**.

Termination by the Solicitor

(4) If the solicitor terminates the agreement under paragraph 7, counsel is entitled to elect between **'Option A'** and **'Option B'**.

Automatic Termination and Counsel taking silk

(5) If the agreement terminates under paragraphs 8 or 10 counsel is entitled only to **'Option B'**.

Challenge to fees

19. If the client or any Litigation Friend wishes to challenge:

a) the entitlement to fees of counsel or the level of such fees following termination of the agreement ;or

b) any refusal by counsel after signing this agreement to accept instructions the solicitor must make such challenge in accordance with the provisions of paragraphs 14 and 15 of the Terms of Work upon which barristers offer their services to solicitors (Annexe D to the Code of Conduct of the Bar of England and Wales).

Return of Work

20. If counsel in accordance with the Bar's Code of Conduct is obliged to return any brief or instructions in this case to another barrister, then:

1) Counsel will use his/her best endeavours to ensure that an appropriate barrister agrees to act for the client on the same terms as this agreement; If counsel is unable to secure an appropriate replacement barrister to act for the client on the same terms as this agreement counsel will not be responsible for any additional fee incurred by the solicitor or client.

2) Subject to paragraph 20(3) hereof, if the case ends in success counsel's fees for work done shall be due and paid on the conditional fee basis contained in this agreement whether or not the replacement barrister acts on a conditional fee basis; but

3) If the solicitor or client rejects any advice by the replacement barrister of the type described in paragraph 5(8) hereof, the solicitor shall immediately notify counsel who shall be entitled to terminate this agreement under paragraph 6(3).

Part seven
Assessment and payment of costs/fees

Costs Assessment

21.

1) If:

(a) a costs order is anticipated or made in favour of the client at an interlocutory hearing and the costs are summarily assessed at the hearing; or

(b) the costs of an interlocutory hearing are agreed between the parties in favour of the client; or

(c) an interlocutory order or agreement for costs to be assessed in detail and paid forthwith is made in favour of the client:
then

(i) the solicitor will include in the statement of costs a full claim for counsel's normal fees; and

(ii) the solicitor will promptly conclude by agreement or assessment the question of such costs; and

(iii) within one month of receipt of such costs the solicitor will pay to counsel the amount recovered in respect of his/her fees, such sum to be set off against counsel's entitlement to normal fees by virtue of this agreement.

Solicitor's Obligation to pay
22.

1) The amounts of fees and expenses payable to counsel under this agreement:
   (a) are not limited by reference to the damages which may be recovered on behalf of the client and
   (b) are payable whether or not the solicitor is or will be paid by the client or opponent.

2) Upon success the solicitor will promptly conclude by agreement or assessment the question of costs and will pay Counsel promptly and in any event not later than one month after receipt of such costs the full sum due under this agreement.

Interest

23. The solicitor will use his best endeavours to recover interest on costs from any party ordered to pay costs to the client and shall pay counsel the share of such interest that has accrued on counsel's outstanding fees.

Challenge to Success Fee

24.
1) The solicitor will inform counsel's clerk in good time of any challenge made to his success fee and of the date, place and time of any detailed costs assessment the client or opponent has taken out pursuant to the Civil Procedure Rules and unless counsel is present or represented at the assessment hearing will place counsel's risk assessment, relevant details and any written representations before the assessing judge and argue counsel's case for his/her success fee.

2) If counsel's fees are reduced on any assessment then:
   a) the solicitor will inform counsel's clerk within seven days and confer with counsel whether to apply for an order that the client should pay the success fee and make such application on counsel's behalf;
   b) subject to any appeal or order, counsel will accept such fees as are allowed on that assessment and will repay forthwith to the solicitor any excess previously paid.

Disclosing the reasons for the success fee

25.

1) If
   (a) a success fee becomes payable as a result of the client's claim and
   (b) any fees subject to the increase provided for by paragraph12 hereof are assessed and
   (c) Counsel, the solicitor or the client is required by the court to disclose to the court or any other person the reasons for setting such increase as the level stated in this agreement,
   he / she may do so.

Reduction on Assessment

26. If any fees subject to the said percentage increase are assessed and any amount of that increase is disallowed on assessment on the ground that the level at which the increase was set was unreasonable in view of the facts which were or should have been known to counsel at the time it was set, such amount ceases to be payable under this agreement unless the court is satisfied that it should continue to be so payable.

Agreement on Fees

27. If the Opponent offers to pay the client's legal fees or makes an offer of one amount that includes payment of Counsel's normal fees at a lower sum than is due under this agreement then the solicitor:

(a) will calculate the proposed pro-rata reductions of the normal and success fees of both solicitor and counsel, and

(b) inform counsel of the offer and the calculations supporting the proposed pro-rata reductions referred to in paragraph (a) above, and

(c) will not accept the offer without counsel's express consent.

If such an agreement is reached on fees, then counsel's fees shall be limited to the agreed sum unless the court orders otherwise.

Part 5
HUMAN RIGHTS

Chapter 36

HUMAN RIGHTS

INTRODUCTION

36.1 Over six years have now elapsed since the Human Rights Act 1998 (the HRA) came into force. Those expecting the HRA to have changed the legal landscape overnight may have been disappointed. Certainly the changes, so far as day-to-day personal injury practice is concerned, have been modest to date. But what changes there have been are significant because they have heralded in a new freedom to challenge longstanding principles or laws. Now a previously insurmountable hurdle to a claim, whether as a matter of substantive law or procedure, *may* be susceptible to challenge under the HRA 1998. In many cases, as set out below, the party seeking to rely on the HRA has failed. In some cases, however, the HRA has provided the key to unlocking the claim. The challenge for the future is to try and determine how the HRA can be applied successfully to other areas of personal injury practice.

THE KEY CONVENTION RIGHTS

36.2 To understand why the HRA has had an impact, which has been significant but at the same time not resounding, it is necessary to consider the nature of Convention rights, which have been incorporated into our law by the HRA (at Sch 1 to the Act). There are two types of rights under the Convention: absolute rights and qualified rights. Absolute rights are of the highest order, such as the right to life (Art 2) and prohibition of torture (Art 3). Inevitably, therefore, their application in the personal injury field is limited. Qualified rights are much more readily applicable, such as the right to a fair trial (Art 6) and the right to respect for private and family life (Art 8). The corollary of that is that, being qualified, the fact that a party is able to show his right is engaged does not necessarily mean that the party can also show his right has been breached.

36.3 In general terms, qualified rights are only breached where a limitation or interference is disproportionate: that is where it does not pursue a legitimate aim and if there is not a reasonable relationship of proportionality between the means employed and the aim sought to be achieved: see, for instance, *Tinnelly & Sons Ltd v UK*.[1]

---

[1] (1998) 27 EHRR 249 at para 72.

36.4 Very often there will be a conflict between the qualified rights of both parties to the litigation, for instance their rights under Art 6. Or it may be that one party's right under Art 8 conflicts with another party's right under Art 6: see, for instance, *Jones v University of Warwick*.[2] Alternatively, there may be a conflict between one party's Convention rights and the general rights or interests of others, not necessarily parties to the litigation. In all these cases, the European Court of Human Rights (ECtHR) has searched out 'a fair balance between the demands of the general interest of the community and the requirements of the protection of the individual's fundamental rights': see *Soering v UK*.[3] The lasting effect of the qualified rights is, therefore, to import the crucial test of proportionality into our law.

Article 6

36.5 Article 6 provides that:

> '1. In the determination of his civil rights and obligations ... everyone is entitled to a fair and public hearing within a reasonable time by an independent and impartial tribunal established by law.'

36.6 Article 6 is the key procedural provision of the Convention. Article 6 only applies where the litigant has a civil right. This is a matter for the domestic law of the state: see *Matthews v Ministry of Defence*.[4] So it is necessary to establish that the civil right is recognised under English law. The classic example, for our purposes, is a cause of action. Whilst the term 'civil right' is an autonomous Convention term, that has more to do with the classification of the right in question, in other words whether the right is to be seen as a civil one, rather than with whether the right itself exists: see *R (Kehoe) v Secretary of State for Work and Pensions*.[5] So, for instance, a doctor's right to practise medicine is a civil right: see *Le Compte, Van Leuven and De Meyere v Belgium*.[6] But a claimant cannot rely on the fact of a civil right being an autonomous term to create a civil right where none exists under domestic law.

36.7 Article 6 is in principle concerned with the procedural fairness and integrity of a state's judicial system. So Art 6 cannot be employed to challenge the content of the substantive law: see *Z v UK*[7] and *Matthews v Ministry of Defence*.[8] Article 6 provides a number of express guarantees: right to a fair trial, right to a trial by an impartial tribunal and so on. It is important to note that both parties to litigation enjoy these rights: it is not a claimant's charter.

---

[2] [2003] 1 WLR 954.
[3] (1989) 11 EHRR 439 at para 89.
[4] [2003] 1 AC 1163.
[5] [2004] QB 1378 per Keene LJ at 109.
[6] (1982) 4 EHRR 1.
[7] [2001] 2 FLR 612.
[8] [2003] 1 AC 1163.

36.8 Equally importantly, it has long been held that it protects the litigant's right of access to the court: see the seminal case of *Golder v UK*.[9] This right is not absolute. A procedural bar on the right of access to the court will be compatible with Art 6 provided that the procedural bar meets the test of proportionality: see *Ashingdane v UK*.[10] Procedural bars include not just physical barriers to bringing a claim (such as in Golder where the prisoner was refused the right to contact a solicitor) but also statutory or common law bars to a cause of action. It can be a vexed question whether the claimant actually had a substantive civil right, thus engaging Art 6, which was barred by a procedural bar or whether the claimant never had a substantive right at all.

36.9 The court is concerned with substance and not form, so that the drafting technique behind any proposed statutory procedural bar should not determine the issue. The ultimate question for the court, when assessing whether a claimant has a civil right such that Art 6 is engaged, is whether the provisions of the national law prevent the dispute which properly belongs in the province of the courts from being so determined: see *Matthews v Ministry of Defence*[11] and *Wilson v First County Trust Ltd (No 2)*.[12]

36.10 At one stage the ECtHR did hold that Art 6 applied even though as a matter of domestic law no cause of action existed: see *Osman v UK*.[13] In that case the claimant's claim in negligence against the police failed on the ground that, following *Hill v Chief Constable of West Yorks Police*,[14] it was not fair, just and reasonable to impose a duty of care on the police. Nevertheless, the ECtHR found that Art 6 was engaged and indeed had been breached. The decision in *Osman* was resiled from in *Z v UK*,[15] in which the ECtHR explained that the decision had been based on a misunderstanding of the English law of negligence. However, in *Matthews v Ministry of Defence*[16] Lord Walker recognised that 'the uncertain shadow of *Osman v UK* still lies over this area of the law': see para 140. Be that as it may, the Court of Appeal in *D v East Berkshire County Council*[17] did not take up the claimant's proposal to 'resurrect' *Osman*. Likewise, in *R (Kehoe) v Secretary of State for Work and Pensions*[18] the majority of the House of Lords showed no willingness to stretch the concept of civil rights. In *Roche v UK*, the applicant made the same challenge to s 10 of the Crown Proceedings Act 1947 as did Mr Matthews. By the narrowest of majorities, the ECtHR has held that Art 6 is not engaged. It can now be conclusively stated that the state's immunity under the 1947 Act is safe from attack under the HRA 1998.

---

[9] (1975) 1 EHRR 524.
[10] (1985) 7 EHRR 528.
[11] Per Lord Hoffmann at para 29.
[12] [2004] 1 AC 816 per Lord Nicholls at para 35.
[13] [1999] 1 FLR 193.
[14] [1989] AC 53.
[15] [2001] 2 FLR 612.
[16] [2003] 1 AC 1163.
[17] [2004] QB 558.
[18] [2006] 1 AC 42.

Article 8

36.11 Article 8 provides that:

'1. Everyone has the right to respect for his private and family life, his home and his correspondence.

2. There shall be no interference by a public authority with the exercise of this right except such as is in accordance with the law and is necessary in a democratic society in the interests of national security, public safety or the economic well-being of the country, for the prevention of disorder or crime, for the protection of health or morals, or for the protection of the rights and freedoms of others.'

36.12 The right to privacy underlies Art 8 though it is worth noting that Art 8 actually protects the right to respect for private life, rather than the right to private life. This, at the same time, makes the right weaker but of wider application: see *Harrow LBC v Qazi*.[19]

36.13 Private life can extend into the workplace: see *Halford v UK*[20] in which it was held that a telephone call from a private telephone line in an office engaged Art 8 as the applicant had a reasonable expectation of privacy. A person does not have to have a lawful interest in a property for it to be his home for the purposes of Art 8: see *Qazi*. Article 8 affords protection to a person's home as an aspect of his right to privacy (not as a possession or as a property right). Article 8 does not guarantee any absolute right to amenities currently enjoyed.

36.14 If the State interferes sufficiently with a person's mental health, that may engage Art 8. So in *Bensaid v UK*,[21] the ECtHR held that 'treatment which does not reach the severity of Art 3 treatment may nonetheless breach Art 8 in its private life aspect where there are sufficiently adverse effects on physical and moral integrity'. And in *Pretty v UK*,[22] the ECtHR said that Art 8 'covers the physical and psychological integrity of a person'.

In *Wainwright v UK*[23] visitors to a prison were subjected to strip searches. Save to the extent that one of them was touched, there was no battery and hence no claim under ordinary English law principles (see *Wainwright v Home Office*[24]). Such a strip search fell within the scope of Art 8. Whilst the search pursued a legitimate aim (of fighting the drugs problem at the prison), the prison authority did not comply strictly with its own safeguards to protect the dignity of those being searched. Accordingly, there was a breach of Art 8. This decision of the ECHR evidences a different approach to that taken by Lord Hoffmann in the same case in the House of Lords. Lord Hoffmann

---

[19] [2004] 1 AC 983.
[20] (1997) 24 EHRR 523.
[21] (2001) 33 EHRR 205.
[22] (2002) 35 EHRR 1.
[23] 26 September 2006, ECHR.
[24] [2004] 2 AC 406.

considered that there was probably not a breach of Art 8 because the defendant's actions had not amounted to an intentional invasion of privacy.

36.15 Article 8 imposes not just a negative obligation but also a more limited positive obligation on the state. Commonly such a positive obligation will have two aspects: (1) to require the introduction of a legislative or administrative scheme to protect the right to respect for private and family life; and (2) to require the scheme to be operated competently so as to achieve its aim: see *Anufrijeva v Southwark LBC*.[25] Before inaction can amount to lack of respect for private and family life, there must be an element of culpability by the state: at the very least there must be knowledge that the claimant's private and family life were at risk: see *Anufrijeva* at para 45.

36.16 The right can be interfered with in the manner set out at Art 8(2). The word 'necessary' imports the test of proportionality inherent in qualified rights. The court has to ask whether the objective of the measure complained of can be achieved by means which are less interfering of an individual's rights. Even if they are necessary in the sense that they are the least intrusive of Convention rights, does the measure have an excessive or disproportionate effect on the interests of affected persons: see *Samaroo v Secretary of State for HO*[26] per Dyson LJ but see also *Lough v First Secretary of State* [2004] 1 WLR 2557 per Pill LJ at para 49.

Article 2

36.17 Article 2 provides that:

'1. Everyone's right to life shall be protected by law . . .'

36.18 Article 2 imposes substantive obligations on a state. There is not just a negative obligation to refrain from the unlawful and intentional taking of life but also a positive obligation to take appropriate steps to safeguard life. In *Osman v UK*[27] the applicants alleged that the police had not taken sufficient steps to prevent a teacher from assaulting and killing members of their family. In this context, the ECtHR accepted that there was a duty on the state but that the applicants must establish that: (a) the authorities knew or ought to have known at the time of the existence of a real and immediate risk to the life of an identified individual or individuals from the criminal acts of a third party; and: (b) the authorities failed to take measures within the scope of their powers which, judged reasonably, might have been expected to avoid that risk. (See para 116.) (For the substantive duties on a state, see also *Keenan v UK*.[28]) Where the risk to life is attendant on some action that a state authority is

---

[25] [2004] QB 1124 at para 16.
[26] [2001] UKHRR 1150.
[27] [1999] 1 FLR 193.
[28] (2001) 33 EHRR 38.

contemplating putting into effect itself, then the threshold is somewhat lower: see *R(A) v Lord Saville of Newdigate*.[29]

36.19 Article 2 also imposes a procedural obligation on a state to initiate an effective public investigation by an independent official body into any death occurring in circumstances in which it appears that one of the substantive obligations under Art 2 has, or may have been, violated and it appears that agents of the state are, or may be, in some way implicated: see *McCann v UK*,[30] *Jordan v UK*[31] and *Edwards v UK*.[32] There should be a thorough and effective investigation capable of leading to the identification and punishment of those responsible for the loss of life. The state should be made responsible for deaths occurring under its responsibility.

36.20 Even if there has been no breach of Art 2, there may be a remedy for a relative who would otherwise have no claim under English law. In *Bubbins v United Kingdom*[33] the ECtHR found that the circumstances in which a man was shot dead by the police involved an arguable case under Art 2 but that there was no breach. Nevertheless, it granted a remedy to the deceased's sister. The ECtHR was mindful that, without such a remedy, the sister could claim only funeral expenses and would not be able to obtain legal aid in order to bring a claim against the police. All this amounted to a breach of Art 13, which protects the right to an effective remedy. Article 13 was not incorporated into the Schedule to the HRA on the basis that the HRA itself provided the mechanism to ensure that individuals had an effective remedy.

Article 3

36.21 Article 3 provides that:

> 'No one shall be subjected to torture or to inhuman or degrading treatment or punishment.'

36.22 The threshold is set relatively high: see *Z v UK*.[34] In the context of a prisoner held by the State, Art 3 requires that the person is detained in conditions which are compatible with respect for their human dignity, that the manner and method of execution of the sentence do not subject the prisoner to distress or hardship of an intensity exceeding the unavoidable level of suffering inherent in detention and that, given the practical demands of imprisonment, the prisoner's health and well-being are adequately secured by, among other things, providing them with the requisite medical assistance: see *McGlinchey v UK*.[35]

---

[29] [2002] 1 WLR 1249.
[30] (1995) 21 EHRR 97.
[31] (2001) 37 EHRR 52.
[32] (2002) 35 EHRR 487.
[33] 17 March 2005.
[34] [2001] 2 FLR 612.
[35] [2003] Lloyd's Rep Med 264.

In *Price v UK*[36] a four-limb deficient thalidomide victim was committed for contempt of court and detained for four days. She was not provided with a suitable bed the first night and had to sleep in her wheelchair. She did not get sufficient nursing care and had the greatest difficulty in going to the toilet or keeping clean. In the circumstances, the court held that the applicant had been subjected to degrading treatment contrary to Art 3.

36.23 As with Art 2, there is not just a negative obligation on public authorities not to engage in inhuman or degrading treatment but also a positive obligation to take steps to prevent others engaging in inhuman or degrading treatment. So in *Anufrijeva v Southwark LBC*,[37] the Court of Appeal recognised that: 'There is a stage at which the dictates of humanity require the state to intervene to prevent any person within its territory suffering dire consequences as a result of deprivation of sustenance.' In *A v UK*[38] the applicant, a 9-year-old, was beaten on more than one occasion with a garden cane by his step-father. The step-father was acquitted on the charge of assault on the basis of reasonable chastisement. The ECtHR found the UK to be in breach of Art 3 for having failed to provide a sufficient deterrence against such serious breaches of personal integrity.

Where a person has suffered injuries whilst under the control of a State body (for instance the police), then the state bears the burden of showing that those injuries were not caused by its agents: see *Corsacov v Moldova*.[39]

Article 1 Protocol 1

36.24 Article 1 of the First Protocol, referred to now commonly as Art1P1, provides that:

> 'Every natural or legal person is entitled to the peaceful enjoyment of his possessions. No one shall be deprived of his possessions except in the public interest and subject to the conditions provided for by law and by the general principles of international law. The preceding provisions shall not, however, in any way impair the right of a state to enforce such laws as it deems necessary to control the use of property in accordance with the general interest or to secure the payment of taxes or other contributions or penalties.'

36.25 A possession can include a cause of action of value (see *Pessos Compania Naviera SA v Belgium*[40]) and contractual rights (see *Wilson v Secretary of State for Trade and Industry* per Lord Nicholls at para 39). Otherwise, the obvious possessions are money or property. So a direct and substantial interference with the value of a litigant's property can be said to

---

[36] (2002) 34 EHRR 53.
[37] [2004] QB 1124 at para 35.
[38] (1999) 27 EHRR 611.
[39] 4 April 2006.
[40] (1995) 21 EHRR 301.

engage Art1P1 (but see per Pill LJ in *Lough v First Secretary of State*[41]). Any such interference will required to be justified, applying the proportionality test.

Article 14

36.26 Article 14 provides that:

> 'The enjoyment of the rights and freedoms set forth in this Convention shall be secured without discrimination on any ground such as sex, race, colour, language, religion, political or other opinion, national or social origin, association with a national minority, property, birth or other status.'

36.27 This is a derivative right. In any Art 14 inquiry, the court will need to consider:

(a) Do the facts fall within the ambit of one or more of the Convention rights?

(b) Was there a difference in treatment in respect of that right between the complainant and others put forward for comparison?

(c) Were those others in an analogous position?

(d) Was the difference in treatment based on one of the grounds proscribed in Art 14?

(e) Was the difference in treatment objectively justifiable, ie did it have a legitimate aim and bear a reasonable relationship of proportionality to that aim? See *Wandsworth London BC v Michalak*[42] and *Ghaidan v Mendoza*.[43]

THE STRUCTURE OF THE HRA 1998

36.28 The various Convention rights under the European Convention on Human Rights are set out at Sch 1 to the HRA 1998. The HRA applies these Convention rights in a number of different ways, as follows:

Direct or indirect impact on legislation

36.29 Section 3(1) provides that:

---

[41] [2004] 1 WLR 2557 at para 51.
[42] [2003] 1 WLR 617.
[43] [2004] 2 AC 557.

'3. **Interpretation of legislation.**

(1) So far as it is possible to do so, primary legislation and subordinate legislation must be read and given effect in a way which is compatible with the Convention rights.'

36.30 Section 4(4) provides that:

'4. **Declaration of incompatibility.**

(4) If the court is satisfied that the provision is incompatible with a Convention right, it may make a declaration of that incompatibility . . .'

36.31 Section 3 is of general application and can apply to litigation between private parties provided a Convention right is engaged. The interpretative obligation is a heavy one: see *Ghaidan v Mendoza*.[44] Words in a statutory provision can be read down. Alternatively, words can be read into a provision. It does not matter greatly if a short form of words to insert into the statutory provision cannot be found – it is the effect that counts.

36.32 The interpretative obligation does have its limits. The interpretation will be permissible if it goes with the grain of the legislation. Where the entire substance of a legislative provision is incompatible with a Convention right, then s 3(1) will not assist. Instead, and as a last resort, it is then open to the court to make a declaration of incompatibility under s 4. This will not affect the proceedings between the parties directly. However, it is not without value for that litigant because he can proceed to the ECHR and seek a remedy there based on the acknowledged interference with his Convention right under English law. Furthermore, the litigant can expect a change in the law to be effected as a result of the declaration of incompatibility.

Duty on public authorities

36.33 Section 6 provides that:

'6. **Acts of public authorities**

(1) It is unlawful for a public authority to act in a way which is incompatible with a Convention right.
(2) Subsection (1) does not apply to an act if (a) as a result of one or more provisions of primary legislation, the authority could not have acted differently; or (b) in the case of one or more provisions of, or made under primary legislation which cannot be read or given effect in a way which is compatible with the Convention rights, the authority was acting so as to give effect to or to enforce those provisions.
(3) In this section 'public authority' includes (a) a court or tribunal, and (b) any person certain of whose functions are functions of a public nature . . .'

---

[44] [2004] 2 AC 557.

36.34 What constitutes a public authority is still a vexed question. Some bodies are 'core' public authorities, that is for all purposes, such as local authorities, the police, the armed forces and central government. Other bodies are 'hybrid' public authorities, that is public authorities when their functions are of a public nature but not otherwise: see HRA 1998, s 6(3)(b) above. Factors to be taken into account in deciding whether a function is public include the extent to which in carrying out the relevant function the body is publicly funded, or is exercising statutory powers, or is taking the place of central government or local authorities, or is providing a public service: see *Aston Cantlow PCC v Wallbank*.[45] See also *Poplar Housing and Regeneration Community Association Ltd v Donoghue*[46] and *R (on the application of Heather) v Leonard Cheshire Foundation*.[47]

36.35 The court is also public authority: see s 6(3)(a) above. The effect of this provision is that the HRA will apply, in some circumstances, horizontally as well as vertically. So, for instance, in *Jones v University of Warwick*[48] the Court of Appeal took no point on the engagement of Art 8 where the claimant's complaint was that the defendant, a private entity, should not be entitled to rely on a video it had obtained of the claimant inside her home.

Claim for damages against public authorities

36.36 Sections 7 and 8 of the HRA provide that:

'**7. Proceedings**

(1) A person who claims that a public authority has acted (or proposes to act) in a way which is made unlawful by section 6(1) may (a) bring proceedings against the authority under this Act in the appropriate court or tribunal, or (b) rely on the Convention right or rights concerned in any legal proceedings, but only if he is (or would be) a victim of the unlawful act.
. . .
(5) Proceedings under subsection (1)(a) must be brought before the end of (a) the period of one year beginning with the date on which the act complained of took place; or (b) such longer period as the court or tribunal considers equitable having regard to all the circumstances, but that is subject to any rule imposing a stricter time limit in relation to the procedure in question.

8. Judicial remedies

(1) In relation to any act (or proposed act) of a public authority which the court finds is (or would be) unlawful, it may grant such relief or remedy, or make such order, within its powers as it considers just and appropriate.
(2) . . .

---

[45] [2004] 1 AC 546 per Lord Nicholls at para 12.
[46] [2002] QB 48.
[47] [2002] 2 All ER 936.
[48] [2003] 1 WLR 954.

(3) No award of damages is to be made unless, taking account of all the circumstances of the case, including (a) any other relief or remedy granted, or order made, in relation to the act in question (by that or any other court), and (b) the consequences of any decision (of that or any other court) in respect of that act, the court is satisfied that the award is necessary to afford just satisfaction to the person in whose favour it is made.

(4) In determining (a) whether to award damages, or (b) the amount of an award, the court must take into account the principles applied by the European Court of Human Rights in relation to the award of compensation under article 41 of the Convention.

(5) ...

(6) In this section 'court' includes a tribunal; 'damages' means damages for an unlawful act of a public authority; and 'unlawful' means unlawful under section 6(1).'

36.37 So, as was recognised by the Court of Appeal in *Anufrijeva* (at para 55):

(a) the award of damages under the HRA is confined to the class of unlawful acts of public authorities identified by s 6(1);

(b) the court has a discretion whether to make an award of damages;

(c) the award must be necessary to achieve 'just satisfaction';

(d) the court is required to take into account the different principles applied by the ECtHR; and

(e) exemplary damages are not awarded.

36.38 Even on this issue, just as with determining whether a qualified right has been infringed, the court is required to draw a balance between the interests of the victim and those of the public as a whole. Who qualifies as a victim? Clearly those claimants who would otherwise have a claim in tort qualify. The ECtHR cases have also included relatives of primary victims regardless of whether those relatives would themselves qualify as secondary victims: see, for instance, the claim by the mother in *Osman v UK*.[49] In *McGlinchey v UK*,[50] the ECtHR awarded damages for a breach of Art 3 in circumstances where no award could have been made under English law as the suffering did not qualify as an injury or illness. Where the unlawful act of the public authority results in personal injury, the Court of Appeal confirmed in *Anufrijeva* that the JSB guidelines may act as a rough guide to the level of damages to be awarded.

36.39 Few claims have been brought under HRA 1998, s 7 and this remains a relatively unexplored but potentially highly fruitful area. One successful claim at first instance under s 7 was *Van Colle v Chief Constable of Hertfordshire Police*.[51] This case has been appealed to the Court of Appeal and, at the time of

---

[49] [1999] 1 FLR 193.
[50] [2003] Lloyd's Med Rep 264.
[51] [2006] 3 All ER 963.

going to print, the outcome of the appeal is awaited. In *Van Colle* the claimant's son, a prosecution witness in a dishonesty criminal charge against a Mr Brougham, was shot dead by Mr Brougham. The court accepted that the police had failed in their duty under Art 2 to protect the claimant's son from Mr Brougham and awarded damages of £50,000 (£15,000 for the son's distress in the weeks leading up to the death and £35,000 for the claimant's own grief and suffering). As set out at HRA 1998, s 7(5) above, it should be noted that the limitation period is 1 year, not 3, from the date of the breach of Convention right (albeit there is a power to extend time). The scope of s 7(5) was considered by the High Court in *Cameron v Network Rail Infrastructure Ltd*.[52]

Not retroactive

36.40 So far as ordinary civil claims are concerned, the HRA is not retroactive. So a claimant cannot bring a substantive claim against the defendant for breach of a Convention right arising out of an event occurring prior to 2 October 2000: see, for example, *Wainwright v Home Office*.[53] Likewise, HRA 1998, s 3 cannot be applied so as to alter parties' existing substantive rights and obligations under a statutory provision: see *Wilson v First County Trust (No 2)*.[54] But Art 6, being a procedural right, can be relied on in all cases after the HRA came into force even where the cause of action preceded that date.

IMPACT OF THE HRA ON SUBSTANTIVE LAW

Law of negligence

36.41 When *Osman v UK*[55] was in its heyday, there was a notable shift in the courts' approach to the existence of a duty of care in novel situations. Whereas, prior to *Osman*, the courts had had little concern in striking out cases on the basis that it was not fair, just or reasonable to impose a duty of care (the third stage of the *Caparo* test), after *Osman* the House of Lords, in a series of cases, has held that it was not appropriate to strike out the claims as a duty of care was owed or, at the least, it was arguable on the facts to be determined at trial that such a duty might be owed: see *Barrett v LB of Enfield*,[56] *W v Essex CC*,[57] *Phelps v Hillingdon BC*,[58] *Waters v Metropolitan Police Commissioner*,[59] *Darker v Chief Constable of West Midlands Police*[60] and *Arthur JS Hall v Simons*.[61]

---

[52] [2007] 1 WLR 163.
[53] [2002] QB 1334, CA.
[54] [2004] 1 AC 816.
[55] [1999] 1 FLR 193.
[56] [2001] 2 AC 550.
[57] [2001] 2 AC 592.
[58] [2001] 2 AC 619.
[59] [2000] 1 WLR 1607.
[60] [2001] 1 AC 435.
[61] [2002] 1 AC 615.

36.42 In the light of *Z v UK*,[62] it is not appropriate to rely on Art 6, a procedural right, in seeking to establish a novel duty of care (see, for example, *Walters v North Glamorgan NHS Trust*[63] in the context of a claim as a secondary victim). However, *Osman* has had a more lasting impact on the approach of the higher courts to strike out applications, once a sizeable industry for personal injury lawyers. The court will still readily strike out a claim where it finds there is not the proximity required to establish a duty of care: see *Palmer v Tees HA*,[64] but the court now takes a more restrictive approach to the exclusion of liability based on the third stage of the *Caparo* test without first ascertaining the precise facts: see per Lord Woolf MR in *Kent v Griffiths*.[65]

36.43 The Crown Proceedings Act 1947 has the effect of preventing a serviceman from suing the Ministry of Defence for any personal injury relating to work. Although the 1947 Act was repealed prospectively in 1987, it still has the effect of barring claims by servicemen for asbestos-related illness due to pre-1987 exposure. In *Matthews v Ministry of Defence*[66] the House of Lords decided that the 1947 Act never conferred any substantive right on the serviceman with the result that Art 6 did not apply. The ECtHR came to the same conclusion in the later case of *Roche v UK*.

36.44 Although Art 6 cannot be relied on to challenge a common law ruling that no duty of care is owed, a substantive Convention right can. So in *JD v East Berks Community NHS Trust*[67] children claimed in negligence against local authorities for their decisions to take the children into care on the basis the children were being subjected at home to abuse. In *X v Bedfordshire CC*,[68] the House of Lords had ruled that decisions by local authorities whether or not to take a child into care were not reviewable by way of a claim in negligence. But since that time the ECHR had found that a wrongful decision by a local authority to take a child into care could amount to a breach of Art 8 (*TP and KM v UK*[69]) and that a wrongful decision by a local authority not to take a child into care amounted to a breach of Art 3 (*Z v UK*[70]). The effect of those decisions, so held the Court of Appeal, was that the rule laid down in *X v Bedfordshire CC* was no longer justified. Accordingly, the Court of Appeal overruled *X v Bedfordshire CC* and dismissed the applications to strike out brought by the local authorities. The Court of Appeal were not held back by the fact that the alleged negligence occurred prior to 2 October 2000 so that the HRA was not applicable.

---

[62] [2001] 2 FLR 612.
[63] [2003] PIQR P2.
[64] [2000] PIQR P1.
[65] [2000] 2 WLR 1158 at 1168H.
[66] [2003] 1 AC 1163.
[67] [2004] QB 558.
[68] [1995] 2 AC 633.
[69] [2001] 2 FLR 549.
[70] [2001] 2 FLR 612.

36.45 In *D v East Berkshire County Council*[71] the House of Lords made no comment on this innovative approach by the Court of Appeal. Its focus was on the question whether a duty of care was owed by social services to the parent as well as the child. The majority held that there was a conflict between the interests of the parent and that of the child so that it was inappropriate to fix social services with such a duty of care. This decision related to actions occurring before the HRA came into force. Where the allegations relate to actions occurring after the HRA came into force, the parents will have a remedy before the ECtHR for breach of Art 3 or Art 8. In those circumstances, they will surely have a remedy under s 7 of the HRA 1998. It is a more vexed question whether such a parent will also have a claim in common law negligence, in other words whether *D* should be treated as binding in respect of post-HRA cases. In *Lawrence v Pembrokeshire CC*[72] the High Court struck out such a claim. The claimant's appeal has been heard by the Court of Appeal and, at the time of going to print, the outcome of that decision is awaited.

36.46 The decision in *JD* is particularly significant because the Court of Appeal was relying on a qualified Convention right (Art 8) to change the common law duty of care. Any assessment under Art 8 necessarily involves applying the proportionality test. It has been suggested that the court should adopt such an approach more generally to the issue of determining whether a novel duty of care exists.[73] The fair balance test inherent in any qualified Convention right echoes the clash of corrective and distributive justice principles (the interests of the victim on the one hand and of society in general on the other) but in a much more focussed way.

Nuisance claims

36.47 Under domestic law, a claim could only be brought in nuisance by a person with a proprietary interest in land: see *Hunter v Canary Wharf Ltd.*[74] By contrast, a claim can be brought under Art 8 in respect of interference with a home by someone who has no proprietary right at all to live there.

36.48 Article 8 can be engaged where severe environmental pollution occurs even when the pollution is not caused by a public authority. So, in *Lopez Ostra v Spain*[75] those living near to a waste treatment plant, which released fumes and smells which caused health problems, established not only that their Art 8 rights were engaged but also that they were breached. And in *Guerra v Italy*[76] the applicants lived near a chemical factory which produced various chemicals. The ECtHR held the state liable for having failed to take steps to prevent the pollution affecting the applicants from being able to enjoy their homes properly. A similar situation arose in England in *McKenna v British*

---

[71] [2005] 2 AC 373.
[72] [2007] PIQR P1.
[73] See 'The mosaic of tort law' Oppenheim [2003] JPIL 151.
[74] [1997] AC 655.
[75] (1994) 20 EHRR 277.
[76] (1998) 26 EHRR 357.

Aluminium Ltd,[77] where the claimants, all children, made claims based on emissions and noise pollution from a nearby factory. The defendant's application to strike out the claims in nuisance and *Rylands v Fletcher* was dismissed. Although the children had no proprietary interest, there was a powerful case for saying that they should be entitled to rely on Art 8.

36.49 Noise nuisance formed the basis of the complaint in *Hatton v UK*.[78] The applicants all lived under the Heathrow flight path and were affected by noise from night-time flights. The ECtHR accepted that an issue could arise under Art 8 where an individual was directly and seriously affected by noise or other pollution. But, in that case, there was no breach of Art 8. Had the applicants been able to establish that their properties were less valuable as a result of the changes to night-time flights, they would also have been able to rely on Art1 P1.

36.50 In *Marcic v Thames Water Utilities Ltd*,[79] the claimant's garden was flooded by backflow from the public authority's surface water sewers. Although the claimant, who claimed a breach of Art 8 and Art1P1, succeeded in the Court of Appeal, the House of Lords rejected his claim. Whilst Art 8 was engaged, the overall statutory scheme for sewerage, entrusting enforcement to an independent regulator, was fair. (However, an issue did remain over the fact that no compensation was payable under the statutory scheme in respect of external flooding caused whilst a householder is waiting for flood alleviation works to be carried out.) The independent regulator was himself a public authority (within the terms of s 6 of the HRA 1998) so that a claim could be brought against him under HRA 1998, s 7 if he failed to act in accordance with a householder's Convention rights.

36.51 In *Andrews v Reading BC*,[80] the claimant complained that the increase in traffic noise caused by a new road scheme implemented by the defendant, had made his life intolerable. He claimed damages for insulation work to his home. The High Court, in dismissing the council's application for summary judgment, held that an increase in traffic noise which seriously affects an individual may engage Art 8. *Marcic* was distinguished on the basis that the local authority appeared not to have considered one of the relevant factors under Art 8(2), namely the availability of measures to mitigate the effects of noise.

Inquests

36.52 The procedural obligation under Art 2 sets minimum standards of investigation into any death which raises Art 2 issues: see *R (Amin) v Secretary of State for the Home Department*.[81] In that case, following a murder of one prisoner by another, inquiries were conducted by the prison service, the police and the Commission for Racial Equality. However, the family were not

---

[77] (2002) Env LR 30.
[78] (2003) 37 EHRR 611.
[79] [2004] 2 AC 42.
[80] [2004] EWHC 970.
[81] [2004] 1 AC 653.

permitted to participate in any of these inquiries, which were conducted in private. The House of Lords held that the state's procedural obligation under Art 2 had not been discharged and that an independent public enquiry, at which the deceased's family would be legally represented, should be held.

36.53 It is not necessary for there to be an independent inquiry in all cases in which Art 2 issues arise. The ordinary mechanism of an inquest by a coroner with a jury will normally suffice. (Where there has been a criminal trial and the defendant has pleaded not guilty and there has been a full exploration of the facts surrounding the death, that trial may well meet the requirements of Art 2.) However, the rules under which the coroner operates have had to be altered to accommodate the more thorough investigation required by Art 2. Whereas previously the jury has only been required to investigate how the deceased died (meaning 'by what means': see *R v North Humberside Coroner ex parte Jamieson*[82]), the jury now has to consider by what means and in what circumstances the deceased died: see *R (Middleton) v West Somerset Coroner*.[83] Appropriate cases for such a wide inquiry are by no means limited to cases involving the use of lethal force by agents of the state. In *Middleton* the House of Lords emphasised that a systemic failure by the state may call for an investigation which may be no less important and perhaps even more complex. No distinction should be drawn between individual and systemic failure. In both types of cases, the jury should express a conclusion, however brief, on any disputed factual issues at the heart of the case.

There will be some cases where the State needs to hold a public inquiry in addition to an inquest in order to meet its Art 2 obligation but such a case is likely to be rare: see *Scholes v Home Secretary* (2006) HRLR 44. In *R (D) v Home Secretary* [2006] 3 All ER 946 a prisoner attempted suicide but did not die. The Secretary of State was obliged to hold an inquiry but the court should not order that the prisoner had the right to cross-examine witnesses. That was a matter for the chairman of the inquiry.

36.54 In *R (Takoushis) v Coroner for Inner North London*,[84] the Court of Appeal confirmed that Art 2 is engaged, in the sense that it gives rise to certain obligations on the part of the state, whenever a person dies in circumstances which give reasonable grounds for thinking that the death may have resulted from a wrongful act of one of its agents. A common example is where there are grounds for thinking that a death may have been caused by negligence on the part of a member of staff in an NHS hospital. The primary obligation on the state is to conduct an effective investigation. The state must set up a system which involves a practical and effective investigation of the facts and the determination of civil liability. As stated in *R (Goodson) v Bedfordshire and*

---

[82] [1995] QB 1.
[83] [2004] 2 WLR 800.
[84] [2005] EWCA Civ 1440.

Luton Coroner[85] and confirmed in *Takoushis,* where the negligence is simple negligence (as opposed to gross negligence), that will not amount to a breach of Art 2.

Other claims under s 7

36.55 Under the common law, there are well known restrictions of the rights of secondary victims to recover damages for pure psychiatric illness (see *Alcock v Chief Constable of South Yorks Police*[86]). A claimant under the HRA is not so constrained provided that he can establish a breach of a substantive Convention right. If, for instance, a parent can establish a breach of Art 8 by a public authority causing injury or death to their child, there may be scope for the parent to claim damages as a 'victim' even if the parent does not meet the *Alcock* criteria.

36.56 A claim under the HRA can be made to provide a remedy where none is available under the domestic law. So in *Wainwright v Home Office*[87] the claimants were subjected to unlawful, humiliating and distressing strip searches by the prison authorities. However, one claimant was not touched and so could not claim in trespass to the person whilst the other claimant suffered psychiatric illness but not as a result of being touched. The House of Lords limited the application of the old tort of *Wilkinson v Downton*[88] and found that (save for the limited claim in trespass to one claimant) the claimants had no cause of action. Had the events occurred after the coming into force of the HRA 1998, Lord Hoffmann indicated that Art 8 may justify a remedy for an intentional invasion of privacy by a public authority even where no damage is suffered other than distress. However, a merely negligent act by a public authority may not suffice to found a claim for damages under the HRA if the claimant's distress falls short of psychiatric illness. Whether such guidance from Lord Hoffmann is right is open to doubt in the light of the decision in *Wainwright v UK*.[89]

36.57 A claimant can rely on Art 2 to bring a claim against the police for its failure to prevent a criminal causing injury to the claimant. The fact that no such claim in negligence will stand (see *Hill v Chief Constable of West Yorkshire Police*[90]) will be no bar to such a claim under the HRA 1998. For a successful claim at first instance (on which the decision of the Court of Appeal is awaited), see *Van Colle v Chief Constable of Hertfordshire Police*.[91] Individual errors alone by doctors will not suffice to bring a claim under Art 2; however, systemic errors by a hospital might: see *Glass v UK*[92] (admissibility decision). It has been held that the threshold for Art 2 in a clinical negligence setting is, at

---

[85] [2005] 2 All ER 791.
[86] [1992] 1 AC 310.
[87] [2004] 2 AC 406.
[88] [1897] 2 QB 57.
[89] 26 September 2006.
[90] [1989] AC 53.
[91] [2006] 3 All ER 963.
[92] [2004] Lloyd's Rep Med 76.

the least, gross negligence of a kind sufficient to sustain manslaughter: *Savage v South Essex Partnership NHS Foundation Trust*.[93]

36.58 The twin cases of *Z v UK* and *TP and KM v UK* open the way to claims being made by children who are taken into care when they should not have been or who are not taken into care when they should have been under Arts 8 and 3 respectively. Such claims would constitute free-standing claims under the HRA although the common law has now been modified to permit claims in negligence founded on such facts to be made. The question remains whether parents, who are accorded a remedy by the European Court, should be entitled to sue now in negligence or only under HRA 1998, s 7: see *Lawrence v Pembrokeshire County Council*[94] (on which the Court of Appeal's decision is awaited). The House of Lords' decision in *D v East Berks NHS Trust*[95] does not resolve this issue because that case concerned facts arising before the HRA came into force.

36.59 Article 3 successfully founded a claim in *McGlinchey v UK*, a case in which Ms McGlinchey, a heroin addict, died shortly after commencing her prison sentence. Her family could not bring any claim under the Fatal Accidents Act 1976 because there was no medical evidence to link the alleged deficiencies in the care of the deceased with her subsequent death. However, her family did establish in the ECtHR that the prison authorities had failed to meet the requisite standards imposed by Art 3. In particular, the prison had not provided adequate means of establishing the reasons for the deceased's weight loss, there was a gap in her monitoring and there was a failure to take more effective steps to treat her condition. Despite the fact that none of these failures caused any personal injury or illness, let alone Ms McGlinchey's death, the court awarded the family a total of EUR 22,900 in damages.

36.60 If similar facts arose now, there would be no need either to try and manipulate an existing cause of action or to go to the ECtHR; the applicant could simply bring a claim under HRA 1998, s 7 for breach of the Convention right by the relevant public authority. It is not clear whether the approach of the ECtHR would be mirrored in a claim by a patient against the NHS.

36.61 In *Glass v UK*,[96] the mother of a seriously ill child refused her consent to his treatment with morphine, which might well have the side-effect of hastening his death, despite which the child was treated anyway. The hospital's failure to seek prior authorisation from the High Court amounted to a breach of Art 8.

---

[93] (2007) *The Times*, 16 February.
[94] [2007] PIQR P1.
[95] [2005] 2 AC 373.
[96] (2004) 39 EHRR 15.

IMPACT OF THE HRA ON PROCEDURAL LAW

36.62 The Convention right most commonly linked with procedural law is Art 6.

Ordinary case management decisions

36.63 The case of *Daniels v Walker* is well known. In it, Lord Woolf made clear that it was not helpful to rely on Art 6 in an application by a party to rely on its own expert rather than a jointly instructed expert. (And see also *Hubbard v LS & L Health Authority*[97] in which the Court of Appeal gave short shrift to the argument that Art 6 had anything to do with a case management decision as to whether experts should hold a without prejudice meeting.) *Daniels v Walker* is evidence not so much of the inapplicability of Art 6 to issues of procedure as to the fact that Lord Woolf had foreshadowed the coming into force of the HRA when creating the CPR. The overriding objective, complete with its express reference to proportionality, broadly meets the requirements of Art 6. So in *Woodhouse v Consignia plc*,[98] the Court of Appeal, whilst considering the narrow question of how the discretion should be exercised on an application to lift the automatic one year stay, made a point of general application: it noted that provided judges make their decisions within the general framework provided by CPR Part 1.1 (and in that case Part 3.9), they are unlikely to fall foul of Art 6.

36.64 A good example of the application of the principle of proportionality comes in *Price v Price*.[99] In this case, the claimant instructed a medical expert with the agreement of the defendant long before proceedings were issued. Having issued the claim form, the claimant then changed experts without telling the defendant and delayed for over a year in providing particulars of claim. The claimant's application to extend time for service of the particulars of claim failed in the county court despite the defendant being hard pushed to identify much actual prejudice referable to the delay. The Court of Appeal considered its final duty was to decide whether it would be a disproportionate response (to the claimant's unimpressive conduct) to stop the case now by refusing the extension of time outright, or whether it may be possible to fashion a more proportionate response. It granted the claimant permission to extend time for service of the particulars of claim but on condition that no claim was made for special or general damages other than what may be substantiated by the pre-action medical report of the first expert.

Bringing more than 1 action

36.65 The Fatal Accidents Act (FAA) 1976 provides at s 2(3) that: 'Not more than one action shall lie for and in respect of the same subject matter of

---

[97] [2002] Lloyd's Rep Med 8.
[98] [2002] 1 WLR 2558 at para 43.
[99] [2004] PIQR P6.

complaint.' In *Cachia v Faluyi*,[100] an action was brought under the FAA 1976 on behalf of all the dependants but never served. Some years later, outside the limitation period for adults but within the limitation period for children, the child dependants brought another action against the defendant. Met with the bar of s 2(3), the claim was struck out at first instance. The Court of Appeal held that Art 6 was engaged as s 2(3) barred the claimants' right of access to the court. Section 2(3) produced an obvious injustice to the claimants and the Court of Appeal had no hesitation in remedying it by interpreting the word 'action' in the most strained fashion to mean 'served process'.

36.66 A claimant cannot complain about a breach of Art 6 where a court requires the claimant to pay the costs of the first action before being permitted to continue with the second: see *Stevens Associates v The Aviary Estate*.[101]

Limitation

36.67 The Walkley principle withstood a challenge under article 6: see *Young v Western Power Distribution (South West) plc*.[102] It then fell on the basis that the House of Lords no longer considered it to be good law: see *Horton v Sadler*.[103] In *Horton* Lord Bingham indicated that he would have needed much persuasion to accept that the Walkley decision violated Art 6.

There is no discretion to extend time for a claim in trespass: see *Stubbings v Webb*.[104] In *Stubbings v UK*[105] the ECtHR was prepared to assume that limitation periods engaged Art 6 but found that the rule under s 2 of the Limitation Act 1980 was Convention-compliant. This has caused some considerable injustice and it remains to be seen whether *Stubbings* is revisited by the House of Lords in the light of the HRA. The HRA only comes into play if the time limit under the Limitation Act expired after the HRA came into force on 2 October 2000: see *A v Hoare*.[106]

SERVICE

36.68 The deemed service provision under CPR 6.7 is not rebuttable by evidence of actual receipt of the claim form by the defendant. Such an interpretation is not incompatible with Art 6: see *Anderton v Clwyd County Council*.[107] The rule on extension of time for service under CPR 7.6.3(a) was construed by the Court of Appeal in a way which protected the claimant's right of access to the court, without recourse to the HRA 1998. The Court of

---

[100] [2001] 1 WLR 1966.
[101] (2001) *The Times*, 2 February.
[102] [2003] 1 WLR 2853.
[103] [2006] 2 WLR 1346,
[104] [1993] AC 498.
[105] (1997) 23 EHRR 213.
[106] [2006] 1 WLR 2320.
[107] [2002] 1 WLR 3174.

Appeal made it clear that, had it been necessary to do so, it would have applied HRA 1998, s 3 so as to read the rule in a way which was compatible with Art 6: see *Cranfield v Bridgegrove Ltd*.[108] In another case concerned with service of claim forms, the Court of Appeal held that a judge's power to determine a matter on paper and without a hearing did not infringe Art 6; the existence of the right of appeal adequately protected the applicant's Art 6 rights: see *Collier v Williams*.[109]

Amendment

36.69 In *Goode v Martin*[110] the claimant brought a claim within the limitation period setting out her version of how the yachting accident in which she had been seriously injured had occurred. After the expiry of the limitation period, she applied to amend her particulars of claim to rely on a new cause of action based on a version of events more recently put forward by the defendant. The claimant's new cause of action arose out of the same facts as already in issue in her claim within the terms of s 35(5) of the Limitation Act 1980. The difficulty for the claimant was that CPR 17.4(2) provided a narrower test for amendment outside of the limitation period which the claimant could not meet, namely that the new claim arose out of the same facts (or substantially the same facts) as a claim in respect of which the claimant had already claimed a remedy. The Court of Appeal had no difficulty in holding that CPR Part 17.4(2) was incompatible with the claimant's right of access to the court under Art 6. Applying s 3 of the HRA 1998, the Court of Appeal interpreted CPR Part 17.4 in line with s 35 of the 1980 Act by inserting the words in italics 'if the new claim arises out of the same facts or substantially the same facts as *are already in issue on* a claim in respect of which the party applying for permission has already claimed a remedy in the proceedings'.

36.70 (The rules on adding a new party under CPR Part 19.5 comply with Art 6: see *Kesslar v Moore and Tibbits*.[111])

Strike out/stay

36.71 Every litigant has a right to a fair trial. The corollary of that is that where a litigant was guilty of conduct that put the fairness of a trial in jeopardy, the court was bound to refuse to allow that litigant to take any further part in the proceedings and, where appropriate, to determine the proceedings against him: see *Arrow Nominees v Blackledge* TLR 7.7.2000.

36.72 It is not consonant with Art 6 or indeed with the basic principles of English justice for a party to be barred from proceeding if the court considered that the claim, though very weak, stood a chance of success: see *Chan U Seek v*

---

[108] [2003] 1 WLR 2441.
[109] [2006] 1 WLR 1945.
[110] [2002] 1 WLR 1828.
[111] [2004] EWCA Civ 1551.

Alvis Vehicles Ltd,[112] Neuberger J. A court can, compatibly with Art 6, and where it is fair, just and proportionate to do so, stay proceedings where a claimant refuses to cooperate in a medical examination: see *James v Baily Gibson*.[113] In *Woodhouse v Consignia plc*,[114] the Court of Appeal admonished judges to 'remember that if a stay remains in place they are depriving the claimant of access to the court'.

Right to go to trial

36.73 The right of access to a court does not mean that the claimant has a right, come what may, to have a trial. If the defendant admits liability, the issue is closed. As obvious as that may seem, it does mean, for instance, that someone seriously injured by the police would not have the opportunity to have the circumstances surrounding his injury openly investigated and exposed. Likewise, a claimant would be hard-pushed to argue that it was reasonable to reject a payment into court, made without prejudice to liability in the usual way, even though for generous damages, on the basis that he was determined to secure a judgment on liability.

36.74 Nevertheless, the court would be acting in breach of Art 6 if it required a party to mediate and refused that party the opportunity, after a failed mediation, to continue on to trial. By extension, the court should hesitate before penalising a party, set on litigating and not mediating, in costs: see *Halsey v Milton Keynes NHS Trust*.[115]

36.75 When a party gets to trial, then the parties are entitled to reasons for the judge's decisions: *English v Emery Reimbold*.[116] The practice of giving no reasons for a decision as to costs could only comply with Art 6 if the reason for the decision was implicit from the circumstances in which the award was made.

36.76 The court's procedures for limiting the rights of a vexatious litigant to bring or appeal claims is Convention-compliant: see *Bhamjee v Forsdick*.[117] Requiring a party to provide security for costs as a condition of bringing or continuing a claim will not necessarily breach Art 6: see *Tolstoy Milslavsky v UK*.[118]

In *Smith v Kvaerner Cementation Foundations Ltd*[119] the claimant sought permission to appeal a judgment four years out of time. The Court of Appeal accepted that the claimant had been denied a hearing at the original trial before an independent and impartial tribunal. That the claimant's Art 6 right had

---

[112] [2003] EWHC 1238.
[113] [2002] EWCA Civ 1690.
[114] [2002] 1 WLR 2558.
[115] [2004] 1 WLR 3002.
[116] [2002] 1 WLR 2409.
[117] [2004] 1 WLR 88.
[118] (1995) 20 EHRR 442.
[119] [2007] 1 WLR 370.

been infringed was the paramount consideration when determining whether to grant an extension of time. The Court of Appeal ordered that there should be a re-trial.

Enforcing a foreign judgment

36.77 The HRA is applicable to foreign judgments which emanate from other countries party to the ECtHR. There is a ready presumption that such judgments will be Convention-compliant. However, on the extreme facts of *Maronier v Larner*,[120] the Court of Appeal refused to enforce a Dutch judgment on the basis to do so would be contrary to Art 6. It was apparent that the judgment against a Dutch national now living in England had been obtained without first giving the defendant any notice that judgment was sought or any opportunity to appeal.

36.78 Article 6 is also capable of being applied to the enforcement in England of a judgment obtained in a non-Convention country such as the United States. However, an extreme degree of unfairness would have to be established, amounting to a virtually complete denial or nullification of Art 6 rights: see *US Govt v Montgomery (No 2)*.[121]

Evidence improperly obtained

36.79 In *Jones v University of Warwick*[122] the defendant instructed an enquiry agent to take a covert video of the claimant inside her home. The video duly obtained by the agent, posing as a market sales representative, was of significant probative value and was seen by both sides' experts. The Court of Appeal held that such evidence was admissible. Although the evidence engaged Art 8(1), the crucial issue was whether, in terms of Art 8(2), it was necessary to admit the evidence in order to meet the public interest that the truth shall out. Provided admission of the evidence met with the overriding objective (for these purposes synonymous with Art 6), then Art 8(2) was satisfied and the evidence should be disclosed. The Court of Appeal marked its disapproval by ordering the defendant to pay the costs of the application and the appeal to the Court of Appeal. The difficulty with the Court of Appeal's approach is that defendants are surely being given the green light to secure evidence from inside a claimant's home. (Even the costs punishment will not be so severe in future cases unless they are appealed). The test for the admission of such evidence ought instead to be whether such probative video evidence could have been obtained by any less invasive means such as by videoing the claimant outside his home and in a public place.

---

[120] [2003] QB 620.
[121] [2004] 4 All ER 289.
[122] [2003] 1 WLR 954.

Disclosure

36.80 Disclosure of confidential documents is likely to engage Art 8. Such disclosure can be justified under Art 8(2) provided the proportionality test is met: see *Z v Finland*[123] and *MS v Sweden*.[124] Disclosure of a patient's records to a health authority, in order to assist its investigation into a GP practice, would be ordered where there was a compelling public interest requiring the disclosure and adequate safeguards against abuse were in place: see *A Health Authority v X and others*.[125]

36.81 In *A v X & B (Non party)*,[126] the defendant wished to examine the claimant's brother's medical records to determine whether his medical disorder was genetic in origin. It was accepted that such an order would infringe the non-party's Art 8 rights. In dismissing the application for disclosure under CPR Part 31.17, the High Court noted that such disclosure would be justified only in a very exceptional factual situation.

36.82 In *Gaskin v UK*,[127] the applicant alleged that he had been ill-treated during his lengthy time in care during his childhood. The failure by local authorities to provide him with disclosure of his records amounted to a breach of Art 8. (See also *McGinley and Egan v UK*[128] in which individuals exposed to nuclear radiation on Christmas island were entitled to disclosure of the radiation level records.) But in *R (Addinell) v Sheffield City Council*,[129] the court held it would be an unwarranted extension of *Gaskin* to permit disclosure to the father of the social services records of his deceased child. If the father brought civil proceedings against the council, disclosure would be dealt with in the usual way during the litigation.

36.83 In an application in civil proceedings for disclosure of financial information set out in an affidavit in ancillary relief proceedings, the court would have to balance the conflicting right of one party under Art 6 to a fair trial against the right of the other under Art 8 to privacy in respect of the information revealed in family proceedings: see *Nayler v Beard*.[130]

Capacity

36.84 Where a person is treated as a patient, he is deprived of civil rights and Arts 6 and 8 are engaged. Accordingly, the courts should always, as a matter of

---

[123] (1997) 25 EHRR 371.
[124] (1999) 28 EHRR 313.
[125] [2001] 2 FLR 673.
[126] [2004] EWHC 447.
[127] (1990) 12 EHRR 36.
[128] (1999) 27 EHRR 1.
[129] 27 October 2000 (Sullivan J).
[130] [2001] 2 FLR 1346.

practice, at the first convenient opportunity, investigate the question of capacity whenever there is any reason to suspect that it may be absent: see *Masterman-Lister*.[131]

Funding

36.85 Article 6 protects the right of access to the court. That right has to be real and effective. So, the state will have to ensure the litigant has funding to enable him to present his case at court if the litigant cannot afford representation and such representation is necessary to ensure a fair trial (see *Airey v UK*[132]). The test under Art 6 was whether the court was put in a position where it really could not do justice in the case because it had no confidence in its ability to grasp the facts and principles of the matter on which it had to rule: see *Perotti v Collyer-Bristow*.[133] The court itself had no power to grant a right to representation; the decision whether or not to fund legal services in civil proceedings was a matter for the Legal Services Commission (see *Perotti*). Where the Legal Services Commission had lavishly supported litigation for five years until just before trial, and there had been no material change in prospects in enforcing any judgment, the decision to withdraw legal aid had denied the claimant effective access to the court and had breached Art 6: see *R v LSC ex parte Alliss*.[134]

36.86 The CICA scheme does not cover the costs of legal representation. However, provided the claimant's right of access to the CICA was recognised and effective, the fact that the applicant would have to commit part of his eventual award to obtaining legal representation did not make the scheme incompatible with Art 6: see *C v Secretary of State for the Home Department*.[135]

36.87 The procedural obligation under Art 2 will, in appropriate cases, impose a duty on the state to provide funding for the family of the deceased so that they can be legally represented at the hearing established to investigate the circumstances surrounding the death: see *R (Khan) v Secretary of State for Health*.[136] In *Khan* a child died at hospital. Neither the police investigation nor the NHS trust's investigation could act as a substitute for an investigation meeting the requirements of Art 2. It was a matter for the Secretary of State whether to provide the family with funding for an inquest or to provide funding for some other type of suitable enquiry; either way, such funding was necessary to ensure that the family could play an effective part in the hearing.

---

[131] [2003] PIQR P20.
[132] (1979) 2 EHRR 305.
[133] (2003) *The Times*, 27 November.
[134] Jackson J 25 September 2002.
[135] (2004) *The Times*, 11 March.
[136] [2004] 1 WLR 971.

INDEX

References are to paragraph numbers.

Acceleration	
general damages, and	9.37
Accommodation	
adaptation of	14.10
damages for	
periodical payments, and	21.27
provision of	
Children Act 1989, and	13.106
Accomodation	
adaptation of existing	15.2
betterment of property	15.4, 15.5
local authority grants and	
assistance	15.6, 15.7
necessity and amenity,	
distinction	15.3
reasonable necessity	15.2
care implications	15.46
changes in care regime	15.49
live-in carers	15.48
minimum requirements	15.47
evidence	15.34
accomodation bought pre-trial	15.35
depletion of capital fund	15.36
expert evidence	15.38
assessment of needs	15.41
broad brush approach without	15.39
costing of works	15.42
disciplines	15.38
estate agent's list	15.40
interim payment based on	
estimate	15.43
heads of claim	15.1
three principle	15.1
housing association	15.37
local authority	15.37
medical evidence	15.44, 15.45
new	
ancillary costs	15.27, 15.28
application of formula	15.14, 15.15,
15.16, 15.17, 15.18, 15.19, 15.20	
cases	15.11, 15.12
deductions from Roberts v	
Johnstone claim	15.21, 15.22,
15.23, 15.24, 15.25	
measuring loss	15.9
more than one move	15.26
test of reasonable necessity	15.13
valuation of	15.8
loss of investment income	15.10

Accomodation—*continued*	
running costs	15.29
council tax	15.31
insurance	15.33
maintenance costs	15.30
utility bills	15.32
Admissions	
children, and	28.34, 28.35
Advocates	
immunity	5.24
Age	
general damages, and	9.45
Aids and equipment	14.1
assessment of past loss	14.27
claims for	14.1
component parts of claim	14.25
associated expenses	14.25
powered wheelchair, claim for	14.26
contingency awards	14.23
evidence, need for	14.7
accommodation	14.10
assistive communication	14.11
care	14.9
information technology	14.14
medical evidence	14.7
occupational therapy	14.8
orthotics	14.13
physiotherapy	14.12
prosthetics	14.13
Speech and Language Therapy	14.11
witness evidence	14.15
future loss, assessment of	14.28
appropriate multiplier	14.32
broad brush/global assessments	14.36
delayed recurrent expenses and	
losses	14.34
general principles	14.29
method for calculating	14.33
one off items	14.30
ongoing items	14.31
periodic multiplier	14.35
periodical payments	14.37
averaging method	14.38, 14.39
exact method	14.40, 14.41
holidays	14.22
overlap with other claims	14.16
accomodation claims	14.17
standard items	14.18
care claims	14.16
purpose of	14.6

Aids and equipment—*continued*			Appeals—*continued*	
responding to claims for	14.42		costs orders, against	33.33
duplication in claims	14.44		Court of Protection, from	17.33
examples	14.45		criminal injuries compensation	22.38
expert evidence	14.43		interim payments, and	20.53
points to consider	14.42		periodical payments, and	21.88
state provision	14.24		procedural	27.118
test for recovert	14.2		recoupment of damages, and	16.37, 16.38, 16.39, 16.40, 16.42
clear benefit	14.4			
item of special damage, as	14.2		procedure	16.41
reasonableness, meaning	14.3		security for costs of	33.53
travel and transport	14.19		Apportionment	
considerations	14.20, 14.21		damages, of	
types of	14.5		tortious and non-tortious, between	3.19, 3.20
Air passengers				
duty of care	1.9		fatal accident claims	31.41
Allocation			Assistive communication	
defending actions	27.68, 27.69, 27.70, 27.71, 27.72, 27.73		aids and equipment, and	14.11
			Asymptomatic conditions	
Alternative dispute resolution	27.29, 32.1, 32.4		general damages, and	9.29, 9.30
			ATE insurance	35.72, 35.73, 35.74, 35.75
clinical disputes	27.44		Attributability	
costs sanctions	32.30, 32.31, 32.32, 32.33, 32.34, 32.35, 32.36		criminal injuries compensation, and	22.22, 22.23
Court of Appeal ruling	32.47			
rules	32.37, 32.49, 32.50			
costs issues at trial	32.44, 32.45, 32.46		Bereavement	
			actions under Fatal Accidents Act 1976	31.14
Court of Appeal ruling	32.48			
Daniels	32.42		Blame	
Halsey	32.40, 32.41		just and equitable test, and	4.33
principles in	32.38, 32.39		Breach of statutory duty	
trial	32.43		limitation	24.10, 24.11, 24.12
CPR, and	32.5		Burden of proof	
definition of ADR	32.10, 32.11		contributory negligence	4.13
mediation	32.13, 32.14		evidential burden	4.16
position post CPR	32.7, 32.8, 32.9		legal burden	4.15
position pre-CPR	32.5, 32.6		Business rent	
round table meetings	32.12		recoupment of damages, and	16.19
how to negotiate	32.15		'But for' test	3.1
adaptability	32.16		alternative sufficient causes	3.5
applicable principles	32.18		cause of action for second event	3.7
authorities and instructions	32.24, 32.25		judicial instinct	3.7
discussion of legal/factual issues	32.20, 32.21, 32.22, 32.23		naturally occuring events	3.8
			omissions	3.6
example of	32.29		simultaneous events	3.9
flexibility	32.16		time between events	3.7
negotiations	32.26		causally irrelevant facts, and	3.3
preliminary matters	32.19		omissions	3.4
stages in negotiation	32.28		reason for breach of duty, and	3.3
starting point	32.26, 32.27		intervening causes, and	3.48
twin purpose of negotiations	32.17		multiple tortfeasors	3.2
meaning	32.3		one tortfeasor	3.2
mediation	32.3		unsatisfactory results from	3.10
resolution of issues	27.30		apportionment of damages, and	3.19, 3.20
type	27.29			
Alternative occupational pension			departure from standard test	3.16, 3.17, 3.18
loss of pension	12.31			
Ancillary benefits			major cases	3.14
loss of earnings, and	11.18		Mason CJ on	3.13
Appeals	27.116, 27.117		material contribution principle	3.16, 3.17, 3.18
awards of general damages, against	9.60			
contributory negligence	4.51			

'But for' test—*continued*
  unsatisfactory results from—*continued*
    materially increasing chance of
      injury   3.21, 3.22, 3.23, 3.24
    materially increasing risk,
      sufficiency of   3.29
    McGhee and multiple
      tortfeasors   3.32, 3.33, 3.34,
      3.35, 3.36, 3.37, 3.38, 3.39, 3.40
    McLachlin J on   3.12
    mesothelioma cases   3.30, 3.31
    number of potential causes   3.25, 3.26, 3.27
    Sopinka J on   3.11
    three causation difficulties   3.15
    Wilsher and McGhee,
      distinction   3.28
Bystanders
  psychiatric injuries   6.54, 6.55, 6.56, 6.57

Cab rank principle
  conditional fee agreements, and   35.18
Capacity
  Human Rights Act, and   36.84
  person lacking   17.14
  test for   17.49, 17.50, 17.51, 17.52, 17.53, 17.54, 17.55, 17.56, 17.57, 17.58, 17.59, 17.60
Car
  adaptation of   14.19
Care, damages for   13.1
  accomodation, and   15.46
  aids and equipment, and   14.9
  availability of Local
    Authority/Social Services
    accommodation and care
      applicable test   13.136
      argument for consideration of   13.123
      courts' approach   13.124
      Crofton v NHSLA   13.125, 13.126, 13.127, 13.128, 13.129, 13.130
      Drury v Crookdale   13.131, 13.132, 13.133, 13.135
      Freeman v Lockett   13.144, 13.145, 13.146, 13.147, 13.148
      Godbold v Mahmood   13.140, 13.141
      'reasonable requirements' test   13.137, 13.138, 13.139
      relevance of   13.123
      Sowden v Lodge   13.131, 13.132, 13.133, 13.134
    Walton v Calderdale Healthcare
      NHS Trust   13.142, 13.143
  basis of claim   13.12
  claimant's need for care   13.12, 13.13, 13.14, 13.15, 13.16, 13.17, 13.18, 13.19, 13.20
  carer's loss of earnings   13.48
  commercial rate and discounting
    adopting commercial rate   13.38, 13.39, 13.40

Care, damages for—*continued*
  commercial rate and
    discounting—*continued*
    appropriate discount to
      commercial rate   13.41
    awarding more than
      commercial rate   13.47
    conventional discount, whether   13.42, 13.43, 13.44, 13.45, 13.46
  contributory negligence, effect   13.66
  differing approaches to   13.68
  early advice   13.67
  evaluation of gratuitous care   13.31
    approach to   13.31
    calculation of value of   13.32, 13.33, 13.34
    serious cases   13.37
    standard discount   13.35
    two approaches to   13.36
  fatal cases, in   13.149
    cases   13.155, 13.156, 13.157, 13.158, 13.159, 13.160
    common law   13.150
    evaluating care of children in   13.161, 13.162, 13.163, 13.164
    Fatal Accidents Act 1976, and   13.152, 13.153, 13.154
    present law   13.149
    substitute care   13.151
  future care, periodical payments for   13.55
  health/local authorities, provision
    of care by   13.69
    Avon CC v Hooper   13.101, 13.102, 13.103, 13.104
    care provided under S21   13.87, 13.88
    Children Act 1989   13.106, 13.107, 13.108
    Health and Social Services and
      Social Security
      Adjudications Act 1983   13.95, 13.96, 13.97, 13.98
    Health and Social Services and
      Social Security
      Adjudications Act 1983,
      claims under   13.121
    indemnities   13.119
    liason between health and local
      authorities   13.115, 13.116, 13.117
    main statutes   13.71
    means taken into account   13.99, 13.100
    National Assistance
      (Residential
      Accommodation)
      (Disregarding of
      Resources)(England)
      Regulations 2001   13.89
    National Assistance Act 1948   13.84
    National Assistance Act 1948,
      claims under   13.120

Care, damages for—*continued*
　health/local authorities, provision of care
　　by—*continued*
　　National Health Service
　　　Act 1977　　　　　　　　　13.105
　　National Health Service and
　　　Community Care
　　　Act 1990　　　　　　　　　13.84
　　NHS, provision of care by　　13.72,
　　　13.73, 13.74, 13.75, 13.76, 13.77
　　protection from recoupment
　　　claims　　　　　　　　　　13.118
　　recoupment　　13.109, 13.110, 13.111,
　　　13.112, 13.113, 13.114
　　recoupment of costs of　　　13.70
　　recoupment of costs of
　　　accommodation　　13.87, 13.88
　　recoupment of costs under
　　　section 29　　　　　　　　13.94
　　residential accommodation/care　13.85,
　　　　　　　　　　　　　　　13.86
　　Section 21　　　　　　13.85, 13.86
　　section 29　　13.90, 13.91, 13.92, 13.93
　　services including home care　13.90,
　　　　　　　　　13.91, 13.92, 13.93
　　social services and local
　　　authorities　　　　　13.82, 13.83
　interest on care　　　　　　　　13.49
　interim payments　　　　　　　　13.51
　less serious cases　　13.27, 13.28, 13.30
　　awards at modest levels　　　13.29
　lump sum damages　　　　13.53, 13.54
　main principles　　　　　　　　13.11
　once and for all damages　　　　13.52
　periodical payments　　　　　　13.52
　principles applied in awards for　13.6
　　gratuitous care　　　13.7, 13.8, 13.9
　　guidelines for calculation　　13.10
　　validity of　　　　　　　　　　13.6
　principles underlying award of　13.2
　　cost to country　　　　　　　　13.5
　　judicial input　　　　　　　　13.3
　　seriousness of case　　　　　　13.4
　recovery for care　　　　　　　13.48
　title to award　　　　　　　　13.50
　tortfeasor, care provided by　13.21, 13.22,
　　　　　13.23, 13.24, 13.25, 13.26
Case management
　impact of Human Rights Act on　36.63
Causation
　Bonnington Castings, McGhee,
　　Wilsher and Fairchild
　　effect of decisions in　　　　　3.43
　'but for' test　　　　　　　　3.1, 3.2
　contributory negligence, and　　4.44
　de minimis exception　　3.44, 3.45, 3.46
　Fairchild principles　3.32, 3.33, 3.34, 3.42
　foreseeability, and　　　　　　　2.38
　fresh intervening acts　　　　　　2.42
　health and safety　　　　7.23, 7.24, 7.25
　intervening causes　　　　　　　3.48
　loss of a chance　　　　　　　　3.47

Causation—*continued*
　material contribution
　　proof of causation, as　　　3.36, 3.37
　material contribution principle　3.16, 3.17,
　　　　　　　　　　　　　　　　　3.18
　materially increasing risk, and　　3.28
　sufficiency of　　3.33, 3.34, 3.35, 3.36,
　　　　　　　　　　　　　　　　　3.37
　meaning　　　　　　　　　　　　3.1
　proof of　　　　　　　　　　　4.45
　Wilsher test　　3.25, 3.26, 3.27, 3.28, 3.29,
　　　　　　　　　3.30, 3.31, 3.42
CFA Lite　　　　　　　　　35.62, 35.63
Champerty
　conditional fee agreements, and　35.6
Children
　compromise of claims involving　28.45
　　costs on settlement　　　　　28.63
　　　circumvention of costs rules　28.70,
　　　　　　　　　　　　　28.71, 28.73
　　　conditional fee agreements　28.69
　　　court's discretion　　　　　28.76
　　　dealing with　　　　　　　28.66
　　　detailed assessment,
　　　　avoidance　　　　　　　28.65
　　　expenses　　　　　　28.75, 28.77
　　　general rule　　　　　　　28.64
　　　insurance and interest　　28.72
　　　purpose of rules　　　　　28.67
　　　redrafting of rules　　　　28.74
　　　Road Traffic Accident cases　28.78,
　　　　　　　　　　　　　28.79, 28.80
　　　summary assessment　　28.68
　　court approval　　　　　　　28.45
　　Fatal Accidents Act 1976, and　28.81,
　　　28.82, 28.83, 28.84, 28.85, 28.86,
　　　　　　　　　　　　　　　　28.87
　　reasons for court approval
　　　requirement　　　　　　　28.47
　　settlement after commencement
　　　of action　　　　　　　　28.48
　　　approval　　　　　　　　28.50
　　　evidence　　　　　　　　28.49
　　　Forms　　　　　　　　　28.52
　　　Part 36 payments　　　　28.50
　　　private hearing　　　　　28.51
　　settlement prior to proceedings
　　　being brought　　28.53, 28.54
　　　approval requirements　　28.56
　　　costs　　　　　　　　　　28.60
　　　judge　　　　　　　　　　28.58
　　　opinon on merits　　　　28.57
　　　Part 8 Claim Form rules　28.55
　　　periodical payments　　　28.62
　　　presence of defendant　　28.59
　　　provisional damages　　　28.61
　　validity　　　　　　　　　　28.46
　contributory negligence, and　　4.25
　　age of child　　　　　　　　4.26
　　child's actions　　　　　　　4.28
　　child's awareness of dangers　4.29
　　special knowledge　　　　　4.27

Children—*continued*
  dealing with money recovered   28.88
    court practice   28.98
    directions   28.88, 28.89
    District Judge as contact point   28.99
    funds paid from court   28.97
    payment to Litigation Friend   28.96
    Practice Direction rules   28.90, 28.91, 28.92, 28.93, 28.94, 28.95
  defendant, as
    default proceedings, in   28.31, 28.32, 28.33, 28.34, 28.35, 28.36, 28.37, 28.38, 28.39, 28.40, 28.41, 28.42, 28.43, 28.44
  delay, and   18.28
  evaluating care of
    fatal cases, in   13.161, 13.162, 13.163, 13.164
  interim payments, and   20.51
  litigation friend   28.4
    appointment by court order   28.18, 28.19, 28.20, 28.21, 28.22, 28.23, 28.24
    appointment without court order   28.13, 28.14, 28.15
    certificate of suitability   28.16, 28.17
    no litigation friend   28.5, 28.6, 28.7
    replacement of by court order   28.25, 28.26, 28.27, 28.30
    termination of appointment   28.28, 28.29
  meaning   28.3
  more stringent foreseeability test   2.26, 2.29
  need, in
    recoupment, and   13.107, 13.108
  proceedings against
    application of provisions   28.10
    provisions   28.8, 28.9
    service of documents   28.11, 28.12
  reaching full age   28.100
    cessation of Litigation Friend   28.100
    liability of Litigation Friend   28.103, 28.104
    procedure for termination of Litigation Friend   28.105, 28.106
    provisions   28.101
    striking out   28.102
  rules for claims involving   28.2
Children Act 1989
  provision of accommodation/care   13.106
  recoupment   13.109, 13.110, 13.111, 13.112, 13.113, 13.114
    children in need   13.107, 13.108
Civil Procedure Rules
  alternative dispute resolution, and   32.5
  experts   5.1
  overriding objective   27.2, 27.4, 27.5
    consideration of appeal   27.7
    judicial discretion   27.3
    meaning   27.2
    need for cooperation   27.6

Claim Form
  contents   27.53
  Guide   27.53
  meaning   27.54
  Practice Direction   27.55
  statement of truth   27.59
Claimant
  death of   9.46
  means of   9.49
  need for care
    damages for care, and   13.12
    previous lifestyle   9.50
Class of person
  duty of care, and   2.11
Clinical disputes
  pre-action protocol for resolution of   27.31
Clinical negligence
  success fees, and   35.41
Clinical negligence claims
  general damages, and   9.34
Collective conditional fee agreements   35.22
Conditional fee agreements   35.1
  assessment of costs   35.67
    additional liability, and   35.67
    formula   35.68, 35.69
    scope   35.70
  ATE insurance   35.72
    deferement of payment for   35.74
    premium, definition   35.73
    recovery of premium   35.75
  collective   35.22
    aim   35.22
    CCFA requirements   35.23
    legislation governing   35.22
    meeting members' liabilities   35.23
    trade union members' liability   35.24
  common law   35.1
    champerty   35.6, 35.7, 35.8, 35.9
    indemnity principle   35.1, 35.2
    maintenance   35.3, 35.4, 35.5
  disclosure   35.71
  duties of legal advisers   35.25, 35.26, 35.27, 35.28
  enforceability   35.52
    before the event insurance,
      existence of   35.55
    breach causing loss, whether   35.57
    compliance with Regulations, and   35.52
    court's jurisdiction   35.59
    disclosure of interests in insurance   35.58
    materially adverse effect, meaning   35.54
    small road traffic accident claims   35.56
    test for   35.53
  primary legislation requirements   35.15
    amount recoverable by way of success fee   35.20
    cab rank principle   35.18

Conditional fee agreements—*continued*
  primary legislation
    requirements—*continued*
      litigant's ability to fund
        litigation, and   35.21
      non-contentious business
        agreement   35.16
      solicitor/counsel agreement   35.20
      success fee   35.17
      success, definition   35.19
  Regulations   35.48, 35.49
    1 November 2005, after   35.60, 35.61
    CFA Lite   35.62, 35.63
    Conditional Fee Agreements
      Regulations 2000   35.50, 35.51
  retrospective agreements   35.64
    backdating   35.65
    common law, and   35.66
    permissibility   35.64
    retrospective variation   35.64
  sources of information   35.77
  statutory provisions   35.10, 35.11, 35.12
    contemplated proceedings   35.14
    definition   35.13
    provision of legal services,
      meaning   35.14
  success fees   35.38
    'additional liability'   35.44
    benefit of hindisght and
      assessment of   35.42
    bundle of documents   35.43
    disclosure of funding
      arrangement   35.46
    fixed uplift regime   35.40
    modest value clinical negligence
      claim   35.41
    rate   35.39
    recovery of additional liability   35.47
    summary assessment at interim
      application   35.45
    two stage uplift   35.38
  success rate   35.29
    cap on   35.29
    fixed success fee   35.30
      employers' liability   35.33, 35.34, 35.35
      employers' liability disease
        litigation   35.36, 35.37
      road traffic accidents   35.30, 35.31, 35.32
  tribunals   35.76
  wasted costs, and   34.19, 34.20
Conditional fee arrangements   27.114
Conduct of parties
  costs, and   33.11
Confidentiality
  experts, and   5.40
Construction (Health, Safety and
  Welfare) Regulations   7.79

Constructive knowledge   24.58, 24.59, 24.60, 24.61, 24.62, 24.63, 24.64, 24.65, 24.66, 24.67, 24.68, 24.69, 24.70, 24.71, 24.72, 24.73, 24.74
  limitation   24.58, 24.59, 24.60, 24.61, 24.62, 24.63, 24.64, 24.65, 24.66, 24.67, 24.68, 24.69, 24.70, 24.71, 24.72, 24.73, 24.74
Contingency awards
  aids and equipment, and   14.23
Contribution
  health and safety   7.23, 7.24, 7.25
Contributory negligence   4.1
  1945 Act   4.52
    application to different torts   4.52, 4.53
  availability of defence   4.8
    claimant not personally at fault   4.10
    definition of fault   4.8
    vicarious liability   4.9
  damages for care, and   13.66
  degree of
    de minimis exception, and   3.46
  fatal accident claims   31.47
  interim payments, and   20.21
  just and equitable test   4.33
    blame   4.33
    causation   4.44, 4.45, 4.46, 4.47
    causative potency   4.44, 4.45, 4.46, 4.47
    caused solely by claimant   4.41
    claimant not expected to take
      precautions   4.39
    decision   4.48, 4.49, 4.50, 4.51
    failure to wear seat belt or
      crash helmet   4.38
    ignoring warning signs   4.36
    intoxicated drivers   4.35
    persons of particular skill   4.43
    policy considerations   4.40
    statutory obligation   4.42
    suicide, and   4.37
  multiple defendants   4.11
    blameworthiness, and   4.12
    causative potency, and   4.12
    totality of defendants' tortuous
      conduct   4.11
  nature of claimant's failure   4.4
    assessing degree of fault   4.7
    availability of defence   4.5
    extent of injuries   4.6
    occurrence of incident   4.6
  objective test   4.21
    application to children   4.25, 4.26, 4.27, 4.28, 4.29
    disabled person   4.22, 4.23
    'normal' objective test   4.24
    'reasonable care for one's own
      safety'   4.22
    rescue or emergency situations,
      application   4.30
  periodical payments, and   21.21

Index

Contributory negligence—*continued*
  pleading and proof requirements   4.13, 4.14
    evidential burden of proof   4.16
    legal burden of proof   4.15
  recoupment of damages, and   16.23
  standard of care   4.17
    carried out work in manner expected   4.20
    claimant acts in contravention of regulations   4.20
    context of claimant's conduct   4.20
    employers' breach of duties   4.20
    foreseeability of harm to oneself   4.17
    freedom to avoid danger   4.20
    'marked' finding   4.20
    reasonable care test   4.18
    reasonable skill and care of others   4.19
    'thrown off guard' by defendant's conduct   4.20
  statutory provision   4.1
    background to statute   4.2
    effect of Act   4.3
Costs   33.1, 33.2
  allocation or re-allocation, following   33.30
  appeal against order for   33.33
  assessment of success   33.25
  award of   33.18
  capping   33.38
  cases where costs orders deemed to have been made   33.31
  conditional fee arrangements   27.114
  conduct of parties   33.11
    conduct, meaning   33.12
    court orders   33.13
  counterclaim   33.40
  Court of Protection   17.34
  courts' powers in relation to misconduct   33.32
  CPR, and   33.1
  detailed assessment   33.74
    base costs   33.77
    interim payment   33.78
    request for hearing   33.76
    time period   33.75
  effect of specific costs orders   33.14
  entitlement to assessment and recovery   33.7, 33.8
    indemnity principle   33.7
    members of trade unions   33.9
  exercise of discretion   33.10
  failure to mediate   33.29
  fast track   27.111, 27.112, 33.66
    basis of assessment   33.70, 33.71, 33.72, 33.73
    conduct of parties   33.69
    counterclaims   33.68
    court's powers   33.67
  fixed costs in road traffic accidents   27.113

Costs—*continued*
  general rule   33.3, 33.5
    CPR   33.4, 33.6
  inflated claims   33.28
    relevance of financial limits   33.28
  interest on   33.79
  interim hearings   33.34
  Judicial Studies Board Guidelines, and   9.15, 9.16
  late amendment   33.27
  legal aid, and   33.26
  Lockley orders   33.39
  LSC funding, and   33.26
  material for exercising discretion   33.20
    failure to recover damages   33.24
    general principles   33.20, 33.21, 33.22, 33.23
  non-parties, against   33.18, 33.19, 34.34
    application in practice   34.52, 34.53, 34.54, 34.55, 34.56, 34.57
    Civil Procedure Rules   34.36, 34.37
    general guidance   34.49
    principles   34.38, 34.39, 34.40, 34.41, 34.42, 34.43, 34.44, 34.45, 34.46, 34.47, 34.48, 34.50, 34.51
    jurisdiction   34.35
  Part 20 proceedings   33.41
    discontinuance of claims   33.42
    general principles   33.41
    multiple parties   33.43
      co-defendants   33.43, 33.44, 33.45
      joint tortfeasors   33.46
  Part 36 offers and payments   33.47
    appeals against orders for costs only   33.54, 33.55
    appeals, and   33.52
    fixed costs   33.56, 33.57, 33.58
    security for costs   33.48
    security for costs of appeal   33.53
    setting aside judgment   33.50
    transfer of proceedings   33.49
    varying order for costs   33.51
  proportionality   27.110
  Protective Costs Orders   33.35, 33.36, 33.37
  reasonableness   27.110
  sanctions for failure to negotiate   32.30
  set off   33.40
  silence as to   33.15, 33.16
  small claims   27.115
  summary assessment of   33.59
    agreement between parties   33.65
    assisted persons   33.63
    circumstances for consideration   33.64
    failure to comply with directions   33.62
    procedure   33.60
    rules   33.59
    statement of costs   33.61
  time for complying   33.17
  wasted costs   34.1
Council tax
  accomodation, and   15.31

Court of Appeal
  experts' liabilities, and   5.27
Court of Protection   17.1
  designated decision makers   17.9, 17.10
  existing practice   17.8
  fees   17.84
    ancillary and related expenses   17.85
    guidance for quantification   17.89
    past and prospective   17.87
    potential heads of damage   17.86
    specialist investment advice   17.88
  independent mental capacity
      advocates   17.26, 17.27
  jurisdiction   17.28
    acting without evidence of
      incapacity   17.45
  nature and function   17.79
    appointment of patient's
      receiver   17.80
    interim payments   17.83
    jurisdiction   17.82
    Master's jurisdiction   17.81
  new powers   17.4
    appeals   17.33
    applications for exercise of
      fundamental powers   17.30
    appointing deputy   17.22
    declarations on capacity   17.21
    fees and costs   17.34
    making decisions on person's
      behalf   17.24
    personal welfare   17.23
    President's directions   17.32
    reports from Public Guardian   17.29
    rules   17.31
  practice and procedure   17.5
  reform of   17.1
  replacement by new   17.4
  subordinate rules and directions   17.6
Criminal injuries compensation   22.1
  amount   22.24
  appeals to CICAP   22.38
  attributability   22.22, 22.23
  case preparation   22.39
  crime of violence   22.17
    definition   22.17
    scope   22.18
  'criminal injury'   22.14
    law enforcement activities   22.16
    offence of trespass on railway   22.15
    principal definition   22.14
  deductions   22.36
    rules   22.36
  eligibility   22.20
    absolute bars   22.20
    discretionary bars   22.21
  fatal cases   22.30
    'qualifying claimants'   22.30, 22.31
    supplementary compensation   22.32
  further appeals   22.45
  future prospects   22.46
  loss of earnings   22.28
  medical evidence   22.41, 22.42, 22.43
  multiple injuries   22.27

Criminal injuries compensation—*continued*
  multipliers for future loss   22.33, 22.34, 22.35
    Ogden Tables   22.33
  procedure at heaaring   22.40
  procedure for claim   22.37
  re-opening cases
    medical deterioration, for   22.44
  secondary victims   22.19
  social basis of   22.3
  sources of information   22.4
  1996 and 2001 tariff Schemes   22.7, 22.8, 22.9
  'common law' Scheme   22.4, 22.5, 22.6
  guides   22.10
  special expenses   22.29
  tariff injury award   22.25, 22.26
  tariff of awards   22.2
  who can recover   22.11
    dead victims   22.12, 22.13
    living victims   22.11
Criminal Injuries Compensation Board
  (CICB)
  tariff for injuries   9.41
Crofton v NHSLA   13.125, 13.126, 13.127, 13.128, 13.129, 13.130
CRU certificates   16.14

Damages
  accommodation, for
    periodical payments, and   21.27
  care, for   13.1
  failure to recover
    costs, and   33.24
  objective   10.2
  provisional   19.1, 27.109
  recoupment   16.1, 16.3
    Act, implementation   16.2
    appeals   16.34, 16.37, 16.38, 16.39, 16.40, 16.41, 16.42
    application of Act   16.5
    basic framework   16.4
    business rent   16.19
    contributory negligence   16.23
    CRU certificates   16.14
    defendant's liability   16.15
    disregard of listed benefits   16.10
    excluded benefits   16.11
    excluded compensation
      payments   16.7
    Fatal Accident Act claims   16.8
    gratuitous care   16.17
    heads of compensation outside
      Sch 2   16.20
    interest on damages   16.21
    interim payments   16.22
    judgments   16.24
    offsetting   16.16
    part 36 payments   16.25, 16.26, 16.27, 16.28, 16.29, 16.30, 16.31, 16.32, 16.33
    'payment', meaning   16.6
    pension contributions   16.18

Damages—*continued*
   recoupment—*continued*
      relevant benefits   16.9
      'relevant period', meaning   16.13
      reviews   16.34, 16.35, 16.36
      Sch 2 heads of compensation   16.17
      statutory sick pay   16.12
      variations of certificates   16.43
Date of knowledge
   limitation   24.17, 24.18, 24.19, 24.20,
         24.21, 24.22, 24.23, 24.24, 24.25,
         24.26, 24.27, 24.28, 24.29, 24.30,
         24.31, 24.32, 24.33, 24.34, 24.35,
         24.36, 24.37, 24.38, 24.39, 24.40,
         24.41, 24.42, 24.43, 24.44, 24.45,
         24.46, 24.47, 24.48, 24.49, 24.50,
         24.51, 24.52, 24.53, 24.54, 24.55,
         24.56, 24.57, 24.58, 24.59, 24.60,
         24.61, 24.62, 24.63, 24.64, 24.65,
         24.66, 24.67, 24.68, 24.69, 24.70,
         24.71, 24.72, 24.73, 24.74, 24.75,
         24.76, 24.77, 24.78, 24.79, 24.80,
         24.81, 24.82, 24.83, 24.84, 24.85,
         24.86, 24.87, 24.88, 24.89, 24.90
De minimis exception   3.44
   causative potency of defendant's
      conduct   3.46
   degree of contributory negligence   3.46
   large number of small exposers   3.46
   level of exposure   3.45
   parameters   3.46
   pleural plaques litigation   3.46
   relative and quantative exposure   3.46
De minimis principle
   psychiatric injuries, and   6.59
Dead victims
   criminal injuries compensation, and 22.12
Death
   claimant, of
      general damages, and   9.46
Death in service benefits
   loss of pension, and   12.38
Default judgment
   interlocutory applications   27.94, 27.95
   setting aside   27.96
Default proceedings
   child as defendant   28.31, 28.36, 28.44
      admissions   28.34, 28.35, 28.37
      agreements between parties   28.42
      Practice Direction   28.33
      procedure   28.32
      rebuttable presumption   28.38
      settlement agreements   28.43
      withdrawal of admission   28.39, 28.40,
                                       28.41
Defendant's Guide   27.16
Defendant's letter
   specimen letters   27.14
Defending actions   27.60
   allocation   27.68, 27.69, 27.70, 27.71,
                                       27.72
      important factors   27.73
   contents of defence   27.61, 27.62

Defending actions—*continued*
   disputing valuation   27.63
   medical report   27.65
   reply   27.67
   Schedule of Special Damages   27.66
   Statement of Truth   27.64
   time limits   27.60
Delay
   interest, and   18.24
   limitation   24.114, 24.115, 24.116, 24.117,
                 24.118, 24.119, 24.120, 24.121
Deputy
   appointing
      Court of Protection, in   17.22
Directors
   loss of earnings, and   11.25
Disability   24.126, 24.127, 24.128
   limitation, and   24.126, 24.127, 24.128
   meaning   24.126, 24.127, 24.128
Disabled persons
   contributory negligence, and   4.22, 4.23
Disclosure
   Human Rights Act, and   36.80
   standard   27.84, 27.85
      disclosure points   27.88
      disclosure statement   27.87
      duty of search   27.86
      taking initiative   27.89
Disclosure of documents
   Personal Injury Protocol, and   27.17
Discretion   24.108, 24.109, 24.110, 24.111,
                              24.112, 24.113
   limitation   24.108, 24.109, 24.110, 24.111,
                            24.112, 24.113
Disease and illness at work claims
   pre-action protocol   27.45
Documents
   service of
      children, on   28.11
Drury v Crookdale   13.131, 13.132, 13.133,
                                       13.135
Duty of care   1.1
   air passengers   1.9
   balancing multiple   1.12
      provision of public services   1.12, 1.13
   breach of duty   2.37
   class of person   2.11
      relationship of proximity, and   2.11
   common law negligence, in   1.1
   employee on loan   1.4
      employer liability   1.4
   employers   1.2
      foreseeability   1.2
      implied   1.3
      tortuous   1.3
   experts'   5.21
   fire brigade   1.11
   foreseeability   1.14, 2.2
   Human Rights Act, and   36.44
   kind of damage   2.12
      concept of   2.15
      duty owed, whether   2.13
      kind of accident   2.16

Duty of care—*continued*
  kind of damage—*continued*
    pure economic loss   2.14
    police   1.10
    primary victims, owed by
      psychiatric injuries, and   6.74, 6.75
    probability required to impose   2.8
    'real risk'   2.8
    rescuers   1.23
    road users
      highway authority   1.8
      other road users, to   1.7
      removal of snow and ice   1.8
    self-employed workers
      element of control   1.6
      foreseeability   1.5
      labour-only sub contract   1.6
      status of worker   1.6
  three part test   2.2
    cases of pure omission   2.4
    foreseeability as only
      requirement   2.3
    'proximity', meaning   2.2
    pwer but no duty to act   2.4
  three-part tests   1.1
    fairness of imposition of duty   1.1
    flexibility   1.1
    foreseeability   1.1
    proximity of parties   1.1
Duty of search
  disclosure, and   27.86

Eggshell skull rule   1.21
Emergency situations
  contributory negligence, and   4.30
  nature of employment   4.32
  unusual demands   4.32
Employee
  loan, on
    duty of care   1.4
Employees
  primary or secondary victim,
    whether   6.63
  psychiatric injuries   6.49, 6.50, 6.51, 6.52, 6.53
Employer
  duty of care
    employee on loan, to   1.4
  statutory liabilities   7.1
    principal health and safety
      Regulations   7.2
Employers
  duty of care   1.2, 1.3
  liability
    conditional fee agreements, and   35.33, 35.34, 35.35
Employers' liability disease litigation
  conditional fee agreements, and   35.36
  fixed success fees   35.36, 35.37
Equipment
  aids and   14.1

European Convention on Human
  Rights
  immunity from suit, and   5.26
European law   8.1
  direct effect   8.11
    application   8.17
    discretion in implementing
      Directives   8.16
    'emanation of the state',
      definition   8.13
    enforcement   8.12
    European Court jurisprudence   8.14
    failure of implementation, and   8.11
    responsibility for
      implementation   8.15
    'vertical' application   8.12
  effective remedies   8.18, 8.19
  English appellate case-law applying   8.27, 8.28, 8.29, 8.30, 8.31
  European Court of Justice   8.21
    case-law   8.21, 8.22
    defective product liability   8.25, 8.26
    derogations   8.24
    working time, and   8.23
  foreign accidents   8.32
  interpretation   8.9
    national judges' duties   8.10
    positive   8.10
  liability of State
    failure to implement Directive,
      for   8.20
  rights and remedies under   8.8
  scope   8.2
    areas of interest   8.3
    four freedoms   8.2
    implementation   8.4
    principal areas   8.2
    rationale behind   8.5
  sources   8.6
    Directives   8.7
    secondary legislation   8.6
European Union law
  uninsured and unidentified drivers,
    and   30.3
Evidence
  accomodation, and   15.34
  aids and equipment, and   14.7
  interim payments, and   20.45
  loss of earnings, for   11.8
  oral
    experts   27.106
    video   26.1
Expert evidence
  loss of earnings   11.11
Experts   5.1, 27.104, 27.105
  aim of reforms   5.3
  Civil Procedure Rules, and   5.1
  Code of Guidance on Expert
    Evidence   5.2
  confidentiality and privilege   5.40, 5.45
  CPR   5.46
  incomplete statement of
    instruction   5.49

Experts—*continued*
  confidentiality and privilege—*continued*
    material instructions, meaning   5.47
    replacement experts   5.50
    statements, letters and documents   5.41
    unenforceable CPR provisions   5.48
    unintentional disclosure of existence of statement   5.42
    waiver   5.43, 5.44
  court's duties   5.51
  different types of   5.34
  duties
    connection with parties   5.11
    daily attendance   5.10
    Ikarian Reefer duties and functions   5.8
    independence   5.7
    medico-legal workers   5.10
    objectivity   5.7
    pre-litigation advisory stage   5.6
    psychiatry and objectivity   5.10
    Stuart Smith LJ on   5.9
    treating clinicians   5.10
  duties of those instructing   5.28
    Code of Conduct   5.29
    covering letter   5.32
    CPR   5.32
    modified preliminary view   5.29
    opinions in report   5.28
    questions to other side's expert   5.33
    'suggested' amendments from counsel   5.30
    weaknesses in report   5.31
  format of expert's report   5.12
    failure to comply with requirements   5.14
    Practice Direction   5.12
    statement of truth   5.13
  liabilities   5.21
    Court of Appeal   5.27
    Court of Appeal review of   5.22
    does not give evidence a trial   5.23
    duty of care   5.21
    European Convention on Human Rights, and   5.26
    immunity of advocates   5.24
    witnesses   5.25
  medical expert evidence   5.35, 5.36, 5.37
  meeting   27.107, 27.108
  meeting of   5.18
    issues discussed at   5.19
    purpose of   5.18
    questions from parties   5.20
  non-medical expert evidence   5.38, 5.39
  oral evidence   27.106
  permission to use   5.4
  Practice Direction   5.2
  restrictions   5.3
  single joint experts   5.15
    appropriateness   5.17
    obligations   5.15
    parties conferring with   5.16

Experts—*continued*
  use of reports at trial   5.5
Extent of damage
  foreseeability   2.36

Fairchild principles   3.42
Fast track   27.51
  application   27.1
  costs   27.111, 27.112, 33.66
  directions   27.74, 27.75, 27.76, 27.77, 27.78
    failure to comply with   27.80
    variation of   27.79
Fatal accident claims   31.1
  actions for benefit of deceased's estate   31.5
    1934 Act, under   31.5
    causes of action   31.8
    loss of expectation of life   31.7
    losses of deceased and past losses distinction   31.6
    past losses   31.9
  causes of action   31.2
  common law   31.1
  Fatal Accidents Act 1976, actions under   31.10
    bereavement   31.14, 31.15
    cause of action   31.10, 31.11, 31.12
    contributory negligence   31.47
    funeral expenses   31.43
    benefits resulting from death   31.44, 31.45, 31.46
    heads of damage   31.13
    interest   31.48
    loss of dependency   31.16
    apportionment   31.41, 31.42
    assessment   31.19
    calculation   31.24
    division of amount recovered   31.18
    double deductions for uncertainty   31.22
    foundation for claim   31.17
    future pecuniary loss   31.20
    hypothesis   31.21
    multiplicand   31.25, 31.26, 31.27, 31.28, 31.29, 31.30, 31.31, 31.32
    multiplier   31.33, 31.34, 31.35, 31.36, 31.37, 31.38
    periodical payments   31.39, 31.40
    relationship of dependency   31.23
  Human Rights Act, actions under   31.49, 31.52
    bereavement damages   31.50
    limitations to   31.51
  statutory rights   31.3
Fatal accidents
  multipliers, and   10.28
Fatal Accidents Act
  general damages, and   9.58
Fatal cases
  claims for care in   13.149

Fear of impending death	
general damages, and	9.42
Fire brigade	
duty of care	
owner of premises	1.11
Foreign accidents	8.32
applicable secondary legislation	8.40
package holidays	8.40, 8.41
road traffic accidents	8.42, 8.43, 8.44
Brussels Regulation	8.33
court first seised	8.38
determination of jurisdiction	8.34
domicile of defendant	8.35
English Courts' jurisdiction	8.33
English defendant	8.37
judgment in foreign court	8.39
tortious claims	8.36
Foreign judgments	
enforcing	
Human Rights Act, and	36.77
Foreseeability	1.14
breach of duty	2.37
causation and damage	2.38
congruence of test	2.39
effect of application	2.41
fresh intervening acts	2.42
liability should reflect	
blameworthiness	2.39
risk principle	2.39, 2.40
class of person	2.11
duty of care	
three part test	2.2
extent of damage	2.36
harm to oneself	4.17
kind of accident	2.16
children	2.26, 2.29
claim resulting from different	
cause	2.24
danger due to state of premises	2.28
defining	2.41
deliberate act	2.27
precise manner of occurence	2.18, 2.19, 2.20, 2.21, 2.23
precise manner of occurrence	2.17
reason for neglecting risk	2.22
remoteness of risk	2.25
statutory duty owed to	
trespassers	2.28
trespassing child	2.28
kind of injury	2.30
depressive illness	2.32
phyisical and psychiatric,	
distinction	2.30
primary victim	2.31
stress at work cases	2.33, 2.34, 2.35
reasonable	
hindsight, and	2.10
objective test, as	2.10
standard of care, and	2.10
sufficiency of	2.43
view of reasonable man	2.10
scope	2.1

Foreseeability—*continued*	
standard of foresight	2.5
degree of foresight of injury	2.7
negligible risk	2.6
'real risk', definition	2.8
'reasonable foresight', meaning	2.5
small risk as real risk	2.9
ubiquitousness of injury, and	2.6
suicide, and	6.61
test of	1.14, 1.15
degree of severity of risk	1.14
incidence of risk	1.14
objective test	1.17
'ordinary prudent employer'	1.17
previous occurence	1.16
vulnerability to injury	1.18
Fraud	
video evidence, and	26.36
Freeman v Lockett	13.144, 13.145, 13.146, 13.147, 13.148
Fresh intervening acts	
causation, and	2.42
Funeral expenses	
fatal accident claims	31.43
Future loss	
assessment of	
aids and equipment	14.28
Future losses	
loss of earnings	11.26, 11.27
Gender	
general damages, and	9.44
General damages	9.1
acceleration	9.37
age, and	9.45
appeals against awards of	9.60
assessment	9.2
awards at top of range	9.5
checklist for	9.61
circumstances of accident	9.52
claimant's previous lifestyle	9.50, 9.51
death of claimant	9.46, 9.47, 9.48
degree of insight into condition	9.4
Fatal Accidents Act claims, in	9.58, 9.59
fear of impending death	9.42
gender, and	9.44
global awards	9.57
Heil v Rankin	9.17, 9.18
individual factors affecting	9.27
interest rates	18.7, 18.8
applicable money values	18.6
Judicial Studies Board Guidelines	9.6, 9.8, 9.13, 9.14
costs, and	9.15, 9.16
intention of	9.12
'real world' cases	9.10
reviews	9.7
status	9.9
total loss of one eye	9.11
loss of amenity	9.32
cases	9.33
meaning	9.32
loss of congenial employment	9.53, 9.54

General damages—*continued*	
loss of enjoyment of holiday	9.56
loss of expectation of life	9.43
loss of leisure	9.55
meaning	9.1
means of claimant	9.49
multiple injuries	9.38
CICB tariff	9.41
Court of Appeal guidance	9.39
overall effect of injuries	9.40
pain and suffering	9.28
asymptomatic conditions	9.29, 9.30
meaning	9.28
mesothelioma cases	9.31
pre-existing condition	9.34
clinical negligence claims	9.34, 9.35, 9.36
updating awards	9.21
awards made after 23rd March 2000	9.23
awards made before 23rd March 2000	9.24, 9.25, 9.26
date of award	9.22
judges' duties	9.21
uplifts	9.19, 9.20
upper limit	9.3
Godbold v Mahmood	13.140, 13.141
Gratuitous care	
evaluation of	13.31
recoupment of damages, and	16.17
Health and safety	
Codes of Practice and Guidance	7.12
applicable Codes	7.17, 7.18
compliance with ACOP provisions	7.15
limitations	7.14
'Regulation' and guidance hybrid	7.13
relevant Code	7.16
Construction (Health, Safety and Welfare) Regulations	7.79
absolute obligations	7.83
cases	7.84
contents	7.82
equipment requirements	7.83
liability	7.83
scope	7.79, 7.80, 7.81
employers' liabilities	7.2
employers' liability	
general points from case-law	7.97
procedural implications	7.96
European Directives	7.8
direct effect, effect of	7.10
effect	7.8
non-implementation of	7.11
'state authority', meaning	7.9
general principles of prevention	7.4
Health and Safety (Display Screen Equipment) Regulations	7.31
cases	7.36
contents	7.35
requirements	7.35

Health and safety—*continued*	
Health and Safety (Display Screen Equipment) Regulations—*continued*	
scope	7.31, 7.32, 7.34
upper limb disorders	7.36
liability	7.19
causation	7.23, 7.24, 7.25
commencement	7.22
contribution	7.23, 7.24, 7.25
defences	7.23, 7.24, 7.25
scope	7.20, 7.21
Lifting Operations Regulations 1998	7.85
borrowed equipment	7.89
contents	7.88
liability for breach	7.89
records	7.89
report of examination	7.89
scope	7.85, 7.86, 7.87
Management Regulations	7.26
cases	7.30
contents	7.28
liability for breach	7.27
requirements	7.28
risk assessments	7.29
Manual Handling Operations Regulations	7.37
'as far as reasonably practicable'	7.42
cases	7.43
contents	7.41
guidelines	7.42
instruction and training	7.42
requirements	7.41
scope	7.37, 7.38, 7.39, 7.40
need to monitor	7.5
Personal Protective Equipment at Work Regulations	7.59
contents	7.64
employers' duties	7.64
maintenance of equipment	7.65
scope	7.59, 7.60, 7.61, 7.62, 7.63
specific needs of job	7.65
principal Regulations	7.2, 7.3
European Directive	7.4
principles of English law	7.6, 7.7
Provision and Use of Work Equipment Regulations	7.44
cases	7.58
contents	7.48
dangerous parts of machinery	7.54, 7.55
general duties	7.49
guards and protection devices	7.56
important regulations	7.51
'maintained'	7.53
'maintaining in an efficient state'	7.57
scope	7.44, 7.45, 7.46, 7.47
specific requirements	7.50
'suitability'	7.52
regulation	7.19

Health and safety—*continued*
   Working Time Regulations   7.90
      contents   7.93
      hours beyond statutory figures   7.95
      scope   7.90, 7.91, 7.92
      standard of normal working
         hours   7.94
   Workplace (Health, Safety and
      Welfare) Regulations   7.66
      appropriateness of building   7.78
      contents   7.71, 7.72
      duties   7.71
      floor construction   7.73, 7.74
      handrails   7.76
      holes   7.75
      loading ramps   7.78
      means of access   7.78
      reasonable practicality   7.77
      scope   7.66, 7.67, 7.68, 7.69, 7.70
      smoke   7.78
      snow and ice   7.78
      'technical maintenance'   7.78
Health and Safety (Display Screen
   Equipment) Regulations   7.31
Health and Social Services and Social
   Security Adjudications
   Act 1983
   claims under s17   13.121
   defences   13.122
   limitation   13.122
Health authorities
   negligence of
      shock induced psychiatric
         injuries, and   6.65
Highway authority
   duty of care   1.8
Hillsborough disaster
   psychiatric injuries, and   6.35
Holidays
   aids and equipment, and   14.22
Home care   13.90, 13.91, 13.92, 13.93
Housing   15.1
Housing association
   accomodation   15.37
Human Rights Act 1998   26.42, 36.1
   enactment   36.1
   fatal accident claims   31.49
   impact on substantive law   36.41
      s7 claims   36.55, 36.56, 36.57, 36.58,
         36.59, 36.60, 36.61
   key Convention rights   36.2
      Article 1 Protocol 1   36.24, 36.25
      Article 2   36.17, 36.18, 36.19, 36.20
      Article 3   36.21, 36.22, 36.23
      Article 6   36.5, 36.6, 36.7, 36.8, 36.9,
         36.10
      Article 8   36.11, 36.12, 36.13, 36.14,
         36.15, 36.16
      Article 14   36.26, 36.27
      conflict between rights of
         parties   36.4
      disproportionate limitation or
         interference   36.3

Human Rights Act 1998—*continued*
   negligence law   36.41
      duty of care   36.44, 36.45, 36.46
      reliance on Art 6   36.42
      servicemen suing MOD   36.43
   nuisance claims   36.47, 36.50
      inquests   36.52, 36.53, 36.54
      noise nuisance   36.49
      severe pollution   36.48
      traffic noise   36.51
   procedural law, impact on   36.62
      limitation   36.67
      multiple actions   36.65, 36.66
      ordinary case management
         decisions   36.63, 36.64
      service   36.68
      amendment   36.69, 36.70
      capacity   36.84
      disclosure   36.80, 36.81, 36.82, 36.83
      enforcing foreign judgments   36.77,
         36.78
      evidence improperly obtained   36.79
      funding   36.85, 36.86, 36.87
      right to go to trial   36.73, 36.74, 36.75,
         36.76
      strike out/stay   36.71, 36.72
   structure   36.28
      claims against public authorities   36.36,
         36.37, 36.38, 36.39
      duty on public authorities   36.33,
         36.34, 36.35
      impact on legislation   36.29, 36.30,
         36.31, 36.32
      retroactive, whether   36.40
   video evidence, and   26.42

Impecunious claimant
   wasted costs, and   34.19, 34.20
Indemnity principle   33.7
   conditional fee agreements, and   35.1
Index linking
   periodical payments, and   13.59, 13.60,
      13.61, 13.62, 13.63, 13.64, 13.65
Inflated claims
   costs   33.28
Information technology
   aids and equipment, and   14.14
Inquests
   Human Rights Act, and   36.52, 36.53,
      36.54
Insurance
   accomodation, and   15.33
   motor
      compulsory   30.25
      periodical payments, and   21.41
Interest   18.1
   costs, on   33.79
   damages, on
      recoupment, and   16.21
      delay   18.24
         active case management, and   18.26
         cases   18.25
         commercial cases   18.27

Interest—*continued*
  delay—*continued*
    court's discretion ... 18.29
    minors ... 18.28
  effect of interim payments on ... 18.18
    complex approach ... 18.23
    complex method ... 18.20
    example ... 18.22
    excessive payments ... 18.21
    simple approach ... 18.19
  fatal accident claims ... 31.48
  payments by volunteers ... 18.30
  procedure ... 18.34
    pleading ... 18.34, 18.36
    requirements ... 18.35
  rates ... 18.5
    general damages ... 18.6, 18.7, 18.8
    special damages ... 18.9, 18.10, 18.11, 18.12, 18.13, 18.14, 18.15, 18.16
    tax ... 18.17
  repayment
    reduction of award on appeal, following ... 18.33
  social security benefits, and ... 18.31
    interim payment ... 18.32
  statutory framework ... 18.1
    court awarding ... 18.3
    Court of Appeal, and ... 18.4
    presumptions ... 18.2
Interim hearings
  costs, and ... 33.34
Interim payments ... 20.1
  adjustment ... 20.32
    discharge ... 20.34, 20.35
    payment as between defendants ... 20.36
    repayment ... 20.33
    variation ... 20.34, 20.35
  appeals ... 20.53
  care, to fund ... 13.51
  children ... 20.51
  Civil Procedure Rules on ... 20.6, 20.7
  court's powers ... 20.2
  definition ... 20.1
  effect on interest ... 18.18
  hearing ... 20.47
  instalments, by ... 20.49, 20.50
  interlocutory applications ... 27.100, 27.101
  judgment and/or liability admitted ... 20.10
    if action proceeded to trial claimant would obtain substantial damages ... 20.11, 20.12, 20.13, 20.14, 20.15, 20.16
  judgment for 'substantial damages' ... 20.19
    amount of interim payment ... 20.22
    contributory negligence ... 20.21
    discretion ... 20.22, 20.25
    evidence ... 20.25
    exercise of discretion ... 20.30
    'level playing field' ... 20.28
    need for interim payment ... 20.24
    prejudice of defendant's position ... 20.26, 20.27
    'reasonable proportion' ... 20.23, 20.29
    small claims ... 20.20

Interim payments—*continued*
  mentally incapable claimants ... 17.68
  mode of application ... 20.44
    evidence ... 20.45, 20.46
    provisions ... 20.44
  multiple applications for ... 20.4
  multiple defendants ... 20.17, 20.18
  Part 36 payments ... 20.52
  patients ... 20.51
  periodical payments, and ... 21.92
  preconditions ... 20.8, 20.9
  recoupment of damages, and ... 16.22
  requirements ... 20.10
  restrictions on personal injury payments ... 27.102
  social security benefits ... 20.31
  split trial ... 20.48
  time period ... 20.3
  timing/ tactics ... 20.37
    application to enter judgment and ... 20.39
    defendant wishing to resist ... 20.43
    liability denied ... 20.40
    liability in dispute ... 20.41
    Part 36 offer and ... 20.42
    time period ... 20.38
  type ... 20.5
Interlocutory applications ... 27.90, 27.91
  Application Notice requirements ... 27.93
  deduction of benefits ... 27.103
  default judgment ... 27.94, 27.95
    setting aside ... 27.96
  interim payments ... 27.100, 27.101, 27.102
  procedure for making ... 27.92
  summary judgment ... 27.97, 27.98, 27.99
Intervening causes ... 3.48
  application of ... 3.48
  extremity of subsequent action ... 3.49
  medical treatment ... 3.49
  time available to intervenor ... 3.49
Intoxicated drivers
  contributory negligence ... 4.35
Involuntary participant
  psychiatric injuries ... 6.28

Judicial Studies Board
  general damages Guidelines ... 9.6
Just and equitable test ... 4.33
  blame ... 4.33
    caused solely by claimant ... 4.41
    claimant not expected to take precautions ... 4.39
    failure to wear seat belt or crash helmet ... 4.38
    ignoring warning signs ... 4.36
    intoxicated drivers ... 4.35
    persons of particular skill ... 4.43
    policy considerations ... 4.40
    statutory obligation ... 4.42
    suicide, and ... 4.37

Just and equitable test—*continued*
   causation and causative potency   4.44, 4.47
      link between behaviour and injury   4.46
      proof of causation   4.45
   decision   4.48
      appeals   4.51
      'discretion'   4.49
      reversal at appeal   4.50

Kind of damage   2.12

Late amendment
   costs, and   33.27
Legal aid
   costs, and   33.26
Letter of claim
   clinical disputes, and   27.36, 27.37
      issuing after   27.39
      status   27.38
   specimen letters   27.12, 27.13
Liability
   health and safety   7.19
Life expectancy
   periodical payments, and   21.33
Lifetime losses   10.19
   expenditure for entire lifetime   10.20
   life expectation   10.19
   loss of pension   10.23
   multipliers for fixed periods   10.26
   one-off future losses   10.24, 10.25
   variations   10.22
   'whole life' multiplier   10.21
Lifting Operations Regulations 1998   7.85
Limitation   24.1, 24.2, 24.3, 24.4, 24.5, 24.6, 24.7, 24.8, 24.9, 24.10, 24.11, 24.12, 24.13, 24.14, 24.15, 24.16, 24.17, 24.18, 24.19, 24.20, 24.21, 24.22, 24.23, 24.24, 24.25, 24.26, 24.27, 24.28, 24.29, 24.30, 24.31, 24.32, 24.33, 24.34, 24.35, 24.36, 24.37, 24.38, 24.39, 24.40, 24.41, 24.42, 24.43, 24.44, 24.45, 24.46, 24.47, 24.48, 24.49, 24.50, 24.51, 24.52, 24.53, 24.54, 24.55, 24.56, 24.57, 24.58, 24.59, 24.60, 24.61, 24.62, 24.63, 24.64, 24.65, 24.66, 24.67, 24.68, 24.69, 24.70, 24.71, 24.72, 24.73, 24.74, 24.75, 24.76, 24.77, 24.78, 24.79, 24.80, 24.81, 24.82, 24.83, 24.84, 24.85, 24.86, 24.87, 24.88, 24.89, 24.90, 24.91, 24.92, 24.93, 24.94, 24.95, 24.96, 24.97, 24.98, 24.99, 24.100, 24.101, 24.102, 24.103, 24.104, 24.105, 24.106, 24.107, 24.108, 24.109, 24.110, 24.111, 24.112, 24.113, 24.114, 24.115, 24.116, 24.117, 24.118, 24.119, 24.120, 24.121, 24.122, 24.123, 24.124, 24.125, 24.129, 24.130, 24.131, 24.132, 24.133, 24.134, 24.135, 24.136,

Limitation—*continued*
   24.137, 24.138, 24.139, 24.140, 24.141, 24.142, 24.143, 24.144, 24.145, 24.146, 24.147, 24.148
   all circumstances of case   24.91, 24.97, 24.98, 24.99, 24.100, 24.101, 24.102, 24.103, 24.104, 24.105, 24.106, 24.107, 24.108, 24.109, 24.110, 24.111, 24.112, 24.113, 24.137
      Horton v Sadler   24.96
      position prior to Horton v Sadler   24.92, 24.93, 24.94, 24.95
   breach of statutory duty   24.10, 24.11, 24.12
   conduct of defendant   24.122, 24.123, 24.124, 24.125
      response to requests by plaintiff   24.122, 24.123, 24.124, 24.125
   date of knowledge   24.17
      attributability   24.44, 24.45, 24.46, 24.47, 24.48, 24.49, 24.50, 24.51, 24.52
      constructive knowledge   24.58, 24.59, 24.60, 24.61, 24.62, 24.63, 24.64, 24.65, 24.66, 24.67, 24.68, 24.69, 24.70, 24.71, 24.72, 24.73, 24.74
      identity   24.53, 24.54, 24.55, 24.56, 24.57
      knowledge of facts   24.18, 24.19, 24.20, 24.21, 24.22, 24.23
      medical or other appropriate advice   24.75, 24.76, 24.77, 24.78, 24.79, 24.80, 24.81, 24.82, 24.83, 24.84
      proviso (s 14 (3))   24.85, 24.86, 24.87, 24.88, 24.89, 24.90
      significance and injury in question   24.34, 24.35, 24.36, 24.37, 24.38, 24.39, 24.40, 24.41, 24.42, 24.43
      significant, meaning   24.24, 24.25, 24.26, 24.27, 24.28, 24.29, 24.30, 24.31, 24.32, 24.33
   delay   24.114, 24.115, 24.116, 24.117, 24.118, 24.119, 24.120, 24.121
      cogency of evidence, and   24.119, 24.120, 24.121
      length of   24.114, 24.115, 24.116, 24.117, 24.118
      reasons for   24.114, 24.115, 24.116, 24.117, 24.118
   disability, and   24.126, 24.127, 24.128
   discretion   24.91, 24.108, 24.109, 24.110, 24.111, 24.112, 24.113
      circumstances
         Horton v Sadler   24.96
         position prior to Horton v Sadler   24.92, 24.93, 24.94, 24.95
      exercise of   24.97, 24.98
   history   24.1, 24.2, 24.3, 24.4, 24.5

Limitation—*continued*
    Human Rights Act 1998, and   36.67
    ignorance of law   24.129, 24.130, 24.131,
                        24.132, 24.133
    knowledge of cause of action   24.129,
                24.130, 24.131, 24.132, 24.133
    mentally incapable claimants, and   17.90
    negligence   24.10, 24.11, 24.12
    nuisance   24.10, 24.11, 24.12
    personal injuries   24.13, 24.14, 24.15,
                            24.16
    policy   24.1, 24.2, 24.3, 24.4, 24.5
    prejudice   24.91, 24.99, 24.100, 24.101,
                    24.102, 24.103, 24.104, 24.105,
                    24.106, 24.107
        Horton v Sadler   24.96
        position prior to Horton v
            Sadler   24.92, 24.93, 24.94,
                         24.95
    primary limitation period 24.6, 24.7, 24.8,
                               24.9
    procedure   24.138, 24.139, 24.140, 24.141,
                 24.142, 24.143, 24.144
    special time limits   24.145, 24.146, 24.147,
                           24.148
    steps taken to obtain advice   24.134,
                                 24.135, 24.136
Litigation friend   17.71
    actions prior to appointment, effect 17.73
    certificate of suitability   17.76, 17.77,
                                  17.78
    children, and   28.4
        appointment by court order   28.18,
            28.19, 28.20, 28.21, 28.22, 28.23,
            28.24
        appointment without court
            order   28.13, 28.14, 28.15
        certificate of suitability   28.16, 28.17
        no litigation friend   28.5, 28.6, 28.7
        replacement of by court order   28.25,
                           28.26, 28.27, 28.30
        termination of appointment   28.28,
                                      28.29
    dispensing requirement for   17.74
    obligation to act   17.75
    procedural requirements   17.72
Litigation services
    definition   35.13
Local authorities
    accomodation   15.37
    adaptation of accomodation, and   15.6,
                                         15.7
    provision of care by   13.82, 13.83
Lockley orders   33.39
Loss
    five categories of   10.12
Loss of a chance   3.47
Loss of amenity
    general damages, and   9.32
Loss of chance
    loss of earnings, and   11.55, 11.56, 11.57,
                             11.58, 11.62, 11.63
        'basic loss', calculation   11.59

Loss of chance—*continued*
    loss of earnings, and—*continued*
        'broad-brush' approach   11.61
        four stages of opportunity   11.60
        'litigation risk'   11.64
Loss of congenial employment
    general damages, and   9.53
Loss of dependency
    fatal accident claims   31.16
Loss of earnings   10.17, 11.1
    adjustments for contingencies   11.43
        accuracy of results   11.44
        example   11.47, 11.48, 11.49
        procedure   11.45
        residual earning capacity   11.46
    ancillary benefits   11.18, 11.19
    calculating   10.17
        variations   10.18
    criminal injuries compensation, and 22.28
    delay entering job market   11.65
    directors   11.25
    entitlement to   11.1
    evidence   11.8
        absence of   11.9
        expert   11.11, 11.12, 11.13, 11.14,
                       11.15, 11.16, 11.17
        under-settlement   11.10
    future losses   11.26, 11.27
    handicap on labour market   11.50, 11.51,
                                 11.52, 11.53, 11.54
    loss of chance   11.55, 11.56, 11.57, 11.58,
            11.59, 11.60, 11.61, 11.62, 11.63,
            11.64
    multiplicand   11.33
        example   11.37
        meaning   11.33
        rate of growth in income   11.35
        residual earning capacity   11.36
        two or more   11.34
    multiplier   11.38
        annual rate of return   11.39
        discount rate   11.41
        influences of   11.38
        investment advice, and   11.42
        working party on   11.40
    partnership   11.22
        husband and wife partnerships   11.24
        'silent partners'   11.23
    period of unemployment   11.3
    periodical payments   11.28, 11.29
        'bottom-up' approach   11.31
        departure from RPI   11.32
        mechanism for calculating   11.30
    self-employment   11.20
        business expenses   11.21
        supporting documents   11.20
    separate heads of claim   11.2
    straightforward claims   11.4
        benefits   11.5
        'cost of earning'   11.6
        living expenses   11.7
Loss of enjoyment of holiday
    general damages, and   9.56

Loss of expectation of life
   general damages, and   9.43
Loss of leisure
   general damages, and   9.55
Loss of pension   10.23, 12.1
   alternative occupational pension   12.31
   average life expectancy short of
      retirement   12.37
   conventional approach   12.1
      binding on pensions   12.3
      Wells v Wells, following   12.2
      wider principles   12.1
   death in service benefits   12.38
   evidential framework   12.20
      additional receipt   12.24, 12.25, 12.26, 12.27, 12.28
      breadth of evidence   12.23
      terms of scheme   12.21
      worked example   12.22
   hybrid personal/employer funded
      schemes   12.35, 12.36
   money purchase plans   12.35
   modern approach   12.4
      Ogden Tables   12.4
   Ogden multipliers   12.6
      further adjustment   12.14, 12.15, 12.16, 12.17, 12.18, 12.19
      multiplicand   12.13
      multiplier   12.10, 12.11, 12.12
      type 1 cases   12.7, 12.8
      type 2 cases   12.9
   personal pension plans   12.34
   tax allowances and relief   12.32, 12.33
   types of claim   12.5
      type 2, worked example   12.39, 12.40
   widow's pension   12.29, 12.30
LSC funding
   costs, and   33.26
Lump sum   10.35
   aids and equipment, and   14.28
   appropriateness   10.35
   damages for care, and   13.53, 13.54

Maintenance
   conditional fee agreements, and   35.3
Maintenance costs
   accomodation, and   15.30
Management Regulations
   health and safety, and   7.26
Manual Handling Operations
   Regulations   7.37
Material contribution principle   3.16, 3.17, 3.18
   materially increasing chance of
      injury, and   3.21, 3.22, 3.24
      mesothelioma cases, and   3.23
   proof of causation, whether   3.36, 3.37
   McGhee test   3.21, 3.24
      establishes legal principle, whether   3.36
      multiple tortfeasors, and   3.32
      number of potential causes   3.25
   single and multiple tortfeasors,
      distinction   3.38, 3.39, 3.40

Meaningful degree, rule of   30.61
Mediation   32.3, 32.13
   failure to mediate
      costs, and   33.29
   meaning   32.13
Medical evidence
   accomodation, and   15.44, 15.45
   aids and equipment, and   14.7
   criminal injuries compensation, and   22.41, 22.42, 22.43
Medical examinations   25.1
   commissioning of medical report   25.17
   all material instructions   25.19
   disclosure of letter of
      instruction   25.18
   Expert Witness Institute   25.23
   interview of witnesses   25.20
   jointly instructed experts   25.21
   medico-legal experience   25.22
   timing of   25.24, 25.25, 25.26, 25.27
   mututal exchange   25.75, 25.76, 25.77, 25.78
   necessity of medical evidence   25.2
   Particulars of Claim, and   25.3
   purpose   25.5, 25.9, 25.11
   case management, and   25.10
   choice of doctor   25.16
   disparity of findings   25.15
   exclusion of   25.6
   fast track   25.8
   nature and severity of injuries   25.12
   relevant expertise   25.13
   scope   25.14
   small claim track   25.7
   refusal to undergo   25.50
      application of reasonableness
         test   25.63, 25.64, 25.65
      cases   25.54, 25.55
      claimant, by   25.57, 25.58
      court considerations   25.53
      defendant, by   25.72, 25.73, 25.74
      granting of stay   25.50
      imposing conditions   25.66
      attending with another
         doctor present   25.71
      attending with companion   25.66, 25.67, 25.68, 25.69, 25.70
      medical tests, refusal to undergo   25.59, 25.60, 25.61, 25.62
      reasonableness of stay   25.51
      reasonableness test   25.52
      substantial ground for
         requirement that party undergo   25.44, 25.45
      cases   25.48, 25.49
      reluctance to submit to   25.46
      unreasonable refusal   25.47
   single expert   25.38, 25.43
      disclosure requirements   25.39, 25.40, 25.41
      reliance on report   25.42
   single joint expert   25.28
      approach to instruction of   25.31
      availability for trial date   25.36

Index

Medical examinations—*continued*
  single joint expert—*continued*
    calling at trial   25.35
    'desktop' report   25.30
    further expert   25.33
    notice requirements   25.37
    opinion   25.34
    proportionality   25.32
    rejection of report   25.29
Medical expert evidence   5.35, 5.36, 5.37
Medical reports
  defences   27.65
Medical research
  Mental Capacity Act 2005, and   17.25
Mental Capacity Act 2005   17.2
  ability to retain information   17.17
  ability to understand information   17.16
  care providers   17.20
  designated decision makers   17.9, 17.10
  determining person's best interests   17.19
  implementation   17.3
  key principles   17.12
  medical research   17.25
  mentally incapable person, definition   17.13
  person lacks capacity, meaning   17.14
  person unable to make decision   17.15
  reforms introduced by   17.11
  relevant information   17.18
  Royal Assent   17.2
  transitory provisions   17.7
Mental capacity advocates
  independent   17.26
    functions   17.27
    powers   17.27
    responsibilities   17.27
Mental illness
  definition   17.40
Mentally incapable claimants   17.35
  limitation, and   17.90
    approach to litigation   17.94
    claimant later becomes patient   17.95
    limitation periods   17.92
    long delays   17.93
    person under disability, definition   17.91
  litigation friend   17.71, 17.72, 17.73, 17.74, 17.75, 17.76, 17.77, 17.78
  patient bringing claim   17.37
  patient procedure   17.46
  patient, meaning   17.36, 17.38
    appointment of receiver   17.43
    at risk claimant   17.62
    categories of mental disorder   17.39
    emergency cases   17.45
    empowerment, and   17.63
    expert medical evidence   17.42
    half-way protective category   17.65
    head injury victims   17.41
    medical certificate   17.44
    mental illness, definition   17.40
    non-patient claimant   17.61
    patient, whether   17.64
    second limb   17.47

Mentally incapable claimants—*continued*
  patient, meaning—*continued*
    subjective approach   17.48
    test for capacity   17.49, 17.50, 17.51, 17.52, 17.53, 17.54, 17.55, 17.56, 17.57, 17.58, 17.59, 17.60
  settlement and compromise   17.66
    code of procedure   17.67
    interim payments   17.68
    periodical payments   17.69
    practice direction   17.70
Mentally incapable person
  definition   17.13
Mesothelioma cases
  cause of disease   3.30, 3.31
  Fairchild principles   3.42
  general damages, and   9.31
  material increase in risk, and   3.23
  multiple tortfeasors   3.33, 3.34, 3.35
  new causation test, and   3.41
Misconduct
  costs, and   33.32
Moeliker v Reyrolle & Co [1977] 1 WLR 132   11.51
Motor vehicles
  uninsured and unidentified drivers   30.1
Multi-track   27.52
Multiple injuries
  general damages, and   9.38
Multipliers   10.1, 10.8
  acturial tables   10.7
  alternatives to   10.35, 10.36, 10.37, 10.38, 10.39, 10.41
    'judicial instinct approach'   10.40
  combining Tables   10.27
  discount rate   10.9
  fatal accident cases and   10.28
    binding nature of Cookson   10.34
    date of death, at   10.30
    gap between death and trial   10.31
    general principle   10.29
    increase in multiplier   10.32
    Ogden Committee proposals   10.33
  fixed periods, for   10.26
  future losses, for   10.11
  ILGS rate of return   10.10
  inflation   10.5
  interest rates, and   10.3
  lifetime losses   10.19
  loss of earnings   11.38
  loss of earnings, calculating   10.17
  objective of damages, and   10.2
  Ogden Tables   10.7
  practice of discounting   10.6
  'prudent investor', concept of   10.4
  Tables, using   10.12
    'contingencies other than mortality'   10.14
    five categories of loss   10.12
    'judicial discout'   10.16
    rejection of capping   10.15
    tables of mortality   10.13
  use of   10.1

National Health Service Act 1977	13.105
Naturally occuring events	
liability, and	3.8
Negligence	
impact of Human Rights Act on	36.41
limitation	24.10, 24.11, 24.12
'Nervous shock'	1.19
discredited phrase, as	6.7
liability for	6.4
controversial nature of law on	6.5
lack of judicial unanimity on	6.6
'primary victims'	1.20
eggshell skull rule	1.21
meaning	1.21
recognised psychiatric illness, need for	1.19
rescuers	1.23
duty of care, and	1.23
'secondary victims'	1.20
meaning	1.22
proximity	1.22
NHS	
provision of care by	
changes in services	13.77
recoupment of costs of, and	13.72, 13.73, 13.74, 13.75, 13.76
relevance of availability of	13.78, 13.79, 13.80, 13.81
Non-medical expert evidence	5.38, 5.39
Non-parties	
costs against	33.18, 34.34
Nuisance	
limitation	24.10, 24.11, 24.12
Nuisance claims	
Human Rights Act 1998, and	36.47
Occupational therapy	
aids and equipment, and	14.8
Offers to settle	29.1, 29.2, 29.3
clinical disputes, and	27.40
non-complying	29.6, 29.7, 29.8, 29.9
court giving effect to	29.6, 29.7, 29.8, 29.9
Offsetting	
recoupment of damages, and	16.16
Ogden tables	10.7
Ogden Tables	22.33
fatal accident claims	31.34
loss of pension	12.4
Omissions	
'but for' test, and	3.4
Once and for all damages	
damages for care, and	13.52
Oral evidence	
experts	27.106
Orthotics	
aids and equipment, and	14.13
Package holidays	
foreign accidents, and	8.40
Pain and suffering	
general damages, and	9.28

Part 20 proceedings	33.41
Part 36 offer	
acceptance	
payment of lump sum and periodical payments	29.26
clarification	29.19
calculation of amount	29.22, 29.23
contributory negligence	29.22, 29.23
information as to recoverable benefit	29.20, 29.21
content	29.12, 29.13, 29.14
future pecuniary loss claims	29.15, 29.16
costs, and	33.47
effect of acceptance	29.30, 29.31
claimant does better	29.38, 29.39, 29.40
claimant fails to do better	29.36, 29.37
offeree does better than proposed	29.32, 29.33, 29.34, 29.35
form	29.12, 29.13, 29.14
future pecuniary loss claims	29.15, 29.16
nature of	29.4, 29.5
non-complying	
court giving effect to	29.6, 29.7, 29.8, 29.9
time for acceptance	29.27, 29.28, 29.29
what may be subject of	29.17, 29.18
when made	29.10, 29.11
withdrawal	29.24, 29.25
Part 36 offers	
interim payments, and	20.42
periodical payments, and	21.73
Part 36 payment	
clarification	29.19
calculation of amount	29.22, 29.23
contributory negligence	29.22, 29.23
information as to recoverable benefit	29.20, 29.21
content	29.12, 29.13, 29.14
future pecuniary loss claims	29.15, 29.16
costs, and	33.47
effect of acceptance	29.30, 29.31
claimant does better	29.38, 29.39, 29.40
claimant fails to do better	29.36, 29.37
offeree does better than proposed	29.32, 29.33, 29.34, 29.35
form	29.12, 29.13, 29.14
future pecuniary loss claims	29.15, 29.16
nature of	29.4, 29.5
time for acceptance	29.27, 29.28, 29.29
when made	29.10, 29.11
withdrawal	29.24, 29.25
Part 36 payments	16.25
calculation of	16.30, 16.31, 16.33

Part 36 payments—*continued*	
cases	16.29, 16.32
defendant's obligations	16.27, 16.28
interim payments, and	20.52
technical aspects	16.26
Particulars of Claim	27.56, 27.57
contents	27.56
Guide to	27.58
medical examinations, and	25.3
Partnership	
loss of earnings, and	11.22
husband and wife parnterships	11.24
'silent partners'	11.23
Past loss	
assessment of	
aids and equipment, and	14.27
Patient	
bringing claim	17.37
interim payments, and	20.51
litigation friend	17.71, 17.72, 17.73, 17.74, 17.75, 17.76, 17.77, 17.78
meaning	17.36, 17.38
appointment of receiver	17.43
at risk claimant	17.62
categories of mental disorder	17.39
emergency cases	17.45
empowerment, and	17.63
expert medical evidence	17.42
half-way protective category	17.65
head injury victims	17.41
medical certificate	17.44
mental illness, definition	17.40
non-patient claimant	17.61
patient procedure	17.46
patient, whether	17.64
second limb	17.47
subjective approach	17.48
test for capacity	17.49, 17.50, 17.51, 17.52, 17.53, 17.54, 17.55, 17.56, 17.57, 17.58, 17.59, 17.60
settlement and compromise	17.66
code of procedure	17.67
interim payments	17.68
periodical payments	17.69
practice direction	17.70
Payments by volunteers	
interest, and	18.30
Payments into court	29.1, 29.2, 29.3
Pension contributions	
recoupment of damages	16.18
Periodical payments	21.1
appeals	21.88
default position	21.89
financial provision for claimant in meantime	21.91
judicial discretion	21.90
appropriate index	21.51
CPR provisions	21.53
default index	21.52
'exceptional circumstances'	21.54
identification of	21.55
uplift	21.56
assessment of future loss, and	14.37

Periodical payments—*continued*	
assignment and right to receive	21.70
factors for court to consider	21.71
scope of provisions	21.72
children, and	28.62
court's approach	21.17
claimant's preference	21.20
contributory negligence	21.21
factors	21.19
obligation to consider	21.17
primary criterion	21.18
'scale' point	21.22
'the nature of any financial advice'	21.23
damages for care, and	13.52
fatal accident claims	31.39
form of Order	21.24
basic payment period	21.25
damages for accommodation	21.27, 21.29
future pecuniary losses	21.30
increase or decrease on future certain date	21.31, 21.32
large awards	21.28
loss of earnings and care costs, distinction	21.26
losses for future	21.25
'other recurring or capital costs'	21.27
future care, for	13.55
application	13.56
continuity of payment	13.56
court's duties	13.56
index linking, and	13.59, 13.60, 13.61, 13.62, 13.63, 13.64, 13.65
practice and procedure	13.57, 13.58
interim payments	21.92
lump sum interim payment	21.93
provision needed for ongoing care	21.94
life expectancy, and	21.33
bottom up approach	21.36
funding of payments	21.37
top down approach	21.34, 21.35
loss of earnings	11.28, 11.29, 11.30, 11.31, 11.32
mentally incapable claimants	17.69
Part 36 offers	21.73, 21.75
acceptance of offer	21.79
appeals, and	21.87
broad based application of discretion	21.86
costs	21.80, 21.84
injustice, and	21.85
judgment more or less advantageous than offer	21.82, 21.83
lump sum	21.74
mixture of lump sum and periodical payment	21.76
requirements	21.77
terms of settlement	21.78
time for acceptance	21.81

Periodical payments—*continued*
  policy behind 21.11
    ability to raise capital 21.15
    advantages 21.12
    alternatives to 21.16
    cases 21.14
    disadvantages 21.13
    linking to index 21.15
    minimum sum 21.15
    money to leave dependants 21.15
    necessary accommodation 21.15
    variation of amount 21.15
  security of payments 21.38
    cases 21.44
    consideration of other methods 21.46
    government bodies 21.45
    insurance, and 21.41, 21.42
    non-protected payments 21.43
    protection by ministerial
        guarantee 21.39
    reasonableness 21.47
    security into far future 21.48, 21.49, 21.50
    statutory protection 21.40
  statutory provisions 21.2
    agreements between parties 21.3
    appropriateness 21.5
    consent order 21.10
    CPR 21.4
    'non-variable' and 'variable'
        payments 21.6
    orders and agreements,
        distinction 21.7
    regulation of agreements 21.9
    'with profits' annuity 21.8
  substantive law 13.55
  variable orders 21.57
    agreements for 21.63
        combination of provisional
            damages and 21.68
        court's permission, and 21.65
        further deterioration 21.67
        improvement in claimant's
            condition 21.69
        invalid agreements 21.64
        provisional damages, and 21.66
    application for variation 21.60
    application to extend period 21.61
    assessment of damages 21.59
    number of applications 21.62
    preservation of documents 21.62
    provisions 21.58
Personal injuries 24.13, 24.14, 24.15, 24.16
  definition 24.13, 24.14, 24.15, 24.16
  limitation 24.13, 24.14, 24.15, 24.16
Personal Injury Protocol 27.11
  alternative dispute resolution 27.29, 27.30
  disclosure of documents 27.17, 27.18
    suggested documents 27.19
  experts 27.21
    amendments to reports 27.25
    clarifying report 27.27
    consequences of unreasonable
        rejection of 27.22

Personal Injury Protocol—*continued*
  experts—*continued*
    exploiting rules 27.26
    instructions to 27.21
    joint selection of 27.21
    medical notes 27.23
    permission to rely upon 27.24
    rehabilitation 27.28
    schedule of damages 27.20
    specimen letters 27.12
        Defendant's Guide 27.16
        defendant's letter 27.14
        letter of claim 27.12, 27.13
        scope of admission 27.15
Personal Protective Equipment at
    Work Regulations 7.59
Physiotherapy
  aids and equipment, and 14.12
Pleural plaques
  depression caused by 6.67, 6.68
  general damages, and 9.29, 9.30
Pleural plaques litigation
  de minimis exception, and 3.46
Police
  duty of care 1.10
Post traumatic stress disorder
  diagnostic criteria 6.66
Practice Direction
  Claim Form 27.55
  failure to comply with 27.80
    fixing the trial 27.82
    pre-trial checklist 27.81
    typical timetable 27.83
Pre-action protocol 27.8
  court's approach 27.9
  disclosure and inspection 27.47
    application 27.48
    inspection 27.49
  disease and illness at work claims,
    for 27.45
    scope 27.46
  penalties for breach 27.10
  Personal Injury Protocol 27.11
  resolution of clinical disputes, for 27.31
    aim 27.32
    alternative dispute resolution 27.44
    defendant's response 27.41
    Guide to 27.42
    experts 27.43
    letter of claim 27.36, 27.37, 27.38, 27.39
    obtaining healthcare records 27.34
    offers to settle 27.40
    status 27.33
    structure 27.31
    time limit for compliance 27.35
Pre-existing condition
  general damages 9.34
Pre-trial checklist 27.81
Prejudice
  limitation 24.99, 24.100, 24.101, 24.102, 24.103, 24.104, 24.105, 24.106, 24.107

Privilege
  experts, and   5.40
  wasted costs, and   34.22, 34.23, 34.24
Procedural appeals   27.118
Prosthetics
  aids and equipment, and   14.13
Protective Costs Orders   33.35
Provision and Use of Work Equipment
  Regulations   7.44
Provisional damages   19.1, 27.109
  children, and   28.61
  courts' power to award   19.2
  legal framework   19.3
    appropriateness   19.9
    exercise of discretion   19.8
    'serious' deterioration   19.5, 19.7
    three-stage test   19.6
    two-stage assessment   19.4
  periodical payments, and   21.66
  procedural requirements   19.10
    CPR   19.10
    period   19.12
    Practice Direction   19.11
    preservation of case files   19.13
Psychiatric illness
  'nervous shock', and   1.19
Psychiatric injuries   6.1
  aftermath   6.69
    clinical negligence, and   6.69
    material contribution   6.71
    negligent act, of   6.70
    particular factual situation   6.73
    sufficient proximity   6.72
  as result of physical injury   6.2
  bystanders   6.54
    assessment of degrees of horror   6.57
    Hillsborough, and   6.56
    'particularly horrific'
      catastrophe   6.55
  duty of care owed   6.60
  employees   6.49, 6.51, 6.52, 6.53
    quasi employment relationship   6.50
  Frost, law following   6.58
  involuntary participant   6.28, 6.29, 6.33
    applications of proposition   6.32
    mediately involved   6.31
    unwilling participant   6.30
  liability for
    Lord Bingham on   6.3
  negligence of health authorities,
    and   6.65
  nervous shock, liability for   6.4, 6.5, 6.6
  pleural plaques, depression caused
    by   6.67, 6.68
  primary and secondary victims   6.59
    categorisation of victims   6.62
    claims by police officers   6.64
    de minimis principle, and   6.59
    employees as   6.63
    foster parents   6.62
    importance of distinction
      between   6.59
    suicide, and   6.61

Psychiatric injuries—*continued*
  primary victims   6.11, 6.12
    distinction from secondary
      victims   6.13
    duty of care owed by   6.74, 6.75
    facts of relevant incident   6.14
    foreseeability, and   6.15
    recovery of damages, and   6.15
  proposals for reform   6.76
    close tie of love and affection   6.78
    Law Commission   6.77
    self-inflicted harm   6.79
  PTSD diagnostic criteria   6.66
  'recongisable psychiatric injury'   6.7, 6.9
    expert medical evidence   6.10
    Lord Bridge on   6.8
  recovering damages for   6.1
  rescuers   6.34, 6.35, 6.36, 6.37, 6.38, 6.39,
                  6.40, 6.41, 6.42, 6.43, 6.44, 6.45,
                                    6.46, 6.47, 6.48
  secondary victims   6.16
    close tie of love and affection   6.19,
                                            6.20
    immediate aftermath, meaning   6.22,
                                       6.23, 6.24
    Law Commission on   6.17
    main requirements   6.18
    means of perception   6.26, 6.27
    physical and temporal
      proximity   6.21, 6.25
Public authorities
  claims for damages against   36.36
  duties
    Human Rights Act, and   36.33
Public funding
  wasted costs, and   34.19, 34.20
Public Guardian
  reports from   17.29
Public services
  provision of
    multiple duties of care, and   1.12, 1.13

Reasonableness
  MIB requirements, of   30.62
Recoupment
  children in need, and   13.107, 13.108
  protection from claims   13.118
Rehabilitation   23.1, 27.28
  Code of Best Practice   23.2, 23.3, 23.4
  aim   23.9
  appropriate qualification to
    conduct assessment   23.22
  assessment   23.20
  assessment process   23.23, 23.25
  assessment report   23.26, 23.27, 23.28,
                              23.29, 23.30, 23.31
  claimant's solicitors duty   23.11, 23.12,
                                23.13, 23.14, 23.15
  independent assessment   23.21
  insurer's duties   23.16, 23.17, 23.18,
                                            23.19
  interview of claimant   23.24

Rehabilitation—*continued*
  Code of Best Practice—*continued*
    Introduction to   23.5, 23.6, 23.7, 23.8,
                                                23.10
      recommendations   23.32, 23.33
    forms of   23.1
    litigant's concerns   23.2
    pursuit of compensation at expense
      of   23.2
    Rehabilitation Code   27.28
Remoteness of damage
  foreseeability, and   2.38
Rescuers
  contributory negligence, and   4.30
    level of urgency   4.30
    reasonable actions test   4.31
    risk of danger   4.30
  definition   6.36
  duty of care, and   1.23
  'function' test   6.47
  narrow definition   6.38
    'being exposed to danger'   6.39
    reference to peril   6.40
  professional   6.48
  psychiatric injuries   6.34, 6.41, 6.42, 6.43,
                                  6.44, 6.45
    Hillsborough disaster   6.35
    secondary victim criteria, and   6.37
    special case, as   6.34
    temporal and physical proximity   6.46
Reviews
  recoupment of damages, and   16.35, 16.36
Risk assessments
  Management Regulations, and   7.29
Risk principle   2.39
  justification of   2.40
Road
  definition   30.40
Road traffic accidents
  conditional fee agreements, and   35.30
    success fee   35.30, 35.31, 35.32
  fixed costs in   27.113
  foreign accidents, and   8.42
  uninsured and unidentified drivers   30.1
Road users
  duty of care   1.7, 1.8
Round table meetings
  alternative dispute resolution, and   32.12

Schedule of damages
  Personal Injury Protocol   27.20
Schedule of Special Damages   27.66
Secondary victims
  criminal injuries compensation, and   22.19
Self-employed workers
  duty of care   1.5, 1.6
Self-employment
  loss of earnings, and   11.20
Self-inflicted harm
  duty of care owed by primary
    victims, and   6.74, 6.75

Sikhs
  crash helmets, and   4.39
Simultaneous events
  'but for' test, and   3.9
Single joint expert
  medical examinations, and   25.28
Single joint experts   5.15
Small claims track   27.50
  costs   27.115
Social security benefits
  interest, and   18.31
  interim payments, and   20.31
Social services
  provision of care by   13.82, 13.83
Sowden v Lodge   13.131, 13.132, 13.133,
                                       13.134
Special damages
  interest rates   18.9, 18.16
    appropriate yardstick   18.10
    continuing loss of wages   18.12
    damages for bereavement   18.13
    half-rate approach   18.14
    hlaf-rate approach   18.15
    period   18.11
Specimen letters
  Defendant's Guide   27.16
  defendant's letter   27.14
  letter of claim   27.12, 27.13
  scope of admission   27.15
Speech and Language Therapy   14.11
Standard disclosure   27.84
Standard of care
  contributory negligence   4.17
  reasonable foreseeability, and   2.10
Statement of truth   27.59
Statement of Truth
  defences   27.64
Statutory sick pay
  recoupment of damages, and   16.12
Stress at work cases
  foreseeability   2.33, 2.34, 2.35
Success fees   35.38
Suicide
  contributory negligence, and   4.37
  psychiatric injuries, and   6.61
Summary assessment
  costs, of   33.59
Summary judgment   27.97
  procedure   27.98, 27.99
Surveillance evidence   26.1

Tax
  interest rates   18.17
Tax allowances
  loss of pension, and   12.32, 12.33
Time limits
  defending actions   27.60
Travel and transport
  aids and equipment, and   14.19

Index

Uninsured and unidentified drivers 30.1
  compulsory motor insurance 30.25
    'caused by, or arising out of' 30.37, 30.38
    employers' liability insurance 30.28, 30.29, 30.30, 30.31, 30.32
    exceptions to general rule 30.26
    general rule 30.25
    'liability' 30.34, 30.35, 30.36
    'liability caused by use of vehicle on road or other public place 30.33
    'or other public place' 30.42, 30.43
    'road' 30.40, 30.41
    'use' 30.39
    vehicles covered by deposit 30.27
    vehicles used by certain public bodies 30.27
  European Union law 30.3
    consequences of failure to implement 30.11
    Directive not of Direct Effect 30.18, 30.19
    Directive of Direct Effect 30.12, 30.13, 30.14, 30.15, 30.16, 30.17, 30.20, 30.21, 30.22, 30.23, 30.24
    framework 30.3
    implementing measures 30.7, 30.8
    interpretation of domestic law, and 30.7, 30.8
    Second Directive 30.4, 30.5
    Third Directive 30.6
    UK failure to implement 30.9, 30.10
  idenitifiable and insured 30.44
  idenitifiable and uninsured 30.44
  unidentifiable 30.44
  uninsured driver/user 30.45
    'Article 75 insurer' 30.50, 30.51
    authority of insurer to act 30.76
      authority from D or court 30.76
      conflict of interest 30.77, 30.78
    compliance with Act and Agreements 30.67
    claimant's 'safe course' 30.67
    European Directive 30.73
    Human Rights Act 30.73
    limitation 30.69, 30.70
    setting aside own steps 30.68
    waiver or estoppel 30.71, 30.72
    interim payment 30.82
    joinder of Act insurer/Art.75 insurer/MIB 30.79, 30.80, 30.81
    no 'Article 75 insurer' 30.52
    recovery from D 30.83
      judgment on quantum 30.85
      Road Traffic Act 1988, under 30.83
      Uninsured Drivers Agreements, under 30.84
    s.151 Road Traffic Act 1988 30.45, 30.46, 30.47, 30.48
    service of proceedings 30.74, 30.75

Uninsured and unidentified drivers—*continued*
  uninsured driver/user—*continued*
    Uninsured Drivers Agreement 1988 30.53
      conditions precedent 30.55
      deductions 30.54
      exclusions 30.56
    Uninsured Drivers Agreement 1999 30.57
      concenssions in Revised Guidance Notes 30.63, 30.64, 30.65
      conditions precedent 30.60
      deductions 30.58, 30.59
      exclusions 30.66
      new procedure 30.61
      reasonableness 30.62
      rule of meaningful degree 30.61
    Uninsured Drivers Agreements 30.49
  'untraced' driver/user 30.86
    Untraced Drivers Agreement 1996 30.87, 30.88, 30.89, 30.90, 30.91
      conditions precedent 30.92
      exclusions 30.94, 30.95, 30.96
      reasonableness 30.93
    Untraced Drivers Agreement 2003 30.97
      exclusions 30.98
Utility bills
  accomodation, and 15.32

Vicarious liability
  contributory negligence 4.9
Video evidence 26.1
  admissibility 26.7
  advances in technology 26.3
  authenticity of recording 26.6
  case management, and 26.10, 26.54
  CPR, under 26.32
    cases 26.38, 26.39, 26.40, 26.41
    flexible costs orders 26.35
    fraud 26.36
    improper conduct 26.37
    parties' conduct 26.33, 26.34
  delaying service of 26.11
  disclosure procedure 26.9
  disclosure rules 26.5
  disclosure surveillance has taken place 26.15
  guidance on post-CPR approach 26.8
  Human Rights Act, impact 26.42, 26.43, 26.44
    cases 26.49
    competing public interests 26.52
    covertly obtained 26.48
    film obtained by breach of Act 26.50
    public body as defendant 26.53
    reliance on wrongly obtained footage 26.51
    right to respect for private life 26.45, 26.46

Video evidence—*continued*
  inconclusive 26.14
  legitimacy of 26.2
  purpose 26.16
    'a day in the life' evidence 26.20
    back-injury claims 26.19
    demonstration of malingering 26.17
    liability issues 26.18
  special reasons for non-disclosure 26.12, 26.13
  status 26.8
  tactics for meeting 26.29
    claimant, by 26.29
      after disclosure of evidence 26.29, 26.30
      anticipatory tactics 26.29
    defendant 26.31
  when to use 26.21
    claimant, by 26.21, 26.22
      advantages 26.23
      disadvantages 26.24
    defendant, by 26.25, 26.26
      advantages 26.27
      disadvantages 26.28

Walton v Calderdale Healthcare NHS Trust 13.142, 13.143
Warning signs
  ignoring
    contributory negligence, and 4.36

Wasted costs 34.1
  appropriateness 34.14, 34.15, 34.16, 34.17
  conditional fees 34.19, 34.20
  CPR r44.14 34.31, 34.32, 34.33
  hopeless cases 34.18
  impecunious claimant 34.19, 34.20
  inherent jurisdiction 34.29
  section 51(1) and (3) 34.30
  statutory jurisdiction 34.2
    amount of costs 34.28
    application in practice 34.7, 34.8, 34.9, 34.10, 34.11, 34.12, 34.13
    CPR rules 34.4
    privilege 34.22, 34.23, 34.24
    reliance on counsel 34.21
    rules applicable to 34.5, 34.6
    Supreme Court Act 1981 provisions 34.3
    three-stage test 34.25, 34.26, 34.27
Wasted costs public funding 34.19, 34.20
Widow's pension
  loss of pension 12.29, 12.30
Wilsher test 3.42
Witness evidence
  aids and equipment, and 14.15
Witnesses
  immunity 5.25
Working Time Regulations 7.90
Workplace (Health, Safety and Welfare) Regulations 7.66